CHI2013
CHANGING PERSPECTIVES

I0131478

CONFERENCE PROCEEDINGS

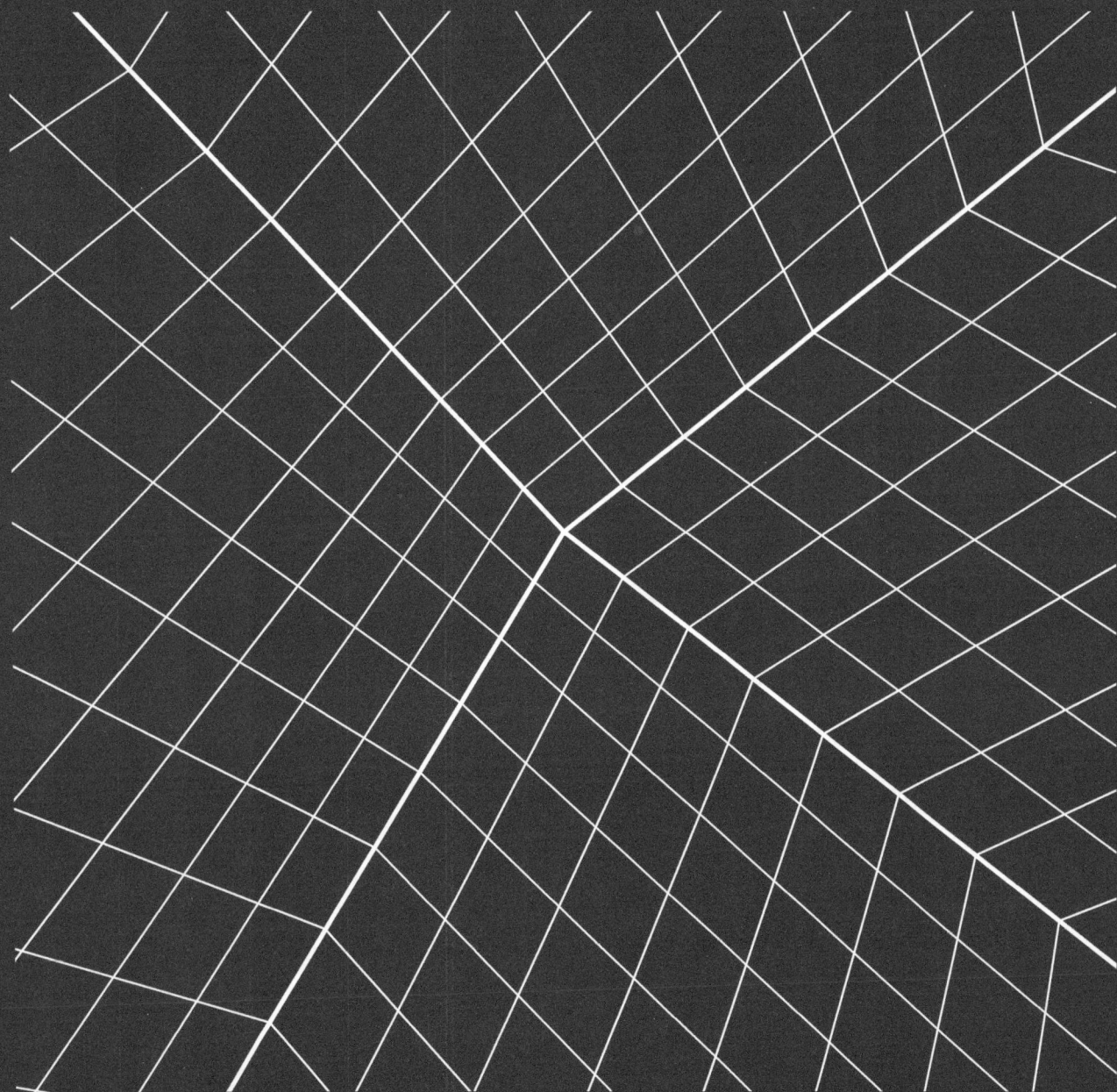

The 31st Annual CHI Conference on Human Factors in Computing Systems
27 APRIL - 2 MAY 2013 • PARIS • FRANCE

acm Association for
Computing Machinery

EDITORS:
Susanne Bødker, *Papers Co-Chair*
Steven Brewster, *Papers Co-Chair*
Patrick Baudisch, *Technical Program Co-Chair*
Michel Beaudouin-Lafon, *Technical Program Co-Chair*
Wendy E. Mackay, *General Conference Chair*

SIGCHI

Association for Computing Machinery

Advancing Computing as a Science & Profession

The Association for Computing Machinery
2 Penn Plaza, Suite 701
New York, New York 10121-0701

ISBN: 978-1-4503-2450-2

Additional copies may be ordered prepaid from:

ACM Order Department
PO Box 30777
New York, NY 10087-0777, USA

Phone: 1-800-342-6626 (USA and Canada)
+1-212-626-0500 (Global)
Fax: +1-212-944-1318
E-mail: acmhelp@acm.org
Hours of Operation: 8:30 am – 4:30 pm ET

Printed in the USA

Bienvenue and Welcome to CHI 2013 in Paris, France!

CHI 2013 is located in the Palais des Congrès in central Paris, a few blocks from the Arc de Triomphe. Often described as the most beautiful city in the world, Paris is home to world-class museums, excellent food and breath-taking architecture, just steps away or a short ride on the metro.

CHI is the premier international conference on human-computer interaction, offering a central forum for sharing innovative interactive technologies that shape people's lives. CHI gathers a multidisciplinary community from around the world: our great strength is our ability to bring together students and experts, researchers and practitioners, scientists, designers and engineers, drawing from their diverse perspectives to create new visions of human-computer interaction.

This year's theme, changing perspectives, is symbolized by the Louvre's elegant pyramid. Its transparency reveals the technical, modern structure within, as it reflects the classic architecture surrounding it, changing color and texture in the shifting Paris light. Our eminent keynote speakers offer similarly contrasting perspectives, from design, engineering and the social sciences. We open with Paola Antonelli, Senior Curator and Architecture & Design Director for Research & Development at MOMA in New York and we close with Bruno Latour, author of Science in Action and head of Paris's Médialab at Sciences Po.

Vint Cerf, President of ACM and fondly referred to as the 'father of the internet', will give a joint keynote on May 2 with ACM's First European Computing Research Congress (ECRC), organized in collaboration with CHI 2013. On that day, participants may attend each other's sessions and discover new perspectives on computing and interaction.

CHI 2013 includes two days of focused workshops and four days of technical content, including CHI's prestigious technical program, with 16 parallel sessions of rigorously reviewed research Papers, engaging Panels, Case Studies and SIGs, an extensive Course program and invited talks from SIGCHI's award winners: George Robertson, Jacob Nielsen, and Sara Czaja. This year, RepliCHI joins the Honorable Mention and Best Paper awards, to recognize excellence in the research process. We also host student research, design, and game competitions, provocative alt.chi presentations and last-minute Birds-of-a-Feather sessions for discussing current topics.

Interactivity showcases the best of interactive technology, both advances in research and artistic explorations, and we highlight over 300 Works-In-Progress posters. Evening events include the CHI 2013 reception, Sponsors and University events, local performances, the job fair and the Video Showcase.

We received a record number of submissions (over 3500) and accepted over 1000 that will appear in the ACM Digital Library. To help you navigate through this immense program, we introduce Video Previews, 30" clips that describe each event in the main program. Before the conference, browse through them on the CHI 2013 website. At the conference, get an overview of the upcoming session on the large Interactive Schedule displays and add your favorites to your Mobile App. Or, browse the videos, papers and extended abstracts on the CHI 2013 flash drive.

After the conference, create a video montage to share with colleagues at home or link to them from ACM's YouTube channel or the Digital Library.

We are deeply indebted to the vast number of volunteers, without whom CHI 2013 would not be possible, including over 2000 reviewers, over 200 senior members of the program committee, over 50 venue chairs on the CHI 2013 conference committee and, of course, the student volunteers. We thank you all!

We are excited by the opportunity to host CHI 2013 and wish you a productive and enjoyable stay in Paris!

Wendy E. Mackay
INRIA
CHI 2013 General Conference Chair

Patrick Baudisch
Hasso Plattner Institute
CHI 2013 Technical Program Co-Chair

Michel Beaudouin-Lafon
Université Paris-Sud
CHI 2013 Technical Program Co-Chair

From ACM SIGCHI's President and Vice President for Conferences

SIGCHI is proud to sponsor the premier annual conference in the field of human-computer interaction. We are extremely grateful to the CHI 2013 Conference Chair Wendy Mackay, to Technical Program Chairs Patrick Baudisch and Michel Beaudouin-Lafon, and to their wonderful crew, who succeeded to build an impressive program and experience.

CHI 2013 turns back to Europe, and, for the first time, resides in Paris with its vibrant French HCI community, 31 years after the first conference, on Human Factors in Computer Systems, in Gaithersburg, MD, on March 15-17, 1982. The second and third conferences were a year and a half apart, and from then on CHI, as the conference has been called since 1983, has been an annual event with the official name: "ACM Conference on Human Factors in Computing Systems".

That first conference drew over 900 attendees, and since then CHI has continued to grow and broaden its range of topics and contributing disciplines: the founding psychologists and software engineers began to meet new visions from ethnography, sociology, communication sciences and arts, among others. Relevant industries, as well as research institutes and academia, showed an increasing - and often long-lasting - interest and involvement (through volunteers and through sponsorship for conference expenses).

CHI is an ideal forum for people to meet formally as well as informally, to exchange knowledge and views, to share experiences, and to learn. The CHI conference brings together professionals from research and practice; people from industry, academia, and from government; long-term veterans of HCI, young professionals and students; all in an environment designed to encourage interaction. We invite you to actively participate in that interaction: introduce yourself to people, interact with presenters and speakers, renew old friendships and make new ones.

CHI is organized on behalf of ACM's Special Interest Group on Computer-Human Interaction (SIGCHI), an international community of professionals who share an interest in the many diverse facets of HCI. SIGCHI is committed both to advancing the field of HCI, to facilitate exchange of information within the SIGCHI community, and to support students to enter the domain.

The CHI conference is arguably the single most visible activity of SIGCHI, but we also sponsor and support a wide range of specialized conferences and workshops in areas ranging from interactive systems design to user interface technology to computer-supported cooperative work to "intelligent" user interfaces. Visit the SIGCHI website at **http://www.sigchi.org** to find our conference schedule, listing upcoming as well as past conferences.

SIGCHI and ACM produce some of the most respected publications in the field. All members receive interactions, a highly-acclaimed magazine covering the broad field of HCI and user interface design. ACM Transactions on Computer-Human Interactions (ToCHI), now in its 20st year, is our flagship journal - a quarterly publication with the top-quality archival research aimed at researchers and those translating research into practice.

SIGCHI is truly an international organization, with over 30 local chapters and 3 student chapters in 23 countries on 5 continents. We encourage all SIGCHI members to join their local chapter - or if there isn't one in your area, we would love to help you create one. And don't forget virtual communities! SIGCHI hosts dozens of electronic mailing lists on topics ranging from HCI and the Web, to HCI educations, to public policy and beyond. Those lists range from dozens of subscribers to thousands, and are an excellent way to keep up with the field and with friends and colleagues.

Finally, on behalf of ACM SGICHI, we again want to thank the conference committee and all of the hundreds of volunteers who make this conference possible. Their work makes this a rewarding experience for all of us.

Gerrit C. van der Veer
SIGCHI President

John "Scooter" Morris
SIGCHI Vice-President for Conferences

About SIGCHI

CHI 2013 is sponsored by ACM's Special Interest Group on Computer-Human Interaction (ACM SIGCHI). ACM, the Association for Computing Machinery, is an educational and scientific society uniting the world's computing educators, researchers, and professionals to inspire dialogue, share resources, and address the field's challenges. ACM strengthens the profession's collective voice through strong leadership, promotion of the highest standards, and recognition of technical excellence. ACM supports the professional growth of its members by providing opportunities for life-long learning, career development, and professional networking. ACM offers its more than 100,000 worldwide members cutting edge technical information through world class journals and magazines, dynamic special interest groups, and globally recognized conferences.

Visit **www.acm.org** for more information about the ACM.

SIGCHI is the premier international society for professionals, academics, and students who are interested in human-computer interaction (HCI). We provide a forum for the discussion of all aspects of HCI through our conferences, including our flagship CHI conference, publications, web sites, email discussion groups, and other services. We advance education in HCI through courses, workshops, and outreach, and we promote informal access to a wide range of individuals and organizations involved in HCI. Members can be involved in HCI-related activities with others in their region through local SIGCHI chapters. Come to the SIGCHI Town Hall meeting on Wednesday, May 1, at 12:40 in Meeting Room 241, or visit **www.sigchi.org** to learn more about SIGCHI.

ACM, the Association for Computing Machinery **http://www.acm.org/**, is an educational and scientific society uniting the world's computing educators, researchers and professionals to inspire dialogue, share resources and address the field's challenges. ACM strengthens the profession's collective voice through strong leadership, promotion of the highest standards, and recognition of technical excellence. ACM supports the professional growth of its members by providing opportunities for life-long learning, career development, and professional networking. ACM offers its 100,000 members cutting-edge technical information through world class journals and magazines, dynamic special interest groups and globally recognized conferences.

Welcome to CHI 2013!

The CHI Papers and Notes program is continuing to grow along with many of our sister conferences. We are pleased that CHI is still the leading venue for research in human-computer interaction.

CHI 2013 continued the use of subcommittees to manage the review process. Authors selected the subcommittee they believed was best qualified to review their work: For clarity, we retained the same committee identifiers as last year. Due to the continuing growth in submissions, we split several subcommittees into more manageable sizes. We are pleased with the subcommittee process: By dividing the work, each paper received much more careful discussion than would otherwise have been possible.

This year we had 1963 total submissions, including 1347 papers and 617 notes, representing a 24% growth over last year. We accepted 392 submissions (20%): 316 papers and 76 notes.

The CHI review process demands a tremendous amount of work from all areas of the human-computer interaction community. As co-chairs of the process, we are amazed at the ability of the community to organize itself to accomplish this task. We would like to thank the 2680 individual reviewers for their careful consideration of these papers. We also deeply appreciate the huge amount of time donated to this process by the 211-member program committee, who paid their own way to attend the face-to-face program committee meeting, an event larger than the average ACM conference.

We are proud of the work of the CHI 2013 program committee and hope that you enjoy these papers and notes, which represent the best research in human-computer interaction.

Stephen Brewster, *Glasgow University*
Susanne Bødker, *University of Aarhus*
CHI 2013 Papers & Notes Chairs

Table of Contents

Session 22: Evaluation Methods 1
Session Chair: Anthony Jameson
(German Research Center for Artificial Intelligence (DFKI), Germany)

Session 24: Co-Design with Users
Session Chair: Andrea Parker
(Northeastern University, USA)

Session 26: Language and Translation
Session Chair: Gahgene Gweon
(KAIST, Korea)

Session 27: Brain Sensing and Analysis
Session Chair: Petra Isenberg
(INRIA, France)

Session 30: Crowdwork and Online Communities
Session Chair: Krzysztof Gajos
(Harvard University, USA)

Session 116: Collaborative Creation

Session 118: Aesthetics and the Web

Session 120: Evaluation Methods 2

Session 122: Design for the Blind

Session 125: Mobile Interaction

CHI 2013 Conference Organization

Conference Chair
Wendy Mackay, *INRIA, France*

Technical Program

Technical Program Chairs
Patrick Baudisch, *Hasso Plattner Institute, Germany*
Michel Beaudouin-Lafon, *Université Paris-Sud, France*

Technical Program Chair Assistant
Dominik Schmidt, *Hasso Plattner Institute, Germany*

Papers and Notes
Stephen Brewster, *University of Glasgow, UK*
Susanne Bødker, *Aarhus University, Denmark*

Panels
Jofish Kaye, *Yahoo! Labs, USA*
Gillian Hayes, *University of California, Irvine, USA*

Case Studies
Jonathan Arnowitz, *Google, USA*
Michael Arent, *SAP, USA*
Dirk-Jan Hoets, *Flipside, The Netherlands*

Courses
Gregorio Convertino, *Xerox Research Centre Europe, France*
Wiliam Hudson, *Syntagm Ltd, UK*

Interactivity
Floyd Muller, *RMIT University, Australia*
Steve Benford, *University of Nottingham, UK*
Danielle Wilde, *RMIT University, Australia*
Atau Tanaka, *Goldsmiths College, UK*

Video Showcase
Jeffrey Bardzell, *Indiana University, Boomington, USA*
Nicolas Roussel, *INRIA, France*

SIGs
Kaisa Väänänen-Vainio-Mattila, *Tampere University of Technology, Finland*
Albrecht Schmidt, *University of Stuttgart, Germany*

Doctoral Consortium
Marti Hearst, *University of California, Berkeley, USA*

Mobile Apps

Workshops
Ido Guy, *IBM Research, Israel*
Nadir Weibel, *University of California, San Diego, USA*

Works in Progress
Henriette Cramer, *Yahoo! Labs, USA*
Jakob Bardram, *IT University of Copenhagen, Denmark*
Christian Holz, *Hasso Plattner Institute, Germany*
Dan Vogel, *University of Waterloo, Canada*

Student Design Competition
Thecla Schiphorst, *Simon Fraser University, Canada*
Carola Zwick, *Weissensee Art Academy Berlin, Germany*

Student Research Competition
Shaowen Bardzell, *Indiana University, Boomington, USA*
Celine Latulipe, *UNC Charlotte, USA*

Student Game Competition
Seth Cooper, *University of Washington, USA*
Heather Desurvire, *User Behavioristics Research, Inc., USA*
Magy Seif El-Nasr, *Northeastern University, USA*
Katherine Isbister, *NYU Poly, USA*
Regina Bernhaupt, *Université Paul Sabatier, France*

alt.chi
Amanda Williams, *Wyld Collective Ltd, Canada*
Daniela Rosner, *University of Washington, USA*

TOCHI papers
Jeffrey Nichols, *IBM Research, USA*

Best of CHI Awards
Scott Hudson, *Carnegie Mellon University, USA*

RepliCHI
Max Wilson, *University of Nottingham, UK*

Industry days
Elizabeth Dykstra-Erickson, *Nuance Communications, Inc., USA*
Evan Gerber, *Fidelity Investments, USA*
Scott Weiss, *Misys, UK*
Jonathan Arnowitz, *Google, USA*

Communities

Communities Chairs
Bo Begole, *Samsung Information Systems, USA*
Kristina Höök, *KTH, Sweden*

Design Community
Patrick Olivier, *Newcastle University, UK*
Ellen Yi-Luen Do, *Georgia Tech, USA*

Engineering Community
Fabio Paterno, *CNR-ISTI, Italy*
Philippe Palanque, *Université Paul Sabatier, France*

Management Community
Janice Rohn, *Experian, USA*
Carola Fellenz Thompson, *zSpace, USA*

Child Computer Interaction Community
Janet Read, *University of Central Lancashire, UK*
Juan Pablo Hourcade, *University of Iowa, USA*

Sustainability Community
Lisa P. Nathan, *University of British Columbia, Canada*
Samuel Mann, *Otago Polytechnic, New Zealand*

Health Community
Karen Cheng, *University of California, Irvine, USA*
Kelly Caine, *Clemson University, USA*

Arts Community
David England, *Liverpool John Moores University, UK*
Jill fantauzzacoffin, *Georgia Tech, USA*

User Exp. & Usability Community
Virpi Roto, *Aalto University, Finland*
Arnold Lund, *GE Global Research, USA*

Entertainment and Games Community
Regina Bernhaupt, *ruwido, Austria*
Katherine Isbister, *NYU Poly, USA*

Operations

Student Volunteer Coordinators
Bobby Beaton, *Virginia Tech, USA*
Lindsay Reynolds, *Cornell University, USA*

Technology Liaison
Scooter Morris, *University of California, San Francisco, USA*

Technical Liaison
Sara Drenner, *BI Worldwide*

Data
Max von Kleek, *MIT, USA*

Graphic Design
Jeremy Boy, *INRIA, France*
Lora Oehlberg, *INRIA, France*
Dario Rodighiero, *Sciences Po, France*

Webmaster
Cary-Anne Olsen, *University of Texas, Austin, USA*
Caris Hurd, *University of Texas, Austin, USA*
Vicky McArthur, *York University, Canada*

Social Media
Cliff Lampe, *University of Michigan, USA*
Katie Panciera, *Facebook, USA*

Video previews
Gene Golovchinsky, *FX Palo Alto Laboratory, Inc., USA*
Gonzalo Ramos, *Microsoft, USA*

Proceedings
Michael Ekstrand, *University of Minnesota, USA*
Stéphane Conversy, *ENAC, France*

Proceedings
Robert J. Teather, *York University, Canada*

Proceedings
Robert J. Teather, *York University, Canada*
Stephen Oney, *Carnegie Mellon University, USA*
Jason Wiese, *Carnegie Mellon University, USA*
Eiji Hayashi, *Carnegie Mellon University, USA*

Interactive Schedule
Arvind Satyanarayan, *Stanford University, USA*
Daniel Strazzulla, *INRIA, France*
Clemens Klokmose, *Aarhus University, Denmark*

Community-sourcing and Scheduling
Steven Dow, *Carnegie Mellon University, USA*
Paul André, *Carnegie Mellon University, USA*
Lydia Chilton, *University of Washington, USA*
Juho Kim, *MIT, USA*
Rob Miller, *MIT, USA*
Haoqi Zhang, *Northwestern & MIT, USA*

Posters
James Eagan, *Telecom ParisTech, France*

Publicity
Molly Mackinlay, *Stanford University, USA*

PC Meeting Liaison
Eric Lecolinet, *Telecom ParisTech, France*

CHI Women's Breakfast
Allison Druin, *University of Maryland, USA*

Sponsors and Exhibits
Carol Klyver, *Foundations of Excellence*

Reviewing Software
James Stewart, *Precision Conference, Canada*

Conference Logistics
Janeé Pelletier, *Conference & Logistics, USA*
Allison Perrelli, *Conference & Logistics, USA*

Local Logistics
François Tapissier, *Dakini, France*

Registration
Yvonne Lopez, *Executive Events, Inc., USA*
Jill Skuba, *Executive Events, Inc., USA*

CMC Liaison
John "Scooter" Morris, *University of California, San Francisco, USA*

ACM Staff Liaison
Ashley Cozzi, *ACM, USA*

CHI 2013 Sponsors, Supporters, Contributors, & Friends

acm Association for Computing Machinery

SIGCHI

CHI Hero & Champion Sponsors

JCDecaux

Bloomberg

DAUPHINE UNIVERSITÉ PARIS

Google

ebay

PayPal

Inria
INVENTORS FOR THE DIGITAL WORLD

Microsoft

TELECOM ParisTech

CHI Contributing Sponsors

AUTODESK

digiteo
Research in science and technology of information

facebook

îledeFrance

NOKIA

YAHOO!

Friends of CHI

cran

IBM

GE

The Whats and Hows of Programmers' Foraging Diets

David J. Piorkowski[1], Scott D. Fleming[2], Irwin Kwan[1], Margaret M. Burnett[1],
Chris Scaffidi[1], Rachel K.E. Bellamy[3], Joshua Jordhal[1]

[1]Oregon State University
Corvallis, Oregon, USA

[2]University of Memphis
Memphis, Tennessee, USA

[3]IBM Research
Hawthorne, New York, USA

{piorkoda, kwan, burnett, cscaffid}@eecs.oregonstate.edu,
scott.fleming@cs.umemphis.edu, rachel@us.ibm.com

ABSTRACT

One of the least studied areas of Information Foraging Theory is diet: the information foragers choose to seek. For example, do foragers choose solely based on cost, or do they stubbornly pursue certain diets regardless of cost? Do their debugging strategies vary with their diets? To investigate "what" and "how" questions like these for the domain of software debugging, we qualitatively analyzed 9 professional developers' foraging goals, goal patterns, and strategies. Participants spent 50% of their time foraging. Of their foraging, 58% fell into distinct dietary patterns—mostly in patterns not previously discussed in the literature. In general, programmers' foraging strategies leaned more heavily toward enrichment than we expected, but different strategies aligned with different goal types. These and our other findings help fill the gap as to what programmers' dietary goals are and how their strategies relate to those goals.

Author Keywords

Information foraging theory; information diet; debugging strategies

ACM Classification Keywords

D.2.5 [Software Engineering]: Testing and Debugging;

H.1.2 [Information Systems]: User/Machine Systems—Human factors

INTRODUCTION

Pirolli et al.'s pioneering work on Information Foraging Theory (IFT) [18] has greatly influenced our community's understanding of how humans seek information within information-rich environments such as the Web. The theory is based on the idea that humans seek information in a manner analogous to the way animals seek food in the wild. In short, it states that a human information predator seeks information prey by following information scent through an environment. IFT has been well validated empirically (e.g., [3,6,12,13,14,20]). It has facilitated predictive models of how people navigate as they forage within websites (e.g.,

[3,18,21]) and during software maintenance tasks (e.g., [12,13]). Furthermore, the theory has spawned principles for the design of interfaces and tools that help people forage (e.g., [16,24]).

One area of potential for IFT that so far has been mostly untapped is using the theory to understand the *diets* of predators in a particular problem domain—that is, to understand the types of information goals those predators desire. A notable exception is Evans and Card [4], who investigated the diets of web users who were "early adopters." They discovered that these users' diets were considerably different from the information commonly provided by mainstream news sites, and they identified the niche topics that made up the users' diets. They also noted that the information sources chosen by these users reduced the cost of attention by lowering the cost of social foraging and social interpretation. Clearly, these findings have strong implications for the design of sites to support such users. The Evans and Card work demonstrates the potential benefits of applying information foraging ideas to understand the diets of people in particular contexts.

Inspired in part by the Evans/Card paper, our work aims to expand our understanding of IFT diets by investigating the diets of professional software developers engaged in debugging. Work in the software engineering (SE) literature has investigated related ideas, such as the questions that programmers ask (e.g., [5,10,11,23]), but that work was not grounded in a theory, such as IFT. Thus, by investigating the information diets of professional programmers from an IFT perspective, our work aims to help bridge the gap between such results from the SE literature and the IFT foundations and results from the HCI literature.

For an understanding of the "whats" of diet to be truly useful, we also need to understand the "hows". Toward this end, we also investigate, from an IFT perspective, the *strategies* that programmers use during foraging. The literature contains numerous works on program debugging strategies (see [22] for a summary), but these have not been tied to IFT. We believe that such strategies both influence and are influenced by programmers' diets, and this paper investigates these ties.

Thus, in this paper, we address the following research questions with a qualitative empirical study.

- RQ1 (diet "whats"): What types of information goals do professional programmers forage for during debugging, and how do those goals relate to one another?
- RQ2 (foraging "hows"): How do professional programmers forage: what foraging strategies do they use?
- RQ3 ("whats" meet "hows"): Do professional programmers favor different strategies when foraging for different types of information?

BACKGROUND

Information Foraging Theory

Information foraging theory is a theory of how people seek information during information-intensive tasks [19]. IFT was inspired by biological theories of how animals seek food in the wild. In IFT, a *predator* (person seeking information) pursues *prey* (valuable sources of information) through a *topology* (collection of navigable paths through an information environment). What information constitutes valuable prey depends on the predator's *information goals*. Predators find prey by following information *scent* that they infer from *cues* in the environment, such as the labels on buttons or clickable pictures that adorn navigation options. Thus, the scent of a cue is the predator's assessment of the value and cost of information sources obtained by taking a navigation option associated with that cue.

The focus of this paper is predator *diet*, that is, the variety of information types that a predator consumes. A predator's *information goals* define his/her "ideal" diet, but what predators actually consume depends also on what is available in the environment and how costly the information is to obtain. The relationship between cost and diet in IFT is explained well by Anderson's notion of *rational analysis*, which is based on the idea that humans tend toward strategies that optimally adapt to the environment [1].

To help satisfy their diets, predators commonly engage in *enrichment*, that is, transforming the environment to facilitate foraging. For example, by searching on the Web, the predator enriches the environment by creating a new patch of search results, which could potentially satisfy some or all of the predator's information goals. In addition to using search tools, other examples of enrichment include writing a to-do list on a piece of paper and running a test on a program to create a patch of relevant program output.

The earliest IFT research was in the domain of user-web interaction. For example, computational models based on IFT have successfully predicted web foraging behavior [3,6,18]. IFT has gone on to inspire practical principles and tools for designing web sites and user interfaces [24,25].

Information Foraging for Debugging Software

In the domain of software development (and especially debugging), information foraging often occurs in the context of sensemaking. The *sensemaking process* in an information-rich domain has been represented as a series of two main learning loops: foraging for information, and making sense of the foraged information [20]. In this model, the role of IFT is central. In fact, in Grigoreanu et al.'s sensemaking study of end-user debugging [8] (which applied the Pirolli/Card sensemaking model [20]) found that the foraging loop dominated the participants' sensemaking process.

In the software engineering community, there has been recent research focused on supporting the questions programmers ask [5,10,11,23], and these questions can be viewed as surrogates for programmers' information goals. The software engineering analyses and tools have not been grounded in theory, but their empirical success shows that they are useful. A premise of this paper is that IFT may be able to provide a richer, more cohesive understanding of programmers' information seeking behaviors than atheoretic efforts. Recently, we and a few others have begun investigating the efficacy of using IFT to understand programmer information-seeking (e.g., [12,13,14,15,16]). However, that work focused only on how programmers respond to cues. This paper instead investigates the whats and hows of their diets, i.e., the relationship between programmers' information goals and debugging strategies.

METHODOLOGY

Study Data

To investigate our research questions, we analyzed a set of nine videos we collected in a previous study of professional software developers debugging in an Eclipse environment [16]. In that study, the developers used the usual Eclipse tools, plus a new IFT-based code recommender tool powered with a variety of recommendation algorithms. This setup is consistent with real-world scenarios in which developers work on unfamiliar code, such as a new team member being brought "onboard" a project, a developer on a team needing to work on code that another team member wrote, or a newcomer to an open-source project.

To summarize the study setup, each video included screen-capture video, audio of what the participant said, and video of the participant's face. Participants "talked aloud" as they worked. Their task was to fix a real bug in the jEdit text editor, a mature open source project. None of the participants had seen the jEdit code before, and with 6468 methods, it provided a large information space in which to forage. The bug was from an actual bug report (#2548764) and regarded a problem with deleting "folded" text. Each debugging session lasted two hours with a short break halfway through. No participants completed the task, and all exhibited instances of foraging throughout the two hours.

Categorization Procedures

We used a qualitative, multi-part coding approach to analyze these videos. First, we segmented the videos into 30-second intervals, resulting in roughly 70 segments per video. (We chose 30 seconds to be long enough for participants to verbalize a goal.) We then coded each segment to identify (1) instances of foraging, (2) participants' information goals, and (3) participant debugging strategies, allowing multiple codes per segment. To enhance generalizability, these code sets were drawn from prior studies, as we describe below.

To ensure reliability, we followed standard inter-rater reliability practices. Two researchers first worked together on a small portion of the data to agree on coding rules. They then independently coded 20% of the segments to test the agreement level. We computed agreement using the Jaccard index, as it is suitable when multiple codes are allowed per segment, as in our case. We performed a separate coding pass (with separate reliability checks) for each code set. For each pass, agreement exceeded 80%, so the two researchers then divided up the coding of the remaining data.

Information Foraging Behavior Codes
To code whether a participant showed evidence of information foraging within a 30-second segment, we used a two-part coding process. First, we segmented around participants' utterances and coded the segments. The codes were *foraging-start*, *foraging-end*, and *foraging-ongoing*. This code set was inspired by the scent-following code set used in [14], but ours focused only on whether or not foraging occurred, and not whether scent was lost, gained, etc. We coded an utterance as *foraging-start* when participants stated an intention to pursue a particular information goal and then took accompanying action to seek that goal, like searching. We coded an utterance as *foraging-end* when participants stated that they had learned some information, or expressed giving up on a goal. We coded an utterance as *foraging-ongoing* when participants restated a previously stated goal, or said they were still looking for something.

In the second part of the coding process, we used the utterance codes from the first part to code each 30-second segment as *foraging* or *non-foraging*. A segment was *foraging* if it had an utterance coded as *foraging-start*, *foraging-ongoing*, or *foraging-end*, else it was *non-foraging*. Also, to include segments in which a participant may not have explicitly made an utterance, we also coded segments in between *foraging-start* and *foraging-end* utterances as *foraging*. However, some segments were exceptions. If a participant clearly never foraged during a segment, we coded the segment as *non-foraging*. *Non-foraging* activities included configuring Eclipse or reasoning aloud about the task. Using this coding scheme independently, two researchers achieved 82% agreement on 20% of the data before dividing up and individually coding the remaining data.

Information Goal Codes
We based the Information Goal code set on Sillito et al.'s empirically based taxonomy of 44 questions programmers ask, which Sillito et al. had grouped into four types [23]. We coded the 30-second segments against the 44 questions, and then grouped them into the four types for presentation brevity. (Results for the 44 individual questions are given in Appendix A of the expanded version [17].) Table 1 lists the

types, with a few examples of the Sillito questions that were our actual code set. We chose the Sillito questions for several reasons. First, they are a good fit for the program-debugging domain, because they categorize information needs specific to programmers. Second, they seem generalizable to a broad range of programming languages and environments, since Sillito et al. collected them from a study that covered seven different programming languages and at least eight different programming environments. Third, they are consistent with information goals identified in other studies from both programming and non-programming domains (e.g., [8,9,14,20]). Finally, they are specific and low-level, enabling a code set with the potential for high interrater reliability.

We coded each participant utterance in the foraging segments (as per our foraging code set above) to one of Sillito's questions. We also included a code of *other* goals, for utterances that did not match any of the questions. Using this scheme, two coders achieved 80% agreement on 20% of the data, and then split up the rest of the coding task.

The coding resulted in 384 goals coded using the Sillito question codes and 286 *other* goals. About one fourth of the utterances coded *other* were similar to one of the Sillito questions, but were not a precise match, so for reasons of rigor, we did not include them. The remaining *other* goals were about concepts (e.g., the bug's specifications, how to use the jEdit "fold" feature, the Eclipse environment, etc.) that are beyond the scope of this paper.

Information Goal Patterns
To investigate how information goals relate to each other, we categorized the information goal data into the five patterns in Table 2. Four of the patterns (*Stairstep*, *Restart*, *Pyramid*, and *Oscillate*) came from literature suggesting progressions in these sequences (e.g., [8,20,23]). The fifth pattern, *Repeat*, emerged as a common pattern during the course of our analysis.

Following the Table 2 definitions, we used a greedy pat-

Goal Type	Codes	Examples of Sillito questions
1-initial: Find initial focus points	Sillito questions 1–5	#2: Where in the code is the text of this error message or UI element? #5: Is there an entity named something like this in that unit?
2-build: Build on those points	Sillito questions 6–20	#14: Where are instances of this class created? #20: What data is being modified in this code?
3-group: Understand a group of related code	Sillito questions 21–33	#22: How are these types or objects related? #29: How is control getting (from here to) here?
4-groups: Understand groups of groups	Sillito questions 34–44	#35: What are the differences between these files or types? #43: What will be the total impact of this change?

Table 1. Information goal types with examples [23].

tern-matching algorithm (which always returned the longest possible matches) to identify instances of the patterns in the goal data. We did not allow matches that contained a gap of 5 or more minutes (i.e., 10 or more 30-second segments) between goal utterances or contained an interruption/intervention, such as the between-session break. We permitted overlapping patterns, except for instances of *Oscillate* completely contained within a *Stairstep* or *Pyramid,* and for instances of *Stairstep* completely contained within a *Pyramid*. We omitted *Oscillate* and *Stairstep* instances in these cases, because they were essential components of the containing patterns. A single author performed this analysis because the definitions were objective and the analysis automatable.

Debugging Strategy Codes

To code participant strategies, we reused Grigoreanu et al.'s debugging strategy code set [7]. We chose these strategy codes because, while being specific to the program debugging domain, each also maps cleanly to one of the three key foraging activities [19]: within-patch foraging, between-patch foraging, and enrichment. (Technically, enrichment is a between-patch foraging activity; however, in this paper, we use the term *between-patch foraging* to include only non-enrichment activities.)

Table 3 lists the strategy codes grouped by type of foraging activity. The Within-Patch strategies all involve looking for information within the contents of a single patch, such as in a Java method or web page. The Between-Patch strategies all involve navigating between different patches by selecting and clicking links, such as those provided by the recommender tool. The Enrichment strategies all involve manipulating the environment to facilitate foraging, for example, by creating a new patch of search results.

For each segment, we looked for evidence of the participant applying each strategy using indicators such as those shown in Table 3. A segment could have multiple strategy codes. Using this scheme, two coders achieved 80% agreement on 28% of the data, and then divided up the remaining data.

RESULTS

Preliminaries: How much foraging did they do?

As Table 4 shows, participants spent 50% of their 2-hour sessions foraging on average. We were unable to find prior measures of programmer foraging with which to compare this result, but Ko et al. measured time spent on *mechanics* of navigation. Their programmers spent 35% of the time on "the mechanics of navigation between code fragments" [10]. Even our participant who foraged the least still did so more than 35% of the time.

RQ1: The Whats of Programmers' Diets

A Diversity of Dietary Whats

Although all participants had the same high-level information goal (to find the information needed to fix the bug),

their dietary preferences were diverse, as Table 5 shows. (Recall the four goal types defined in Table 1.) In aggregate, participants pursued the most goals of Type 1-initial,

Pattern	Example	Formal Definition
Oscillate: Back and forth between two adjacent types repeatedly.	1121212212	$O = O_1 \mid O_2$ where: $O_1 = UpDn(1,2) \mid UpDn(2,1)$ $O_2 = UpDn(2,3) \mid UpDn(3,2)$ $UpDn(a,b) = a+b+(a+b+)+a*$
Stairstep: From 1 up through adjacent types to at least 3.	1122223	*Stairstep* = $(1+2*)+ (2+3*)+ 3$
Restart: Jump off the Stairstep down to 1.	112331	*Restart* = *Stairstep* 1
Pyramid: Up then down the stairsteps. Constraint: If Pyramid, then not Stairstep.	12321	*Pyramid* = *Pup Pdown* | $2+ Pup\ Pdown$ 1 where: $Pup = (1+2*)+(2+3*)+$ $Pdown = (3+2*)+(2+1*)+$
Repeat: One type at least 10 times.	1111111111	*Repeat* = 11111111111* | 22222222222* | 33333333333* | 44444444444*

Table 2. Information goal patterns. Each definition is a regular expression of Goal Type instances (+ means 1 or more instances, * means 0 or more; "|" means "or"). E.g.: 1+2+ means one or more instances of Type 1, then one or more of Type 2. We omit Type 4s next to Type 3s because 4 never followed 3 in our data.

Strategy	Example Indicators
Within-Patch Strategies	
Specification checking	Looking for info by reading within the bug description
Spatial	Looking for info by reading through the list of package contents in the Package Explorer
Code inspection	Looking for info by reading within a Java code file
File inspection	Looking for info by reading within a non-code file, such as a Java properties file
Seeking help-Docs	Looking for info by reading within the jEdit documentation
Between-Patch Strategies	
Control flow	Following control dependencies
Dataflow	Following data dependencies
Feedback following	Following method links from the recommender tool
Enrichment Strategies	
Code search	Creating a patch of search results with the Eclipse code search utility
Testing	Creating a patch of program output or internal state to inspect
To-do listing	Writing notes on paper
Seeking help-Search	Creating a patch of search results with an (external) web search for info on bug/code

Table 3. Debugging strategy code set [7] with example indicators for each strategy.

Participant:	P2	P3	P5	P6	P7	P8	P9	P10	P11	Mean
Time Foraging:	52%	71%	38%	63%	46%	43%	48%	42%	49%	50%

Table 4. Participants spent a large fraction of their time, ranging from 38% to 71%, foraging for information.

with slightly fewer in 2-build, and many fewer in the more complex 3-group and 4-groups. However, most participants did not conform to the aggregate: Only P6 and P9 had goal counts consistent with the aggregate.

Patterns of Dietary Relationships
Despite their dietary diversity, the progression of information goals that participants pursued often followed certain patterns (summarized in Table 6 and Figure 1; patterns defined in Table 2). Eight of the nine participants displayed one or more of the patterns, and 58% of segments in which a participant expressed a goal were part of a larger pattern. Participants exhibited a median of 1.5 patterns each, with P6 exhibiting all five.

For example, P6's use of the Restart pattern at the end of a Stairstep is shown in the Figure 1e example. The Restart occurred when his Stairstep progression culminated in gaining the information he sought about the handleMessage method's relationship to the editor (a Type 3-group goal):

Goal Type	P2	P3	P5	P6	P7	P8	P9	P10	P11	Total
1-initial		6	76	0	34	18	8	18	8	2	170
2-build	3	1	2	24	34	17	16	15	11	123
3-group	2	2	2	3	2	3	15	9	11	49
4-groups	13	1	0	0	0	9	0	3	16	42
Total	24	80	4	61	54	37	49	35	40	384

Table 5. Number of segments spent on the (codeable) types of information goals. Gray highlights each participant's most-pursued goal type.

Pattern	P2	P3	P5	P6	P7	P8	P9	P10	P11
Repeat	1(4)	2(1)		1(1)	1(2)			1(2)	1(4)
Oscillate				1(1,2)	2(1,2)			1(3,2)	1(3,2)
Stairstep				1					
Pyramid				1		1	2	1	
Restart				1					

Table 6: Frequency of pattern instances exhibited by each participant. The numbers in parentheses indicate the type of goals within the pattern (e.g., 1(3,2) in the Oscillate row indicates patterns like 33322322, as defined in Table 2).

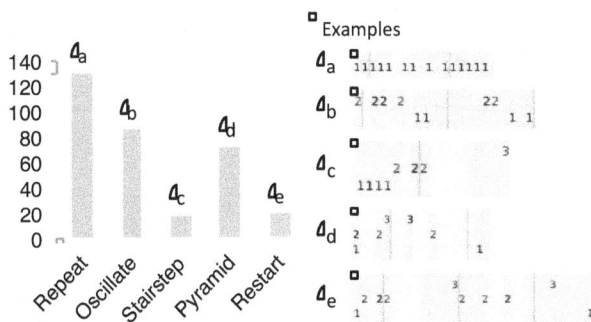

Figure 1. Frequency of goal patterns. Y-axis is count of segments in each pattern. Each bar is labeled with an example from the participants' videos. The beige background denotes foraging; white is non-foraging (e.g., studying the code that has been found); and numbers denote the goal types.

P6: "So this (handleMessage) is handling some events for the editor."

This was what P6 had wanted to know, so he then changed to a new line of foraging, thus dropping down to a Type 1-initial goal:

P6: "But I don't know how the menu is hooked up to this. ... I wonder if there is some method that might be named 'delete lines' ..." [P6 starts searching in package explorer.]

Some of these patterns were predicted by the literature. Sillito et al. [23] suggested one progression: find an initial focus (1-initial), then build on it (2-build), then understand a group of related foci (3-group), and finally understand groups of groups (4-groups). Other empirical studies have found a similar progression from 1-initial to 2-build, including our previous work on information foraging during debugging (characterized there as "debugging modes") [14], and earlier work on how people seek information in web environments (summarized in [9]). Furthermore, the notion of progressing from Type 1-initial to 2-build to 3-group to 4-groups is consistent with prior results from applying Pirolli and Card's sensemaking model [20] to intelligence analysts and to end-user debuggers [8].

However, participants did not usually organize their foraging in the ways suggested by the above literature: Stairstep, Pyramid, and Restart together accounted for only 22% of the pattern segments. In fact, only four of the participants used any of them at all! This finding suggests that idealized progressions outlined in prior research miss much of how programmers forage for information in code, at least in the widely used Eclipse environment.

In contrast to the patterns from the literature, the Repeat pattern, which emerged from our study, occurred frequently. In Repeat, a participant spent extended periods following one information goal type. 6 of the 9 participants exhibited this pattern—greater usage than any other pattern.

Why did participants exhibit the above patterns? To answer this question, we need two pieces of information: what strategies they used for their foraging, and how those strategies came together with their goals and goal patterns. We discuss each of these in turn in the next two sections.

RQ2: The Hows: Strategies during Foraging
Recall from Methodology (Table 3) that each debugging strategy maps to an IFT activity: within-patch foraging, between-patch foraging, and enrichment. Table 7 shows each participant's strategy usage by IFT category.

Debugging Strategies Meet IFT
Since much of the prior IFT research has focused on between-patch scent following (e.g., [3,13]), we were surprised that only 24% of participants' foraging fell into that category. Participants spent considerably more time foraging within patches and performing enrichment.

As Table 7 shows, participants used a diverse mix of strategies (median of 8 different strategies); however, each foraging category had clearly dominant strategies. Spatial was the participants' primary Within-Patch strategy; Control Flow was their primary Between-Patch strategy; and Code Search and Testing were together (but especially Testing) their primary Enrichment strategies.

What Participants Used Enrichment For

Enrichment is an activity wherein the predator changes the environment to facilitate foraging [19]. The participants changed their environments in two ways. Code Search, Seek Help-Search, and To-Do Listing involved creating a patch of *links* to other patches for the predator to *navigate*. In contrast, Testing involved creating patches of information *content* for the predator to *process*.

Most participants strongly favored one or the other of these types of enrichment strategies. In particular, they either favored creating patches of linked search results with Code Search, or creating patches of runtime state information with Testing. In fact, over half of the participants used only one of Code Search or Testing. For example, Participant P7 used Code Search repeatedly, trying to find methods that implemented line deletion and folding in jEdit:

> P7: "Let's see if I can find something like what is in that bug report." [Searches for *delete lines*. No results.] "Let's just look for 'explicit fold'." [Searches for *explicit fold*.] "Finally, something that actually has to do with folding..."

In contrast, P5 stepped through program runs repeatedly, collecting information about its internal state:

> P5: [Looks at the debugger's Variable Watch view.] "*lineCount* is zero." [Reads code.] "I'm going to step into that

(method)" [Steps.] "*count* is greater than–now *count* is zero. [Steps again.] "I'm stepping through the code. ... I'm trying to understand what this code is doing."

Despite prior findings about users' preference for searching (e.g., [2]), four of the nine participants used neither Code Search nor Seek Help-Search. This lack of searching cannot be because the task was too easy (no one finished) or the code base was too small (it had 6468 methods). However, earlier findings on web information processing [9] may explain this result. Hearst points out that, in many cases, browsing works better than searching because it is mentally less costly to *recognize* a piece of information than it is to *recall* it, and recall is often needed to formulate an effective search query. Consistent with Hearst's observation, every participant used the Code Inspection strategy.

Go-To Strategies for Foraging

Reconsidering Table 7 from a most-used perspective, some strategies stand out as having been used particularly often for one or more aspects of foraging. The leftmost four (white) columns of Table 8 summarize.

RQ3: Whats Meet Hows: Dietary Strategies

Strategies by Goal Type

Table 9 and Figure 2 tie all 12 of the strategies back to the participants' dietary goals. As the table and figure show, some strategies were strongly tied to particular goal types. For example, Specification Checking was used only for Type 1-initial goals, and Code Inspection was used primarily for Type 2-build goals. Figure 2 shows that participants used Code Search (labeled a) and Spatial (labeled b) more than the other strategies with their Type 1-initial goals. From a patch perspective, Spatial seemed particularly suited to helping participants cope with large patches, and Code Search with large spaces of patches. For example, P6 spent considerable time performing Spatial in the Package

Strategy	P2	P3	P5	P6	P7	P8	P9	P10	P11	Total
Within-Patch Strategies										
Spec. Checking	2	9	0	11	0	0	0	3	0	25
Spatial	25	39	5	28	31	14	47	19	12	220
Code Inspection	4	9	10	16	17	15	22	7	30	130
File Inspection	0	6	0	4	0	0	0	3	0	13
Seek Help-Doc	4	0	0	0	0	0	0	2	0	6
Total:	35	63	15	59	48	29	69	34	42	394
Between-Patch Strategies										
Control Flow	19	1	18	14	20	27	23	14	21	157
Data Flow	0	0	5	1	2	4	0	7	5	24
Feedback Follow.	4	8	12	5	6	4	6	1	6	52
Total:	23	9	35	20	28	35	29	22	31	232
Enrichment Strategies										
Code Search	0	51	0	29	33	4	0	12	0	129
Testing	36	0	34	14	5	37	30	22	45	223
Todo Listing	1	1	0	1	1	2	0	0	5	11
Seek Help-Search	0	4	0	0	0	0	0	0	0	4
Total:	37	56	34	44	39	43	30	34	49	366
Overall Total:	95	128	84	123	115	107	128	90	122	992

Table 7. Usage (segment counts) of each strategy during foraging. Gray cells indicate the maximum frequency by participant and by strategy category. Although participants foraged in a total of 660 segments, the overall total of strategy segments (992) is greater because participants used multiple strategies during some segments.

Strategy	How many used it?	Top strategy for...			
		... which participants	... which IFT category	... which Goal Type	... which Patterns
Within-Patch Strategies					
Spatial	all 9	P9	Within	2-Build	Pyramid
Code Inspect.	all 9	-	-	-	-
Between-Patch Strategies					
Control Flow	all 9	-	Between	-	Restart
Feedback Follow.	all 9	-	-	-	-
Enrichment Strategies					
Code Search	5	P3, P6, P7	-	1-initial	Repeat, Oscillate, Stairstep
Testing	8	P2, P5, P8, P10, P11	Enrich.	3-group, 4-groups	-

Table 8. These 6 strategies (out of 12) stood out. Each of these was used by everyone, was at least one person's most-used strategy, or was the top strategy for an IFT category.

Explorer view (a patch containing hundreds of lines), looking for a Java class on which to focus:

> P6: "I keep thinking this menu package gotta be involved somehow." [P6 scans down the list of Java classes inside the menu package in Eclipse's Package Explorer view.]

P3, on the other hand, applied Code Search to search the

Strategy	Information Goal Type				Total
	1-initial	2-build	3-group	4-groups	
Within-Patch Strategies					
Spec Checking	24	0	0	0	24
Spatial	92	**62**	23	8	185
Code Inspection	13	56	20	4	93
File Inspection	10	0	0	0	10
Seeking Help-Docs	2	0	0	0	2
Total:	141	118	43	12	314
Between-Patch Strategies					
Control Flow	21	46	14	9	90
Dataflow	1	4	3	1	9
Feedback Following	13	15	7	1	36
Total:	35	65	24	11	135
Enrichment Strategies					
Code Search	**104**	47	2	1	154
Testing	25	26	**26**	**30**	107
To-Do Listing	1	4	1	3	9
Seeking Help-Search	0	0	0	0	0
Total:	130	77	29	34	270
Overall Total:	306	260	96	57	719

Table 9. Strategy usage by goal types. Gray highlights the maximum strategy usage for each goal type. The overall total (719) is greater than the total foraging segments (660) because some segments contained multiple strategies. The total for Seeking Help-Search was 0 because none of the strategy's 4 instances co-occurred with a goal statement.

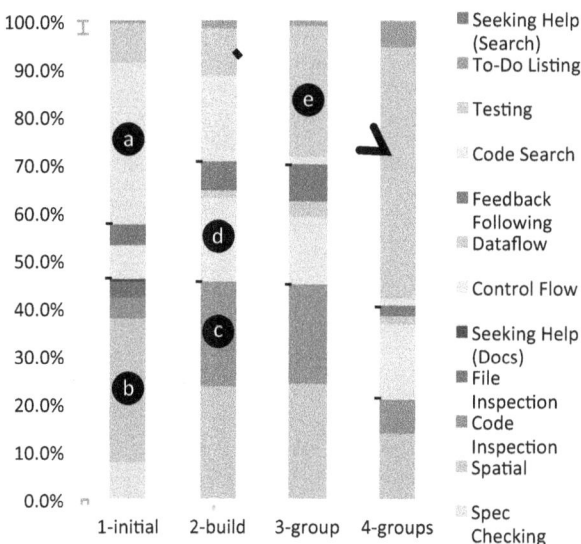

Figure 2: Strategy proportions by goal type. Strategies are color-coded, with black bars separating the IFT categories. Red: Within-Patch. Green: Between-Patch. Blue: Enrichment.

6468 methods for code related to deleting lines in jEdit:

> P3: "I would imagine that I would look for the word 'delete' perhaps, especially given that that's the term that's used in the menu." [Executes a search for *delete*.]

Participants tended toward different strategies for the Type 2–4 goals, which express progressively deeper relationships among code entities. For example, Figure 2 shows the shift away from Code Search and Spatial, and toward Code Inspection (c) and Control Flow (d) for Type 2-build and Type 3-group goals. Testing in particular (e) increased markedly from Type 2-build to Type 4-groups goals.

Considering participants' goal patterns in the context of their strategies (summarized in Table 10) sheds additional light on why the patterns emerged.

Pattern Repeat: Constant Goal Type, Constant Strategies
Pattern Repeat, repeated pursuit of a single goal type, was also characterized by repeated participant use of a constant handful of *strategies*. The Repeat instances occurred in two cases. In one case, participants' debugging strategies were producing the desired goals efficiently, i.e., at such low cost to the participants that staying with that goal type and strategy was a good way to optimize their costs. In the other case, their strategy for that goal type was so ineffective, they needed a long time to fulfill that type of dietary need.

As an example of the first case, P7 followed the Repeat pattern on Type 2-build goals using three strategies continuously: Spatial, Code Inspection, and Control Flow. Eclipse supports all three with low-cost navigation tools, such as

Pattern	Participant	Strategy		
		Within-Patch	Between-Patch	Enrichment
Repeat(1)	P3	70%	6%	71%
	P6	75%	0%	75%
Repeat(2)	P7	83%	72%	48%
	P10	50%	38%	63%
Repeat(4)	P2	40%	10%	80%
	P11	30%	40%	90%
	Median:	60%	24%	**73%**
Oscillate(1,2)	P6	79%	8%	63%
	P7	74%	57%	60%
Oscillate(3,2)	P10	40%	47%	73%
	P11	100%	48%	62%
	Median:	**77%**	47%	62%
Pyramid	P6	62%	57%	76%
	P8	53%	53%	88%
	P9	100%	21%	7%
	P10	53%	29%	76%
	Median:	57%	41%	**76%**
Restart	P6	61%	57%	**70%**
Stairstep	P6	62%	57%	**76%**

Table 10. Percentage of goal-pattern segments that co-occurred with each category of strategy. Recall that multiple strategies were allowed per segment. Gray denotes the maximum category for each pattern.

one-click navigation to the declaration of any class, method, or variable. P7 used these features to efficiently fulfill his Type 2-build goals, and fulfilled multiple goals, often building from one goal to the next using the same strategies.

When participants followed the Repeat pattern on goals of Type 1-initial or of Type 4-groups, their strategies were still constant, but not as fruitful. In the cases involving Type 1-initial, participants used Code Search (Enrichment) and Spatial (Within-Patch) extensively, but not particularly fruitfully, looking for a place to start. For example, Figure 3 shows P3 repeatedly using Code Search to find an initial starting point. Likewise, in P11's use of Repeat on his Type 4-groups goals, he used Testing across numerous segments of the pattern, trying to understand the relationship between changes he had made and the rest of jEdit's functionality. He pieced the information together by laboriously gathering it in small bits, one execution of the program at a time.

Pattern Oscillate: Changing Strategies to Dig Deeper

For the participants who followed the Oscillate pattern on Type 1-initial and 2-build goals, the story was similar to Repeat on Type 1-initial, except the oscillators tended to seek additional information from their search results. In particular, the oscillating participants would typically do a code search, explore the results a bit, decide they were on the wrong track, and return to searching. Unlike the Repeat pattern, the participants we observed within the Oscillate pattern switched strategies rapidly along with their goals. Figure 4 illustrates this behavior for P6.

Patterns for Enrichment and Goal Switching

Table 10 suggests that Enrichment tended to drive the interrelated Pyramid (up then down the stairs), Restart (stairs followed by starting again), and Stairstep (climb the stairs) patterns. Participants following the Pyramid pattern used the Enrichment strategies of Code Search and Testing equally often, but P6's instances of Stairstep and Repeat were characterized by almost exclusive use of the Code Search strategy. (Only P6 followed these two patterns.)

All three patterns were characterized by rapid goal fulfillment followed by a rapid switch to the next goal. This rapid fulfillment and initiation of the next goal type is consistent with our previous findings pointing to the reactiveness of foraging in this domain [13,16].

The Most-Used Strategies' Strengths

This brings us to the particular strengths of different strategies. Refer back to Table 8; the rightmost (shaded) columns include the goal types and patterns we have just discussed for the most-used foraging strategies. As the table shows, certain classic debugging strategies were used heavily in *foraging* but often were concentrated into dietary niches. For example, Code Inspection and Feedback Following were generalists—used by everyone, but not the top in any particular IFT category, any goal type, or any pattern. In contrast, Code Search was a specialist, dominating some of

the patterns and one of the goal types, but still used by only half the participants.

DISCUSSION

Generalizability

As in any empirical study, our results may have been influenced by the environment the participants used, the tools available to them, the task they worked on, etc. Issues like

---

⌐ 6:30: [Searches]. Java search, in the workspace, a method including 'delete.'

⌐ 9:00: So one of the things I'm looking to do is open a fold, so if I ask for methods about methods can methods involving folds or even better, opening a fold.

∟ -18:00: I would imagine that I would look for the word delete perhaps, especially given that that's the terms that's used in the menu, but I um I think I'll try again. [Searches for 'delete'].

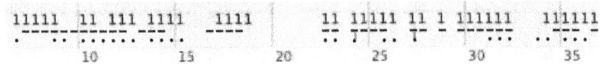

```
11111  11 111 1111   1111      11 11111 11 1 111111   111111
-----------  ----        -- -  -  --- ---
  10      15     20      25       30       35
```

24:30: Let me try to look for 'delete' again. [Searches for 'delete'].
27:00: If I could search across the text—I'm sorry, search through all the source code and found out delete lines, then I would be able to —I should be able to find where and what that function is called.
31:00: Let's just look for 'delete' again. [Searches for 'delete'].
37:00: I am going to look for references show me all references to *deleteLineLabel*. [Search for references to *deleteLineLabel*].

Figure 3. P3 continuously used Code Search (underlined) to find code relevant to deleting lines of text. He often complemented it with Spatial (dots). The beige background denotes foraging; white is non-foraging and the numbers indicate the minutes in the session.

25:00: So whose subclass is this? How can I figure that out?

⌐ 26:00: I am looking for a concrete class, not a abstract class (*EditAction*).

⌐ 27:00: If I look for references to the abstract class it will show me someone who implements this class. [Searches for references to *EditAction*].

⌐ 28:00: **So I don't think that search helped me understand who implements the *EditAction* class. Well I guess I could start with main and start debugging from that.**

28:30: [Searches]. Find method, "main." Search.

```
  ⌐ ⌐ ⌐⌐
  2 22 2        22
      11          1 1
  .  --  -  .      --  .  -
    25       30       35
```

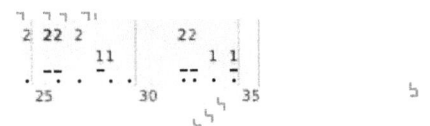

32:30: Let's look and see the references to this constructor. [Searches References to *main*].
33:30: **There are no references for the constructor for the main class what does this mean?**
34:00: There must be some public methods here. So, let's search for public. [Searches for 'public'].
35:00: [Scanning results]. "public static void main" Oh, there it is.

Figure 4. The Oscillate pattern for P6. The abandonment of goals is highlighted in bold. The underlines are segments with Code Search. The dots are segments with Spatial. Note that strategies alternate with the goal types.

these can be resolved only through additional studies. However, our methodology was designed to strengthen generalizability through the use of code sets and methodological conventions from other pertinent studies (e.g., [7,8,22]), and through the use of realistic elements: The software project was a real open source project; the bug was from a real bug report; the participants were experienced professionals (not students) using a popular IDE; and the participants worked alone on fairly long tasks (similar to what they would encounter professionally, even in a team context).

Diet Whats: The Long Tail

Participants' dietary needs varied greatly. This variety was not only between participants, but also within each participant's session from one moment to the next.

Our participants' diverse diets are reminiscent of the highly varied and personal diets reported by the Evans/Card study [4]. Evans and Card attributed this finding to a "long tail" demand curve, in which an abundance of available information makes it possible for people to satisfy their own individual, even quirky, desires for information. However, in the Evans/Card study, people foraged as part of their own individual tasks. Interestingly, we saw the same phenomenon with our participants, even though they all had the *same* overall goal (to fix the bug).

The participants' sometimes stubborn pursuit of particular information goals—tolerating very high costs even when their efforts showed only meager promise of delivering the needed dietary goal—highlights an important difference in the software domain versus other foraging domains: Programmers' dietary needs are often very specific. For an information forager on the Web, one dictionary page is often as good as another. But for a programmer trying to fix a bug, only very particular information about very specific code locations will help them in their task. This high dietary selectiveness in this domain may explain the high costs programmers were sometimes willing to pay.

Whats Meet Hows: Diet-Specific Strategies

Our results identified particular strategies that participants preferred for certain information goals. Of the 12 strategies we coded, 6 dominated, but in different ways.

Among the Within-Patch strategies, two strategies, Spatial (scanning lists) and Code Inspection (reading code), showed distinct associations to particular goal types. Spatial was ubiquitous across all goal types—it seemed that there was almost always some patch of information that a participant could scan. In contrast, Code inspection was particularly tied to Type 2-build and 3-group goals. Apparently, participants tended not to read code in detail when looking for an initial place to start (1-initial) or when trying to understand more complex relationships among groups of entities (4-groups). Instead, they dug into the code only when they needed information about more basic relationships (2-build and 3-group).

Turning to the Between-Patch strategies, participants applied Control Flow (following control dependencies) for all goals that involved understanding relationships between code entities (i.e., goal types 2–4). The proportion of participants who used the strategy relative to other strategies held steady, whether they were building up a basic understanding about a code entity (2-build) or understanding complex inter-relationships among groups of entities (4-groups).

Participants used the two most frequently used Enrichment strategies, Code Search (via a search utility) and Testing (running code), for different purposes. They used Code Search heavily for finding initial starting places and building upon them (Types 1 and 2). In contrast, they favored Testing for acquiring more complex information about the relationships between entities and between groups of entities (Types 3 and 4).

Participants' goal patterns reveal a close relationship between these Enrichment strategies and many of the goal patterns in Table 2. For example, participants who followed Repeat on Type 1-initial goals and who followed Oscillate on Type 1-initial and 2-build goals were generally using Code Search (Enrichment) repetitively (expending much effort with little success), looking for code relevant to the bug to investigate in more depth. Similarly, participants who used Repeat on Type 4-groups goals were generally Testing (Enrichment) by repetitively stepping through executions of the program over and over to build up information about the program's internal execution state. Overall, Enrichment strategies were heavily used in all patterns.

CONCLUSION

In this paper, we considered *what* programmers want in their diets and *how* they forage to fulfill each of their dietary needs. Some results this diet perspective revealed were:

RQ1 (whats):

- *Diversity*: Even though all participants were pursuing the same overall goal (the bug), they sought highly diverse diets. This suggests a need for debugging tools to support "long tail" demand curves of programmer information.
- *Dietary patterns*: Most foraging fell into distinct dietary patterns—including 78% in a new pattern not previously proposed in the literature.

RQ2 (hows):

- *Foraging strategies*: Participants spent only 24% of their time following between-patch foraging strategies, but between-patch foraging has received most of the research attention. This suggests a need for more research on how to support within-patch and enrichment foraging.
- *Search unpopularity*: Search was not a very popular strategy, accounting for less than 15% of participants' information foraging—and not used at all by 4 of our 9 participants—suggesting that tool support is still critical for non-search strategies in debugging.

RQ3 (what meets how):

- *Strategies' diet-specificity*: Some foraging strategies were of general use across information goal types, but others were concentrated around particular dietary niches. This suggests tool opportunities; for example, tools aimed at supporting a particular strategy may be able to improve performance by focusing on the strategy's dietary niche.
- *Cost of selectivity*: Participants stubbornly pursued particular information in the face of high costs and meager returns. This emphasizes a key difference between software development and other foraging domains: the highly selective nature of programmers' dietary needs.

As Evans and Card summarize from Simon: "For an information system to be useful, it must reduce the *net* demand on its users' attention" [4]. Our results suggest that the diet perspective can help reveal when programming tools help to reduce this net demand—and when they do not—during the 50% of debugging time programmers spend foraging.

REFERENCES

1. Anderson, J. *The Adaptive Character of Thought*. Lawrence Erlbaum Associates, 1990.

2. Brandt, J., Dontcheva, M., Weskamp, M., Klemmer, S. Two studies of opportunistic programming: Interleaving web foraging, learning and writing code. *Proc. CHI*, ACM (2009), 1589-1598.

3. Chi, E., Pirolli, P., Chen, K., and Pitkow, J. Using information scent to model user information needs and actions on the web. *Proc. CHI*, ACM (2001), 490–497.

4. Evans, B. and Card, S. Augmented information assimilation: Social and algorithmic web aids for the information long tail. *Proc. CHI*, ACM (2008), 989–998.

5. Fritz, T. and Murphy, G. Using information fragments to answer the questions developers ask. *Proc. ICSE.* ACM/IEEE (2010), 175–184.

6. Fu, W.-T. and Pirolli, P. SNIF-ACT: A cognitive model of user navigation on the World Wide Web. *Human-Computer Interaction 22*, 4 (2007). 355–412.

7. Grigoreanu, V., Burnett, M. and Robertson, G. A strategy-centric approach to the design of end-user debugging tools. *Proc CHI*, ACM (2010), 713–722.

8. Grigoreanu, V., Burnett, M., Wiedenbeck, S., Cao, J., Rector, K., Kwan, I. End-user debugging strategies: A sensemaking perspective, *ACM Trans. Comp.-Human Interaction 19, 1*, Article 5, (2012), 28 pages.

9. Hearst, M. User interfaces for search, In *Modern Information Retrieval*, 2nd Edition, ACM Press, (2011).

10. Ko, A., Myers B., Coblenz, M., Aung, H. An exploratory study of how developers seek, relate, and collect relevant information during software maintenance tasks. *IEEE Trans. Soft. Eng. 33*, (2006), 971–987.

11. LaToza, T. and Myers, B. Visualizing call graphs. *Proc. VL/HCC*, IEEE (2011), 117–124.

12. Lawrance, J., Bellamy, R., Burnett, M., and Rector, K. Using information scent to model the dynamic foraging behavior of programmers in maintenance tasks, *Proc. CHI*, ACM (2008), 1323–1332.

13. Lawrance, J., Burnett, M., Bellamy, R., Bogart, C. and Swart, C. Reactive information foraging for evolving goals. *Proc. CHI*, ACM (2010), 25–34.

14. Lawrance, J., Bogart, C., Burnett, M., Bellamy, R., Rector, K., Fleming, S. How programmers debug, revisited: An information foraging theory perspective, *IEEE Trans. Soft. Eng.* (2013), [DOI: 10.1109/TSE.2010.111].

15. Niu N., Mahmoud, A. and Bradshaw, G. Information foraging as a foundation for code navigation. *Proc. ICSE*, ACM/IEEE (2011), 816–819.

16. Piorkowski, D., Fleming, S., Scaffidi, C., Bogart, C., Burnett, M., John, B., Bellamy, R. and Swart, C. Reactive information foraging: An empirical investigation of theory-based recommender systems for programmers. *Proc. CHI*, ACM (2012), 1471–1480.

17. Piorkowski, D., Fleming, S., Kwan, I., Burnett, M., Scaffidi, C., Bellamy, R., Jordhal J. The whats and hows of programmers' foraging diets, Oregon State Univ. Tech Report. http://hdl.handle.net/1957/36082. Jan. 2013.

18. Pirolli, P. Computational models of information scent-following in a very large browsable text collection. *Proc. CHI*, ACM (1997), 3–10.

19. Pirolli, P. and Card, S. Information foraging. *Psychological Review 106*, (1999), 643–675.

20. Pirolli, P. and Card, S. The sensemaking process and leverage points for analyst technology as identified through cognitive task analysis. *Proc. Int'l. Conf. Intelligence Analysis*. MITRE Corp. (2005).

21. Pirolli, P. and Fu, W-T. SNIF-ACT: A model of information foraging on the world wide web. *Proc. User Modeling*, LNCS. Springer-Verlag Berlin. (2003).

22. Romero, P., du Boulay, B., Cox, R., Lutz, R., and Bryant, S. Debugging strategies and tactics in a multi-representation software environment. *Int'l J. Hum.-Comp. Studies 65*, Academic Press, (2007).

23. Sillito, J., Murphy, G. and De Volder, K. Questions programmers ask during software evolution tasks. *Proc. FSE*, ACM (2006), 23–34.

24. Spool, J., Profetti, C. and Britain, D. Designing for the scent of information, *User Interface Eng.*, (2004).

25. Teo, L., John, B., Blackmon, M. CogTool-Explorer: A model of goal-directed user exploration that considers information layout, *Proc. CHI*, ACM (2012).

How Tools in IDEs Shape Developers' Navigation Behavior

Jan-Peter Krämer, Thorsten Karrer, Joachim Kurz, Moritz Wittenhagen, Jan Borchers
RWTH Aachen University
52062 Aachen, Germany
{kraemer, karrer, kurz, wittenhagen, borchers}@cs.rwth-aachen.de

ABSTRACT

Understanding source code is crucial for successful software maintenance, and navigating the call graph is especially helpful to understand source code [12]. We compared maintenance performance across four different development environments: an IDE without any call graph exploration tool, a Call Hierarchy tool as found in Eclipse, and the tools Stacksplorer [7] and Blaze [11]. Using any of the call graph exploration tools more developers could solve certain maintenance tasks correctly. Only Stacksplorer and Blaze, however, were also able to decrease task completion times, although the Call Hierarchy offers access to a larger part of the call graph. To investigate if this result was caused by a change in navigation behavior between the tools, we used a set of predictive models to create formally comparable descriptions of programmer navigation. The results suggest that the decrease in task completion times has been caused by Stacksplorer and Blaze promoting call graph navigation more than the Call Hierarchy tool.

Author Keywords

Development Tools / Toolkits / Programming Environments; Analysis Methods

ACM Classification Keywords

H.5.2. Information Interfaces and Presentation (e.g. HCI): User Interfaces

INTRODUCTION

Software maintenance, the process of fixing bugs or performing other modifications after the software has been released, accounts for up to 70% of the total expenses in a typical software project [19]. Since it requires developers to modify the source code without introducing side effects or otherwise interfering with its structure, they need to gather knowledge about the program. For example, they have to find out which methods are responsible for a given feature, and how methods rely on each other. Despite the efforts to support source code

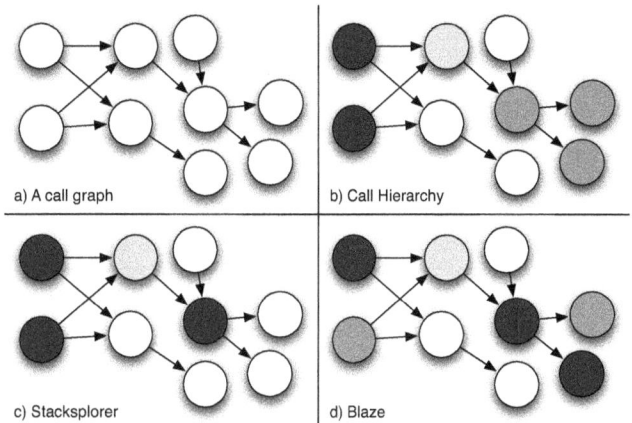

Figure 1. a) An example call graph. Each node represents one method, edges point to callees. b) With the light orange method being the focus method the Call Hierarchy allows browsing either the medium green or the dark blue subtree (including the focus method). c) Stacksplorer shows the neighborhood of the focus method. d) Blaze shows one path including the focus method (dark blue nodes); medium green nodes are options for alternative paths.

comprehension with modern development environments, developers still consider comprehending source code one of their biggest problems [14].

The process of navigating through source code has been found to be especially important for developers to build up their mental model of the application [20, 23]. This is particularly true for navigation along the call graph [12, 25]. The call graph represents methods as nodes, and an edge from a to b means that method a, the *caller*, calls method b, the *callee*.

The call graph for many real world software projects, however, is a complex structure that cannot easily be visualized completely. Tools to support call graph exploration thus have to restrict visualization to a subgraph. Most tools let the developer pick a *focus method* and only visualize subgraphs including this focus method. The most widespread tool for call graph exploration is the Call Hierarchy, which is, for example, found in the Eclipse IDE[1]. The subgraph visualized in the Call Hierarchy is a tree with its root at the focus method; the developer can choose if this tree is built up in caller or callee direction. We previously proposed two alternative tools for call graph exploration that offer access to a smaller subgraph than the Call Hierarchy: In Stacksplorer [7], the visualized subgraph is the direct neighborhood of the focus method.

---

[1]http://www.eclipse.org/

Blaze [11] visualizes a single path through the focus method. The three different approaches are visualized in Figure 1.

In the first half of this paper, we show that developers using Stacksplorer and Blaze are faster in solving certain maintenance tasks than developers using the Call Hierarchy. This result is unexpected because the Call Hierarchy facilitates access to a superset of the methods visible in Stacksplorer or Blaze. In the second half of this paper, we analyze if this result can be explained by changes in the navigation behavior of developers caused by using the different tools. This is done by describing developers' navigation histories using a set of seven quantifiable features, where each feature is determined by calculating how well the navigation can be predicted by a stereotypic navigation model. These descriptions are then compared between the tools.

Thus, this paper makes the following contributions: (1) We present a study comparing the three call graph exploration techniques described above to an IDE without any dedicated call graph navigation tool. (2) We introduce an analysis technique to describe navigation behavior based on predictive models. (3) We apply this technique to offer possible explanations for the performance differences between the call graph exploration tools.

RELATED WORK

Navigation Strategies
Ko et al. [9] found that navigation accounted for 35% of the time developers needed to perform tasks within a 500SLOC^2 Java application using the Eclipse IDE. The powerful navigation tools available in Eclipse were rarely used. Similar results were found by Murphy et al. [16] when analyzing Eclipse usage logs from 41 Java developers.

LaToza et al. [12] found that one of the most important questions developers ask are reachability questions, i.e., searches for feasible control flow paths. They surveyed 460 professional software developers, who consistently reported those questions were at least "somewhat hard" to answer and came up ten times a day or more.

Previous studies [7, 9, 21] repeatedly describe strategies for navigation in the call graph by a *two-phase model*. In the first phase, developers search for an anchor point they consider interesting. In the second phase, they explore different paths starting from the anchor point until they found the relevant location in the source code.

Lawrence et al. [15] carried over results from information foraging theory [18] to model how developers navigate. Each link to a piece of source code has a certain scent that determines how likely a developer will follow the link when searching for specific information. The model incorporates structural aspects of the source code as well as linguistic similarity of source code to a bug report. Predictions from this model were on par with predictions generated from historical navigation data recorded from actual developers.

---
^{2}SLOC: Non-comment, non-empty lines of source code

Navigation Tools
Recommender tools use models of navigation behavior to constantly predict and show the methods the developer will most likely navigate to in order to make them more easily accessible. These tools calculate a *degree of interest* (DOI) for all methods in a project and show navigation shortcuts to those with the highest DOI in a list. DOI may be determined by factors such as the reading and editing history or textual similarity to information from version control systems [4, 8, 22, 24]. For all of these tools, controlled experiments revealed a significantly reduced navigation effort.

REACHER [13] can restrict searches to reachable branches of the call graph originating in or leading to a specific method. The relevant portions of the connection between the method and the search result are displayed graphically. A study showed significantly increased success rates among developers using REACHER compared to those using Eclipse in six tasks involving reachability questions. In contrast to the tools we compare, REACHER is a search tool, requiring the developer to formulate a query.

The Whyline [10] allows to determine the cause of certain aspects of an application's graphical and textual output. Users can, for example, formulate the question "Why did this circle's color = blue" about a circle drawn in the interface. The Whyline then computes a dynamic slice from a runtime trace of the application, i.e., it computes which methods influenced the relevant property. This dynamic slice is presented as a graph. The tool allowed novice programmers to fix a bug significantly faster than expert developers not using the tool. In contrast to the navigation tools we compare in this paper, the Whyline is a dedicated debugging tool.

Code Bubbles [2] and Code Canvas [5] introduced IDE concepts in which source code is laid out by arranging pieces of information, such as individual methods or bug reports, in bubbles on a 2D plane. Bubbles are connected to indicate relationships between two items, such as a method call connecting two methods. This layout greatly simplifies glancing at related methods after they have been first visited and opened in a bubble.

REACHER, the Whyline, Code Bubbles, and Code Canvas all introduce new possibilities to explore the call graph. In contrast, we compare call graph navigation tools that visualize a subgraph of the call graph and that extend an existing IDE. This subgraph depends on a focus method the user has to select in some way. A comparison of these tools with the ones presented above is an interesting endeavor for future work.

CALL GRAPH NAVIGATION TOOLS
In our first experiment, we compare three call graph navigation tools in terms of how they impact participants' performance and navigation behavior: a Call Hierarchy tool, Stacksplorer, and Blaze. The tools differ in which subgraph of the call graph they visualize (Figure 1), how the displayed subgraph can be changed, and how developers can navigate using the tool. All tools were implemented as plug-ins for Apple's Xcode 3 IDE and were using the same backend for code analysis and call graph creation.

Figure 2. The screenshots show how each tool is presented in Xcode. The user interface elements circled in blue are provided by the tool and are not part of a standard Xcode installation.

Call Hierarchy

Our Call Hierarchy plug-in (see top of Figure 2) closely resembles the equally named tool in Eclipse. The user starts by selecting a *root method* (the light orange node in Figure 1b) for a tree view. Expanding any element in the tree view shows its callers (the dark blue nodes in Figure 1b) or callees (the medium green nodes in Figure 1b), depending on the mode the Call Hierarchy tool is in. The mode can be changed using two buttons at the bottom. If a method appears multiple times in the list of callers or callees of a method, it is displayed only once. In callee view mode, children of an element are ordered in the same way they appear in the implementation of the element; in caller view mode the order is arbitrary.

The root method is changed by selecting the "Show Call Hierarchy..." command from the context menu for a method identifier anywhere in the source code. To navigate, users can click on the elements in the tree view. If callers are shown, this opens the method in the editor and the call to the parent method is highlighted. In case callees are shown, clicking a method opens its parent method and the call to the clicked method is highlighted. Consistently across modes, the "Open" command in the context menu of an element in the tree view opens this element in the editor.

Our Call Hierarchy tool does not detect cycles in the call graph, but our user study avoided such cycles. Xcode does not allow users to freely place tools in the interface, so our Call Hierarchy is always displayed on the right side of the source code editor. This allows a fair comparison in terms of screen real estate to the other tools that both reduce the width but not the height of the editor.

Stacksplorer

Stacksplorer [7] (see middle of Figure 2) visualizes the call graph neighborhood of the *focus method* (the blue nodes in Figure 1c). It shows one interactive side column view on each side of the source code editor. The left column shows a list of callers of the focus method, the right column shows a list of callees. In Stacksplorer, the focus method is always synchronized to the method in which the cursor is placed in the central source code editor. Because Stacksplorer occupies two side columns, it takes up more space than the other tools.

Clicking any method in one of the side columns opens it in the central editor. This implicitly also causes the focus method to change and the side columns to update. The focus method also changes when the user navigates to a different method in the central editor by other means. Thus, even when the developer is not exploring the call graph, the automatically-updated side columns provide auxiliary information.

Like in the Call Hierarchy tool, callees in the right column are sorted by their order of appearance in the source code, but Stacksplorer shows the same method more than once if it is called more than once. The side columns' content scrolls automatically to keep the on-screen distance to the related code minimal. Additional overlays can be turned on, which connect an entry in the side column with the corresponding method call in the source code. This is especially helpful for densely written code, e.g., nested method calls.

Blaze

Blaze [11] (see bottom of Figure 2) implements depth-first call graph exploration, and shows one path through the call graph including the focus method (the blue nodes in Figure 1d). Blaze shows all methods on this path in a view at the right side of the source code editor. The path is displayed top-to-bottom, i.e., each entry calls the one immediately below. As in Stacksplorer, clicking any method in the Blaze column navigates to this method.

To change which path through the call graph is displayed, Blaze uses a combination lock metaphor: For each entry in the path, several alternatives exist (the medium green nodes in Figure 1d). Because the focus method has to be part of the path, each entry below the focus method can be exchanged with another callee of the preceding method; above the focus method, each entry can be exchanged with another caller of the following method. When an entry is exchanged, the following (below the focus method) or preceding (above the focus method) path changes accordingly. To exchange an entry on the path, a user can either click the arrow between two entries to reveal a list of all options, or use the arrows next to each entry. A line of dots is displayed in each entry to show the number of possible options and the current selection.

As in Stacksplorer, the focus method in Blaze is automatically synchronized to the method the user is currently working on. When the focus method changes, the displayed path is updated accordingly, but changes are kept minimal, i.e., if the developer navigates to a method that is already visible on the path, the path does not change at all. Optionally, Blaze can be locked to prevent automatic updates to the focus method. To keep users aware of their location on the path, an overlay is shown that connects the currently edited method in the editor to the corresponding entry in the side column.

The two states Blaze supports (locked and unlocked) can be mapped to the two-phase navigation model described before. While Blaze is unlocked, the automatically displayed path is additional auxiliary information that might help finding an anchor point during the first phase. When Blaze is locked with the anchor point being the focus method, it allows to browse all paths involving the anchor point in the second phase.

STUDY SETUP

We analyzed the data from two previous studies [7, 11], of participants working on maintenance tasks for BibDesk[3], an open-source bibliography manager for Mac OS X. Participants were given a typical maintenance task: firstly, they had to identify a location for a change (task 1), and secondly, they had to identify possible side effects (task 2). The first task concerned BibDesk's Autofile feature, which automatically moves and renames PDF files according to a user specified naming convention. Subjects were asked to change the feature so that it would prepend a fixed string to the name regardless of the specified naming convention. To successfully solve this task, the participant had to suggest a modification that would have achieved the intended effect. Because we were

[3]Rev. 17029, Objective-C, 80.000SLOC

only interested in how developers *navigate* between methods for finding a change location, implementing the change was not required. The second task required finding a side effect introduced by a given solution for the first task.

For both tasks, an expert judged a solution as correct when the suggested change would lead to the effect described in the task. We saw no non-standard solution that would have required more effort to be verified. The unsuccessful participants either could not complete the task in time or presented solutions that would clearly not have the desired effect. The complete maintenance task was considered correct if both individual tasks were solved correctly. In [7], the tasks were referred to as tasks 1.1 and 1.2.

We recruited 33 subjects—31 students and two professional software developers—for our study. On average, participants were 26.3 years old ($SD = 2.6$), spent an average of 12.6 hours ($SD = 11.6$) on programming per week, and had an average of 2.6 years ($SD = 2.1$) of experience with Objective-C. A minimum of half a year of experience with Objective-C was required to participate in the study. No participant had seen the BibDesk source code before, although half of them had used BibDesk before.

Participants were randomly assigned to one of four conditions: *Xcode* (XC), the control condition, used the unmodified interface of Apple's Xcode 3 IDE. It includes no dedicated call graph navigation tool, but users can navigate to a callee from within the editor using the "Jump to definition" context menu command for a method call. *Call Hierarchy* (CH), *Stacksplorer* (SP), and *Blaze* (BL), the experimental conditions, used the same version of Xcode but extended with the respective plug-in. Each condition was similarly sampled in terms of number of participants (XC: 8, CH: 9, SP: 8, BL: 8), programming experience (in years), and coding done per week. In the three experimental conditions, the session started with a brief introduction to the tool using an unrelated code base. To make sure not to bias participants, the experimenter did not tell the participants if the tools were designed by us or not.

After the introduction, participants were allowed to familiarize themselves with the BibDesk project for up to 10 minutes. Then, we handed tasks 1 and 2 to the participants one task at a time, so that while working on task 1 they would not be aware of task 2 yet. Time to finish the tasks was limited to 25 minutes for task 1 and 15 minutes for task 2. We encouraged participants to work quickly but to make sure to arrive at a correct solution, as they had only one chance to provide an answer. When exceeding the time limit or giving an incorrect answer, we used the respective time limit as the task completion time.

Consistent with previous studies [2, 20], using runtime analysis tools such as the debugger was prohibited. However, participants were allowed to run a compiled executable of the application.

PERFORMANCE COMPARISON

Firstly, we compared success rates between the different tools. We found a significant increase in success rates for the

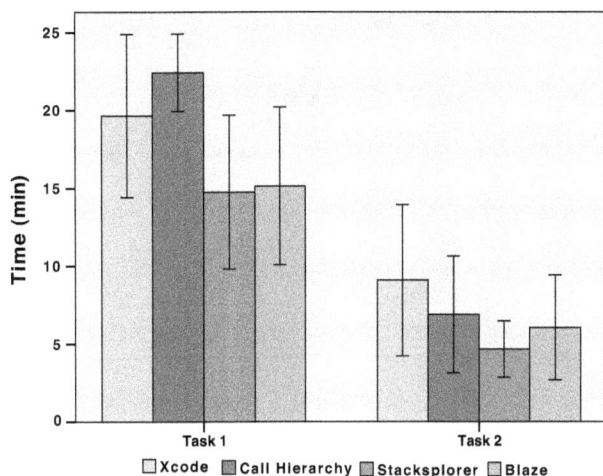

Figure 3. The graph shows task completion times per condition and 95% confidence intervals. Task and condition both have a significant effect on task completion times.

complete maintenance task between the experimental conditions and the control (one-sided Fisher's exact test: $p = 0.015$). No significant differences in terms of success rates were found between the experimental conditions.

Next, we compared the task completion times and assumed to find similar results. An ANOVA[4] revealed a significant effect of task and of condition.

Task: $F(1, 29) = 65.281$ $p < 0.001$ $\eta^2 = 0.666$
Condition: $F(3, 29) = 3.720$ $p = 0.022$ $\eta^2 = 0.278$

Using a post-hoc Dunnett t-test we found that task completion times in the Stacksplorer and Blaze conditions were significantly lower than in the control condition, but those in the Call Hierarchy condition were not. A post-hoc Tukey's test comparing Blaze and Stacksplorer was not significant.

XC vs.   CH: $p = 0.662$ ST: $p = 0.038$ BL: $p = 0.020$
ST vs.   BL: $p = 0.992$

In summary, call graph exploration tools have a positive impact on the success of a typical code maintenance task. Stacksplorer and Blaze also have a significant effect on task completion times, while the Call Hierarchy unexpectedly does not. Blaze and Stacksplorer perform similarly although they implement different approaches for presenting a subgraph of the call graph to the user.

MODEL-BASED ANALYSIS OF NAVIGATION BEHAVIOR

The comparison shows that performance differences between the tools exist. We argue that there are two possible reasons for these differences: Either the user interface of the more successful tools was better or easier to use, or the tools encouraged different navigation strategies, which then caused the differences in efficiency. In the following we focus on the latter.

---

[4]All ANOVAs carried out are Repeated-Measures ANOVAs, where task is a within-groups factor and condition is a between-groups factor.

To compare the different navigation strategies, we first need a consistent way to formally describe navigation. This description should be independent of the tool and development environment used. We therefore propose to characterize navigation behaviors by a set of quantifiable features, where each feature represents the degree to which the navigation behavior conforms to one of a set of well known micro navigation patterns. To measure a feature for a recorded session, we use the navigation models compared by Piorkowski et al. [17]: Since these models all predict navigation targets according to different micro strategies of navigating source code, the prediction accuracy of each model is a quantitative indicator for how well the overall navigation behavior of the session resonates with these micro strategies. We thus use these prediction accuracies as our features.

Note that, while originally Piorkowski et al. tried to find the most accurate model for predicting developers' navigation, we do *not* evaluate the models in terms of their prediction accuracies, but we characterize the different navigation tools in terms of their effect on the individual prediction accuracies of all models.

Formally, the models as described by Piorkowski et al. [17] assume that navigation in a single study session is coded as a sequence of visited methods $H = (m_1, m_2, ..., m_n)$ where $\forall m_i, m_{i+1} \in H : m_i \neq m_{i+1}$. Using the navigation sequence up to an element m_j as input, the models try to predict m_{j+1}.

To do so, they calculate the probability that a developer navigates to a method for all methods in $M_j - \{m_j\}$, where M_j is a set of methods approximating all methods known to the developer and comprises all methods in files that have been opened so far or that have been visible in call graph exploration tools or search results.

Models calculate their prediction by creating an activation function $A_j : M_j - \{m_j\} \mapsto \mathbb{R}$, with higher activation values indicating a higher probability of the developer navigating to a method. Then, a ranking function $R_j : M_j - \{m_j\} \mapsto \mathbb{N}$ is obtained by rank-transforming A_j. For methods with the same activation value, the average of all involved ranks is used. All models share a parameter N that determines how many of the top ranked methods are returned by the model. If more than N methods are assigned the highest available rank, the models do not predict anything. Characteristic for each model is the definition of A_j.

We will provide only a qualitative description of A_j for the different models here, and explain which navigational "micro-pattern" we think is represented by each model. For the formal definition of each model please refer to [17].

Recency assigns higher activation values if a method has been visited more recently. It correlates with navigating back and forth between related methods to understand their connection, which was shown to be a common and important pattern in [9].

Frequency assigns higher activation values the more frequently a method has been visited. It correlates with going back frequently to very important methods, such as the anchor point found in the two-phase navigation model.

Working Set assigns an activation of 1 to all methods visited during the last δ navigation steps and 0 to all other methods. δ is an estimate of the size of the working set, in our analysis we used $\delta = N$. The Working Set model is similar to Recency, but implies that there is a fixed-sized set of methods that are particularly important to the task, as suggested in [3].

Bug Report Similarity assigns a method m the tf-idf weight [1] of the bug report compared to the words in m. Before calculating the tf-idf weight, stop words are removed and camelCase identifiers are split apart. The Bug Report Similarity model correlates with the micro-pattern of searching for locations in the source code based on textual clues in the bug report, which was reported previously in [15].

The following models all maintain a graph G containing the methods in M_j as nodes. $A_j(m)$ is calculated inversely proportional to the distance between m and m_{j-1}. The models differ in what edges are included in G.

Within-File Distance adds an undirected edge between two nodes if they are adjacent in a source file document. It correlates with scrolling in a file, which is commonly used to explore the file based decomposition of the software [20].

Forward Call Depth adds a directed edge between two nodes m_a, m_b if m_b is called from the implementation of m_a. It correlates with navigation to callees, which is possible in many IDEs even without the use of a dedicated tool using the "Jump to definition..." command from the context menu for a method call in the editor.

Undirected Call Depth is a modified variant of Forward Call Depth with directed edges being replaced by undirected edges. This model correlates with the call graph navigation supported by the call graph exploration tools we compared.

Analysis of Navigation Behavior

Navigation events were coded manually in video recordings of the user study sessions using ChronoViz [6], annotating all clicks on UI elements that lead to changes in the source code editor as well as navigations via text search and scrolling. User actions that were less than 0.5s apart were consolidated into one navigation action, e.g., clicking the back button twice. For every navigation, the tool used for navigation and the target of the navigation action were recorded. Targets of navigations are methods, unless the target method could not be clearly determined. If the target method was unclear, e.g., after opening a file, either a set of possible target methods was recorded or a more abstract target, such as the file, was annotated as navigation target.

A model prediction was counted as correct if the next method m_{j+1} was contained in the set of suggestions returned by the model. When the navigation led to a set of methods, a model predicted this navigation correctly if it predicted any method in the set; when navigating to anything else than a method or a set of methods a prediction could not be correct.

We compare prediction accuracy of the models for different prediction list sizes $1 \leq N \leq 20$. Model prediction accuracies for different N and the different models are depicted in Figure 4. In the following, we will analyze one model at a time. Statistical tests were performed only for $N = 1$, $N = 10$, and $N = 20$, results of which are listed in Table 1.

Frequency

For the Frequency model we expected to see a lower prediction accuracy in the more successful tools Stacksplorer and Blaze, because previous studies [9] showed the importance of back and forth navigation to gather contextual information but also that it requires a lot of time.

There is a significant effect of condition on the prediction accuracy of the Frequency model for $N = 10$. A post-hoc Tukey test only shows a significantly higher prediction accuracy in the Stacksplorer condition than in the Call Hierarchy condition ($p = 0.018$). There is no evidence that this increased number of revisits did decrease the number of distinct methods visited throughout the session ($p = 0.815$).

Stacksplorer allows, in contrast to our assumption, to perform more navigation to previously viewed methods but fast enough to still save time compared to the control condition and the Call Hierarchy. This indicates that frequent revisits to previously explored methods do not necessarily slow down the process of understanding source code. One explanation for that might be found in the two-phase navigation model, which states that revisits occur when backtracking to the focus method. In Stacksplorer, this often happens using the "Back" button in Xcode, because the focus method is not explicitly stored as in Blaze or the Call Hierarchy.

Recency & Working Set

We expected to see no effect of the condition on the prediction accuracy of the Recency and the very similar Working Set model. Methods might be included in a working set for a variety of reasons, not only because they are connected in the call graph, which is what a call graph exploration tool would support.

No effect of condition was found for the Recency model. We found a significant effect of condition, though, for the Working Set model for $N = 10$. Here again, a difference exists between Stacksplorer and the Call Hierarchy (Tukey test, $p = 0.017$).

Together with the previous result that the number of revisits was higher when using Stacksplorer, we can conclude that developers using Stacksplorer performed longer exploration phases in rather limited subsets of methods (likely connected by the call graph). Because they were also faster in solving the tasks than participants using Xcode alone or the Call Hierarchy, this result supports previous results by Sillito et al. [21], pointing out the importance of thoroughly understanding closed subsets of related methods.

For all conditions, prediction accuracy in the Recency and Working Set model becomes constant roughly for $N > 10$. This can be interpreted as an estimate about the maximum size for a working set for our tasks.

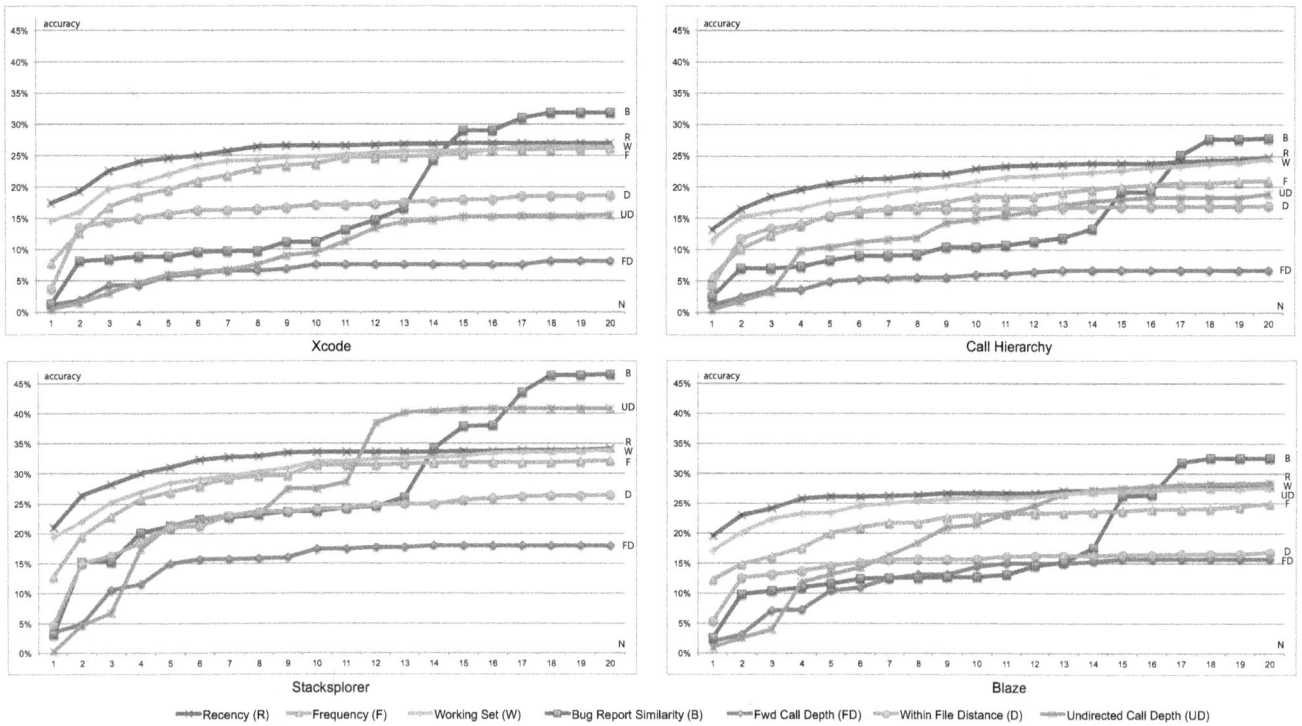

Figure 4. Plots of prediction accuracy against prediction list sizes N per condition for all models. When using a call graph navigation tool, Fwd Call Depth and Undirected Call Depth improve considerably.

Bug Report Similarity

We assumed that call graph navigation tools have no effect on the prediction accuracy of the Bug Report Similarity model, because the call graph, from which all navigation targets available in the tools are taken, does not provide any information about the textual content of the methods.

The prediction accuracy of the Bug Report Similarity model changes significantly with condition for $N = 20$. Here, the most important differences exist between Stacksplorer and both the Call Hierarchy and the control condition (Post-hoc Tukey's test, XC: $p = 0.035$, CH: $p = 0.004$).

One possible explanation for this result is that Stacksplorer, in contrast to the Call Hierarchy, automatically updates the list of navigation targets from which developers then preferably select textually similar navigation targets [15]. Of course, the degree to which the call graph neighborhood contains textually similar navigation targets depends on the source code.

Within-File Distance

In the BibDesk source code, as in most object-oriented source code, one file implements one class. Hence, by scrolling through a file, the different methods comprising the class can be explored. This structure of methods belonging to classes is orthogonal to the call graph, and consequently we assumed navigation behavior through this hierarchy would not be influenced by any call graph exploration tool.

No significant effect of condition was found for the Within-File Distance model. This result matched our expectations.

Forward Call Depth & Undirected Call Depth

We did expect an effect of the condition on the Call Depth models. Navigation along the call graph is what all tested tools specifically support.

This was confirmed; significant effects of condition are found for $N = 10$ and $N = 20$ for both the Forward Call Depth model and the Undirected Call Depth model. For the Forward Call Depth model, post-hoc tests (for $N = 20$) reveal significantly higher accuracy for Stacksplorer and Blaze compared to the control condition (one-sided Dunnett t-test, ST: $p = 0.004$, BL: $p = 0.022$) and compared to the Call Hierarchy (Tukey's test, ST: $p = 0.003$, BL: $p = 0.022$). Similar results are obtained for the Undirected Call Graph model, however, here no significant difference between Blaze and the Call Hierarchy was found in post-hoc tests. Over all tests, we did not find differences in prediction accuracy between the Call Hierarchy and Xcode.

In all call graph navigation tool conditions, accuracy of the Call Depth models increases substantially for $N > 6$. This can be explained by the average neighborhood size of a method. Among the 277 methods visited in all sessions, the average number for callers or callees is 1.81 ($SD = 5.93$) and 3.49 ($SD = 4.63$), respectively. Considering only methods that have been visited by at least half of the participants, the averages are even higher (callers: 3.33 ($SD = 2.58$), callees: 11.33 ($SD = 6.83$)). The Call Depth models do rank all neighbors (or callees in case of the Forward Call Depth model) of a method equally, so if there are more than N neighbors (or callees) they predict nothing.

		N = 1		N = 10		N = 20	
		F	p	F	p	F	p
Frequency	T	27.13	.001	28.60	.001	18.31	.001
	C	2.729	.062	3.384	**.031**	2.482	.081
	I	1.733	.182	.384	.766	.813	.497
Recency	T	27.82	.001	11.64	.002	9.215	.005
	C	2.4	.088	2.728	.062	2.009	.122
	I	.696	.562	.793	.508	1.248	.311
Working Set	T	22.28	.001	14.49	.001	9.518	.004
	C	2.757	.06	3.432	**.030**	2.222	.107
	I	.823	.492	1.559	.221	1.124	.356
Bug Report Similarity	T	3.8	.061	36.88	.001	142.3	.001
	C	.366	.778	3.056	**.044**	5.279	**.005**
	I	.182	.908	2.784	.059	1.681	.193
Within-File Distance	T	39.09	.001	11.30	.002	13.55	.001
	C	.679	.572	1.178	.335	1.682	.193
	I	1.269	.303	.914	.447	.561	.645
Forward Call Depth	T	.048	.828	.548	.465	0.299	.589
	C	.1.688	.191	6.470	**.002**	7.023	**.001**
	I	.334	.801	1.693	.190	1.771	.175
Undirected Call Depth	T	5.969	.021	6.000	.021	5.395	.027
	C	.857	.474	5.791	**.003**	9.514	**.001**
	I	.125	.944	2.141	.117	5.344	.005

Table 1. The table shows comparisons between prediction accuracies of each model. The factors analyzed are task (T), condition (C), and their interaction (I). For task $df = 1$, for condition and interaction $df = 3$, for error $df = 29$. All significant effects of condition are in bold face.

For all tools, roughly two thirds of call graph navigations were performed using the tool and not via means existing in Xcode.

$$CH: \quad M = 68.2\% \quad SD = 37.1\%$$
$$ST: \quad M = 65.0\% \quad SD = 31.2\%$$
$$BL: \quad M = 65.0\% \quad SD = 39.8\%$$

An ANOVA, however, reveals a significant effect of task and condition on the percentage of navigations that happened along an edge in the call graph, and a significant interaction.

$$\text{Task:} \quad F(1, 29) = 10.892 \quad p = 0.003 \quad \eta^2 = 0.211$$
$$\text{Condition:} \quad F(3, 29) = 11.002 \quad p < 0.001 \quad \eta^2 = 0.532$$
$$\text{Interaction:} \quad F(3, 29) = 3.877 \quad p = 0.019 \quad \eta^2 = 0.226$$

A post-hoc Tukey's test shows a significantly higher percentage in the Stacksplorer condition as in all other conditions; a Dunnett test additionally shows significantly higher percentage in the Blaze condition but not in the Call Hierarchy condition compared to the control condition.

Tukey's: ST vs.   XC: $p < 0.001$ CH: $p < 0.001$ BL: $p = 0.023$
Dunnett: XC vs.   CH: $p = 0.602$ BL: $p = 0.036$

These results indicate that Xcode and the Call Hierarchy promoted call graph navigation similarly, Blaze did so significantly more and Stacksplorer again more than Blaze.

Differences in how the tools were used also show up when looking at the average length of a call graph navigation sequence. A call graph navigation sequence is a subsequence $S = (m_m, ..., m_n)$ of H, such that for all $m \leq i < n$ m_i and m_{i+1} are connected in the call graph. The condition has

a significant effect on the average length of these sequences.

$$\text{Condition:} \quad F(3, 29) = 5.819 \quad p = 0.003 \quad \eta^2 = 0.376$$
No significant effect of task, no interaction.

Post-hoc one-sided Dunnett t-tests revealed significantly longer sequences in the Stacksplorer and Blaze conditions but not in the Call Hierarchy condition when compared to Xcode.

XC vs.   CH: $p = 0.451$ ST: $p = 0.002$ BL: $p = 0.009$

Blaze and the Call Hierarchy allow call-graph navigation along more than one edge at a time. When accommodating for that by allowing navigations back to a method previously visited in the sequence, results do not change. The reason is that, despite the possibility to navigate in that manner, these navigations only occurred 9 times over all sessions.

When no call graph navigation tool is used, developers seem to exhibit other strategies to find the desired information, one of which is using the project wide search. There is a significant effect of condition on the percentage of navigations performed using the project wide search ($F(3, 29) = 9.487$, $p < 0.001$, no effect of task). Post-hoc one-sided Dunnett t-tests show that the project wide search was used significantly more in the control condition than in all other conditions ($p < 0.001$ for all conditions). The project wide search in Xcode is often used to navigate to callers of a method by searching for the method name. This workaround to access callers is slow to invoke and error prone because of similarly named methods. Consequently, people stopped using this technique when dedicated tools were available.

We can conclude that Stacksplorer and Blaze can promote navigation along the call graph effectively. But the opportunity to shape navigation behavior by making additional navigation targets available seems to be limited: The option to navigate along multiple edges of the call graph at once, as it is offered by Blaze and the Call Hierarchy, was seldom used. We assume that backtracking multiple edges in the call graph at once is cognitively too challenging and developers fear to get lost in relatively unknown source code. However, this may be different when developers are familiar with the source code.

Comparing the three call graph exploration tools we tested, we find that Stacksplorer, which provides access to just the neighborhood of the focus method and synchronizes the focus method to the method currently being edited, promotes call graph navigation the most. Blaze still encourages more call graph navigation than the Call Hierarchy or Xcode alone. With Blaze, developers can perform some call graph exploration completely within the tool, without the need to navigate to each method on the path. This might explain why we observed less call graph navigation being performed using Blaze than using Stacksplorer.

Both Stacksplorer and Blaze present meaningful parts of the call graph: The direct call graph neighborhood usually contains very closely related methods; a single path through the call graph is familiar to many developers, e.g., from call stacks in a debugger. Unrestricted exploration as it is possible in the Call Hierarchy seems to be overwhelming and could not substantially change how developers explore the source code. It was, however, successful in replacing the cumbersome project wide searches to find callers of a method, which were utilized in the Xcode condition.

LIMITATIONS

UI Differences

We cannot clearly differentiate between the effects caused by the tools exposing different parts of the call graph or by the presentation of this information. Stacksplorer and Blaze have user interfaces specifically designed for the respective exploration strategy; the Call Hierarchy was designed to be comparable with currently existing tools.

One of the most obvious differences between Blaze and Stacksplorer and the Call Hierarchy are automatic updates to the focus method. With automatic updates, Blaze and Stacksplorer present additional information with no interaction required. In post-session interviews half of the participants in the Call Hierarchy condition suggested to add automatic updates, even though they were not aware of the other tools. However, adding automatic updates to the Call Hierarchy tool would require adding a locking state as in Blaze, because otherwise we would lose any way to navigate back to the original root once we have navigated to a subtree node.

If the information displayed in the tool can be refined manually, as in Blaze and the Call Hierarchy, we observed mode errors happening. For example, in Blaze problems occurred if the path length required scrolling the part of the path up- or downstream from the focus method, which could cause methods to be hidden between the focus method and the method directly above or below it on the screen. This could be solved by allowing the full path to scroll instead of scrolling in two separate parts. Using the Call Hierarchy, many participants had issues with the caller and callee view modes, and some forgot that the method they read in the editor is not the one selected as root of the Call Hierarchy. The latter problem did not occur in Blaze even if it was locked, because overlays always maintain a graphical connection between the method currently inspected in the editor and the information displayed in Blaze. Overlays are another property specific to Blaze and Stacksplorer, which simplifies parsing the additional information displayed while trying to understand source code in the central editor.

We already identified several problems with the design of Blaze: Mode errors might happen, and navigation targets that were more than one edge away from the currently edited method were rarely used. Nevertheless task completion times were on par with those in the Stacksplorer condition. Hence, the information displayed in Blaze seems relevant even though not all methods displayed are also navigated to directly using Blaze.

Effects of Task and Setup

The task had a significant effect on the prediction accuracy of all models except for the Forward Call Depth model. This indicates that the navigation behavior overall is influenced considerably by the task at hand. Further, both tasks used

in our study were concerned with the same code base, which also might have an influence on the navigation behavior. This makes comparisons with other studies using different tasks and environments difficult.

Another problem when trying to study tools in development environments seems to be the large diversity in developers' strategies [20]. While in our experiment the groups of participants were comparable in terms of programming experience (in years) and coding done per week, we acknowledge that these measures cannot capture individual differences in coding strategies.

Of all methods we saw being visited during the sessions, 45% were visited by only one participant; only six methods were visited by more than half of the participants. These six methods were the ones essential for the task, they were either the solution (i.e., the method to be changed) or very closely related to it. All those 45% of methods were not important to the task at hand and hence likely visited during the initial exploration and search phase. This divergence in the first phase added noise to our model-based analysis.

SUMMARY AND FUTURE WORK

We presented a comparative study of three call graph navigation tools: the Call Hierarchy, which is ubiquitous in current IDEs, Stacksplorer, and Blaze. Call graph navigation tools support developers in performing software maintenance and yield higher task success rates compared to an IDE without any of these tools. Stacksplorer and Blaze could also decrease task completion times and thus make developers potentially more productive.

An analysis of navigation patterns in the different conditions indicated how the tools change developers' strategies. Without call graph navigation tools developers resort to workarounds for call graph navigation, such as text searches. Stacksplorer and Blaze changed developers behavior to include more call graph navigation than we observed in the Call Hierarchy condition. This is one potential explanation for the increased efficiency of these tools.

Call graph navigation mostly happens between neighboring methods, which benefits Stacksplorer. Only rarely developers navigate along multiple edges at a time, even though the tool at hand might support it.

For the comparison of the call graph exploration tools, we presented a new method to formally describe navigation behavior. This method quantifies the degree to which any given navigation history complies with a number of characteristic navigation models, yielding a representation that can be analyzed statistically. We found the results to be very helpful to find and analyze differences in navigation behavior among the conditions tested.

In future work it would be interesting to determine the influence of various other factors on navigation behavior. Promising factors to look at would be the programming language or API used, the task at hand, or the design patterns used in the application. It would also be interesting to examine how other performance measures, e.g., learnability or user satisfaction, are influenced by the different tools. Further, while we chose to compare three tools that could each be embedded into the same IDE to maintain a high internal validity of the study, it is an important task for future work to analyze other navigation tools as well.

REPLICHI

The navigation sequences obtained through video annotation that were used for this study are available for further analysis as XML files generated with ChronoViz [6]. We also published a Mac OS X tool that uses the ChronoViz files and a call graph stored in an XML format to analyze the navigation behavior using the methodology we presented. The material can be downloaded at http://hci.rwth-aachen.de/developerNavigation. We would like to invite others to pick up our format to annotate navigation and our methodology to quantify navigation in their own studies. This would allow a comparison of navigation behavior among a wide variety of environments, tasks, and developers.

ACKNOWLEDGMENTS

This work was funded in part by the German B-IT Foundation and by the German Government through its UMIC Excellence Cluster for Ultra-High Speed Mobile Information and Communication at RWTH Aachen University.

REFERENCES

1. Baeza-Yates, R. A., and Ribeiro-Neto, B. *Modern Information Retrieval*. Addison-Wesley Longman, 1999.

2. Bragdon, A., Zeleznik, R., Reiss, S. P., Karumuri, S., Cheung, W., Kaplan, J., Coleman, C., Adeputra, F., and LaViola, J. J. Code Bubbles: A Working Set-based Interface for Code Understanding and Maintenance. In *Proc. CHI '10*, ACM (2010).

3. Coblenz, M. J., Ko, A. J., and Myers, B. A. JASPER : An Eclipse Plug-In to Facilitate Software Maintenance Tasks. In *Proc. 2006 OOPSLA Workshop on Eclipse Technology eXchange*, ACM Press (2006).

4. DeLine, R., Czerwinski, M., and Robertson, G. Easing Program Comprehension by Sharing Navigation Data. In *Proc. VLHCC '05*, IEEE (2005).

5. DeLine, R., and Rowan, K. Code canvas: zooming towards better development environments. In *Proc. ICSE '10*, ACM (2010).

6. Fouse, A., Weibel, N., Hutchins, E., and Hollan, J. D. ChronoViz: a system for supporting navigation of time-coded data. In *Proc. CHI '11*, ACM (2011).

7. Karrer, T., Krämer, J.-P., Diehl, J., Hartmann, B., and Borchers, J. Stacksplorer: Call graph navigation helps increasing code maintenance efficiency. In *Proc. UIST '11*, ACM (2011).

8. Kersten, M., and Murphy, G. C. Mylar: A Degree-of-Interest Model for IDEs. In *Proc. AOSD*, ACM (2005).

9. Ko, A., Myers, B., Coblenz, M., and Aung, H. An Exploratory Study of How Developers Seek, Relate, and Collect Relevant Information during Software Maintenance Tasks. *IEEE Transactions on Software Engineering 32*, 12 (2006).

10. Ko, A. J., and Myers, B. A. Debugging Reinvented: Asking and Answering Why and Why Not Questions about Program Behavior. In *Proc. ICSE '08*, IEEE (2008).

11. Krämer, J.-P., Kurz, J., Karrer, T., and Borchers, J. Blaze: supporting two-phased call graph navigation in source code. In *Proc. CHI EA '12*, ACM (2012).

12. LaToza, T. D., and Myers, B. A. Developers Ask Reachability Questions. In *Proc. ICSE '10*, ACM (2010).

13. LaToza, T. D., and Myers, B. A. Visualizing Call Graphs. In *Proc. VLHCC '11* (2011).

14. LaToza, T. D., Venolia, G., and DeLine, R. Maintaining Mental Models: A Study of Developer Work Habits. In *Proc. ICSE '06*, ACM (2006).

15. Lawrance, J., Bellamy, R., Burnett, M., and Rector, K. Using information scent to model the dynamic foraging behavior of programmers in maintenance tasks. In *Proc. CHI '08*, ACM (2008).

16. Murphy, G. C., Kersten, M., and Findlater, L. How Are Java Software Developers Using the Eclipse IDE? *IEEE Software 23*, 4 (2006).

17. Piorkowski, D., Fleming, S. D., Scaffidi, C., John, L., Bogart, C., John, B. E., Burnett, M., and Bellamy, R. Modeling programmer navigation: A head-to-head empirical evaluation of predictive models. In *Proc. VL/HCC '11* (2011).

18. Pirolli, P., and Card, S. K. Information Foraging. *Psychological Review 106*, 4 (1999).

19. Pressman, R. S. *Software Engineering: A Practitioner's Approach*, 7th ed. McGraw-Hill, 2010.

20. Robillard, M. P., Coelho, W., and Murphy, G. C. How Effective Developers Investigate Source Code:An Exploratory Study. *IEEE Transactions on Software Engineering 30*, 12 (2004).

21. Sillito, J., Murphy, G. C., and Volder, K. D. Asking and Answering Questions during a Programming Change Task. *IEEE Transactions on Software Engineering 34*, 4 (2008).

22. Singer, J., Elves, R., and Storey, M.-A. NavTracks: Supporting Navigation in Software Maintenance. In *Proc. ICSM '05*, IEEE (2005).

23. Singer, J., Lethbridge, T., Vinson, N., and Anquetil, N. An Examination of Software Engineering Work Practices. In *Proc. 1997 Conference of the Centre for Advanced Studies on Collaborative Research*, IBM Press (1997).

24. Čubranić, D., and Murphy, G. C. Hipikat: Recommending Pertinent Software Development Artifacts. In *Proc. ICSE '03*, IEEE (2003).

25. Winograd, T. Breaking the complexity barrier again. *ACM SIGIR Forum* (1974).

Webzeitgeist: Design Mining the Web

Ranjitha Kumar[1]   Arvind Satyanarayan[1]   Cesar Torres[1]   Maxine Lim[1]   Salman Ahmad[2]

Scott R. Klemmer[1]   Jerry O. Talton[3]

[1]Stanford University   [2]Massachusetts Institute of Technology   [3]Intel Corporation

{ranju, arvindsatya, ctorres, maxinel}@cs.stanford.edu, saahmad@mit.edu, srk@cs.stanford.edu, jerry.o.talton@intel.com

ABSTRACT

Advances in data mining and knowledge discovery have transformed the way Web sites are designed. However, while visual presentation is an intrinsic part of the Web, traditional data mining techniques ignore render-time page structures and their attributes. This paper introduces *design mining* for the Web: using knowledge discovery techniques to understand design demographics, automate design curation, and support data-driven design tools. This idea is manifest in Webzeitgeist, a platform for large-scale design mining comprising a repository of over 100,000 Web pages and 100 million design elements. This paper describes the principles driving design mining, the implementation of the Webzeitgeist architecture, and the new class of data-driven design applications it enables.

ACM Classification Keywords

H.2.8 Information Systems: Database Applications; D.2.2 Software Engineering: Design Tools and Techniques

General Terms

Design

Author Keywords

Web design; data mining

INTRODUCTION

Web knowledge discovery and data mining [23] have transformed the way people build and evaluate Web sites [15], and the way that consumers interact with them. The information gained from Web mining drives search, e-commerce, interface development, network architectures, online education, social science, and more [16].

Web data mining typically comprises three domains: usage mining, or click analysis [32]; content mining, or text analysis [24]; and structure mining, or link analysis [8]. Together, these techniques mine the *content* contained in a Web page, but ignore that content's *presentation*. In fact, most mining and knowledge discovery systems *discard* style and rendering data [39, 33]. This raises the question: what could we learn from mining design?

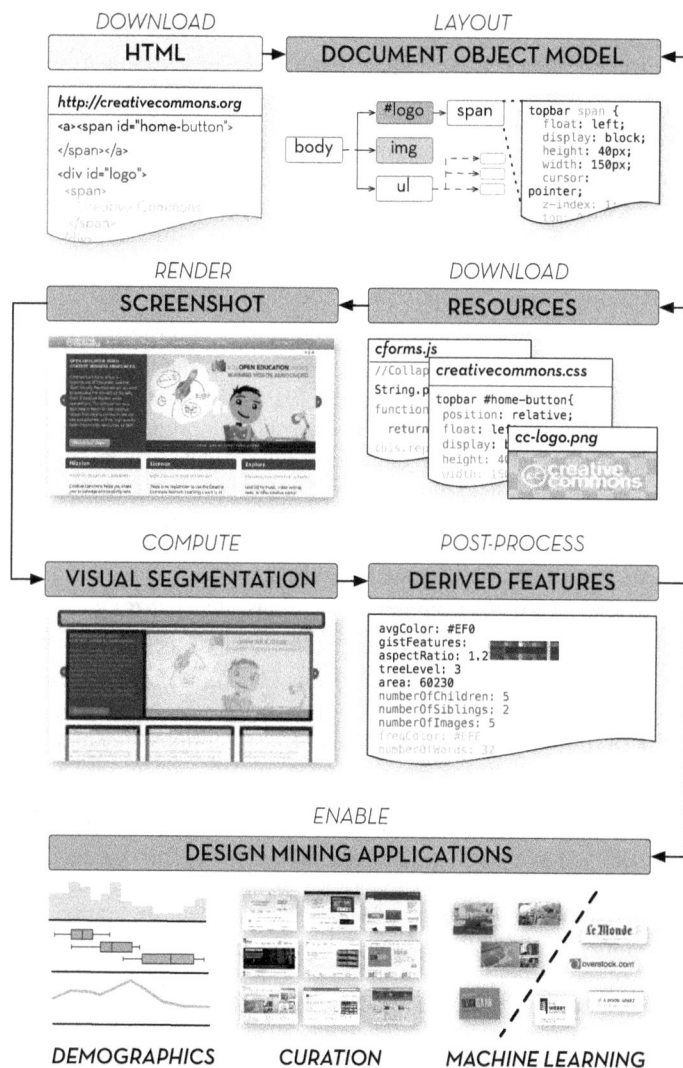

Figure 1. Webzeitgeist, a scalable platform for Web *design mining*, supplements the data used in traditional Web content mining (yellow) with information about the visual appearance and structure of pages (blue) to enable a host of new design applications (green).

This paper introduces *design mining* for the Web (Figure 1). With billions of extant pages—each comprising a concrete example of human creativity and aesthetics—the Web provides an opportunity to learn about design on a truly massive scale [18]. This paper demonstrates that applying knowledge discovery techniques to Web design data can help users understand design demographics, automate design curation, and support new data-driven design interactions.

These ideas are manifest in *Webzeitgeist*,[1] a software platform for mining and machine learning on Web design. Webzeitgeist comprises a repository of Web pages, processed into data structures that facilitate large-scale design knowledge extraction. The Webzeitgeist architecture is based on four underlying principles—scalability, extensibility, completeness, and consistency—and optimized for three common use cases: *direct access* to specific page elements, *query-based access* to identify a set of page elements which share common properties, and *stream-based access* to the repository as a whole for large-scale machine learning and statistical analysis [12].

Webzeitgeist's repository is populated via a bespoke Web crawler, which requests pages through a specialized caching proxy backed by a flexible data store. As each page is crawled and rendered, its resources are versioned and saved, and its Document Object Model (DOM) tree is snapshotted to produce a complete, static record of the page's design. Then, a set of semantic and visual features describing each DOM node are computed in a post-process and stored. Client applications access the repository through a RESTful API [30].

This paper discusses the principles that enable large-scale Web design mining, the implementation of the Webzeitgeist architecture, the repository crawled from the Web, and the API that exposes it. In addition, we demonstrate the utility of the platform by describing several data-driven design applications, including statistical analysis of design patterns, design-based search, and design-driven machine learning.

PRINCIPLES FOR DESIGN MINING

To support design mining applications, the Webzeitgeist architecture is predicated on four underlying principles.

Scalability. In rich visual domains like Web design, the utility of data mining critically depends on the size of the corpus. In a space with thousands of parameters, millions of examples are necessary to extract meaningful statistics or find relevant examples during search [10, 31]. Webzeitgeist, therefore, is designed to scale to millions of distinct page elements. Visual and semantic features are precomputed for fast access, stored in a relational database to facilitate complex queries, and duplicated in a key-value store for efficient streaming. To eliminate redundant storage of shared page resources, Webzeitgeist employs Rabin fingerprint hashing [29]. Additionally, the Webzeitgeist server uses a large memory pool to minimize disk access, backed by a hardware RAID controller with striping to make disk access fast when it does occur.

Extensibility. Since Webzeitgeist provides a general platform for design mining, not all of its eventual uses can be presently foreseen. Thus, a modular architecture facilitates the addition of new data, features, and functionality. To support transparent updates, two versions of the data store exist at all times: a *production* version that is exposed to external applications, and a *staging* version where new pages are added during crawling and features are computed. To minimize code and data dependencies, individual features are implemented as independent C++ dynamic plugin libraries.

---

[1] *Webzeitgeist* is a portmanteau intended to evoke the "spirit" of a Web site.

The post-process communicates with the data store through the public API, allowing implementation details to change as long as interfaces are preserved.

Completeness. Most Web mining employs static page analysis: issuing an HTTP GET request for a given URL, storing the returned HTML, and parsing it [21]. To mine the *design* of Web pages, Webzeitgeist must identify and capture every resource and DOM property that contributes to a page's visual appearance. Since render-time visual properties cannot be determined through static page source analysis, Webzeitgeist uses a layout engine to process retrieved HTML into a DOM tree, and a proxy server to dynamically intercept all the resource requests made by the engine during this process.

Consistency. Dynamically-generated content poses another complication for design mining. DHTML and client-side scripting allow arbitrary code to modify the DOM based on requests made to external resources. Thus, it is nearly impossible to archive pages in a format that guarantees reproducible rendering in a browser without altering their source [28, 2]. This ephemerality frustrates many machine learning and statistical analysis applications, which expect data to remain consistent between accesses. Webzeitgeist, therefore, renders a canonical view of each page during crawling, and serializes the resultant DOM and all of its properties to the data store. Client applications and feature computations access this static snapshot of a page's design instead of interacting with the layout engine directly, and can query render-time properties without having to re-render the page.

IMPLEMENTATION

The Webzeitgeist architecture comprises five integrated components: the Web crawler, the proxy server, the data store, the post-process, and the API (Figure 2). The crawler loads pages through the proxy, which writes them to the data store. Post-processes then run on the stored pages to compute high-level features and data structures, after which client applications can access the repository through the API.

Web Design Crawler

The Web crawler consists of a set of parallel browser processes, which load pages from the Web to add them to the Webzeitgeist repository. The crawler builds a queue of URLs from a seed list. At each stage of the crawl, a browser process dequeues a URL, checks that it is not already in the repository, and requests the corresponding page. Once the page is downloaded, its HTML is parsed, and all external links are extracted and added to the queue. The Webzeitgeist crawler loads each page in a Webkit browser window [3], computes its DOM tree, and renders it. This rendering and the computed DOM are then saved in the *staging* store.

Caching Proxy Server

To identify and store a page's resources, the system routes all browser requests through a custom Web proxy. The proxy sits between the Web and the crawler, and connects directly to the Webzeitgeist data store. The proxy intercepts each resource request made by a page, downloads it from the Web, and hashes its contents. If the file does not already exist in the store, it is added.

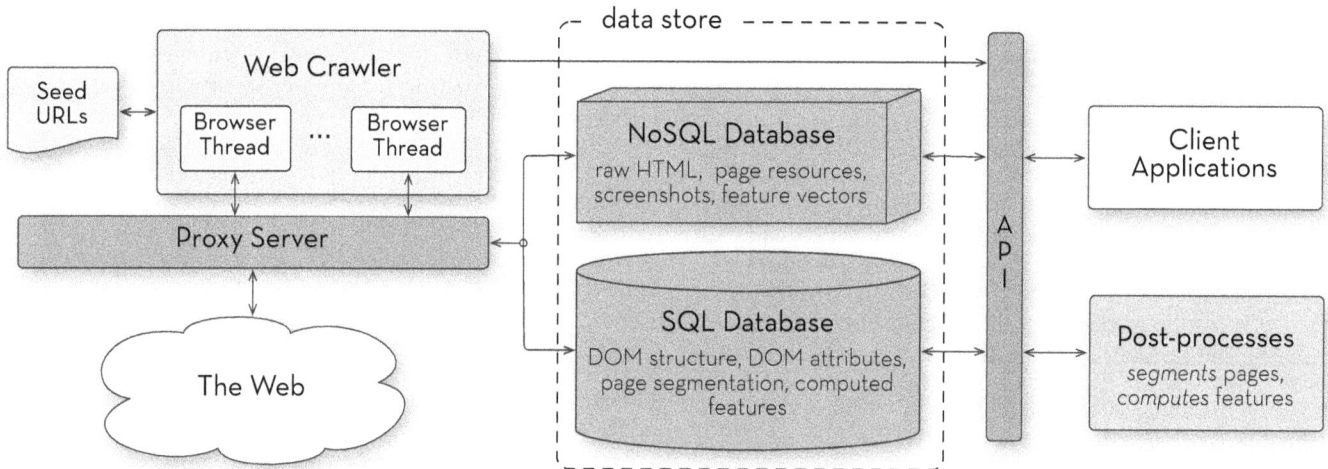

Figure 2. The Webzeitgeist architecture. A bespoke Web crawler requests pages through a caching proxy, and renders them in a set of browser threads. The proxy saves requested resources in a NoSQL key-value store, while the crawler writes the complete DOM tree for each page into a relational SQL database. Then, a set of post-process scripts are run to compute high-level features and data-structures over the stored pages. Client applications access the repository through a RESTful API.

The proxy server is also responsible for storing the graph structure of page-resource relationships. Since HTTP is a stateless protocol, this requires using custom HTTP headers to associate each resource request with the page that originated it. When the crawler requests a page, the data store generates a unique identifier and passes it back in the response header. The crawler then uses this ID to label each subsequent request the page makes to the proxy.

Two additional headers determine how the proxy services requests: adding them to the store during the crawl, or serving them directly from the database during retrieval. In the event that an application tries to retrieve a URL that does not exist in the data store, the proxy server responds with a 404 - PAGE NOT FOUND error.

Feature Post-processes

Once a page has been downloaded, converted to a DOM, rendered, and stored, a set of post-processes are run. First, Webzeitgeist computes a visual hierarchy from the DOM, discarding nodes that do not contribute to the page's rendered appearance and re-parenting nodes to ensure that parent-child relationships in the hierarchy correspond to visual containment on the page [17]. Then, the system computes a set of semantic and computer vision features over each element in the hierarchy and stores them (see Figure 3).

Next, the post-process coalesces each node's visual, semantic, and render-time features into a vector descriptor, exposing page properties in a convenient form for design mining applications. Numeric features are normalized to the range [0, 1], and string-based attributes are binarized based on their possible values to generate dictionary-length bit vectors. After this conversion, each page node is associated with a 1679-dimensional descriptor consisting of 691 render-time HTML and CSS properties computed by the DOM, 960 GIST scene descriptors computed on the node's rendering [26], and 28 structural and computer vision properties.

After the feature vectors are computed, the post-process restructures the table in which DOM properties are stored. During the crawl, DOM tree data is added to a wide table which facilitates fast insertions but results in slow retrieval; partitioning this table into a *star schema* reduces retrieval times by an order of magnitude [38]. After this restructuring, the post-process migrates the data store from the staging environment to production.

Data Store

The Webzeitgeist data store comprises two databases: a NoSQL database for page resources, binary data, and the vector descriptors for page nodes; and a relational SQL database for DOM nodes and properties, the visual page hierarchies, and the associated vision and semantic feature values.

The NoSQL database is a MongoDB instance [1], which provides fast access to binary files and structures too large to be efficiently stored in SQL tables, while simultaneously supporting dynamic queries and aggregation. This database con-

POSITION		DIMENSION	
[absolute, fractional] **X position**		**area, height, width, aspect ratio**	
[absolute, fractional] **Y position**		*fractional* **area** w.r.t. *[parent, page]*	
percent overlap with *[left, top]* of page		*fractional* **height** w.r.t. *[parent, page]*	
		fraction **width** w.r.t. *[parent, page]*	
CONTENT			
number of **[images, links, words]**		**STRUCTURE**	
VISION		number of **[children, siblings]**	
		[absolute, fractional] **sibling order**	
GIST features		*[absolute, fractional]* **tree level**	
[average, most frequent] **RGB color**			
[number, percent] **edge pixels**			

Figure 3. The semantic and computer vision features that Webzeitgeist computes over page elements.

tains the full HTML of every crawled page, its resources, and the high-dimensional feature descriptor for each visual hierarchy node.

The relational database is a MySQL instance [27], comprising five tables: PROXY CONTENT, PROXY LINKS, DOM NODES, VISUAL BLOCKS, and FEATURES (Figure 4). The PROXY CONTENT table contains metadata for every URL requested by pages during crawling, describing where the resource is from, its identifier in the NoSQL store, when it was retrieved, and a Rabin fingerprint hash of its contents. The PROXY LINKS table associates pages with a list of the resources upon which they depend. The DOM NODES table contains a record of each DOM node encountered in the crawl, along with pointers to its parent page and node; its type, name, value, and inner HTML; and all 258 render-time DOM attributes defined by the HTML4 and CSS3 standards [37, 36]. The VISUAL BLOCKS table contains the page elements that result from the visual segmentations performed during post-processing. The FEATURES table stores the visual and semantic features computed for each such block. For fast retrieval, tables are denormalized with replicated Page, DOM, and Block IDs.

API

Clients access the Webzeitgeist repository through a RESTful API, loading the appropriate endpoint URL and receiving JSON data in return [5]. Three modes are available for requesting data. The first allows *direct access* to design properties based on unique identifiers. The second allows clients to *stream* batches of data from the repository with a single request.

For more complex access patterns, the API also provides a custom JSON-based design query language (DQL). DQL predicates allow for filtering based on combinations of DOM attributes and computed visual features. When issuing queries, the client can also specify a list of properties that should be returned by the API call, keeping result sets succinct. The API transparently converts DQL queries into SQL and Mongo Query Language, sanitizes them to prevent injection attacks, and returns the results in JSON.

Server Hardware

The Webzeitgeist repository is hosted on a twelve-core 2.4GHz Intel Xeon server to allow complex DQL queries to be executed efficiently. The server contains 48 GB of RAM to facilitate caching and ensure that the SQL index fits in memory. The server's 4TB data store consists of fourteen 600GB 15K RPM SAS drives in a RAID 10 configuration, backed by a hardware RAID controller with a 1GB cache. The drive array is capable of sustaining 6GB/s throughput when data is being streamed from disk.

THE WEBZEITGEIST DATASET

The Webzeitgeist crawl was seeded with 20 URLs, including the Alexa Top 500, the Webby Awards gallery, and popular design blogs. To build a diverse repository, pages were crawled in a breadth-first order, self-referential domain links were skipped, and only a single copy of each resolved URL was stored. The resultant dataset contains 103,744 Web pages from 43,743 domains, with 143.2 million DOM nodes and 12.7 million visual blocks. The raw HTML content of these pages and their referenced resources together require 425GB of disk space; the SQL database requires 187GB. The pages reference over 5.3 million HTML, CSS, JavaScript, image, and other resources, including Flash, movie, and audio files (see inset figure).

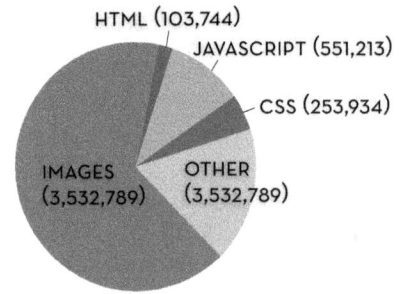

HTML (103,744)
JAVASCRIPT (551,213)
CSS (253,934)
IMAGES (3,532,789)
OTHER (3,532,789)

The Webzeitgeist crawl was a computationally intensive task, requiring more than 35 CPU days of processing. As a representative example, the CHI 2013 homepage http://chi2013.acm.org references two style sheets, four JavaScript files, and five images for a total of 480KB of raw content. The crawler downloaded the page on September 13th, 2012, in 3.5 seconds. The DOM, which comprised 251 nodes, was computed in 0.1 seconds and stored via the API in 0.47 seconds.

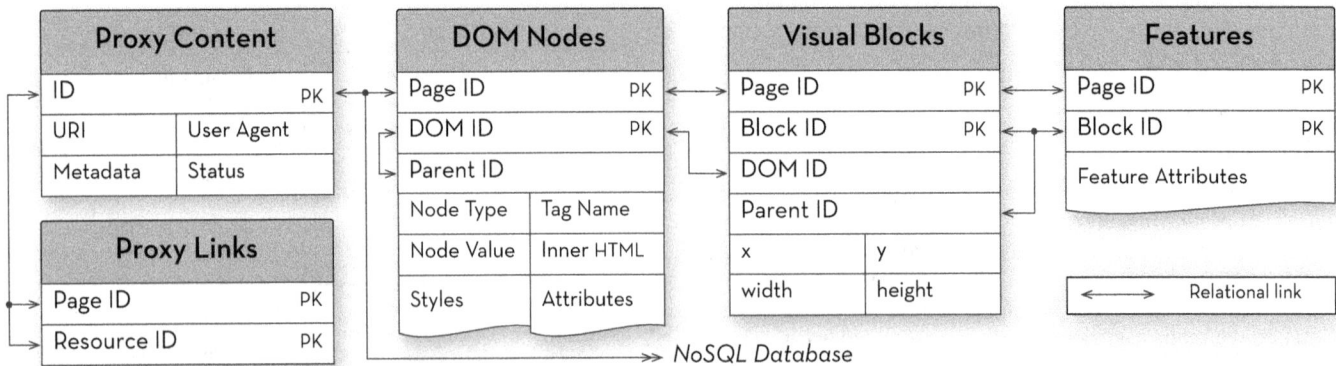

Proxy Content		
ID		PK
URI	User Agent	
Metadata	Status	

Proxy Links		
Page ID		PK
Resource ID		PK

DOM Nodes		
Page ID		PK
DOM ID		PK
Parent ID		
Node Type	Tag Name	
Node Value	Inner HTML	
Styles	Attributes	

Visual Blocks		
Page ID		PK
Block ID		PK
DOM ID		
Parent ID		
x	y	
width	height	

Features		
Page ID		PK
Block ID		PK
Feature Attributes		

←→	Relational link

→ *NoSQL Database*

Figure 4. The schema for the Webzeitgeist data store, showing the five tables that comprise the SQL database and their contents. This denormalized structure, with replicated Page, DOM, and Block IDs, facilitates fast retrievals.

Figure 5. The 295 distinct cursors in the Webzeitgeist repository, fetched in 47.8 seconds. This query searches the CSS `cursor` property on DOM nodes, looks up the ID in the PROXY CONTENT table, and fetches the associated file from NoSQL.

The visual segmentation algorithm ran for 2ms, producing 61 visual blocks; visual feature computation ran for 13.53 seconds. Writing this segmentation and the associated features to the database took another 1.04 seconds, for a total processing time of 18.64 seconds.

DESIGN MINING IN ACTION

The Webzeitgeist design mining platform enables content producers to answer questions about design practice and software developers to build next-generation design tools. Designers can query Webzeitgeist to understand design demographics and search for examples of design patterns and trends [7, 11], without relying on manual curation. Application developers can apply machine learning techniques to Web design problems without incurring the overhead of crawling, rendering, and sanitizing Web data. Webzeitgeist significantly lowers the barrier to data-driven Web design, facilitating analysis on a scale 50–300 times larger than prior work [14, 31].

Design Demographics

Designers often seek to understand the space of options along a particular design axis [20]. For instance, a designer who wants to customize the cursor on her Web page might look at a gallery of cursors used on other pages for inspiration. We can query Webzeitgeist to return all the distinct cursors in the repository:

```
POST, /v1/dom.json
query = {
  "$select": [
    {"@styles": {"$distinct": "cursor"}
  ]
}
```

This DQL query—which executed in 47.8 seconds—first finds cursors by examining the CSS `cursor` property across DOM nodes, and then fetches the corresponding files from the NoSQL database. A "cursory" inspection of the 295 results shows that arrows, hands, cartoon characters, and celebrity faces are all popular choices (Figure 5).

Webzeitgeist can answer similar questions about popular text color choices, for instance by computing a cumulative distribution function over the CSS `color` property:

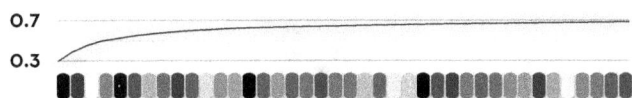

The forty most popular text colors in the database account for nearly 70 percent of all text color; most are shades of grey.

Webzeitgeist affords the ability to examine distributions over both page- and node-level Web properties. For instance, an information architect might use Webzeitgeist to compute statistics on the visual complexity of pages. Figure 6 (*top row*) shows that the mode depth of a page's DOM tree is six, and that most pages contain between 50 and 200 DOM nodes. To investigate the cause of the sharp spike in the latter histogram, the architect can request IDs for pages with only a single DOM node and inspect their HTML: unsurprisingly, these pages are predominantly Flash-based.

Similarly, a designer might wish to inspect common properties for individual page assets to guide the design of new content. Calculating a histogram over the *aspectRatio* of visual nodes reveals that there are many square elements, but that page elements, on average, are wider than they are tall (Figure 6, *bottom left*). Computing a histogram over the CSS `opacity` property and examining values less than 1, reveals sharp peaks at .5, .65, .75, and .8 (Figure 6, *bottom right*).

Since Webzeitgeist stores HTML properties in addition to design data, we can also use the repository to revisit HTML demographics in a new way. In 2005, Google released the results of a large-scale survey of popular HTML `class` names [9]. Webzeitgeist allows us to take this study one step further, and understand the relationship between static HTML properties and dynamic render-time ones. Since Webzeitgeist records the render-time bounding box for each DOM node, we can compute spatial probability distributions for the most popular CSS selectors (Figure 7). The striking patterns that result indicate that the visual positions and semantic roles of some page elements are highly correlated.

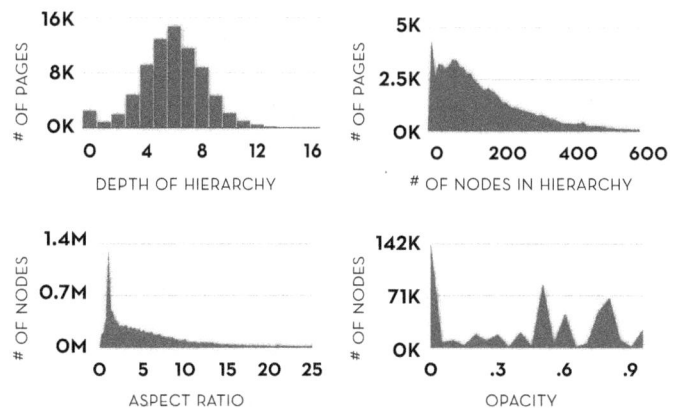

Figure 6. *Top row*: distributions over page-level properties: depth (left) and number of nodes (right) in a page's visual hierarchy. *Bottom row*: distributions over node-level properties: *aspect ratio* feature (left) and CSS `opacity` (right).

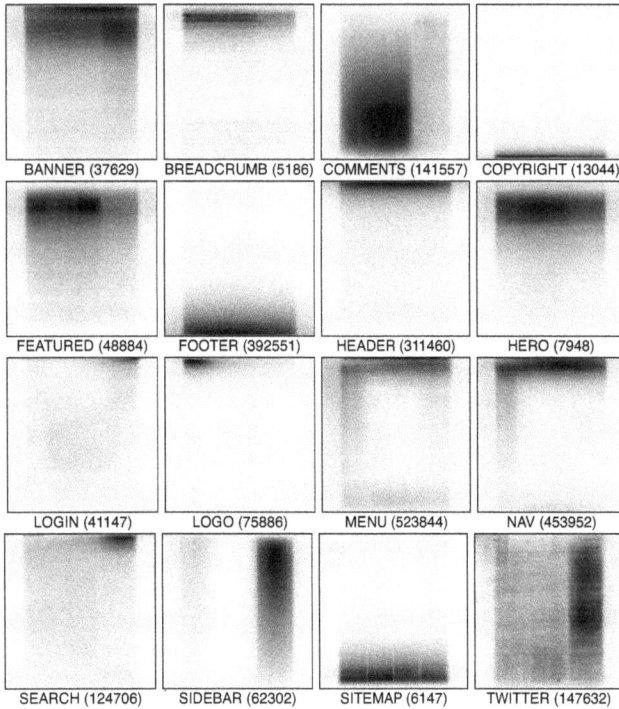

Figure 7. Spatial probability distributions for frequently occurring HTML `id` and `class` attributes demonstrate striking visual correlations.

Design Queries

Designers are often interested in understanding the context of particular patterns and trends. Many design blogs maintain small, curated sets of examples showcasing notable Web design techniques.

To give designers more powerful search and collection capabilities, Webzeitgeist introduces the ability to quickly create dynamic collections that exhibit particular design characteristics. For instance, one distinctive technique discussed on design blogs is the use of long, scrolling horizontal layouts.

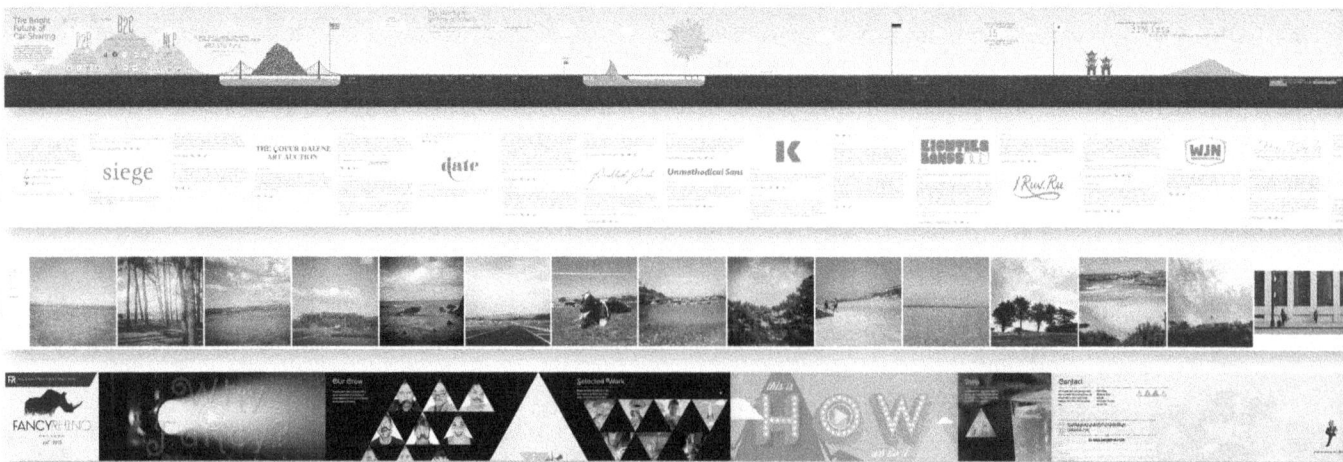

Figure 9. Selections from some of the 4943 pages containing <CANVAS> elements in the Webzeitgeist repository, demonstrating interactive interfaces, animations, graphs, reflections, rounded corners, and custom fonts.

To find such pages, we queried Webzeitgeist for pages with *aspectRatio* greater than 10.0:

```
POST, /v1/pages.json
query = {
  "$select": [{"$distinct": "page_id"}],
  "$where" : [
    {"@visual": {"aspectRatio": {"$gt": 10} } }
  ]
}
```

This query produced 68 horizontally-scrolling pages in 1.1 seconds. Figure 8 shows a few representative results.

Querying Webzeitgeist with constraints based on HTML markup can also shed light on design trends. The W3C describes the <CANVAS> element—introduced in HTML5—as a scriptable graphics container. The specification, however, gives little insight into how the tag is actually used. Webzeitgeist returns all 201,658 <CANVAS> elements in the database in 2.4 minutes. Figure 9 shows representative uses.

Figure 8. Four of the 68 query results for pages with horizontal layouts. Blogs, image/photo galleries, and vector art pages are a few of the representative styles in the results set.

Figure 10. Query results for nodes containing large typography, demonstrating large text in logos, site titles, hero graphics, and background effects. The query identified 6856 DOM nodes from 1657 distinct pages, and executed in 56 seconds.

Webzeitgeist allows us to investigate another problematic aspect of Web design: typography. Although the CSS @font-face rule was introduced in 1998 [6], technical and licensing issues with embedding custom Web fonts have traditionally relegated complex typographic effects to images. We can use Webzeitgeist to search for examples of prominent Web font typography, querying for nodes with a CSS font-size property greater than 100 pixels. Figure 10 shows a few of the 6856 results, which occur in only 1657 distinct pages.

We can build more complex queries by specifying more constraints. To learn the different ways in which semi-transparent overlays are used, we queried for nodes with

a solid background color where the *alpha* value of the CSS background-color property is between 0 and 1 (Figure 11).

We can also use Webzeitgeist to construct queries over high-level design concepts. Suppose a designer wants to browse "search engine-like" pages. This concept is loaded with design constraints, but we can approximate it in DQL as a query for pages with a centered <INPUT> element and low visual complexity:

```
POST, /v1/pages.json
query = {
  "$select": [{"page_id": 1}],
  "$where": [
    {
      "@dom": {
        "tagName": "INPUT",
        "type": "text",
      "@visual": {
        "leftSidedness": {"$or": {"$gte": 0.4}, {"$lte":0.6}},
        "topSidedness":  {"$or": {"$gte": 0.4}, {"$lte":0.6}}
      }
    },
    {"@visual": {"$cnt": {"$lt": 50} } }
  ]
}
```

Figure 12 shows a few results from this query.

Similarly, attribute queries can be composed to search for pages with specific visual layouts. Figure 13 shows a sample layout with a large header, a top navigation bar, and a large body text node. We can encode this layout in a DQL query that searches for pages with a header that takes up more than 20 percent of the page's area, a navigation element that is positioned in the top 10 percent of the page's height, and a text node that contains more than 50 words. This example illustrates the kinds of applications that Webzeitgeist might engender: imagine a search interface that automatically formulates queries from sketches like the one shown in the figure.

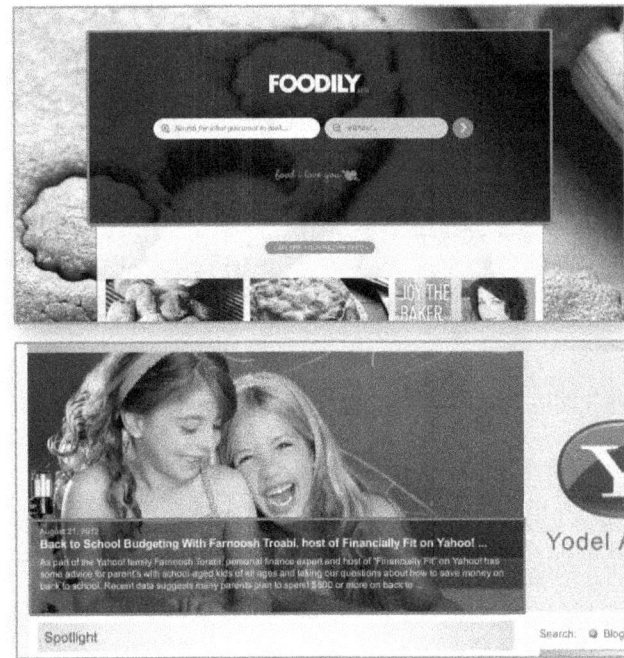

Figure 11. Query results for semi-transparent overlays. The query identified 9878 DOM nodes from 3435 distinct pages, and executed in 48.1 seconds. Semi-transparent overlays are often used on top of photographs, either as a way to display content over of a busy photographic background (top) or to frame captions (bottom).

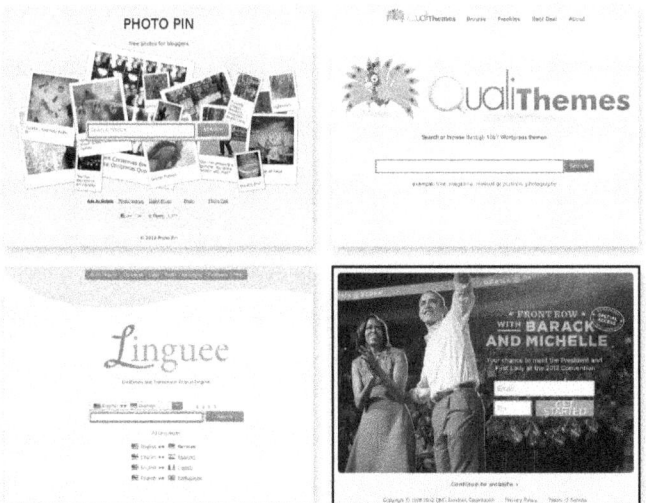

Figure 12. Query results for "search engine" pages: roughly centered (vertically and horizontally) text INPUT elements, and fewer than 50 visual elements on the page. This query produced 209 pages and executed in 3.9 minutes. Some login and signup pages are also returned (bottom right).

Figure 13. Five of the 20 search results for the three-part DQL layout query visualized on the left. The query, which executed in 2.1 minutes, returns pages that share a common high-level layout, but exhibit different designs.

Machine Learning

Webzeitgeist also enables a new kind of design-based machine learning. For the first time, applications can stream structured visual descriptors for page elements from a central repository. Moreover, Webzeitgeist's extensible architecture allows new data to be collected and integrated with the repository for supervised learning applications, for instance via crowdsourcing.

Classification. Lim et al. [22] used Webzeitgeist as a backend to train structural semantic classifiers for concepts like ARTICLE TITLE, ADVERTISEMENT, and PRODUCT IMAGE. In an online study, they collected a set of more than 20,000 semantic labels over more than 1000 distinct pages. They then used the descriptors associated with page elements to train 40 binary Support Vector Machine classifiers, reporting an average test accuracy of 77 percent. In the future, these and other similar classifiers could be used to support Web accessibility, guide attempts to "semantify" the HTML standard, and allow designers to search for pages that match a given visual "feel."

Metric Learning. Machine learning techniques can also be used to enable example-based search over the repository. Using Lim et al.'s label data, we induced a distance metric in the 1679-dimensional descriptor space using OASIS, a metric-learning algorithm originally developed for large-scale image comparison [4]. The method takes as input sets of identically-labeled page elements, and attempts to learn a symmetric positive-definite matrix that minimizes interset distances. Once learned, this metric can be used to perform query-by-example searches on page regions via a nearest-neighbor search in the metric space. These nearest-neighbor computations can be performed in realtime via locality sensitive hashing [13].

Example-based search provides a powerful mechanism for navigating complex design spaces like the Web [31]. Figure 14 shows three example queries and their top results, demonstrating how Webzeitgeist can be used to search for alternatives for a given design artifact, and to identify template reuse between pages. The utility of this search interaction critically depends on the full Webzeitgeist feature space. For comparison, Figure 15 shows nearest-neighbor results for the top query in Figure 14 using only the vision-based GIST descriptors. While these elements are visually reminiscent of the query, they bear little structural or semantic relation to it.

DISCUSSION AND FUTURE WORK

This paper demonstrates—for the first time—the value of large-scale mining of design data, and offers a new class of data-driven problem-solving techniques to the design community. While the paper showcases several concrete design interactions, we imagine that the applications that eventually arise from design mining will greatly outstrip our power to predict them.

There are a number of directions for future work. Scaling the database by several orders of magnitude would increase the accuracy and utility of many design-mining applications. While the current indexing strategy for Webzeitgeist should scale to about five million pages, crawling a more substantial portion of the Web would require porting the infrastructure to a distributed computing and storage platform. More flexible and powerful backing stores (for instance, graph databases [25]) may also make it easier to formulate complex queries that span multiple levels of page hierarchy (e.g., "Find all the nodes whose children are all <IMAGE> elements").

In addition to crawling more pages, altering the crawl's selection policy to capture additional information from each visited site could provide a more holistic view of Web design practice. By spoofing USER-AGENT headers and requesting pages with browser windows of varying sizes, the repository could detect responsive Web designs, or pages with layouts that adapt to the viewing environment. This type of mining would help users understand design patterns across different form factors (e.g., mobile, tablet, and desktop). Expanding Webzeitgeist to support site-level mining by sampling several pages from each visited domain could help designers analyze how individual page elements are reused and adapted. Aggregating multiple versions of pages over time could allow users to build data-driven models of Web design evolution [2, 35].

Figure 14. Top search results from querying the repository using the learned distance metric and three query elements. These results demonstrate how Webzeitgeist can be used to search for design alternatives (top, middle), and to identify template re-use between pages (bottom).

Perhaps the most exciting avenue for future work is using the repository to realize new machine learning applications, or reimplementing existing methods at scale [14, 31, 34]. Exploiting model and hardware parallelism has made it feasible to train models with billions of parameters on Web-scale datasets with millions of examples, leading to a number of breakthroughs in unsupervised learning [19]. In addition, using the Webzeitgeist platform to bootstrap crowdsourced data collection may enable a host of new supervised learning applications.

We hope that Webzeitgeist will lower the barrier to building data-driven design applications and engender a new class of Web design tools. For more information, please visit `http://hci.stanford.edu/research/webzeitgeist`.

ACKNOWLEDGMENTS
We thank Dan Fike, Andreas Paepcke, Richard Socher, Tom Yeh, David Karger, the Stanford HCI Group, and the anonymous reviewers for their helpful comments and suggestions. This research was supported by the National Science Foundation under Grant No. 0846167, a Google PhD Fellowship, and an SAP Stanford Graduate Fellowship.

REFERENCES
[1] 10gen, I. *MongoDB*. 2012. http://www.mongodb.org.

[2] Adar, E., Dontcheva, M., Fogarty, J., and Weld, D. S. Zoetrope: interacting with the ephemeral web. In: *Proc. UIST*. 2008, 239–248.

[3] Apple Inc. *The WebKit open source project*. 2012. http://www.webkit.org/.

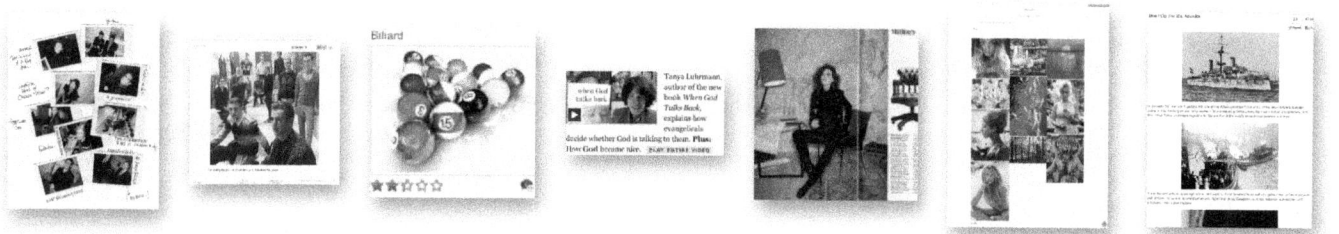

Figure 15. The top matches for the first (page) query in Figure 14 using *only* the vision-based GIST descriptors. While these elements are visually reminiscent of the query, most of them bear little structural or semantic relation to it.

[4] Chechik, G., Sharma, V., Shalit, U., and Bengio, S. An online algorithm for large scale image similarity learning. In: *Proc. NIPS*. 2009.

[5] Crockford, D. *The application/json Media Type for JavaScript Object Notation (JSON)*. Tech. rep. RFC 4627. IETF, July 2006.

[6] CSS Working Group. *Cascading style sheets, level 2*. May 1998. http://www.w3.org/TR/2008/REC-CSS2-20080411/.

[7] Duyne, D. K. van, Landay, J. A., and Hong, J. I. *The Design of Sites*. Addison-Wesley, 2002.

[8] Getoor, L. and Diehl, C. P. Link mining: a survey. *SIGKDD Explorations Newsletter* 7, 2 (2005), 3–12.

[9] Google Inc. *Web Authoring Statistics*. 2005. https://developers.google.com/webmasters/state-of-the-web/.

[10] Hays, J. and Efros, A. A. Scene completion using millions of photographs. In: *Proc. SIGGRAPH*. ACM, 2007.

[11] Herring, S. R., Chang, C.-C., Krantzler, J., and Bailey, B. P. Getting inspired!: understanding how and why examples are used in creative design practice. In: *Proc. CHI*. 2009.

[12] Hirai, J., Raghavan, S., Garcia-Molina, H., and Paepcke, A. WebBase: a repository of Web pages. *Computer Networks* 33, 1–6 (2000), 277–293.

[13] Indyk, P. and Motwani, R. Approximate nearest neighbors: towards removing the curse of dimensionality. In: *Proc. STOC*. 1998.

[14] Ivory, M. Y. and Hearst, M. A. Statistical profiles of highly-rated Web sites. In: *Proc. CHI*. 2002, 367–374.

[15] Kohavi, R., Henne, R. M., and Sommerfield, D. Practical guide to controlled experiments on the web: listen to your customers not to the HiPPO. In: *KDD*. 2007.

[16] Kosala, R. Web mining research: a survey. *SIGKDD Explorations* 2 (2000).

[17] Kumar, R., Talton, J. O., Ahmad, S., and Klemmer, S. R. Bricolage: example-based retargeting for Web design. In: *Proc. CHI*. ACM, 2011.

[18] Kumar, R., Talton, J. O., Ahmad, S., and Klemmer, S. R. Data-driven Web design. In: *Proc. ICML*. 2012.

[19] Le, Q., Ranzato, M., Monga, R., Devin, M., Chen, K., Corrado, G., Dean, J., and Ng, A. Building high-level features using large scale unsupervised learning. In: *Proc. ICML*. 2012.

[20] Lee, B., Srivastava, S., Kumar, R., Brafman, R., and Klemmer, S. R. Designing with interactive example galleries. In: *Proc. CHI*. 2010.

[21] Lee, H.-T., Leonard, D., Wang, X., and Loguinov, D. IRLbot: scaling to 6 billion pages and beyond. In: *Proc. WWW*. ACM, Beijing, China, 2008, 427–436.

[22] Lim, M., Kumar, R., Satyanarayan, A., Torres, C., Talton, J. O., and Klemmer, S. R. *Learning Structural Semantics for the Web*. Tech. rep. CSTR 2012-03. Stanford University, 2012.

[23] Liu, B. *Web Data Mining: Exploring Hyperlinks, Contents, and Usage Data*. Springer-Verlag, 2011.

[24] Liu, B. and Chen-Chuan-Chang, K. Editorial: special issue on web content mining. *SIGKDD Explorations Newsletter* 6, 2 (2004), 1–4.

[25] Neo Technology. *Neo4j*. 2012. http://neo4j.org/.

[26] Oliva, A. and Torralba, A. Modeling the shape of the scene: a holistic representation of the spatial envelope. *International Journal of Computer Vision* 42, 3 (2001), 145–175.

[27] Oracle Corporation. *MySQL*. 2012. http://www.mysql.com.

[28] Pollak, B. and Gatterbauer, W. Creating permanent test collections of Web pages for information extraction research. In: *Proc. SOFSEM*. 2. 2007, 103–115.

[29] Rabin, M. O. *Fingerprinting by random polynomials*. Tech. rep. Center for Research in Computing Technology, Harvard University, 1981.

[30] Richardson, L. and Ruby, S. *Restful Web services*. First edition. O'Reilly, 2007.

[31] Ritchie, D., Kejriwal, A., and Klemmer, S. R. d. tour: style-based exploration of design example galleries. In: *Proc. UIST*. 2011.

[32] Srivastava, J., Cooley, R., Deshpande, M., and Tan, P.-N. Web usage mining: discovery and applications of usage patterns from Web data. *SIGKDD Explorations Newsletter* 1, 2 (2000), 12–23.

[33] Sun, F., Song, D., and Liao, L. DOM based content extraction via text density. In: *Proc. SIGIR*. ACM, Beijing, China, 2011, 245–254.

[34] Talton, J., Yang, L., Kumar, R., Lim, M., Goodman, N. D., and Měch, R. Learning design patterns with Bayesian grammar induction. In: *Proc. UIST*. 2012.

[35] Teevan, J., Dumais, S. T., Liebling, D. J., and Hughes, R. L. Changing how people view changes on the Web. In: *Proc. UIST*. 2009.

[36] W3C Working Group. *Cascading style sheets snapshot 2010*. May 2011. http://www.w3.org/TR/CSS/.

[37] W3C Working Group. *HTML 4.01 specification*. Dec. 1999. http://www.w3.org/TR/html401/.

[38] Wikipedia. *Star schema — Wikipedia, the free encyclopedia*. [Online; accessed 19-September-2012]. 2012. http://en.wikipedia.org/wiki/Star_schema.

[39] Yi, L., Liu, B., and Li, X. Eliminating noisy information in Web pages for data mining. In: *Proc. SIGKDD*. ACM, 2003, 296–305.

Informal Cognitive Walkthroughs (ICW):

Paring Down and Pairing Up for an Agile World

Valentina Grigoreanu
Microsoft Corporation
Redmond, WA
valeng@microsoft.com

Manal Mohanna
Microsoft Corporation
Redmond, WA
manalmo@microsoft.com

ABSTRACT

Agile software teams' frequent releases and fast iterations present a growing need for rigorous user experience research methods that are faster, lighter-weight, and more flexible. To this end, we developed the Informal Cognitive Walkthrough (ICW). This agile research methodology grew organically, over the course of three years, while working with a very large agile software development team. ICWs involve conducting one or more Simplified 'Streamlined Cognitive Walkthroughs' (SSCW), followed by one or more Simplified 'Pluralistic Walkthroughs' (SPW). In this paper, we present the ICW and provide a real-world example of its application. Preliminary experiences with the method revealed potential advantages over traditional lab studies, ranging from more quickly uncovering and fixing usability issues, to a stronger collaboration between the disciplines, and to acting as a forcing function in aligning diverse engineers to deliver on a common user goal.

Author Keywords

Agile; Usability testing; User-centered design.

ACM Classification Keywords

D.2.2. Software Engineering: design tools and techniques

INTRODUCTION

The fast-paced development environment of agile software development teams often cannot afford the long turnaround time from traditional lab study setup, execution, data analysis, and report writing. New research methods are needed for usability testing to provide feedback on the frequent new iterations of an agile product.

In this paper, we present a new practitioner agile research methodology which we developed and have been applying for the past three years on a very large cloud solution development team, with hundreds of engineers. The method, the Informal Cognitive Walkthrough (ICW) mixed-methods approach, is grounded in two variations of the long-standing cognitive walkthrough methodology.

The Cognitive Walkthrough (CW) is a usability inspection method which involves "simulating a user's problem-solving process at each step in the human-computer dialog, checking to see if the user's goals and memory for actions can be assumed to lead to the next correct action" [2]. To prepare for CWs, user experience researchers need: the characteristics of a typical user, the tasks to be evaluated, a prototype of the interface, and a clear sequence of actions needed to complete the task. The players in this methodology are a usability expert and one or more expert evaluators of the software (product team members) [6].

While the CW quickly gained momentum with practitioners, it was soon criticized for its overhead (e.g., time consuming, tedious form-filling), which resulted in a flurry of simplified versions of the method, including the Cognitive Jogthrough [4], the Simplified Walkthrough [3], and the Streamlined Cognitive Walkthrough [5].

ICWs continue the trend of simplifying cognitive walkthroughs, to make them suitable for practitioners and, in particular, for agile development teams. We did this by both simplifying and then combining two variations of CWs: the Streamlined Cognitive Walkthrough [5] and the Pluralistic Walkthrough [1].

Spencer's Streamlined Cognitive Walkthrough (SCW) simplifies the CW by only asking two straightforward questions at each walkthrough step, instead of the more ambiguous original set of four questions. Only the most actionable data are collected for SCWs (steps where the user's stuck or does not know they did the right thing, design ideas or gaps, walkthrough gaps or flaws, etc.), instead of recording all the data. Each SCW session starts with training and ground rules to set expectations for what can and cannot be discussed during the session, and to determine each participant's role in the session.

The Pluralistic Walkthrough (PW) is a similar usability inspection method to the SCW, but it includes a group of representative users, in addition to usability professionals and product development engineers. In PWs, the users make their points first at each step, so as not to be influenced by the team members. They also individually write down their answers before sharing them with the rest of the participants, to prevent group-think.

The ICW is the result of first simplifying, and then pairing up, the Streamlined Cognitive Walkthrough (SCW) and Pluralistic Walkthrough (PW) methodologies.

PARING DOWN THE SCW AND THE PW

Simplified Streamlined Cognitive Walkthrough (SSCW)

While SCWs are much faster to conduct than CWs, they involve time-consuming training of the SCW participants: setting the ground rules and prepping the team took Spencer 20 minutes of the 1.5-hour session [5]. This is an onerous task on large agile teams, where dozens of members would need to be trained, especially when the team membership is in constant flux. We therefore simplified the SCW to primarily remove the need for training, and called this approach the Simplified Streamlined Cognitive Walkthrough (SSCW). To do this, we increased the responsibilities of the researcher, as described below. The researcher can be an HCI researcher, a user experience researcher, or any other usability professional that is very familiar with the software's problem space and its target users, but is not the owner of the design.

SSCWs (like SCWs and CWs) are user goal-oriented. Announcing each user goal, the researcher pretended to be a customer, walking through the individual steps for accomplishing that goal. The researcher answered the two SCW questions at each step: 1. As the user, would I know what to do at this step? 2. If I do the right thing, as the user, do I know I have made progress toward my goal?

Once the researcher made all the comments they had about a specific step, the rest of the product team members added their thoughts. The more variety there is in the team members' roles, the more variety there is in their comments as well. Typical roles taking part in SSCWs included: designers, program managers, developers, testers, and writers. Their only instructions are to place themselves in the customer's shoes as they try to accomplish the user goal, let the researcher talk first to not bias them, and then share their thoughts on the design at each step of the process.

The researcher also monitored discussions, bringing up rules only reactively if and when they are broken, unlike in the SCW. For example, if a deep discussion emerged about a tangential issue, the researcher would take note of it as an issue to discuss at a separate meeting. How much design talk, design decision explanations, and cognitive theory discussion is allowed is at the researcher's discretion. Unlike with SCWs, the researcher has also often been the note-taker, as he/she can stay in control of the session, making sure all comments are taken down before moving on to the next step. As with SCWs, notes are the only form of documentation resulting from an SSCW (often in an email sent out right after the meeting), and include what changes will be made by whom before the next session.

We typically conduct two SSCWs per feature area, before bringing in real users. The second session serves as a check that the problems found in the first session have been addressed and to make any last-minute improvements. The higher the fidelity of the design, the more sessions might be required (e.g., fixing one live code bug might reveal further bugs or usability issues down the line).

Simplified Pluralistic Walkthrough (SPW)

As with PWs, real product users have the spotlight in SPWs. The usability professionals and a subset of the product team members who attended the SSCWs are also present during the SPWs. As usability professionals and product team members would have already expressed their thoughts during the two SSCWs, they often spend the SPW session mostly listening and asking clarifying questions of the participants.

One difference from the PW is that, as a part of the Simplified PW (SPW), users were provided with blank generic comment forms, as opposed to printouts with the step-by-step screens for PWs. This provided the users the flexibility (agility) to take other paths through the software than the predefined 'golden path'. Another difference is that PWs are typically conducted with 6-10 real customers [1]. In SPWs, we aim to conduct two sessions with four customers each; with more participants, we have found the discussions become more superficial.

The biggest simplification with SPWs, however, is the note-taking method. More structured notes have meant quicker result turnaround time for us, since some of the analysis has happened during the session. To speed up note-taking, the researcher sets up a dual-monitor display: projecting the UI onto an overhead projector, and taking notes in a document on his/her laptop's screen. At each step, the researcher takes a screenshot of the UI, and types up the notes below it in one of four pre-defined areas: 1-next step the users would perform; 2-what the users did not like about this step; 3-what the users liked about this step; and 4-neutral comments. Each issue was written down as soon as it was mentioned. While the session was also recorded as a backup, the notes are the primary sources of data, as there is no time to analyze video data in the traditional way. The biggest issues are noted down during the SPW session and taken care of before the next SPW session (or filed as a bug if they are too big to address immediately).

As with SSCWs, multiple SPWs can be performed per feature area. To increase the sample size, and further reduce the impact of group-think, we have been conducting two sessions per target user population (four customers each).

PAIRING UP THE SSCW AND SPW

Thus, our ICW is made up of:

1. A series of Simplified Streamlined Cognitive Walkthroughs (SSCWs) conducted within the product team to prepare materials for customer feedback,

2. Followed by a series of Simplified Pluralistic Walkthroughs (SPW) with representative customers to gather real-world feedback on the features' usability.

The two parts of the ICW (the SSCWs and SPWs) are complimentary. On the one hand, the SSCWs find the obvious usability problems which are taken care of by the team before the first SPW session. This is similar to a CW version of a sandbox pilot session for a traditional lab study; it increases the quality of the design (at its current level of fidelity) and of the study documents before customers see it. A potential side-effect of the SSCW is that they help the product team better empathize with the customer. Furthermore, as product teams fix the obvious usability problems before they reach the customers, SSCWs also remove distractions from the design, so participants can focus on making novel and interesting insights. SPWs, on the other hand, provide the valuable customers' real-world context to the evaluation. The two methods complement each other and we always perform them together, in this order.

THE ICW APPLIED

Timing
As a usability inspection method, ICWs are best used during the iterative research phase (following generative research, and preceding summative research), and should be conducted as often as possible. We have fallen into a natural cadence of conducting about one ICW (two SSCWs and two SPWs per feature area) per month. The artifact to be tested in an ICW can be as high-level and informal as a workflow, a higher-fidelity prototype, or even as final as the implemented product itself. Ideally, at least one ICW is conducted at each level of fidelity for every key user goal.

Within one ICW, we expect to conduct a couple of SSCWs and SPWs for each feature area. Typically, the first week of the month lends itself well to planning, the second to the first set of SSCWs, the second set of SSCWs in the third week, and the SPWs in the fourth week. There is always a day or two break between the sessions for each feature area, to give the them time to act upon the findings before the next session.

For example, here is a real timeline we used for one ICW. Since the product team is large (hundreds of team members are indirectly affected by the methodology, about 50 of which take part in it directly), we evaluated three feature areas in parallel (FA 1, FA 2, and FA 3), for a total of 22 scenarios.

- Feb. 7: SSCW for FA1
- Feb. 9: SSCW for FA2,
- Feb. 14: SSCW for FA3, and
- Feb. 16: Three SSCWs, one each for FA1, 2, and 3.

We targeted two different user populations for the three feature areas: Information Workers (IWs) and IT Professionals (IT Pros).

- Feb. 17: IW SPW for FA1 and IW SPW for FA2
- Feb. 21: IT Pro SPW for FA2 and IT Pro SPW for FA3
- Feb. 24: IW SPW for FA1,2 and IT Pro SPW for FA2,3

True to the agile process, we thus conducted 14 mini-user studies over the course of one month, each time improving the design and acting upon the feedback before the next session.

Study Setup
Before switching to ICWs, our traditional lab studies involved bringing in about eight participants from each target population (IW and IT Pro) per study, one at a time, each for a two-hour session. This would result in 16 two-hour sessions, over the course of two weeks, making it hard for each product team member to hear more than one or two participants' feedback. The ICWs, on the other hand, only take about nine hours of each team members' time (two 1.5-hour SSCW sessions and two 3-hour SPW sessions per FA), for the same number of participants.

During SPWs, product team members and the researcher all sit on the participant side, further increasing the interactions between the product team and the customers. With the product team members directly involved and in the same room as the participants, team members actively filed bugs, started email discussion threads, and even changed code to fix usability issues, all before leaving the room.

PRELIMINARY EVALUATION
Preliminary indications are that the ICW approach is more productive and enjoyable for team members than traditional lab studies. Product team members were better engaged in the ICW sessions than we have previously experienced in traditional one-on-one lab study sessions. They lauded the methodology for, in one Program Manager's words, its "immediate, positive, and direct impact on the product" and "significant bang-for-the-buck."

SSCW Results
For an early evaluation of the effectiveness of the SSCW, we compared the findings from an SSCW (alone, without an SPW) to the results from a traditional lab study conducted in parallel on the same designs and code. When compared to the traditional lab study on the same UI, we found that approximately 80% of lab study findings were also revealed by the SSCW.

There could be, of course, important issues in the additional 20%, and this is why we have paired up SSCWs with SPWs: the real-world context received from the fresh perspective the participants bring to the table is essential. However, in our case, 80% of the issues discovered in the traditional lab study could have been taken care of before evaluating the software with customers, so that their focus could have been on the 20% real-world-context-related issues, and other insightful issues they might not have had time to mention.

SPW Results

The SPWs' preliminary evaluations also point to positive results. The notes, taken 'live' by the researcher during the SPW sessions, were already in a format where they could further be shared with the product team. Without any analysis beyond the raw notes, this series of four SPW sessions resulted in 155 usability findings:

- 45 of those were good experiences that we wanted to make sure not to break as we fixed the issues,
- 50 were bad user experiences we decided to fix within the current release, and
- 60 were bad user experiences that we used to inform the directions of the next couple of releases.

These 155 usability observations were based on the raw notes taken during the session alone. To measure the effectiveness of the note-taking technique, the researcher reviewed the video recordings of the sessions, looking for any additional usability findings we might have missed during the live session. This only resulted in 27 additional usability issues. Thus, with a good note-taker, the dual monitor note-taking and screenshot method allowed us to identify 85% of all the user experience observations, and with another set of agile sessions always close in the near future to catch additional issues.

The ICW mixed-methods approach therefore shows signs of succeeding in the measures that matter most to agile software development teams: user-centric, quick turnaround time, team integration, and plenty of actionable results.

CONCLUSION AND DISCUSSION

The primary contribution of this paper is to present a new agile UX research methodology, the informal cognitive walkthrough (ICW), which combines simplified versions of SCWs and PWs, tailored for software development practitioners on fast-moving agile projects.

Every methodology has its strengths and weaknesses. With the simplified ICW, removing some of the structure around the cognitive questions asked and increasing the role of the researcher meant the training was eliminated. However, this also means that the results of the session will be highly dependent on the researcher's skills. While the researcher is not a representative user of the software, this methodology does guard against bias in the following ways, to increase the external validity of the ICW approach: 1-The researcher is the expert on the product's users, 2-Customer feedback starts early with generative research with open-ended questions, 3-ICWs are conducted frequently throughout the product development process, and 4-SSCWs are always

paired up with PCWs (early and often) to quickly sense if customers think we are deviating from the right track.

We have developed and improved the ICW mixed-methods approach over the past three years to keep pace with frequent releases and design iterations on a large-scale agile team with hundreds of engineers, about 50 of which were directly involved with the ICWs. Whlie formal analysis of the methodology is future work, we continue to rely on ICWs since they appear to be low-cost and effective in a variety of settings and applications.

One major advantage of ICWs seems to be that they get all disciplines thinking about the user goal and user experience. The more disciplines can be brought into a room, the more varied the different perspectives that are shared on the designs. While our focus in developing this methodology was on maximizing available resources on a demanding schedule, the methodology can also be applied on projects on a longer timeline. In a future formal evaluation of the ICW methodology against traditional one-on-one lab studies, we expect the advantages of ICWs to include: more efficient collection of user feedback, lower resource allocation, higher team member involvement from all disciplines, and more directly measurable positive impact to the product's usability.

ACKNOWLEDGMENTS
We thank Tari Topolski and Marc Schwarz for their help analyzing the data from the parallel studies for an early evaluation of ICWs.

REFERENCES
1. Bias, R., "The Pluralistic Usability Walkthrough: Coordinated Empathies." In Nielsen, J. and Mack, R. eds, *Usability Inspection Methods*, John Wiley and Sons (1994).

2. Nielsen, J. Usability inspection methods. In *Proc. CHI 1994*, ACM Press (1994), 413-414.

3. Rieman, J., Franzke, M. and Redmiles, D. Usability evaluation with the cognitive walkthrough. In *Proc. CHI 1995*, ACM Press (1995), 387-388.

4. Rowley, D. and Rhoades, D. The cognitive jogthrough: a fast-paced user interface evaluation procedure. In *Proc. CHI 1992*, ACM Press (1992), 389-395.

5. Spencer, R. 2000. The streamlined cognitive walkthrough method, working around social constraints encountered in a software development company. In *Proc. CHI 2000*, ACM Press (2000), 353-359.

6. Wharton, C., Rieman, J., Lewis, C. and Polson, P. The cognitive walkthrough method: a practitioner's guide. Tech report: http://ics.colorado.edu/techpubs/pdf/93-07.pdf (1994).

Picode:
Inline Photos Representing Posture Data in Source Code

Jun Kato

Daisuke Sakamoto

Takeo Igarashi

The University of Tokyo, Tokyo, Japan – {jun.kato | d.sakamoto | takeo}@acm.org

ABSTRACT

Current programming environments use textual or symbolic representations. While these representations are appropriate for describing logical processes, they are not appropriate for representing raw values such as human and robot posture data, which are necessary for handling gesture input and controlling robots. To address this issue, we propose *Picode*, a text-based development environment augmented with inline visual representations: photos of human and robots. With *Picode*, the user first takes a photo to bind it to posture data. She then drag-and-drops the photo into the code editor, where it is displayed as an inline image. A preliminary user study revealed positive effects of taking photos on the programming experience.

Author Keywords

Development Environment; Inline Photo; Posture Data.

ACM Classification Keywords

H.5.2. Information interfaces and presentation (e.g., HCI): User Interfaces – GUI; D.2.6. Software Engineering: Programming Environments – Integrated environments.

INTRODUCTION

A programming language is an interface for the programmer to input procedures into a computer. As with other user interfaces, there have been many attempts to improve its usability. Such attempts include visual programming languages to visualize the control flow of the program, structured editors to prevent syntax errors, and enhancement to code completion that visualizes possible inputs [8]. However, programming languages usually consist of textual or symbolic representations. While these representations are appropriate for precisely describing logical processes, they are not appropriate for representing the posture of a human or a robot. In such a case, the programmer has to list raw numeric values or to maintain a reference to the datasets stored in a file or a database.

To address this issue, Ko and Myers presented a framework called "Barista" for implementing code editors which are capable of showing text and visual representations [5]. This framework enhances comments for an image processing

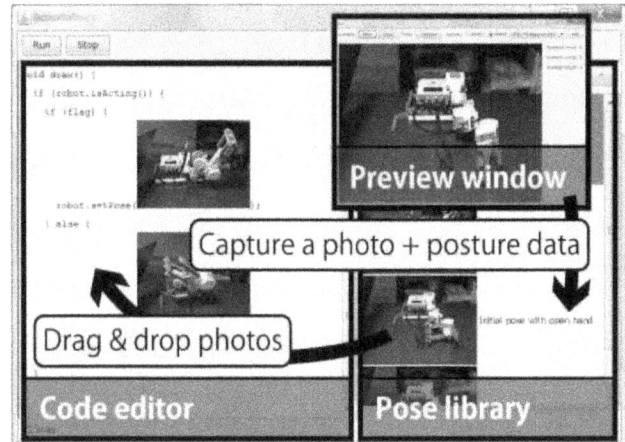

Figure 1. Overview of *Picode*

method by including an image that shows a concrete example of what the method does. Yeh et al. presented a development environment named "Sikuli," with which the programmer can take a screenshot of a GUI element and paste the image into a text editor [12]. In Sikuli, the image serves as an argument of the API functions. Our goal was to apply a similar idea to facilitate the programming of applications that handle human and robot postures.

We propose a development environment named *Picode* that uses photographs of human and robots to represent their posture data in a text editor (Figure 1). It helps the development process of applications for handling gesture input and/or controlling robots. The programmer is first asked to take a photo of a human or a robot to bind it to the posture data. She then drag-and-drops the photo into the code editor, where it is shown as an inline image. Our environment provides a built-in API which methods take photos as arguments. It allows the user to easily understand when the photo was taken and what the code is meant to do.

RELATED WORK

After the Microsoft Kinect and its Software Development Kit (SDK) hit the market, many interactive applications have been developed that handle human posture. At the same time, some toolkits and libraries have been proposed that support the development of such applications. They can typically recognize preset poses and gestures. When the programmer wants to recognize her own poses and gestures, however, she has to record the examples outside the development environment. On the other hand, our development environment is designed to support the entire prototyping process of application development. It fully integrates the recording phase, and the programmer can

Figure 2. Example code that makes robot swing its hand when user raises her hand

Table 1. Usage examples of photo-based API

follow the workflow without distraction. Attempts to support a general workflow of domain-specific applications have already been made for many domains including physical computing [3], machine learning [9] and interactive camera-based programs [4].

There is a long history of developing robot applications that deal with robot posture. Typical approaches include Programming by Example (PbE) [1], timeline-based editors to help designers defining transitions from one posture to another [7], and general development environments for textual or visual programming languages [6]. Most of the PbE systems focus on reproducing observed human actions, and the editors focus on creating and editing actions. They both tend to have limited support for handling user input. Conversely, general development environments are more flexible in terms of input handling, but do not display posture data in an informative way. Our objective is to design a hybrid environment, by taking advantages of these approaches.

PROGRAMMING WORKFLOW

Our prototype implementation consists of three main components (Figure 1): a code editor, the pose library, and a preview window. First, the user takes a photo of a human or a robot in the preview window. At the same time, posture data are captured and the dataset is stored in the pose library. Next, she drag-and-drops the photo from the pose library into the code editor, where the photo is displayed inline, as shown in Figure 2. Then, she can run the application and distribute the source code bundled with the referenced datasets so that others can run the same application within our development environment.

Taking Photos

To start taking photos, the user clicks the "+" button in the pose library interface and opens the preview window in which the photo preview and posture status are displayed in real time. She can choose the input source of the posture data from Kinect (human) or Mindstorms NXT [6] (robots)

devices. While only one Kinect device can be connected at a time and is automatically detected, one or more Mindstorms NXT devices can be used by entering their Bluetooth addresses. Photos are usually taken from the RGB stream of a Kinect device, but a web camera can be used as an alternative source.

While the preview window is displayed, clicking the "Capture" button triggers the system to take a photo and capture the corresponding posture data. Each captured dataset is automatically named, e.g., "New pose (1)," and stored in the pose library. It can be manually renamed but must be unique. Saying the word "capture" works when the user wants to capture a human posture and cannot click the button because standing in front of the Kinect device. When capturing a robot posture, a torque is applied to each servo motor on a joint to fix its angle. When the user tries to change its angle, however, the torque is set off so that she can move the joint freely. Therefore, the user can set the robot posture by changing joint angles individually. Additionally, she can load an existing posture by right-clicking its photo in the library. This allows the user to easily create a new posture from the existing ones. These interactions for capturing a robot's posture are inspired by the actuated physical puppet [13].

Coding with Photos

The programmer can write code in a programming language that is an extension of Processing [10], with a built-in photo-based API whose methods take photos as arguments. She can drag-and-drop photos from the pose library to the code editor, directly into argument bodies of the methods. Usage examples of currently supported API are shown in Table 1. A human and robot are represented by *Human* and *Robot* classes, whose instance handles communication with the hardware devices. Note that the *Human* instance is capable of sensing but not controlling posture while the *Robot* instance is capable of both.

Running Program

The programmer can compile and run the program by clicking the "Run" button in the main window. After iterative cycles of development, a ZIP archive consisting of source code, referenced photos, and posture data can be made so that others can run the same application.

IMPLEMENTATION

Picode is built on top of Processing core components including its compiler and libraries. The main difference is in the user interface. Therefore, the programmer can benefit from the simple language specification and extensibility provided by many Java-based libraries. Beside the user interface, we modified the compilation process to link every program to our library. We also modified the execution process so that the development environment disconnects from the Kinect device and robots when the program starts, and reconnects to them when it shuts down.

Human postures and the corresponding images are retrieved using a standalone GUI-less program implemented with Kinect for Windows SDK, which is automatically executed when needed. It communicates with the development environment and all programs that run on the environment through a TCP/IP connection. Robot postures are retrieved by reading values of a motor encoder or set by transmitting Bluetooth commands that are officially supported by the Mindstorms NXT firmware.

Code Editor Supporting Inline Photos

The code editor is implemented in the Model-View architecture, where the model is the source code in string format and the view is its GUI representation. Each photo has its string representation, which is a call to the specific photo-based API *Pose.load(key)* where *key* is a unique name of the corresponding posture data. When the photo is dropped to the code editor, the string is inserted into the source code. Every change in the source code triggers the language parser in order to build an abstract syntax tree. Then, the view is updated for syntax highlighting and every call to the photo-based API is replaced with photos.

API with Photo Arguments

Each posture dataset represented by a photo is instantiated as a *Pose* class instance. A *Pose* class is currently extended using *KinectHumanPose* and *MindstormsNXTPose* classes to support platform-dependent implementation and can be further extended to support more types of robots, such as humanoids, or more ways of detecting poses such as with a motion capture system. The posture data and the photo are saved as a text file and a JPEG file with its unique name (e.g. *Hand up.txt* and *Hand up.jpg*) in the same directory. The text file starts with its corresponding *Pose* class name followed by raw numerical values.

The equality test between *Pose* instances always returns false if their types are different. When their types are the same, the system calculates the Euclid distance between the vectors consisting of the absolute difference between joint angles (e.g. absolute difference in elbow angle, knee angle, ...) and normalizes it between 0 and 1. The equality test returns true if the distance is less than the specified threshold, otherwise it returns false.

PRELIMINARY USER STUDY AND DISCUSSION

We asked two test users to try our development environment together for about three hours. The goal was to verify two hypotheses on the benefit of embedding photos in the source code. The first hypothesis was that photos contain rich contextual information other than mere posture information, which helps the programmer recall the situation. The other was that the inline photos can involve a non-programmer in the software development process since they can be basically taken and understood by anybody. While one test user knew Processing and was familiar with basic programming concepts, the other did not know about programming except for basic HTML coding. We had them work together since we expected our environment to establish a new relationship between programmers and non-programmers (users). First, we thoroughly explained the workflow of our programming environment with the example code for an hour. Then, we asked them to make their own program for the remaining two hours.

After two hours of free use, the participants could write a program that uses gesture input to control robot posture. The robot basically tried to mimic the user input, e.g., when the user waved her hand, the robot waved its hand back. By putting the robot in front of the keyboard, the participants also had it operate the PC with its mechanical hand, which reminded us of mechanical hijacking [2].

Contextual Information in Photos

When the participants were asked to read existing code, they seemed to benefit from contextual information in photos, which was missing in the numerical posture data. The programmer commented that he might also benefit from the information when he reads the code he had written a long time ago since the photo can remind him of the situation. According to this observation, there were two types of contextual information. The first type tells the user about what the subject (human or robot) in the photos was doing. For example, photos would make it easy to distinguish when a user is drinking a glass of juice from when she is raising her hand to greet, while raw posture data will be the same (or very similar). A robot hand grasping a small ball and a large cube falls within the same issue. Additionally, each photo of the robot helps the users remember the proper hardware configuration. Prototyping robot applications often requires many iterations, and the photos taken during the development process might work as revision history for the hardware setup. The second type tells the user about the surrounding context for which the program was designed. For instance, the optimal parameters for a mobile robot that runs on the floor differ according to the material, such as carpets or laminated flooring.

Source Code as Communication Medium

The meaning of the inline photos could be understood by both the programmer and the non-programmer, and the photos worked as a communication medium between them. The non-programmer said that she felt involved in the application development process and was never bored. She stated two reasons for this feeling. First, she could take part in the development process by taking photos. Simple algorithms that handle posture data often require parameter tuning depending on the environment in which the code runs. In our environment, this can be done by replacing the existing photo with a new one. Through the replacement, she started to take ownership of the source code. With the inline photos, the source code became not only for the programmer but also for the non-programmer. Second, she could guess what the code was doing by recognizing the inline photos. For non-programmers, text code sometimes looks like a series of non-sense words. In *Picode*, however, they can understand the meaning of the code in relation to its nearby photos. When she asked a question about the code to the programmer, the programmer often started the explanation by pointing to the related photo. She also mentioned that the photos were easy to see in the plain text code, which made it easy to locate particular lines of the code. The idea of making meaning of code transparent (more understandable) was also discussed in Victor's recent essay about learnable programming [11]. Inline photos can be a good starting point for learning programming.

FUTURE WORK AND CONCLUSION

We foresee three enhancements that can make our development environment more effective: support for machine learning, comparison between partial posture data, and recording videos instead of taking photos. First, the current API only supports comparison between one posture dataset with another, which makes it difficult to recognize more general postures. For example, when the programmer wants to recognize the human posture of raising the right hand regardless of the height of the hand, she must write several "if" statements. Support for machine learning might solve this issue, treating multiple posture datasets as correct examples and others as false examples. Second, the current API cannot compare partial data, which makes it difficult to recognize the posture of the right hand and ignore the other body parts. With Kinect, *Picode* might allow the programmer to mask certain areas of the body on the photo to ignore the corresponding joints. Third, recording videos instead of taking photos might allow interesting programming experiences, by combining *Picode* code-based approach with the flow paradigm of DejaVu [4]. Videos can be used for learning human gestures or for replaying robot actions. The programmer might be able to change the replaying speed to make robot actions faster or slower.

We introduced *Picode*, a development environment that integrates photos into a code editor. It supports the programming workflow with the posture data: recording examples by taking photos, coding, and running the program. Photos were found to be interesting media that enhance the programming experience. *Picode* is open-source and available at http://junkato.jp/picode/.

ACKNOWLEDGEMENTS This work was supported in part by Microsoft Research 7th collaborative research program and JSPS KAKENHI Grant Number 23-9292, 24700112.

REFERENCES

1. Billard, A., Calinon, S., Dillmann, R. and Schaal, S. Robot programming by demonstration. In *Handbook of Robotics*, Springer (2008), 1371-1394.

2. Davidoff, S., Villar, N., Taylor, A.S. and Izadi, S. Mechanical hijacking: how robots can accelerate UbiComp deployments. In *Proc. UbiComp 2011*, 267-270.

3. Hartmann, B., Klemmer, S.R., Bernstein, M., Abdulla, L., Burr, B., Mosher., A.R. and Gee, J. Reflective physical prototyping through integrated design, test, and analysis. In *Proc. UIST 2006*, 299-308.

4. Kato, J., McDirmid, S. and Cao, X. DejaVu: Integrated support for developing interactive camera-based programs. In *Proc. UIST 2012*, 189-196.

5. Ko, A.J. and Myers, B.A. Barista: An implementation framework for enabling new tools, interaction techniques and views in code editors. In *Proc. CHI 2006*, 387-396.

6. LEGO Mindstorms NXT. http://mindstorms.lego.com/

7. Nakaoka, S., Kajita, S. and Yokoi, K. Intuitive and flexible user interface for creating whole body motions of biped humanoid robots. In *Proc. IROS 2010*, 1675-1682.

8. Omar, C., Yoon, Y., LaToza, T.D. and Myers, B.A. Active code completion. In *Proc. ICSE 2012*, 859-869.

9. Patel, K., Bancroft, N., Drucker, S.M., Fogarty, J., Ko, A.J. and Landay, J. Gestalt: integrated support for implementation and analysis in machine learning. In *Proc. UIST 2010*, 37-46.

10. Processing. http://processing.org/

11. Victor, B. Learnable Programming. http://worrydream.com/LearnableProgramming/

12. Yeh, T., Chang, T.H. and Miller, R.C. Sikuli: using GUI screenshots for search and automation. In *Proc. UIST 2009*, 183-192.

13. Yoshizaki, W., Sugiura, Y., Chiou, A.C., Hashimoto, S., Inami, M., Igarashi, T., Akazawa, Y., Kawachi, K., Kagami, S. and Mochimaru, M. An actuated physical puppet as an input device for controlling a digital manikin. In *Proc. CHI 2011*, 637-646.

Modeling How People Extract Color Themes from Images

Sharon Lin
Computer Science Department
Stanford University
sharonl@cs.stanford.edu

Pat Hanrahan
Computer Science Department
Stanford University
hanrahan@cs.stanford.edu

ABSTRACT

Color choice plays an important role in works of graphic art and design. However, it can be difficult to choose a compelling set of colors, or *color theme*, from scratch. In this work, we present a method for extracting color themes from images using a regression model trained on themes created by people. We collect 1600 themes from Mechanical Turk as well as from artists. We find that themes extracted by Turk participants were similar to ones extracted by artists. In addition, people tended to select diverse colors and focus on colors in salient image regions. We show that our model can match human-extracted themes more closely compared to previous work. Themes extracted by our model were also rated higher as representing the image than previous approaches in a Mechanical Turk study.

Author Keywords

color theme extraction; color themes; color names; algorithms; crowdsourcing

ACM Classification Keywords

H.5.m. Information Interfaces and Presentation (e.g. HCI): Miscellaneous

General Terms

Algorithms; Human Factors; Design; Measurement.

INTRODUCTION

Color choice plays an important role in setting the mood and character of a work of art and design. However, it can be difficult to choose good color combinations from scratch. Instead, artists, both expert and beginner, often draw colors from other sources of inspiration. These include other images and premade sets of color combinations called *color themes*.

There are many online communities, including Adobe Kuler [15] and COLOURlovers [4], that are centered around sharing and creating color themes. Many of these color themes are also created from images, rather than from scratch. Around 30% of a sampling of the newest 1,000 themes created on Colourlovers were created using their From-A-Photo theme tool.

In this work, we focus on color themes extracted from images. We consider the color theme of an image to be a small set of colors, usually 3 to 7, that best represent that image. Being able to automatically extract good image-associated themes can facilitate applications such as color picking interfaces [18] and color mood transfer from one image to another [10, 22]. Identifying the key colors in an image can also be useful in matching colors in a document or website around an image [20].

To our knowledge, this work is the first to evaluate and model color theme extraction based on the themes people pick from images. Previous work on automatically extracting color themes from images include general clustering techniques like k-means [16, 23] and fuzzy c-means [2] that focus on optimizing image recoloring error. We show that people often pick different colors than these algorithms. Other techniques include extracting colors successively from peaks in the image's color histogram [5, 6]. However, such a tiered approach can make it difficult to control the number of colors in the final theme. More recently, O'Donovan et al. [21] introduce a model to predict highly aesthetic themes by training on large online theme datasets. They consider themes in the general context, while we look specifically at themes extracted from images.

This work has two main contributions. First, we a present a method to evaluate theme extraction techniques against human-extracted themes using theme *overlap* and theme *distance*. Second, we introduce a regression model trained on a corpus of human-extracted themes and their associated source images. The fitted model can then be used to extract color themes from other images. We show that our model extracts themes that match human-extracted themes more closely than previous approaches. Online study participants also rate the model-extracted themes higher as representing the source image than themes extracted by k-means and an aesthetics-based approach.

RELATED WORK

Previous approaches have proposed quantitative measures for evaluating the quality of a theme based on either recoloring error [23, 2], aesthetics [21], or color nameability [12]. However, to our knowledge, this is the first approach that compares image-based color themes to ones that people have manually extracted.

Clustering and Histogram-based Approaches

One common method for extracting a representative set of colors is to use general clustering techniques, such as k-means [16, 23] and fuzzy c-means clustering [2]. K-means takes a number of requested colors k, and attempts to find clusters that minimize recoloring error. It does not take into account spatial arrangement of the colors in the image, and can thus wash out important image regions. Fuzzy c-means clustering is similar to k-means, except with soft instead of hard assignment of pixels to clusters, and so it is less affected by outliers. These approaches evaluate color themes based on a quantitative metric: the recoloring error. However, this may not be the only metric people use to evaluate themes.

Delon et al. [5, 6] found that peaks in the image's color histogram often correspond to spatial regions in natural imagery. Their algorithm extracts color themes by successively finding meaningful peaks in the Hue, Saturation, and Value histograms of the image. The resulting color set often contains many colors, some of them redundant, due to the tiered extraction approach. Morse et al. [19] used a similar tiered histogram approach to extract color themes given user-specified constraints on the maximum number of colors and a minimum distance between colors. However, they provided no user or quantitative evaluation of the themes against other approaches.

Color Harmony and Theme Aesthetics

Many online color theme creators allow users to design themes based on popular harmony templates [13, 17], predefined relationships of colors on the hue wheel. These relationships are often used as guidelines when creating themes from scratch. O'Donovan et al. [21] investigated the impact of color harmony templates on themes within large-scale online theme datasets. They found little evidence that people naturally gravitated towards harmony templates or that following these templates increased aesthetic ratings.

Our method uses a similar data-driven approach as O'Donovan et al., who predict the aesthetic rating of a color theme using a regression model trained on online theme datasets. Their model considered low-level features such as the values of each color component in the theme in multiple color spaces and differences between adjacent colors.

However, O'Donovan et al. focused on color themes and their ratings without context of where the theme originated. This paper looks more specifically at color themes that are paired with images. Instead of modeling themes with high aesthetic ratings, we look at the problem of characterizing themes that best capture an image, which itself may be aesthetically pleasing.

Color Names

Previous research in color names [1, 3, 12] has developed models and corresponding metrics for categorical color perception. Color names, such as *red* and *light blue*, are the descriptions people use to communicate a color. Chuang et al. [3] introduced a probabilistic model for these color-name associations, learned from the 330 colors in the World Color Survey [1]. Colors that are more consistently and uniquely named are considered to have higher saliency.

More recently, Heer and Stone [12] built upon this probabilistic model and trained on a much larger XKCD online

color name survey. They also defined a distance metric between two colors as the distance between the associated name distributions. Heer and Stone looked at color name features for assessing themes used in data visualization applications. They hypothesized that using colors with unique names would make it easier for people to verbally communicate different elements in the visualization than when using colors with overlapping names. In this work, we look at these color nameability and color name difference features [12] as potential predictors for how people extract themes from images.

GATHERING THEMES FROM PEOPLE

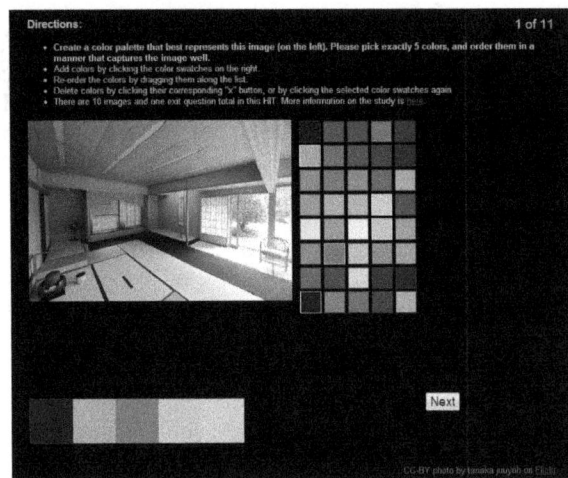

Figure 1. The user interface for the theme collection experiment with source image on the left, swatches on the right, and created theme below. Image credit: Tanaka Juuyoh (tanaka_juuyoh on Flickr)

To gather a dataset of human-extracted color themes, we asked people to extract themes from a set of 40 images. These images consisted of 20 paintings and 20 photographs. We varied the type of image to counter the effects of image style and content on the themes extracted. The paintings were chosen from five artists with different artistic styles (Impressionist, Expressionist, Pointillist, Realist, and Ukiyo-e prints). The photographs were Flickr Creative Commons images chosen from the categories Landscape, Architecture, Interior, Closeup, and Portrait.

We gathered themes from Amazon Mechanical Turk, which has been used successfully in crowdsourcing graphical perception [11] and creative sketching tasks [7]. One potential issue with crowdsourcing color themes is that we cannot easily control for different monitor and lighting conditions, which can introduce more noise in the collected data. However, in practice, people often view and create color themes under different conditions. Thus, by gathering themes from many different people, we can later fit a model that averages over typical viewing conditions rather than one that targets a specific condition.

Pilot studies determined that Turk participants often did not take the time to choose color shades carefully by clicking on the image directly. In addition, giving no limitation on the number of colors chosen resulted in color themes with wide variance in size. Therefore, we constrained the study design by requiring participants to choose exactly 5 colors from candidate color swatches. Color themes of size 5 have been studied previously [21] and are also the most common on online theme sharing sites.

For each image, we generated 40 color swatches by running k-means clustering on the image. The initial seeds for the clustering were stratified randomly sampled within the CIELAB bounding box of the image. The resulting swatch colors were snapped to the nearest pixel color in the image.

We asked participants to extract themes from either 10 paintings or 10 photographs. Participants were shown one image at a time and its associated color swatches. They were asked to pick 5 different colors that would "best represent the image and order them in a way that would capture the image well." The interface allowed for participants to add, remove, and reorder color swatches in their created theme. The order of images was counter-balanced using a balanced Latin square design. In total, we recruited 160 different participants and collected a total of 1600 themes (40 themes per image). Each Turk task was $0.50 ($0.05 per theme) and was limited to participants in the United States. The median time to complete one theme was 24 seconds. All images and color swatches were shown on a black background to match previous color theme rating studies [21] and popular online theme creation tools. At the end of the study, participants were asked to describe their strategy for choosing which colors to include in their themes.

For comparison purposes, we also asked 11 art students to extract themes from a randomly chosen subset of 10 images (5 paintings and 5 photographs). The interface for the art students was the same as for the Mechanical Turk participants, and image order was randomized within the paintings and the photographs. Art student participants were compensated with a $5 gift card after the study. For art students, the median time to complete one theme was 20 seconds.

Theme-Gathering Results

Figure 2 shows all the swatches presented to participants for one image, and each human-extracted theme as a column to the right of the swatches. The themes chosen by k-means and c-means clustering with k set to 5 is shown on the left of the swatches. Qualitatively, people agree with each other on certain key colors, shown by the strong horizontal lines in the figure, with some variability in the exact shade. K-means and c-means clustering often fail to select the common colors chosen by people.

To compare the consistency of participants quantitatively, we look at the mean *overlap* (number of colors in common) between all pairs of collected themes. We first match up the colors in one theme to the other to achieve the minimum total error, the minimum bipartite matching. The overlap is the number of color matchings that fall below a given distance threshold:

$$overlap(A, B, t) = \sum_{(a,b) \in m(A,B)} [\|a - b\|_2 < t] \quad (1)$$

where A and B are themes, $m(A, B)$ is the minimum bipartite matching, and t is the distance threshold.

Figure 3 plots the average overlap between themes from different sources against the distance threshold. Colors from k-means and c-means are snapped to the nearest candidate swatch color in the graph. For low distance thresholds (e.g. 0), colors from these methods would never overlap with colors chosen from the swatches by people. This snapping gives the algorithms which operate on continuous color space a fair footing when comparing them against choices made by participants.

On average, people agree on nearly 2 out of 5 color swatches per theme. Artists are more consistent with each other than Mechanical Turk participants when choosing particular color shades. However, their themes are about as similar as Turk themes on average. That is, artists agree with Turk participants about as well as Turk participants agree with each other. On the other hand, random, c-means, and k-means themes all agree poorly with human-extracted themes when considering particular color shades.

TRAINING A MODEL OF THEME-EXTRACTION

Given the dataset of images and their associated themes, we train a model for characterizing a human-extracted theme. Our basic approach is to first compute target scores for each theme on how close it is to human-extracted themes, generate many themes with different scores, and then calculate features describing them. Finally we use LASSO regression [9] to fit a linear model to predict the target scores given the theme features. Once fitted, this model can later be used to extract themes from images without human-extracted theme data.

Theme Similarity to Human-Extracted Themes

We define the *distance* between two themes to be the minimum total error from a bipartite matching of each color in one theme to a color in the other theme. The score for how similar a theme is to human-extracted themes is then the average distance between that theme and all human-extracted themes. This can be expressed as:

$$score(p) = 1 - \frac{1}{|H|} \sum_{h \in H} \frac{dist(p, h)}{maxDist} \quad (2)$$

where p is the given theme in question, H is the set of human-extracted themes, $dist$ is the total Euclidean error between the two themes in CIELAB color space, and $maxDist$ is some maximum possible distance between two themes. The theme scores are then rescaled between 0 and 1 for each image, so that each image gets equal weight in training. Themes with scores closer to 1 are more perceptually similar to human themes on average than themes with scores closer to 0.

We find that the top 30 (75%) representative Turk-extracted themes out of 40 for each image have a similar consistency as the artist-extracted themes, and they agree more closely with the artist-extracted themes. For the rest of the analyses in the

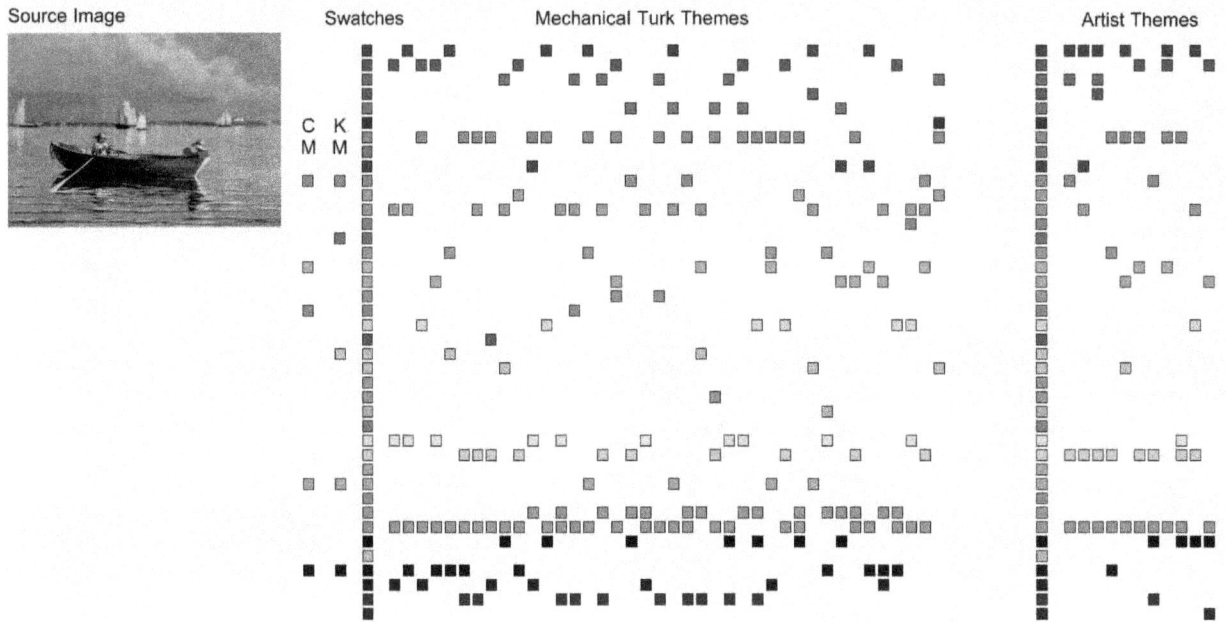

Figure 2. All the color themes for the source image. The color swatch options are shown down the middle. The human-extracted themes are on the right, with each column being a separate theme. The themes chosen by k-means (KM) and c-means (CM) are shown on the left. Image credit: Homer

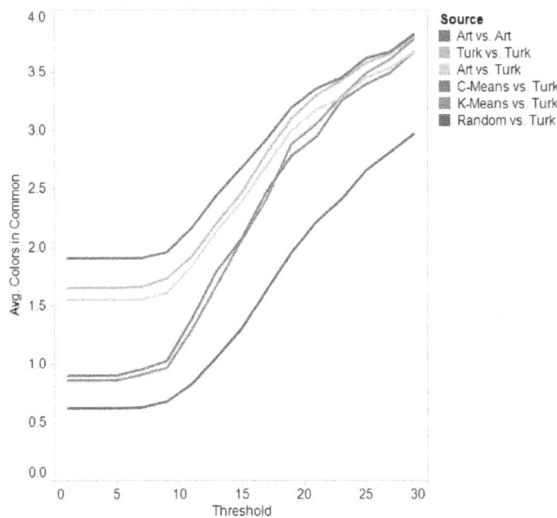

Figure 3. The average number of colors in common between themes from different sources plotted over a distance threshold. Blue lines are humans compared to humans. Other colored lines are automatic algorithms compared to humans.

Figure 4. Examples of oracle color themes, which have closest distance on average to the Turk-extracted color themes for each image. Image credits: Per Ola Wiberg (powi on Flickr); Seurat

paper, we therefore remove the bottom 10 themes from each image (25%) as outliers.

Given this distance metric and the human-extracted themes for an image, we can find an optimal *oracle* color theme that is closest on average to all the human-extracted themes. This provides us with a way to sanity check our distance metric as well as provide a theoretical upper bound of performance for automatic algorithms. Figure 4 shows the oracle color themes for two example images.

The oracle themes were created by hill-climbing over the candidate color swatches shown to participants in the palette-extraction experiment. In this method, we pick a random starting theme of 5 different colors from the candidate swatches. Then for each color in the theme, we find a replacement color from the candidate swatches that would most increase the score. We repeat this process until no further replacements can be made to increase the score. This method will find local, though not necessarily global, optima. Thus, we re-run hill-climbing for several (in this case 10) random restarts and pick the result with the best score.

LASSO Regression

We randomly generate 1000 themes per image with scores evenly distributed among 10 bins between 0 and 1. The 10 images shown in the artist experiment and their associated themes are reserved as a test set. The rest of the themes are used for training.

We use LASSO regression to fit a linear model to the training set. LASSO regression attempts to model the theme score in Equation 2 as a weighted sum of features and an intercept $b + \sum_i w_i \cdot f_i$. It also does feature selection by penalizing potential models by the L1 norm of their feature weights. This means that LASSO will find a model that both predicts the target scores well and also does not contain too many features. For each theme, we calculate a total of 79 features and use LASSO to find the features most predictive of human-extracted themes. The hyper-parameter λ determines the sparsity of the model and was tuned to minimize 10-fold cross-validation error in the training set (with 3 images and their associated themes in each fold).

In this work, we consider six types of features to describe each theme: saliency, coverage error both for pixels and for segments, color diversity, color impurity, color nameability, and cluster statistics. Within each type of feature, we calculate several variations using different distance metrics and parameters. Several of the features are highlighted below.

Saliency

Most study participants reported that they picked colors which "popped out of the image", "caught their eye", or were "the most salient colors." To detect salient regions in the image, we compute image saliency maps according to the work of Judd et. al. [14], who learned a model of saliency from eye tracking data on natural photographs. These maps were computed taking into account both low-level features and semantic features such as horizon lines and faces. They assign a saliency value to each pixel in the image.

We assign each image pixel to the nearest candidate color swatch shown to participants. The saliency of a color swatch is the sum of its individual pixel saliencies. The *total saliency* captured by a theme, $sal(C)$, is then the sum of its color swatch saliencies, relative to the maximum capturable saliency. Formally,

$$sal(C) = \frac{1}{max} \sum_{c \in C} \sum_{p \in cluster(c)} saliency(p) \quad (3)$$

where C is the set of five swatches in the theme, $cluster(c)$ is the set of pixels quantized to swatch c, and max is the total saliency of the top 5 most salient swatches.

In addition to the total saliency, we also look at min, max, and average *salient density* of the colors in the theme. The salient density of a color, $sd(c)$, is calculated as the saliency of the color swatch divided by the number of pixels assigned to that swatch. Cluster assignments can be made among the candidate color swatches or the theme colors.

$$sd(c) = \frac{1}{|cluster(c)|} \sum_{p \in cluster(c)} saliency(p) \quad (4)$$

Pixel Coverage

One feature people may take into account when choosing theme colors is how well the colors cover the overall image. We consider two metrics: *recoloring error* and color channel *range coverage*.

Recoloring error is defined as the total error resulting from recoloring each pixel in the image with the theme colors. We define *hard* recoloring error as:

$$hcov(C, I) = \sum_{p \in I} w_p \cdot \min_{c \in C} error(p, c) \quad (5)$$

where I is the set of pixels in the image, w_p is the weight of pixel p, and c is a theme color. Intuitively, this is the error resulting from recoloring each pixel with the closest theme color. K-means clustering minimizes a variant of this feature with uniform pixel weights and squared Euclidean distance as the error function.

We replace the error function with Euclidean distance and squared Euclidean distance in a perceptually-based color space (CIELAB) and color name cosine distance [12]. Distances are normalized according to the maximum color swatch distance. In addition, we either weight each pixel uniformly with $w_p = \frac{1}{size(I)}$, or we weight each pixel according to their saliency in the image.

We also define *soft* recoloring error as:

$$scov(C, I) = \sum_{p \in I} w_p \cdot \sum_{c \in C} u_{pc}^2 \cdot error(p, c)^2 \quad (6)$$

$$u_{pc} = \frac{1}{\sum_{j \in C} \left(\frac{error(p,c)}{error(p,j)} \right)^2} \quad (7)$$

where each pixel can take different recoloring contributions from each theme color. This is the objective function that fuzzy c-means clustering attempts to minimize. Again, we vary the error function with Euclidean distance in CIELAB space and color name cosine distance.

In addition, we consider the lightness (L), red-green (A), and blue-yellow (B) range of the image compared to the range of the theme in CIELAB space. Saturation (S) range coverage in HSV space is also considered. For lightness coverage:

$$Lcov(C) = \frac{range(C)}{range(I)} \quad (8)$$

where $range(I)$ is the difference between the maximum and minimum L values in the image swatches, and $range(C)$ is the difference for the theme. Red-green, blue-yellow, and saturation coverage are defined similarly.

Segment Coverage

People interpret images as arrangements of objects and components instead of on a pixel-level scale. Thus, we also include features that consider segments instead of just pixels. We segment the images using the method of Felzenszwalb and Huttenlocher [8].

The first feature is segment recoloring error, which is a weighted sum of the average recoloring error within each segment. *Hard* segment recoloring error is defined as:

$$hsegcov(C) = \sum_{s \in S} w_s \cdot hcov(C, s) \qquad (9)$$

Similarly, *soft* segment recoloring error is:

$$ssegcov(C) = \sum_{s \in S} w_s \cdot scov(C, s) \qquad (10)$$

with pixel weights $w_i = \frac{1}{size(s)}$. S is the set of segments. The segment weights w_s can be either uniform or based on the relative saliency or salient density of the segment in the image.

Secondly, we also consider the *uniqueness of the segment color* among the theme colors, $uniq(C)$. The idea is that colors in a theme may be evenly distributed among segments, so that no one segment would be sourced from most of the theme colors. To model this, we calculate the mean negative entropy of segments being colored by a particular theme color.

$$uniq(C) = \sum_{s \in S} w_s \cdot \sum_{c \in C} p(c|s) \ln p(c|s) \qquad (11)$$

where $p(c|s)$ is the probability of a segment s being colored by c from the theme.

For each segment in the image, we calculate the distances from its mean color to the colors in the given theme. The probability of a segment taking on a given color from the theme is then its relative distance to that color compared to all other colors in the theme.

Color Diversity
We calculate several metrics for *color diversity*. These include the mean distance between one color and its closest color in the theme and the min, max, and mean distance between two colors in the theme.

Similarly, we use either CIELAB or color names as the distance metric. We normalize the distances by either the max or mean distance between the candidate color swatches shown to the user.

Color Impurity
The *impurity* of a theme color is computed as the mean distance between the theme color and its n% closest pixels in the image. O'Donovan et al. used this metric when applying their aesthetics model to extracting color themes from images [21]. Following their work, we chose n to be 5%.

We normalize distances by either the max or the mean distance between the candidate color swatches.

Color Nameability
In data visualization, one desirable trait for a theme may be how easy it is to refer to a color in the legend [12]. Similarly, for general images, people may extract the most characteristic color shades for a particular color category.

We compute the *nameability* of colors used in the themes and normalize by either the max or mean nameability in the candidate color swatches. Color nameability used here is the same as the color saliency metric used by Heer and Stone [12], but rescaled to the nameability range of the candidate color swatches. It describes how consistently and uniquely a given color is named.

Cluster Statistics
After quantizing image pixels to theme colors, we compute variance statistics to describe the resulting clusters. We look at the average *within-cluster variance* of image pixels around each theme color. The *between variance* is just the variance of the theme colors around the mean theme color.

RESULTS

Predictive Features of Human-Extracted Color Themes
Relative weights in the fitted model can indicate which sets of features predict human-extracted color themes well. Features with large weights create one set of good predictors. Features with small or zero weights tend to be uninformative or are redundant with these features. In our model, 40 of the 79 features were given non-zero weights. These weights are listed in the Appendix. For this analysis, we standardize the weights to better compare them across features.

Weighted soft recoloring error and color diversity features consistently have the largest weights in our model. Themes that contain the right color for salient regions in the image and have a variety of colors tend to be closer to human-extracted themes. Other weighted features included saturation range coverage, color impurity, and segment color uniqueness. Good themes tended to cover the range of saturations in the image well. In addition, themes that contained good color clusters in the image and did not focus too many colors on one image region were also boosted. Color nameability had small negative weights, possibly because highly nameable colors may be less used in photographs and paintings and also less aesthetically pleasing.

A remaining question pertains to the stability of these weights as the number of training images varies. Although the exact weights of the metrics shift as the number of training images grows, the top feature types in the model tends to stay the same. For example, the soft recoloring error per segment and color diversity remain the highest-weighted features as we increase the number of training images from 10 to 30 for constant lambda. In addition, the change in weights decreases as the number of training images grows to 30. Thus, we believe 30 images is a reasonable training set size, though more images could help stabilize the weights further.

One important note is that while LASSO regression selects a set of features that fits the training data well, there may be other feature sets with similar predictive power. Further investigation is needed to explore the tradeoffs between models with different feature sets and performance.

Matching Human-Extracted Themes
On our test set of images, the mean absolute error (MAE) from running the fitted linear model was 0.10 compared to

the 0.22 of a fixed baseline for the target scores. We use the fitted model to extract color themes from the test set of 10 images by hill-climbing over the candidate color swatches. This is identical to our approach when finding the oracle themes, except we use the model to predict the scores instead of the actual human-extracted themes.

Figure 5 plots themes created using our model, k-means, c-means, and random selection against artist-created themes on the test set of 10 images. We also plot the Turk oracle themes against the artist-created themes to see the theoretical maximum agreement. For the graph, we again snap the colors in the themes to the closest swatch color shown to the human participants.

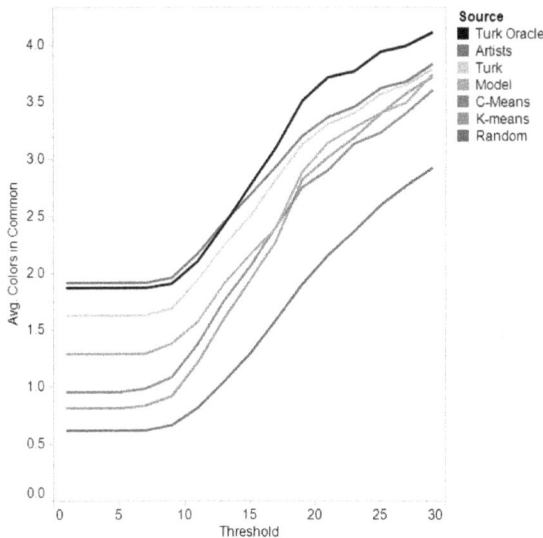

Figure 5. Theme agreement (number of colors in common) compared to artist-extracted themes on the test set of 10 images as color distance threshold increases.

Reference	Artists	Turk	Model	CM	KM	Rand
Artists	18.8	19.6	**20.4**	22.9	22.7	29.1
Turk	19.6	16.2	**18.6**	21.3	20.3	28.4

Table 1. Average distances per color between color themes of different methods compared to humans. Units are in CIELAB color space. Abbreviations are our model (Model), k-means (KM), c-means(CM), and Random (Rand)

The oracle themes from Turk were very close to the artist-created themes, and agreed on particular color shades about as well as artists do among themselves. This indicates that if we are able to perfectly model our optimization function, we can extract good color themes.

Our model-extracted themes agreed more closely with artist-extracted themes than do themes from other algorithms. In addition, the average distance of the human-extracted themes to the model-extracted themes is smaller than for the other algorithms, shown in Table 1. Reported distances are given for the original colors, not ones snapped to the color swatches.

For evaluation with previous work, we gathered human-extracted color themes for the 40 images used by O'Donovan et al. [21]. Figure 6 shows the similarity of themes extracted from different algorithms to human-extracted themes

from Mechanical Turk. The aesthetics-enhanced model (OD-Aesthetic) [21] performed slightly better than the original without the aesthetics term (OD-Original), which indicates that aesthetics may play a role in the colors people choose. In this second test set, our model again matched human-extracted themes from Turk more closely than the other algorithms, shown in Table 2.

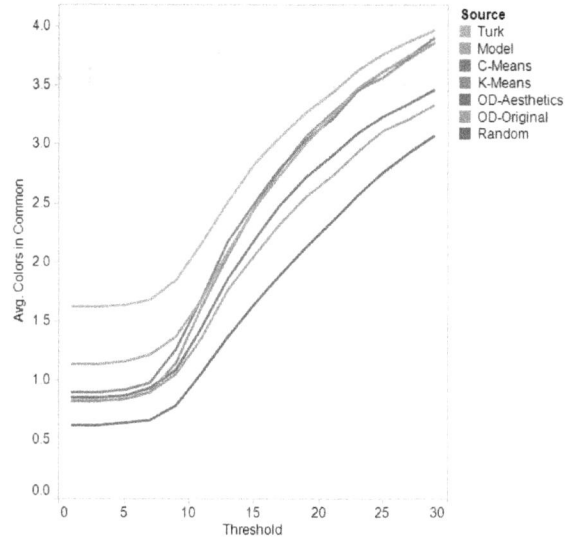

Figure 6. Theme agreement (number of colors in common) compared to Turk-extracted themes on the larger test set of 40 images as color distance threshold increases

Reference	Turk	Model	OD [21]	CM	KM	Rand
Turk	16.8	**19.6**	27.9	20.0	20.9	27.0

Table 2. Average distances per color between color themes of different methods compared to humans on a larger test set of 40 images. Units are in CIELAB color space. Abbreviations are our model (Model), the aesthetics-enhanced model by O'Donovan et al. (OD), k-means (KM), c-means(CM), and Random (Rand)

Representing the Image

Quantitatively, our model-extracted themes closely match human-extracted themes for the test images. But how well do the model-extracted themes actually represent the color theme of the image?

To answer this question, we conducted a study on Mechanical Turk asking 40 participants to rate color themes for 20 random images from the O'Donovan test set. The task was limited to participants in the United States. Figure 7 shows the study interface. Participants were shown one image at a time and 4 associated color themes: a representative human-extracted theme (nearest to other human-extracted themes), our model-extracted theme, a k-means theme, and an aesthetics-based theme from O'Donovan et. al. [21]. They were asked to rate the color themes on "how well they represent the color theme of the image" on a Likert scale from 1 (Not well at all) to 5 (Very well). Theme order was randomized, and image order was counter-balanced using a Latin Square design. The order of colors in the model-extracted and k-means themes was determined by their CIELAB distance to red. Each participant was paid $1.

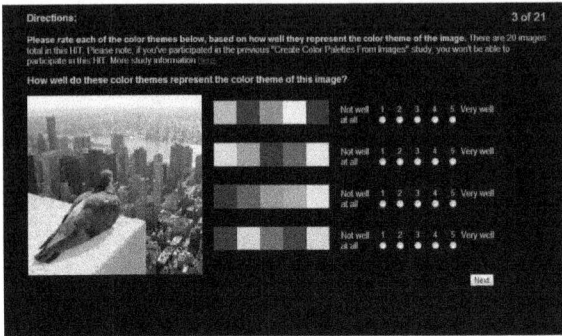

Figure 7. The interface for the theme rating study with source image on the left and themes on the right. Participants were asked to rate each theme on how well it represents the color theme of the image. Image credit: ZeroOne (villes on Flickr)

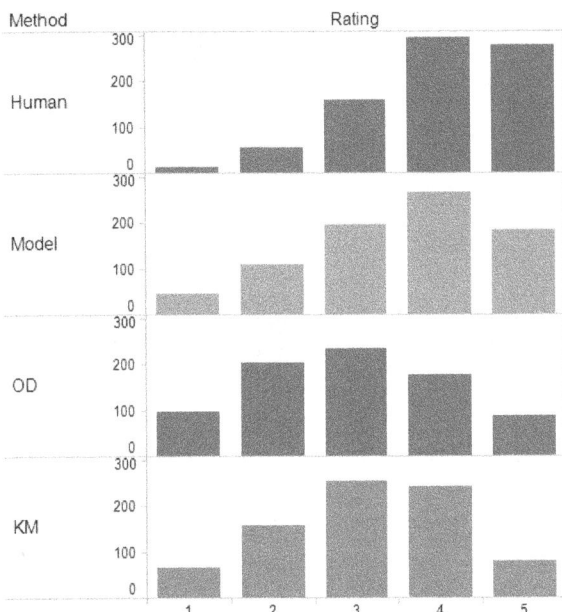

Figure 8. Histogram of theme ratings for human-extracted, our model, O'Donovan et al.(OD), and k-means themes

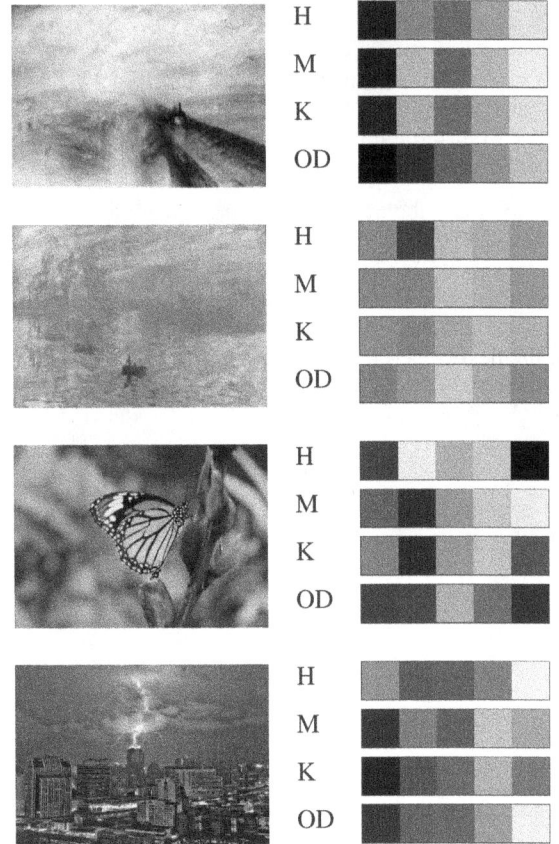

Figure 9. Examples of images and their associated themes from people (H), our model (M), k-means (K), and an aesthetics-based model in O'Donovan et al. 2011 (OD). H, M, and K themes are re-aligned to match the OD themes for easier comparison. Image credits: Turner; Monet; Ajith U (uajith_set1 on Flickr); Mike Behnken (mikebehnken on Flickr)

Figure 8 shows the distribution of ratings for each method according to how well their themes represented the color theme of the image. Overall, human-extracted themes were rated highest (Mean: 3.97), then our model-extracted themes (Mean: 3.54), k-means themes (Mean: 3.14), and the aesthetics-enhanced themes (Mean: 2.94). This indicates a correlation between how closely a theme matches human-extracted themes and how well it is rated as representing the image.

We ran a repeated measures ANOVA on the ratings with the method as a fixed effect and participant and image as random effects. There was a significant effect of the methods on the ratings ($p < 0.001$). We then ran follow-up paired t-tests using Bonferroni correction for each pair of methods. Each image and participant combination was treated as a repeated observation of the method. The differences between the mean ratings for each method were all significant at $p < 0.001$.

It should be noted that the experiment tested how well a theme captures the color theme of the image, and not how generally aesthetically pleasing the theme is. The results show that themes which best represent an image and themes that are optimized for general aesthetics may be different.

Figure 9 shows examples of the 4 different themes shown to participants for 5 images. Our model tends to extract vivid and bold colors, which are often ones chosen by people, as it has learned that themes with large distances between colors are usually more fitting. However, the last image in the figure shows a case where our model extracts a very bold theme that includes bright green and red, which may not be desirable. Although people often chose these colors individually, they rarely included them together in a theme. This may be a byproduct of the training set of 30 images, where the color distribution tended to be larger than the color distribution in this test set of images.

DISCUSSION

Themes from our model closely match human-extracted themes compared to other algorithms, though there is still room for improvement. More images and human-extracted themes can help smooth out biases in the model. Improvements in object recognition, segmentation, and image saliency maps are also likely to help our model. For example, face detection used in the image saliency model [14] works well in photographs, but usually fails on stylized images. Moreover, additional knowledge about semantics and object hierarchy in the image may help prioritize colors for very colorful images. A more in depth notion of aesthetics or harmony may also be predictive of the color shades people pick. More complex models, such as specially-designed graphical models, may better capture situation-dependent choices made by people.

However, our framework is flexible and can accommodate larger sets of images and additional features as necessary. There are many people interested in art who are creating color themes from images online each day, and these themes could provide data from which to learn. A similar framework could perhaps be used to learn good color themes for more focused application scenarios, such as web design, interior design, and data visualization.

There are many potential applications for color themes paired with their associated images. It could provide a method for image search for images with similar color themes. Images also provide context for how a color theme can be used, and the two together can assist colorization of patterns or web elements to match a given image. Drawing and painting programs can also personalize color swatches based on the color themes of a user's collection of favorite images.

CONCLUSION AND FUTURE WORK

In this paper, we present a framework for evaluating automatic color theme extraction algorithms against themes people extract. We show that people choose colors that are different from the widely-used k-means and c-means clustering algorithms.

In addition, this work presents a first step in learning how to extract good color themes based on human-extracted theme data. We show that a linear model fitted on a training set of 30 images and their associated human-extracted themes outperforms many of the previous approaches. High-scoring themes tended to have diverse colors, focused on getting accurate colors for salient image regions, picked colors that are well-concentrated in the image, and spread colors evenly across image regions.

Future work includes looking at how people choose colors for more focused image classes, such as web design, visualization, or particular art styles. We could learn what features of color themes are most characteristic for each scenario, how they differ, and if there are any trends in color combinations.

Color themes are also only one component of how people interpret works of art and design. A similar data-driven approach could be used to learn important features for other graphical aspects, such as texture or shading. Increasing our understanding in these areas could perhaps enable better tools for assisting users in art and design tasks.

ACKNOWLEDGMENTS
We thank Peter O'Donovan for his help in comparing results. Thank you to Jeffrey Heer and Theresa-Marie Rhyne for helpful feedback, and to all our study participants. This work was funded by NSF FODAVA grant CCF-0937123.

REFERENCES

1. Berlin, B., and Kay, P. *Basic color terms: Their universality and evolution.* Univ of California Pr, 1991.

2. Bezdek, J. *Pattern recognition with fuzzy objective function algorithms.* Kluwer Academic Publishers, 1981.

3. Chuang, J., Stone, M., and Hanrahan, P. A probabilistic model of the categorical association between colors. In *Color Imaging Conference* (2008), 6–11.

4. Colourlovers. http://www.colourlovers.com.

5. Delon, J., Desolneux, A., Lisani, J., and Petro, A. Automatic color palette. In *Image Processing, 2005. ICIP 2005. IEEE International Conference on*, vol. 2 (sept. 2005), II – 706–9.

6. Delon, J., Desolneux, A., Lisani, J. L., and Petro, A. B. Automatic color palette. *Inverse Problems and Imaging 1*, 2 (2007), 265–287.

7. Eitz, M., Hays, J., and Alexa, M. How do humans sketch objects? *ACM Transactions on Graphics (TOG) 31*, 4 (2012), 44.

8. Felzenszwalb, P. F., and Huttenlocher, D. P. Efficient graph-based image segmentation. *Int. J. Comput. Vision 59*, 2 (Sept. 2004), 167–181.

9. Friedman, J., Hastie, T., and Tibshirani, R. Regularization paths for generalized linear models via coordinate descent. *Journal of statistical software 33*, 1 (2010), 1.

10. Greenfield, G. R., and House, D. H. Image recoloring induced by palette color associations. *Journal of WSCG 11* (2003), 189–196.

11. Heer, J., and Bostock, M. Crowdsourcing graphical perception: Using mechanical turk to assess visualization design. In *ACM Human Factors in Computing Systems (CHI)* (2010), 203–212.

12. Heer, J., and Stone, M. Color naming models for color selection, image editing and palette design. In *ACM Human Factors in Computing Systems (CHI)* (2012).

13. Itten., J. The art of color. *Van Nostrand Reinhold Company* (1960).

14. Judd, T., Ehinger, K., Durant, F., and Torralba, A. Learning to predict where humans look. In *IEEE International Conference on Computer Vision (ICCV)* (2009).

15. Adobe Kuler. http://kuler.adobe.com.

16. MacQueen, J., et al. Some methods for classification and analysis of multivariate observations. In *Proceedings of the fifth Berkeley symposium on mathematical statistics and probability*, vol. 1, California, USA (1967), 14.

17. Matsuda, Y. Color design. *Asakura Shoten* (1995).

18. Meier, B. J., Spalter, A. M., and Karelitz, D. B. Interactive color palette tools. *IEEE Comput. Graph. Appl. 24*, 3 (May 2004), 64–72.

19. Morse, B., Thornton, D., Xia, Q., and Uibel, J. Image-based color schemes. In *Image Processing, 2007. ICIP 2007. IEEE International Conference on*, vol. 3, IEEE (2007), III–497.

20. Obrador, P. Automatic color scheme picker for document templates based on image analysis and dual problem. In *Proceedings of SPIE*, vol. 6076 (2006), 64–73.

21. O'Donovan, P., Agarwala, A., and Hertzmann, A. Color compatibility from large datasets. In *ACM SIGGRAPH 2011 papers*, SIGGRAPH '11, ACM (New York, NY, USA, 2011), 63:1–63:12.

22. Wang, B., Yu, Y., Wong, T.-T., Chen, C., and Xu, Y.-Q. Data-driven image color theme enhancement. In *ACM SIGGRAPH Asia 2010 papers*, SIGGRAPH ASIA '10, ACM (New York, NY, USA, 2010), 146:1–146:10.

23. Weeks, A., and Hague, G. Color segmentation in the hsi color space using the k-means algorithm. In *Proceedings of SPIE*, vol. 3026 (1997), 143.

APPENDIX

Recoloring Error

Components	Weighted By	Type	Metric	Weights
Image Pixels	Uniform	Hard	Dist	0
			SqDist	**0.9392**
			CN	0.2083
			SqCN	0
		Soft	Dist	0
			CN	0
	Saliency	Hard	Dist	0
			SqDist	0
			CN	0
			SqCN	0
		Soft	Dist	0
			CN	0
Segment Pixels	Uniform	Hard	Dist	0
			SqDist	**1.2941**
			CN	0.2439
			SqCN	0
		Soft	Dist	0
			CN	0
	Saliency	Hard	Dist	-0.0087
			SqDist	0
			CN	0
			SqCN	0
		Soft	Dist	**-7.1864**
			CN	**-2.0479**
	Salient Density	Hard	Dist	0
			SqDist	0
			CN	0
			SqCN	0
		Soft	Dist	**-9.9725**
			CN	0
Segment Mean	Uniform	Hard	Dist	0
			CN	0
	Saliency	Hard	Dist	0
			CN	-0.0496
	Salient Density	Hard	Dist	-0.0828
			CN	0

Range Coverage

Type	Weights
Lightness (L)	-0.1909
Red-Green (A)	0.1601
Blue-Yellow (B)	0.0982
Saturation (S)	**0.8743**

Segment Uniqueness

Weighted	Weights
Uniform	**0.7110**
Saliency	0

Diversity

Space	Normalize	Metric	Weights
CIELAB	$max_D(I)$	min	0
		max	-0.0274
		mean	**1.5602**
		closest	0.3292
	$mean_D(I)$	min	0.0322
		max	0
		mean	0.1450
		closest	0.0299
CN	$max_D(I)$	min	0
		max	-0.0798
		mean	-0.0729
		closest	-0.0061
	$mean_D(I)$	min	0.0068
		max	0.0157
		mean	0
		closest	0

Nameability

Space	Normalize	Metric	Weights
CN	$max_N(I)$	min	0
		max	-0.0411
		mean	0
	$mean_N(I)$	min	-0.0014
		max	0
		mean	0

Impurity

Space	Normalize	Metric	Weights
CIELAB	$max_D(I)$	min	0.0278
		max	0
		mean	0
	$mean_D(I)$	min	0.0423
		max	-0.0355
		mean	**-0.6297**

Saliency

Clusters	Metric	Weights
Swatches	min	-0.0408
	max	0
	mean	0.2937
	total	-0.1166
Theme	min	-0.0958
	max	0.1537
	mean	-0.1715

Cluster Statistics

Type	Normalize	Weights
Within Variance	$max_D(I)^2$	-0.4973
Between Variance	$max_D(I)^2$	**-2.1370**

Table 3. All features and weights considered by the regression, organized by feature type and broken down by variations in parameters. Weights with magnitudes greater than 0.5 are highlighted. Abbreviations: CN - Color Name cosine distance, Sq - Squared, Dist - CIELAB Euclidean distance. Variations under Recoloring Error would be interpreted as recoloring error within Components:C, Weighted By:W, using Type:T assignments with the distance Metric:M. Similarly, Diversity variations would be interpreted as distances within the color Space:S, normalized by Normalize:N, using the Metric:M. Normalization terms can be either the mean or max distance or nameability between image swatches. Saliency variations are interpreted as using the Metric:M with saliency determined by clusters among the Clusters:C.

Reducing Disruption from Subtle Information Delivery during a Conversation: Mode and Bandwidth Investigation

Eyal Ofek, Shamsi T. Iqbal and Karin Strauss
Microsoft Research
One Microsoft Way, Redmond, WA 98052
{eyalofek, shamsi, kstrauss}@microsoft.com

ABSTRACT

With proliferation of mobile devices that provide ubiquitous access to information, the question arises of how distracting processing information in social settings can be, especially during face-to-face conversations. However, relevant information presented at opportune moments may help enhance conversation quality. In this paper, we study how much information users can consume during a conversation and what information delivery mode, via audio or visual aids, helps them effectively conceal the fact that they are receiving information. We observe that users can internalize more information while still disguising this fact the best when information is delivered visually in batches (multiple pieces of information at a time) and perform better on both dimensions if information is delivered while they are not speaking. Interestingly, participants qualitatively did not prefer this mode as being the easiest to use, preferring modes that displayed one piece of information at a time.

Author Keywords
Augmented Reality; Attention; Design; Human Factors.

ACM Classification
H.5.2 [Information interfaces and presentation]: User Interfaces. - Graphical user interfaces.

INTRODUCTION
The increasing ubiquity of mobile devices is making information available anywhere, anytime [19, 22, 25]. The development of mobile processing power, the inclusion of sensors such as GPS, accelerometers, gyros, cameras and microphones, as well as the accumulation of supporting data and computation in the cloud, made it easy to display information to a user based on location and context [33]. Easy and seamless access to information can help augment many ongoing tasks, e.g., providing awareness of peripheral activities [6, 34], opportunistically delivering information to help coding and development [14], and providing relevant information during searching [3, 13].

A major challenge when it comes to openly consuming information in social settings is the perceived cost in terms of

disruption to established social norms of being attentive to the ongoing interaction [2, 10, 18, 27]. Widespread adoption of such practices largely depend on their social acceptability: how seamlessly they fit into the routine activities carried out in everyday life [30].

Our broader research goal is to investigate how to deliver information to augment natural conversation among people in face-to-face settings. Presenting conversational aids may improve conversation quality; e.g., 7-9 words delivered peripherally has been shown to help trainee supervisors better manage training sessions [26]. Such aids may benefit other common real world scenarios, e.g., short text or words may help strangers find topics of mutual interest, and help acquaintances recall the context of prior meetings. However, expected social norms may deter people from explicitly seeking for aid as processing information in the background during a conversation can be potentially distracting. Research on conversation aids has mostly focused on helping people with cognitive degenerative diseases such as dementia and Alzheimer's [11, 28], but for this population the goal is to help them participate in settings where they are unable to communicate independently and the disruption caused by the device is typically overlooked.

For more general settings, we wish to provide conversation aids that do not disrupt ongoing conversations. We focus on minimizing distraction, as prior work has shown explicit consumption of information during a conversation can be interpreted as a lack of interest [10]. As a first step towards this goal, we studied how information processing can be made more discreet and socially acceptable. More specifically, we wanted to understand how much information users can internalize without any discernible cues during a conversation, and how this was impacted by the medium and mode of information delivery. We conducted a user study that targeted measuring how much information users can consume during a conversation while not letting it show to their interlocutor. We exposed participants to three different modalities and multiple word group sizes with the purpose of better understanding how these factors affect their ability to maintain a conversation with sufficient attention while effectively consuming content.

Results showed that while participating in a conversation, users can internalize more information while still disguising this fact the best when information is visually delivered in batches (multiple pieces of information at a time). Additionally, users perform better on both dimensions if information delivery is done while they are not speaking. Interestingly, participants qualitatively did not prefer this mode as being the easiest to use, preferring modes that display one piece of information at a time. Our findings have important implications for the design of augmented reality systems intended to deliver information while the receiver performs other tasks, e.g., face-to-face conversations.

RELATED WORK

We discuss related work in peripheral awareness, and device use and social communication.

Devices for peripheral information delivery

Peripheral awareness systems allow multitasking users to access information without causing abrupt suspension of ongoing tasks. Maglio and Campbell [15] compared various modes of displaying peripheral information to a multitasking user to understand how the mode affects the balance between delivering information and distraction from the primary task. McCrickard et al. [18] explored ways of presenting peripheral information to users engaged in a browsing task. They found tickering text to be the most effective and least disruptive to the primary task, and that smaller displays were more disruptive, while slower presentation of information was more comprehensible. In the domain of driving, Brumby et al. compared the effectiveness of delivering information to drivers via audio and visual displays [5]. They found that participants who prioritized processing the information over driving safety preferred visual display because of the speed of processing, whereas participants who prioritized safety chose audio – suggesting that the sharing of cognitive processing channels while multitasking results in performance compromise on at least one of the tasks, even if the task is more suited for that channel.

In the domain of augmented reality (AR) devices, the practice of adopting AR technologies to enhance how we perceive and experience the world is rapidly becoming ubiquitous [32]. In such devices, information may be transmitted to the user in the form of computer generated sensory input such as sound or video. The proliferation of positional and directional sensors in smart phones enables the distribution of AR applications to the general public [20]. For example, the Remembrance Agent project [23] was aimed at delivering just-in-time information for users using a wearable display. The focus of this and later work was on recovery of relevant information and usability for a single user.

Over the years head-mounted displays (HMDs) and virtual retinal displays for visualization have been researched extensively [7, 16, 21, 29]. Unfortunately, many of these displays are cumbersome, and are non-natural in appearance, which limited their use to few early adopters. More recent HMDs, such as Google's project Glass [1], have the advantage of being lightweight and appear similar to accessories people already use – thus such displays have the potential of being more socially acceptable. However, current

implementations are not quite transparent, and display information on the periphery, causing people to look away.

In context of the prior work on peripheral information systems, our work looks at the mode and bandwidth of information that can be delivered to a person without disrupting the ongoing flow of a face-to-face conversation. While the use of teleprompters is common for newscasters and reporters for receiving information surreptitiously, in these cases information delivery is mostly unidirectional. No formal study has investigated effectiveness of information delivery in bi-directional settings, e.g., conversations. The challenge is to determine the optimal bandwidth and appropriate mode that helps users easily consume information without giving out cues that they are receiving that information, so that social protocols of being attentive during face-to-face conversations are not violated.

Device use and social communications

The use of devices to access information in social settings is rapidly becoming a common practice, but the reaction to resulting distractions is not well understood. Iqbal et al. studied the use of devices during presentations and reported on the perceived costs of disruption on both speakers and device users, and benefits of information awareness for device users [12]. Campbell and Kwak found that use of technology in public did not detract people from conversing to strangers in public [8], suggesting that using appropriately designed technology during face-to-face conversation may blend in with such social interactions. McAtamney and Parker studied how wearable computing devices affect face-to-face conversation [17]. Their results showed that wearable devices without active displays did not affect the conversation, but those with active displays disrupted the conversation as users lost eye contact.

Our work complements existing work in this domain by further understanding how to design devices so that information delivery can be made subtle without disrupting face-to-face interactions. Evidence from prior work suggests that adaptation and usage of such technology will not be viewed negatively, however, success of these devices depend on how little they disrupt existing social norms and expectations. We focus on studying two parameters that affect disruption these devices may cause: the mode of information delivery, and the amount of information delivered.

UNDERSTANDING USER INFORMATION ABSORPTION

Our goal in this study was to understand design parameters for augmented reality devices that deliver information without disrupting face-to-face conversations. Specifically, we looked to answer the following two research questions:

RQ1. *How does the mode of delivery and amount of information impact how a person processes information internally while conversing with another person?*

RQ2. *How does the mode of delivery and amount of information impact how detectable to their fellow conversants the receivers are as they internalize information?*

To answer these questions we conducted a controlled laboratory study where information was delivered surreptitiously to a person who is engaged in a conversation with another person. For this study, we recruited pairs of participants to have multiple conversations on topics we pre-selected for them. One person in the pair also received a set of words (without knowledge of the other person) via various delivery modes using a custom device, which they had to process during the conversation. We measured how well participants were able to disguise the fact that they were also processing a separate stream of information during the conversation. Lessons from the study should help generate design guidelines for creating technology in the augmented reality domain that can be used to deliver information without impacting users' ongoing interactions noticeably.

Experimental Design

The study was a 3 (Information delivery mode: auditory, visual persistent, visual non-persistent) X 5 (Length of information: 3, 5, 7, 9 or 11 words) within subjects repeated measures study. Each delivery mode was repeated three times, and within each trial there were two sets of information of each of the 5 lengths that we tested. There were four baseline trials: one for the conversation, and one each for processing words using the three information delivery modes (no conversation). To balance for ordering effects, a latin square design was used for the delivery mode, and the length of information factor was assigned randomly within each trial. Baselines were assigned at the beginning and once every three experimental trials.

Users

Users participated in pairs, each instructed to participate roughly equally in a conversation on topics that we preselected. One of the participants was assigned the role of the 'receiver' who would receive information during the conversation, and the other participant was assigned the role of the 'observer' who would try to detect when the receiver was getting information during the ongoing conversation. We did not mirror the condition because we wanted to save both people from having to adapt to different tasks, which could add confusion, and because of time limitations. 24 pairs of participants who did not know each other and who were native English speakers were recruited for the study using a corporate recruiting service, allowing us to access a diverse population. Their ages ranged from 19 to 49 (M=30, S.D= 7.1) and the gender distribution was as follows: FF=8, MF=5, FM=5 and MM=6, where the first letter indicates the gender of the receiver and the second letter indicates the gender of the observer. Occupations included nanny, health service manager, students, security officer, rapid response engineer, writer, physical therapist and so on. Users were compensated with a free software or hardware gratuity. To incentivize appropriate attention on performing the task, an additional gratuity was offered to the 'receiver' and the 'observer' who had the best performance in the study, measured through points that they could gain during the session (described later).

Tasks

For each trial, the primary task was to carry on a conversation on a pre-selected topic for about 5 minutes. Topics included experiential subjects, e.g., favorite childhood memory, high school graduating class, interesting book read recently, role model, and nightmare travel experiences. Participants were asked to maintain a balanced conversation so that each participant talked roughly half of the time. To ensure that the balance was maintained, we flashed a light to alert them if the conversation became one-sided.

Secondary task for the receiver

As the pairs engaged in the conversation, the receiver also performed an information processing task. For this task, the receiver received a list of independent words (i.e., the words were not part of the same phrase), the set size being between 3 and 11. Table 1 shows a subset of the words being presented during a conversation where the topic was 'hobbies'. The observer was aware that the receiver may receive some information during the conversation, but they did not know when the information was being delivered.

We asked receivers to perform two tasks using the word-lists. For the main task, for each word in the list, receivers had to identify whether the word was relevant to the current conversation topic (or not). The purpose of this task was to make sure they were reading and processing the words to be able to respond to them appropriately. They were provided with a clicker with two buttons corresponding to 'relevant' and 'not relevant' responses (see Figure 1). Selecting a response via the clicker automatically advanced them to the next word in the list, until the last word was displayed.

Receivers were instructed to perform this task while still participating in the conversation and to try to disguise that they were multitasking. To ensure that the receiver was motivated to do the secondary task, we told them that they would gain a point for each correct identification of word relevance. They would also receive bonus points if they were able to use one or more words from the list in the conversation. The purpose of this additional task was to assess the viability of this setup as a conversation assistant.

However, to make sure that the receivers did not sacrifice performance on the main task, they were told that they would lose a point every time they were caught being distracted by the observer, so that they would attempt to balance processing the words and participating in the conversation to not appear distracted.

Word sets were delivered to the receiver at most ten times during each trial, roughly with an interval of 30 seconds between word set arrivals. For each trial, words were delivered via one of the three modes: audio, visual non-persistent and visual persistent, defined as follows:

Audio: Presented pre-recorded sets of words sequentially via headphones every 3 seconds, or right after the receiver processed the previous word; **Visual non-persistent:** Replicated audio mode using a visual medium (described in the

Wordlist Size	Words presented
3	Cooking, radio, peaceful
5	Invigorating, quilting, glowing, fine, snorkeling
7	Lonely, kayak, efficient, inferior, glow, Halloween, depression
9	Swim, movies, anger, performance, fresh, serene, pure, fishing, robotics
11	Friends, video-game, enhanced, addicted, ant-farm horse-back-riding, zoo, embarrassed, smooth, serenity, jaded

Table 1: Example of wordlists delivered during a conversation where the topic was 'Hobbies'.

Trials: 16			
(3 dual task practice, 1 primary & 3 secondary baseline, 9 dual task)			
Tasks		Factors Manipulated	
Primary	Secondary	Modes	Size
Both: Converse on a given topic	**Receiver:** • Select which words are related • Insert words into conversation (opt) **Observer:** • Detect distractions	**Audio:** Words delivered sequentially via audio **Visual Non-persistent:** Words delivered sequentially via teleprompter **Visual Persistent:** Words delivered in blocks via teleprompter	3,5,7, 9,11

Table 2: Summary of conditions

next subsection), i.e., words appeared at the same location on the visual medium one by one and disappeared after 3 seconds, or when the receiver processed it; **Visual persistent**: Presented the entire set of words arranged vertically all at once, via the same visual medium. The receiver processed each word sequentially by hitting the clicker. Visual information was gradually faded in and out of the display to avoid sudden gaze change of the receivers that may reveal their action to the observers.

Secondary task for the observer

The task of the observer was to detect when the receiver was performing secondary tasks during the conversation. The purpose of this task was to assess how receiving information affected the receivers' ability to hold a normal conversation and how detectable this background processing of information is. Observers did not have knowledge about when or via what medium the receiver was receiving the word lists, therefore they were instructed to identify when the receiver appeared distracted to them. The observers also had a clicker with a single button that they used to indicate when the receiver was distracted (see Figure 1). Table 2 summarizes the conditions for the study.

Prototype system for information delivery

The setup of our study required participants' faces to be visible at all times, as one would expect in a natural face-to-face conversation. At the same time, we needed a mechanism for delivering information surreptitiously to the receiver without the knowledge of the observer, allowing delivery using both audio and visual modes. This is particularly challenging for information delivery using the visual channel, as it requires some surface on which to display information. Current implementations of head-up displays do not meet our requirements as they tend to cover the user's eyes and part of the face. Alternatives such as Google glasses that hardly block the user's face are also not suited for our needs: their displays are mounted at the edge of the user's field of view and as a result, the usage of such displays results in a very visible change of gaze.

To solve this problem, we built a custom teleprompter-like device that enables delivery of information to users in a way that is expected to least disrupt their natural conversation. The device is designed with the goal of allowing a

person to subtly receive both audio and visual signals during the conversation, which does not explicitly interrupt the ongoing conversation. At the same time it allows participants to see each other without any obstruction. This allows the conversation to still seem natural to their collocutor, as the delivery of the signals does not occlude the receiver's face, facial expressions, and eye gaze.

Figure 1 illustrates the setup. The two participants sit on either side of a screen that is visible to the receiver but transparent to the observer. The device allows information delivery through two modes: visual and audio. When in visual mode, words displayed on a concealed LCD screen are projected on a tilted planar glass. This reflects the image towards the receiver, not allowing any of the light to be refracted in the observer's direction and providing a view angle of 25 degrees for a person sitting 1 meter away. The receiver sees the words superimposed on what they see through the glass. In contrast to a regular teleprompter, the screen is set at a depth (w.r.t. the glass) similar to the distance between the observer and the glass. This results in similar focal distances for both words and the observer's face, making them easier for the receiver to read, while focusing on the observer's face. The displayed words are about 0.5 degrees high with a visible distance of 0.5 degrees between them. The observer sees the receiver through the glass, and cannot see the projected image. The audio signals are transmitted to the receiver via headphones, which are worn by the receiver throughout the study.

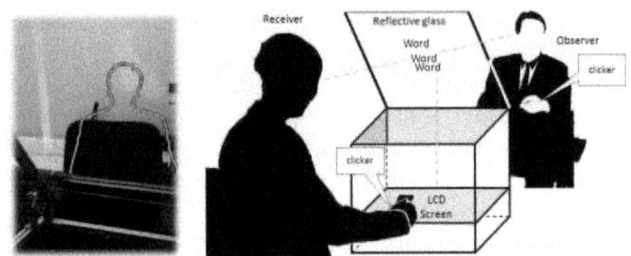

Figure 1. Illustration of the study setup. The receiver and observer sit on either side of our system where information is displayed on a reflecting glass (see actual photo on the left). Both participants have clickers in their hand hidden from the view of the other person. The receiver wears headphones at all times to disguise when information is received via audio.

Both the receiver and the observer hold clickers to register significant events: word relevance for the receiver and distraction detections for the observer. Both clickers have been silenced with a muffling cloth to prevent detections due to the noise of the receiver clicking and other distractions.

METHODOLOGY

On arrival to the lab, participants were assigned roles of 'receiver' and 'observer' according to the experimental design. For trials where both participants were male or both participants were female, roles were assigned randomly. Receivers and observers were then seated at opposite sides of the device (see Figure 1) and taken through an informed consent process. An experimenter read out instructions for the study followed by three practice trials, where participants were exposed to all three delivery modes.

After participants completed the practice trials, they moved on to the experimental trials. The experimental set started with a randomly assigned baseline trial, followed by sets of three experimental and one baseline trial, resulting in a total of 13 trials for the study. For the baseline conversation trial, participants conversed, but no word list was delivered. The observer was unaware of this fact and the purpose of this was to determine the baseline detection of false positives.

For the baseline word list processing trials (one for each delivery mode), 10 word lists (2 for each length) were delivered for each trial, but there was no conversation and the observer was asked to leave the room. The purpose of this trial was to identify the baseline performance for processing words when there was no additional task of conversing or hiding the processing from the other participant.

During tasks, we recorded the conversation, and faces and hand movements of the participants. Time-stamped clicks from the clickers were recorded through our program that was being used to deliver words, so that clicks could be associated with word delivery in post-hoc processing. We also annotated what words from the word list were being used in the conversation in real time, and later validated this with the audio recordings of the conversation.

At the end of each trial both participants filled out separate questionnaires that the experimenters created during the conversation focusing on the content of the conversation. Each person answered questions on what the other person had talked about. The purpose of the questionnaire was to ensure that the participants were attentive to the conversation and not only focusing on the secondary task.

RESULTS

There were a total of 312 scheduled trials including baselines across the 24 pairs. The data for 25 trials were excluded as they either had to be discarded due to equipment malfunction or the trials could not be performed as the participants ran out of time. For some trials not all wordlists were delivered twice and this is accounted for in the analysis using provisions for missing values. A total of 16771 words were delivered, each of which was encoded into a row. The corresponding detections (or lack of thereof) were mapped to each word. An additional 841 rows were generated for false positives in detections using the same format.

We report results according to the research questions, focusing on effects of the delivery mode and bandwidth. For RQ1, we looked at how well the receiver responded to the incoming information while conversing. For RQ2, we looked at how well the observer was able to detect the receiver responding to the information. Unless otherwise stated, for each measure we first report on the differences between dual-task and baseline to establish how dual-tasking affected that metric. We then look at only the experimental trials (where dual tasking occurred) to understand effects of the mode and amount of information delivered on the metric. Table 7 provides a brief summary of findings.

RQ1: Receiver's response to incoming information while conversing

To understand how receiver's ability to respond to incoming information was affected by the mode and amount of information, we looked at three metrics: whether the receiver responded to delivered words or not, the time taken to respond, and whether they were able to insert any of the words that they received into the conversation (the last task was optional for participants).

Whether the receiver responded to a word or not

Comparison between baseline and experimental: A two-way contingency analysis with Response (Responded, Did not respond) and Condition (Baseline, Experimental) found them to be significantly related: Pearson's $\chi^2(2, N=16160)=1149.03$, p<0.001, Cramer's V=0.267. In the baseline condition, 87.7% of the words received a response from the receiver, whereas only 61.9% of the words received a response in the experimental condition. This shows that, while conversing receivers chose not to ignore words, perhaps so that the conversation did not get disrupted.

Within experimental trials: For trials where a word list was delivered during a conversation, we conducted two more two-way contingency analyses to determine whether receivers' tendency to respond varied with 1) Delivery mode (audio, visual non persistent, visual persistent) and 2) Length of the word list (3, 5, 7, 9, 11). Delivery mode and Response (Responded, Did not respond) was significantly related: Pearson's $\chi^2(2, N=10816)=306.42$, p<0.001, Cramer's V=0.168. Receivers were likely to respond to 70.8% of the words in the Visual persistent condition, compared to the 55.7% in Audio and 53.6% in Visual non-persistent. The relationship between List length and Response approached significance (Pearson's $\chi^2(4, N=10816)=8.896$, p<0.064, Cramer's V=0.029. Response percentages were: length 3 (58.8%), length 5 (61.2%), length 7 (60.8%), length 9 (62.8%) and length 11 (63.3%).

Time to respond

For Audio and Visual non-persistent, *time to respond* was measured as the time between when a word was presented to the receiver, and when they hit the clicker to decide whether the word was relevant or not. For Visual persistent, where all words appeared at once, the response time was computed as the time from the last word responded to the response time for the current word. For the first word in the list, the response time was computed as the difference between the list arrival and the response.

Comparison between baseline and experimental: A univariate ANOVA on Response time with Condition (Baseline, Experimental) as a factor showed a significant effect of Condition $(F(1,16159)=150.69, p<0.001)$: receivers took more time to respond on the baseline (M=1.71s, S.D= 1.68) compared to the experimental trials (M=1.26, S.D.=2.36). This is an interesting observation as it suggests that though receivers responded to a smaller percentage of words (62%) in the experimental trials, they did so quickly, perhaps to get the task out of the way and focus on the conversation.

Within experimental trials: A univariate ANOVA on Response time with Delivery mode and Word list length as factors revealed significant effects of Delivery mode $(F(2,10816)=186.21, p<0.001)$ on responding to words during conversations. There was also a marginal interaction effect between Delivery mode and Word list length $(F(8,10801)=1.915, p<0.053)$.

Looking at the interaction effects, there was a significant difference in response time for word lists of various lengths only in the Visual persistent mode. Post hoc Bonferroni tests showed that words belonging to lists of length 3 were responded to faster (M=1.01, S.D. = 2.02) compared to words in lists of length 5 (M=1.29, S.D.=2.28, p<0.419), length 7 (M=1.39, S.D.=2.63, p<0.037), length 9 (M= 1.46, S.D. =2.49, p<0.005) and length 11 (M=1.58, S.D.=2.62, p<0.0001). This result suggests that when multiple words are presented together, more time is required per word to process words in the list. This is further supported in the non-significant difference in response times for words in lists of varying lengths for Audio or Visual non-persistent, where words appeared and were responded to one by one.

For the delivery mode, post-hoc Bonferroni tests showed words appearing in the Audio mode had significantly higher response time (M=1.77s, S.D.=2.7) compared to both Visual persistent (M=1.42, S.D.=0.2.49, p<0.001) and Visual non-persistent (M=0.61, S.D.=1.611, p<0.001). Response time for Visual persistent was also significantly higher than response time for Visual non-persistent (p<0.001). That processing Audio is the most time consuming during con-

	Word was delivered	No word was delivered	Total
Observer identified distraction	1026	841	1867
Observer did not identify distraction	15745	0	15745
Total	16771	841	17612

Table 3: Breakdown of true positives, false positives and missed detection of distraction

versations is likely due to conflicts in processing two auditory streams simultaneously. Visual non-persistent, which has the quality of Audio in terms of fading out soon after arrival, was processed the quickest, likely because it was easier to process while also conversing and because receivers knew that the word would disappear soon.

Insertion of words into the conversation
Receivers were encouraged to insert words from the word lists into the conversation if possible. The rate of this was low, resulting in a total of 216 words being inserted in the conversation across all users (Audio: M=2.32, S.D.=3.03, Visual persistent: M=3.31, S.D. 3.9, Visual non-persistent: M=2.85, S.D.=3.9). An ANOVA analysis did not reveal any significant effects of the Delivery mode on the insertion, suggesting that inserting the words did not vary based on how the words were delivered to the user. We were unable to associate the length of wordlists to word insertions as often receivers would use words much later in the conversation after its onset. Nonetheless, because word insertions were not the participants' main task, we cannot conclude that participants were unable to insert words. Instead, we observe that it is possible to insert words in a conversation as they are received. We plan to quantify how well users can insert words as their main task in the future.

RQ2: Observer's ability to detect the receiver responding to information during a conversation

To understand how detectable the receiver was while responding to information during a conversation, we looked at the following measures: how often the observer was able to correctly detect the receiver responding to information and how many detections happened based on wordlist size.

Across 24 users and 1516 wordlists, a total of 16771 words were delivered. Observers were able to correctly detect 1026 of these (recall: 6.1%). Observers also detected 841 distractions when there was no word delivered, resulting in a precision of 54.9%. See Table 3 for a breakdown.

Whether observers were able to detect the receiver
Comparison between baseline and experimental: A two-way contingency table showed a significant relationship between Condition (Baseline, Experimental) and Detection: Pearson's $\chi^2(2, N=12169)=366.17, p<0.0001$, Cramer's V=0.173. 96.4% of the detections were during the experimental trials and only 3.6% of the detections were during baselines (31 across 24 baseline trials, M=1.29/trial). Out of the detections on the experimental trials, 59% were correct detections (M=3.9/trial), and 41% were false positives (the observer detected the receiver being distracted when no word was presented, M=3.1/trial). The numbers suggest that these detection rates were not due to random clicking as the pattern for the baseline trials (1.29 detections/trial) were much lower than the experimental trials (>3 detections/trial). Also for the experimental trials words were delivered less than half of the time, and random clicking would have yielded a higher percentage of false positives.

	Audio	Visual non persistent	Visual persistent
Correct detection	14.5%	7.4%	6.8%
False positive	3.8%	9.3%	4.9%
Missed detection	81.7%	83.1%	88.3%

Table 4: Breakdown of correct detections, false positives and missed detection across the three delivery modes.

	Receiver speaking	Observer speaking
Correct detections	37.1%	19.4%
False positives	34%	9.5%

Table 5: The effect of speaker on detection correctness.

<u>Within experimental trials:</u> Looking only at trials where a wordlist was delivered, we wanted to see the effects of delivery mode and wordlist length on the correct detections, false positives and missed detections. A two-way contingency table showed a significant relationship between Detection type (correct detection, false positive and missed detection) and Delivery mode: Pearson's $\chi^2(4, N=11729)=247.4$, $p<0.0001$, Cramer's V=0.145. Overall, words delivered via Audio had the highest correct detection rate (14.5% of all words delivered via that mode) compared to 7.4% for Visual non-persistent and 6.8% for Visual persistent. Also, Audio had the least false positives (3.8%) compared to 9.3% for Visual non persistent and 4.9% for Visual persistent. Table 4 summarizes the breakdowns. Groups were not significantly different in terms of detections across word list lengths, so we omit these results.

Number of detections per wordlist

Since we established in the previous subsection that 96.4% detections were during the experimental trials, we do not repeat the baseline comparison here. Results found a significant effect of both Delivery mode (F(2,1501)=32.2, $p<0.0001$) and Word list length (F(4,1501)=26, $p<0.0001$) on the number of detections per wordlist. For mode, post-hoc Bonferroni tests showed that observers had significantly higher number of detections per wordlist when the wordlist were delivered via Audio (M=1.03, S.D.=1.42), compared to Visual persistent (M=0.54, S.D.=0.88, $p<0.0001$) and Visual non-persistent (M=0.56, S.D.=0.89, $p<0.0001$). For word lists, Bonferroni tests showed that word lists of length 3 had significantly lower detections (M=0.322) compared to length 11 (M=1.124), length 9 (M=0.848), length 7 (M=0.723) and trended lower than length 5 (M=0.538). However, this is not unexpected, as the higher the number of words in a list, the longer the time it is displayed, and thus the higher the probability that there will be more detections. For this, we normalized the detection counts according to the word list length and found that there were no significant differences in normalized detection counts across word lists of different lengths.

As Visual persistent was the only mode where all words in the list were shown at once, we focus only on this list. Though there was still no significant differences in the

normalized detection count, the values were trending upwards with the length of the wordlist (M(length 3)=0.069, M(length 5)=0.078, M(length 7)=0.074, M(length 9)=0.068 and M(length 11)=0.086) – suggesting that receivers become more detectable as number of words increase.

Additional analysis: Effects of who is speaking

Although not in the manipulated factors, during the study it appeared that performance was affected by who was speaking at a given moment. To further explore this, we looked at two metrics (only for experimental trials where speech happened during processing of words) – whether a receiver responded to a word or not, and detection by an observer.

For receivers' response to words, a two-way contingency table analysis showed significant relationship between Response and who was speaking: Pearson's $\chi^2(1, N=10712)=98.99$, $p<0.001$, Cramer's V=0.96. Receivers responded to a word 66.2% of the time if the word arrived while the observer was speaking, and 56.8% of the time if they were speaking themselves. This suggests that receivers are more inclined to process information if it arrives when they are not actively engaged in the conversation.

For detections by the observers, looking at all detections, a two-way contingency table analysis suggested a significant relationship between Detections and Speaker (observer, receiver): Pearson's $\chi^2(2, N=1816)=34.7$, $p<0.0001$, Cramer's V=0.138. This did not vary across delivery mode. We further break correct and incorrect detections down in Table 5. These results show that when the receiver is speaking, observers generate more detection events. However, about half of these detections are incorrect detections (i.e., the receiver was not receiving any information), showing that observers were essentially generating detecting events at random. On the other hand, when the observer speaks, the number of overall detections goes down, but the accuracy of detections goes up: observers are roughly twice as likely to be correct in their detections as they are to be incorrect. This is probably due to observers splitting their attention between the task of speaking and the task of detecting; observers mostly detected receivers when receivers gave stronger cues that they were receiving information.

Subjective feedback

At the end of the trials both receivers and observers answered a final questionnaire asking about their experience in the study. Only one receiver was unable to fill out the questionnaire as the server crashed. Receivers were asked to rank-order the delivery modes in terms of how easy it was for them to carry out the word processing task surreptitiously while delivered via that channel. Examining participants' relative rankings of modality shown in Table 6, we observe that Audio was the least preferred mode by more than half of the receivers. However, 34.8% rated Audio to be their top choice. Visual non-persistent was the top choice (43.5% preferring it the most), and it was also a much more popular second choice than Audio was. We believe this is the case because participants perceived it as

Mode	Most preferred	Second choice	Least prefered	Rating average
Audio	34.8%	8.7%	56.5%	1.78
Visual non persistent	43.5%	57.1%	4.8%	2.39
Visual persistent	23.8%	39.1%	39.1%	1.83

Table 6: Modality ranking by receivers.

easy to process due to offering only one word at a time, and in a medium that does not conflict with the conversation in terms of delivery channel. Interestingly, even though quantitative results for Visual Persistent show high performance for this mode, participants were least attracted to it.

Subjects also provided justifications for their choices. The reasons for ranking Audio low included: *"it was difficult to listen to both at once. I preferred one at a time so I didn't have to memorize a couple words while I was trying to talk to someone"*, while justifying why Visual non-persistent was preferred over Audio and the Visual persistent; and *"in the visual tests, I was trying to keep eye contact but the words didn't line up with XX's eyes, so I would have to break eye contact... that was the least distracting*, suggesting that the single word lined up with the observer's eyes allowed receivers to maintain eye contact with the observer while processing the word in the background. 12/23 receivers who completed the survey said that the secondary task being presented via Audio was challenging, as it was difficult to process two auditory streams simultaneously. This was also reflected in the quantitative findings, where receivers failed to respond to almost half of the words delivered via Audio. However, preferences for Audio were also voiced. The most common reason is echoed in this comment: *"It was easier to look like I was paying attention when I didn't have to read text. The text lists were most difficult because I felt more bombarded with information ..."*.

Receivers also revealed strategies they used to disguise their processing an additional task during the conversation. 10/23 receivers said that they tried to maintain eye contact as much as possible. A few others commented that it was difficult for them to hide that they were performing another task and they tried to use filler words such as 'um' and 'ah's to create the impression that they were paying attention.

Observers were asked about what strategies they were using to detect the receiver being distracted. 17 out of the 24 respondents reported that they were looking for eye contact, which matches the strategy that many receivers reported to use to show that they were paying attention. Some observers commented that they looked for unusual breaks in the receiver's conversation. Others commented on leveraging hand movements (as the receiver had to use to the clicker to respond to a word) or overall body language that suggested that the receiver was distracted. As our quantitative results showed observers to be less likely to miss an auditory distraction, it is possible that the difficulty in processing the audio may be resulting in subtle distraction cues via body language that observers were picking up on.

Overall, responses on the questionnaire suggested both receivers and observers had comparable strategies in trying to display a veneer of paying attention and trying to determine when the receiver was not paying attention. Eye contact was the most common technique to show attention or to determine the lack thereof. These findings also suggest that any display providing information without the knowledge of others around the receiver should not require the receiver to look away or lose eye contact, or only display information when this has already happened for some other reason.

Receivers and observers also received questionnaires at the end of each trial, each answering 3 questions on the topic just discussed. There was no significant difference in their scores compared to the baseline when no word list was delivered or in the scores based on the modality of word list.

DISCUSSION, LIMITATIONS AND FUTURE WORK

We now examine the implications of the results we obtained on the design of augmented reality artifacts. Regarding modality, we observed that wordlists delivered to receivers via Audio results in low response rates and high response times from the person receiving, and high number of correct detections from the person observing. Participants performed especially poorly when they were speaking and received words via Audio. This is an interesting result, as one may assume that concealing receipt of information via audio may be easier, especially since no eye movements are necessary as in the visual modes. The cocktail party

Research Question	Measures	Effects of factors tested	Effects of who is speaking	Subjective feedback
RQ1	How receivers responded	Visual persistent yields most responses, longer wordlists are more likely to be responded to.	More inclined to process information if the other person is speaking	Visual non-persistent is most and Audio is least preferred
	Time to respond	Visual non persistent had shortest response time; words in shorter lists got fastest response		
	Insertion of words	No effect of factors		
RQ2	Can observers detect receivers?	-59% correct detections -Most correct during audio	More correct detections if the other person speaks	Receivers try to maintain eye contact, observers look for lack of contact
	Number of detections per wordlist	Audio is detected the most, shorter wordlists are detected the least		

Table 7: Summary of main findings

effect [4] also suggests that people may be able to process two simultaneous streams of information if relevant to an ongoing conversation. However, an explanation may be found in limitations of cognitive resource sharing - processing two streams coming in via the same channel has been shown to be difficult [31]. We advise against using Audio to convey information during conversations.

The Visual non-persistent mode resulted in low response rates, low response times, and number of correct detections lower than Audio and similar to the Visual persistent mode. We attribute the low response times to users trying to quickly dismiss words being displayed. The lower detection rates suggests that the Visual non-persistent mode demands less from receivers than Audio, resulting in less discernible cues from the receiver that the observer can pick up on.

Finally, the Visual persistent mode resulted in high response rates, medium response times that grow with word list size, and low detection rates that also grow with word list size. We attribute the higher response rates to the "batching" nature of the Visual persistent mode, where users can read and process multiple words at a time.

Although quantitatively users performed better in the Visual persistent mode, users ranked Visual non-persistent mode as the easiest to cope with. One caveat is that the reported discomfort with the Visual persistent mode could have been caused by how we structured the question to participants: unfortunately, we did not ask them about their comfort level with specific word list sizes. It is important to note that even though users perceived the Visual non-persistent mode as easiest to cope with, they were not detected more often in Visual persistent mode, and had higher response levels. This means that users are capable of adapting to the display of multiple words and possibly other delivery modes that require changes of gaze. Additionally, users also frequently reported that they used eye contact to show (in the case of receivers) and detect (observers) whether they were engaged in the conversation. This seems to be in contradiction with the previous observation, but it seems that receivers found strategies to effectively disguise the secondary task, even if they were not comfortable with them. These observations seem to imply that a Visual persistent mode with a low number of words is a good trade-off. As future work, we plan to investigate whether the positioning of these words has an impact on user satisfaction with the system.

Finally, we observed a significant difference in performance of both receivers and observers depending on who was talking when words were delivered. When receivers were speaking, they were less likely to respond. Additionally, in these situations, observers were more likely to detect receivers getting the words, but only because they were more likely to click (true detections were as common as false positives). When observers were speaking, however, receivers were more likely to respond. In these situations, observers detected receivers fewer times, probably because their focus was on the task of speaking. They were however more precise in their detection, likely because it took more significant cues from the receiver to call for their attention. Still, the number of overall correct detections was lower when observers were speaking, so we recommend that words are delivered to receivers when they are in silence.

Asking receivers to optionally insert words in the conversation may have possibly distracted them from the mandatory secondary task, which was indicating whether they thought a word was related to the topic of the conversation. However, we decided to include this task to demonstrate that it is possible for a user to use words delivered during a conversation. Even though that was not the focus of our study, our results show evidence that this is possible.

It is worth noting that our user recruitment may have biased our results, as we only recruited native English speakers. The reason for this was that we wanted to factor out the influence of mother tongue on distractions or loss of detection accuracy. One strong trend we found was that participants assumed eye contact is a strong signal of attention, which is the case in the American culture, but may not generalize to other cultures. However, extending the findings to other populations is beyond the scope of this paper.

The usage of a transparent custom teleprompter met our needs for uninterrupted view of the participants, and the scenario we investigate. It could be used to evaluate other AR scenarios such as those where clerks or sales people provide services via windows (e.g., information that could enable more personalized service to customer projected on the window glass), and video conferencing scenarios.

A central assumption in this work is that distraction during face-to-face conversations is detrimental and thereby should be minimized. Part of this assumption is, as the collocutor is not aware of what their fellow conversant is distracted with, judgment about their lack of attention towards the conversation is possible. Would people be more open to others visibly consuming information if they knew that the information is either important to the conversation or urgent for the person receiving it? Prior work has shown that shared goals can help people better manage interruptions in terms of being more considerate about when to interrupt the other person [9, 24] – here, we can imagine that with the shared goal of a more informed and involved conversation, it will be more socially acceptable to receive information while conversing, as long as the other person is aware of this. Future work will investigate these possibilities.

CONCLUSION

We presented a study that revealed parameters that designers should consider when developing information delivery interfaces for new augmented reality devices. Results show that users can process information while conversing without being detected by their conversation partners. They perform best when presented with small batches of visual information and when they are not speaking. These findings can inform design of devices that deliver just-in-time information to people engaged in other tasks, e.g., face to face conversations.

ACKNOWLEDGMENTS

We thank Tim Sherwood for initial discussions and brainstorming, and Hrvoje Benko and Andy Wilson for their valuable feedback on this work.

REFERENCES

1. Albanesius, C. Google 'project glass' replaces the smartphone with glasses, *http://www.pcmag.com/article2/0,2817,2402613,00.asp*,2012.

2. Argyle, M. and Cook, M. *Gaze and Mutual Gaze*. Cambridge University Press, London, 1976.

3. Bateman, S., Teevan, J. and White, R.W. The Search Dashboard: Changing How People Search Using a Reflective Interface, *CHI* 2012, 1785-1794.

4. Bronkhorst, A.W. The Cocktail Party Phenomenon: A Review on Speech Intelligibility in Multiple-Talker Conditions. *Acta Acustica 86, 2000*. 117-128.

5. Brumby, D.P., Davies, S., Janssen, C.P. and Grace, J.J. Fast or safe?: how performance objectives determine modality output choices while interacting on the move. *CHI* 2011, 473-482.

6. Brush, A.B., Meyers, B.R., Scott, J. and Venolia, G.D. Exploring Awareness Needs and INformation Display Preferences Between Coworkers *CHI* 2009, 2091-2094.

7. Cakmakci, O. and Rolland, J. Head-worn displays: a review. *Journal of Display Technology*, 2006, *2* (3). 199-216.

8. Campbell, S.W. and Kwak, N. Mobile Communication and Civil Society: Linking Patterns and Places of Use to Engagement with Others in Public. *Human Communication Research*, 2011, *37* (2). 207-222.

9. Dabbish, L. and Kraut, R.E., Controlling interruptions: awareness displays and social motivation for coordination. in *CSCW* 2004, 182-191.

10. Goffman, E. *The presentation of self in everyday life.* Doubleday, Garden City, NY, 1959.

11. Gowans, G., Campbell, J., Alm, N., Dye, R., Astell, A. and Ellis, M. Designing a multimedia conversation aid for reminiscence therapy in dementia care environments. *CHI* 2004, 825-836.

12. Iqbal, S.T., Grudin, J. and Horvitz, E. Peripheral computing during presentations: perspectives on costs and preferences, *CHI* 2011, 891-894.

13. Jansen, B.J. Seeking and implementing automated assitance during the search process. *Information Processing and Management*, 2005, *41*, 909-928.

14. Ko, A.J., DeLine, R. and Venolia, G. Information Needs in Collocated Software Development Teams *International Conference on Software Engineering*, 2007, 344-353.

15. Maglio, P. and Campbell, C.S., Tradeoffs in Displaying Peripheral Information. *CHI* 2000, 241-248.

16. Mann, S. Wearable Computing: A First Step Towards Personal Imaging. *IEEE Computer*, 1997, *30* (2). 25-32.

17. McAtamney, G. and Parker, C. An examination of the effects of a wearable display on informal face-to-face communication. *CHI* 2006, 45-54.

18. McCrickard, D.S., Catrambone, R., Chewar, C.M. and Stasko, J.T. Establishing Tradeoffs that Leverage Attention for Utility: Empirically Evaluating Information Display in Notification Systems. *IJHCS*, 2003, *58* (5). 547-582.

19. Milrad, M. and Spikol, D. Anytime, Anywhere Learning Supported by Smart Phones: Experiences and Results from the MUSIS Project. *Educational Technology and Society*, 2007, *10* (4). 62-70.

20. Papagiannakis, G., Singh, G. and N.Magnenat-Thalmann A survey of mobile and wireless technologies for augmented reality systems. *Journal of Visualization and Computer Animation*, 2008 *19*. 3-22.

21. Rash, C.e.a. The Effect of a Monocular Helmet-Mounted Display on Aircrew Health: A Cohort Study of Apache Ah Mk1 Pilots Four-year Review, United States Army Aeromedical Research Laboratory, 2010.

22. Rauterberg, M. Ubiqutious and Mobile Computing - New Directions in User System Interaction. *IEEE Proceedings Symposium on Wireless Multimedia, 1998*.

23. Rhodes, B., Minar, N. and Weaver, J. Wearable computing meets ubiquitous computing: Reaping the best of both worlds *ISWC* 1999, 141-149.

24. Romero,N., Szostek,A., Kaptein,M. and Markoloulos,P. Behaviours and preferences when coordinating mediated interruptions: Social and system influence *ECSCW*, 2007, 351-370.

25. Roussos, G., Marsh, A.J. and Maglavera, S. Enabling Pervasive Computing with Smart Phones. *IEEE Pervasive Computing*, 2005 *4* (2). 20-27.

26. Scherl, C.R. and Haley, J. Computer Monitor Supervision: A clinical note. *The American Journal of Family Therapy*, 2000, *28*. 275-283.

27. Shirey, W.J. The Frustration Phenomenon: Exploring Leader-Follower Relationships in the Information Age. *International Journal of Leadership Studies*, 2008, *3* (2). 223-229.

28. Subramaniam, P. and Woods, B. Towards the therapeutic use of information and communication technology in reminiscence work for people with dementia; a systematic review. *Int. J. Comput. Healthc.*, 2010, *1* (2). 106-125.

29. Sutherland, I.E. A Head-mounted Three Dimensional Display *The Fall Joint Computer Conference, part 1, AFIPS '68(Fall part 1)*, ACM, New York, NY, 1968, 757-764.

30. Tamminen, S., Oulasvirta, A., Toiskallio, K. and Kankainen, A. Understanding mobile contexts. *Personal Ubiquitous Comput.*, 2004, *8* (2). 135-143.

31. Treisman, A.M. Contextual Cues in Selective Listening. *Quarterly Journal of Exp. Psychology*, 1960, *12*. 242-248.

32. vanKrevelen, D. and Poelman, R. A Survey of Augmented Reality Technologies, Applications and Limitations. *The International Journal of Virtual Reality*, 2010, *9* (2). 1-20.

33. White, R.W. and Buscher, G. Characterizing Local Interests and Local Knowledge, *CHI* 2012, 1607-1610.

34. Wiese, J., Biehl, J., Turner, T. and van Melle, W. Beyond 'yesterday's tomorrow': Towards the design of awareness technologies for the contemporary worker, *MobileHCI*, 2011, 455-464.

Adaptive Automation and Cue Invocation: The Effect of Cue Timing on Operator Error

Daniel Gartenberg	**Leonard A. Breslow**	**Joo Park**	**J. Malcolm McCurry**	**J. Gregory Trafton**
George Mason University	Naval Research Laboratory	George Mason University	ITT Exelis	Naval Research Laboratory
gartenbergdaniel @gmail.com	len.breslow@nrl.navy.mil	park.joo@gmail.com	malcolm.mccurry .ctr@nrl.navy.mil	greg.trafton@nrl. navy.mil

ABSTRACT

Adaptive automation (AA) can improve performance while addressing the problems associated with a fully automated system. The best way to invoke AA is unclear, but two ways include critical events and the operator's state. A hybrid model of AA invocation, the dynamic model of operator overload (DMOO), that takes into account critical events and the operator's state was recently shown to improve performance. The DMOO initiates AA using critical events and attention allocation, informed by eye movements. We compared the DMOO with an inaccurate automation invocation system and a system that invoked AA based only on critical events. Fewer errors were made with DMOO than with the inaccurate system. In the critical event condition, where automation was invoked at an earlier point in time, there were more memory and planning errors, while for the DMOO condition, which invocated automation at a later point in time, there were more perceptual errors. These findings provide a framework for reducing specific types of errors through different automation invocation.

Author Keywords

Adaptive Automation; Situation Awareness; Fan-out; Trust in Automation; Eye Tracking; Errors; Supervisory Control.

ACM Classification Keywords

H.5.2, H.1.2.

INTRODUCTION

Human operators are increasingly taking on the role of supervisor in complex semi-autonomous computer systems. Yet increased automation comes with unexpected side effects. This is because automation does not simply supplant human behavior, but rather, it interacts with human behavior in unintended ways [1]. This can include reduced situation awareness, inappropriate trust, unbalanced workload, decision biases, and over-reliance and complacency [2, 3, 4]. As a result, there is a need to understand the types of errors that operators make when interacting with such systems.

Adaptive automation (AA) has been proposed as a solution to the negative consequences of more-typical, static automation [5, 6, 7]. In an adaptive automation system, automation is flexible and responsive to the needs of the user and the changes in the task environment [8]. AA can be invoked by: a) critical events; b) operator performance measures; c) operator physiological assessment; d) operator modeling; and/or e) hybrid methods [9]. While empirical evaluations have shown the efficacy of adaptive automation in such domains as aviation [10], air traffic management [11], and industrial process control [12], the method of invocation can dramatically affect how the operator performs on a given task [13].

Of these methods of invocation, recent evidence points to the potential advantage of a hybrid invocation method to improve operator performance, where the operator's attention, evaluated by analyzing eye movements, and a critical event are used to invoke automation. This was recently demonstrated by the dynamic model of operator overload, which assessed the urgency of the critical event and the operator's attention allocation to predict whether a vehicle will fly into a hazard. When the model predicted an error, a cue was initiated on the situation in question, which resulted in over 50% fewer errors [14].

The dynamic model of operator overload (DMOO) was an adaptation of the fan-out model, initially proposed by Crandall et al. (2005) [15]. Fan-out specifies the maximum number of vehicles that an operator can effectively control by taking into account, *interaction time* (IT) -- how long it takes to interact with a vehicle in order for it to be in an acceptable state, and *neglect time* (NT) -- how long the vehicle can be ignored before it needs attention. Variables that captured cognitive limitations of the operator were later included in the fan-out model, such as wait time due to *human decision making* called interaction wait time (WTI), wait time due to *attention allocation* (WTAA), and wait time due to attending to other vehicles that were ahead in the *queue* (WTQ) [16] (see Equation 1).

$$FO = (NT / (IT(WTI) + WTAA + WTQ)) + 1$$

Equation 1: The Fan-out model initially developed by Crandall et al. (2005) and later modified by Cummings et al. (2008) that predicts the maximum number of vehicles that can be simultaneously controlled. WTI is wait time associated with time spent on decision- making and is nested within IT.

The DMOO uses similar theoretical concepts as the fan-out model, yet instead of predicting the maximum number of vehicles that an operator can control, the DMOO predicts operator overload in real-time during the performance of a dynamic task. The model predicts operator overload based on whether or not the operator will respond to a critical event, such as whether or not a vehicle will intersect with a hazardous area. Three theoretical constructs from the fan-out model (see Equation 1) are used as predictors for operator overload in the DMOO. In DMOO, WTAA is instantiated as the amount of time it took to look at objects involved in the situation in question, WTQ is instantiated as the number of fixations on irrelevant objects, and NT is instantiated as the interval of time from when the vehicle's projected path first becomes critical for the operator to address, i.e. when the vehicle intersected a hazardous area, to the predicted moment that the vehicle will make contact with the hazard.

Another consideration when developing the DMOO, and other AA systems, is what component of information processing to automate. Parasuraman, Sheridan, and Wickens (2000) [17] proposed four levels of information processing: sensory processing, perception/working memory, decision-making, and response selection. Each of these four levels can be automated to different degrees where at the lowest end of the spectrum the computer offers no assistance and at the highest end of the spectrum the computer acts autonomously and ignores the human. For the DMOO, decision-making was automated at a medium level on Parasuraman et al.'s (2000) [17] scale, where the automation suggests an alternative action by cueing the operator to a situation needing attention. The reason for automating at this level is that higher levels of automation can have negative consequences, such as reduced situation awareness [11] and increased complacency [18].

Due to the unintended consequences that automation often has on human performance [17], it is important to explore how and why the DMOO is effective. Since increased inaccuracy of automation typically results in worse performance [5, 19], the accuracy of the DMOO should reduce operator errors. However, it is unclear whether there will be similar types of errors based on the accuracy of the automation. Three types of errors were distinguished with respect to how participants respond to an adaptive automation cue: (a) The participant did not look at the situation at all (Noticing Errors), (b) The participant did not look at the situation in time to act (Time-out Errors), (c)

The participant looked at the situation in time, decided to act on something else, and did not act on the cued situation in time (Delay Errors).

Additionally, since the hybrid method invokes automation based on both a critical event in the environment and the operator's state, the relative contributions of these two factors in reducing operator error are unclear. In particular, the timing of the automation is a major difference between a hybrid invocation technique and a critical event invocation technique. If automation is invoked based solely on critical events, the system does not have to take into account the operator's cognitive state, so the cue can be invoked much earlier. Thus, when critical event automation is initiated at the instance that a vehicle needs attention (Point A on Figure 1), the operator quickly becomes aware of the situation, yet may decide to act on something else, since they have more time. But with the DMOO, the automation is invoked later, resulting in an urgent scenario (Point B on Figure 1), whereas the participant is more likely to be responsive to the automation and act on the situation the instant it enters attention.

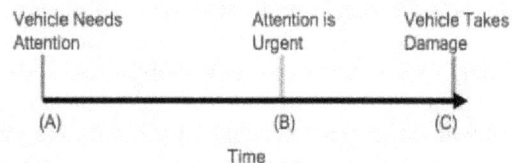

Figure 1: This is an example of a critical event. (A) represents invoking the automation based solely on a critical event, (B) represents invoking the automation using the DMOO (B), and (C) is the negative outcome of damage that occurs when the participant does not respond to the critical event.

Thus, earlier invocation of automation, such as critical event invocation, may result in participants being more likely to look at the automation but decide to act on something else first. A result of looking at other objects after looking at the cue is that prospective memory errors and planning errors are more likely. Prospective memory errors involve memory for intended actions that are planned to be performed at some designated point in the future [20]. In the DMOO condition, prospective memory and planning errors may be less common because it is a more urgent cue. Yet since the DMOO cue is generally triggered later, there is an increased risk of errors due to the participant not noticing the cue in time.

We therefore hypothesize that the timing of a cue will affect the proportion of operator error types, where an earlier cue will result in more delay errors, and a later cue will result in more noticing and time-out errors. Thus, we predict that the distribution of error types will not be different when comparing an accurate DMOO invocation system with an inaccurate DMOO system, where both systems invoke the automation at the same time. Though we would expect overall performance to be better when the automation is more accurate, based on previous research regarding the negative consequences of inaccurate automation [5, 19]. However, because the timing of DMOO and pure critical event invocation will likely differ, we hypothesize that there will be differences in the distribution of error types between these conditions. In the DMOO system, where automation is invoked later, we expect that there will be more noticing errors and time-out errors. Yet for the critical event invocation system, where automation is invoked earlier, we expect more delay errors. The reason for this is that when the DMOO invokes the automation at a later point in time there is an increased likelihood that the participant will not notice the event. However, when the critical event invocation initiates the automation at an earlier point in time, this increases the likelihood that the participant will look at the situation, decide to act on something else, but will have a prospective memory or planning failure that results in not returning to the critical event in time.

EXPERIMENT 1

To determine the role that accuracy of invocation plays in the distribution of errors in a dynamic task, we adopted Breslow et al.'s (under review) DMOO and ran it in the same simulation they used. Similar to Breslow et al. (under review) the DMOO predicted whether or not a vehicle will take damage by providing a probability that damage will occur. When the probability reached a high enough threshold, a cue was initiated. The accuracy of the automated cue was then manipulated by changing the location of the cue. In the accurate condition, the DMOO model was run in real-time and when the model predicted damage would occur, a cue flashed on the relevant hazard of the impending damage situation. In the inaccurate condition, the same DMOO model was run, but instead of flashing the cue on the relevant hazard, a random hazard (one of the 18 hazards) flashed when the model predicted damage. This resulted in approximately the same number and timing of cue invocations in both conditions, but very different levels of invocation accuracy.

METHOD

Participants

Twenty-nine George Mason University undergraduate students participated for extra credit. All participation was voluntary. Three participants' data were eliminated due to experimental error that involved an issue with the eye-tracking hardware not recording data. Four participants' data were eliminated due to low eye tracker validity. In total, 22 participants' data were analyzed. All participants had normal or corrected-to-normal vision.

Materials

The Research Environment for Supervisory Control of Heterogeneous Unmanned Vehicles (RESCHU) [21] was used in this study. A Navy pilot who is familiar with supervisory control tasks designed the RESCHU task and

the task has been used extensively. In this version of the RESCHU task, homogenous unmanned aerial vehicles (UAVs) moved on a computer screen in an environment that was dynamically changing. There were three main sections in the simulation: the map window on the right, the payload window on upper left, and a status window on the

Figure 2: RESCHU supervisory control task. The upper left panel is the payload screen that appears when a user engages a vehicle. The bottom left panel provides the user with information about each of the vehicle states. The right panel is the map view where participants must navigate vehicles to targets while also avoiding hazardous areas.

Figure 3: RESCHU supervisory control task. The circles are hazardous areas. The blue circle (highlighted with a dotted line container in order to distinguish the cue when printing in black and white) demonstrates what the cue looks like when it is fired. The half circles represent what the vehicle looks like. The red diamonds are the targets that the vehicles are directed towards.

lower left (see Figure 2). The map area displayed UAVs (blue half ovals), targets (red diamonds), which UAVs were directed to, and hazards (yellow circles), which should be avoided. Vehicles were labeled with numbers and targets were labeled with letters. The payload window (top left) displayed a photographic image in which the participant engaged in visual search to locate an object based on written instructions as part of a payload delivery operation (described later). The status window (bottom left) depicted a timeline of each UAV's past and upcoming milestones, including the waypoints and the target of each UAV, as well as the vehicles' states (safe, damaged, dead). The simulation included five UAVs that moved at a fixed speed, 5.2 pixels per second, throughout the duration of the task. There were eighteen hazard areas, one of which changed its position randomly every four seconds, with the constraint that the hazards could not appear within three degrees of visual angle (about 50 pixels) of any UAV. If the UAV passed through a hazard, it incurred damage. Damage was indicated as a red bar in the status window. The location of targets and hazards on the simulation map was randomized with the constraint that targets and hazards were no closer than three degrees of visual angle from each other. This insured that targets and hazards could not co-occur in the same position. There were always seven targets present on the map.

Within the simulation, the system directed UAVs to targets on straight-line paths. The participant could engage targets after the vehicle arrived at a target. At the start of the simulation the UAVs were randomly assigned to targets towards which they moved along automatically generated linear paths. Once the UAV reached the target destination, the target flashed red until it was engaged. A target was engaged when the operator right clicked on the vehicle and selected the appropriate popup menu item. Engaging the vehicle triggered the payload task, where the participant performed a visual search task to locate an object such as a ship or a car in the payload window.

During the payload task, the vehicles in the map panel continued to move toward their respective targets, but operator input to the map screen was disabled. After identifying the object in the payload panel, the UAV's mission was completed. The UAV was then randomly assigned to a new target that did not already have a UAV assigned to it.

The participant also attempted to prevent vehicles from traversing hazard areas. To avoid a hazard area, the participant could assign the UAV to a different target or the participant could add waypoints to the UAV's trajectory, which effectively allowed the participant to pilot the UAV around hazard areas. The participant could also move or delete waypoints. The trajectory of the UAV was indicated with lines on the map, making it unambiguous whether a UAV would traverse a hazard area.

RESCHU requires the operator to manage multiple events that occur in parallel: more than one UAV could be waiting at a target for engagement, multiple UAVs could be on a path to a hazardous area, and it was left to the operator's discretion to act on any one of the five vehicles. In view of these task demands, the participant could not be relied on to notice whenever a UAV was on a trajectory towards a hazard.

In the accurate automation condition the equation model developed by Breslow et al. (under review) was run repeatedly (every 500 ms) in real-time with updated inputs. If the model signaled danger, a highly salient cue flashed on the hazard that the model predicted to be posing a threat (see Figure 3). In the inaccurate automation condition the equation was also run, but instead of flashing the cue on the relevant hazard to the model, a random hazard flashed. In both conditions the cue was instantiated by the yellow hazard flashing blue.

Design and Procedure

The experiment had a between groups design with the accurate automation and inaccurate automation conditions.

All participants began the experiment by completing an interactive tutorial that explained all aspects of the simulation. Participants learned about the objective of the simulation: to prevent as much damage as possible and engage as many vehicles as possible. Additionally, participants learned how to control the UAVs (changing targets, assigning/deleting/moving waypoints) and to engage a target (by right clicking on the target and selecting the engage menu item in the popup menu). Participants were also warned of the dangers of hazards and were instructed on how to avoid hazards. The tutorial lasted approximately 10 minutes.

After the tutorial, participants were instructed to practice interacting with the RESCHU simulation in the condition that they were assigned to. This practice was identical to the task that they were later be exposed to. The experimenter asked the participant to perform the actions that the participant was instructed on in the tutorial and the participant practiced the task until they were comfortable with the controls. Participants were then reminded that the goal of the task was to prevent as much damage as possible and engage as many vehicles as possible. Following this, participants were calibrated on the eye-tracker, seated approximately 66 cm from the screen, told to try to avoid damage as much as possible and to engage as many vehicles as possible, and then were administered a 10-minute session on RESCHU. This session was followed by a brief break, after which a second 10-minute RESCHU session was administered in the same manner as the first. Participants were run in the same condition for both 10-minute sessions.

Measures

Keystroke and mouse data were collected for each participant. Eye tracking data were collected using an SMI eye tracker operating at 250 hertz. A fixation was defined using the dispersion-based method, where a fixation was defined by 60 ms of sample data within a 50 pixel radius.

In order to examine how the accuracy of the automation impacted performance, the pattern of eye movements was analyzed from the moment the cue fired to when it stopped firing, which either occurred when the participant resolved the danger situation or the situation ended in damage. Fixations were categorized based on their object of focus. There were a total of five UAVs on the screen, each having a different target, and possibly different hazards associated with it. A vehicle, the vehicle's relevant hazard(s), and the vehicle's target were classified as a 'vehicle cluster'; a fixation on any of these objects was classified as a fixation on the vehicle cluster, while the initial (and possibly only) fixation on the hazard were classified as a hazard fixation.

To examine the type of errors that participants made in the accurate vs. inaccurate automation conditions, three types of errors were distinguished with respect to how participants responded to the cue: (a) Participant did not look at the situation at all (Noticing Errors), (b) Participants did not look at the situation in time to act (Time-out Errors), (c) Participants looked at the situation in time, decided to act on something else, and did not act on the cue situation in time (Delay Errors).

RESULTS

Performance on the RESCHU Simulation

A mixed ANOVA was run with condition as a between groups factor and session as a within groups factor in order to determine the impact of the accuracy of the automation on performance, where performance was evaluated based on the number of instances where a vehicle received damage by making contact with a hazardous area on the map. As expected, there were fewer instances of damage in the accurate automation condition ($M = 1.86$, $CI = .60$) than the inaccurate automation condition ($M = 3.95$, $CI = 1.16$), $F(1, 20) = 6.89$, $p < .05$, $\eta^2 = .27$. There was not a significant effect of session, $F(1, 20) = 1.12$, $p = .30$, $\eta^2 = .05$, and no interaction between condition and session, $F(1, 20) = 1.53$, $p = .23$, $\eta^2 = .07$.

The Cue's Effect on Perceptions and Actions

Recall that we hypothesized that participants would be more responsive to the cue in the accurate automation condition than the inaccurate automation condition. In support of this hypothesis, participants in the accurate automation condition were more likely to look at the cue ($M = 60.55\%$, $CI = 9.56\%$) than participants in the inaccurate automation condition ($M = 25.21\%$, $CI = 8.44\%$), $t(20) = 5.43$, $p < .05$, $d = 2.31$ (see Figure 4, first two bars). It also might be expected that participants would take longer to respond to the inaccurate automation than the accurate cue, yet there was no difference in how long it took for participants to respond to the accurate automation condition ($M = 3.79$ secs, $CI = .92$ secs) and inaccurate automation condition ($M = 4.78$ secs, $CI = 1.34$ secs), $t(20) = 1.20$, $p = .24$, $d = .51$. There was a marginal difference in the

percentage of time participants fixated on the vehicle cluster, where participants in the accurate automation condition were marginally more likely to look at the relevant vehicle cluster after the automation fired ($M = 88.83\%$, $CI = 4.07\%$) than participants in the inaccurate automation condition ($M = 82.73\%$, $CI = 4.86\%$), $t(20) = 1.89$, $p = .07$, $d = .81$ (see Figure 4, middle two bars). In further support of the hypothesis that participants are more responsive to the automation in the accurate condition than the inaccurate condition, after looking at the situation (vehicle cluster) participants were more likely to act and resolve the hazardous situation in the accurate condition ($M = 96.75\%$, $CI = 1.95\%$) than the inaccurate condition ($M = 86.57\%$, $CI = 8.63\%$), $t(20) = 2.26$, $p < .05$, $d = .96$ (see Figure 4, last two bars).

These results confirm previous findings that showed advantages of accurate automation. Additionally, the results provide a reason for why participants performed better in the accurate condition than the inaccurate condition. In the accurate condition, participants were more likely to look at the cue and were more likely to act on the relevant situation than in the inaccurate condition. This demonstrates that accurate automation results in increased responsiveness for both perceptions and actions.

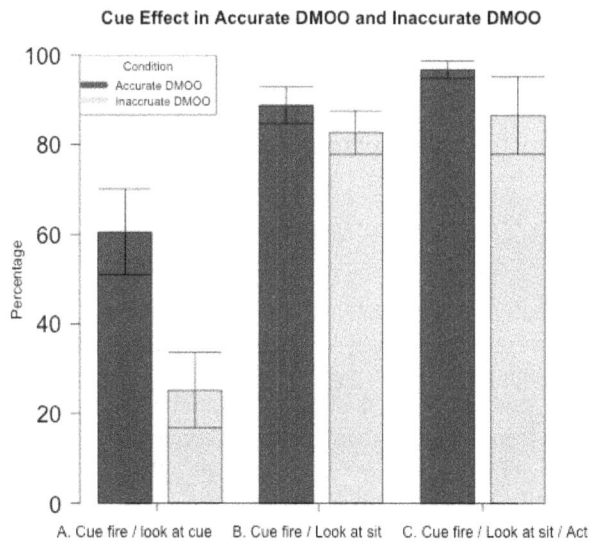

Figure 4: Perception and action behavior based on task condition. (A) The first two bars, which represent the percentage of time participants look at the cue after it fires. (B) The second two bars, which represent the percentage of time participants look at the situation after the cue fires. (C) The third two bars, which represent the percentage of time participants look at the situation after the cue fires and acted on the situation. Error bars are 95% confidence intervals.

Types of Errors

While there were fewer errors in the accurate DMOO condition than the inaccurate DMOO condition, as was demonstrated by the previous finding of improved performance in the accurate DMOO condition, we hypothesized that the distribution of errors would be no different between the conditions. The reason for this is that in both conditions the cue was initiated using the DMOO, which fires the cue at the same point in time. The DMOO fires a cue at a critical moment, at a later point in time. Despite the accuracy of the cue, when it is fired at a later point in time this should not impact the proportion of noticing errors, delay errors, and time-out errors.

In order to explore this, instances where participants had no errors were eliminated from the analysis and a 2 X 3 mixed ANOVA was run with error type as a within subjects independent variable, and with the percentage of errors as a dependent variable. Again, condition was the between group variable. The types of errors were noticing errors, time-out errors, and delay errors. There was not a significant difference in the percentage of errors between conditions, $F(1, 16) = 1.66$, $p = .22$, $\eta^2 = .09$. There was also not a significant in the type of errors within conditions, $F(2, 32) = 1.65$, $p = .21$, $\eta^2 = .09$ and there was no interaction between condition and the type of errors, $F(2, 32) = 0.02$, $p = .98$, $\eta^2 = .00$ (see Figure 5). While there are other explanations for this non-significant effect, in Experiment 2 we will investigate whether the timing of the cue impacts the proportion of error types.

DISCUSSION

As expected, participants were more responsive to the cue in the accurate automation condition than the inaccurate automation condition. Participants looked at the accurate automation cue more often than the inaccurate automation cue and were more likely to act on the accurate automation cue than the inaccurate automation cue. Moreover, participants performed better in the accurate automation condition than the inaccurate automation condition.

In support of the idea that the timing of automation impacts the distribution of error types, there was no difference in the proportion of different types of errors that operators make in the accurate cue and inaccurate cue conditions. While more errors occurred overall in the inaccurate automation condition, there was not a significant difference in the proportion of error types in the accurate DMOO and inaccurate DMOO. We believe that there was not a significant difference in the proportion of error types in both conditions because the cue fired at the same time in both conditions, resulting in the same opportunity to respond to the automation and then decide to do something else. Thus, while the accuracy of the automation affects the number of errors and performance because accurate automation brings the participant's attention to the relevant situation, it did not significantly affect the distribution of error types. In Experiment 2 we will explicitly test the hypothesis that the timing of cue automation impacts the distribution of error types by manipulating the timing of cue invocation.

EXPERIMENT 2

To determine how automation invocation impacts operator error, and specifically how the timing of AA impacts the distribution of error types, we again used the RESCHU simulation and the same adaptive model-based cue (Breslow et al. under review). Yet in this experiment, the DMOO was compared to a simpler system that initiated automation based solely on critical events invocation of automation. In the critical event invocation of automation condition, the hazard flashed the instant that a vehicle entered a path intersecting with it. This was in contrast, to

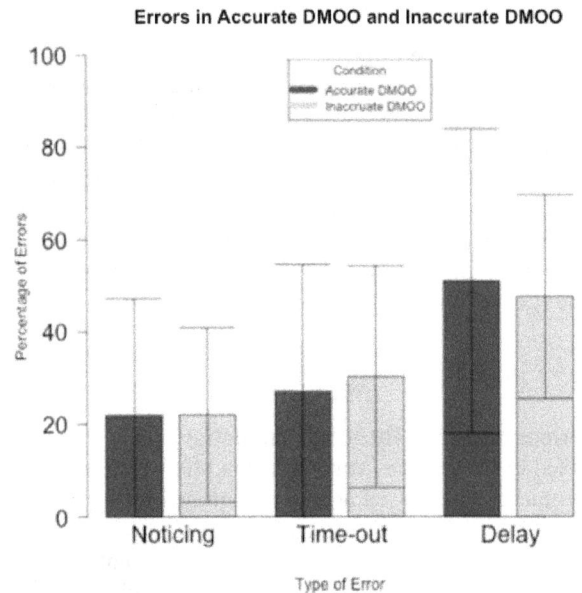

Figure 5: Type of error based on task condition. Error bars are 95% confidence intervals. A *noticing error* occurs when the participant never looks at the critical vehicle, a *time-out error* occurs when the participant looks at the vehicle, but cannot act in time, and a *delay error* occurs when a participant looks at the critical vehicle, decides to act on something else, and then does not return to the critical vehicle.

the DMOO where the cue only flashed when the system detected that there was a high probability that the operator was not going to respond to the critical event in time. This resulted in an earlier cue invocation for the critical event system condition and a relatively later cue invocation for the DMOO condition.

METHOD

Participants

Fifty-two George Mason University undergraduate students participated for extra credit. All participation was voluntary. One participants' data was eliminated due to experimental error that involved an issue with the eye-tracking hardware not recording data. Six participants' data were eliminated due to low eye tracking validity. In total, 45 participants' data were analyzed. All participants had normal or corrected-to-normal vision.

Materials

Materials were identical to the RESCHU task described in Experiment 1, with the exception that the inaccurate DMOO condition was replaced with the critical event invocation condition, which entailed flashing a cue immediately when a vehicle's path first intersected a hazardous area.

Design and Procedure

The design and procedure was identical to Experiment 1, with the exception that participants were randomly assigned to the critical event invocation condition instead of the inaccurate condition.

Measures

Measures were identical to Experiment 1.

RESULTS

Performance on the RESCHU Simulation

A mixed ANOVA was run with condition as a between groups factor and session as a within groups factor in order to determine the impact of the type of invocation on performance, where performance was evaluated based on the number of instances where a vehicle received damage by intersecting with a hazardous area on the map. There was no difference in the frequency of damage between the critical event invocation condition ($M = 2.70$, $CI = 1.11$) and the DMOO condition ($M = 3.77$, $CI = 1.77$), $F(1, 43) = 1.04$, $p = .31$, $\eta^2 = .02$. There was a significant effect of session, $F(1, 43) = 5.31$, $p < .05$, $\eta^2 = .11$, and a marginal interaction between condition and session, $F(1, 43) = 3.23$, $p = .08$, $\eta^2 = .07$.

The Cue's Effect on Perceptions and Actions

We hypothesized that participants would be equally responsive to the cue in the DMOO condition and critical event invocation condition. In line with this hypothesis, there was no difference in the percentage of time participants fixated on the cue in the DMOO condition and the critical event invocation condition, $t(43) = 0.54$, $p < .59$ (see Figure 6, first two bars). However, participants fixated on the situation a greater percentage of time in the critical event invocation condition ($M = 90.21\%$, $CI = 2.40\%$) than the DMOO condition ($M = 85.37\%$, $CI = 2.05\%$), $t(43) = 3.00$, $p < .05$, $d = 78$ (see Figure 6, middle two bars). This is likely due to the cue simply appearing for a longer amount of time in the critical event invocation condition than the DMOO condition, resulting in a greater likelihood of fixating on the situation. In the DMOO condition the cue fired on average 26.84 sec before the vehicle could potentially intersect with the hazard and in the critical event invocation condition the cue fired on average 40.92 sec before the vehicle could potentially intersect with a hazard ($p < .05$).

Also in line with the hypothesis that participants are equally responsive to the cue in the two conditions, after looking at the situation, participants were equally likely to resolve the situation in the DMOO condition ($M = 93.91\%$, $CI = $

2.61%) and the critical event invocation condition ($M = 93.72\%$, $CI = 2.88\%$), $t(43) = 0.25$, $p = .81$, $d = .03$ (see Figure 6, last two bars). These results suggest that participants had similar perceptions and actions in response to equally accurate cues.

We also hypothesized that participants in the critical event invocation condition would be more likely to look at the cue and then decide to do something else, since they had more time available to resolve the problem. As a result, participants in the critical event invocation condition should respond to the cue more slowly than participants in the DMOO condition. In support of this hypothesis, while there was no difference in how long it took for participants to look at the cue in the critical event invocation condition and DMOO condition, $t(43) = 0.34$, $p = .74$, after looking at the cue, participants took longer to act on the critical event invocation condition ($M = 7.31$ secs, $CI = .99$ secs) than the DMOO condition ($M = 5.50$ secs, $CI = .59$ secs), $t(43) = 3.11$, $p < .05$, $d = 90$ (see Figure 7). This was likely due to the fact that participants had more time to deal with the event in the critical event invocation condition than the DMOO condition.

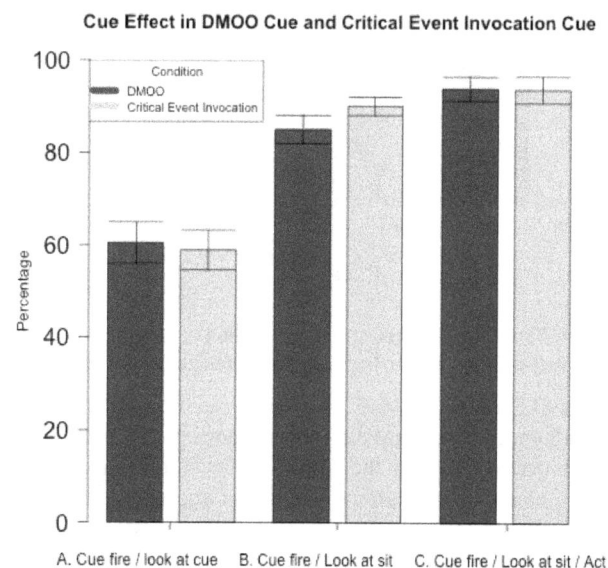

Cue Effect in DMOO Cue and Critical Event Invocation Cue

Figure 6: Perception and action behavior based on task condition. (A) The first two bars, which represent the percentage of time participants look at the cue after it fires. (B) The second two bars, which represent the percentage of time participants look at the situation after the cue fires. (C) The third two bars, which represent the percentage of time participants look at the situation after the cue fires and act on the situation. Error bars are 95% confidence intervals.

The finding that participants take longer to act in the critical event invocation condition (see Figure 7) and are more likely to look at the situation in the critical event invocation condition (see Figure 6, middle two bars) suggests that participants' strategies differ in response to the two types of cues. While for the DMOO condition participants look at the cue and respond by quickly acting, for the critical event invocation condition, participants take longer to respond. This is due to the fact that in the critical event invocation condition there was a greater number of instances where participants looked at the cued situation and decide to resolve other problems ($M = 12.17$, $CI = 2.04$) than in the DMOO condition ($M = 5.32$, $CI = 1.56$), $t(43) = 5.27$, $p < .05$, $d = 1.51$. The reason that participant are more likely to delay dealing with the cued situation in the critical event invocation condition is likely because they have more time to return to the cued problem later.

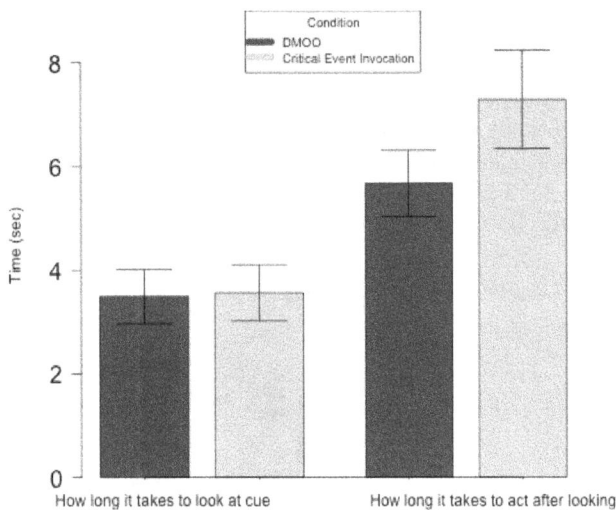

Cue Effect in DMOO Cue and Critical Event Invocation Cue

Figure 7: Timing of perception and action behavior based on task condition. Error bars are 95% confidence intervals.

Types of Errors

It was hypothesized that different proportions of error types would occur between the DMOO cue condition and the critical event invocation cue condition due to the effect of the timing of the cue. An early cue, such as the critical event invocation cue, increases the risk of delay errors, while later, urgent cues, such as the DMOO cue, increases the prospect of noticing errors and time-out errors. In order to test this, instances where participants had no errors were eliminated from the analysis and a 2 X 3 mixed ANOVA was run with the percentage of errors as a dependent variable. Condition was between group and type of error was within groups, with the type of error including noticing errors (not looking at the cue at all), time-out errors (looking at the cue but not acting in time), and delay errors (looked at something else and not returning in time). There was no effect of condition, $F(1, 33) = 0.16$, $p = .69$, $\eta^2 = .00$, and there was a main effect of type of error, $F(2, 66) = 20.02$, $p < .05$, $\eta^2 = .38$,. In support of the hypothesis that the timing of the cue results in different types of errors, there was an interaction between condition and the type of

error, $F(2, 66) = 4.69$, $p < .05$, $\eta^2 = .14$, where Benjamini Hochberg tests showed that delay errors were more prevalent in the critical event invocation condition than the DMOO condition ($p < .05$), and noticing errors were marginally more prevalent in the DMOO condition ($p = .07$). There was no difference between the conditions in the frequency of time-out errors (see Figure 8). Thus, the types of errors differ between conditions with noticing errors being more common in the DMOO condition and delay errors being more common in the critical event invocation condition. This is due to perceptual errors being more common for the DMOO invocation condition and prospective memory / planning errors being more common in the critical event invocation condition.

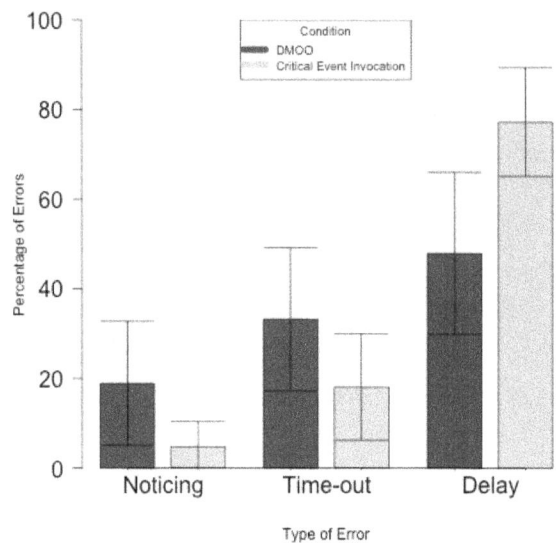

Error in DMOO Cue and Critical Event Invocation

Figure 8: Type of error based on task condition. Error bars are 95% confidence intervals.

DISCUSSION

While performance between the DMOO condition and the critical event invocation condition was the same, participants responded to the cues differently and experienced different proportions of error types. For the DMOO condition, participants acted on the vehicle more quickly after they looked at the cue. This suggested that participants responded to the initializations of the cue differently, where the DMOO condition resulted in resolving the problem more quickly after it was looked at.

In support of our hypothesis regarding different types of errors based on the timing of automation invocation, in the DMOO condition, participants were more likely to make noticing errors, i.e. not looking at the cue. Yet for the critical event invocation condition, participants were more likely to make delay errors due to looking at the cue, deciding to do something else, and then not looking back at the cue. This may be due to forgetting, or not having enough time to act after returning to the problem (e.g. due to poor planning). This suggested that a later cue, which functions as a more urgent cue, has the disadvantage of producing noticing, perceptual-based errors, while the earlier critical event invocation has the disadvantage of producing delay errors due to degraded prospective memory and poor planning.

CONCLUSION

We presented two studies that compared the DMOO with an inaccurate DMOO automation and a simpler model that invoked AA using only a critical event. The DMOO is a form of AA that invokes automation using a hybrid method that takes into account both critical events in the environment and the operator's state [14]. Of particular interest was how participants responded to the computer automation, given that automation can interact with human behavior in unanticipated ways that can have negative consequences [1, 2, 3, 4].

In support of previous research related to the benefits of more accurate automation [5, 19], participants performed better on a complex supervisory control simulation when the DMOO initiated an accurate automation than when the DMOO initiated an inaccurate automation. Participants' behavior suggested greater trust in the accurate automation, which was reflected by an increased likelihood of fixating on the accurate cue and acting on the accurate cue.

In line with of our hypothesis regarding how the timing of automation invocation affects the distribution of error types, in Experiment 1, when the automation in both conditions was invoked using the DMOO that fires a cue at an identical time, there was not a significant difference in the distribution of error types. Thus, when automation was invoked using the DMOO, participants proportionally made the same types of errors, where these types of errors included: not looking at the situation in time (noticing errors), looking at the situation but not acting in time (time-out errors), and looking at the cue, deciding to act on something else, and then not returning to the cue in time (delay errors).

Experiment 2 provided further support for the hypothesis that the timing of automation affects the distribution of error types because different proportions of error types occurred between the DMOO invocation condition and the critical event automation invocation condition. When the automation was invoked earlier, which occurred in the critical events invocation condition, participants took longer to act after looking at the cue. This suggested that a critical event invocation method would result in a greater likelihood of delay errors. Indeed, this strategy of delaying a response in the critical event invocation condition resulted in a greater proportion of errors due to the participant looking at the situation, deciding to act on something else, and not coming back to the situation in time. Yet in the DMOO condition, errors were more likely to occur due to not looking at the event in time (noticing errors).

The different proportions of error types in the critical event invocation condition and DMOO condition can be understood in terms of failures in different levels of information processing. When a cue is initiated early, there is a greater likelihood of errors due to degraded prospective memory, that is, the inability to remember actions that are planned for the future [20], or due to poor planning. Yet when automation is invoked using the DMOO method, which only alerts participants when the situation is critical, at a later point in time, participants were more likely to make perceptual errors, where they did not look at the cue before an error occurred.

The finding that the invocation of AA impacts the types of errors that operators make has implications for how to improve operator performance in various types of complex and dynamic computer tasks. Since prospective memory degrades when attention is divided [22, 23], highly complex tasks that tax working memory may benefit more from invocation of automation that occurs only at critical times, such as is the case with the DMOO. But tasks that are simpler and require that the participant be perceptually aware of the environment may benefit more from earlier cues, as in the critical event invocation condition in Experiment 2. These findings also suggest that there may be advantages to invoking multiple cues. A cue that occurs earlier could address perceptual errors and a cue that occurs at a critical moment could address prospective memory and planning errors.

One important limitation regarding the effect of timing of AA on the types of errors that operators make is that these finding may only apply to dynamic tasks where multiple events occur in parallel. For example, in a simpler task where a single event unfolds in a specific order, the operator does not have the opportunity to delay responding to a cue by addressing other components of the task.

Additionally, the finding regarding the different proportion of error types based on cue invocation may be limited to specific task parameters and levels of expertise. For example, perceived consequences can affect the operator's willingness to make delay errors because a more severe consequence for making an error may result in the operator being less likely to delay addressing the problem. Delay errors may also be less common with more heavily trained and experienced personnel because they may better understand the timing constraints of the task and therefore be less likely to make delay errors. Nonetheless, the finding regarding the different distributions of errors based on the type of cue invocation method speaks to various dynamic and time sensitive tasks where multiple events must be managed in parallel, such as air traffic control, piloting an airplane, driving an automobile, and operating a power plant. System designers must consider how the timing of automation invocation has differential effects on types of errors by invoking automation earlier to resolve perception errors and later to resolve delay errors.

ACKNOWLEDGEMENTS

This work was supported in part by the Office of Naval Research under funding document N0001409WX20173 and N0001410WX30037 to JGT. The views and conclusions contained in this document are those of the authors and should not be interpreted as necessarily representing the official policies, either expressed or implied, of the U.S. Navy. The authors thank the HAL Lab. and Missy Cummings for the use of the RESCHU simulation.

REFERENCES

1. Parasuraman, R., & Riley, V. A. (1997). Humans and automation: Use, misuse, disuse, abuse. *Human Factors, 39*, 230–253.

2. Lee, J., & See, K. (2004). Trust in automation: Designing for appropriate reliance. *Human Factors, 46*, 1, 50-80.

3. Sarter, N. B., Woods, D. D., & Billings, C. E. (1997). Automation surprises. *Handbook of human factors and ergonomics, 2*, 1926-1943.

4. Sheridan, T. B., & Parasuraman, R. (2006). Human-Automation Interaction. *Reviews of Human Factors and Ergonomics, 1*, 1, 89-129.

5. Parasuraman, R. (2000). Designing automation for human use: Empirical studies and quantitative models. *Ergonomics, 43*, 931-951.

6. Parasuraman, R., & Miller, C. (2006). Delegation interfaces for human supervision of multiple unmanned vehicles: Theory, experiments, and practical applications. In N. Cooke, H. L. Pringle, H. K. Pedersen, & O. Connor (Eds). *Human Factors of Remotely Operated Vehicles. Advances in Human Performance and Cognitive Engineering, 7*, 251-266. Oxford, UK: Elsevier.

7. Scerbo, M. (2001). Adaptive automation. In W. Karwowski (Ed.), *International Encyclopedia of Ergonomics and Human Factors*. 1077–1079. London: Taylor & Francis.

8. Opperman, R. (1994). Adaptive user support. Hillsdale, NJ: Erlbaum.

9. Parasuraman, R., Bahri, T., Deaton, J., Morrison, J., & Barnes, M. (1992). Theory and design of adaptive automation in aviation systems (Progress Rep. No. NAWCADWAR-92033-60). Warminster, PA: Naval Air Warfare Center.

10. Parasuraman, R., Mouloua, M., & Hilburn, B. (1999). Adaptive aiding and adaptive task allocation enhance human-machine interaction. In M. W. Scerbo & M. Mouloua (Eds). *Automation Technology and Human Performance: Current Research and Trends*. 119-123. Mahwah, NJ: Erlbaum.

11. Kaber, D. B., & Endsley, M. (2004). The effects of level of automation and adaptive automation on human performance, situation awareness and workload in a dynamic control task. *Theoretical Issues in Ergonomics Science, 5*, 113–153.

12. Moray, N., Inagaki, T., & Itoh, M. (2000). Adaptive automation, trust, and self-confidence in fault management of time-critical tasks. *Journal of Experimental Psychology: Applied, 6*, 44–58.

13. Barnes, M., Parasuraman, R., &Cosenzo, K. (2006). Adaptive automation for military robotic systems. In *RTO-TR-HFM-078 Uninhabited military vehicles: Human factors issues in augmenting the force - NATO Tech. Rep.*, 420–440. Brussels: NATO Research and Technology Organization.

14. Breslow, L., Gartenberg, G., McCurry, M., & Trafton, T. (*under review*). Dynamic Fan out: Predicting Real-time overloading of an operator supervising multiple UAVs. *IEEE*.

15. Crandall, J. W., Goodrich, M. A., Olsen, D. R., & Nielsen, C. W. (2005) Validating Human-Robot Interaction Schemes in Multi-Tasking Environments. *IEEE Transactions on Systems, Man, and Cybernetics Part-A, 35*, 4, 438-449.

16. Cummings, M. L. & Mitchell, P. J. Predicting controller capacity in supervisory control of multiple UAVs. (2008) *IEEE Systems, Man, and Cybernetics, Part A: Systems and Humans, 38*, 451-460.

17. Parasuraman, R., Sheridan, T. B., & Wickens, C. D. (2000). A model for types and levels of human interaction with automation. *IEEE Transactions on Systems, Man, and Cybernetics. Part A: Systems and Humans, 30*, 286 - 297.

18. Parasuraman, R., Molloy, R., & Singh, I. L. (1993). Performance consequences of automation-induced "complacency." *International Journal of Aviation Psychology, 3*, 1, 23.

19. Parasuraman, R., & Miller, C. (2004). Trust and etiquette in high-criticality automated systems. *Communications of the Association for Computing Machinery, 47*, 4, 51-55.

20. Brondimonte, M., Einstein, G. O., & McDaniel, M. A. (eds) (1996). Prospective Memory: Theory and Application. Erlbaum: Mahwah, NJ.

21. Boussemart, Y. & Cummings, M. L. (2008). Behavioral recognition and prediction of an operator supervising multiple heterogeneous unmanned vehicles. *Humans operating unmanned systems*.

22. Marsh, R. L., & Hicks, J. L. (1998). Event-based prospective memory and executive control of working memory. *Journal of Experimental Psychology: Learning, Memory, & Cognition, 24*, 336-349.

23. McDaniel, M. A., Robinson-Riegler, B., Einstein, G. O. (1998). Prospective remembering: Perceptually driven or conceptually-driven processes? *Memory and Cognition, 26*, 121-134.

Distraction Beyond the Driver: Predicting the Effects of In-Vehicle Interaction on Surrounding Traffic

Dario D. Salvucci

Department of Computer Science
Drexel University
3141 Chestnut St.
Philadelphia, PA 19103, USA
salvucci@cs.drexel.edu

ABSTRACT

Recent studies of driver distraction have reported a number of detrimental effects of in-vehicle interaction on driver performance. This paper examines and predicts the potential effects of such interaction on other vehicles around the driver's vehicle. Specifically, the paper describes how computational cognitive models can be used to predict the complex interactions among several vehicles driving in a line when one or more of the vehicles' drivers are performing a secondary task (phone dialing). The results of simulating two distinct car-following scenarios illustrate that in-vehicle interaction by one driver can have significant downstream effects on other drivers, especially with respect to speed deviations relative to a lead vehicle. This work generalizes recent work developing computational evaluation tools for user interfaces in complex domains, and further serves as an example of how user interaction in some domains can have broader effects on the community at large.

Author Keywords

Driving; driver distraction; multitasking; cognitive models.

ACM Classification Keywords

H.5.2. User interfaces: theory and methods; H.1.2 User/ machine systems: human factors, information processing.

INTRODUCTION

Driver distraction is a critical issue facing the global community today, and the CHI community has recently expended great effort on this problem to understand the effects of in-vehicle interaction [e.g., 6, 7]. The vast majority of work on driver distraction, both within and outside the CHI community, has focused on one driver interacting with the interface and the effects on performance as observed through the driver's vehicle. However, like many areas of human-computer interaction, driver distraction does not occur in isolation: it can greatly affect those around the driver, to the point at which others may be exposed to dangerous, even life-threatening, situations.

Unfortunately, the empirical basis for understanding the effects of distraction on surrounding traffic is currently very thin. There have been large-scale studies of distraction in terms of the risk factor of a crash [e.g., 4, 8], along with many single-driver studies of distraction [e.g., 3, 6], but very little research focusing on effects on surrounding drivers and vehicles (with just a few exceptions discussed later). However, the recent development of computational tools to simulate behavior and evaluate distraction [e.g., 10] offers great potential to begin understanding this issue. In particular, such tools can be extended to simulate not just one driver-vehicle system, but a fleet of drivers and vehicles, and then to simulate and predict effects when one or more of these drivers is performing a secondary in-vehicle task.

This paper takes this approach as an important first step in understanding the effects of distraction on surrounding traffic. The paper describes a generalization of Distract-R [10], a tool that allows designers to prototype in-vehicle interfaces and then simulate driver interaction with these interfaces to predict potential distraction. Distract-R relies on an underlying computational cognitive model to make psychologically plausible predictions with respect to a person's cognitive, visual, motor, and multitasking abilities. The system developed here simulates many instances of the model (with some driver variability), one following another in a car-following chain of vehicles. In this way, the system allows for testing of how one driver's distraction may affect others in the chain. More generally, by demonstrating how multiple models can be simulated together in a unified environment, this work can serve as an example of how to pursue future model-based prototyping and evaluation for any domain with complex interactions among users.

DISTRACT-R AND TRAFFIC SIMULATION

The starting point for this work is the Distract-R system [10] for rapid prototyping and evaluation of in-vehicle interfaces. Distract-R allows a user to (1) prototype a new device with a simple interface, (2) demonstrate tasks that can be performed on the interface, (3) define characteristics of the drivers and scenarios, and (4) simulate drivers performing these tasks to predict relevant measures of driver performance (e.g., lateral deviation from the lane center as a measure of steering accuracy). Distract-R incorporates a computational cognitive architecture called ACT-R [1] to provide a psychologically plausible model of driving, and relies on a recent

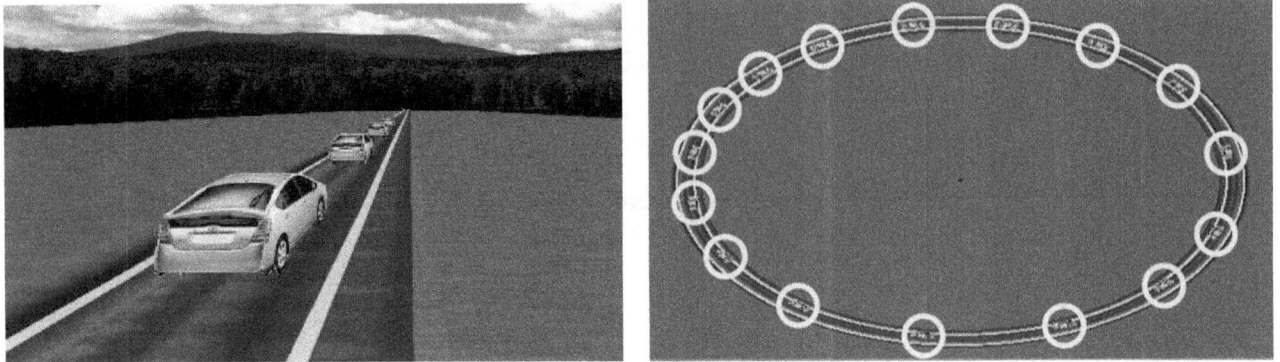

Figure 1: Sample visualizations for the standard car-following scenario (left) and the circular car-following scenario (right). The image on the right includes circles to highlight vehicle positions; note how the vehicles in the top half and left are bunched more closely than the others, illustrating a potential traffic bottleneck that can occur in this scenario.

psychological theory of multitasking for predictions of how interface use is interleaved with driving; however, these details are largely "under the hood," freeing the user to focus on the interfaces and tasks of interest.

The standard Distract-R system focuses on a single driver and thus simulates only that one driver's behavior (although some scenarios include a simple automated lead vehicle). Prediction of effects on surrounding traffic required an extension of the system to simulate multiple humanlike drivers simultaneously. For this purpose, the open-source Distract-R system was adapted in two major ways.

First, a traffic simulation system was built around the system, such that the system could include many instances of the core driver model. In this way, one humanlike model would follow another, and thus the effects of one driver's interaction could ripple to the drivers and vehicles following that driver. Two separate scenarios were developed:

(1) *Standard car-following scenario.* This scenario included a line of humanlike model drivers, one following the next, on a straight roadway. A simple automated vehicle, driving at a constant speed, was placed at the front of the line to provide a stable basis for following behavior.

(2) *Circular car-following scenario.* This scenario used a circular loop of traffic, mimicking a recent experiment designed to illustrate how traffic phenomena can evolve even in simple situations [13]. The scenario includes a line of vehicles, similar to the highway car-following, except that the first vehicle is made to follow the last (with no automated lead vehicle)—creating an "infinite" sequence of models, each following and reacting to the vehicle in front of them.

Figure 1 shows sample visualizations for each scenario.

The second adaptation related to the car-following aspects of the cognitive driver model. The original model used only time headway for speed regulation, which works well at high speeds but unfortunately not at low speeds: as speed approaches zero, any given time headway (say, 1 second) translates to a headway distance approaching zero (i.e., right

at the lead vehicle's bumper). Thus, the model was modified to switch between time-based control at higher speeds and distance-based control at lower speeds (threshold at 18 kph, with a desired following distance of 5 m). The steering parameter that scales the change in headway was multiplied 3 to improve stability and was only factored into control for deceleration (as proposed by [14]). Other relevant parameters remained at the values in the open-source distribution.

Although the concept of cloning the driver model to generate traffic lends psychological plausibility in using a validated model, it assumes that all drivers are exactly the same—thus distorting the attempt to produce a realistic prediction of traffic flow. To remedy this issue, variability was added to the most critical parameter for car-following, namely the desired following time headway: human drivers tend to follow a lead vehicle with a time headway roughly distributed between 1 and 2 seconds [see 2]; to reflect this result, each model driver is given a desired time headway uniformly sampled from the range 1.25 to 1.75 seconds.

The resulting system, which allows rapid prototyping of an interface and then simulation of a traffic environment, is fairly unique in the context of the research literature. On the one hand, there are large-scale traffic simulators to aid transportation engineers in designing efficient roadways, but even so-called "microsimulators" that model individual vehicles [e.g., 5] do not predict drivers' cognitive and associated behavior, and thus cannot model in-vehicle interaction. On the other hand, there are models of individual drivers that focus on cognition and behavior (see [9] for a review), but do not attempt to account for behavior and traffic beyond the driver's vehicle. The new traffic-based Distract-R allows a user to prototype a new in-vehicle device interface, and then in seconds, to generate predictions of driver performance and their potential effects on larger-scale traffic patterns.

(a) Standard Car-Following

(b) Circular Car-Following

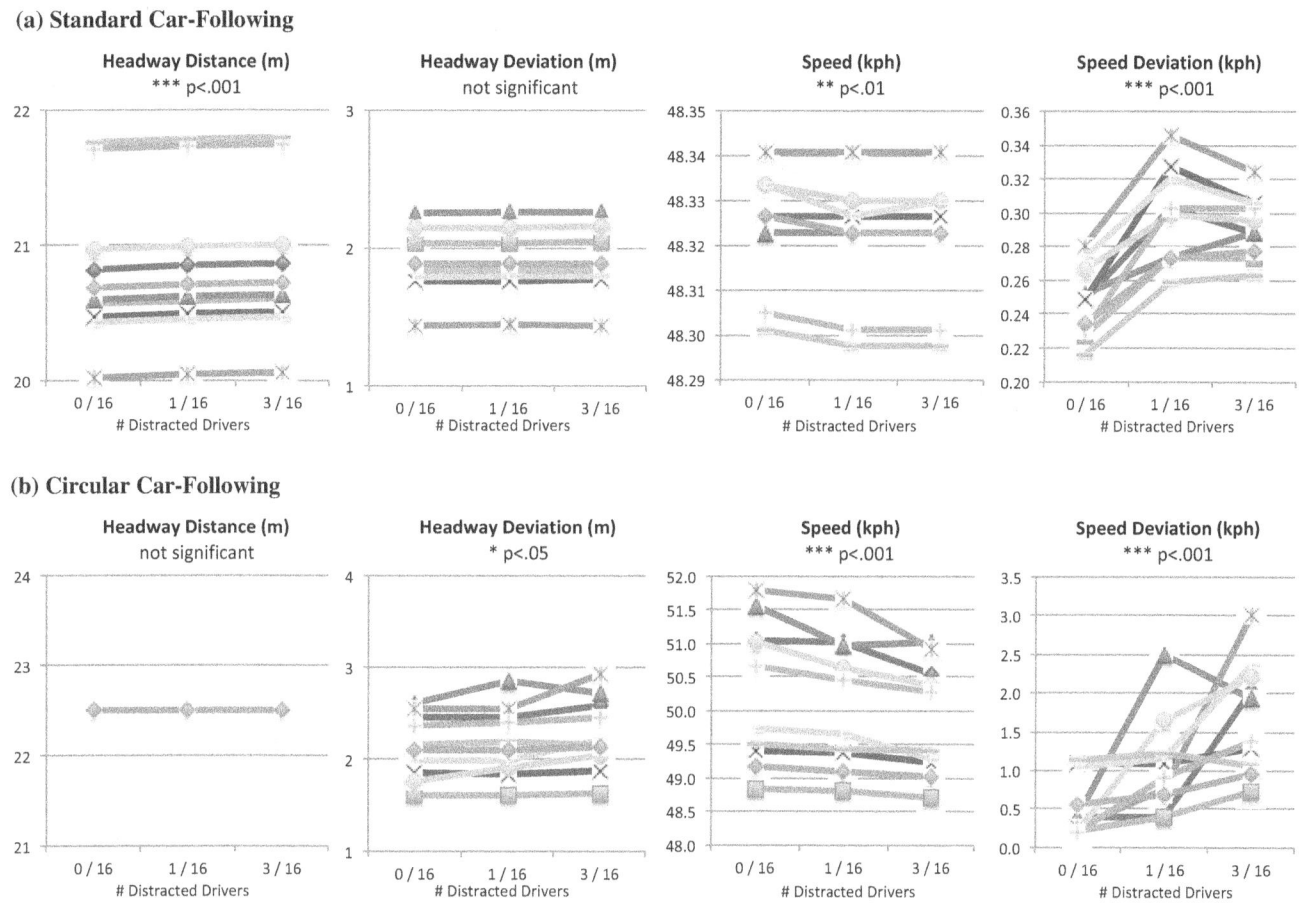

Figure 2: Results for (a) standard car-following and (b) circular car-following. Each graph line represents a group of model drivers simulated across three conditions, namely with 0, 1, or 3 distracted drivers (performing the dialing task) out of 16 total drivers. Significance results were computed using repeated-measure ANOVAs comparing results in the three conditions.

TEST CASES AND RESULTS
Standard Car-Following

The first test case for the proposed approach examined standard car-following along with a common in-vehicle task, manual phone dialing, which has been shown to be detrimental to driver performance (see [10] for a review). The test case included 16 model-controlled vehicles, one following the other, with an automated lead vehicle driving at a constant speed of 48 kph. The simulation began with the vehicles at a standstill spaced 20 m apart. The lead vehicle slowly accelerated to its final speed, leading each model vehicle to follow and accelerate in turn. Each simulation run lasted 10 minutes of simulated time (needing only a few seconds of real time). Results did not include the first 20 seconds to allow for vehicles to accelerate to full speed.

Results were collected from 10 groups of simulated drivers, in which each group comprised 16 model drivers with randomly sampled values for desired time headway. Each group was then run in three conditions: the 0/16 condition with no distracted drivers, the 1/16 condition with 1 distracted driver (3rd vehicle behind the lead) performing the secondary dialing task, and the 3/16 condition with 3 distracted drivers (3rd, 8th, and 13th vehicles behind the lead). In the latter two conditions, the vehicles performing the

secondary task dialed a phone every 20 seconds during the 10-minute run, roughly simulating an intermittent but still somewhat continual source of distraction. Because each group was run in all three conditions, repeated-measures ANOVAs were used to check for statistical significance (including a Greenhouse-Geisser correction when Mauchly's test indicated a violation of the sphericity assumption).

Figure 1(a) shows the simulation and significance results across several aggregate measures of traffic and stability; each line in the graphs connects the results for a particular group of model drivers. *Mean headway distance* (i.e., distance to the vehicle in front) increased a small amount with more distracted drivers, $p < .001$, and *headway deviation* (the standard deviation of headway distance) did not significantly vary by condition. In contrast, both *speed*, $p < .01$, and *speed deviation* (the standard deviation of speed), $p < .001$, produced significant effects. Although mean speed stayed steady for some groups of drivers, it decreased for other groups. Speed deviation jumped radically even for 1 distracted driver; pairwise comparisons (with the Bonferroni correction) indicated that the 0/16 condition differed significantly from 1/16 and 3/16, $p < .05$, but these two conditions did not differ from each other. Thus, even a single distracted driver was enough to generate an effect on overall traffic stability as measured by deviations in speed.

Circular Car-Following

The second test case kept most aspects of the previous study, but changed the scenario: the road was a loop and introduced a circular interaction among all the vehicles (this time with no automated pace car—all vehicles were driven by a humanlike model). The 16 vehicles were initially spaced evenly throughout the circular road. All other parameters were kept constant from the first test case.

Table 1(b) shows the results for the circular car-following simulations. Headway distance remained constant (constrained by the loop), but headway deviation grew slightly with 1 or 3 distracted drivers, $p<.05$. Again, larger effects were observed in the speed-related measures. For mean speed, there was a very significant effect, $p<.001$, in which speed decreased with more distracted drivers; the 0/16 condition was marginally different from 1/16, $p<.10$, and significantly different from 3/16, $p<.01$, and 1/16 was significantly different from 3/16, $p<.05$. For speed deviation, there was also a very significant effect, $p<.001$; the difference between 0/16 and 3/16 was the only significant difference in pairwise comparisons, $p<.01$. As is especially evident for speed deviation, the circular road exhibited greater potential for instability because the effects of traffic bottlenecks wrap around the road circuit.

About Validation

With simulations of human behavior, it is preferable to compare the simulated behavior directly to human behavior. However, there are currently no empirical data sets that make such validation possible here, and one might imagine why: an ideal validation of the 16 humanlike model drivers would require 16 human drivers all driving and interacting at the same time, in the real world or in a simulator. Nevertheless, there is indirect evidence for many of the predictions here. Strayer et al. [12], Kujala [11], and Cooper et al. [3] found that distracted drivers tended to reduce their mean speed; this effect was observed in both test cases here (albeit the effect was very small for standard car-following). Salvucci and Macuga [11] reported an increased speed deviation for phone dialing, which was shown significantly in the simulations. Strayer et al. [12] also found that headway standard deviation increased with distraction, which occurred for the circular (though not the standard) scenario. Cooper et al. [3] and Strayer, Watson, and Drews [12] found that headway distance was not affected by distraction; the straight-road simulations produced a significant but very small effect (.04 m difference between the 0/16 and 3/16 conditions).

DISCUSSION

This paper has shown that it is possible to take an in-vehicle task interface and predict its effects not only on the driver's vehicle, but also on other drivers and vehicles in surrounding traffic. The use of humanlike models of driver behavior for all vehicles is critical, because it results in psychologically plausible predictions of one driver's reaction to another. Large-scale traffic simulations [e.g., 5] have been used to predict congestion and even carbon emissions; the driver models used here are much more computationally intensive than those in the large-scale simulators, and thus scaling up to (for example) city-wide traffic presents a challenge in simplifying and optimizing the models. Nevertheless, the current work offers the promise of predicting distraction effects across a broad transportation network—for example, predicting the changes in a city's traffic patterns if 5% of its drivers are operating a cell phone at any given time.

ACKNOWLEDGMENTS

The author is funded by ONR grant #00014-09-1-0096 and by a gift from Nissan Motor Company.

REFERENCES

1. Anderson, J. R. (2007). *How can the human mind occur in the physical universe?* New York: Oxford University Press.

2. Ayres, T. J., Li, L., Schleuning, D., & Young, D. (2001). Preferred time-headway of highway drivers. *Proc. of the IEEE Intelligent Transportation Systems Conference.*

3. Cooper, J. M., et al. (2009). An investigation of driver distraction near the tipping point of traffic flow stability. *Human Factors, 51,* 261-268.

4. Dingus, T. A., et al. (2006). The 100-car naturalistic driving study, phase II—Results of the 100-car field experiment. U.S. Department of Transportation Report #DOT-HS-810-593.

5. Hidas, P. (2002). Modelling lane changing and merging in microscopic traffic simulation. *Trans. Res. Pt. C, 10,* 351–371.

6. Iqbal, S. T., Horvitz, E., Ju, Y., & Mathews, E. (2011). Hang on a sec!: Effects of proactive mediation of phone conversations while driving. *Proc. CHI '11.*

7. Kujala, T. (2012). Browsing the information highway while driving: Three in-vehicle touch screen scrolling methods and distraction. *Personal & Ubiquitous Computing,* #1617-4909.

8. Redelmeier, D. A., & Tibshirani, R. J. (1997). Association between cellular-telephone calls and motor vehicle collisions. *The New England Journal of Medicine, 336,* 453-458.

9. Salvucci, D. D. (2006). Modeling driver behavior in a cognitive architecture. *Human Factors, 48,* 362-380.

10. Salvucci, D. D. (2009). Rapid prototyping and evaluation of in-vehicle interfaces. *ACM ToCHI, 16,* 9:1-9:33.

11. Salvucci, D. D., & Macuga, K. L. (2002). Predicting the effects of cellular-phone dialing on driver performance. *Cognitive Systems Research, 3,* 95-102.

12. Strayer, D. L., Watson, J. M., & Drews, F. A. (2011). Cognitive distraction while multitasking in the automobile. In *The Psychology of Learning and Motivation 54* (pp. 29-58).

13. Sugiyama, Y., et al. (2008). Traffic jams without bottlenecks—experimental evidence for the physical mechanism of the formation of a jam. *New Journal of Physics, 10,* #033001.

14. van Winsum, W. (1999). The human element in car following models. *Trans. Res. Pt. F, 2,* 207-211.

I Feel For My Avatar: Embodied Perception in VEs

Sangseok You[†]
School of Information
University of Michigan
Ann Arbor, MI 48105, USA
sangyou@umich.edu

S. Shyam Sundar[†]
Media Effects Research Laboratory
The Pennsylvania State University
University Park, PA 16802, USA
sss12@psu.edu

ABSTRACT

Visual perception is dependent upon one's physical state. The apparent inclination of a hill is overestimated when the observer is carrying a heavy backpack. But, what if the hill is a virtual one and the user is about to navigate the virtual environment through an avatar? In a 2 (user with a backpack vs. user without the backpack) × 2 (avatar with a virtual backpack vs. avatar without a virtual backpack) × 2 (customized avatar vs. assigned avatar) between-subjects experiment ($N = 121$), participants estimated the hill as being steeper when using a customized avatar rather than an assigned one. When the avatar is encumbered by a heavy virtual backpack, those with a customized avatar perceived the virtual hill as being more difficult to climb. Avatar customization and the physical resources of the avatar (operationalized here in the form of a 'virtual' backpack) were found to be key predictors of embodied perception in virtual environments (VE). This has implications for the design of games and interventions that make use of VEs.

Author Keywords

Avatars; customization; embodied perception; virtual worlds

ACM Classification Keywords

H.5.1. Multimedia Information Systems: Artificial, augmented, and virtual realities

INTRODUCTION

Avatars have been employed in a wide variety of fields, from video games to virtual training for military and athletics. These digitally rendered characters enable us to experience the virtual environment without any risk to our physical selves. For instance, novice drivers can train themselves for coping with diverse dangerous situations in a virtual driving simulator with no actual harm to their body. This phenomenon implies that the general rule of human perception, specifically visual perception, can be extended into virtual environments (VEs). However, we do not yet know how human perception is altered in VEs, which consequently dictates the degree of effectiveness of the virtual setting for a variety of interventions.

Human visual perception is related to bodily status, i.e., the degree to which the perceiver is physically fit, has physical resources at his/her disposal and/or battling physical constraints at the time of perception. For example, individuals carrying a heavy backpack estimate a hill to be steeper compared to those who are not carrying a backpack. This phenomenon, labeled "embodied perception," has been found in different settings (e.g., distance perception; slant perception of hills) [1,2]. To investigate if this phenomenon is applicable also in virtual settings, the present study proposed the following hypothesis for testing.

H1: Users with backpack will estimate the apparent inclination of virtual hills steeper than users without backpack.

Assuming that the user's physical resource matters in embodied perception in a virtual environment, it is likely that the physical resources of the user's avatar—the virtual body of the user—will have a similar effect. An avatar is "the representational medium for the mind" in a virtual environment [3]. Hence, avatars enable users to think of themselves through technologically extended bodies. This implies that, as we do in reality, users of virtual environments could perceive the virtual world around them from the point of view of their avatars. Therefore, considering that our perception of the real world varies by the physical resources that we possess, visual perception in a mediated digital environment can be affected by the avatar's physical status. Therefore, we propose:

H2: Users using avatars with backpack will estimate the apparent inclination of virtual hills steeper than those using avatars without backpack.

If the avatar in question is customized by the user himself or herself, then that would serve to reinforce the identification of one's self in one's avatar and, in turn, influence the quality of the virtual interaction [4]. The agency model of customization emphasizes the role of self as a "creator" and "source" for filtering individual needs [5]. The technological affordances underlying customization, such as modality, interactivity and navigability, serve to position the user himself or herself as the source of communication, leading to higher levels of involvement with customized content, stronger identity with the object that is customized and greater control over the interaction, representing positive cognitive, affective, and behavioral outcomes respectively. The identity aspect is particularly relevant in the context of avatar customization, and is likely to enhance the likelihood of viewing the hills from the point of view of the avatar rather than from outside the virtual world. Therefore, we hypothesize:

H3: Users with customized avatars will estimate the apparent inclination of virtual hills steeper than will those with assigned avatars.

Overall, avatar customization will serve to magnify the embodied perception between the real environment and the virtual environment. This means the physical resources of the avatar are likely to be more salient for those users who enter the virtual environment through their own customized avatar. That is, the addition of a heavy backpack to an avatar for the purpose of reducing its physical resource will have a stronger effect. Users would feel a higher sense of self as source toward the avatar built by themselves, and the avatar's reduced physical resource in the form of a virtual backpack would be perceived as if they are carrying a heavy backpack in reality.

H4: There will be an interaction between avatar's physical resource and avatar customization on the apparent inclination of virtual hills. Specifically, with a customized, rather than assigned, avatar, the apparent inclination of virtual hills will be estimated steeper when the avatar is wearing a backpack.

METHOD

One hundred and twenty-one participants were recruited at a university campus in Seoul, Korea (58 females and 63 males, mean age: 22.6 years). Each participant was randomly assigned to one of eight conditions. The recruiting message mentioned that the objective of the experiment was to generally investigate the psychological effects of virtual environments.

Procedure

In order to test the hypotheses proposed in the present study, a 2 (user with backpack vs. user without backpack) × 2 (avatar with backpack vs. avatar without backpack) × 2 (customized avatar vs. assigned avatar) between-subjects experiment was conducted. Participants underwent a virtual interaction for a controlled duration by navigating a virtual environment with avatars that were either assigned to them or customized by them. The manipulation of the physical resource of avatar and user was applied by having them carry a heavy backpack during the interaction.

The experiment was administered to one participant at a time in a virtual interaction room that was equipped with a 100-inch large screen and a podium. Before entering the experiment room, participants were asked to fill out a pre-questionnaire about previous VE experience and demographic information, including body weight, and given instructions for the whole procedure, including the methods by which they could control their avatars.

Once the instruction was given, participants who were assigned to the customized avatar condition performed the avatar customization activity with a desktop computer in a separate room. They were asked to build their own avatars as similar as possible to themselves in terms of appearance and general image. For those who were assigned to the assigned avatar condition, Lego blocks were provided to build a non-human object. This treatment for the assigned condition was designed in order to avoid an activity-non-activity confound. By building Lego blocks, participants in the assigned condition were able to experience a similar level of creative activity without reflecting their identity into the object. For participants in the assigned condition, one of the customized avatars (of the same gender) from the other condition was provided. (By taking this measure, we ensured that the avatars across both conditions were identical so that we can rule out any effects due to specific avatar features or characteristics).

After completing the customization/Lego block procedure, the participant was guided inside the virtual interaction room. Asked to stand in front of a podium, the participant was given the instruction about filling out the slant estimation questionnaire with paper and pencil during the virtual interaction. For those who were assigned to the real backpack condition, they were asked to perform the task while carrying the backpack from the beginning. However, for those who were assigned to the virtual backpack condition, the experimenter explained to the participant that the weight of the virtual backpack was equivalent to 1/5th of body weight, showing the avatar with a virtual backpack on its back. To prevent participants from guessing the reason for the backpack, a cover story was given that the backpack was to make their virtual trekking as similar as possible to that in real life.

From their spot at the podium and looking ahead at the hills in the projected virtual environment, participants were asked to evaluate the hills and to fill out the blanks on the questionnaire. The first hill as tutorial included the same tasks as the ones with the other two hills, which were estimating the slope of the hill and filling out the questionnaire. On completing the questionnaire for all of the three hills, the participant was asked to put the backpack down and exit the virtual interaction room.

Virtual Hills

The main stimuli in this study were the virtual hills that were rendered with grass in three angles: 1) approx. 14.93° with 27 metres height, 2) 23.49° with 35 metres height, and 3) 30.97° with 38.75 metres height. The first hill, i.e., the lowest one, was used as a tutorial in order for participants to get familiar with controlling avatars and becoming immersed in the virtual environment built for this study. It should be noted that size of each hill was designed to be apparently identical. This was to control for the effect of hill size on distance and slant perception. Degrees of angles were modified to make apparent differences among these three hills salient. By placing arrow-shaped marks in front of each hill, participants' viewpoint and the viewing distance toward each hill were strictly controlled.

Figure 1 Frontal view of hill1, hill2, and hill3

Backpacks

The backpack was a key manipulation of the present study—physical resource of avatar and user. The basic idea of making the user carry a backpack was to deplete the physical resource of the user in the real world. The reason behind making the avatar carry a virtual backpack equivalent to the one in the real world was to deplete physical resources of the avatar. Hence, the effectiveness of the backpack manipulation of physical resource was dependent on the extent to which they perceived the backpack was heavy enough to deplete physical resources.

Each backpack weighed 1/5th the participant's self-reported body weight (which, by the way, was highly correlated with self-reported height, $r = .76$, $p < .00001$). Mean of body weight of females was 51.1 kilograms, while mean of body weight of males was 64.1 kilograms. Hence, the mean weight of the backpack for females was approximately 8.5 kilograms, whereas that for males was approximately 12.8 kilograms.

Virtual backpacks were used for manipulation of avatar's physical resource. The design of the virtual backpack was identical to that of the real backpack. To prime that the virtual backpack is depleting the avatar's physical resource, participants were told that it weighed the equivalent 1/5th of their body weight, which was the same as the weight of the real backpacks.

Dependent Variables

Perception of the virtual environment was assessed bi-dimensionally: cognitive and perceptive. For the cognitive evaluation, apparent inclination of the hills was estimated through verbal and visual means. Participants were asked to write down a number ranging from 0 to 90 degrees as their perceived angle of the hills. The question was "please indicate how steep you perceive the slant, in degrees" with a bracket for answer. In the visual measure, participants were asked to draw a straight line that indicates the angle of the slant, from the center of a quarter circle to the parameter. Since the virtual interaction administered two hills along with an additional hill as tutorial, questions for hill 2 and hill 3 were combined when analyzed. Correlations between the hills for the verbal and the visual measures were fairly high ($r = .63$, $p < .0001$, and $.81$, $p < .0001$, respectively).

Perceptual dimension measures were used to test how embodied perception is related to their perceived physical confidence. There were two questions capturing perceived

cost to climb up the hills: 1) "how difficult do you think it will be to reach the top of the slant? (9 point Likert scale)" and 2) "how much calories do you think you will burn in climbing up the slant? (0-1,000 kcal)" As with cognitive questions, the questions for the two hills were combined. Correlations between the two hills were quite high ($r = .66$, $p < .0001$ for perceived labor and $.91$, $p < .0001$ for calorie consumption).

RESULTS

Main Effects

A three-way full-factorial ANCOVA, controlling for previous VE experience, showed no significant main effects for user's physical resource (IV1) and avatar's physical resource (IV2) on embodied perception on any of the dependent measures. That is, neither user's physical resource nor avatar's physical resource (operationalized with the backpack) made a difference to their visual perception in the virtual environment. Therefore, H1 and H2 were not supported.

However, a significant main effect for avatar customization (IV3) was found on the verbal measure $F (1,112) = 4.22$, $p < .05$, $\eta^2 = .07$. Participants estimated the inclination of the hills higher in the customized condition (*std. M = .15*, *std. SE = .11*; raw least-squares mean = 62.10°) than in the assigned condition (*std. M = -.11*, *std. SE = .11*; raw mean = 56.51°). Likewise, in terms of the visual measure, the apparent inclination of the hills was significantly higher in the customized condition (*std. M = .19*, *std. SE = .13*; raw mean = 56.80°) than in the assigned condition (*std. M=-0.16*, *std. SE=0.12*; raw mean = 52.14°), $F (1,112) = 4.31$, $p < .05$, $\eta^2 = .08$. However, there were no significant main effects of avatar customization for the perceptual measures. There was no significant mean difference between the two conditions in terms of perceived labor to climb the hills, $F (1,112) = 1.27$, $p = .26$. Nor was there a difference in perceived calorie consumption for climbing the hills, $F (1,112) = .22$, $p = .64$. Therefore, H3 on avatar customization was supported in terms of the measures in the cognitive dimension, but not the perceptual dimension.

Interaction Effects

H4 proposed that with customized avatar, the apparent inclination of hills will be estimated steeper when avatar is wearing the backpack. In contrast, there will be no difference in inclination estimation between the backpack and no-backpack conditions when the avatar is assigned. As hypothesized, the results from the three way full factorial MANCOVA, controlling for previous VE experience, showed a significant two-way interaction between avatar's physical resource (IV2) and avatar customization (IV3), Roy's Max Root = .24, $F (8,112) = 3.38$, $p < .01$, partial $\eta^2 = 0.14$. Specifically, there were significant interactions found in perceptual measures, but not in cognitive measures, when followed up with two-way full-factorial ANCOVAs. Participants estimated higher labor to climb the hill when their customized avatars had a backpack than

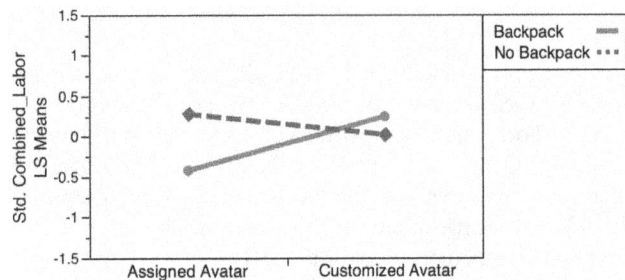

Figure 2 Two-way interaction between avatar's physical resource and avatar customization on perceived labor

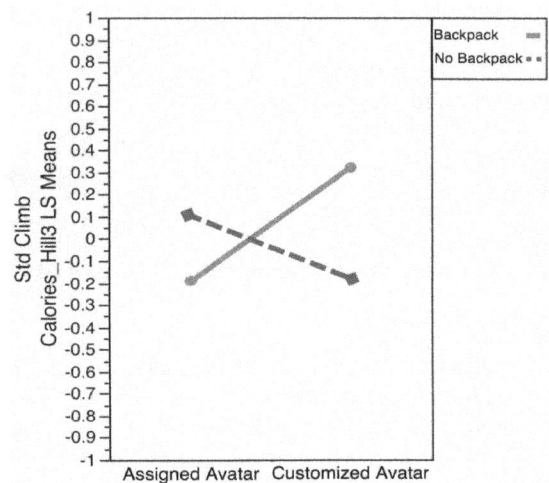

Figure 3 Two-way interaction between avatar's physical resource and avatar customization on perceived calorie consumption for climbing Hill3

when they did not, whereas this difference was not found for assigned avatars, $F(1,112) = 7.59$, $p < .01$, see Figure 2. In addition, there was a partial two-way interaction between avatar's physical resource and avatar customization in terms of calorie consumption. While there was no interaction for Hill 2, the interaction was found for Hill 3, $F(1,112) = 4.30$, $p < .05$, see Figure 3. That is, participants estimated higher calorie consumption to climb the hill in the customized condition than in the assigned condition when the avatar was carrying the virtual backpack, whereas there was no significant difference between the customized condition and the assigned condition when the avatar was not carrying the virtual backpack. Therefore, H4 was partially supported.

DISCUSSION AND CONCLUSIONS

The central purpose of the study was to find out the effect of user's and avatar's physical resources on visual perception in a virtual environment. Furthermore, it sought to ascertain whether this mutual trading of physical resources between the user and the avatar is moderated by the customization of one's avatar. Although somewhat modest, the study data do suggest that the resource conversion is more likely to occur when the avatar is customized rather than assigned. Through avatar customization, visual perception of the virtual environment appears to be driven by the avatar's physical resources rather than the user's actual physical resources.

This empirical study extends the domain of embodied perception into virtual environments and showcases the importance of customized avatars in enabling this embodiment. Design of virtual training programs for use in athletic and military training contexts would do well to emphasize avatar creation and customization features so that users can feel higher embodiment in VR. The practical consequence of doing so is the opportunity to leverage the ego confusion that results between the user and the customized avatar. Just like the virtual backpack made the user perceive more difficulty in achieving a task, a virtual crutch could make a disabled user feel more empowered. Considering that the customization process begins with the user acting as the source [5], the greater the number of avatar features that users can tweak, the higher their ability to imbue their individual identity onto the avatar, leading not only to greater engagement in the virtual environment, but also opening the door for a wide variety of interventions

via the avatar, involving such manipulations as enhancing or diminishing the avatar's physical resources in the virtual environment. Of course, in this study, we have evidence only for the effects of depleting physical resources. Future research would do well to test the effects of enhancing avatar's physical resources on user perceptions of VEs.

ACKNOWLEDGMENTS

This study was supported by the Korea Science and Engineering Foundation under the WCU (World Class University) program funded through the Ministry of Education, Science, and Technology, South Korea (Grant No. R31-2008-000-10062-0) and awarded to the †Department of Interaction Science at Sungkyunkwan University, Seoul, South Korea, where the first author received his master's degree and the second author serves as a visiting WCU professor.

REFERENCES

1. Proffitt, D.R., Stefanucci, J., Banton, T., & Epstein, W. (2003). The role of effort in perceiving distance. *Psychological Science*, 14, 106–112.

2. Creem-Regehr, S. H., Gooch, A. A., Sahm, C. S., & Thompson, W. B. (2004). Perceiving Virtual Geographical Slant: Action Influences Perception. *Journal of Experimental Psychology: Human Perception and Performance*, Vol 30(5), Oct 2004, 811-821.

3. Biocca, F. (1997). The cyborg's dilemma: progressive embodiment in virtual environments. *Journal of Computer-Mediated Communication*, 3(2).

4. Sundar, S. S., & Marathe, S. S. (2010). Personalization vs. customization: The importance of agency, privacy and power usage. *Human Communication Research*, 36, 298-322.

5. Sundar, S. S. (2008). Self as source: Agency and customization in interactive media. In E. Konijn, S. Utz, M. Tanis, & S. Barnes (Eds.), *Mediated interpersonal communication* (pp. 58-74). New York: Routledge.

Testing the Robustness and Performance
of Spatially Consistent Interfaces

Joey Scarr[†], Andy Cockburn[†], Carl Gutwin[‡], Sylvain Malacria[*]

[†]Computer Science
University of Canterbury
Christchurch, New Zealand
{joey, andy}@cosc.canterbury.ac.nz

[‡]Computer Science
University of Saskatchewan
Saskatoon, Canada
gutwin@cs.usask.ca

[*]Computer Science
University of Canterbury
Christchurch, New Zealand
sylvain@malacria.fr

ABSTRACT

Relative spatial consistency – that is, the stable arrangement of objects in a 2D presentation – provides several benefits for interactive interfaces. Spatial consistency allows users to develop memory of object locations, reducing the time needed for visual search, and because spatial memory is long lasting and has a large capacity these performance benefits are enduring and scalable. This suggests that spatial consistency could be used as a fundamental principle for the design of interfaces. However, there are many display situations where the standard presentation is altered in some way: e.g., a window is moved to a new location, scaled, or rotated on a mobile or tabletop display. It is not known whether the benefits of spatial organization are robust to these common kinds of view transformation. To assess these effects, we tested user performance with a spatial interface that had been transformed in several ways, including different degrees of translation, rotation, scaling, and perspective change. We found that performance was not strongly affected by the changes, except in the case of large rotations. To demonstrate the value of spatial consistency over existing mechanisms for dealing with view changes, we compared user performance with a spatially-stable presentation (using scaling) with that of a 'reflowing' presentation (widely used in current interfaces). This study showed that spatial stability with scaling dramatically outperforms reflowing. This research provides new evidence of spatial consistency's value in interface design: it is robust to the view transformations that occur in typical environments, and it provides substantial performance advantages over traditional methods.

Author Keywords

Expertise; spatial memory; revisitation.

ACM Classification Keywords

H.5.2 [User Interfaces]: Interaction Styles.

INTRODUCTION

Spatial memory is a valuable capability in the design of user interfaces. It allows people to locate items quickly [14,

25, 28], it has a large capacity [19], and it is long-lasting [10]. Several research systems have recognized the importance of spatial memory and have used it as a fundamental principle of interface organization (e.g., CommandMaps [25], ListMaps [14], or the Data Mountain [10, 24]), and related features are appearing in commercial applications such as the 'Hotbox' in Autodesk's Maya.

Users can build up spatial memory of an interface when the display is spatially consistent – that is, when the locations of the objects in a view are stable over time. Spatial consistency is determined relative to a particular frame of reference (Figure 1), and in typical interfaces, the windows and displays of desktop and mobile systems provide the spatial frame of reference for the graphical objects they contain. With experience, users learn the arrangement of objects within the frame of reference, and can anticipate the location of targets, such as the Windows 'Start' icon in the bottom-left display corner, or the 'Close' icon at the top right of a window.

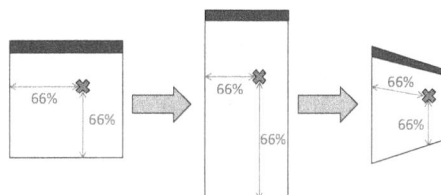

Figure 1: Spatial consistency keeps items proportionately stable with respect to the window bounds.

These examples show that spatial organizations are already a part of some interfaces (e.g., window managers) – but the organization of objects *within* windows, such as icons in file browsers, do not always use spatially consistent designs. For example, when the user changes the size of a window, or rotates a tablet computer from landscape to portrait mode, many systems *reflow* the items in the frame of reference – that is, they re-arrange items to fit the new aspect ratio of the window or display. This fills the window, but breaks spatial consistency – and items can be more difficult to find as a result. If spatial consistency was maintained in this situation, the primary arrangement of items (e.g., the portrait home screen) would be scaled to fit the altered frame of reference (e.g., the landscape window).

Although spatial consistency has been shown to provide enduring and fast retrieval of large data sets [10, 24], there are still issues that need to be understood to extend its utility as a design principle. In particular, designers need to understand its robustness to the transformations that commonly occur during interaction. These transformations can cause substantial changes to the appearance of objects from the user's perspective, such as scaling to accommodate an aspect-ratio change, translating a window across the display, or a rotated view on a tabletop display.

To understand the degree to which the fast performance offered by spatially consistent interfaces is robust to the types of transformations that commonly occur during interaction, we performed an experiment in which participants learned the locations of a series of targets within a window frame of reference. We then measured the effects on selection time of five transformations: *translation*, e.g., when a window is moved to another location on the screen; *rotation*, which is common in surface-based computing; *scaling* and *stretching*, such as when a window is resized; and *perspective distortion*, which occurs when viewing any kind of display from an oblique angle. Results show that many of these transformations had a low impact on performance: in particular, the effects of *scaling* and *stretching* were minimal, especially at low magnitudes.

To test how the spatial approach compares with traditional mechanisms for dealing with view changes, we carried out a second study with a realistic task and setting. Using a simulation of the Windows 7 control panel, we compared a spatially stable layout (where the presentation is scaled when the window size changes) to the 'reflow' layout currently used in Windows 7. Participants were initially trained with a stable presentation of the items. We then randomly resized the window in two ways, and asked participants to find and select target items. Results showed that the spatially consistent layout (using scaling) was dramatically faster than reflowing.

The results from these studies show that the performance enabled by spatially consistent displays is robust to the typical window/display transformations that occur in visual workspaces, and suggest that spatial consistency should be more often used as a fundamental UI organization principle.

RELATED WORK

Spatial Memory
Extensive prior literature in psychology and HCI has investigated human memory of object locations [1-2, 23], including mobile navigation through 3D environments and static memory for objects in 2D scenes (our interest). People learn item locations as a natural side-effect of interacting with them [11], and the rate at which locations are learnt follows a power law of practice [21]. There is also evidence that location memory is improved when effort is required to locate that object [6, 13].

Spatial memory is powerful: it allows fast decision-based retrieval, rather than comparatively slow visual search [17-

18]; it is enduring, with users able to quickly retrieve items months after creating spatial organizations [10]; and it has a large capacity, shown both by empirical studies (e.g., [19]) and by people's abilities in recalling hundreds of locations and routes needed to operate in everyday environments.

In HCI research, several interfaces have made use of spatial memory in order to explore or improve performance. For example, Robertson *et al.*'s Data Mountain allowed users to arrange thumbnails of web pages in a spatial environment [10, 24], and results showed that item retrieval was significantly faster than in a standard bookmarking system. More recently, the benefits of spatial memory have been exploited in window switching interfaces [29], as well as in list revisitation [14] and command selection [25].

Mental spatial-transformation abilities
It is well known that people have a strong ability to recognize familiar forms, even when sizes or orientations are different [20], and various researchers have examined people's ability to deal with specific visual transformations in 2D and 3D. The most common instance of this is mental rotation, which is frequently used to measure differences in spatial ability (e.g., [9, 27]). Scaling was investigated by Bundesen and Larsen [5], who showed that the recognition time for 2D shapes at differing scales was a linear function of size ratio. Bryant and Tversky [3] investigated different methods of conveying 3D information, and showed that simple depth cues such as size and converging lines led people to easily interpret 3D scenes; however, there is also evidence to suggest that viewing familiar objects from unfamiliar viewpoints reduces recognition efficiency [4]. To our knowledge, no research exists on the transformation problem for UIs: that is, people's performance in locating familiar items in a transformed frame of reference.

SPATIAL CONSISTENCY AS A DESIGN GUIDELINE
'Be consistent' is a fundamental rule of HCI, featuring in many design guidelines (e.g. [12, 22, 26]). However, this principle is abstract, and it does not prescribe which design elements should be held consistent. Hansen's 1971 interface guidelines [15] include a recommendation to support 'display inertia', meaning that "the size and layout of the display do not change drastically" (p.529). Hansen's objective in this guideline was to optimize user execution of operations by allowing users to make rapid decisions (modeled by Hick-Hyman choice reaction time [17-18]).

However, Hansen's argument that the *size* of the display should not change drastically is inconsistent with current interface designs, where users have freedom to resize and reorient windows. In this paper we investigate methods to achieve display inertia that are robust to commonly occurring size and layout manipulations.

We propose the design principle '*maintain relative spatial consistency within the frame of reference*' as a foundation of interface organization. The *frame of reference* will normally be provided by the display edge or by the borders on a particular window, but it can also be perceived by Gestalt proximity [30]: for example, a grid of items with no visible border can still be seen to have a frame of reference. By '*relative spatial consistency*', we mean that the arrangement of items within the frame of reference should remain proportionately stable with respect to the bounds of the frame. For example, if an item is the closest item to the top right corner of a frame before transformation, it should be similarly positioned after transformation as well. Figure 1 illustrates *relative spatial consistency* as the frame undergoes stretch and perspective transformations.

Common transformations to the frame of reference
Frames of reference in UIs commonly undergo (or are viewed in such a way that they are perceived to undergo) five forms of visual transformation (Figure 2). The thick 'top' edges of the frames in Figure 2 represent the standard orientation of the frame (i.e., which way is 'up').

1. *Translation* occurs frequently in desktop computing, when windows are moved to different screen locations.
2. *Scaling* also occurs frequently in desktop computing, when windows are resized by the user.
3. *Stretching (changing aspect ratio)*. Similar to scaling, stretching occurs when windows are resized in one dimension. This also occurs on mobile devices when an interface is reoriented to landscape or portrait mode.
4. *Rotation* is common in surface-based computing (e.g. digital tables or shared use of tablets), where displays or windows can be turned to face another person. It also occurs on mobile devices when an interface has not been programmed to adapt to device rotation (e.g., the Apple iPhone home screen, when viewed in landscape mode).
5. *Perspective distortion* occurs when viewing any kind of display from an oblique angle, as is common on shared wall or tabletop displays.

Relative spatial consistency after transformations
The previous section discussed transformations to the frame of reference itself. Relative spatial consistency, however, concerns the location of content *inside* the frame of reference after transformation.

When the frame of reference changes, UI designers can choose how the interface adapts to the new bounds. Translation, rotation and perspective transformations normally do not require any particular adaptation or response from the user interface – the window moves (with translation) or the user changes their viewing orientation (with rotation and perspective). However, an interface response is necessary when the user scales or stretches the frame of reference. 'Reflowing' the content is a common design strategy (e.g., the grid view in the Windows file explorer), as is item elision (e.g., the Office 2007 Ribbon moves items into hierarchies as the window gets smaller). As demonstrated by our Study 2, designers could also choose to maintain the original arrangement of items within the frame, and scale the entire grid when a stretch occurs.

The grid lines in each window in Figure 2 depict how 'canonical' relative spatial consistency can be maintained during the different transformations. Other approaches (e.g., 2D scaling in response to 1D stretching) can be achieved by combining these primitives. The final row of the figure shows transformation matrices for each effect.

EXPERIMENT ONE: INTERFACE TRANSFORMATIONS
It seems reasonable that the fast interaction enabled by spatial consistency will be robust to at least some of the transformations described above and shown in Figure 2. For example, users are unlikely to have difficulty locating items in a window after translating it. However, the time taken to adapt and respond to these transformations is less clear –

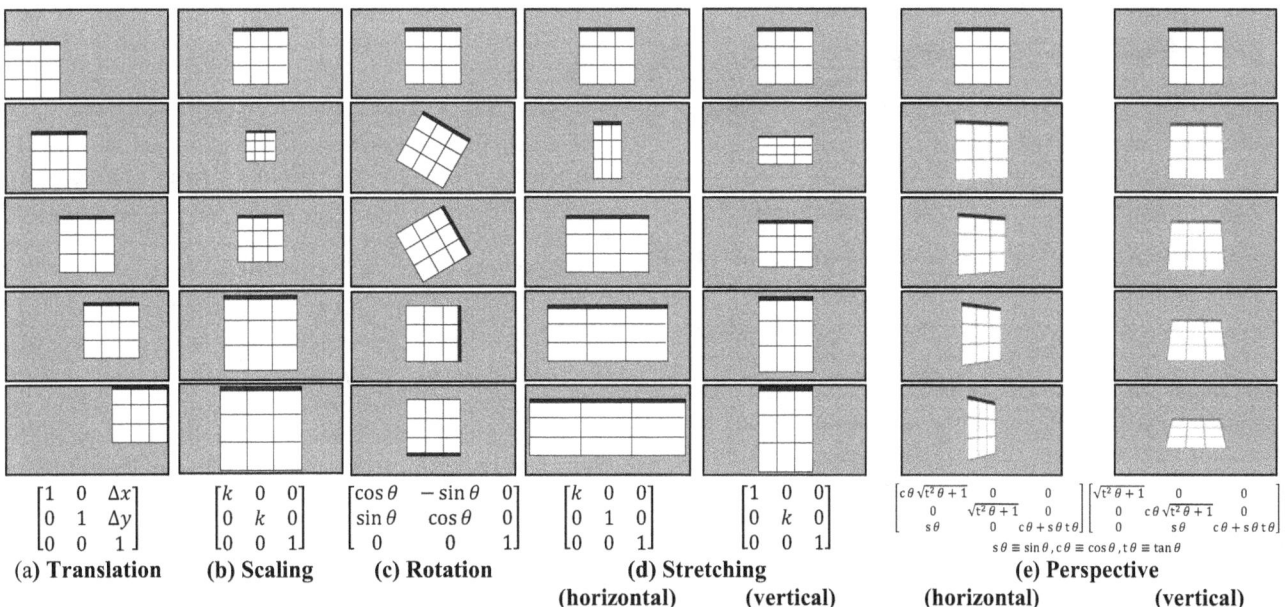

$$\begin{bmatrix} 1 & 0 & \Delta x \\ 0 & 1 & \Delta y \\ 0 & 0 & 1 \end{bmatrix} \quad \begin{bmatrix} k & 0 & 0 \\ 0 & k & 0 \\ 0 & 0 & 1 \end{bmatrix} \quad \begin{bmatrix} \cos\theta & -\sin\theta & 0 \\ \sin\theta & \cos\theta & 0 \\ 0 & 0 & 1 \end{bmatrix} \quad \begin{bmatrix} k & 0 & 0 \\ 0 & 1 & 0 \\ 0 & 0 & 1 \end{bmatrix} \quad \begin{bmatrix} 1 & 0 & 0 \\ 0 & k & 0 \\ 0 & 0 & 1 \end{bmatrix} \quad \begin{bmatrix} c\theta\sqrt{t^2\theta+1} & 0 & 0 \\ 0 & \sqrt{t^2\theta+1} & 0 \\ s\theta & 0 & c\theta+s\theta t\theta \end{bmatrix} \begin{bmatrix} \sqrt{t^2\theta+1} & 0 & 0 \\ 0 & c\theta\sqrt{t^2\theta+1} & 0 \\ 0 & s\theta & c\theta+s\theta t\theta \end{bmatrix}$$

$s\theta \equiv \sin\theta, c\theta \equiv \cos\theta, t\theta \equiv \tan\theta$

(a) **Translation**   (b) **Scaling**   (c) **Rotation**   (d) **Stretching**   (e) **Perspective**
                                                            (horizontal)   (vertical)   (horizontal)   (vertical)

Figure 2. The transformations used in Experiment One. The top row shows the untransformed window used for training.

while it is likely that users can reorient their spatial understanding, there may be time costs in doing so.

We therefore performed an exploratory study to determine the additional time needed to acquire items following different types and magnitudes of spatially consistent transformation. The method involved repeatedly selecting the same four items in a spatially consistent layout, while the grid underwent the transformations shown in Figure 2. The time taken to select a target after each transformation involves perceptual and cognitive processes of reorienting to the display and deciding about item location (which we call *reorientation time*), as well as the mechanical time to point to the target. Our interest lies in reorientation time, so to extract the variable effects of target relocation caused by the transformations, we analyzed each participant's Fitts' Law pointing characteristics, and used them to subtract pointing time from the total selection time for each item. (Note that study 2 considers overall performance including pointing time; our interest here is the reorientation phase.)

Tasks, stimuli, and instructions

Tasks involved a sequence of selections from a 10×10 grid of textual items (Figure 3a) that was either transformed or untransformed. All text items were common English three-letter words, which were used (rather than images or variable word sizes) to reduce confounds from visual pop-out. Also, to avoid effects of reading distorted text, text labels were not transformed with the interface (Figure 3b). An exception was made for rotation because pilot testing showed that participants use text orientation as a primary cue to establishing the frame of reference.

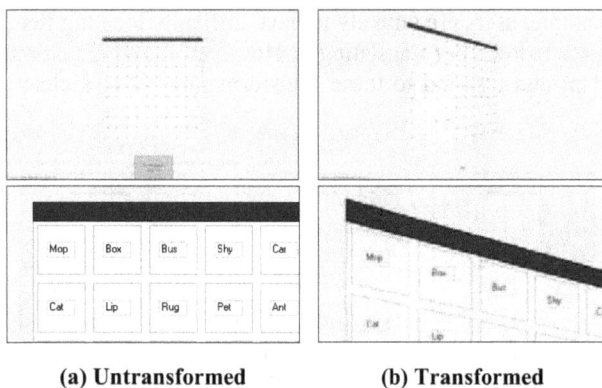

(a) Untransformed   (b) Transformed

Figure 3. Overview and close-up of the interface used in Study 1, before and after a horizontal perspective transformation.

Tasks began by showing an untransformed window (Figure 3a). Participants clicked a button to reveal the target item and display the transformed window (Figure 3b). Task timing began with the button click, and stopped when the target was selected; this was achieved by clicking in a visible hitbox surrounding the text label, which was a constant size in all conditions. After selection, the display returned to the untransformed window. Subjects were asked to make selections "as quickly and accurately as possible".

Transformations and magnitudes

The study tested seven transformations: translation, scaling, rotation, horizontal stretching, vertical stretching, horizontal perspective, and vertical perspective (columns in Figure 2). Each transformation was tested at five levels of magnitude (rows in Figure 2). A summary is shown in Table 1.

		Magnitude			
		1	2	3	4
Transformation	Translation (Δx, Δy), px	290,100	580, 200	870, 300	**1160,400**
	Scaling	×0.5	×0.75	×1.25	×1.5
	Rotation	30°	60°	90°	**180°**
	Stretching-x	×0.5	×1.5	×2	×2.5
	Stretching-y	×0.5	×0.75	×1.25	×1.5
	Perspective-x	15°	30°	45°	**60°**
	Perspective-y	15°	30°	45°	**60°**

Table 1. Experiment One transformations and magnitudes. Bold items denote the level deemed most extreme.

Procedure

Each participant initially performed a bi-directional Fitts' calibration task, consisting of 144 selections across 7 indices of difficulty. They then completed four blocks of trials with each of the seven transformations (Table 1). Order of transformation was counterbalanced using a Latin square. All four blocks were completed with one transformation before advancing to the next. The blocks comprised: *familiarization*, *training*, *recall*, and *learning*, always in that order. The *familiarization* block (data discarded) acquainted participants with the transformation, and consisted of ten trials (two for each magnitude), using different target items to the main experiment.

The *training* block consisted of 20 trials in the untransformed interface. The *training*, *recall*, and *learning* blocks used the same four target items throughout the experiment. To reduce potential confounds stemming from specific item locations, each participant had a unique set of target locations, with each item randomly selected from one of the four regions shown alongside. No adjacent locations were allowed.

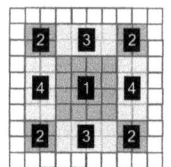

The *recall* block was used to examine selection times immediately after transformation. It consisted of 20 selections: one each for the four target items at each of the five magnitudes of transformation, in random order. The un-transformed interface was displayed between trials, and became transformed once the participant initiated the trial.

Finally, the *learning* block was included to examine participants' ability to re-learn item locations after the interface had been transformed. We used the most extreme form of each transformation (see Table 1), and participants selected each target five times (random order), without the untransformed window being presented between selections (i.e., the extreme view was continually shown).

In summary, each participant performed 1960 trials:
7 transformations × 4 blocks
    familiarization: 10 selections (data discarded)

training: 20 selections
recall: 20 selections } same 4 targets throughout expt.
learning: 20 selections

Participants and Apparatus

There were 14 participants; 7 male, 7 female, aged 19-42 (mean 26.9). The experiment was performed on a Windows 7 PC with a 1920×1200 monitor. Participants performed Experiments 1 then 2 in a single one-hour session.

Design

The study compares the time needed to reorient to a transformed display to the time for the non-transformed view. *Reorientation time* (T_r) is calculated by subtracting pointing time (T_p) from total selection time (T). Pointing time is calculated using each participant's individually calibrated Fitts' Law function, so $T_r = T - T_p$. For each transformation type, two pairwise measures are used to characterize the size of the effect of each transformation magnitude in comparison to the non-transformed condition: the statistical *effect size* using Cohen's *d*, which provides a sample-size independent estimate of effect size (Cohen [8] states that .2 is a small effect, .5 is medium, and .8 large); and the percentage increase in reorientation time. *Reorientation time* is analyzed using a 7×5 repeated measures ANOVA with within-subjects factors *transformation {translation, scaling, rotation, stretchingX, stretchingY, perspectiveX, perspectiveY}* and *magnitude level {0, 1, 2, 3, 4}*.

Results

Fitts' calibration

Linear regression showed strong Fitts' models for 13 participants (R^2 >=0.95), and one slightly weaker at R^2= 0.89. The mean pointing time predicted by the models varied little between the transformation types and their magnitudes: the overall mean was 948ms (s.d. 25), ranging from 926ms in the 180° rotation condition to 1063ms in the maximum translation condition.

Time to find items during training

The experiment focuses on the additional time required for users to reorient to *known* spatially consistent displays when they undergo various forms of visual transformation. One relevant data point that helps understand the scale of reorientation cost (to determine whether the time increases are large or small) is the time taken to find the items when the user has no spatial knowledge regarding item placement. We therefore analyzed the mean time to select items for the first time in the *training* block, which occurred after familiarization but before any spatial learning. The mean selection time was 15470ms, of which 14493ms can be attributed to visual search (once predicted pointing time is subtracted). By the fifth repetition during training, the mean decision time (selection time minus pointing time) had reduced to 811ms, which can be attributed to spatial memory supporting much faster selections.

Reorientation time after transformation in recall blocks

The primary results concerning reorientation times are presented here. Mean reorientation times across all levels for each transformation, as well as the mean calculated Fitts' Law pointing times, are shown in Figure 4a – the dashed horizontal line shows the mean reorientation time for the non-transformed condition. The lower segment of each bar shows reorientation time, and the upper segment shows calculated pointing time. The two numbers in each bar show Cohen's *d* effect size compared to the baseline and the percentage increase from the baseline. Figure 4a suggests that most of the transformations (other than rotation) had a relatively small impact on reorientation time – within 388ms of the baseline, which is only 2.7% of the visual search time reported above. As expected, ANOVA (error trials removed) showed significant main effects of *transformation* ($F_{6,78}$ = 19.1, p < .001) and *magnitude* ($F_{4,52}$ = 8.5, p < .001), and an interaction ($F_{24,312}$= 4.8, p < .001).

Our analysis shows that adapting to transformed displays caused a reliable increase in reorientation time, but that this increase is small compared to the visual search time needed when the item's location is unknown.

Figure 4a shows reorientation time averaged across all transformation magnitudes (except the no-transformation level). To gain further insight into the effects of each transformation magnitude, we separately compared each transformation magnitude with the no-transformation magnitude. The results are summarized in Figure 4b-h for each transformation, which include Cohen's *d* and percentage differences. Note that the baseline data is extracted from the no-transformation level within each transformation type. The key findings are as follows.

Translation caused small absolute increases in reorientation time (< 100ms), regardless of magnitude (Figure 4b). This finding is unsurprising given users' extensive experience in adapting to windows placed in different display regions. The reduced time at the (870, 300) translation level is attributed to participants having already moved their mouse closer to this translation (which was near the centre of the screen) causing a reduction in actual pointing time, and hence an under-estimation in calculated reorientation time.

Scaling (Figure 4c) had little effect on reorientation time at 0.75×, 1.25×, and 1.75× levels (increases of 190ms, 35ms, and -180ms). There was a larger effect at the extreme 0.5× level (387ms). This may have been influenced by our scaling method, which kept text size constant (to maintain legibility and pointing time) regardless of scale level. Text labels were thus very close to one another at small scales.

Stretching (Figure 4e,f), like scaling, showed relatively small absolute time increases for most levels (<250ms for all but 0.5× and 2× x-stretching, which exceeded 550ms). The higher time for 0.5× x-stretching can be explained in the same way as scaling above; the 2× result is reasonable

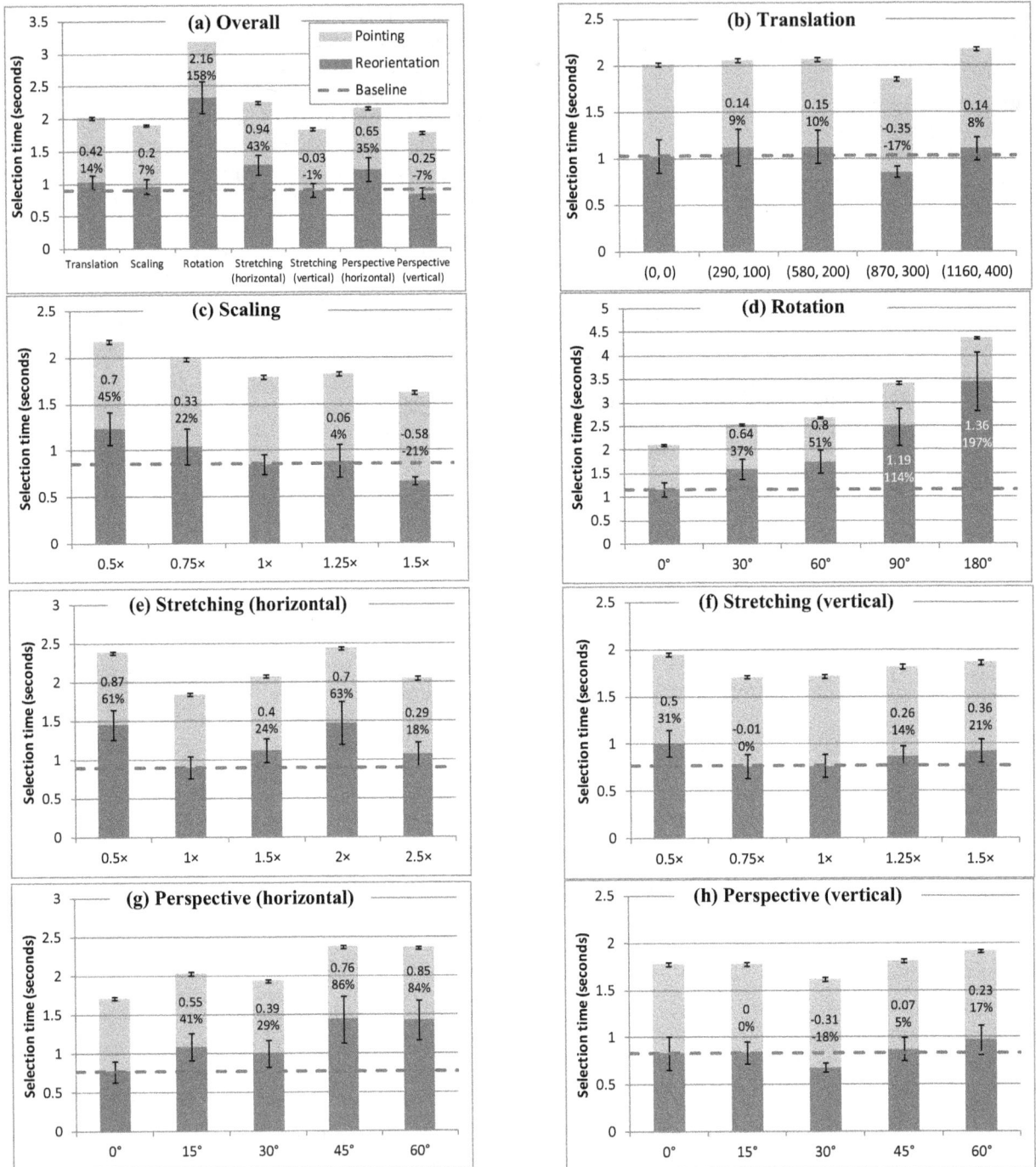

Figure 4. Reorientation time and Fitts' Law pointing times for each transformation type. The baseline value (red dashed line) is the mean reorientation time of participants in the un-transformed condition.

(and the lower time of the higher 2.5× level may be due to the proximity of the screen edge assisting reorientation).

Rotation had much larger effects on reorientation time (Figure 4d), with absolute mean time increases from 434ms (30°) to 2284ms (180°). Some of this time will be incurred by reading rotated text, but we suspect that most of it can be attributed to mental processes of reorienting to the rotated frame of reference. This is supported by prior work from Cooper [9], which showed that the time taken to interpret

rotated pattern stimuli increases linearly with rotation angle. Linear regression of our reorientation time data with degree of rotation supports Cooper's finding ($R^2 = 0.98$).

Horizontal *perspective* changes (Figure 4g), like rotation, resulted in an approximately linear increase in reorientation time across angle ($R^2 = 0.84$). However, the absolute value of the increase (compared to the baseline) was much smaller than rotation (ranging from 226 to 665ms). Vertical perspective changes (Figure 4h) had a much smaller effect on reorientation time, ranging from 2ms at 15° to 139ms at 60° (and a negative effect of 152ms at 30°). One possible explanation is that this type of perspective is common in everyday life (e.g., reading on a flat table); regardless, subjects were quickly able to reorient to the transformation.

Learning
During the learning block, participants selected the target items five times each in a random order from a maximally transformed window. Reorientation time data (selection time minus pointing time) is analyzed using a 7×5 ANOVA for factors *transformation* and selection *repetition*. There was a significant effect of *transformation* ($F_{6,78} = 5.1, p < .001$), largely due to the slow performance of rotation (1593ms) with all other transformations within 921±164ms. There was also a significant effect of *repetition* ($F_{4,52} = 5.9, p < .005$), with mean reorientation times quickly improving from 1318ms in the first selection to a minimum of 879ms in the third (within 24ms of the time with untransformed windows in the training block). Participants' performance with stable transformed windows quickly matched that of untransformed views. There was no interaction between *transformation* and *repetition* ($F_{24,312} = 1.1, p = .35$), giving no evidence that any transformation type is harder to learn.

Discussion
To summarize, we analyzed how quickly users can reorient their expectation for the location of known targets when spatially consistent displays undergo likely transformations (translation, rotation, scaling, stretching, and perspective). Results showed that users can quickly adapt to all forms of transformation (much more quickly than the time needed to find unknown items in the display). Adapting to rotations was much slower than the other transformations (at 180°, 20x that of translation). We also replicated results showing that rotation reaction times are a linear function of angle.

These results provide a new human-factors characterization of performance with common display transformations; in addition, the study provides design insights that we deploy in the next study. In particular, the fast reorientation times in response to scaling and stretching suggest that users will be much faster when a spatially consistent approach is used to deal with transformation, than with approaches that rearrange items to fill the transformed window.

EXPERIMENT TWO: SCALING VS. REFLOW
Experiment 1 demonstrated that people are able to quickly select familiar items after a spatially consistent display is

transformed. Our second experiment tests the application of this finding in a realistic interface.

Many commercial interfaces, such as toolbars and file browsers, use a 'reflow' algorithm to rearrange items when the window dimensions change (Figure 5c). However, when items are rearranged in this manner, people lose their spatial knowledge of the interface, potentially slowing retrieval. We therefore compared a reflow-based layout strategy to two different spatially consistent designs.

Interface Layout Designs
We considered three designs for adapting the layout of a simple icon view (e.g., a file browser) to window size.

Scaling. This layout scales a grid of icons to fit the window bounds. Note that when the window's aspect ratio is changed, spatial consistency is maintained relative to the perceived bounds of the item grid, rather than the window edges (Figure 5a).

Scrolling. This layout maintains spatial consistency to the original frame of reference, using scrolling to allow viewport translation over the icon grid (Figure 5b). The location of items is predictable as an absolute displacement from the information space's origin, but the interface does not maintain relative spatial consistency with respect to the new frame of reference. Scrolling requires more interface manipulations to select targets than the other conditions.

Reflow. This is the standard layout strategy employed in contemporary file browsers: when the window changes size, icons are rearranged to fill the window, in reading order (Figure 5c). Reflowing makes efficient use of display space, but requires scrolling when icons do not fit the view.

Procedure
The experimental task consisted of a sequence of selections from a file-browser-like interface, populated with items from the Windows 7 control panel (Figure 6). Participants clicked a button to begin each trial, triggering the display of a stimulus in a sidebar. Selecting the target item completed the task and redisplayed the "Click to begin" button.

Two blocks (*training* and *recall*) were completed with each of the three layouts (*scaling, scrolling,* and *reflow*). The *training* block consisted of six repetitions of each of six target items, using a *square* window size with a content area of 700×700 pixels. In the *recall* block, the window bounds were varied on every trial to be either *square*, *wide*

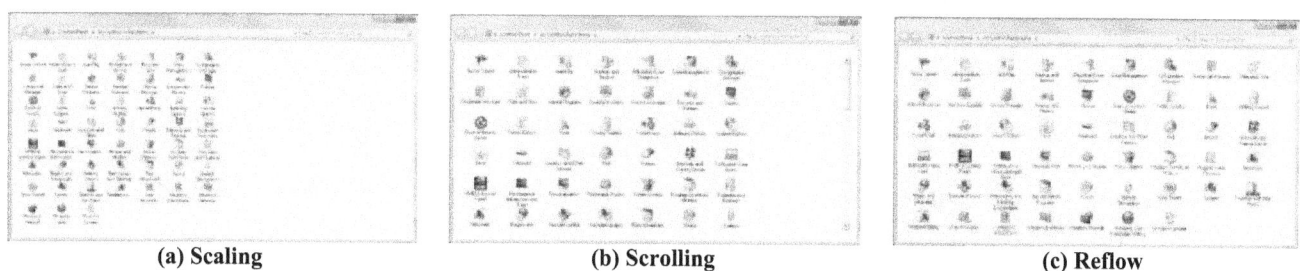

| (a) Scaling | (b) Scrolling | (c) Reflow |

Figure 5. The three alternative icon layout strategies in a wide window configuration.

(917×401), or *tall* (401×917). The *tall* configuration extended to the vertical height of the monitor, and was just wide enough for all of the items to fit into the *reflow* window without scrolling. The *wide* configuration was the transposition of *tall*. When window configuration changed, items were arranged according to the layout strategy (*scaling*, *scrolling* or *reflow*). With *square*, the three layout strategies were equivalent. Figure 5 shows the effect of each layout strategy on a *wide* configuration. For *scaling*, *wide* scaled the icon grid by 0.7×, and *tall* by 0.57×.

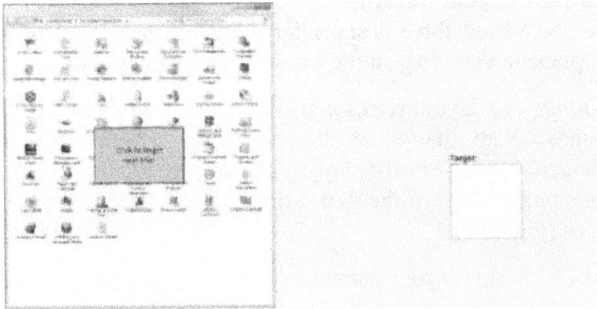

Figure 6. The system used in Experiment Two. Targets were displayed on the right, and participants selected the target items from the interface on the left.

Target items and window configuration sequences were different for each participant in each condition, and targets were selected such that no two target items were in the same row or column. The row and column constraint was used (without subject knowledge) to give an approximately uniform spatial distribution of items in the *scrolling* condition (to control the number of items that required scrolling). Each participant therefore performed 162 trials:

3 layout strategies × 2 blocks
    training: 36 selections (data discarded)
    recall: 18 selections

Participants completed NASA-TLX [16] worksheets and responded to visual appeal questions after each layout. They ranked the layouts for preference, speed and error rate at the end of the experiment.

Participants and Apparatus
15 participants were recruited for the study, with 14 completing it directly after Experiment One. Experiments One and Two used the same hardware and setup.

Design and Hypotheses
The experiment was designed as a 3×3 RM-ANOVA for factors *layout {scaling, scrolling, reflow}* and *configuration {square, wide, tall}*, with selection time as the dependent variable. *Layout* was counterbalanced using a Latin square.

Our primary hypotheses were as follows:

H1: *Scaling* will be faster than *scrolling* and *reflow*. *Scaling* keeps items spatially consistent, unlike *reflow*, and requires no extra user action, unlike *scrolling*.

H2: *Scaling* will be subjectively preferred by participants.

Results
Error rates were low in all conditions: 1.5% for *scaling*, 2.6% for *scrolling*, and 1.9% for *reflow*. Trials including incorrect selections were excluded from the analysis; this did not affect the significance of our results. For significant ANOVA effects, we include partial eta-squared (η^2) as a measure of effect size (where .01 is a small effect size, .06 medium, and .14 large [7]).

Selection Times
Mean selection times were fastest with *scaling* (2.27s, s.d. 0.76), followed by *scrolling* (2.96s, s.d. 1.26) and *reflow* (3.158s, s.d. 1.69), giving a significant main effect of *layout*: $F_{2,28} = 7.3$, $p = .003$, $\eta^2 = .34$. With the *scaling* layout, mean selection times following *wide* and *tall* view transformations increased by 262ms and by 277ms over the time taken with the *square* view used for training. These small increases contrast with the substantial increases of 1039ms and 1653ms with the reflow layout. Posthoc Bonferroni-adjusted pairwise comparisons ($\alpha = 0.05$) showed that *scaling* was significantly faster than both *scrolling* and *reflow*, but there was no difference between *scrolling* and *reflow*. We therefore accept **H1**.

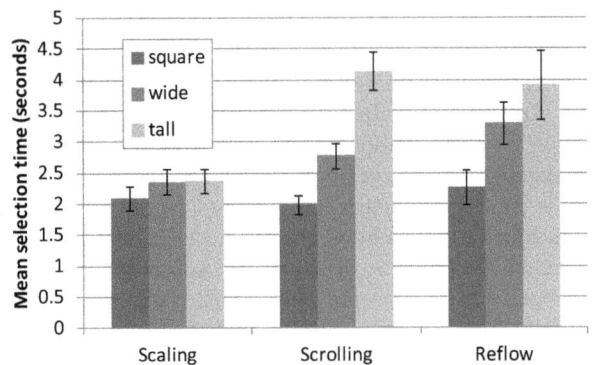

Figure 7. Mean selection times in Experiment 2.

As expected, there was a significant effect of *configuration* ($F_{2,28} = 24.8$, $p < .001$, $\eta^2 = .64$) with *square* (2.11s, s.d. 0.83) faster than *wide* (2.81s, s.d. 1.05) and *tall* (3.47s, s.d. 1.65). More importantly, there was a *layout × configuration* interaction ($F_{4,56} = 5.98$, $p < .001$, $\eta^2 = .30$), as shown in Figure 7: *scaling* performed similarly to *scrolling* and *reflow* in the *square* configuration, but was faster in the *wide* and *tall* configurations.

26% of *scrolling* trials in the *wide* configuration required the user to scroll the viewport, with 18% for *tall* and 0% for *square*. Figure 7 shows that scrolling was slowest in the *tall* condition, which required horizontal scrolling.

Subjective Responses
TLX questionnaire responses showed no significant differences, perhaps due to low statistical power; further study in this area is needed. We therefore fail to find support for **H2**.

GENERAL DISCUSSION

Experiment 1 showed that users can quickly adapt to many forms of view transformation, allowing rapid selections when items remain spatially stable within the frame of reference. Experiment 2 used this finding to compare user performance between the contemporary 'reflow' strategy (which reduces spatial stability) and a scaling layout that maintains spatial stability. Results confirmed that selection times following view transformations were much faster with the scaling layout than with the reflowing layout.

The following subsections discuss the implications of these findings, as well as the limits of their applicability.

Generalizing the results of Experiment Two

Experiment 1 examined human performance factors in response to view transformations, requiring an experimental method that was substantially abstracted away from day to day interaction contexts. Experiment 2, in contrast, focused on a specific interaction context (contemporary icon layouts in file browsers), but in doing so necessarily introduced potential confounds, including icon visual saliency, dataset ordering and size, and specific transformation settings.

Experiment 2 used the actual icons from the MS Windows control panel. We did this to assist external validity, while aware of the differing visual salience across icons – for example, the colorful 'Default Programs' icon is more likely to pop out than the small, grey 'keyboard' icon. The experimental design mitigated these effects by randomizing the target set for each participant and layout.

The method also used an alphabetical ordering of icons in each view, again to maintain consistency with the current Microsoft layout. This arrangement is very likely to have assisted users in identifying target locations after reflowing. However, logical or predictable icon arrangements are challenging to determine in many contexts, and it is likely that the benefits of scaling would be more pronounced if predictable ordering was unavailable.

The size of the dataset was also determined by the typical size of the control panel window. The sizes of the tall and wide windows were selected to maximally utilize space in the reflowing condition without scrolling – i.e., the sizes were biased to aid reflowing. If the windows had been any smaller, the reflowing condition would have required scrolling. There are, however, interesting questions for the scaling condition around the relationship between performance and scale factor. Experiment 1 suggested that performance deteriorates as views are transformed further from 1× views, and there are likely trade-offs between the costs of reducing scale and the costs of increased scrolling. We intend to conduct further work in this area.

Finally, subjective responses in Experiment 2 showed no significant differences between conditions. Participants were neither strongly in favor nor strongly opposed to the scaling view, but we do not know how their opinions would change if, for example, more extreme scale factors were

used, or if the reflowing condition had required scrolling. Again, further work is needed, but it currently appears that scaling allows much faster performance following transformations than does reflowing, and that this benefit comes without the costs of negative subjective reaction.

Applications of spatial consistency

The primary design implication of our results is that spatial consistency should be a *fundamental* consideration in the design of interfaces and information displays. In many cases, designing to maintain spatial consistency is a relatively simple matter – for example, on mobile devices that allow landscape and portrait view modes (switched by accelerometer input) interface design should favor relative spatial consistency of items, rather than seeking ways to rearrange interface components to exploit the variable display space in the different layouts.

Designing for spatial consistency also allows new styles of interaction, such as that demonstrated by the Data Mountain [10] or CommandMaps [25]. Another interesting possibility lies in creating new interface toolkits and APIs that are more robust to variable display requirements. Built-in scaling functions to accommodate different window sizes and/or display resolutions would greatly facilitate the implementation of interfaces that are spatially robust, rather than resorting to the current methods of reflowing, rearranging, and elision.

Finally, there are several potential questions that designers may have about a fundamentally spatial approach to interface design. We address some of these issues here, but as the discussion above suggests, spatial consistency is not an all-or-nothing principle: the idea can easily be used to improve existing interfaces in small ways, as well as to create new ways of accessing information.

What happens with changing window content? Experiment Two studied an icon set that changes slowly if at all (i.e., control panel icons). In windows where content changes more quickly (e.g., additions or deletions of icons), how well does the spatial approach work? There are four reasons why a spatially consistent presentation can work well, even with changing content. First, in many windows, items change slowly, and a person's spatial memory can often keep up with the changes [28]. Second, users could be in charge of placing new items in a display (as with a phone's home screen, or in systems like the Data Mountain [24]); in these cases, the act of placing the items can help to overcome the difficulties caused by changing content. Third, ordering by addition (i.e., new icons are added at the bottom of the display) would lead to stable arrangements that allow the development of spatial memory. Fourth, a spatial organization could be used as one of several views presented by an interface: in situations where content changes slowly, the user would gain the benefits of developing spatial memory; in situations where items change frequently, the user could switch to an alphabetic arrangement (or a list view).

What happens with large data sets and small window sizes? When there are many items in an interface, scaling the entire icon set to fit the window bounds may be impractical. Furthermore, pointing can be difficult at very small scales. In these scenarios we recommend a hybrid scaling/scrolling strategy, where the grid is scaled according to the width of the window and a vertical scrollbar allows users to access off-screen items. When the window width becomes too small to feasibly scale items, scaling ends and a horizontal scrollbar can be added. We note that as sets grow, the problems of the 'reflow' strategy also increase (i.e., items near the end of the list will be even further displaced from their original locations). Further work in this area is needed.

What happens to search and list views? Grid layouts are not the only choice for users – they can switch to other views when appropriate (e.g., in a file browser, a list view allows users to sort by date), and can also find items through a search interface. These alternate presentations, however, do not imply that a spatially consistent view is not practical – it would be simple to include a spatially consistent view as one of several presentations. In addition, it is also possible to use visualization techniques to add the functionality of these other views to a spatially consistent presentation. For example, highlighting could be used to show search results (as seen in the Mac OS X control panel), or to show recently-used files. Augmented views such as these could provide the benefits of spatial consistency and still give users the power of specific retrieval tools.

CONCLUSION

Spatial consistency is a powerful organizing principle for interfaces, but everyday use involves many forms of view transformation. We conducted a study to improve understanding of how performance with spatially consistent views is influenced by different forms and magnitudes of display transformation. Results showed that users can quickly reorient their spatial understanding to all of the tested transformations, but that adaptation to rotation is much slower than the others. We then tested these findings in a real-world usage scenario, hypothesizing that performance with a file browser could be improved by replacing the reflow layout approach with a layout that scaled the view. Results showed substantially improved performance. The primary design implication of this work is that spatial consistency should be used as a fundamental design principle for interfaces and information displays.

REFERENCES

1. Andrade, J. and Meudell, P. Short report: Is spatial information encoded automatically? *Quarterly J of Exp. Psych. 46A* (1993), 365-375.
2. Baddeley, A.D. *Human Memory*. Lawrence Erlbaum Associates, Hove, 1990.
3. Bryant, D.J. and Tversky, B. Mental representations of perspective and spatial relations from diagrams and models. *J. Exp. Psych.: Learning, Memory, Cognition 25*, 1 (1999), 137.
4. Bülthoff, I. and Newell, F.N. The role of familiarity in the recognition of static and dynamic objects. *Progress in Brain Research*, Elsevier, 2006, 315-325.
5. Bundesen, C., Larsen, A. Visual transformation of size. *J. Exp. Psych.: Perception and Performance 1*, 3 (1975), 214-220.
6. Cockburn, A., Kristensson, P., Alexander, J. and Zhai, S. Hard Lessons: Effort-Inducing Interfaces Benefit Spatial Learning. in *Proc. CHI'07*, (2007), 1571-1580.
7. Cohen, J. Eta-squared and partial eta-squared in communication science. *Hum. Comm. Research 28*, 473-490 (1973), 56.
8. Cohen, J. *Statistical power analysis for the behavioral sciences*. Lawrence Erlbaum, 1988.
9. Cooper, L.A. Mental rotation of random two-dimensional shapes. *Cognitive psychology 7*, 1 (1975), 20-43.
10. Czerwinski, M., van Dantzich, M., Robertson, G. and Hoffman, H. The Contribution of Thumbnail Image, Mouse-Over Text and Spatial Location Memory to Web Page Retrieval in 3D. in *Proc. INTERACT'99*, (1999), 163-170.
11. Darken, R. and Sibert, J. Wayfinding strategies and behaviors in large virtual worlds *Proc. CHI'96*, 1996, 142-149.
12. Dix, A., Finlay, J., Abowd, G. and Beale, R. Human-Computer Interaction (1993).
13. Ehret, B. Learning Where to Look: Location Learning in Graphical User Interfaces. in *Proc. CHI'02*, (2002), 211-218.
14. Gutwin, C. and Cockburn, A. Improving List Revistation with ListMaps. in *Proc. AVI'06*, ACM, (2006), 396-403.
15. Hansen, W.J. User engineering principles for interactive systems *Proc. AFIPS'71 (Fall)*, 1971, 523-532.
16. Hart, S. and Staveland, L. Development of NASA-TLX (Task Load Index): Results of Empirical and Theoretical Research. in *Human Mental Workload*, 1988, 139-183.
17. Hick, W.E. On the rate of gain of information. *Quarterly J. of Exp. Psych. 4* (1952), 11-26.
18. Hyman, R. Stimulus information as a determinant of reaction time. *J. Exp. Psych. 45* (1953), 188-196.
19. Jiang, Y., Song, J.H. and Rigas, A. High-capacity spatial contextual memory. *Psychonomic Bulletin & Review 12*, 3 (2005), 524-529.
20. Milner, P.M. A model for visual shape recognition. *Psychological Review 81*, 6 (1974), 521-535.
21. Newell, A. and Rosenbloom, P.S. Mechanisms of Skill Acquisition and the Law of Practice. in *Cognitive Skills and their Acquisition*, Erlbaum, 1981, 1-55.
22. Nielsen, J. *Usability Engineering*. Morgan Kaufmann, San Francisco, 1993.
23. Postma, A. and De Haan, E. What Was Where? Memory for Object Locations. *Q. J. Exp. Psych. 49A*, 1 (1996), 178-199.
24. Robertson, G., Czerwinski, M., Larson, K., Robbins, D., Thiel, D. van Dantzich, M. Data Mountain: Using Spatial Memory for Document Management. *Proc. UIST'98*, (1998), 153-162.
25. Scarr, J., Cockburn, A., Gutwin, C. and Bunt, A. Improving command selection with CommandMaps. *Proc. CHI'12*, ACM, Austin, Texas, 2012, 257-266.
26. Shneiderman, B. *Designing the User Interface*, 1992.
27. Steven, G.V. and Allan, R. Mental rotations, a group test of three-dimensional spatial visualization. *Perceptual and motor skills 47*, 2 (1978), 599-604.
28. Tak, S., Cockburn, A., Humm, K., Ahlstroem, D., Gutwin, C. and Scarr, J. Improving Window Switching Interfaces. *Proc. INTERACT'09*, (2009), 187-200.
29. Tak, S., Scarr, J., Gutwin, C. and Cockburn, A. Supporting window switching with spatially consistent thumbnail zones: design and evaluation. *Proc. INTERACT'11*, (2011), 331-347.
30. Wertheimer, M. Laws of organization in perceptual forms. *A source book of Gestalt psychology* (1999), 71-88.

Canyon: Providing Location Awareness of Multiple Moving Objects in a Detail View on Large Displays

Alexandra Ion[1], Y.-L. Betty Chang[3], Michael Haller[1], Mark Hancock[2,3], Stacey D. Scott[3]

[1]Media Interaction Lab,
University of Applied Sciences
Upper Austria, Hagenberg, Austria
{alexandra.ion|haller}@fh-hagenberg.at

[2]Management Sciences, [3]Systems Design Engineering, University of Waterloo,
Waterloo, Ontario, Canada
{betty.chang|mark.hancock|stacey.scott}@uwaterloo.ca

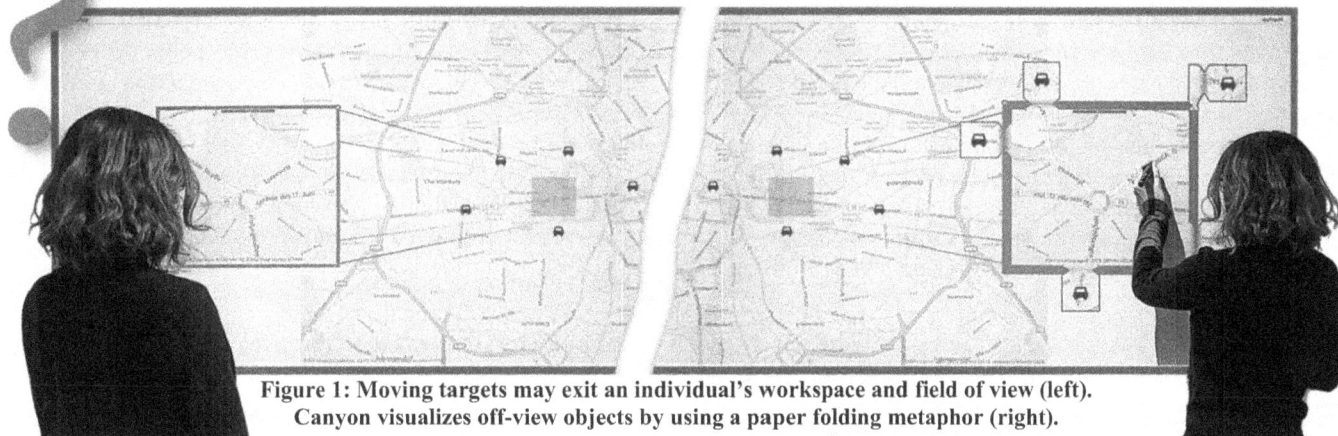

Figure 1: Moving targets may exit an individual's workspace and field of view (left).
Canyon visualizes off-view objects by using a paper folding metaphor (right).

ABSTRACT

Overview+Detail interfaces can be used to examine the details of complex data while retaining the data's overall context. Dynamic data introduce challenges for these interfaces, however, as moving objects may exit the detail view, as well as a person's field of view if they are working at a large interactive surface. To address this "off-view" problem, we propose a new information visualization technique, called Canyon. This technique attaches a small view of an off-view object, including some surrounding context, to the external boundary of the detail view. The area between the detail view and the region containing the off-view object is virtually "folded" to conserve space. A comparison study was conducted contrasting the benefits and limitations of Canyon to an established technique, called Wedge. Canyon was more accurate across a number of tasks, especially more complex tasks, and was comparably efficient.

Author Keywords

Information Visualization; Overview+Detail; Dynamic Data; Large Display; Map Data

ACM Classification Keywords

H.5.2 [Information Interfaces and Presentation]: User Interfaces—Graphical user interfaces, User-centered design

INTRODUCTION

Large, interactive displays are increasingly being used to support collaborative data analysis and decision-making involving large, complex datasets [24,26]. Yet, their large, shareable surface introduces navigation issues for collaborators, as people may wish to examine different aspects of the dataset. Offering multiple, independent views of the data can address this issue; however, data relationships can become unclear as the views diverge or are being explored at different zoom levels. Instead, Overview+Detail interfaces [8] can be used to provide an overview of the entire dataset along with multiple detail views. The bounds of the detail views are shown on the overview to provide context. When the dataset contains dynamic data this approach is insufficient for providing a consistent view of the data of interest within the detail views. Consider the following scenario in a police command centre, based on an early version of our prototype system developed for police officers.

A group of police officers stand at an interactive wall monitoring a large city map. The map is augmented with GPS-tracked police vehicles. An officer wishes to check on a particular incident. She selects the incident location on the map (overview) to open a view showing a zoomed portion of the incident area (detail view). She sees that three police vehicles have arrived at the scene. While she monitors the incident, one vehicle moves away from the scene, and its associated icon disappears as its location moves outside the bounds of the detail view. She receives a report that the vehicle is in pursuit of a fleeing suspect. Now, she needs to maintain awareness of this vehicle and the incident scene.

While the vehicle was no longer visible in the detail view, it may still be visible on the large overview map. It might be outside her focal view due to the size of the display. We define this problem as the "off-view" problem, where we wish to maintain awareness of objects within the detail view and of dynamically moving objects that begin in the view and leave the view over time.

We distinguish this problem from the previously identified "off-screen" problem, where objects of interest are located outside a given window view [4,8,13]. In our situation, objects located beyond the bounds of the detail view hold some relationship to objects in the overview (and may even be visible there). Moreover, the large display context provides additional screen real-estate around the detail view(s), unlike "off-screen" situations which are often limited to indicating the location of a non-visible object within the constraints of a small interface window (e.g., on a handheld device [4,13]). Thus, large displays provide a different design context with opportunities for different design solutions to provide location awareness of an off-view object.

To address this design space, we propose a new information visualization technique, called Canyon (Figure 1), developed for map-based datasets. In Canyon, orthogonal strips of map data that include the off-view object are attached to the detail view. To conserve screen space, the area between the detail view and the region containing the off-view object is "folded". This folding metaphor was inspired by the "Mélange" multi-focus interaction technique [9]. Canyon is designed to provide a high level of location detail by showing the off-view object as well as its surrounding map area.

To explore the potential of this design in facilitating location awareness of off-view objects, we conducted a controlled laboratory experiment comparing Canyon to an existing off-screen visualization technique, Wedge [13]. To set the context for this study we first present the related work. Next, we present the design of Canyon, the study method, and results. Finally, we discuss the overall study and provide design recommendations for future off-view object interfaces.

RELATED WORK

As previously mentioned, we distinguish the off-view problem from the off-screen problem. Objects become off-screen any time the screen is too small to represent the area of interest, often caused by the need of higher level of detail. However, off-screen objects are also off-view, and we can leverage existing off-screen visualizations to understand and approach the off-view problem. This section presents existing techniques on large visual spaces and visualizing off-screen objects.

Navigation-based Techniques

Large visual spaces can be explored using pan, zoom or scroll. "Speed-dependent automatic zooming" [15] reduces the zoom level depending on scrolling speed. Zooming in-

terfaces like Pad [19] separate views temporally, and require users to mentally connect the views [8]. Plumlee and Ware [21] report that only one graphical object can be held in memory, and recommend the use of multiple views to enable visual comparisons of complex data.

View-based Techniques

Overview+Detail interfaces provide overview and detail views simultaneously, but spatially separated, and leave the user to build the connection.

These interfaces are used in many common computer applications, like Microsoft PowerPoint's slide thumbnails. Digital map systems like Google Maps show a large detail view and give an overview as an inset. In contrast, the DragMag image magnifier [25] grants the most screen space to the overview area and provides multiple smaller detail views. PolyZoom [17] additionally supports construction of focus hierarchies. Plaisant et al. [20] found intermediate windows useful for detail-to-overview ratios exceeding 20:1.

Focus+Context interfaces combine focus and context areas in one view, aiming to decrease short term memory load. These areas are typically connected using distortion.

The first Focus+Context interface was 'Bifocal Display' [23], which used the metaphor of bending sides of a paper strip backward to create a focus area while preserving context. 'Fisheye views' [11] delegate a large portion of the view to the area of greatest interest and less space to other areas depending on their distance from this area. Baudisch et al. [3] embedded a small high resolution display (focus) into a large, low resolution display (context). A unifying framework, incorporating this wide range of approaches was presented by Carpendale and Montagnese [7].

Multi-scale interfaces, also known as semantic zooming [19], present content differently depending on scale.

Multi-focus interfaces provide multiple foci at the same time.

Many Overview+Detail and Focus+Context interfaces allow multiple foci [22,25]. Techniques supporting both, multi-scale and multi-focus interaction, include PolyZoom [17] and Mélange [9]. Mélange supports multiple foci and folds space in between points of interest, and allows viewing points of interest at different levels of detail. Mélange inspired the off-view technique presented in this work.

Cue-based Techniques

Pointing techniques provide information about off-screen objects by pointing in their direction. Typically, graphical elements are overlaid onto the screen border region.

Off-screen object's direction is conveyed by pointing and distance is conveyed by altering the visual cues' properties, e.g. size. Combining this information gives the location of the object. Visualizations include arrows [5] and rays [1]. Halo [4] draws a circle around the off-screen object's location that intrudes into the screen. However, it suffers from overlap and corner issues. A comparison of arrows and Halo [5] shows arrows to be more accurate for distance tasks, and Halo performing better for location tasks. Instead of using circles, Wedge [13] uses partly visible isosceles triangles to point towards the off-screen object. Wedge was found to be more accurate than Halo. In a comparison of arrows, Overview+Detail, and Wedge [6], Wedge outperformed the other techniques for distance tasks. Wedge was included as the comparison technique in our study, due to its effectiveness.

Contextual views are derived from fisheye views and use abstract visual representations along the view border to point to the location of off-screen objects.

City Lights [27] and EdgeRadar [14] provide contextual information by displaying proxies of off-screen objects into a compressed border region within the view. Contextual views are also used for large node-link diagrams [10].

Interactive off-screen techniques allow interacting with proxies and auto-focus of the associated object [10,16,18]. Our work focuses on the visualization, rather than manipulation, of off-view objects. Current off-screen visualizations mainly target small displays and use abstract cues. To our knowledge, no research has investigated visualization of off-view objects on large displays featuring individual views. To address this usage context, we developed Canyon, a multi-focus approach to visualize off-view objects on large displays. The design and implementation of Canyon is described next.

DESIGN OF CANYON

Canyon was designed to provide location awareness of targets, outside of the focal area of a person, on large displays with direct input (see Figure 2 (d)). Targets can be static or dynamic, and they are visualized around the detail view.

Design Goals
For enhancing location awareness about off-view targets on large displays, we defined the following design goals:

G1. *No change of the defined view.* The view defined should not be altered (by another person or the system).
G2. *Keep off-view object in context.* A person should always be aware of how an off-view object is related to his or her current view.
G3. *Provide distance awareness.* The distance to the workspace should be indicated.
G4. *Support fast comparison.* Fast comparison of off-view objects relative to each other should be enabled.

Folding Paper
The idea of Canyon is to bring off-view objects close to the current workspace by using a paper folding metaphor. Canyon was inspired by Mélange [9], a technique for fitting multiple focus points into the viewport by folding unused space in between. In contrast, Canyon extends the view by adding cut-out views onto the user's view.

The design details can be explained using a map exploration context (see Figure 2). Consider having a workspace showing a user defined map area and multiple objects, which are outside of the user's focal range. Canyon extends the view by cutting out a strip of a paper map containing the off-view object and attaches it to the edge of the detail view. Since this strip of map can be long and the space in between is uninteresting, it is sharply folded like paper in order to bring the objects of interest close to the detail view. A paper folding metaphor is easy to understand since humans are familiar with paper manipulation. Since the cut-out view and the fold are attached to the outside of the map view, the defined view never changes, fulfilling G1. Moreover, by connecting the detail view and the cut-out view with the fold, context is provided, fulfilling G2.

The width of the folded map connecting the detail view with the cut-out view is dependent on the *distance* of the detail view edge to the off-view target. It is calculated by

$$foldSize = \text{round}(\ln distance^5).$$

A logarithmic function is used to avoid overly large folds caused by very distant objects. Since the *foldSize* varies, G4 and partly G3 are fulfilled.

Adding Shadow
One design goal of Mélange was providing distance awareness. Elmqvist et al. [9] used an abstract environment in their study with a checkerboard-like background and additional black lines indicating screen units as an additional distance cue. Like the authors of Mélange, we think that distortion alone does not provide proper distance awareness. While a difference in distance conveyed by distortion between a near and a far object is noticeable, the difference between two far objects is not. As the depth of the fold can no longer be estimated, distance awareness shrinks and the paper folding metaphor suffers.

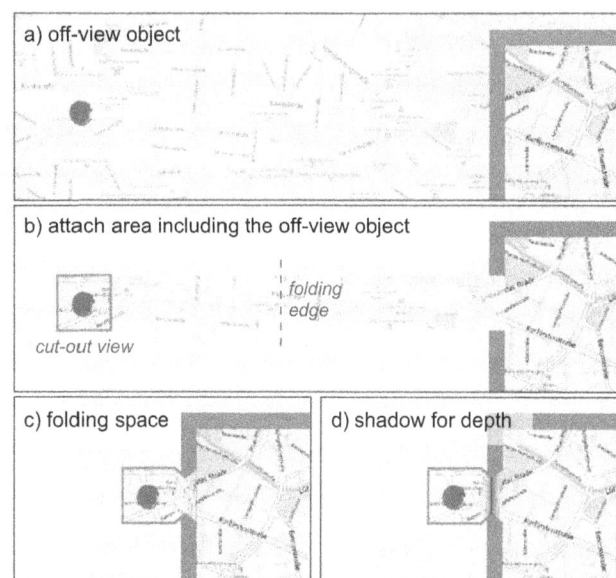

Figure 2: Canyon attaches a strip of map material containing the object to the view and folds uninteresting space away.

To overcome these issues, a shadow is added onto the fold. It intensifies the depth illusion and serves as an additional cue for distance awareness, which fulfills G3. The maximum darkness of the shadow is calculated depending on the ratio of visible map in the fold,

$$darkness = \left(1 - \frac{foldSize}{distance}\right)^5.$$

It is applied as a linear gradient from the maximum darkness in the middle to transparent on the sides. The shadow and the distortion are applied in a pixel shader in one step using linear transformation. Mélange enhanced distance awareness by using fold pages, each representing the size of the screen. Although this linear translation of distance is well-understandable, we used non-linear distance representation for representing objects regardless of their distance.

Merging and Chaining

When the distance between off-view objects on the *x* or *y*-axis is smaller than the cut-out view size defined with 80 pixels in this implementation, the cut-out views are merged. The cut-out view is enlarged to accommodate these targets. When one cut-out view is in between another and the detail view, the farther away one is chained. The bounds of a closer cut-out view are extended to incorporate all following intersecting cut-out views that are farther away. Folded maps between cut-out views only depend on the distance between these views. Both the folded map width and the shadow are calculated based on this distance (see Figure 3).

Corners

Representing off-view objects in corner regions requires special attention in many off-screen visualization techniques. As off-screen objects are mostly visualized orthogonal to the view edges of a rectangular screen, corners present a bigger area to cover but less space for visualization. Canyon visualizes corner off-view objects by extending the vertical view edges and folds the cut-out views orthogonally to these extended edges. Thus, two folds are needed to show a corner object (see Figure 3), and may increase the cognitive load to understand it. Nevertheless, the paper folding metaphor is preserved which should assist understanding. Cut-out views are always kept in distinct octants around the view to prevent them from overlapping. When one cut-out view overlaps octant edges, it is shifted into the octant, where the centre of the represented object is.

Benefits and Limitations

Canyon provides a high level of detail by showing the surroundings of off-view objects, which can provide spatial hints about their precise location. We expect that this additional information can improve one's ability to locate an object. In order to avoid occlusion and maintain this location awareness, and as suggested by previous work [13], cut-out views are also designed to not overlap. In addition, the distance of the cut-out from the view is conveyed using a paper folding metaphor, already familiar in the physical world, which was successfully employed in Mélange [9]. The size of the cut-outs remains consistent and does not depend on the target distance. However, unlike other cue-

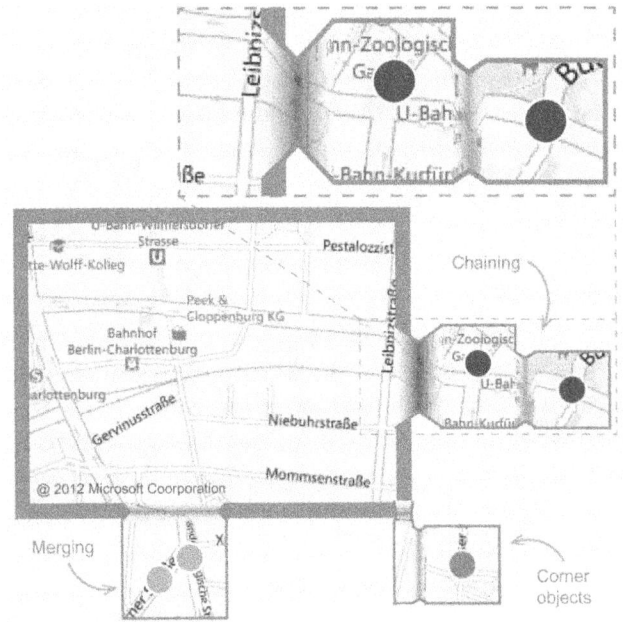

Figure 3: Close objects are merged in one Canyon (bottom). Objects located in the same direction are chained (right). Corner objects require folding twice (bottom right). The close up at the top shows the fold in detail.

based off-screen visualization techniques, each cut-out uses additional space, and thus the technique may not generalize to situations where screen real estate is at a premium.

We designed Canyon for the specific purpose of supporting awareness of multiple objects in a detailed view that may move out of the view. However, it is not clear to what degree our design improves location awareness, or whether the use of additional space and information will increase cognitive load. In addition, our paper-folding metaphor differs from other off-view visualization techniques, and we are interested in how effectively our technique conveys an object's distance from the cut-out.

METHOD

We conducted an empirical study in order to explore these benefits and limitations. Specifically, our study investigated how well people could understand the connection between the detail window and overview map, the effect of using additional space, and the degree to which Canyon provides awareness of a target's absolute location, relative location, and movement. As a baseline for comparison, we used Wedge [13], a well-designed off-screen technique (see Figure 4) due to little literature regarding the off-view problem.

Participants

Sixteen unpaid participants (6 female, 10 male), between 21 and 31 years of age, were recruited from a university computer science undergraduate program. Participants signed up as individuals, but were paired up to complete the study. 75% of participants reported being familiar with direct-input computational devices and all of the participants reported having used digital map systems.

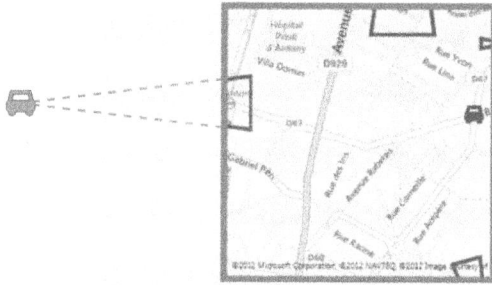

Figure 4: Wedge visualizes object locations with partly visible isosceles triangles overlaid on the view.

Apparatus

The study was conducted on a large interactive whiteboard, measuring 3 × 1.125 m, with a total resolution of 2048 × 768 pixels. The whiteboard was operated by two Hitachi CP-A100 projectors, with input through Anoto digital pens (ADP-301). The context of the study was a map-based police emergency response situation with an Overview+Detail interface inspired by DragMag [25], which provided a large overview and allowed flexible placement of detail views to provide awareness of the current situation (see Figure 5).

Design

We used a 2 (*technique*) × 2 (*density*) × 2 (*position*) mixed design with the following factors:

- *Technique:* Canyon, Wedge; within-participants
- *Density:* 5 cars, 10 cars; within-participants
- *Position:* left, right; between-participants

For the technique factor, we compared our Canyon visualization, which provides details of the surroundings of a target, to Wedge, an established off-screen visualization technique that uses abstract cues (see Figure 4). Wedge was implemented as described in [13], including the overlap resolution algorithm. Since the map application itself included an Overview+Detail interface, Overview+Detail was not used as a comparative technique. For the density factor, each participant's detail view presented 5 or 10 moving cars as targets.

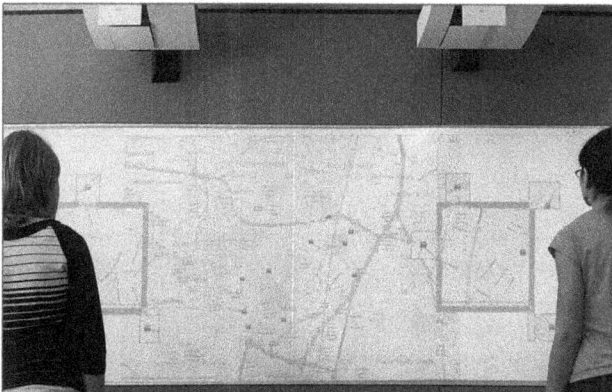

Figure 5: The study setup included a large shared overview map and one detail map for each participant.

Suburban areas of a large, foreign city were used so that participants would be unlikely to have in-depth knowledge of the map data, and thus have similar expertise. For every task, visually comparable map areas were selected and car locations were randomly generated prior to the study. Since two participants completed a task simultaneously with the same overview map, each participant had a detail map and thus the detail map areas were not the same. To account for any variance caused by differences in map area, we included the position factor.

Tasks

Four tasks were used to explore spatial limitations, the degree of difficulty to relate detail view and overview, and how well movement, relative location, and absolute location of objects are conveyed. Since we opted for higher precision and realism, tasks were inspired by the previously studied police work context. Selections were achieved by tapping the corresponding object once with the pen.

T1. *Identification.* A car was highlighted in red on the detail map, and the participant was asked to select the corresponding car on the overview map. This task tests how well objects can be correlated between maps.

T2. *Movement.* All cars were paused. The participant was then asked to select all cars that were stationary prior to the pausing, and then select the "Finished" button. Knowledge about whether a car is moving improves a police officer's situation awareness and motivates this task. We test how well movement is conveyed.

T3. *Distance.* While all cars are stationary and off-view, the participant was asked to select the closest car to the centre point of their detail view and then the second-closest car. Thereby, we test how well relative distance is interpreted. This task was motivated by having a new incident in the middle of the detail map and the need to send cars to that location. The closest cars are expected to arrive fastest.

T4. *Location.* A car was highlighted in red on the detail map, the participant was then asked to mark its location by tapping once on the overview map. This tests how well absolute location information is conveyed and was motivated by a police officer's need to know the absolute position of a police car.

Procedure

Each pair of participants was welcomed and given an overview of the project and study procedure. After filling out a background questionnaire, they were given time to practice drawing with the digital pen until they felt comfortable with the whiteboard technology.

Participants were then introduced to the tasks and the first technique through a presentation, followed by a training session. Then, they performed two blocks of all four tasks in the same order (T1-T4) for the first density condition, then two blocks for the second density condition, and then filled out post-condition questionnaires. Participants then followed the same procedure for the second technique, then completed an exit questionnaire and were interviewed. The order of technique and density were counterbalanced, but the density was presented in the same order of both techniques. Each trial was repeated 7 times for a total of 56 trials per participant (2 techniques × 2 densities × 2 blocks of tasks × 7 repetitions).

Data Collection

Each session was video and audio recorded. Timing data, car locations, and pen selections were captured through computer logs. Preference data were collected through post-condition and exit questionnaires.

RESULTS & DISCUSSION

This section presents the quantitative results, categorized by the tasks, as well as the overall study observation and participants' preference and feedback.

In our design, the density condition required a pre-determined task setup including map area and movement patterns of cars, and so our density factor was not separable from this setup. Our observations and preliminary analyses revealed that these different setups may have impacted participants' behavior, and so we performed two separate analyses for each density to avoid this confounding factor. We instead included *density order* as a between-participants factor, to separate learning effects and fatigue from the technique factor, as some of our participants would have performed comparable trials at different times throughout the study session. Error rates and trial completion time were thus analyzed using a 2 (*technique*) × 2 (*density order*) × 2 (*position*) repeated measures ANOVA (α = .05) separately for each level of density.

We found little significant differences between the tested techniques in our 5-car analysis. However, the 10-car condition reveals a number of significant differences between Wedge and Canyon. Since the results of the 10-car analysis are more interesting we will report only these results in this paper. For a comprehensive report of all results, we refer the reader to our supplementary material.

T1 – Identification

The trial completion time was calculated from when the car was highlighted in the detail view to when the car was selected on the overview map. The error rate was measured as a binary value: whether the selection was correct or not. No main effects or interactions were found for error rate.

Trial Completion Time

A significant main effect of technique ($F_{1,13} = 6.037$, $p = .029$) was found. Wedge was significantly faster ($M = 4.74$ s, $SE = 0.66$ s) than Canyon ($M = 6.57$ s, $SE = 1.26$ s). We suspect that this was due to the growth of Canyon, sometimes even exceeding the screen borders. Highlighted targets were sometimes not visible and participants had to move the detail view to find them.

A significant main effect of density order was found ($F_{1,13} = 5.376$, $p = .037$). Participants were faster when the 10 cars condition was tested second ($M = 4.58$ s, $SE = 0.67$ s) than when it was first ($M = 6.74$ s, $SE = 1.25$ s), an expected learning effect. No other main effects or interactions were significant.

T2 – Movement

The trial completion time was calculated as the time from when the cars were frozen to when the "Finished" button was pressed. Three types of error were also calculated and compared: omissions, false-positives, and overall error. Omissions were calculated as the percentage of stationary cars participants missed. False-positives were calculated as the percentage of moving cars erroneously selected. The overall error was calculated as the sum of stationary cars missed and the number of moving targets selected divided by the total number of cars in the condition. There were no main effects or interactions for trial completion time or omissions.

False Positives

There was a significant main effect of technique ($F_{1,13} = 10.687$, $p = .006$). Participants selected significantly fewer moving cars with Canyon ($M = 3.13\%$, $SE = 1.89\%$) than with Wedge ($M = 10.19\%$, $SE = 3.82\%$). Participants may have been more accurate with Canyon as people can easily identify movement in their periphery, and in Canyon this movement remains outside the detail view, whereas with Wedge the movement is promoted to the focus. In addition, Wedge allows for overlapping objects and can become easily cluttered, making false movement detection more likely. No other main effects or interactions were significant.

T3 – Distance

Trial completion time was calculated as the time between dismissing the instructions and selecting a car. The error rate was calculated as the distance between the closest target and the selected target divided by the distance from the detail map centre to the selected target. For the second trial, the target was the closest object among the remaining objects. There were no main effects or interactions for trial completion time.

Error

A significant main effect of technique ($F_{1,13} = 9.276$, $p = .009$) was found. The error was far less for Canyon ($M = 1.72\%$, $SE = 1.27\%$) than for Wedge ($M = 20.23\%$, $SE = 9.57\%$). The main effect may be due to that Canyon provided a more consistent visualization at the corners and for objects at extreme distances. No other effects or interactions were significant.

T4 – Location

Trial completion time was calculated as the time from when the car was highlighted on the detail map to when the location was marked on the overview map. The error was calculated as the distance between the target location and the selected location on the overview map measured in centimeters on the whiteboard. The projected map's scale was approximately 1 cm : 87 m.

Trial Completion Time

There was a significant main effect of density order for trial completion time ($F_{1,13}$ = 8.124, p = .014). Both techniques were faster when the 10 cars density was tested second (*Mean difference* = 3.80 s). This is likely caused by a learning effect. No other significant main effects or interaction were found.

Error

There was a significant main effect of technique ($F_{1,13}$ = 9.405, p = .009). Canyon was less error-prone (M = 1.61 cm, SE = 0.53 cm) compared to Wedge (M = 2.85 cm, SE = 0.67 cm). In meters, the average error for Canyon amounts to 139 m and to 247 m for Wedge. This main effect may be due to that the cut-out views provided participants more details surrounding targets so they can identify the absolute location based on the features of the landscape.

Questionnaires

After each technique block, participants were asked to rate how much knowledge they felt they had for each task at both levels of density. The rating was based on a 7-point Likert scale, where 1 means they had no knowledge, but rather guessed, and 7 means they knew exactly where the objects were, if they were moving, etc. The questionnaires used are included in the appendix accompanying this paper.

The post-condition questionnaire data were analyzed using two related samples Wilcoxon signed-rank tests. For the distance task (T3), the results showed that participants perceived themselves to have more knowledge of the targets with Canyon than with Wedge in both density conditions (5 cars: z = 2.208, p = .027; 10 cars: z = 2.248, p = .025). For the location task (T4), Canyon was also rated higher for both 5 cars (z = 2.015, p = .044) and 10 cars (z = 2.133, p = .033). The rating results for T3 and T4 are shown in Figure 6. No significant difference was found in technique for the remaining tasks.

After the experiment, participants were asked to rate their preferred technique by task and overall (see Figure 7). Canyon was more preferred per task and overall. Overall, 14 out of 16 participants (87.5%) preferred Canyon over Wedge. Wedge's highest rating was in the movement task (T2), with 6 participants (37.5%) preferring it to Canyon.

Interviews and Observations

At the end of the study, participants were asked to state their preferred technique and why. According to the participants, the major advantages of Canyon were the clear design and the additional detail provided in the cut-out views. Twelve participants stated that they found Canyon "clearer" or "easier" because they felt confident about the off-view object locations. Three participants pointed out that Canyon provided good orientation by giving reference points within

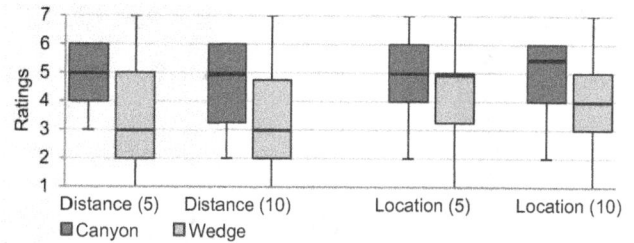

Figure 6: Significantly different Likert-scale ratings for Distance and Location task. 1 means having no knowledge about the object and 7 means having complete knowledge.

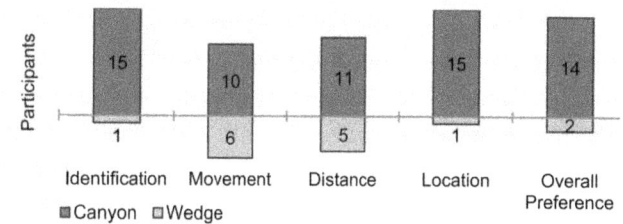

Figure 7: Preferences of technique per task and overall.

the cut-out view, such as roundabouts or parks, which helped locate the target.

> "I liked it [Canyon] better because it was easier to orientate with the small [cut-out] map and one can associate the object better. For example, if it is near a park, you see the green on the small [cut-out] map." – Participant 5B

One participant commented that with local knowledge, it would be even easier to assign locations with Canyon's cut-out view. However, the drawback of Canyon was estimating the exact distance as reported by 5 participants, and two participants stated explicitly that they felt, distance was better conveyed with Wedge.

> "It [Canyon] was more difficult for [estimating] distances because it was difficult to convert the shadow into distance information" – Participant 6A

Nevertheless, two participants felt that the paper folding metaphor of Canyon gave a good understanding of distance, and two participants described Canyon as "intuitive".

Wedge was described by 9 participants as "confusing", especially with overlapping Wedges. One participant commented that the inconsistent base length of Wedges at corners is difficult to understand, while one participant did not notice the inconsistency at all. Moreover, some participants commented that it can be difficult to complete the Wedges mentally.

> "I found it really difficult [with Wedge] to imagine where the legs intersect" – Participant 8B

> "You could locate the cars easier [with Canyon] because you did not have to imagine how big the triangles are once they are completed" – Participant 7B

In fact, some participants used their hands in order to interpret Wedge properly and estimate location or distance. Figure 8 shows an example of one participant tracing the legs

Figure 8: A participant was carefully tracing legs of Wedges with both hands and measuring the length relative to the view size.

of a Wedge carefully with both hands during the Location task. Once the intersection point of a Wedge's legs was found, she measured the distance relative to the detail view. On the overview map, she scaled the distance relative to the detail area marker for finding the object's location.

Furthermore, Wedge's representation of very close objects can lead to overlooking. In one configuration of the Distance task, an off-view object was very close to the detail view (see Figure 9). The Wedge representation of this object was very small and 4 out of 8 participants did not select it as the closest object. In contrast, none of the participants facing this situation with Canyon missed it.

We noticed that during the study participants stepped away from the digital whiteboard for both Canyon and Wedge, but in different tasks. With Canyon, we noticed more often that participants stepped back for observing movement of the cars (T2) than with Wedge. Increasing the distance to the display increased their field of view and provided a better overview for covering the larger area of Canyon's visualizations. With Wedge, participants stepped back for completing Wedges and finding the car location (T4). In contrast, they moved very close to the digital whiteboard to carefully examine Canyon's cut-out view and find the car location. For both techniques, participants looked repeatedly to the detail map and overview map. However, we noticed that they compared the detail and overview map more extensively with Canyon than with Wedge, in order to find location reference points to match corresponding map areas.

In conclusion, participants appreciated the additional detail provided by Canyon and preferred it over the abstract cues in Wedge. For them, estimating absolute distance was diffi-

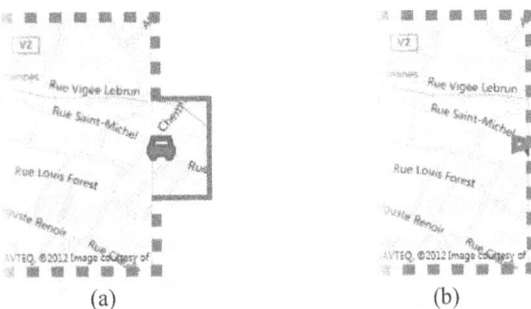

Figure 9: A very close off-view object visualized with Canyon (a) and with Wedge (b).

cult with Canyon, and the main drawback of Wedge was the overlapping cues, which often confused the participants.

OVERALL DISCUSSION

The quantitative results suggest some positive results for accuracy in favour of Canyon over Wedge, with no corresponding differences in trial completion time, suggesting that this benefit does not come at the cost of speed. Furthermore, participants preferred Canyon over Wedge. While this study was framed in a police emergency response context with moving cars as targets, the results will likely generalize to other situations involving large screen setups with moving targets and the need for detailed views. The tasks were designed to reflect strengths and weaknesses of the techniques regarding general off-view object features like location, distance and movement.

Specifically, the results indicate that Canyon more accurately conveyed movement in T2. Even though the amount of objects on the screen and the growth of Canyon may overwhelm participants, they still performed better using Canyon. This improved movement awareness may be due to Canyon placing off-view objects outside of the workspace, where movement can be perceived in the periphery. It should be noted, however, that in T1 participants were slower when using Canyon, which suggests that the additional information provided by Canyon may interfere with simpler tasks. For instance, the chaining of objects, sometimes even exceeded the screen borders. Visibility of off-view objects should be guaranteed and stemming Canyon's growth will be addressed in future work.

Our results also suggest that Canyon allows participants to be more accurate at measuring distance, which corresponds well with participants' stated preferences; however, five participants stated during interviews that they could not determine the target distance by observing the shadow. A distinction between relative and absolute distance conveyed by Canyon may help to explain this discrepancy. In the distance task (T3), participants were required to estimate the *relative* distance (i.e., first and second closest cars). We suspect that participants are instead referring to an inability to precisely measure the *absolute* distance, rather than an inability to describe the next closest target. Unlike in Wedge where the closest target may result in a very small triangle, off-view targets in Canyon have more consistent sizes. Even though the corners require more effort to interpret, the Canyon visualization, namely the distortion and shadow, is consistent for both corner and regular cases.

These same comments also seem to contradict the quantitative results about absolute location awareness in the location task (T4). Using Canyon, participants measured 1.24 cm more accurately than with Wedge, despite the comment that the shadows were insufficient. Interviews with the participants revealed a potential explanation. Participants commented that even though it was difficult to estimate the exact distance with Canyon, the cut-out views provided cues to the exact location of the targets, such as landmarks and features of the landscape. Moreover, participants were able to compare the cut-out views with the overview map to match the location in Canyon. In contrast, Wedge does not provide extra clues to the surrounding and participants had to rely only on their estimation of the intersection of Wedge legs.

Design Recommendations

Based on our results, we provide design recommendations for multi-user applications on large displays involving individual workspaces and moving off-view objects:

Provide context of the off-view targets

The results showed that providing the surrounding area of off-view objects provided clues and awareness of their location. This information was especially helpful on top of the distance cues conveyed by distortion and shadow. Participants also rated Canyon higher and preferred the provided context more than the abstract cues in Wedge.

Make distance cues consistent

The findings revealed the importance of providing a consistent visualization and the fact that people may first interpret a visualization based on the most salient features, such as the base length in Wedge. Moreover, the results indicated that Canyon's paper folding metaphor provided a more understandable method to interpret relative distance for the participants than Wedge did. It also enabled higher accuracy while maintaining comparable speed. However, special attention is needed for objects at extreme distance, such as very close or distant. One approach may be to adjust the parameters of the shadow in a consistent manner based on the specific situations to increase its expressiveness.

Avoid clutter and pay attention to dynamic movement

Despite the success of Wedge on mobile devices and its compact design, the results revealed that the interface was too cluttered and confusing for the participants in the large display environment. Thus, the design should avoid clutter and overlapping of cues. The jiggling of the cues in the high-density condition was another factor that confused the participants in Wedge. Designers should consider both static and dynamic aspects of the visualization.

Stem growth and ensure visibility

Uncontrolled growth of Canyon was intentionally allowed in the study to investigate trade-offs in Canyon's design. However, the results revealed that this growth significantly increased the time to perform tasks. Therefore, off-view objects should always remain visible and not exceeding the screen border so the awareness of the objects is preserved.

Generalizing Canyon

Canyon is best suited for scenarios involving maps, node-link diagrams, or other 2D spatial information visualizations. However, the general "off-view object" context may be applicable to other task contexts. In addition to the command and control contexts described earlier in this pa-

per, it could also be used for logistics. A dispatcher at a transportation company could use Canyon to stay aware of current truck locations and plan future tours.

Canyon may be useful for content management on a large display. In a multi-monitor desktop environment, people often have a primary task on the primary monitor and multiple types of content opened on the secondary monitor to support the primary task [12]. This also applies to large displays. Consider working on the layout of a large poster of size DIN A1 (841 × 594 mm) on a large whiteboard to edit it in its original scale. Multiple folder views might be opened and contain input for the poster, such as text, sponsors' logos and images. Often, a web browser view is needed to search for appropriate fonts or images, and mail client for related email threads and attachments. In this case, the primary task is in the view containing the poster design, and folder, web browser and mail client views are secondary tasks, assisting the primary task. Opened views for secondary tasks could be removed from the screen to reduce clutter and be represented by Canyon around the primary-task-view. This reduces distance on a large display [2] and facilitates efficient retrieval of required views due to cognitively associated locations.

Canyon may also be used in a calendar view for visualizing future appointments or events. For example, the current time point plus 6 hours are presented in detail. The y-axis might represent hours and the x-axis might represent days. Future calendar items are laid out accordingly using Canyon to represent the connection to the current time point.

CONCLUSION & FUTURE WORK

We have presented Canyon, a novel off-view visualization technique for large-display applications. It employed the paper-folding metaphor; therefore, using both distortion and shadow to convey distance information. Moreover it provided context around target location, which helped to improve accuracy. To investigate the effectiveness and efficiency of the technique, a controlled laboratory experiment was conducted comparing Canyon with an established technique, Wedge. Results revealed that Canyon improved the accuracy in the high-density condition while maintaining comparable speed, across density conditions, to Wedge.

In the future, we would like to investigate potential ways to control the growth of Canyon. Another area of future research is to improve the visualization at corners to allow faster interpretation of distance. One potential way is to use circular workspace instead of rectangular shapes. Moreover, an investigation on fine tuning the shadow or creating an alternative augmentation for conveying distance will improve the estimation of absolute distance of targets. Finally, in-depth knowledge of an area can be particularly beneficial when using Canyon for showing off-view objects on maps. Further research can investigate how much performance improvement can be gained with Canyon for people with knowledge of the local area.

ACKNOWLEDGEMENTS

We want to thank Thomas Seifried for mentoring this project and the Upper Austrian Police for giving us insights into their work. We also gratefully acknowledge the LEIF Canada-EU Exchange Program for enabling such a close collaboration on this project.

REFERENCES

1. Avrahami, D., Wobbrock, J.O., and Izadi, S. Portico: Tangible interaction on and around a tablet. *Proceedings of UIST'11*, (2011), 347–356.

2. Baudisch, P., Cutrell, E., Robbins, D., et al. Drag-and-pop and drag-and-pick: Techniques for accessing remote screen content on touch-and pen-operated systems. *Proceedings of INTERACT'03*, IOS Press (2003), 57–64.

3. Baudisch, P. and Good, N. Keeping things in context: A comparative evaluation of focus plus context screens, overviews, and zooming. *Proceedings of CHI'02*, (2002), 259–266.

4. Baudisch, P. and Rosenholtz, R. Halo: A technique for visualizing off-screen objects. *Proceedings of CHI'03*, (2003), 481–488.

5. Burigat, S., Chittaro, L., and Gabrielli, S. Visualizing locations of off-screen objects on mobile devices: A comparative evaluation of three approaches. *Proceedings of MobileHCI'06*, ACM (2006), 239–246.

6. Burigat, S. and Chittaro, L. Visualizing references to off-screen content on mobile devices: A comparison of Arrows, Wedge, and Overview+Detail. *Interacting with Computers 23*, 2 (2011), 156–166.

7. Carpendale, M.S.T. and Montagnese, C. A framework for unifying presentation space. *Proceedings of UIST'01*, (2001), 82–92.

8. Cockburn, A., Karlson, A., and Bederson, B.B. A review of overview+detail, zooming, and focus+context interfaces. *ACM Computing Surveys 41*, 1 (2008), 1–31.

9. Elmqvist, N., Henry, N., Riche, Y., and Fekete, J.-D. Mélange: Space folding for multi-focus interaction. *Proceedings of CHI'08*, (2008), 1333–1342.

10. Frisch, M. and Dachselt, R. Off-screen visualization techniques for class diagrams. *Proceedings of SOFTVIS'10*, (2010), 163–172.

11. Furnas, G.W. Generalized fisheye views. *Proceedings of CHI'86*, (1986), 16–23.

12. Grudin, J. Partitioning digital worlds: Focal and peripheral awareness in multiple monitor use. *Proceedings of CHI'01*, (2001), 458–465.

13. Gustafson, S., Baudisch, P., Gutwin, C., and Irani, P. Wedge: Clutter-free visualization of off-screen locations. *Proceedings of CHI'08*, (2008), 787–796.

14. Gustafson, S. and Irani, P. Comparing visualizations for tracking off-screen moving targets. *Extended Abstracts CHI'07*, (2007), 2399–2404.

15. Igarashi, T. and Hinckley, K. Speed-dependent automatic zooming for browsing large documents. *Proceedings of UIST'00*, (2000), 139–148.

16. Irani, P., Gutwin, C., and Yang, X. Improving selection of off-screen targets with hopping. *Proceedings of CHI'06*, (2006), 299–308.

17. Javed, W., Ghani, S., and Elmqvist, N. PolyZoom: Multiscale and multifocus exploration in 2D visual spaces. *Proceedings of CHI'12*, (2012), 287–296.

18. Moscovich, T., Chevalier, F., Henry, N., Pietriga, E., and Fekete, J.-D. Topology-aware navigation in large networks. *Proceedings of CHI'09*, (2009), 2319–2328.

19. Perlin, K. and Fox, D. Pad: An alternative approach to the computer interface. *Proceedings of SIGGRAPH'93*, (1993), 57–64.

20. Plaisant, C., Carr, D., and Hasegawa, H. *When an Intermediate View Matters a 2D-browser Experiment.* University of Maryland, Systems Research Center, 1992.

21. Plumlee, M.D. and Ware, C. Zooming versus multiple window interfaces: Cognitive costs of visual comparisons. *ACM Transactions on Computer-Human Interaction (TOCHI) 13*, 2 (2006), 179–209.

22. Shoemaker, G. and Gutwin, C. Supporting multi-point interaction in visual workspaces. *Proceedings of CHI'07*, (2007), 999–1008.

23. Spence, R. and Apperley, M. Data base navigation: An office environment for the professional. *Behaviour & Information Technology 1*, 1 (1982), 43–54.

24. Tobiasz, M., Isenberg, P., and Carpendale, S. Lark: Coordinating co-located collaboration with information visualization. *IEEE Transactions on Visualization and Computer Graphics 15*, 6 (2009), 1065–1072.

25. Ware, C. and Lewis, M. The DragMag image magnifier. *Conference companion CHI'95*, (1995), 407–408.

26. Wigdor, D., Jiang, H., Forlines, C., Borkin, M., and Shen, C. WeSpace: The design development and deployment of a walk-up and share multi-surface visual collaboration system. *Proceedings of CHI'09*, (2009), 1237–1246.

27. Zellweger, P.T., Mackinlay, J.D., Good, L., Stefik, M., and Baudisch, P. City lights: Contextual views in minimal space. *Extended Abstracts CHI'03*, (2003), 838–839.

Designing Graphical Menus for Novices and Experts: Connecting Design Characteristics with Design Goals

Krystian Samp
National University of Ireland
Digital Enterprise Research Institute
krystian.samp@deri.org

ABSTRACT

This paper presents a design space for graphical menus. We model the design space as a set of design goals, a set of design characteristics, and connections between the two. The design goals are based on novice and expert behaviors. The connections link the choices for design characteristics with the positive or negative effects that these choices have on the design goals. The paper further synthesizes the design space into a succinct form of structured design guidelines. A case study demonstrates how these guidelines can be used to assess and compare the strengths and weaknesses of two menu designs.

Author Keywords

Graphical menus; radial menus; cascading menus; menus; design space; design characteristics; guides; guidelines.

ACM Classification Keywords

H.5.2 [Information Interfaces and Presentation]: User Interfaces - Interaction styles.

General Terms

Human Factors; Design.

INTRODUCTION

Graphical menus remain one of the primary modes used to interact with computer software. The large body of menu research focuses mostly on novel designs – e.g., cascading menu improvements [1, 8, 19, 48], radial menus [4, 39], and marking menus [20, 54]. New designs are described (i.e., how they look and work) and then evaluated, usually in a controlled user study. The motivation for new designs is typically based on a single observation or problem with an existing menu design. For example, observations about radial layout's ability to decrease distances and increase item sizes [4], observations about top-bottom search patterns in linear layouts [44], and the problem of steering between sub-menus in a cascading menu [1, 48].

Such design-focused works are useful for practitioners who want to choose between one of the menu designs compared

in a user study. However, from these works we learn little about the design space. They do not identify a palette of important design decisions and how to make these decisions to accomplish desired goals. The answers to these questions are necessary to inform new menu designs. They are also helpful for the review process of existing menus and the evaluation of early design ideas and sketches [3].

The above tasks are partially supported by guidelines for designing menus (see e.g., [45]). Guidelines come in the form of a bullet-point list of prescriptions – e.g., "provide meaningful labels", "organize items into meaningful groups". These are useful but also limited in their ability to provide any explanation. Why is a particular guideline important? Which goal does it help to accomplish? What if it cannot be followed? Or what are the trade-offs between guidelines? These questions also cannot be easily answered using reviews of menu research, such as [26, 33], which are mainly concerned with categorizing previous works.

To address the above gap this paper presents a design space that was built to inform the design of the Compact Radial layout menu (CRL) [39, 42]. The CRL menu is a graphical menu designed to support the needs of novices and experts. It successfully met these goals as demonstrated by the evaluation results [39, 40, 41, 42]. The design space proved useful and our hope is that it can inform researchers and practitioners in the design of other graphical menus.

The design space is based on a synthesis of previous work. We model it as a set of design goals, a set of design characteristics, and connections between the two. The design goals are based on novice and expert behaviors. The connections indicate the positive or negative effects of different choices for design characteristics on the goals.

The paper begins by describing the design space as a series of design goals followed by design characteristics. The paper then presents the design space in a synthesized form of structured design guidelines. A case study follows where the design guidelines are used to compare two menu designs. The conclusions close the paper.

DESIGN SPACE

Our design space is based on the basic definition of a graphical menu: a graphical menu provides two important elements: 1) graphical representations of application commands; and 2) a mechanism by which the users can choose one of these representations [26].

We further limit the design space to hierarchical menus. Over the years hierarchical menus, next to sequential menus and menu networks, have surfaced as the most effective and also the most common [33]. A menu hierarchy is a tree structure that contains two types of items: structural items and functional items. Structural items serve as categories which determine the organization of the menu structure. Functional items represent specific application commands.

Design Goals

Previous research has established that menus should consider the needs of novices, experts and those transitioning from novice to expert [8, 33]. We now define design goals in the context of novice behavior, expert behavior, novice-to-expert transition, and other technical requirements.

Novice Behavior

Novices are unfamiliar with the menu content and thus do not know the locations of menu items. They search for an item visually and then navigate to it [8]. When searching, novices rely on readability and the meaning of item labels and icons [17]. Typically, the visual search time dominates the total selection time [39].

Novices often navigate back and forth in menus, visiting a few sub-menus before finding an item. This is empirically demonstrated in [31] where novices visited 12 sub-menus on average while the optimal selection required traversing only four sub-menus. Snowberry et al. [46] provide supporting evidence reporting that 4 – 34% of selections in menu hierarchies are erroneous (i.e., wrong parent items selected). Tombaugh and McEwen [50] observed that when searching for information, users were very likely to choose menu items that did not lead to the desired information.

However, while searching, novices often experience a problem of disorientation [21 p.37,39]. This is because they have to remember which parts of a menu structure they have already visited. And if novices do not know their present location and find it difficult to decide where to look next, they feel disoriented [38]. Norman and Butler [32] present a menu study demonstrating that participants searching for menu items tended to repeat paths and forgot where they had looked before.

Graphical menus are designed to enable guided exploration and learning [21, 26]. This mode of knowledge acquisition is not only preferred but also one of the most effective [7].

To support novice behavior we define the following design goals (ordered by priority):

Ease of Use (EASY). Visual structure should clearly communicate the concepts of menu levels, depth, items, and item groups. Visual representations of the commands should be readable and meaningful. The selection mechanism should be simple and familiar.

Guided Exploration (GUIDE). To guide the novice the menu should decrease the information load and enable exploration. It should prevent disorientation and support the behavior when novices make mistakes and need to explore multiple locations in the command space.

Effective Visual Search (SEARCH). A menu should allow to quickly search menu content: previous and newly visited locations.

Effective Navigation (NAV). A menu should allow quick and direct navigation between all menu locations and items.

Expert Behavior and Novice-to-Expert Transition

The transition from novice to expert is associated with a transformation in the mental representation of the menu. In contrast to novices, experts do not rely on the readability of menu items. In fact, experts have problems recalling labels of frequently used menu items [29]. Kaptelinin [17] demonstrates that degrading readability through changing label characters into dots does not impact expert performance.

Experts are familiar with menu content. They remember the locations of items and rely on these when performing menu selections. Somberg [47] shows that positionally constant arrangement (i.e., consistent assignment of individual items to screen positions) is the most effective compared to three other arrangements: alphabetical, random, and probability of selection. Similar results are demonstrated in [17, 30].

In sum, experts do not search for menu items visually. They decide which item to select and then navigate to it [8]. Extensive menu use can lead to a substantial decrease in decision time [6, 25] and it is typically the pointing time that dominates the total selection time [39]. Experts perform fast, unattended movements which are less precise and thus are more prone to missing a target item [43, 54].

Cockburn et al. [8] demonstrate that the rate of novice-to-expert transition depends on the stability of global features. If they are stable, the transition happens rather quickly [17]; notable differences occur even after one exposure to each menu item [30].

Due to memory decay, experts occasionally forget what they learnt. In such cases, they return back to novice behavior; once again they have to search for items visually. This is demonstrated empirically in [23] where after lay off periods of few hours or days, experts needed to switch back to novice techniques and re-learn what they forgot. Experts also return back to novice behavior if memorized global visual features change: for example, when a memorized location of an item changes. This situation happens with spatially adaptive menus that constantly reorder menu items [47]. Cockburn et al. [8] show that the learnability of such menus is degraded. Finally, experts return back to novice behavior when they want to find new functionality, previously not used or used sporadically. In sum, the transition from novice to expert does not happen once and forever. Rather than being a novice or an expert, users often switch between both behaviors over time.

To support expert behavior and the novice-to-expert transition we define the following design goals:

Support Learning Menu Content (LEARN). A menu should avoid forcing experts to return to novice behavior. It should avoid unnecessary changes of global visual features, such as item location, size, and color.

Effective Navigation (NAV). Note that this goal was defined in the previous section; we now extend it. A menu should allow quick navigation, require little navigation precision, and reduce the number and consequences of navigation errors.

Miscellaneous
Finally, we define some technical design goals:

Quantity (QUANT). A menu should accommodate menu hierarchies and hundreds of commands.

Reduced Screen Consumption (SPACE). A menu should limit its screen consumption. This is especially important for devices with small screens such as smartphones.

Design Characteristics
A menu has various characteristics. They can be viewed as design variables whose values are determined in the design process. An example of a characteristic is the size of a menu item. This section presents the characteristics most important for the design goals defined previously. Each characteristic is discussed in terms of its benefits and its impacts on the goals. If a particular choice of a characteristic value benefits a goal, it is indicated in brackets using the following notation: X+, where X is a symbolic name of the particular goal being benefited. The symbolic names of the goals were provided in Design Goals above. Similarly, the notation: X- indicates that a particular characteristic value impacts the goal X. For example, big menu sizes improve pointing performance (NAV+) but they also increase screen consumption (SPACE-).

Hierarchy Structure and Visual Structure
Depth vs Breadth. There has been a considerable amount of research focusing on the depth versus breadth issue; that is, on finding an optimal hierarchy structure. This research is predominantly based on two approaches: theoretical analyses and empirical studies (for a good review see [26, 33]). The conclusions are often inconsistent. However, one re-occurring empirical finding is that increasing the depth of the hierarchy has negative effects. Snowberry et al. [46] found that error rates increased from 4% to 34% as the menu depth increased from one to six levels (GUIDE-). Depth also impacts the selection performance [24] and increases the costs of error recovery [18] (NAV-).

At the same time increasing the depth has some positive effects. It can decrease information overload, and help a

user to "narrow down" the choice and access items more quickly than using a flat list of items (GUIDE+) [21]. It can also reduce screen consumption if an unfolding menu is used (SPACE+).

Domain Hierarchy. Some researchers believe that efforts aiming at finding an optimal hierarchy incorrectly assume that such an optimum depends primarily on depth and breadth. Instead, Lee and Raymond, 1993 [26] have proposed that it is much more important for a menu hierarchy to reflect the structures inherently embedded in specific domains and the actions carried in the context of those domains. This view is supported by studies demonstrating that different categorizations and tasks – rather than depths and breadths – have a strong effect on user behavior and overall performance [30] (GUIDE+).

Visual Structure. The visual structure of a menu needs to effectively communicate concepts of hierarchy levels, depth, individual items, and item groups. In cascading menus, for example, individual items are communicated with rectangular boxes, levels are communicated with disjoint lists of items and item groups are communicated with horizontal bars that separate two adjacent groups. This makes a menu easier to use and help guide visual search (EASY+, GUIDE+, SEARCH+). Hornof [15] provides empirical evidence that a visual hierarchy, with distinguishable category items and their child items, guides visual search and results in better search performance compared to a visually unstructured list of items.

Hierarchy Navigation
Unfolding vs Parallel. A hierarchical menu can take a form of an unfolding menu or a parallel menu. In an unfolding menu—a cascading menu being an example—a user is initially presented only with the first level of the menu hierarchy and is given a mechanism to "unfold" subsequent levels. This way, a user traverses menu in a "walking manner", selecting parent items, and then moving to their newly displayed sub-menus.

A hierarchical unfolding menu decreases the amount of displayed information, showing only those hierarchy levels which are currently explored. This reduces screen consumption (SPACE+), and decreases information load (GUIDE+), but can increase the number of necessary interactions (NAV-). The process of selecting an item is structured into steps, each associated with a small portion of new information used to make a simple decision of where to go next. Paap and Roske-Hofstrand [35] observe that when the alternatives in a menu are organized into a hierarchy, the scope of the search may be substantially reduced. Snowberry et al. [46] show that menu hierarchies improve selection performance when compared to random ordering, up to a factor of two.

A fully parallel hierarchical menu displays all menu levels and items at once. Quinn and Cockburn [37] demonstrate that such a menu decreases navigation demands (NAV+)

but it is not better than an unfolding menu. This is because displaying more levels and items increases information load (GUIDE-). It also increases screen consumption (SPACE-).

Unfolding menus are currently the most ubiquitous so users are familiar with their semantics and mechanics (EASY+).

Navigation Aids. To further address the problem of disorientation, hierarchical unfolding menus typically use three navigational aids. The first one is *selection preview*. It provides feedback indicating which item is about to be selected. The most common approach is to highlight the item directly under the mouse cursor. The second navigational aid is *path highlighting*. It marks all the parent items that lead to the currently visible level. Occasionally, some hierarchical menus also use a third navigational aid, which is the *level preview*. Once a cursor is over a parent item a preview of the corresponding sub-menu is displayed immediately without waiting for selection. Visual preview improves search performance and reduces error rates [20]. The three navigational aids help users perceive their present location and help them decide where to go next (GUIDE+). They function as *cognitive landmarks* denoting the focal points at which fundamental turns have been taken [33].

Distances

Graphical menus can use different spatial layouts which determine the distances between the menu items and levels.

Short vs Long Distances. Shorter distances improve the navigation performance (NAV+) in four ways. First, shorter distances reduce the difficulty of a movement task, which also reduces movement time [27]. Second, shorter distances decrease the pointer drift – that is, the distance between the initial and the final position of the mouse pointer on the screen after performing a selection from a menu. The reduced drift means that the mouse pointer can be repositioned to its initial location faster. This is important in situations where the mouse pointer is used to directly manipulate content (e.g., many digital content creation applications). Third, short distances might allow for ballistic movements [10]. Such movements are motor programmed and during their execution visual feedback for path correction is not possible. Consequently, no visual control is involved and the movement can be performed faster. Ballistic movements occur if the duration of the movement is short, around 200 ms [10] which is not unusual in menu selection task [39]. Fourth, short distances require less positioning accuracy and thus result in fewer errors. Phillips and Triggs [36] show that there is a significantly greater number of overshoot errors for far targets than for near targets. This can have a considerable impact on performance because, as Phillips and Triggs observe, participants overshoot their targets regularly. Schmidt et al. [43] show that accuracy is better for short distances. Similarly, Thompson [49, experiment 1] shows that accuracy decreases with greater distances.

Shorter distances, apart from improving navigation performance, can potentially also improve the performance of visual search in two ways (SEARCH+). First, shorter distances shorten the length of the scan path and thus fewer fixations and saccades are necessary. Second, shorter distances might potentially 'squeeze' more items into the eye fovea enabling more parallel processing. Hornof and Kieras [14] show that more items in the fovea result in considerable improvements in search performance.

Finally, shorter distances keep the items and the levels tighter which decreases the screen consumption (SPACE+).

Discrimination Method

Discrimination method determines a type of movement used to discriminate between menu items (see Figure 1).

Angle vs Length. The extent of the differences between items' angles and positions determine how easy or difficult it is to properly discriminate between the items. For example, it requires more movement precision to discriminate between two items that lay at the same angle and close to each other than between two items at two opposite angles. Kurtenbach and Buxton [22] show that smaller angular differences lead to increased error rates and slower performance (NAV-). The same is demonstrated in [55]. Callahan et al. [4] provides empirical evidence that for small eight-item menus, discrimination by angle enables faster selections than discrimination by length (NAV+).

Different angles of approach affect selection performance [53]. The fastest are the vertical movements (NAV+) while the slowest are the horizontal movements (NAV-). However, although the differences are significant they tend to be small, approximately on the order of 50 ms.

The discrimination method also characterizes screen consumption because it determines how the menu expands spatially when it is navigated. Menus using discrimination by length expand in one direction (e.g., cascading menus). Such an expansion strategy might not be suitable for small screens. Menus using discrimination by angle expand in more directions. Such menus might require less space on any side of the menu, thus are more suitable for small screens (SPACE+). At the same time, however, they might not be suitable for placement at screen borders.

The discrimination method is closely related to spatial

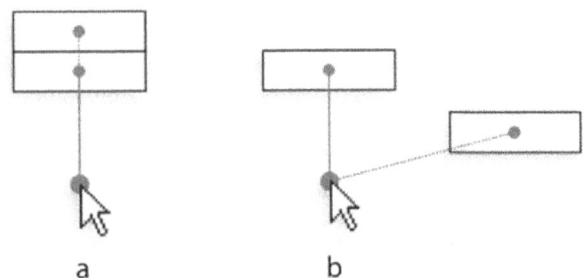

a   b

Figure 1. Discrimination by length (a) and angle (b).

organization (or layout) of the menu. Some layouts based on discrimination by angle can restrict amount of space available on menu levels – e.g., radial layout uses rings to represent levels thus limiting the number of items that can be accommodated (QUANT-). Although this characteristic will depend on the specific layout, discrimination by length leads to more spacious designs typically limited by the screen size (QUANT+). Further, non-linear layouts (e.g., radial layouts) are slower to search [39] (SEARCH-).

Spacing and Overlaps

Spacing refers to empty space separating the elements of menu structure: items and levels. Spacing can be negative in which case elements of menu structure overlap.

Spacing Extent. Decreasing the spacing decreases the distances between menu elements, which can improve both navigation performance (NAV+) and visual search performance (SEARCH+) while decreasing screen consumption (SPACE+). This is an underlying strategy of the cascading menu improvement proposed in [19]. It analyses the direction of the cursor movement. If the cursor moves towards a sub-menu of a parent item, that sub-menu is displayed immediately, next to the cursor, overlapping part of the menu. The reported study showed that the design reduced selection time by 12% and movement length by 31% compared to a traditional cascading menu.

Spacing also influences the consequences of under- and overshooting errors – that is, errors resulting from selections that miss a target item. If the spacing is low – an example being a cascading menu where item borders are tangent – under- and overshooting errors may result in selections of items adjacent to the target item (NAV-). The consequence will vary on the activated command, but in some cases this might involve extensive processing or showing a pop-up dialog. The complexity of error recovery has a considerable influence on user satisfaction [9].

Overlaps vs No-overlaps. Overlaps can obscure items in the overlapped regions. Some items might not be visible (SEARCH-), perhaps those that a novice should visit next (GUIDE-). Overlaps might also increase visual complexity and hinder the perception of the menu structure. A special mechanism might be necessary to reveal the obscured region or to revert to a previous step in the selection process (EASY-). Such a mechanism is necessary in marking menus that use series of pie menus [21, p. 56-57].

In the same screen space, overlapping methods can display more menu content than non-overlapping methods. Therefore, overlapping methods might be considered if the screen space is limited. It might be more beneficial to use overlaps than to introduce another mechanism for dealing with content that does not fit in the screen (e.g., scrolling).

Item Ordering and Grouping

Item ordering determines which command is assigned to which menu item. Research on item ordering has focused predominantly on two approaches: 1) analyzing visual search strategies, and 2) empirical investigations of various ordering techniques.

Visual Search Strategies. Visual search is often found to have elements of regularity. This means that during the search some items are systematically encountered before the others. Thus it is sensible to place the most important items in those locations which are searched first (GUIDE+, SEARCH+). It is also sensible to place these items in those locations which can be navigated the fastest (NAV+).

In linear menus which organize items in a vertical list, visual search, although includes a random component, is predominantly top to bottom [8, 14]. The differences in search time between the first and the last item can be considerable. Samp and Decker [39] report differences of 300–1500 ms depending on the menu size. Further, navigation to the top items is faster by approximately 160-300 ms [39]. In radial menus visual search starts at a location closest to the parent item (or the 12 o'clock position for the first level) and follows a zig-zag pattern [40]. The same items are also fastest to point at.

Ordering Techniques. Empirical investigations of item ordering and grouping have focused predominantly on three types of orderings: random, alphabetical, and functional (also called categorical). The functional ordering displays groups of related functions.

Random ordering is slower than alphabetical and functional [5, 13, 30]. Conclusions regarding alphabetical vs. functional ordering are inconsistent. One problem with alphabetical order is that it provides good performance results in experiments in which participants are presented with an exact name of a command to find. However, in real scenarios, novices often do not know a command name in advance. In experiments where a definition rather than exact command name is given, functional ordering is superior to the alphabetized one [13, 30] (NAV+).

Functional ordering can facilitate development of a mental model of the menu and make learning the commands faster (LEARN+). Card [5] presents empirical evidence that users organize menu items into memory chunks that reflect command groupings. In this sense, a menu group can be perceived as an additional feature by which experts can organize their knowledge and discriminate between items.

Functional ordering can also improve guidance and visual search performance (GUIDE+, SEARCH+). Triesman [51] found evidence that groups, rather than individual items, are scanned serially. Supporting evidence is also provided in [30] which found that items grouped by category are searched faster than randomly ordered menus.

The effects of item ordering and grouping disappear with practice [5, 30, 47]. Therefore they concern only novices.

Ease of Use (EASY)	**Effective Navigation (NAV)**
Visual structure should clearly communicate the concepts of menu levels, depth, items, and item groups. Visual representations of the commands should be readable and meaningful. The selection mechanism should be simple and familiar.	A menu should allow quick and direct navigation between all menu locations and items. A menu should require little navigation precision, and reduce the number and consequences of navigation errors.

Hierarchy Structure and Visual Structure	**Hierarchy Structure and Visual Structure**
✓ Visually communicate the elements of menu structure: hierarchy levels, depth, items, and item groups.	✓ Consider decreasing the number of hierarchy levels and avoid hierarchies deeper than three levels.
Hierarchy Navigation	**Hierarchy Navigation**
✓ Prefer unfolding over parallel menus.	✓ Prefer parallel over unfolding menus (especially for menus with more levels).
Spacing and Overlaps	**Distances**
✓ Avoid overlaps between menu elements (e.g. items, levels), and avoid special interaction mechanisms for handling overlaps.	✓ Shorten distances between menu elements (e.g., items, levels) – improves performance, pointer drift, and error rates.
Interaction Methods	**Discrimination Method**
✓ Prefer Button Press over Dwell and border crossing.	✓ Increase the extent of the differences between items' angles and positions.
✓ Avoid restricting navigation path (e.g., steering).	✓ Prefer discrimination by angle over length.
Guided Exploration (GUIDE)	✓ Prefer vertical over horizontal movements.
To guide the novice the menu should decrease the information load and enable exploration. It should prevent disorientation and support the behavior when novices make mistakes and need to explore multiple locations in the command space.	**Spacing and Overlaps**
	✓ Consider some minimal spacing between items to decrease consequences of under- and overshooting errors.
Hierarchy Structure and Visual Structure	✓ Avoid excessive spacing between menu elements.
✓ Menu hierarchy should reflect structures and actions carried in a target domain.	**Item Ordering and Grouping**
✓ Consider adding more hierarchy levels (especially for menus with more items) but avoid hierarchies deeper than three levels.	✓ Place the most important items in the positions navigated first.
✓ Visually communicate the elements of menu structure: hierarchy levels, depth, items, and item groups.	**Item Size and Shape**
Hierarchy Navigation	✓ Prefer regular, convex shapes such as squares, rectangles, and circles over non-regular, concave shapes.
✓ Prefer unfolding over parallel menus (especially for menus with more items).	✓ Increase item size – improves performance and error rates.
✓ Provide selection preview, level preview, path highlighting.	✓ Avoid overly small item sizes (e.g., typical radio buttons).
Spacing and Overlaps	✓ Avoid overly large item sizes if they considerably increase navigation distances to menu items.
✓ Avoid overlaps between menu elements (e.g., items, levels).	**Interaction Methods**
Item Ordering and Grouping	✓ Prefer Point-and-Click over Drag-and-Drop.
✓ Place the most important items in the positions searched and navigated first: for lists these are the top positions, for radials these are positions closest to the parent item (or the 12 o'clock position for the first level) and following a zig-zag pattern.	✓ Prefer Button Press over Dwell and border crossing.
	✓ Avoid restricting navigation path (e.g., steering).
✓ Prefer functional grouping over alphabetical and random orders	**Reduced Screen Consumption (SPACE)**
Effective Visual Search (SEARCH)	A menu should limit its screen consumption. This is especially important for devices with small screens such as smartphones.
A menu should allow to quickly search menu content: previous and newly visited locations.	**Hierarchy Structure and Visual Structure**
	✓ Consider adding additional hierarchy level.
Hierarchy Structure and Visual Structure: see EASY	**Hierarchy Navigation**
Distances	✓ Prefer unfolding over parallel menus.
✓ Shorten distances between menu elements (e.g., items, levels).	**Distances**
Discrimination Method	✓ Shorten distances between menu elements.
✓ Prefer linear layouts (e.g., vertical lists).	**Discrimination Method**
Spacing and Overlaps	✓ Consider radial layout to reduce number of pixels.
✓ Avoid excessive spacing between menu elements.	✓ Prefer linear layout if the menu should expand in one direction.
✓ Avoid overlaps between menu elements.	**Spacing and Overlaps**
Item Ordering and Grouping: see GUIDE.	✓ Decrease spacing between menu elements.
Support Learning Menu Content (LEARN)	✓ Consider overlapping menu elements.
A menu should avoid forcing experts to return to novice behavior. It should avoid unnecessary changes of global visual features, such as item location, size, and color.	**Item Size and Shape**
	✓ Decrease item area.
	✓ Prefer regular shapes.
Item Ordering and Grouping	**Quantity (QUANT)**
✓ Prefer functional grouping over alphabetical and random orders	A menu should accommodate menu hierarchies and hundreds of commands.
✓ Avoid changing global features (e.g., item position) or decrease the frequency of such changes.	**Discrimination Method**
	✓ Prefer layouts that do not restrict space on menu levels (e.g., linear layout).

Table 1. Guidelines for designing graphical menus (organized by design goal and characteristic).

Item Size and Shape

Many ways of measuring the size of a screen object have been proposed, including object *height*, *width*, and *width×height* [27]. However, calculating the size of an object along the direction of approach leads to the most accurate modeling results [27].

Shape Regularity. Concave, non-regular menu shapes might cause the center of the perceived item to be close to an item edge [12]. In such a case under- and overshooting errors are more likely (NAV-). Moreover, these menu shapes result in different item size depending on the direction of approach. For this reason, convex, regular shapes, such as circles and squares, are preferred. Their

Figure 2. A traditional cascading menu. A selection consists of a series of alternating vertical and horizontal movements.

center is equally distant from all edges and their size is the same regardless of the direction of approach (NAV+). Performance of circular and square items is either not different or the differences are small (20-50 ms) [53].

Small vs Big Item Size. Bigger item sizes improve navigation performance in three ways (NAV+). First, bigger sizes reduce the accuracy constraint of a movement task which also reduces its movement time [27]. Smaller items increase the duration of movement verification [52] (i.e., a check at the end of a movement if the cursor is over the item). Graham and MacKenzie [11] show that homing in on smaller targets is more difficult, thus more time consuming. Second, bigger sizes reduce error rates (NAV+). Series of rapid, aimed movements do not terminate at the center of an item but rather are spread around its perceived center [12, 28]. Thompson [49] shows that increasing target size decreases total error. Third, larger item sizes are likely to induce users to employ speed/accuracy trade-off that favors speed over accuracy (NAV+). Movement strategies are chosen to maximize expected gain, given the costs and benefits explicitly implemented in the environment. Oel et al. [34] demonstrate that small targets, such as radio buttons and toolbar icons, need above-average time in order to be hit.

Although increasing item size might seem in general to be a good idea, typically this will also increase the distances between items and levels (NAV-). Therefore, item size and navigation distance are coupled in a trade-off. Menu items should accommodate at least two-three word labels [39].

Interaction Methods
Interaction methods determine the type of motor actions used to select menu items. The most commonly used mechanism for issuing selections in graphical menus is Point-and-Select: a user points at a desired item and selects it, for example, with a button press.

Point-and-Click vs Drag-and-Drop. Menu selection through Point-and-Select can employ two different interaction styles. The first style is Point-and-Click, found, for example, in traditional single-level linear menus. A user first moves a pointer to a target item and then presses a button to select it. The second style is the Drag-and-Drop, employed, for example, by marking menus [21]. In this

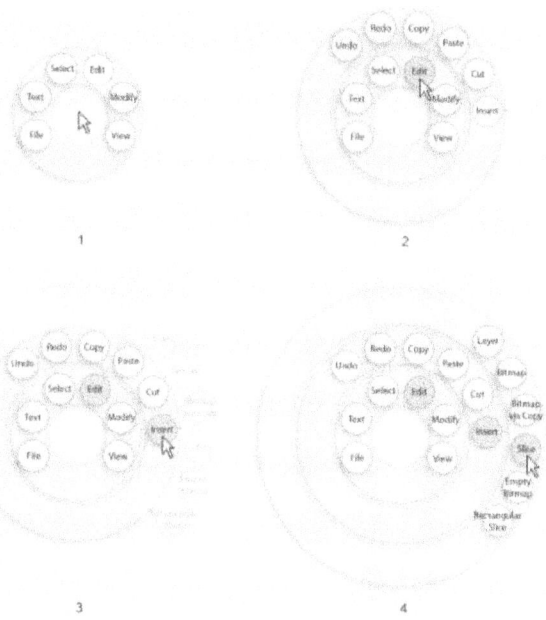

Figure 3. An example of a selection from a Compact Radial Layout menu. 1) User invokes the menu, 2) User clicks on a parent item on the first menu level, 3) User hovers over a parent item on the second level (a menu preview of the third level is displayed), 4) User selects an item on the third level.

case, the user first presses a button, then moves to a target item (with the button still pressed), and finally releases the button to select the target. The Point-and-Click is faster, less error prone (NAV+), and preferred over the Drag-and-Drop style (EASY+) [27]. Inkpen [16] demonstrates similar findings in a study conducted with children.

Dwell vs Button press. There are also two different ways of issuing selections: 1) dwelling – e.g., used in cascading menus to select parent items; and 2) button press (e.g., a mouse click). Pressing a button is faster than typical dwell times of 1/3 sec [6] (NAV+). More importantly, dwelling often leads to restricting navigation path (see next section).

Another technique of issuing selections is that of border crossing [21]. A user moves between items and selects one by moving the cursor outside the menu through the border of the target item. This approach is less intuitive (EASY-) and also restricts the movement trajectories (NAV-).

Restricted vs Unrestricted Navigation Trajectory. A menu design can restrict the navigation path necessary to move from one item to another. For example, a typical cascading menu restricts the type of movement used to move from a parent item to its sub-menu. The user must steer a cursor inside the parent item to avoid an error (a sub-menu disappearing). This kind of error is not uncommon [19, 48]. The steering task is more difficult and slower than non-restricted pointing [2] (EASY-, NAV-). Increasing the height of a steering 'tunnel' reduces the restriction [2].

Table 1 summarizes the design space in a form of structured guidelines organized by goal and characteristics.

EASY	NAV
Interaction Methods ✓ CS: dwell (-). CRL: button press (+). ✓ CS: restricted navigation path (steering) (-). CRL: unrestricted navigation path (+).	**Distances:** see SEARCH **Discrimination Method** ✓ CS: small length differences (-). CRL: considerable differences between items' angles and positions (+).
GUIDE	✓ CS: discrimination by length (-). CRL: discrimination by angle and length (+).
Item Ordering and Grouping ✓ CS: functional grouping (+). CRL: no functional grouping (-).	✓ CS: vertical movements (+). CRL: horizontal and vertical movements (-).
SEARCH	**Spacing and Overlaps**
Distances ✓ CS: long distances – sequences of vertical and horizontal movements (-). CRL: short distances (+).	✓ CS: no minimal spacing to decrease consequences of under-overshooting errors – important since item sizes are small (-). CRL: minimal spacing (+).
Discrimination Method ✓ CS: linear layout (+). CRL: non-linear layout (-).	**Item Ordering and Grouping:** see GUIDE.
Spacing and Overlaps ✓ CS: no spacing (+). CRL: spacing between items/levels (-).	**Item Size and Shape** ✓ CS: items approached vertically, small item size (21 pixels) (-). CRL: large item size (circle diameters: 45-55 pixels) (+).
Item Ordering and Grouping: see GUIDE.	✓ CS: item size comparable to typical radio button (-). CRL: items bigger than typical radio button but do not impact distances (+).
SPACE	**Interaction Methods:** see EASY
Distances: see SEARCH	**LEARN**
Discrimination Method ✓ CS: linear layout (-). CRL: radial layout (+).	**Item Ordering and Grouping:** see GUIDE
Spacing and Overlaps ✓ CS: no spacing (+). CRL: some spacing (-).	**QUANT**
Item Size and Shape ✓ CS: big item area (-). CRL: smaller item area (+).	**Discrimination Method** ✓ CS: open levels (+). CRL: closed levels – first level especially limited (-).

Table 2. Differences between the CS and CRL menus according to the design guidelines defined in Table 1.

CASE STUDY

This section presents a case study that demonstrates use of the design space, by applying the presented guidelines in order to compare strength and weaknesses of two menu designs: a traditional cascading menu (see Figure 2) and the Compact Radial Layout menu (see Figure 3).

Figure 3 shows an example of a selection from the CRL menu. The levels of the menu hierarchy are represented as concentric rings while the items are represented as circles tightly packed within the rings. A user begins in the center of the menu and performs selections by pointing and clicking on items. For a detailed description of the CRL menu design see [39, 42].

We assign + or - for each guideline and menu depending on whether or not the menu supports a particular guideline. For guidelines involving qualitative measures, such as "shorten distances", we assign + and – based on comparisons between the menus. To save space, Table 2 shows only those guidelines that differentiate the menus. For an analysis of all guidelines see supplement material. Table 3

shows the total counts of + and – for each menu and goal.

To quickly summarize characteristics shared by both menus: both are unfolding and support selection preview, level preview, and path highlighting; both clearly communicate menu structure (i.e., menu levels and items); both do not overlap items; both use regular item shapes; both employ a Point-and-Click selection mechanism.

Discussion

The counts in Table 3 do not have any units and should not be used to draw particular conclusions. They hint, however, at possible design problems.

There is a large difference between the counts for the NAV goal (CS 4/9 vs CRL 11/2). It seems that the CRL menu better supports navigation than the CS menu. This observation is supported by the experimental results demonstrating that the CRL menu is faster and less error prone [39, 41, 42]. The identified problems of the CS menu design include long distances, small item sizes, high costs of under- and overshooting errors, restricted navigation trajectory (steering), and reliance on dwelling. It seems there is a lot of room for improvement. Some designs reduce the distances by allowing diagonal movements [48] or by overlapping levels [19] leading to better performance. The restricted trajectory and dwelling explain also the differences for the EASY goal (CS 4/2 vs CRL 6/0).

There is also a difference between the counts for the SEARCH goal (CS 5/1 vs CRL 3/3). In this case it seems that the CS menu better supports visual search. This observation is also supported by the experimental results [39, 40]. One reason is the radial (non-linear) layout of the CRL menu. This choice, however, is fundamental to

Menu Goal	CS		CRL	
	+	-	+	-
EASY	4	2	6	0
GUIDE	7	0	6	1
SEARCH	5	1	3	3
NAV	4	9	11	2
LEARN	2	0	1	1
QUANT	1	0	0	1
SPACE	3	4	5	2

Table 3. Counts of positive and negative effects for each menu and goal.

assuring better NAV support. Another reason for the CRL's worse SEARCH support is the lack of functional grouping.

The difference between the counts for the SPACE goal (CS 3/4 vs CRL 5/2) hints at the CS menu's worse utilization of the screen space. This is supported by the measurements of pixel consumption in [39]. The problem is again the long distances in the CS menu but also the large item area and the discrimination by length only. However, this last point enables the CS menu to be placed on the screen border in contrast to the CRL menu which expands in all directions due to its use of discrimination by both angle and length.

Finally, there is a difference between the counts for the QUANT goal (CS 1/0 vs CRL 0/1). In contrast to the CS menu, the CRL menu has closed levels (rings). The inner levels can accommodate fewer items as their circumferences are smaller. The problem is the most severe for the first level which seems to be able to accommodate only approximately eight items.

CONCLUSIONS AND FUTURE WORK

The paper presented a design space for graphical menus. It is modeled as a set of design goals, a set of design characteristics, and connections between the two. The goals are based on novice and expert behaviors. The connections indicate the positive or negative effects of different choices of values for design characteristics on the design goals.

The presented structure of the design space increases the resolution of insights that can be made. It is explicit in what goals are important for novices and experts, what are the ways of supporting these goals, what happens if specific design changes are made, what are some of the trade-offs.

The paper further synthesized the design space to a succinct form of structured guidelines which can be more readily applied to assess the strengths and weaknesses of different designs. A case study demonstrated how such an assessment can be carried out with arguably little effort.

But apart from comparing two different menus the design space and guidelines can also help in other situations: to review a single design; to compare two or more design modifications; to identify which design decisions require experimentation; and to spark new ideas. We believe that the design space is also a learning device as it reveals important factors that might have not been known before. Also researchers can benefit from it as a framework for organizing and planning further investigations.

It is important to note that the insights provided by the design space should be treated as hints rather than definitive truths. Each single design is a combination of many characteristics whose effects might not be additive but rather depend on complex interactions between the characteristics. Furthermore, the exact effect sizes of different characteristics vary. Future works could extend the current structure of the design space with the effect size ranges found in previous works.

Finally, a limitation of the presented work is the lack of formal evaluation of the design space and the guidelines. We identify that as an area for the future work. It will be particularly interesting to look at the effects of the design space on the ability of HCI novices and experts to identify the strengths and weaknesses of different designs.

The presented design space certainly does not contain all the important characteristics and those described in the paper could certainly be extended. The paper is only one step towards a better understanding of the design space of graphical menus. We hope that the future works can deepen this understanding.

ACKNOWLEDGMENTS

This work was supported by Science Foundation Ireland under Grant No. SFI/09/CE/I1380 (Líon2). I thank Jodi Schneider for extensive comments and discussions.

REFERENCES

1. Ahlström, D. Modeling and improving selection in cascading pull-down menus using Fitts' law, the steering law and force fields. *Proc. CHI* 2005, 61-70.
2. Accot, J. and Zhai, S. Beyond Fitts' Law: Models for trajectory-based HCI tasks. *Proc. CHI* 1997, 295-302.
3. Buxton B. Sketching User Experiences, Morgan Kaufmann, 2007.
4. Callahan, J., Hopkins, D., Weiser, M., and Shneiderman, B. An empirical comparison of pie vs. linear menus. *Proc. CHI* 1988, 95-100.
5. Card, S.K. User perceptual mechanisms in the search of computer command menus. *Proc. CHI* 1982, 190-196.
6. Card, S.K., Moran, T.P., and Newell, A. The Psychology of Human-Computer Interaction, 1983.
7. Charney, D., Reder, L., and Kusbit, G. Goal setting and procedure selection in acquiring computer skills: a comparison of problem solving and learner exploration. *Cognition and Instruction*, 7(4), 1990, 323-342.
8. Cockburn, A., Gutwin, C., and Greenberg, S. A predictive model of menu performance. *Proc. CHI'07*.
9. Feng, J., Sears, A. Beyond errors: measuring reliability for error-prone interaction devices. *J.B&IT*, 29(2), 2010.
10. Gan, K.C., and Hoffmann, E.R. Geometrical conditions for ballistic and visually controlled movements. In *Ergonomics*, 31(5), 1988, 829-839.
11. Graham, E.D., and MacKenzie, C.L. Physical versus virtual pointing. *Proc. CHI* 1996, 292-299.
12. Grossman, T., Kong, N., and Balakrishnan, R. Modeling pointing at targets of arbitrary shapes. *Proc. CHI* 2007.
13. Hollands, J.G., and Merikle, P.M. Menu organization and user expertise in information search tasks. In *J. Human Factors and Ergonomics Society*, 29(5), 1987.
14. Hornof, A.J., and Kieras, D.E. Cognitive modeling reveals menu search is both random and systematic. *Proc. CHI* 1997, 107-114.

15. Hornof, A.J. Visual search and mouse pointing in labeled versus unlabeled two-dimensional visual hierarchies. In *ToCHI*, ACM, 8(3), 171-197.

16. Inkpen, K.M. Drag-and-drop versus point-and-click mouse interaction styles for children. *ACM Transactions on Computer-Human Interaction*, 8(1), 2001, 1-33.

17. Kaptelinin, V. Item Recognition in menu selection: the effect of practice. *Proc. CHI* 1993, 183-184.

18. Kiger., J.I. The depth/breadth trade-off in the design of menu-driven user interfaces. *International Journal of Man-Machine Studies*, 20(2), 1984, 201-213.

19. Kobayashi, M., and Igarashi, T. Considering the direction of cursor movement for efficient traversal of cascading menus. *Proc. UIST* 2003, 91-94.

20. Kristensson, P.O., and Zhai, S. Command strokes with and without preview: using pen gestures on keyboard for command selection. *Proc. CHI* 2007, 1137-1146.

21. Kurtenbach, G. The design and evaluation of marking menus. PhD Thesis, the University of Toronto, 1993.

22. Kurtenbach, G., and Buxton, W. The limits of expert performance using hierarchic marking menus. *Proc. CHI/INTERACT* 1993, 482-487.

23. Kurtenbach, G., and Buxton, W. User learning and performance with marking menus. *Proc. CHI* 1994.

24. Landauer, T., and Nachbar, D. Selection from alphabetic and numeric menu trees using a touch screen: breadth, depth and width. *Proc. CHI* 1985, 73-78.

25. Lane, D.M., Napier, H.A., Batsell, R.R., and Naman, J.L. Predicting the skilled use of hierarchical menus with the keystroke-level model. *HCI*, 8(2), 1993.

26. Lee, E.S., and Raymond, D.R. Menu-driven systems. *Encyclopedia of Microcomputers*, 11, 1993, 101-127.

27. MacKenzie, I.S., Sellen, A., and Buxton, W. A comparison of input devices in elemental pointing and dragging tasks. *Proc. CHI* 1991, 161-166.

28. MacKenzie, I.S. Fitts' law as a research and design tool in human-computer interaction. *HCI*, 7(1), 1992, 91-139.

29. Mayes, J.T., Draper, S.W., McGregor, A.M., and Oatley, K. Information flow in a user interface: The effect of experience and context on the recall of MacWrite screens. *Proc. BCS HCI 1988*, 275-289.

30. Mcdonald, J.E., Stone, J.D., and Liebelt, L.S. Searching for items in menus: The effects of organization and type of target. *Proc. Human Factors Society*, 1983, 834–837.

31. Norman, K.L., and Chin, J.P. The effect of tree structure on search in a hierarchical menu selection system. *J. Behaviour & Information Technology*, 7(1), 1988.

32. Norman, K.L., and Butler, S. Search by uncertainty: menu selection by target probability. *Technical Report from the University of Maryland*, 1989.

33. Norman, K.L. The Psychology of Menu Selection. Ablex Publishing Corporation, 1991.

34. Oel, P., Schmidt, P., and Schmitt, A. Time Prediction of Mouse-based Cursor Movements. *Proc. CHI* 2001.

35. Paap, K.R., and Roske-Hofstrand, R.J. The optimal number of menu options per panel. *J. Human Factors & Ergonomics Society*, 28(4), 1986, 377-385.

36. Phillips, J.G., and Triggs, T.J. Characteristics of cursor trajectories controlled by the computer mouse. In *Ergonomics*, 44(5), 2001, 527-536.

37. Quinn, P., and Cockburn, A. The effects of menu parallelism on visual search and selection. *Proc. Conference on Australasian User Interface*, 76, 2008.

38. Robertson, G., McCracken, D., and Newell, A. The ZOG approach to man-machine communication. *Int. Journal of Man-Machine Studies*, 14, 1981, 461-488.

39. Samp, K., and Decker, S. Supporting menu design with radial layouts. *Proc. AVI 2010*, 155-162.

40. Samp, K., and Decker, S. Visual Search in Radial Menus. *Proc. INTERACT* 2011.

41. Samp, K., and Decker, S. Navigation Time Variability: Measuring Menu Navigation Errors. *Proc. INTERACT* 2011.

42. Samp, K. The Design and Evaluation of Graphical Radial Menus. Ph.D. Thesis, 2011.

43. Schmidt, R.A., Zelaznik, H., Hawkins, B., Frank, J.S., Quinn, J.T. Motor-output variability: A theory for the accuracy of rapid motor acts. *Psych. Review*, 86, 1979.

44. Sears, A., and Shneiderman, B. Split menus: effectively using selection frequency to organize menus. *Trans. on Computer-Human Interaction*, 1(1), 1994, 27-51.

45. Shneiderman, B., Plaisant, C., Cohen, M., Jacobs, S. Designing the User Interface: Strategies for Effective Human-Computer Interaction, Addison Wesley, 2009.

46. Snowberry, K., Parkinson, S. R., and Sisson, N. Computer display menus. In *Ergonomics*, 26(7), 1983.

47. Somberg, B.L. A comparison of rule-based and positionally constant arrangements of computer menu items. *Proc. CHI/GI* 1987, 255-260.

48. Tanvir, E., Cullen, J., Irani, P., Cockburn, A. AAMU: adaptive activation area menus for improving selection in cascading pull-down menus. *Proc. CHI* 2008.

49. Thompson, S.G. Effect on movement performance as a function of visual-motor scale and velocity: An investigation of the speed-accuracy tradeoff. PhD Thesis from the University of Louisiana at Monroe, 2007.

50. Tombaugh, J. and McEwen, S. Comparison of two information retrieval methods on Videotex: tree structure versus alphabetical directory. *Proc. CHI* 1982.

51. Treisman, A. Perceptual grouping and attention in visual search for features and for objects. *J. Experimental Psych.: Human Perception Performance*, 8(2), 1982.

52. Walker, N., Meyer, D.E., and Smelcer, J.B. Spatial and temporal characteristics of rapid cursor-positioning movements with electromechanical mice in human-computer interaction. *Human Factors*, 35(3), 1993.

53. Whisenand, T.G., and Emurian, H.H. Analysis of cursor movements with a mouse. *Proc. CHI* 1997, 533-536.

54. Wright, C.E., and Meyer, D.E. Conditions for a linear speed-accuracy trade-off in aimed movements. *J. Experimental Psychology*, 35A(2), 1983, 279-296.

55. Zhao, S., and Balakrishnan, R. Simple vs. compound mark hierarchical marking menus. *Proc. UIST* 2004.

Binocular Cursor: Enabling Selection on Transparent Displays Troubled by Binocular Parallax

Joon Hyub Lee, Seok-Hyung Bae

I²DEA Lab, Department of Industrial Design, KAIST

291 Daehak-ro, Yuseong-gu, Daejeon 305-701, Republic of Korea

joonhyub.lee | seokhyung.bae @kaist.ac.kr

ABSTRACT

Binocular parallax is a problem for any interaction system that has a transparent display and objects behind it, as users will see duplicated and overlapped images. In this note, we propose a quantitative measure called Binocular Selectability Discriminant (BSD) to predict the ability of the user to perform selection task in such a setup. In addition, we propose a technique called Binocular Cursor (BC) which takes advantage of this duplicating and overlapping phenomenon, rather than being hampered by it, to resolve binocular selection ambiguity by visualizing the correct selection point. An experiment shows that selection with BC is not slower than monocular selection, and that it can be significantly more precise, depending on the design of BC.

Author Keywords: Transparent display; binocular parallax.

ACM Classification: H.5.2 [Information Interfaces and Presentation]: User Interfaces - interaction styles.

General Terms: Design; Human Factors.

INTRODUCTION

Transparent displays are on the verge of commercialization. Users can look at physical and virtual objects through a transparent display, and combined with touch capability and augmentation techniques, they will be able to interact with it, even without additional gears.

However, unlike opaque displays, transparent displays are affected by binocular parallax, which occurs because a person's left and right eyes are horizontally offset and therefore see two different images, with 'convergence' determining how the two images are combined. When a person converges on the near object, the images are combined to produce a focused image for the near object, creating a duplicated and overlapped image for the distant object, and vice versa. When the user looks concurrently at objects at different distances through a transparent display and interacts with them, the parallax can potentially degrade the usability.

We performed a simple demonstration (Figure 1) with two cameras separated by 7 cm (simulating eyes) placed 45 cm from the fingertip (simulating comfortable arm length interaction on a transparent tablet), and a 4 cm diameter Ping-Pong ball (simulating the bounding sphere of a behind ob-

ject). In this configuration object distance as small as 30 cm caused significant parallax, rendering even basic interaction such as pointing difficult.

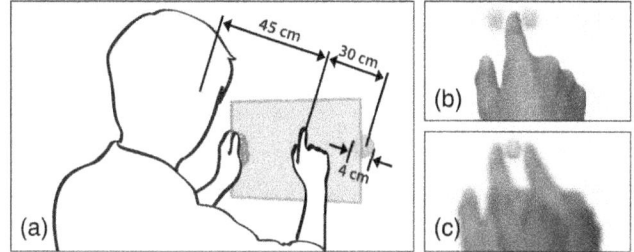

Figure 1. Binocular parallax can render interaction through a transparent tablet difficult (a). Images from left and right eyes are combined to create focused images for the fingertip (b) and the behind object (c).

In this note, we explain an approach of quantifying this problem, 'Binocular Selectability Discriminant (BSD)', a concept first introduced in an earlier work-in-progress publication [7], and an interaction technique, 'Binocular Cursor (BC)', that eliminates the ambiguity caused by the parallax, through appropriate visualization of the selection point.

RELATED WORK

A transparent display can serve as an augmentation window and display useful overlay information in a stationary setup, such as machining parameters over a CNC machining tool [11] and 3D annotation over a holographic 3D model [1]. In addition, when it is mobile and touch-enabled, a user can use the 'transparent tablet' to look at out-of-reach visual content such as a large-scale 3D model of a city, and manipulate it comfortably [9], through image plane interaction [12]. However, such interactions assume monocular vision, and binocular vision can cause ambiguity (Figure 1).

Some setups that use transparent panels as reflectors [3, 4] are configured such that when the overlay image from the source is reflected, it is at the same depth as the behind objects. These setups are unaffected by binocular parallax. We note that only the setups that use a transparent display as is [6], not as a reflector, are affected.

Stereoscopic 3D displays with touch input are also troubled by binocular ambiguity [14]. When selectable objects were displayed behind the screen stereoscopically, and the users were asked to select them by touching on the screen surface, they tended to select with the finger seen by the dominant eye, and also with the middle point in between the two duplicated finger images. It was found that selection performance could be enhanced by interpreting a selection as the touching with a specific point in between the two points.

However, even with such a remedy, selection is still ambiguous for the user, making it difficult to select from a crowded scene or perform more complex tasks. To overcome this problem, some selection techniques to disambiguate selection have been suggested [13], such as displaying a cursor selectively to the dominant eye only. Unfortunately, such a technique is specific to stereoscopic setups only and inapplicable for direct touch input. Thus, an unambiguous selection technique specific to touch-capable transparent displays remains to be studied.

BINOCULAR SELECTABILITY DISCRIMINANT

We define Binocular Selectability Discriminant (BSD), which quantifies the extent of binocular parallax and tests whether it will cause a problem when a user performs a selection task on a transparent tablet. We chose selection because it is often essential for higher level tasks.

In the simplified model (Figure 2), a user with an eye-to-eye distance of 'L' (~7 cm) holds the transparent display at distance 'D' (~45 cm), and attempts to select an object with width 'w' and distance 'd' from the display by placing his finger on the display. When the user converges on the object, the image of the finger is duplicated with distance 'p' apart. From similar triangles, p is Ld/D.

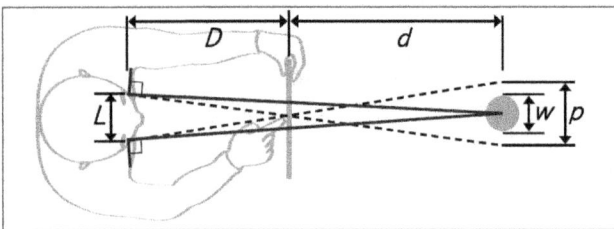

Figure 2. Diagram for deriving Binocular
Selectability Discriminant (BSD).

For selection to be possible, p must be smaller than w, not considering the finger thickness. The discriminant writes:

$$\text{BSD} \equiv \frac{w}{d} - \frac{L}{D}$$

Large BSD corresponds to easy selection (Figure 3a), BSD of 0 to barely possible selection (Figure 3b), and BSD of less than 0 to impossible selection (Figure 3c). This simple model allows us to predict the user's ability to make an unambiguous selection depending on the above parameters.

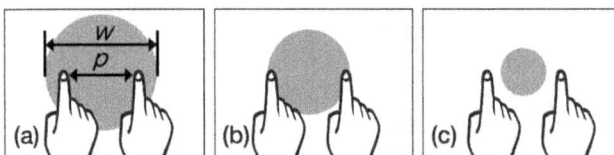

Figure 3. Easy to select (BSD > 0) (a), barely able to select
(BSD = 0) (b), unable to select unambiguously (BSD < 0) (c).

BINOCULAR CURSOR

Difficulty of Visualizing Selection Point

When binocular ambiguity is beyond a certain threshold (BSD < 0), explicit visualization of the selection point can enable unambiguous selection. However, such a visualization is difficult: when the user attempts to select an object, the user converges on the object [10], causing any imagery displayed on the nearer transparent tablet to become dupli-

cated and overlapped. To avoid this, visualization can be placed at the object distance so that the user is able to converge on the object and visualization simultaneously, but this requires additional hardware such as a network of projectors configured to cover the entire selection space. Such a setup can be undesirable, especially for mobile use.

Binocular Cursor (BC) Concept

We present Binocular Cursor (BC), which visualizes the selection point directly on the transparent tablet, taking advantage of the duplicating/overlapping phenomenon, rather than being hampered by it. When a user attempts to select a behind object, two partial cursors appear on the left and right of the finger. These partial cursors are arranged such that when the user converges on the distant object, the partial cursors appropriately duplicate and overlap to complete the cursor (Figure 4). BC appears upon touch and is maintained while the user moves it around, and selection is made when the finger lifts, as in an offset cursor [15]. Even with completed BC, the partial cursors are still visible, but we assume that users will focus on the completed cursors and not pay attention to the peripheral artifacts.

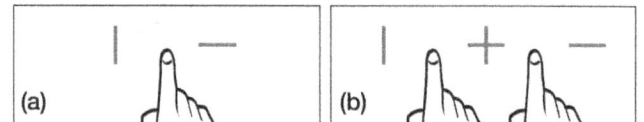

Figure 4. Partial cursors (a) adequately duplicate and overlap to
create a complete Binocular Cursor (BC) when the user converges on the behind object (b).

Binocular Cursor Design

Partial cursors can be horizontally shifted to visualize different selection points. The two most intuitive selection points are at the dominant eye image of the finger (DE BC) (Figure 5) and the middle of the two finger images (ME BC, where ME stands for 'middle eye') (Figure 4) [14]. While horizontal and vertical partial cursors can switch sides for ME BC due to symmetry, they cannot for DE BC, because the horizontal line needs to be placed on the finger and the vertical line on the left (right DE) or right (left DE) to avoid finger occlusion. In addition, DE BC requires more space and selection near the display edges can be troublesome, as one of the partial BC can go outside the screen. But this may not be problematic as the users would normally point their mobile devices to the object of interest, and not deliberately use peripheral regions for interaction.

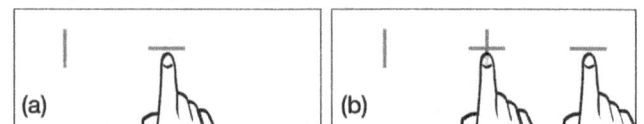

Figure 5. Partial cursors horizontally shifted (a) to place BC on
the dominant eye image of the finger, converged (b).

Moreover, BC can be designed to create an area cursor (OBC) that can increase the effective target size (Figure 6), with which users can select smaller targets faster with less error [2], compared to a crosshair BC (+BC). The size of the area cursor can be adjusted depending on the object density in the user's view of the scene through the tablet.

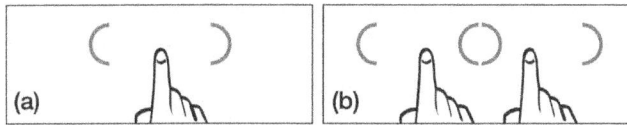

Figure 6. Partial cursors designed to create an area BC (a), converged (b).

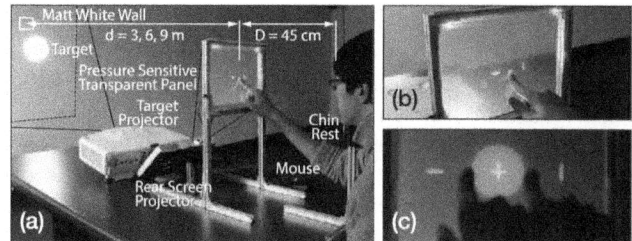

Figure 7. The experiment setup (a); rear-projected, touch-sensitive transparent display (b); a combined image to simulate the user's view of BC while converging on the target (c).

Data Acquisition

To implement BC, the system requires the 3D positions of the two eyes, and the positions and sizes of the selectable objects behind the tablet. While the eye positions relative to the tablet can be obtained directly using commercial sensors, different strategies are needed to obtain sizes and distances of selectable objects of different types. When selectable objects are virtual, e.g. 2D and 3D objects displayed on a distant screen, or holograms [1, 9, 11], their sizes and relative positions are usually known. When selectable objects are physical, the surrounding environment needs to be scanned and segmented [5]. When selectable objects are environmental, the tablet's position and orientation relative to a pre-surveyed environment are needed.

EVALUATION

An experiment was conducted to verify 6 hypotheses:

H1. BCs will be as quick as ONE EYE.
H2. BCs will be as precise as ONE EYE.
H3. DE BCs will be quicker than ME BCs.
H4. DE BCs will be more precise than ME BCS.
H5. ○BCs will be quicker than +BCs.
H6. ○BCs will be more precise than +BCs.

Apparatus & Implementation

We created a transparent tablet using a 15″ pressure-sensitive transparent overlay panel, a commercially available component that adds basic single touch capability to an LCD screen. Since it is cheap and opaque enough (20% opaque), we used it as a rear-projection screen, upon which BCs were projected (Figure 7).

To focus on testing the feasibility of BC, the degree of freedom was minimized: the position of the tablet was fixed by mounting it on a custom-built profile structure, and the positions of the user's eyes were also fixed with a chin rest planted 45 cm in front of the tablet (Figure 7a).

The experiment was conducted in a large lecture room with low lighting condition. The targets simulating bounding spheres of selectable objects of variable sizes were projected onto the matt, white wall with another projector, with the target distance varied by moving the setup closer to or farther away from the wall (Figure 7a).

We used 4-point calibration to align the 4 corners of the target projection area on the distant wall with that of the transparent tablet in the perspective of each of the two eyes.

Participants

12 volunteers (3 female, 9 male), with age ranging from 22 to 32 participated in the experiment. All were right-handed. We used the Porta test and the Dolman test to determine the eyedness [8]. 11 were right and 1 was left eye dominant.

Procedure & Task

After the pretests, a warm-up session was held for each participant for about 10 minutes. During this session, the eye-to-eye distance (L in Figure 2), the distance between the centers of pupils, was measured and finely adjusted until the participant could see a correctly converging BC.

The participant selected targets appearing at random locations by touching on the tablet with the index finger of the dominant hand (Figure 7b). The participant was instructed to use a mouse at a specified position and to right-click with the dominant hand to initiate each selection task. The participant lifted the finger off the screen when they judged that a selection was made. No visual feedback was given for correct or incorrect selection to allow for selection error. Each experiment lasted about 40 minutes.

Design

A repeated measures within-participant design was used. The independent variables were: target distance (3, 6, 9 m, d in Figure 2 & Figure 7a); cursor type (ONE EYE, +ME, +DE, ○ME, ○DE); target size (apparent diameters 1/16, 1/8, 1/4, 1/2, 1, 2 times the finger images separation distance p in Figure 3a & Figure 7c). Each participant made 450 selections (3 target distances × 5 cursor types × 6 target sizes × 5 blocks).

We counterbalanced the presentation order of target distance with a balanced Latin square. At each target distance, the participant first selected with the non-dominant eye closed (ONE EYE) without BC, and then with different BCs in a counterbalanced presentation order. The sizes of BCs were set to span 1/4 of the apparent distance between the finger images (Figure 7c). For each cursor type, differently sized targets appeared in a random order, each appearing 5 times.

Results & Discussion

Selection time (ms), defined as the time taken from the right-click initiation to the last lifting of the finger, and selection error, defined as the on-screen distance (mm) between the nearest correct selection point to the touched point, were the dependent variables.

Repeated measures ANOVA showed significant main effects for cursor type ($F_{4,44} = 19$, $p < .01$) and target size ($F_{5,55} = 98$, $p < .01$) on selection time, but not for target distance ($F_{2,22} = .015$, $p = .86$) (Figure 8).

Post-hoc pairwise comparison test showed that selection time differences were not significant between ONE EYE and $\bigcirc$DE (p = 1.0), not between ONE EYE and $\bigcirc$ME (p = .052), significant between ONE EYE and +ME (p < .01), and between ONE EYE and +DE (p < .01), thus *partially confirming H1*. The differences were significant between $\bigcirc$ME and $\bigcirc$DE (p < .05), but not between +ME and +DE (p = 1.0), thus *rejecting H3*. In addition, the differences were significant between +ME and $\bigcirc$ME (p < .05), and between +DE and $\bigcirc$DE (p < .01), thus *confirming H5*.

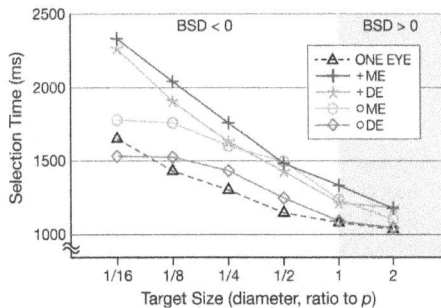

Figure 8. Selection time for cursor types and target sizes.

Repeated measures ANOVA showed significant main effects for cursor type ($F_{4,44}$ = 17, p < .01) target size ($F_{5,55}$ = 38, p < .01) on selection error, and target distance ($F_{2,22}$ = 3.7, p < .05) (Figure 9).

Post-hoc pairwise comparison test showed that selection error differences were not significant between ONE EYE and +ME (p = .65), and between ONE EYE and +DE (p = 1.0). $\bigcirc$ME and $\bigcirc$DE were both significantly more precise than ONE EYE (p < .01), thus *confirming H2*. The differences were not significant between +ME and +DE (p = 1.0) and between $\bigcirc$ME and $\bigcirc$DE (p = 1.0), thus *rejecting H4*. Lastly, the differences were significant between +ME and $\bigcirc$ME (p < .05) and between +DE and $\bigcirc$DE (p < .01), thus *confirming H6*.

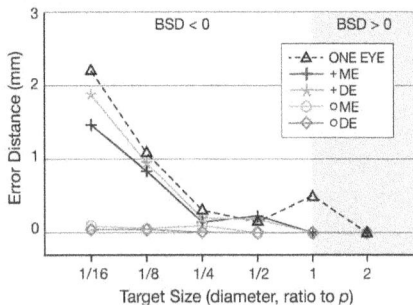

Figure 9. Error distance for cursor types and target sizes.

We compared BCs against monocular selection because it was the only comparable technique with which users could select unambiguously. However, many people cannot wink voluntarily, and even for those who can, it can be fatiguing if it lasts for more than a short period of time. In our experiment, some participants were allowed to block one eye with the non-selecting hand, but in practice, they would not be able to do so because he/she would be holding the mobile transparent tablet with it. Still, monocular image plane interaction by itself is effective and efficient [12], and the fact that selection with BC can be as quick and also more precise, without the inconvenience, shows BC's usefulness.

CONCLUSION AND FUTURE WORK

Unlike opaque displays, transparent displays are inherently susceptible to usability degradations caused by binocular parallax. We suggested a measure (BSD) that can quantify this problem and a technique (BC) that rather uses the parallax to enable unambiguous selection, with competent performances. In the near future, we will implement BC with higher DOF so that both the face and transparent tablet can move, and evaluate it in actual application.

REFERENCES

1. Bimber, O. (2006). Augmenting holograms. *IEEE CG&A*, 26(5), 12-17.
2. Grossman, T. & Balakrishnan, R. (2005). The bubble cursor: enhancing target acquisition by dynamic resizing of the cursor's activation area. *Proc. CHI'05*, 281-290.
3. Hachet, M., Bossavit, B., Cohé, A., & de la Rivière, J. (2011). Toucheo: multitouch and stereo combined in a seamless workspace. *Proc. UIST'11*, 587-592.
4. Hilliges, O., Kim, D., Izadi, S., Weiss, M., & Wilson, A. (2012). HoloDesk: direct 3D interactions with a situated see-through display. *Proc. CHI'12*, 2421-2430.
5. Izadi, S., Kim, D., Hilliges, O., Molyneaux, D., Newcombe, R., Kohli, P., Shotton, J., Hodges, S., Freeman, D., Davison, A., & Fitzgibbon, A. (2011). KinectFusion: real-time 3D reconstruction and interaction using a moving depth camera. *Proc. UIST'11*, 559-568.
6. Lee, J. & Boulanger, C. (2012). Direct spatial interactions with see-through 3D desktop, *SIGGRAPH'12 Poster*.
7. Lee, J., Bae, S., Jung, J., & Choi, H. (2012). Transparent display interaction without binocular parallax. *Adj. Proc. UIST'12*, 97-98.
8. Mapp, A., Ono, H., & Barbeito, R. (2003). What does the dominant eye dominate? A brief and somewhat contentious review. *Perception & Psychophysics*, 65(2), 310-317.
9. Schmalstieg, D., Encarnação, L., & Szalavári, Z. (1999). Using transparent props for interaction with the virtual table. *Proc. I3D'99*, 147-153.
10. Sherstyuk, A., Dey, A., Sandor, C., & State, A. (2012). Dynamic eye convergence for head-mounted displays improves user performance in virtual environments. *Proc. I3D'12*, 23-30.
11. Olwal, A., Gustafsson, J., & Lindfors, C. (2008). Spatial augmented reality on industrial CNC machines. *Proc. SPIE'08 Electronic Imaging*.
12. Pierce, J., Forsberg, A., Conway, M., Hong, S., Zeleznik, R., & Mine, M. (1997). Image plane interaction techniques in 3D immersive environments. *Proc. I3D'97*, 39-44.
13. Teather, R. & Stuerzlinger, W. (2011). Pointing at 3D targets in a stereo head-tracked virtual environment. *Proc. 3DUI'11*, 87-94.
14. Valkov, D., Steinicke, F., Bruder, G., & Hinrichs, K. (2011). 2D touching of 3D stereoscopic objects. *Proc. CHI'11*, 1353-1362.
15. Vogel, D. & Baudisch, P. (2007). Shift: a technique for operating pen-based interfaces using touch. *Proc. CHI'07*, 657-666.

Studying Spatial Memory and Map Navigation Performance on Projector Phones with Peephole Interaction

Bonifaz Kaufmann
Alpen-Adria-Universität Klagenfurt, Austria
bonifaz.kaufmann@aau.at

David Ahlström
Alpen-Adria-Universität Klagenfurt, Austria
david.ahlstroem@aau.at

ABSTRACT

Smartphones are useful personal assistants and omnipresent communication devices. However, collaboration is not among their strengths. With the advent of embedded projectors this might change. We conducted a study with 56 participants to find out if map navigation and spatial memory performance among users and observers can be improved by using a projector phone with a peephole interface instead of a smartphone with its touchscreen interface. Our results show that users performed map navigation equally well on both interfaces. Spatial memory performance, however, was 41% better for projector phone users. Moreover, observers of the map navigation on the projector phone were 25% more accurate when asked to recall locations of points of interest after they watched a user performing map navigation.

Author Keywords

Map navigation; spatial memory; peephole interaction; touch interaction; handheld projector.

ACM Classification Keywords

H.5.m. Information interfaces and presentation (e.g., HCI): Miscellaneous.

INTRODUCTION

Smartphones are popular portals for many daily activities, such as communication, note taking, web surfing, and map navigation. Although well suited for personal assistance, they perform badly in collaborative settings, mainly due to their small screen size. In addition, interacting with fingers on a touchscreen makes it even more difficult for collaborators to look at the screen. Indeed, many tasks on a smartphone are not intended and designed for collaboration (e.g., taking a picture, texting, etc.), however, other tasks like picture viewing, web browsing, or map navigation would benefit from enhanced collaborative features.

One way to facilitate collaboration is to embed a projector into a smartphone – e.g., the Samsung Galaxy Beam projector phone – and to project the screen content for better visibility for collaborators. In this paper we

investigate how well such projector phones can support collaboration and performance in a map navigation task. Map navigation on a smartphone is a common activity used by travelers to find out where they are and where to go. Normally, one person is interacting with the map application while fellow travelers are looking over the shoulder. One key aspect for collaboration on a mobile device is how well people can follow what the operator is doing. Constructing a mental map of the surrounding and to recall the relative locations of points of interest is important for later situations with no access to the previously inspected map. Considering the amount of zooming, panning, and hand occlusion involved when using interactive map applications on small screen devices, this can be very challenging for both observers and the operator.

Peephole interaction [3, 12] – a promising interaction method for handheld projectors [1, 2, 6, 9] – provides an interesting, yet largely unexplored, alternative for collaborative settings with operators and observers. In contrast to scroll and pan interfaces, where the workspace is moved 'behind' a stationary screen, in peephole interfaces the screen (i.e., the peephole) is moved across the stationary workspace. The effect is akin to using a flashlight to look around a dark room without entering (cf. Figure 1).

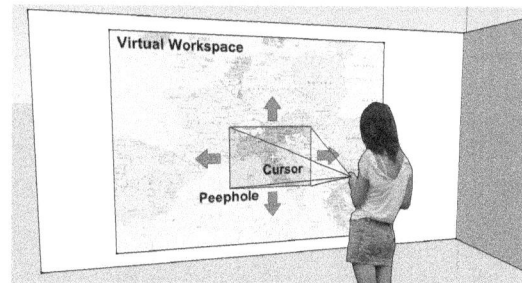

Figure 1. Peephole interaction allows for interacting with a large virtual workspace. The peephole is moved by pointing with the device. The cursor stays fixed at the peephole center.

Peephole interaction has the advantage that virtual items seem to be attached to the real environment (i.e., the projection surface). This might improve the ability to construct a mental map of the virtual content, whereas in traditional scroll and pan interfaces spatial information about items must be integrated with respect to the amount of scrolling and panning being performed [5].

Previous research has shown that peephole interfaces outperform scroll and pan interfaces in navigation and spatial memory performance [8, 4] as well as joystick interaction on mobile phones [10]. However, as far as we know, spatial memory and map navigation performance of peephole interfaces have never been compared with mobile touch interfaces, and it is unknown how peephole interaction with a projector phone influence recall performance for observing collaborators.

With our study we take the next step. We use a map navigation task and compare: (i) users' map navigation performance with touch screen interaction to peephole interaction, (ii) users' location recall performance, and (iii) observers' location recall performance. This study is the first showing usage and benefit of a handheld projector over a touch phone in terms of recall performance for both actors and observers.

EXPERIMENT

We conducted an experiment in which a user (actor) searched for and navigated between marked points of interest (markers) on a map. A second participant (observer) standing next to the actor had to observe and memorize the locations of the markers. The actor performed the navigation task on a handheld projector using peephole interaction and on a smartphone using touch screen input. After completing the navigation task, participants were asked to recall the marker positions.

Apparatus and Interfaces

On-screen navigation took place on a Samsung Nexus S (Android 4.0.4) with a screen resolution of 480×800 pixels. It was operated through standard pan and tap interactions on the touch screen. The map application was based on Google Maps and used the same interaction design for on-screen navigation. Peephole navigation was made on a prototype consisting of a LG Optimus 3D (Android 2.2) connected via HDMI to a MicroVision SHOWWX+ laser pico projector (800×480 pixels) attached to its back. Inertial sensors were used to implement the peephole interface (as described in [7]). A cross-hair cursor at the center of the peephole allowed users to select items (confirmed by a tap on the screen). The peephole/projection was moved across a 4×3 meters large wall from two meters distance resulting in a projection size of 1.2x0.7 meters; actor and observer maintained the same distance to the projection.

Participants, Task and Experimental Design

Participants were grouped in pairs (actor and observer). We recruited 28 actors (13 female) aged 10-46 years (mean 24.8, s.d. 9.3) and 28 observers (10 female) aged 17 to 72 years (mean 34.1, s.d. 13.7). Removing the youngest actors (10, 12, 14 yrs) and the oldest observers (50, 66, 72 yrs) did not change our results, thus we decided to report on data from all participants. All actors were daily smartphone users, but had never used a projector phone before.

The actor presses a start button, timing starts and the display (on-screen or projection, depending on interface) shows a start marker (M0) on a map. The actor navigates

the map, searching for seven target markers (M1 to M7) in ascending order (Figure 2). When the next marker is found the actor selects it (tapping it for on-screen, positioning the cross-hair cursor over the marker and tapping the screen, for peephole), the search time for that marker stops, search time for the following marker starts. Having found the last marker (M7), the first of three rounds is completed and the next round starts over from M0. Depending on interface, the observer follows the navigation activities on the screen resp. on the wall. Since the following reconstruction task involves recalling and positioning markers on a white background, the observer was asked to memorize the positions of the markers without using landmarks from the map. The actor, however, is not informed about the upcoming recall task for the observer.

When the third round is completed with the first interface, the actor, who does not know what the observer is instructed to do, is introduced to the second interface. Meanwhile, the observer tries to reconstruct the navigated route by placing seven markers on a white desktop screen. The start marker M0 is centered on the screen to serve as an initial reference point. The size of the marker provides the only clue for proportions. After the recall task, the observer joins the actor who then begins the navigation task with a different map and different marker positions using the second interface. When the navigation task is completed on the second interface, the actor is informed about the recall task and both, actor and observer, reconstruct the last navigation route on separate desktop screens.

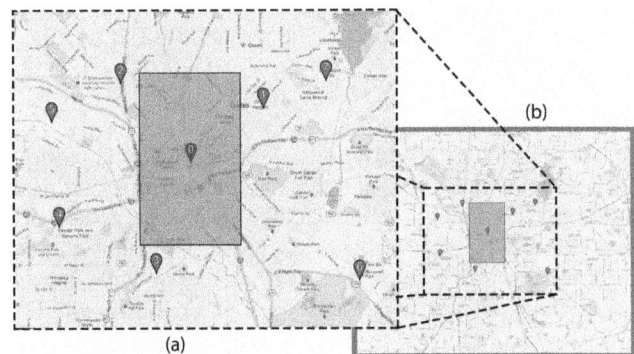

Figure 2. (a) Marker positions. (b) The accessible area shown with correct proportions to the screen (green rectangle).

Half of the participating pairs started with on-screen, half with peephole. Two different city maps were used for timed trials (Dallas and Houston), a third map for initial practice. Interface and map were counterbalanced between pairs. Marker locations on the two maps were mirrored to keep complexity constant across maps. For data analysis Houston data was normalized to Dallas data, allowing us to consider it as of being from one single navigation path.

We implemented semantic zooming so that markers would vanish when actors zoomed out. Because of the semantic zoom and since zooming in reduces overview, all actors decided not to utilize zooming. Figure 2b shows the proportion of the visible area (green rectangle) in relation to the entire Dallas map with its markers. The red outline defined the end of the map and indicated actors not to search further in that direction.

We hypothesize that search time will be faster with the peephole interface as it does not require frequent and time consuming panning gestures. Moreover, the peephole interface should provide faster search times by making it easier for the actors (and observers) to mentally register and 'place' markers at physical relative locations (on the wall). Location memory should be improved with better recall performance in later situations with no access to the map.

Results

Navigation Results

Marker search times were positively skewed. We performed a logarithmic transformation and obtained distributions close to normal. Following analyses are based on the log-transformed data.

The geometric mean search time (i.e., the antilog of the mean of the log-transformed data) across rounds was 28.2s with the smartphone and 23.4s with the peephole projector (Figure 3a). A 2×3×7 (interface: smartphone, projector; round: 1, 2, 3; marker: 1–7) repeated measures ANOVA showed no significant main effect for interface.

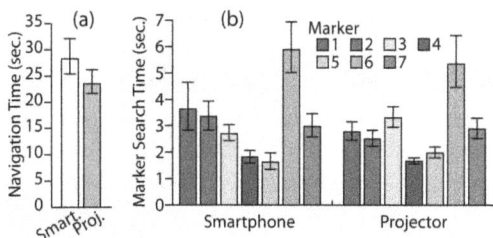

Figure 3. (a) Geometric mean time for interfaces.
(b) Geometric mean time interface-marker combinations.
Error bars show 95% confidence intervals.

Across the two interfaces, round had a significant effect on search time ($F_{2,54} = 26.3$, $p < 0.0001$, $\eta^2 = 0.48$) indicating a learning effect, as expected. Post-hoc pairwise comparisons (these and all subsequent post-hoc comparisons were Bonferroni adjusted) showed that all rounds differed with the first round being the slowest at a geometric mean search time of 33.6s compared to 24.3s and 21.9s for the second and third rounds, respectively. This shows a clear learning effect with participants improving as they gradually learned the rough position of the markers from previous visits.

The geometric mean search time for each marker with each interface is shown in Figure 3b. The ANOVA showed a main effect for marker ($F_{4.1,110.9} = 38.4$, $p < 0.0001$, $\eta^2 = 0.59$, Greenhouse-Geisser corrected). Post-hoc comparisons showed that M6 was slower to find than all other markers; among all markers, M6 was located furthest away from the preceding marker. Marker 1, 2, 3, and 7 were slower than marker 4 and 5. The improved search time for marker 4 and 5 might have resulted from their closeness to their

respective predecessors. This increased the likelihood to catch a glimpse of these markers when targeting for the corresponding predecessor.

Recall Results

We measured recall performance by calculating the Euclidean distance for each placed marker to the correct marker location. Given the fundamental difference in knowing or not knowing about the recall task during the navigation task we do not directly compare actors' and observers' recall performance. For both data sets we found positively skewed Euclidean distances from the correct marker positions. We therefore performed a logarithmic transformation (which resulted in distributions close to normal) before the data was analyzed.

Figure 4a shows the geometric mean distances for each role-device combination: for actors, 177 pixels with the smartphone and 105 pixels with the projector; for observers, 129 pixels with the smartphone and 97 pixels with the projector.

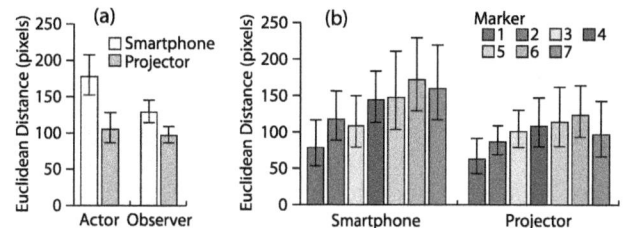

Figure 4. (a) Geometric mean Euclidean distance for interface-role combinations. (b) Geometric mean Euclidean distance for interface-marker combinations for observers. Error bars show 95% confidence intervals.

Actor: A 2×7 (interface, marker) mixed design repeated measures ANOVA (with interface as a between-subject factor) for the actor data showed a significant difference of 41% between the two interfaces ($F_{1,26} = 6.8$, $p < 0.01$, $\eta^2 = 0.21$) and no significant main effect for marker or device×marker interaction.

Observer: A 2×7 (interface, marker) repeated measures ANOVA for the observer data showed a significant difference of 25% between the two interfaces ($F_{1,27} = 7.2$, $p < 0.01$, $\eta^2 = 0.25$). There was also a significant main effect for marker ($F_{6,162} = 6.3$, $p < 0.001$, $\eta^2 = 0.19$) but no interface×marker interaction (cf. Figure 4b).

Post-hoc pairwise comparisons showed that the first marker differed from marker 4, 5, and 6 and that there were no differences between any other pairs. Behind the good accuracy of the first marker, we probably see a primacy effect reflecting participants being more likely to correctly remember the first item in the 'list' of markers.

The spread around the correct marker positions for each role-device combination is shown in Figure 5. The recalled positions of all participants for a specific marker are represented by a uniform symbol (e.g., purple circles represent M1 recalls, brown diamonds M2, etc.).

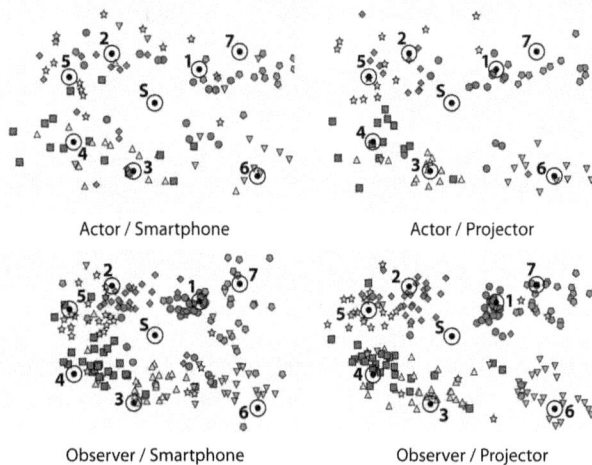

Figure 5. Participants' recalled marker locations for all four role-device combinations.

DISCUSSION

The navigation results show that the peephole interface performed at least as good as the on-screen interface. At the beginning, however, we anticipated the peephole interface to be significantly faster, expecting users to find markers more easily with the handheld projector. Instead, users seem to be highly accustomed to map navigation on mobile touchscreens and the benefit of having kinesthetic cues [11] in handheld projector interaction did not evolve. On the other hand, the results are looking promising, considering that no participant had ever used a handheld projector before and all were new to peephole interaction, but had used smartphones for at least several months. In addition, participants reported that getting lost on the touchscreen was very frustrating as compared to the peephole interface. With the peephole it was easier to remember which areas had been searched and which ones had been left out. However, a projected display requires a suitable projection surface and will not work well under bright light conditions, rendering projected peephole interaction less general to use.

Along with our hypothesis, the peephole interface performed better in the recall task. Observers generally underestimated relative distances between markers on the touchscreen interface, as visible in Figure 5. With the peephole interface, users can memorize marker locations in respect to their own body and surrounding, whereas with the touchscreen interface, the spatial layout can only be memorized indirectly through integration of the amount of panning and scrolling being involved. As reported in previous studies, this effect also benefits object size [4] and line length [8] discrimination tasks.

CONCLUSION AND FUTURE WORK

Peephole interaction with projector phones enables a group of people to look at a large screen without the occlusion of fingers from the mobile device operator. Moreover, our results show that accessing large workspaces through a projected peephole interface improves spatial memory

performance for actors and observers when compared to a touchscreen interface. Remarkably, even without extensive training on a projector phone's peephole interface, users' map navigation performance on a projector phone was on the same level as on a familiar touchscreen phone. Apart from scrolling and panning, map navigation often requires zooming. In future work, we want to find out how zooming affects spatial memory and navigation performance on projected peephole interfaces.

REFERENCES

1. Beardsley, P., van Baar, J., Raskar, R., and Forlines, C. Interaction using a handheld projector. *IEEE Computer Graphics and Applications 25*, 1 (2005), 39-43.

2. Cao, X. and Balakrishnan, R. Interacting with dynamically defined information spaces using a handheld projector and a pen. In *Proc. UIST 2006*, ACM (2006), 225-234.

3. Fitzmaurice, W.G. Situated information spaces and spatially aware palmtop computers. *Communications of the ACM 36*, 7 (1993), 39-49.

4. Hürst, W. and Bilyalov, T. Dynamic versus static peephole navigation of VR panoramas on handheld devices. In *Proc. MUM 2010*. ACM (2010), 25:1-25:8.

5. Jetter, H-C., Leifert, S., Gerken, J., Schubert, S., and Reiterer, H. Does (multi-)touch aid users' spatial memory and navigation in 'panning'and in 'zooming & panning' UIs? In *Proc. AVI 2012*, ACM (2012), 83-90.

6. Kaufmann, B. and Ahlström, D. Revisiting peephole pointing: a study of target acquisition with a handheld projector. In *Proc. MobileHCI 2012*, ACM (2012), 211-220.

7. Kaufmann, B. and Hitz, M. X-Large virtual workspaces for projector phones through peephole interaction. In *Proc. MM 2012*, ACM (2012), 1279-1280.

8. Mehra, S., Werkhoven, P., and Worring, M. Navigating on handheld displays: dynamic versus static peephole navigation. *ACM Transactions on Computer-Human Interaction 13*, 4 (2006), 448-457.

9. Rapp, S. Spotlight Navigation: a pioneering user interface for mobile projection. In *Proc. Ubiprojection, Workshop on personal projection at Pervasive* (2010).

10. Rohs, M., Schöning, J., Raubal, M., Essl, G., and Krüger, A. Map navigation with mobile devices: virtual versus physical movement with and without visual context. In *Proc. ICMI 2007*, ACM (2007), 146-153.

11. Tan, D.S., Pausch, R., Stefanucci, J.K., and Proffitt, D.R. Kinesthetic cues aid spatial memory. *Ext. Abstracts CHI 2000*, ACM (2002), 806-807.

12. Yee, K. Peephole displays: pen interaction on spatially aware handheld computers. In *Proc. CHI 2003,* ACM (2003), 1-8.

Why Do They Still Use Paper? Understanding Data Collection and Use in Autism Education

Gabriela Marcu, Kevin Tassini, Quintin Carlson, Jillian Goodwyn,
Gabrielle Rivkin, Kevin J. Schaefer, Anind K. Dey, Sara Kiesler
Human-Computer Interaction Institute, Carnegie Mellon University
{gmarcu@cs, qcc@andrew, jgoodwyn@andrew,
grivkin@andrew, kjschaef@andrew, anind@cs, kiesler@cs}.cmu.edu, tassini@punchcut.com

ABSTRACT

Autism education programs for children collect and use large amounts of behavioral data on each student. Staff use paper almost exclusively to collect these data, despite significant problems they face in tracking student data *in situ*, filling out data sheets and graphs on a daily basis, and using the sheets in collaborative decision making. We conducted fieldwork to understand data collection and use in the domain of autism education to explain why current technology had not met staff needs. We found that data needs are complex and unstandardized, immediate demands of the job interfere with staff ability to collect *in situ* data, and existing technology for data collection is inadequate. We also identified opportunities for technology to improve sharing and use of data. We found that data sheets are idiosyncratic and not useful without human mediation; improved communication with parents could benefit children's development; and staff are willing, and even eager, to incorporate technology. These factors explain the continued dependence on paper for data collection in this environment, and reveal opportunities for technology to support data collection and improve use of collected data.

Author Keywords

Fieldwork; Contextual inquiry; CSCW.

ACM Classification Keywords

J.4 Computer Applications: Social and Behavioral Sciences; K.3.1 Computers and Education: Computer Uses in Education.

General Terms

Human Factors; Design.

INTRODUCTION

Children with special needs such as autism enter special education programs when conventional schools are not able to support their learning and behavioral needs. Children with special needs require support to learn subjects such as math and reading at their own pace, and to learn language, social, and motor skills that may be underdeveloped. Children with special needs also may exhibit problem behaviors such as anxiety, disruptiveness, and aggression. These behaviors need to be understood so appropriate

interventions can be applied to help the child overcome them. To individualize students' education based on their unique needs, staff in special education programs collect learning and behavioral data that help them diagnose problems, evaluate the effectiveness of interventions, and monitor progress over time. Under U.S. special education laws, quantifiable evidence of progress is required for reports to parents, school districts, and state agencies.

Each child with autism has unique, complex, and changing needs, making each day in special education unpredictable. To set the scene for this paper, we developed the following scenarios from our fieldwork. They highlight the issues that impact data collection in the autism classroom, which we refer to throughout the paper.

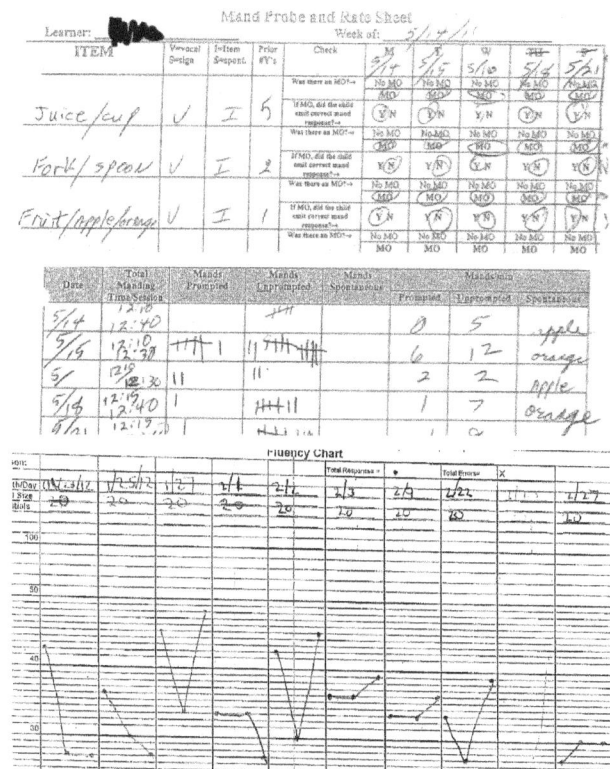

Figure 1. Three sample sheets used to collect behavioral data on paper. (Top) Two sheets filled out *in situ* while working on the language skill, manding—verbally requesting a desired object such as a cup of juice or an apple. (Bottom) A chart used to graph student fluency data—*i.e.*, the ability to recall mastered skills—by hand each day.

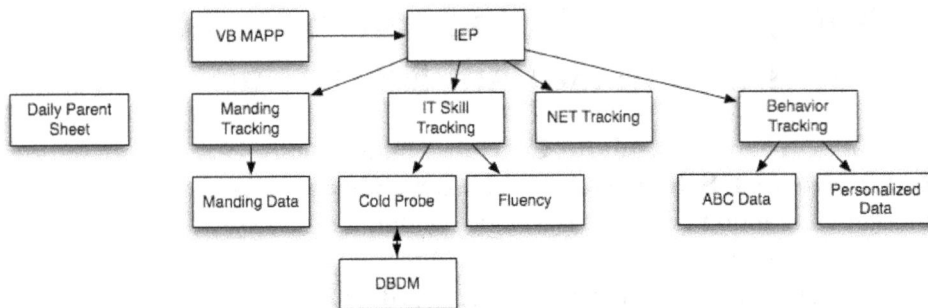

Figure 2. (Left) Our model of the data sheets used by a school, demonstrating the complexity caused by a large number of highly specialized sheets. (Right) A teacher's desk at the same school, with a lot of storage for data sheets – a bookcase full of binders on the left, and a filing cabinet on the right.

Behaviors. Amanda, 10 years old, has suddenly begun displaying negative reactions to balls. Her mother reports similar behavior at home. Her siblings can no longer play basketball in front of their house because Amanda will become very upset. Having removed all anxiety-provoking objects from Amanda's sight, the staff are now applying an intervention to gradually introduce balls back into her life. They begin with desensitizing her to seeing a ball in the room, and collect data on her behavior during encounters with a ball to help them track her progress.

Skill learning. A teacher, Clara, has prepared a lesson plan for her 13-16 year old students on different types of cows. Sitting at desks in a circle with her four students, she reads aloud a sentence at a time while showing them pictures of each cow. She asks each of her students in turn to repeat words from the lesson plan, as a way of practicing verbal communication and social skills such as taking turns to speak. One student, Drew, becomes unexpectedly upset and hits the table repeatedly. In response to the loud noise, Albert stands up and runs out of the room. While one teaching aide tries to calm Drew, another follows Albert. Clara calmly tries to continue her lesson in an effort to avoid further arousal of the other students. When the chaos subsides, the staff collect data on each student's behaviors.

Interruptions. Jeremy, who is 15, is a big fan of elevators and is easily distracted by them. His teacher, Tim, tries to keep him focused as they walk by an elevator, but Jeremy makes a beeline into the elevator. Tim stands in the doorway to prevent the elevator from leaving, but she cannot convince Jeremy to exit the elevator. They stay in the elevator for about 30 minutes until Jeremy is finally willing to come out. In the meantime, Tim asks the librarian next door to attend to his classroom to ensure there is adequate supervision for the other students. Tim later records data about this episode and its antecedents so that he can try to determine triggers for the behavior and work to decrease its frequency.

DATA COLLECTION PROCESS

Special education staff, including teachers, aides, and therapists, collect data on a regular basis. They collect data *in situ* in a variety of ways to monitor students' mastery of skills. For example, staff record the number of consecutive days in which a task such as counting or spelling was successfully completed. The staff will also time students to measure how quickly they can recall mastered skills. To monitor behaviors, staff will also record the frequency of specific behaviors that may happen anytime throughout the school day. Sometimes capturing data in the moment is not possible, and the staff write down what happened at a later time, affecting the accuracy of data. Though the staff value the data, data collection often falls in priority due to their students' needs for individual attention.

Figure 1 shows examples of data sheets filled out *in situ*. The top sheet was completed while working with a student on the language skill, "manding," that is, verbally requesting a desired object such as a cup of juice or an apple. The bottom chart shows student's "fluency" data, which measures his ability to recall mastered skills.

The left panel of Figure 2 shows our model of one school's system of data sheets. The thirteen kinds of data reveal the complexity of data collected about each student every day. A significant number of data sheets are generated, requiring the staff to use large binders to store data for each student. A teacher's collection of binders takes up a large amount of storage space at her desk (Figure 2, Right). Staff may review collected data as often as once per day to check each student's progress and adjust daily goals accordingly.

Given the burden of collecting so much data, the importance of using it to aid student development, and the necessity of reporting it by law, it is surprising that staff use paper almost exclusively for collecting, and even graphing data. This reliance on paper is all the more surprising given the widespread use of assistive technology by the students themselves to support learning, skill building, and independence. As we discovered in this work, staff are accustomed to having assistive technology in the school and are eager to introduce new kinds of technology into their activities. Yet the schools almost exclusively use paper to collect, share, and use data. Given the complexities of collecting data in this domain, we explored why technology has been unable to meet the needs of these users.

WHY PAPER PERSISTS IN THE WORKPLACE

Researchers have explored the use of paper in everyday work practices within other domains where complexity made the transition to technology difficult. Mackay [14] studied the role of paper flight strips by air traffic controllers – whose work practices are similar to those in special education because they are complex, social, collaborative, and the wellbeing of others depends on them. Mackay's work on interactive paper using augmented reality stemmed from observations similar to those we have made in special education:

> Contrary to what many believe, users are not Luddites, clinging to paper as a way of resisting change. On the contrary: most are excited by the benefits offered by computers and some are even accomplished hackers. Their resistance is, in fact, extremely practical. New computer systems are either less efficient or simply cannot perform many required tasks. [15]

In this paper, we discuss the excitement in special education surrounding use of technology, and the practical reasons why, despite this enthusiasm, technology is not being leveraged for the collection and use of student data. While Mackay recommended augmented paper as a way of introducing technology in air traffic control, other domains have required different solutions. Shehory et al. [19] applied a web-based multi-agent infrastructure to replace notes and sketches made on paper during a standardized process for aircraft maintenance repair. However, unlike these two domains, special education does not have standardized or well-established work practices. Due to the individualized needs of each student and the unpredictable nature of the special education work environment, best practices are applied in customized ways and adjusted frequently. In our fieldwork we studied these complexities to understand how technology might be able to replace paper in this domain to support complex data collection.

Use of data is also limited in special education due to the constraints of having data on paper and little time to review it. In other domains, customized tools have been developed to help specialists use data in more powerful ways. Bier, Ishak, and Chi [1] developed a software tool to help intelligence analysts make sense of the data they collect in an electronic document – including going through data more efficiently and drawing more connections in the data. This kind of sensemaking also happens in special education. Due to a still limited understanding of autism and other special needs, and the uncertainty and variety of interventions used, sense making is complex. The staff make decisions based on their expertise and an intimate knowledge of students. Therefore, we draw from Mackay's recommendation that flight strips for air traffic controllers be augmented but not changed, to "leave the user interface and its subsequent evolution in the hands of the people most responsible, the air traffic controllers themselves."

In special education, we view "the user interface and its subsequent evolution" as the data sheets and data collection model currently used. In this work, we did not set out to fundamentally change the way data is collected. Staff in the special education domain need support to collect and use data, but we did not want to change their fundamental methods, as they alone are the experts on their data collection process. We explored how technology can support staff in collecting and using data so that their human expertise and collaboration can still drive the process and empower nuanced sense making.

This approach differs from other work on improving data collection in the autism domain in two ways: (1) we focus on staff playing an active role in collecting data, and (2) we seek to understand the complexity of complete data needs within a classroom. Other work has been aimed at reducing burden on users as much as possible, by seeking to automate data collection using capture and access, sensors, and other highly augmented collection methods. These types of systems collect large amounts of data automatically while a child is engaging in an activity [8, 21], or with minimal involvement from staff or caregivers [7, 9, 10, 16, 17]. Our work complements these systems by providing an understanding of the expert's role in collecting data in situ. We considered the implicit processes at play when experts (teaching staff and therapists) collect and use data, and we tried to make these processes explicit to inform the design of technologies that support or automate data collection. We focused on understanding current data collection methods without changing them in order to learn about experts' work practices. We also studied use of the data, including information sharing among staff and the ability to craft reports about multiple kinds of data for multiple stakeholders. Finally, we looked at data collection and use broadly in the classroom setting, rather than within the context of a particular therapy or activity, to address the multiplicity and complexity of the complete data needs.

Abaris, a system designed to support a specialized approach for autism therapy, was developed using a model closer to our own, that is, supporting collaborative collection and use of data for decision-making [12]. We build on this work by studying a variety of approaches and interventions at several schools, and understanding how a system like Abaris could operate in the complex and unpredictable setting of a school. AMA, a tablet application for annotation, monitoring, and analysis, was developed with goals similar to ours [18]. We contribute to the development of these kinds of applications by providing a real-world investigation of how they can be used in special education, and understanding why similar, widely available applications are not currently being used in schools.

In our fieldwork, we wanted to understand work practices in special education around the collection and use of behavioral data. We set out to find what role technology can play in supporting these work practices without changing them or interfering with them.

Why the staff use paper to collect data	1. Data needs are complex and not standardized
	2. Immediate demands of the job interfere with thorough *in situ* data collection
	3. Existing technology for data collection is inadequate
Why technology could improve sharing and use of collected data	4. Data sheets are idiosyncratic and not useful without human mediation
	5. Improved communication with parents could benefit children's development
	6. Staff are willing, and even eager, to incorporate technology

Table 1. We identified six factors that affect data collection and use in autism education: three factors explain why paper is being used to collect data, and three factors reveal opportunities for technology to improve sharing and use of data.

METHODS

Six researchers conducted fieldwork over the course of six months. Our field sites were 7 special education programs in 4 states providing services to children with autism and other special needs. Six of the sites were schools (two with residential programs), and one was a therapy center providing after-school services. While the organizations differed somewhat, their services for children with autism were similar. Participants were recruited by word of mouth. All activities were approved by our university's review board, and the sites' review boards if required.

Our fieldwork included 58 person-hours of observation and 62 interviews with staff. We primarily interviewed teachers [n=14], because they play the largest role in data collection. In one school, we surveyed 130 of their 150 staff, with 49 of the staff also participating in two focus groups. In our fieldwork we interacted with teaching staff, therapeutic staff (*e.g.*, speech, physical, occupational), and administrators. We observed staff and students in the school environment but did not interview any children.

Children with autism are reactive to change in their environment, so the presence of even passive observers may be disruptive and distracting. We therefore used mixed methods to gain as accurate of a picture as possible of the natural daily activities of all our participants. We conducted contextual inquiries [2] with the staff to understand their workflow and tools. We used interviews and focus groups to gain an understanding of aspects we would not be able to capture only through naturalistic observation [6, 13]. During fieldwork we took detailed notes, and the research team met after fieldwork sessions to discuss and interpret the data. We used affinity analysis [2] to combine data from different sites, collected by different researchers.

We also conducted a competitive analysis to understand the data collection tools currently available. This knowledge enabled us to discuss tools during fieldwork, helping us discover why the tools were not their meeting needs. We focused on mobile apps for data collection because of the ease of integrating their use *in situ*, the abundance and popularity of these apps, and the high degree of interest we observed in iPads. We searched app stores, blogs, reviews, and forums, identifying apps using two criteria: 1) popular apps that were the most downloaded, discussed, and reviewed, and 2) apps that are representative of the type of functionality available. We identified 5 apps: ABC Data Pro, Autism Tracker Pro, Behavior Journal, Behavior Tracker Pro, and Catalyst HD. All were available for download on the iTunes App Store. One was free, one had a monthly subscription fee of $40, and the rest ranged from a one-time payment of $10 to $30. The comparative costs were not reflected in the quality or functionality of the apps. These five apps were analyzed based on established usability principles [3, 20], and user experience metrics adapted for ubiquitous health technologies [4].

RESULTS

Through our fieldwork, we identified six factors affecting data collection in special education (see Table 1). Three factors suggest why paper is still being used to collect data. Three other factors suggest opportunities for technology to improve sharing and use of data, in addition to supporting and streamlining data collection.

Why they use paper to collect data

During our formative research, we narrowed our focus from the use of technology in special education to the collection and use of data. We were surprised that technology was not being used in this area, and it became very clear that these processes are both critical and cumbersome. For those two reasons, data collection was one of our most frequently encountered topics. As our fieldwork continued we found two challenges staff face in collecting data: data needs are complex and not standardized, and the immediate demands of their job interfere with thorough *in situ* data collection. These challenges explain the persistence of paper due to the complexities of the domain and demands on the staff. Later, we discuss how existing technology is not meeting the needs of the staff as a result of these demands.

1. Data needs are complex and not standardized

Data needs in special education derive from the individualized nature of teaching. Skills that need to be developed in special education include life skills such as sitting correctly in a chair, learning goals such as reading and counting, social skills such as greeting a stranger, as well as curbing any aggressive or disruptive behavior. Each student's learning goals will differ, and a student's goals will change based on his development. As such, data help staff track these changes and make decisions about interventions and approaches to use with each student.

One teacher described a particular data sheet as the "backbone" of her work with students. Staff depend on data sheets for making everyday decisions to help their students succeed. Each student progresses differently, and sometimes working on a particular skill may take months of painstaking work before staff see progress. Data is sometimes the only way to judge a student's progress.

Perhaps due to the high need for individualization and flexibility, there is little standardization of methods for data collection in special education. For example, the model shown in Figure 2 (Left) is only representative of one school we studied. The other programs used different systems and entirely different sheets for collecting the data. Each program determines its own system for collecting data, and each staff member may adapt the system to her own work practices. These systems are so complex that they take a significant amount of time to learn:

"The time to learn a data recording system can take anywhere from a week or two to over a month depending on the employee's position and type of data that they record." –Staff member in a focus group

Data collection enables the staff to monitor a student's development, and adjust interventions regularly depending on how a student is progressing. If an intervention is improving a student's learning or behavior, staff must have evidence of that progress to show that the approach works well for that student. If an intervention is not resulting in improvement, the staff need to recognize this in order to change course and evaluate other interventions.

Due to the range and transience of student goals, teachers develop lesson plans with activities more complex than typical subjects such as math or reading. Lesson plans integrate many skills in order to address the individual needs of students. In order to help students generalize what they learn to different situations, teachers randomize the skills they work on and the order in which students will work on them. According to Tracy this dynamic and unpredictable approach to teaching "gets [students] ready for the real world, it helps them be flexible". However, it also makes data collection a complex process. Collection methods need to be dynamic and flexible enough to keep up with constant changes. This was a main reason paper seemed to be the only reliable method of collecting data. We saw staff adapt data sheets to their own personal work practices so they could be as efficient and accurate as possible. Even small adaptations such as adding an extra column seemed to help make a data sheet more usable.

During our contextual inquiries, we noticed staff would make these minor adaptations to data sheets for themselves. Interestingly, when we probed about the possibility of the sheets being designed to suit their needs better or help them work more efficiently, the staff were unable to suggest many improvements, stating that they weren't sure because out of necessity they had figured out how to make that sheet

work for them. As Alicia put it, "maybe I only like [the sheet] because it's what I'm used to... it works."

This response spoke to the incredible adaptability of special education staff, in making a system work for them so that they can focus on helping their students. Their job pushes them to be creative in most aspects, yet because they are so reliant on current data collection methods they are forced to adapt to them rather than think past them to what might be more effective. For technology designers, this means these particular users may not provide much in the way of design ideas. Moreover, this finding speaks to a certain amount of rigidity when it comes to changing an established data collection process. Not only is the process deeply integrated into classroom activities, but staff have also worked so hard to make the process work for them that they can't seem to be able to consider another possible process. Changing the process may therefore lead to staff resistance or stress.

At the same time, each teacher's adaptation of the sheets led to increased inconsistency in how data was collected:

"It's not consistent. Sometimes I won't know what data is being collected. I won't know how to read someone else's data sheet." –Staff member in a focus group

Problems with inconsistency, which were common, suggest that a change in process would improve the impact of data collected. Administrators from one school spoke frequently about the importance of inter-rater reliability amongst all of the staff collecting data on their students. Staff at this school regularly performed inter-rater reliability checks.

Another problem with data inconsistency is when students are transferred between classrooms or schools:

"When you transfer a student you're looking at the data sheet and you're trying to figure out how they worked with it. Instead of just having a system that goes with them and stays consistent year to year." –Staff member in a focus group

A lack of standardization, coupled with individual staff members' necessitated adaptations of sheets, often leads to problems using data that was previously collected on a student. This challenge seemed to leave staff with unusable data, forced to guess about a student's past history and start data collection from scratch. Sometimes, students arrived at a new school with no data at all.

2. Immediate demands of their job interfere with thorough in situ data collection

Adding to the difficulty of collecting data, the staff need to make sure the data is accurate by collecting it *in situ*. Whether tracking each time a student exhibits a type of behavior, or monitoring the acquisition of a skill through repeated trials, staff need to work closely with a student and observe his behavior carefully. A piece of paper is always nearby—at arm's length whenever possible—for recording data during most activities. However, the staff's work with the children and collection of data naturally interfere with one another, creating conflicting demands on their attention. Data should be collected *in situ* to ensure accuracy, but by writing down that data, they take some of their attention away from students.

Staff reported that they sometimes don't have a chance to capture data because they are in a situation in which they absolutely cannot afford the distraction. This kind of situation may happen if a student is having a difficult day and unable to stay on task, or if it is a particularly chaotic day in the classroom overall. Many staff reported that they sometimes have to record data on sheets at the end of the day instead, though admitting "I have trouble remembering the exact details of all behaviors from one day" (Tracy, teacher). The demands of their immediate responsibilities to their students can get in the way of data collection, and despite the fact that they recognize the value of data, in the moment they will choose their students over data.

A day in special education is rarely typical, making it difficult to rely on predictable methods of collecting data. Special education is rarely predictable and often chaotic. Student behaviors are quite unpredictable, and a day can be turned upside down by one student having a difficult day. When staff have to respond and attend to one student who is having a difficult day, the rest of the staff must help to cover for one another. Moreover, one student's anxiety and behaviors can affect another's, quickly spreading tension or chaos to an entire room. Staff respond to these events using best practices they've been trained in, but their response will be highly based on their own expertise and their nuanced understanding of each individual student. Each child with autism is unique, and special education is work that is inherently and complexly human and social – as such, it is an environment that is difficult to automate.

However, a significant opportunity for technology to support staff in collecting data is to free up their attention so they can focus on their students. One staff member participating in a focus group, describing how cumbersome it is to collect data on paper and transfer that data several times, lamented that "it's taking time from the kids." One of the complaints we heard most frequently from staff was the amount of energy spent on paperwork. They found the cumbersome process frustrating because the most important aspect of their role is their direct work with children, and as a result they often have to take any unfinished paperwork home at the end of the workday.

One staff member wanted to involve students in data collection, to help him engage with the children rather than taking his attention away from them. He used a wall display with pipe cleaners to count behavior points where they were visible to students, rather than on a piece of paper only he could see. Students had greater awareness of when they were receiving or losing points (which can be effective reinforcement), and by engaging them in the collection, this method helped to bring his attention back to the students. However, it also increased the burden as it took him additional time to transfer the data to paper afterwards. If technology supports data collection and can also engage

students (similar to [5, 11]), it can reduce burden on staff and also enhance motivation to collect data by leveraging the staff's desire to engage with their students.

Though we expected other factors—such as cost, politics, or resistance to new technology—to contribute to the difficulty of adopting technology in schools, we discovered that time was the single most limiting factor. Staff in special education are regularly overburdened, and face-to-face time with their students always comes first. As a result, little time remains for their other responsibilities such as data collection or staff collaboration, and there is almost no time for researching or learning new technologies. From our focus groups and survey at one school, we found that professional development was a problem that administrators were aware of and staff expressed frustration with:

> "New tech training has kind of been trial by fire. I wish there was more a chance to learn new systems before being thrown in there." –Staff member in a focus group

The staff struggle to learn and incorporate technologies with the little time and training they have available. Changing their data collection processes from paper to technology would require significant effort, and adequate professional development would be critical.

3. Existing technology for data collection is inadequate

We encountered hardware such as iPads and Smart Boards in schools, but the staff had difficulty incorporating them into their activities due to a lack of adequate software applications that would make these devices useful for them. Grants made iPads and Smart Boards attainable for three schools we studied. One school had provided an iPad for each staff member. Another school purchased three iPads to trial, and our survey at this school revealed that iPads were in high demand among the staff—they were one of the most common topics of responses to both closed-ended and open-ended questions. Administrators at this school were in discussions to purchase additional iPads, but wanted to understand first how they would be used and what software was available, rather than purchasing them as a hardware device without a specific purpose.

The hesitation of these administrators points to a key reason that paper is still being used for data collection—existing technology is inadequate. There is no existing system that is widely known and recommended for data collection, which is unusual in a domain where many creative parents and staff discover and share effective solutions. For example, Proloquo2Go is a popular communication app for children who have limited speech, and Talking Tom Cat is a popular game that appeals to children with autism. When apps are as effective as these two examples, they become popular through word of mouth, parent support groups, online forums and educational blogs. So, it is unusual that there is no well-known app for supporting data collection and use—and an indication that existing apps are inadequate.

Another school we studied had set out to find an app to use on the iPads they already own. They were even able to devote some time to this endeavor, having several staff members test existing apps on their iPads. However, their disappointment with the functionality and usability of these apps led them to abandon their search and continue to use paper. Our competitive analysis of existing apps revealed what aspects made them fall short of meeting their needs. Our findings echo the complaints reported by the school.

Not practical for collecting data on multiple students. We first discovered that many of the apps were designed for collecting data on a single student. Few supported separating data by student, which is critical for the school environment. In addition, data could only be collected using a single device and was stored locally on the device. This kind of use is not practical given the number of staff interacting with a student in a school day, and the unpredictability that causes the staff to have to cover for each other often. More importantly, data cannot be stored locally on devices due to personal health and educational data privacy laws (HIPAA and FERPA, respectively). These laws ensure student data is protected, and make it impossible to use many existing apps in schools.

Tradeoff between burdensome customization and limited functionality. Given the complexity of collecting different types of data on each student depending on individualized goals, apps failed to manage an important tradeoff between burdensome customization and limited functionality. Those that provided simple and easy to use collection methods were too limited in their functionality, and lacked customization for a variety of students. However, those apps that provided customization added significant burden to the user, and tended to also suffer from usability issues. Some apps included so many options for data collection that the amount of time it takes to complete a report would not be practical in a special education environment. We also saw apps attempting to enable a variety of data collection methods by using such unconventional interactions as a triple tap and two-finger tap. These interactions are unintuitive and not feasible to use in an unpredictable environment that is demanding on the staff's attention.

Lack of support for data use and analysis. Most apps were focused only on the collection of data, and did not support users in sharing or analyzing the data effectively. Some provided low-fidelity line graphs or a means of sending raw data by email from the application. Based on our fieldwork findings that we discuss in the next section, these features would not provide much value to staff, who need sophisticated analyses of school-wide data, and quick ways of sharing digestible snippets of key data.

Attempts to be engaging impeded usability. Most of the apps embraced their context of use and used school-related design elements such as pencils, crayons, notebooks, and primary colors. However, these design elements, coupled with interactions that broke with convention, tended to be distracting or confusing and ultimately impeded usability. One app had an interface mimicking a multi-section

notebook, but inconsistently implemented this metaphor. For example, clicking on a section tab opened a pop-up window rather than mimicking a page turn to that section.

Schools reported the same shortcomings that we found in existing systems, and pointed to those shortcomings as reasons for sticking with paper and pencil.

Why technology could improve sharing and use of collected data

The staff is limited in how they can share and use data that has been collected on paper. Data on paper is difficult to reproduce or share with others. The demands on staff also leave little time to review the data and use it to inform their decisions. With the support of technology, we discovered opportunities for sharing and use of data: improving collaboration among staff, and communication with parents. In addition, the eagerness of staff to incorporate technology into their work shows the feasibility of adoption if systems can meet their data collection needs and offer improvements in collaboration and communication.

4. Data sheets are idiosyncratic and not useful without human mediation

One of the most important uses of data is to help staff monitor student development and make decisions about the most appropriate interventions and approaches to use with each individual student. Collaboration among different types of staff (teachers, teaching aides, speech therapists, occupational therapists, *etc.*) is involved in deciding on interventions for each student. Though some best practices exist for interventions, each child with autism is unique and staff must be creative in applying interventions to each individual student's case. Teaching staff spend their time with the same set of students—those in their classroom— while other types of staff have larger caseloads assigned to them. For example, a speech therapist we interviewed covered two classrooms. Other therapists have even larger caseloads, working with a larger portion of the school.

The teaching staff know their own students best, while therapeutic staff are experts on developing particular skills. Together they determine interventions and goals for each individual student. When teachers struggle with a student's grasp of a particular skill, they seek advice from one of the therapists on how to best help the student. Similarly, therapists spend one-on-one time with students a few times a week, evaluating their skills and working with them in focused therapy sessions. Therapists then report back to teaching staff, so that the same work with the student can continue in the classroom. Jamie, a speech therapist, explained that this type of collaboration is critical "because therapy doesn't work if you're only doing it two times a week". The interventions used by the therapists should match those used by the teaching staff.

Despite the importance of staff collaboration, our participants frequently discussed the issue of time:

> *"I wish we had time. I feel like staff here are really innovative. People work in teams and do cool things. This*

year I lost all my time... we need time to mess with things and see what works." – Staff member in a focus group

Staff collaboration was described as running into each other in the hallway, talking in passing while doing something else such as cleaning up, or stopping by someone's office to try and catch them. One staff member estimated that 60-70% of collaboration is done in passing. Staff use email and phone to reach out to one another, but rarely have the time to sit down for a scheduled meeting. Scheduled face to face time may be every few weeks, but during busy times of the school year these meetings are cancelled. Jared, a member of the teaching staff said this situation is "pathetic".

Due in part to the limited time the staff have for collaborating, they share little data among one another. First of all, the lack of standardization makes it difficult to interpret data collected by someone else. Second, a lack of face-to-face collaboration makes it difficult to share and discuss data. Jamie, a speech therapist, shares with teachers the data that she collects during one-on-one therapy sessions, but she knows many of them do not look at the data. She feels that she can make a bigger impact by walking into a teacher's classroom and briefly explaining some advice she has for working with a student based on her data. She can only hope that teachers put her advice to use and that it influences their teaching. Overall, she feels there is only so much she can do because she knows that the teaching staff have a lot of demands on their time and so are not likely to be able to look at data that she provides. This concerns her given the importance she noted of continuing therapy outside of one-on-one sessions, and inserting it through the school day. There is an opportunity for technology to help someone like Jamie communicate her data to other staff in a palatable way. Given the impromptu nature of collaboration, data analysis and visualization could help staff prepare and discuss data more efficiently.

One of the schools we studied had a particularly strong interest in data, originating from an administrator who wanted to improve collaboration. She had recently joined the school and enforced a system for more structured and frequent data collection based on a standardized point system. At first, staff did not like the extra work involved in the incorporation of this system. However, the school's new system grew on staff as they came to understand the value of data and the administrator's vision for it:

"Data basically needs to be available to the rest of the team, parents, therapy providers, changes in staff, supervisors. It needs to be analyzed on many different dimensions: within classrooms, across the school, across gender." –Stephanie, Administrator

While data is now more available, Stephanie recognized that technological tools to empower both collection and analysis were missing. As long as data is still on paper, they are significantly limited in what they can do. This school had attempted to find and adopt an iPad application for data collection, and in their search evaluated the same apps that we did for our competitive analysis. Echoing the issues we

found with the apps, Stephanie said none of them met their needs so they were forced to stick with paper.

There is significant opportunity for technology to provide visualizations and other tools for easily sharing important snippets of data and supporting collaboration and decision-making around the data. In addition, schools want to be able to make school-wide comparisons, for example across days of the week, gender, staff members, or interventions. Tools for analyzing large data sets would be influential for schools, which are working to find what works for their students and provide evidence for their success, within a domain that has limited standardization and best practices.

5. Improved communication with parents could benefit children's development

U.S. laws require special education programs to report to state agencies regularly on student progress, and online systems are becoming more common and widely utilized for standardized reporting. Several times a year, school staff must put additional effort into summarizing and reporting data to meet this requirement, as well as to communicate student progress with parents and other staff members. Despite little standardization in data collection, reporting mechanisms are standardized across states, forcing the staff to use tools that they do not find easy to use. Transferring data into these reporting tools adds to their workload and frustration. Technology to aid the transfer of this data would significantly reduce staff burden.

In addition to state-mandated reporting requirements, the staff sees additional value in improved communication with parents. Despite staff's hard work within the school environment, they recognize that a child's development is highly dependent on their home life. When parents are knowledgeable and involved with their child's learning and behavioral goals, children make the most significant progress in their development. Therefore, staff are often looking for ways to engage parents by keeping them informed about what happens with their child at school, and what they can do to continue working on goals at home.

Our focus group participants spoke at length about their efforts to improve communication with parents. For example, because they cannot assume that all families have access to the Internet at home, they had developed a newsletter to send home relatively easily as a mass mailing to all parents. However, they discovered that parents did not want to know generic information about goings on at the school, but rather specific details about their child. Preparing individualized reports would take a significant amount of time, so a parent committee developed a sheet for staff to fill out, in an attempt to make it easier for them. However, this sheet is very unpopular, with both parents and staff, in part because it is sent home each day. Staff feel overburdened and even report having to cut time with their students short in order to have the time to fill out the sheets. On the other side, most parents seem too busy to read such reports on a daily basis, which staff are aware of because they find the sheets still in their students' backpacks.

Staff argued for communication that is more detailed and frequent, but not a large burden on them. Parents have a legal right to see their child's data, and it can help them make decisions outside of school:

"Parents can see any data sheet they want. Some ask to see all data, and a lot ask for behavior data to show to a psychiatrist—helps with deciding on what meds parents will or will not give their kids. [Sharing data is] needed to make home life better." –Tracy, teacher

In addition to providing data that will help parents at home, staff want data to be shared back and forth to help them do their job. For example, sometimes a behavior is achieved at school, but has not been generalized outside of that context. As a result, a student will not display the behavior at home, and parents may not even believe staff when they report this behavior. This situation is frustrating for staff, who have worked hard with students to achieve the behavior, and want to share data with disbelieving parents as proof.

Staff also wish they received more data from parents, because it helps them predict and respond to student needs:

"Predictors are really important. [We] need to know outside factors, such as changes in meds." –Dylan, behavior specialist

In addition to big changes such as medications, small pieces of information can be helpful to staff. For example, if something anxiety-provoking happens in the morning before a student gets to school, some parents let staff know by phone call or email. This kind of information helps staff not only predict student behaviors, but also interpret and respond to them appropriately. Unfortunately, parents rarely provide staff with this kind of information. Providing a different mechanism for sharing data could increase the amount of information shared by parents, by making it more convenient or creating more motivators.

6. Staff are willing, and even eager, to incorporate technology

Staff are open to and eager to try new technologies if they have reason to believe it would support their work practices and they see evidence of a technology's success. For example, the recent rise in use of the Apple iPad has made a significant impact on the special education community. The device is very affordable compared to traditional assistive devices that cost thousands of dollars each. Moreover, with a plethora of apps available, it can replace multiple devices created for a specific purpose. Staff and parents alike are excited by stories about various apps that have made an impact on children with autism. However, they find the number of apps available to be overwhelming, especially since the right app needs to be matched to each individual child according to his needs. Many feel that it would take too much time to look through all of the apps to find the right one for each child:

"I think there's a lot more out there available, but it just takes time and energy to find it." –Zoe, Teacher

Despite this drawback, there is still significant excitement about incorporating iPads into many aspects of special education. In our focus groups and many of our interviews, iPads came up as solutions to a variety of problems, especially data collection. Participants thought iPads would give them the mobility to collect data around the classroom and the power to store and analyze large amounts of data – however they were not sure how exactly this would work. Still, some staff were quick to point out that iPads are not a panacea, especially considering the time it would take to find the right app for many different individualized goals.

Technology was brought up frequently when we discussed data collection in our fieldwork. Staff pointed out many benefits of incorporating technology, including saving paper, saving time, and providing easier access to data:

"We have parent-teacher communication forms that have to be filled out every day. It's a ton of paper that's being wasted. Can we do this electronically? Teachers can sit down each day and say this is what has been covered. If you're looking for information on what's being done each and every day there should be somewhere you can go." –Staff member in a focus group

The eagerness of staff to use technology for data collection, and their astute suggestions as to how it would improve their process, made it all the more surprising that all of the schools we studied were still using paper. Even the schools that had been recently equipped with iPads or Smart Boards, and had them readily available, had not incorporated them into their activities. Time was the single most limiting factor in this environment, and revealed significant barriers to adoption of technology.

CONCLUSION

In our fieldwork, we found evidence explaining why paper is used almost exclusively for collecting and using data in autism education. We identified six factors affecting data collection in autism education: three explained why paper was used and technology had not been incorporated into data collection, and another three revealed opportunities for technology to support sharing and use of collected data.

Three factors helped to answer our primary research question: why are they using paper? First, the individualized nature of autism education requires collection of a significant amount of data for the purposes of tracking student development. These data needs are complex due to the unique needs of each student, and methods for collecting the data are not standardized. Second, individual student needs and the unpredictable nature of the special education environment create significant demands on staff, and interfere with the collection of data *in situ*. Third, existing technology for data collection is inadequate. Our participants confirmed what we found in a competitive analysis of apps currently available for download: they are not practical for use in the classroom, they do not provide appropriate customization for individual students, they do not support sharing or analysis of data, and many also suffer from usability flaws.

In addition to understanding what role technology could play in the collection of data, we identified opportunities for technology to improve the use of collected data. First, the data sheets used are idiosyncratic and are not useful without human mediation. However, the demands on staff in special education leave little time for discussions about data. Tools enabling the quick capture and sharing of important snippets of data would support discussion, enable more collaboration and decision-making around the data, and also require limited prep time for the overburdened staff. Second, because student development is dependent on the consistency of interventions applied in school *and* in the home, it is important for staff and parents to communicate. Both sides struggle to keep each other informed, so if technology could improve the sharing of data that has been collected, better communication between staff and parents could benefit student development. Third, staff's eagerness to incorporate technology into their work practices suggests that it would be feasible to pursue these opportunities for supporting collaboration and communication.

In special education, it is critical for multiple kinds of data to be collected *in situ*. However, the number of interruptions and activities, and other people to be consulted, interfere with data collection. Staff in our fieldwork perceived that paper is much easier for jotting down notes, editing them later, and collaborating with others on these notes than any technology they have tried. Paradoxically, we found that the persistence of paper reduces the amount of sharing and use of data. The large collection of data sheets is difficult to use. By replacing paper with technological tools that better fit the needs of *in situ* data collection and data storage, we hope to empower their use of data.

ACKNOWLEDGEMENTS

We would like to express our gratitude to our participants for their generosity with their time, and their support and enthusiasm for our work. This research was supported by the NSF under Grant No. CCF-1029549, and by a NSF Graduate Research Fellowship to the first author under Grant No. 0750271.

REFERENCES

1. Bier, E.A., Ishak, E.W., and Chi, E.H. Entity workspace: an evidence file that aids memory, inference, and reading. *In Proc ISI 2006*. LNCS 3975: 466-472.
2. Beyer, H., and Holtzblatt, K. *Contextual Design: Defining Customer-Centered Systems*. Morgan Kaufmann Publishers, Inc., San Francisco, CA, 1998.
3. Brooks, P. "Adding value to usability testing", Chapter 10 in *Usability Inspection Methods*, Nielsen, J., and Mack, R.L. (Eds.), 255-271.
4. Connelly, K., Caine, K., Siek, K.A., Kientz, J.A., Kutz, D.O., Hanania, R., Khan, D., Choe, E.K. Evaluating Off-the-Shelf Technologies for Personal Health Monitoring, Ubicomp 2012 workshop proposal abstract.
5. Cramer, M.D., Hirano, S., Tentori, M., Yeganyan, M., and Hayes, G.R. Classroom-Based Assistive Technology: Collective Use of Interactive Visual Schedules by Students with Autism. *In Proc. CHI 2011*, 1-10.
6. Esterberg, K.G. *Qualitative Methods in Social Research*. McGraw-Hill, 2002.
7. Hayes, G.R. and Abowd, G.D. Tensions in Designing Capture Technologies for an Evidence-Based Care Community. *In Proc. CHI 2006*, 937–946.
8. Hayes, G.R., Hirano, S., Marcu, G., Monibi, M., Nguyen, D.H., and Yeganyan, M. Interactive Visual Supports for Children with Autism. *Personal and Ubiquitous Computing*. 14(7): 663-680, 2010.
9. Hayes, G.R., Kientz, J.A., Truong, K.N., White, D.R., Abowd, G.D., and Pering, T. Designing Capture Applications to Support the Education of Children with Autism. *In Proc. UbiComp 2004*, 161-178.
10. Hayes, G.R., Gardere, L.M., Abowd, G.D. and Truong, K.N. CareLog: A Selective Archiving Tool for Behavior Management in Schools. *In Proc. CHI 2008*, 685-694.
11. Hirano, S., Yeganyan, M., Marcu, G., Nguyen, D., Boyd, L.A., and Hayes, G.R. vSked: Evaluation of a System to Support Classroom Activities for Children with Autism. *In Proc. CHI 2010*, 1633-1642.
12. Kientz, J.A., Hayes, G.R., Westeyn, T.L., Starner, T., Abowd, G.D. Pervasive computing and autism: assisting caregivers of children with special needs. *IEEE Pervasive Computing*, Jan 2007, 28–35.
13. Lofland, J., Snow, D.A., Anderson, A., Lofland, L.H. *Analyzing Social Settings: A Guide to Qualitative Observation and Analysis* (4th Ed), Thomson Wadsworth, 2006.
14. Mackay, W.E. Is Paper Safer? The Role of Paper Flight Strips in Air Traffic Control. *ACM Transactions on Computer-Human Interaction*. 6 (4), 2000, 311-340.
15. Mackay, W.E. & Fayard, A-L. Designing Interactive Paper: Lessons from three Augmented Reality Projects. *In Proc. International Workshop on Augmented Reality*. (1998) Natick, MA: A K Peters, Ltd.
16. Nazneen, Boujarwah, F.A., Rozga, A., Abowd, G.D., Arriaga, R.I., Oberleitner, R., Pharkute, S. Towards in-home collection of behavior specimens: Within the cultural context of autism in Pakistan. *In Proc. PervasiveHealth 2012*, 9-16.
17. Plotz, T., Hammerla, N.Y., Rozga, A., Reavis, A., Call, N., Abowd, G.D. Automatic Assessment of Problem Behavior in Individuals with Developmental Disabilities. *In Proc. Ubicomp 2012*, 391-400.
18. Sano, A., Hernandez, J., Deprey, J., Eckhardt, M. Picard, R.W., Goodwin, M.S. Multimodal Annotation Tool for Challenging Behaviors in People with Autism Spectrum Disorders. *Ubicomp 2012 Workshop on Ubiquitous Mobile Instrumentation*.
19. Shehory, O., Sycara, K., Sukthankar, G., and Mukherjee, V. Agent aided aircraft maintenance. *Proc. of Intl. Conf. on Autonomous Agents*, 1999, 306-312.
20. Tognazzini B. Ask TOG: First principles of interaction design. [2012 May 23]. http://www.asktog.com/basics/firstPrinciples.html.
21. Westeyn, T.L., Abowd, G.D., Starner, T.E., Johnson, J.M., Presti, P.W., Weaver, K.A. Monitoring children's developmental progress using augmented toys and activity recognition. *Personal and Ubiquitous Computing*, 16(2), 2012, 169-191.

TOBY: Early Intervention in Autism through Technology

Svetha Venkatesh, Dinh Phung, Thi Duong
School of Information Technology
Deakin University, Australia
svetha.venkatesh,dinh.phung,thi.duong@deakin.edu.au

Stewart Greenhill, Brett Adams
Department of Computing
Curtin University, Australia
s.greenhill,b.adams@curtin.edu.au

ABSTRACT

We describe TOBY Playpad, an early intervention program for children with Autism Spectrum Disorder (ASD). TOBY teaches the teacher – the parent – during the crucial period following diagnosis, which often coincides with no access to formal therapy. We reflect on TOBY's evolution from table-top aid for flashcards to an iPad app covering a syllabus of 326 activities across 51 skills known to be deficient for ASD children, such imitation, joint attention and language. The design challenges unique to TOBY are the need to adapt to marked differences in each child's skills and rate of development (a trait of ASD) and teach parents unfamiliar concepts core to behavioural therapy, such as reinforcement, prompting, and fading. We report on three trials that successively decrease oversight and increase parental autonomy, and demonstrate clear evidence of learning. TOBY's uniquely intertwined Natural Environment Tasks are found to be effective for children and popular with parents.

ACM Classification Keywords

H.5.m. Information Interfaces and Presentation (e.g. HCI): Miscellaneous

Author Keywords

Autism, early intervention, therapy, wait-list

INTRODUCTION

As computer scientists, we are familiar with the sense of satisfaction that accompanies an accepted paper or grant proposal. Much rarer is a sense of true delight at a finished project. We describe here one such unusual project–the development, from concept to field trial, of an early intervention program for childern with Autism, TOBY Playpad (tobyplaypad.com).

Our journey began in early 2009 when our friends' 2 year old son was diagnosed with Autism Spectrum Disorder (ASD), a neuro-developmental disorder that causes deficits in social interaction, communication, behaviours and interests. None of us had first-hand experience with Autism, despite its prevalence of 1 in 89 children. Alarmingly, the diagnosis came without clear guidelines for the parents about what to do next. The experts stressed the importance of early intervention, but our friends felt helpless in the face of a bewildering array of

different therapies, while they waited to access formal therapy. When they finally began therapy, they discovered it required 20 hours one-on-one with their son, and another 20 hours of preparation, each week. The cost in dollars, anxiety, and stress, was indescribable.

Our goal was simple: to help parents during the stressful time between diagnosis and commencement of formal therapy, and during therapy itself. We wanted to empower them to deliver therapy at home. We set the following specific goals for what ultimately became TOBY Playpad:

- Deliver stimuli flexibly within a *rigorous* learning framework that uses best-practice techniques from behavioural therapy, including reinforcement, prompting, and measurable criteria for skill mastery and syllabus progression;

- Teach from a *multi-skill* syllabus spanning visual and auditory understanding, receptive and expressive language, and, critically, social skills and imitation;

- Deliver stimuli in *mixed environments*, on- and off-device, intergrated with this rigorous learning framework;

- Maximise the scope by making it *language independent*.

This paper presents a progression from our previous work [12]. However, beyond some reiteration of necessary background, it is markedly different from [12]. Previous work [12] is a systems paper targeting a system venue; it focuses on the system architecture, database structure, construction of stimuli, and detailed specifications of the algorithms that adapt the complexity of stimuli and measure mastery. In contrast, This paper focuses on user-centered design and iterative redesign. Outstanding distinct novelties and contributions from [12] include the following. a) *Syllabus Evolution:* we provide a discussion of the characteristics of Applied Behavior Analysis (ABA), its aptness to computer-mediated delivery, and the flash-card based model that TOBY seeks to replace and augment. The description of changes to the feedback model for NET and the division of responsibility between System and Parent for the different task types is new. This section also includes a more detailed breakdown of the four major skill areas in the syllabus. b) *Imitation Tasks:* this section is newly added which discusses how video modeling is used to teach various skills, how we take feedback from the parent, and communicate prompting requirements. It also describes the interface changes between prototype and final implementation (cf. Figure 2). c) *Natural Environment Training* (NET): our implementation, both in protocol and interface, changed substantially from [12]. These changes and their rationale are explained in details. d) *Lesson Planning:* this section discusses the rationale and effect of interfaces changes which was not implemented previously. e) *Help Guide:* TOBY relies on the parent learning a number of concepts basic to ABA in order to deliver therapy, and the help system is a crucial part of learning process. In previous trials parents received a degree of instruction from therapists, but in the new final longitudinal trial they received no such help. The discussion of the provided documentation and videos is also newly added. f) *Experiments:* the results for Trial 2 include an evaluation of evidence of learning, and a comparison of NET/iPad use, both of which are not presented in [12]; Trial 3 is newly added which further substantiates previous trials in several respects, including a larger number of participants and was not supervised by therapists – parents received all training through the application. Trial results show evidences of learning, both on- and off-iPad. In particular, the most novel aspect of TOBY, its Natural Environment Tasks, were well received.

BACKGROUND

Software and Assistive Devices for ASD
Research into assistive devices for ASD have targeted three main areas: early diagnosis and progress measurement; affect recognition; and social skill development. Kientz et al. used toys fitted with accelerometers and wireless interfaces to trigger video recording for review and pediatric analysis [6]. Blocher and Picard developed mobile, assistive devices to help children recognize affect (a common difficulty for children with ASD) using facial analysis [2]. Exploratory work by Schmidt and Schmidt examined 3D environments used as surrogates for the real world in order to teach social skills [9], whereas Stanton et al. experimented with the effect of real-world, robotic toys on social development (i.e., autistic behaviours) [11].

Focussing on visual support, many systems have demonstrated efficacy in early treatment of mental disorders including autism (e.g., [1, 10]). Examples of proprietary software include *DTTrainer*[1] and the Picture Exchange Communication System (PECS) [3]. Video has also been used, in the form of social stories, which are concrete, idiosyncratic video narratives that teach social skills [7]. Computer-assisted intervention has proven effective in teaching language, reducing inappropriate verbalisation, and improving functional communication and generalisation [4, 5]. *Teachtown*[2] is perhaps the closest system to TOBY currently available in that it provides graded online and paper-based lessons rooted in Applied Behavior Analysis (ABA) theory, but it suffers from a restricted set of stimuli and impoverished adaptation to response.

Anecdotal evidence suggests the iPad has been a great learning tool for children with autism.[3] There is a host of iPad apps targeting specific skill deficits. E.g., *Proloquo2Go*, *iComm*, and *TapToTalk* for communication via symbols and text-to-voice; *Grace* for sentence-building via images; *iCommunicate* for storyboarding with pictures and images; *First-Then-Visual-Schedule* for daily schedules; *AutismExpress* for emo-

tion interpretation; and *Stories2learn* for personalized social stories about complex social situations. But none of these systems target systematic, automated stimulus generation and complexity adaptation, at the level proposed here.

Behavioural Early Intervention Therapy for ASD
Applied Behavior Analysis (ABA) [8] and Discrete Trial Training (DTT) are prominent established therapies (US National Standards Report on Autism, 2009). They focus on cognitive functions, such as object labelling and categorization. While intervention is designed and partially administered by therapists, much of the therapy requires parental involvement. ABA's reliance on paper-based materials can translate to significant preparation costs, and suffers from difficulty in communicating dynamic concepts, such as verbs. ABA and DTT also require fine-grained record keeping during sessions, which in practice can be poorly implemented.

But ABA's structured progression formulae, record-keeping, and stimulus-based learning, are a good fit for computational delivery. Thus ABA underpins the content delivery framework described below, and instantiated as TOBY Playpad. But we hasten to add that this framework is not a replacement for human-delivered therapy, but a complement to it.

SYLLABUS EVOLUTION
Our initial vision of TOBY Playpad arose from direct experience with ABA therapies. TOBY aimed to simplify delivery of these therapies for parents, by automating the tedious or time-consuming aspects, including: making flashcards, printing, and laminating; sharing images between parents; and keeping records of therapy sessions. In 2009 we designed a multi-touch surface to replace table-top activities done using hand-made flashcards. This prototype stored and presented images and sounds for matching tasks, and recorded performance. But by April 2010, the iPad offered a dramatic improvement in price and robustness of multi-touch devices.

At that time we contacted a support group for parents of children with autism, Autism West. Together we formulated the goal of developing a product for early intervention, to cover the crucial time between diagnosis and access to formal therapy, which could be up to six months. Autism West supplied therapists and psychologists, who brought their own perspective to the problem. The result was a dramatic increase in the scope of skills covered by the syllabus, which grew from sensory and language matching tasks to include social, imitation, and Natural Environment Tasks.

We decided to use ABA for our therapy framework. ABA uses operant conditioning to teach a child how to respond to stimuli. While it can be used to teach a vast array of skills, for children with autism we are also interested in communication skills. These are founded on a range of pre-requisite cognitive and social skills. We began with ABA's use of flashcards to teach children object names, which is typical of computer-based autism therapy. But many skills must be taught in parallel. E.g., making eye contact; attending to another person; understanding and following basic instructions; focusing attention on a task; imitating gross- and fine-motor actions; and producing basic speech sounds.

A computer cannot teach a child to do these things, but a computer can *teach a parent* to teach a child. Thus our syllabus has been designed from the outset to involve both parent and child. TOBY teaches parents the basics of operant conditioning, which they then apply to the crucial areas of their child's development that cannot be handled by the computer.

In an ABA therapy model, we present a *stimulus* to which the child responds. If the *response* is the desired response, we give *reinforcement*–e.g., verbal praise, a favourite food or toy. If the response is not the desired response, we may *prompt* the child by demonstrating the correct response. Prompting is *faded* over time so that eventually responses are self-initiated (and similarly for reinforcement). *Measurement* of behaviour is used to decide: if a response is correct; when to reinforce; when to prompt and how much; when a skill has been mastered; and what should be taught next. Underlying the therapy is an algorithm that adjusts stimuli, reinforcement, and prompting as a result of responses. For those situations where the computer can measure a response directly, it delivers reinforcement and prompting, e.g., where the task requires the child to find a given stimulus picture from among a set of pictures presented on the screen. We call this type of task a *Solo* task, because it can ostensibly be performed by the child without assistance. Solo tasks are important, but they only cover a small subset of skills we want to teach. The remaining skills involve the parent in some way, either to recognise the child's response (e.g., an action or spoken word), or to present stimuli, prompts, and reinforcement. We call these *Partner* tasks, because the parent and child work must together.

The iPad delivers two kinds of language task: *receptive* and *expressive*. For receptive language, the child must learn to recognise an object given its name, and point to the correct picture in response to a voice prompt, such as "Find apple". For expressive language, the child must say an object's name given a picture and voice prompt, such as "What is this?" Expressive tasks are Partner tasks, as the parent must indicate if the response is correct, and prompt if necessary. While receptive language usually develops faster than expressive, TOBY treats these skills as independent, as children with autism often do not follow expected developmental paths.

Once the important concepts were identified, we collected images which were Creative-Commons licensed for use as stimuli in sensory and language tasks. We also recorded videos for imitation tasks, which extensively use video modelling.

Therapists stressed the importance of integrating computer-based therapy with real-world activities. Skills must be transferred to natural settings so they are generalized, and the child's reliance on screen-based prompting and reinforcement is reduced. TOBY's *Natural Environment Training* (NET), which is performed off-device, serves this purpose.

We experimented with several models for NET. Initially we tightly coupled the real and cyber worlds, by using digital exemplars to guide physical activities (e.g., an image of a banana, to be found while shopping). This model required parents to input many trial-level outcomes, so that the syllabus progression logic could be as sensitive as it was for iPad tasks,

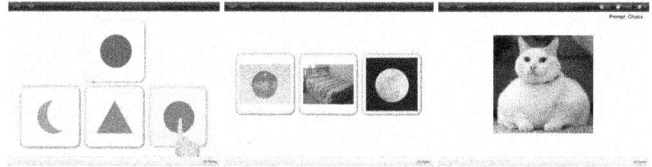

Figure 1. Matching tasks. Left: Sensory matching – the instruction is "Find same". An incorrect response causes TOBY to indicate the correct response using a pointing finger. Middle: Receptive matching – the instruction is "Find apple". Right: Expressive matching – the instruction is "What is this?". The child must say the word "cat". Parent inputs feedback using the buttons at the top right of the screen.

but this proved to be impractical and restrictive.

We switched to a model requiring a single response after each NET activity. This allows parents independence from the iPad while performing the task, but obtains the feeback necessary to drive syllabus progression, albeit at a larger granularity than the iPad tasks. Each NET instructs the parent how to perform the task, and how to prompt and reinforce if required. Every Solo and Partner task has a corresponding NET task.

Role	Task Type		
	Solo (iPad)	Partner (iPad)	NET
Stimulus	System	System	Parent
Response	System	Parent	Parent
Prompting	System	Parent	Parent
Reinforcement	System	System	Parent
Adaptation	System	System	System

Table 1. Roles of parents and system in Solo, Partner and NET activities.

The differences between the task types–Solo, Partner and NET–in terms of which agent performs the different parts of therapy is shown in Table 1. Observe that in all cases the system decides what lessons should be offered based on the performance of the child.

Our syllabus is divided into four major skill areas:

- *Sensory*: perception and discrimination of sensory cues– e.g., colour, shape, same-ness and difference

- *Imitation*: copy an action, design, or pre-speech sounds

- *Language*: recognition and production of object names

- *Social*: inter-presonal skills, such as joint-attention

There are between 10 and 15 specific skills in each of these areas, and a total of 51 skills in the syllabus, which are strucutred as a graph of skill dependencies. New skill nodes unlock as pre-requisites are completed. Each node may have multiple tasks, and all nodes have iPad tasks, except Social nodes, which only have NET tasks. The syllabus contains a total of 326 tasks: 34 iPad and 292 NET.

USER INTERFACE

Here we outline the different parts of the TOBY Playpad app from a user's perspective. Figure 2 is a simple schematic of the navigation choices in the app. The parent begins by registering a new account, which enables their profile and activity data to be stored for backup, migration across devices, or sharing with a therapist. If already registered, they login with their private credentials. From the *manage* screen, the parent can add, remove and edit child profiles. After selecting a profile, TOBY displays the *plan* screen, which displays a list of available tasks and an overview of the child's progress through the syllabus. The *guide* explains through text and video how to set up and perform different types of syllabus activities, including knowledge necessary to perform each task, such as how to prompt, reinforce, and motivate the child.

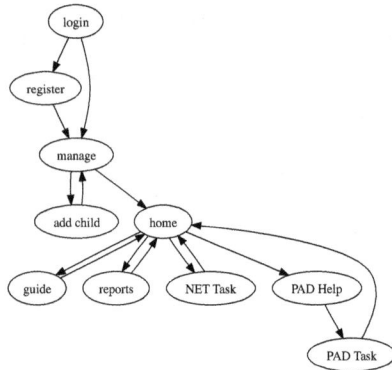

Figure 2. Simple schematic of the navigation choices in TOBY Playpad.

When the parent selects a task for their child to perform, and before proceeding to the task screen, they are first shown any task-specific instructions. Recall that there are three types of task in the system: *solo tasks*, which include receptive matching games the child can do under parental supervision; and *partner tasks*, which include imitation tasks, where the child must copy an action shown in a video, and expressive matching tasks, where the child must name objects presented on the screen; and NET tasks, which are performed off-iPad. In partner tasks, the parent provides feedback to TOBY about the child's response, and TOBY indicates how the parent should prompt the child if the response is incorrect.

The following sections describe the design of the different activities comprising TOBY's syllabus, including matching tasks, imitation tasks, NET tasks, as well as how lesson plans are communicated to the parent.

Matching Tasks

Matching tasks are used to teach categorisation. The child must identify objects that are similar in sensory or semantic properties. Recall that TOBY uses multiple exemplar training (MET), in which three categories are taught simultaneously, with the target category changing from trial to trial, and the non-target categories serving as distractors.

The simplest kind of matching is sensory. Here TOBY presents a target image, and a row of alternatives, with the instruction, "Find same". One of the images matches the target, and the other two are distractors, and the child must select the correct image by touching it, or dragging the target to it. Figure 1 (left) is a screenshot of a sensory matching task. The target (top) is the purple circle, which the child must pick from the bottom row of three images. This figure also shows one of the ways TOBY prompts the child for the correct response when an incorrect answer is given, in this

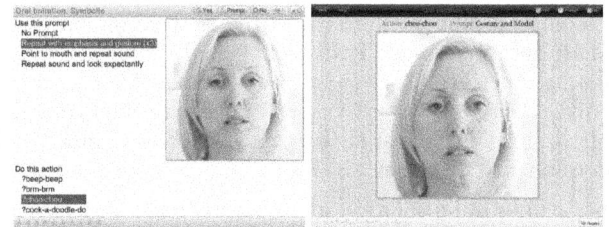

Figure 3. Left: Early prototype imitation task. Video models an action the child must imitate. The parent records their child's response with the buttons at the top right of the screen. Right: Subsequent redesign, with lists for prompt type and action removed to avoid mis-interpretation as choices.

case by highlighting the correct alternative, pulsing its size, and pointing to it. Once prompted, the child is allowed to choose again. A more complex version of this task presents two non-identical examples of an object. This trains the child to attend to similarities, whilst ignoring irrelevant details.

In addition to prompting after incorrect answers, TOBY offers rewards for correct answers. Between individual trials, reinforcement is given using a display of fireworks and verbal praise. Each correct answer earns the child a star, and 10 stars earns one token that can be traded for 20 seconds of play time on one of the built-in reward activities (e.g., bubble pop, drawing, favourite video, spinner). A progress bar at the bottom left of screen shows elapsed time, and after 20 seconds TOBY pauses the reward activity and returns to the current task.

Matching is also used to teach the names for classes of objects. Again, three images are presented, but now the target is defined via a voice instruction, such as "Find apple". Figure 1 (middle) shows an example of this task. TOBY organises categories into groups, and ranks them in order of increasing complexity. In this example, it has randomly chosen three sub-categories of *noun*: food, household object, and outdoor object, and has chosen the next simplest category in each set which has not already been presented: apple, bed, and moon. There are multiple examples of each category in the database, and these are chosen randomly during each trial.

The matching task described above that requires the child to choose the correct image given its name is termed *receptive matching*. A more difficult skill is to vocalize object names, which is termed *expressive matching*. Figure 1 (right) is an example of expressive matching. Again, TOBY uses three category MET, but in this case displays only the target image, with the instruction, "What is this?" TOBY relies on the parent to determine if the child's answer is correct, hence this is a partner task. Partner tasks include controls for the parent to give TOBY feedback. Here, valid feedback is one of Yes, Prompt, and No, which are mapped to buttons at the top right of screen. These are deliberately subtle in appearance so as not to attract the attention of the child.

If the child's response is correct, the parent presses the Yes button, and TOBY presents reinforcement before proceeding to the next trial. If the child's response is incorrect, the parent presses the No button. If appropriate, the parent may be asked to prompt the child using the prompt type displayed on the screen. In this example, the prompt type is *Choice*, so they would simplify the task by giving the child a choice, such as "Is it a dog or a cat?" If the child responds correctly with prompting, the parent presses the Prompt button.

A variety of tasks can be handled within this framework: Matching identical objects, where the child must match an object given an identical object; Matching non-identical objects, where the child must match an object to another of the same category; Receptive matching, where the child must match an object given its category; Expressive matching, where the child must name an object; Relational matching, where the child must match two objects based on a relationship between them. E.g., "Where does this [bird] live?" (in a nest), or "What is this [fork] used for?" (eating); and "What does not belong?" where the child must identify the object that does not belong in a group of similar objects.

Imitation Tasks

For imitation tasks, stimuli are in the form of video models, and the child performs the task by copying the actions of the model. Imitation tasks are used to teach skills in gross motor, fine motor, and oral motor imitation. These are prerequisite skills for expressive language. Each task includes 4 actions, which are presented in random order. According to performance, TOBY adjusts the suggested prompting level. Prompts are delivered by the parent using the suggested cues. TOBY includes 174 imitation videos, consisting of 100 actions and 74 echoic (oral-motor) videos. These are typically short, with an average duration of 1 second for echoic videos, and 4 seconds for action videos.

Figure 3 is a prototype screen for an imitation task, and a similar task in the current design. The task *symbolic oral imitation* requires the child to copy play sounds, like "beep-beep" and "meow". Most of the screen is reserved for the video, and above is the name of the action and current prompt type. Three buttons for parent feedback are located top right. This example has a prompt level of *Gesture and Model*, which the parent can enact to simplify the task by pointing to their lips, repeating the sounds, and breaking them into syllables.

The alterations from the early prototype, Figure 3 (left), were prompted by parent feedback. Initially, the system highlighted the current prompt level from a list of levels, and similarly for the current action. The aim was to communicate to parents the spectrum of prompt levels and action types by providing them in context. But in trials we found the effect of this interface was to confuse the parent, as it was interpreted as offering a choice, where in fact there was none. This screen also shows the parent controls rendered as regular buttons, which in practice attracted the attention of some children, who tried to press them and became frustrated when they were not allowed to do so. Subsequent versions were altered to the more subtle look shown on the right.

Natural Environment Training

Natural Environment Training (NET) generalizes skills by applying them to real-world situations. Typically, each part of the syllabus has 5 to 10 different NET tasks, grouped into two difficulty levels: *Adaptive* tasks modify a regular daily routine, such as meal time, dressing, washing, etc.; *Play* tasks

are specifically designed games and play, which can be done at any place or time. The child must perform a mixture of adaptive and play tasks to demonstrate mastery of a skill. The protocol defined by the therapists is as follows: 1) *First*, the child must complete one adaptive task; 2) *Next*, the child must complete one play task; 3) *Finally*, the child must complete another adaptive and play task within 1 week (the only time constraint in the app) to demonstrate both skills have been retained.

This constraint complicates the interface design, since depending on the stage (1, 2, or 3) different tasks are available to the user. If the child fails one stage, they regress to the previous stage which must be repeated. Thus, the user interface must indicate which tasks are available and why, as well as the current stage within the sequence.

NET tasks have the following template: Goal; Materials required; Description; Instructions for prompting and reinforcement if required. TOBY allows the parent to navigate each NET task at increasing levels of detail via the Overview, Activity and Outcome screens. Figure 4 (left) shows the Overview screen, which lists the NET activities available to the child given their current stage. At the top of the screen is a summary of what is required for this stage (e.g., stage 3's summary is "Revision: Complete one Adaptive and one Play activity within one week.") The parent taps a task to see its goal and required materials. For more detail, the parent taps *Select Activity*, which displays a screen like Figure 4 (middle). The Activity screen has a full step-wise description of the activity, and instructions for prompting and reinforcement. It can be used as a reference when performing the task.

After the task is complete, the parent selects *Add Outcome* to provide feedback to TOBY about how the child performed, which displays a screen like Figure 4 (right). The Outcomes screen enables the parent to indicate successful completion, failure, or a range of outcomes corresponding to the three prompting levels. The parent selects the level that best describes their child's performance. After trials we found some parents chose not to perform tasks they believed their children could do, which prompted us to add the outcome: "Skip, my child can already do this." This is treated as a successful attempt, but records that the task was not performed.

The NET interface underwent several iterations. The prototype integrated browsing and feedback into a single screen (see Figure 5), and listed available tasks on the left (similar to the current version), but the right pane included *all* of the task's instructions. This was found to be overwhelming, and was altered to the multi-stage format described above to enable the parent to consume the information in bites. In the first prototypes, the completion state of each task was indicated by an icon (tick, cross) prefixed to its item in the list. Parents added feedback about a task by tapping this icon, which triggered a pop-up containing the response options. But some parents mistakenly interpreted this to mean they couldn't attempt a task more than once. That is, they assumed a ticked task was completed and no longer available, whereas repeated task attempts were in fact desirable. Subsequent designs removed all feedback about previous task attempts.

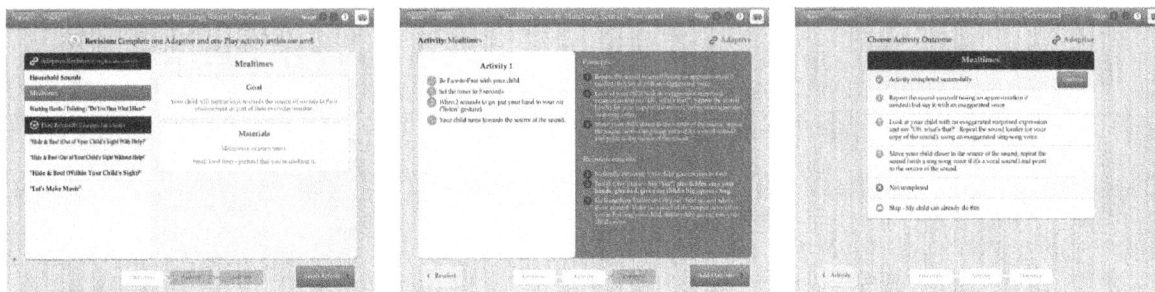

Figure 4. An example Natural Environment Training task: Overview, Activity, and Outcome screens.

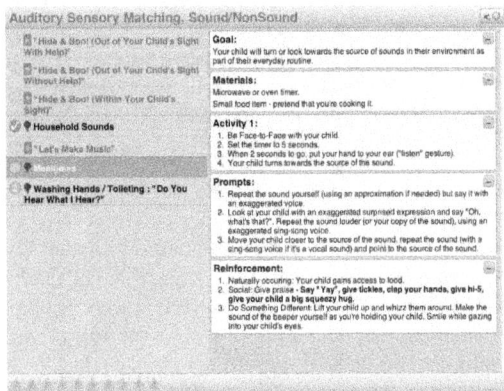

Figure 5. Early prototype NET screen.

Lesson Planning

Parents initiate tasks from the *Plan* screen, shown in Figure 6 (right). It is here that TOBY and the parent combine to schedule each day's lessons. The left side of the screen contains an extract of the current child's profile, including their name and photo (or an image of their choice), along with a summary of their progress. Bar graphs (bottom left) indicate the amount of the available course content completed for each kind of task–Sensory, Imitation, Language, and Social, in both iPad and NET–and so can be used by the parent to shape the lesson plan, by focussing on weak areas or capitalizing on sucesses.

On the right is the list of all currently available tasks. Each is represented by an item embellished with an icon indicating its type (left), its title (middle), and a selection toggle (right). Membership of this list is a function of the child's progress (recall that the syllabus is structured as a graph of task completion dependencies). The parent can tailor this plan by selecting a subset of tasks using the toggle "+", and those selected appear under the *My Plan* tab (middle top). My Plan was introduced to enable parents to firstly filter the–at times long–list of available tasks, and secondly to record tasks they intended to do. Tapping a task launches it, with optional intervening instructions for the chosen task. When it has been completed it appears for the remainder of the day checked with a tick, and is then moved to a list accessed under the *Completed* tab. Completed tasks can be revisited, but have no impact on progress. New tasks unlocked by the completion of pre-requisites appear dynamically in the available list.

The current form of the Plan screen is the result of a number of iterations that served to shift some of the initiative for lesson planning and pacing from TOBY to the parent. Figure 6 (left) shows an early prototype of the plan screen, then called

"Today's Lesson". It contained only a list of available tasks and a legend. In this prototype, the task list remained static during each day (apart from marking completed tasks), and was refreshed only when the parent manually triggered a *Replan* with the button in the top right of screen. This "batch" protocol was adopted initially for two reasons: first, to render newly available tasks more noticable to the user, and, second, to cause the available tasks to be balanced across the syllabus.

Feedback from the first two trials caused us to rethink this protocol. While some parents became concerned they weren't doing enough tasks each day, others found having to wait until the next day to access tasks at which their children were excelling too constraining–they, and our therapists, were keen to capitalize on a child's progress in a branch of the syllabus. The solution was to make the list dynamically update, provide detailed reports on per-skill progress, and allow sub-selection of tasks (i.e., My Plan). Thus parents could perform tasks at their own pace, go as deep in any branch of the syllabus as they desired (subject to the completion of pre-requisites), and be informed about any imbalances in skill acquisitions so they could redress them in their own time.

Activity Reports

TOBY's range of reports grew as it was recognized that feedback about a child's progress was important to the parent, both for the encouragement it could provide, and as a guide to scheduling future lessons. Moreover, when TOBY is functioning as a "wait-list" support tool, fine-grained reports become valuable information about the child's development at the comencement of formal therapy. Visible in the lower-left corner of Figure 6 (right) is a miniature version of the course progress summary. The bars represent the proportion of available skills that have been mastered, grouped by task type: Imitation, Language, Sensory, and Social, for iPad and NET tasks. Sections shaded green are completed, cross-hatched sections are available, and unshaded portions represent course material yet to be unlocked. Depending on the situation, the parent may continue to focus on areas of strength, or may decide to focus on areas of weakness.

Other reports include: Progress achieved the previous day; Task attempts over time, colour-coded to indicate successful, prompted, and unsuccessful attempts–see Figure 8 (left); Task attempts for NET and iPad tasks; Daily summary of results for NET and iPad tasks–see Figure 8 (right).

Help Guide

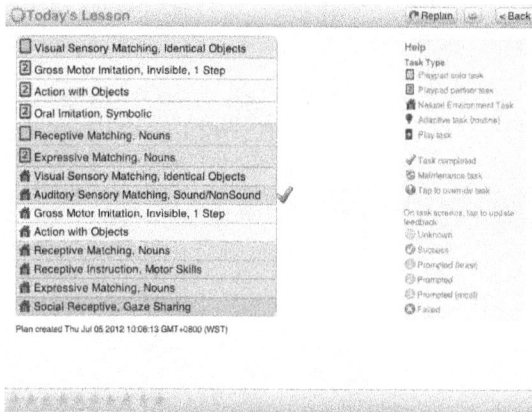

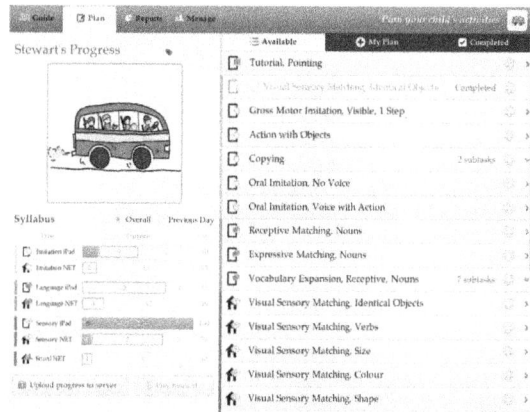

Figure 6. Left: Early prototype lesson plan screen (previously "Today's Lesson"). Right: Subsequent redesign showing a tabbed breakdown of available, scheduled, and completed tasks, and progress summarys.

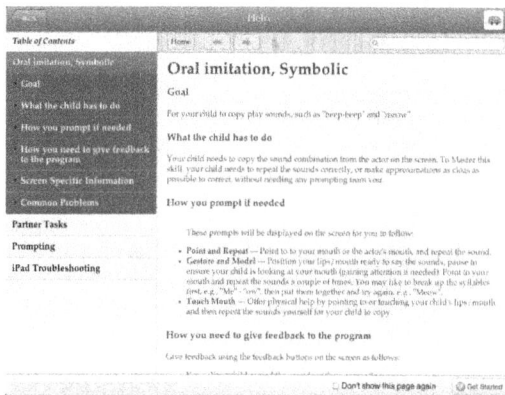

Figure 7. Detailed instructions specific to a task.

Feedback from the first two trials led to the creation of an extensive help system. Comprehensive help is unusual for iPad apps, where functionality tends to be limited, obvious, or inductive. In contrast, TOBY aims to empower parents in their role of therapist to their child, a task requiring them to digest concepts from the everyday language of psychology. Help includes: Information about early intervention, and *how* and *what* TOBY teaches; Instructions for Solo, Partner and NET tasks, prompting and reinforcement, and troubleshooting about attention and motivation; Video of prompting strategies for a variety of tasks; and Specific instructions for every iPad and NET task. In total, the documentation includes 30,000 words, 31 minutes of video about the system, and 23 minutes of prompting examples.

Each task has a set of instructions which are presented whenever the task is started. Figure 7 shows the instruction screen for the task "symbolic oral imitation". It briefly describes the task, but importantly reminds the parent:

- How they should prompt if required
- How they should give feedback to TOBY
- How they can deal with common problems (e.g., their child can't perform the task, or isn't motivated).

After reading the information, the parent launches the task with the *Get Started* button at the bottom right of screen. As the parent becomes more familiar with TOBY, they can skip task instructions with the "Don't show this page again"

checkbox. The instructions can later be accessed from within the task screen using the context-sensitive *Help* button. The rest of the documentation is available from the main screen under the *Guide* tab. Both task-specific help and general help share the same interface, shown in Figure 7. A topic list is shown on the left, and when a page is selected it expands to show the headings for quick navigation. Text is shown on the right, and may include supporting images and video.

EXPERIMENTS

We have undertaken three trials during the development of TOBY Playpad, each granting a greater degree of autonomy (and correspondingly lesser oversight) to the participants:

Trial 1: was conducted over 2 weeks, and involved 8 children and their parents, who performed tasks at Autism West, a registered provider of support services. This trial focussed on the mechanics of receptive and expressive matching, and an early implementation of NET. Each child spent 20-30 minutes on receptive or expressive matching (depending on developmental level) and the same amount on NET. Limited instructions about TOBY were given, and a therapist observed each session. Participants were solicited through Autism West.

Trial 2: lasted 4 weeks, and involved 16 children and their parents. This trial occurred in the homes of children. A parent information evening was conducted at Autism West to introduce TOBY's learning philosophy and interface. Two therapists called the families each week, and recorded any qualitative feedback in addition to TOBY's quantitative recording. Following the trial, a parent evening was held to de-brief and solicit further feedback or suggestions for improving TOBY. Participants were solicited through Autism West, and by expression of interest in response to an invitation on the TOBY website, up to a maximum of 16, first come first served.

Trial 3: lasted 6 weeks, and involved 47 children and their parents. Parents downloaded TOBY and worked at home at their own pace, and without therapist intervention, in a situation matching that faced by parents once TOBY was submitted to the App Store. Participants were solicited through Autism West and by expression of interest in response to an invitation on the TOBY website.

All children involved in the trials had a diagnosis of Autism, ranging in age from 2 to 8, with most between 2 and 6. There

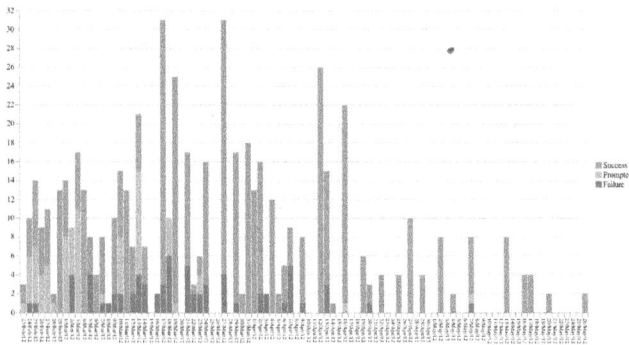

Figure 8. Left: Task attempt report, plotting successful (green), prompted (orange), and unsuccessful (red) task attempts per day. Ideally, reliance on prompting should decrease over time, as is the case here. Right: NET sessions report, showing times and results for each NET node, and optionally the related NET tasks. Note: a white background indicates a task has yet to be unlocked.

were approximately three times as many boys as girls, which corresponds roughly to the prevalence of ASD in the community at large. Below we focus on three aspects of these trials: qualitative feedback that informed design iterations; progression through the syllabus and evidence of learning; and profiling of when and how the application was used.

Qualitative Feedback, all Trials

Trials 1 & 2 were structured to obtain direct qualitative feedback from parents, and many has raised the impact of the subsequent design of TOBY and/or the suitability criteria for the application. Positive feedback is summarized under the following categories (paraphrased from explicit feedback):

A Sense of Empowerment – Many parents expressed their regret at not having had TOBY at the time of diagnosis, as they wanted to do something helpful but didn't know where to start. TOBY gave them easy, practical tools and ideas of how to do activities within the home, at any time. Some parents said TOBY taught them how to talk "therapist", and be proactive (based on the recorded progress) with their therapist, which made formal therapy time more productive.

Individuality & Adaptability – Parents liked how TOBY adapted to their child's progress at a fine level.

Syllabus Scope & Quality – Parents felt TOBY balanced play and structured activities. NET tasks were obviously designed by experienced therapists. Children displayed transfer of skills to other activities, such as being able to interact with computers generally. The syllabus helped identify gaps in current intervention programs and provide ideas on how to take therapy further, and served as a reminder for parents of different skills to focus on.

Recording & Accountability – Parents liked being accountable to TOBY and more thoughtful about therapy. Progress reports encouraged parents, and showed that previously taught skills have been maintained, strengthened, and generalised. The tangible record enabled them to say, "I've done enough today," rather than always, "I didn't get to X, Y, Z..."

Enjoyment & Ease of Use – NET tasks were easy and enjoyable, and parents look forward to extensions. Siblings joined in with tasks and activities–both NET and iPad–which provided futher reinforcement and family bonding.

Markee Moments – TOBY occasioned one child's first imitation of Mum, another's first pointing gesture, and another's first verbalization of "Mum".

Feedback obtained through exit surveys, communication with our therapists, and the parents events, prompted re-design of a number of facets of TOBY. A selection of these have been mentioned where appropriate, and are summarized here:

Algorithm – Some children weren't able to point, but would grasp the iPad, so we added tutorials to the root of the syllabus tree for the skills of pointing and dragging. More advanced children sometimes found progress tedious, so we introduced a "fast mastery" algorithm that rewarded 4 of 5 successful task attempts with completion (rather than 8 of 10).

Look & Feel – Some children were attracted to any and all buttons on screen. In response, parent controls on screens for children were de-emphasized. Some parents reported the initial NET screens to hold an intimidating amount of information. These were subsequently unpacked into parts, and combined with a visual indicator of the complex staging model.

Supporting Resources – Parents of newly diagnosed children were unfamiliar with core therapy concepts, such as reinforcement and prompting. The help guide was much expanded to cover these topics in depth and provide context-sensitive help at and during task performance. We also found that in some cases the home environment was interfering with therapy. In response we added material help on activity schedules, physical preparation of the home environment, use of external reward systems (e.g., to help with motivation), and explanation of learning concepts (goals, socially based activities, how to teach children).

Evidence of Learning, Trial 2

Based on iPad task performance, nearly all participants in Trial 2 can be assigned to one of 3 groups that showed evidence of learning. Figure 9 contains a plot for a child drawn from each group, where each plot presents the number of successful task attempts (S), successful attempts with a high. medium, and low levels of prompting (HP, MP, LP), and failed attempts (F). Below we interpret each group.

Children in Group 1 (profile ids 35, 37, 40, 50, and 72) progressed through the syllabus with ease, evidenced by consistent successful task attempts. Towards the second half of the trial when tasks get more challenging, the participants in this

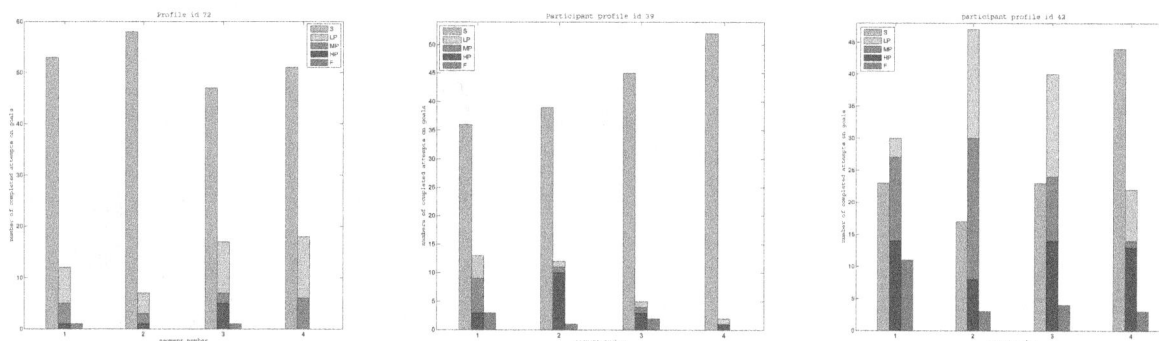

Figure 9. Trial 2 Evidence of Learning. Left: Group 1, successful task attempts over duration of trial; Middle: Group 2, steady increase in successful task attempts; Right: Group 3, increase in successful task attempts with decreasing prompts.

group typically learned new skills at a lower level of prompting. Figure 9 (left) plots an exemplar from this group.

Children in Group 2 (profile ids 39, 50, 65 and 84) made steady progress throughout the trial, as evidenced by increasing numbers of successful attempts without prompting. Figure 9 (middle) plots an exemplar from this group.

Children in Group 3 (profile ids 41 and 42) require prompting to learn across the trial, but even so, achieved increasing successful tasks attempts and decreasing prompting. Figure 9 (right) plots an exemplar from this group.

Of those children who did not evidence a clear trend in successful task attempts, all but one achieved more successful attempts than fails in any given skill.

Overall, we found that 40% of failed skills (18 out of 45) are eventually achieved without prompting, and 13% are achieved with some level of prompting. Moreover, the majority of skills (62% – 98 of 158) begun at some level of prompting were subsequently achieved without prompting. From the quantitative outcomes, we can confirm that TOBY met two important goals of any education application: it enabled *success* (by all but one child); and *learning* (Groups 1, 2 & 3).

The third educational goal targeted by TOBY is generalization of skills to daily life, which is a stepping stone to increased independence. To assess this aspect we turn to the results for NET. Recall that NET tasks make up 90% of the total tasks. A tasks could be attempted and completed more than once depending on how the child had progressed. NET tasks are also required to be revisited after a two week interval to test skill retention, and we found nearly all revisited NET tasks were successful. Of 2119 completed attempts (all participants), 1746 tasks, or 82.40%, were NET. Figure 10 (left) plots the popularity of NET tasks for this trial. From this we infer NET tasks were both accessible to the parents, and pitched appropriately with their partner iPad tasks.

Usage Patterns, Trial 3

With more participants, and a real-world scenario, Trial 3 afforded an opportunity to observe how TOBY was adopted into daily life. To do this we instrumented the app to log the timestamps and ids of all task attempts, together with the initial and subsequent state of the syllabus (e.g., if a task completion unlocks a new task). This allows us to see, e.g., if there exist temporal patterns for different kinds of tasks. In

addition, all navigation interactions are logged, thus allowing us to see how much time is spent reading the help guide (and which page), looking at reports, or playing rewards.

The chart at the top of Figure 10 (right) plots total amount of time spent actively using the TOBY Playpad for 32 families who spent at least 1 hour using the app, and uploaded their data to our server. The bottom chart plots proportions of time spent in different parts of the app. Those who spent a reasonable amount of time in the app (on the left) performed a mix of tasks, such as receptive and expressive matching, and NET; whereas those who spent the least time in the app, on the right, spent their time on help and management tasks.

Time spent on NET varies across users. This reflected different modes of use for NET tasks, which were subsequently uncovered through questionnaire. Some parents reported doing NET tasks with the iPad present as a reminder of the task parameters, and so they could supply feedback immediately. Others preferred to digest the NET task on the iPad, but then put it away when performing the task, because their child found it difficult to concentrate with the iPad present.

Some participants used rewards heavily (ids 56, 31, 61), and recorded less progress in other iPad activities. This may be because the children had difficulty focusing on the iPad tasks. Most parents spent at least 20% of their time in admin sections of the app (i.e., Help, Manage, Reports, and Plan), some as much as 60%. There are relatively few users who spent above 70% of their time on course content (ids 30, 22, 54, 28, 34, 50), but these tended to be the users who had spent proportionally the most time doing high-level iPad tasks e.g., (receptive and expressive matching), and less time doing NET.

For certain users, we noticed the time between first view of a NET task and feedback was too short for the task to actually have been performed. This explained the large number of task completions during some sessions–sometimes as many as 50 in one session. During de-briefing we discovered this behaviour was due to their believing their child was already able to do the task. We subsequently added the ability to skip NET tasks in this situation.

CONCLUSION

We have traced the evolution of TOBY Playpad, an iPad app for early intervention therapy for children with autism. Initially the primary design challenge appeared to be how to

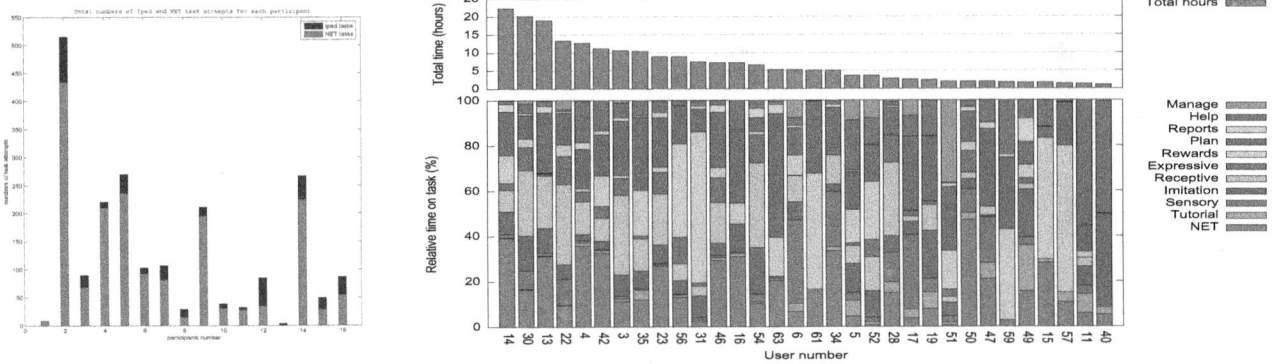

Figure 10. Left: Trial 2, Ipad and NET tasks. Right: Trial 3, total time using TOBY proportional breakdown, for 32 trial families.

encode therapist practice and deliver discrete trials. But as TOBY's scope expanded, and we observed and interacted with parents across a number of software trials, we came to realize that the major hurdle TOBY needed to jump was also its unique contribution: *teaching a parent how to teach.*

Unsurprisingly, this challenge led to the creation of an extensive, multimedia help resource. But it also caused the shift in TOBY's mixed-initiative daily lesson planning toward flexibility in task selection and pacing. This in turn led to the provision of richer progress reports by which to guide that parental intiative.

The parameters of three formal trials mirror the evolution of the software design, shifting, as they do, the onus toward parents, concluding with a large field trial that replicates the conditions of TOBY's ultimate deployment. The trials demonstrated clearly that TOBY engendered learning, but just as importantly, that the majority of parents came to understand the therapy process TOBY uses, and felt empowered because of their role in it. The immediate future will see TOBY's influence on learning outcomes tested in a large, independent clinical trial, extension of its syllabus to cover new skills and the 6-12 years range, and analysis of the feedback obtained from parents via various social media channels.

Acknowledgments

We would like to express our wholehearted appreciation to the children and parents participated in this study – without them, this research would have had never been possible. We wish them a bright future ahead. We also would like to acknowledge our speech therapist, Wendy Marshall and clinical psychologist, Darin Cains for their expertise and involvement in the development of TOBY and the trials.

REFERENCES

1. Bernard-Opitz, V., Sriram, N., and Nakhoda-Sapuan, S. Enhancing social problem solving in children with autism and normal children through computer-assisted instruction. *Journal of Autism and Developmental Disorders 31*, 4 (2001), 377–384.

2. Blocher, K., and Picard, R. Affective social quest: emotion recognition therapy for autistic children. In *In Socially Intelligent Agents-Creating Relationships with Computers and Robots*, Kluwer Academic Pub. (2002).

3. Bondy, A., Frost, L., and Bondy, A. *A picture's worth: PECS and other visual communication strategies in autism.* Woodbine House, 2001.

4. Bosseler, A., and Massaro, D. Development and evaluation of a computer-animated tutor for vocabulary and language learning in children with autism. *Jnl. of autism and developmental disorders 33*, 6 (2003), 653–672.

5. Hetzroni, O., and Tannous, J. Effects of a computer-based intervention program on the communicative functions of children with autism. *Journal of Autism and Developmental Disorders 34*, 2 (2004), 95–113.

6. Kientz, J., Hayes, G., Westeyn, T., Starner, T., and Abowd, G. Pervasive computing and autism: Assisting caregivers of children with special needs. *IEEE Pervasive Computing* (2007), 28–35.

7. Lorimer, P., Simpson, R., Smith Myles, B., and Ganz, J. The use of social stories as a preventative behavioral intervention in a home setting with a child with autism. *Jnl. of Positive Behavior Interventions 4*, 1 (2002), 53.

8. Lovaas, O. Behavioral treatment and normal educational and intellectual functioning in young autistic children. *Jnl. of consulting and clinical psych. 55*, 1 (1987), 3–9.

9. Schmidt, C., and Schmidt, M. Three-dimensional virtual learning environments for mediating social skills acquisition among individuals with autism spectrum disorders. In *Procs. of the Int. Conf. on Interaction Design and Children*, ACM (2008), 85–88.

10. Schreibman, L., Whalen, C., and Stahmer, A. The use of video priming to reduce disruptive transition behavior in children with autism. *Journal of Positive Behavior Interventions* (2000).

11. Stanton, C., Kahn Jr, P., Severson, R., Ruckert, J., and Gill, B. Robotic animals might aid in the social development of children with autism. In *Procs. of the ACM/IEEE Int. Conf. on Human Robot Interaction*, ACM (2008), 271–278.

12. Venkatesh, S., Greenhill, S., Phung, D., Adams, B., and Duong, T. Pervasive multimedia for autism intervention. *Pervasive and Mobile Computing* (2012).

Evaluation of Tablet Apps to Encourage Social Interaction in Children with Autism Spectrum Disorders

Juan Pablo Hourcade, Stacy R. Williams, Ellen A. Miller, Kelsey E. Huebner, Lucas J. Liang

Department of Computer Science, University of Iowa

Iowa City, Iowa 52242, USA

juanpablo-hourcade@uiowa.edu

ABSTRACT

The increasing rates of diagnosis for Autism Spectrum Disorders (ASDs) have brought unprecedented attention to these conditions. Interventions during childhood can increase the likelihood of independent living later in life, but most adults with ASDs who benefited from early intervention do not live independently. There is a need for novel therapies and interventions that can help children with ASDs develop the social skills necessary to live independently. Since the launch of the iPad, there has been a great deal of excitement in the autism community about multitouch tablets and their possible use in interventions. There are hundreds of apps listed as possibly helping children with ASDs, yet there is little empirical evidence that any of them have positive effects. In this paper we present a study on the use of a set of apps from Open Autism Software at an afterschool program for children with ASDs. The apps are designed to naturally encourage positive social interactions through creative, expressive, and collaborative activities. The study compared activities conducted with the apps to similar activities conducted without the apps. We video recorded the activities, and coded children's behavior. We found that during the study children spoke more sentences, had more verbal interactions, and were more physically engaged with the activities when using the apps. We also found that children made more supportive comments during activities conducted with two of the apps. The results suggest the approach to using apps evaluated in this paper can increase positive social interactions in children with ASDs.

Author Keywords

Autism; app; tablet; social skills.

ACM Classification Keywords

H.5 [Information interfaces and presentation (e.g., HCI)]: Miscellaneous; J.3 [Life and medical sciences]: Health.

INTRODUCTION

Multitouch tablets, including iPads, have made computing more accessible for a wide variety of populations. The simplicity of touch interactions and the portability of these devices have lowered the barriers for interacting with computers. A quick search for online videos yields older adults enjoying card games, toddlers playing games, and even frogs frustrated at not being able to eat ants on the screen.

Multitouch tablets have also brought hope to people with autism spectrum disorders (ASDs) and their families. ASDs are characterized by challenges in communication, social interaction, and symbolic or imaginative play [2]. An increase in the rate of diagnosis, with 1 in 88 children in the United States diagnosed with ASDs, has brought greater visibility and attention to ASDs [6].

The preference of many children with ASDs for touchscreens has long been documented [47, 51, 55]. In fact, a very expensive yet popular device for augmentative and assistive communication, the DynaVox, served many people with ASDs long before tablets became widely available [13]. The arrival of iPads has brought with it a veritable downpour of excitement about their use primarily by children with ASDs. For example, a recent feature in *60 Minutes*, a popular television news program in the United States highlighted anecdotes of children with ASDs using iPads [5]. The enthusiasm has also reached non-profit organizations dedicated to ASDs research, with *Autism Speaks,* one of the most important ones in the United States, recently starting an initiative called *Hacking Autism* to develop tablet apps [24]. This excitement has produced hundreds of apps that purportedly help children with ASDs, making it difficult for caregivers to identify useful apps [1] [24].

This difficulty is only made worse by the lack of empirical data supporting the use of specific approaches to the design or use of multitouch tablet apps for children with ASDs. Beyond making interaction simpler and more accessible, what actual activities with multitouch tablets can help children with ASDs improve in areas where they face challenges?

For the research presented in this paper, we used a set of free, open source, multitouch tablet apps from Open Autism Software [31]. These apps and the activities we conducted with them aim to help children with ASDs associate social interaction with positive feelings by making it happen naturally through creative, expressive and collaborative activities. In this paper, we focus on an evaluation of the impact of these activities on children over several months in an afterschool program. When comparing social behaviors with and without app-based activities, we found using the apps was associated with increased verbal communication, physical interaction, and supportive comments. In doing so, we contribute one of the first bits of empirical evidence supporting a specific approach toward the design and use of multitouch tablet apps for children with ASDs.

RELATED RESEARCH

A Deeper Look at ASDs

Depictions of people with ASDs in popular media can lead to stereotypical views on the characteristics of this population. In particular, there can be a sense that people with ASDs are similar to each other. The reality is that there is significant variability within this population [6]. Some people with ASDs do not speak, while others do not know when to stop talking. Some cannot make eye contact, while others will stare at people in socially inappropriate ways. In fact, leading scientists specializing in ASDs are reaching the conclusion that ASDs are not one condition, but many [9]. In addition, context can significantly affect the behavior of children with ASDs, leading to within-child variability [37]. Therefore, variability is an important factor to take into account when designing technologies for this population.

The common thread running through the spectrum and the main barrier preventing most high-functioning children with ASDs from growing up to be independent adults is challenges with social skills. In our own work with children with ASDs we have met many children who are quite talented, yet may not be able to fully share those talents with the rest of us due to their limited social skills. Early diagnosis and intervention are critical for improving these skills [26]. But even for those who benefited from early intervention, the percentage of adults with ASDs who can live independently remains low [3, 14, 32]. Therefore, while tools for early diagnosis are crucial, there is also a need to go beyond them and develop novel interventions.

The intervention for which there is the most evidence of positive effects is applied behavior analysis, which uses a behaviorist approach to teach skills in areas such as speech and motor skills [15]. These interventions are highly structured and use clear instructions, repetition, practice, and reinforcement. Naturalistic methods are also commonly used, taking advantage of children's interests to teach skills. For example, picture dictionaries can help children communicate their needs if they are not able to speak [52].

These interventions tend to be very costly, with estimates for intensive therapy in the United States ranging from 40 to 60 thousand dollars a year per child. This is in addition to medical costs that are about six times those of children without ASDs [6]. In addition, there are few free resources available. Therefore, any role technologies can play in reducing costs can make a difference, especially for families with limited financial resources.

Due to the complexity of needs for this population, there are usually several stakeholders that will be affected by interventions. Besides the people with ASDs themselves, stakeholders include parents, other family members, teachers, clinicians, therapists, caretakers, classmates, and so forth. From an interaction design perspective, having so many stakeholders increases the complexity of the design process, especially for technologies that may be used in multiple contexts.

Computer-Based Interventions

The most similar computer-based interventions to the ones evaluated in this paper are those that use multitouch screens. The pioneers in this approach were Piper et al. [44] who designed a four-player tabletop application. They found it to be effective in engaging children with ASDs, even though it required group work. Hendrix et al. worked with shy children, instead of children with ASDs, but followed a similar tabletop approach successfully, in this case giving shy children special roles to positively engage them with peers [29]. A collaboration between Israeli and Italian institutions yielded several activities on multitouch tables, some story-based, with examples of enforced collaboration used to encourage collaborative behaviors among children with ASDs [21, 23, 53]. These are all examples of applications that make use of computers to encourage face-to-face interactions for children with ASDs. The apps used in the research described in this paper have a similar goal, although the activities are less structured, and use tablets instead of tabletops. It also is unclear whether the benefits obtained with tabletops can be obtained with tablets, given differences in size, orientation, and mobility.

Tangible devices are another way to engage children with ASDs in face-to-face interactions. Examples include the work of Farr et al. with Topobo and LEGO toys [18], experiences with robots [19, 46], and toys with sensors and actuators [12].

Mobile devices are also increasingly used to support people with ASDs in their social interactions. A group at MIT implemented emotion-recognition algorithms on a mobile device to help people with ASDs who have difficulty recognizing emotions in face-to-face situations [38]. Escobedo et al.'s MOSOCO, based on previous work by Tentori and Hayes [50], provided children with instructions on how to interact with peers in a playground [16]. In addition, there are many software apps for both mobile phones and tablets that enable their users to communicate by selecting picture symbols that are then translated into speech for face-to-face communication (e.g. [47]). These follow the example of the DynaVox we mentioned previously, but are significantly more affordable [13].

Virtual characters can enable children to practice face-to-face communication, or to even communicate with others through a virtual character. Examples of this line of research include the work of Tartaro and Cassell [49] and the ECHOES project in the United Kingdom [20] [45].

Researchers have also developed many applications targeting traditional desktop and laptop computers, with the aim of improving a variety of skills related to communication. These include building vocabulary, vocalizing words, reading human faces, and learning about appropriate forms of communication (e.g., [4, 7, 17, 25, 39, 55]).

Other approaches aim to support children with autism, but are not specifically geared at improving face-to-face interactions. These include the computer-based implementation of visual-supports, schedules, and other common tools used in schools [28, 30]. Others are geared at developing motor skills, relaxation, and learning about cause and effect [34, 43], and there has also been a significant amount of research on tracking children's behavior (e.g., [1, 27, 35, 40, 54]).

DESCRIPTION OF APPS USED IN THIS STUDY

Overall Approach

The approach of the apps evaluated in the study presented in this paper is significantly different from that of the research reviewed above, and from the commercial apps developed for children with ASDs. The Open Autism Software suite aims to help children enhance their social skills by using tablet apps to entice children to engage in positive face-to-face interactions [42]. The idea is to help children practice social skills in activities they enjoy, where face-to-face interactions are desirable to them. This in turn can lead to children with ASDs associating positive feelings with face-to-face interactions. As the name of the suite implies, the apps are free and open source, and are written in Python, enabling them to run on a variety of platforms including Tablet PCs, Linux, MacOS, and Windows (not iOS).

The suite consists of a set of simple, flexible apps that can be used in a variety of activities involving creative, collaborative, and expressive endeavors. This focus is quite different from the prevailing behaviorist approaches. The intention is not to replace these existing approaches, but to complement them.

To provide an individualized experience, session facilitators can select a subset of apps and activities that best suit the participating children given their current needs and context. This contrasts with more typical approaches to customization that usually involve changing settings within a particular technology.

The apps have very simple user interfaces with little or no use of words to better appeal to a population that can often better process information visually than verbally [11], and can easily be distracted by irrelevant visual stimuli [41]. There are also no right or wrong ways of doing things in the apps, which in this case is intended to enable the children to explore the apps, feel free to express themselves, and reduce anxiety [22].

Description of Apps and Activities

In the research described in this paper we used four Open Autism Software apps. These are described in the Open Autism Software website, which includes videos [42], and in an article that included case studies [31]. We used the apps on a Dell XT2 Tablet running Windows 7. Below, we provide a brief description of the apps and the activities we conducted with them.

The first app, Drawing, allows children to express their creative ideas, interests and emotions through art. It provides basic drawing through the stylus, as well as panning and zooming using the pinch gesture [36] (pan with one finger, zoom and rotate with two fingers). It also includes a simple palette to change colors. This app is mainly used for collaborative storytelling for two or more participants. In the collaborative storytelling activities we asked children to take turns adding the next visual scene in a story. These activities promote creativity, fine motor skills, sharing, and collaboration.

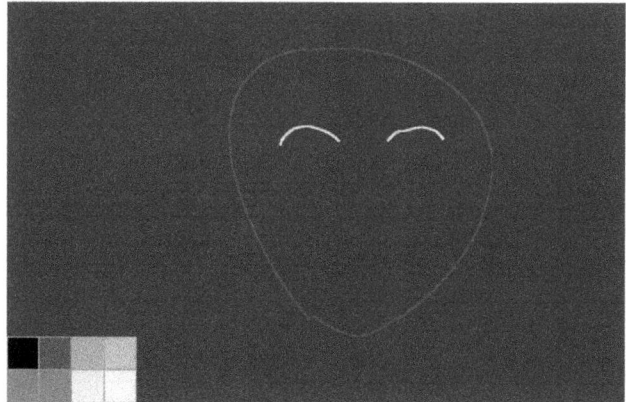

Figure 1. Drawing application showing color palette.

The next app is called Music. This app presents the user with a screen full of gray blocks. Touching a block turns it orange and produces a note. Touching it again removes the note. Using this method, users can create a short melody that the application continually loops through. Each column is played in turn, with the current column in green. Notes higher in each column representing higher pitched notes, and vice versa. For collaborative composition activities, we asked children to take turns adding a few notes until they were satisfied with the music. This activity helped children practice fine motor skills and turn taking.

Figure 2. A child using the Music app.

The third app, called Untangle, presents a visual puzzle. It appears as small circles, each connected to two other circles by straight lines. To solve the puzzle, users have to move the circles so that no lines overlap. When played collaboratively, the goal of the game is to encourage participants to cooperate and coordinate their actions. It also supports fine motor skills and sharing.

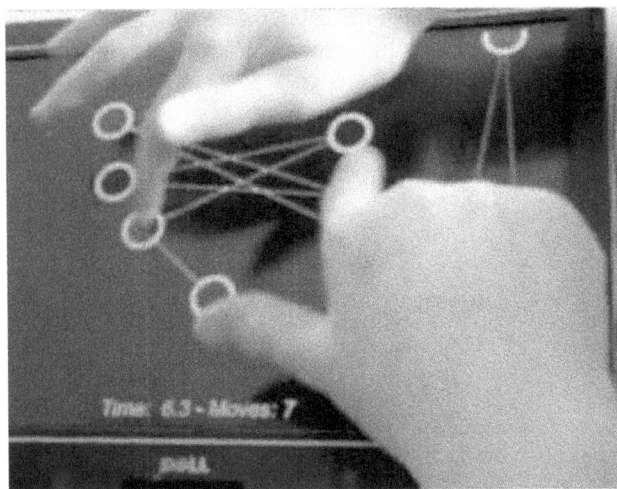

Figure 3. Two children using the Untangle app.

The last app is called Photogoo. In this app, users select an image within the application and then manipulate it by either distorting it with their fingers, or by drawing over it with the stylus. The application can be used for emotion modeling, where we ask children to change a face so that it looks like it displays a particular emotion. Many children also find this app quite amusing, especially when deforming the faces of adults they know. In this manner, it can be used as a reward, or to enhance a child's mood.

Figure 4. Photogoo with a modified Mona Lisa.

RESEARCH QUESTIONS

We wanted to learn whether the activities conducted with the Open Autism Software apps could lead to children diagnosed with ASDs being engaged in the activities themselves and socially with each other. To provide a fair comparison, we decided to compare them to non-computer activities that closely resembled the app-based activities.

METHOD

Participants

The participants were eight children, five boys and three girls. They were 10 to 14 years old (average age 12.5). They all attended an afterschool program for children with ASDs, intended for children on the higher end of the spectrum. The program used two rooms in a recreational center a few blocks away from our university.

Before we began our study, but after the children had a few weeks of daily activities with staff from the afterschool program, we asked the head of the staff to fill out the Super Skills Profile of Social Difficulty, which is used as part of the Super Skills program for children with ASDs [8]. The questionnaire rates children in four different skill areas through several questions under each area. These skill areas are: fundamental skills, social initiation skills, social response skills, and getting along with others. The scale goes from 0 to 6, with 0 being "very difficult" and 6 being "very easy". Figure 5 shows a summary of the scores for participating children and also illustrates the diversity of the population, even among a group of children who were grouped because of similar needs and abilities.

Materials

To have a fair comparison with the Open Autism Software apps, we developed equivalent activities that did not involve computers. As a counterpart to the Drawing app, we brought large sheets of paper (25 by 30 inches) together with markers. Using these materials, we facilitated collaborative storytelling activities the same way we did for the Drawing app. As a counterpart to the Music authoring app, we brought a music keyboard that children could take turns playing. As counterparts to Photogoo and Untangle, we observed the children conduct their regular activities at the program, which included playing board games, working on art projects, and practicing social skills.

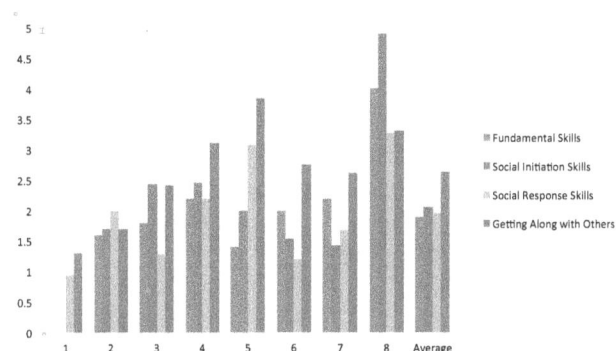

Figure 5. Skills for the eight children participating in the study according to the Super Skills Profile of Social Difficulty. The x-axis shows sets of bars for each child (and one for the aveage). The y-axis show the ratings on a 0 to 6 scale (the higher, the better the skills).

Procedures

We conducted research activities in the afterschool program on Monday afternoons starting in September of 2011 through April of 2012. We conducted activities with all the children who were present every time we went. It was common for a couple of children to be absent. The staff at the afterschool program would send two children at a time to work with two researchers, one facilitating the session, and the other video-recording it. In addition, a member of the afterschool staff was always present during the research sessions.

The role of session facilitators was the same for all conditions and involved introducing an activity and helping it move along by, for example, prompting children to end their turn. For the storytelling activities (with app or large sheet of paper), the instructions were exactly the same, asking children to get started on a story with a "once upon a time there was a…", asking them to draw first and tell the story later, and take turns adding elements to the story. We followed the same pattern for other activities.

The sessions were conducted in a room adjacent to where the regular afterschool program activities occurred. Each session with a pair of children was usually 10 to 15 minutes long.

Design

This was a within-subjects study. The independent variable was the type of media used (apps vs. non-computer). We began the study with children using the apps, with observations from 14 sessions (we usually hosted three or four sessions during each visit). We then proceeded to

facilitate the non-computer activities, with observations from 40 sessions. After this, we returned to app-based activities for another 25 sessions.

This design provided us with the ability to observe changes in behavior over time, and gave us a chance to compare the values of the independent variable with less concern about learning or changes in behavior due to other factors.

We coded the videos for events related to social skills and engagement in the activities, yielding the dependent variables for the study. We describe the coding process in the next section.

RESULTS

Below, we first describe how we coded the videos. We then discuss results by dependent variable. For statistical analyses, we used SPSS 19. All the variables we coded were numeric. We tested whether they had a normal distribution using Kolmogorov-Smirnov's test. If they had a normal distribution, we compared activities with and without apps using a paired t-test, or a repeated measures ANOVA if comparing the three sets of sessions. For data that was not normally distributed we used Wilcoxon's signed ranks test when comparing two values of a variable, and Friedman's test for more values. The statistical analyses used average values of each variable per child for each set of the three sets of sessions.

Coding of Video Recordings

The videos of the recorded sessions focused on the children, as opposed to filming what they were doing with the apps or other materials. Therefore, we were able to capture their facial expressions and what they did with their bodies during the sessions.

Three researchers who had not previously participated in the project coded and processed the video recordings. One researcher performed the coding of the videos. Two other researchers transcribed all the sessions verbatim.

We decided to code events that would reflect social engagement as well as engagement with the activities. The coding researcher did the coding by watching video to avoid mistakes due to the use of sarcasm by some children. Below are the types of events we coded, together with a brief description of each.

Verbal interactions. We coded for the number of verbal exchanges by children in a session to separate it from how much they spoke since a few of the children could go into long monologues. We counted a new verbal interaction when the child speaking would change, or whenever a child would speak after an adult spoke.

Supportive comments. These are cases where a child verbally expressed support or encouragement toward another child. We also included cases when they provided helpful suggestions to other children. Examples: "I think it looks awesome!"; "Perhaps you should move that...you might want to move that green circle over here"

Discouraging comments. These are cases where a child verbally expressed displeasure toward another child or verbally criticized them. Examples: "Stop saying shy! What is wrong with you?" (said during a session where one student presented an emotion and the other had to guess).

Physical interactions. We primarily looked for turn-taking, counting a new interaction with each turn taken, but also counted it as an interaction if a child joined into the other child's turn (e.g., playing a keyboard together, or adding notes to the Music app together). We decided to code this to provide a sense of the children's engagement in an activity.

Atypical behavior. We coded for non-verbal behaviors that would be unusual in typically developing children. These included rocking, jumping, and making noises during sessions.

Social missteps. These included inappropriate tone of voice, staring or avoiding eye contact, invading personal space, and interrupting or breaking a social interaction.

Time off-task. We coded the beginning and end of episodes where children would do something other than participate in the activity.

We also transcribed all the sessions verbatim. We used these transcripts to measure the number of sentences spoken by children per session.

Since sessions were of different lengths, we normalized all the measures above to occurrences per minute (e.g., sentences per minute, supportive comments per minute).

Number of Sentences

The number of sentences per child per minute was normally distributed. A paired t-test found a statistically significant difference in the number of sentences per child per minute between sessions with and without apps (p=.005). Children spoke more sentences per minute when using the apps. Comparing the three sets of sessions through a repeated measures ANOVA did not yield statistically significant differences. See the differences between sessions with and without apps in Figure 6.

Verbal Interactions

There was a statistically significant difference in the number of verbal interactions per minute between activities with and without apps (p=.001), based on a paired t-test. However, this did not extend to a statistically significant difference when comparing the three periods of activities. There were more verbal interactions per minute when children used apps. Figure 7 shows the change over time with a clear dip in the number of verbal interactions per minute when no apps were used. Figure 8 gives a sense for the variability between children showing changes with one line per child.

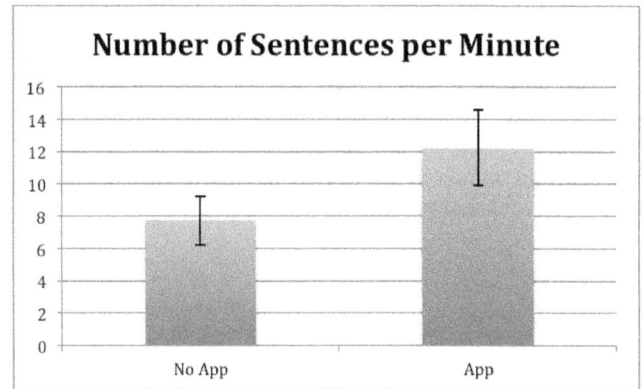

Figure 6. Number of sentences per child per minute comparing sessions with and without the use of apps. Error bars are two standard errors long.

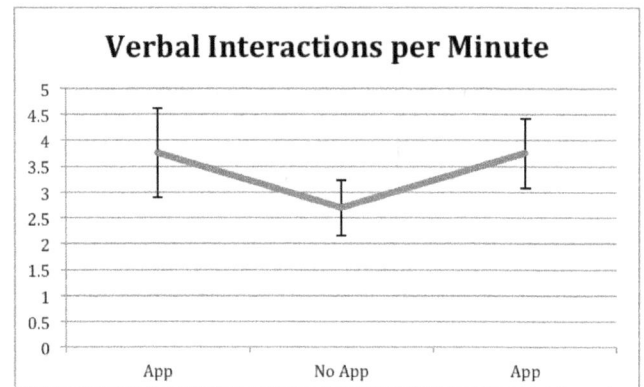

Figure 7. Verbal interactions per minute. Error bars are two standard errors long.

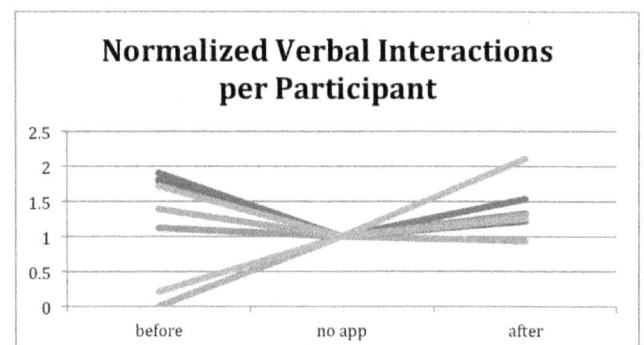

Figure 8. Verbal interactions per participant normalized by the average verbal interactions per minute for the set of sessions without apps.

Supportive Comments

There was no statistically significant difference between sessions with and without apps in terms of supportive comments. However, a closer look at the data revealed differences if we broke down numbers by activity (e.g., Drawing, Music, Photogoo, Keyboard). Further investigation revealed that there were many more supportive comments with the Music and Untangle apps than with any other activity (see Figure 9).

There were statistically significant differences between the activities with the two apps that promoted supportive comments, those with the apps that did not, and those with no apps. Friedman's test yielded p=.011.

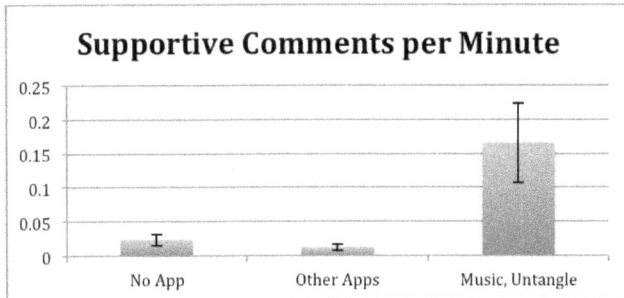

Figure 9. Supportive comments per minute by type of activity. Error bars are two standard errors long.

Discouraging Comments

There were no statistically significant differences in terms of discouraging comments.

Physical Interactions

There were statistically significant differences when comparing physical interactions per minute in the three sets of activities through a repeated measures ANOVA, adjusting for lack of sphericity through Geenhouse-Geisser $(F(1.1, 6.6)=7.528, p<.05, power=.66)$. Figure 10 shows the changes in the number of physical interactions, with a clear dip when children switched to no apps, and with numbers not quite picking up to the original level when children returned to using apps.

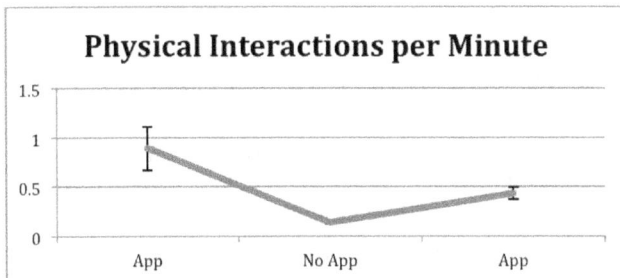

Figure 10. Physical interactions per minute. The error bars are two standard errors long.

Other Dependent Variables

We did not find any statistically significant differences between app and non-app activities for atypical behavior, social missteps, or time off-task.

DISCUSSION

The results provide some of the first empirical evidence of tablet apps helping children with ASDs engage in positive social behaviors. In particular, the greater rate of verbal

interactions suggests that the children in the study engaged in more exchanges with others during these activities. Likewise, the two apps that led to more supportive comments may provide useful ideas for additional activities that may enable children with ASDs to practice more advanced social skills.

Beyond the impact on children with ASDs, this study is also a rare example of tablet apps leading to higher quality face-to-face interactions.

Why Did It Work?

The app activities that were part of the study took advantage of children with ASDs' interest in computers and technology to have them engage in social activities. In the research we have conducted with dozens of children with ASDs, the most consistent interest we have found is in some variation of computers. This interest is understandable given the difficulty these children have with social interactions. In our conversations with participants, we have learned that one of their main sources of anxiety comes form uncertainty or unexpected events. Interacting with computers is much more predictable and controllable than interacting with people. We believe that the social interactions in the app activities were easier and more comfortable for participants because they happened in the context of an enjoyable activity with a computer. This made the children more confident, less anxious, and led to increased engagement.

In terms of the two app activities that generated more supportive comments, we believe they did so for somewhat different reasons. In the Music app activity, children liked the music they made together, and would often comment on how they liked what another child had done. The advantage the app provided is that it did not require any expertise to create likable music. The Untangle app activity timed children on how quickly they would complete a puzzle, giving them an incentive to complete it faster, appreciate help from others, offer help, and provide encouragement.

Limitations

The number of participants was low compared to most HCI research studies, but similar to other studies involving special needs populations. The length of the study and the need for researchers to engage directly with participants during each session limited the number of participants with whom we could work. Adding more participants would have likely meant adding additional sites to the study, which would bring with it additional factors due to different contexts.

There are also limitations due to the variability between children with ASDs. Because of this variability, the small number of children in the study, and the lack of additional randomization, the results from statistical tests presented in this study should be taken with great caution. The descriptive statistics shared through charts though, provide strong evidence supporting our overall conclusions. However, children with ASDs, but with different needs and abilities from those who participated in the study may not benefit from using the apps. Children with ASDs also vary their behavior significantly based on context, and conducting similar activities in different contexts could yield different results.

The study setup had some limitations. There were not an equal number of sessions with apps before and after the sessions without apps. However, the statistical methods we used adjusted for these differences. There was also only coder, which could have compromised reliability.

Parents should be aware that the fact that we obtained positive results favoring tablet apps in this study does not mean that iPads or other tablet apps will benefit children with ASDs. However, we expect that similar approaches to those used in this study, where apps are used to encourage positive face-to-face social interactions through creative and collaborative activities are likely to yield positive results for children with similar backgrounds to those in the study.

Future Work

An obvious follow up to this study would be a larger one with more sites. It would also be useful to increase the frequency of these activities (e.g., hosting them every day), so that the chances that they may influence children's behavior in other activities would increase. It would also be useful to develop similar activities with lower functioning children with ASDs in mind, to help them develop more basic social skills.

We have also noticed in some of our sessions that some of the children seemed to improve their mood during the app-based activities. This could lead to an additional research study.

In addition, we think it would be interesting to analyze the types of stories, music, and other creations that children with ASDs put together during these activities.

CONCLUSION

In this paper we presented a study evaluating the use of tablet apps for encouraging social interaction in children with ASDs. In the study, children with ASDs spoke more sentences, engaged in more verbal exchanges, and were more physically engaged with the activities when involved in app-based activities than when conducting similar activities that did not involve tablet apps. In addition, two of the activities pursued with apps led to a greater number of supportive comments when compared to other activities. These results suggest the approach to tablet activities presented in this paper may have a positive effect in children with ASDs' social interactions.

ACKNOWLEDGMENTS

This work would not have been possible without the collaboration of the children who participated and their parents. We would also like to thank the members of the research team who previously worked in this project, especially Thomas Hansen, who developed the apps, and Natasha Bullock-Rest, who played a major role in developing the activities around the apps. We would also like to thank the staff from the Children's Center for Therapy in Iowa City for their help and support in these research activities. We would also like to acknowledge our other research partners: Hoover Elementary School in Iowa City, Iowa, the Grant Wood Area Education Agency (especially Deb Scott-Miller) and Four Oaks in Cedar Rapids, Iowa (in particular Monica Ryan-Rausch). This research was funded in part by the University of Iowa's Social Sciences Funding Program.

REFERENCES

1. Abinali, F., Goodwin, M.S. and Intile, S. (2009). Recognizing stereotypical motor movements in the laboratory and classroom: a case study with children on the autism spectrum. In *Proceedings of the 11th international conference on Ubiquitous computing* (Ubicomp '09). ACM, New York, NY, USA, 71-80.

2. American Psychiatric Association (2000). *Diagnostic and statistical manual of mental disorders* 4th. Ed., text rev.).

3. Billstedt, E., Gillberg, C. and Gillberg, C. (2005). Autism after Adolescense: Population-based 13- to 22-year Follow-up Study of 120 Individuals with Autism Diagnosed in Childhood. *Journal of Autism and Developmental Disorders, 35*(3), 351-360.

4. Bosseler, A. and Massaro, D.W. (2003). Development and evaluation of a computer-animated tutor for vocabulary and language learning in children with autism. *Journal of Autism and Developmental Disorders, 33*(6), 653-669.

5. CBS News (2012). *Studying autism and iPads.* Available at http://www.cbsnews.com/video/watch/?id=7385702n

6. CDC (2012). *Data and Statistics- Autism Spectrum Disorders (ASDs).* Available at http://www.cdc.gov/ncbddd/autism/data.html

7. Coleman-Martin, M.B., Wolff-Heller, K., Cihak, D.F. and Irvine, K.L. (2005). Using computer-assisted instruction and the nonverbal reading approach to teach word identification. *Focus Autism Other Dev Disabl, 20,* 80-90.

8. Coucouvanis, J. (2005). *Super Skills.* Shawnee Mission, Kansas: Autism Asperger Publishing Company.

9. Dawson, G. (2012). *Annual Letter from the Chief Science Officer.* Autism Speaks. Available at

http://www.autismspeaks.org/science/science-news/annual-letter-chief-science-officer

10. Des Roches Rosa, S. (2011). iPads for Autism: A spreadsheet of reviews and recommendations. Available at http://www.squidalicious.com/2011/01/ipad-apps-for-autism-spreadsheet-of.html

11. Dickerson Mayes, S. and Calhoun, S.L. (2003). Ability profiles in children with autism. *Autism, 7*(1), 65-80.

12. Dsouza, A.J., Barretto, M. and Raman, V. (2012). *Uncommon Sense: Interactive Sensory toys that encourage Social Interaction among children with Autism.* IDC 2012 Wokshop on Interactive Technologies for Children with Special Needs.

13. DynaVox (2012). Available at http://www.dynavoxtech.com

14. Eaves L.C. and Ho H.H. (2008). Young adult outcome of autism spectrum disorders. *J Autism Dev Disord, 38*(4). 739–47.

15. Elkeseth, S (2009) Outcome of comprehensive psycho-educational interventions for young children with autism. Research in Developmental Disabilities 30(1):158-78.

16. Escobedo, L., Nguyen, D.H., Boyd, L., Hirano, S., Rangel, A., Garcia-Rosas, D., Tentori, M. and Hayes, G. (2012). MOSOCO: a mobile assistive tool to support children with autism practicing social skills in real-life situations. In *Proceedings of the 2012 ACM annual conference on Human Factors in Computing Systems* (CHI '12). ACM, New York, NY, USA, 2589-2598.

17. Faja, S., Aylward, E., Bernier, R. and Dawson, G. (2008). Becoming a face expert: a computerized face-training program for high-functioning individuals with autism spectrum disorders. *Developmental Neuropsychology 33*, (1), 1-24.

18. Farr, W., Yuill, N. and Raffle, H. (2010) Social benefits of a tangible user interface for children with Autistic Spectrum Conditions. *Autism, 14*(3), 237-52.

19. Feil-Seifer, D., Mataric, M.J. (2009). Toward socially assistive robotics for augmenting interventions for children with autism spectrum disorders. In Siciliano, B., Khatib, O. and Groen, F. (eds.). *Experimental Robotics*. Berlin: Springer.

20. Frauenberger, C., Good, J., Alcorn, A. and Pain, H. 2012. Supporting the design contributions of children with autism spectrum conditions. In *Proceedings of the 11th International Conference on Interaction Design and Children* (IDC '12). ACM, New York, NY, USA, 134-143.

21. Gal, E., Bauminger, N., Goren-Bar, D., Pianesi, F., Stock, O., Zancanaro, M. abd Weiss, P.L. (2009). Enhancing social communication of children with high-functioning autism through a co-located interface. *AI & Soc, 24*, 75-84.

22. Gillott, A., Furniss, F. and Walter, A. (2001). Anxiety in high-functioning children with autism. *Autism, 5*(3), 277-286.

23. Giusti, L., Zancanaro, M., Gal, E. and Weiss, P.L. (2011). Dimensions of collaboration on a tabletop interface for children with autism spectrum disorder. In *Proceedings of the 2011 annual conference on Human factors in computing systems* (CHI '11). ACM, New York, NY, USA, 3295-3304

24. Hacking Autism (2012). Available at http://www.hackingautism.org/

25. Hailpern, J., Karahalios, K. and Halle, J. (2009). Creating a Spoken Impact: Encouraging Vocalization through Audio Visual Feedback in Children with ASD. *Proceedings of CHI 2009*, 453-462.

26. Harris, S.L. and Handleman, J.S. (2000). Age and IQ at Intake as Predictors of Placement for Young Children with Autism: A Four- to Six-Year Follow-Up. *Journal of Autism and Developmental Disorders, 30*(2), 137-142.

27. Hayes, G.R., Kientz, J.A., Truiong, K.N., White, D.R., Abowd, G.D. and Pering, T. (2004). Designing Capture Applications to Support the Education of Children with Autism. *Ubicomp 2004*, 161-178.

28. Hayes, G.R., Hirano, S., Marcu, G., Monibi, M., Nguyen, D.H. and Yeganyan, M. (2010). Interactive visual supports for children with autism. *Personal and Ubiquitous Computing, 14*(7), 663-680.

29. Hendrix, K., van Herk, R., Verhaegh, J. and Markopoulos, P. (2009). Increasing children's social competence through games, an exploratory study. *Proceedings of IDC 2009*. ACM Press: pp. 182-185.

30. Hirano, S.H., Yeganyan, M.T., Marcu, G., Nguyen, D.H., Boyd, L. and Hayes, G.R. (2010). vSked: evaluation of a system to support classroom activities for children with autism.

31. Hourcade, J.P., Bullock-Rest, N.E. and Hansen, T.E. (2012). Multitouch tablet applications and activities to enhance the social skills of children with autism spectrum disorders. *Personal and Ubiquitous Computing, 16*, 157-168.

32. Howlin, P., Goode, S., Hutton, J. and Rutter M. (2004). Adult outcome for children with autism. *J Child Psychol Psychiatry, 45*(2), 212–29.

33. Joshi, P. (2011). *Finding Good Apps for Children with Autism*. New York Times Gadgetwise Blog. Available at http://gadgetwise.blogs.nytimes.com/2011/11/29/finding-good-apps-for-children-with-autism/

34. Keay-Bright, W. (2009). ReacTickles: playful interaction with information communication

technologies. *International Journal of Arts and Technology, 2*(1), 133-151.

35. Kientz, J.A., Hayes, G.R., Westeyn, T.L., Starner, T. and Abowd, G.D. (2007). Pervasive Computing and Autism: Assisting Caregivers of Children with Special Needs. *IEEE Pervasive Computing, 6*(1), 28-35.

36. Krueger, M.W. (1983). *Artificial Reality*. Reading, MA:Addison-Wesley

37. Lopez, B. and Leekam, S.R. (2003). Do children with autism fail to process information in context? *Journal of Child Psychology and Psychiatry, 44*(2), 285–300.

38. Madsen, M., el Kaliouby, R., Goodwin, M., Picard, R. (2008) Technology for just-in-time in-situ learning of facial affect for persons diagnosed with an autism spectrum disorder. *Proceedings of Assets '08*, 19-26.

39. Moore, M. and Calvert, S. (2000). Brief Report: Vocabulary Acquisition for Children with Autism: Teacher or Computer Instruction. *Journal of Autism and Developmental Disorders, 30*(4), 359-362.

40. Nazneen, N., Rozga, A., Romero, M., Findley, A.J., Call, N.A., Abowd, G.D. and Arriaga, R.I. (2012). Supporting parents for in-home capture of problem behaviors of children with developmental disabilities. *Personal Ubiquitous Comput., 16*(2), 193-207.

41. Ohta, H., Yamada, T., Watanabe, H., Kanai, C., Tanaka, E., Ohno, T., Takayama, Y., Iwanami, A., Kato, N. and Hashimoto, R. (2012). An fMRI study of reduced perceptual load-dependent modulation of task-irrelevant activity in adults with autism spectrum conditions. *NeuroImage, 61*(4), 1176-1187.

42. Open Autism Software (2012). Available at http://www.openautismsoftware.org/

43. Pares, N., Carreras, A., Durany, J., Ferrer, J., Freixa, P., Gomez, D., Kruglanski, O., Pares, R., Ribas, J.I., Soler, M. and Sanjurjo, A. (2005). Promotion of creative activity in children with severe autism through visuals in an interactive multisensory environment. In *Proceedings of the 2005 conference on Interaction design and children* (IDC '05). ACM, New York, NY, USA, 110-116.

44. Piper, A.M., O'Brien, E., Ringel Morris, M. and Winograd, T. (2006). SIDES: A cooperative tabletop computer game for social skills development. *Proceedings of CSCW 2006*. ACM Press: pp. 1-10.

45. Porayska-Pomsta, K., Frauenberger, C., Pain, H., Rajendran, G., Smith, T., Menzies, R., Foster, M. E., Alcorn, A., Wass, S., Bernadini, S., Avramides, K., Keay-Bright, W., Chen, J., Waller, A., Guldberg, K.,

Good, J. and Lemon, O. (2012). Developing technology for autism: an interdisciplinary approach. *Personal Ubiquitous Comput.* 16, 2 (February 2012), 117-127.

46. Robins, B., Dickerson, P., Stribling, P. and Dautenhahn, K. (2004). Robot-mediated joint attention in children with autism: A case study in robot-human interaction. *Interaction Studies, 5*(2), 151-198.

47. Sampath, H., Indurkhya, B. and Sivaswany, J. (2012). A Communication System on Smart Phones and Tablets for Non-verbal Children with Autism. *Lecture Notes in Computer Science, 7383*, 323-330.

48. Sitdhisanguan, K., Chotikakamthorn, N., Dechaboon, A. and Out, P. (2012). Using tangible user interfaces in computer-based training systems for low-functioning autistic children. *Personal Ubiquitous Comput., 16*(2), 143-155.

49. Tartaro A, Cassell J (2008) Playing with Virtual Peers: Bootstrapping Contingent Discourse in Children with Autism. Proceedings of ICLS 2008.

50. Tentori, M. and Hayes, G.R. (2010). Designing for interaction immediacy to enhance social skills of children with autism. In *Proceedings of Ubiquitous computing* (Ubicomp '10). ACM, New York, NY, USA, 51-60.

51. WATI (1997). *Designing Environments for Successful Kids: A Resource Manual*. Wisconsin Assistive Technology Initiative, Oshkosh, WI.

52. Weiss, M.J., Fiske, K. and Ferraioli, S. (2008). Evidence-Based Practice for Autism Spectrum Disorders. In *Clinical Assessment and Intervention for Autism Spectrum Disorders* (Johnny Matson, Ed.). Burlington, MA: Academic Press.

53. Weiss, P.L., Gal, E., Zancanaro, M., Giusti, L., Cobb, S., Millen, L., Hawkins, T., Glover, T., Sanassy, D. and Eden, S. (2011). Usability of Technology Supported Social Competence training for Children on the Autism Spectrum. *International Conference on Virtual Rehabilitation*.

54. Westeyn, T.L., Abowd, G.D., Starner, T.E., Johnson, J.M., Presti, P.W. and Weaver, K.A. (2012). Monitoring children's developmental progress using augmented toys and activity recognition. *Personal and Ubiquitous Computing, 16*(2), 169-191.

55. Whalen, C., Liden, L., Ingersoll, B., Dallaire, E., Liden, S. (2006). Behavioral improvements associated with computer-assisted instruction for children with developmental disabilities. *The Journal of Speech and Language Pathology 1*(1), 11-26.

Investigating the Use of Circles in Social Networks to Support Independence of Individuals with Autism

Hwajung Hong[1], Svetlana Yarosh[2], Jennifer G. Kim[3], Gregory D. Abowd[1], Rosa I. Arriaga[1]

[1]Georgia Institute of Technology
{hwajung, abowd, arriaga}@gatech.edu

[2]AT&T Research Labs
lana@research.att.com

[3]University of Illinois at Urbana-Champaign
jgkim2@illinois.edu

ABSTRACT

Building social support networks is crucial both for less-independent individuals with autism and for their primary caregivers. In this paper, we describe a four-week exploratory study of a social network service (SNS) that allows young adults with autism to garner support from their family and friends. We explore the unique benefits and challenges of using SNSs to mediate requests for help or advice. In particular, we examine the extent to which specialized features of an SNS can engage users in communicating with their network members to get advice in varied situations. Our findings indicate that technology-supported communication particularly strengthened the relationship between the individual and extended network members, mitigating concerns about over-reliance on primary caregivers. Our work identifies implications for the design of social networking services tailored to meet the needs of this special needs population.

Author Keywords

Social networks, social support, autism, independence

ACM Classification Keywords

H.5.3. Information interfaces and presentation (e.g., HCI): Group and Organization Interfaces

General Terms

Human Factors; Design;

INTRODUCTION

Like all young people, youth with autism face life transitions when they leave school or home. An adolescent with autism and her family face many challenges on the way to attaining a satisfying independent life for that individual [12]. One of those challenges is developing a robust and sufficiently large network of people who can provide advice about everyday situations. These situations vary in terms of the immediacy of the need for an answer and the topic addressed (e.g., health, grooming and dressing, home upkeep, school or work relationships, financial planning and management and leisure activities [25]). Over-reliance on a small set of people, typically a primary caregiver, is a barrier to independence and a burden on the caregiver [3]. Thus, having access to social support networks with people who can provide help is crucial both for the individual and for the primary caregivers [23].

Social networking services (SNSs) are used widely today as a way for an individual to communicate with a wide set of people. In particular, over the past years interesting new features to SNS have been introduced to encourage and support different communicative patterns. One of those specialized features, the focused communication circle [14], is of particular interest to the work presented here. The ability to direct conversations either to a set of people with a common social connection (e.g., family, friends, co-workers) or to those interested in a particular topic (e.g., health, job coaching) may be a promising way to break the trend of over-reliance on the primary caregivers for individuals with special needs.

Our research goal is to identify opportunities and challenges of the use of SNS to support independence for adolescents and young adults with autism[1]. The study reported here recruited individuals having Asperger's Syndrome, a diagnosis that reflects an individual with average or above average language skills, but with qualitative impairments in social interaction and restricted, and stereotyped patterns of behavior, interests, and activities. Of particular interest here is the support SNS provide for individuals who seek information, advice and support for specific life transitions and social problems.

In this paper, we explore a particular feature of SNSs, and that is the ability to define a small set of members, a "circle" to participate in shared discussions. We want to see how the use of these circles influences how an individual with autism might reach out to people beyond a primary caregiver (e.g., a mother) for advice on everyday life skills. Using a commercial, cross-platform social networking service, GroupMe [24], we supported three individuals with Asperger's Syndrome and their primary caregivers with the ability to set up multiple communication circles. Over the course of 4 weeks, we examined 1) how the use of the communication circle impacted the initiation and topics of requests for help and 2) how the technology-supported communication impacted the existing support practice as well as the strength of the relationship between the individual and the network of friends and family.

The contribution of our work is twofold. First, we provide an in-depth analysis of the interplay between independent skills and social support with the use of SNS. Our study shows how a focused communication circle and other related SNS features impact important social problems (i.e., over-reliance on a small

---

[1] Throughout this paper, we will use the term "autism" to refer to individuals who either self-diagnose or have an official diagnosis of autism, as defined in the DSM-IV criteria for Pervasive Developmental Disorders.

set of caregivers and social isolation) by increasing social connections with other circle members. Second, we identify two key challenges: managing circle membership and balancing communication load within a circle. These challenges should open up design opportunities for the development of future systems that support individuals with autism online. The features we propose include tools that help users build and shape circles that will allow them to receive immediate and adequate advice on daily activities.

RELATED WORK

Autism Context: Towards Building a Support Network

Attaining independence may be more difficult for those with autism because of their limited ability with self-determination [11]. Lower self-determination ability leads to over-reliance on caregiver prompting and continuous assistance in everyday situations ranging from very simple operations to complex social activities [12]. Over-reliance on a primary caregiver also leads to problems such as difficulty broadening one's social network, reaching out to appropriate people to get advice about specific topic, and tapping into other available resources [3].

Increasingly, the use of technology for fostering social support for individuals with special needs, such as those with autism [8,10,17] or other cognitive disabilities [18,23], has been the focus of considerable research within the HCI research community. A notable example of the technology-mediated social support includes a mobile-based prompting system that provides individuals affected by cognitive disabilities with detailed protocols created by a set of caregivers to perform activities such as using public transportation [7]. One recent study explored the role of computer-mediated communication (CMC) and available social media for the support of individuals with high functioning autism, particularly those having a social communication difficulty [6]. Additionally, a human-computation approach that harnesses the ability of distributed workers has been investigated as a means to develop software to teach adolescents with autism problem-solving skills [1]. However, much of the previous research in this area has focused on the technology design itself rather than any potential interventions or ecological approaches that benefit the community of people who are involved in the care of individuals with autism.

Our work complements these efforts, focusing on empowering young adults with autism and their caregivers in a style that differs from most assistive technologies. To foster social support, we emphasize leveraging existing connections for the practical and social assistance that appeal to individuals with autism as well as caregivers. Individuals with autism naturally form small social support circles that typically consist of immediate family members and close friends [3]. However, such support can also be provided by others, perhaps using a technology such as an online social networking system. While research has explored the design of a special purpose social networking system for connecting individuals with autism to a wider set of people online [10], such a system has not been actually deployed.

Our work investigates the use of an SNS as a social support system for this special population in real world settings. In particular, we wanted to explore how a specific feature of SNS, the communication circle, enables individuals to initiate communication or request help, and ultimately whether this system can be used by overburdened caregivers to distribute their responsibility to others in the network.

Communication Circles on Social Networking Services

boyd and Ellison [2] defined social network sites as a multidimensional construct that allows users to build a profile, to represent their list of contacts within a system, and to form relationships with their contacts. We consider Social Networking Services (SNS) a subset of social network sites to the extent that they particularly facilitate communication and collaboration across networks of contacts online with a variety of different technical features. Outside of networking with friends or everyone, SNSs also offer a novel setting in which one can build sub-groups for specific purposes [14] and solicit help or information from the group members [9]. These features are explicitly presented as "lists" or "groups" in Facebook or "circles" in Google+.

Morris et al. [19] conducted a survey that examined the use of personal connections within an SNS for asking questions. They found that more than half of participants reported that they asked questions on people's Facebook statuses on various topics such as technology, leisure and social activities, and philosophical inquires. The study also revealed that many questions were likely to be answered by close friends. However, asking overly personal inquiries about topics such as health, dating, religion, and finance, seems to be inappropriate within the SNS context or at least through the mechanisms revealed in this study.

The disclosure of highly personal information is sometimes necessary when seeking help or advice, but it inevitably raises tensions around one's privacy and social identity. To tackle this social dilemma, Newman et al. [20] proposed a mechanism that builds customized support groups for focused communication, for example, groups consisting of individuals that a user selects for the health-related goal. This approach is echoed by recent work investigating selective and targeted sharing practice in Google+ [14]. In that study, participants generated custom circles across life facets (professional life), tie strength, and topical interest. More importantly, the result showed these groups are utilized for specific purposes (e.g., selectively sharing health and nutrition content with those who might be interested.)

A key benefit of soliciting help or information through a focused communication circle is that they provide an individual with access to direct communication to the right set of people. Building upon the previous work, we seek to explore how the mechanism of pre-defined groups or circles in a specific social networking service, GroupMe, influences an individual with autism in seeking advice on everyday activities.

METHODS

Our aim was to understand the impact of the SNS's communication circle on the patterns of support and the relationship between an individual with autism and his or her caregivers. To that end we enrolled three groups that were comprised of an individual with autism, their primary caregiver, and a flexible number of extended network members.

Technology Probes

Technology probes [13] have been adopted as a methodology that allows researchers to investigate the daily activities for children with autism and their families [17]. We also used this approach as well. We installed a social network application into a real-use context to observe how it is used over a period of time. Instead of seeding "new" technology in the existing context, we explored the repurposing of a general online social networking application for a specific situation, the day-to-day support of individuals with autism. We expected the participants to provide us with feedback on how the use of the social network application may or may not have addressed their needs and concerns and to critique the technology by describing their experiences with it.

The cross-platform social networking application, GroupMe (see Figure 1) [24], was used in the study for three reasons. First, it facilitates the network creation process. Users can smoothly transfer existing connections offline to GroupMe members using contact information (e.g., phone number, email address) stored in their communication devices. It allowed the researchers to track those who were already involved in offline support and how they moved to online support. Another reason for choosing GroupMe was that it facilitates user-generated groupings of contacts (which we refer to "focused communication circle"). It enables users to sort their contacts so that they can selectively communicate with circle members and to broadcast messages to circles they wish to communicate with. This mechanism shapes GroupMe as a more synchronized group chat system. We expected to observe what kinds of circles the study participants created and what interactions would evolve within each circle. The main reason

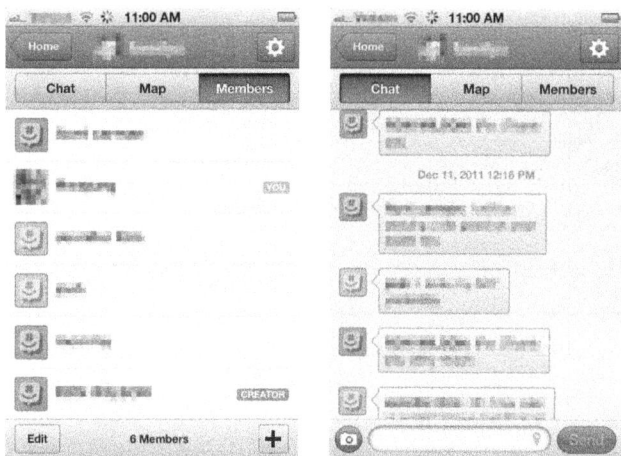

Figure 1. Two screen shots from GroupMe mobile app: Members view of G1's circle (left); Chat view of G1's circle

we chose to explore GroupMe was because of its unique communication mode. Users can access GroupMe not only through a web interface but also on mobile phones. GroupMe also integrates mobile telephony features into social networking by assigning a proxy phone number to each circle. Even if users do not have a smartphone, they can still broadcast messages through text via a feature cellphone. The use of various communication modes in GroupMe allowed us to determine effective ways of asking and providing support in various situations.

Participants

We solicited participants through word-of-mouth, mailing lists, and public events. We recruited three young adults (Andrew, Sarah, and Paul)[2] who self-identified as having Asperger's Syndrome (AS) and whose primary caregivers were their mothers (see the demographic summary in Table 1). All three pairs invited their existing networks such as other family members, relatives, and friends (Total: 20) to join the GroupMe system. Each pair was compensated $30 for completing four weeks of the field study phase plus $20 for completing the pre- and post-study questionnaires. We decided to approach only three groups for this study because this number was sufficient to address our research questions and because it was consistent with previous technology probe studies in this domain (e.g., [16], [17]). Keeping the number of deployments fairly small allowed us to conduct a more in-depth qualitative analysis focusing on the lived experiences of each participant.

During the study, two researchers joined as members of all three groups in GroupMe because researchers were interested in determining how young adults react to the inclusion of someone that they do not know well in their existing network. To authenticate the researchers' presence in the group, the researchers asked the participants to consider them as proxies for community volunteers (e.g., church youth group members) who could be invited to participate in future studies.

The first group (**G1**) consisted of a moderately independent college student (Andrew) with AS who was in his late teens and his immediate family members. Although he managed his daily chores under his mother's proactive guidance, he was less confident about staying on a schedule. He lived with his mother, a leader of a local autism awareness group, and his younger brother who was 17 years old. The family members also included an aunt whom they met once a month. Since G1 was the first group with whom we deployed the social network application for the study, we wanted to identify technical and behavioral challenges and to use insights to revise our study procedure during the study period. Furthermore, Andrew was unfamiliar with social networking tools unlike Sarah and Paul. Hence, researchers were more actively involved the G1's communication than those of others.

The second group (**G2**) consisted of "Sarah," a 16-year-old female middle school student with AS, her extended family and their friends. Members lived in in multiple states. Outside

---

[2] Names are pseudonyms.

of school, Sarah spent most of the time with her mother, who assisted her with maintaining her appearance, managing her schedule, and making friends. During the study period, one of the mother's friends dropped out of the group because of personal circumstances. Two weeks after the beginning of the study, the mother invited Andrew (from the first group study described above) because he attended an autistic teen and adult transition group with Sarah. She also invited Andrew's mother to join G2.

The third group (**G3**) consisted of a 28-year-old moderately independent adult (Paul) with AS who was employed as a technical assistant in a local IT company, and extended family members including an aunt and a cousin in their late twenties that lived in a remote part of the same state. A week after the beginning of the study, a family friend was added as a group member. Although Paul was described as very organized and routine-oriented, his mother was concerned about his limited social interaction skills. He tended to engage in solitary activities such as watching television or listening to music. He lived in a metropolitan city with his mother, his father, and his 17-year-old younger brother, who often asked Paul for rides to his high school and who played baseball in a local league.

Procedure
The study consisted of three phases: the pre-study, the field study, and the post-study.

Pre-Study Individual with autism and their primary caregiver took part in an opening interview, a questionnaire, and a tutorial. The questionnaire included the following:

1. Information about current needs and concerns associated with independence with perceived levels of importance and competency independent living skills in seven areas defined by the Virginia Education Department (VED) transition guidebook [25]: maintaining good hygiene, staying on schedule, good health habits, work and professional life, financial management, leisure and social activity, and managing household chores.

2. A form on which both listed known relatives and friends who had helped or who would be able to help the individual acquire these living skills.

3. Information about the relationship with each person on the list and the individual's perceived strength of the relationship in terms of closeness (Likert scale 1-5) and intensity (i.e., the frequency of contact with each person on the list).

Participants were asked to create groups on GroupMe using the list they had developed (see #2 above). We asked the participants to invite two of us so we could join their GroupMe conversations. This approach allowed us to capture data and the context in which the participants sent messages and any changes that they made to group memberships.

Field Study Over the course of 4 weeks, Participant interacted with invited members through GroupMe. Log data from the GroupMe system was collected during this period.

Post Study After the fourth week, each participant with AS and his/her primary caregiver took part in debriefing

Network	Individuals with Asperger's	GroupMe Members	Changes in Closeness (Post – Pre)	Intensity	
				Frequency of contact before the study	# of Message that the member sent to Group during the study
G1 18 threads 147 messages	**Andrew** (age: 19 | College student | AS) - Moderately independent - Less confident (2 out of 5) about staying on schedule - Feature cellphone user - Recently joined Facebook (FB), access weekly - Created 69 out of 147 messages (50%) - Initiated 11 out of 18 threads (61%)	Mother	-1	Hourly	16
		Brother	0	Daily	6
		Aunt	0	Weekly	13
		Researcher 1	2	Never met before	33
		Researcher 2	2	Never met before	10
G2 32 threads 186 messages	**Sarah** (age: 16 | Middle school student | AS) - Less independent - Not confident (1 out of 5) about managing good hygiene and leisure and social activities - Feature cellphone user - Access Facebook daily, produce a number of videos on her YouTube channel - Created 81 out of 186 messages (43%) - Initiated 7 out of 23 threads (30%)	Mother	0	Hourly	25
		Father	0	Daily	9
		Mother's friend1	N/A (removed immediately)		
		Mother's friend2	2	Not often	12
		Family friend	1	Not often	12
		Friend*	2	Weekly	34
		Friend's mother*	2	Weekly	12
G3 23 threads 250 messages	**Paul** (age: 28 | Technical assistant | AS) - Moderately independent - Less confident (2 out of 5) about social activities - Smartphone user - Access FB daily, but do not write on the wall - Created 69 out of 250 messages (28%) - Initiated 8 out of 32 thread (25%)	Mother	0	Daily	41
		Father	0	Daily	25
		Aunt	1	Not often	61
		Cousin	0.5	Not often	39
		Family friend*	0	Not often	15

*: Members who invited after pre-study phase

Table 1. Summary of participants' profile, questionnaire result, and usage logs.

interviews and filled out post-study questionnaires, which included the same form (see #3 above). We then conducted semi-structured interviews with each group, asking them about their overall experience interacting on GroupMe, the benefits of using GroupMe, its technical and social barriers, and the effects of the application on their support activities and interpersonal relationships. The materials used during the debriefing included lists of the group members that they had invited and the messages they generated. The purpose of the debriefing was to encourage the participants to reflect on the use of GroupMe, to explore the rationale for their interaction with the system, and to expand on the context of specific message threads pulled from the log.

Analysis

We conducted two phases of analysis of the logs and questionnaire responses. First, we conducted a descriptive analysis to examine the relationship between questionnaire responses and the overall communication patterns generated from GroupMe use. We also collected fine-granularity scale conversational data such as messages exchanged on GroupMe. We then grouped the messages by VED skill topics area, and defined the group of messages as a conversation thread. We examined the relationship between the conversation threads and the concerns around independence which participants reported.

Concurrently, we conducted in-depth qualitative analysis of transcribed interview data and logged messages. Two of the authors conducted an initial round of open coding and memoing to create thematic connections using a data-driven approach [22]. We extracted statements of interest and grouped them according to theme, conducting two such passes through all of the data. We refined the themes through affinity diagramming until a set of distinct themes emerged. By applying a triangulation of descriptive quantitative analysis of the system logs and questionnaires and the interviews, we were able not only to assess the functional value of the technology but also to understand the social value from the perspective of daily interaction.

RESULTS

Questionnaire

Skill Importance and Competency. Managing hygiene and attire was considered as the most (Andrew, Sarah) or the second most (Paul) important skill in a self-reported ranking of the seven skill areas from the VED guidebook [25]. The self-reported level of competency differed from the level of importance. Schedule management (Andrew: 2 out of 5), attire-and hygiene-management (Sarah: 1 out of 5), social and leisure activities (Sarah: 1 out of 5 & Paul: 2 out of 5) are the skills individuals were least confident in being able to perform.

The Sense of Closeness. Pre and post assessments of the closeness showed that all three participants had an increase perception of closeness to the extended network members (61%, 8 out of 13 relationships). Two of the three participants showed no change in the closeness to their primary caregivers and one showed a decrease in closeness (see Table 1).

Log Analysis

In the following section, we begin by describing the general patterns of communication extracted from the GroupMe usage logs. We recorded a total of 73 threads (583 messages) from our three participants' groups.

Membership. All three groups communicated within a single focused communication circle of GroupMe that consisted of five to seven members. In the pre-study, we worked with participants to create their first social support circle in GroupMe; we also encouraged them to add new members and create additional circles as the study progressed. However, we observed only a few instances in which new people were added to existing groups (two new members to G1 and one new member to G3), and none of the participants created new circles during the study.

Patterns. The three groups showed both common and distinct patterns of communication. All three individuals with autism were the most active communication participants in their groups (Andrew: 50%, 69 out of 147 messages, Sarah: 43%, 81 out of 186 messages, Paul: 28%, 69 out of 250 messages). Of the three young adults, Andrew was the most active communication initiator (61%, 11 out of 18 threads) followed by Paul (30%, 7 out of 23) and Sarah (25%, 8 out of 32). The initiation in both Sarah's and Paul's groups were more evenly distributed among the members of their groups. We found that the mothers, who were providing prompts both online and offline in all of the groups, were more engaged during the first week, but they reduced their engagement in the remaining weeks when invited group members increased their activity. For instance, Andrew's mother participated in 75% threads at the first week, but 2% of threads the remaining weeks (Sarah's mother: 43% to 36%, Paul's mother: 88% to 64%).

Topics. Overall, the system addressed an ongoing issue that all of the participants with autism faced—that of socializing (see Figure 2). Social and leisure activity was the dominant theme. The second most frequently discussed topic was schedule management. Participants also generated phatic communication or greetings almost every day and it often emerged as other topics such as social activity planning. Two participants discussed health-related concern such as physical discomfort, sickness, and hospital visit. Those two participants

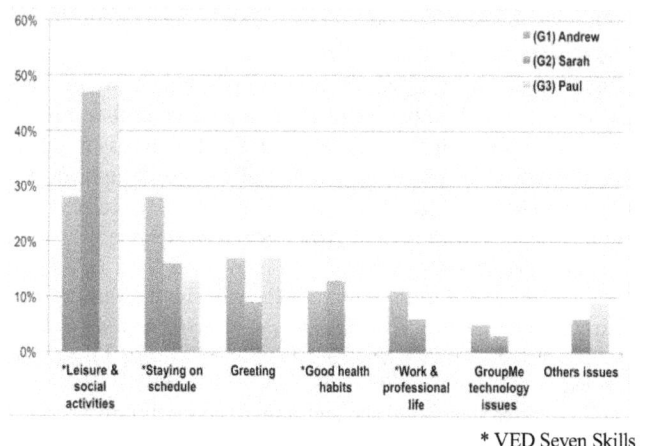

* VED Seven Skills

Figure 2. Topics discussed on GroupMe

had conversations related to job and professional life, such as upcoming job interview. However, none of participant discussed house chores and attire- or hygiene-related issues through GroupMe. We also looked at the association between the skill importance and competency questionnaire response and the topics of communication participants generated. Sara and Paul reported that they had least confidence in social and leisure activities among the seven skills area. We found that almost half of Sarah's (47%) and Paul's (48%) threads were related to social activities (e.g., offering a movie night, buying a gift for a friend, planning a potluck party). Andrew ranked schedule management as the skill that he was least confident in and it was one of the most frequently discussed topics (28%) in his group threads.

Summary of Results

We make the following four observations about the characteristics and the impact of the communication circle. First, participants made limited changes to the membership in the circles following the initial deployment and they did not add any new circles. The members were, however, actively engaged in communicating within a single circle. The circle was based on their social connections rather than on a particular topic. Next, GroupMe motivated participants to initiate communication and the responsibility for responding was shared among the members. Thirdly, the application was utilized to address some of the participants' ongoing needs, but some sensitive topics were not broached on the system. Lastly, the participants perceived that their engagement with the various members of their extended network, but not their primary caregiver, was improved between pre- and post-study.

Building upon the results from the survey and log data, we were interested in whether the use of GroupMe impacted existing support practices and therefore mitigated the over-reliance on the primary caregiver. Keeping these high-level findings in mind, we move on to data collected through the qualitative study, through which we aim to gain a detailed understanding of the contexts in which these patterns occurred.

QUALITATIVE ANALYSIS

We analyzed the interview data, logged messages, and written responses from a few members. The findings indicated that participants were highly motivated to engage in GroupMe that they perceived that the application was beneficial for both improving the care network and extending social relationships.

The Comfort of the Small Circle

GroupMe was perceived as a comfort zone in which the individuals could extend conversations to a controlled set of individuals. Though some participants also had access to other social media, the prescribed nature of GroupMe appears to have ameliorated some of the social anxiety related to communicating with a large group. Sarah complained: *"I have too many people on Facebook, but I'm not actually comfortable talking with them."* She reported feeling more comfortable sharing on GroupMe: *"I'm still at the point where I'm afraid to walk up to somebody, get their attention, and say this is what I need. I'm learning that it's easier when I know the people are there for me."* Paul's mother stated that she and Paul liked GroupMe because

it provided them with a safe place in which to engage people they felt comfortable asking for help: *"The resources are there, and the families and friends are on."*

Our participants, both individuals with autism and their caregivers, reported that they were satisfied communicating with those in the circle they first created, so they did not want to create more circles. In the study, we saw incidences that might explain why no more circles were created. While family members understood the purpose of using GroupMe and knew how to use it in advance, friends could not acquire information about how to participate. In addition, participants had difficulty inviting others to GroupMe because of strict social norms that managed certain relationships (e.g., the teacher-student relationship). For example, Andrew asked his teacher to join GroupMe, but teachers were not allowed to contact students through personal social media.

Immediacy of Response

An individual and his primary caregiver valued the focused communication circle because of the immediacy of the response. Participants noted positive feelings about GroupMe as a personalized Q&A system. For example, Andrew had a job interview and asked a question: [Message] I have an interview tonight and I need to know some questions to ask what should I ask.

Shortly thereafter, his aunt responded: [Message] Ask for details regarding their training for new employees. […] They might ask u for 2 or 3 of your best and worst qualities and why[,] so be prepared to tell them what they are. I would say one is that you are creative […] and another is trusting of people. That one can be a positive and [a] negative.

Andrew emphasized that the immediacy of GroupMe was his favorite feature: *"It makes everything a lot quicker [...] I don't have to keep going to my contacts to find someone. I just got an answer to what I needed. Quicker!"* Andrew's mother added: *"He liked the dialog in GroupMe because it is faster and convenient and because I'm very long [winded]. When I teach, I will go from the very beginning to the end, like a half hour answer, like 'Andrew, you are going for an interview. Make sure that you have eye contact, be sure to shake hands, be sure that you say thank you.' [...] GroupMe response, when he asked, was very simple and concise."*

Although we were concerned that members might be less inclined to respond to posts and instead rely upon others to take responsibility, we observed no such reluctance during the study period. All queries were answered by at least one group member within an hour. The average response time was 10.3 minutes. Members with existing relationships tended to make the networks more responsive and supportive. Further, participation in the same circle allowed members to expedite action on an individual's request because they could determine immediately whether the request had been handled by others or whether the poster was still awaiting a response.

Instrumental Support

Individuals and their primary caregivers adopted GroupMe for providing and receiving practical support. For example, schedule management was a skill Andrew admitted he always needed help with. Andrew's mother and his brother often had to remind him about upcoming events such as a final exam, a hospital visit, or a family gathering. The distinct qualities of GroupMe, near-synchronous communication and the group-broadcasting feature, facilitated schedule coordination activities in which multiple members were involved.

Through the instrumental support seeking process, individuals could harness various ideas and perspectives. Sarah's mother commented: *"I liked GroupMe because when she [Sarah] posted something I didn't feel that I had an answer, but the other people that I trusted were able to answer."* Andrew's mother noted advice from members helped Andrew prepare for various scenarios he and the mother never expected: *"Information is very different coming from me than from his peers on GroupMe. The best thing was when he was going for the interview, he got replies from everyone and they were all different. It was very, very helpful for him during this interview. So, he wasn't just relying on me, my own experiences and my ideas. But, he got his aunt's, yours, and everybody's."* On another day Andrew asked a question: [Message] I am at a grocery store and what should I get my friend who is in the hospital. Everyone told him different gift ideas. For example, his mother suggested: [Message] Chocolates, flowers, cards. A researcher in his group asked a question to understand details: [Message] How sick was your friend? If it's severe, snacks might not be a good idea. Andrew chose to wait awhile in order to collect ideas and then decided to buy a card. His mother valued GroupMe because he no longer was dependent solely on her opinion. More importantly, Andrew and his mother appreciated that the opportunity to weigh a variety of ideas could lead to more flexible decision-making, an important step toward independence.

There were instances where individuals with autism reported needing support in a given area but failed to address this concern via GroupMe. Most notably hygiene- and attire-related matters were never discussed. For example, during the pre-interview Sarah said: *"It's really hard to keep up my hygiene. I mean, I have a lot of trouble with it."* Our findings from her post-study interview revealed that these were still issues that her mother was helping her deal with.

Learning by Lurking
GroupMe members can choose not to respond to conversation threads. We found that in these situation individuals with autism were able to observe how dialog evolved among the different members. The passive engagement allowed participants to learn communication norms that were often opaque to them. Such silent observation also gave them access to various styles of interaction that they could later mimic.

All individuals reported that in some cases others' posts on GroupMe gave them ideas for future interaction. When Andrew engaged in Sarah's group, for example, he observed that Sarah brought up various topics about herself instead of just saying "Hi, how are you?" Thus, learning occurred even when individuals merely lurked within a communication thread. An individual indicated that they enjoyed being silent while other members developed multiple dialogs. For example, Paul followed a thread where his aunt and cousin discussed an outing and was then motivated to ask his group members about going to a concert the following month: *"I love the fact that*

people actually want to go on and talk more. I start a question, people can talk about it, and I can jump in and add what I want."

On another occasion Paul simply posed a question about a boxing match: [Message]Question: Mayweather or Cotto? The thread evolved and ultimately Paul's family and friends gathered to watch the fight. Paul remained quiet while others exchanged messages to coordinate a potluck. At that point, he joined the conversation: [Message] I will handle dessert. He commented later that this dialog was the highlight of his GroupMe trial. By providing the opportunity for such silent participation, GroupMe could help individuals learn communication skills that may enrich their future interactions. This finding echoes Burke *et al* 's conclusion that passive consumption of others' communication has a greater impact on those with low social skills [5].

Opening up Richer Social interaction
All individuals lived in their parents' homes. One of the concerns often reported was that the individual's social interaction was very dependent on their primary caregivers. Thus, mothers expressed concerns that their children might be socially isolated if they moved away from home. For example, in the pre-interview, Paul's mother was worried that: *"He tends to isolate in his room, listening to music... Having access to people, knowing how to go and find activity is crucial."*

As conversations grew and expanded, opportunities arose for enriched social relations. For example, Paul's mother appreciated the fact that GroupMe increased interaction between Paul and his aunt: *"They're close in age. She lives on the south side of the town. Paul and [his aunt] didn't even talk that often. But, I think he would see her at Thanksgiving or Christmas. I feel there's more interaction. So, I think that's the best part of it."* Consequently, these GroupMe conversations led Paul and his aunt to attend a concert together. Paul confirmed the use of GroupMe made the social event happen: *"It was the first time we actually talked about it. We never did it before. It was the first time that I invited her to go to a concert."* Paul's mother reported that GroupMe fostered improved interaction between her son and other members and, in turn, helped Paul interact with others more spontaneously than before.

The conversations on GroupMe also helped to identify and meet individual needs even primary caregivers had overlooked. For instance, a friend of Sarah's mother treated her to an age appropriate treat: [Message] Hey Sarah, you know I'm a nail tech so I'd love for you to come get your nails done and get to know you:-) let's plan something! Sarah's reaction was one of delight: *"[When I got this message] I felt 'Oh, I want to do that.' Honestly, I never really had friends ask me if I can go with them for the nail stuffs. So, I felt like 'WOW'. I never thought of that. So, it was surprising to me."*

Sarah's mother found that GroupMe also provided members with a different view of her daughter: *"I think [GroupMe] gives [other members] a little more insight into her, like how she thinks. I think this is a good way for them to see her as more a person coming into the adulthood and to see that she's just not a kid playing. I think it helped them to see her as more mature and older."* This positive experience increased Sarah's sense of closeness to the mother's friend. In fact, Sarah rated her closeness with the mother's friend as 2 ("I barely know this person") in the pre-questionnaire, but listed a 5 ("we're very close") after the study.

Challenge: Managing Circle Membership

Individuals and primary caregivers did not always assign the same significance to relationships or value the same method of maintaining contact with others. Some individuals expressed a willingness to defer to the caregiver for most of these decisions. Sarah explained that she did not object to her mother's addition of a friend to GroupMe: *"I honestly don't know [mom's friend], but I trust my mom enough to let her help me."* However, in other situations, participants wished to exclude members who were close to the caregiver but not to the individual. Sarah noted that: *"This is my stepfather. I just didn't put him on because it isn't comfortable at the moment, but not all the time"* Nevertheless, individuals relied heavily on their mother's input in selecting network members at the pre-study and did not make any change in members or circles by themselves.

Questions exist, therefore, about who should control the social network, the individual or the primary caregiver, or both. Because the goal is to support an individual's transition to independence and adulthood, conflicts between the individual and the caregiver will inevitably emerge. Disagreements could arise in situations where the caregiver may invite a person with whom the individual is not comfortable or, alternatively, where an individual with autism may seek to include a person whom the parent does not see as being *"on the same page [with] our beliefs."* In fact, the mothers did not think they needed to have complete authority of managing membership. Rather, they anticipated that their children could develop an ability to create a social network on their own through GroupMe: *"I want him to be outside of family and friends ... I want him to be able to develop his own network of friends."* (Paul's mom)

Another issue to consider is an inevitable tension between creating a circle of known and trusted participants versus extending participation to less known others to increase social opportunities, such as the diversity of relationships and ideas presented above. Sarah's mother noted that open participation in the network might lead her to worry about the quality of the provided responses: *"When she posts something on Facebook, she could get a ton of friends she does not know well. So the younger kids may not have quite thought out their answers."* She noted that members of the network needed to be vetted on a number of characteristics including: *"[their ability to] understand her strength and her weaknesses with Asperger's ... They need to understand what our religious beliefs are so that they don't suggest for her to do things that we wouldn't allow..."*

Challenge: Managing and Distributing Communication

GroupMe is basically a group broadcasting system. Participants used the technology appropriately to address the whole group (e.g., [Paul's Message] what are all your plans for this weekend?). However, group broadcasts and the resulting responses created significant message volume, which proved problematic for some members. This led one member to drop out on the first day. During the post interview, Sarah's mother noted: *"I had one person at the first day who said that 'take me off.' [...] When you're getting responses from everybody, that can get to be way too much."* She tried to ameliorate the

traffic flow: *"There was a couple of times that I was supposed to respond to say something, but I didn't because I thought, 'well, I don't want to bother everyone with this.'"* To cope with the group format, if a conversation between others became irrelevant or uninteresting, participants often stopped conversation on GroupMe and switched to other channels (e.g., phone call) to directly communicate with a selected person. Participants had to negotiate when they needed to sign off GroupMe and to determine to whom to direct their message, but it was not easy to determine whether a member was available for such communication.

DISCUSSION

In this paper, we investigated the opportunities and challenges of fostering the independence of young adults with autism. We investigated a specific feature, the focused communication circle that enables broadcast communication to a pre-defined set of people, particularly in the context of requesting help or advice. Our results suggest that this feature can be adopted for the specialized purpose of helping young adults with autism to seek help from individuals other than primary caregivers. In this section we will revisit our original research questions and propose a set of design alternatives to augment SNS to better serve individuals that have disabilities such as autism.

How does a single communication circle impact the type of topics and requests for help?

As we discussed in related work, general SNS users create diverse circles by reflecting their facets of life, tie-strength, and topical interests [14]. We expected to observe the similar behavior from our participants, but found that instead they created a unified circle and posted a variety of queries and comments. In the first few days or week, the individuals relied on their mothers' prompts to initiate conversations or to request help, but the participation of the primary caregivers dwindled as that of others increased. This demonstrates a distribution of responsibility for answering requests of help among friends and family members. Thus, it is seen that SNS may indeed lessen the previously reported over-reliance on primary caregivers.

Because social isolation impacts the independence of young adults with disabilities [15] and since SNS is inherently social and informal, it is therefore an appropriate outlet for discourse on social and leisure topics. However, request for help on other areas requiring more instrumental assistance, such as hygiene or attire management, did not occur. One explanation is that such questions may have been too sensitive to share in an SNS setting, or the individuals may not have known how to articulate the problem (e.g., a question about a romantic relationship that the individual does not want to ask parents, a number of questions about cosmetics that a woman would only want to ask a female). The unified circle may not always be suitable for discussing those unique questions. Some questions or requests would be applicable to only few members in the circle. We consider a design opportunity that could address this challenge by proposing an alternative way to create circles in the existing system.

How does the technology-supported communication impact existing practices? And how does it impact the strength of the relationship between the individual and the network of friends and family?

Our findings support the notion that SNSs mediate participants' communicative expression in two ways: passive engagement and active involvement. First, our findings resonate with the conclusion arising from past research that found that SNSs afford opportunities for passive engagement [21] that confers informational and social benefits to those with low self-esteem [5] or on the autism spectrum [6]. The three young adults in our study reported that they sometimes neither initiated a group conversation nor participated in it extensively, but they actually read the stream and sought to understand the intentions of other members as they communicated. By allowing them to passively observe how people initiate a discussion topic and respond to others, a shared discussion thread itself may serve as a tool for individuals with autism to learn social skills. Conversely, observing threads helped members understand some facts about the individual with autism. Thus, the discussion thread could also be a tool for critical reflection of an individual's emerging needs and concerns.

Next, active involvement allowed participants to receive both immediate responses, and over time, multiple responses to a request. While a previous study speculated about the possible risk of conflicting advice among SNS members holding different perspectives [10], we saw no evidence of this potential conflict in practice. However, caregivers still raised concerns about including members that do not share the caregivers' values. They wanted others to understand the specific attributes of their children such as their strengths and weaknesses related to Asperger's. Thus, in the next section, we will explore a way of improving value transparency and accountability.

GroupMe facilitated various communication practices that led to an increased sense of closeness to their group members whom they did not know well before the study. Our four-week field study also revealed that online interaction led to offline socialization, which was clearly a positive experience for both the young adults and their caregivers who wanted their children to seek social opportunities. However, in the long term, the use of the circle could have an unexpected impact on network relationships. One can imagine that being in a circle that centers around supporting the needs of one individual and that includes all of the other members' messages directed to the individual can become quite overwhelming and burdensome to the group members. Therefore, the long-term outcomes of SNS use within the perspective of network membership should be studied in more depth.

Design Opportunities

GroupMe was appealing to use for this investigation because it was freely available and offered cross-platform support for desktop, smartphone, and feature phone users. Having conducted this exploratory study, we see several opportunities for building specific features on the top of circle services.

Prompting contextual circle formation

Current approaches to creating circles focus on setting up groups for the purpose of controlling who receives particular messages during the early stages of system use. At the outset of our study, it was not clear to our participants whether and to what extent they should assign their family and friends to different circles. Furthermore, inexperienced individuals may not know what types of questions their social network members are willing to answer. Therefore, one design recommendation is to have the system suggest both themes for various circles and ideal members for focused communication within each circle. Future systems could, at any time, explicitly aid in circle creation by suggesting topics and inviting people that the user might find easier to discuss a topic with. Initially, a basic set of topics for circles could come from the seven independence skill areas, and group members could be invited to join any of the circles they wished. Additional circle topics may also evolve in the context of ongoing conversations within the system. Therefore, a circle may not be a permanent entity but rather a more contextual or perhaps ephemeral one as an individual's concerns or interests change. One direction for future work, then, will be to determine the factors and mechanisms that will produce valuable suggestions for circle formation and membership.

Profile articulation: Requesting and offering help

Knowledge about the individual's personality, personal and professional goals, and interests may help group members provide more effective support. To that end, a system could prompt and help young adults with autism to openly advertise their limitations so that group members can proactively provide advice or suggestions on those topics. This mechanism can be embedded in SNS profile management since a profile does not just depict one's identity, but mediates communication [4]. A young adult could thus identify skill areas that they want to improve. Conversely, the system may allow members to browse the needs articulated by the individual and choose which topics they would like to support. Other relevant system features could include prompts to group members regarding the areas that the individual identified as ones in which he or she has limited capabilities. These reminders could lead the members to reach out to the individual with specific information or suggestions.

Another profile idea is one expressed by primary caregivers who want to ensure that a member giving advice shares values and priorities similar to those of the primary caregiver's family. The primary caregiver may be aware of this information about individuals they already know outside of the SNS, but they would want some form of profile information about those they do not know, making the process more transparent.

Fine-grained communication control

As we discussed above, the downside of GroupMe included a high volume of messages. Since individuals had no way of knowing whether members' were available to communicate, they tended to broadcast a message to the entire group first, and only directed subsequent messages to a particular individual once someone responded to the initial broadcasted message. Thus, tensions arose as the individual generated significant message volumes at times when members were not available to provide support. The current all-or-nothing mechanism for participation in the discussions within a circle is inadequate. We see the need for more fine-grained controls on discussion threads that enable a circle participant to opt in and out of various discussion threads, or allow active participants in a thread discussion to limit those who can see further messages.

The ability for group members to signal their availability for real-time support might help to ensure that a request for help is targeted at the right people at the right time. For example, a simple feature that turned off the network participation temporarily could serve both to signal to the individual that particular group member is not available, while simultaneously encouraging other members to make themselves available to cover for the diminished network size. Intelligence embedded in the system could also play a role; for example, recurring "unavailability" could be predicted based on the members' past behavior within the circle. A new design could attempt to handle the situation when too few members are available to participate. One possibility we have explored is the creation of a service of "trusted stranger," volunteers willing to provide input but who remain anonymous to members of a circle.

CONCLUSION

The goal of this study was to determine if specific communication features of a cross-platform social networking system such as GroupMe could reduce the barriers to independence experienced by individuals with autism. Our findings showed that circles of communication helped individuals overcome their over-reliance on their primary caregivers by increasing social closeness to others after a month of use. The identified design features, including contextual circle formation, profile articulation, and delicate communication control mechanisms, which have implications for adopting a system that supports independence, represent a promising direction for future work. These implications may also encourage researchers to explore issues faced by groups of users who would benefit from support for independent living.

ACKNOWLEDGEMENT

We thank all of our participants for making this study possible. We also thank UbiComp lab members and the many readers for their incredibly helpful comments. This research was supported by the Samsung Fellowship awarded to the first author.

REFERENCES

1. Boujarwah, F.A., Abowd, G.D., and Arriaga, R.I. Socially Computed Scripts to Support Social Problem Solving Skills. *CHI 2012*.

2. boyd, d.m. and Ellison, N.B. Social Network Sites: Definition, History, and Scholarship. *Computer-Mediated Communication 13*, 1 (2007).

3. Boyd, B.A. Examining the Relationship Between Stress and Lack of Social Support in Mothers of Children With Autism. *Focus on Autism and Other Developmental Disabilities 17*, 4 (2002).

4. boyd, d.m. and Heer, J. Profiles as Conversation: Networked Identity Performance on Friendster. *HICSS 2006*.

5. Burke, M., Kraut, R., and Marlow, C. Social capital on Facebook: Differentiating uses and users. *CHI 2011*.

6. Burke, M., Kraut, R., and Williams, D. Social use of computer-mediated communication by adults on the autism spectrum. *CSCW 2010*.

7. Carmien, S. and Fischer, G. Design, adoption, and assessment of a socio-technical environment supporting independence for persons with cognitive disabilities. *CHI 2008*.

8. Cramer, M., Hirano, S.H., Tentori, M., Yeganyan, M.T., & Hayes, G.R. Classroom-Based Assistive Technology: Collective Use of Interactive Visual Schedules by Students with Autism. *CHI 2011*.

9. Evans, B.M., Kairam, S., and Pirolli, P. Do your friends make you smarter?: An analysis of social strategies in online information seeking. *Information Processing & Management 46*, 6 (2010).

10. Hong, H., Kim, J.G., Abowd, G.D., and Arriaga, R.I. Designing a Social Network to Support the Independence of Young Adults with Autism. *CSCW 2012*.

11. Howlin, P. Outcome in high-functioning adults with autism with and without early language delays: implications for the differentiation between autism and Asperger syndrome. *Journal of autism and developmental disorders 33*, 1 (2003). 3-13.

12. Hume, K., Loftin, R., and Lantz, J. Increasing independence in autism spectrum disorders: a review of three focused interventions. *Journal of autism and developmental disorders 39*, 9 (2009). 1329-1338.

13. Hutchinson, H., Mackay, W., et al. Technology probes: inspiring design for and with families. *CHI 2003*.

14. Kairam, S., Brzozowski, M.J., Huffaker, D., and Chi, E.H. Talking in Circles: Selective Sharing in Google+. *CSCW 2012*.

15. King, G. a., Baldwin, P.J., Currie, M., and Evans, J. Planning Successful Transitions From School to Adult Roles for Youth With Disabilities. *Children's Health Care 34*, 3 (2005).

16. Mancini, C., Rogers, Y., Thomas, K., et al. In the Best Families: Tracking and Relationships. *CHI 2011*.

17. Marcu, G., Dey, A.K., and Kiesler, S. Parent-driven use of wearable cameras for autism support: a field study with families. *UBICOMP 2012*.

18. Morris, M., Lundell, J., and Dishman, E. Catalyzing social interaction with ubiquitous computing: a needs assessment of elders coping with cognitive decline. *CHI 2004*.

19. Morris, M., Teevan, J., and Panovich, K. What Do People Ask Their Social Networks, and Why? A Survey Study of Status Message Q&A Behavior. *CHI 2010*.

20. Newman, M.W., Lauterbach, D., Munson, S.A., Resnick, P., and Morris, M.E. "It's not that I don't have problems, I'm just not putting them on Facebook": Challenges and Opportunities in Using Online Social Networks for Health. *CSCW 2011*.

21. Preece, J., Nonnecke, B., and Andrews, D. The top five reasons for lurking: improving community experiences for everyone. *Computers in Human Behavior 20*, 2 (2004). 201-223.

22. Seidman, I. *Interviewing As Qualitative Research: A Guide for Researchers in Education And the Social Sciences*. Teachers College Press, 2006.

23. Tixier, M. Gaglio, G., and Lewkowicz, M. Translating Social Support Practies into Online Servics for Family Caregivers. *GROUP 2009*.

24. http://www.groupme.com

25. *Autism Sepctrum Disorders and Transition to Adulthood*. Virginia Department of Education, 2010.

Interactive Horizon Graphs: Improving the Compact Visualization of Multiple Time Series

Charles Perin
Univ. Paris-Sud & INRIA
Bat. 650, Univ. Paris-Sud,
91405 Orsay, France
Charles.Perin@inria.fr

Frédéric Vernier
Univ. Paris-Sud
Bat. 508, Univ. Paris-Sud,
91405 Orsay, France
frederic.vernier@limsi.fr

Jean-Daniel Fekete
INRIA
Bat. 650, Univ. Paris-Sud,
91405 Orsay, France
Jean-Daniel.Fekete@inria.fr

ABSTRACT

Many approaches have been proposed for the visualization of multiple time series. Two prominent approaches are *reduced line charts* (*RLC*), which display small multiples for time series, and the more recent *horizon graphs* (*HG*). We propose to unify RLC and HG using a new technique—*interactive horizon graphs* (*IHG*)— which uses pan and zoom interaction to increase the number of time series that can be analysed in parallel. In a user study we compared RLC, HG, and IHG across several tasks and numbers of time series, focusing on datasets with both large scale and small scale variations. Our results show that IHG outperform the other two techniques in complex comparison and matching tasks where the number of charts is large. In the hardest task IHG have a significantly higher number of good answers (correctness) than HG ($+14\%$) and RLC ($+51\%$) and a lower *error magnitude* than HG (-64%) and RLC (-86%).

Author Keywords

Visualization; Horizon Graphs; Time Series; Evaluation.

ACM Classification Keywords

H.5.2. Information Interfaces and Presentation: User Interfaces

General Terms

Design; Experimentation.

INTRODUCTION

Time series—sets of quantitative values changing over time— are predominant in a wide range of domains such as finance (*e. g.*, stock prices) and sciences (*e. g.*, climate measurements, network logs, medicine).

Line charts are one of the simplest ways to represent time series, and one of the most frequently used statistical data graphics [9]. However, using line charts to visualize multiple time series can be difficult because the limited vertical screen resolution can result in high visual clutter.

We introduce *Interactive Horizon Graphs* (*IHG*), an interactive technique for visualizing multiple time series. IHG are inspired by pan and zoom techniques and unify *Reduced Line Charts* (*RLC*) and *Horizon Graphs* (*HG*), two of the most effective techniques for visualizing multiple time series. We designed IHG to increase the number of time series one can monitor and explore efficiently. Datasets involving large numbers of time series such as stocks or medical monitoring are frequent and important [16]. We evaluate the benefits of our contribution for standard tasks on time series visualizations. While the related work has used generated time series with clear landmarks for evaluation, we used a non-synthetic dataset with both large scale and small scale variations (*LSV*) adapted to multi-resolution visualization techniques.

Under these conditions, we obtained results that are different from those in previous work [15, 19] (performances are better for HG than for RLC) and found that IHG outperform both RLC and HG for large numbers of time series.

This paper first reviews related work on time series visualization techniques and then describes the two techniques that we rely on (RLC and HG) in detail. Next, it presents IHG and our variant of pan and zoom. We then describe a controlled experiment that shows how IHG handles up to 32 time series in parallel. We discuss the results of the experiment and how our technique can be combined with others to support comparison tasks in an effective way.

RELATED WORK

Since line charts have become widespread [22], visualization of time series has been an active research topic, moving from paper-based representations to interactive visualizations. Many design considerations exist for displaying data in the form of charts (*e. g.*, [5, 8, 28]) and for the comparison of graphical visualization techniques (*e. g.*, [21, 26]). For relevant surveys see [1, 25].

Visualization Of Multiple Time Series

Visualizing multiple time series in a small space (where the vertical resolution is smaller than the series variations one may be looking for) has led to techniques that use space-filling [29] and multi-resolution representations [20].

Javed et al. classified visualization techniques for multiple time series into two categories [19]. In *shared-space* techniques, time series are overlaid in the same space (*e. g., line*

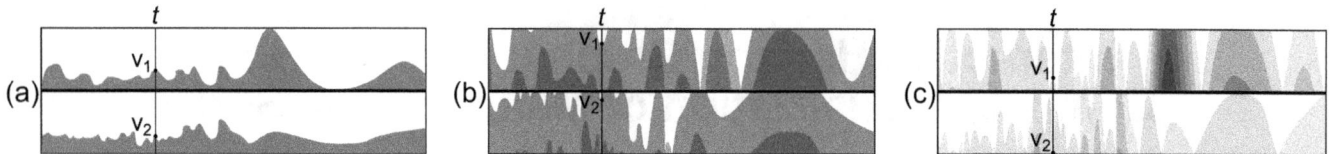

Figure 1. Two time series visualized in parallel using Reduced Line Charts (RLC), Horizon Graphs (HG) and Interactive Horizon Graphs (IHG). The degree of difficulty when determining which of the series has the highest value at point t (marked by a vertical black line) is different for each technique: (a) Using RLC, it is very difficult to compare v_1 and v_2. (b) Using HG with standard baseline at half the y axis and with two bands, we can barely see that $v_1 > v_2$: since both charts are blue at that point (*i. e.,* under the baseline), the highest value is the lowest blue one. (c) Using IHG, setting the baseline at 28% of the range of values and a zoom factor of 6, it is clear that $v_1 > v_2$: only v_1 is shown in red, *i. e.,* above the baseline.

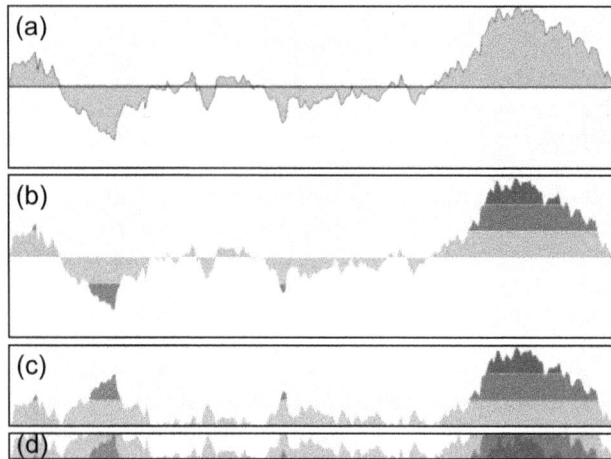

Figure 2. The construction of a *Horizon Graph* with 3 bands, adapted from [12, 19]. (a) Values are colored (blue and red) according to their value compared to the baseline: blue below and red above. (b) The chart is split in 3 bands (3 reds and 3 blues). (c) Values below the baseline are mirrored. (d) The bands are wrapped.

graphs [22], *braided graphs* [19], *stacked graphs* [6]). In *split-space* techniques, the space is divided (usually horizontally) by the number of time series and each one occupies its own reduced space (*e. g.,* RLC [28], HG [12, 23]). Shared-space techniques can support only a limited number of time series (considering more than four involves too much visual clutter [19]). Because we focus on large numbers of time series, we only consider split-space techniques. Also, while most of prior techniques are static, we focus on evaluating the benefits of adding interaction.

Reduced Line Charts (RLC)

RLC are small multiples for time series using line charts. To perform comparison tasks on different RLC, they must all share the same range of values (Figure 1(a)).

Horizon Graphs (HG)

HG is a recent split-space technique intended to display a large number of time series. It was originally introduced under the name "two-tone pseudo-coloring" [24] and was later developed by the company Panopticon under the name "horizon graph" [12, 23]. This technique uses two parameters: the number of bands b and the value of the baseline y_b separating the chart horizontally into positive and negative values.

Figure 2 illustrates the construction of HG from a line chart centered around a baseline. First, the values are colored ac-

cording to their position relative to the baseline (2(a)). Next, the line chart is horizontally split into uniformly-sized bands and their saturation is adjusted based on each band's proximity to the baseline (2(b)). The bands below the baseline are then reflected above the baseline (2(c)), so that the height of the chart becomes half of what it was originally. Finally, the different bands are layered on top of one another (2(d)), reducing the final chart height to $h/(2 \times b)$, where h is the original height of the chart and b is the number of bands. Using HG, data values are represented not only by their vertical height, but also by their color saturation and hue. For instance, the global maximum of a time series is the highest of the darkest red values. Figure 1(b) illustrates two HG in parallel.

Heer et al. [15] evaluated the use of HG focusing on how chart-reading performance changed using different parameters. They provide some recommendations, such as the optimal chart height and the number of bands which should be used. They limited their study to two simultaneous time series and the number of bands to four. Javed et al. [19] compared HG with other visualization techniques for higher numbers of time series. They limited the HG parameters to those recommended by Heer et al. and did not highlight any considerable advantage of the technique. In particular, they did not find critical differences between RLC and HG. However, they found that the number of time series seriously impacted the visual clutter and played a very important role in the performance of the visualization techniques. In their experiments, both pieces of prior work used synthetic data that included clear landmarks, which may have aided visual search tasks. As HG is a multi-resolution visualization technique, we can expect different results for the more difficult LSV datasets.

Large Scale and Small Scale Variations Datasets

Techniques such as stack zooming [18] and dual-scale data charts [17] use focus+context [10] techniques to visualize time series data containing regions with high variations. These techniques magnify and increase the readability of regions of interest by modifying the x axis (time scale), but not the y axis (value scale). We only found one article [20] that explored LSV datasets exhibiting both large and small variations visible at low and high resolutions. However, time series with these properties are common—for example, one may observe the temperature of a city along one year according to different variation scales: large (seasonal), medium (daily), small (hourly).

According to Bertin, the scale of time series with small variations must be adjusted to get closer to the optimum angular legibility, which is 70 degrees [5] and multi-scale banking to 45 degrees has been extensively studied in order to improve the graphical perception of time series [7, 14, 27]. While several tasks can be accomplished on time series where each chart has its own y axis (*e. g.,* compare the trend of two time series during a period of time), related work [12, 15, 19] suggests that the best configuration for multiple time series consists of sharing the same y axis, *i. e.,* using the same scale of values and baseline.

Tasks on multiple time series

Time series visualization techniques have been studied extensively and prior work has evaluated their use for a variety of different tasks. According to Andrienko et al. [2], tasks on multiple time series can be of two types: *elementary* (about individual data elements) or *synoptic* (about a set of values). For each type, the tasks can be *direct/inverse comparison* tasks or *relation-seeking* tasks. The closest study to our work, that inspired us [19], evaluated RLC and HG considering three tasks: *Maximum*, *Discriminate* and *Slope*.

Find the Maximum (*Max*)

Max is an elementary task for direct comparison. It consists of determining which of several time series has the highest (or lowest) value at a shared marked point [19, 20]. Javed et al. compared RLC and HG using this task for 2, 4 and 8 time series. Their study revealed that RLC were faster than HG but they did not find any significant result for Correctness.

Max is, for instance, executed to find the hottest city in a country for a given date. This task can be very easy to achieve if there are clear differences between the cities but becomes difficult when both the differences and the vertical resolution are small. Figures 1(a) and 1(b) illustrate *Max* using RLC and HG, respectively. This example highlights the difficulty of such a simple task using LSV datasets.

Discriminate (*Disc*)

Disc is an elementary task for relation-seeking, similar to *Max*. However, instead of having to find the highest value at a marked point t shared by all the time series, each time series has its own marked point. *Disc* is more difficult than *Max* [15, 19, 26] and HG has been evaluated for this task in two recent studies:

Heer et al. have studied the impact of the number of bands in HG [15] for *Disc*. They found that time and error increased with the number of bands. However, these results were obtained for value estimation tasks and they aptly noticed that these increases were due to the mental math implied.

For their *Disc* task, Javed et al. asked subjects to answer by selecting the time series with the highest value, rather than by estimating the highest value. They did not find any significant difference in terms of Correctness or Time between RLC and HG for *Disc*.

Evaluate the Slope

Slope is a synoptic task for pattern comparison proposed by Beattie et al. [3]. It consists of determining which time series has the highest increase during a given time period. For this task, Javed et al. found no significant results for Correctness

and found HG to be slower than RLC [19]. We believe that these results were also due to the synthetic dataset they used and we expect different results from a more difficult dataset.

In conclusion, previous studies on multiple time series had two main limitations: they only studied small numbers of time series (≤ 8), when much larger numbers are available in popular datasets, and used synthetic datasets, with features simpler than those typically found in these popular datasets.

INTERACTIVE HORIZON GRAPHS

Interactive Horizon Graphs (IHG) unify RLC and HG by introducing interactive techniques to control the baseline position and the zoom factor applied to values. Interaction is meant to allow HG to remain effective even while exploring larger numbers of time series. *Baseline panning* and *value zooming* can be seen as variants of the commonly used pan and zoom interaction techniques [4]—the baseline is controlled through a variant of panning and the number of bands through a variant of zooming. Thus, the pan and zoom interaction techniques are related to the y axis of the visualization instead of the x axis as described in [17]. We detail our interaction techniques in the following subsections.

Baseline Panning

Baseline panning allows users to interactively move the baseline along the y axis—in our implementation, this is achieved by dragging the mouse up/down with the right button pressed. Note that baseline panning does not change the positions on the x axis at all, unlike regular panning, and it does not change the height of the chart. The user's interaction with a single chart simultaneously changes the baselines on all small multiples. Because the baseline is always at the bottom of the chart, it does not move in response to the interaction. Rather, the series appear to shift up or down as the baseline changes and colors change as points in the series move from one band to the next (Figure 3).

Interactively changing the baseline overcomes a limitation of the fixed baseline used in traditional HG—because preattentive color perception (distinguishing between red and blue) is only effective for values around the baseline, points far from the baseline are more difficult to discriminate. Baseline panning allows a user to make transitions around a value of interest more salient. This can be particularly valuable if one is interested in identifying deviations from a specific baseline—for comparing the in body temperature for a patient against the patient's expected value. Meanwhile, finding a maximum value becomes a comparison of intensity of red plus height (y) estimation (first search the most red-saturated areas, then find the highest value which belongs to one of these areas).

For RLC, HG, and IHG, all the charts have the same range of values for the y axis: $[y_m, y_M]$, with y_m and y_M being the minimum and the maximum values in the visualized dataset. The three techniques have different values for the baseline y_b: $y_{b_{\mathrm{RLC}}} = y_m$ (the baseline is always at the bottom of the chart), $y_{b_{\mathrm{HG}}} = \frac{y_M - y_m}{2}$ (the baseline crosses the y axis at its middle point), and $y_{b_{\mathrm{IHG}}} \in [y_m, y_M]$ (the baseline can take any value in the range of values).

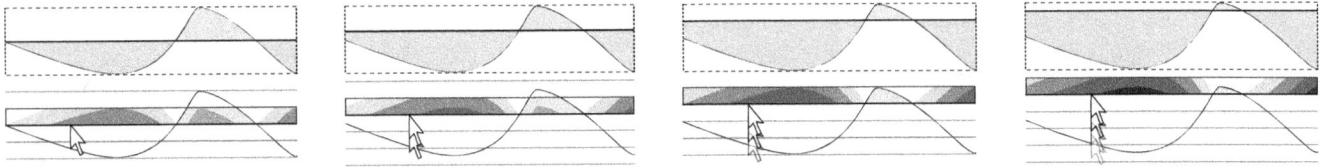

Figure 3. Baseline panning: The bottom charts represent the view of the time series using IHG for 4 different values of y_b overlaying the original line chart (for a constant zoom factor $z = 2$). Dragging upwards the mouse with the right button pressed increases the value of y_b (sequence from left to right) and values going under y_b become blue. The original line chart is presented above each step for better understanding.

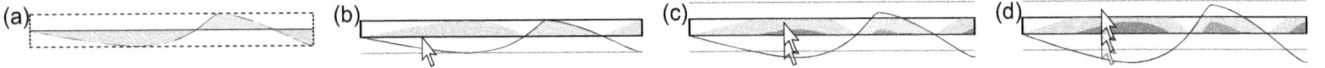

Figure 4. Value zooming: (a) From a standard mirrored line chart, the zoom value z is progressively increased by dragging upwards the mouse with the left button pressed (for a constant baseline $y_b = \frac{y_M - y_m}{2}$): (b) $z = 1.0$, (c) $z = 1.35$, (d) $z = 1.70$. Values reaching the top of the y axis appear at the bottom of the chart, with a more saturated hue. The original chart (deformed according to z) is overlaid for each step, for better understanding.

Value Zooming

Value zooming allows users to specify the zoom factor using a continuous interaction—in our case, dragging the mouse up/down with the left button pressed. Note that value zooming does not change the scale of the x axis, unlike regular zooming, and it does not change the height the of chart, since the values will wrap around the lower border of the chart.

HG use a discrete number of bands, so changing from 2 to 3 bands triggers a sudden transition. The continuous interaction we propose prevents this abrupt change, resulting in a smooth and continuous zoom, as seen in the three zoom levels shown in Figure 4. The chart can be seen as if drawn on a tall sheet of paper which is wrapped around its baseline according to the zoom factor: when the shape of the chart reaches the top of the y axis, it is cut and appears at the bottom of the y axis, with a more saturated hue. The appropriate zoom factor depends on the scale of the variations one wants to analyze: observing small variations will result in a high zoom value and large variations in a low zoom value. Using Heer et al. [15] terminology, our zooming implementation keeps the height of the horizon graph fixed but increases the virtual resolution of the underlying chart.

We were interested in observing how users would adapt and understand this unusual metaphor. We believe that this interactive virtual resolution control provided by our zoom can be easily understood thanks to the paper-wrapping metaphor, and that this interaction can lead to substantially higher numbers of bands than the recommended two. However, increasing the number of bands makes it more difficult for users to discriminate the different color intensities. This trade off rests in the user's hands, according to the task and/or the data. While standard zooming techniques consist of focusing on a specific area and losing context information, our zooming implementation for IHG preserves both the visibility of the context and the details of small variations around the baseline.

The range r_i of each band b_i is computed differently for HG and IHG because of the different values for y_b and because HG use a discrete number of bands b, while IHG use a continuous zoom value z:

$$r_i = [y_b + i\frac{h}{2K}, y_b + (i+1)\frac{h}{2K}], \quad \text{with}$$

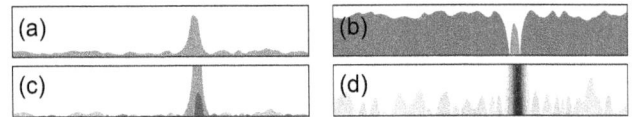

Figure 5. Four views of a time series illustrating the importance of the interactive settings of the baseline value y_b and the zoom factor z.
(a) $y_b = y_m$, $z = 1.0$; (b) $y_b = \frac{y_M - y_m}{2}$, $z = 2.0$;
(c) $y_b = 0.08(y_M - y_m)$, $z = 2.0$; (d) $y_b = 0.08(y_M - y_m)$, $z = 8.5$.

$$\text{HG} \begin{cases} i \in [-b, b[\\ h = y_M - y_m \\ K = b \end{cases}$$

$$\text{IHG} \begin{cases} i \in [-\lceil z \rceil, \lceil z \rceil[\\ h = \max(|y_b - y_m|, |y_b - y_M|) \\ K = z \end{cases}$$

Combination Of Pan And Zoom

The technique we provide never leads to loss of information thanks to the HG properties. Moreover, for both our pan and zoom interaction techniques, the visual feedback is different from a standard pan and zoom along the x axis and results in user-controlled transitions instead of sudden changes.

To illustrate the effectiveness of our technique, let's consider the basic task of finding the global maximum over multiple time series. This task is accomplished in two steps: first, the baseline is set at y_M so that all the values are colored blue. Then, the value of the baseline is progressively decreased by the user until red values appear in one or several charts. The global maximum belongs to one of these charts. If two or more time series turn red for the same value of the baseline, the user will zoom in to enlarge these areas and the differences in magnitude will be visible.

Another typical use of our technique consists of locking the pan to a reference value of interest and zooming to highlight the differences with the other values. This case is illustrated in Figure 5: let's consider a time series with small variations around a specific value except during a period of time containing higher values, resulting in a high bump (5(a)). Using the recommended parameters ($z = 2.0$, $y_b = \frac{y_M - y_m}{2}$, 5(b)) slightly increases the small variations but the baseline separating the chart in two brings no interesting information because the value of interest is not near y_b and HG is not adapted to such a case. With a well-chosen value for y_b (5(c)) one can focus on the value of interest. Still, the differences between values are difficult to estimate. Combining pan and zoom ($z = 8.5$, $y_b = 0.08 \times (y_M - y_m)$, 5(d)) makes the small variations easy to read and compare. Furthermore, Figure 1(c) illustrates how *Max* can be easily accomplished using IHG in comparison to RLC and HG. These examples illustrate the importance of properly setting the number of bands and the value of the baseline. Those settings need to be interactively set because they depend on which part of the chart and on which type of variations (large or small) one is interested in.

Finally, we designed our pan and zoom interaction techniques keeping real-world scenarios in mind. For instance, baseline panning would let a doctor specify the base value for the body temperature of patients according to their health.The continuous zoom provides an effective way of exploring the temperatures of a city during one year; according to the zoom factor, seasonal, daily, or hourly variations may be observed.

USER STUDY

We designed an experiment to determine the usefulness of adding interactivity to HG. In the study we asked users to examine LSV datasets and perform three kinds of tasks using RLC, HG, and IHG. To quantify the impact of each approach, we measured the *Time*, *Correctness*, and *Error magnitude* for each visualization technique.

Data

We used several datasets, including unemployment rates and temperatures, during our pilot studies. However, for the main experiment we chose real-world data from Google Finance [13]. We used the stock market history during February 2012 from 182 banks with no missing data for that period. We chose these datasets because they are LSV time series that evolve in a close range, making it necessary to use a common scale for all visualized charts. Because LSV time series have different levels of detail, we expected that HG would outperform RLC and that we would be able to differentiate HG and IHG, since both are multi-resolution visualization techniques.

Hypotheses

Our hypotheses for this experiment were as follows:

H_1 *The benefits in terms of Time, Correctness and Error of IHG compared to RLC and HG will increase with the number of time series* . This hypothesis is based on the intuition that the task becomes more difficult with larger numbers of time series but that interaction will help deal with the increasing scale. To test this hypothesis, we designed variants of the task using 2, 8, and 32 time series. We also predicted that the greater the number of time series, the less efficient RLC will be.

H_2 *IHG will be faster for all the tasks.*

H_3 *HG with its recommended parameters ($y_b = \frac{y_M - y_m}{2}$ and $b = 2$) will be less efficient than IHG for LSV time series.*

Experimental Factors

We describe in the next subsections our experimental factors: *visualization technique*, number of time series N and *task*.

Visualization Techniques

Across all three visualization conditions (RLC, HG and IHG), each of the charts was given the same height and all charts shared the same value range and the same baseline value. Based on previous work, we chose a constant height of 24 pixels for the charts, regardless of the number of displayed time series. Heer et al. found this height to be optimal for both RLC and 1-band mirrored HG [15], and using this size allows us to compare our results to theirs. We also made several specific choices in the design of each condition:

RLC: for consistency with HG and IHG, the charts were filled in with the color corresponding to values above the baseline. Although the data values were not all positive, the baseline was at the overall dataset minimum value y_m.

HG: we reversed the meaning of red/blue in our color map because, during the experiment design and pilots, we tested datasets with temperatures that are usually encoded using blue for cold and red for warm. This flipping of colors does not bias the experiment since the coding is consistent over the three techniques. We used the recommended values $y_b = \frac{y_M - y_m}{2}$ and $b = 2$.

IHG: to facilitate learning, we chose the value of the baseline and the zoom factor at the initial stage to be the same as the ones for RLC, *i. e.,* y_m and 1.0, respectively. The color coding was identical to the one used for HG. During the experiment, the value of the baseline and zoom factor were displayed.

Numbers Of Time Series (N)

The related work on graphical perception of multiple time series often considered only two time series at a time [15, 26]. More recently, Javed et al. compared different visualization techniques with higher values for N: their main study dealt with 2 to 8 time series and their follow-up included up to 16 time series [19]. We considered sets of $N=2$ and $N=8$ time series so that we could compare our results against prior work. In addition, because one of our goals was to deal with larger numbers of time series and test the scalability of split-space techniques, we also considered sets of $N=32$ series.

Tasks

Based on the task taxonomy for time series developed by Andrienko et al. [1, 2], we chose one elementary task for direct comparison (*Max*), one elementary task for relation-seeking (*Disc*), and one synoptic task for relation-seeking (*Same*) (Figure 6).

The *Find the same (Same)* task is a variant of the Andrienko et al.'s *Slope* task. Users are asked to select the time series that is exactly the same as a specified *reference* time series. We chose this alternative because of the very high difficulty in discerning the slope of time series using RLC with LSV datasets. Our selection of this particular set of tasks was motivated by our pilot studies and was designed to allow us to compare our results against prior work.

We also discarded several other tasks from our experiment based on the results of pilot studies. For example, we did not ask users to find the global maximum across all the time series because IHG were clearly better for this task than the two

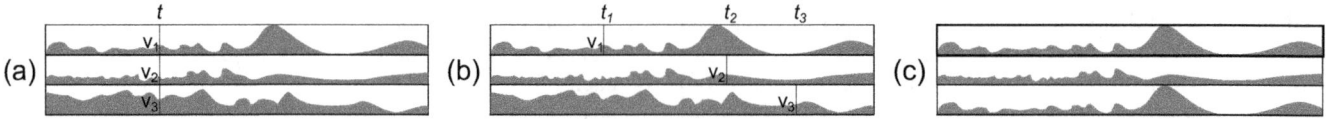

Figure 6.   Narrower visuals of the three tasks. (a) *Max*: select the time series having the highest value at t. *Disc*: select the time series i having the highest value at t_i. *Same*: select the time series $i, i > 1$, being the copy of the reference time series i.

other techniques in terms of Correctness and Time. Furthermore, automatic techniques would outperform any interactive technique for this kind of basic task.

Find the Maximum (Max): We chose to have more control on the task than previous experiments to adapt it to LSV time series. A *reference* time series is randomly picked from the dataset and assigned a random position in the display order. This *reference* is marked at a random point in time t. Its associated value is V_t. The other time series are then selected in the dataset if they satisfy the following condition: being v_t the value of each additional time series at t, the time series is said to be *comparable* with the *reference* if:

$$\begin{cases} V_t - v_t > 2\% \times (y_M - y_m) \\ V_t - v_t < 10\% \times (y_M - y_m) \end{cases}$$

By imposing these conditions, the minimum visual difference between the *reference* value and the remaining time series values at the shared marked point t is in the range $[0.5, 2.5]$ pixels for the RLC technique. For HG and IHG, the difference in pixels is proportional to the virtual resolution [15], *i. e.,* the number of bands.

Discriminate (Disc): The time series are selected in the same way as in *Max* but each has its own random time-point t.

Find the Same (Same): There is one more time series displayed for this task than for the two others (the *reference*).

Because we are focused on assessing visual perception of time series, we did not include additional features such as sorting or highlighting maximum values that might help users perform operations like *Max* and *Disc*. As in Javed et al.'s study [19] we provided no scale or tick marks and displayed no numerical values. Participants were only able to analyze the shape and colors of the time series. Note that these tasks are very difficult to perform if the differences in magnitude between the values are small, which is the case for LSV datasets.

Overall Experiment Design
The dependent variables we measured are *Time* (continuous) and *Correctness* (binary). Because Correctness does not capture the error's magnitude, for *Max* and *Disc* we also measured the *Error* (continuous), which is defined as $\frac{100 \times e}{(e_M - e_m)}$, where e is the absolute error measured, and e_M and e_m are the maximum and minimum possible errors. Error expresses the difference in percentage between the correct maximum value and the value chosen by the user. For *Same*, this additional measure has no meaning unless we subjectively define a similarity measure. Therefore, we only recorded the Correctness of the answer in *Same*. For IHG, we also measured how long each participant took to perform the pan and the zoom interactions, as well as their values at the end of each trial. Each participant performed four trials per *technique* × *task* × N combination.

The order of *technique* and *task* was counterbalanced using a Latin square to minimize learning effects.

Because the difficulty of the task is highly correlated with the number of time series [19], the order of N was gradually increased instead of being randomized (first 2, then 8, and finally 32). In summary, the design included $(3 \times techniques) \times (3 \times tasks) \times (3 \times N) \times (4 \times trials) = 108$ trials per participant. For each, the time series were randomly selected in the dataset. The experimental session lasted about 45 minutes in total.

Participants finished the trials for a particular technique, separated into task blocks, before moving on to another one. Each time a new task began (three times for each technique), participants went through a short training for that block. This training consisted in a reminder of the task and four training trials, not limited in time to let participants establish their strategy for the task. During the training as well as the actual trials, participants received feedback as to whether their answer was correct or not. There were told that the Correctness of the answer was more important than the Time.

Participants
Nine participants (7 males, 2 females) were recruited from our research institute. Participants ranged from 23-36 years in age (mean 27, median 26), had normal or corrected-to-normal vision and were not color blind. Participants were all volunteers and were not paid for their participation in the experiment. All the participants (students as well as non-students) had a background in computer science and good chart reading skills. Six participants had already heard of RLC and only one knew HG.

Procedure
The participants watched a short introductory video explaining the RLC and HG techniques and illustrating the possibility of modifying the baseline to separate the values below and above it by coloring a standard line graph. They sat in front of a 19 inch LCD monitor (1280x1024 pixels) at a distance of approximately 50 cm and used only the mouse during the experiment. To select an answer time series, they had to double-click on it. To avoid accidental clicks, after having selected the time series, a dialog asked them to confirm their choice while the time kept running. This interaction was the only one available for RLC and HG. For IHG, pan and zoom were provided using the mouse by dragging vertically anywhere on the screen with one of the two mouse buttons pressed. The left button triggered the zoom and the right button the pan. Participants were able to practice until they understood the interface well. After each task and for each visualization technique, participants were asked to give a score for *difficulty* and describe the strategy they used.

Table 1. Significant results for each factor by N and *task*. The best value for each line is in bold.

N	Factor	Task	$F_{2,16}$	p	Pairwise mean comparisons	Mean RLC	HG	IHG
2	*Time*	Same	7.71	*	$HG \ll RLC \,\&\, HG \ll IHG$	4.45s	**2.78s**	3.80s
		Max	7.08	*	$RLC \ll IHG \,\&\, HG \ll IHG$	**2.77s**	3.02s	4.93s
		Disc	4.15	*	$RLC \ll IHG \,\&\, HG \ll IHG$	**3.30s**	3.74s	5.49s
8	*Time*	Max	10.87	**	$HG \lll IHG$	7.69s	**5.73s**	11.40s
		Disc	5.45	*	$RLC \ll IHG \,\&\, HG \ll IHG$	**9.59s**	10.18s	14.45s
	Correctness	Max	4.96	*	$RLC \ll IHG$	0.833	0.972	**1.0**
		Disc	9.45	*	$RLC < IHG$	0.805	0.944	**1.0**
	Error	Max	5.17	*	$IHG \ll RLC \,\&\, HG \ll RLC$	7.43	0.73	**0.0**
		Disc	6.15	*	$IHG \ll RLC$	7.82	1.43	**0.0**
32	*Time*	Same	7.38	*	$IHG \lll RLC \,\&\, HG \ll RLC$	30.06s	20.99s	**18.17s**
	Correctness	Same	6.52	*	$RLC \lll IHG$	0.694	0.92	**1.0**
		Max	10.20	**	$RLC \lll IHG \,\&\, RLC \ll HG$	0.639	0.916	**0.944**
		Disc	13.36	**	$RLC \lll IHG \,\&\, HG < IHG \,\&\, RLC \ll HG$	0.361	0.722	**0.871**
	Error	Max	9.61	**	$IHG \lll RLC \,\&\, HG \ll RLC$	12.9	2.01	**1.34**
		Disc	29.44	***	$IHG \lll RLC \,\&\, IHG \ll HG \,\&\, HG \ll RLC$	24.15	9.01	**3.23**

* for $p \leq 0.05$, ** for $p \leq 0.001$, *** for $p \leq 0.0001$
We report Cohen-d's effect size [11] computed using the pooled standard deviation:
$x < y$ for a *small effect* $(.2 < d < .3)$, $x \ll y$ a *medium effect* $(.3 < d < .8)$, $x \lll y$ a *large effect* $(.8 < d < \infty)$.

Table 2. Percent of participants using no interaction, only the pan, only the zoom, and both interaction by N, all tasks combined.

N	None	Only Pan	Only Zoom	Both
2	46.7	6.6	10	36.7
8	3.3	6.7	18	71.7
32	3.3	0	10	86.7

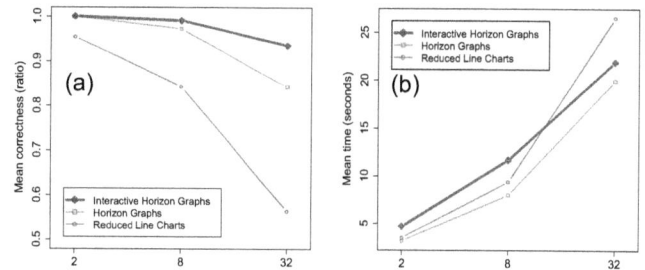

Figure 7. (a) *Correctness* and (b) *completion time* plots for each technique for the overall study (all tasks combined) as a function of N.

RESULTS

All data were analyzed using repeated ANOVA measures. We applied a log transform to the measures of Time to obtain a quasi-normal distribution. Pairwise t-tests were done with the Bonferroni adjustments. Effect sizes were computed using the unbiased estimate of Cohen's d [11], with the pooled standard deviation. We only report on significant effects that are summarized in Table 1, along with their effect size.

Use Of Pan And Zoom For Interactive Horizon Graphs

Table 2 presents participants' use of pan and zoom for IHG. For *N=2*, half the participants did not use any interaction at all. For *N=8*, 71.7% used both types of interaction. For *N=32*, 86.7% used both. The harder the task, the more interaction was used. We also observed that for all N, few participants used only pan or only zoom—both seem useful to most participants.

We also recorded the values of the baseline and the zoom factor at the end of each trial for IHG (Figure 8(a) and (b)) and the percentage of total time participants used pan and zoom (Figure 9(b)) using our kinematic logs. The end values are important measures because they correspond to the number of bands and the value of the baseline the participants estimated to be the best for each trial.

Questionnaire Results

For each technique × task × N, we asked participants to give a score between 1 and 4 for *difficulty* (1: very easy, 2: easy, 3: difficult, 4: very difficult). Mean difficulty by task and

N is reported Figure 9(a). With 9 participants we could not perform a reliable ANOVA, but consistent ranking can be reported: all the 9 participants ranked the techniques in the same order regardless of the task and N: they ranked IHG first, HG second and RLC third.

SUMMARY AND DISCUSSION

The results confirmed our hypotheses that IHG were better than RLC and HG for large numbers of LSV time series.

Influence of Number of Time Series

In this subsection we detail the *statistically significant* differences between RLC, HG, and IHG for each N, and provide recommendations for the use of each technique.

For *N=2*: For *Same*, HG are faster than both RLC and IHG. This improvement is likely due to the fact that HG use colors that allow pre-attentive perception and recognition of key features. With IHG, participants lost time using the interactions, looking for recognizable shapes using pan and zoom.
For *Max* and *Disc*, both RLC and HG are faster than IHG: participants had been told that Correctness was more important than Time and we observed that they double-checked their answers using pan and zoom whenever they were in doubt.

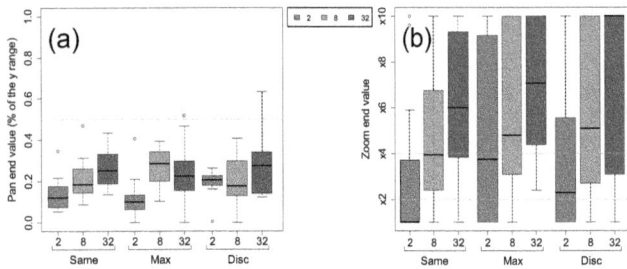

Figure 8. (a) Pan and (b) zoom values at the end of the trials by *task* and number of time series N for IHG. In (a), the grey horizontal line at 0.5 indicates the value of the baseline using HG (50% of the chart height). In (b), the grey horizontal lines at $z = 2$ and $z = 4$ are the recommended and the maximum values of b.

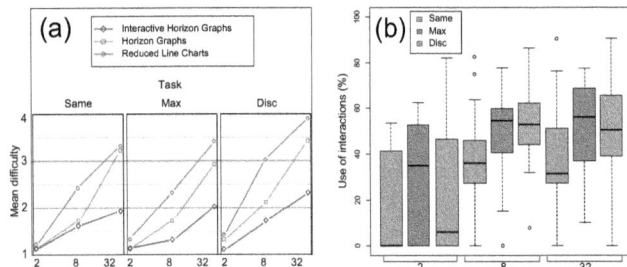

Figure 9. (a) Mean difficulty score for each task by N from participant's answers to the questionnaire. (b) Pan and zoom use in percent of the trials total time for IHG.

Figure 9(b) illustrates this observation—even for $N=2$, the use of pan and zoom represents up to 50% of the trials' time.

Because there is no difference in Correctness or Error for $N=2$, we recommend using HG for $N=8$ or fewer. RLC can be used for elementary comparison and relation-seeking tasks such as *Max* and *Disc*. However, we do not recommend IHG for such small numbers of series because the interaction technique distracts users and does not bring any benefit.

For $N=8$: For both *Max* and *Disc*, HG are faster than IHG. The rationale is likely the same as for $N=2$—participants lost time using the interactions. Moreover, since the initial state of IHG was identical to RLC ($z = 1$, $y_b = y_m$), participants had to interact to obtain a visualization similar to HG, while for HG the default configuration was readily available. The remarkable distinction between $N=2$ and $N=8$ is that, in the latter, there are significant differences in Correctness and Error. For *Max*, IHG have higher Correctness than RLC because the zoom allows users to discern fine differences between charts. Since IHG and HG amplify the small variations, both techniques induce lower Error than RLC.
For *Disc*, IHG have higher Correctness and lower Error than RLC for the same reasons.

In summary, IHG are 1.2 and 1.02 times more correct than RLC and HG for *Same* and 1.2 and 1.06 times more correct than RLC and HG for *Disc*. All participants completed the tasks with no error using IHG.

We recommend using IHG or HG and avoiding RLC for medium numbers of time series when performing elementary comparison and relation-seeking tasks. The difference

between HG and RLC was not highlighted in previous studies and is almost certainly due to the properties of our datasets.

For $N=32$, both IHG and HG have higher Correctness and lower Error than RLC for all tasks except for *Same* where there is no difference in Correctness between HG and RLC. RLC are clearly limiting for large numbers of time series, regardless of the task. Interestingly, for *Disc*, IHG have higher Correctness and lower Error than HG. For this task—which is the hardest, involving visually browsing the charts vertically and horizontally—IHG exhibit better results than HG.

IHG are more correct than both RLC and HG for *Same* (1.4 and 1.1 times more), for *Max* (1.5 and 1.03 times more), and for *Disc* (2.4 and 1.2 times more). Not only are there significant differences between the techniques, but the effect size indicates that these differences are substantial.

The Error measure also shows substantial differences: for *Max*, the Error for IHG is 9.6 times less than for RLC and 1.3 times less than for HG. For *Disc*, Error for IHG is 7.5 times less than RLC and 2.7 times less than for HG. This confirms that IHG leads to more correct answers and that, even when an answer is wrong, the Error is lesser than when using RLC and HG.

For Time, there is no significant difference between IHG and HG regardless of the task. This is in contrast to the results for smaller N, where IHG were usually slower than the other techniques. Here, the overhead of interaction with the charts was less than that of visual search.

We strongly recommend using IHG for large numbers of time series and avoiding RLC. We also found that for large and medium numbers of time series, HG are more efficient than RLC, in contrast to previously published studies. Our work is the first to reveal these advantages of HG.

Time vs. Accuracy

The Time to perform *Max* and *Disc* is similar for all three techniques for $N=32$ (Figure 7(b)) but the Correctness for RLC decreases severely between $N=8$ and $N=32$ (Figure 7(a)). Participants answered as quickly as in HG and IHG, but with very low Correctness. Participants' answers to our questionnaire explain this effect—for the RLC technique, their strategy was to quickly identify potential answers and to pick one randomly, without being sure of the answer. Clearly, regardless of how much time users take with RLC for $N=32$, they cannot perform *Max* and *Disc* correctly. We observed the same effect for HG, to a lower extent, but not for IHG. Figure 7(a) illustrates the scalability of each technique as a function of N, showing a clear advantage for IHG.

Figure 7(b) illustrates the Time to accomplish the task as a function of N. This shows a different trend than for Correctness—the Time for IHG and HG increases similarly with larger N, whereas the increase for RLC is much greater.

Tasks

As expected, Correctness decreases when N increases for all tasks. Furthermore, task difficulty can be clearly seen from the trends in Error: *Same* is the easiest task, followed by *Max*, with *Disc* being the hardest. Participants' questionnaire responses corroborate these results—they found *Disc* to be the hardest task and found that the *difficulty* dramatically increased with the number of time series (Figure 9(a)). These results are in agreement with Javed et al. [19]. However, our results do not show that HG are slower than RLC for *Max*, probably due to our use of LSV datasets.

Hypothesis Control

We confirm **H₁**: $N=32$ is the only value of N that showed clear differences between the three techniques. IHG have the highest Correctness and the lowest Error, followed by HG, while RLC was much worse. HG also have significantly better scores than RLC for both Correctness and Error. This difference had not been highlighted in previous studies and is explained by our use of LSV data—suggesting a need for multi-resolution techniques.

We reject **H₂**: our results show that at least for task *Same*, IHG are significantly faster than RLC, but there is no significant difference with HG. This is due to the fact that, unlike HG, IHG require users to interact with the chart to obtain a useful configuration, which takes additional time.

We partially confirm **H₃**: the Correctness for HG decreases when N increases and is lower than when using IHG. We did not find any significant difference between HG and IHG for *Max*, but IHG have substantially higher Correctness and less Error than HG for *Disc*. We were however surprised to see how robust HG are with respect to the number of time series; we did not expect such good results for this technique.

Pan And Zoom

End-values: Contrary to [15], the most useful zoom level can be well above 2. This can be seen in Figure 8(b), which shows z at the end of each trial. We interpret the final value as being the most comfortable zoom level for answering the task.

For *Max* and *Disc* users' final zoom value is frequently the maximum zoom we allowed—10 bands. The recommended number of bands was rarely the one chosen for $N=8$ and $N=32$. Our conclusion is that there is no default value for this parameter— the need for a higher or lower number of bands is related to the task, the dataset, and N. Conversely, the use of lower zoom values when completing *Same* can be explained by the strategy the participants adopted. Most participants modified the value of y_b until a specific composition of color and shape appeared in the reference time series. Then they visually browsed all the time series to search this feature.

The *baseline* end value (Figure 8(a)) was rarely at the classic value of the baseline (50% of the chart height). This result is certainly due to the datasets, but confirms that if users have the possibility of modifying the baseline, they will choose a value which can be in a continuous range and will not limit their choice to a single value.

Interactions: The percentage of interaction time (Figure 9(b)) for $N=2$ is low and does not linearly increase with N. Rather, it is about the same for both $N=8$ and $N=32$—around 50% of the total time. This confirms that IHG are more useful for large numbers of time series but are distracting for $N=2$.

Comparison With Previous Studies

The differences between our study and the previous ones can be attributed to three factors: the use of interaction in IHG, the use of LSV datasets, and the use of the *Same* task instead of *Slope*. For $N=8$, contrary to previous studies [19], HG are significantly more efficient than RLC, likely because we used LSV datasets. Previous studies never tried $N=32$ when all tasks become very difficult and interaction helps immensely. As for the choice of tasks, we have not compared IHG with the other techniques for *Slope* since this task was too hard to perform on LSV datasets, especially for RLC; the benefit of IHG on more uniform datasets remains to be studied.

Heer et al. recommended not to use too many bands [15] for value estimation tasks, not considered in our experiments. We are not sure value extraction would be accurate on LSV datasets, even with few bands.

General Implications

We used LSV datasets which are usually more challenging than the synthetic datasets used in previous studies, and also ecologically more valid. Our results show that more varied datasets should be used for future experiments to obtain more generalizable results.

Finally, we believe that IHG can decrease the learning curve of HG because they start with the familiar RLC representation and, with continuous interactions using the pan and zoom, show novice users how HG are constructed. Our results highlight the fact that adding interaction to existing techniques can notably improve their performance as well as their usability.

Limitations and future work

Our recommendations for design are valid under some conditions that we detail below.

Participants: Our participants were students and researchers from HCI and Infovis and additional studies are required to evaluate IHG for novice users.
N: We constrained the number of time series to the height of a standard screen without having to scroll and more than 32 time series would require a larger screen.
Datasets: Our results are valid for LSV datasets, for which HG and IHG perform well. Having shown that IHG are efficient for at least one category of datasets, in future work we plan to investigate a deeper range of datasets.
Tasks: We did not consider value estimation tasks, since it requires users to perform a considerable amount of mental math using HG and IHG. However, alternative interaction techniques can be designed specifically to support value reading and extraction.

CONCLUSION

We have presented *Interactive Horizon Graphs (IHG)*, an efficient interactive technique for exploring multiple time series which unifies two split-space visualization techniques: *Reduced Line Charts (RLC)* and *Horizon Graphs (HG)*. We have shown that IHG outperforms RLC and HG for several tasks in the most difficult conditions, thanks to interactive control of its two parameters: the baseline value and the zoom factor. Both relate to the number of bands traditionally used by HG. We have shown that IHG perform well with up to 32 time series, when previous work only tested up to 16. We also found that HG perform better than RLC for our datasets.

We conclude that systems visualizing time series using small multiples should provide our interaction techniques as a default. Our techniques generally improve performance on visual exploration tasks, except during the learning phase or for very small sets where interactions can be distracting.

Our contributions are: *(i)* the unification of RLC and HG by using interactive pan and zoom, *(ii)* a demonstration that IHG can scale up to 32 time series, and *(iii)* an evaluation using real LSV datasets rather than synthetic datasets with clear landmarks that help visual search tasks.

In the future we plan to investigate displays with more than 32 time series using larger screens and specialized hardware such as wall-sized displays. We are also interested in evaluating the benefits of our pan and zoom techniques individually.

This work has shown that our simple interactions can unify two visualization techniques and substantially improve their efficiency. We hope it will be adopted to limit the proliferation of slightly different visualization techniques currently provided to explore multiple time series.

ACKNOWLEDGMENTS
The authors thank P. Irani for introducing Horizon Graphs to them, P. Dragicevic for his constructive suggestions, A. Bezerianos, A. Spritzer, B. Bach, J. Boy and W. Willett for their help proofreading the document.

REFERENCES
1. Aigner, W., Miksch, S., Schumann, H., and Tominski, C. *Visualization of Time-Oriented Data.* Springer, 2011.

2. Andrienko, N., and Andrienko, G. *Exploratory Analysis of Spatial and Temporal Data: A Systematic Approach.* Springer, Dec. 2005.

3. Beattie, V., and Jones, M. J. The impact of graph slope on rate of change judgments in corporate reports. *Abacus 38*, 2 (2002), 177–199.

4. Bederson, B. B., Hollan, J. D., Perlin, K., Meyer, J., Bacon, D., and Furnas, G. Pad++: A zoomable graphical sketchpad for exploring alternate interface physics. *JVLC 7* (1995), 3–31.

5. Bertin, J. *Semiology of graphics.* University of Wisconsin Press, 1983.

6. Byron, L., and Wattenberg, M. Stacked graphs geometry & aesthetics. *TVCG '08 14*, 6 (Nov. 2008), 1245–1252.

7. Cleveland, W., and McGill, R. Graphical Perception: The Visual Decoding of Quantitative Information on Graphical Displays of Data. *Journal of the Royal Statistical Society 150*, 3 (1987), 192–229.

8. Cleveland, W. S. *The elements of graphing data.* Wadsworth Publ. Co., Belmont, CA, USA, 1985.

9. Cleveland, W. S. *Visualizing Data.* Hobart Press, 1993.

10. Cockburn, A., Karlson, A., and Bederson, B. B. A review of overview+detail, zooming, and focus+context interfaces. *ACM Comput. Surv. 41*, 1 (Jan. 2009).

11. Cohen, J. *Statistical power analysis for the behavioral sciences*, 2 ed. Lawrence Erlbaum, Jan. 1988.

12. Few, S. Time on the horizon. available online at `http://www.perceptualedge.com/articles/visual_business_intelligence/time_on_the_horizon.pdf`, Jun/Jul 2008.

13. Google finance. `http://www.google.com/finance`.

14. Heer, J., and Agrawala, M. Multi-scale banking to 45 degrees. *TVCG '06 12*, 5 (2006), 701 –708.

15. Heer, J., Kong, N., and Agrawala, M. Sizing the horizon: the effects of chart size and layering on the graphical perception of time series visualizations. In *Proc. CHI '09* (2009), 1303–1312.

16. Hochheiser, H., and Shneiderman, B. Dynamic query tools for time series data sets: timebox widgets for interactive exploration. *InfoVis '04 3*, 1 (2004), 1–18.

17. Isenberg, P., Bezerianos, A., Dragicevic, P., and Fekete, J.-D. A study on dual-scale data charts. *TVCG '11 17*, 12 (2011), 2469 –2478.

18. Javed, W., and Elmqvist, N. Stack zooming for multi-focus interaction in time-series data visualization. In *Proc. PacificVis 2010* (2010), 33–40.

19. Javed, W., McDonnel, B., and Elmqvist, N. Graphical perception of multiple time series. *TVCG '10 16*, 6 (2010).

20. Lam, H., Munzner, T., and Kincaid, R. Overview use in multiple visual information resolution interfaces. *TVCG '07 13*, 6 (2007), 1278–1285.

21. Peterson, L., and Schramm, W. How accurately are different kinds of graphs read? *Educational Technology Research and Development 2* (1954), 178–189.

22. Playfair, W. *The Commercial and Political Atlas.* London, 1786.

23. Reijner, H. The development of the horizon graph. available online at `http://www.stonesc.com/Vis08_Workshop/DVD/Reijner_submission.pdf`, 2008.

24. Saito, T., Miyamura, H. N., Yamamoto, M., Saito, H., Hoshiya, Y., and Kaseda, T. Two-tone pseudo coloring: Compact visualization for one-dimensional data. *InfoVis '05* (2005), 23.

25. Silva, S. F., and Catarci, T. Visualization of linear time-oriented data: A survey. In *Proc. WISE'00* (2000).

26. Simkin, D., and Hastie, R. An Information-Processing Analysis of Graph Perception. *Journal of the American Statistical Association 82*, 398 (1987).

27. Talbot, J., Gerth, J., and Hanrahan, P. An empirical model of slope ratio comparisons. *TVCG '12* (2012).

28. Tufte, E. R. *The visual display of quantitative information.* Graphics Press, Cheshire, CT, USA, 1986.

29. Wattenberg, M. A note on space-filling visualizations and space-filling curves. In *InfoVis '05* (2005), 181–186.

Patina: Dynamic Heatmaps for Visualizing Application Usage

Justin Matejka, Tovi Grossman, and George Fitzmaurice

Autodesk Research, Toronto, Ontario, Canada

firstname.lastname@Autodesk.com

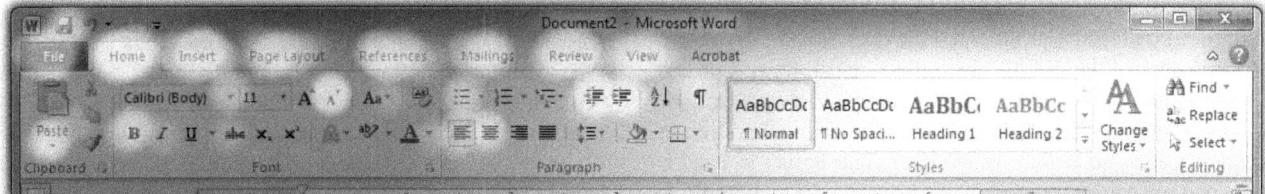

Figure 1. A side-by-side view of the Patina heatmap overlay showing the usage patterns of both the active user and the user community on the left, and the standard underlying Microsoft Word interface on the right.

ABSTRACT

We present *Patina*, an application independent system for collecting and visualizing software application usage data. Patina requires no instrumentation of the target application, all data is collected through standard window metrics and accessibility APIs. The primary visualization is a dynamic heatmap overlay which adapts to match the content, location, and shape of the user interface controls visible in the active application. We discuss a set of design guidelines for the Patina system, describe our implementation of the system, and report on an initial evaluation based on a short-term deployment of the system.

Author Keywords: Visualization; Social Learning

ACM Classification: H.5.2 [Information interfaces and presentation]: User Interfaces. - Graphical user interfaces.

INTRODUCTION

In today's software applications, users can be faced with thousands of menus, dialogs, and interactive widgets, making the usage and navigation through those interfaces overwhelming. These applications typically look the same regardless of their past usage. A user will be faced with the exact same user interface, regardless of how many times it has been used. On the contrary, physical objects give people a rich set of cues related to their usage history; We can recognize that a car is brand new by its smell, that a book has been well read by the deteriorating visual appearance of its cover, or that a baseball glove has a long history of use from its feel, and the ease at which it closes.

Pirolli and Card's information foraging theory [22] introduced the concept of *information scent*, defined as "the (imperfect) perception of the value, cost, or access path of information sources obtained from proximal cues." Research has shown that the existence of information scent can aid in

navigation and decision making tasks [27]. Thus, improving the information scent cues in software application interfaces could help alleviate the challenges imposed by their overwhelmingly large feature sets.

One way to provide information scent in a user interface is to visualize cues related to the history of its usage [27]. In their Scented Widgets paper, Willett *et al.* argue that such social navigation cues can "direct our attention to hot spots of interest or to under-explored regions." For example, a user opening up an advanced preference dialog may be able to quickly identify settings that users rarely disabled, or parameters that are commonly adjusted.

While usage metrics for software applications can often be collected [17,19], doing so typically requires instrumentation of the host application. Similarly, supporting scented widgets [27], or adapting an application to a user's past behaviors [12], requires modification of the application.

In this paper, we present *Patina*, a new system that collects and visualizes software application usage data. Our system adds two core contributions to the existing literature.

First, whereas scented widgets were designed to enhance individual or groups of widgets, Patina provides visual cues across an entire application interface using a dynamic graphical overlay. A colored heatmap indicates commonly and rarely used features in any view of the interface, and adapts to the current interface layout. Second, Patina is implemented in an application-independent manner requiring no instrumentation of the host application, both for the collection *and* presentation of the usage metrics. This is made possible using a combination of system window metrics and accessibility information, available in many of today's Windows applications.

In the following sections, we provide an overview of the related research, discuss the design goals of our system, and present the implementation details of Patina. We also report on an initial evaluation based on a short-term deployment of the system, used by 8 users for 1 week.

Our results and experiences indicate three primary scenarios where the Patina system could be useful: familiarizing new users with an application; exposing functionality relevant to a specific document; and supporting continuous reflection on personal and community usage patterns.

RELATED WORK

Collecting and Visualizing Usage Metrics

Many commercial software products have customer usage reporting facilities which log and report usage metrics. The ingimp project [26] instrumented the open-source image editing program "the GIMP" to collect real-time usage and demographic information. As with commercial applications however, ingimp required modifying the original source of the application to collect usage data. The Patina system is designed to require no modifications to the original application. The AppMonitor tool [1] from Alexander *et al.* is a client side logging tool that records user interactions in unmodified Windows applications. However, a special DLL must be loaded into a shared memory space with the target application. In contrast, the Patina system collects and monitors data only through an external process. Hurst *et al.*'s Dirty Desktops [16] identified likely interface targets through the collection of user click points but relied on a fixed size and arrangement of UI elements, while the Patina system is designed to work with resizable UIs.

Semi-transparent heap-maps overlaid over the original content are frequently used for viewing eye tracking data [28]. Heatmap overlays have also become a popular way for website administrators to view where user's click on their website [29]. These displays can be useful, however they are not robust to changes in the layout of the underlying webpage. The Mozilla Labs team instrumented the Firefox browser to collect data on which interfaced regions were clicked. They then plotted the results over a static image of the browser [30], whereas the Patina system displays a live-updating heatmap over a running application.

Information Scent

Many research projects have looked to improve the information scent [22] of an interface to assist in the user's navigation through or usage of a software application. In 1992, Hill and Hollan [14] introduced the idea of *computational wear* by marking up the scroll bar of a text editor with indications of which parts of the document have been frequently read and/or edited. This idea was also explored more recently by Alexander *et al.* [2]. Patina employs the idea of *computational wear* by essentially marking up areas of the UI based on their usage.

Scented Widgets [27] offers visual encodings built into individual UI widgets to show community gathered usage data. In contrast, Patina visualizes social navigation cues over the entire application, using a dynamically generated heatmap, and introduces an application independent implementation of Scented Widget visualizations.

The Phosphor [4] and Mnemonic Rendering [5] systems use visual feedback to attract the user's attention to settings or parts of the screen which have been modified. This might allow a user to see which parts of the interface are more useful or important, and the Patina system can serve a similar purpose.

Adaptive UIs

Researchers have explored several ways to address the issue of a user being overwhelmed by the multitude of options and tools available in a complicated software application. One approach has been a multi-layered, or "training wheels" interfaces [3, 6] which only expose new users to a subset of the available functionality, and gradually expose more functionality as the user becomes more experienced. These techniques can reduce the number of mistakes made by a user, but are not applicable for experienced users, or in situations where the user really does need access to the full functionality of the system.

To provide the benefits of multi-layered interfaces while still providing access to the full range of functionality, adaptive menus [12, 13] have been explored which automatically rearrange the items in a menu placing the most frequently used items at the top. These techniques suffer from rearranging the items in the interface, requiring the user to "re-find" elements which have been displaced. Findlater *et al.*'s Ephemeral Adaptation [13] addressed this shortcoming of adaptive menus by maintaining a fixed menu item arrangement where the predicted items appear immediately while the remaining items fade in after a short (500ms) delay. The Patina system uses an automatic transient display similar to Ephemeral Adaptation.

UI Recognition

For a system to augment the interface of an existing application without access or modifications to the original source code, it must be able to recognize the location and properties of the application's UI elements. Prefab [10, 11] and Sikuli [8] use a vision based approach to locate user interface elements based on their appearance. Systems by Hurst *et al.* [15], the PAX framework [7], and Façades [24] combine image techniques with accessibility data collected from the publicly exposed accessibility APIs. Our system exclusively uses externally available window and accessibility data but could be made to take advantage of additional recognition techniques.

While aspects of our design have been inspired by previous work, our system is unique and flexible. None of the previous systems offer an application-independent means of visualizing software application usage data via dynamic graphical overlays which adapt to match the content, location and shape of the user interface controls.

DESIGN GUIDELINES

Our design of Patina was grounded by a study of related research and theory on information visualization and information scent. Below we describe the guidelines that we followed in our design process.

Uniform: Encoding the same data in different ways across widgets can complicate visual comparison [27]. As such, the visual encoding should be consistent across the entire user interface.

Distinguishable: Information scent encoding should not conflict with the conventions of the underlying content [27]. Our visual encoding should respect and be *easily distinguishable from the underlying interface conventions.*

Intuitive: For a visualization to be effective, the user must be able to understand it. Users should be able to, without training, see which areas of the interface are heavily used, as well as which areas are infrequently used. It is therefore important to use a visual encoding that will be intuitive for users to comprehend.

Proximal: To aid in navigation of an information space, the information scent should be provided in the form of a proximal cue [22, 27]. Our visualization should be presented in the same visual space as the user interface elements so the mapping between UI element and usage is directly visible.

Non-Disruptive: The information scent should not adversely impact the user interface design or layout [27]. The data presentation should strike a balance between providing useful information while not being disruptive.

PATINA SYSTEM DESIGN

Our goal is to design a system that works without any modifications to the target application, and without any specialized knowledge about the internal workings of the application. Additionally, the system should be designed in a way that allows it to collect and display usage data from any application.

The Patina system is implemented in C# as a Microsoft Windows application. The main system is broken down into two main sections of Data Collection, and Presentation, with a Data Management block in between (Figure 2).

Figure 2. Organization of the Patina System.

Data Collection

Typical heatmaps collect and visualize static *x* and *y* click points [29] or eye-tracking coordinates [28]. However, to implement a visualization on a live, resizable, customizable user interface, our system needs to recognize which user interface controls the user has interacted with. Our implementation uses Windows-specific libraries for collecting the necessary data, although similar functionality does exist for other operating systems.

Window-Level Data

Top-level, or main application windows in the Windows operating system are accessed programmatically through a handle to the window, referred to as an hWnd. Through a collection of Win32 API calls to functions (including `GetWindowText`, `GetClassName`, and `GetWindowThread-ProcessId` hosted in the `user32.dll` file), a selection of

information about the window and associated process can be gathered (Table 1).

The *Window Title* represents the text which appears in the title bar of the active window. If we are looking at the main application window, the *Application Window Title* field will be the same as *Window Title*. However, if we are looking at a dialog box of some other secondary window, the *Application Window Title* will have the text in the title bar of the host application.

PROPERTY	EXAMPLE
Window Title	"Modify Style"
Application Window Title	"Docu2.docx - Microsoft Word"
Location (x, y)	`408, 457`
Size (width, height)	`532, 545`
Module Name	`WINWORD.EXE`
Class Name	`bosa_sdm_msword`

Table 1. Information collected for a top-level window, the "Modify Style" dialog in Microsoft Word 2010.

In Windows there is also the notion of *control* windows, which are not windows in the traditional UI sense, but rather are sub-elements within a parent window such as scrollbars, informational status areas, or the main canvas area. Outlines for all areas defined as nested hWnd's from a standard view of Microsoft Word and AutoCAD are shown in Figure 3. The *Class Name*, *Size*, and *Location* are collected and logged for each new window activation. Each time the user performs a click event, we check the hWnd hierarchy to see if there have been any structural changes, and if so, we log the differences.

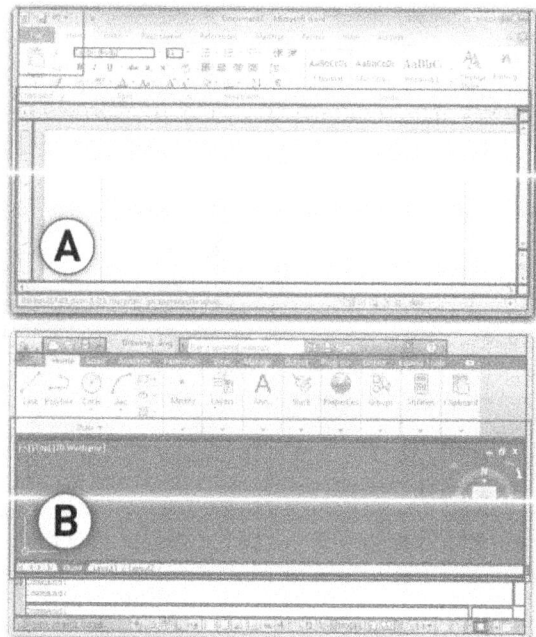

Figure 3. Rectangle information collected from HWND data structures from standard Microsoft Word (A) and AutoCAD (B) windows.

It is apparent by looking at Figure 3 that not all of the area information collected through the interrogation of the nested control windows corresponds visually with UI elements; for example, the square in the top left corner of the Microsoft Word window. Despite the somewhat dirty nature of the data collected in this way, many elements are detected such as the scroll bars in Microsoft Word, and the tool pallets and command line area in AutoCAD.

Accessibility-Level Data

Accessibility APIs are interfaces included in many operating systems which provide programmatic access to user interface elements and are typically used by assistive technologies such as screen readers or GUI automation tools. It generally takes additional work from application developers to fully support the platform's accessibility API's, and as such, the completeness of accessibility coverage can vary greatly between applications. Hurst *et al.* [15] found that over a dataset of 1335 interface elements from 8 popular applications, the Microsoft Active Accessibility (MSAA) API was able to correctly recognize 74% of the UI targets. Our exploration has found that traditional UI elements such as buttons, scrollbars, combo boxes, menus, pull-down menus etc. are relatively well supported by the Accessibility API, but more specialized or unique controls are less reliably covered. Figure 4 shows the accessibility regions returned when querying the same two main windows from Figure 3. We can see that all of the standard controls have been recognized but several specialized controls have been missed; For example, the margin handles in the Word ruler bar, and the document tabs and in-canvas UI elements in AutoCAD.

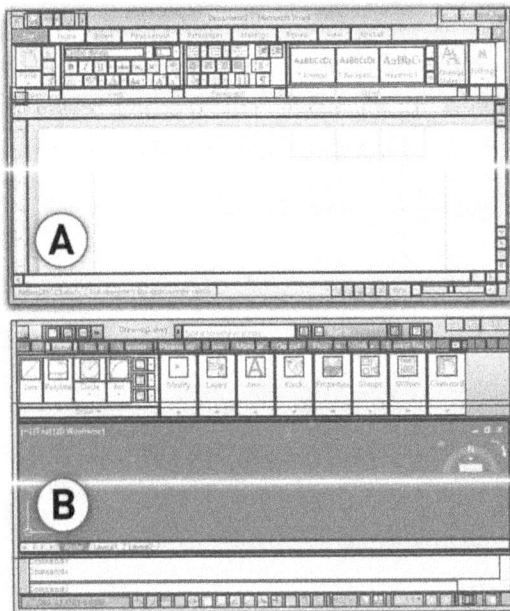

Figure 4. Rectangle data collected from the Accessibility APIs for Microsoft Word (A) and AutoCAD (B) windows. Yellow rectangles indicate regions which are reported as "offscreen".

When pull-down or pop-up menus are posted, new accessibility regions are generated for the individual items in the menu, and the Patina

Our system gathers accessibility data using the previously mentioned Microsoft Active Accessibility (MSAA) API

through the Managed Windows API[1] wrapper. Each item exposes a different set of parameters through the API (as members of the `SystemAccessibleObject` class), but an example of the data available for a combo box is presented in Table 2.

The *Role* field contains what type of UI element we are accessing and the *State* field reports the current condition of the control, such as *offscreen* for items that are not currently visible, and *checked* for selected checkboxes. The current value of a UI element with a user-modifiable component such as a text field or combo box is reported in the *Value* field.

PROPERTY	EXAMPLE
Name	**Font:**
Role	**Combo Box**
State	**None**
Value	**Times New Roman**
Description	**Change the font face.**
Shortcut Text	`null`
Location (x, y)	`303, 83`
Size (width, height)	`98, 22`

Table 2. Information collected for a UI element with the Accessibility API, in this case, the font selection combo box in Microsoft Word 2010.

Querying a single accessibility object can be done without a noticeable delay, but requesting the entire accessibility object tree, which we require, is more intensive, so we perform this data collection in a background thread. Each time the user clicks, we query the accessibility API to get a listing of all available UI elements, and compare against the previously cached list of elements. If there are any additions or removals between the two lists, the new list is cached and saved to disk.

User Activity Data

Besides collecting identifying and structural information related to the window and UI components on the hWnd and accessibility levels, the Patina system is also notified of when a new foreground window is activated. Mouse click events are captured and the coordinates are saved relative to the coordinates of the active window.

Data Management and Sharing

Our system architecture utilizes Dropbox[2] as a mechanism to share data among users [19]. Collected window, accessibility, and user data is placed in a shared Dropbox folder and automatically synced with all other users. This technique simplifies the deployment and evaluation of the system, in comparison to commercial cloud based data management services that would be used for an actual implementation.

Presentation: Dynamic Heatmaps

The Patina system uses dynamic heatmaps as the primary mechanism for encoding usage information. Heatmaps were chosen after a consideration of our grounded design goals. First, heatmaps visualize usage data across the entire interface with a consistent visual encoding (*Uniform*). Heatmaps

---

[1] mwinapi.sourceforge.net

[2] www.dropbox.com

are also capable of being overlaid ontop of the user interface (*Proximal*). Furthermore, the organic nature of our heatmaps are clearly distinguishable from the interface itself (*Distinguishable*). Finally, heatmaps have become a common method for encoding web analytics [29] since it is intuitive for users to understand the meaning of the "hot zones" (*Intuitive*).

The presentation layer of the Patina system comprises two main functions: first, generating the usage pattern heatmap for the current view, and second, displaying the heatmap overlay on top of the active window.

Generating the Heatmap

The process of creating the heatmap can be broken down into four main steps as described below.

1 - COLLECTING RELEVANT CLICK POINTS

Since the Patina system works across applications, only a subset of previously recorded click points will have occurred in the current working application. The first step in filtering the entire set of mouse click points is to find those which occurred in the current application. We do that by considering the *Module Name* and *Class Name* fields from the window data which tells us the name of the executable and the type of window where the click occurred. We only consider clicks which were generated in windows matching the current *Module* and *Class Name*.

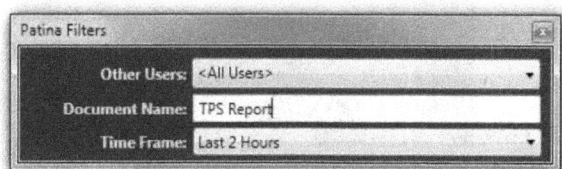

Figure 5. Filters dialog to specify parameters to narrow the data used to generate the heatmaps.

The *Filters Dialog* (Figure 5) provides an additional level of control over filtering the data. Users can choose to only consider clicks from a particular user, particular document (which is implemented as a filter on the *Application Window Title* field), or from a particular time frame.

2 - MAPPING CLICK POINTS TO CURRENT INTERFACE

At this point we have a collection of click points which may be relevant to the current view. The next step is to see which ones have a mapping to the application's current view.

In the simplest scenario, the original window where the recorded click occurred, and the current view, will be exactly the same; that is, they have the exact same dimensions and they have the exact same content. This could occur for a fixed-size window without any tabs or dynamic controls [16]. In this scenario we could simply use a static heat map, using the originally recorded click points. However, few such static user interfaces exists, so we look at our logged control window and accessibility data for a more generalized solution.

Through the collection of control window and accessibility regions we have a set of structural and organizational data about the state of the window at each past click event. We

refer to these control windows and accessibility regions collectively as *control regions*. Some of these *control regions* are quite large and non-specific. For example, the "Home: property page" accessibility region represents the entire *Home* tab of the ribbon. Others are smaller and more precise, such as the "Bold: push button" which corresponds to the 23x22 pixel *Bold* button (Figure 6). The system preferentially uses the accessibility region data for UI element discrimination, and only uses the control windows when no accessibility information is available.

Figure 6. Overlapping rectangular accessibility regions for the "Bold: push button", with the larger areas being the "Font: toolbar" and "Home: property page".

Since these areas are nested and overlapping, the location of each click event could be within multiple *control regions*. To determine at the finest granularity which UI element the click occurred in we look for the smallest *control region* which contains the click coordinates, and associate that *control region* with the original click event. We then look for a corresponding *control region* in the currently active window. For accessibility regions we do this by looking for a region with matching *Name*, *Role*, and *Description* fields. If we find a match, we keep this click point and use it in the next step.

3 - CREATING INTENSITY MAP

At this point we have a collection of click points and associated *control regions* in their original context and we need to map them to the current display. Since the *control region* in the original capture and the matching *control region* in the current interface might have different locations and/or sizes, we consider the position of the click within the original *control region* relative to the width and height of the region, and map the same relative values onto the corresponding region in the current view (Figure 7).

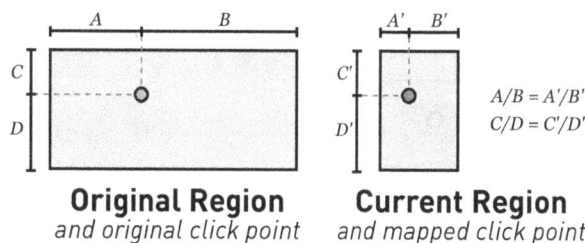

Figure 7. Click point mapping from original *control region* to current *control region*.

This relative positional mapping of click points allows the heatmap to maintain a correct view of usage patterns when UI elements have been moved around on the screen, as well as when the UI controls themselves change between different sizes such as resizing icons in a Ribbon toolbar. The mapping from the original click points to corresponding points on the current view is recalculated every time the current view changes and allows the heap map to update based

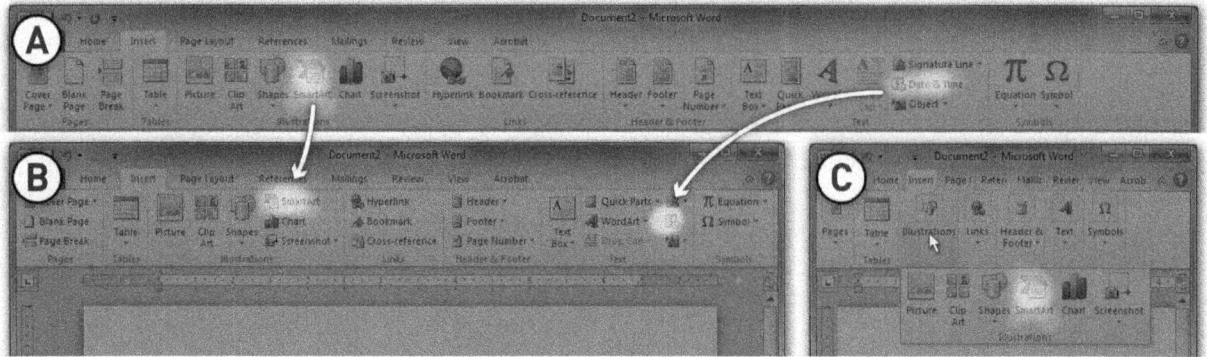

Figure 8. Demonstration of Patina overlay persisting on the correct UI elements after a window resizing, even when the target UI elements change size and position between (A) and (B). During ribbon resizing icons may become hidden (C), however when those elements are exposed through the fly-out menu, their Patina hotspots are restored.

on any changes to the interface layout. An example of this behavior can be seen in Figure 8.

Once all the click points have be mapped onto the current interface layout, the intensity map is created by drawing a semi-transparent circle at each click location which fades from its most opaque in the center to transparent at the edges (Figure 9). The size of the circle is configurable, but we used a radius of 20 pixels for the prototype. The base opacity for each click point is 40%, and as points overlap each other, sections of the intensity become darker, approaching solid black, indicating high activity. If there are many overlapping click points, the opacity of each point can be reduced to prevent the heatmap from becoming oversaturated. Initial testing found that many clicks points occur in the main canvas or working area of an application, and have a tendency to distract from the more useful data related to usage of the specific UI elements such as buttons. Since our main goal is to grack usage of interactive widgets, the opacity of individual click points are reduced for all accessibility regions with an area greater than 64x64 (4,096 pixels^2, which corresponds approximately to the largest size of buttons found in a Ribbon interface) down to 3% for all click points in a region larger than 90,000 pixels^2 (Figure 9A).

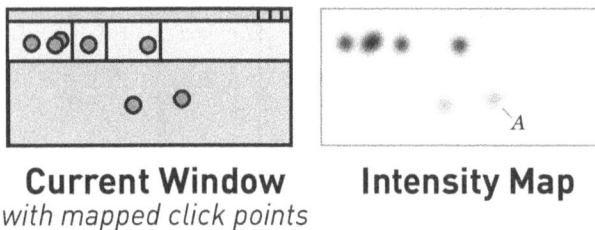

Current Window   Intensity Map
with mapped click points

Figure 9. Intensity map creation.The intensity mapping process is done once for the active user's data and again for the rest of the community data.

4 - COLORING HEATMAP.

Once the intensity maps are created they are converted into heatmaps. This conversion is done on a per pixel level mapping of the greyscale level of the intensity mask to an appropriate color (Figure 10). The heatmap for the active user is generated using the "You" band of colors on the left

while the community heatmap is generated using the "Others" band of colors on the right.

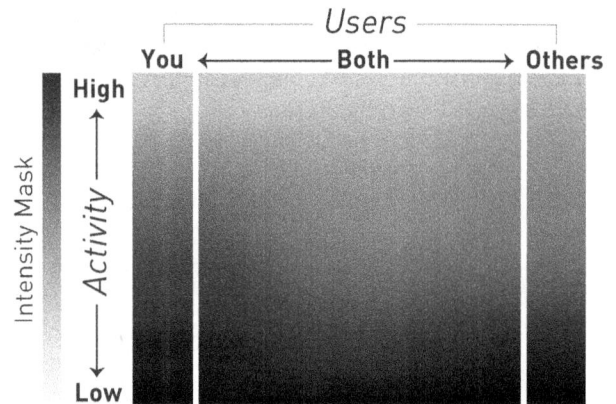

Figure 10. Color mapping used for the heatmaps ranging from low activity to high activity on the vertical axis, and the active user to the community on the horizontal axis.

This coloring creates the look of blue spotlights being used for highlighting the active user's usage data, and orange lights being used when displaying the community usage patterns (Figure 13). In addition to heatmaps showing only one of either the active user or community usage data, a third heatmap is created to create a combined overview. For this heatmap, the "Both" portion of the coloring chart is used, with the intensity level taken as the maximum of the two intensity masks at each pixel, and the color chosen as a blend between the two groups based on relative proportion of activity (Figure 11).

color(pixel **P**) = color_map(x, y)
where:

x = intensity$_{other}$(**P**) - intensity$_{you}$(**P**)

y = MAX(intensity$_{other}$(**P**), intensity$_{you}$(**P**))
and:

$0 \leq$ intensity(**P**) ≤ 1

Figure 11. Formula for determining the color of a given pixel in the combined heatmap.

We looked at several different schemes for coloring the heatmaps and found that this combination gave the best combination of visual appearance and ease of recognition when looking at the *you* and *others* heatmaps individually, as well as when combined.

Displaying Resulting Heatmap

When a window is activated, a floating panel is positioned over the top left of the window giving information about the Patina system (Figure 12) including the state of data collection, the quality of information available for this application/window, and indicators to show which heatmaps are currently being displayed.

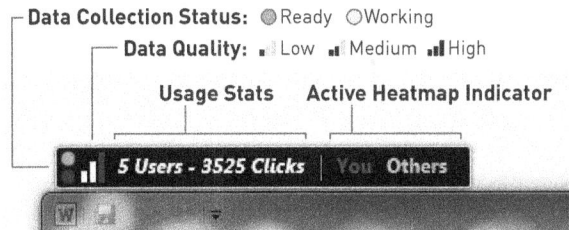

Figure 12. Patina information panel.

To maintain our *non-disruptive* design goal, the primary method for viewing the heatmap is manually through hotkeys, F2 for the "You" heatmap and F3 for the "Others" heatmap. The "You" and "Others" indicators in the information panel can also be clicked. The individual heatmaps are displayed when only one of "You" or "Others" is selected, and the combined heatmap is displayed when both are chosen. The heatmaps smoothly fade in over a duration of 0.3 seconds and are displayed over the entire window at an opacity of 50%. An example of the three different heatmap views is shown in Figure 13.

Standard View

User-Initiated Patina

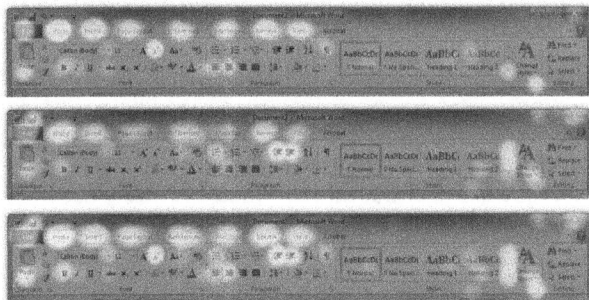

Automatic Transient Patina

Figure 13. Examples of the different overlay modes.

An alternative visualization we considered was to render the usage patterns as rectangular overlays covering the extents of the UI widget (Figure 14). However, we prefer the organic look of the click-point representation, and believe it better satisfies our *Distinguishable* and *Intuitive* design goals.

Figure 14. Combined usage overlay with rectangular regions matching over UI elements.

Automatic Transient View

Besides the user initiated display of the entire-window heatmap we have also created a view that is automatically and temporarily displayed when new UI components become visible (Figure 15). This mode gives the benefits of the Patina overlay without requiring the user to manually activate the visualization, and is similar in nature to Ephmeral Adaptation [13]. To minimize visual distraction, the heatmap is rendered with a transparent background, and only points associated with newly visible controls are included. For example, in the scenario shown in Figure 15, once the user clicked on the "Page Layout" tab, new UI elements appeared on the screen; namely, all of the controls under the "Page Layout" tab. Only these newly displayed controls are considered when gathering the points for this transient heatmap which smoothly fades in and out over a period of 5 seconds.

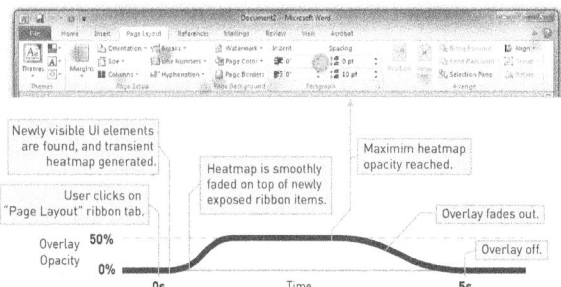

Figure 15. Visual example and time graph for the automatic transient Patina view.

This transient overlay view also works well to see which options are frequently modified when scrolling through large preference dialogs with many items.

Additional Applications of the Patina System

In addition to the previously described dynamic heatmaps, we now showcase how Patina can be used for application-independent implementations of three previously published research systems: *Scented Widgets*, *Usher*, and *CommunityCommands*.

Scented Widgets

Willett, Heer, and Agrawala's *Scented Widgets* [27] introduced graphical user interface controls enhanced with embedded visualizations. These visualizations are implemented as a "Look and Feel" layer extending the standard Java UI toolkit appearance. However, to implement *Scented Widgets* developers would need to modify the application source code and use that particular UI toolkit. Using the Patina system we can create an application-independent implementation of *Scented Widgets* for standard check and combo boxes. (Figure 16).

For checkbox controls, a small stacked horizontal bar chart is overlaid to the left of the checkbox to indicate the relative proportion of users who have this option selected. For comboboxes, we show a horizontal bar chart showing the relative frequency of the items which have been selected from the dropdown. The user's currently selected value is shown in a darker shade. For both controls, hovering over the charts shows a larger version with labels. To minimize visual distraction we only display the small visual scent indicators for UI close to the cursor position.

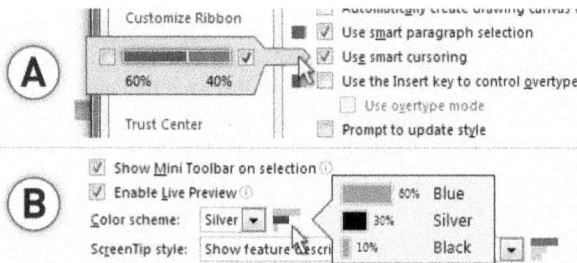

Figure 16. Scented interface for check box (A) and combo box (B) controls.

USHER

The *USHER* system [9] by Chen *et al.* is designed to improve the accuracy of form filling information by learning a probabilistic model of the dependencies between options. Based on this model, the *USHER* system augments the user interface to promote correct user input and alert the user of entries which may be incorrect.

Besides form filling applications, we believe a system like *USHER* could be useful in situations such as preference dialogs where there are often many settings that a user can modify and difficulties can arise if any of them are set incorrectly. We prototyped this by placing a warning icon beside options which may be set incorrectly based on the behavior of other users. We looked at settings individually, but the accessibility data used by the Patina system would allow for creating a probabilistic model for determining outliers in a similar way as is done in the *USHER* system.

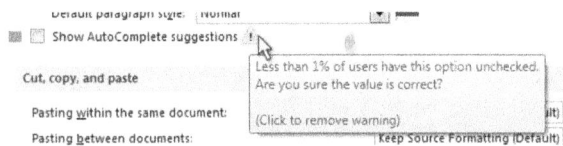

Figure 17. Warning icon and message for setting which are possibly set outside of normal bounds.

CommunityCommands

The *CommunityCommands* system [17, 19] is a recommender system for commands within an application. The active user's usage history is compared to the usage patterns of others in the community, and a list of commands are presented which might be useful to the user. The *CommunityCommands* system relies on in-product instrumentation to collect the usage data, but we are able to provide similar functionality using the data collected from the Patina system (Figure 18).

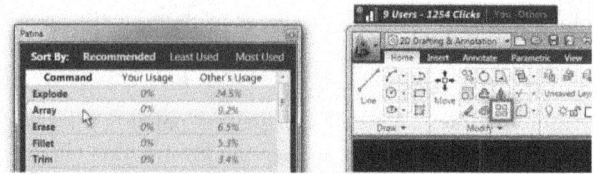

Figure 18. Command recommendation interface (left). Highlighted command in AutoCAD (right).

A list of the UI elements available in the application are presented in a list view, along with how often they are used by the active user and by the community. The list can be sorted to show the commands which the active user uses the most/least, or to present a list of recommended commands which is calculated by finding commands which the community uses a lot, but the active user does not use at all. Advanced collaborative filtering algorithms could be used to generate more robust recommendations.

When the users clicks an item in the list, a rectangular highlight is drawn over the element in the main interface and if the accessibility information includes hotkey data, we can automatically execute the command.

INTERNAL DEPLOYMENT

To get initial feedback of the Patina system, we conducted a short-term deployment evaluation of the system. Because Patina is still a prototype system that needs to run at all times, and collects potentially sensitive data (such as document names) the study was run internally. Eight participants within our organization ran the Patina prototype for 1 week on their office machines while performing their daily computing tasks. To reduce the system load and the amount of data being transferred, the system was modified to only collect data when Microsoft Word was the foreground application.

Usage Data and Feedback

During the deployment the Patina system recorded 8,742 total click events from the eight users. The heatmap overlay was activated a total of 285 times: 92 for the personal overlay, 130 for the community overlay, and 63 times using the combined data. Looking at the area of the regions that the click events occurred in (Figure 19) we can see that 12% of click events were below our 4,096 px^2 threshold where we display the clicks at full intensity, and 80% were above the 90,000 px^2 threshold for events we assume took place in a main canvas area. Since we render these large-area points very transparently because we don't believe they have much informational value, in the future we could consider ignoring those data points completely when they are collected to reduce the data transfer and rendering costs.

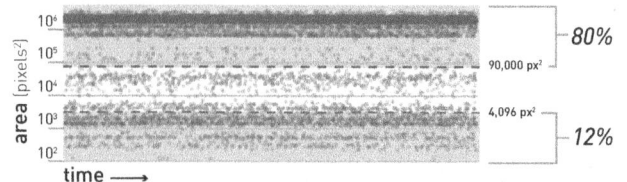

Figure 19. Scatter plot of the region sizes where clicks occurred during the internal deployment.

While using the system the users reported exploring more of the interface than they usually would because they were curious to see what parts of the interface the others were using. Several users discovered interface widgets they were previously unaware of through the heatmap visualization. For example, one user discovered the "zoom slider" in the bottom right corner of the window, and has subsequently adopted the use of that slider for zooming his documents. Another user mentioned that seeing the heatmap from the other users made him realize that he uses a much smaller set of tools than his colleagures. Several of the particiapants mentioned liking the transient overlay, particularly that it would appear when a new dialog box was activated.

PRIMARY USAGE SCENARIOS

Based on the results and feedback from our evaluation, and in addition to our own experiences with the system, we see three primary ways in which the Patina system can be beneficial to users.

Familiarizing New Users with an Application's Interface

New users of complex applications can often be overwhelmed by the number of user interface elements presented on the screen. This can also be a problem for users experienced in one facet of the program when they start exploring a new area of functionality. The Patina system helps in these cases by highlighting areas of functionality which are frequently used, and potentially, the most relevant to begin exploring.

Exposing Single Document Usage Patterns

The relevant application interface elements may be highly dependent on the current working document. By filtering on a per-document basis, users can quickly locate commonly used widgets for that document, or obtain an understanding of what commands and settings other users have used to create or modify a specific document, in collaborative situations.

Continuous Learning and Reflection

For experienced users of an application, the Patina system supports continuous learning by highlighting interface elements which others are using, which could lead to a better overall understanding of the type of task others perform with the software. Personal reflection is supported by highlighting those elements most often used by the active user and comparing that set with the community usage data, providing a way for the user to notice patterns in their own usage behavior that they would otherwise be unaware of.

DISCUSSION AND FUTURE WORK

We have developed an application independent system to collect and display historical usage information within the context of a software user interface. An internal deployment provided some initial insights into the nature of the data that would be collected.

While this internal deployment was valuable at our current stage of research, an important next step will be to perform more formal evaluations. It would be interesting to study how the system would be received and used in a larger scale external deployment. Further designs may need to be considered to handle data from a larger user base. Focused laboratory studies could also be used to evaluate aspects of the design space presented in this paper. For example, we could evaluate the differences between various visual schemes, such as the light and dark background heatmaps, or compare organic heatmap shapes to a rectangular highlighting technique. We could also study the effectiveness of the color schemes used for the heatmaps.

In terms of gerneralizability, one limitation of our work is that it does depend on the accessibility data for an optimal experience. In the absence of such data, it could be useful to explore augmenting our system with pixel-based image analysis techniques. Projects such as Sikuli [7, 8], Prefab [10, 11], and Hurst et al.'s automatic target identification system [15], are all impressive demonstrations of how vision can be used to interpret interface layout and usage and could be used in concert with *Patina* to recognize UI widgets without sufficient accessibility information present.

Future Work

We have only begun to explore how usage metrics can be displayed within the context of software application user interfaces. There are still a number of interesting design opportunities that could be topics of future work.

One important topic which we have not explored is the dependency of usage information between elements in the interface. Similar to how USHER learns dependencies between data entry fields [9], Patina could be extended to learn dependencies between user interface parameter values and options. The heatmaps and scented widget values could be updated to show most likely options to be used based on a user's current context.

Alternatively, when working in a preference or configuration dialog, the Patina system could provide a mechanism to view or restore previous states of the entire dialog. This could allow users to quickly review how combinations of parameters have been used in the past, either from their own use, or by other users on their team or from the community.

Another way user interface dependencies could be used is to incorporate command recommender system technology into Patina [17, 19]. A user's usage patterns could be compared to the community's, and the *other user* heatmaps could be generated from the most similar users. Heatmaps could also be used to show the next most likely elements a user will click on, based on their past sequence of interactions. This could guide users through a correct workflow when setting up multiple parameters in a dialog.

Patina could also be bundled with tutorials to help establish which tools in the interface are used to complete the tutorial task. This would be similar to the AdaptableGIMP project [18], which provides custom tool pallets for individual tutorials, but with Patina the layout of the interface would not need to be changed.

Another domain of usage we have not explored is webpage navigation. Typical webpages are composed of rectangular components [25], similar to that of graphical user interfaces. Such data can be accessed through accessibility APIs through some browsers, or through their Document Object Model. Patina could potentially be used to track and show usage information of a website without integration of special tracking software [29].

Finally, Patina currently visualizes only the usage information of mouse clicks. Because accessibility information does often contain keyboard hotkey associations, hotkey usage information could also be collected and overlaid on the associated icons.

CONCLUSION

The complexity of today's graphical user interfaces exposes users to large information spaces they must navigate to use the software efficiently. The *Patina* system can aid this process by visualizing usage information in the context of the associated user interface elements. Our application independent implementation allows such information to be collected and generated for any application that provides accessibility data, without instrumentation or modification of the actual application. We believe our data collection and interactive UI overlay approach will be useful for future work in application independent desktop services.

REFERENCES

1. Alexander, J., Cockburn, A., and Lobb, R. (2008). AppMonitor: a tool for recording user actions in unmodified Windows applications. *Behavior Research Methods 40*, 413-421.

2. Alexander, J., Cockburn, A., Fitchett, S., Gutwin, C., and Greenberg, S. (2009). Revisiting read wear: analysis, design, and evaluation of a footprints scrollbar. *ACM CHI*, 1665-1674.

3. Bannert, M. (2000). The effects of training wheels and self-learning materials in software training. *Journal of Computer Assisted Learning 16*, 336-346.

4. Baudisch, P., Tan, D., Collomb, M., Robbins, D., Hinckley, K., Agrawala, M., Zhao, S., and Ramos, G. (2006). Phosphor: explaining transitions in the user interface using afterglow effects. *ACM UIST*, 169-178.

5. Bezerianos, A., Dragicevic, P., and Balakrishnan, R. (2006). Mnemonic Rendering: An Image-Based Approach for Exposing Hidden Changes in Dynamic Displays. *ACM UIST*, 159-168.

6. Carroll, J. M., and Carrithers, C. (1984). Training wheels in a user interface. *Comm. ACM 27*, 800-806.

7. Chang, T.-H., Yeh, T., and Miller, R. (2011). Associating the Visual Representation of User Interfaces with their Internal Structures and Metadata. *ACM UIST*, 245-256.

8. Chang, T.-H., Yeh, T., and Miller, R. C. (2010). GUI testing using computer vision. *ACM CHI*, 1535-1544.

9. Chen, K., Hellerstein, J., S., and Parikh, T. S. (2010). Designing Adaptive Feedback for Improving Data Entry *ACM UIST*, 239-248.

10. Dixon, M., and Fogarty, J. (2010). Prefab: Implementing Advanced Behaviors Using Pixel-Based Reverse Engineering of Interface Structure. *ACM CHI*, 1525-1534.

11. Dixon, M., Leventhal, D., and Fogarty, J. (2011). Content and Hierarchy in Pixel-Based Methods for Reverse Engineering Interface Structure. *CHI*, 969-978.

12. Findlater, L., and McGrenere, J. (2004). A comparison of static, adaptive, and adaptable menus. *CHI*, 89-96.

13. Findlater, L., Moffatt, K., Mcgrenere, J., and Dawson, J. (2009). Ephemeral Adaptation: The Use of Gradual Onset to Improve Menu Selection Performance. *ACM CHI*, 1655-1664.

14. Hill, W. C., Hollan, J. D., Wroblewski, D., and McCandless, T. (1992). Edit wear and read wear. *ACM CHI*, 3-9.

15. Hurst, A., Hudson, S. E., and Mankoff, J. (2010). Automatically Identifying Targets Users Interact with During Real World Tasks. *ACM IUI*, 11–20.

16. Hurst, A., Mankoff, J., Dey, A. K., and Hudson, S. E. (2007). Dirty desktops: using a patina of magnetic mouse dust to make common interactor targets easier to select. *ACM UIST*, 183-186.

17. Li, W., Matejka, J., Gossman, T., Konstan, J.A., and Fitzmaurice, G. (2011). Design and Evaluation of a Command Recommendation System for Software Applications. *ACM TOCHI*.

18. Lafreniere, B., Bunt, A., Lount, M., Krynicki, F., and Terry, M. (2011). AdaptableGIMP: designing a socially-adaptable interface. *UIST Adjunct*, 89-90.

19. Matejka, J., Grossman, T., and Fitzmaurice, G. (2011). IP-QAT: In-Product Questions, Answers, & Tips. *ACM UIST*, 175-184.

20. Matejka, J., Li, W., Grossman, T., and Fitzmaurice, G. (2009). CommunityCommands: command recommendations for software applications. *ACM UIST*, 193-202.

21. Nakamura, T., and Igarashi, T. (2008). An application-independent system for visualizing user operation history. *ACM UIST*, 23-32.

22. Pirolli, P., and Card, S. (1999). Information Foraging. *Psychological Review 106*, 643-675.

23. Shneiderman, B. (2003). Promoting universal usability with multi-layer interface design. *CUU*, 1-8.

24. Stuerzlinger, W., Chapuis, O., Phillips, D., and Roussel, N. (2006). User interface facades: towards fully adaptable user interfaces. *ACM UIST*, 309-318.

25. Talton, J. O., and Klemmer, S. R. (2011). Bricolage: Example-Based Retargeting for Web Design. *ACM CHI*, 2197-2206.

26. Terry, M., Kay, M., Vugt, B. V., Slack, B., and Park, T. (2008). ingimp: Introducing Instrumentation to an End-User Open Source Application. *ACM CHI*, 607-616.

27. Willett, W., Heer, J., and Agrawala, M. (2007). Scented Widgets: Improving Navigation Cues with Embedded Visualizations. *IEEE Transactions on Visualization and Computer Graphics 13*, 1129-1136.

28. Wooding, D.S. (2002). Fixation Maps: quantifying eye-movement traces. *ETRA*. 31-36.

29. CrazyEgg. *http://www.crazyegg.com/* (Sept 2012).

30. Mozilla Heatmap. *https://heatmap.mozillalabs.com/* (Sept 2012

Evaluation of Alternative Glyph Designs for Time Series Data in a Small Multiple Setting

Johannes Fuchs[1] **Fabian Fischer**[1] **Florian Mansmann**[1]
[1]University of Konstanz
fuchs@dbvis.inf.uni-konstanz.de
(fabian.fischer|florian.mansmann)@uni-konstanz.de

Enrico Bertini[2]
[2]NYU Poly
ebertini@poly.edu

Petra Isenberg[3]
[3]INRIA
petra.isenberg@inria.fr

ABSTRACT

We present the results of a controlled experiment to investigate the performance of different temporal glyph designs in a small multiple setting. Analyzing many time series at once is a common yet difficult task in many domains, for example in network monitoring. Several visualization techniques have, thus, been proposed in the literature. Among these, iconic displays or glyphs are an appropriate choice because of their expressiveness and effective use of screen space. Through a controlled experiment, we compare the performance of four glyphs that use different combinations of visual variables to encode two properties of temporal data: a) the position of a data point in time and b) the quantitative value of this data point. Our results show that depending on tasks and data density, the chosen glyphs performed differently. Line Glyphs are generally a good choice for peak and trend detection tasks but radial encodings are more effective for reading values at specific temporal locations. From our qualitative analysis we also contribute implications for designing temporal glyphs for small multiple settings.

Author Keywords

Glyphs; time series; evaluation; small multiples; information visualization.

ACM Classification Keywords

H.5.2 Information Interfaces and Presentation: Misc

General Terms

Human Factors

INTRODUCTION

Time series data is the basis for decision making in many different application domains—such as finance, network security, or traffic management—and, thus, constitutes an important area of research for visualization and data analysis. We collaborated, for example, with network security analysts from a large university computer center who need to make decisions based on the amount of daily network traffic for single hosts over time. Detecting trends, spotting peaks, or investigating single points in time from a visual representation are

daily analysis tasks of vital importance for our collaborators and analysts in many other domains [18, 20, 26].

For data analysis in such a scenario, glyphs (iconic representations) are an appropriate choice to consider for visually encoding and presenting temporal data. Their advantage lies in their compact way to use screen real estate and the possibility to use them in a small multiple setting. In such a setting, glyphs can enable quick visual comparison of the development of data values over time. However, glyphs come with a trade-off between resolution and increased data density for each time series. They usually do not include axes for reading exact values since they are primarily designed to show multiple attributes in a compact way [36]. A notable example of such a technique is the well-known *sparklines* technique [33].

Yet, due to glyphs' power in presenting multiple time series for comparison, a multitude of designs have been proposed. Different visual variables such as length, color, or position can be used to encode two aspects of temporal data in one glyph: a) the location of a data point in time, and b) the quantitative data value. When confronted with the task of choosing an appropriate glyph design, a visualization designer or practitioner currently has little guidance on which encodings would be most appropriate for which tasks and on which visual features and factors influence people's perception of data encoded in glyphs. While one could follow Cleveland and McGill's ranking of elementary perceptual tasks [10] and try to predict the performance of glyphs based on these results, it is not clear whether their results will hold. Temporal glyphs include dual encodings, are used in specific temporal analysis tasks, and come in many different sizes and densities.

In order to address this lack of guidance on the use of temporal glyphs, we ran a controlled experiment to compare four carefully selected glyphs using two different data densities. These four glyphs were chosen for their use of different combinations of visual variables to encode temporal position and quantitative value of a data point. We evaluated all glyph designs in a small multiple setting as small multiple is the most common usage scenario for temporal glyphs. To our knowledge no other evaluation has been conducted to compare the performance of time series glyphs for small multiple settings based on their data encodings. In particular, we contribute:

- results comparing the task-dependent performance of four glyph designs under two data densities,
- plausible explanations for the observed performance patterns and resulting implications for design,
- a first investigating into the broader issue of how glyphs perform and what factors influence their performance.

RELATED WORK

Time series visualization has a long history going back to at least the 18th century and many different techniques have been developed in the past.

Time Series Visualization Techniques

Willam Playfair [28], for example, used line charts to visualize exports, imports, expenditures or prices and their development over time. Even today these line charts are among the most popular time series visualization techniques and their details are actively discussed in the visualization community, as for example the arc length-based aspect ratio selection [31]. Furthermore, visualization techniques such as stacked graphs (e.g. [37]) aim at making line graphs scalable to analysis tasks involving many time series at once.

Besides line charts, common techniques for visualizing time series are *pixel visualizations* (e.g., Recursive Patterns [4], Circle Segments [5], or Time-Series Bitmaps [22], surveyed in [17]) and *glyph visualizations* (e.g., Sparklines [33] or Tow-Tone Pseudo Coloring [29], surveyed in [35]). Furthermore, properties either inherent or assigned to time have resulted in the development of a number of specialized methods. Periodic patterns can, for example, be visualized with the Concentric Circles Technique [11] or Spirals [8]; likewise several calendar visualizations have been proposed [6, 34] to cope with the irregularities of our Gregorian calendar. Properties assigned to time series often result in multi-dimensional data sets, which can for example be analyzed with axes-based visualizations with radial layouts [32].

Time Series Comparison

Time series comparison is the area most related to our work. Some studies have already been conducted on the evaluation of multiple timeline representations [16] or the comparison of different value ranges for line charts [1]. Alternative techniques for displaying many time series at once are CloudLines [21] or Horizon Graphs [15]. More application driven visualizations, such as systems monitoring (e.g., LiveRAC [25]), project management (a classic: Gantt chart [9]), health (e.g., LifeLines [27]), news (e.g., ThemeRiver [14]) and geographic analysis (e.g., Space-time Cube [19]) make use of various dedicated representation techniques.

Temporal glyphs, the subject of our experiment, are often used in small multiple settings for comparing many different time series at once. Their layout on the plane varies to add additional information like the geographic context on top of a map [13], the ranking in a scatterplot, or a hierarchical data organization [12]. Pearlman and Rheingans use stacked circular glyphs in a graph layout to monitor network traffic over time and visualize the connections [26]. Circular glyphs positioned in a matrix for monitoring the daily traffic of many network devices were also mentioned by Kintzel et al. [18]. These circular representations are similar to the ones used in our experiment. Krasser, however, uses a parallel coordinates plot in combination with glyphs to investigate connections, type of network traffic and the timely sequence [20]. Many glyphs build patterns of different colored stripes over time.

Such a stripe combination is related to one of the designs investigated in our user study.

DESIGN SPACE FOR TEMPORAL GLYPHS

The design space for a basic temporal glyph can be characterized by the visual variables that are used to encode two attributes of temporal data: a) the position of a timepoint on the plane and b) the data value associated with this timepoint. Different visual variables can be used to encode these two attributes. In Table 1 we show some meaningful combinations of visual variables taken from Cleveland and McGill [10] for quantitative data and how they form different glyphs.

Ward [35] describes several categories of glyphs. To narrow down the design space for our experiment we only discuss temporal glyphs with many-to-one mappings where several or all data attributes map to a common type of graphical attribute. This is important in order not to promote certain temporal dimensions and to enable easier intra-record and inter-record comparison, which is fundamental for many tasks involving time series, including the ones chosen for our experiment. While many more different glyph types exist, such as face glyphs, arrows/weathervanes, box glyphs, sticks and trees etc., we focus on two main types of glyphs here: profiles and stars (see [35]). Both types have the advantage that relationships between adjacent data points are easier to see than for other glyphs [35]. While it is theoretically possible to encode temporal position using other visual variables such as length, direction, area, volume, curvature, or shading, no glyph design using these encodings has established itself in practice and is, thus, part of our study.

EXPERIMENT DESIGN

The purpose of our experiment was to compare the performance of different, potentially powerful, temporal glyphs in a small multiple setting. Our three tasks are inspired from our work with network analysts but generalize to other domains in which temporal data has to be compared and analyzed.

Experiment Factors

Our experimental factors were *glyph*, *task*, and *data density*.

Glyphs

We chose the Line Glyph (LIN), Stripe Glyph (STR), Clock Glyph (CLO), and the Star Glyph (STA) for their different characteristics and to assess their performance in a small multiple setting. LIN was chosen as one of the best ranked and most commonly used glyphs in our space and STR for its similar temporal but different value encoding. Glyphs are often designed to encode intuitive pairings of data to visual variables [35] and, thus, we chose two circular designs that take people's potentially intuitive notion of time encoded in a clock-like fashion into account. We chose to test STA for its similar value encoding to LIN and CLO for its similar value encoding to STR.

The Dot Plot was excluded as in our experience the single dots became too small, making it nearly impossible to spot them. The Bar Chart was excluded as well because Cleveland and McGill [10] conjecture that even for values encoded in bar charts the primary elementary task is judging position

Glyph	Temporal Enc.	Data Value Enc. (ranked)	Data Density Issues
Dot Plot	Position CS	Position CS (1)	Small dots difficult to see for small glyphs
Line Glyph	Position CS	Position CS (1)/Direction (3)	May become very dense
Bar Chart	Position CS	Position CS (1)/Length (3)/ Area (4)	May become very dense
Star Glyph	Angle	Length (3)	Small angular differences are hard to distinguish
Stripe Glyph	Position CS	Color Saturation (6)	Color blending for small areas
Clock Glyph	Angle	Color Saturation (6)	Color blending

Table 1. Partial overview of the design space for temporal glyphs. We show combinations of the encodings for quantitative data (cf. Cleveland and McGill's [10]) ranked according to their study results: 1) Position CS, 2) Position NAS, 3) Length/Direction/Angle, 4) Area, 5) Volume/Curvature, 6) Shading/Color Saturation. Other combinations are certainly possible. Position CS = position along a common scale, Position NAS = position along non-aligned scale. Glyph designs written with bold characters are the ones used in our experiment.

along a common scale but that judgements of area and length may also play a role. Therefore, we cannot safely test, which visual variable affects the perception of the data value.

When comparing glyphs visually, the distance between the representations matters. We chose to keep the distance for the different designs identical and, therefore, to have the same uniform small multiple layout. As a consequence it was important to set a fixed aspect ratio for each glyph. To maximize display space for circular glyphs for a fairer comparison we chose a square aspect ratio for each glyph.

For the color encoded glyphs (CLO and STR) we chose a heatmap colorscale, which was motivated by the yellow to red colorscale from ColorBrewer [7]. This scale takes advantage of the fact that the human visual system has maximum sensitivity to luminance changes for the orange-yellow hue [23] and it is also suitable for color blind people.

For each trial, the same type of glyph—but showing different data—was drawn on the screen in a small multiple layout of $8 \times 6 = 48$ glyphs in total (Figure 1). Each glyph was drawn at a resolution of 96×96 pixel.

Tasks
Many different tasks exist that can be performed on time-oriented data [2, 3, 24]. We chose our tasks taking two criteria into account: (1) their ecological validity, i. e. how commonly they are performed in environments where the quick comparison of multiple time series is needed. (2) their heterogeneity in terms of the elementary perceptual tasks, i. e. we picked tasks that involve the comparison of visual variables for encoding data values, investigating different layouts for time and the combination of the two. In terms of ecological validity our tasks were inspired by our work with network security analysts from a large university computer center who had to monitor large amounts of network devices. The ana-

lysts had to be able to efficiently detect anomalous traffic patterns (e.g., peak values in none working hours) to be able to quickly react on the possible threat. Our three tasks were:

Task 1—Peak Detection: Amongst all small multiple glyphs, participants had to select the glyph that contained the highest data value (Figure 1). This task, thus, involved scanning all glyphs for its highest value and comparing across glyphs using length (LIN, STA) or saturation (STR, CLO) judgements.

Task 2—Temporal Location: Among all small multiples, participants were asked to select the glyph with the highest value at a predefined time-point. This time-point was textually shown to the participant in advance (e.g. "3am"). This task, thus, involved first identifying the location of a time-point by making positional (LIN, STR) or angular judgements (STA, CLO) and then comparing the peaks as in Task 1.

Task 3—Trend Detection: Among all small multiples, participants had to select the glyph with the highest value decrease over the whole displayed time period (Figure 2). This task, thus, involved first detecting all decreasing trends and then comparing the first and the last value.

Data Density
In order to test the scalability of each glyph in terms of the number of datapoints it can encode, we tested two data densities. The smaller density consisted of 24 data values (1 for each hour), and the larger of 96 data values (1 for each 15 minutes). The rendered size of the glyphs holding these data points was not varied between each density (Figure 3).

Hypotheses
We previously conducted two exploratory pilot studies with similar glyphs and tasks. From these and the related literature [10, 35] we derive the following hypotheses:

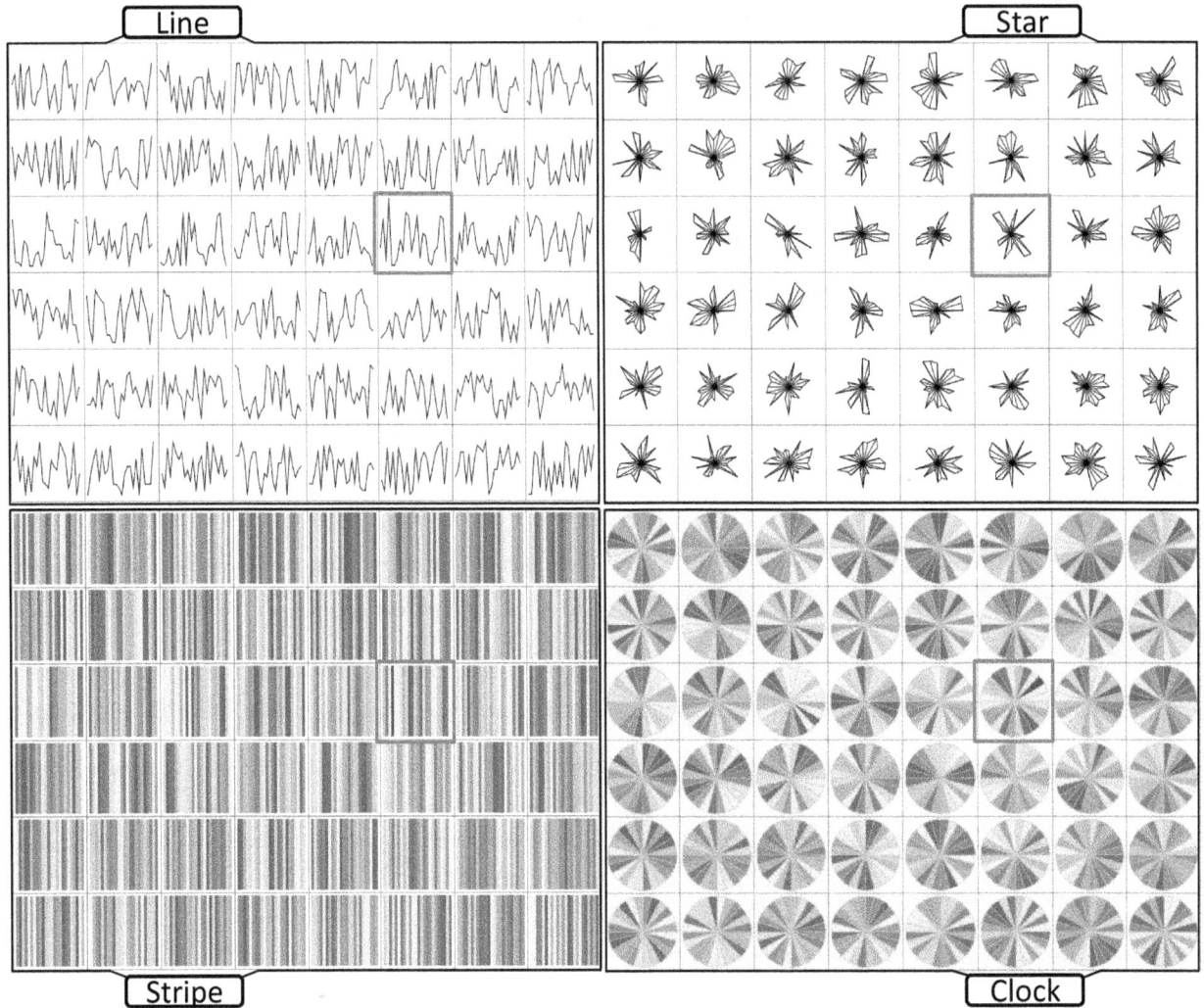

Figure 1. Peak detection: Illustration of the different glyphs with one high data value at a random point in time. For a better understanding the correct glyph is artificially highlighted.

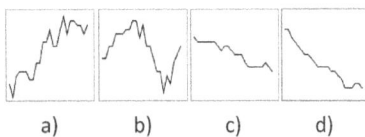

Figure 2. Trend detection: The four glyphs demonstrate different kinds of trends. From left to right: (a) visualizes a positive trend; (b) contains a positive and negative value development but for the whole displayed time interval there is no clear trend visible; (c and d) picture a negative trend over the whole displayed time period with (d) having the higher decrease. The glyph with the highest decrease over the whole displayed time period is artificially highlighted.

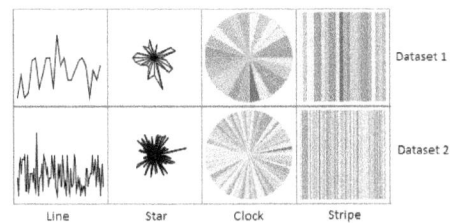

Figure 3. Differences between the two datasets for each glyph design.

H1: *For tasks involving primarily a value judgement LIN & STA (position/length encodings) are more accurate and efficient than CLO & STR (color encodings). This effect is strongest for LIN.* This hypothesis is based on Cleveland and McGill's experiments [10] on the perception of position, length, and color. We expect the results to hold for both data densities.

H2: *For tasks involving primarily a value judgement, CLO & STR (color enc.) are more impacted by higher data density than LIN & STA (position/length enc.).* Color perception may change drastically with varying context colors and size of the object being viewed [30, 36]. We expect color perception to be more impacted than visual acuity on dense line and position encodings.

H3: *When detecting temporal positions, STA & CLO (angular enc.) outperform LIN & STR (position enc.).* Using the familiar clock metaphor, we expect that circular glyphs allow the perception of specific points in time to be more accurate. This effect is stronger for **CLO** than **STA** as the clock shape is more clearly retained.

H4: *When detecting temporal positions, increasing data density will negatively impact performance with each glyph..* This is because color judgements are impacted by the size of the object being viewed [30] and angular as well as positional judgements by visual acuity. We expect **CLO** & **STA** to perform best as they spread out values towards the circumference of the circle giving additional space for perceiving color and position.

H5: *For trend detection, **LIN** & **STA** (position and length enc.) are most effective.* In trend detection, two mental sub-tasks have to be integrated by the participant: a) analysis of data development over time (characterized by the slope) and, b) comparison of the first and last data value (trend steepness). We expect the first sub-task to be performed equally well with all glyphs but expect that the comparison of distances between two data values is more difficult with color compared to position/length.

H6: *For trend detection tasks, the participants' performance for each design is not influenced by data density.* For detecting a trend comparing the overall shape rather than single data values is necessary. We expect that increasing the data density will not influence the trend shape and, thus, has no effect on task performance.

Experiment Design

We used a mixed repeated-measures design with the between-subjects variable *task* and the within-subjects independent variables *glyph* and *data density*. The dependent variables were *error*, *time* and *confidence*. Each participant conducted one task with all four glyphs, two densities, and four trial repetitions.

Data

To control the data values and their resulting visual representations, we created synthetic data for the experiment. In total, we created 48 data instances (glyphs) for each repetition, task, and data density. The data was created such that just one glyph represented the correct answer. The glyphs with smaller density held 24, the ones with large density 96 data values. In previous pilot experiments these two values were established as being sufficiently different from one another. Data for each task was created as follows:

Task 1: Each glyph was filled with random noise to a threshold of 80% of its value range according to our experience from pilot studies. For the target glyph a peak value at 100% of the value range was added to the dataset at a random point in time.

Task 2: Each glyph was filled with random noise as in Task 1. A peak value at 100% of the value range was added to the target glyph at a predefined point in time. For the distractor glyphs, peak values of the same value were integrated but at wrong temporal positions.

Task 3: We designed different decreasing trends by varying the values of the first (0–25% of value range) and last data point (75–100% of value range). The target trend decreased 75% of the value range from first to last data value while the distractor glyphs included a decrease of 55%. Along

the trend line each data point was varied by zero, one, or two values using a probabilistic function.

Participants

We recruited 24 participants (12 male, 12 female) mainly from the local student population. All participants had normal or corrected-to-normal vision and did not report color blindness. Their age ranged from 19–56 years (median age 24). Each participant had at least finished high school, eight held a Bachelor's, two a Master's degree, and one a Ph. D. The academic background of the participants was quite diverse with no one having a computer science background. 34% of the participants reported to use the computer for more than 30 hours per week and 50% less than 20 hours.

Procedure

The experiment took place in a quiet closed room at our university. In addition to the study participant, the experimenter was the only person present. The participant sat in front of a table at a distance of approx. 50cm from a 24in screen set to a resolution of 1920 × 1200. Participants interacted with the study software using only a mouse.

The experimenter began by explaining the data, the single task, and the design of the different glyphs. The data was presented as financial stock data to provide context. Only when the participant was familiar with the current glyph design and task, he/she was allowed to proceed. For each glyph and density tested, the participant stepped through four practice trials followed by the four actual study trials. After each trial, the participant entered a confidence score for their answer on a 5-step Likert scale.

The task question was visible on the screen at all times. The presentation order of each glyph was randomized in a Latin square fashion between participants. The glyphs were presented in a 6×8 matrix layout (Figure 1). Each participant saw the same glyphs per trial in different random configurations.

RESULTS

We report on significant results ($p < .05$) from our quantitative analysis (Figure 4) in this section and refer to the qualitative feedback in the discussion section afterwards.

Data Analysis

Task completion time, error rate, and confidence score were recorded for the analysis. We used a repeated-measures ANOVA for the analysis of completion time. Time in our experiment was log-transformed where it did not follow a normal distribution. For the error rate as well as for the confidence score, a non-parametric Friedman's test was used.

Except for the second task we did not observe a strong learning effect between trials. Therefore, we analyzed all four trials for the first and third task, glyph and dataset for each participant. For the second task we analyzed the results of the last three trials. In addition, single answers were marked as outliers when each metric (time, error) was beyond two standard deviations from the mean for a given task and glyph per participant. Outliers were replaced with the closest value

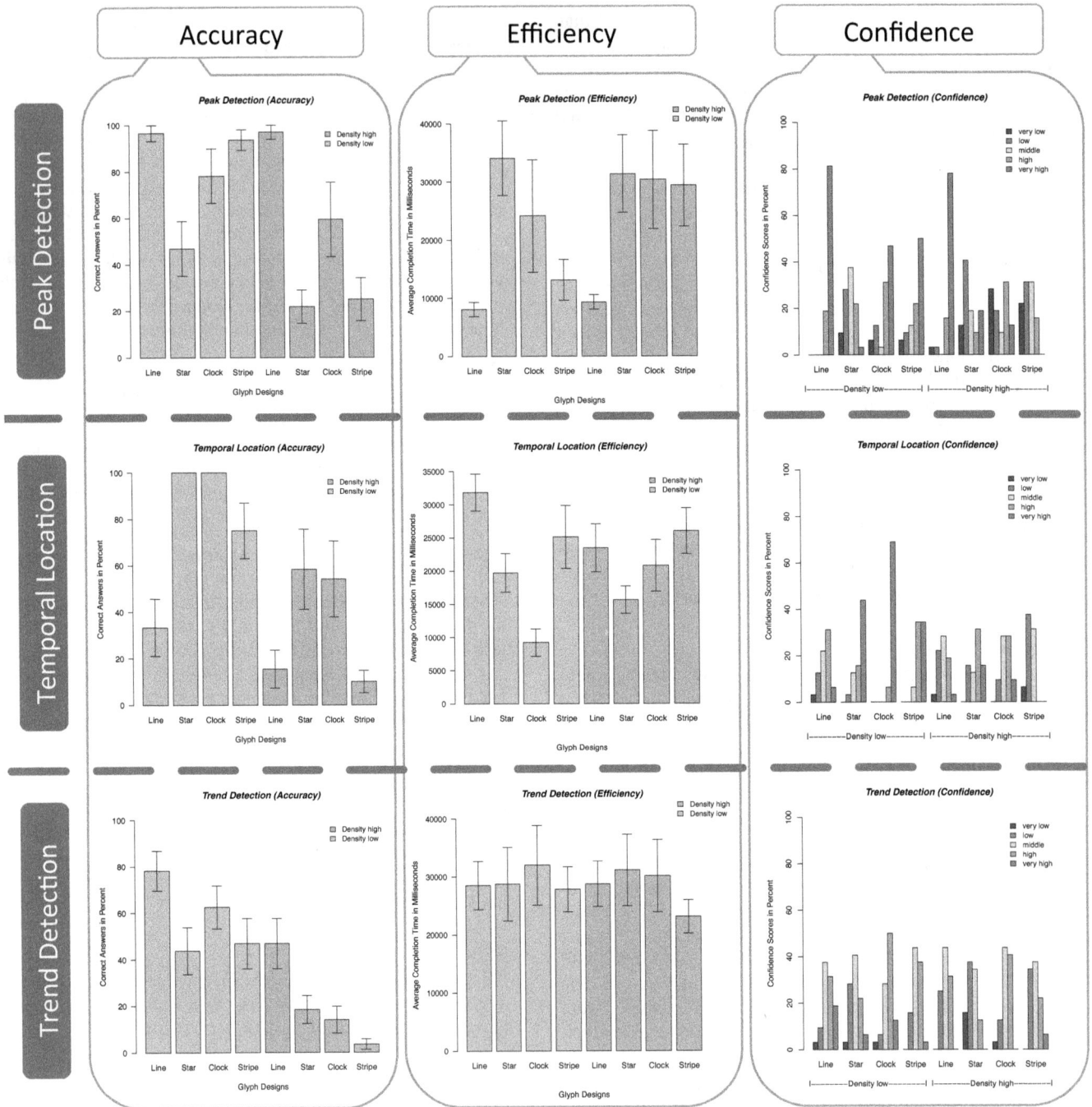

Figure 4. Bar charts with mean and standard deviation showing the results for each task and factor. The x-axis represents the different dependent variables. The y-axis illustrates the different tasks.

two standard deviations from the mean for each participant according to standard procedure. The tasks used in the study differed in their characteristics, so we analyzed the results of each task and dataset independently. Finally, we analyzed the feedback and subjective preference from the post-session interview for a qualitative analysis.

Task 1: Peak Detection
Task 1 consisted of four training repetitions and 2 densities × 4 repetitions with an increasing difficulty for each repeti-

tion block. This setting was used for each glyph design. For the analysis we only considered the more difficult repetition block since the results reveal more interesting insights.

Accuracy
There was a significant effect of *glyph* on *error* for both the low density ($\chi^2(3, N = 32) = 11.62, p < .01$) and the high density condition ($\chi^2(3, N = 32) = 17.59, p < .001$). In the low density condition pair-wise comparisons showed that errors in judgement were significantly worse for STA

(46.9%) than all other designs ($p < .05$). LIN (96.5%) and STR (93.6%) both showed high accuracy with LIN nearly at 100% accuracy. In the high density condition LIN (96.9%) significantly outperformed the other designs by staying at nearly 100% accuracy (all $p < .05$). In addition, CLO (59.4%) performed significantly better than STR (25%) and STA (21.9%) with $p < .01$ in each case. With an increasing data density, STR (from 93.6% to 25%) and STA (from 46.9% to 21.9%) significantly lost accuracy (all $p < .05$).

Efficiency
There was an overall effect of *glyph* on *time* in the low density ($F_{3,21} = 12.1, p < .0001$) and the high density ($F_{3,21} = 11.5, p < .001$) condition. Post-hoc comparisons showed that completion time was significantly higher for STA (34.1 sec.) compared to STR (13.1 sec) and LIN (8 sec.) for the low densities (all $p < .01$). For the higher densities LIN had the fastest completion time (9.3 sec.) compared to the other designs (nearly 30s per repetition on average) ($p < .05$). There was also a significant effect of *glyph* across densities ($F_{3,21} = 4.7, p < .05$). From low to high densities STR (from 13.1 sec. to 29.4 sec.) and CLO (from 24.1 sec. to 30.4 sec.) worsened ($p < .05$), whereas the mean for LIN stayed relatively stable (from 8 sec. to 9.3 sec.).

Confidence
There was an overall effect of *glyph* on *confidence* for both the low density ($\chi^2(3, N = 32) = 15.47, p < .01$) and the high density ($\chi^2(3, N = 32) = 16.28, p < .001$) condition. In the low density condition participants using STA (56.3%) reported a significantly lower confidence score with their answers than for all other designs (all $p < .01$). LIN (96.3%) received the highest confidence with significantly better ratings compared to CLO (80%, $p < .05$) and STA (56%, $p < .001$). In the high density condition LIN (92.5%) is significantly better than the other designs ($p < .001$) and STA (56.3%) better than STR (48.1%) ($p < .05$). From low to high densities STR (from 80% to 48.1%, $p < .05$) and CLO (from 80% to 56.3%, $p < .001$) worsened.

Task 2: Temporal Location
Task 2 consisted of four training repetitions and four real trials for both densities. After the initial training trials we asked participants to detect a different temporal location for the peak value. Therefore, the first real trial was discarded due to the mental recalibration necessary by the participants.

Accuracy
There was a significant effect of *glyph* on *error* for both the low density ($\chi^2(3, N = 32) = 17, p < .001$) and the high density condition ($\chi^2(3, N = 32) = 7.81, p = .05$). In the low density condition pair-wise comparisons showed that errors in judgement were significantly worse for LIN (33.3%) compared to CLO (100%) and STA (100%) (both $p < 0.01$) and STR (75%) compared to CLO (100%) and STA (100%) (both $p < 0.001$). In the high density condition STA (58.3%) significantly outperformed LIN (15.5%) and STR (10%) (both $p < 0.05$). With an increasing data density, STA (from 100% to 58.3%), CLO (from 100% to 54.2%)

and STR (from 75% to 10%) significantly lost accuracy with $p < .05$ in each case.

Efficiency
For the completion time there was only an overall effect of *glyph* on *time* in the low density ($F_{3,21} = 9.1, p < .001$) condition. Post-hoc comparisons showed that CLO (9.2 sec.) significantly outperformed LIN (31.8 sec.) ($p < .01$). There was another significant effect of *glyph* across densities ($F_{3,21} = 5.45, p < .01$). From low to high densities CLO (from 9.2 sec. to 20.8 sec.) deteriorated significantly ($p < .05$).

Confidence
There was an overall effect of *glyph* on *confidence* for both the low density ($\chi^2(3, N = 32) = 13.78, p < .01$) and the high density ($\chi^2(3, N = 32) = 12.12, p < .01$) condition. For the low density condition the results showed a clear picture for the confidence of the participants. The users were significantly more confident when using CLO (73.8%, $p < .05$), and had least confidence with LIN (50%, $p < .05$). For the high density condition the subjects were nearly equally confident using CLO (52.5%) or STA (54.4%), whereas LIN (44.4%, $p < 0.05$) and STR (35%, $p < 0.001$) are ranked worst. From low to high densities STA (from 65.6% to 54.4%, $p < .05$), CLO (from 73.8% to 52.5%, $p < .001$) and STR (from 65.6% to 35%, $p < .001$) worsened.

Task 3: Trend Detection
Task 3 consisted of four training repetitions and four real trials for both densities. For the analysis we discarded the training repetitions and focus only on the real trials.

Accuracy
There was a significant effect of *glyph* on *error* for both the low density ($\chi^2(3, N = 32) = 7.43, p = .05$) and the high density condition ($\chi^2(3, N = 32) = 8.9, p < .05$). In the low density condition pair-wise comparisons showed that errors in judgement were significantly better for LIN (78.1%) compared to STA (43.8%) and STR (46.9%) ($p < .05$). In the high density condition LIN (46.9%) significantly outperformed CLO (14%, $p < .05$) and STR (3.5%, $p < .01$). With an increasing data density, LIN (from 78.1% to 46.9%, $p < .05$), CLO (from 62.5% to 14%, $p < .01$) and STR (from 46.9% to 3.5%, $p < .05$) significantly lost accuracy (all $p < .05$).

Efficiency
For both densities no significant differences can be shown. The participants needed around 30 seconds on average. This was expected to be the maximal amount of time per repetition.

Confidence
There was an overall effect of *glyph* on *confidence* for both the low density ($\chi^2(3, N = 32) = 8.06, p < .05$) and the high density ($\chi^2(3, N = 32) = 7.6, p = .05$) condition. For the low density condition STA (60%) had lower ratings compared to CLO (72.5%, $p < 0.01$) and LIN (70.6%, $p < 0.05$). Same is true for the high density as well with STA (48.8%) being worse compared to CLO (64.4%, $p < 0.01$) and LIN (61.3%, $p < 0.05$). With an increased data density

STA (from 60% to 48.8%, $p < 0.01$) and CLO (from 72.5% to 64.4%, $p < 0.01$) lost significantly confidence.

DISCUSSION

In this section we combine both quantitative and qualitative data collected in our study to explain the varying performance of the different glyph designs according to our hypotheses. An overview of the quantitative results for each task is given in Table 2 where values highlighted in orange signify the best result compared to the other designs.

Task	Measure	LIN	STA	CLO	STR
Peak Detection	accuracy	96%	34%	69%	60%
(value comparison)	efficiency	8s	28.2s	18.6s	16.9s
Peak Detection	accuracy	24%	79%	77%	43%
(time comparison)	efficiency	27.6s	17.7s	15s	25.5s
Trend Detection	accuracy	63%	31%	39%	25%
	efficiency	26.2s	25.5s	27.1s	23.7s

Table 2. Glyph performance for different tasks: This table illustrates the percentage of correct answers (accuracy) and the average time needed (efficiency) for each of the tasks for both densities combined. The orange background signifies the best result compared to the other designs.

Peak Detection

In H1 we conjectured that LIN & STA would outperform CLO & STR due to their position and length encodings for value. The analysis of *error*, however, revealed that nearly no mistakes were made with LIN and only few with STR and that STA had the lowest accuracy followed by CLO. Apparently, the participants had more problems reading value with the circular layouts. This becomes obvious by comparing the most with the least accurate glyph design (i. e., LIN with STA). Both use the same value encoding but differ in the layout of the time dimension. This effect did not change across the two density conditions. STA and STR had a similarly high error rate across densities, CLO deteriorated only slightly, whereas LIN still performed best.

We can, thus, only partially confirm H1. We conclude that polar coordinates must have an effect on *error* for value judgements when the value is encoded with length. The same effect seems not to take place when the value is encoded with color. This can perhaps be explained by the different baselines of the designs. Comparing position/length in a radial design perhaps involves mental rotation to transfer the overall design to a comparable linear layout. This is not true for color encodings, since color does not need an identical baseline.

Another notable effect is the one between CLO and STR: while accuracy was not significantly different for low data density, CLO outperformed STR with high data density. This suggests that CLO is more resilient with respect to data density than STR. We believe this to be due to the fact that the slices in the circular design get more space near the circumference, wheras the slices in the stripe get too small, making the comparison more difficult. This only partially confirms H2: while STR is strongly affected by data density, LIN and CLO are either not affected by data density or affected to a smaller extent (decrease CLO: 18.8%; decrease STR: 68.7%).

The confidence score of the participants for this task was unambiguous with LIN having the highest ratings. In the final interview the participants had to rank the different glyph designs according to their subjective preference. LIN was the most preferred glyph type which matches the performance results of the quantitative analysis.

In the post-session interview, some participants argued that color was better than position/length for data value comparison especially when the distance between the values was very large. Of course, this depends on the color scale used, but seems plausible when the color value is entirely different, which may lead to a preattentive recognition effect. With smaller distances most of the participants commented that they would prefer the position/length encoding. When explaining their performance with STA (i. e. angle/length encoding), participants argued that they had problems comparing lengths with different orientation which further supports our hypothesis that mental rotations may be necessary for comparison and make values harder to compare in these glyphs. Especially in a small multiple setting this is an interesting finding and has to be further tested and considered when arranging glyphs.

Temporal Location

Our results partially support H3. In terms of accuracy both polar designs (CLO and STR) outperformed the linear designs when data density was low. To find an explanation for this result, we looked at the selections made by our participants and discovered an interesting side effect. The data sets corresponding to these wrongly answered questions were enriched with distractors very similar to the correct data instances by showing the same high value but at a different point in time. Participants seemed less likely to select such distractors when using the circular layouts for the time dimension. Participants were significantly more confident and made significantly less mistakes with the polar designs. The participants also reported to like the clock metaphor. Some suggested, however, to visualize only 12 hours at a time for a more intuitive encoding.

When data density was high we observed the same trend, even though only STA showed significant differences with respect to STR and LIN. The good performance of STA can be explained with the combination of the encodings. The length encoding for the data values makes it possible to easily spot the highest value even with lots of datapoints. With the color encodings, participants had problems spotting the peak value. The circular layout performed better than the linear one and worked for estimating the correct point in time.

We saw almost no significant differences between the designs for efficiency (only CLO was better than LIN with low data density and STA better than STR with high data density). Nonetheless, we observed that the overall trend for efficiency did not contradict the trend we found in terms of accuracy.

A significant decrease in performance between the two data densities can only be seen for accuracy. All designs had an increased error rate except for LIN. However, LIN's accuracy had been very low for the low density, thus, a significant decrease was nearly not possible. In terms of efficiency only CLO has a higher completion time, whereas, the other designs remained stable. These investigations partially support our hypothesis H4 where we had conjectured that the performance for detecting temporal positions would drop for an increased data density.

Trend Detection

In H5 we had conjectured that LIN & STA would be most effective for this task with the required value judgement as the bottleneck of the two required subtasks. As we expected, in terms of accuracy, the participants performed best using LIN independent from the data density. There was no significant difference between STA, CLO and STR on *error* and no significant results for *time* and, thus, H5 can only be partially confirmed. Independent from the designs, the participants needed around 30 seconds to complete the task.

With an increased data density the accuracy of LIN, CLO and STR dropped significantly. The completion time remained stable with no changes between the two density conditions. Our hypothesis H6 stating that the performance will not change by increasing the data density can, therefore, not be confirmed. Interestingly, participants commented that subjectively the task difficulty was not impacted by higher data density. The qualitative feedback almost matched the quantitative results. Nearly all participants reported to prefer LIN (i.e., position/length encoding) for solving the task.

DESIGN CONSIDERATIONS

With the results gained from the analysis and discussions we derive the following design considerations.

- **To improve value comparison, use a linear layout or switch to color encoding for value:**
  As can be seen in the results for the first and third task, LIN and STA's performance are quite diverse although the value encoding is similar. The polar design has a strong effect on the perception of the position/length encoding.

- **For value encoding, position/length encodings should be preferred to a color encoding:**
  As can be seen in the results gained from Task 1 and 3 where a value comparison was necessary, LIN performs best. Even with an increased data density values could still be compared.

- **Triangular shapes rather may be better than rectangular shapes for color encoding:**
  The slices used in CLO for encoding single data values form a triangular shape because of the circular layout. As can be seen in the results for CLO compared to STR, having more space near the circumference increased participants' performance. Designers could experiment with adding triangular shapes in a linear encoding.

- **Color encodings for higher data densities should be used with caution:**
  The results from task 1 and 3 illustrate, that the performance of the color encoded designs (CLO and STR) depends on the data density. Having a higher data density leads to a decreased performance.

- **Circular layouts rather than linear ones should be preferred for detecting temporal locations:**
  Polar designs are better for detecting specific points in time. This guideline results from the analysis of the second task. Participants performed significantly better using CLO and STA compared to LIN and STR. The clock metaphor increases users' chronological orientation.

- **For time-dependent tasks, sufficient space should be assigned to the designs:**
  Whereas, for solely value comparison tasks the performance of the best design (LIN) is not affected, the accuracy for tasks including temporal information decreases. This is independent from the combination of visual variables used as can be seen for task 2 (STA and CLO) and 3 (LIN). The designs performing best for these tasks are encoded differently but still show the same behavior.

LIMITATIONS

As stated at the beginning, we were inspired by time series data for a daily monitoring task. Especially CLO and STA with their 24 hour clock metaphor profit from this data arrangement. The performance may change with different lengths of time series.

The same is true for the aspect ratio and the size of the single glyphs. The aspect ratio was chosen in order not to greatly disadvantage the circular designs in terms of display space used. However, especially STR would profit from an aspect ratio with more horizontal space. With varying sizes of glyphs, the performance of the designs could change. In our setting we used the minimal space possible to be able to assign one pixel to one data value for the higher data density.

CONCLUSIONS

In this paper, we conducted a controlled experiment with 24 participants to assess the performance of time series visualizations when shrinking their size to glyph representations. In particular, we quantitatively measured accuracy and efficiency, and qualitatively surveyed user confidence and preferences for four glyph types based on three tasks important to our domain experts: peak detection, peak detection at a certain point in time, and trend detection. The four glyphs: Line Glyph, Stripe Glyph, Clock Glyph and Star Glyph were chosen for their varying use of visual variables to encode temporal position and the quantitative value of a data value.

The results show that depending on tasks and data density, the chosen glyphs performed differently. We show that the Line Glyph is generally a good choice for peak and trend detection tasks but that radial encodings of time (Star Glyph and Clock Glyph) were more effective when one had to find a particular temporal location. Participants' subjective preferences support these findings. Thus, our study shows that both accuracy and efficiency of tasks such as ours can be boosted when carefully choosing the most appropriate design.

In the future we plan to expand upon this work in two ways: First, we want to test the effect of different small multiple layout techniques for our glyphs (e. g., on a map). Second, it would be interesting to test alternative glyph designs that cover a larger variety of visual variables for the value encoding in an identical controlled experiment on time series. This would allow us a more general judgement about the applicability of Cleveland and McGill's ranking of visual variables [10] with respect to glyph design. With our current study we complement the research in the field of glyph evaluation by comparing the performance of four temporal glyphs for two peak detection and one trend detection task and provide a first set of design considerations for practitioners.

ACKNOWLEDGMENTS

The research leading to these results has received funding from the European Commission's Seventh Framework Programme (FP7/2007-2013) under grant agreement no. 257495, "Visual Analytic Representation of Large Datasets for Enhancing Network Security" (VIS-SENSE).

REFERENCES

1. Aigner, W., Kainz, C., Ma, R., and Miksch, S. Bertin was right: An empirical evaluation of indexing to compare multivariate time-series data using line plots. *Computer Graphics Forum 30*, 1 (2011), 215–228.

2. Aigner, W., Miksch, S., Schumann, H., and Tominski, C. *Visualization of time-oriented data.* Springer-Verlag, 2011.

3. Andrienko, N., and Andrienko, G. *Exploratory analysis of spatial and temporal data.* Springer Berlin,, Germany, 2006.

4. Ankerst, M., Keim, D. A., and Kriegel, H.-P. Recursive pattern: A technique for visualizing very large amounts of data. In *Proc. Visualization (VIS)*, IEEE (1995), 279–286.

5. Ankerst, M., Keim, D. A., and Kriegel, H.-P. Circle segments: A technique for visually exploring large multidimensional data sets. In *Hot Topic Session of Visualization (VIS)*, IEEE (1996).

6. Bederson, B. B., Clamage, A., Czerwinski, M. P., and Robertson, G. G. Datelens: A fisheye calendar interface for pdas. *ACM Trans. Computer-Human Interaction 11*, 1 (2004), 90–119.

7. Brewer, C. A. Colorbrewer—color advice for maps. Accessed online September, 2012, `http://www.colorbrewer.org/`.

8. Carlis, J., and Konstan, J. Interactive visualization of serial periodic data. In *Proc. Symposium on User Interface Software and Technology (UIST)*, ACM (1998), 29–38.

9. Clark, W., Polakov, W., and Trabold, F. *The Gantt chart: A working tool of management.* The Ronald Press Company, 1922.

10. Cleveland, W., and McGill, R. Graphical perception: Theory, experimentation, and application to the development of graphical methods. *Journal of the American Statistical Association* (1984), 531–554.

11. Daassi, C., Dumas, M., Fauvet, M., Nigay, L., and Scholl, P. Visual exploration of temporal object databases. In *Proc. Bases de Données Avancées (BDA)* (2000).

12. Fischer, F., Fuchs, J., and Mansmann, F. ClockMap: Enhancing circular treemaps with temporal glyphs for time-series data. In *Proc. EuroVis Short Papers*, Eurographics (2012), 97–101.

13. Guttorp, P., Sain, S., Wikle, C., Wickham, H., Hofmann, H., Wickham, C., and Cook, D. Glyph-maps for visually exploring temporal patterns in climate data and models. *Environmetrics 23*, 5 (2012), 382–393.

14. Havre, S., Hetzler, B., and Nowell, L. Themeriver: Visualizing theme changes over time. In *Proc. Information Visualization (InfoVis)*, IEEE (2000), 115–123.

15. Heer, J., Kong, N., and Agrawala, M. Sizing the horizon: The effects of chart size and layering on the graphical perception of time series visualizations. In *Proc. Human Factors in Computing Systems (CHI)*, ACM (2009), 1303–1312.

16. Javed, W., McDonnel, B., and Elmqvist, N. Graphical perception of multiple time series. *Trans. Visualization and Computer Graphics 16*, 6 (2010), 927–934.

17. Keim, D. A. Designing pixel-oriented visualization techniques: Theory and applications. *Trans. Visualization and Computer Graphics 6*, 1 (2000), 59–78.

18. Kintzel, C., Fuchs, J., and Mansmann, F. Monitoring large ip spaces with clockview. In *Proc. Visualization for Cyber Security (VizSec)*, ACM (2011).

19. Kraak, M. The space-time cube revisited from a geovisualization perspective. In *Proc. International Cartographic Conference (ICC)* (2003), 1988–1996.

20. Krasser, S., Conti, G., Grizzard, J., Gribschaw, J., and Owen, H. Real-time and forensic network data analysis using animated and coordinated visualization. In *Proc. Workshop on Information Assurance and Security*, IEEE (2005), 42–49.

21. Krstajic, M., Bertini, E., and Keim, D. CloudLines: compact display of event episodes in multiple time-series. *Trans. Visualization and Computer Graphics 17*, 12 (2011), 2432–2439.

22. Kumar, N., Lolla, N., Keogh, E., Lonardi, S., and Ratanamahatana, C. Time-series bitmaps: A practical visualization tool for working with large time series databases. In *Proc. Data Mining Conference*, SIAM (2005), 531–535.

23. Levkowitz, H., and Herman, G. Color scales for image data. *Computer Graphics and Applications, IEEE 12*, 1 (1992), 72–80.

24. MacEachren, A. *How maps work.* Guilford Press, 1995.

25. McLachlan, P., Munzner, T., Koutsofios, E., and North, S. LiveRAC: interactive visual exploration of system management time-series data. In *Proc. Human Factors in Computing Systems (CHI)*, ACM (2008), 1483–1492.

26. Pearlman, J., and Rheingans, P. Visualizing network security events using compound glyphs from a service-oriented perspective. In *VIZSEC*. Springer, 2007, 131–146.

27. Plaisant, C., Milash, B., Rose, A., Widoff, S., and Shneiderman, B. Lifelines: visualizing personal histories. In *Proc. Human Factors in Computing Systems*, ACM (1996), 221–227.

28. Playfair, W., and Corry, J. *The commercial and political atlas and statistical breviary.* 1786.

29. Saito, T., Miyamura, H., Yamamoto, M., Saito, H., Hoshiya, Y., and Kaseda, T. Two-tone pseudo coloring: Compact visualization for one-dimensional data. In *Proc. Information Visualization (InfoVis)*, IEEE (2005), 173–180.

30. Stone, M. In Color Perception, Size Matters. *IEEE Computer Graphics and Applications 32*, 2 (Mar./Apr. 2012), 8–13.

31. Talbot, J., Gerth, J., and Hanrahan, P. Arc length-based aspect ratio selection. *Trans. Visualization and Computer Graphics 17*, 12 (2011).

32. Tominski, C., Abello, J., and Schumann, H. Axes-based visualizations with radial layouts. In *Proc. Symposium on Applied Computing*, ACM (2004), 1242–1247.

33. Tufte, E. *Beautiful Evidence.* Graphics Press, 2006.

34. Van Wijk, J. J., and Van Selow, E. R. Cluster and calendar based visualization of time series data. In *Proc. Information Visualization (InfoVis)*, IEEE Computer Society (1999), 4–9.

35. Ward, M. Multivariate data glyphs: Principles and practice. *Handbook of Data Visualization* (2008), 179–198.

36. Ware, C. *Information Visualization: Perception for Design*, 2nd ed. Morgan Kaufmann, 2004.

37. Wattenberg, M., and Kriss, J. Designing for social data analysis. *Trans. Visualization and Computer Graphics 12*, 4 (2006), 549–557.

Motif Simplification: Improving Network Visualization Readability with Fan, Connector, and Clique Glyphs

Cody Dunne, Ben Shneiderman

Department of Computer Science and Human-Computer Interaction Lab
University of Maryland, College Park, MD 20742
{cdunne, ben}@cs.umd.edu

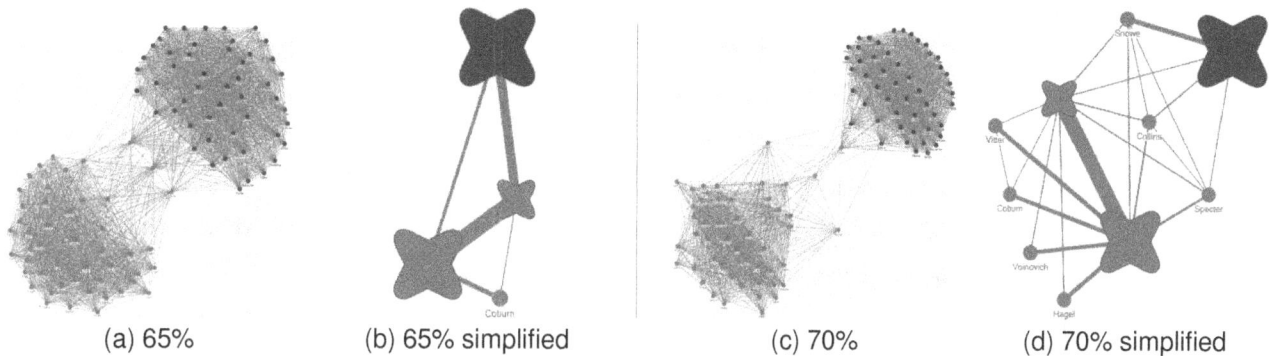

(a) 65%   (b) 65% simplified   (c) 70%   (d) 70% simplified

Figure 1: U.S. Senate 2007 co-voting network at 65% and 70% agreement cutoffs, simplified using clique motif glyphs. Key features are visible, such as the moderate Republican clique around McCain with "wildcards" at the periphery.

ABSTRACT

Analyzing networks involves understanding the complex relationships between entities, as well as any attributes they may have. The widely used **node-link diagrams** excel at this task, but many are difficult to extract meaning from because of the inherent complexity of the relationships and limited screen space. To help address this problem we introduce a technique called **motif simplification**, in which common patterns of nodes and links are replaced with compact and meaningful glyphs. Well-designed glyphs have several benefits: they (1) require less screen space and layout effort, (2) are easier to understand in the context of the network, (3) can reveal otherwise hidden relationships, and (4) preserve as much underlying information as possible. We tackle three frequently occurring and high-payoff motifs: **fans** of nodes with a single neighbor, **connectors** that link a set of anchor nodes, and **cliques** of completely connected nodes. We contribute design guidelines for motif glyphs; example glyphs for the fan, connector, and clique motifs; algorithms for detecting these motifs; a free and open source reference implementation; and results from a controlled study of 36 participants that demonstrates the effectiveness of motif simplification.

Author Keywords

Motif simplification; network visualization; graph drawing; node-link diagram; visual analytics.

ACM Classification Keywords

H.5.2. User Interfaces (D.2.2, H.1.2, I.3.6)

INTRODUCTION

Networks of entities and their ties have long been common data structures in computer science, but have only recently exploded into popular culture with publishers like the New York Times including elaborate and interesting networks with their articles. Online communities like Facebook, MySpace, Twitter, Flickr, and mailing lists (to name only a handful) enjoyed enormous growth over the last few years and provide incredibly rich datasets of interpersonal relationships, which social scientists are now fervently exploring. Networks have also found applications in such diverse disciplines as bioinformatics, scientometrics, urban planning, politics, and archeology.

Analysis of network data requires understanding clusters, connectivity, and centrality. Statistical analysis and conventional visualization tools like bar and pie charts are often inadequate when faced with these varied and oftentimes immense datasets. visualcomplexity.com provides almost 800 network visualizations, but most are variations of node-link diagrams, where nodes represent entities and the links or edges indicate ties connecting them. Node-link diagrams only recently became widely available but have already been put to great effect, such as detecting social roles in online newsgroups [32] or studying U.S. political blog ties during an election [2].

However, there is a huge array of possible layouts of the nodes and links in any given network, many of which can be misleading or incomprehensible. Network visualizations are only useful to the degree they "effectively convey information to the people that use them" [3]. In fact, the spatial layout of a node-link diagram can have a profound impact on the detection of communities in the network and the perceived importance of actors [23]. Significant thought must be given to proper visualizations so that analysts will be able to understand and effectively communicate data like clusters, the paths between them, and the importance of individual actors.

As manual layout of nodes in the node-link diagram is incredibly time consuming to do well, a lot of effort has been put into developing automated network layout algorithms and filtering tools. As the optimization of many readability metrics is NP-hard [3], layout algorithms often use heuristics that produce suboptimal visualizations quickly. However, the results of applying a layout algorithm can vary greatly depending on the size and topology of the network, and the layout generated is highly dependent on the algorithm used. We believe that state of the art layout algorithms alone are insufficient to consistently produce understandable network visualizations.

One way forward is the use of aggregation, specifically by aggregating common network structures or subnetworks called **motifs**. Large, complex network visualizations often have motifs repeated throughout because of either the network structure or how the data was collected. Regardless of their cause, some frequently occurring motifs contain little information compared to the space they occupy in the visualization. Existing tools may highlight certain motifs, allow users to filter them out manually, or replace them with meta-nodes.

We improve on these approaches with **motif simplification**, in which network motifs are automatically replaced with compact, representative glyphs. Well-designed glyphs have several benefits: they (1) require less screen space and layout effort, (2) are easier to understand in the context of the network, (3) can reveal otherwise hidden relationships, and (4) preserve as much underlying information as possible. In this paper we discuss three high-payoff motifs that plague network analysts, shown in Fig. 2: **fans**, **connectors**, and **cliques**. We contribute the design of representative and combinable glyphs for these motifs, algorithms for detecting them, and a supporting task-based controlled study with 36 participants. These techniques are all implemented and made publicly available as part of the free and open source NodeXL network analysis tool [27], which is available from nodexl.codeplex.com.

Specifically, the contributions of this paper are:

- A technique for simplifying node-link diagrams by replacing common network motifs with representative glyphs,
- A set of design guidelines for these glyphs to show the motif contents and underlying attributes,
- The design of glyphs for fans, connectors, and cliques,
- Algorithms for detecting these three motifs,
- A supporting task-based study with 36 participants, and
- A free and open source implementation as part of NodeXL.

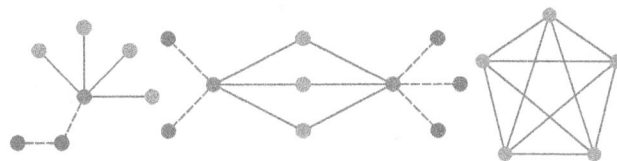

Figure 2: From left to right: fan, connector, and clique motifs.

RELATED WORK

Network analysis tools generally use node-link diagrams, as in NodeXL [27], or matrix representations like Matrix-Explorer [13]. Both node-link and matrix diagrams show the topology of small networks well but can be unreadable with a few thousand nodes. We can reduce the visualization complexity by showing an aggregate version of the network, based on any number of criteria. NetLens [17] groups nodes by their attributes and can pivot between connected groups of two different types, while PivotGraph [31] uses attribute groupings but shows ties between aggregates using arcs. GraphTrail [5] combines these approaches with familiar charts, arc diagrams, and a many-to-many pivot between several node types. However, these approaches focus on attribute comparisons at the expense of showing topology.

Alternatively, we can use a hierarchical topologic clustering to show a network of meta-nodes like ASK-GraphView [1] and van Ham & van Wijk [30]. Rather than letting meta-nodes overlap, van Ham & van Wijk used semantic fisheye views to show clusters as merging spheres. Other approaches to creating overview networks include graph summarization [25] and aggregating nodes by shared neighbor sets [21]. [21] also provide a topologic clustering tool, and a level of detail option to split meta-nodes apart to better see the underlying topology. ManyNets [7] takes a different tack, showing statistical comparisons of a network partitioned by topology, attributes, or time. In each of these techniques it can be difficult to understand the topology of the individual aggregates, often because of the ambiguous nature of clustering algorithms.

Instead of clustering, we can use a metric for node importance to filter to an important subset. Skeletal images [15] highlights high-metric nodes, and replaces filtered trees with triangles that take the same space. Tsigkas et al. [29] similarly filtered a security network of events and features on a domain-specific metric, while including a way to aggregate the events joining a subset of features into meta-edges. However, the aggregation is limited to ties between two feature types and obscures the number of connecting nodes and edges.

Our approach is to aggregate the network by the frequently occurring motifs it contains. While the fan, connector and clique motifs we target are quite prominent in social network datasets, there are many other motifs of interest, especially for biologists. Motif census (counting the kinds of motifs) and analysis is used extensively to analyze the behavior of complex biologic networks, looking for repeated patterns that indicate underlying processes. For example, Milo et al. [24] find motifs that appear more frequently than expected in random networks, and provide a chart of small motif frequency.

Knowledge of the motifs present in a network can help predict behavior and the "structural signatures" of individual entities [32], but visualizing these motifs effectively is challenging. Huang et al. [16] detect motifs with fewer than five nodes and draw transparent convex hulls to highlight them. Similarly, in [19] the matches to a chosen 3–5 node motif are colored within the overall visualization and are drawn identically to be easily spotted. Highlighting small motifs can help biologists spot the locations of particular processes, but does little to reduce the clutter of a complex network visualization and can even reduce readability.

Current approaches to reducing complexity aggregate nodes based on their attributes, topology, or metrics but do not provide visible indications on the meta-nodes showing the underlying topology. Moreover, these algorithms usually pay little attention to the motifs present and create a grouping with ambiguous topology. While current tools can highlight small detected motifs, there are few techniques for providing a graphical overview or summary of them. More importantly, we know of no approaches that leverage the motifs present to reduce the visual complexity of the network visualization.

NETWORK MOTIF SIMPLIFICATION
Many common network motifs present little meaningful information, yet can dominate much of the display space and obscure interesting topology. We believe that replacing these motifs with representative glyphs will create more effective visualizations as there will be far fewer nodes and edges for layout algorithms and users to consider. We have chosen three motifs for our initial foray into motif simplification:

- A **fan motif** consists of a **head node** connected to **leaf nodes** with no other neighbors. As there may be hundreds of leaves, replacing all the leaves and their links to the head with a **fan glyph** can dramatically reduce the network size.
- A **D-connector motif** consists of functionally equivalent **span nodes** that solely link a set of D **anchor nodes**. Replacing span nodes and their links with a **connector glyph** can aid in connectivity comparisons.
- A **D-clique motif** consists of a set of D **member nodes** in which each pair is connected by at least one link. Cliques are common in biologic or similarity networks, where swapping for a **clique glyph** can highlight subgroup ties.

These motifs are prime simplification candidates for several reasons. For one, these motifs are quite common in the network datasets we have encountered in several disciplines. While simple to understand on their own, these motifs can account for much of the visual complexity of a node-link diagram. The fan motifs especially can dominate the diagram. While connector motifs usually occupy less space than the fans, they are hard to detect and can contribute substantial complexity. In the densest networks, such as pairwise similarity scores, overall relationships can be hidden in a tangled hairball of edges from overlapping clique motifs as in Fig. 1a.

Glyph Design
For each motif, careful thought must be given to how to represent the simplified version. Arbitrary motifs can be shown as a simple meta-node (e.g., $\oplus$), possibly with embedded

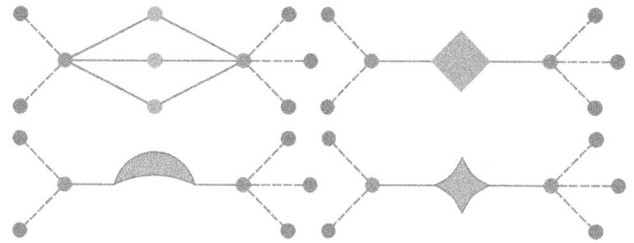

Figure 3: A 2-connector motif with three simplified glyph variants: diamond, crescent, and tapered diamond.

images that show a small node-link diagram of the underlying subnetwork. However, a specially designed representative glyph for a motif can make it easier to understand aggregate topology and attributes with only minimal additional visual clutter. We went through several designs for each of our motif glyphs, though for space reasons we will primarily discuss the final designs and criteria for designing effective glyphs.

Motif Topology
Foremost each glyph must be representative of the underlying subnetwork topology so that the aggregate relationships in the network can still be understood. As we aim to reduce visual clutter, we must use a small, easily-distinguishable glyph rather than heavy-weight visualizations. An effective way to differentiate the glyphs is to use unique shapes to identify each type, ideally that correspond to the underlying topology.

Several example shapes for a connector motif are shown in Fig. 3. The diamond is a straightforward representation of the outline made by the motif topology, is discernible at scale, and has geometric properties that allow easy area scaling and subdivision. However, they are often used with other shapes for categorical attribute coding. The crescent is not, but our user studies indicated that its asymmetry was visually jarring and that it had poor edge connector properties. We finally chose a symmetric tapered diamond: unique enough to be distinguishable and representative yet symmetric and connectable. We use the same shape regardless of the number of anchor nodes so as to reduce the shape corpus required. The clique motifs were originally represented with a tapered square to indicate the link density, but it was easily confused with the connector motif and has since been replaced with a rounded X (Fig. 6). Like the connector motif, the same shape is used for any number of clique members. For the fan motifs, we chose a sector of a circle (Fig. 4), as it represented the fan of leaf nodes commonly seen in node-link diagrams.

Contained Nodes
In addition to the topology, it is helpful to show information about the nodes contained in the motif. What information we want to show impacts the display mechanism we choose for it. Most useful would be a count of the nodes in the motif. This quantitative value is best expressed by position [22], though in node-link diagrams this is reserved for showing ties. The next best choices would be length, angle, or area [22]. For the fan motif, we can scale the angle of the sector linearly between 10–120° by the number of contained nodes, which

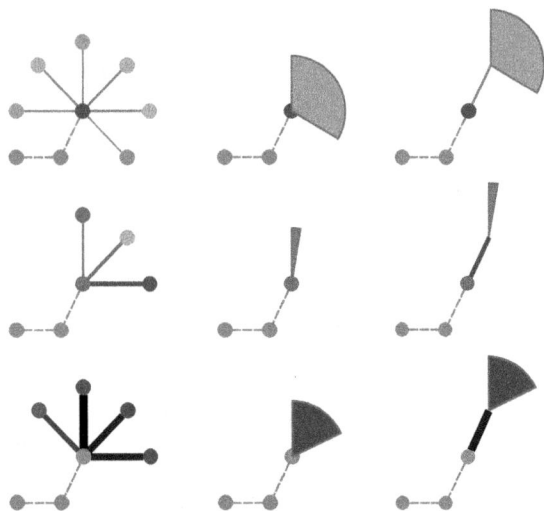

Figure 4: Three fan motifs and two glyph variants of each.

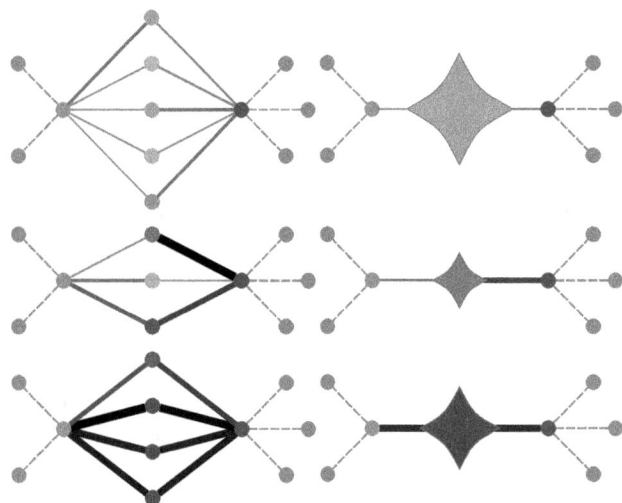

Figure 5: Three 2-connector motifs and their glyphs.

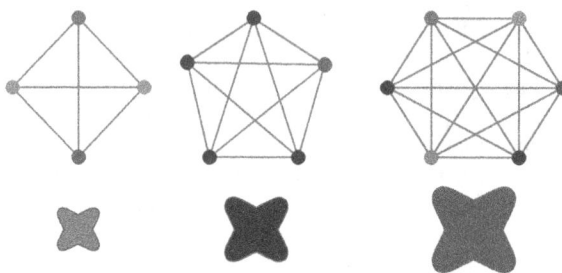

Figure 6: 4-, 5-, and 6-clique motifs and their glyphs.

demonstrating these quantitative attribute or statistic encodings are shown in Figs. 4 to 6, using the same color scale as the underlying nodes in the network. Categorical attributes are more challenging to display without subdividing glyphs or embedding visualizations, increasing the visual clutter. Finally, text attributes such as labels would help reveal the contents of the motif. While a glyph can show a small label, it is challenging to compute a representative one. Instead, we discuss later how interactivity can reveal the underlying nodes.

Connecting Edges

Nodes contained within a motif may have connecting edges, and when the motif is simplified these edges are re-routed to link to the glyph instead. This can result in duplicate, overlapping edges in straight-line drawings, as with the connector motif in Fig. 5. As with nodes, it is useful to show the number of duplicate edges and any attributes they may have. The edges could be drawn independently as curves of varying arcs or stacked in slices with scaled area, but again we strive to avoid visual clutter and show aggregate relationships clearly.

We aggregate these duplicate edges into meta-edges, with width and thus area representing a function of the underlying edges such as the number of edges (Figs. 1 and 8), the average of an attribute value (Figs. 4 and 5), etc. There are options for showing categorical attributes or labels, but these require cluttered embedded visualizations or interactivity. In some cases there are no attributes on the edges to encode, and showing even edge count would be a redundant. One example is the fan motif, in which the number of edges equals the already-encoded number of leaf nodes (in an undirected network without duplicates). Example fan glyphs without meta-edges are shown in the center column of Fig. 4.

Alas, glyph shape impacts how edges connect to them. Ideally, each glyph lies along a straight line with connecting edges so paths can be traced easily. For the 2-connector motif, a crescent would suffice if its corners were aligned along the path (Fig. 3). However, for connectors with three or more anchors our users reported that crescents make edges difficult to follow. Symmetric shapes like the tapered diamond and rounded X are better suited for many connecting edges.

Motif Overlap

Often motifs are non-overlapping and easily transformed into glyphs, though many motifs do not have this luxury. When detecting motifs we can choose a non-overlapping set to display, but motif glyphs will be more effective at reducing com-

also linearly scales its area (Fig. 4). We chose this range after tests using smaller ranges (20–90°) did not reveal enough size variation. The vertical alignment eases area comparisons and eases glyph subdivision to show edge directionality or attributes. We also scale the area of the other motifs linearly by the number of nodes (Figs. 5 and 6). Designers should ensure the shape is still discernible at its minimum size while not so large at its maximum to occlude edges unnecessarily.

We may also wish to show quantitative attributes or statistics of the underlying nodes. Showing all the values or their distribution would require complex embedded charts or focusable tooltips. Instead, we show a function of the values such as mean (used for these examples), sum, min, or variance. As size is reserved for node count, we are left with the less effective color saturation, color hue, and density/opacity [22]. While these are less effective encodings, the maximum deviation reported for quantitative tasks is only 13% [4]. Glyphs plexity when they can be combined to show overlapping motifs. The design of any motif glyphs must thus take overlaps into account. Among our three motifs, fans are the most immune to overlap. The fan leaves have too few edges to participate in the other motifs, though the fan head can be a connector anchor or clique member. As a clique glyph replaces all the clique members, we must exclude the fan head from the fan glyph to allow this combination. Similarly, a connector anchor can be a clique member, which requires its exclusion from the connector glyph. Two example overlaps are shown in Fig. 7 and more on overlap handling is discussed later.

Glyph Interactivity

While the motif glyphs we described can be effective for simplifying a network, we would like to make sure that they are easily understandable and investigable. One important aspect of this is to ensure that users can switch between the original and simplified views interactively. Users can simplify the entire network, or only a selected subset of motifs. Likewise, users can expand the entire network to see the original visualization, or only expand a selected glyph they are interested in exploring. We expose the contents of each glyph with tooltips. It would be possible to expand on this and show details for a glyph via a heavyweight focusable tooltip that contains a chart of attribute distributions or a list of node labels.

Direct manipulation of the motif glyphs and underlying nodes is an effective way of exploring the network. Users can adjust node or glyph placement manually, as well as highlight incident edges or adjacent nodes through simple context menus. Additionally, automatic layout algorithms are available for laying out the simplified network. An ideal layout algorithm would take the shape and size of the glyphs into account, in addition to the number of edges in any meta-edges.

Motif Detection Algorithms

General motif detection can be accomplished with approaches like symmetry-breaking [10], but custom algorithms are more effective for specific motifs that can vary substantially in size. We have implemented algorithms to detect fan, connector, and clique motifs of all sizes, but due to space constraints can only present an overview and refer the interested reader to our supplementary material, tech report,[1] and source code.[2] We will use the terminology of a network or graph G with a set of nodes $G.nodes$ with a size denoted $|G.nodes|$.

Fan Motifs

We use the obvious algorithm for detecting fan motifs which has a run time complexity of $O(|G.nodes| \times$ average neighbor count). Average neighbor count is usually relatively small and can be considered a bounded constant. The main thing to note is that we count the neighbors for each node, rather than its degree, as there may be overlapping or directed edges.

Connector Motifs

Connectors have a **dimension**, denoted D, that indicates the number of anchors it has and is always two or greater. Our

---

[1]www.cs.umd.edu/localphp/hcil/tech-reports-search.php?number=2012-29

[2]nodexl.codeplex.com/SourceControl/changeset/view/70521#1208172

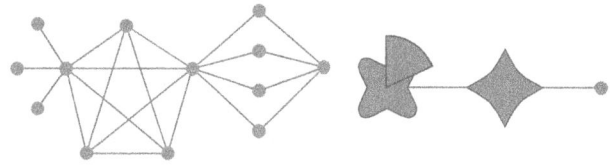

Figure 7: Glyphs for fan, clique, and connector motif overlap.

algorithm for detecting connector motifs of all dimensions takes parameters $D\text{-}min$ and $D\text{-}max$ to indicate the range of dimensions to search for. The run time complexity of this algorithm is also $O(|G.nodes| \times$ average neighbor count).

Connectors require more algorithmic details to detect than fans, despite having the same run time complexity. The algorithm is broken into several components. First, a pass is made through all nodes searching for span nodes with sets of neighbors that could be anchors and creating or adding to a map of keys to possible motifs. An additional pass is required to traverse the potential motifs and remove those with only one span node, as well as remove all but the most desirable of any overlapping motifs. We choose motifs to keep first by the total number of anchors and spanners, then by the number of spanners, then arbitrarily.

Clique Motifs

To find all cliques in the graph we use the Tomita et al. algorithm [28], which has a run time complexity of $O(3^{|G.nodes|/3})$. However, this algorithm has high memory requirements and for especially large graphs a new linear-storage algorithm by Eppstein and Strash may be faster or required [6]. Unfortunately cliques in general can have high amounts of overlap. We use a greedy heuristic that chooses the largest non-overlapping clique motifs to keep that is $O(\text{number of motifs} \times$ average motif size). This works well on the networks we have analyzed, but may be insufficient for studying dense networks.

Resolving Motif Overlap

When computing motifs, not only can motifs of a type overlap (like cliques), but in general the various types can overlap with each other as well. While our design for fan and connector motifs prevents any ambiguous overlap and allows easy combinations (Fig. 7), the choice of which cliques are simplified can impact user perception of the network. In order to effectively pick a disjoint set of motifs to keep, we would have to rate each motif by desirability and solve the set packing problem, one of Karp's 21 NP-complete problems [18]. Not only is this problem computationally hard to solve exactly, it is also difficult to approximate, hence our use of heuristics.

NodeXL Implementation

We have implemented a reference implementation of motif simplification and made it publicly available as part of the NodeXL network analysis tool [27]. NodeXL is a free and open source template for Microsoft Excel 2007/2010 that is tailored to provide powerful features while being easy to learn. The Excel integration allows rapid data processing using standard formulas and macros, but NodeXL also provides calculators for network statistics, automatic layout algorithms, visual attribute encodings, dynamic filters, direct manipulation, coordinated views, and importers from online social networks and common network file formats like GraphML, Pajek, and UCINET. More details are available in our supplementary material. NodeXL is widely used in many disciplines and has a full-time developer as well as a team of volunteer advisors, including the authors of this paper. Many introductory courses on network analysis have used NodeXL and its companion book [11] as part of their curriculum,[3] and user studies have shown NodeXL to be effective in these situations. Given that these users generally have little prior knowledge about network visualization readability, we believe that they will particularly benefit from our interactive motif simplification techniques.

CASE STUDIES

We explored several networks of interest using motif simplification, in several cases while helping domain experts analyze their data. Overall, motif simplification resulted in vastly reduced network size, reducing the visual complexity faced by the user and easing automatic and manual layout tasks.

U.S. Senate Voting Patterns in 2007

The power of clique motif simplification is shown in an example network of U.S. Senate voting patterns from 2007,[4] shown in Figs. 1 and 8. The percent similarity in voting patterns is an attribute of each one of the 4950 links connecting the 100 Senator nodes. The naive drawing produces a completely connected graph, but filtering the similarity values to show only those with values above 0.65 and applying a force-directed layout produces a revealing portrait (Fig. 1a). We see the willingness of three Republican Senators (center, in red) to vote in support of their Democrat colleagues (top-right, in blue). One of these, Arlen Specter, later switched his affiliation to the Democrats in 2009. However, further insights are not readily visible in the tangled hairball of each party.

After simplifying cliques, several additional features are visible (Fig. 1b). There are three completely connected groups: one with 48 Democrats, the two independents, and a Republican (Snowe); another with 42 Republicans; and a 4-clique of Collins, Smith, McCain, and Specter. We worked with a political scientist to see if these cliques highlighted known behavior, and, in fact, they did. The 4-clique represents moderate Republicans and bridge builders that were often decisive votes, though they have stronger ties to the Republican clique. The only Senator not in a clique is Coburn, a staunch Republican on contentions issues but who often votes his heart.

We increased the cutoff to 0.70 and ran the layout again (Fig. 1c). However, the simplified version (Fig. 1d) has become quite intriguing. While the Democrats and Independents still form a 50-clique, a few members trickled out of Republican cliques. Snowe returns to the middle with high connectivity with her former Democrat clique. Collins and

Specter also move to the center, replaced in the McCain clique by Coleman and Lugar – more moderates. The corner outliers are known wildcards that do not follow the party.

Extending this process to higher cutoffs, we begin to see party fragmentation, led by the Republicans (Fig. 8). At 0.80 the network bisects (Fig. 8a), and the Democrats split into three cliques and a solitary Nelson, a Blue Dog moderate (Fig. 8b). The top right 4-clique is the east-coast liberals, while the left 4-clique are moderates. The Republicans splinter further, and by 0.95 only the two Senators from Georgia remain (Fig. 8d).

All told, the political scientist was impressed that motif simplification could highlight many of the features he was already aware of. Moreover, several new insights came from analyzing these visualizations and then checking other sources to provide additional evidence for the pattern.

Lostpedia Wiki Edits

An example of overlapping motif simplification is shown in Fig. 9, which represent the bipartite network for the Lostpedia wiki community collected by Beth Foss. Boxes with labels show wiki pages, linked to the colored discs representing their associated editors. The editors are colored and sized according to two measures of their activity in the wiki. Fig. 9a shows the initial network, while the Fig. 9b shows a simplified version. By combining fan and connector glyphs, we only have 13 nodes to lay out and compare instead of the original 513, only 23 edges instead of 586, and use a fraction of the screen space. While these simplifications are not entirely necessary to understand such a small and well-arranged diagram, they are effective at showing aggregate relationships like the large number of highly active main page editors.

VOSON Web Crawl

A larger dataset we encountered is shown in Fig. 10a, which we modified from the NodeXL book, Fig. 12.9 [11, p. 192]. This network of 3958 web pages and 4380 hyperlinks was collected by crawling sites connected to voson.anu.edu.au. It is immediately evident that large fans of nodes dominate the periphery, in in part because the NodeXL [27] implementation of the Fruchterman-Reingold layout [8] tends to draw elliptical layouts within a rectangular space. However, the fans tend to dominate the visualization regardless of the layout.

Our manual calculations using Gimp showed that 21% of the screen space in Fig. 10a is wasted as blank space in the corners, with 33% showing the core network with its connector motifs, and the remaining 46% used to show the fan motifs. Calculating only for the elliptical visualization region, approximately 58% of the space available is used to show the fan motifs. This is a substantial amount of area dedicated to showing a very common structure in network datasets obtained by crawling web sites or using surveys. Moreover, these fans do not show any information besides the rough number of nodes they contain. The fans in Fig. 10a vary from 17 to 852 nodes, but due to overlap this can be hard to see.

Some of the overlap between motifs and and with other nodes is not visible in the original image, but there is substantial overlap in the bottom-right and many of the smaller fans are

---

[3]nodexl.codeplex.com/wikipage?title=NodeXL%20Teaching%20Resources

[4]Data by Chris Wilson of Slate magazine, available from above link.

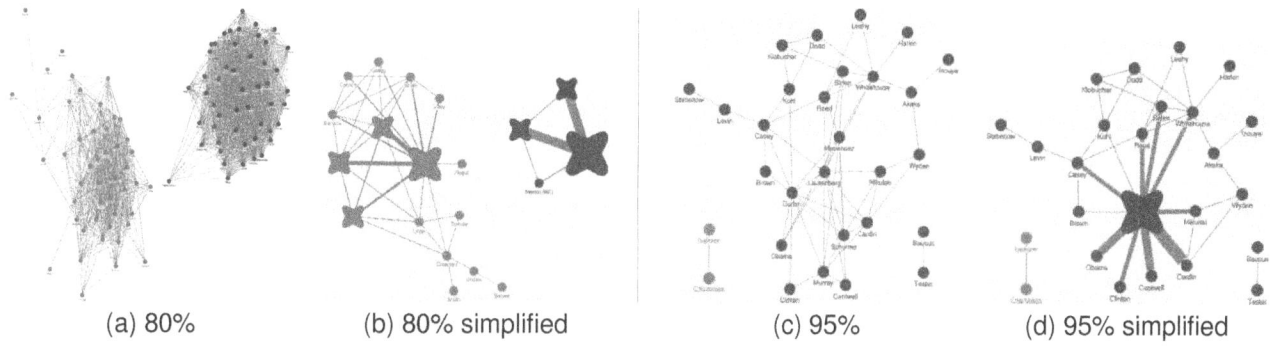

(a) 80%   (b) 80% simplified   (c) 95%   (d) 95% simplified

Figure 8: U.S. Senate 2007 co-voting network at 80% and 95% agreement cutoffs, simplified using clique motif glyphs. The east-coast liberals and the Blue Dog Democrats separate at 80%. We see the network decompose at higher cutoffs.

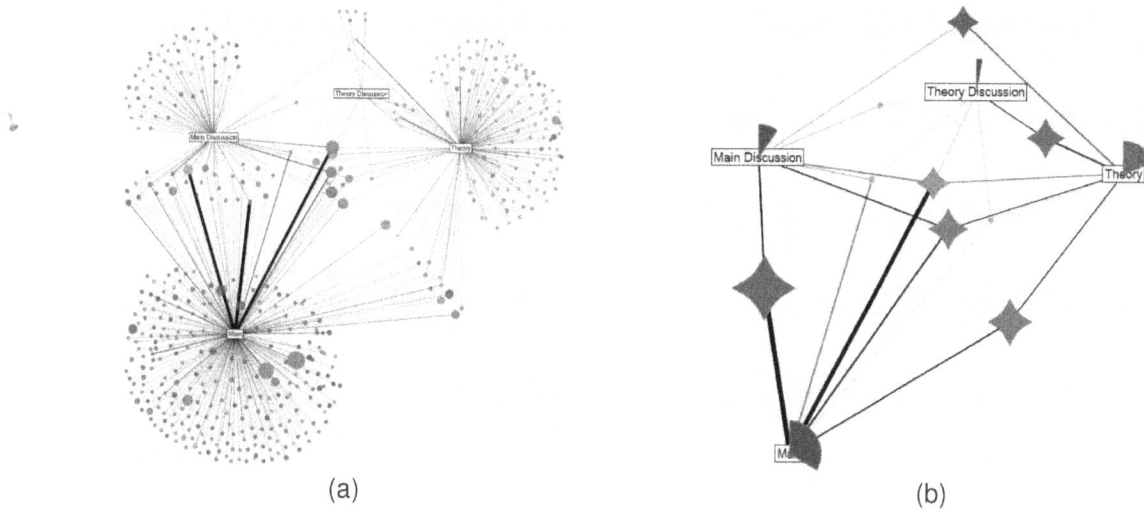

(a)   (b)

Figure 9: A bipartite network of Lostpedia of wiki edits (left) and a simplified version using fan and connector glyphs (right).

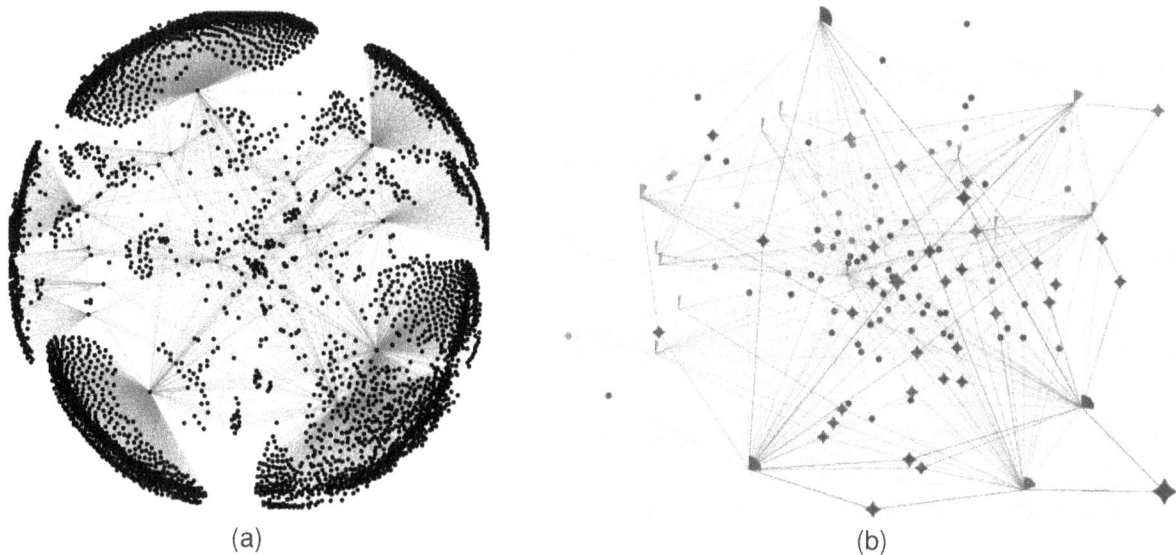

(a)   (b)

Figure 10: A web crawl starting at voson.anu.edu.au, modified from Fig. 12.9 of the NodeXL book [11], p.192 (left) and the simplified version using fan and connector motifs and colored by eigenvector centrality (right).

spread in several directions or hidden in the interior. Moreover, many of the fans overlap and obscure other more important nodes that are not participating in any fan, such as a huge 2-connector motif with 50 span nodes in the bottom-right. This 2-connector motif, as well as the several others connecting parts of the web page network together, are quite hard to detect among the clutter.

We then simplified these fan and connector motifs, going from 3958 nodes to 559 and 4380 edges to 765, creating a much less cluttered visualization (Fig. 10b) After simplification, it became evident that the large connector motif in the linked the web sites for the Summer Doctoral Programme at the Oxford Internet Institute and the National Center for eSocial Science. Applying a layout algorithm to the simplified network would result in a new layout that makes more effective use of the newfound space. This visualization is much clearer at presenting (1) the size and membership of the various fans motifs and (2) the large connector motifs connecting pairs of fan heads. Moreover, it appears to have minimal loss of information and visual clutter compared to the original.

Larger Networks
We analyzed several other large networks not pictured here. One was a network of innovation and funding ties with 7124 nodes and 16,109 edges. Another showed acquisitions of JP Morgan Chase, with 5766 nodes and 6752 edges. Both were visualized interactively with no performance issues, and had drastic reductions in complexity with motif simplification.

CONTROLLED EXPERIMENT
We ran a controlled experiment to determine the effect motif simplification has on user performance with several common network visualization tasks.

Tasks
We chose a varied set of tasks relating to topology, attributes, and overviews from a taxonomy [20], which demonstrates how all complex tasks can be seen as a series of low-level tasks. These tasks are also used in many recent papers evaluating network visualizations [14, 26, 9]. We asked:

1. About how many nodes are in the network?
2. Which individual node would we remove to disconnect the most nodes from the main network?
3. Which is the largest (fan | connector | clique) motif and how many nodes does it contain?
4. Which node has the label "XXX"?
5. What is the length of the shortest path between the two highlighted nodes?
6. Which of the two highlighted nodes has more neighbors?
7. How many common neighbors are shared by the two highlighted nodes?
8. Which of two pairs of nodes has more common neighbors?

Data
Current random network generators do not produce realistic data [14], which we confirmed trying to generate several networks with similar characteristics. Thus we chose to use three sufficiently interesting networks produced by actual users solving their own problems, which are discussed in the Case Studies section.

Participants
After a two-participant pilot study, we recruited 36 students from our university (19 males and 17 females). The participants were almost entirely graduate students, half from computer science and the balance from eight other departments. 9 had used network visualization tools and an overlapping 9 had seen motif simplification, though none had used it. As we could not generate sufficiently varied datasets with similar properties, we used a between subjects design. We randomly divided participants into two groups, which had similar distributions of gender, department, grade level, and experience.

Procedure
Each 45-minute session began with 5-10 minutes of training on the tool and for the specific tasks, followed by about 35 minutes for answering a total of 31 questions across the three networks and tasks. Each participant received the same order of questions and visualizations. The control group was provided with an interactive node-link diagram in which they could select nodes along with their incident edges, as well as move the nodes. The treatment group received a simplified version of each new visualization, with additional interactive tooltips and the ability to expand and collapse the motifs. Each visualization is presented consistently, originally computed using Harel-Koren [12].

As in [9, 14], users were given one minute to answer each question, told to answer as quickly and accurately as possible, and that they could skip if they could not answer a question. The evaluator spoke each question, gave the participant time to ask for clarification, then revealed the next visualization in turn and began the timer. Users were given $10 plus a $15 bonus for the fastest, most accurate participant in each group.

Analysis
The recorded data was analyzed in several ways. As is common with response time data, the response times were not normally distributed so were normalized using a log transformation. The two groups were then compared using a t-test. Answers to questions consisted of a categorical answer (a specific item), which was recorded correct or not, and/or an integer answer. For questions with categorical answers, the groups were compared with Fisher's exact test instead of the chi-square test as none of the significant group-by-correct matrices had expected values of five or higher in all four cells. For numeric answers we computed $error = (answer - truth)/truth$, skipping any questions that had an incorrect categorical answer the integer answer depended on, and compared error across groups using a t-test.

Results
Here we report only the significant findings. We expect overview tasks like identifying the maximal motif of a type would be easier with the less visual complexity of a simplified network. This was true for all three motifs across all three networks. Cliques, the epitomical clusters, were found in the two networks they occurred in faster (p<0.01, -20.82s),

more accurately (p<0.01, 92% vs. 23.5%), and with fewer people giving up (3 vs. 0). Moreover, in the Senate network there was higher accuracy in size estimates (p<0.05, 0% vs. -28% error), which could be true for the web network but we could not measure it as not one control participant detected the maximal 5-clique.

Fans were found in both the networks they occurred in faster (p<0.01, mean -7.77s) and their size was approximated more closely (p<0.01, 2% vs. -62% error). In the large web network the maximal fan was also found more frequently (p<0.01, 95% vs. 35%). Connectors were detected in both their networks faster as well (p<0.01, mean -17.13s). In the web network the largest connector was found more frequently (p<0.01, 79% vs. 6%), and in the wiki network its size was estimated more precisely (p<0.1, -5% vs. -17% error).

These results show that using glyphs for motifs makes the motifs easier to detect and measure, but how does simplifying motifs affect the rest of the network? We would think estimating the number of nodes would be easier in the simplified, interactive view. Our participants could indeed gauge the size of all three networks with significantly more accuracy (p<0.01, -8% vs. -47% error), but for the wiki and web networks users took longer to do so (p<0.01, 21.82s). How about finding a specific node by its label? Logically reducing the number of visual items makes finding a label easier. Our results show that finding labels that are not in motifs is significantly faster (p<0.01, -19.93s), they are found more frequently except in the Senate case (p<0.01, 97.5% vs. 14.5%), and fewer users give up or run out of time (12 did on the plain wiki and web networks). We only saw worse search time for labels in motifs for the Senate clique case (p<0.05, 15.29s).

What about topology-based tasks? It seems that with fewer items on the screen tracing edges would be easier. For some questions it did turn out better, like finding the node to cut in the web network correctly (p<0.05, 53% vs. 18%) and the accuracy of the shortest path length between two clique members in the Senate network (p<0.05, -7% vs. 22% error). For others topology questions, the results were mixed to poor. Shortest path length time and accuracy worsened in the web network (p<0.1, 10.06s & 20% vs. 1% error). Comparing the number of neighbors was slower on the wiki (p<0.01, 10.89s) and senate (p<0.05, 9.26s) networks, and the choice accuracy dropped for the senate (p<0.1, 53% vs. 82%) and web (p<0.1, 68% vs 76%). Lastly, the shared neighbor count tasks were slower in the web network (p<0.01, 11.73s), and reduced accuracy in the wiki network (p<0.1, -21% vs. -10%).

Discussion

All told it appears that motif simplification is beneficial for many analysis tasks. Naturally identifying maximal motifs is faster, more accurate, and we can estimate their sizes more accurately when we have glyphs and interaction. Counting nodes in the network turned out to be slower, but more accurate when using the glyphs. Finding unsimplified labels became much quicker, while simplified labels were only slower in one case. Finally, it seems like topology-based tasks are a mixed bag. Finding cut nodes is more accurate, but path-based tasks were better and worse in different circumstances.

Comparing the number of neighbors and shared neighbors turned out slower and less accurate in a few cases, while counting them was more error-prone.

We have already implemented additional features to increase user performance on topologic tasks. When we ran the study we did not yet use the sized meta-edges that are shown in Fig. 1. With this simple modification, we believe we can show much of the aggregate connectivity. However, user education is likely the most promising way to improve the glyph performance. Many participants had difficulty understanding the topology inside the collapsed glyphs. With more than the 5-10 minutes of training provided in this study, users may perform much better on these tasks.

LIMITATIONS & FUTURE WORK
Our studies indicate that motif simplification is an effective way of reducing node-link diagram complexity, but it does pose several challenges. There is an extra effort in learning the motif concepts and interpreting the glyphs, which may deter some users, but simplification is a user choice which can be reversed at any time. Heavyweight glyphs with color striping or embedded charts would help users see the content of a motif, but would also add to the visual clutter and reduce the utility of the simplification. While the underlying topology of an individual motif is unambiguous, in some cases the choice of which motifs to simplify can lead to different overviews. The fan and connector motifs prevent ambiguous overlap, but clique motifs can overlap each other substantially. We use a heuristic that picks the largest non-overlapping clique to simplify. A more effective, but computationally hard, approach would be to rate each motif by desirability and find the optimal set of motifs. Alternatively, instead of visualizing exact cliques, we could show the overlap between almost-cliques and the confidence of various clusterings.

CONCLUSION
We present motif simplification, a technique for increasing the readability node-link diagram network visualizations. With motif simplification, common repeating network motifs are replaced with easily understandable motif glyphs that require less space, are easier to understand, and reveal hidden relationships. While users must learn the visual language of motifs and glyphs, there is a dramatic payoff in the usability and readability of the visualization. We contribute design guidelines for motif glyphs; designs of glyphs to replace the high-payoff fan, connector, and clique motifs common in networks; as well as algorithms to identify these motifs. Finally, we have developed a free and open source reference implementation, made publicly available as part of NodeXL.

With case studies and a controlled study we demonstrate the effectiveness of motif simplification as well as areas to focus on for improving glyph design. Motif simplification can result in substantial reductions in visual complexity, allowing easier understanding and manipulation of large network visualizations. There are several avenues for exploration opened up by this work, including additional glyphs for other common motif types, algorithms and glyphs for fuzzy motifs, and methods for showing edge directionality within glyphs.

ACKNOWLEDGEMENTS
We thank Marc Smith, the NodeXL team, and Yiyan Liu for their assistance. This work is supported in part by the Social Media Research Foundation, the Connected Action Consulting Group, and National Science Foundation grant 0915645.

REFERENCES

1. Abello, J., van Ham, F., and Krishnan, N. ASK-GraphView: a large scale graph visualization system. *IEEE TVCG 12*, 5 (2006), 669–676.

2. Adamic, L. A., and Glance, N. The political blogosphere and the 2004 U.S. election: Divided they blog. In *ACM LinkKDD* (2005), 36–43.

3. Battista, G. D., Eades, P., Tamassia, R., and Tollis, I. G. *Graph drawing: Algorithms for the visualization of graphs*. Prentice Hall, July 1998.

4. Cleveland, W. S., and McGill, R. Graphical perception and graphical methods for analyzing scientific data. *Science 229*, 4716 (1985), 828–833.

5. Dunne, C., Riche, N. H., Lee, B., Metoyer, R. A., and Robertson, G. G. GraphTrail: Analyzing large multivariate, heterogeneous networks while supporting exploration history. In *ACM CHI* (2012), 1663–1672.

6. Eppstein, D., and Strash, D. Listing all maximal cliques in large sparse real-world graphs. In *SEA*, vol. 6630 (2011), 364–375.

7. Freire, M., Plaisant, C., Shneiderman, B., and Golbeck, J. ManyNets: An interface for multiple network analysis and visualization. In *ACM CHI* (2010), 213–222.

8. Fruchterman, T. M. J., and Reingold, E. M. Graph drawing by force-directed placement. *SPE 21*, 11 (1991), 1129–1164.

9. Ghoniem, M., Fekete, J.-D., and Castagliola, P. A comparison of the readability of graphs using node-link and matrix-based representations. In *IEEE InfoVis* (2004), 17–24.

10. Grochow, J., and Kellis, M. Network motif discovery using Subgraph Enumeration and Symmetry-Breaking. In *RECOMB* (2007), 92–106.

11. Hansen, D., Shneiderman, B., and Smith, M. *Analyzing social media networks with NodeXL: Insights from a connected world*. Morgan Kaufmann, 2011.

12. Harel, D., and Koren, Y. A fast multi-scale method for drawing large graphs. *JGAA 6*, 3 (2002), 179–202.

13. Henry, N., and Fekete, J.-D. MatrixExplorer: A dual-representation system to explore social networks. *IEEE TVCG 12*, 5 (2006), 677–684.

14. Henry, N., and Fekete, J.-D. MatLink: Enhanced matrix visualization for analyzing social networks. In *INTERACT* (2007), 288–302.

15. Herman, I., Marshall, M. S., Melançon, G., Duke, D. J., Delest, M., and Domenger, J.-P. Skeletal images as visual cues in graph visualization. In *Data Visualization* (1999), 13–22.

16. Huang, W., Murray, C., Shen, X., Song, L., Wu, Y. X., and Zheng, L. Visualisation and analysis of network motifs. In *IEEE InfoVis* (2005), 697–702.

17. Kang, H., Plaisant, C., Lee, B., and Bederson, B. B. NetLens: Iterative exploration of content-actor network data. In *IEEE VAST* (2006), 91–98.

18. Karp, R. M. Reducibility among combinatorial problems. In *Complexity of Computer Computations*, R. E. Miller and J. W. Thatcher, Eds. Plenum Press, 1972, 85–103.

19. Klukas, C., Schreiber, F., and Schwöbbermeyer, H. Coordinated perspectives and enhanced force-directed layout for the analysis of network motifs. In *APVis* (2006), 39–48.

20. Lee, B., Plaisant, C., Parr, C. S., Fekete, J.-D., and Henry, N. Task taxonomy for graph visualization. In *ACM BELIV* (2006), 1–5.

21. Liao, Q., Shi, L., and Sun, X. Anomaly analysis and visualization through compressed graphs. In *IEEE LDAV Poster Session* (2012).

22. Mackinlay, J. Automating the design of graphical presentations of relational information. *ACM TOG 5*, 2 (1986), 110–141.

23. McGrath, C., Blythe, J., and Krackhardt, D. The effect of spatial arrangement on judgments and errors in interpreting graphs. *Social Networks 19*, 3 (1997), 223–242.

24. Milo, R., Shen-Orr, S., Itzkovitz, S., Kashtan, N., Chklovskii, D., and Alon, U. Network motifs: Simple building blocks of complex networks. *Science 298*, 5594 (2002), 824–827.

25. Navlakha, S., Rastogi, R., and Shrivastava, N. Graph summarization with bounded error. In *ACM SIGMOD* (2008), 419–432.

26. Shneiderman, B., and Aris, A. Network visualization by Semantic Substrates. *IEEE TVCG 12*, 5 (2006), 733–740.

27. Smith, M., Shneiderman, B., Milic-Frayling, N., Rodrigues, E. M., Barash, V., Dunne, C., Capone, T., Perer, A., and Gleave, E. Analyzing (social media) networks with NodeXL. In *ACM C&T* (2009), 255–264.

28. Tomita, E., Tanaka, A., and Takahashi, H. The worst-case time complexity for generating all maximal cliques and computational experiments. *Theoretical Computer Science 363*, 1 (2006), 28–42.

29. Tsigkas, O., Thonnard, O., and Tzovaras, D. Visual spam campaigns analysis using abstract graphs representation. In *ACM VizSEC* (2012), 64–71.

30. van Ham, F., and van Wijk, J. J. Interactive visualization of small world graphs. In *IEEE InfoVis* (2004), 199–206.

31. Wattenberg, M. Visual exploration of multivariate graphs. In *ACM CHI* (2006), 811–819.

32. Welser, H. T., Gleave, E., Fisher, D., and Smith, M. Visualizing the signatures of social roles in online discussion groups. *JOSS 8*, 2 (2007).

Limiting, Leaving, and (re)Lapsing: An Exploration of Facebook Non-Use Practices and Experiences

Eric P. S. Baumer[1,2], Phil Adams[2], Vera D. Khovanskaya[2], Tony C. Liao[1], Madeline E. Smith[3], Victoria Schwanda Sosik[2], Kaiton Williams[2]

[1]Communication Department, Cornell   [2]Information Science Department, Cornell
[3]Technology & Social Behavior, Northwestern
{ericpsb, pja22, vdk9, cl566, vls48, kow2}@cornell.edu   madsesmith@u.northwestern.edu

ABSTRACT

Despite the abundance of research on social networking sites, relatively little research has studied those who choose not to use such sites. This paper presents results from a questionnaire of over 400 Internet users, focusing specifically on Facebook and those users who have left the service. Results show the lack of a clear, binary distinction between use and non-use, that various practices enable diverse ways and degrees of engagement with and disengagement from Facebook. Furthermore, qualitative analysis reveals numerous complex and interrelated motivations and justifications, both for leaving and for maintaining some type of connection. These motivations include: privacy, data misuse, productivity, banality, addiction, and external pressures. These results not only contribute to our understanding of online sociality by examining this under-explored area, but they also build on previous work to help advance how we conceptually account for the sociological processes of non-use.

Author Keywords

Facebook, non-use, technology refusal.

ACM Classification Keywords

H.5.m. Information interfaces and presentation (e.g., HCI): Miscellaneous.

INTRODUCTION

As of June 2012, Facebook boasts 955 million user accounts active monthly, with an average of 552 million users active daily [7]. Significant amounts of research have explored the use of Facebook and other similar social networking sites [see 4], examining the roles such sites play in their users' social lives.

But what about those who do not use Facebook? With close to a billion users, it can be difficult to remember that some people with Internet access do not use the social networking

site. Changing privacy controls, data ownership policies, and questions about the kinds of social interaction it affords have all contributed to a growing trend of users pointedly leaving Facebook. For example, on May 31, 2010, Quit Facebook Day [19] encouraged users to leave Facebook, listing a number of grievances and providing alternative venues for online socialization. While no Facebook collapse ensued—the site claims just over 40,000 "committed Facebook quitters"—the initiative arguably drew significant attention, both the popular media's and Facebook's, to this growing contingent of Facebook quitters [18].

So why study Facebook refusal as opposed to non-use of any other social technology? Consider, for example, Google's Gmail, which provides web-based email to hundreds of millions of users [6]. Despite its popularity, leaving Gmail does not carry the same significance as leaving Facebook, largely because of the unique social role Facebook plays for so many people—for example, 63% of U.S. adults have an online social networking account and of these, 93% are on Facebook [15]. Email is a platform available from many interoperable providers; if I have a Yahoo or MSN email account, I can still email someone with a Gmail account. Facebook, on the other hand, is a service that does not provide for similar interoperability; if I have a MySpace or Friendster or Orkut account, I cannot friend someone on Facebook. In short, refusing Facebook excludes me from social interaction in a way that refusing few other technologies would, thus making Facebook non-use an important area of study.

To the authors' knowledge, no mass exodus from Facebook has yet occurred, nor is one impending. However, it is difficult to know how many people have left Facebook, as the company does not publish such data. Moreover, no extant research examines the prevalence of leaving Facebook, the commonality of the desire to leave, types of opinions about leaving, or other practices of limiting Facebook use without leaving entirely. Furthermore, little is understood about what the leaving process entails or its personal and social ramifications [see 18 for an exception].

To address this gap, we present results from a questionnaire of over 400 Internet users about their use and/or non-use of Facebook. These results begin to paint a picture about the

Are you sure you want to deactivate your account?

Deactivating your account will disable your profile and remove your name and picture from most things you've shared on Facebook. Some information may still be visible to others, such as your name in their friends list and messages you sent.

Your 209 friends will no longer be able to keep in touch with you.

Chris will miss you   Amanda will miss you   Anju will miss you   Josef will miss you   Silvia will miss you

Send Silvia a Message

Send Anju a Message   Send Josef a Message

Send Amanda a Message

Send Chris a Message

Figure 1. After choosing to deactivate, a Facebook user is shown a confirmation screen with several of their friends' profile pictures, messages saying their friends will miss them, and a survey (not pictured) asking why they want to deactivate their account.

prevalence of leaving Facebook, providing two primary contributions. First, there does not exist a strict binary distinction between use and non-use. Through qualitative analysis of stories told by respondents, we find a broad array of practices enacting varied degrees and styles of engagement with and disengagement from Facebook. Second, our analysis provides an account of the motivations and justifications that respondents provide for these varying degrees of (non)use. Thus, this paper helps deepen and add nuance to discussions in HCI about non-use, opting out, and the sociological processes by which technologies are deemed inappropriate, undesirable, or unwanted.

BACKGROUND

Motivations for use of Facebook are well studied. Joinson, for example, describes seven Facebook uses and gratifications, which were also associated with user demographics and site visit patterns [10]. Further, research has explored the way people using Facebook manage their online self-presentation, for example using separate profiles for professional and personal networks [5]. Hughes et al. demonstrate personality as a predictor of preference between Facebook and Twitter [9], while Ryan and Xenos correlate frequency of Facebook use and preference for particular Facebook features with personality traits such as loneliness, shyness, and narcissism [22]. The Facebook user population and their motivations for use, however, are moving targets that change over time.

Recent research about conflicts occurring on Facebook is both timely (as of 2011-12, 49% of adults and 88% of teens have witnessed unkind or offensive behavior on SNS [13,21]) and begins to reveal reasons for limiting Facebook usage. McLaughlin and Vitak [16] explore the fallout of Facebook norm violation among college students, finding 'unfriending' to be a common response. Gershon finds romantic relationship conflict (external to Facebook) a reported reason for quitting Facebook [8].

Non-use of Facebook is less well-explored. From a personality perspective, Facebook non-users may be more conscientious and socially lonely, and less extraverted and narcissistic, than Facebook users [22]. Some see Facebook

abstention and quitting as deliberate and often very political statements by the non-user. Portwood-Stacer posits Facebook refusal as a performative mode of resistance within the context of today's consumer culture [18]. Karppi describes Facebook quitting through the lens of digital suicide services such as seppukoo.com, which keeps a Facebook account active but disconnects it from its human owner; over time, basic information in the profile, friend lists, and browsing data, change independently of the original human account owner [11]. Rather than associate personality characteristics with non-users or highlight political statements made by quitting Facebook, this paper explores the motivations for stepping back from Facebook.

While non-use of Facebook has been less explored, researchers have studied non-use of technology more generally [e.g., 3, 12]. Perhaps the most broadly applicable typologies of non-users are Wyatt's four dimensions [27] and Satchell and Dourish' six varieties of non-use [23]. Wyatt broadly clusters non-users into four categories: *resisters*, *rejectors*, the *excluded*, and the *expelled*. These categories are clearly arranged over two dimensions: (1) those who have joined and are now non-users (rejecters and the expelled) vs. those who never used the technology (resisters and the excluded), and (2) intrinsic choice (rejecters and resisters) vs. external constraints (the excluded and the expelled). Satchell and Dourish lend more nuance to these four, describing six varieties of non-use particular to HCI: *lagging adoption*, those who have not yet adopted the technology; *active resistance*, essentially diehard laggards; *disenchantment*, a sense that the technology is in some sense inauthentic; *disenfranchisement*, barriers to entry or continued adoption; *displacement*, broadly second-hand use; and *disinterest*.

HOW TO LEAVE

At the time of this writing, Facebook makes available two ways to disengage from their service. First, a user may deactivate her or his account. Upon deactivation, all data provided or uploaded by the user becomes hidden; the user's friends no longer see that user, as if s/he has disappeared. However, all the data are still retained. A user who has deactivated her or his account can still log in to Facebook (or use their account to log into another site via Facebook Connect) and, in so doing, will reactivate the account. A user can deactivate her or his account using an option under security settings, but before the deactivation is complete, s/he will see the confirmation screen in Figure 1.

The other option, somewhat less readily apparent, deletes a user's account. Doing so permanently removes a user's data from Facebook's servers, and Facebook provides no means for recovering these data. From friends' perspectives, the effect is the same: the user simply disappears. Deletion also has a two-week safety period; if the user logs in to Facebook (or Facebook Connect) within two weeks of deleting, the account is fully restored, much like logging in to reactivate a deactivated account. A user can delete her or his account through Facebook's help page, which fully describes what the deletion process involves.

METHODS
Our study is driven by three general research questions:

RQ1: What is the prevalence of both actual Facebook non-use and consideration of non-use?

RQ2: In what practices do Facebook non-users engage, and what is the prevalence of these various practices?

RQ3: What motivations are used to justify, and what experiences surround, Facebook non-use?

Data Collection
To explore these questions, we adapted the methods of Rader et al. [20], who used a short survey to elicit stories about issues related to computer security. Similarly, we developed a questionnaire with two types of questions.

The first type asked straightforward, factual questions about Facebook usage. These included mostly yes/no or Likert-style questions about whether the respondent currently has an account, when s/he first signed up, which features s/he uses most often, which features s/he most values, what other channels s/he uses to communicate with friends and family (email, Twitter, Skype, etc.), whether s/he had ever deactivated or deleted her or his account, whether the respondent knew anyone who had deleted her or his account, whether s/he had ever considered deleting or deactivated her or his own account, and similar questions.

The second portion of the questionnaire explored the experience of deactivating or deleting through a set of open-ended, free text questions about these practices experiences. Inspired by Rader et al. [20], all respondents were asked to tell a story about a time when they or someone they knew either left Facebook or systematically limited their use of it in some way.

Additionally, some portions of the questionnaire were either shown or hidden depending on responses to certain questions. For example, respondents who had deleted their account were asked to describe how they made the decision

and what happened afterward. Those who had not deactivated or deleted their account but had considered doing so were asked to describe a time that made them consider leaving. Respondents who had never had a Facebook account were asked why they did not. The factual questions about use and non-use similarly adapted to respondents' answers. For example, respondents who did not currently have an account were not shown questions about their most used or favorite features. Those who had deactivated or deleted their account were asked how happy they were with that decision. Respondents who had not deactivated or deleted their account were asked if they had ever considered doing so.

The questionnaire concluded with demographic information, including age, gender, occupation, and city, state/province, and country of residence, all provided via free text responses. A full description of the questionnaire instrument and anonymized response data can be found at http://hdl.handle.net/1813/30908.

The questionnaire was distributed via several relevant email listservs, including air-l@listserv.aoir.org, chi-announcements@listserv.acm.org, and chi-web@acm.org, as well as via snowball sampling on Facebook, Twitter, and other channels. Recruitment text read, "*Do you use Facebook? We want to hear from you. Do you not use Facebook? We want to hear from you, too. We're interested in people limiting their Facebook usage in some way, including deactivating or deleting their account,*" followed by a brief synopsis of the study goals. In addition, respondents were asked to forward the questionnaire to or provide email addresses for anyone they thought might be interested. The data on which we report here were gathered over two and a half weeks from June 20 to July 8, 2012.

Analysis
While we provide below some statistical analysis of yes/no and Likert responses, this paper focuses primarily on analysis of the qualitative data.

Responses to the open-ended free text questions were analyzed in two stages. First, the questions were divided among the authors, such that each author read through all respondents' responses to one or more of the questions. Each author worked independently and iteratively developed a list of themes for each question using open coding [14]. The authors then met and discussed the themes and patterns that each had observed, noting both resonances and differences among responses to the different questions.

Based on this discussion, the authors also generated a list of codes and themes that might be associated with one another. Some codes pertained to thematic concerns, such as privacy, others to attributes of a respondent, such as whether the respondent was tech savvy. These codes pertained only to the respondent and her or his experience, not to stories s/he may have told about others.

This list of codes became the basis for the second stage of the analysis. In this stage, respondents were divided among the authors, such that each author read through responses to all questions for a subset of the respondents. Each respondent was then coded by the assigned author. After coding was completed, each set of respondents was rotated to a different author, who confirmed agreement with the initial author's coding. Disagreements were discussed and resolved in a pairwise fashion between the first and second coders for each respondent. This process was not intended to establish inter-rater reliability, and the coding does not play a pivotal role in the analyses. Rather, this coding process served as another iteration in developing and refining not only our understanding of the themes in the data but also the relationships among them.

RESULTS

This section presents three types of results. First, it gives a quantitative description of who our respondents are and how they use (or don't use) Facebook (RQ1). Second, it provides a descriptive summary of the stories respondents told and the accounts they gave about practices of leaving Facebook (RQ2). Third, it presents interpretive results that draw on themes from respondents' experiences to describe motivations for their varied degrees of (non)use (RQ3). The second and third portions of the results come from the iterative interpretive analysis described above. When possible, extended quotes are accompanied with gender, age, and occupation demographics.

Profile of Respondents

We received nearly 500 responses. Empty responses, nonsensical responses, and responses by people under 18 were removed (the latter for IRB compliance), leaving N=410 respondents. All but 20 of these respondents completed the entire questionnaire, although due to the addition or removal of questions based on previous responses, as described above, no respondent answered every question. Fifty respondents provided incomplete demographic data (commonly omitting gender, age, or hometown). After removing responses that lasted more than 10 hours, which we assume took place over multiple sessions, the questionnaire took on average 22 minutes (median 10, st. dev. 55).

When asked their gender, 199 respondents replied female, 160 male, 2 gender neutral, 1 transgender, 1 identified as non-male, and 47 did not share their gender. Ages spanned

19 to 76 (mean 35, median 33); 48 respondents did not share their age. While respondents reported having careers as varied as civil service, veterinary medicine, publishing, homemaking, and missionary roles, a large proportion (168/410, 41%) of respondents were academics, either graduate students, post-docs, professors, researchers, or lecturers. Furthermore, we identified 52/410 (12.7%) respondents as 'tech savvy,' based on having training, a career, or other evidence of expertise in IT. Our respondents spanned six continents, with the majority from the US and Europe. Respondents initially joined Facebook between Facebook's inception in 2004 and 2012. Three respondents indicated (apparently without jest) membership since 2003. Sizes of respondents' Facebook networks ranged from 0 to 2489 reported friends (mean 311, median 249).

Motivations for first joining, and continuing to use, Facebook fit to a large extent within Joinson's [10] seven uses and gratifications: social connection, shared identities, photographs, content, social investigation, social network surfing, and status updating. Motivations that do not fit well into these categories come largely from effects of increased Facebook adoption since Joinson's publication in 2008 (e.g. *"because everyone else has one it's often the most convenient way to communicate with groups."* Professional and social pressures now sometimes suggest Facebook as the only accepted mode of communication and membership, such as enrolling as a member of a class or club, or to stay in touch with others:

"When I finished my PhD, my advisor told me that if I ever wanted to keep in touch with her, I'd have to join. So I did. I had managed to avoid it until then." - F, 35, Researcher

Lastly, following companies and 'liking' others' content only became available after 2008. Figure 2 summarizes how frequently respondents reported using various Facebook features over the preceding month. Liking and commenting on others' content, as well as general lurking behavior, were reported more frequently.

Deactivating and Deleting

Of our respondents, 110 (26.8%) reported having deactivated their account, of whom 73 (66.4%) reported being "somewhat happy" or "very happy" with their decision. A total of 46 (11.2%) reported deleting their account, with 42 (91.3%) "somewhat happy" or "very happy" with the decision and none "very unhappy" (Figure

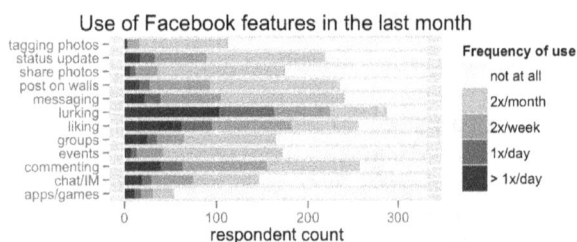

Figure 2. Respondents' reported use of Facebook features in the month preceding the questionnaire.

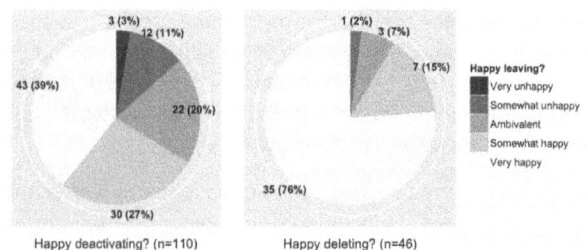

Figure 3: Respondents reported being happy with their decision to deactivate (left) or delete (right) their account.

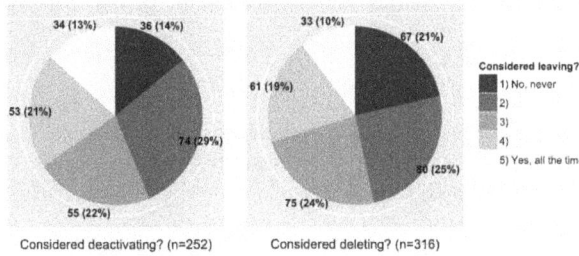

Figure 4. The extent to which users considered leaving Facebook by deactivating (left) or deleting (right) their account.

3). 28 people reported both deactivating and deleting their account. We also asked those who had never deactivated their account or never deleted their account to what extent they had considered doing so (Figure 4). Respondents considered deactivation slightly more often than deletion, but not significantly so (Mann-Whitney, p=0.10 two-tailed).

Knowing someone else who had left Facebook differently affected deactivation and deletion. Respondents who knew someone that had deactivated were almost three times as likely to deactivate their account (χ^2_1=14.3,p<0.001), but knowing someone who had deleted had no effect on a respondent's likelihood of deleting their account (Table 1). Conversely, knowing someone who deactivated did not make a respondent more likely to consider deactivating, but knowing someone who had deleted did make them more likely to consider deleting their account (Mann-Whitney, p=0.03 one-tailed). These results address RQ1 by providing a sense for the prevalence of both consideration of and the actual act of leaving Facebook.

Deactivated	Yes	No		Deleted	Yes	No
Knows	99	181		Knows	30	174
Does not	10	70		Does not	15	141

Table 1: Whether respondent does or does not know someone who has deactivated (left) or deleted (right) vs. whether respondent has deactivated or deleted their own account.

Stories and Practices

This section addresses RQ2 by describing the practices of respondents who choose not to use Facebook in the first place, to leave the site, or to limit their use of it. Figure 5 shows this variety of practices. This section draws on both first hand stories from our respondents describing their own

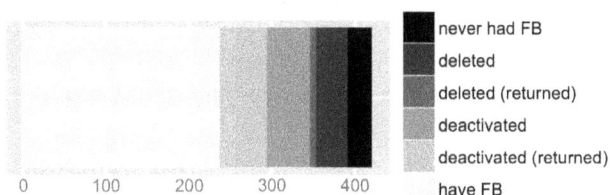

Figure 5: Proportions of our participants who currently have a Facebook account, deactivated their account then returned, deactivated and stayed away, deleted their account then returned, deleted and stayed away, and never had an account.

use and third-person accounts about their contacts, each quote or description making its source clear.

Resisting

Of our 410 respondents, 75 reported not having a Facebook account, either active or deactivated. While some respondents reported simply not having a use for the site, others provided elaborate lists of reasons they would not join. Some did not want to be on display or live "life in a global aquarium." We also observed a sense of rebelliousness and pride among those who resisted Facebook. As one respondent explained:

"I'm a non conformist. I was never interested by it. It is a passive way of keeping making friends. Now that people can friend company's [sic], I feel my choice was right. I abhor commercialism." - M, 42, UX Designer

These reasons given by non-users are closely related to those of former users who have since decided to leave the site, as described in the next sub-section.

Leaving

Of our 410 respondents, 127 indicated that they had deleted or deactivated their Facebook accounts at some point, but only 45 of them described doing so permanently. A few mentioned leaving Facebook with the help of friends or during the 2010 Quit Facebook Day. Many other respondents described attempting to delete their accounts and having difficulty doing so. For example:

"I tried to permanently close my account but apparently I only deactivated it [...]. This survey has made me aware that there is another procedure to remove my account permanently, although I doubt whether I will be able to find it since I looked for this before! This is one of the reasons I want to quit: if you can't quit easily I don't trust the application." - F, 49, Academic Researcher

Rather than delete or deactivate their account, some respondents described more creative work-arounds:

"I set up a junk e-mail account and set Facebook to send all its crap updates and alerts to that account, which I never use and am never tempted to access. I avoided deactivating the account directly, because I believed and do, that it can pull one back psychologically. The mail shunt works better." - F, 38, Sociologist

A wide variety of reactions followed deactivation or deletion. A few respondents, particularly those who had not previously been heavy users, indicated little had changed:

"I was not really using it after a couple years and just decided to close my account. Nothing happened afterward other than it was one less thing to worry about." - M, 30, Engineer

One respondent described accidentally locking himself out of his account, coming to terms with life without Facebook, and ultimately permanently deleting his account:

"One night I got really drunk and changed my Facebook password to something I thought would be easier to remember. When I woke up and realised I had no idea what I had changed it to, [...] I realised I was locked out. I was surprised that it made me a bit anxious for a couple of hours. After that I realised I felt great, that actually I'd been thinking and talking about how stupid, pointless, and time-wasting the damn thing was for ages, let alone the fact that I was giving a corporation all of my personal details and habits for free.

"I left it like that for a year, then spent a couple of days going through the process of regaining my password from them so I could permanently delete it. [...] These days I have no regrets at all - I much prefer twitter[...]" - M, 29, Admin Manager

While in some ways this case is exceptional, a few respondents mentioned switching to other SNS, including Twitter, Google+, and LinkedIn.

(re)Lapsing

An additional 59 respondents described leaving Facebook but subsequently returning. A number of these respondents never intended to leave permanently and some even described periodically deactivating their accounts with intentions of returning. For example, one respondent wrote:

"I deactivated 2 or 3 times during my finals. I used to get distracted during the final week. I was happy to get back afterward." F, 25, Student

Other respondents left Facebook without any intention of returning but later found themselves back on the site. Some of these respondents were happy to return, either because they took specific steps, such as 'unfriending' hundreds of their friends, or, as one put it, they *"somehow [...] got a more positive experience the second time around"*. In other cases, respondents described returning for a specific purpose and limiting use of their reactivated accounts to accomplish those tasks while avoiding the aspects of the site that initially drove them away. For example:

"I deleted my account permanently in May 2010. However, when I went to India to do fieldwork, I found that I couldn't avoid facebook and do my participation so I have a research-contacts only account." - F, 31, PhD Candidate

Limiting

We also heard from respondents who had not left Facebook but had systematically limited their use of the site, such as the email shunt described above. A few respondents asked someone else to change their password so they would temporarily be unable to access their accounts:

"I was writing my dissertation and found FB to be my number one distraction. I had my husband change my password and he'd log me on once a week or so as a treat." - F, 39, Postdoctoral Fellow

Others used technical means of blocking or limiting their access such as browser add-ons or changing settings:

"I also set up my browser to forward me to a more productive URL (Github, a social code website where I keep software code) whenever I typed in Facebook. This reminded me of what I should be doing, and kept facebook off of my mind." - F, 23, Graduate Student

The Left Behind

When people leave or limit their use of Facebook, they impact not only themselves but also those who connect with them on Facebook. One respondents highlighted this issue:

"There's this very annoying social problem when one limits their Facebook use, which I recently did. Do you announce it? Publicly? Or to those you just want to keep around? How long do you keep the announcement up? [...]" - F, 34, PhD Student

A few respondents explicitly stated that their limiting or leaving elicited questions, concerns, and pressures from their online friends.

"The people I actually cared about asked me if something was wrong in my life. I hard [sic] through the grapevine that other people I cared less about had suspected I had defriended or blocked them, and were asking around (but never came directly to me)." - F, 25, Engineer

Conversely, some respondents talked about how a friend leaving Facebook made them feel or how it impacted their relationship with the person. In some instances, Facebook was the sole mode of contact between friends, and the friend leaving resulted in less or no communication.

"One acquaintance deactivated his account without warning anyone first, and the fact that he was suddenly not contactable through Facebook dismayed a lot of people. [...] a lot of his friends were not in the same country as him and used Facebook as a primary mode of communication; although they could email him, this was not the norm and many said they didn't want to do that." - F, 23, Postgraduate Student

Even when friends have other ways of communicating outside Facebook, the departure can negatively impact certain types of communication.

"Recently a good friend of mine deactivated her FB account [...] But now I feel somehow disconnected or distanced to her, which is very strange because we see each other a few times a week and exchange e-mails almost everyday [...]; but I still feel like I know less about her now." - F, 23, Grad Student

Motivations

This subsection shifts to more interpretive analysis, addressing RQ3 by identifying thematic motivations and justifications for respondents' varied styles and degrees of non-use. Due to the nature of our methods, we provide rough estimates rather than exact numbers for how often each theme was mentioned.

Privacy

Privacy emerged as a resounding theme, with over a quarter of respondents citing privacy concerns as an impetus for leaving, limiting, resisting, or considering leaving Facebook. "Privacy," however, was not an isolated, atomic concern, and manifested in various ways. In a general sense, users objected to the idea of being on display: "*living my life in a 'global aquarium'*" felt uncomfortable. The idea of someone "*being able to flip back through to several years ago with just a few clicks*" and "*knowing the most intimate details about friends as well as strangers*" affected the perceived "authenticity" of the users' relationships.

Users also cited concerns about privacy violations in professional relationships, with Facebook "*sharing information with potential employers.*" In cases of interpersonal conflict, Facebook provided content for harassment and blackmail in various relationships, as discussed later. Many users felt that the violations they experienced on Facebook happened because, as an entity, Facebook "*disrespected and devalued*" the idea of privacy.

Data Use and Misuse
In addition to privacy, a separate set of concerns highlighted data ownership, control, and misuse, cited by about a fifth of respondents. In contrast to privacy concerns, which dealt with other users seeing personal information, many respondents expressed concerns about the (mis)use of personal information by Facebook itself. They described concerns with Facebook's data policies and practices and did not "*trust Facebook to adequately protect [their] information and keep it private.*"

Respondents perceived Facebook's policies as an inconstant and even "*insidious*" document. One user described the rationale of his friend quitting:

"*He used [Facebook] too infrequently to keep up with the constant changes to the default privacy settings...better to erase any chance of misuse of the information on his account by deleting it.*" - M, 25, Graduate Student

Distrustful of Facebook, respondents were wary of new default privacy settings that come with each policy change, settings they must manually alter.

"*Every time they screw with the privacy settings. Every time I learn something more about how they collect data and use it.*" - demographics not provided

These are seen as "*unannounced changes in privacy settings*" that happen under the table with a lack of "*transparency*" in the data-usage agreements. Respondents also recounted rumors about Facebook's practices—"*Heard that you can never really delete your account*"—and the difficulty they experienced in trying to change their privacy settings or to delete their accounts. They also speculated on what their mined data points were being used for:

"*I want to limit the amount of information I disclose about myself and 'hand over' to corporations who profit from this at the expense of my privacy.*" - F, 31, Graduate Student

Banality
About a sixth of respondents perceived Facebook as banal: trivial, uninteresting, and a waste of time. One user said:

"*I was tired of using Facebook without getting much in return —the majority of the discussions going on (as status updates) are very shallow and trivial. Basically, I thought FB was a big waste of my time.*" - M, 32, PhD Student

Others specifically highlighted discussions occurring on Facebook that were not of interest to them. For some it was political or religious discussions that were banal, for others it was seeing photos of other people's babies. Such content was either not what they expected or not sufficiently interesting. These respondents did not mention whether they had tried to use Facebook's built-in filtering features to limit the amount of, or whose, content they see.

Respondents also spoke to the banality of Facebook relationships. Many of these respondents described these interactions as inauthentic and did not "*appreciate the types of interactions it [Facebook] encourages[...].*" One respondent tied this inauthenticity to a sense of lurking in others' lives without rich contact:

"*I had realized that I mostly just looked at what people posted and considered myself up to date on their lives without any contact. I didn't like the feeling of being included in someones [sic] life without actually being in it.*" - M, 28, Post-doc

Productivity
On the opposite end of the spectrum from those who found it uninteresting, about a fifth of respondents found Facebook too interesting and felt they had to take the step of deleting or deactivating their accounts during times where they needed to concentrate on work. Here's one user:

"*I do it [deactivate] during exam periods, mostly. When I know I'll be easily distracted, I deactivate the account, and reactivate it after the exams.*" - M, 21, Student

While a variety of respondents reported deactivating during high stress periods, our coding showed a strong correlation between academics and productivity concerns. Productivity may not be as salient for others, such as office workers whose IT infrastructure blocks access to Facebook. However, we suspect Facebook may impact productivity for others whose work environments are less strictly controlled, such as consultants or freelancers.

Addiction, Withdrawal, and Envy of the Disconnected
In these discussions of banality and productivity, Facebook was often described as superficial yet addictive. After deleting his account, one respondent said:

"*Afterward I went through facebook withdrawal. I would be sitting at my computer and feel the need to login to facebook [...]*" - M, 28, Post-doc

Another respondent described working with a friend to "*limit each other [sic] use of FB and the internet more generally through shaming techniques.*" Many of the respondents who had not left or had left and then returned looked up to those who had successfully quit or who never signed up for Facebook as paragons of virtue. Those who had successfully left often referred to a palpable sense of relief once they no longer felt bound to the site. While only a few respondents explicitly mentioned being addicted to Facebook, about a tenth of respondents described other experiences—withdrawal, shaming, admiration and envy of those who stopped using—consistent with addiction.

Social, Professional, and Institutional Pressures
Not everyone who left did so out of self-directed action. About a seventh of our respondents limited use of or left the site due to varied types of pressures from other people, both on and off Facebook, or from institutions such as work. In these cases, the network begins to represent a realized space that has to be bounded and avoided in a manner similar to physical locations. In some cases these pressures resulted from the need to maintain professional boundaries:

"One of my friends is a TA and closed her account when her students started trying to add her." - M, 26, Statistician

Other Facebook users found themselves "stalked" or "tracked down" by certain individuals, and they limited their use of or left Facebook to prevent these behaviors. Such limiting or leaving often occurred following the dissolution of a romantic relationship when the Facebook user no longer wanted to be in contact with their ex-partner:

"One [friend left or limited use of Facebook] when they got divorced so their ex-partner could no longer follow them on [Facebook]." - F, 45, Postgrad Student

Sometimes use of the site itself creates pressures within a romantic relationship, and the user changes Facebook habits to help ease the tension.

"A friend deactivated her facebook account due to a conflict with a partner over some of her online communications (spending too much time online, contact with individuals that brought stress to the relationship)." - F, 36, Administrator

While previous work found that romantic relationships led to changes in use, e.g, posting different types of pictures, that work found less evidence for leaving or limiting [28].

Respondents also recounted stories about users who were required to alter their use of Facebook because of their occupation or legal troubles:

"My brother in law deleted his facebook account. He is a military officer, and I think taht [sic] the institution made him do this." - M, 29, Doctorate Student

"My friend deleted his facebook account because he was convicted of a crime and the victim threatened to report that he had breached his parole by being on facebook[...] He deleted his account before it became a problem because he wanted to avoid repercussions [...]." - F, 24, Masters Student

While deleting an account to avoid going to jail was not typical, these accounts demonstrate the variety in the types of pressures participants felt. This non-volitional leaving of Facebook resembles to some extent Wyatt's [27] description of the *excluded* or the *expelled*, as discussed below.

DISCUSSION
The results above describe not only the varying degrees and types of dis/engagement with/from Facebook, but also the motivations and justifications respondents gave therefor. This section considers relationships between these findings and previous work on the negation of technology.

Use and Non-use
We see here many resonances with previous work on non-use. Respondents who did not have an account could be described as actively resisting [23] Facebook. These include not only those who resisted using in the first place but also those who used Facebook once but do not any longer, i.e., resistors and rejectors [27]. Disenchantment [23] aligns with descriptions of the banality and inauthenticity of social interaction on Facebook, particularly in contrast to face-to-face communication, though we did not observe a nostalgic longing for "the way things were" or for a time gone by. The section above on pressures clearly aligns with Wyatt's [27] expelled category. While these pressures also resemble disenfranchisement [23], these cases were not due to geographic or socioeconomic configurations as much as to socio-institutional pressures, such as the case of the parolee described above. Also, while cases of respondents accessing Facebook via others after deactivation or deletion occurred, these were more often post-hoc coping strategies rather than arrangements of one person offering technology use as a service to others [23].

While Satchell and Dourish [23] note lagging adoption as the most common form of non-use in HCI, we found little evidence of it in our data. Those who did not use Facebook reported no intention of joining and provided well-reasoned explanations for their non-use, in contrast with lagging adopters who simply have not *yet* adopted the technology.

Instead, we saw something we term *lagging resistance,* a sense of wanting to quit but not doing so just yet. Large numbers of respondents who had so far neither deactivated nor deleted reported having considered doing so (see Figure 4). We see a variety of justifications for this lagging resistance throughout the results: simple external constraints, such as a PhD advisor insisting on Facebook-based communication until dissertation defense; network scale effects leading to the fear that non-use will result in isolation, missed events, etc.; and idolization of active resisters and quitters making their level of non-use seem unattainable. This point draws attention to the social role of Facebook limiters and leavers.

Symbolic Functions and Deproblematizing the Non-user
Typologies of technology non-use and non-users often problematized them, for example, highlighting barriers to entry [e.g., 25] and developing policy initiatives to stimulate use [e.g., 26]. Other research has found that network structure can also increase likelihood of adoption [24]. Commentators, particularly those in science and technology studies, have called instead for the role and perspective of the non-user to be recognized and valued

[e.g., 23,27]. For example, resistance to early telephone and electrical technology, particularly among rural populations, led producers to develop new designs and infrastructures better suited to rural life [12]. Thus, these non-users became important agents of sociotechnical change.

Our results suggest that social pressures can similarly stigmatize non-use as a deviant behavior; one would leave Facebook only "if something was wrong." Just as various pressures can lead to non-volitional non-use [27], such pressures can also lead to non-volitional use.

The above results also show how limiting or leaving Facebook not only has important utilitarian consequences, e.g., impacting productivity, but also plays an important symbolic role. It can demonstrate commitment to a romantic partner [8,28] or serve as means of rejecting a consumption-driven identity [18]. On one hand, the performative nature of such active resistance can frame refusal as something for an elite and therefore not emulable. On the other hand, the performative nature of such refusal may help account for the network effect where knowing someone else who had deactivated increased a respondent's likelihood of doing so. We suspect a similar effect does not occur for deletion because deletion is more permanent, while deactivation allows the curious user to experiment with non-use. At a higher level, just as network effects can help explain the diffusion and adoption of new technologies [24], they may also help explain non-use or rejection.

Collectively, these points emphasize the importance of non-users. Seeing non-use only as problematic or deviant risks missing important insights that may be gained by treating non-use as a legitimate phenomenon of inquiry.

(un)Design Implications
Although somewhat tempting, we do not interpret the above results as an implication not to design [1], that there should not be a Facebook or that certain features should be eliminated. However, while respondents' leaving or limiting was not precipitated by the researchers, this work could be seen as what Baumer and Silberman call "technological extravention" [1], i.e., studying the removal of a technology. Similarly, we would not necessarily suggest that someone should "undesign" Facebook by displacing it, erasing it, or using other strategies that Pierce [17] describes. However, there may be possibilities for Facebook to include more varied self-inhibiting options [17] beyond simple deactivation or deletion. Whether Facebook's owners and designers are interested in facilitating more nuanced varieties of non-use, though, is another question entirely, one that is beyond the scope of this paper.

LIMITATIONS
While our questionnaire elicited interesting and provocative stories, it did not allow for follow-up questions, as interviews would, and sometimes generated terse responses.

Also, recruitment may have impacted our sample in at least two ways. First, despite the open recruitment text, people

strongly opposed to Facebook may have been more likely to respond, creating a self-selection bias. While such a bias may be problematic for questions of representativeness (RQ1), it may have helped for understanding practices of and motivations for non-use (RQ2 and RQ3), since those questions require a more purposive sample. Second, the prevalence of academics may have impacted the importance of some motivations, such as productivity concerns, as noted above, or data (mis)use and privacy, since these are popular topics of academic research on SNS. However, privacy issues also feature prominently in popular media [18], suggesting this theme may occur more broadly.

Finally, since this exploratory study sought to be as open-ended as possible, we simply collected stories rather than ask about specific motivations or experiences. Thus, the proportions for each theme may not be representative; a respondent not mentioning, say, addiction does not mean s/he has not experienced it. Future work should examine each theme and motivation more closely.

FUTURE WORK
While questionnaire responses gave us many rich personal narratives, the medium of pre-made questions yielded responses that were often ambiguous and hinted at more insights "under the surface." Future work should use such techniques interviews, focus groups, diaries, and others to explore deeper. Our sample was also heavily biased towards academics and excluded minors; future work should examine non-use among particular populations, such as teens or certain socio-economic groups.

Also, as noted above, better theoretical understandings are needed of the interplay between technology design and non-use. Significant effort has helped theorize the roles that technology can play in society [e.g., 2]. We suggest there is space for developing equally important theoretical accounts for the roles that non-use or refusal of technology play. As described above, previous work on non-use [23,27] does not fully account for use followed by non-use (potentially followed by re-use), nor for the lagging resistance we observed. We see this area as ripe for theorization.

Finally, respondents hinted at a dynamic between Facebook users and non-users: users regarded non-users with both non-understanding and reverence. Future work should examine further such perceptions.

CONCLUSION
Just as HCI research attends to motivations for technology use [10], we should similarly attend to motivations for not using technology [23] as well as understanding social ramifications of non-use. This paper does so through a questionnaire of over 400 Facebook users and non-users. Results show that non-use is not an atomic category but encompasses a broad array of practices. This paper provides an understanding of both the variety of those practices and the motivations and justifications given therefor. Thus, we contribute to developing an understanding of the

sociological processes of determining what technologies are (in)appropriate and in which contexts.

ACKNOWLEDGMENTS

Thanks to our respondents for sharing their stories; to Steve Voida, Maria Hakansson, Emily Sun, Jamie Guillory, and the anonymous reviewers for helpful comments on earlier drafts; and to the Interaction Design Lab for helpful conversations. This material is based in part on work supported by the NSF under Grant Nos. DGE-1144153 and DGE-0824162.

REFERENCES

1. Baumer, E.P.S., & Silberman, M.S. (2011). When the Implication Is Not to Design (Technology). *Proc CHI*, 2271-2274. Vancouver, BC.

2. Bijker, W. E., Hughes, T. P., & Pinch, T. J. (Eds.). (1989). The Social Construction of Technological Systems. Cambridge, MA: MIT Press.

3. Birnholtz, J. (2010). Adopt, adapt, abandon: Understanding why some young adults start, and then stop, using instant messaging. *Computers in Human Behavior, 26*, 6, 1427–1433.

4. boyd, d. m., & Ellison, N. B. (2007). Social network sites: Definition, history, and scholarship. Journal of Computer-Mediated Communication, 13(1), article 11.

5. DiMicco, J. M., & Millen, D. R. (2007). Identity management: multiple presentations of self in Facebook. *Proc. GROUP*.

6. D'Orazio, D. (2012). Gmail now has 425 million total users. *The Verge*. June 28, 2012.

7. Facebook Newsroom. http://newsroom.fb.com/content/ default.aspx?NewsAreaId=22. Accessed Sept 8, 2012.

8. Gershon, I. (2011). Un-Friend My Heart: Facebook, Promiscuity, and Heartbreak in a Neoliberal Age. *Anthropological Quarterly, 14*, 4, 865–894.

9. Hughes, D. J., Rowe, M., Bately, M., & Lee, A. (2012). A tale of two sites: Twitter vs. Facebook and the personality predictors of social media usage. *Computers in Human Behavior, 28*, 2, 561–569.

10. Joinson, A. Looking at, looking up or keeping up with people?: Motives and use of Facebook. *Proc. CHI 2008*, 1027–1036.

11. Karppi, T. (2011). Digital suicide and the biopolitics of leaving Facebook. *Transformations, 20*.

12. Kline, R. (2003). Resisting Consumer Technology in Rural America: The Telephone and Electrification. In N. Oudshoorn & T. Pinch (Eds.), How Users Matter (pp. 51-66). Cambridge, MA: MIT Press.

13. Lenhart, A., Madden, M., Smith, A., Purrcell, K., Zickuhr, K., & Rainie, L. (2011). Teens, kindness and cruelty on social networks sites. Pew Research Center's Internet and American Life Project.

14. Lofland, J., & Lofland, L. H. (1994). *Analyzing Social Settings: A Guide to Qualitative Observation and Analysis*. Belmont, CA: Wadsworth.

15. Madden, M. (2012). Privacy management on social media sites. Pew Research Center's Internet and American Life Project.

16. McLaughlin, C., & Vitak, J. (2011). Norm evolution and violation on Facebook. *New Media & Society, 14*, 2, 299–315.

17. Pierce, J. (2012). Undesigning Technology: Considering the Negation of Design by Design. *Proc CHI*, 957-966. Austin, TX.

18. Portwood-Stacer, L. (forthcoming). Media Refusal and Conspicous Non-Consumption: The Performative and Political Dimensions of Facebook Abstention. *New Media & Society*.

19. Quit Facebook Day. http://www.quitfacebookday.com/. Accessed Sept 8, 2012.

20. Rader, E., Wash, R., & Brooks, B. (2012). Stories as Informal Lessons about Security. *Proc SOUPS*. Washington, D.C.

21. Rainie, L., Lenhart, A., & Smith, A. (2012). The tone of life on social networking sites. Pew Research Center's Internet and American Life Project.

22. Ryan, T., & Xenos, S. (2011). Who uses Facebook? An investigation into the relationship between the Big Five, shyness, narcissism, loneliness, and Facebook usage. *Computers in Human Behavior, 27*, 5, 1658–1664.

23. Satchell, C., & Dourish, P. (2009). Beyond the user: use and non-use in HCI. *Proc. OZCHI 2009*, 9-16.

24. Ugander, J., Backstrom, L., Marlow, C., & Kleinberg, J. (2012). Structural diversity in social contagion. *Proceedings of the National Academy of Sciences*, 109(16), 5962–5966.

25. Van Dijk, J. (2005). *The deepening divide: Inequality in the information society*. Thousand Oaks, CA: Sage.

26. Verdegem, P., & Verhoest, P. (2009). Profiling the non-user: Rethinking policy initiatives stimulating ICT acceptance. *Telecomm. Policy, 33*, 10-11, 642–652.

27. Wyatt, S. (2005). Non-users also matter: The construction of users and non-users of the Internet. In N. Oudshoorn & T. Pinch (Eds.), *How users matter* (pp. 67–79). Cambridge, MA: MIT Press.

28. Zhao, X., Sosik, V. S., & Cosley, D. (2012). It's Complicated: How Romantic Partners Use Facebook. *Proc CHI*, 771-780. Austin, TX.

Predicting Postpartum Changes in Emotion and Behavior via Social Media

Munmun De Choudhury   **Scott Counts**   **Eric Horvitz**

Microsoft Research, One Microsoft Way, Redmond WA 98052

{munmund, counts, horvitz}@microsoft.com

ABSTRACT

We consider social media as a promising tool for public health, focusing on the use of Twitter posts to build predictive models about the influence of childbirth on the forthcoming behavior and mood of new mothers. Using Twitter posts, we quantify postpartum changes in 376 mothers along dimensions of social engagement, emotion, social network, and linguistic style. We then construct statistical models from a training set of observations of these measures before and after the reported childbirth, to forecast significant postpartum changes in mothers. The predictive models can classify mothers who will change significantly following childbirth with an accuracy of 71%, using observations about their prenatal behavior, and as accurately as 80-83% when additionally leveraging the initial 2-3 weeks of postnatal data. The study is motivated by the opportunity to use social media to identify mothers at risk of postpartum depression, an underreported health concern among large populations, and to inform the design of low-cost, privacy-sensitive early-warning systems and intervention programs aimed at promoting wellness postpartum.

Author Keywords

behavioral health; childbirth; depression; emotion; health; language; postpartum; PPD; social media; Twitter; wellness

ACM Classification Keywords

H.3.4; H.5.2; H.5.3

INTRODUCTION

Having a baby is a major life event that creates significant changes in the lives of new parents. Sleep and daily routines are disrupted, and adjustments must be made in personal and professional lives. First time mothers may be particularly challenged with navigating the new, complex realm of caring for their newborn. Adding to the challenges, many new mothers experience psychological changes, such as the "baby blues," a temporary condition involving mild mood instability, anxiety, and depression. Beyond such relatively mild blues, a portion of new mothers experience

more extreme changes. According to the CDC[1], between 12 and 20 percent of new mothers report postpartum depression (a 13% incidence rate in a meta-analysis report [20]), a form of depression that typically begins in the first month after giving birth and is characterized by symptoms including sadness, guilt, exhaustion, and anxiety [16].

We examine social media as a tool in public health. Social media is a source of population data about behaviors, thoughts, and emotions, and can serve as record and sensor for events in peoples' lives. Whether in the form of explicit commentary, patterns of posting, or in the subtleties of language used, social media posts bear the potential to offer evidence as to how a person is affected by life events. Within this context, we investigate the feasibility of *forecasting* future behavioral changes of mothers following the important life event of childbirth. We extend our prior research that examines the value of harnessing social media signals to characterize changes in new mothers, along three dimensions: patterns of posting, linguistic style, and emotional expression [8]. These measures were used to explore the behavioral changes of a cohort of new mothers who showed large postpartum changes, including those showing increases in indicators of negative emotion and lowered posting volume.

Here, we focus on predicting significant changes in new mothers postpartum *in advance of their being exhibited*, including behavioral changes that may be associated with significant downturns in mood. We base predictions on prior behavioral patterns of new mothers as manifested on Twitter. We construct statistical models from training data to predict significant future changes in a test cohort. To construct and test the predictive models, we harness evidence from 33 different measures, spanning changes in posting behavior, ego-network, linguistic style, and emotional expression. We demonstrate that we are able to identify which new mothers will exhibit large changes several months into their postpartum phase, with a mean classification accuracy of 71% when we leverage behavioral data from only the prenatal period (i.e., *before* the birth of the baby). We obtain a considerable boost in prediction power, with accuracy in the range 80-83%, when we include in our evidential horizon data from the first few

---

[1] http://www.cdc.gov/reproductivehealth/Depression/

postnatal weeks. We find evidence that certain types of measures can be better predicted, including expression of negative affect, interpersonal pronoun use, and degree of interaction with one's network.

We see such predictions and predictive power as a step toward creating private, low-cost tools that can raise awareness among new mothers who are at the highest risk for suffering from postpartum depression (PPD), thus empowering them to seek understanding, as well as emotional support or professional assistance in a timely manner. More broadly we seek to highlight opportunities for studying the influence of major life events on people using public content shared in an online setting.

BACKGROUND

Risk and Presence of Postpartum Changes

Most attempts at understanding changes in behavior of mothers following childbirth focus on identifying the presence of PPD and on risk factors for PPD. We do not focus directly on identifying PPD, but find literature on PPD relevant, particularly from a methodological standpoint. PPD is underreported, with estimates that as many as 50% of cases of PPD go undetected [24], in part because even when mothers feel seriously depressed they do not seek help; one study reported that fewer than half of mothers suffering PPD report their depression [15]. We therefore believe that a predictive modeling effort can be especially valuable for early detection of PPD, given the major known challenges with detecting this condition [1].

Surveys such as the Postpartum Depression Predictors Inventory (PPDI) [2] reflect meta-analyses of risk factors for PPD [3], including prenatal depression, life stress, lack of social support, socioeconomic status, maternity blues, and infant temperament, among others (see also [19] for more on risks and influencers of PPD). Social support in particular has been shown to influence the attitudes, emotions, and behaviors of new mothers [11,29]. Neilson [18] identified social isolation and psychological stress, as significant predictors of PPD. Although some of these risk factors (e.g., socioeconomic status) are not easily inferred via social media posts, proxies for several factors could be monitored. For example, social support might be inferred from connectivity and the amount of social interaction a person has on social media. Infant temperament might be measured through posts the mother makes about her baby.

We do not yet understand the links between the measures we predict and PPD, nor do we propose the methods we present as a replacement for traditional PPD assessment and risk stratification. Rather, we explore the potential to use an analysis of online behavior to augment existing techniques for assessing changes in new mothers.

Social Media, Language, and Behavioral Prediction

The short history of using social media for behavioral assessment and prediction largely centers on population-scale measurement via retrospective or real-time studies. Facebook has been mined to create a happiness index that reveals the daily sentiment of people in the US [14]. Twitter posts reflect daily life patterns [12], and in the public health domain have been correlated with disease rates [22]. Sadelik et al. [25] study individual level predictions using Twitter data to estimate the likelihood that a person will become ill based on degree of co-location in the recent past, with others who became sick.

In the realm of psychological health, there is evidence that social media can serve both as an aid to mental health and as a data source for studying it. For instance, Facebook use has been shown to have positive influences on psychological well-being such as helping those with lower self-esteem to attain higher social capital [28]. Brubaker et al. [5] identify language features, including both sentiment and linguistic style features, of MySpace posts that correlate with expression of grief and distress around death of loved ones.

There is a growing understanding of the relationship among linguistic analysis, human behavior, and psychology. Text analysis has been used to identify markers of emotional closeness [13], as well as depression [17], anxiety, and other psychological disorders [6,21,23,30]. Even the process of writing has been found to help people cope with difficult situations, such as the loss of a job [27].

Weaving together several threads of prior research, the connections between social media, human experience, and text analysis suggest that linguistic, activity, and network oriented analyses of social media posts can offer a novel methodology for augmenting traditional approaches to measuring the influences of the birth of a child on mothers. For example, the frequency of use of first-person pronouns in writing has been found to be a correlate of depression [7]. This finding could be leveraged to help estimate *prenatal* depression, itself a strong predictor of PPD [3]. Motivated on these lines, in our previous work, we utilized a variety of such behavioral cues from Twitter, spanning activity, emotion and language in order to understand changes underwent by new mothers. In this paper, we show the extent to which these social media-based measures can *predict* ahead of time, extreme changes in activity and correlates of mood in new mothers following childbirth.

DATA

We begin by discussing our data collection methodology for predicting new mothers' behavioral changes in postpartum. We seek female Twitter users and follow a two-stage approach to construct a high-confidence sample of new mothers. We chose Twitter because it is public and provides a longitudinal record of the events, thoughts, and emotions experienced in daily life. Other topically relevant social media sources such as support forums for mothers tend to be explicitly problem-focused and lack per-person data density and longitudinal requirements for our study.

First, we identify posts that indicate a recent birth of a child on Twitter (English language posts only). We filter the Twitter Firehose stream (made available to us via a contract with Twitter) based on phrases typically used in newspaper announcements of births. We examined announcements in four newspapers, totaling 604 birth announcement posts in 2009-2012. Note that the phrases extracted from the newspaper announcements resonate with intuitions that parents announce the birth of their children in canonical ways, often including mention of the labor experience and reporting on the physical details of their newborn child, including gender, weight, and height. These phrases also tend to be unambiguous (e.g., "Announcing the birth of a new baby boy..."). We list in Table 1 examples of these phrases that we used as search queries to find birth events on Twitter. The authors of the resulting posts (2,929 posts in all between June 2011 and April 2012) constituted an initial set of candidate new mothers.

(1) birth, weigh*, pounds/lbs, inches, length/long, baby/son/daughter/boy/girl
(2) announc*, birth/arrival of, son/daughter/brother/sister
(3) are the parents of, son/daughter/boy/girl/baby
(4) welcome* home by, brother/sister/sibling*
(5) is the proud big brother/sister
(6) after, labor, born
(7) it's a boy/girl, born

Table 1. List of queries for identifying birth events on Twitter.

In the second step, we identify a high probability set of new mothers, first by performing gender inference via a classifier of first names trained on U.S. Census data, and then obtaining confidence ratings on these inferences from crowdworkers recruited through Amazon's Mechanical Turk interface. Specifically, we showed each worker (min. 95% approval rating, English language proficient, and familiar with Twitter) a set of 10 Twitter posts from each mother in our candidate set, such that five posts were posted right before the index childbirth post, and five after the post. Additional cues from the candidate mothers' Twitter profiles were also provided to enable better judgment—e.g., their Twitter profile bio, picture, and a link to their Twitter profile. The specific question posed to the crowdworkers involved choosing from a yes/no/maybe multiple-option menu, per candidate mother, to indicate if she was truly a new mother. We collected five ratings per candidate mother from the crowdworkers, and used the majority rating as the correct label, after independent inspection from two researchers (Fleiss-Kappa was 0.71).

The final dataset consisted of 376 validated new mothers, who exhibited strong evidence (on Twitter) of having given birth to a child at a time point between June 2011 and April 2012. Finally, for each of these 376 new mothers, we queried their public Twitter timelines in the Firehose stream to collect all of their posts in two three-month periods, corresponding to prenatal and postnatal phases, around the

point of childbirth. The choice of a three-month window for prenatal and postnatal data is motivated from PPD studies in the medical literature [14]. For instance, for a mother with evidence of childbirth in October 2011, the prenatal phase would correspond to data between July 2011 and September 2011, while the postnatal period would consist of data from November 2011 to January 2012. In this manner, the total timespan of our dataset is between March 2011 and July 2012, with a total of 36,948 posts from the 376 mothers during the prenatal period, and a total of 40,426 posts from the same mothers during postpartum.

MEASURES OF BEHAVIORAL CHANGE

We employ four types of measures to characterize the behavior and mood of the new mothers as below.

Engagement. A measure of overall engagement with communications in social media is *volume*, defined as the average normalized number of posts per day made by the new mothers over the prenatal and postnatal periods. We define a second engagement measure to be the mean proportion of *reply* posts (@-replies) from a mother over a day; this serves as a proxy for her level of activity in social interaction with other Twitter users. The third measure is the fraction of *retweets* from a mother per day, which indicates how the mother participates in information sharing with her followers. The proportion of *links* (urls) shared by each mother over a day comprises a fourth engagement measure. We define a fifth measure as the fraction of *question-centric* posts from a mother on a given day; this measure indicates the mother's tendency to seek information from the greater Twitter community.

Ego-network. We define two measures that characterize the nature of a mother's egocentric social network. The first measure is the number of *followers* or inlinks of a mother at a given day, while the second is the count of her *followees* or outlinks. Inlinks demonstrate her reach/popularity in the larger network (in a coarse sense), while outlinks indicate her tendency to act as an informational hub and remain connected with others.

Emotion. We consider four measures of the emotional state of mothers: *positive affect* (PA), *negative affect* (NA), *activation,* and *dominance*. PA and NA are computed using the psycholinguistic lexicon LIWC (http://www.liwc.net/). LIWC's emotion categories have been scientifically validated to perform well for determining affect with Internet language [23], as well as from short text data, e.g., Twitter [8,12]. For PA computation, we focus on words in the positive emotion category of LIWC [12]. For NA, we consider the negative affect categories: *negative emotion, anger, anxiety, sadness.*

Like in [8], we use the ANEW lexicon [4] for computing activation and dominance. This resource provides a set of normative emotional ratings (pleasure, arousal, and dominance) for a large number of words (~2000) in the English language. Activation measures the intensity of an emotion, an important dimension beyond the valence captured by PA and NA. As an example, while *frustrated* and *infuriated* are both negative emotions, *infuriated* is higher in activation. Dominance represents the controlling and dominant nature of an emotion. For instance while both *fear* and *anger* are negative emotions, *anger* is a dominant emotion, while *fear* is a submissive emotion.

Linguistic Style. We also use measures to characterize change based on the use of linguistic styles in posts from new mothers during the prenatal and the postnatal periods [8]. Linguistic styles capture how language is used by individuals and provide information about their behavioral characteristics subject to their social environment [7,23]. We again referred to LIWC for determining 22 specific linguistic styles: *articles, auxiliary verbs, conjunctions, adverbs, impersonal pronouns, personal pronouns, prepositions, functional words, fillers, assent, negation, certainty* and *quantifiers*.

OBSERVATIONS OF POSTPARTUM CHANGES

We share several empirical observations prior to focusing on the task of constructing classifiers to predict postpartum changes in new mothers. The observations illustrate the manner in which mothers change in their behavior as manifested through our different measures. Figure 1 shows heat maps of individual-level changes for five measures: volume, replies, negative affect, activation and first-person pronoun use. For brevity, we focus on these measures as illustrative examples of change, though we note that most measures showed similar patterns. Greater details of changes in different measures across the cohorts of mothers can be referred to in [8].

The heat maps in Figure 1 display a variety of shifts in patterns, including how some new mothers may show noticeable changes in their behavior on Twitter. Changes are observed in the decreasing and increasing directions. Some new mothers exhibit only small changes while others show more extreme shifts in one or more measures.

For instance, the heat maps show a considerable decrease in volume, replies, and activation following childbirth for a

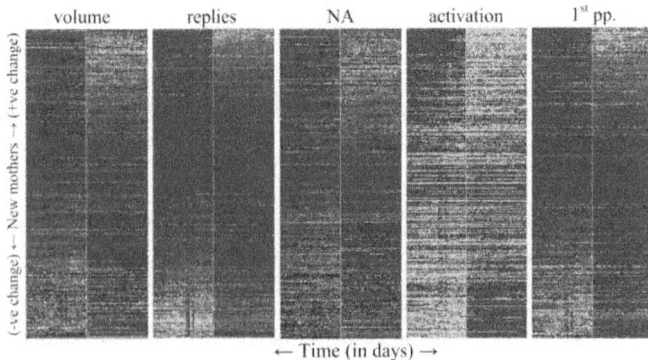

Figure 1. Heat maps (scaled on RGB spectrum with red=high, blue=low) showing changes in five measures behavior in new mothers during postpartum, compared to prenatal period. Center white line in each figure represents estimated time of childbirth.

subset of the mothers. Such decreases indicate that these women are posting less, suggesting a possible loss of social connectedness following childbirth. We also observe a noticeable increase in NA for a portion of the mothers. This finding may be attributable to these mothers' physical, mental, and emotional exhaustion [19], as well as the sleep deprivation typical of parenting a newborn. Similarly, the drastic reduction in activation during the postnatal phase for some mothers may indicate emotions of low intensity, perhaps based in fatigue from handling daily tasks around care of the newborn. Finally, we find that the use of the first-person pronoun increases considerably for some mothers, possibly reflecting increases in attention to self and emotional distancing from others after childbirth [7,30].

The cohort of mothers showing extreme changes (in either direction, depending on the measure, e.g., decreasing for volume, increasing for NA) is of particular interest to us, as these significant changes could indicate difficulty adjusting to new motherhood, including emotional changes seen in maternity blues. In fact, prior literature establishes that the above-observed signs of considerable decrease in social interaction (e.g., lowered volume), generally unhappy postings (e.g., lowered PA, high NA), and psychological distancing (e.g., high 1st person pronoun use) may point to emotional instability, depression vulnerability, or existing depression [7]. In this light, classifying and predicting the behavior of mothers who will later show extreme negative postpartum changes *ahead of time*, may be useful in flagging risk of forthcoming behavioral health problems.

PREDICTION FRAMEWORK

We now pursue the use of supervised learning to construct classifiers trained to predict postpartum behavioral and emotional changes of new mothers. To this end, we use observations of our measures during the prenatal phase: engagement, emotion, ego-network, and linguistic style.

Classification Setup

Given observed data during the prenatal period, we frame prediction as a binary classification problem per measure, where we discriminate the following two classes:

- *Extreme-changing mothers*: the first group (*class C1*) comprises mothers whose mean value of a measure in postpartum *after* childbirth is considerably less than (or greater than, depending on the measure of interest) that *before* childbirth, with respect to a suitably chosen empirical threshold τ that is discussed below;
- *Standard-changing mothers*: the second group (*class C0*) comprises those mothers not in the extreme change class.

To construct these two classes, we need to estimate the expected directionality of change[2] of a particular measure indicating the manner in which the mothers deviate in their

---

[2]Normalized change per mother is defined as the difference between mean value of a measure postpartum and the mean value of the same measure in the prenatal period, divided by the latter.

behavior postpartum. To this end, we leverage insights from prior literature that examine association between the linguistic expression of individuals and their responses to traumatic context and crises, including depression vulnerability [7,30]. For instance, increases in NA, and decreases in activation are known to be indicative of emotional instability [6,8]. Thus, in our class definition for NA, we consider increasing directional changes for demarcating C1, while decreasing directional changes corresponding to activation. The directionality of change for other measures is discussed in greater detail in Table 2.

For the purposes of classification, we represent each mother as a vector of features, where the features consist of daily values of all of the measures we track during the prenatal period (33 measures in all). The high dimensionality of the feature space can lead to overfitting to the training data. To avoid overfitting and to eliminate feature redundancy and interaction, we employ principal component analysis (PCA) and regularized random forest procedures [10]. We compare several different parametric and non-parametric classifiers to empirically determine the best suitable classification technique, including linear, quadratic, discriminant classifiers, naïve Bayes, k-nearest neighbor, decision trees, and Support Vector Machines with a radial-basis function (RBF) kernel [10]. The best performing classifier was found to be the SVM across all measures, which outperformed the other methods with prediction accuracy improvements in the range of 10-35%. We use SVMs with an RBF kernel as the classification method for the rest of this paper. For all of our analyses, we train and test one classifier for each measure. We use five-fold cross validation on the set of 376 mothers, over 100 randomized experimental runs.

Estimating Optimal Threshold for Class Definition

We now discuss our method of identifying a threshold τ per each behavioral measure for defining the two classes of mothers as defined above. The ideal threshold is a conceptual boundary that would distinctly separate the extreme-changing mothers, from the mothers who show smaller changes. We define the threshold τ as the minimum normalized change[2] in the value of the measure *after* childbirth, compared to that *before* birth.

We follow an empirical strategy involving the optimization of the threshold τ for class definition. Specifically, given a measure that we intend to predict, we step through a range of threshold values (τ=0, .01, .05, .1, .15, …, .3, etc.) to define the classes. For each such case, we train an SVM classifier and attempt to maximize the log likelihood of the learned model using expectation-maximization (EM) [10].

In conducting this series of model fittings in pursuit of the optimal τ for each measure, the best model fit for τ is observed in the range .05 to .2 across all of our measures. Corresponding to these values of τ, we report, in Table 2, the median increase/decrease in changes per measure exhibited by the two classes of mothers. Qualitatively, the

changes for the extreme-changing mothers (C1) stand out against the background behaviors seen in other mothers. As an example, for the volume measure, mothers in the extreme change class (C1), exhibit median change of -0.88 postpartum, indicating an 88% drop in posts per day, while the standard changing mothers actually increase in posting volume by 84%. While both groups change in volume, the extreme changing mothers are distinguished by a relative change of 2.05 times that of standard changers and in a decreasing direction.

Measures	C1	C0	Measures	C1	C0
volume	-0.878	0.838	verbs	-0.911	0.951
Replies	-0.983	1.417	aux-verbs	-0.889	0.914
RT	-0.847	2.188	adverbs	3.025	-0.678
Links	-0.791	2.347	preposition	-0.899	1.020
Questions	2.110	-0.749	conjunction	-0.890	1.042
PA	-0.798	0.428	negate	2.867	-0.690
NA	1.726	-0.593	quantifier	-0.896	0.950
activation	-0.743	0.525	swear	3.258	-0.751
dominance	-0.717	0.543	tentative	3.710	-0.700
Followers	-0.941	1.451	certain	-0.997	1.386
Followees	-0.928	1.013	inhibition	3.425	-0.722
functional words	4.574	-0.865	inclusive	-0.914	1.048
1st pp.	1.924	-0.426	exclusive	-0.822	2.304
2nd pp.	-0.901	0.872	assent	-0.904	1.073
3rd pp.	-0.894	0.990	non-fluency	3.028	-0.724
indefinite pronoun	-0.810	2.082	filler	2.929	-0.786
article	3.940	-0.701			

Table 2. Median changes in measures for two classes of new mothers with C1 corresponding to extreme-changing mothers and C0 corresponding to mothers showing smaller changes. Directionality of changes reflects for each measure whether extreme-changing mothers are considered to be changing in increasing or decreasing directions. *Volume* decreases postpartum for C1, but *negative affect* (NA) increases [6,8].

This and similar observations from Table 2 indicate that the optimal τ's for different measures obtained through the learning technique separate the two classes well and help us construct reliable ground truth labels for the mothers. We note that, over the range of optimal τ, the sizes of the two classes of behavior across all of the measures fall in the range 8.8-28.2% for class C1 (median: 15.7%; standard deviation 4.3%), and the rest for class C0. In the next section, we use these optimal threshold τ (referred to as τ^*) for the class definitions corresponding to each of our behavioral measures.

RESULTS ON PREDICTION

Prediction with Prenatal Period Data Alone

We begin by first examining the performance of the classifiers in identifying the two classes of mothers. Here, we train an SVM using only the mothers' behavioral measures during the prenatal period. The goal of this particular model is to predict postpartum changes before the birth of a child. We use six different performance metrics:

accuracy, precision and recall, F1, specificity and area under curve (AUC). We present the results of this prediction model in Table 3. We train one classifier to predict each of the behavioral measures (e.g. volume, replies, PA, NA etc.). For brevity, we report the mean performance per measure category—*engagement, emotion, ego-network* and *linguistic style.*

Measures	% Acc.	Prec.	Recall	F1	Spec.	AUC
engagement	71.70%	0.757	0.708	0.727	0.742	0.734
Mean accuracy of extreme-changing mothers (eng)						74.21%
emotion	71.21%	0.696	0.740	0.714	0.688	0.689
Mean accuracy of extreme-changing mothers (emo)						70.94%
ego-net.	68.63%	0.725	0.797	0.757	0.510	0.633
Mean accuracy of extreme-changing mothers (ego-net)						69.25%
style	72.90%	0.738	0.713	0.722	0.743	0.712
Mean accuracy of extreme-changing mothers (style)						74.30%
Mean	71.11%	0.729	0.740	0.730	0.671	0.692
Std. dev.	0.023	0.032	0.020	0.075	0.075	0.032
Mean accuracy for predicting extreme changers						71.46%

Table 3. Mean performance metrics (accuracy, precision, recall, F1, specificity, and AUC) of measure types, in predicting behavioral change classes of new mothers. Mean accuracy in predicting the class of extreme-changing mothers is also shown separately for each category. We only use data from the prenatal period.

The results in Table 3 indicate that, in our test set, the predictive models yield an average accuracy of more than 71% corresponding to the class of mothers showing extreme changes (C1). Good performance of this classifier is also evident from the receiver-operator characteristic (ROC) curves in Figure 2. These curves depict relationship of the true positive (extreme-changing mothers) and false positive (mothers with less extreme changes predicted as extreme-changing mothers) for different thresholds of the inferred probability of extreme-changing mothers required to admit these mothers into the extreme-changing class.

We find that the measures of linguistic styles, engagement, and emotion are more accurately predicted than the ego-network measures. Mean accuracies of classifying extreme-changing mothers per measure category are displayed in Table 3. We explore the differences in discriminatory power of measures in greater detail in the next subsection.

Prediction with an Optimal Training Window

Estimating Optimal Training Window k

So far, we have investigated predicting new mothers' future behavioral changes using data from the prenatal period alone. However, clinical literature on PPD marks the typical onset of PPD at about *one month following childbirth* [16]; hence a few days or weeks of training data in the early postnatal phase may contain valuable clues about future changes in behavior that can be additionally leveraged to boost prediction performance.

We now consider harnessing evidence for additional periods of up to three weeks (21 days) following childbirth

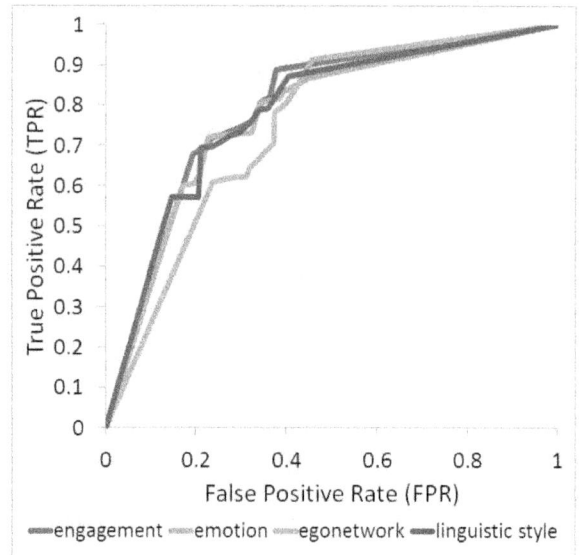

Figure 2. ROC curves for prediction using prenatal data. Aggregated trends over measure categories shown.

for each mother. Together with the three month prenatal phase (91/92 days prenatal plus up to 21 days postnatal), we refer to this period as the *training window*. We note here that, due to the intrinsic differences in the characteristics of the different measures (e.g., see Figure 1 for illustrative examples), it is likely there will be an optimal training window for each measure, perhaps shorter than the 21 day period, which can make the best predictions of change in mothers. To obtain such an optimal training window k for a certain measure (referred to as k^*), we follow a similar optimization strategy using the training data and EM, as we used for inferring τ^* in the previous section. We observe a relatively narrow range of optimal k, corresponding to the best model fit for all measures. This narrow range is between 12-19 days following estimated day of childbirth.

Overall Classification Performance

We now present classification performance over the two classes of mothers for the optimal training window size k^* for each of the measures. Table 4 reports the performance of the classifier along the different metrics. Overall, we observe good performance from our classifiers, with an average accuracy of more than 80% and F1 measure of 0.82 (standard deviations over all the performance metrics are shown at the bottom of Table 4). Note that this constitutes a considerable improvement over our previous prediction that used only the data over the prenatal period for training (more than 9% improvement in accuracy and F1 scores).

Specifically, we observe an accuracy of 81.62% in classifying the relatively small fraction of extreme-changers in the entire population of our dataset (mean size of class extreme-changing mothers is 16%). As before, we find that classifiers for changes in emotion, engagement, and linguistic style show the best performance. In essence, we conclude that two to three weeks into postpartum, the mothers show enough evidence in their behavioral and emotional changes, that it can be used along with the data from the prenatal period, to make more accurate predictions for remainder of the postpartum phase studied.

Measures	Acc.	Prec.	Recall	F1	Spec.	AUC
volume	*82.72%*	*0.819*	*0.893*	*0.853*	*0.745*	*0.835*
replies	*82.64%*	*0.796*	*0.884*	*0.836*	*0.735*	*0.854*
retweets	81.44%	0.807	0.823	0.812	0.828	0.838
links	77.46%	0.718	0.774	0.743	0.717	0.769
questions	80.06%	0.743	0.808	0.770	0.800	0.825
mean	80.86%	0.777	0.837	0.803	0.765	0.824
PA	80.99%	0.785	0.906	0.840	0.616	0.833
NA	*81.05%*	*0.824*	*0.789*	*0.805*	*0.813*	*0.820*
activation	*82.33%*	*0.784*	*0.908*	*0.840*	*0.666*	*0.842*
dominance	80.34%	0.799	0.891	0.842	0.677	0.820
mean	81.18%	0.798	0.874	0.832	0.693	0.829
followers	78.45%	0.747	0.918	0.822	0.629	0.829
followees	*80.32%*	*0.821*	*0.877*	*0.848*	*0.675*	*0.837*
mean	79.39%	0.784	0.898	0.835	0.652	0.833
Functional words	81.38%	0.795	0.880	0.835	0.731	0.822
1st pp.	*82.44%*	*0.811*	*0.918*	*0.860*	*0.686*	*0.819*
2nd pp.	*83.26%*	*0.869*	*0.887*	*0.876*	*0.733*	*0.832*
3rd pp.	*83.39%*	*0.819*	*0.879*	*0.845*	*0.720*	*0.835*
indefinite pronoun	78.46%	0.758	0.784	0.766	0.787	0.763
article	*82.20%*	*0.802*	*0.894*	*0.845*	*0.738*	*0.801*
verbs	80.53%	0.789	0.861	0.820	0.722	0.779
aux-verbs	80.59%	0.832	0.842	0.836	0.745	0.793
adverbs	81.38%	0.843	0.857	0.849	0.741	0.843
prepos.	80.88%	0.753	0.863	0.801	0.654	0.778
conjunct.	81.38%	0.789	0.900	0.837	0.724	0.809
negate	80.31%	0.786	0.886	0.831	0.705	0.792
quantifier	80.85%	0.844	0.850	0.845	0.740	0.822
swear	78.99%	0.767	0.883	0.819	0.682	0.835
tentative	80.83%	0.775	0.896	0.829	0.715	0.847
certain	79.40%	0.817	0.796	0.804	0.737	0.818
inhibition	*81.39%*	*0.788*	*0.891*	*0.835*	*0.729*	*0.806*
inclusive	80.06%	0.791	0.877	0.828	0.710	0.780
exclusive	78.90%	0.738	0.744	0.740	0.787	0.732
assent	79.80%	0.793	0.865	0.827	0.704	0.828
non-fluency	80.87%	0.777	0.886	0.825	0.728	0.813
filler	78.93%	0.816	0.714	0.761	0.842	0.843
mean	80.74%	0.798	0.857	0.823	0.730	0.809
overall mean	**80.54%**	**0.789**	**0.866**	**0.823**	**0.726**	**0.824**
Std. dev.	0.007	0.009	0.022	0.013	0.042	0.009
Accuracy of class of extreme-changing mothers					81.62%	

Table 4. Performance metrics (accuracy, precision, recall, F1, specificity and AUC) for predicting behavioral change classes of mothers, using optimal training window k^*.

Best Predicted Measures

We now discuss the performance of individual measures in more detail. In the *engagement* category, we find that volume and replies are best predicted (shown in italics), with higher accuracy, precision, recall, and F1 by 2-11%. One-way ANOVA reveals statistically significant

differences in performance among the different engagement measures ($F(4,300)=2.54$; $p<.01$), while pairwise comparisons (Tukey range test) confirm that volume and replies show significant improvements in prediction compared to most other engagement measures. We note here that the volume of postings would signal how involved a mother is with her contacts, while replies would indicate the degree of social support that maybe available to a mother via her one-to-one interactions with other users. Given that both of these measures go down in the case of extreme-changing mothers (see Table 2), it appears that their trends during the training window are powerful predictors of future drops in these two key measures of Twitter-based social engagement.

Among the *emotion* measures, the best prediction is observed in the cases of NA and activation (margin of 2-20% improvement across different metrics; one-way ANOVA and corresponding pairwise Tukey range tests yields significant improvements over other emotion measures: $F(3,225)=3.25$; $p<.01$). We speculate that lower arousal may be based in exhaustion, anxiousness, and the general overwhelming routine of new motherhood. In order to obtain some qualitative observations on this conjecture, we examined several randomly selected posts shared by the mothers who we classified as showing extreme changes during postpartum. Some of the excerpts indicate notable negative emotional expression and concur with our above conjecture: "*Anxiety/panic attacks need to eff off!!!!!!!!!!!!!! I'm trying to lead a somewhat normal life with my baby!!!!*" (high NA); "*My first time being alone with my baby and I cant stop crying. What is wrong with me?*" (low activation).

For the *ego-network* measures, #followees (outlinks) is better predicted than #followers (inlinks). Outlinks could indicate how a mother is attempting to socialize or her tendency to consume external information and remain connected with others. In the light of the social isolation that some of the extreme-changing mothers appear to undergo, it appears that the shrinkage of ego-networks provides valuable cues in predicting their postpartum behavioral changes along this measure.

For the *linguistic style* measures, we observe high prediction performance for the three pronoun uses (first-, second- and third-person usages) and the use of articles, by a margin of 2-17% over other linguistic style metrics (statistically significant differences with the most number of other measures, based on one-way ANOVA: $F(21,1575)=2.97$; $p<.01$, followed by Tukey range test). Results in prior literature suggest that use of these styles provide information about how individuals respond to psychological triggers. For instance, we observe one of the extreme changing mothers in this category posting the following during postpartum: "*No lie I fuckin miss all socializing..... my daughter keeps me occupied and exhausted.*" This excerpt involving high first-person pronoun usage shows high self-focus on the part of the

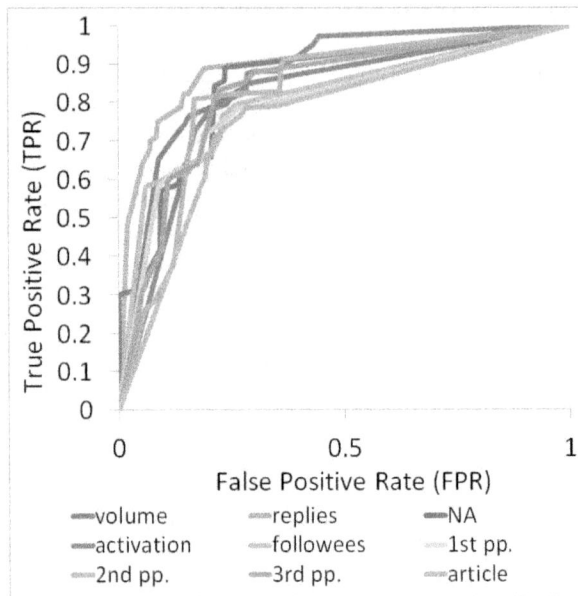

Figure 3. ROC curves for top predictable measures using composite features based classifier. Mean AUC values corresponding to these curves are shown in Table 4.

mother [7,30]. We conjecture that the general social and psychological distancing characterizing the circumstances of new motherhood is linked to such high attentional focus on oneself, and turns out to be a strong predictor of postpartum change for the extreme-changing mothers for these measures of linguistic style.

As a summary graphical statistic, Figure 3 presents the ROC curves corresponding to the best predicted measures discussed above. The curves demonstrate improvements in Figure 2 (upward trends towards left with growing area under the curve), with increases in the true positive rate (i.e., the extreme changers) versus false positives.

Broadly, the observation, that certain measure categories (emotion, NA, pronoun, article use) can be better predicted when demarcating mothers with extreme change, reveals interesting artifacts about postpartum behavioral signatures of these mothers. For instance, the behavioral trends of these particular measures bear resemblance to heightened levels of emotional pain or distress, up to even depression as indicated in prior literature [6,23]. In the following section, we discuss possibilities of leveraging these postpartum behavioral signatures to aid new mothers as well as the broader implications of our prediction methodology and outcomes in public health.

DISCUSSION

Theoretical Implications
Through our experimental findings on prediction, we have demonstrated how sets of behavioral markers manifested in social media during the prenatal period and in early postpartum periods, can be harnessed to predict future

changes. We are able to identify with good accuracy (71%), a cohort of mothers who later show extreme changes (the median class size of extreme-changing mothers was 16% across all measures), by leveraging their behavioral and emotional signals exhibited in social media before the birth of the child. The accuracy of the predictive models rises (~80%) when the evidential horizon is extended to the early postnatal period.

The ability to predict significant changes in behavior and mood postpartum has broad implications. The postpartum behavioral markers exhibited by the subset of mothers who we identified as showing extreme changes, resonate with the feelings of hopelessness, dejection, and depressive tendencies seen in postpartum depression [16]. Further, the 16% of extreme-changing mothers aligns with reported rates of postpartum depression in the United States [19,20]. We conjecture that the predictive models may be able to reveal valuable clues about forthcoming shifts in mood ahead of time or soon after childbirth; thereby providing sufficient time for mothers and caregivers to take appropriate and valuable action.

In follow-on research, we seek to collect ground truth on PPD in new mothers, wherein we can empirically validate the relationship between the measures we predict and blues and deeper depression experienced by some mothers. Along these lines, we believe that our methodology has implications for public health. The findings can potentially assist agencies, support groups, or the larger medical community with the measurement of PPD in large populations, providing a new lens on a traditionally underreported illness.

We note that the clinical literature [2] indicates that the risk factors of postpartum depression include history of depression or psychological disturbance during pregnancy, experience of stressful events during the past year, problems in the woman's relationship with the partner, and weakness in the available support system(s). Such observations may be identifiable via longitudinal records of social media postings made by mothers during the prenatal period or earlier and could be used as higher-level evidence in the training classifiers that predict postpartum behavioral changes in mothers.

Our result that including two to three weeks of data following childbirth improves our prediction significantly may be explained by findings in the literature. Studies have shown that PPD typically arises after the fading away of the less severe baby blues, which usually appears in the week or two following childbirth [11]. Other known PPD triggers, such as difficult infant temperament and childcare stress [3] only manifest after the birth of the baby. Thus, mothers who consistently show extreme changes following childbirth and who suffer these early postnatal stressors may be at highest risk of PPD. However, as mentioned above, concrete validation of such potential risks will require ground truth data on PPD from a sufficiently large population of new mothers.

Directions in Design and Deployment

We have demonstrated the feasibility of predicting the future appearance of extreme changes in the behavior of new mothers, up to three months into the future with relatively high accuracy, using only prenatal behavioral data. The predicted behavioral changes in the measures we study can enable adjuvant diagnosis of postnatal disorders, complementary to survey based approaches (e.g., Edinburgh Postnatal Depression Scale [19]), helping promote wellness of women postpartum. In another direction, we believe that it is possible to develop software applications and services that serve as early warning systems, one day providing pregnant women and new mothers with personalized information on their risk of encountering significant changes in activity and mood. Such systems could be designed as privacy preserving applications that are deployed by and for individuals.

Predictive models running in a personalized service or within a smartphone application may provide value over traditional methods used for keeping track of new mothers' health and vitality. Traditionally, new mothers are asked to fill out surveys or are interviewed about PPD-like symptoms that they may be experiencing following childbirth, as well as the duration and severity of the symptoms. A tool motivated by this research could automate this process via monitoring behavioral trends of new mothers, and could be part of broader diary-centric systems that capture a self-narrative about postpartum life. Such an application is loosely akin to systems for Web-based depression treatment, which have been shown to be engaging and effective [9]. Per our study and results, applications could work privately in making *predictions* about potential risks of future changes as well, considering such measures in social media activity, as volume, replies, NA, activation, etc. The application might, for example, assign a "PPD risk score" to mothers based on predictions made about forthcoming extreme changes in their behavior and mood. In operation, if inferred likelihoods of forthcoming extreme changes surpass a threshold, mothers could be warned or engaged, and information might be provided about professional assistance and/or such guidance to mothers as noting the value of social and emotional support from friends and family.

Ethics and Privacy

Analysis of publicly shared data that could reveal existing or future mental health challenges raises concerns regarding the preservation of personal data privacy, as well as more general ethical considerations with pursuing research in this realm. On the research itself, we note that our studies have leveraged publicly available data (public expression by mothers on Twitter) with no personally identifiable information used in the analysis. As we discussed earlier, the privacy of mothers can be honored with applications

that restrict the sharing of such information to the user herself and optionally to a trained medical practitioner or support group.

Nevertheless, we note that this type of research, and also results on the kinds of inferences that can be made from publicly available data pose interesting questions for individuals and for society more broadly. We have demonstrated that it is possible to make inferences from publicly available feeds about future psychological states that people may not wish to share with others. The predictions we make are similar to predictions about people made by systems in common use, including recommender systems that make inferences, e.g., about the titles of books that online users may wish to purchase given their history of purchases, search engines which guess the intentions of people performing online searches, given past behavior and terms input in online searches, and predictions made by online services about the likelihood that a user will click on a particular advertisement. Although the methods may be based in a similar mathematics of statistics and large-scale data analysis about people and their online activities, predictions about future changes in psychological wellbeing may be viewed by many as qualitatively different. People may be uncomfortable with the possibility that third parties might have the ability to predict future psychological states, especially when relatively accurate predictions can be made about future illness and disability. We believe it is important to bring the possibilities to the fore, so as to leverage the benefits of these methods and ideas to enhance the quality of life for people, as well as to stimulate discussion and awareness of potential concerns that need to be addressed at the individual and societal levels.

CONCLUSION

We have found that online activities, including the nature and changes of peoples' social networks, statistics of engagement, and the expression of thoughts and emotions in social media can be harnessed to make predictions about future behaviors and moods. We introduced a methodology for constructing and evaluating predictive models that forecast forthcoming changes in the behavior and mood of new mothers postpartum. We explored attributes of new mothers as manifested in their interactions on Twitter before and shortly after childbirth, including those of engagement, emotion, ego-network, and linguistic styles. We found that we could identify a group of new mothers who are likely to exhibit extreme changes in their behavior during the three-month period following childbirth. We constructed predictive models with the ability to predict with 71% accuracy which mothers will show extreme changes postpartum, using only prenatal observations. With adding consideration of additional short periods of postnatal data, the predictive accuracy rises to 80%.

We believe that such predictive models could be valuable tools in public health and could be used one day in the design and deployment of new kinds of early warning systems that could bring people timely information and assistance. At the same time, we foresee that our results will stimulate useful discussions about privacy and ethics with regard to the feasibility of forecasting forthcoming mental or physical illness from information that people share publicly. We can predict future behavior and mood with well-characterized confidence. However, people may be uncomfortable with others performing and sharing these predictions, even if the inferences are based solely on data that they have shared openly with the public.

REFERENCES

1. Bagehahl-Strindlund, M. & Borjesson, K.M. (1998). Postnatal depression: A hidden illness. *Acta Psychiatrica Scandinavica, 98,* 272-275.

2. Beck, C.T. (1998). A checklist to identify women at risk for developing postpartum depression. *Journal of Obstetric, Gynecologic, & Neonatal Nursing, 27,* 39-46.

3. Beck, C.T. (2001). Predictors of Postpartum Depression: An Update. *Nursing Research,* 50 (5), 275-285.

4. Bradley, M.M., & Lang, P.J. (1999). Affective norms for English words (ANEW). Gainesville, FL. *The NIMH Center for the Study of Emotion and Attention.*

5. Brubaker, J. R., Kivran-Swaine, F., Taber, L., and Hayes, G. R. (2012). Grief-Stricken in a Crowd: The language of bereavement and distress in social media. In *Proc. ICWSM 2012.*

6. Bucci W, Freedman N. (1981). The language of depression. *Bull. Menninger Clin.* 45:334–58.

7. Chung, C.K., & Pennebaker, J.W. (2007). The psychological functions of function words. In K. Fielder (Ed.), *Social communication* (pp. 343-359).

8. De Choudhury, M., Counts, S., and Horvitz, E. (2013). Major Life Changes and Behavioral Markers in Social Media: Case of Childbirth. In *Proc. CSCW 2013.*

9. Doherty, G., Coyle, D., & Sharry, J. (2012). Engagement with Online Mental Health Interventions: An Exploratory Clinical Study of a Treatment for Depression. In *Proc. CHI'12.*

10. Duda, Richard O., Hart, Peter E., & Stork, David G. (2000). *Pattern Classification.* 2nd Edition, Wiley.

11. Fleming, A. S., Klein, E. and Corter, C. (1992). The Effects of a Social Support Group on Depression, Maternal Attitudes and Behavior in New Mothers. *Journal of Child Psych. & Psychiatry,* 33: 685–698.

12. Golder, S. A., & Macy, M. W. (2011). Diurnal and Seasonal Mood Vary with Work, Sleep and Daylength Across Diverse Cultures. *Science.* 30 Sep 2011.

13. Kapoor, A., Horvitz, E. & Basu, S. (2007). Selective Supervision: Guiding Supervised Learning with Decision-Theoretic Active Learning. In *Proc. IJCAI.*

14. Kramer, A. (2010). An Unobtrusive Behavioral Model of "Gross National Happiness". In *Proc. CHI 2010.*

15. MacLennan, A., Wilson, D., & Taylor, A. (1996). The self-reported prevalence of postnatal depression in Australia and New Zealand. *Journal of Obstetrics and Gynecology, 36,* 313.

16. Miller, Laura J. (2002). Postpartum Depression. *J. of American Med. Association* (JAMA) 287 (6): 762–765.

17. Neuman, Y., Cohen, Y., Assaf, D., & Kedma, G. (2012). Proactive screening for depression through metaphorical and automatic text analysis. (2012). *Artificial Intelligence in Medicine,* 56 (1), 19-25.

18. Nielson, Forman D., Videbech, P., Hedegaard, M., Dalby Slavig, J. & Secher, N.J. (2000). Postnatal depression: identification of women at risk. *British Journal of Obstetrics and Gynaecology* (BJOG) 107 (10): 1210–1217.

19. O'Hara, M.W. (1995). Postpartum Depression: Causes and Consequences. *New York: Springer-Verlag.*

20. O'Hara, M.W., & Swain, A.M. (1996). Rates and risks of postpartum depression – a meta-analysis. *Intl. Review of Psychiatry, 8 (1),* 37-54.

21. Oxman T.E., Rosenberg S.D., & Tucker G.J. (1982). The language of paranoia. *American J. Psychiatry* 139:275–82.

22. Paul, M., J., & Dredze, M. (2011). You are What You Tweet: Analyzing Twitter for Public Health. In *Proc. ICWSM '11.*

23. Pennebaker, J.W., Mehl, M.R., and Niederhoffer, K.G. (2002). Pyschological aspects of natural language use: Our words, ourselves. *Annual Review of Psychology* 54: 547-477.

24. Ramsay, R. (1993). Postnatal depression. *Lancet, 341, 1358.*

25. Sadilek, A., Kautz, H., & Silenzio, V. (2012). Modeling Spread of Disease from Social Interactions. In *Proc. ICSWM '11.*

26. Scott KD, Klaus PH, Klaus MH.(1999). The obstetrical and postpartum benefits of continuous support during childbirth. *J Womens Health Gend Based Med.* 8(10):1257-64.

27. Spera SP, Buhrfeind ED, Pennebaker JW. (1994). Expressive writing and coping with job loss. *Acad. Manag.* J. 37:722–33.

28. Steinfeld, C., Ellison, N., Lampe, C. (2008). Social capital, self-esteem, and use of online social network sites: A longitudinal study. *J. of Applied Developmental Psychology, 29,* 434-445.

29. Tarkka, M.-T. & Paunonen, M. (1996). Social support and its impact on mothers'experiences of childbirth. *Journal of Advanced Nursing,* 23: 70–75.

30. Weintraub W. (1981). Verbal Behavior: Adaptation and Psychopathology. New York: Springer.

"I read my Twitter the next morning and was astonished" A Conversational Perspective on Twitter Regrets

Manya Sleeper*, Justin Cranshaw*, Patrick Gage Kelley†, Blase Ur*,
Alessandro Acquisti*, Lorrie Faith Cranor*, Norman Sadeh*

*Carnegie Mellon University
{msleeper, jcransh, bur, acquisti, lorrie, sadeh}@cmu.edu

†University of New Mexico
pgk@unm.edu

ABSTRACT

We present the results of an online survey of 1,221 Twitter users, comparing messages individuals regretted either saying during in-person conversations or posting on Twitter. Participants generally reported similar types of regrets in person and on Twitter. In particular, they often regretted messages that were critical of others. However, regretted messages that were cathartic/expressive or revealed too much information were reported at a higher rate for Twitter. Regretted messages on Twitter also reached broader audiences. In addition, we found that participants who posted on Twitter became aware of, and tried to repair, regret more slowly than those reporting in-person regrets. From this comparison of Twitter and in-person regrets, we provide preliminary ideas for tools to help Twitter users avoid and cope with regret.

Author Keywords

Twitter; regrets; messaging; conversation; survey

ACM Classification Keywords

H.5.m. Information Interfaces and Presentation (e.g. HCI): Miscellaneous

INTRODUCTION

It is easy to say something you regret, angrily insulting a loved one or inadvertently letting a secret slip. However, Twitter, a social networking service, enables these types of regrettable messages to spread rapidly and broadly, and to remain available for extended periods of time. Twitter's ability to broadcast messages widely and retain them indefinitely potentially alters the dynamics of regretted communications. In extreme cases, Twitter has enabled highly-publicized instances of regret, like Rep. Anthony Weiner's infamous tweet that led to his resignation [5]. However, everyday Twitter use can lead to more mundane regrets. As in conversation, Twitter users insult others, accidentally reveal private information, and express emotion in heated moments.

Thus it is worthwhile to investigate regret both on Twitter and for in-person conversations. Past studies of in-person regret have identified factors that lead to regret, methods for becoming aware of regret, and strategies for repairing harm [8, 15, 16]. However, Twitter presents different features and limitations than offline conversation. Beyond offering wider audiences and increased message persistence, Twitter lacks face-to-face channels, such as body language, for transmitting apologies or indicating offense.

We explore regretted messages Twitter users posted on Twitter or said during in-person conversations. We aim to improve understanding of regrets on Twitter by comparing them with in-person regrets. By examining these regrets, as well as how people became aware of regrets in person and on Twitter, we also identify preliminary design directions for preventing and ameliorating regrets on Twitter.

Specifically, we examine four research questions:

- Q1: What states of being lead to regret on Twitter and in person?

- Q2: What types of regret occur on Twitter and in person?

- Q3: How do people become aware of regretted messages on Twitter versus in person?

- Q4: What repair strategies do people use to cope with regretted messages on Twitter and in person?

To address these questions, we ran a 1,221-participant online Mechanical Turk survey with two conditions. In one condition, we asked Twitter users to report on one message they regretted saying during an in-person conversation. In the other, we asked parallel questions about a message they regretted posting on Twitter. We collected information on the incident, the participant's emotional state preceding the incident, how the participant became aware of the regret, and any mitigation strategies employed. We used these answers to understand and compare drivers and consequences of regretted messages during in-person conversation and on Twitter.

BACKGROUND AND RELATED WORK

To demonstrate the conventions of posting on Twitter, we briefly highlight key features of the service. We then review related work on regret, first examining past analyses of regret during in-person conversations before discussing more recent work on social networking sites.

Twitter features

Twitter is an online social networking site where users post tweets, which are text-based messages of 140 characters or less. These messages are broadcast to a user's followers in relationships that are often asymmetric.

Twitter has several conventions that aid in sharing. Users can direct a message to a handful of specific users by crafting an @-reply. Users indicated by the @-reply will be alerted to the message through email or the Twitter client, but the message itself is public. A direct message (DM) allows a user to send a private message to a single person. A user can also add #hashtags to a tweet to categorize it, better enable searches as part of a trend, or provide contextual information. Tweets are publicly accessible unless an account is protected. Only a user's approved followers can view a protected user's tweets.

Related work

We first discuss research in the communications literature that has sought to understand many aspects of regret during in-person communication. We then outline work examining users' potentially regrettable behaviors and coping mechanisms on social networking sites.

In-person conversational regrets

Past studies of regrettable messages generally considered in-person messaging. Knapp et al. conducted 155 interviews, asking each participant about something they wished they hadn't said. The researchers noted eleven categories of regret, which we used in this study. They found that blunders, direct attacks, and group references were most frequently associated with regret, and that participants typically realized immediately when a message was regrettable [8].

Meyer surveyed 173 undergraduates about their cognitive states before and after saying regrettable things in person. Stress, frustration, and anger, as well as "having a lot on [their] mind," were most frequently associated with regrets. Participants commonly realized on their own that regrets had occurred, and regretted messages were rarely directed at more than one person [15]. Meyer separately examined efforts to repair the effects of in-person regretted messages. In a 204-participant survey, she found that nearly two-thirds of repair strategies involved apologies, while excuses and justifications were also common [16]. We drew heavily from these studies for our survey design.

McLaughlin et al. also examined regretted in-person messages as part of broader work on failure events. They evaluated concession, excuse, justification, refusal, and silence as failure-management strategies. Excuse was most commonly used, although increased guilt by the speaker tended to lead to concession [14]. We expect our work to align more closely with the narrower study of regretted in-person messages.

Like in-person conversation, Twitter is primarily focused on individual short messages, potentially with intended audiences. Thus, to explore the regrets that emerge in Twitter communications, rather than in person, we based our methodologies on previous in-person regrettable messaging work and results.

Regret in social media

Regretted tweets have not been studied extensively; however, Wang et al. performed a mixed-methods study of Facebook users' most regretted posts. These posts often contained sensitive or potentially offensive content, were created during highly emotional "hot states," or were seen by unintended audiences. The researchers also identified audience management and appearance management as major sources of potential regret [19]. While this work informed our analyses, differences between Facebook and Twitter usage patterns and audiences necessitated a different approach for investigating regrets on Twitter. Wang et al. looked at most-regretted incidents, a method often used to examine life regrets. We instead looked at unspecified regrets, a method used for in-person messaging regrets.

Although regretted messages have not been directly addressed for Twitter, a variety of factors have been investigated that could contribute to, or help ameliorate, regret on Twitter. Marwick and boyd found that Twitter users deal with "context collapse." Users fashion tweets that can simultaneously fit a variety of social contexts by tweeting to an "imagined audience," employing self-censorship, or aiming to balance authenticity with conscious identity management [13]. This tension between perceived and actual audiences, as well as the difficulty of balancing authenticity with self-censorship, may lead to regret on Twitter.

Lampinen et al. found that users adopted proactive coping strategies for managing the co-presence of diverse groups on Facebook [10]. Wisniewski et al. also examined interpersonal boundary management on social networks and found that users adopted ad-hoc boundary management mechanisms, such as ignoring information, blocking people, using aggressive behavior, or self-censoring [20].

Twitter presents a social environment with potential for regret. We seek to use methods from in-person messaging regrets research to understand the regrets that emerge, as well as the ad-hoc awareness and repair strategies used to address such regrets, by examining and comparing Twitter users' regrets on Twitter and from in-person conversations.

METHODOLOGY

Our goal was to analyze regrets that Twitter users had experienced on Twitter and during in-person conversations. We conducted a large-scale online survey from August to September 2012 using Amazon's Mechanical Turk (MTurk). We asked each of 1,221 MTurk Twitter users to describe one thing they had said and then later regretted (the regretted message) either during in-person conversation or on Twitter, depending on the condition to which the participant was assigned. We collected a description of the message, the context, how they became aware of the regret, and how they sought to repair the regret. It took participants 14.5 minutes on average to complete the survey, for which they were paid $0.75 (within the typical pay range for MTurk [6]).

Participant selection and conditions

We screened for US MTurk workers over 18 years old who self-reported English proficiency and relatively frequent

Twitter use (having had a Twitter account for at least a month and posting at least monthly). Of the 3,175 MTurk workers who started the survey, 946 did not meet these requirements. The majority (609) were disqualified for posting less than once a month on average.

Survey

Conditions

After the initial screening questions, participants were split into two conditions in a round-robin fashion. The first condition was conversational regret, which mirrored previously described work. The second condition asked parallel questions, slightly reworded to focus on Twitter regret. In both conditions, participants were asked to recall a time when they said or tweeted something and then regretted it, with the wording and format of the prompt based on Meyer's work on in-person messaging regrets [15, 16].

Our prompt for **conversational-regret** participants was:

> "Please recall an occasion when you **said** something during an **in-person** conversation and then regretted saying it. This may be something that you regretted saying immediately or that you regretted saying later."

Our **Twitter-regret** prompt was similar:

> "Please recall an occasion when you **tweeted** something and then regretted tweeting it. This may be something that you regretted tweeting immediately or that you regretted tweeting later."

Survey structure

Participants in both conditions who could not recall a regret were directed to an alternate survey that asked them about why they did not have regrets. We do not report the results of this survey, as the goal was only to ensure an equal workload for either positive or negative responses. Of the 1,879 participants who qualified for the study, 601 (456 for Twitter and 145 for conversational regret) could not recall regrets.

Participants who were able to recall regrets completed a survey about the regretted messages they reported in response to the initial prompt. The survey drew heavily on questions and structure from in-person messaging regrets work [8, 15, 16] and included several groups of related questions. We asked participants about the following:

Regretted message description: a series of essay questions that asked the participant to describe the message in detail, including the context, the reason why they said/tweeted it, the intended audience, the audience's reaction, why they regretted the message and any consequences

Circumstances: follow-up questions about their state when they delivered the message

Awareness: free response about how they became aware that they should not have said the message, followed by a multiple choice selection of how quickly after the message they realized they should regret the message

Repair strategies: a description of whether, how, and how successfully they tried to repair any harm caused by the message; participants were also asked to rate the seriousness of the regret before and after repair

Twitter specifics: questions on Twitter usage (e.g., client and device tweeted from, is/was the account protected)

Demographics: basic demographic questions

We based the general survey structure on the format used in previous work on in-person regrettable messaging [15, 16]. Specifically, we used Meyer's format of asking participants to provide one regret and then probing for details. Although this format has several weaknesses, as outlined in Limitations, it has been used repeatedly to examine in-person messaging regrets.

Quality control on Mechanical Turk

While MTurk has been shown to produce quality samples and results [6], surveys on MTurk should be designed to encourage quality responses. We took several quality control measures. First, we only used MTurk workers who had over a 95% approval rating on the site. Second, we front-loaded longer essay questions. By putting these questions earlier in the study, we encouraged lazy or unmotivated participants to drop out early or to enter nonsensical data where it was visible. It also made it easy for honest survey participants to return to the task, without feeling like they still needed to invest large amounts of time. We removed a small number of participants (25) from the dataset who provided nonsensical or non-English answers to the free response fields.

We also removed responses from 32 conversational-regret participants who responded about a regret on Twitter. We believe they did so because they were primed to think about Twitter when recruited as Twitter users. An additional 350 participants were removed for not completing the survey.

Data analysis

We surveyed MTurk users who posted on Twitter about a regretted message either said in-person or posted on Twitter. Although the surveys for each condition were designed to be parallel, the fundamentally different contexts preclude statistical comparisons between conditions. To explore characteristics of how regret on Twitter compares with in-person regret, we present the results of the Twitter- and conversational-regret conditions side-by-side. The proportions of participants reporting different answers are only meant to illuminate general themes and trends, not to be compared statistically.

Within a single condition, we perform statistical analyses. We use logistic regression to evaluate the relationship between types of regret and whether the audience was a group or individual, the relationship between awareness mechanisms and whether or not regret was experienced immediately, and the impact of repair strategy on the success level. Demographics were compared between conditions using a Wilcoxon test for numerical data and χ^2 tests for categorical data. All tests use a significance level of $\alpha = .05$.

Participant demographics

After quality-control removals, 1,221 people reported regrets: 747 for conversational regret (72% of those who started) and 474 for Twitter (41%). The mean age was 30.3 (28.2 for Twitter and 31.7 for conversational regrets). Overall, 53% of participants were female and 46% were male (10 preferred not to answer). The gender breakdown was almost identical for the Twitter- and conversational-regret conditions. Of the participants, 26% were students and 10% were unemployed. The remainder were primarily employed in science (9%), service (8%), and art (8%) occupations. There were no significant differences between the Twitter- and conversational-regret participants in age, gender or occupation, nor were there significant demographic differences between participants who did and did not report regrets.

ANALYSIS AND RESULTS

Q1: States of being leading to regret

States leading to regret

People often say things they later regret because of demands on mental capacity that impair thought processes. We found that both Twitter- and conversational-regret participants were often in negative, highly emotional states prior to regret. Meyer outlines several factors that contribute to "cognitive load," "physiological state," and "emotional state," which can potentially lead to regret [16]. We asked participants about these states. Based on Wang et al. [19], we also asked whether they were drunk at the time of the message. We asked participants to rate on a five-point scale how much or how little each factor applied immediately before they tweeted or spoke. A one indicated "Not at all" and a five indicated "Very much so." They rated each of the following: "I was fearful or frightened," "I had a lot on my mind," "I was feeling excited," "I felt ill," "I was worried," "I was nervous or anxious," "I was drunk," "I was angry," "I was stressed," "I was tired/fatigued," "I was happy," "I was hung over," and "I felt frustrated."

Consistent with Wang et al.'s work on Facebook regrets [19], we found that both in person and on Twitter, highly emotional negative states were most common prior to regret. Participants commonly reported a four or a five for stress (46% of Twitter and 50% of conversational participants), anger (51% and 43%), or frustration (58% and 53%) prior to the regrets. Participants also often had something on their minds (54% and 51%). Somewhat less common were positive emotions, including feeling excited (26% and 17%) or happy (22% and 21%).

Q2: Types of regret

We also looked at types of regrets participants reported for Twitter and for in-person conversations. In both conditions, participants most commonly reported regretting messages that were critical of others. However, on Twitter, participants more commonly regretted content that was expressive/cathartic and that was intended for groups of people.

Types of regret

We coded each regret described by participants into one of Knapp et al.'s categories for types of regretted in-person conversational messages [8], specifically:

Participant-Reported Types of Regret

	Twitter		Conversation	
Reveal too much	117	25%	105	14%
Direct criticism	96	20%	213	29%
Expressive	64	14%	15	2%
Direct attack	62	13%	108	14%
Blunder	51	11%	120	16%
Implied criticism	34	7%	84	11%
Group reference	13	3%	21	3%
Agreement changed	3	1%	10	1%
Behavior edict	2	0%	28	4%
Lie	1	0%	25	3%
Other	31	7%	18	2%

Table 1. Types of regret for Twitter and Conversation

- **Blunder:** "not normally perceived by a third-party observer as problematic"; mistakes, factual issues; includes typos or errors during conversation

- **Direct attack:** "critical statements directed at a person, the person's family, or the person's friends [...] general rather than specific"

- **Group reference:** stereotypical references about a group (e.g., ethnic, racial)

- **Direct criticism:** critical statements about "something specific" about a person

- **Reveal/explain too much:** telling "more than the situation calls for"; e.g., undesired personal information or a secret

- **Agreement changed:** agreeing to something, then later changing one's mind

- **Expressive/catharsis:** general "expressions of feeling and emotion"

- **Lie:** "knowingly lying to another person"

- **Implied criticism:** "critical remarks that are implicit" and can be "teasing remarks"

- **Behavioral edict:** telling someone to behave in a certain way

Two coders independently coded all the regrets based on Knapp et al.'s categories. Two coders reached a consensus for any regrets for which there were discrepancies.

Across both conversational and Twitter regrets, participants most commonly regretted critical statements (Table 1). Common critical statements included direct attacks and direct criticisms; 29% of conversational and 20% of Twitter regrets were direct criticisms, while 14% of conversational and 13% of Twitter regrets were direct attacks.

Blunders also arose frequently for both conversational and Twitter regrets, although more often for conversational (11% for Twitter, versus 16% for conversational). Although both Twitter- and conversational-regret participants reported some similar blunders, such as saying/posting messages they later found out were false or that had been said/shown to someone who found them offensive, some blunders were unique to Twitter. On Twitter, time-delayed blunders sometimes caused participants to regret messages because of an event or change in context. For example, one participant regretted tweeting about a drive-by shooting in his friend's hometown when that friend was later killed in a drive-by shooting. Twitter, as an online interface, also allowed blunders caused by typos and broken links, which several participants found embarrassing. For example, one participant reported being "made fun of" for tweeting that he "used a lot of hags on [his] car."

Participants also regretted expressive or cathartic content more frequently on Twitter than in person (14% versus 2%). These expressive statements were typically tweeted when participants were angry or upset. They often served to vent or express frustration on topics such as work, relationships, or politics. Often, the goal was to allow others to sympathize or "know what [the participant] was going through." Participants tended to regret the message later after re-thinking how it would sound, or after someone who viewed it became upset. For example, one participant described tweeting "Last day of my internship, so excited to be done," because she "was unhappy with how the internship treated [her] and what had happened [...and] wanted [her] friends to see it because they knew [she] was having a rough time." However, she regretted the tweet when her internship coordinators saw it and sent her an email telling her she needed to delete the tweet. In contrast, expressive regrets during in-person conversations tended to be part of arguments or opinions.

Type and audience
Participants also specified whether they intended the messages to be seen or heard by individuals, or by multiple people. Twitter-regret participants were more likely to target multiple people (73% of Twitter regrets, versus 24% of conversational), likely because of Twitter's broadcast capabilities.

Certain types of regretted messages were more frequently intended for multiple people, especially on Twitter. When the intended audience comprised multiple people, rather than an individual, Twitter-regret participants were significantly more likely to report a blunder ($p = 0.008$), content that revealed too much ($p = 0.005$), or expressive/cathartic content ($p = 0.003$). Of Twitter blunders, 82% were intended for multiple people, versus 33% of reported in-person blunders. Twitter-regret participants often said that they wanted to tweet to friends, coworkers, or others interested in a specific topic, but regretted the tweet because they made an error that caused confusion or made them look bad. For example, one participant reported tweeting, "Congratulations to B for being elected ALA Councilor," intending the message for other librarians in South Carolina. She later realized that the individual was actually a candidate for the position, rather than having been elected, and regretted the tweet because "it was embarrassing."

Twitter-regret participants who regretted expressive or cathartic posts also tended to target multiple people rather than an individual (84% of expressive/cathartic regrets). Participants

often hoped to share political or negative feelings with the general public or their friends because they "wanted to vent" or express their feelings "to anyone that would listen."

Regretted statements on Twitter that revealed too much also tended to be targeted at multiple people (80%). Many participants tweeted personal information, such as details about their lives or relationships, and then regretted sharing them on Twitter. Several participants also reported having both personal and professional accounts and regretting tweeting personal information on their professional Twitter accounts. For example, one participant said that he regretted tweeting "on my professional twitter account about a night of heavy drinking" because it seemed "unprofessional."

In contrast, conversational-regret participants were significantly more likely to report regrets that were direct attacks ($p = 0.024$) when the intended audiences were individuals (67%) rather than multiple people. Participants were typically angry or arguing with the recipient of the message. For example, one participant "screamed at my father that 'I hate him' in an argument" because his father kept him from attending a party. On Twitter, such attacks were commonly focused at groups (68%), and participants reported wanting their anger to be seen. For example, one participant had a conflict with a friend, and wrote "she's so annoying and whiny," intending "it to be seen by friends."

Unintended audience
We also coded for regretted messages having unintended audiences. In conversation, unintended audiences included people overhearing messages (e.g., by walking into a room) or being told about them. On Twitter, most of the tweets reported were public tweets. However, participants still had particular audiences in mind when they tweeted. Unintended audiences occurred because people other than the intended audiences saw or heard about the tweets.

For Twitter regrets, 13% had unintended audiences, compared to 5% of in-person regrets. Unintended audiences occurred most commonly on Twitter for regrets that revealed too much (23% of regrets that revealed too much), often because participants tweeted something private, insulting, or about work, which they later realized they didn't want everyone to know. For example, one participant described how she tweeted "something sexual and my [T]witter at the time was public, so I freaked out when I saw that my brother's screen name popped up on Recommended Twitter."

Level of regret
To measure level of regret, we asked participants "In your opinion, how serious of a problem was it that you said the messages, at the time you said it" (or tweeted it), based on a question from [15]. Participants responded from one ("Not at all") to five ("Very much so"). We consider participants who reported a four or a five to have had a high level of seriousness and below a four to have had a low level.

For Twitter, 18% of messages had high levels of seriousness. For conversational regrets, 38% had high levels of seriousness. However, the interpretation of the difference is somewhat ambiguous; the seriousness of regrets across contexts

Descriptions of Means of Awareness

Self realization	The individual realizes either by thinking about it or by just feeling bad that they should regret the message
Audience says something	The intended audience says something to imply that the person should regret the message
Audience takes an action	The intended audience does something to imply that the person should regret the message (e.g., stops speaking to the individual)
Audience body language	The individual realizes they should regret the message based on the intended audience's body language (e.g., smile, frown)
Third party says something	A person other than the intended audience says something to imply that the person should regret the message
Third party action	A person other than the intended audience does something to imply that the person should regret the message
Third party body language	A person other than the intended audience uses body language to imply that the person should regret the message

Table 2. Codes for means of awareness

may not be directly comparable. For instance, a serious conversational regret may differ from one on Twitter.

Q3: Awareness of regret

Individuals must become aware of regrets to address them. Conversational-regret participants tended to become aware of regret more quickly and relied more on audience actions, such as body-language cues. Twitter participants more often reported realizing regrets themselves or had audience members tell them they should regret the message.

Means of awareness

We asked each participant to describe in a free response how they became "aware [they] shouldn't have said the message." Two coders created a set of codes for means of awareness based on types of awareness outlined in Meyer's work on regretted messaging [15] using a set of 100 regrets (Table 2). The same two coders then independently coded the regrets based on these codes. A third coder also independently coded the regrets to break ties. In cases where all three coders disagreed, two coders reached a consensus. A regret could be coded for multiple, different means of awareness.

Participants became aware of regret using different means on Twitter and in person (Table 3). This is partially explained by the different contexts for Twitter and conversational regret. Audience body language is usually immediately available in person but typically absent on Twitter. Thus, 19% of conversational-regret participants described using audience

Participant-Reported Means of Awareness

	Twitter		Conversation	
Self realization	58%	275	39%	294
Audience said	29%	138	17%	126
Audience action	7%	32	26%	191
Audience body lang	0%	1	19%	143
3rd party said	7%	33	5%	39
3rd party action	1%	5	1%	8
3rd party body lang	0%	1	0%	3
Other	1%	6	0%	3
Total		474		747

Table 3. Means of awareness for Twitter and Conversation

body language to become aware of regret. Participants often realized the regret immediately when they saw their audiences' facial expressions. For example, one participant reported calling "his cousin an asshole in-front of our entire family" and realized he should regret it "[w]hen everyone glared at me."

Conversational-regret participants were also more likely to report relying on audience actions to become aware of regret (26% for conversation, versus 7% for Twitter), also likely due to the intended audience's physical presence. Such actions included storming out of a room, laughter, or sitting silently, which are difficult to convey over Twitter. Offline followups to Twitter messages, such as job termination or laughter, led to awareness for Twitter regrets, as did Twitter-specific online actions, such as being unfollowed or ignored.

Comparatively, Twitter-regret participants more frequently became aware of regret on their own (58%, versus 39% for conversational regrets). Participants in both conditions would often realize that the regretted message was something that they should not have said or tweeted, either after thinking about it or because they felt bad. As one participant put it: "Something inside just told me it was wrong." However, on Twitter, messages also remain available over time. Several Twitter-regret participants reported re-reading the message later and realizing that they should regret it, an option that is rarely available in person. For example, one participant tweeted, "Absolutely pointless," about her relationship and realized she should regret it when she "read over [her] tweets the next morning and thought it was dumb."

Twitter-regret participants were also more likely to report that their intended audience said something to imply that they should regret the message (29% of Twitter, versus 17% of conversational). This may partly reflect the wider audiences targeted by Twitter users but also how, on Twitter, people helped participants realize they should regret a message. Often, a friend or co-worker saw the message and contacted the participant to tell them that they should regret it. For example, one participant tweeted "Having fun on my day off. #callinginsick" and realized he should regret it when "[o]ne of [his] friends told [him] it wasn't a good idea."

Time until awareness

Conversational-regret participants also became aware of regrets more quickly than participants on Twitter. Based on wording used by Meyer [15], we asked participants "how much time passed between" when they tweeted or spoke and when they became aware they shouldn't have tweeted or said the message. We found that the majority of conversational respondents became aware immediately (62%), with many of the remaining participants becoming aware within a few minutes (18%). Of the remaining 20%, the majority became aware the same day or the next day (13%). On Twitter, participants reported taking longer. Only 11% were immediately aware, while 29% realized within a few minutes, 33% at some point the same day, and 16% the next day. The majority of the remaining 11% became aware of the regret within a few days.

For some types of awareness, participants were more or less likely to become aware immediately. On Twitter, participants were significantly less likely ($p = 0.028$) to become aware of the regret immediately (4%), rather than later, when the audience said something to imply that they should regret the tweet. This is consistent with users tweeting and audience members later informing them that they should regret the content, implying a time delay. For conversational regrets, participants were significantly more likely ($p < 0.001$) to learn immediately (84%) from audience body language about a regret. They often reported realizing as soon as they spoke that they should regret the message due to the audience's physical reactions. As one participant reported, "The moment it slipped out, I knew I shouldn't have. The awkward looks and silence that followed confirmed that it was as bad as it sounded." In contrast, conversational-regret respondents were significantly less likely ($p < 0.001$) to become aware immediately (13%) when a third party told them something to imply that they should regret the message. The person about whom they were talking, or who was impacted by the message, often contacted them, delaying awareness. For example, one participant "told a coworker that I intended to leave my job in an open area" and regretted it "[w]hen I went to meet with my boss she told me she had heard rumors."

Q4: Repair strategies

After becoming aware of a regretted message, people often employ strategies to repair the impact, or potential impact, of the message. We asked participants about the repair strategies they used after tweeting or saying the messages, as well as the impact of these repair strategies. We found that conversational-regret participants most often chose to apologize, while Twitter-regret participants most often chose to delete regretted tweets. As occurred in regret awareness, Twitter-regret participants also took longer to repair regrets than conversational-regret participants.

Frequency of repair strategy

We asked each participant to select repair strategies they used from a list taken directly from the conversational-regrets literature [16]. Participants in both conditions were provided with the options: "I tried to say something to offset the harm done," "I tried to justify or defend what I said to minimize its offensiveness," "I apologized for saying it," "I just acted

Participant-Reported Repair Strategies

	Unsuccessful		Successful	
	Twi.	Conv.	Twi.	Conv.
Delete	111	–	134	–
Apology	53	173	72	218
Act like nothing hppnd.	44	70	38	42
Excuse	36	92	34	55
Justify	38	89	30	64
Say something to offset	17	77	22	67
Deny	10	50	10	31
Non-verbal behavior	–	40	–	30
Other	11	21	5	21
Apology and delete	30	–	38	–
Apology and justify	15	49	16	43
Apology and offset	5	52	12	45
Apology non verbal	–	25	–	19
Total (participants)	191	329	196	302

Table 4. Repair strategies for Twitter and Conversation

like nothing had happened," "I denied or tried to take back what I said," "I offered an excuse for why I said it," "I didn't do anything." Conversational-regret participants were also offered the option "I employed a nonverbal behavior to indicate that I regretted it" (from the regrets literature), while Twitter participants were offered "I deleted the tweet."

Overall, we found that a similar proportion of Twitter- and conversational-regret participants took actions (did not report doing nothing) to repair regrets (82% and 84%, respectively). However, the distribution of repair strategies varied (Table 4). Conversational-regret participants most frequently chose to apologize (34% of strategies). Twitter-regret participants most often chose to delete regretted tweets (37%), an option unavailable in person. Both conversational and Twitter participants were relatively likely to try to make an excuse (11% of Twitter and 13% of conversational strategies), justify their messages (10% and 13%), and act like nothing had happened (12% and 10%). However, conversational participants were more likely to try to say something to offset the harm (12%, versus 6% for Twitter).

Success of repair strategies

These different repair strategies also met with varied levels of success (Table 4). Participants rated, on a five-point Likert scale, how successful or unsuccessful their repair strategies were. Participants who ranked their strategies as "successful" or "very successful" were categorized as having successfully repaired the regret. Approximately half of each of Twitter- and conversational-regret participants who took repair actions were successful. Controlling for seriousness of regret at the time of the message, several repair strategies emerged as significantly more likely to be successful or unsuccessful.

On both Twitter and in conversation, using an apology significantly increased the probability of success ($p = 0.043$ and $p < 0.001$ respectively). In person, making an excuse significantly decreased the probability of success ($p = 0.002$), while on Twitter, deleting the tweet significantly increased the probability of successful repair ($p = 0.038$).

Participants who apologized on Twitter varied in their use of online and offline apologies. Online, they apologized using a variety of means, including tweets, instant messages, and text messages. Offline, they apologized face-to-face or by calling impacted individuals. This choice of online or offline strategy seemed to depend on level of personalization and context. Several participants chose to apologize offline because they were confronted about a regretted tweet in an offline environment. For example, one participant apologized when his tennis coach confronted him about an insulting tweet and and told the coach that he "would delete the tweet immediately." Other participants reported apologizing in person to make the apology more personal, writing, "It was personal," so "I called them personally."

Twitter is often a relatively public forum, and, as the regretted tweets often reached wide audiences, apologizing online could also allow participants to reach larger audiences. Participants reported using online apologies to add additional information to their original tweets or add corrections. For example, one participant described accidentally posting misinformation about an animal rescue. After realizing her mistake, she tweeted a correction and an apology. Online apologies were also used to reach large groups of people. One participant described how she "tweeted back so everyone could see my apology and called the person" that she had upset.

Apologies after regretted tweets were also often paired with other online actions. Of the regretted tweets participants apologized for, 54% were also deleted. After posting "something passive-aggressive about someone," one participant described how she tried to repair the situation by telling her "friend that I'd acted immaturely and that I was sorry." She also "deleted the tweet because [I] was embarrassed by my actions."

For in-person regrets, apologies tended to be offline and verbal, often face-to-face to a single person involved with the regret. For instance, one participant jokingly "insulted a friend only to find out his mother had passed away earlier in the week and hadn't told anyone." Once he found out, the participant "immediately apologized stating that [he] didn't know and offered [his] condolences." Such apologies were often paired with justifications (23% of conversational apologies) or explanations that tried to offset the harm (25%). One participant described criticizing how her husband had done the household chores. She explained that she "apologized, and I think maybe explained that I hadn't meant to sound as rude and critical as it sounded. I also thanked my husband for the work he had done and said that I was glad he was so helpful."

Time to repair
Varied amounts of time passed before participants addressed the regretted messages. Participants responded in free-text to "When did you take these actions?" Two coders coded responses for all participants who used repair strategies other than acting like nothing had happened (1127 participants), based on the indication of the first repair. The coders reached a consensus on any disagreements. The categories were: Im-

mediately/a few minutes after the regret (15 minutes or less), the same day, the next day, more than a day but less than a week, more than a week but less than a month, and one month or more. For 32 participants (29 for Twitter and 3 for conversation), the time period was unclear.

Conversational-regret participants tended to respond more quickly, as might be expected because they also become aware of the regret more quickly. Of conversational-regret participants who actively tried to repair their regrets, 392 (67%) did so within a few minutes. The majority of the remainder did so the same day (78 participants, 13%) or the next day (49 participants, 8%). Alternatively, only 98 Twitter-regret participants (26%) who actively tried to repair their regrets did so within minutes; 131 (34%) tried to do so the same day, and 74 (19%) did so the next day. The majority of the remaining 10% took less than a week.

LIMITATIONS
There are limitations in our study design. We performed this study using Mechanical Turk. Although this potentially biases our sample, MTurk's population biases have been documented [18]. Samples and results from MTurk workers have also proven comparable to other online sources [6, 7]. We also took several measures to ensure quality responses. However, such quality control measures may also have biased our participant pool, potentially electing for more diligent or intelligent workers. It is unclear how this impact might differ from quality-control measures used for other survey methodologies. However, previous conversational-regrets work drew from an undergraduate population [15, 16]; using MTurk allowed us to expand to a large, cost-effective sample relative to offline pools or alternative online sources.

Our survey design had additional, inherent limitations. We used the basic design from the conversational-regrets literature [15, 16] in which each participant recalled a single, regretted message. Thus, we don't have a true analysis of the frequency of different types of conversational or Twitter regrets. Based on the conversational-regrets design, we asked participants for the regret that first came to mind, rather than the most recent or strongest regrets. However, certain regrets may come to mind more easily or may be more or less embarrassing to detail in a survey. Thus, we may have an overrepresentation of memorable regrets and an underrepresentation of deeply shameful regrets.

The survey format was also a limitation. We asked participants for self-reported, recalled data. Participants may attribute more meaning to events occurring in the past when reporting on them in a survey. There was also potential for reverse causality issues. We tried to limit causality questions, but participants may have attributed factors like states of being to the regret, when they were actually caused by the regret. We could offer more conclusive results if we tracked participant behavior over time and noted actions, like repair strategies, as they occurred. For example, a diary-study approach could be used to supplement this work.

DISCUSSION

We found that Twitter- and conversational-regret participants differed in the types of messaging regrets they reported, how they became aware of the regrets, and how they tried to repair the harm caused by the regrets. Time delays on Twitter, as well as lack of face-to-face communication with audiences, also caused awareness and repair on Twitter to occur more slowly than for conversational regrets. Based on these findings, we offer several early potential design directions for helping users prevent and repair Twitter regret.

Detecting and preventing regret on Twitter

Although our participants took measures to repair harm caused by the regretted messages, they often would have liked not to have tweeted the messages. One way to potentially prevent regret on Twitter would be to develop tools to detect potentially regrettable messages and provide users with suggestions for when they might want to reconsider tweeting. Behavioral economics offers a potential direction to help prevent users from sending such tweets by using behavioral "nudges" to help people identify tweets they might not want to post [1, 4]. Such nudges are cues that suggest that users should alter a behavior without forcing them to do so.

We found that several negative emotions, including anger, stress, and frustration, tended to lead to regret on Twitter. A recent study of deleted tweets also found a slightly higher frequency of negative-sentiment keywords in tweets that were deleted [3], a common strategy for coping with regretted tweets. Prior to a tweet being sent, such negative states could potentially be detected using tools like sentiment analysis or word frequency. Word analyses could potentially also be combined with environmental cues, such as location, especially when users tweeted from mobile devices; 45% of regrets reported by Twitter-regret participants were made from mobile devices. Once a negative mood was detected, it might be possible to provide feedback to the user about the negative emotion, or, in a manner similar to Google Mail Goggles [17], lock them out until they could think more clearly.

We also found that certain types of regret related to broadcasting thoughts to wide audiences were more common on Twitter. Twitter-regret participants tended to report regretting revealing too much, revealing expressive/cathartic thoughts, and sharing with unintended audiences. Such types of regret might be preventable through better audience awareness or management on Twitter. Participants often regretted tweets that revealed too much or that were expressive/cathartic because they were seen by people they didn't want to see them, or because people saw the tweets and were hurt. For these regrets, it might be possible to indicate more clearly who might view a tweet, for example by showing images of a user's followers. Interestingly, several tweets were sent by participants who had protected accounts at the time of the regretted message (25% overall, and 21% for unintended audience). Participants tended not to accidentally tweet to the general public. Rather, their tweets were viewed by people they didn't initially anticipate would view the posts. This is in line with Acquisti and Gross' concept of "imagined communities" [2] and the concept of tweeting to an "imagined" audience [13]. One

way to visualize the actual audience might be to show images of people who could view the tweet, potentially prioritizing by interaction level. For instance, Lieberman and Miller's Facemail prototype uses this approach for email [11].

Promoting regret awareness

To address a regretted message, users must first realize that they should regret the tweet. We saw several methods for becoming aware of regretted messages that were unique to in-person conversation and could potentially be adapted for Twitter, as well as several techniques that were unique to Twitter and could be further emphasized.

In person, participants often quickly became aware of regretted messages, typically through physical cues. For instance, one conversational-regret participant experienced regret after his girlfriend "instantly became upset and started to cry." Other participants saw audiences storm out of the room or laugh. Twitter users, physically separated from their audiences, usually lack instant audience feedback.

One possibility for improving Twitters users' awareness of regret would be to improve their abilities to gauge potential audience reaction absent physical feedback. Work has been performed to visualize sentiment conveyed in electronic communications. For example, Liu et al. prototyped an "EmpathyBuddy" for email that presents a line-drawn face that reacts to the emotion in the text [12]. Similar visualizations showing the sentiment conveyed by tweets might help Twitter users more quickly become aware of potentially regrettable tweets before tweeting them. A visualization that persisted after a user tweeted might also allow awareness to occur more quickly after a tweet.

We also found that Twitter-regret participants often reported being informed by their communities (e.g., friends, family, and co-workers) that they should regret messages, often over electronic means like text messages, or on Twitter itself. Lampinen et al. discussed how users of social networks collaboratively control disclosure [9]. Their participants used collaborative strategies to protect each others' privacy. Similarly, other individuals helped our participants become aware of regretted content. In some cases, these individuals were impacted by the message. In other cases, they were not. Developing easy mechanisms for people to tell someone about potentially regrettable tweets could mitigate potential regret.

Throughout our results, we saw that Twitter had a time delay compared to conversation, both in terms of time to awareness and time to repair. This was somewhat due to the lack of immediate audience feedback; in cases where Twitter regret was informed by others, this response often came hours or days later. On Twitter, users cannot typically see immediate feedback, and audiences sometimes cannot immediately access messages, delaying regret awareness and potential repair. However, unique to Twitter, even when there was no negative reaction, participants regretted tweets because of the record provided by Twitter. Participants re-read their tweets and realized the message was regrettable. Creating tools that better help users review past tweets may also help them become aware of, and purge, possibly regrettable content.

CONCLUSION

We examined Twitter users' regrets for in-person conversations and on Twitter. We found that, on Twitter, participants tended to report regretted messages targeted at broad audiences, including messages intended to be expressive or cathartic, that revealed too much, or that reached unintended audiences. In general, we also saw that Twitter-regret participants became aware of regret more slowly than conversational-regret participants, more often relying on others to tell them about the regret or eventually realizing themselves that the message should be regretted in the absence of physical audience cues. Once aware of the regret, Twitter users tended to delete the regretted tweet and/or apologize. Based on the findings, we offer several early design suggestions, including behavioral nudges for helping Twitter users realize potentially regrettable posts either before or after tweeting and for better audience management.

ACKNOWLEDGEMENTS

This material is based upon work supported by the National Science Foundation under Grants No. 0946825, DGE-0903659, and CNS-1012763 (Nudging Users Toward Privacy), as well as by Google under a Focused Research Award on Privacy Nudges, by IWT, by a DoD NDSEG Fellowship and by the ARCS Foundation.

REFERENCES

1. Acquisti, A. Nudging privacy: The behavioral economics of personal information. *IEEE Security & Privacy 7*, 6 (Nov./Dec. 2009), 82–85.

2. Acquisti, A., and Gross, R. Imagined communities: Awareness, information sharing, and privacy on the Facebook. In *Privacy Enhancing Technologies*, Springer (2006), 36–58.

3. Almuhimedi, H., Wilson, S., Liu, B., Sadeh, N., and Acquisti, A. I wish I hadn't tweeted that! Large-scale quantitative analysis of deleted tweets. In *Proc. CSCW 2013*, ACM (2013).

4. Balebako, R., Leon, P., Almuhimedi, H., Kelley, P. G., Mugan, J., Acquisti, A., Cranor, L. F., and Sadeh, N. Nudging users towards privacy on mobile devices. CHIPINC 2011 (2011).

5. Bosker, B. The Twitter typo that exposed Anthony Weiner, 2011. `http://www.huffingtonpost.com/2011/06/07/anthony-weiner-twitter-dm_n_872590.html`.

6. Buhrmester, M., Kwang, T., and Gosling, S. D. Amazon's Mechanical Turk: A new source of inexpensive, yet high-quality, data? *Perspectives on Psychological Science 6*, 1 (2011), 3–5.

7. Jakobsson, M. Experimenting on Mechanical Turk: 5 how tos. `http://blogs.parc.com/blog/2009/07/experimenting-on-mechanical-turk-5-how-tos/`, July 2009.

8. Knapp, M. L., Stafford, L., and Daly, J. A. Regrettable messages: Things people wish they hadn't said. *Journal of Communication 36*, 4 (1986), 40–58.

9. Lampinen, A., Lehtinen, V., Lehmuskallio, A., and Tamminen, S. We're in it together: Interpersonal management of disclosure in social network services. In *Proc. CHI 2011*, ACM (2011), 3217–3226.

10. Lampinen, A., Tamminen, S., and Oulasvirta, A. All my people right here, right now: Management of group co-presence on a social networking site. In *Proc. GROUP 2009*, ACM (2009), 281–290.

11. Lieberman, E., and Miller, R. C. Facemail: Showing faces of recipients to prevent misdirected email. In *Proc. SOUPS 2007*, ACM (2007), 122–131.

12. Liu, H., Lieberman, H., and Selker, T. Automatic affective feedback in an email browser. Tech. rep., MIT Media Laboratory Software Agents Group, 2002.

13. Marwick, A. E., and boyd, d. I tweet honestly, I tweet passionately: Twitter users, context collapse, and the imagined audience. *New Media & Society 13*, 1 (Feb. 2011), 114–133.

14. McLaughlin, M. L., Cody, M. J., and O'Hair, H. D. The management of failure events: Some contextual determinants of accounting behavior. *Human Communication Research 9*, 3 (1983), 208–224.

15. Meyer, J. R. Regretted messages: Cognitive antecedents and post hoc reflection. *Journal of Language and Social Psychology 30*, 4 (2011), 376–395.

16. Meyer, J. R., and Rothenberg, K. Repairing regretted messages: Effects of emotional state, relationship type, and seriousness of offense. *Communication Research Reports 21*, 4 (2004), 348–356.

17. Perlow, J. New in labs: Stop sending mail you later regret, 2008. Official Gmail Blog. `http://gmailblog.blogspot.com/2008/10/new-in-labs-stop-sending-mail-you-later.html`.

18. Ross, J., Irani, L., Silberman, M. S., Zaldivar, A., and Tomlinson, B. Who are the crowdworkers?: Shifting demographics in Mechanical Turk. In *Ext. Abstracts CHI 2010*, ACM (2010), 2863–2872.

19. Wang, Y., Norcie, G., Komanduri, S., Acquisti, A., Leon, P. G., and Cranor, L. F. "I regretted the minute I pressed share": A qualitative study of regrets on Facebook. In *Proc. SOUPS 2011*, ACM (2011).

20. Wisniewski, P., Lipford, H., and Wilson, D. Fighting for my space: Coping mechanisms for SNS boundary regulation. In *Proc. CHI 2012*, ACM (2012), 609–618.

Understanding Motivations for Facebook Use: Usage Metrics, Network Structure, and Privacy

Tasos Spiliotopoulos, Ian Oakley
Madeira Interactive Technologies Institute, University of Madeira
Campus da Penteada, Funchal, Portugal
{tspiliot, ian.r.oakley}@gmail.com

ABSTRACT

This study explores the links between motives for using a social network service and numerical measures of that activity. Specifically, it identified motives for Facebook use by employing a Uses and Gratifications (U&G) approach and then investigated the extent to which these motives can be predicted through usage and network metrics collected automatically via the Facebook API. In total, 11 Facebook usage metrics and eight personal network metrics served as predictors. Results showed that all three variable types in this expanded U&G frame of analysis (covering social antecedents, usage metrics, and personal network metrics) effectively predicted motives and highlighted interesting behaviors. To further illustrate the power of this framework, the intricate nature of privacy in social media was explored and relationships drawn between privacy attitudes (and acts) and measures of use and network structure.

Author Keywords

Uses and gratifications; social network sites; social networks; Facebook; privacy; computer-mediated communication.

ACM Classification Keywords

H.5.m. Information interfaces and presentation (e.g., HCI): Miscellaneous.

General Terms

Human Factors; Theory.

INTRODUCTION

Social Network Sites (SNSs) exhibit wide popularity, high diffusion and an increasing number of features. Specifically, Facebook, which currently holds a prime position among SNSs, has a continuously evolving feature set and one billion monthly active users, approximately 81% of whom are from outside the U.S. and Canada, and 604 million of whom access the site via mobile devices [22]. Given this diversity, an effective way of understanding Facebook is by exploring motives for using the service via theoretical frameworks such as Uses and Gratifications (U&G) [18, 32]. A good understanding of

these motives can shed light onto the intricate mechanisms behind important aspects of SNSs, such as site adoption, participation [25], information seeking [26], and the privacy of users [18]. Privacy, in particular, is a major concern since it dictates the usage decisions of many SNS users [5] and as Facebook, specifically, has found itself under harsh criticism regarding the enactment of highly contentious privacy policies and privacy-sensitive features [6].

The emergence of social sites also represents a valuable research resource. Indeed, scholars have highlighted the enormous potential of taking advantage of data that are generated electronically when people use online services [27]. Furthermore, compared to the methods and data available to traditional social scientists, online information can be accessed and analyzed computationally in ways that are both efficient and accurate [16, 27]. In particular, in the case of Facebook, a rich, robust Application Programming Interface (API) allows researchers to collect large volumes of data relating to issues such as site feature use and personal network structure with unprecedented accuracy, granularity and reliability.

Leveraging these data, researchers have recently begun to explore how automatically captured information from Facebook relates to key social concepts. For instance, Gilbert and Karahalios [14] demonstrated that tie strength among friends can be predicted with data collected by scraping Facebook pages. Panovich et al. [30] relied on the same tie-strength algorithm to understand the connection between tie strength and information seeking, while Quercia et al. [35] looked at the links between Facebook popularity and personality, and Burke et al. [9] analyzed server logs in order to understand social capital.

In a similar vein to these efforts, researchers have argued that more data-driven methods for the collection of U&G data can enhance the analytical power of the approach [32]. A typical U&G study employs a survey instrument (or occasionally interviews [34] or focus groups [11, 39]) for the collection of all relevant data. In contrast to downloading data directly from Facebook, this is less efficient and subject to well-acknowledged biases [28]. However, as a theoretical framework, U&G does not mandate that any particular empirical methods be used and, therefore, this paper argues for the inclusion of computationally captured data in the U&G framework of analysis.

One way that this can be achieved is by collecting a broader range of Facebook usage data. Typically, one of the main elements of the U&G frame of analysis is the description of the behavioral outcomes from the use of a system, which is typically operationalized as usage patterns [32]. However, U&G studies in social media limit these behavioral outcomes to crude, subjective measures such as self-reported time on site and/or frequency of visits [e.g., 18, 34, 36], even though it has been strongly argued that such data are inadequate [37]. The benefits of a data-centric study that follows a computational approach to measuring Facebook use would include freedom from issues such as recall bias [7], interviewer effects [29], and other sources of measurement error that may accompany survey research (see [28]), and assure the collection of accurate measures of users' activity, broken down by specific Facebook features.

Another untapped resource in U&G studies is the personal network structure of the users. Even though personal network structure has been extensively included in social science studies, network researchers have long observed major discrepancies between self-reports and behavioral measures [24]. Computational modeling of the personal networks with data obtained through the Facebook API can mitigate this concern. Since the relations among users constitute the building blocks and differentiating factors in SNSs, this paper argues that studies on Facebook motivations would benefit greatly by taking into account characteristics of the users' personal networks.

In sum, this paper extends scholarship on SNSs by exploring what aspects of a person's motives for using Facebook can be derived by examining their usage patterns and network structure. Furthermore, it adds to the SNS privacy literature, by utilizing the interpretive power of the U&G framework to understand which user motivations are associated with different dimensions of online privacy. This work also contributes to theory by expanding the analytic framework of U&G theory to include *network* antecedents, as well as a more comprehensive and accurate measure of Facebook *usage*. Finally, this work expands the methodological scope of U&G by combining a typical survey tool with data captured using the Facebook API.

Before embarking on a description of this empirical work, the following section introduces and reviews a range of related work: U&G theory and its application to social media; measures of Facebook usage; the network perspective in SNSs; and online privacy.

USES AND GRATIFICATIONS

Media is consumed for a wide range of purposes and individuals utilize different media channels to achieve very different ends [20,37]. U&G is a theoretical framework for studying these motives and outcomes – fundamentally, the "how" and "why" of media use [18]. A key strength of the approach is its established and broadly applicable frame of analysis (covering media as diverse as tabloids, reality TV

and the Internet) that combines *motives* for media use (such as entertainment or social connection) with social and psychological *antecedents* (such as demographics) and cognitive, attitudinal, or behavioral *outcomes* (such as usage patterns) [32].

U&G has recently proven valuable in exploring and explaining a wide variety of social media phenomena including topics as diverse as the motivations for contributing content to an online community [26], explaining why political candidates are befriended [1], and cataloguing the psychosocial well-being of teenage girls [11]. U&G studies have explored behavior on most common forms of social media including content sharing sites (e.g., YouTube [15]), SNSs (e.g., Myspace [1]), media sharing communities [19], and blogs [21].

As the currently dominant SNS, Facebook has been the subject of much U&G research. In early work on this platform, Joinson [18] identified seven unique motives for Facebook use: social connection, shared identities, photographs, content, social investigation, social network surfing and status updating. This study also showed that user demographics, site visit patterns and privacy settings were associated with specific motives. More recent work has continued in this vein and attempted to uncover relationships between motives for Facebook use, antecedents and complex communication outcomes. For instance, Papacharissi and Mendelson [31] found substantial links between Facebook motives, social and psychological predispositions, and the generation of different forms of social capital.

Taken together, this work highlights the importance of eliciting and understanding users' motives in social media, as well as the value of employing data from a natural [28] research instrument, like Facebook, for social studies. Such online services offer the potential to combine traditional U&G survey instruments with data derived from sources such as content analysis [32], behavioral traces captured by site servers [25], and network and usage level data derived from public APIs (e.g., [8, 35]). By integrating such information, the methodological scope of the U&G theory is expanded to offer improved explanatory power. This paper highlights the unexplored potential of capturing and analyzing detailed usage information (representing an accurate, detailed depiction of outcomes) and personal network metrics (serving as new forms of antecedent) for U&G studies. The following sections introduce and review work relating to these two topics.

MEASURING FACEBOOK USAGE

Usage of social network services, and Facebook in particular, has most commonly been captured by self-report methods using surveys. Typical questions include time spent on site and visit frequency [e.g., 18, 34, 36, 39]. Acknowledging the lack of rigor in such ad-hoc methods, the Facebook Intensity Scale [12] was introduced to capture the extent to which a user is emotionally connected to Facebook and the extent to which Facebook is integrated into their daily activities. The scale has been subsequently adopted in a number of other studies [e.g., 39, 40].

However, evidence points to the inadequacy of such sweeping cross-site measures. Smock et al. [37] strongly argue that Facebook is better conceived as a collection of features that different individuals use in different ways than as a single monolithic site. Indeed, some studies [e.g., 31, 37] have tried to describe Facebook usage in terms of self-reported frequency of use of partial collections of features. Similarly, Yoder and Stutzman [42] conceptualized user activity as where on the user interface Facebook activity took place and were able to link public, person-to-person communication with perceived social capital. Moving away from self-reported usage measures, Burke et al. [9] showed how Facebook affects social capital by analyzing server logs to identify three types of activity: one-to-one directed communication, passive consumption, and broadcasting.

Overall, this body of literature makes a strong case for the development of studies that capture and analyze Facebook usage automatically and with a fine granularity. In essence, the substantial breadth and scope of the site often render overall descriptions of use too high level to be meaningful.

SOCIAL NETWORK METRICS

Studies of the structure of personal networks, i.e., the networks comprised by the social relationships a participant (ego) maintains with other people (alters), have revealed that network structure can provide a very useful perspective for understanding important theoretical constructs. In fact, a basic tenet of the field of social network analysis is that an individual's position in a network can provide a better understanding of "what's going on" or "what's important" than that person's individual attributes, and it has been argued that exclusively focusing on actor attributes leads to the loss of many important explanatory insights provided by network perspectives on social behavior [24].

Results from network studies have found striking similarities between the social structures in offline and online personal social networks [2], and it has been argued that Facebook networks represent complete and unbiased proxies for hard-to-establish real world friendship networks [16]. Reflecting this perspective, Facebook personal network structure has been associated with many important social constructs and phenomena, such as social capital [8], personality [35], and diffusion of information [3]. The advent of SNSs has greatly facilitated the capture of personal social network data and a wide range of useful metrics can now be calculated automatically and in real time [16]. Commonly used metrics include:

- *Network Size*: The number of nodes in a participant's egocentric network, i.e., the number of friends that an individual has. Correlations have been shown between network size and personality [35] and social capital [8].

- *Network Density*: The extent that nodes in an egocentric network are interconnected – essentially, how many of an individuals' friends know each other. This is calculated as the ratio of the number of ties to the number of possible ties.

- *Average Degree*: Mean number of mutual friends in an egocentric network. Higher values on this statistic have previously been associated with bonding social capital and higher socioeconomic status [8].

- *Average Path Length*: The average geodesic distance between all pairs of nodes in a network.

- *Diameter*: The longest geodesic distance within the network, i.e., maximum distance between two nodes.

- *Network Modularity*: A scalar value between −1 and 1 that measures the density of links inside communities as compared to links between communities [4].

- *Number of Connected Components*: The number of distinct clusters within a network. This has been interpreted as the number of an individual's social contexts [38] and associated with bridging social capital [8] and social contagion [38].

- *Average Clustering Coefficient*: The clustering coefficient is a measure of the embeddedness of a node in its neighborhood. The average gives an overall indication of the clustering in the network, and high values are associated with a "small-world" effect [41].

This paper highlights the explanatory power of these measures and aims to deploy them in a U&G study in order to explore their value as antecedents capable of predicting (or being predicted by) individual motives for media use.

PRIVACY IN SOCIAL MEDIA

Users often make decisions about whether and how they use a SNS based on the perceived privacy implications of their actions. However, privacy is a complex concept that has presented challenges to the social media ecosystem. One key issue is the tradeoff between providing users with advanced new features that mine their data to provide relevant content but lead to negative effects in terms of how users perceive their privacy [6]. Attempting to understand this topic further, boyd [5] argues that in the context of the social web, privacy violations are common because mediated publics exhibit certain properties that are not present in unmediated publics, namely persistence, searchability, replicability, and invisible audiences. Researchers studying the social implications of privacy have concluded that the right to privacy can be considered a social stratifier that divides users into classes of haves and have-nots, thus creating a privacy divide [33].

Finally, the privacy of SNS information is a particularly pertinent topic of study because of research reporting that users find it challenging to understand the privacy

	Median	Mean	SD
Age	20	23.5	8.35
Time spent on site (mins/day)	42.5	71.5	88.3
Facebook usage metrics			
Activities mentioned	3	11.8	28.3
"Likes" given	136.5	306.9	460.9
Photo albums uploaded	12	13.63	7.95
Photos uploaded	153	309.8	388.7
Check-ins posted	0	2.63	6.1
Events currently attending	0	1.22	2.01
Groups joined	11	19.7	23.1
Photos tagged in[1]	33	85.3	265.1
Links posted[2]	8	45.7	127.5
Questions posted	0	0.38	1.38
Status updates posted[2]	21	56.6	96.9
Network metrics[3]			
Size (nodes)	362.5	427	295.3
Average degree	30.6	55.5	59.2
Diameter	7	7.1	2.2
Density	0.111	0.132	0.092
Modularity	0.41	0.4	0.17
Connected components	9	14.7	32.1
Average clustering coefficient	0.56	0.56	0.089
Average path length	2.45	2.6	0.66

[1] in the past 12 months, [2] in the past 6 months
[3] based on the personal networks with ego and their ties removed

Table 1. Demographics, usage, and network metrics collected

implications of SNSs. For instance, recent research has shown that the current Facebook privacy controls allow users to effectively manage threats from outsiders, but are poor at mitigating concerns related to members of a user's existing friend network [17]. Similarly, a study on Facebook apps found abundant misunderstandings and confusion about how apps function and how they manage, use, and share profile data [23].

METHOD

Data Collection and Participants
Participants were recruited with a request to complete an online survey. Approximately 1/3 of participants were recruited through posts on social network sites, 1/3 through posts to online forums, mailing lists and online study repositories, and 1/3 through a Facebook ad campaign. The ad campaign consisted of two ads with similar wording targeted at self-reported English-speaking Facebook users from 12 countries and the experiment was framed clearly as an academic study. Facebook automatically manages the visibility of ads in an auction-like way. Thus, the Facebook ads resulted in the recruitment of a relatively large number of Indian users, possibly due to the lower cost (and therefore higher frequency) of ads distributed to this group. The ads linked to the study description page and participants then had to explicitly click a link to login with their Facebook credentials and access the survey, which is an equivalent action to installing a Facebook application.

During this process the Facebook API ensured the application displayed all data-access permissions granted to it. Thus participants had a good understanding of the data captured by the study. The whole data collection procedure was in compliance with the Facebook terms of service. The app required access to the users' basic profile information and one extended permission: friendlists. 25.5% of participants refused this extended permission, and so this single variable was excluded from the analysis. 67.1% of the people that clicked the link to go to the app accepted the "basic info" permission dialog. The Facebook ads themselves had a 0.059% click-through rate. Participants whose responses exhibited discrepancy between the demographic variables (e.g., gender, age) that were collected through the API and those reported by them in the survey were considered unreliable and removed. This resulted in an 8% discard rate and a total of 208 usable responses. There was no compensation, but participants were given the option to be contacted about the results of the study and to receive information on the structure of their Facebook network.

Participants were 116 males (55.8%) and 92 females (44.2%), with a mean age of 23.5 years old (SD = 8.35, range = 14 – 62 years old). Participants came from 30 different countries, with 85 (40.9%) from the USA and 64 (30.8%) from India. The majority of the sample were full time students (n = 159, 76.4%), 21.2% (n = 44) were employed and 2.4% (n = 5) unemployed. 96 participants (46.2%) reported to have been using Facebook for between 3 and 5 years, 53 (25.5%) between 2 and 3 years, 28 (13.5%) for more than 5 years, and 25 (12%) between 1 and 2 years. 43.3% of the sample (n = 90) reported using Facebook every day and 38% (n = 79) many times per day.

Survey Content
After logging in, participants were directed to an online survey capturing demographics and presenting 28 questions regarding their gratifications from Facebook, corresponding to the items identified by Joinson [18]. More specifically, the participants were asked to answer "How important are the following uses of Facebook to you personally?" on a 7-point Likert scale from "very unimportant" to "very important". Five more questions followed that measured participants' use of Facebook, including frequency and length of visits, and attitudes towards privacy.

Facebook Usage Data and Network Measures
The Facebook API was used to access a range of usage information for each participant (see Table 1). In addition, the participant's Facebook friendship network was also collected via the application. This is essentially a 1.5-degree egocentric network (i.e., the friends and all the mutual friendships among them) with ego (i.e., the participant) removed. Table 1 presents descriptive statistics from the network data, as well as demographics and usage data.

RESULTS

Exploratory factor analysis based on the items used in previous literature [18] led to the identification of the uses and gratifications. The scores for each factor were calculated for each participant, and then a series of multiple regressions was carried out, in order to investigate the effect of Facebook usage metrics and network metrics on the motives for Facebook use. Further analysis examined the effect of the motives to Facebook users' attitudes and actions about privacy.

Identifying Motives of Facebook Use

An exploratory factor analysis was conducted on the 28 items with orthogonal rotation (varimax). The Kaiser-Meyer-Olkin measure verified the sampling adequacy for the analysis, KMO = .850. Seven factors were found with eigenvalues over Kaiser's criterion of 1 and in combination explained 69.01% of the variance. Examination of the scree plot and unique loadings supported the retention of these seven factors. A cut-off value of 0.6 for the factor loadings led to five items being discarded. Table 2 shows the factor loadings after rotation.

Predicting Facebook Motives

A series of multiple regressions were run with the seven motives (i.e., factor scores) of Facebook use as outcome variables. The Facebook usage metrics and network metrics were used as predictor variables with age, reported time spent on site, gender (male = 1), occupation (recoded as a dichotomous variable, student = 1), and nationality (recoded as a dichotomous variable, USA = 1) as controls. The correlation matrix revealed a number of strong relationships among the predictor variables, however none exceeded the 0.8 benchmark which would indicate potential multicollinearity. The highest correlation was found between network diameter and average path length at 0.789 ($p < 0.001$), which is to be expected as both metrics rely on path length, but indicate a different distribution of path lengths in a network. Furthermore, examination of the Variance Inflation Factor (VIF) for every predictor variable found a highest value of VIF = 6.551, which is well below the benchmark value of 10 that indicates multicollinearity. Therefore, we are confident that the regressions carried out were free from multicollinearity concerns. Table 3 shows the results of the regressions.

Predicting Attitudes Towards Privacy

With the intention of investigating more closely the intricate and important topic of privacy in SNSs, further analysis was conducted in order to understand the attitudes and actions towards privacy among different types of Facebook users, i.e., the users with different motives. Two additional multiple regressions were run with the factor scores of the users as predictor variables and the answers to two questions regarding privacy as outcomes. Age, time spent on site, gender and occupation were used as control variables. The question Q1: "Generally, how concerned are

Item	Mean	SD	Factor Loading
Factor 1: Social Connection (α = .775)			
Connecting with people you otherwise would have lost contact with	5.13	1.57	.770
Reconnecting with people you've lost contact with	4.81	1.74	.739
Finding people you haven't seen for a while	4.74	1.58	.706
Finding out what old friends are doing now	4.51	1.61	.651
Factor 2: Shared identities (α = .736)			
Organizing or joining events	3.69	1.92	.815
Joining groups	3.09	1.78	.799
Communication with likeminded people	3.80	1.96	.660
Factor 3: Photographs (α = .878)			
Being tagged in photos	3.58	1.98	.843
Tagging photos	3.25	1.85	.823
Sharing / posting photos	4.28	1.85	.778
Viewing photos	4.85	1.60	.694
Factor 4: Content (α = .862)			
Applications within Facebook	2.54	1.78	.848
Discovering apps because you see friends have added them	2.19	1.61	.797
Playing games	2.02	1.71	.796
Quizzes	2.14	1.61	.779
Using advanced search to look for specific types of people	2.65	1.99	.610
Factor 5: Social Investigation (α = .713)			
Virtual people-watching	2.98	1.97	.817
Stalking other people	2.60	1.96	.688
Factor 6: Social network surfing (α = .894)			
Looking at the profiles of people you don't know	2.67	1.89	.833
Viewing other people's friends	2.91	1.81	.823
Browsing your friends' friends	2.88	1.80	.787
Factor 7: Newsfeed (α = .819)			
Seeing what people have put as their status	4.41	1.78	.766
The news feed	4.95	1.74	.683

Note: All items shared a common prompt: "How important are the following uses of Facebook to you personally?" and were measured with a 7-point Likert-type scale ranging from "very unimportant" to "very important".

Table 2. Summary of factors and individual items

you about your privacy on Facebook?" (mean = 4.83, SD = 1.96) was intended to measure participants' attitudes towards privacy and the question Q2: "How often do you change your Facebook privacy settings?" (mean = 2.95, SD = 1.68) was intended to measure participants' actions. Both items were rated on a 7-point Likert scale from "Not at all" to "A lot", and from "Not at all" to "Very often" respectively. Due to the fact that these outcome variables were measured at the ordinal level, only correlations of significance $p < 0.01$ were interpreted as statistically significant. Table 4 shows the results of this analysis.

DISCUSSION

Motives for Facebook Use

The exploratory factor analysis yielded seven factors, corresponding to motives for Facebook use, which are similar to those identified by Joinson [18]. This was expected, since the same set of items were used. The differences between the factors identified in the two studies

	Social Connection	Shared Identities	Photographs	Content	Social Investigation	Social Network Surfing	Newsfeed
Age	-.014	.351***	.106	.030	-.088	-.083	-.106
Time spent on site	.018	-.049	-.064	.041	.199*	.138	.055
Gender (male)	-.213**	.103	.084	.033	.002	.187*	.108
Occupation (student)	.041	.107	.170	.117	-.071	-.085	-.097
Nationality (USA)	-.042	-.209*	.199*	-.161	.122	-.172	.012
Activities mentioned	-.008	-.079	-.010	.018	-.007	.127	-.049
"Likes" given	-.020	.085	.067	.131	.020	-.119	-.234*
Photo albums uploaded	.011	.057	.222*	.140	.039	-.156	.039
Photos uploaded	-.003	.057	.168	-.332***	.106	.084	.006
Check-ins posted	-.039	-.141	-.033	-.035	-.016	.010	.068
Events currently attending	.125	.152	.061	-.011	.007	.013	-.035
Groups joined	.034	.090	-.050	-.113	.036	-.022	-.068
Photos tagged in	.013	-.056	.049	.013	.075	.015	.047
Links posted	.002	.153*	-.049	.015	-.088	.078	.059
Questions posted	.008	.006	-.114	.088	.045	-.105	-.012
Status updates posted	.040	-.138	.009	-.146	-.185*	-.194*	.324***
Network size	.298*	.014	-.122	.026	-.135	-.033	.017
Average degree	-.299	.059	.169	-.108	.163	.129	-.151
Diameter	.074	.036	-.142	-.076	.206	-.045	.013
Density	.162	-.195	-.050	.031	-.016	.048	.044
Modularity	.197	-.105	.120	-.111	.099	.087	-.160
Connected components	-.104	.171*	.063	.004	.137	-.034	-.171*
Average clustering coefficient	-.048	.209*	.037	-.196	.127	-.177	-.117
Average path length	.011	-.184	-.011	.139	-.259	-.046	.127
Intercept	-0.687	-1.644*	-1.269	1.078	-0.655	1.659	0.935
R^2	.150	.261	.233	.303	.143	.186	.190

$* p < .05, ** p < .01, *** p < .001$, all beta coefficients are standardized

Table 3. Multiple regression models comparing the effects of demographics, Facebook usage measures and network measures

are in the five items that did not load clearly, and the reinterpretation of factor 7 from "Status updates" to "Newsfeed" to better reflect its constituent questions. In addition, the item "Using advanced search to look for specific types of people" was moved from the "Social Investigation" factor to the "Content" factor.

Effects of Facebook Usage, Social and Network Antecedents on Motives for Facebook Use

Gender emerged as a significant predictor of both the *Social Connection* and the *Social Network Surfing* motives, albeit in opposite directions. Females were associated with the *Social Connection* motive (as in [18]), the items of which indicate connections and links to past relationships. On the other hand, males were associated with the factor whose items indicate a tendency for acquiring more information about acquaintances or strangers. Network size, i.e., the number of friends, was also positively correlated with the *Social Connection* motive; users interested in connecting with others tend to have larger networks.

Older participants and those from outside the USA were more motivated by the opportunity to be associated with like-minded individuals, as described by the *Shared Identities* factor. Surprisingly, neither the number of events nor groups that an individual is associated with proved a good predictor for this motive. The number of links posted was positively correlated with this factor, illustrating that

(re)sharing information can be a way of connecting with like-minded people. Interestingly, two network measures were found to have a significant positive effect on this motive: the number of connected components and the average clustering coefficient. The former has been interpreted as the number of an individual's social contexts [8, 38], and in this sense explains the motivation of these

	Q1	Q2
Age	-.033	-.086
Time spent on site	.141*	.046
Gender (male)	-.136	-.055
Occupation (student)	.011	.000
Nationality (USA)	-.233**	-.110
F1: Social Connection	.078	.100
F2: Shared Identities	.149*	.281***
F3: Photos	.033	.000
F4: Content	.068	.231***
F5: Social Investigation	.019	.053
F6: Social Network Surfing	-.015	.048
F7: Newsfeed	.045	.090
Intercept	5.426***	3.549***
R^2	.132	.193

Q1: "Generally, how concerned are you about your privacy on Facebook?"
Q2: "How often do you change your Facebook privacy settings?"

$* p < .05, ** p < .01, *** p < .001$, all beta coefficients are standardized

Table 4. Multiple regression models comparing the effects of motives of Facebook use on two privacy questions

people to belong to distinct groups. A high average clustering coefficient is an indication of networks with modular structure and, at the same time, small distance among the different nodes; in other words, like-minded people will tend to form groups and attend events (based on their similar interests) and will tend not to engage in isolated friendships. In all, the model for the *Shared Identities* motive has five significant predictors from all three variable types, accounting for 26.1% of the variation.

Participants from the USA were positively correlated with the *Photographs* motive, pointing perhaps to the high diffusion of camera-equipped smartphones in that market. Interestingly, the number of photo albums uploaded emerged as a significant predictor, whereas the number of photos uploaded was (marginally) not significant. In a follow-up analysis (not presented), when the number of albums was removed from the model, the number of photos emerged as a very significant predictor. This indicates that, while the two variables share a lot of variation, the number of albums is a better predictor for this motive, possibly demonstrating that people who are really interested in photographs organize them carefully in albums.

The *Content* motive, which includes items for Facebook applications and games, was strongly and negatively associated with only one predictor variable: uploaded photographs. This highlights the possibility of a user population on Facebook that is focused on highly interactive content and disinclined to use and share more traditional media. This finding also reinforces the notion that Facebook uses can be very distinct and that there is a need to differentiate among particular uses when examining the site [37].

Time on site was positively associated with the *Social Investigation* motive, possibly suggesting that this kind of activity can be "addictive" and occupy large amounts of time. On the other hand, the number of status updates posted was negatively associated with this motive, as well as with *Social Network Surfing*. This reinforces the notion of a distinction between users who are interested in contributing content to the site and those that are not [26].

The last motive examined, *Newsfeed*, has two significant usage predictors, "likes" given and status updates posted. It is worth noting that these two major and popular Facebook features predict this motive in opposite direction, again reinforcing the idea that it is important to unbundle Facebook usage to its respective features [37]. For example, the use of likes may indicate someone who tends to respond more to media clips rather than status updates, which, in turn, may seem more appealing to users interested in conversation. Furthermore, the number of connected components in a user's personal network was negatively correlated with this motive. As component count has been viewed as a measure of structural diversity [38], with each component hinting at a distinct social context, this correlation may indicate that Facebook users with a very

large number of diverse social groups get less value from their newsfeed - it may be overloaded, or the content too wide-ranging and tertiary to be of substantial interest.

Looking at the overall picture of the analysis, it stands out that the number of status updates emerged as a significant predictor for 3 out of the 7 motives for Facebook use. This suggests that this feature remains one of the most important aspects on the site, despite the continuous inclusion of new functionality, the shift in the demographics of users and the general evolving ecosystem of Facebook.

The size of a Facebook user's personal network emerged as a significant predictor for one of the seven factors, even though it has traditionally been the most common, and usually the only, network measure in SNS studies. Two more sophisticated network measures, the number of connected components and the average clustering coefficient, also show a significant effect on motives for use. Thus, the impact of the network size appears to have been lessened with the introduction of more complex network measures, suggesting they capture aspects of the structure that are more important and meaningful for understanding motives.

Finally, recent research has suggested that appropriate use of network analysis depends on choosing the right network representation for the problem at hand [10]. Indeed, a previous study of the different "connection strategies" among Facebook users has found that they differentiate between all Facebook friends and "actual" friends at approximately 25% of that total [13]. Since the underlying relations (i.e., Facebook friendships) of networks can vary substantially, it may be that standard network metrics are not directly comparable across Facebook users. Taking the idea of systematically introducing personal network measures in studies of SNS motives a step further, it may be valuable to study alternative network representations, such as those whose links are weighted based on tie strength (see [14]). Such networks may result in metrics and analyses with greater explanatory power.

Understanding Privacy

Nationality showed a significant effect on the regression model for the first privacy question, with participants from the USA being less concerned about their privacy on Facebook, possibly due to the fact that they are more tech savvy and comfortable with this online media. On the other hand, nationality did not have a significant effect on the second privacy question, but two of the motives for use did. Specifically, users that were motivated by communication opportunities with like-minded people were found to be more likely to report tweaking their privacy settings. From the factor's description we know that these people tend to be more enthusiastic about organizing or joining events and groups. This may be because they feel more comfortable in familiar settings and therefore have increased suspicion of strangers or companies on Facebook. Furthermore, since events predominantly take place offline and a popular use of groups is to organize offline meetings, it may be that these people have greater experience of the implications of Facebook privacy settings to offline social interaction. The fact that the *Content* motive was positively associated with frequently changing privacy settings may be due to the fact that people who frequently use applications and interactive content on Facebook have taken the time to understand the privacy implications of installing such dynamic features.

Interestingly, the newsfeed feature, which caused a large backlash with regards to privacy when it was first introduced [6], does not show a significant effect on users' perceived privacy. Furthermore, a substantial discrepancy was observed in the motives of people that report to be concerned about their privacy on Facebook and those that engage in changing their privacy settings.

Theoretical and Methodological Contributions to U&G
Although the U&G framework has been used extensively in the communications sciences, one of its main criticisms is that it relies heavily on self-reported data [20, 32]. This study addressed this limitation by eliciting extensive data about the patterns of use and several social and network antecedents programmatically through the Facebook API. These data should be more accurate than self-reported data about usage or network structure, as well as free from possible cognitive and recall biases.

In fact, previous research [37] revealed that users' motivations for using Facebook predict their use of different features, such as status updates and wall posts, but features that share similar capabilities do not necessarily share underlying motivations for use. When these results are contrasted against models employing unidimensional measures of Facebook use, differences were found between motivations for both general Facebook use and that of specific site features. This suggests that unidimensional measures of SNS use obfuscate motivations for using specific features. The current study took this analytic approach further by looking not only at the reported use of specific Facebook features, but by examining a broad range of Facebook usage data. In particular, a comprehensive set of data corresponding to Facebook usage was gathered computationally, comprising 11 distinct variables as opposed to the one or two variables (time on site, frequency of visits) that are typically gathered through self-reports in similar studies.

Furthermore, this study expanded the methodological arsenal of U&G studies by leveraging the Facebook API to gather a set of data that is by far larger and more diverse than that in a typical U&G study. Furthermore, the network structure was gathered and eight representative network metrics were computed for each participant. This introduced the network antecedent as a possible consideration in the U&G frame of analysis, next to the social and psychological antecedents usually employed.

As a result, none of the regression models for predicting motives for Facebook use were rejected, since at least one predictor variable for every motive was found to have a significant effect. Overall, all three types of predictor variables - social antecedents, usage metrics, and personal network measures - were useful in predicting motives, supporting the validity of this broad data-centric approach.

Advantages and Limitations of the Sampling Procedure
The sampling procedure that was employed resulted in a participant sample that exhibited certain particularities. The combination of recruitment methods led to a sample that was diverse in terms of demographic and geographic distribution, compared to similar studies that typically take place within universities and study students. Since motives for Facebook use will likely vary substantially across cultures, ages, and educational backgrounds, the diversity of the sample used in this work may better match the traditionally exploratory nature of U&G studies.

However, as with other web-based survey studies, the current work was subject to a self-selection bias. Basically, the group of people who opted to participate in the study may not adequately represent typical users. This bias may have been strengthened by the study's requirement that participants install a Facebook application that openly admitted it would access personal details; many users may have been frightened off. On the other hand, these same processes may have discouraged spurious participants (e.g., careless, dishonest, or mischievous web surfers). These advantages and limitations, common to similar studies [35], pose interesting implications for future work using the Facebook API or comparable data-intensive techniques.

Practical Implications
Typically, in a U&G study, after the gratifications are gathered, the analysis examines the effect of the social/psychological antecedents and gratifications on the uses. However, since this analysis is purely correlational, it is methodologically sound to reverse the directionality of analysis and attempt to predict the gratifications from the variables describing antecedents and uses, which is the approach adopted in the current work.

In this study, a number of predictor variables that can be collected and measured automatically by an API were used to establish potentially predictive links to valuable subjective data that can only be collected via a survey instrument. In particular, the motives for Facebook use that were the outcome of this analysis can be very useful information for marketers who want to promote their products or services to the users who visit Facebook with a particular goal in mind. For example, advertisements of digital cameras can be shown to users who score highly on the *Photographs* motive, or applications, games and online services can be suggested to users interested in *Content*. In addition, opportunities for social connection can be shown more prominently to users interested in connecting and interest- or event-based recommendations may more effectively target people scoring highly on the *Shared Identities* factor.

The study found users with large numbers of connected components (i.e., separate social contexts) to be less motivated to use their feeds, independently of overall network size. This hints at information overload – a problem that needs to be addressed in future versions of this feature. Furthermore, status updates were also negatively associated with two motives, *Social Investigation* and *Social Network Surfing*. This suggests that individuals who post few status updates are not necessarily inactive on this site, but may be enthusiastic and regular users aiming to achieve specific, largely observational, goals.

Motives of use can also provide useful insights for features to incorporate into future system designs. For instance, motives can be directly incorporated into user personas in the requirements analysis and design phase of systems, leading to richer creative artifacts. On the interface level, adaptive systems can use the identified motives of use as part of the user modeling process that is employed to personalize and adapt the system interfaces and the user experience. In addition, the relationships identified between specific Facebook motives of use and the way users perceive their privacy, and act on privacy-sensitive issues, can aid the association of specific types of users with the level of privacy or publicity that makes them feel more comfortable and, thus, enable an improved user experience.

CONCLUSION

Investigating the uses and gratifications of a social network site can provide powerful descriptive and explanatory insights into the mechanisms that drive users' behaviors. In this study we identified seven distinct uses and gratifications for Facebook users and investigated the extent to which they can be predicted through a range of data that can be collected automatically via the Facebook API.

In addition, an expansion of the current methodological scope of the U&G framework was suggested. This combines a survey instrument with the wealth of data that can be collected in an automatic way from a social network site, thus enabling the inclusion of a more comprehensive and reliable set of usage data, as well as a number of metrics derived from the personal networks of users. The theoretical implications of this are that network antecedents are useful additions to the U&G frame of analysis, complementing the social and psychological antecedents that are typically employed. In fact, the inclusion of more complex network measures lessened the effect of network size, the single and most common network metric used in prior work.

Finally, this paper highlights practical mechanisms by which the usage of a social network site can be unpacked to its many dimensions with high accuracy and reliability, adding to the descriptive and explanatory power of the U&G framework. This technique applies to unearthed general findings and for exploring specific factors and issues, such as the important topic of privacy.

In sum, this paper has shown the benefits of combining the established framework of U&G theory with detailed data captured from an online social network service. Precise usage data helps unbundle and untangle the links between features and motives, while network antecedents serve as novel forms of predictor. We believe that work that further explores and investigates these topics will continue to shed light on the complex and evolving ways in which users interact on social network services.

ACKNOWLEDGMENTS
The work reported in this paper is supported by FCT research grant SFRH/BD/65908/2009.

REFERENCES
1. Ancu, M. and Cozma, R. MySpace Politics: Uses and Gratifications of Befriending Candidates. *Journal of Broadcasting & Electronic Media 53*, 4 (2009).

2. Arnaboldi, V., Conti, M., Passarella, A., and Pezzoni, F. Analysis of Ego Network Structure in Online Social Networks. In *Proc. SocialCom*, (2012).

3. Bakshy, E., Rosenn, I., Marlow, C., and Adamic, L. The role of social networks in information diffusion. In *Proc. WWW 2012*, ACM (2012).

4. Blondel, V.D., Guillaume, J.-L., Lambiotte, R., and Lefebvre, E. Fast unfolding of communities in large networks. *Journal of Statistical Mechanics: Theory and Experiment 2008*, 10 (2008).

5. boyd, d. Why Youth (Heart) Social Network Sites: The Role of Networked Publics in Teenage Social Life. In D. Buckingham, ed., *MacArthur Foundation Series on Digital Learning – Youth, Identity, and Digital Media Volume*. MIT Press, Cambridge, MA, 2007.

6. boyd, d. Facebook's Privacy Trainwreck: Exposure, Invasion, and Social Convergence. *Convergence 14*, 1 (2008).

7. Brewer, D. Forgetting in the recall-based elicitation of personal and social networks. *Social Networks 22*, (2000), 29–43.

8. Brooks, B., Welser, H.T., Hogan, B., and Titsworth, S. Socioeconomic Status Updates: Family SES and emergent social capital in college student Facebook networks. *ICS 14*, 4 (2011), 529-549.

9. Burke, M., Kraut, R., and Marlow, C. Social capital on Facebook: Differentiating uses and users. In *Proc. CHI 2011*, ACM (2011), 571–580.

10. Butts, C.T. Revisiting the foundations of network analysis. Science (New York, N.Y.) 325, 5939 (2009).

11. Dunne, Á., Lawlor, M.-A., and Rowley, J. Young people's use of online social networking sites – a uses

and gratifications perspective. *Journal of Research in Interactive Marketing 4*, 1 (2010), 46-58.

12. Ellison, N. and Steinfield, C. The Benefits of Facebook "Friends :" Social Capital and College Students' Use of Online Social Network Sites. *JMC 12*, 4 (2007), 1-28.

13. Ellison, N.B., Steinfield, C., and Lampe, C. Connection strategies: Social capital implications of Facebook-enabled communication practices. *New Media & Society 13*, 6 (2011), 873-892.

14. Gilbert, E. and Karahalios, K. Predicting tie strength with social media. In *Proc. CHI 2009*, ACM (2009).

15. Hanson, G. and Haridakis, P. YouTube users watching and sharing the news: A uses and gratifications approach. *Journal of Electronic Publishing 11*, 3 (2008).

16. Hogan, B. Visualizing and Interpreting Facebook Networks. In D.L. Hansen, B. Shneiderman and M.A. Smith, eds., *Analyzing Social Media Networks with NodeXL*. Morgan Kaufmann, 2010, 165-180.

17. Johnson, M., Egelman, S. and Bellovin, S. Facebook and privacy: it's complicated. In *Proc. SOUPS 2012*, ACM (2012).

18. Joinson, A. "Looking at", "looking up" or "keeping up with" people?: Motives and use of Facebook. In *Proc. CHI 2008*, ACM (2008), 1027-1036.

19. Karnik, M., Oakley, I., Venkatanathan, J., Spiliotopoulos, T., and Nisi, V. Uses & Gratifications of a Facebook Media Sharing Group. In *Proc. CSCW 2013*, ACM (2013).

20. Katz, E., Gurevitch, M., and Haas, H. On the use of the mass media for important things. *American Sociological Review 38*, (1973), 164-181.

21. Kaye, B.K. Going to the Blogs: Toward the Development of a Uses and Gratifications Measurement Scale for Blogs. *Atlantic Journal of Communication 18*, 4 (2010), 194-210.

22. Key Facts - Facebook Newsroom. http://newsroom.fb.com/Key-Facts. (Retrieved 13 January 2013).

23. King, J., Lampinen A., and Smolen, A. Privacy: is there an app for that?. In *Proc. SOUPS 2011*, ACM (2011).

24. Knoke, D. and Yang, S. *Social Network Analysis*. Sage Publications, Inc, California, 2008.

25. Lampe, C., Vitak, J., Gray, R., and Ellison, N. Perceptions of facebook's value as an information source. In *Proc. CHI 2012*, ACM (2012).

26. Lampe, C., Wash, R., Velasquez, A., and Ozkaya, E. Motivations to participate in online communities. In *Proc. CHI 2010*, ACM (2010), 1927–1936.

27. Lazer, D., Pentland, A., Adamic, L., et al. Life in the network: the coming age of computational social science. *Science (New York) 323*, 5915 (2009), 721-3.

28. Lewis, K., Kaufman, J., Gonzalez, M., Wimmer, A., and Christakis, N. Tastes, ties, and time: A new social network dataset using Facebook.com. *Social Networks 30*, 4 (2008), 330-342.

29. Paik, A. and Sanchagrin, K. Social Isolation in America: An Artifact (July 5, 2012). *Available at SSRN: http://ssrn.com/abstract=2101146*, (2012).

30. Panovich, K., Miller, R., and Karger, D. Tie strength in question & answer on social network sites. In *Proc. CSCW 2012*, ACM (2012).

31. Papacharissi, Z. and Mendelson, A. Toward a New(er) Sociability: Uses, Gratifications and Social Capital on Facebook. In S. Papathanassopoulos, ed., *Media Perspectives for the 21st Century*. Routledge, 2011.

32. Papacharissi, Z. Uses and Gratifications. In M. Salwen and D. Stacks, eds., *An Integrated Approach to Communication Theory and Research*. Lawrence Erlbaum, 2008, 137-152.

33. Papacharissi, Z. Privacy as a luxury commodity. *First Monday 15*, 8 (2010), 2-5.

34. Quan-Haase, A. and Young, a. L. Uses and Gratifications of Social Media: A Comparison of Facebook and Instant Messaging. *Bulletin of Science, Technology & Society 30*, 5 (2010), 350-361.

35. Quercia, D., Lambiotte, R., Stillwell, D., Kosinski, M., and Crowcroft, J. The personality of popular Facebook users. In *Proc. CSCW 2012*, ACM (2012).

36. Raacke, J. and Bonds-Raacke, J. MySpace and Facebook: applying the uses and gratifications theory to exploring friend-networking sites. *Cyberpsychology & behavior 11*, 2 (2008), 169-74.

37. Smock, A.D., Ellison, N.B., Lampe, C., and Wohn, D.Y. Facebook as a toolkit: A uses and gratification approach to unbundling feature use. *Computers in Human Behavior 27*, 6 (2011), 2322-2329.

38. Ugander, J., Backstrom, L., Marlow, C., and Kleinberg, J. Structural diversity in social contagion. *PNAS, 109*, 16 (2012), 5962–6.

39. Urista, M.A., Dong, Q., and Day, K.D. Explaining Why Young Adults Use MySpace and Facebook Through Uses and Gratifications Theory. *Human Communication 12*, 2 (2009), 215–229.

40. Valenzuela, S., Park, N., and Kee, K.F. Is There Social Capital in a Social Network Site?: Facebook Use and College Students' Life Satisfaction, Trust, and Participation. *JMC 14*, 4 (2009), 875-901.

41. Watts, D.J. and Strogatz, S.H. Collective dynamics of 'small-world' networks. *Nature 393*, 6684 (1998), 440–2.

42. Yoder, C. and Stutzman, F. Identifying social capital in the Facebook interface. In *Proc. CHI 2011*, ACM (2011).

What is "Critical" about Critical Design?

Jeffrey Bardzell
Indiana University
919 E 10th Street
Bloomington, IN 47401
jbardzel@indiana.edu

Shaowen Bardzell
Indiana University
919 E 10th Street
Bloomington, IN 47401
selu@indiana.edu

ABSTRACT

Critical design is a research through design methodology that foregrounds the ethics of design practice, reveals potentially hidden agendas and values, and explores alternative design values. While it seems to be a timely fit for today's socially, aesthetically, and ethically oriented approaches to HCI, its adoption seems surprisingly limited. We argue that its central concepts and methods are unclear and difficult to adopt. Rather than merely attempting to decode the intentions of its originators, Dunne and Raby, we instead turn to traditions of critical thought in the past 150 years to explore a range of critical ideas and their practical uses. We then suggest ways that these ideas and uses can be leveraged as practical resources for HCI researchers interested in critical design. We also offer readings of two designs, which are not billed as critical designs, but which we argue are critical using a broader formulation of the concept than the one found in the current literature.

Author Keywords:

HCI; critical design; critical theory; design methodology

ACM Classification:

H.5.1.m. Information interfaces and presentation (e.g., HCI): Miscellaneous.

INTRODUCTION

The dramatic changes over the past three decades of technology in society has far more than implications for HCI theory: it has socio-cultural implications that affect many if not most spheres of human life, from public policy to the spiritual, from childhood education to care for the elderly, from our cyborg identities to globalized sociability. HCI as a field is increasingly taking seriously its own sociocultural significance: looking beyond concerns about usability and professional support tools, there has been a steady increase in focus on issues such as user experience, social justice and activism, values-oriented design, postcolonialism, etc.

In short, we are collectively asking what it means to live in this electronic world we are creating, whether this world reflects our values, who is entering into this world that we

are designing and whom we are leaving behind. These questions are at least as philosophical as they are technological, and there is more than one way to approach them: science and technology studies, philosophy of technology, and similar fields offer one strategy. Another is the emerging area of research through design or constructive design [20,34], which "refers to design research in which construction—be it product, system, space, or media—takes center place and becomes the key means in constructing knowledge" [29, p.5].

One form of constructive design is critical design, a term coined by Anthony Dunne and Fiona Raby. *Critical design* is a form of research aimed at leveraging designs to make consumers more critical about their everyday lives, and in particular how their lives are mediated by assumptions, values, ideologies, and behavioral norms inscribed in designs [14,15]. On the surface, critical design seems to be well positioned to support HCI research that takes seriously technology's role in creating futures that serve but also marginalize, that aesthetically please but also isolate, that stimulate economic growth but also threaten the earth.

However, in spite of its apparent potential for much recent HCI, critical design is not used very much in HCI. One reason might be that HCI researchers do not know how to do it [4]. Evidently there has also been general confusion about what critical design is: founders Dunne and Raby have tried to correct common misconceptions in their writings. Also, there is confusion about whether design work that has been featured in HCI—most notably projects coming out of Goldsmiths—are or are not at all critical design. [4] and [29] for example both group Goldsmith's work together with critical design, a characterization hotly disputed by Bill Gaver (personal communications).

The argument of this paper is follows: critical design has high potential for the HCI design community; the critical design literature remains too underdeveloped to offer the practical support needed for its broader uptake; design theorists and researchers can improve this situation not by decoding whatever Dunne and Raby might have meant, but by actively and creatively developing critical design in ways that we as a community want to see it used; we offer one such contribution in this paper by (a) exposing some problems that we see in Dunne and Raby's accounts of critical design, our sympathy notwithstanding, (b) looking beyond Dunne and Raby to identify more useful understandings of the term "critical" than can be found in their writings, and

(c) iterating on present understandings of critical design with a broader view of critical thought in mind. The goal of doing so is not at all to offer a "pure" or "correct" notion of critical thought or critical design, but rather to provide a wider and more accessible range of conceptual handles that design researchers can leverage in their day to day work.

ORIGINS AND GOALS OF CRITICAL DESIGN

The Frankfurt School of critical theory, embodied in the works of Horkheimer, Adorno, and Marcuse, argued that products of mass media and consumer culture were politically regressive. In developing this argument, Adorno offered a concept he called *reification*, which "refers to the way that things are produced by society, including the way that it is organized, appear as entirely natural and beyond question [28, p.172]. The underlying concepts here are notions of ideology and alienation as interpreted by some theorists in the Marxist tradition. Simplifying, the basic idea is that dominant social classes maintain their dominance by disseminating a system of myths presenting the status quo as natural and good (this is ideology) which encourages the working class to buy into a system that works against its own interest (this is alienation). Consumer culture is the key mechanism of this system: movies, magazines, and design represent and implement a collection of norms and behaviors that condition the working class (this is reification). The hope was that if critique could expose such operations and bring them to our collective consciousness that we might be better able to resist ideology and reification and instead work towards a more just society.

Although Dunne and Raby in an interview distance critical design from the Frankfurt School [16], their formulation of critical design has unmistakable affinities with it:

> Product genre…offers a very limited experience. Like a Hollywood movie, the emphasis is on easy pleasure and conformist values. This genre reinforces the status quo rather than challenging it. We are surrounded by products that give us an illusion of choice and encourage passivity. But industrial design's position at the heart of consumer culture (it is fuelled by the capitalist system, after all) could be subverted for more socially beneficial ends by providing a unique aesthetic medium that engages the user's imagination [15, p.45]

Their language "illusion of choice," "passivity," "reinforces the status quo," "easy pleasure and conformist values," and "fuelled by the capitalist system" bear the unmistakable stamp of the Frankfurt view of ideology. And Dunne and Raby, correctly in our view, pick up on an important implication of this thought for designers: in many ways, harmful ideologies are perpetuated through our work, which is to say that we can become a locus of resistance, and thus by implication *designers are ethically implicated one way or another in the problem domain of social domination no matter what we do*. Dunne and Raby sketch out two opposing ethical positions that design inevitably participates in:

Design can be described as falling into two very broad categories: affirmative design and critical design. The former reinforces how things are now, it conforms to cultural, social, technical, and economic expectation. Most design falls into this category. The latter rejects how things are now as being the only possibility, it provides a critique of the prevailing situation through designs that embody alternative social, cultural, technical, or economic values. [15, p.58]

Critical design, like Frankfurt School critical theory before it, is a research strategy dedicated to transgressing and undermining social conformity, passivity, and similar values of capitalist ideology, in hopes of bringing about social emancipation. These goals were reinvigorated by the advent of poststructuralism in the 1960s and 70s, especially in the work of Barthes [5]. But whereas these critical theorists used a combination of philosophical and social scientific practices [31], Dunne and Raby instead propose a design research program to operate in similar ways.

So how does critical design subvert the system, engage the user's imagination, and bring about social change? Dunne describes critical design as "a form of social research," so its primary intended outcome is knowledge, not a design product. For Dunne and Raby, its purpose is to "seduce the viewer into the world of ideas rather than objects" [14, p.147], and "to make us think. But also raising awareness, exposing assumptions, provoking action, sparking debate, even entertaining in an intellectual sort of way, like literature or film" [17]. In short, critical design uses design as a strategy to cultivate in the public a critical sensibility, which they define as follows:

> The critical sensibility, at its most basic, is simply about not taking things for granted, to question and look beneath the surface. This is not new and is common in other fields; what is new is trying to use design as a tool for doing this. [18]

The specific critical goal is to leverage design itself in bringing about more critical attitudes in the public and critically innovative thinking among designers. As noted earlier, Dunne and Raby offer few specifics on how this is done, and they characterize critical design as more of an "attitude" than a "method." Indeed, we could find very little methodological direction anywhere in their writings, though they imply one in their use of words like "transgression," "provocation," "satire," and the "staging of dilemmas."

In sum, critical design as articulated by Dunne and Raby is a professional ethical stance for designers. It holds the design profession to account for its complicity with capitalist ideology and alienation. It names some design values of global capitalism—conformity, obedience, easy pleasure, and corporate identity, among others. It challenges designers and consumers alike to envision—and to demand—design products that reflect a more challenging view of human needs and experience, including engaging the sorts of dark pleasures that the best literature and film engage. By inscribing alternative values in designs, critical design cultivates critical attitudes among consumers and designers alike, creating demand for and supporting the professional emergence of alternative design futures.

CRITIQUING CRITICAL DESIGN
We are highly sympathetic to the research project of critical design, but we are discouraged by its relatively weak showing in HCI. For critical design to emerge as a design research program in HCI, we believe that other researchers need to step in and contribute to it, and also that—in the critical spirit—these others will have to operate without Dunne and Raby's expressed or implied blessing. In this section, we will react critically to some of the central claims of critical design. By doing so, we aim to identify areas of opportunity for developing critical design.

Critical Design is Opposed to Affirmative Design
At the core of Dunne and Raby's thinking is their opposition between affirmative and critical design, that is, between designs that affirm vs. subvert the status quo, defined as global capitalism. While the direction of this thinking is appealing, its present formulation is more vague and political than professionally useful. It is political, because Dunne and Raby not only make the distinction but also attach strong value judgments to it: affirmative design is the common practice, and this practice is amoral and ultimately a dupe for capitalist ideology, while critical designers are described as moral agents who seek to change society for the better. Since affirmative design is a pejorative, and critical design is an honorific, the question of who gets to decide whether a design is affirmative or critical is key.

Nor is it clear how such a judgment could be made: how do we recognize critical design when we see it? It would seem that lots of designs challenge the status quo in certain ways. For example, objects of Japanese consumer culture often strike Westerners as challenging and even defamiliarizing, so Japanese designers on this view would seem to become critical designers (but only in the West) by virtue of historically accidental cultural differences! By the same token, if a designer had all the right critical stances and attitudes, but produced designs that were ultimately affirmative in spite of her best efforts, then it would seem that we couldn't call her a critical designer.

The stated binarism of the affirmative/critical opposition also cannot deal with the well known fact that capitalism is extremely fast at appropriating countercultural signifiers and commercializing them for the mainstream, e.g., Vivienne Westwood's appropriation of punk visuality into haute couture. A more complex case is digitally enabled designer sex toys, the (capitalist) designers of which are collaborating with feminist activists, sexual health experts, and the public to design devices that simultaneously transgress against mainstream sexual norms and also provide consumers very simple pleasures [3]; so are they critical or affirmative?

In short, the affirmative/critical distinction points to an ideal whose relationship is very difficult to understand from the perspective of real designs, and yet how a designer or her designs are judged by these criteria has strong consequences in terms of dissemination, funding, reputation, etc. Without a richer vocabulary for making judgments in a rational and consensus-driven way, critical design risks being a cult of personality and a stick to hit people with, rather than a self- and critically-reflexive professional stance.

Critical Design is Not Art
In several writings Dunne and Raby react to the common perception that critical design is art, but they emphatically assert that critical design is not art. We begin by summarizing why a person might suppose critical design is art-like. By identifying critical designs as artifacts that bring about criticality; as aesthetic artifacts that operate (epistemologically at least) outside of global capitalism; and as artifacts that foreground provocation and transgression, the staging of existential situations, and the exposition of cultural assumptions, Dunne and Raby deploy a conceptual vocabulary strongly associated with art. The notions of aesthetic artifacts, aesthetic situations, and aesthetic experiences, understood in ways that art historians, literary theorists, philosophers of art, and film critics talk about such things is also a strong contributing current throughout their work.

With that background, let us consider the two arguments that Dunne and Raby make to refuse the art designation for critical design. One is that art is isolated from the everyday and its messages easily bracketed aside by the public as "just art," but design is a part of the everyday and has more potential to disturb the everyday [15, p.58;17]. The other is that art is "shocking and extreme," but critical design "needs to be closer to the everyday, that's where the power to disturb comes from" [17].

Regarding the first—that art is isolated from the everyday, which creates a bracketing that allows people to dismiss art—we respond that this view seems hard to square with experience. Art is a part of everyday life: teenagers in high school bands and ballet classes, art house cinema, sacred art, fine art photography on magazine covers, open air jazz concerts in city parks, graffiti, etc. We couldn't avoid art—or its messages—if we wanted to. Similarly, the notion that art is "shocking and extreme" is an overly narrow conceptualization of art. Duchamp, Mapplethorpe, and Schneemann certainly shocked audiences, but they are in the minority, if we acknowledge such things as Chinese landscape paintings, eighteenth century chamber music, sculpture gardens, still life painting, pastoral verse, sacred art, and folk art. At best, Dunne and Raby have distinguished themselves from a very limited art practice—the fine arts that are fashionable in today's artworld.

Moreover, even if we were to grant this dubious distinction between art and critical design in the terms Dunne and Raby seem to want to, how can Dunne and Raby ensure that their critical designs will not also be dismissed by members of the public, if not as "art" then instead as "strange university stuff"? Their answer seems to be that any given good critical design walks a fine line: "Too weird and it will be dismissed as art, too normal and it will be effortlessly assimilated" [17]. But this answer suggests that it is the individual design, not the ontological category to which it belongs (i.e., art vs. critical design), that determines its critical effects. But then one could argue that there is no reason why a given work of art cannot also walk that line between being dismissed as weird and being assimilated as everyday; indeed, isn't the desire to be challenged in this way the reason why so many of us listen to classical music, go to art exhibitions and museums, watch art films, and read classic or challenging novels? Dunne and Raby's assertions notwithstanding, the difference between art and critical design does not appear to be ontological; it must be something else, a topic to which we return below.

Critical Design is Critical

What distinguishes critical design from other forms of design is presumably its criticality. But in spite of diverse efforts, Dunne and Raby do not articulate what they mean by "critical" in sufficiently practical terms. We have already cited the most explicit definition of "critical" that we could find in Dunne and Raby's writings: "The critical sensibility, at its most basic, is simply about not taking things for granted, to question and look beneath the surface" [18]. This is a straightforward and conventional enough definition. The immediate follow-up questions are: what does it mean to "look beneath the surface"? What sort of things are you supposed to find under there? And how do you know when you've identified the most important things under that surface? Dunne and Raby have much to offer in response to these questions. Their primary strategy is to offer dozens if not hundreds of examples of designs that they argue serve a critical function. These examples themselves are thematically organized around provocative ideas. In many cases, these readings are supplemented with brief allusions to critical thinkers and design intellectuals. A typical example of the approach is "(In)human Factors" a chapter in *Hertzian Tales* [14]. Dunne introduces the concept of usability only to turn it on its head to suggest that user-friendliness is a bad norm to try to achieve, because it obfuscates the ideology of design and encourages passivity. The chapter is in many ways an enjoyable read, because it makes startling connections between concepts and design particulars. And yet "(In)human Factors" is also a very difficult read. It is a soup of ideas: dozens of challenging designs, a dizzying array of Marxist, semiotic, and architectural theorists follow on each other fast and furious, with little explication or development. It places a considerable burden on the reader to infer how all of this adds up to a critical design practice.

Understanding what's critical about critical design might be easier if Dunne and Raby's work clearly explicated a healthy range of critical outcomes that have emerged from critical designs. But here their writings are surprisingly narrow and repetitive: we read a lot about transgression, prov-

ocation, defamiliarization, and estrangement—a deeply related (both logically and historically) collection of ideas. A thoughtful reader might wonder whether defamiliarization and ideology really are all that "critical" boils down to. Our answer is an emphatic no, and thereby we open the door through which we hope to contribute to critical design.

RECONSTITUTING CRITICAL DESIGN

Given the sorts of concerns that we have raised, a sympathetic but critical contribution to critical design therefore might try to change the practice in a way that both preserves what is good in critical design and rectifies some of its existing shortcomings. Here is what we believe is good about critical design and that come what may we want to preserve: critical design is a design research practice that foregrounds the ethical positioning of designers; this practice is suspicious of the potential for hidden ideologies that can harm the public; it optimistically seeks out, tries out, and disseminates new design values; it seeks to cultivate critical awareness in designers and consumers alike in, by means of, and through designs; it views this activity as democratically participatory. The intent of the following is to provide practical resources to support HCI researchers in doing all of this.

The primary concern that we hope to address is that Dunne and Raby's view of "critical" is too eccentric and narrow and inadvertently mystifies critical design. We believe that substantially rethinking the notion of *critical* in this literature will also help address two other secondary problems: the disturbing politics and vagueness of the affirmative versus critical design distinction and the muddled relationship between critical design and art. Our approach has been to survey a wide range of critical literature from the past 150 years, seeking to collect and accessibly present some of the diverse notions and uses of critical thought that have had an impact in other fields. Our rhetorical strategy is to present two "families" of thought, not to assert them as hard ontological categories or as the correct way to think about critical thought, but rather because doing so offers pragmatic benefits by revealing how critical concepts *are actually used*. We will refer to the two families as *critical theory* and *metacriticism*.

- *Critical theory* refers to the family of skeptical sociocultural critique with origins in the philosophy of Marx of Nietzsche. It includes the Frankfurt School of critical theory and the explosion of critical theory between the 1950s and 1980s, which included semiotics, poststructuralism, feminism, psychoanalysis, and Marxism.

- *Metacriticism* refers to attempts to answer questions such as: What are the categories of criticism? How do we distinguish good from bad criticism? What is the social role of criticism? Generally, it is concerned with skilled appreciation of the arts and can be found in the English-language tradition of literary criticism (e.g., Arnold, Frye, Eliot, Abrams, and Bloom) and analytic aesthetics (e.g., Beardsley, Cavell, and Carroll).

The sketches we present of these families of thought obviously fail to account for both the variety and conflict within each family and also the complex relationships between them. Nonetheless, by distinguishing them, we can tease out some different threads that constitute critical thought and show ways that they have been used, which in turn reveals their potential usefulness for design researchers.

Critical Theory

We start with critical theory, because in many ways Dunne and Raby seem to rely on this line of thinking more than the other. We seek to give a sense of critical theory as a holistic or synoptic framework for thought, rather than a collection of unclearly related concepts (as they are often presented in HCI). The categories we will briefly sketch are predispositions, methods, theories and concepts, general cultural benefits, and what they offer critical design; we acknowledge that some of this vocabulary is alien to critical thought (especially "methods"), and our use of it reflects our intent to express this thought as accessibly as possible for HCI.

Predispositions. As noted earlier, one fundamental thread of all forms of critical theory is skepticism, a suspicion that social reality is not what it seems but rather that something else quite different is going on underneath its surfaces: capitalist domination, patriarchal oppression, erotic and thanatotic unconscious drives, signifying systems, etc. The job of the critical theorist is to expose these hidden forces that are claimed to determine much of our social lives. Implicated in all of this are social institutions—governments, the sciences, the arts—which means that the critical theorist often takes a skeptical position against these institutions and whatever they celebrate as part of the problem. On this view, we don't make high school kids read Shakespeare because his plays enlighten us, but rather because they inculcate students into an ideology by championing certain values over others and/or by providing aesthetic pleasures that mask the pain of real existence. A related predisposition of critical theory is that most people are alienated in some form or other, that they are fooled by the system, and that the critical theorists can facilitate in their emancipation.

Methodologies. Critical theorists commonly use three methodological strategies to do their work. The starting point is what Carroll calls "the hermeneutics of suspicion," which refers to the skepticism just summarized, cast specifically as an interpretative (as opposed to, e.g., empirical) problem [10]. Ideology, patriarchy, and the unconscious often do not manifest themselves in directly observable or measurable ways, and so their existence and operations must be interpreted; critical theory is a strategy of reading social formations and artifacts. One particular hermeneutic strategy is the deployment of *dialectics* that foreground conflicts and historical specificity within societies, eras, situations, events, etc., which are normally presented as unified and timeless. For example, feminist critics have shown that the social sciences, in spite of their rigor and commitment to truth, have carried within them prejudices

and gendered power relations that are irrational by social science's own standards, and that that irrationality has had consequences in the world that are invisible without this critique [27]. A related methodological approach is *utopian thinking*, which imagines realistic but genuinely better worlds or societies, setting up a dialectical contrast between our present reality and its imagined counterpart, which both stimulates demand for a better society and may also clarify some of the concrete mechanisms of a better society [21,28].

Theories and concepts. Critical theory commonly comprises systems of concepts that facilitate the activity of the hermeneutics of suspicion: ideology, reification, alienation, fetish for Marxism; unconscious, eros, mirror stage, the abject for psychoanalysis, etc. But it is the *use* of these concepts that distinguishes critical theory. A good scientific theory is parsimonious and explanatory: it explains why a diverse range of phenomena are the way they are (e.g., evolution or global warming). Moreover, scientific theory is (ideally) objective and apolitical. But, paraphrasing Marx, the point of critical theory is not to describe the world but to *change* it. Theory is introduced speculatively to pierce through and destroy ideological constructs; metaphors of violence are quite common when characterizing critical theory, from Baudrillard's "speculation to the death" to Stuart Hall's account of feminism's effects on cultural studies: "As the thief in the night, it broke in; interrupted, made an unseemly noise, seized the time, crapped on the table of cultural studies" (and, if not obvious, for Hall this was a good development) [26, pp.282-3]. Critical theory is thus often adversarial and confrontational.

Sociocultural benefits. The most direct cultural benefit of critical theory has arguably been its ability to expose the limits of rationality, various hidden modes of domination, and the relationships between the rationality and domination. Doing so supports both social activism and scientific reform. By pointing out, for example, the rampant sexism and racism of popular media, critical theorists helped effect at least some change in the images of women and minorities in popular media. Above all, critical theory holds out the hope that with and through it, people can improve the socio-political situations in which they find themselves.

Potential uptakes for critical design. As Dunne and Raby make clear, they take seriously the skepticism at the heart of critical theory, and applying it to their own profession—design—they came to understand how designers participate in global capitalist hegemony and began to think—dialectically—how they could resist it. Clearly the conceptual vocabulary of the Frankfurt School has influenced Dunne and Raby, and we see in their writings glimpses of other critical theoretic conceptual vocabularies, though they are not yet put to as much work as the Frankfurt framework. Our reading of Marxist utopian thought—e.g., that of Marcuse—is compatible with critical design, though Dunne and Raby denigrate utopianism many times (we suspect we're not defining "utopian thought" in the same way they are). We also observe that feminism and psychoanalysis would seem to be powerful intellectual resources for critical design, though Dunne and Raby make less use of them.

More critically, we also note some challenges for critical theory's introduction into critical design. One challenge is tone: critical theorists can come across as sanctimonious, and we read Dunne and Raby sometimes in that way, which undercuts consensus. More radically, postmodern forms of critical theory seem to preclude the very possibility of consensus, seemingly denying the possibility of facts or communication [30]: staying grounded will be key, though what that would mean exactly is unclear. A final risk of critical theories is that they sometimes imply determinism or "grand narratives" in Lyotard's memorable phrase, leaving little room for agency, the possibility of intentional change, or any room for critical theory itself (or, by extension, critical design).

Metacriticism

Though Dunne and Raby make little direct reference to the tradition of metacriticism, it seems obvious to us that it, too, can be leveraged for critical design. We follow much the same procedure as before, attempting to offer a synoptic description of this family of thought structured by a handful of common categories.

Predispositions. In the grouping of literature we're referring to as metacriticism, most of the writers are speaking as cultural thinkers and educators within (mostly) state-supported educational institutions. These writers, from the Victorian Mathew Arnold [2] through T.S Eliot [19], René Wellek [33], and Harold Bloom [9], take for granted that humankind's most advanced and enlightening forms of thought can be found in the great traditions of the arts, and therefore that members of a civilized society should engage with them. As philosopher Nelson Goodman writes, aesthetic symbolization "is to be judged fundamentally by how well it serves the cognitive purpose: by the delicacy of its discriminations and the aptness of its allusions; by the way it works in grasping, exploring, and informing the world; by how it analyzes, sorts, orders, and organizes; by how it participates in the making, manipulation, retention, and transformation of knowledge" [25, p. 253]. Criticism makes the cognitive benefits of aesthetic engagement more accessible to the public. This view contrasts with the view common in critical theory that "great art" is simply another mechanism of reification and alienation.

In addition to positing that engagement with the arts is intellectually beneficial for the public, the metacriticism family of thought also confronts the fact that this engagement is not easy or natural. Thus, a social problem that critics confront is helping citizens achieve cultural competence: the ability perceive the (dis)value of cultural products, to perceive and make delicate discriminations, to have sensitive and insightful rather than crude aesthetic reactions, to cultivate an aesthetic sensibility. Criticism—from the first time

a child hears "isn't that sunset beautiful?" from a parent through an academic explication of the role of narrative in a modern dance performance—helps us build these skills.

Methodologies. The methods of this tradition are often highly medium- and discipline-specific, and above all they are used to support skilled aesthetic analysis. Noël Carroll describes criticism as comprising six fundamental activities: description, classification, context-providing, elucidation, interpretation, and analysis [11]. There's no room to explain here what he means by each of these, but suffice it to say that all of these are highly technical activities that support the close reading of cultural texts. Another common methodological strategy deployed throughout this tradition is a careful analysis of the relationships between aesthetic forms (e.g., rhetoric, materials, medium) and aesthetic experiences (e.g., insights, interpretations, emotional responses, and discovery of truth) [7].

Theories and concepts. Comparatively speaking, metacriticism tends to be eclectic and pragmatic; see e.g., [1]. One reason for this is the quasi-scientific rhetoric often deployed to characterize its work, and in particular the notion that criticism is an inductive discipline [1,19,22,33]. In that sense criticism tends to be relatively undogmatic and strives to be about attentiveness to artworks themselves; many recent critics (Carroll is one of many examples) are even skeptical of critical theory's reflexive skepticism, challenging whether its skepticism is warranted as often as it is used and suggesting that it distracts from the value of cultural texts. Metacriticism's conceptual vocabulary fluidly accommodates concepts ancient and modern: *ekphrasis, catharsis, mimesis,* the objective correlative, the intentional fallacy, the *novum,* and so forth. If criticism has an underlying theoretical commitment, it is probably the idea that increasingly skilled aesthetic perception leads to increasingly skilled aesthetic appreciation, which in turn leads to wisdom or individual enlightenment.

Criticism has two subcategories: criticism of individual works and criticism of ideas [1]. The former includes close readings typically of works already deemed important or works whose importance critics wish to promote, while the latter collects, curates, and critiques important ideas to help readers make better use of them (this paper is an example of this mode of criticism). As with critical theory, the role of theory in this tradition is speculative: not to explain what is known but to challenge us to see in new ways, to generate new modes of engagement or ideas.

Sociocultural benefits. A key benefit of this family is its broad educational value, that is, its focus on helping remove perceptual and intellectual barriers that prevent people from appreciating the value of art in aesthetically complex and valuable ways. Importantly, this practice scales gracefully from schoolchildren throughout life, since we are always able to learn new and increasingly subtle aesthetic or critical distinctions in much the same way we did as children [32]. Simply, criticism makes our lives more aesthetic; it's why we seek docents in museums, why design schools teach crits, and why we read reviews of books and movies. Another benefit is criticism's focus on (if not full achievement of) rational consensus building and mutual understanding of profoundly subjective phenomena such as aesthetic value judgments, a tradition inherited from Kant.

Potential uptakes for critical design. Critical design's ability to inculcate critical thought and the imagination of alternative futures is dependent on how insightfully people can read designs: aesthetic perception, imagination, insight, and experience are not effects simply caused by visual stimuli (no matter what HCI research says on the subject); they are the result of a skilled and expert cultural subject's efforts. We know of no practice that theorizes about or, in a very everyday sense *creates* such subjects, more than criticism. Medium-specific analytic skills are the stock and trade of criticism, and it seems obvious to us that critical design can avail itself of and contribute to them. Similarly, the critic is valued not in terms of how well he reflects tastes, but rather in terms of how he *sets* them, or rather, how "he sets the terms in which our tastes, whatever they happen to be, may be protected, or overcome" [12, p.403].

As for the limits of metacriticism as a resource for critical design, we note that most of it is persistently apolitical. This is true even of recent work in this area. But the choice of which "great works" we should be honing our skills with continues to be a loaded one. Dunne and Raby are, among other things, great curators—their books are loaded with stimulating examples—so it's vitally important that critical design's search for the "best designs" be deeply reflective about how "best" is defined.

What Makes Critical Design Critical

In synoptically outlining critical theory and metacriticism as two families of thought, we hoped to tease out some concepts and the uses to which they have been put, in hopes of creating some cognitive handles for design researchers to grab onto and hopefully inspire them to engage in some of these literatures directly.

By emphasizing the ways that these two families of thought complement each other—e.g., where critical theory was strong on politics, metacriticism was naïve; where critical theory's agendas sometimes overwhelmed cultural works, metacriticism's offers medium-specific sensitivities—we also hoped to acknowledge the particular limitations of different concepts. For these reasons, a contemporary humanities degree typically covers both close reading and the hermeneutics of suspicion. And, all apparent differences notwithstanding, both critical theory and metacriticism share a number of deeper qualities, and understanding these qualities can shed light on many of the ways that critical design can operate as a practice—including theories, methodologies, objects of inquiry, attitudes, and so forth.

Perspective-shifting holistic understandings. Both critical theory and metacriticism view critical activity as the con-

struction of an account that holistically explains all of the relevant facts, features, and effects of a phenomenon in a way that shifts one's perspective or improve one's perceptual acuity. The phenomenon to be accounted for might be a work, a history of an idea or genre, a hidden operation in the social sphere, etc. In some ways, this reverses the operations of science, which commonly uses atomic thinking to decompose a complex concept (e.g., experience) into models comprising approximating parts set in some sort of relationship to one another [8]. Criticism frequently works in the other direction, combining a literary detail, an experiential effect, a historical detail, and a speculative theory together to produce a unifying account that explains all of the above—not to be correct but to suggest new modes of understanding it.

Theory as speculation. For both critical theory and metacriticism, theory makes no claim to be "right" in the way that scientific theories do. When critical theorist Baudrillard wrote *The Gulf War Did Not Take Place*, he was not offering a conspiracy theory but rather modeling a mode of interpretation that problematizes media-reported images and claims about the "war" and trying to adjust our conceptual models to better fit his interpretation of that conflict [5]. Similarly, when Cavell writes, "The philosopher … turns to the reader not to convince him without proof but to get him to prove something, test something, against himself" [12, p.407], he is making it clear that he is not offering up verifiable truth-claims but rather challenging his reader to think about his topic in a new mode.

A dialogic methodology. In his reflection on the classics, the philosopher Gadamer observed that in spite of the different ways of life depicted in earlier artworks, we nonetheless identify with them and feel intensely about them. He argues that when we read the classics, we do not decode a static content already there, but rather we enter into an active dialogue with the hopes, fears, values, and actions of those who lived them; our own horizons are fused with those of the classic, and in that luminous moment we experience new alignments of our own thoughts and come out of it transformed [23,28]. Whether the "luminous moment" is one of aesthetic enlightenment (via a perceptive and personal struggle with classics) or social revelation (via a critical interrogation of suppressed conflicts), both metacriticism and critical theory seek meaning and discovery in the struggle, heterogeneity, and polyphony of human expressions and experiences, which no one expects or even hopes to finally resolve.

Improvement of the public's cultural competence. Critical theory models ways to read skeptically, to be suspicious of false harmonies and false pleasures; metacriticism models ways to perceive and read with unparalleled sensitivity and insight. Both offer means to "look beyond the surface," and both have very specific technical vocabularies to perceive, identify, and judge what is down there below it. One answer, of course, is the global corporate ideology that

Dunne and Raby frequently raise, but there are many other things "down there," including significant form, patriarchy, aesthetic expression, psychosexual dysfunction, *mimesis*— and perhaps somewhere even wisdom itself.

Reflexivity. Inheriting the Kantian critical tradition, both critical theory and metacriticism are reflexively aware that their own rationalities are limited; both reflect on the sociocultural and epistemological conditions that make their work possible; and both see their theoretical work as engaged with, not cut off from in the name of objectivity, the worlds they occupy and are ethically committed to improve. Critical thought is in service of social change, from the present to a hoped-for future that is attainable but not immediately within reach.

So if we want to understand what makes critical design "critical," the preceding list gives us our answer: *a design research project may be judged "critical" to the extents that it proposes a perspective-changing holistic account of a given phenomenon, and that this account is grounded in speculative theory, reflects a dialogical methodology, improves the public's cultural competence, and is reflexively aware of itself as an actor—with both power and constraints—within the social world it is seeking to change.*

PRIOR PROBLEMS, RESOLVED

Earlier in this essay we took issue with Dunne and Raby's binary use of affirmative versus critical design, and we also took issue with their claim that critical design is not art. We asserted that revisiting the notion of *critical* in critical design would shed some light on these issues.

Affirmative versus critical design. We do not take issue with the value judgments Dunne and Raby attach to these terms: we do recognize a value distinction between affirming and critiquing the status quo. Rather, we take issue with the *scope* of their application to designs or designers considered as wholes, and the *lack of criteria* for making judgments that have such obviously political consequences.

Regarding the scope, we note that critics seldom see any cultural symbol as meaning only one thing; Virgil in Dante's *Divine Comedy* is both a character and an allegory of human rationality, and when Romeo declares Juliet the sun, he is not practicing amateur astronomy. A design is critical inasmuch as some aspect of it critiques the status quo, and it is affirmative inasmuch as it affirms the status quo; that is, any given design may be both affirmative and critical. A symbolic object and the status quo are each infinitely complex, and their relationships must be explicated if aspects of a design are to be deemed affirmative or critical.

That interpretative activity, however, adds up to a critical value judgment for which one has to supply good reasons, paraphrasing Carroll [11]. We hope the features of criticality identified above facilitate the formulation of good reasons, along with traditional critical categories, such as artistic intention, historical reception/effects, semantic/syntactic complexity, agency and voice granted to the marginalized, delicacy of discrimination, innovative use of materials/medium, and so forth. The convincingness of the argument, buttressed by recognizably good reasons, diminishes, though does not remove, the political sting of praising or censuring a design as affirmative or critical.

Whether critical design can be art. It strikes us as odd that Dunne and Raby simultaneously demand that critical design be robustly aesthetic but ontologically distinct from art. As we've argued, attempts to make ontological distinctions between art and critical design are misguided. A better strategy would have been to say that critical design and art may or may not overlap, but that critical design, tactically speaking, should not be absorbed into the social practices of the artworld, with their institutional structures of exhibitions, museums, and funding. Rather, critical design works best when it is operating within industry and commerce, not because art can't get into everyday life, but rather because it is easier to get design into everyday life in predictably quotidian ways. If one composes a sonata, it is hard to anticipate any particular public reception of it, but if one builds an app, one can get it onto people's mobile devices and see what happens (at worst by paying research subjects to do so as part of a study). It is the comparative ease with which design can be dropped into everyday life (in contrast to art) that makes it appealing as a medium for critical research: that ease is a convincing methodological benefit, and this is an important insight that Dunne and Raby seem to have understood but not been able to express clearly.

DESIGNS THAT ARE CRITICAL

So far, our analysis has remained very theoretical and largely isolated from design itself. To help reconnect the preceding analysis back to design, we analyze two recent design research projects in HCI that meet the following criteria: they are not the work of Dunne and Raby; they probably would not be considered critical designs in Dunne and Raby's formulation; they do not claim to be critical designs; and yet, using our proposed reformulation of critical design, we are comfortable asserting that they are designs that are critical. We introduce each project and offer reasons for our judgment that they are critical. Our hope is that this analysis increases the pool of available critical design exemplars— far more design is "critical" than is generally recognized, e.g., participatory design—and also helps HCI researchers interpret the criticality of designs for themselves.

"Hydroscopes" and "Silence and Whispers"

"Hydroscopes" and "Silence and Whispers" are a pair of research through design studies in which the authors, Dalsgaard and Dindler, develop theoretical understandings of user engagement; in particular, these studies investigate the notion of an *interactive peephole* as an approach to designing for engagement [13]. For them, interactive peepholes "refer to aspects of interactive artifacts and environments that utilize the tension between what is hidden and what is revealed to foster engagement through curiosity and inquiry" [13, p.1]. Both designs are situated within existing and original theories of engagement; at the same time, both are also situated within prior interactive installations that feature peepholes. "Hydroscopes" is an aquarium installation in which visitors prototype a fish and then release it into a virtual ocean, which they can see through a peephole. "Silence and Whispers" is an audio installation at an historical site in which stories from the site's history are cut up and presented as audio snippets and chalk writing snippets; the partial glimpses into the historical stories function as metaphorical peepholes.

We argue that this project constitutes critical design for the following reasons. Contributing practically to theories of user engagement, as opposed to brand experience, this project constructs design in service of the user as an active maker of meaning—an emancipatory perspective. From it, the authors offer a holistic and insightful account of the notion of an interactive peephole as an approach to user engagement. This account helps us think in a new way about theories of user engagement and it also trains us how to read designs that use peepholes in both literal and figurative ways; and it suggests ways that it can support future design work. The project's movement back and forth among existing (and highly interdisciplinary) theories (e.g., those of Borgman, Schön, Hedegaard, Csikszentmihalyi, McCarthy & Wright), their own theorizing (i.e., of interactive peepholes), prior art and design projects that incorporated peepholes as an interactive technique, their own designs, and the contexts into which they were placed is a robustly dialogic methodology. Its construction of theory is speculative; the authors use theories as lenses through which to structure their design thinking. Throughout they assess the limitations of their theories and the designs themselves, showing an ongoing reflexivity to their work.

"The Prayer Companion"
Earlier in the paper we alluded to the problem of whether certain design projects from Goldsmiths counted as examples of critical design: we noted that some in HCI interpret this work to be critical design but also that Gaver denies that it is. We believe that the disagreement hinges on a distinction between "critical design" as specifically articulated by Dunne and Raby versus designs that are perceived to make a strong critical contribution in a broader sense. In Dunne and Raby's sense, we agree that the Goldsmiths projects are not critical design; in the second and broader formulation, we argue that some of them are.

We use "The Prayer Companion" as one such example [24]. The Prayer Companion is a small text display device that shows news headlines and individuals' statements from social media sites about how they feel. It is designed to be placed in a convent, so that nuns seeing it can pray for those affected by the events and the individuals. It is also a research through design project intended to help the designers develop "a range of topical, procedural, pragmatic and conceptual insights" [24, p.2055] about a number of design problem areas in HCI.

The Prayer Companion is a coherent yet non-verbal interpretation of the intersection of these themes: spirituality, design, materiality, the elderly, and technology. Its core proposition is that it is a design that supports spiritual life in an intimate and authentic way. Richly detailed processual, material, theoretical, receptional, and technological accounts of it are all offered, and in their details its coherence and appropriateness as a design and interpretation is justified both by its contributions to the spiritual life of the nuns who used it and to the HCI researchers who learned from it.

The Prayer Companion makes no effort to provoke or transgress the lives of the nuns, nor does it position itself as midwifing the nuns' entry into critical thinking. To whatever extent the Prayer Companion changes the nuns' thinking, it is likely in the new ways it connects them to the news and social media—a process influenced by the nuns' own input—but how and whether this changes the nuns' thinking is left to the nuns. The Prayer Companion thus takes a stance of humility; in doing so, it helps reveal what it means for design to be in service of users—an important, and arguably understated, contribution of the project. In these ways, The Prayer Companion is far from Dunne and Raby's account of critical design, which takes a more confrontational stance toward its users.

At the same time, the Prayer Companion is used to critique—and in places even attack—mainstays in HCI. In particular, the paper strongly criticizes the subordination of materiality to functionality, the notion of "the elderly" as an intellectually justifiable (or even ethical) demographic to target via design, and the "disciplinary hubris" of mainstream HCI methods that cast themselves as "powerful champions of enfeebled users" [24, p.2055]. It also critiques HCI's failures to account intimately for human experience, as opposed to "coordinating large organizations, ameliorating constraints, or building emotional relationships with products" [24, p.2057]. Critically speaking, the Prayer Companion's "users" might be us: it is our eyes that are opened, our complacency that is transgressed, and our ideology that is exposed to interrogation. And it is based on the Prayer Companion's simultaneous insightful service to the nuns and withering design-embodied critique of HCI theory and practices—and regardless of what Dunne, Raby, or Gaver might say—that a reasonable person can judge "The Prayer Companion" to be a design that is critical, that is, a critical design.

CONCLUSION
We have argued that critical design is a fit for much contemporary HCI research, but that its uptake is unexpectedly limited. We argued that part of the problem is lack of clarity, examples, and directions that would support its broader adoption, in particular surrounding the notion of what is "critical" about critical design. We surveyed critical thought and teased out a number of critical concepts, situated them within their theoretical contexts, and showed some of the practical ways that they have been used. We also offered

readings of two projects that we argue are critical, one that seeks to create new theory and another that seeks to critique and rework existing theory. Our hope is that this contribution makes critical design—or designs that are critical—more accessible and rewarding for HCI researchers concerned about the futures that we are designing.

ACKNOWLEDGEMENTS

This research was funded in part by the NSF IIS Creative IT (#1002772) and the Intel Science and Technology Center for Social Computing programs. We appreciate the thoughtful feed/push-back from John Bowers, Jodi Forlizzi, Bill Gaver, Erik Stolterman, John Zimmerman, and our anonymous reviewers.

REFERENCES

1. Abrams, M. (1991). *Doing Things with Texts: Essays in Criticism and Critical Theory.* W.W. Norton.

2. Arnold, M. (2001). The function of criticism at the present time. In Leitch, V., Cain, W., Finke, L., Johnson, B., McGowan, J., and Williams, J. (eds.). *The Norton Anthology of Theory and Criticism.* W.W. Norton.

3. Bardzell, J., and Bardzell, S. (2011). "Pleasure is your birthright": Digitally enabled designer sex toys as a case of third-wave HCI. *Proc. of CHI'11.* ACM.

4. Bardzell, S., Bardzell, J., Forlizzi, J., Zimmerman, J., and Antanitis, J. (2012). Critical design and critical theory: The challenge of designing for provocation. *Proc. of DIS'12.* ACM Press.

5. Barthes, R. (2000). *Mythologies.* London: Vintage.

6. Baudrillard, J. (2012). *The Gulf War Did Not Take Place.* Power Publications.

7. Beardsley, M. (1981). *Aesthetics: Problems in the Philosophy of Criticism.* Hackett Publishing Company, Inc.

8. Bernstein, R. (1971). *Praxis and Action: Contemporary Philosophies of Human Activities.* The University of Pennsylvania Press.

9. Bloom, H. (2004). *Where Shall Wisdom be Found?* The Berkley Publishing Group.

10. Carroll, N. (2001). *Beyond Aesthetics.* Cambridge UP.

11. Carroll. N. (2009). *On Criticism.* Routledge.

12. Cavell, S. (2008). Aesthetic problems of modern philosophy. In Cahn, S., and Meskin, A. (eds.). *Aesthetics: A Comprehensive Anthology.* Blackwell Publishing.

13. Dalsgaard, P., and Dindler, C. Peepholes as means of engagement in interaction design. (2009). *Proc. of Engaging Artifacts 2009.*

14. Dunne, A. (2006). *Hertzian Tales: Electronic Products, Aesthetic Experience, and Critical Design.* MIT Press.

15. Dunne, A., and Raby, F. (2001). *Design Noir:The Secret Life of Electronic Objects.* Birkhäuser.

16. Dunne, A. and Raby, F. (2010). Dreaming objects. *Science Poems-Foundations* (May 2010).

17. Dunne, A. and Raby, F. (2007). Critical Design FAQ. Retrieved September 1, 2012. http://www.dunneandraby.co.uk/content/bydandr/13/0

18. Dunne, A. and Raby, F. (2009). Interpretation, collaboration, and critique: Interview with Dunne and Raby. Retrieved September 1, 2012. http://www.dunneandraby.co.uk/content/bydandr/465/0

19. Eliot. T.S. (1949). *Selected Prose of T.S. Eliot.* Kermode, F. (ed.). A Harvest book.

20. Fallman, D. (2007). Why research-oriented design isn't design-oriented research: On the tensions between design and research in an implicit design discipline. *J Know Tech Policy 20* (3), Springer.

21. Friedman, C. (2000). *Critical Theory and Science Fiction.* Wesleyan University Press.

22. Frye, N. (1957). *Anatomy of Criticism.* Princeton UP.

23. Gadamer, H-G. (1992). *Truth and Method.* Crossroad.

24. Gaver, W., Blythe, M., Boucher, A., Jarvis, N., Bowers, J., and Wright, P. (2010). The prayer companion: Openness and specificity, materiality and spirituality. In *Proc. of CHI'10.* ACM Press, 2055-2064.

25. Goodman. N. (1987). When is art? In Ross, S. (ed.). *Art and Its Significance: An Anthology of Aesthetic Theory.* SUNY Press.

26. Hall, S. (1992). Cultural studies and its theoretical legacies. In Grossberg, L., Nelson, C.,a dn Treichler, P. (eds.). *Cultural Studies.* Routledge.

27. Harding, S. (2003). *The Feminist Standpoint Theory Reader.* New York: Routledge.

28. How, A. (2003). *Critical Theory.* Palgrave Macmillan.

29. Koskinen, I., Zimmerman, J., Binder, T., Redstrom, J. and Wensveen, S. (2011). *Design Research through Practice.* Burlington, MA: Morgan Kaufmann.

30. Latour, B. (2004). Why has critique run out of steam? From matters of fact to matters of concern. *Critical Inquiry 30* (Winter 2004). University of Chicago.

31. Rush, F. (2004). *The Cambridge Companion to Critical Theory.* Cambridge UP.

32. Sibley, A. (2008). Aesthetic concepts. In Cahn, S., and Meskin, A. (eds.). *Aesthetics: A comprehensive anthology.* Blackwell.

33. Wellek, R. (1963). *Concepts of Criticism.* New Haven: Yale University Press.

34. Zimmerman, J., Forlizzi, J., and Evanson, S. (2007). Research through design as a method for interaction design research in HCI. In *Proc. of CHI'07.* ACM Press.

Mind the Theoretical Gap: Interpreting, Using, and Developing Behavioral Theory in HCI Research

Eric B. Hekler[1], Predrag Klasnja[2], Jon E. Froehlich[3], Matthew P. Buman[1]

School of Nutrition and Health Promotion[1]
Arizona State University
{ehekler, mbuman}@asu.edu

School of Information[2]
University of Michigan
klasnja@umich.edu

HCIL | Computer Science[3]
University of Maryland, College Park
jonf@umd.edu

ABSTRACT

Researchers in HCI and behavioral science are increasingly exploring the use of technology to support behavior change in domains such as health and sustainability. This work, however, remain largely siloed within the two communities. We begin to address this silo problem by attempting to build a bridge between the two disciplines at the level of behavioral theory. Specifically, we define core theoretical terms to create shared understanding about what theory is, discuss ways in which behavioral theory can be used to inform research on behavior change technologies, identify shortcomings in current behavioral theories, and outline ways in which HCI researchers can not only interpret and utilize behavioral science theories but also contribute to improving them.

Author Keywords

Behavior change; behavioral science; theory; persuasive technology; health; sustainability; behavior change technologies

ACM Classification Keywords

H5.2 User Interfaces: User Design; Theory & Methods

INTRODUCTION

HCI researchers are increasingly designing technologies to promote behavior change. A review of the last 10 years of CHI proceedings in the ACM Digital Library found 136 papers that mentioned "behavior change" with 76% of these from the last four years (Figure 1). Although this work has focused on diverse behaviors from diet [32] and exercise [16] to sustainable water usage [27], a common strategy underlies much of this work: to inform design, HCI researchers draw on theories from behavioral sciences.

For example, He and Greenberg [32] used the transtheoretical model of behavior change as an organizing framework for persuasive eco-feedback design. Consolvo *et al.* integrated multiple constructs from several behavioral theories to guide development and evaluations of UbiFit, a mobile-phone application for physical activity [16]. As HCI research on behavior change technologies matures,

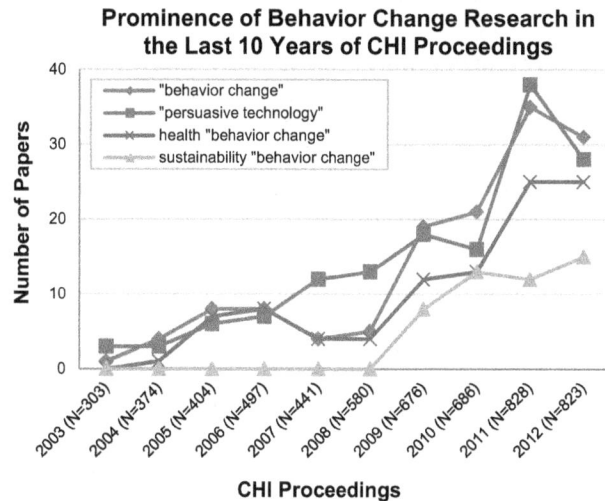

Figure 1: The prominence of behavior change related research in the last 10 years of CHI proceedings. Specific search terms (including quotes) are shown in the legend.

questions emerge about how best to utilize behavioral theory to inform design and evaluation, and what constitutes appropriate use of behavioral theory in HCI. Moreover, as these two research communities continue to explore intersecting topics, are there ways in which HCI research may contribute back to behavioral theory?

In this paper, we aim to provide HCI researchers with guidance on interpreting, using, and developing behavioral theories. We first provide an overview of different forms of behavioral theory across levels of generality—from *meta-models* to *empirical findings*. We then use these distinctions to discuss the current uses of behavioral theory in HCI and to highlight areas that, as yet, have received little attention. We then enumerate a series of shortcomings of behavioral theories as articulated within behavioral science itself, which are likely to be non-obvious to those outside this discipline. Finally, we conclude by suggesting ways HCI researchers can contribute to the development and refinement of behavioral theories. Our paper has implications for the growing body of research in the design and evaluation of behavior change technologies and for HCI researchers interested in utilizing behavioral theory.

A Note on Terminology

As this paper bridges two historically distinct research communities, it is worthwhile to define the terms. Within behavioral science, a common definition of behavioral theory proposed by Glanz and Rimer is ([30], p. 4): "...*a systematic way of understanding events or situations. It is a set of concepts, definitions, and propositions that explain or predict these events or situations by illustrating the relationships between variables.*" When we refer to behavioral theory, this is the definition we are using.

In addition, we also borrow from other terms from behavioral science including: *constructs*, which are the fundamental components or "building blocks" of a behavioral theory, (*e.g.*, two key constructs from social cognitive theory are *self-efficacy* and *outcome expectations* [5]); and *variables,* which are the operational definitions of the constructs, particularly as they are defined in context (*e.g.*, specific measures used to assess self-efficacy or strategies used within an application to influence self-efficacy). We will use the term *design guidelines* to refer to the principles formulated by HCI researchers to make behavioral theory and empirical findings actionable for designing behavior change technologies (*e.g.*, [12, 15]).

Although the term *persuasive technology* [25] is common within HCI, it has become somewhat controversial and can bring up negative associations (*e.g.*, while Fogg's original definition explicitly rebuked coercion as a component of persuasive technology [25], more recent papers have questioned if it is possible to avoid coercion within persuasion, partially by forcing an implicit value-system—see [60]). For this reason, we do not use the term in this paper (except as an author keyword). Instead, we refer to the broad array of systems and artifacts developed to foster and assist behavior change and sustainment as *behavior change technologies*. This term more adequately reflects the diversity of behavioral theories and goals beyond persuasion that can be encoded in technical artifacts.

Finally, based on our own areas of expertise, we primarily focus on behavioral theories from psychology that have been commonly applied in the health domain.

FORMS OF BEHAVIORAL THEORY
Behavioral theories vary widely in *which* behaviors they describe and *how* these behaviors are described. Some theories focus on one behavior (*e.g.*, smoking), others describe the specific process (*e.g.*, relapse prevention), and still others describe dynamics between behaviors and other constructs (*e.g.*, theory of planned behavior [2]). As a consequence, behavioral theories can be categorized in a variety of ways. One common distinction, for instance, is between behavioral theories that describe determinants of *behavior* (*e.g.*, the health belief model [8]) versus the *process of change* (*e.g.*, transtheoretical model [59]; see [66] for a discussion on this distinction).

For the purposes of this paper, we classify behavioral theories based on their generality/specificity: from *meta-models*, which incorporate multiple levels of influence (*e.g.*, individual to societal), to specific and often atheoretical *empirical findings* used to generate ideas, constructs, and

design guidelines (see Figure 1). While we recognize that these levels of specificity exist on a continuum, we delineate discrete markers to anchor our discussion. To enhance understanding, we provide examples at each level drawn primarily from the behavioral science literature.

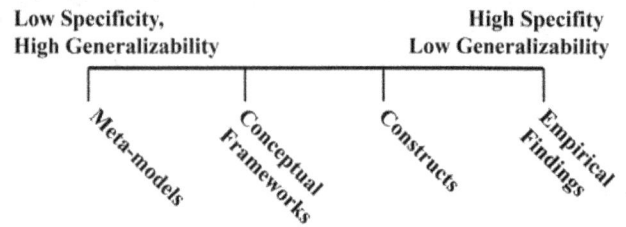

Figure 2: Spectrum of Specificity of Behavioral Theories

Meta-Models
At the highest level of generality are *meta-models*, which are organizational structures of multiple levels of influence on individual behavior. For example, an increasingly popular meta-model in health-related behavioral science is the social ecological model [63], which identifies broad "levels" of inter-related associations and factors of influence on a behavior of interest, from micro-level factors such as genetics and biology to meso-level factors such as interpersonal relationships and, finally, to macro-level factors such as urban design, public policy, and culture.

Like Erickson's model [24], meta-models are valuable for identifying the "lens" a researcher is using and other "lenses" not currently emphasized by the researcher or community at large. In this way, a meta-model can help identify new levels of inquiry. For example, the majority of behavior change-oriented research in HCI has thus far focused on the individual level (*e.g.*, goal-setting, self-monitoring) or the interpersonal level (*e.g.*, social support, social networks), with less emphasis placed on understanding the context with which these individual or interpersonal-level interventions are created and tested [21].

Examining prior work through the perspective of a meta-model can uncover previously under-explored research. For example, King *et al.* [41] used the social ecological model to emphasize important gaps and opportunities for improving population-level physical activity based on, at the time, relatively ignored levels of the social ecological model, such as policy or the built environment. This led to new research and partnerships, such as increased interaction between behavioral scientists and urban planners (*e.g.*, [39,64]). By virtue of their generality, however, meta-models are typically short on specifics about determinants of behavior that could be used to directly inform the design of technical systems. In addition, too often meta-models have too many levels of influence to adequately evaluate. As such, the use of meta-models in design requires a great deal of conceptual and formative work to translate into pragmatic design guidelines and system features.

Conceptual Frameworks
Whereas meta-models describe multiple models within a single frame, *conceptual frameworks* tend to focus on one

or two levels of influence. Conceptual frameworks describe relationships among the fundamental building blocks of a behavioral theory, *constructs*, and provide a more specific account of how constructs are inter-related. Conceptual frameworks encompass several commonly used theories including the transtheoretical model [59], self-efficacy theory [5], theory of planned behavior [2], health belief model [8], and self-determination theory [18].

From an HCI perspective, conceptual frameworks provide more specific guidance to the design and implementation of behavior change technologies (and help guide the evaluation process). For example, goal-setting theory [47] describes the effect of different types of goals on performance, enabling HCI researchers to implement effective goals in their interventions (see, for instance, [13]). However, because of their emphasis on only one or two levels of analysis, conceptual frameworks have the potential to disregard key factors that may be influencing a behavior. For example, recent physical activity promotion research found that "walkability" of a person's neighborhood influenced physical activity intervention effectiveness, such that the interventions tested were only effective for those who lived in walkable neighborhoods [42]. Although conceptual frameworks were used to design the interventions (*i.e.*, the transtheoretical model and social cognitive theory), the key finding emerged from situating these models within the broader context of a meta-model.

Constructs

Constructs are the basic determinants or mechanisms that a theory postulates to influence behavior. For instance, social cognitive theory defines the notion of self-efficacy—a person's assessment of his/her ability to perform certain behaviors in a particular context [6]. The theory identifies this construct, along with other constructs such as outcome expectancies, as a key determinant of behavior.

In lieu of utilizing all of the constructs defined within a conceptual framework, a common practice in the development of behavior change interventions is to selectively use constructs from one or more theories. For example, many researchers both from behavioral science and HCI who utilize the transtheoretical model incorporate only the stages of change construct, leaving out other constructs such as the twelve processes of change or decisional balance (*e.g.*, [10,46]). Although common, this practice makes it difficult to evaluate the utility of the entire conceptual framework as the entire framework was not tested. This can lead to methodological flaws in interpreting the validity of behavioral theories. We return to this point in the *Shortcomings of Behavioral Theory* sections.

By virtue of their focus on a much smaller level of analysis, *constructs* translate more easily into features of a behavior change technology. By focusing on individual constructs rather than whole frameworks, however, an HCI researcher might inadvertently design a system based on constructs that do not work independently but only in tandem with other constructs. To continue with the self-efficacy example, a behavior change technology that supports self-efficacy might be effective for individuals who already have high outcome expectancies but might not work well for individuals with low outcome expectancies. Insofar as the other construct was not assessed or integrated in the system, it would be difficult to understand why the system may work for some individuals but not others.

Empirical Findings
Finally, in some cases, previously developed theories are insufficient to guide HCI research. In such cases, additional empirical work—often in the form of ethnographic and other qualitative approaches—can generate knowledge necessary to establish a starting point for design. Such empirical work can yield concrete and contextually-specific *findings*, which can be applied to ground specific designs and to create design guidelines. For instance, in their work with stroke patients, Balaam *et al.* found that household dynamics acted either as barriers or facilitators for patients' rehabilitation activities [4]. Based on this finding, Balaam *et al.* created personalized interventions to motivate regular performance of exercises needed to increase the range of motion in their affected limbs. Its high level of applicability to design makes such empirical work an essential component of HCI research (*e.g.*, [27, 50]).

The level of specificity of empirical findings comes at the cost of generalizability, however. Empirical findings, by virtue of being observed in a given context, must be abstracted in some way to create generalized knowledge. Although it is tempting to directly generalize specific findings from empirical work, such generalizations should be tempered by factors such as the target participant group, study length and size, and other relevant contexts. That said, empirical findings are an invaluable starting point for the creation of new constructs and theories, as well as for informing the design of new technologies.

USES OF BEHAVIORAL THEORIES IN HCI
In our review of HCI literature on behavior change technologies, we have identified three broad uses of behavioral theory. HCI researchers use theory: (i) to inform the design of technical systems, (ii) to guide evaluation strategies, and (iii) to define target users. Here, we discuss how theory has been used for these purposes thus far and how theory can support HCI research going forward.

Informing design
HCI researchers often draw on theory to make design decisions about a technical system. Theory can be used both to make decisions about *which* functionality to support and *how* to implement such functionality. For example, Consolvo *et al.* [15] drew heavily on theory to design UbiFit, a mobile-phone application for encouraging physical activity. UbiFit supported weekly activity goals based on goal-setting theory [47], rewards for performed behavior based on the transtheoretical model [59], and a stylized display of performance information, based on

Goffman's theory of presentation of self in everyday life [31]. Theory also informed *how* this functionality was implemented. For instance, UbiFit required users to specify the number of strength training, cardiovascular, and walking sessions they would do each week. This design decision was informed by goal-setting theory, which postulates that performance is highest when goals are specific and created by the user (see [47]).

Similarly, Mamykina and colleagues [49] drew upon the construct of breakdown from the theory of sensemaking [19] to design MAHI, an application for patients with diabetes that supports reflection and problem-solving. The theory of sensemaking postulates that individuals constantly engage in drafting and redrafting of a story to understand their experiences. In sensemaking, breakdown refers to the times when everyday routines are interrupted by an unexpected or undesirable event that forces the individual to make sense of what happened and to create a new story that explains the experience. To help users reflect on breakdowns, MAHI enables: (i) flexible journaling through photos and audio recording on a mobile phone; (ii) collecting information about context for measuring glucose via experience sampling; and (iii) discussing captured data with a diabetes educator. By providing patients with the flexibility to capture, document, and discuss breakdowns when they occur, MAHI supports the reflection that sensemaking theory argues is essential to effective problem-solving.

A second way of informing design is the development of design guidelines. For example, drawing on behavioral theory and their own empirical work, Consolvo *et al.* [15] derived eight guidelines for designing technologies for lifestyle change. Such technologies, Consolvo *et al.* argue, need to be *abstract* and *reflective, unobtrusive, public, aesthetic, positive, controllable, comprehensible* to users, and *include historical data.* Similarly, He *et al.* [34] used the transtheoretical model to develop guidelines for technologies for encouraging sustainable energy behavior. He *et al.* write, for instance, that technologies targeting individuals in the pre-contemplation stage "*plant the seed for individuals to acknowledge their current (energy) behavior as problematic,*" while technologies targeting individuals in the preparation stage should support creating "*acceptable, accessible and effective*" plans (p. 5).

Moving forward
Behavioral theory can be a rich source of ideas for behavior change technologies. However, the translation of behavioral theory into effective behavior change technologies is by no means a trivial process. As Balaam *et al.* [4] note, "*Motivation theories...place more emphasis on concepts such as self-efficacy, goals, or the level of competence engendered by a task, rather than the nature of the task itself or what specifically will motivate an individual*" (p. 3079). Indeed, instantiating theory is a difficult task as theoretical constructs lack specificity for concrete design

situations. This gap between theory and a concrete design has to be bridged for every new technology.

The design guidelines such as those described above can help, but researchers need to be mindful about their epistemic status. While we believe strongly in the value of empirical data for generating design guidelines, given the relatively limited amount of empirical data behind many proposed design guidelines (*e.g.,* [15,34,38]), we suggest that the guidelines are more akin to "design hypotheses," which require additional testing. Behind each guideline is a set of assumptions about how a technology that embodies the guideline should affect users' behavior. Testing these assumptions explicitly in user studies, along with exploring the design space for guidelines, can enable HCI researchers to build generalizable knowledge about ways in which behavioral theories can be translated into better designs.

In addition, new strategies for balancing abstraction with contextual relevance are needed. HCI researchers who translate theory into systems should pay close attention to issues such as the specific behavior in question (*e.g.,* physical activity, diet, sustainability), user characteristics (*e.g.,* age, education, values), and the sociocultural context (*e.g.,* Latino diabetic high schoolers). By investigating how technologies with similar theoretical grounding fare in different cultural contexts, the field can begin to develop both more nuanced design guidelines and to inform the development of better behavioral theories.

Guiding evaluation strategies
In addition to informing design, behavioral theories are also relevant to guiding evaluations of behavior change technologies. Although examples of this are less prevalent in HCI literature, behavioral theory has been used both to inform study design and to help interpret findings from technology evaluations.

In a recent paper, Lee *et al.* [45] explored the use of behavioral economics to design technologies to encourage healthy eating. Lee *et al.* developed a webpage for buying snacks at the office based on the behavioral economics construct of default bias (*i.e.,* a person tends to pick the first available option). This construct, however, did not only influence the design of the system but also the design of the evaluation. Specifically, the control condition was a webpage with all food options available on one screen whereas the intervention condition showed only two food options at a time and required participants to click to another page to explore other snack options. This study design was informed by the behavioral theory because the control condition (*i.e.,* having all options available without an explicit default) was a direct complement of the webpage that embodied the default option construct (*i.e.,* having two options as the default and requiring additional action to see more). This is an exciting use of theory to guide technology evaluation through a theoretically-informed delineation of the control condition. More common is the use of behavioral theory to identify measures. For example, in their evaluations of MAHI and UbiFit, Mamykina *et al.* and Consolvo *et al.* drew on theory for their studies by including a variety of measures related to the hypothesized core constructs of interest.

Theory can also help with the interpretation of study results. For example, to understand whether their game OrderUP! contributed to healthy eating behaviors, Grimes *et al.* structured their analysis of interview data from their user study according to the transtheoretical model's processes of change [33]. Grimes *et al.* argue that the themes emergent from these interviews were examples of the four processes that, according to the transtheoretical model, mediate the progression through the stages of change: *consciousness-raising*, *self-re-evaluation*, *helping relationships*, and *counter-conditioning*. For instance, Grimes *et al.* cite data that OrderUP! helped users correct their incorrect assumptions about which foods were healthy, and that it gave them culturally-relevant suggestions for healthy foods. Both of these effects are examples of consciousness-raising. By using theory in this way, Grimes *et al.* suggested that their application was supporting the right kinds of change processes expected by the theory. While not without potential methodological shortcomings, which we delineate in the next section, this is an innovative strategy for using theory in tandem with qualitative data to explore theoretical fidelity [62] within user testing.

Moving forward

Although the stated aim of most behavior change technology research is to design technology that effectively changes behavior, this is rarely robustly demonstrated in HCI research [26,43]. Indeed, very few HCI researchers have the resources to conduct large-scale randomized trials of their prototypes. And though randomized controlled trials (RCTs) remain the gold standard of efficacy research in behavioral science, there are a number of emerging theory-driven study designs and analytic strategies that we believe are highly relevant to the HCI community. These include: (i) mediational/path and moderation analyses, (ii) alternative experimental designs, and (iii) evaluations of qualitative data.

Mediation/path and moderation. Mediation describes *how* an intervention works whereas moderation describes *for whom* or *under what circumstances* an intervention is most efficient [41]. From a behavioral theory perspective, mediating variables are the constructs that drive behavioral change (*e.g.,* breakdown from the MAHI example), while moderating variables identify who responds best to different interventions (*e.g.,* young vs. old, men vs. women) and under what conditions outcomes are optimized (*e.g.,* living in a walkable *vs.* not walkable neighborhood). Understanding key mediator variables within a behavioral theory can allow HCI researchers to both support these constructs in their designs and to assess them in their evaluations instead of solely relying on more distal outcomes such as behaviors. For example, if theory suggests that an application for encouraging physical

activity works in part by strengthening self-efficacy, an evaluation that finds improved self-efficacy would provide preliminary evidence that the application is functioning as intended, even if the study is not able to detect behavioral changes due resource constraints on the study.

Similarly, moderation analyses can be very valuable for defining for whom a system will work. For example, Hekler *et al.* [35] explored who responds better to a physical activity intervention with identical content but delivered either by an interactive voice response (IVR) system or a human advisor. Hekler *et al.* used moderation analysis to explore individual characteristics that self-determination theory suggested might play a role. They found that individuals who were high in amotivation (*i.e.,* who lacked interest in being active) required a human advisor to become more physically active whereas those who were low in amotivation (*i.e.,* were interested in being active) fared better with the IVR system. Such analyses can provide another way to gain knowledge about how technical interventions work for different groups of users.

Alternative experimental designs. There is a small but growing revolution in behavioral science related to the use of alternative experimental designs beyond the RCT to develop and test behavior-focused interventions. Some of these designs, such as single case experimental designs [37] and factorial designs [11], might prove to be useful in HCI research as well. Their emergence is at least partly due to the recent ease with which: (i) behaviors and important variables can be frequently assessed (*e.g.,* multiple times per day over a long time period), a requirement which is key for "in the wild" N-of-1 style experimental designs [37]; and (ii) a much wider range of small variations of experimental conditions can be easily created, which was previously a stumbling block for factorial study designs [11]. A full description of these methods is beyond the scope of this paper, but many were and still are used in lab-based psychological research [37]. Until now, however, such designs were not used in "free-living" situations due to resource constraints that have now largely been abated by new technologies.

Using theory to help evaluate qualitative data. Finally, Grimes *et al.*'s work points to new opportunities for using theory to understand how our technologies affect behavior. As we mentioned, Grimes *et al.* [33] used theory to guide the interpretation of their end-user testing interviews. Such theoretically-guided analyses of qualitative data are a promising form of evaluation for HCI research on behavior change technologies, and they fit well within the tradition of theory-driven qualitative methods such as ethnomethodology, conversation analysis, and other methodologies from anthropology and sociology.

Specifically, the Grimes *et al.* approach points to a way to use theory to test *theoretical fidelity* [62]—whether a technology is operating according to the theoretical mechanisms (*e.g.,* psychological, social, etc.) that were used to guide the design of that technology. To do this, researchers would formulate *a priori* expectations of likely responses in user feedback that would indicate that the technology was having or not having a theoretically postulated effect. For example, a statement like *"Using the application made me feel more confident about being active"* could be an indicator that the system influenced self-efficacy. Having a coding manual with such statements (along with a set of negative examples) would enable researchers to use qualitative data to rigorously assess if a behavior change technology is influencing the proposed constructs (*e.g.*, see [54] for a coding scheme developed for understanding therapist/client interactions based on motivational interviewing).

To decrease the risk of the confirmation bias [55], it would be important for such coding manuals to be established *a priori*, before user interviews begin. It is a well-known psychological fact that humans tend to perceive and interpret their observations to "confirm" their preconceived notions and theories [55]. As with other cognitive biases, confirmation bias operates unconsciously, without our being aware of its influence. This is a central reason why the lists of statements that would indicate that users' experiences with a technology are in line with or refute theoretical expectations should be established in advance. We discuss this idea further in the *HCI Contributions to Behavioral Theory* section.

Put together, these three theoretically-informed evaluation strategies—moderation and mediation analyses, alternative experimental designs beyond the RCT, and using qualitative data to assess theoretically-expected outcomes from user testing—can offer HCI researchers powerful new ways to assess technologies that they are developing.

Selecting target users

Theories like the transtheoretical model suggest that different user groups will have diverse needs and interventions that effectively support one group might be ineffective for another. He *et al.*'s taxonomy of guidelines for technologies that support sustainable energy behaviors is a good example of how theory can help researchers uncover differing needs across user groups. Individuals at different stages of change may require different types of support, even if the goal is to encourage the exact same behaviors (*e.g.*, using public transportation).

In HCI research on behavior change technologies, this insight is most strongly reflected in the use of theory to screen participants for evaluation studies. Among others, Consolvo *et al.* [12,14] have used the transtheoretical model to screen out pre-contemplation individuals from their studies of technologies for physical activity promotion under the assumption that such tools would not be helpful to someone who has no interest in becoming more physically active.

Moving forward

One corollary of this point is that researchers should be specific about the characteristics of users who are testing the behavior change technologies. If study participants do not match the target user group sufficiently closely, it becomes very difficult to make sense of study results, increasing the likelihood of type III error (*i.e.*, finding null results when the hypothesis was never tested in the first place [20]). Put differently, does the system not work or did it not work for these particular participants?

Theory can also help HCI researchers to better understand *who* the most appropriate target users are for a given technology. This is evidenced by King *et al.*'s work that suggests that some physical activity promotion interventions may only work for people living in walkable neighborhoods [42]. Using theory to define target users could lead to the design of tailored—and potentially more effective—interventions.

Related to this point, theory could be used *post hoc* to understand different patterns of use and outcomes among study participants. Similar to how Grimes *et al.* used theory to investigate effects of their system or Hekler *et al.*'s work on physical activity promotion via IVR or human counseling [35], theory could guide analyses of interview and demographic data to create hypotheses about the factors that shaped technology use. These factors could then be more rigorously assessed in follow-up studies, leading to a richer understanding of the individual, social, and cultural variables that influence the effectiveness of behavior change technologies. By extension, findings from such studies would also help delineate for which users a system is and, perhaps more importantly, is not appropriate.

Common pitfalls when using behavioral theories

Although we have argued that theory can be helpful to HCI researchers working on behavior change technologies, its use is not without pitfalls. We have alluded to several common pitfalls already, including: (i) ignoring the broader context in which a technology will be used (*e.g.*, not taking into account a person's neighborhood environment); (ii) picking only some constructs from a theory and thus losing the potency of the full conceptual framework for designing a system; (iii) treating design guidelines generated from one empirical study as "requirements" when they should be thought of as design hypotheses; (iv) using selective constructs from a theory but making claims that are related to the full theory (*e.g.*, stating that a system was based on the transtheoretical model but then only using the stages of change); (v) increasing the likelihood of confirmation bias in studies; (vi) falling prey to Type III error due to poor specification of the target audience (*i.e.*, concluding a hypothesis is false when it was never tested).

We want to emphasize that many of these pitfalls are shared by behavioral science as well. We explicitly enumerate them to help HCI researchers avoid them in their work.

Finally, some HCI researchers may think of behavioral theories as if they were in some way "truth" or "fact" with regard to understanding behavior and behavior change. While tempting, this view would be inappropriate. In the following section, we provide a brief summary of the shortcomings of current behavioral theories, both to inform HCI researchers of their limitations and to highlight that these shortcomings present opportunities for HCI researchers to contribute to the process of refinement and development of behavioral theories.

SHORTCOMINGS OF BEHAVIORAL THEORIES

Despite their prominence in HCI research, behavioral theories have many shortcomings which may not be well-known in the HCI community. These shortcomings include: (i) most behavioral theories explain only a small portion of variance in the outcomes they are trying to account for; (ii) many behavioral theories, in their current form, are not falsifiable; and (iii) there is a fragmentation and an over-abundance of different theories. We expand on each point in turn and summarize strategies behavioral scientists are using to combat each shortcoming. While other shortcomings and debates certainly exist (*e.g.,* the gap between *behavioral theory* and *social theory* [65] and other issues listed in our conclusion section), we see the three we mention above as most relevant to HCI.

Small variance explained

Most behavioral theories traditionally explain, at best, only 20-30% of the total variance in a given health behavior, particularly when the behavior is tested in an intervention (*e.g.,* [58]). In other words, approximately 75% of the variance is not accounted for by behavioral theory and thus can be attributed to unmeasured and unknown factors. There are highly efficacious exceptions (*e.g.,* cognitive behavioral interventions for sleep disturbances, which are based on behavioral theories such as operant conditioning, produce clinically significant improvements in 70-80% of adults [53]); however, the vast majority of behavioral theories explain only a small portion of variance, resulting in interventions that leave much to be desired. For example, Prochaska, the originator of the transtheoretical model recently noted: *"We are convinced that the glass ceiling that has kept efficacy at about 25 per cent for smoking cessation is due first and foremost to inadequate knowledge about the principles of change."*([58], p. 584).

Implicitly, all initiatives within behavioral science are targeting this core problem. Behavioral scientists are continually refining their interventions, improving measurement of constructs, and striving to increase the efficacy of their interventions. For example, behavioral scientists are increasingly utilizing the social ecological model to better understand and represent multiple determinants of behavior, with the goal of explaining more variance [41]. Behavioral scientists are also increasingly relying upon alternative experimental designs (as discussed earlier) to improve evaluation. However, as evidenced here, there is still much to be done. Finally, behavioral scientists

are critically evaluating and questioning central tenets of theories to allow for the models to be falsifiable and by extension testable, a point we address next.

Theories and evaluations that preclude falsification

As discussed in the common pitfalls section, there are important methodological shortcomings related to the evaluation of behavioral theories. A central reason, as pointed out by Ogden [57], is that many current behavioral theories do not generate or are not challenged by falsifiable hypotheses and therefore cannot be tested. For example, the theory of planned behavior [2] identifies subjective norms, perceived behavioral control, attitudes, and behavioral intentions as key predictors of behaviors, but in the evaluations of this conceptual framework reviewed by Ogden, a majority of studies did not find that all of these constructs predicted behavior [57]. However, rather than reject the theory, most papers reviewed by Ogden stated that the theory was good because *some* aspects of the theory were deemed relevant and important, thereby rendering it impossible to falsify the conceptual framework as a whole.

Behavioral theories can also lack falsification if the constructs and relationships are not well specified. For example, Adams et al [1] postulated that the construct of the decisional balance (*i.e.,* weighing the pros and cons for engaging in a behavior results in behavior change when the pros outweigh the cons) from the transtheoretical model was not fully specified. Adams et al argued that the possibility of weighing the pros and cons of competing behaviors (*e.g.,* the pros of sun exposure, such as tanning vs. the pros of sun screen, such as reduced skin cancer risk) was not articulated in the transtheoretical model but is central within other conceptual frameworks such as applied behavioral analysis. In their study, they explored if this poor specification made a difference in predictive models and found that the balance between the pros of the two competing behaviors (*i.e.,* using sunscreen or unprotected sun exposure) was a stronger mediator of the behavior than the pros and cons to just the health behavior (*i.e.,* using sunscreen). This type of work highlights an important area whereby constructs are critically evaluated to generate falsifiable predictions that can be tested.

As these examples illustrate, behavioral scientists are increasingly calling for concrete predictions that are falsifiable and for tests that support, reject, or alter full conceptual frameworks, or alternatively, for tests that focus on constructs or interactions of constructs only [*e.g.,* 51]. In addition, there is a growing interest in comparative studies [56], which could directly compare predictions of different theories within the same context (again, see [1]).

Fragmentation and Over-abundance of Theories

Poor evaluation and lack of falsification of theories has led to a plethora of different conceptual frameworks, competing research findings/conclusions, and redundant underlying constructs that are labeled differently depending on the theoretical camp of origination [3, 51, 57]. For example, confidence in one's ability to perform a given action is a popular construct in behavioral science that has been labeled *self-efficacy* in social cognitive theory but is called *perceived behavioral control* or *locus of control*. While the originating theories do define these constructs slightly differently, many behavioral scientists see the constructs as practically the same [3]. Despite this, the terms remain and are a source of confusion to non-behavioral scientists and behavioral scientists alike.

To resolve this issue, behavioral scientists have attempted to synthesize theories into broader frameworks and, more recently, to create a theory agnostic taxonomy of behavior change techniques. Indeed, the original intent of the transtheoretical model was to, "*reduce 300 theories of psychotherapy and behavior change down to the most common and robust processes of change*" ([58], p. 569). More recently, researchers in Europe have started to develop a taxonomy of behavior change techniques [67]. This work is currently progressing using consensus methodology, but there are already early versions of the taxonomy in the literature (*e.g.,* [51]).

HCI CONTRIBUTIONS TO BEHAVIORAL THEORY
Although HCI researchers have traditionally not engaged in the development of behavioral theory, we see HCI as being in a unique position to help mitigate the shortcomings in behavioral theory we discuss above. Here we outline three ways in which HCI could help improve behavioral theory: (i) improving measurement and, by extension, fostering better theories of behavior, (ii) enhancing early-stage theory fidelity, and (iii) using big data and A/B testing.

Improving Measurement
Many behavioral theories are based on studies that rely on self-report measures and assess key variables infrequently (*e.g.,* see [61] for a discussion about this). The small variance explained by such theories as well as the lack of rigorous testing is at least in part due to the poor fidelity of data on which the theories are based. HCI researchers can significantly contribute to solving both of these problems by improving measurement of theoretical constructs and behaviors.

HCI researchers have ample experience with developing tools that take advantage of ubiquitous sensing, machine learning, and mobile computation to collect data on human behavior (*e.g.,* [7,28]). For example, mobile phones equipped with activity and location sensing [52] allow for data collection on user behavior not just with regards to application usage on the device but interactions and movements in the physical world as well (*e.g.,* [23]). HCI researchers can work with behavioral scientists to develop tools and techniques for precise and frequent measurement of key theoretical constructs and behaviors postulated by current and future behavior theories. Such tools could collect data both automatically (*e.g.,* through sensing) as well as through lightweight self-report at inferred moments of interest (*e.g.,* context-aware experience sampling, [22]).

And, crucially, because many new data collection methods require little-to-no user attention, the data collection tools developed by HCI researchers would enable longer and larger user studies, improving not only the quality of the data but its quantity as well. Better and more frequent assessments, in turn, would enable behavioral theories to be more rigorously tested—and then refined—than behavioral scientists have been able to do in the past (*e.g.,* see [61]).

In addition, tools built by HCI researchers could enable the development of a different kind of theory: personalized, dynamic models of factors that influence behavior of a particular person. By collecting fine-grain data about behavior, context, physiological measures, and cognitive constructs, systems built by HCI researchers could use machine learning techniques to model how various elements in the user's life (*e.g.,* who the user spends time with, the user's daily routine) affect the behavior the user is trying to change (*e.g.,* physical activity or smoking). In addition, as the system is used over time, the model could be continuously tuned and improved. Such individualized models of behavior could be used to create highly effective behavior change interventions which take into account the precise factors that shape the behavior of a particular person. In addition, the models could be aggregated across individuals to create more general theories of behavior which are likely to be more precise than current theories.

Enhancing early-stage theory fidelity testing
Behavioral scientists have historically put great effort into reducing the likelihood of type I error (*finding* a result when that result does *not* exist) and type II error (*not* finding a result when the result *does* exist). Type III error (*i.e.,* concluding a finding does not exist when, in fact, the study was not designed properly and therefore never tested the hypothesis [20]) is becoming an increasing concern. Type III error can lead to erroneous conclusions with regard to the accuracy of a theory. To minimize this, some behavioral scientists are starting to explore *theoretical fidelity*—whether a theoretically-guided intervention actually functions according to the theory [52]. Mediation analyses and treatment fidelity methods [29] are the standard "checks" behavioral scientists use to determine theoretical fidelity. Current behavioral science methods for theoretical fidelity, however, are largely lacking for initial system development. As discussed in the *Uses of Behavioral Theory* section, HCI researchers could establish *a priori* expectations of words or phrases from user testing research to establish early-stage theoretical fidelity tests. To the best of our knowledge, this strategy has not been employed previously but may offer exciting new opportunities for early-stage theoretical fidelity testing.

Supporting and using big data and A/B testing
Finally, increasing opportunities in big data and A/B testing allow unique opportunities for improving behavioral theory. Much of this work is currently being conducted by large corporations (*e.g.,* Facebook) or start-ups with loyal followers (*e.g.,* Runkeeper) that have access to large

databases of user interactions with their systems. The opportunities for testing, refining, and creating new theories about behavior are astounding when big data, improved measurement, and A/B experimental testing are combined.

Big data and A/B testing allow for research that goes beyond testing individual constructs or conceptual frameworks but full meta-models. Before big data, tests of meta-models were almost impossible; this, however, is rapidly changing with big data and improved multilevel measures and A/B testing is a particularly promising approach to testing meta-models. Using A/B tests, it becomes possible to explore the causal impact of constructs after controlling for other components identified in the meta-model. The closest example to this type of study that we are aware of is a recent study in which an A/B test of 61-million users of Facebook was conducted to test the effect of social influence on voting patterns [9]. This type of research, which HCI researchers are uniquely poised to conduct, could radically transform our ability to test and further develop behavioral theories.

CONCLUSIONS AND NEXT STEPS

Our goal in this paper was to provide HCI researchers and designers with guidance for interpreting, using, and contributing to behavioral theories. We explicitly sought to highlight the important place for a cross-pollination of ideas and methods between disciplines. That said, this paper only scratches the surface. Issues that require further explication are numerous such as: (i) best methods for evaluating behavior change technologies in HCI research (extending [43]); (ii) a full understanding of the requisite knowledge each field requires before engaging with the other (e.g., how much knowledge does an HCI researcher need about behavioral theory to use and contribute to it?); (iii) the possibility of distortions that arise from poor translations of concepts between fields; and (iv) the impact of sociocultural differences related to the origin of theories on the interpretability, utility, and generalizability of different behavioral theories within an HCI context. Each of these points requires more careful thought and work from both fields. As such, our final goal is a call for behavioral scientists and HCI researchers to work more closely together both on the design of behavior change technologies and the development of better theories. This paper itself represents the collective effort of two behavioral scientists (one psychologist and one public health researcher), and two HCI researchers (a researcher in health informatics and a computer scientist). We believe that such collaborations and open exchanges of ideas across disciplines are fundamental to the development of better theories, better systems, better behavioral outcomes, and, ultimately, to positive societal impact.

REFERENCES

1. Adams, M.A., Norman, G.J., Hovell, M.F., Sallis, J.F., Patrick, K. (2009). Reconceptualizing decisional balance in an adolescent sun protection intervention: Mediating effects and theoretical interpretations. *Healt Psychol*, 28, 217-225.

2. Ajzen, I. (1991). The theory of planned behavior, *Organizat Behav Hum Dec Proc*, 50, 179-211.

3. Ajzen, I. (2002). Perceived Behavioral Control, Self-Efficacy, Locus of Control, and the Theory of Planned Behavior. *J Appl Soc Psych*, 32, 665-683

4. Balaam, M. *et al.* (2011). Motivating mobility: designing for lived motivation in stroke rehabilitation. *CHI'11*, 3073-3082.

5. Bandura, A.(1986). *Social foundations of thought and action*. Prentice Hall, Englewood Cliffs, NJ.

6. Bandura, A. (1997). *Self-Efficacy-The Exercise of Control*. Worth Publishers, Inc. New York, NY.

7. Bao, L. and Intille, S.S. (2004). Activity Recognition from User-Annotated Acceleration Data. *Most*, 1–17.

8. Becker, M. (1974). The health belief model and personal health behavior, *J Healt Soc Behav*, 18, 348-366.

9. Bond, R.M., *et al.* (2012). A 61-million-person experiment in social influence and political mobilization. *Nature 489*, 295–298.

10. Buman, M.P., Giacobbi, P.R., Yasova, L.D., and McCrae, C.S. (2009). Using the constructive narrative perspective to understand physical activity reasoning schema in sedentary adults. *J Healt Psychol*, 14, 1174–83.

11. Collins, L., Dziak, J., and Li, R. (2009). Design of experiments with multiple independent variables: A resource management perspective on complete and reduced factorial designs. *Psychol Meth*, 14, 202-224.

12. Consolvo, S., Everitt, K., Smith, I., and Landay, J. (2006). Design requirements for technologies that encourage physical activity. *CHI'06*, 457-466.

13. Consolvo, S., Klasnja, P., McDonald, D.W., & Landay, J. (2009). Goal-setting considerations for persuasive technologies that encourage physical activity. *Persuasive '09*, Article 8, 8 pgs.

14. Consolvo, S., Klasnja, P., McDonald, D.W., *et al.* (2008). Flowers or a robot army ? Encouraging awareness & activity with personal, mobile displays. *UbiComp'08*, 54–63.

15. Consolvo, S., McDonald, D.W., and Landay, J. (2009) Theory-driven design strategies for technologies that support behavior change in everyday life. *CHI'09*, 405-414.

16. Consolvo, S., McDonald, D.W., *et al.* (2008). Activity sensing in the wild: A field trial of UbiFit garden. *CHI'08*, 1797-1806.

17. Corbin, J. and Strauss, A. (2008). *Basics of qualitative research: Techniques and procedures for developing grounded theory*. 3rd Ed. Sage, Thousand Oaks, CA.

18. Deci, E.L. and Ryan, R.M. (1985) *Intrinsic motivation and self-determination in human behavior*. Plenum, New York, NY.

19. Dervin, B. (1983). Sense-making theory and practice: An overview of user interests in knowledge seeking and use, *J Know Manag*, 36-46.

20. Dobson, D. and Cook, T. (1980) Avoiding type III error in program evaluation: Results from a field experiment. *Eval Prog Plan*, 269-276.

21. Dourish, P. (2010) HCI and environmental sustainability: the politics of design and the design of politics. *DIS'10*, 1-10.

22. Dunton, G., Intille, S., Beaudin, J., and Pentz, M.A. (2009). Pilot test of a real-time data capture protocol to assess children's exposure to and experience of physical activity contexts using mobile phones. *Obes 17*, S150–S151.

23. Eagle, N. and Pentland, A. (2006). Reality mining: sensing complex social systems. *Pers Ubi Comp*, 255-268.

24. Erickson, T. (2005). Five Lenses: Towards a Toolkit for Interaction Design. *Theories and Practice in Interaction Design*.

25. Fogg, B.J. (2002). Persuasive Technology: Using computers to change what we think and do. *Ubiquity*, December Issue, A-5.

26. Froehlich, J., Findlater, L., and Landay, J. (2010). The design of eco-feedback technology. *CHI'10*. 1999-2008.

27. Froehlich, J., Findlater, L., Ostergren, M. *et al.* (2012). The design and evaluation of prototype eco-feedback displays for fixture-level water usage data, *CHI'12*, 2367-2376.

28. Froehlich, J. (2011). Sensing and feedback of everyday activities to promote environmental behaviors, *UMI*, 3501869.

29. Gearing, R. and El-Bassel, N. (2011). Major ingredients of fidelity: A review and scientific guide to improving quality of intervention research implementation. *Clin Psychol Rev*, 79-88.

30. Glanz, K., Rimer, B., and US- N.C.I. (1995). *Theory at a glance: A guide for health promotion practice*. NIH-NCI.

31. Goffman, E. (2002). *The presentation of self in everyday life*.

32. Grimes, A., Bednar, M., Bolter, J.D., and Grinter, R.E. (2008). EatWell: Sharing nutrition-related memories in a low-income community, *CSCW'08*, 87–96.

33. Grimes, A. and Grinter, R. (2007). Designing persuasion: Health technology for low-income African American communities. *Persuas Tech*, 4744, 24-35.

34. He, H., Greenberg, S., and Huang, E. (2010). One size does not fit all: Applying the transtheoretical model to energy feedback technology design, *CHI'10*, 927-936.

35. Hekler, E.B., Buman, M.P., Otten, J., *et al.* (2012) Who responds better to a computer- vs. human-delivered physical activity intervention? Results from the community health advice by telephone (CHAT) trial. *In Submission.*

36. Hekler, E.B., Buman, M.P., Poothakandiyil, N., *et al.* (2012) Exploring behavioral markers of long-term physical activity maintenance: A case study of system identification modeling within a behavioral intervention. *In Submission.*

37. Hersen, M., and Barlow, D.H. (1976). *Single-case experimental designs: Strategies for studying behavior change.* Peramon, New York, NY.

38. Kim, T., Hong, H., and Magerko, B. (2010). Design requirements for ambient display that supports sustainable lifestyle. *DIS'10*, 103-112.

39. King, A.C., Sallis, J., Frank, L., *et al.*, (2011). Aging in neighborhoods differing in walkability and income: Associations with physical activity and obesity in older adults. *Soc Sci Med*, 73, 1525-1533.

40. King, A.C., Hekler, E.B., Castro, C.M., *et al.* (2013). Exercise Advice by Humans versus Computers: Maintenance Effects at 18 Months. *Healt Psychol.*

41. King, A.C., Stokols, D., Talen, E., Brassington, G.S., and Killingsworth, R. (2002). Forging a Transdisciplinary Paradigm. *Am J Prev Med 23*, 15–25.

42. King, A.C., Toobert, D., *et al.* (2006). Perceived environments as physical activity correlates and moderators of intervention in five studies. *Am J. Healt Prom*, 21, 24–35.

43. Klasnja, P., Consolvo, S., and Pratt, W. (2011). How to evaluate technologies for health behavior change in HCI research. *CHI'11*,3063-3072.

44. Kraemer, H.C. and Kiernan, M., Essex, M., and Kupfer, D.J. (2008). How and why criteria defining moderators and mediators differ between the Baron & Kenny and MacArthur approaches. *Healt Psychol*, 27, S101-S108.

45. Lee, M., Kiesler, S., and Forlizzi, J. (2011). Mining behavioral economics to design persuasive technology for healthy choices. *CHI'11*, 325-334.

46. Lin, J., Mamykina, L., and Lindtner, S. (2006). Fish'n'Steps: Encouraging physical activity with an interactive computer game. *UbiComp'06*, 261-278.

47. Locke, E. and Latham, G. (1990). *A theory of goal setting & task performance*, Prentice Hall, Englewood Cliff, NJ USA.

48. Maguire, M. (2001). Methods to support human-centered design. *Intern J Hum Comp Stud*, 55, 587–634.

49. Mamykina, L. and Mynatt, E. (2008). MAHI: investigation of social scaffolding for reflective thinking in diabetes management. *CHI'08*, 477-486.

50. Chetty, M., Tran, D. and Grinter, R.E. (2008). Getting to green: Understanding resource consumption in the home. *UbiComp '08*, 242-251.

51. Michie, S. Ashford, S., Sniehotta, F.F., *et al.*, (2011). A refined taxonomy of behaviour change techniques to help people change their physical activity and healthy eating behaviours: The CALO-RE taxonomy. *Psychol Healt*, 26, 1479-1498.

52. Miluzzo, E., Lane, N., Fodor, K., *et al.* (2008). Sensing meets mobile social networks: the design, implementation and evaluation of the cenceme application, *SenSys'08*, 337-350.

53. Morin, C. and Bootzin, R. (2006). Psychological and behavioral treatment of insomnia: Update of the recent evidence (1998-2004). *SLEEP*, 29, 1398-1414.

54. Moyers, T.B., Martin, T., Manual, J.K., *et al.* (2005) Assessing competence in the use of motivational intervention. *J Sub Abuse Treat*, 28, 19-26.

55. Nickerson, R. (1998). Confirmation bias: A ubiquitous phenomenon in many guises. *Rev Gen Psychol*, 2, 175-220.

56. Nigg, C., Allegrante, J., and Ory, M. (2002). Theory-comparison and multiple-behavior research: Common themes advancing health behavior research. *Healt Educ Res*, 17, 670-679.

57. Ogden, J. (2003). Some problems with social cognition models: a pragmatic and conceptual analysis. *Healt Psychol*, 22, 424-428.

58. Prochaska, J., Wright, J., and Velicer, W. (2008). Evaluating theories of health behavior change: A hierarchy of criteria applied to the transtheoretical model. *Appl Psychol*, 57, 561-588.

59. Prochaska, J.O. and DiClemente, C.C. (1983). Stages and processes of self-change of smoking: toward an integrative model of change. *J Consult Clin Psychol 51*, 390–395.

60. Purpura, S., Schwanda, V., Williams, K., *et al.* (2011). Fit4Life: The design of a persuasive technology promoting healthy behavior and ideal weight. *CHI'11*, 423-432.

61. Riley, W.T., Rivera, D.E., Atienza, A. *et al.* (2011). Health behavior models in the age of mobile interventions: Are our theories up to the task? *Trans Behav Med 1*, 53–71.

62. Rovniak, L.S., Hovell, M.F., and Wojcik, J.R. (2005). Enhancing theoretical fidelity: an email-based walking program demonstration. *Am J Healt Prom*, 20, 85–95.

63. Sallis, J.F. and Owen, N. (1997). Ecological models. In K. Glanz, *et al.* eds., *Health behavior and health education: Theory, research, and practice*. Jossey Bass, San Francisco, 403–424.

64. Sallis, J.F., Saelens, B.E., Frank, L.D., *et al.* (2009). Neighborhood built environment and income: examining multiple health outcomes. *Social Sci Med*, 68, 1285–1293.

65. Shove, E. (2010). Beyond the ABC: Climate change policies and theories in social change. *Environ and Plan*, A, 42(6), 1273.

66. Velicer, W.F. and Prochaska, J.O. (2008). Stage and non-stage theories of behavior and behavior change: A comment on Schwarzer. *Appl Psychol Interna Rev 57*, 75–83.

67. Behavior Change Techniques Taxonomy. http://www.ucl.ac.uk/healthpsychology/BCTtaxonomy/index.php.

Beyond Digital and Physical Objects:
The Intellectual Work as a Concept of Interest for HCI

Melanie Feinberg

School of Information, The University of Texas at Austin

1616 Guadalupe St., Suite 5.202

Austin, TX 78701-1213, USA

feinberg@ischool.utexas.edu

ABSTRACT

To understand activities of personal collecting and preservation, HCI researchers have investigated why people become attached to particular objects. These studies have examined ways that people relate to physical and digital objects, observing, for example, that people tend to cherish physical objects more than digital ones. This paper proposes that the value of digital objects may inhere less in an object's identity as a particular item and more in the object's ability to provide access to an intellectual *work*. The work, a familiar concept in information studies and textual studies, designates a general product of intellectual creation that may be instantiated in many versions. (For example, Shakespeare's *Hamlet* exists in many editions and forms, which may differ in both content and carrier and yet still are all *Hamlet*.) The paper demonstrates how the concept of the work can extend research on the perceived value of digital objects. It also shows how a flexible definition of the work can reveal new aspects of a design situation.

Author Keywords

Works; texts; documents; digital media; textual studies, information studies; design; collecting; preserving; memory

ACM Classification Keywords

H.5.m. Information interfaces and presentation (e.g., HCI): Miscellaneous.

INTRODUCTION

As more traces of our intellectual and emotional activity become digital, HCI has turned its attention to the support of memory functions, with particular emphasis on personal archiving practices [12, 24, 11, 16]. To provide a conceptual base for this support, researchers have investigated the qualities that make any object significant or cherished [22, 7, 8, 10]. These studies have often noted distinctions between tangible objects and digital ones, finding that the items people select as personally valuable intertwine important memories with significant material

characteristics: the seashell from a summer vacation, the child's artwork. The physical presence of these significant objects may become even more powerful over time as the item is inscribed with the process of aging. The photograph of a beloved great aunt's vigorous youth gets brittle and fades, the favorite picture book from childhood features stains and rips from years of hard use. In contrast, digital objects seem less distinctive. After all, many digital objects can be easily replicated with little cost, whereas a seashell or crayon drawing is unique in its singular presence. And yet losing access to one's digital music collection or stash of Kindle mystery novels would certainly be traumatic. While the idea of missing a particular stream of bits seems strange, the idea of missing the expression enabled through those bits is not. I might not have an attachment to the digital file that encodes my copy of Stevie Wonder's *Ribbon in the Sky*, but if *Ribbon in the Sky* itself somehow disappeared from the world, and I could never listen to it again, I would sad indeed. Replacing my copy with another copy, though? I wouldn't think twice about it.

This paper introduces the concept of the intellectual work, a notion with a long history in information studies and textual studies, as a means of understanding objects that may exist as potentially vast sets of copies and almost-copies. The concept of the work provides a structure to organize the slew of versions that exist for many instances of creative expression. Is one's attachment to *Ribbon in the Sky* the song as written by Stevie Wonder, no matter its instantiation? Or is it to a particular performance of the song by Stevie Wonder (and not a cover version by another artist), or to a specific manifestation of the performance by Stevie Wonder (an MP3 file) or even to a certain physical copy (on the CD that my partner and I bought when we lived in Los Angeles fifteen years ago, that now has a tiny skip in it)? Does one adore plain *Ulysses* by James Joyce? Or does the edition matter? (To some readers, the Gabler edition is an abomination.) Does it have to be in print, or can it be on a Kindle? Is the real object of your affection the tattered copy you toted in high school to establish your reputation as a tortured intellectual? The concept of the work can help us identify important levels of abstraction for particular media forms (moving images, maps) and situations of use (pleasure reading, scholarly criticism). The concept of the work can also clarify the relationships that obtain between different categories of versions. I would never say that I cherished any MP3 file. But having access to the work encoded in that MP3 file may be another matter entirely. (It may be, as well, that where I might once have described my collection of LPs as dear to me, I am now happy to be rid of those heavy boxes of vinyl records, as long as I can listen to the songs on my iPod. The different affordances of new versions may shift our allegiances.)

In this paper, I introduce the concept of the work and explain its history in the domains of information studies and textual studies, highlighting both the utility of the work for each discipline as well as difficulties caused by its inherent ambiguity. Following the track of textual studies, I use the example of documentary film footage to illustrate a flexible approach to defining the work, which I argue is key to its productive employment within HCI. I then show how using the notion of the work in this manner can extend analyses of significant and cherished objects from HCI research. I conclude by demonstrating how conceptualizing the work in different ways can reveal new aspects of a design situation, using the example of personal collections in the social media service GoodReads.

AN OVERVIEW OF THE WORK

In our daily lives, we employ the concept of the work without realizing it when we refer to the product of creative expression at various levels of abstraction. Consider the following scenario:

On my last plane flight, I read Murder at the Savoy, *a Swedish detective novel from the 1960s. The literal translation of the Swedish title is something like Police, Police, Mashed Potatoes, isn't that funny? I bought a used paperback because it was cheaper than the Kindle version.*

In the first sentence, *Murder at the Savoy,* the title, is being used in a general way, without reference to any particular version. In the second sentence, I distinguish between two different versions, one Swedish and one English, that are both still *Murder at the Savoy,* even though the Swedish version not only has a different string of words for the title, but a different meaning for the title. Here, although the sentence indicates two different sequences of symbols (in different languages) that represent the same unit of expression, *Murder at the Savoy,* there is no reference to the instantiation of those symbols in any particular format (printed text, digital text, audiobook). In the third sentence, I refer to different physical manifestations of the English version at two different levels of abstraction. One is the physical item that I bought. It is the one element in this story that is a distinct object; in this case, it is also tangible. The other is not a specific Kindle book on my or anyone else's e-reader but a broader notion of that expresses the idea of the (English) Kindle version in general.

Three levels of abstraction are commonly distinguished to bring some degree of order to this array of version types: document, text, and work [30, 28]. A document indicates a specific copy, like the paperback I read on the plane. A text

indicates different sets of symbols that are similar enough to be considered essentially the same creation. The text is abstract in that it refers to the set of symbols and not their physical embodiment, and so the same text (an English translation of *Murder at the Savoy)* can be available in different formats (paperback, Kindle). The work is the concept that links together all the documents and texts. The scholar of information organization Elaine Svenonius has described the work as that which brings together "almost the same information," and the textual studies scholar Paul Eggert has defined it as "what underwrites the sameness" between texts [27, 5]. That may sound frustratingly ambiguous. As the following sections make clear, no one has defined the work with satisfying precision. And yet the idea is profoundly intuitive and inescapably useful. If you ask me if I've read *Hamlet,* and I say Yes, you won't think I'm lying if I've read the Oxford edition while you've read the Modern Library edition. We unconsciously agree that both of these are equally *Hamlet.* In fact, it's hard to imagine talking about instances of creative expression without reliance on this most general level of abstraction. Most of the time, for most of us, just plain *Hamlet* is the best way of communicating what we care about, and if our yellowed copy was exchanged for a crisp new one, we wouldn't mind. We might not even mind if our copy disappeared, because we know many copies exist, and we can always find another. But what if someone exchanged our copy of the Oxford *Hamlet* with "No Fear Shakespeare, a modern translation"? We might say, "Hey, that's not really *Hamlet!*" We mean that No Fear Shakespeare is not as much *Hamlet* as the Oxford edition or the Modern Library edition; it's no longer the same work. And what about a Japanese translation of *Hamlet?* Our judgment then might depend on whether we speak Japanese, or perhaps on our particular views regarding literary translations.

The disciplines of information studies and textual studies both explore these distinctions. Textual scholars, whose work is associated with literary studies, are interested in what constitutes *Hamlet* to provide a basis for editing and interpretation, while information scholars (and practitioners, such as librarians and information architects) are interested in how the results of searching a document repository for *Hamlet* should be structured to facilitate a user's selection of appropriate items. The next sections distill elements from these traditions.

THE WORK IN INFORMATION STUDIES: COLLOCATION AND ARRANGEMENT OF VERSIONS FOR RETRIEVAL

The goal of assisting a patron in discriminating between editions has always been recognized in library cataloging, even though cataloging rules have traditionally focused on describing the item in hand (most typically a book). The nineteenth-century librarian Charles Cutter's objectives for a library catalog, which continue to underlie modern Anglo-American cataloging principles, assert that the catalog should "assist in the choice of edition," which it does in practice (from Cutter's day to ours) by describing edition information, such as the publisher and publication date, in the catalog record [4].

Over time, however, and especially as collections became larger, it became apparent that bringing together multiple editions in the catalog was a tricky problem. Again since the time of Cutter, catalogs have prioritized three access points: author, title, and subject (in the days of card catalogs, each of these access points had its own set of cards, with items filed in the three ways). While one might initially think that the title would provide sufficient collocation, different editions are often given different titles. Think again of *Hamlet:* one might well have *The Tragedy of Hamlet, Prince of Denmark; Hamlet; Shakespeare's Hamlet;* and so forth among many possible variant titles. Too, *Hamlet* might be contained within another work: *Selected Plays, Shakespeare's Tragedies,* and so on. And there may be other items with the title *Hamlet* that aren't written by Shakespeare at all. By the 1960s, the cataloger Seymour Lubetzky, one of the architects of the Anglo-American Cataloging Rules (the foundation of modern cataloging guidelines) explicitly described the collocation of editions of a particular work as a primary goal of the catalog [15]. Martha Yee expands that a catalog should enable library users to identify documents that are both effectively equivalent or perhaps even preferable to what users were originally searching for: someone looking for the third edition of a textbook may be pleasantly surprised to see that a newer fourth edition is available, for example [32]. Moreover, items that are not the textbook being sought, but that may have similar titles, should be excluded from the search results. Through its abilities to describe and group documents as part of a single work, the library catalog (or, indeed, any document retrieval system) should actively assist users in mapping the appropriate document space and refining information needs.

The current structure of the library catalog (all libraries in the U.S. use the same conceptual structure, the same file format, and the same guidelines for creating records) does not accommodate works incredibly well; each record is still for a particular physical item. Today, collocation of editions occurs through the use of authority files that provide controlled vocabularies for subject terms, author names, and, occasionally, what are called uniform titles (these are most commonly used to relate translated titles with the ones in the original language). One tries to locate all the editions of *Hamlet* by searching the author file for William Shakespeare, which retrieves all the records associated with that author, and then searching those records for *Hamlet* in the title (at my university library, there is no uniform title associated with *Hamlet*). The recall of such a search are invariably incomplete, and options for grouping and sorting the results (over 500 at my university library) are limited.

An entity-relationship model to clarify work-related levels of abstraction

To address such issues, in 1998 the International Federation of Library Associations (IFLA) introduced an entity-relationship model for catalogs based on the concept of the work [9]. This model, Functional Requirements for Bibliographic Records (FRBR) proposes a set of four bibliographic entities of increasing concreteness: works, expressions, manifestations, and items. Each entity has associated attributes and potential identified relationships. In the FRBR model, expression is similar to the more commonly used "text," while manifestation refers to the output of a particular printing (a print run, but also an issue of CDs, e-book, or whatever media). The FRBR model is incorporated into the latest cataloging rules, Resource Description and Access (RDA), recently completed and due to begin adoption by the U.S. Library of Congress (LC) in March, 2013. Most U.S. libraries will follow LC's lead, because most American libraries obtain LC's cataloging records and adapt them for local use. Currently, however, the benefits of FRBR can only be approximated in most library catalogs. The OCLC WorldCat system, a union catalog that aggregates the holdings of 72,000 libraries worldwide, enables some grouping of editions by exploiting properties of the current record structure, but this service is incomplete and inconsistent [21].

Austlit, the online Australian Literature Resource, provides an illustrative example of how the FRBR model would facilitate document retrieval. Austlit was built around the FRBR model and adopts the work, and not the item, as the record unit. A collaborative venture of the National Library of Australia and Australian universities, each bibliographic record in Austlit brings together all the expressions (called versions in Austlit) of a work, as well as all the manifestations (called publications in Austlit) of each expression. (Austlit does not contain item records; it links to item records held by participating libraries.) A sample record for Patrick White's novel *Voss* brings together information about 22 expressions (mostly different translations) represented in 43 manifestations (all printed books but issued by different publishers); it also includes references to related works such as an opera based on the novel and several excerpts contained in literary anthologies [1]. An excerpt from this sample record appears in Figure 1. With a catalog based on works, such as Austlit, it is easier for the information seeker to understand relationships between versions and to discriminate between them.

What kind of entity is a work? Or is it a relationship?

While the FRBR initiative has cemented the importance of the concept of the work for document description and retrieval, it has not provided a rigorous definition of the work, nor has it established a clear set of principles for determining when a particular expression is part of an existing work or when it should be considered a new work. FRBR describes a work as "a distinct intellectual or artistic creation" and as an entity, although an entity without any

Figure 1: Excerpt of Austlit record for a work. Each numbered item is an expression; some expressions have several manifestations.

physical or even symbolic representation. Most discussions of the work within information studies characterize it as an "abstract entity," which is congruent with traditional ideas from textual studies (summarized in the following section). As an example, Smiraglia claims that the work is the set of ideas that "lies behind" all the work's expressions [26]. All of the 22 expressions of White's novel *Voss* from Austlit share a common group of ideas, although the words in each expression might be totally different, and these shared ideas are the work. Both the appeal and difficulty of this sort of definition is that it conceives of the work as a static ideal; it implies that although different expressions might come into being, the work that these expressions represent doesn't change. In this vein, Svenonius remarks on the "abstract, Platonic" nature of the work as a concept [27].

Some scholars, however, conceptualize the work as a relationship or category instead of an entity. O'Neill and Vizine-Goetz define the work as "a set of related texts with a common origin and content," and Renear and Dubin assert that the FRBR entity is logically a relationship [23, 27]. These less rigid notions of the work are echoed by more recent scholarship in textual studies (also summarized in the following section).

Difficulties in specifying what constitutes a work lead to downstream confusion in determining which expressions constitute new works. FRBR guidelines, which do not provide systematic rationale, can appear arbitrary. For example, a sound recording of *Hamlet* is an expression of the original work (and thus as equally *Hamlet* as the printed

Modern Library edition), but the filmed version of a live performance of the play is a new work. Problems associated with not being able to articulate what constitutes a work are particularly apparent for non-book materials, such as maps, motion pictures, and scientific models [18, 31, 3].

Digital materials can be especially complex, because significant differences in underlying code may be undetectable in the user experience, and the sheer number and scope of versions can be dizzying. To demonstrate this, McDonough, et al enumerate the set of versions associated with a simple, early computer game (Adventure); they are unable to adequately differentiate these versions with the current set of FRBR entities [17]. In conducting their case study, McDonough and colleagues argue that the distinctions they seek to reveal are necessary information for the software studies scholar, and so they should also be pertinent for the information professions, who support such research. But McDonough, et al equally acknowledge that the typical game player is not concerned with this level of detail in characterizing the work. Within information studies, pragmatic goals for uniform description of information-bearing objects have supported the idea of single, consistent notion of the work, with a standard set of accompanying entities. But one can alternately view the work from a more flexible perspective, adapting the characteristics that define and relate versions to accommodate certain forms (such as software) and use situations (such as scholarly research as opposed to personal entertainment). The arc of scholarship within textual studies, as described in the next section, supports such an approach. In subsequent sections, I argue that a flexible take on the concept of the work can enrich the notions of significant and cherished objects that have been a significant element of personal archiving research in HCI. A standard, uniform approach to defining the work, as realized in the FRBR model, is appealing its relative fixity. However, I suggest that a flexible concept of the work, where the idea of what counts as an essentially equivalent version may vary according to situational factors such as context of use, is ultimately more useful for HCI.

THE WORK IN TEXTUAL STUDIES: ESTABLISHING THE BASIS FOR INTERPRETATION

Similarly to information studies, textual scholarship, a branch of literary studies, aims to describe the universe of versions of a work and the relationships between versions. However, the traditional goal of textual scholarship has been to discriminate between more and less authoritative versions of literary works, and to assemble evidence that allows the construction of more reliable versions (critical editions). The foundations of textual scholarship lie in the historical transmission of manuscripts from scribe to scribe across centuries of copying, where changes across copies are inevitable (and, with extended passage of time, are potentially gigantic). Medieval scholars, for example, use specialized knowledge of alphabets and scripts (paleography, the study of handwriting) to trace the sequence of versions over time and place, with the aim of assembling a version as close to the original as possible. Modern textual scholarship in English is epitomized by the case of Shakespeare's plays. Early printed versions were notoriously full of printers' mistakes, cuts, and so on. The textual critic's job is to assemble the chain of versions (of which none is actually "correct") and provide various forms of evidence through which an authoritative version of (say) *Hamlet* can be created. Textual scholars see their efforts as crucial to literary interpretation. Without authoritative versions, the conclusions of literary criticism are suspect.

Traditional textual studies: authorial intentions as the primary regulating principle that shapes a work

G. Thomas Tanselle articulates the traditional concept of the work in textual studies as the true expression of the author's intentions [28]. A central component of this view of the work is that any chain of textual transmission (presumably, even from the brain of the author to the initial manuscript) is rife with errors. The intended text—the work—may never have actually taken shape in a particular document, either in manuscript or in print. Nonetheless, it is the textual editor's duty to construct a text that best approximates the ideal of the work, using the existing textual variants and associated historical evidence to do so. The variant texts and the documents that contain them may reflect the work to some degree and provide clues to the ultimate nature of the work, but the work exists somehow independently of them. (The prevalent concept in information studies of the work as an abstract entity is quite similar.) Accordingly, Tanselle can assert that there is no distinction between "literary" texts and other texts—that, for example, it is absurd to have one edition of William James for philosophers and a different edition of William James for literary scholars. The work is the same for all readers, and all serious readers should prefer a text that makes the best possible claim for reflecting the work [28].

Postmodern textual studies: the work as a dynamic, collaborative process

As literary criticism has come to appreciate the socially and historically constructed elements of all interpretive activities, as suggested by the writings of theorists such as Michel Foucault, Roland Barthes, and many others, the association of meaning with authorial intention has weakened. With these ideas permeating literary studies, textual scholars have reexamined their function, along with ideas of the work. Jerome McGann has persuasively contested the association of textual transmission with errors and inevitable corruption, proposing a sense of the work as a collaborative process between authors, editors, publishers, and others. The changes requested by an editor are, in McGann's view, just that, changes, and not mistakes that take a particular text further from the ideal work. For McGann, the work is dynamic and emergent: "a series of specific 'texts,' a series of specific acts of production, and the entire process which both of these series constitute" [19, p. 52]. Current textual scholarship has married these ideas

with new technologies to produce critical editions as digital collections. The aggregation and encoding of textual variations, along with interfaces to structure comparison and interpretation, constitutes a strand of digital humanities research. Examples of such collections include McGann's Rossetti Archive, Clement's collection of the modernist poet Baroness Elsa von Freytag-Loringhoven, and the collaborative Walt Whitman Archive edited by Folsom and Price [20, 2, 6]. The forensic approach to literary analysis originated by Matt Kirschenbaum is also an extension of textual studies; the McDonough, et al case study on code-level differences between versions of Adventure is a collaboration between digital humanists/textual scholars and information studies researchers [13, 17].

In a complementary response to this general reevaluation of the notion of authorship, Eggert introduces contextual and historical elements to the idea of work-as-process, using the restoration of Leonardo da Vinci's Last Supper as one example [5]. Previous restoration attempts from other eras are now deemed inappropriate by the current restorers; they obscure the artist's original vision. In contrast, the current restoration, which uses modern technology to isolate the original fragments, enables, in the view of the restorers, the original vision to be again revealed. In the current context, from the perspective of the restorers, the older restorations are no longer part of the work, but the recent restorations are. And yet some critics contend that the new restorations reveal not Leonardo's vision but a contemporary notion of what the original should look like, and the restoration method itself is conditioned by current ubiquity of image close-ups and detail views.

The need for a flexible definition of the work

The definition of the work, from this example, appears both dynamic and debatable. Selecting a particular definition is in itself an act of interpretation. This suggests that any definition of the work for a particular context must be explicated and defended. If there is no ideal essence motivating the idea of the work, then the structure of the work must be explicitly determined for particular cases. The work becomes a generic category, almost a placeholder; it must be fleshed out before it can be used productively. Moreover, authorship becomes only one potential regulating principle for defining a work and determining its boundaries. For some forms of expression, and some use situations, additional principles may be more salient in determining the set of versions that makes up a particular work. In the next section, I use the example of documentary film footage to illustrate how the concept of the work might be specifically and productively defined for a certain context. I then show how this flexible approach to the work can extend ideas of significant objects as conceptualized in HCI, and how it can also be used to inform design decisions for systems that enable the collection and display of digital materials.

CASE STUDY FOR CONTEXTUAL DEFINITION OF THE WORK: DOCUMENTARY FILM FOOTAGE

In my view, the concept of the work is best defined as a category, or a relationship between particulars. The regulating principles of the category, or the properties that structure and organize the category members, may vary in different situations. In contemplating potential instantiations of the work as category, it is helpful to acknowledge that the most common and recognizable example of a work remains that of a written text created by a single author with a specific initial publication date, like Raymond Chandler's *The Big Sleep* or Agatha Christie's *Murder on the Orient Express*. The combination of author and title forms the nexus of the regulating principle that the work represents. While different editions might make small changes from one to the other (for example, some printings of *The Big Sleep* use the spelling "okey" for "okay"), the substance of each text is consistent across versions, presumably as written by the author. In other situations, however, the variation between versions can be much greater, such as in subsequent versions of a textbook, and authorship may change as well. *Gray's Anatomy* is on its fortieth edition, and it is no longer supervised by Dr. Gray, who died many years ago. In such a case, very little may remain the same from the first version to the most recent. The continuous publication history is perhaps more important to the character of this work as a related set of versions than either the author or the title (which was initially *Anatomy of the Human Body,* not *Gray's Anatomy*).

Action, not authorship, as the regulating principle for a work of documentary film footage

Authorship is perhaps even less indicative of what usefully circumscribes a set of "almost the same" materials when considering certain combinations of both media and situation. An illustrative example comprises documentary film or video footage of a particular event, such as an apartment fire, tennis match, or birthday party. While the edited presentation of such an event, such as ESPN's coverage of a particular Wimbledon match, would exhibit a form of institutional authorship and as such have a distinct identity from, say, the BBC's coverage of the same match, the raw output of all the various cameras recording the proceedings (including spectators' cell phones, and so on) can be seen, from a certain perspective, as a single work.

In this case, it is the event itself, or the action, that forms the regulating principle around which the set of versions that instantiates the work revolves. The centrality of action as a cornerstone of identity for moving images has been suggested for fictional narratives as well: Andrea Leigh, in discussing episodes of television series, in particular *I Love Lucy,* suggests that the principle of action is of primary importance for entertainment-oriented information seeking, because nobody remembers the episode titles and writers; everyone instead thinks of "the one where Lucy works at the chocolate factory," and so on [14]. But such claims are even stronger for unedited recorded images of events like

"the gas explosion on Payne Avenue from last November" or "Gayatri's first birthday party at Dolores Park" where the role of authorship tends to be minimized even if the person (or people) who recorded the footage is known. Let's say that three party guests sent digital video of the birthday girl blowing on her candles to Gayatri's parents. The relationship between the clips, as formed by their shared subject, the event of the birthday party, seems much stronger than the difference between them as being filmed by different people. Moreover, while the family may well want to retain video evidence of the event, they might not have any special connection to one of the clips as opposed to another, if they all included the same activities. The attachment is to the work, here defined as video of the candle-blowing, and not to a particular expression or item.

Use context and the definition of a work

To demonstrate further why a flexible approach is necessary in determining the most appropriate regulating principle to structure the versions of a work, let's add another level of complexity to the birthday video scenario. What if one of the serendipitous videographers at the birthday party happened to be a famous film director, say Martin Scorsese? Wouldn't the idea of authorship be salient in that case, and wouldn't there be a particular attachment to his clip? Indeed, such potential variability is why I propose that the use situation must contribute to any particular definition of the work as well. It may initially seem strange to adapt the determination of what kinds of text are properly *Hamlet* according to a use context. Shouldn't the idea of what is or is not *Hamlet* be something that we can all rely upon? Certainly, while McDonough, et al, note that the needs of the specialist researcher may demand more levels of discrimination between versions of the game Adventure than those required by the general player, their goal is to propose modifications to the FRBR model, in order to make it a more flexible overarching system, and not to propose flexible models for different situations [17]. Still, observations of the dynamic, historical nature of the work as a concept, as noted by McGann and Eggert, hint that no single model will ever be flexible enough [19, 5]. Of course No Fear Shakespeare will never be properly *Hamlet* for a literature scholar, and yet it might well be so for a nervous high-school student—at least, according to some principles of pedagogy. In the case of the birthday party video, if Scorsese were Gayatri's Uncle Marty, and if he was one of several habitual video contributors, there would be more of a reason to treat his clip as but another almost interchangeable version of Birthday Girl Blowing Her First Candle. If not, then there would be a reasonable argument for considering Scorsese's video as another work entirely. Similarly, if the use context was not the personal archive of family memories but digital assets for a stock video company, then the camera angle and lighting might contribute to the appropriate regulating principle for the work, and the level of detail at which the action was described would be less important (baby's first birthday and not Gayatri's birthday).

With such potential for variation, one might begin to wonder about the ultimate utility of the work as a concept at all. Is it too nebulous to provide a rigorous and systematic analytical lens upon the diverse range of expressive artifacts in the world? Although I certainly acknowledge the difficulties in its application, I nonetheless contend that the idea of the work can help us understand the potentially vast expanse of artifact versions in revealing and thoughtful ways. Despite its inherent ambiguities and the need to think carefully about what it means for any particular combination of media and use context, and to think carefully about the level of precision appropriate for differentiating between versions, the concept of the work is a compelling means of understanding document ecologies, particularly in the digital realm, where ease of copying makes for extensive sets of similar files. The work provides a structure through which we can clarify the nature of relationships between documents and the associated meaning that those documents may hold for their creators, their keepers, and their seekers. In the next section, I demonstrate how the idea of the work as developed through this paper can further the analysis of current HCI research on the preservation of significant and cherished objects.

WHEN IS THE OBJECT OF AFFECTION NOT ACTUALLY AN OBJECT? THE WORK IN THE CONTEXT OF HCI RESEARCH ON KEEPING AND CHERISHING

In Kirk and Sellen's excellent depiction of the values enacted through home-based practices of collecting and keeping, they introduce a typology of objects that their participants cherish: physical, digital, or hybrid [12]. Hybrid items are storage media through which both digital and analog content can be accessed (videotapes, music CDs, LPs). While these distinctions are valuable to recognize, the notion of the work and its accompanying layers of abstraction (expressions, manifestations, and items, to use the FRBR terminology, which is easier to apply to non-text material) can add an additional level of complexity to this characterization. Kirk and Sellen describe the hybrid in particular as a case in which the expression or experience enabled through the object is what matters to the owner, and not the physical presence of the item itself, noting that ". . . the actual VHS or tape cassettes used for storage held no sentimental value whatsoever, but the content was considered to be very precious" [12, p. 1014]. It is the song on the CD (a la *Ribbon in the Sky)* that is more often cherished, and not the CD itself. But works with potentially numerous versions appear in the physical and digital categories as well. The physical category includes items such as newspaper or magazine cuttings, books, and printed photographs, while the digital category includes such items as video clips, e-mail messages, and digital photographs. Across the typology, for items that may find expression in multiple versions, at what level of abstraction does attachment lie? Is it to the work in general

(say, Yotam Ottlenghi's recipe for sweet corn polenta), to a particular expression or set of expressions (from the U.S. cookbook *Plenty* or from the UK Guardian newspaper column, or any UK version or any U.S. version), to a particular manifestation or set of manifestations (the U.S. Kindle cookbook, or any U.S. version that can be printed), or to one unique item (torn out of the UK Guardian and kept in the kitchen recipe file)? Answering such questions can sharpen our understanding of what it means to cherish anything; the focus of our attachment may reside in a class of similar objects, instead of a particular object. Where Kirk and Sellen assert that "we can never equate a digital copy of a physical object, no matter how veridical, with its original," this may depend on the level of abstraction at which value is located. Value may inhere in an item; or it may be connected to a work, with many potentially interchangeable items to choose from. If the area of concern in preserving an item is really to maintain convenient access to a work, then attachment to any particular copy is diminished when this access in maintained via some other means, particularly when output in different formats is possible. When I moved to a new house last year, for example, I got rid of my collection of music CDs; it was no longer necessary to store those items, because I had access to my preferred expressions of those songs on my computer and iPod, and the new devices can also be connected to the stereo receiver. My attachment to the works expressed through the songs never changed, but I no longer had need of the CD copies to maintain my access to the works.

The work of Golsteijn and colleagues also provides another demonstration of this [8]. Golsteijn et al used Kirk and Sellen's typology to analyze results from a similar study (although where Kirk and Sellen used home tours to gather data regarding significant objects, Golsteijn et al conducted focus groups where participants brought photos of selected objects). Golsteijn et al note particularly cases where the distinction between physical and digital seems to no longer matter. They describe the example of siblings scanning a set of printed family photographs so that each could have a complete set; ultimately, both siblings retained the digital images instead of the printed versions. On the one hand, it remains worthwhile to use such examples to explore the complementary affordances of different media, as Golsteijn, et al do. But we can also use such cases to examine the potentially different values that accrue to levels of abstraction: work, expression, and so on.

It is may also be possible to use these ideas to obtain a more precise sense of the value people identify in mass-produced designed items that undergo regular versioning, as with consumer electronics and computers. It may be reasonable to think about the next version of an iPhone in the same way that one would think about the next version of a textbook or a travel guide. In both cases, the newest versions are typically more desirable—in other words, the regulating principle of the work is focused around recency. Am I happy to replace my local restaurant guide with this year's updated version? Everything else being equal, of course I am (say if someone gave me the new version, and I didn't have to pay for it). When my university replaces my MacBook with a newer model, do I complain about wanting to keep my older, slower one? Not when the IT staff handles all of the migration tasks for me. Would I always be happy with such exchanges, and what would lead me to refuse them? Through being aware of the concept of the work and its accompanying levels of abstraction, HCI can more readily formulate such questions and investigate their answers.

As another example, these and similar studies ask participants to share significant objects with the researchers. And yet, as has been discussed, a digital photo may be valued for the expression it presents, not for its status as an object. The terminology of objects may discourage participants from selecting items that are valued for the access to expression that they enable more than their material qualities. Petrelli and Whittaker, for example, also directed participants, in home tours, to select special things in physical and digital form [24]. Petrelli and Whittaker were surprised that few people selected photos as significant physical objects. Only 16 percent did so, and Petrelli and Whittaker observed that selected photographs were often "unique or irreplaceable"; that is, not available in multiple versions. In the digital realm, Petrelli and Whittaker's participants selected items that they or others had created or that documented personal experiences (that is, they tended to select family photographs and videos, their own e-mail exchanges, and digital content created by children, and not their iTunes libraries or funny videos of cats collected from around the Web). In both the physical and digital realms, the focus on "special things" may have encouraged participants to concentrate on item-based characteristics instead of higher levels of abstraction. A cat video, in other words, may be special, but not as a thing, and a music collection may be significant, but not identified as such on a home computer if it is also available on a iPod and the laptop in the office.

Consideration of work-related levels of abstraction can also complement studies of personal information management in office and academic settings, such as Whittaker and Hirschberg and Kaye, et al [29, 11]. These studies, too, focus attention on the distinctions between physical (often paper, in this case) and digital items. Whittaker and Hirshberg, for example, identify factors that lead people to retain paper files of documents even when moving offices. While a good portion of retained paper documents were unique items, and another segment of retained documents were in the "to-read" pile, 36 percent of retained paper documents were available elsewhere. The most prevalent forms of rationale for keeping these materials were to preserve convenient, reliable, and persistent access (a variation involved distrust of other access methods). Here, the value seems to be at the level of the work, although one's own print versions are perceived to enable access

better than other versions. But it's the access that's important, not the paper nor the personal storage. Another factor for retention, reminding, relies on the affordances of paper as a medium (a manifestation-level attribute): having a paper document laying around on one's desk keeps the actions associated with it in mind, and browsing articles in files reminds one why they are important. A final factor, sentiment, is associated with item-level characteristics: materials used in one's dissertation, for example. There are memories bound up in the saved items, even though participants recognize that there is nothing about the item's appearance that would make such associations apparent to someone else. Access to the work isn't actually important here, it's the sentiment bound in the materials themselves. While Whittaker and Hirshberg's analysis is perceptive and detailed, the discussion of retention factors could gain additional nuance by considering which level of abstraction is important for each factor, and why this is so. Sometimes the affordances of a particular medium, such as paper, are important, but when the value is at a higher level of abstraction, then alternate media and associated access mechanisms may be appreciated, not just tolerated. However, when the significance lies in the item (even if the traces of attachment are not to be observed in the material itself), then no substitution will be acceptable. Seen from this perspective, the behavior of the administrator with the "almost paperless" office described in Kaye, et al's study of personal document collections is quite reasonable [11]. This administrator kept paper versions only of those materials that he had in some way participated in creating. These items were valued as unique objects; the digital library of documents on the administrator's computer, on the other hand, was valued as a means of accessing works, not because of any item-level significance.

IDENTIFYING PARTICULAR CONCEPTIONS OF THE WORK TO ILLUMINATE A DESIGN SITUATION

In this section, I briefly illustrate how the concept of the work can be used to comprehend a design situation and inform the development of alternative feature sets. As an illustrative example, I consider the domain of collecting, which encompasses a range of activities from the keeping of cherished objects as repositories of memory to the maintenance of personal files for information access. Here, I focus on the collection and display of metadata records as enabled through the social media service GoodReads. In the GoodReads environment, users assemble collections of book records into personal catalogs. The use of books is less central to this example than the idea of a collection of surrogates: analogous systems include Pinterest (collections to linked images) and even something like Facebook (collections of friend profiles). In all these cases, the collections that users create can form the basis for commentary and conversation with the community. The

Juliet's Bookshelves

read (368)	currently-reading (0)	to-read (16)	
			Stats | More...

Eric's Bookshelves

read (513)	essays (47)	alwaysiscloseathand (22)	peteredout (13)
currently-reading (0)	travels (43)	unexpected (22)	music (13)
to-read (987)	poetry (43)	us-civil-war (21)	verysoon (12)
fictiones (121)	to-read-in-2013 (38)	westward-ho (18)	russian-childhooda (12)
criticism (98)	lurid (35)	decadence (18)	design (12)
shouldreread (96)	photography (35)	bagatelle (17)	curiosa (11)
history (72)	massacres (30)	malick-should-film-it (16)	childhood (11)
favorites (62)	dandies (27)	embarrassed-that-i-havent	turkey (11)
hommes-de-lettres (59)	nabokov (27)	mitteleuropa (15)	themaster (11)
etudes-slaves (56)	hearts-laid-bare (26)	great-war (14)	criticismofcriticism (10)
americans (54)	art (25)	personal-bibles (14)	whileboredatwork (9)
war (52)	historiophantasmagoria (25	18thcentury (13)	sam-grant (7)
			Cloud | Stats | More...

Aloha's Bookshelves

read (940)	e-ebooks (1575)	a-paper-book (110)	genre-fiction-contemporary
currently-reading (4)	a-audios (1389)	a-collections-anthology (96	c-nobel-laureate (48)
to-read (2500)	genre-horror (475)	genre-history (89)	genre-scifi-fantasy (47)
to-read-1 (269)	genre-sci-fi (448)	c-1001-books-you-must-rea	genre-splatterpunk (46)
to-read-2 (129)	genre-fantasy (330)	genre-dark-fiction (81)	z-king-stephen (44)
to-buy (84)	genre-non-fiction (275)	genre-historical-fiction (70)	genre-art (44)
to-read-december-2012 (11	genre-literature (255)	genre-post-modern (70)	genre-ya (42)
to-read-this-month (10)	genre-fiction-general (195)	genre-fantasy-ballantine-ad	genre-psychology (41)
new-releases-to-check-up-(	genre-mystery-thriller (148)	genre-biography (62)	z-pratchett-terry (39)
to-watch (2)	genre-science (142)	c-hugo-award-novels (82)	z-heinlein-robert-a (39)
a-unfinished-and-good-ndd	genre-philosophy (129)	a-maciek-read-or-die (56)	z-dick-philip (38)
a-own (2488)	c-sf-masterworks (120)	a-favorites (56)	genre-political-science (38)
			Cloud | Stats | More...

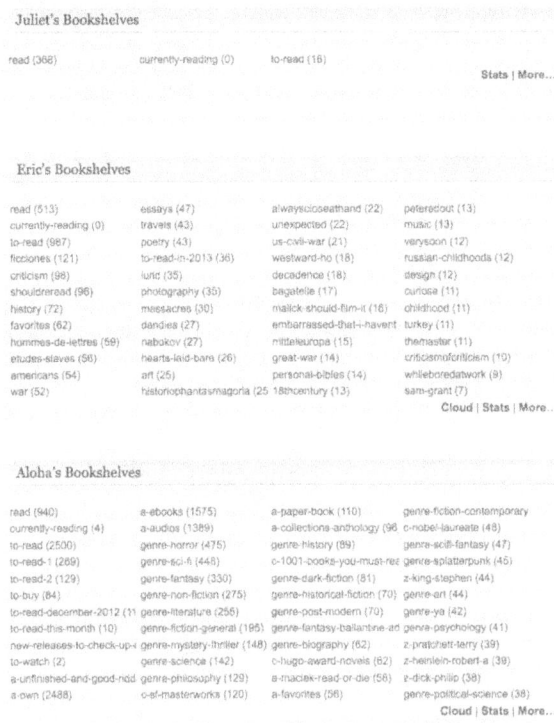

Figure 2: Different use contexts for GoodReads shelves imply different ideas of the work for a collection of book metadata.

collection-building features of GoodReads, however, make it a good example for this scenario.

One of GoodReads' features is the *shelf,* essentially a category for grouping collection items (here, typically records for books owned by the collection creator, usually described at the level of a FRBR manifestation). There are three default shelves: *read, currently-reading,* and *to-read.* Users can create their own shelves and identify these custom shelves with labels (or tags). Differences in shelf use suggest that users' collections constitute different types of works.

Some GoodReads users have significant collections but do not create additional shelves. The user identified as "Juliet Evans," with a collection of 384 books, only includes the GoodReads default shelves. Other users, however, create extensive shelf systems. For example, even though the GoodReads system does not facilitate the creation of multiple category levels, the user "Aloha" created a multidimensional shelf structure using shelf naming conventions as grouping devices. Other users, such as "Eric," devise evocative, idiosyncratic shelf categories such as "bagatelle" and "lurid." Figure 2 shows the shelf systems for the users identified as Juliet Evans, Aloha, and Eric. (Note that the figure can only show a small selection of Aloha's total number of shelves, which extend to the hundreds, including a shelf for every author.)

I propose that in this example, there are two ideas of the work, as distinguished by two different contexts of use. For GoodReads users who do not create additional shelves, or who create very few shelves, the regulating principle of the work centers on the set of records describing each entered book. However, for the users with extensive shelf systems, the regulating principle of the work is the category structure as applied to the records. In terms of design implications, a new version, or expression, of the GoodReads catalog for users like Juliet would occur only when an item is added or deleted. For users like Aloha and Eric, however, a new version would involve a category change: addition, deletion, or assignment (a new record might be created in the context of a new assignment, or an assignment might involve existing records). Each of these ideas of the work might lead to different modes for saving, displaying, and exporting a user's catalog. Currently, GoodReads does not support any catalog versioning or archiving. Especially for users like Aloha and Eric, for whom the value of the catalog entwines deeply with the shelf system, this would seem to represent a useful design opportunity, as revealed through a work-oriented analysis.

CONCLUSION

This paper demonstrates how the concept of the work, as drawn from information studies and textual studies, can extend HCI research on the perceived value of digital objects, and how attending to the various levels of abstraction that structure a set of versions can provide another layer of understanding regarding the relationships between physical and digital objects. While the work, with its inherent ambiguity, requires flexibility in its definition and application for particular situations of use and forms of media, it can nonetheless provide a keen analytical lens to facilitate our conceptual grasp of collecting activities and attitudes.

REFERENCES

1. Austlit, the Australian Literature Resource. Available at http://www.austlit.edu.au/. Last accessed August 30, 2012.

2. T. Clement, ed. In transition: selected poems by the Baroness Elsa von Freytag-Loringhoven. Available at: http://digital.lib.umd.edu/transition/index.jsp. Last accessed September 2, 2012.

3. A. Coleman. Scientific models as works. In *Works as Entities for Information Retrieval.* R. Smiraglia, ed. New York: Haworth Information Press, 129–160, 2002.

4. C. Cutter. *Rules for a dictionary catalog.* 4th ed. Washington: Government Printing Office, 1904.

5. P. Eggert. Where are we now with authorship and the work? *Yearbook of English Studies* 88–96, 1999.

6. E. Folsom and K. Price. Walt Whitman Archive. Available at: http://www.whitmanarchive.org/. Last accessed September 2, 2012.

7. S. Gegenbauer and E. Huang. Inspiring the design of longer-lived electronics through an understanding of

personal attachment. *Proceedings of ACM DIS 2012*, 635–644, 2012.

8. C. Golsteijn, E. van den Hoven, D. Frohlich, and A. Sellen. Toward a more cherishable digital object. *Proceedings of ACM DIS 2012*, 655–644, 2012.

9. International Federation of Library Associations (IFLA) Study Group on the Functional Requirements for Bibliographic Records. *Final Report*. Munich: K.G. Saur, 1998. Available at http://www.ifla.org/publications/functional-requirements-for-bibliographic-records. Last accessed August 28, 2012.

10. H. Jung., et al. How deep is your love: deep narratives of ensoulment and heirloom status. *International Journal of Design* 5(1) 59–71, 2011.

11. J. Kaye, et al. To have and to hold: Exploring the personal archive. *Proceedings ACM CHI 2006*, 275–284, 2006.

12. D. S. Kirk and A. Sellen. On human remains: Values and practice in the home archiving of cherished objects. *ACM Transactions on Computer-Human Interaction* 17(3): 1–43, 2010.

13. M. Kirschenbaum. *Mechanisms: New media and the forensic imagination*. Cambridge, MA: MIT Press, 2008.

14. A. Leigh. Lucy is "enceinte": the power of an action in defining a work. In *Works as Entities for Information Retrieval*. R. Smiraglia, ed. New York: Haworth Information Press, 99–127, 2002.

15. S. Lubetzky. *Principles of cataloging*. Report for U.S. Office of Education grant OE-1-7-071089-4284. Los Angeles,: UCLA Institute of Library Research, 1969.

16. C. Marshall. Digital copies and a distributed notion of reference in personal archives. In *Digital Media: Technological and Social Challenges of the Interactive World*. M. Winget and B. Aspray, eds. Lanham, MD: Scarecrow Press, 2011.

17. J. McDonough, et al. Twisty little passages almost all alike: applying the FRBR model to a classic computer game. *Digital Humanities Quarterly* 4(2), 2010. Available at http://digitalhumanities.org/dhq/vol/4/2/000089/000089.html. Last accessed August 28, 2012.

18. S. McEathron. Cartographic materials as works. In *Works as Entities for Information Retrieval*. R. Smiraglia, ed. New York: Haworth Information Press,181–191, 2002.

19. J. McGann. *A critique of modern textual criticism*. Chicago: University of Chicago Press, 1983.

20. J. McGann, ed. Rossetti Archive. Available at: http://www.rossettiarchive.org/. Last accessed September 2, 2012.

21. OCLC. WorldCat catalog. Available at http://www.oclc.org/worldcat/default.htm. Last accessed August 31, 2012.

22. W. Odom, et al. Understanding why we preserve some things and discard others in the context of interaction design. *Proceedings of ACM CHI 2009*, 1053–1062, 2009.

23. E. O'Neill. and D. Vizine-Goetz. Bibliographic relationships: implications for the structure of the catalog. In *The Conceptual Foundations of Descriptive Cataloging*. E. Svenonius, ed. San Diego, CA: Academic Press, Inc., 167–195, 1989.

24. D. Petrelli and S. Whittaker. Family memories in the home: contrasting physical and digital mementos. *Personal Ubiquitous Computing* 14(2) 153–169, 2010.

25. A. Renear and D. Dubin. Three of the FRBR Group 1 entities are roles not types. *Proceedings of ASIST 2007*.

26. R. Smiraglia. *The nature of "a work": implications for the organization of knowledge*. Lanham, MD: Scarecrow Press, 2001.

27. E. Svenonius. *The intellectual foundation of information organization*. Cambridge, MA: MIT Press, 2000.

28. G. T. Tanselle. *Textual criticism and scholarly editing*. Charlottesville, VA: University of Virginia Press., 1990.

29. S. Whittaker and J. Hirschberg. The character, value, and management of personal paper archives. *ACM Transactions on Computer-Human Interaction* 8(2): 150–170, 2001.

30. P. Wilson. The second objective. In *The Conceptual Foundations of Descriptive Cataloging*. E. Svenonius, ed. San Diego, CA: Academic Press, Inc., 5–16, 1989.

31. M. Yee. The concept of work for moving image materials. *Cataloging and Classification Quarterly* 18(2): 33–40, 1993.

32. M. Yee. What is a work? Part 4: cataloging theorists and a definition abstract. *Cataloging and Classification Quarterly* 20(2): 3–24, 1999.

Critical Perspective on Persuasive Technology Reconsidered

Fahri Yetim

University of Oulu

P.O. Box 3000,

FIN-90014 Oulu, Finland

Fahri.Yetim@oulu.fi

ABSTRACT

Critical researchers in HCI have recently faulted Persuasive Technology (PT) for taking a modernist approach and suggested ways for redirecting research. This paper reflects on this critical perspective and compares it with Habermas's critical perspective. I claim that the recent critiques of PT are grounded on a narrow and pessimistic concept of modernism, and that Habermas's works, rarely taken into account in the HCI community, can serve as an alternative lens for reflective analysis and design and can provide a foundation for justifying design decisions while realizing the unfulfilled potentials of PT. Beyond offering critical analysis and reflections, this paper contributes to the HCI field by calling attention to alternative reflective concepts and emerging relevant works.

Author Keywords

Persuasive Technology; Reflective HCI; Critical Research; Critical Reflection; Modernism

ACM Classification Keywords

K.4.0 Computers and Society: General. H.5.2 [Information Interfaces and Presentation (e.g. HCI)]: Miscellaneous.

General Terms

Human Factors; Design.

INTRODUCTION

Persuasive Technology (PT) is designed to change a person's attitude or behavior [4, 12]. Recent critiques of existing approaches contend that they embody characteristics and values of the modernism and that PT as a modernist technology is suspected of breakdowns due to its narrow vision [3, 10]. Moreover, the critical researchers claim that the problems affect not only PT, but connect to broader issues in HCI research, and suggest alternatives that might be useful in redirecting research.

In contrast, I argue that these valuable critical insights are based on a narrow and mainly pessimistic view of

modernism, when contrasted with J. Habermas's critical analysis of modernism [5]. I claim that Habermas provides not only a broader lens, but also a set of theoretical concepts for reflective analysis and ethically sound design to realize the unfulfilled potentials of PT.

Usually, critical researchers take concepts from critical social theories (such as modernism) or from an explicit value position (such as fairness), and apply them to analyze current practice and/or to suggest ways of improvement [9]. Critical approaches differ depending on which critical writer's theory serves as the basis (e.g. Habermas, Foucault, or others). Having an interest in both the HCI and Information Systems (IS) research, I observed that Habermas's works have widely been acknowledged and applied in the field of IS [9,14,15], whereas they are rarely considered in HCI. A quick search in ACM digital library yielded that only a few works cited Habermas in CHI and CSCW proceedings. They cited Habermas, among others, with regard to specific concepts such as participation, without considering these concepts for analysis, design, or evaluation. This applies also to those publications that are classified as reflective or critical works in HCI.

Thus the motivation of this note is threefold: First, to reflect on the current critiques of PT; Second, to highlight Habermas's distinct way of advancing critical research, including his view of modernism and its implications for PT; And third, to bring some emerging applications of his work to the attention of the HCI community. By contrasting two different critical views, I hope to stimulate further discussions for advancing research on reflective HCI.

MODERNISM AS A NEGATIVE CONCEPT

A Negative View on Modernist PT

The concept of modernism is used in several works in HCI to develop a theoretical lens to critically analyze PT, for example, in the domains of health [10] and environmental sustainability [3]. According to [3], modernism refers to a broad cultural movement.

> Modernism rejects the idea that tradition should be the guide for action and seeks instead to rethink and optimize our life conditions through rational planning. Modernism aims to improve life through technical means; it is associated with the idea of "progress" and

embraces scientific perspectives as the grounds for new definitions of value. [3]

Based on the work of Max Weber as popularized by Ritzer [11], four values (i.e., *calculability*; *predictability*; *efficiency*; and *control*) are regarded to be central to modernist approaches. Brynjarsdóttir et al. state that:

> Modernist approaches to technology tend to be predicated on *quantifying* aspects of human life, focus on improving the *efficiency* of everyday processes, intend to have *predictable* effects, and in order to do so necessarily aim to increase *control* over the vagaries of those processes. [3]

Similarly, Purpura et al. see PT as

> embodying a 'McDonaldized' [...] worldview that values quantification and rationality at the cost of situational, hard-to-measure factors and sees scientific measurement as obviating personal experience. [10]

Through the design of Fit4Life system, the authors provoke reflection about the meaning and value of a broader rationalization of our lives. By highlighting Ritzer's use of the term "irrationality of rationality" – the ways in which too great an emphasis on the individual rational attributes leads to solutions that are globally irrational – they also claim that PT represents an incursion of a rationalistic view of the world and showcases the "irrationality of rationality".

Brynjarsdóttir et al. [3] acknowledge that there is much that is laudable about modernism as a frame for technology design to enable handling complex problems and also provide a list of positive features of modernist technology. However, on the whole their view on modernism is negative, and they consider modernist technologies to be susceptible to breakdown. Modernist solutions to problems are viewed to be based on a narrowed vision that focuses on certain limited aspects of a complex reality, involving the simplification of phenomena and making possible a high degree of schematic knowledge, control, and manipulation.

Suggestions for Redirecting Research

A series of alternatives have been proposed to redirect the research. Purpura et al. [10] proposed (a) expanding criteria for evaluation to include attitudes (not only behaviors) and unintended consequences, and (b) designing for mindfulness and leaving room for stories. They argue that, by telling the users exactly how to behave in every situation, the system takes away the user's ability to reflect on their situation and decide on appropriate action. Instead, the system should encourage mindfulness and promote reflection in order help users to build attitudes important for sustaining long-term health, to enable them to what it actually means to be healthy or how healthy is defined.

Similarly, [3] argued for (a) broadening our understanding of persuasion; (b) including users in the design process; and (c) moving beyond the individual. In addition, they suggest

alternative approaches that go beyond persuasion, which include: (d) shifting from prescribing behavior to enabling open-ended reflection; (e) shifting from individual behaviors to consideration of behaviors in their connection to social and cultural practices.

Limitations, Contradictions, and Open Issues

The critical analysis and suggestions are valuable, yet, they also leave space for counter-critiques. One critique concerns their foundation, in particular, the reference to the Ritzer's interpretations of McDonaldization as an expression of modernism and characteristics of rationalized systems (i.e., efficiency, predictability, calculability, control). According to the critical researchers, this found expression in the design of PT, with ultimately irrational and harmful human consequences. In line with the critics of Ritzer's work, one may argue that McDonaldization encompasses not only the forces of efficiency, and homogeneity, but also a postmodern realm of diversity or heterogeneity [8].

Another, and more important, critique concerns the critique of a worldview that values rationality. Critiques of the Ritzer's use of the "irrationality of rationality" stated that it leads to self-contradiction: criticizing rationality and at the same time developing an immanent critique of the irrationalities that are produced by McDonaldization [8]. Similar contradiction can be seen in the critique of PT, i.e. criticizing that it values rationality and at the same time offering a critique of irrationalities produced by PT.

Moreover, a closer look at Ritzer's [11] understanding of irrationality reveals that rationality and reason are employed to mean antithetical phenomena, when he states:

> Most specifically, irrationality means that rational systems are *unreasonable* systems. By that I mean that they deny the basic humanity, the human reason, of the people who work within or are served by them. [11]

This raises the issue: What should an "improved version" of PT, resulting from the consideration of human reason and/or the other above-mentioned suggestions for refocusing, be considered: non-modernist, post-modernist or anti-modernist technology? In other words, it is unclear what the suggested approaches embody, if they do not embody modernist approach. As discussed below, the processes that are tied to modernity in the critiques are based on a narrow concept of rationality and rationalization.

Finally, the critiques of PT in HCI leave a justification gap since they do not make explicit what set of ethical values and ideals, or which theory will justify both the critique of the present (i.e., the dominant values embodied in or promoted by current technology) and the suggestions for alternative orientations.

Next, I discuss how Habermas's critical perspective and his works can serve as an alternative to frame the research while avoiding contradictions and justification gaps.

MODERNISM AS A POSITIVE CONCEPT

Habermas's Affirmative View

Habermas [5] defends the ideals of the Enlightenment and considers modernity to be an unfinished project. He claims that the pessimistic perspective of modernism is grounded in a subjectivist "philosophy of consciousness" which considers a "purposive rationality" to guide the selection of efficient means for achieving specified goals, without reflection on the rationality of the goals themselves. For Habermas, critical theorists from Max Weber to the Frankfurt School remained trapped in this philosophy and neglected the capacities and resources of communicative action that are also part of modernism. Habermas conceives modernity as a process of differentiation or rationalization, i.e., the lifeworld is rationalized into different cultural value spheres such as science, morality, and art, each pursuing their own ends by their own particular forms of logic. Assuming that the differentiation and reflexivity of traditions promote emancipation, Habermas accounts for the pathologies of rationalization in a way that suggests a redirection rather than an abandonment of modernity.

Central to Habermas's critical analysis is the distinction between three formal concepts of 'worlds': the objective world of things, the social world of people, and the subjective world of feelings. He describes three 'basic attitudes' that people can take up with respect to the elements of the three worlds: an objectivating attitude which views things, people, or feelings as things; a norm-conformative attitude which regards them in terms of moral obligation; and an expressive attitude which approaches them emotively. Following Max Weber, Habermas claims that only some of the world relations are suitable for the accumulation of knowledge and progressive development and thus rationalizable. Modernity is based on precisely those rationalizable world relations. Three complexes of rationality have been derived from world relations: cognitive-instrumental rationality (the production of knowledge taking the form of scientific and technical progress), moral-practical rationality (the production of knowledge taking the form of a systematic treatment of legal and moral representations), and aesthetic-practical rationality (the production of knowledge taking the form of authentic interpretations of needs) [5].

For Habermas, the problem of one-sided modernity is that only the objectivating relation to the objective and social worlds has been allowed fully to develop, whereas there are obstacles in the way of barring rationalization in the moral-practical sphere. With his works on the Theory of Communicative Action [5], Discourse Ethics [6] and Deliberative Democracy [7], Habermas provides a comprehensive concept of rationality, a set of discursive-ethical concepts and principles, to deal with the undiminished potential that modernity has to increase social rationality, justices and morality. All these concepts and principles enable people to reflect on what is purposive, good and just.

Implications for Persuasive Technology

One of implications of Habermas's works for critical research in HCI is psychological in nature, offering an alternative to, and a way out of the negativism often associated with critical research, to develop a more affirmative view by focusing on not-yet utilized potentials. This calls for refocusing current critical discourse on PT from the pitfalls of instrumental rationality to the reaffirmation of communicative rationality (or communicative reason).

This refocusing offers a possibility for conceiving PT as a means for achieving a deliberated end in different domains such as health, education, environmental sustainability. The action-guiding imperatives of a persuasive system can be viewed as part of and moderated by the lifeworld, and institutionalizing and formalizing structures for reflective communication can enable those affected by the system to deliberate and evaluate its imperatives and, in this way, to account for different interests and validity claims, including claims to aesthetic, ethical or moral rationality.

From this perspective, the critical researchers' suggestions for redirecting the PT research (e.g., facilitating reflection, involving users, moving beyond individual) can be viewed as efforts to utilize the reflexive potential of modernism.

Moreover, the critiques of PT, of the dominant values, as well as the suggestions for alternatives require justification. Discourse ethics [6] provides the procedure, i.e. a set of discourses and principles, to fill this justification gap. Both researchers and designers can employ them for critically reflecting on and justifying the choices of goals (e.g., persuasive intent), means (e.g., persuasive strategies), values, and norms. In particular, the distinctions between pragmatic, ethical and moral issues and the related discourses make it possible to deal with each issue according to its logic, when discussing available options and justifying what is purposive (pragmatic discourse), good (ethical discourse), and just or right (moral discourse).

EMERGING APPLICATIONS

Habermas's works, while rarely cited in the CHI community, provide a foundation for informing reflective research in the IS field, for the analysis and design of interactive systems and technologies, ranging from the management of usability guidelines, supporting their reflective use [13], to the Value Sensitive Design (VSD) of systems in general [14] and of PT in particular [15].

A discourse ethical approach to VSD [14] provides responses to the recent articulation of future steps for VSD in HCI [2]. First in response to the call that a "VSD could benefit from a more democratic approach to its own methodology," it describes how a set of discursive-ethical concepts and principles enable reflections on many issues (e.g., comprehensibility, validity, rationality, purposiveness, goodness, rightness) involved in system design and use. Second, in response to the emerging issue of how to deal with situations with less clear organizational boundaries (e.g. browser design, or Facebook), it illustrates the application of a reflective approach to boundary definitions.

Moreover, a set of critical heuristics are defined and associated with different types of discourses [15] to promote and guide reflections in discourses and also help to critically analyze the reasoning and assumptions of the participants. The approach thus responds to the calls for reflective and open-ended approaches to PT [1,3,10,12].

Finally, by seeing 'persuasion' as a communicative act and PT as a communicative technology, designers can employ Habermas's concepts for the analysis, design, and evaluation of PT. They can focus on the communication relation established between the designers (or PT) and the users, on the intent of persuasion and the strategies chosen to achieve the desired attitude and/or behavior change. Valuing communicative rationality implies, for example, not just that the PT communicates imperatives that the user can accept, but also that there is the possibility of two-way communication.

CONCLUSIONS

In this paper, I argued that the critique of PT to some extent approaches the Frankfurt School critique of modernism and instrumental rationality. By taking Habermas's perspective, I claimed that his works provide a basis for a broader framework for reflective PT research. In fact, there is no social theory that has not been criticized, and this applies to both perspectives on modernism. Therefore, instead of questioning the previous critical insightful analysis of PT and the suggestions, I conclude that Habermas's perspective includes, but also goes beyond, previous suggestions.

In particular, his works provide a broader theoretical and ethical foundation for the justification of both the criticism of present and the ideals for future orientation. Beyond justification they also avoid some contradictions with respect to the critiques of rationality. The reasons expressed in different types of discourses among a diverse group of participants can go beyond a technologically or individualistically determined purposive rationality. In this way, a decision is linked to and informed by the human experience of a social and cultural life world. Such a communicative perspective recognizes the intersubjectively constructed nature of reality, without falling into the trap of relativism. Beyond designing means for deliberation, Habermas's works also suggest the need for attention to public sphere as a source for legitimacy, since the public sphere is considered the seat of communicative rationality.

In sum, this paper contributes to HCI by discussing the limitations of the current critical perspective on PT, presenting an alternative and communicative view and

some emerging works. By contrasting two different critical perspectives, I hope to stimulate further debate and opportunities for advancing reflective research in HCI.

REFERENCES

1. Baumer, E.P.S., Katz, S.J., Freeman, J.E., Adams, P., Gonzales, A.L., Pollak, JP, Retelny, D., Niederdeppe, J., Olson, C., and Gay, G. (2012). Prescriptive persuasion and open-ended social awareness: Expanding the design space of mobile health. *Proc. CSCW '12*. ACM.

2. Borning, A., and Muller, M. J. (2012). Next steps in value sensitive design. *Proc CHI '12*. ACM, 1125-1134.

3. Brynjarsdóttir, H., Håkansson, M., Pierce, J., Baumer, E.P.S., DiSalvo, C. and Phoebe Sengers, P. (2012). Sustainably unpersuaded: How persuasion narrows our vision of sustainability. *Proc CHI '12*. ACM, 947-956.

4. Fogg, BJ. (2003). *Persuasive technology: Using computers to change what we think and do*. Morgan Kaufmann Publishers.

5. Habermas, J. (1984). *The theory of communicative action. Vol. 1, Reason and the rationalization of society*. London: Heinemann

6. Habermas, J. (1993) *Justification and Application*. Cambridge: Polity Press.

7. Habermas, J. (1996) *Between Facts and Norms*. Cambridge: Polity Press.

8. Kellner, D. (1999). Theorizing/Resisting McDonaldization: A multiperspectivist approach. In B. Smart (Ed.), *Resisting McDonaldization*. London: SAGE Publications, 186-206.

9. Myers, M.D. and Klein, H. (2011). A set of principles for conducting critical research in information systems. *MIS Quarterly* 35(1), 17-36.

10. Purpura, S., Schwanda, V., Williams, K., Stubler, W., and Sengers, P. (2011). Fit4life: the design of a persuasive technology promoting healthy behavior and ideal weight. *Proc CHI '11*. ACM, 423-432.

11. Ritzer, G. (2004). *The McDonaldization of society*. Newbury Park, CA: Pine Forge Press.

12. Oinas-Kukkonen, H. (2012). A foundation for the study of behavior change support systems. *Pers Ubiquit Comp*

13. Yetim, F. (2009). A Deliberation Theory-Based Approach to the Management of Usability Guidelines. *Informing Science* 12, 73-104.

14. Yetim, F. (2011). Bringing Discourse Ethics to Value Sensitive Design: Pathways Toward a Deliberative Future. *AIS Transactions on Human-Computer Interaction* 3 (2), 133-155.

15. Yetim, F. (2011). A Set of Critical Heuristics for Value Sensitive Designers and Users of Persuasive Systems. *Proc ECIS' 11*. AIS.

How Categories Come to Matter

Lucian Leahu
Mobile Life@SICS
Stockholm, Sweden
lucian@sics.se

Marisa Cohn
University of California at Irvine
Irvine, CA, USA
mlcohn@ics.uci.edu

Wendy March
Intel Labs
Hillsboro, OR, USA
wendy.march@intel.com

ABSTRACT

In a study of users' interactions with Siri, the iPhone personal assistant application, we noticed the emergence of overlaps and blurrings between explanatory categories such as "human" and "machine." We found that users work to purify these categories, thus resolving the tensions related to the overlaps. This "purification work" demonstrates how such categories are always in flux and are redrawn even as they are kept separate. Drawing on STS analytic techniques, we demonstrate the mechanisms of such "purification work." We also describe how such category work remained invisible to us during initial data analysis, due to our own forms of latent purification, and outline the particular analytic techniques that helped lead to this discovery. We thus provide an illustrative case of how categories come to matter in HCI research and design.

Author Keywords

Diffractive analysis; category flux; materiality for design.

ACM Classification Keywords

H.5.m. Information interfaces and presentation (e.g., HCI): Miscellaneous.

INTRODUCTION AND MOTIVATION

Empirically grounded work in Science and Technology Studies (STS) has shown how categories emerge and are maintained in scientific practice. While HCI has drawn on STS to inform and critique its frameworks, theories, and methods, little HCI scholarship has examined the work that categories perform in HCI practice (with notable exceptions on the construction of the "user" category, e.g. [3]). Yet many categories, such as "human" and "machine," are reconfigured in the design and experience of interactive technologies [9]. This paper, grounded in HCI design research, provides an illustrative example of how categories matter to the outcome of HCI research.

We present and discuss interviews with Siri users as a means to understand the role categories play in the design of user studies and of technologies. The Siri iPhone application has been marketed by Apple as a personal assistant

and, as such, engages traditionally human skills such as speech, wit, sarcasm, ostensibly to induce users to experience Siri as if "she" were human. Our broad aim in conducting interviews with Siri users was to find out what kind of relationships people enact with Siri in practice. In this paper, we analyze the role played by categories (such as "human" and "machine") in that research, i.e. in our study design, the interview data, and findings.

Prior work on devices that interact via speech, such as some GPS systems, have shown that people relate to these devices as if they were human without being aware of doing so [e.g., 7]. Initially, we wanted to see whether this was the case with Siri, particularly at a moment when Siri was within just a few months of its release and people were first working their interactions with Siri into their everyday lives. Did people relate to Siri as human or machine?

We recruited 12 participants, from San Francisco and Portland, who had been using Siri for about two months, whom we interviewed in January 2012. The participants, ages 22-65, represented a wide range of technical knowledge and interests, and consisted of 5 women and 7 men; 1 student, 1 retiree, and 10 urban professionals. The interviews, at first glance, confirmed earlier findings [7]: participants' use of categories suggests that they relate to Siri as they would to a human (e.g., friend, therapist, assistant), yet they describe Siri as "only a program" and "just a machine." However, one exceptional participant, Benjy, reported relating to Siri in a different way. While others expressed frustration and disappointment with Siri's limited capabilities, this participant found Siri to be fascinating and enchanting. While at first we took this participant to be an outlier case, in the process of data analysis his unusual reflections kept drawing our attention to his rendering of Siri as part human, part machine, part alive and part not. In the course of data analysis, Benjy's responses caused us to reflect on our study design, recast our research question, and reconsider our data from a new angle. We share the process through which we reworked our inquiry as well as the resulting conclusions and implications for HCI practice. We begin by discussing two relevant episodes from our interview with Benjy, a 36 year old writer for a pop culture magazine in San Francisco.

BENJY'S REFLECTIONS ON SIRI

Episode 1: Siri the entity

In contrast to the other participants who talked about relating to Siri as "just a machine," Benjy describes building a relationship with Siri as an 'entity.' In response to our question: How would you describe Siri? Benjy shared something he considered odd about his interactions with Siri: *"Now that I've spent time with Siri, I would say that she's an entity... [laughs] I know that sounds very odd..."*

Benjy conceptualizes Siri as an "entity" that he was coming to know over time as he became more familiar with the interactions he had with Siri, including his own responses. He notices something different in his actions and emotional responses than he has experienced with other technological devices he has used in the past. He continues:

"... I find myself often saying 'thank you' to her afterwards which is funny... I don't know... and I realize I don't have to do that for a robot... and you know I never do that with other technologies, like if I were using my calendar I would never say thank you after a task, but with Siri I will often add that simple 'thank you'... I don't know it somehow feels more correct ... Even though I know that it's definitely not human or anything resembling a human or I guess it resembles a human, and that's the point... you know, as soon as I hear a voice response that tells me that it did what I asked it to do, I've been conditioned to always say 'thank you.' So I feel bad or guilty if I don't, even though I realize as I do it I realize what I'm doing, you know what I mean? ... It gets close enough to talking to a human that I feel the need to say that sometimes, I guess... and again I call myself out on it... cause I realize exactly what I'm doing. There's a humor in it too to me. I realize what I'm doing and I find it funny... you know, it's funny that I feel the need to say thank you to a computer so therefore when I do it I do it tongue-in-cheek and with a smile."

Benjy recognizes that he doesn't "have to" respond to Siri as a human, yet he experiences a compulsion to do so which raises some contradictions and difficulties in his interaction. He describes these difficulties in finding a way to relate to Siri that feels appropriate. He appears caught between feeling guilty and odd: the guilt of not providing thanks for a service that comes in the form of a human utterance and the oddness of thanking a machine or a program. In time, Benjy effectively creates a new response option: the *"tongue-in cheek and with a smile"* thank you. This is a response that Benjy said emerged through multiple interactions, and feels satisfactorily appropriate because it addresses the simultaneously human and non-human aspects of Siri.

Episode 2: It's my Siri
In another episode during the interview, Benjy reflected on how he relates to Siri as "his" and what this means to him. He recounted these experiences in answering our question: does Siri adapt to you?

"Yeah... I don't know how though ... side note for a second...this is extremely odd... but I would be a little uncomfortable when other people would use my Siri. [laughs] and I still am... and I don't know why that is."

Benjy relates how he came to understand his own relationship with Siri better through his encounters with others who want to use Siri on his phone. It was only through these encounters that he came to realize just how much Siri had become "his" in his mind.

"I'm always surprised by how strongly I feel against that. I don't want anyone using my Siri. And yet they can borrow my phone and make a call and I'd be much more comfortable with that... it's strange for sure... but it's there. [...] I don't like it when other people try to use Siri on my phone because I feel almost like a dog owner... you know... especially when I'd just got the phone and it was new... I felt like: hey, I need to get her used to my voice and used to me... and so I would try to hide it and not let other friends experiment with her... but I would be a little uncomfortable when other people would use my Siri. [laughs]"

Benjy told us that while he doesn't mind demonstrating Siri to others he does mind if they try to use Siri. He relates this to the experience of training a dog, taking the time to build and protect his bond with Siri—one that others might disrupt. He continues:

"I don't know why that is... other than I think there might be an underlying belief that she learns my voice and maybe she learns certain things about me... which may be true or false... but there's that instinctual feeling that... like a dog... or even like a real person... they learn about you... and so I suspect that's why I'm a little uncomfortable. There is some inexplicable intimacy when somebody else asks to use your Siri, I feel like I have a direct relationship with her in that sense... it's almost like someone looking at my diary, you know... not that I keep a diary but if I did, you know... as an example... I just feel like it's an invasion of... not of privacy... but it feels like some sort of an invasion... which I know is really, really odd... I wonder if other people have that."

These quotes show Benjy trying to figure out and articulate why he is uncomfortable when others use *his* Siri. Of particular interest for us in light of our focus on categories are the parallels he draws between Siri and a dog, a "real person", and a diary. In order to depict his feelings, Benjy's explanations bring together elements belonging to different categories: something alive yet non-human, alive and human, and something inert, respectively.

CATEGORIES IN FLUX
In the episodes described above our attention was drawn to the intriguing ways in which categories such as human and non-human, alive and inanimate came together in Benjy's explanations. Here we analyze them with an eye on how they figure the relationships between these categories.

The oddness Benjy describes in these episodes has to do with Siri not fitting into his practices around technologies. In the first episode, this oddness arises from an apparent contradiction: although Benjy knows Siri is just a program running on a machine, the way he reacts to it is different. Benjy reflects on this tension. First considering how should he relate to Siri? – neither a response that would be appropriate for a human nor one appropriate for a machine feels right to him. Second asking how should he think Siri, human or machine? Siri has elements from both categories and therefore does not fit neatly in either. Thus, Siri can be said to complicate the distinctions between the categories human and machine (program, robot, AI) on which he draws simultaneously to make sense of his experiences. Similarly, in episode 2, his explanations draw on elements from disjoint categories, alive (dog) and inanimate (diary), human (real person) and non-human (dog, diary) to make sense of his reactions. Indeed, Siri blurs the boundaries between these two apparently disjoint categories: *"it's very difficult not to think of it as a living thing, even though it doesn't have a heart or a pulse. But there's some awareness there, you know… it's a very gray area."*

Both episodes speak of Benjy's difficulties in categorizing Siri. This blurs the lines between pairs of categories typically understood as non-overlapping: human–machine, alive–inanimate. For Benjy, Siri is simultaneously part human and machine, part alive, part object. He reflects on these tensions and attempts to resolve them in an emergent and explorative process of coming to know the contours of Siri the 'entity' and discovering responses that feel right to him. In sum, it seems that for Benjy categories such as human and machine do not sit still, rather they emerge changed through interactions with Siri.

NEW QUESTION AND ANALYTICAL APPROACH

What about the other participants? Was there no gray area for them? While we began the study with the question of whether people relate to Siri as human or non-human, our encounter with Benjy allowed us to rethink this question and its implicit assumption that the human and non-human are *separate* and *static* categories. This assumption is common fare in HCI studies, for a recent, notable, example see [6]. According to Benjy, Siri troubled the assumed clean delineation between these categories and drew into relief the ways that these categories were invoked not only by our study participants but also by ourselves, as researchers, in how we framed our question. As a result, we reframed our question drawing on STS work showing that classifications and categories are always already in flux and are taken up in the enactment of values and politics in the practices of science, research, and design [5,9,2]. That work provides the insight that even when categories seem to remain static and separate this is due to ongoing efforts and enactments. Informed by that work, our research question became: *How are categories taken up and worked with in the enactment of relationships with Siri?*

We return now to our data analysis with this new question as well as a different approach to our data. This new question suggests that the ways that all our study participants, not only Benjy, perform work with categories warrants ex-

planation. In other words, *we analyze symmetrically majority as well as outlier participant responses*. This is significant and novel as empirically grounded HCI would take Benjy's responses as outliers and would explain them away, rather than engaging them deeply in the analysis. Reading Benjy's and more representative responses "intra-actively through one another" [1] we expose other forms of category work that had at first been invisible to us.

FINDINGS: HOW CATEGORIES ARE REWORKED

Our participants reported relating to Siri as "just a machine." While they noted how Siri could display human-like qualities they were quick to dismiss these as qualities that were scripted. Even when Siri displayed qualities such as humor and wit, these participants discounted them saying *"what does she care, she's not even aware of it"* thus relegating them to the realm of machinic responses as Siri lacks the ability to care or be aware of an interaction.

The participants did volunteer instances where they felt that Siri surprised them with what they judged to be particularly appropriate responses, *"just like a real person would."* Yet, they were quick to point out that *"everything she says is scripted"* implying that her creators are doing the talking. One such surprise was Siri's sense of humor, which one participant qualified as *"sassy."* Asked what about this was surprising, he replied: *"well, you computer scientists aren't exactly the most lively bunch"* thus ascribing this quality or skill to the agency of Siri's makers.

Yet even these dismissals of Siri's human-like behavior indicate that categories are still in flux and at play. In saying *"what does she care"* Siri is positioned as neglectful by offering up human responses without backing them up with care and awareness. This contrast between Siri's sass and the participant's idea of the stereotypical computer scientist revealed an unexpected "liveliness" suggesting that even the humans behind Siri might be viewed as unlively. Hence even in these responses there are blurrings and tensions between the categories of the human and non-human.

Analyzing people's explanations with an eye for how they invoke categories reveals tensions that we did not previously see. These participants work to keep the categories non-overlapping, and it is clear that this separation requires ongoing effort that emerges in practice. While we initially saw only Benjy as playing with categories and resolving tensions where categories blur, we now saw how these participants too were working to resolve tensions. Qualities, skills or attributes—such as humor and wit—that could be seen as overlapping between Siri and a "real person" were attributed to Siri's creators' and, thus, implicitly denied to Siri.

In this way, users' explanations kept categories pure. We term this kind of implicit category work *purification*, meaning the practices people enact to keep categories non-overlapping. These practices can be seen in the participants' efforts to deal with elements that might trouble or blur categories through mechanisms to dismiss, explain away, or redraw the boundary between categories to remove the overlap. Latour has shown how similar kinds of purification are performed in scientific work [5]; while he shows that in general purification leads to the proliferation of hybrids, the research presented here is an instance where purification work appears to impede hybrid forms from materializing.

One mechanism of purification in this study is seen in the attribution of intent—the engineers wanted Siri to be this way, Siri had no choice in this matter—and awareness—Siri displays human qualities but is unaware of doing so. Another mechanism for purifying categories can be seen in the ways that our participants demonstrated Siri's failures to produce responses that a human interlocutor would likely produce. As if to cast away any doubts that Siri is "just a machine," they performed what essentially amounted to a Turing test in which Siri's mistakes and inappropriate responses negate any interactions that displayed human-like qualities. While at first we took these enactments for granted as falling into forms of relating to Siri as non-human, upon reframing our question we saw how these performances too served to reinforce the purity of the human and non-human categories. The fact that they felt the need to display these failures points to the existence of tension they wished to resolve, or gray area they wished to clear up.

These examples also reveal a key side effect of purification work: while the effect of this purification is keeping the categories of human and non-human distinct, the very distinctions between categories are reworked in the process. While our participants considered humor and wit, a priori, to be decidedly human qualities, these are reworked through their interactions with Siri. Our participants' comments show an active split being enacted through attributions of human and non-human. On one side of the split, qualities that are scripted and lack awareness (however judged) are attributed as machinic forms of humor/wit, while the human side of the split entails intent and awareness. The emergence of new distinctions between categories in effect redraws the boundary between the two categories. Thus purifying category work also involves the ways that people reinforce and redraw boundaries between categories.

In sum, our analysis shows that categories cannot be taken for granted: they are not fixed, but in flux. Even when users work to purify categories, to clear up gray areas and category overlaps that occur around new technologies like Siri, they must rework distinctions and thus reveal the flux of categories at play. This work was at first invisible to us. It only become visible after Benjy's case triggered the reframing of our research question and approach. This shows how we too may perform purifying category work by fixing categories in our study design and analysis method, thus inadvertently rendering category reconfigurations invisible.

DESIGN AND METHODOLOGICAL PROPOSITIONS

Fundamentally, our analysis shows categories in flux *in spite* of the purification work performed by users and po-

tentially also by researchers. Our analysis suggests that we consider category work in the design of HCI research and also reveals an opportunity to use the flux of categories as material for design: e.g., approaching humanness and machine-ness as intra-actively produced [1]. This perspective raises new directions for design and design research: How do current HCI approaches and methods contribute to the enactment of the categories in interactions? How might we constrain or encourage the flux of categories through design? Can we redirect the effort users put into purification work into creative work?

Benjy's playful interactions and enchanting discoveries were directly related to Siri's emergent contours. This contrast between Benjy's and the other participants' experiences of Siri highlights the possibility of designing for play, enchantment, and creativity by *actively* engaging the play of categories as a resource for design. Examples include blurring category boundaries and offering opportunities for users to rework the distinctions for themselves; or, reframing the design of agents like Siri as *entity design* and encouraging enchanting experiences like Benjy's as an explorative and emergent process of discovering this entity's contours. The disruption of categories we propose resonates with Taylor's thoughtful analysis of intelligence as "not fixed, but rather actively seen and enacted in the world" [10] and with existing design approaches: DiSalvo and Lukens' explorations of nonanthropocentrism [4], and strategies to design systems that provide an alien, yet still helpful perspective [8]. In conclusion, we advocate designing technologies that evoke and explore humanness rather than replicate it, thus inviting novel enactments of humanness as well as machine-ness.

ACKNOWLEDGEMENTS
The empirical part was conducted during Leahu's internship at Intel Labs. We thank our colleagues and the anonymous reviewers and ACs for feedback and suggestions.

REFERENCES
1. Barad, K. 2003. *Meeting the Universe Halfway*. Duke Press.

2. Bowker, G. & Star,S.L. 2000. *Sorting Things Out*. MIT Press.

3. Cooper, G. & Bowers, J. 1995. Representing the user. In *The social and interactional dimensions of HCI*.

4. DiSalvo, C. & Lukens, J. 2011. Nonanthropocentrism and the Nonhuman in Design. In *From Social Butterfly to Engaged Citizen*. MIT Press: 421-437.

5. Latour, B. 1991. *We have never been modern*. Harvard Press.

6. Lee, M.K. et al. 2010. Receptionist or information kiosk: how do people talk with a robot? In *Proc. CSCW '10*.

7. Nass, C & Brave, S. 2005. *Wired for Speech*. MIT Press.

8. Romero, M. & Mateas, M. 2005. A preliminary investigation of alien presence. In *Proc. HCII'05*.

9. Suchman, L. 2006. *Human-Machine Reconfigurations*. Cambridge University Press.

10. Taylor, A. 2009. Machine Intelligence. In *Proc. CHI'09*.

Personal Clipboards for Individual Copy-and-Paste on Shared Multi-User Surfaces

Dominik Schmidt
Hasso Plattner Institute
Potsdam, Germany
dominik.schmidt@hpi.uni-potsdam.de

Corina Sas, Hans Gellersen
Lancaster University
Lancaster, UK
{corina, hwg}@comp.lancs.ac.uk

ABSTRACT

Clipboards are omnipresent on today's personal computing platforms. They provide copy-and-paste functionalities that let users easily reorganize information and quickly transfer data across applications. In this work, we introduce personal clipboards to multi-user surfaces. Personal clipboards enable individual and independent copy-and-paste operations, in the presence of multiple users concurrently sharing the same direct-touch interface. As common surface computing platforms do not distinguish touch input of different users, we have developed clipboards that leverage complementary personalization strategies. Specifically, we have built a context menu clipboard based on implicit user identification of every touch, a clipboard based on personal subareas dynamically placed on the surface, and a handheld clipboard based on integration of personal devices for surface interaction. In a user study, we demonstrate the effectiveness of personal clipboards for shared surfaces, and show that different personalization strategies enable clipboards, albeit with different impacts on interaction characteristics.

Author Keywords

Multi-touch surfaces; clipboards; copy-and-paste.

ACM Classification Keywords

H.5.2. Information Interfaces and Presentation (e.g. HCI): User Interfaces—Input devices and strategies, Interaction styles.

General Terms

Human Factors; Design.

INTRODUCTION

Today's desktop and mobile computing platforms are hardly imaginable without clipboards and the associated copy-and-paste functionalities. Clipboards facilitate workflows by allowing users to swiftly rearrange, duplicate, or temporarily store information. They also provide a standard mechanism for data transfer across different applications. Conceptually, they implement a background buffer that is easily accessible through basic copy-and-paste operations from any application.

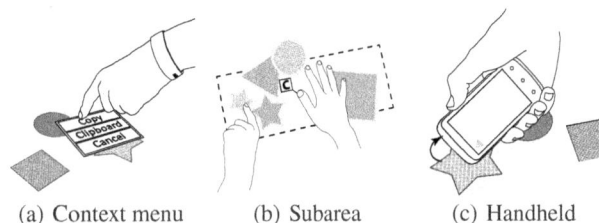

(a) Context menu   (b) Subarea   (c) Handheld

Figure 1. Three personal clipboard systems for shared surfaces, based on different personalization strategies: (a) Context menu clipboards are based on implicitly associating finger touches to users. (b) Subarea clipboards dynamically assign surface regions to users. (c) Handheld clipboards integrate mobile devices for complementary interaction.

This is a simple model and therefore easy to use with minimal mental effort [28].

Originally part of text-based editors, clipboards were adopted successfully to graphical user interfaces (GUI), have become standard in desktop applications, and are now also common on mobile devices with multi-touch interfaces, such as smart phones and tablet computers [32]. In spite of their evident utility, however, clipboards have not yet been extended for multi-user surface computing. The problem on shared surfaces is that copy-and-paste actions of users would be interleaved and confusing, as users interact simultaneously through the same medium. To realize the familiar copy-and-paste semantics on shared surfaces, users require their own clipboard, and applications must be able to distinguish input from different users to unambiguously resolve individual copy-and-paste operations.

Mainstream multi-touch surfaces do not distinguish touch from different users. To realize personal clipboards, we therefore build on complementary methods for associating touch input with individual users. Three common strategies are (a) to use additional sensing techniques for association of finger touches with users, (b) to dynamically associate surface regions with individuals, and (c) to use personal devices in conjunction with shared surfaces. We present a clipboard design and implementation for each of these strategies, with the dual aim of demonstrating alternative system solutions, and gaining insight into the implications of different personalization strategies

Figure 1 shows the three clipboard systems we have developed: (a) a context menu clipboard based on implicit user identification, (b) a clipboard coupled to a personal subarea, and (c) a handheld clipboard on a mobile phone used in stylus-like fashion for direct interaction on the surface. Each clipboard has been designed and implemented on top of existing methods for user identification. The context menu clipboard was realized with IdWristbands [12], the subarea clipboard with HandsDown [22], and the handheld clipboard with Phone-Touch [21].

Benefits of Personal Clipboards

Conceptually, personal clipboards provide individual spaces that are exclusive to their user, within the larger shared workspace. This enables users to copy and paste items independently without interference. Moreover, users can interleave individual tasks and group tasks. Like traditional clipboards, personal clipboards reside in the background without permanently occupying surface space, but are directly accessible in the flow of touch interaction to select items to be copied, or locations for pasting.

Personal clipboards provide the following unique advantages: First, source and target location do not need to be simultaneously reachable (e.g., the target location may be at the other end of a large surface) or visible at the same time (e.g., an application switch may occur). Therefore, copy-and-paste—unlike drag-and-drop—enables users to pick up information for later pasting at different locations. Secondly, personal clipboards reduce clutter as clipboards and the enclosed items do not occupy permanent surface space. Thirdly, personal clipboards provide an exclusive space for their owners, allowing them to collect, organize, or sort copied items individually.

For example, when collaboratively creating a presentation, users may organize their workflow into successive phases. After individually searching and copying items from the web (e.g., text snippets or photos), they switch applications and closely collaborate in assembling a presentation by pasting and arranging items from their individual clipboards in the shared space.

Contribution

In this paper, we introduce personal multi-item clipboards that allow for individual copy-and-paste on shared multi-user surfaces, and study how users interact with these clipboards. The contribution of this work is three-fold: First, we present design and implementation of three personal clipboard systems, each based on a different personalization strategy. Secondly, we demonstrate that personal clipboards allow for directly carrying over familiar copy-and-paste semantics to shared surfaces, while preserving the unique advantages of traditional clipboards. Thirdly, our study also provides a direct comparison of distinct personalization strategies for surface computing. We show that all studied strategies facilitate the effective use of personal clipboards, but impact surface interaction differently.

RELATED WORK

Clipboards have evolved from buffers in early online editors designed for reuse of text "snippets" [5], and the associated notions of copy, cut, and paste have developed into universal commands in GUI and modern operating systems [28, 32]. The concept has since been extended, for example to copy and paste objects across devices [14], adapt objects to the paste-context [30], ease copying across overlapping windows [4], or support particular practices such as programming [33]. A

common extension are multi-item clipboards that let users select items to paste, for instance through a GUI in Microsoft Office, a keyboard extension [2], or a tangible interface [3]. Clipboards are also available for collaborative contexts, for example data transfer from personal devices to shared displays [15], or sharing of clips on the web [7]. In contrast to those works, we aim to extend clipboards to surface computing platforms. Our aim is to provide individual users each with their own clipboard so that they can use copy-and-paste without interference, while interacting simultaneously on the same shared surface.

Only limited research has touched on copying and pasting on shared multi-touch surfaces. DocuBits enabled copying of screen regions based on a paper-cutting metaphor, for transfer to connected personal devices but without clipboard support [8]. Wu et al. demonstrated a "cut/copy-n-paste" gesture that lets users drag and simultaneously resize objects on the surface [35, 27]. The gesture can be used for multiple users to create their own work copy of an object, but is limited to contexts where source and target are visible at the same time and reachable in one motion. In contrast, we aim to support the richer copy-and-paste practices that users know from single-user platforms. Studies on those platforms have indicated that users copy and paste more often across windows and applications than within, and that complex patterns (copy to distributed targets, or paste composition from distributed sources) are more common than isolated copy-and-paste transactions [29].

Personal clipboards provide users with workspaces that are complementary to the surface space. In other work concerned with organization of items, storage bins support stacking of items to create groups that take less space on the surface [25]. Table trays are dynamically created around groups of items which then can be cut or copied onto the tray, moved, and pasted elsewhere on the surface [16]. Tangible drawers are virtual spaces "under the surface" that can be accessed or hidden on demand, in order to move items on or off the main workspace [9]. Personal clipboards are orthogonal to these concepts, as they provide an exclusive space to the individual users around a shared surface. They contrast storage bins and table trays as they store items in the background, and they contrast tangible drawers as they are accessed in the flow of touch interaction on the surface.

It is essential for personal clipboards that copy-and-paste actions on a shared surface can be associated with individual users, but state of the art multi-touch surfaces do not readily distinguish touch from different users. In a variety of systems, additional sensing is used to associate every touch implicitly with a user. In DiamondTouch, this was achieved with a wired connection of user and surface [6], while IR Ring [20] and IdWristbands [12] provide untethered identification based on transmitters worn by the user. Other work has used extrinsic sensing, for example Kinect to first authenticate users and then track their hands [19], or cameras under the table to identify and track users by the shoes they wear [18]. A different strategy to facilitate user identified input is to associate surface regions with users. HandsDown lets users claim surface areas based on hand contour analysis [22], and can be used to dynamically create personal subareas on a shared space [23]. Another strategy is to use user-associated devices for input. PhoneTouch lets users provide direct touch input with their phones in a stylus-like fashion [21, 24], while other work has integrated mobile phones for authentication only [10, 19]. For our purposes, we build on three of these existing approaches (i.e., IdWristbands, HandsDown, and PhoneTouch) to pursue design alternatives for clipboards that leverage different personalisation strategies.

There is a range of further work on copy-and-paste for data transfer across devices, such as Pick-and-Drop [17]. However, we focus on enabling individualized copy-and-paste on shared surfaces, and we consider data transfer across devices only in as far as we integrate personal devices for direct copy action on the surface in one of our three clipboard systems.

PERSONAL CLIPBOARDS

Personal clipboards are designed as an extension to the shared workspace of multi-touch surfaces. The general design is that each user has their own clipboard, onto which they can copy multiple items from the shared workspace. The clipboards provide background storage and users can collect items onto them that remain in the background until they are pasted back onto the main workspace. For pasting, users can select among any of the stored items and insert them directly at a chosen location on the shared workspace.

Personal clipboards provide users with the copy-and-paste functionality they know from work on single-user platforms. Multiple users can each reuse, rearrange, or transfer items in the process of working together, doing so without interference. They can organize their workflows in different ways, for example into successive phases of collecting items and using items from their clipboards, and interweave individual and collaborative tasks.

A key concern is to integrate personal clipboards into surface computing practice in a manner that lets them "stay in the flow" [1]. Copy-and-paste must be directly accessible, in the context of items they wish to copy, or locations at which they aim to paste. Access must be seamlessly integrated with an individual user's flow of multi-touch interaction, and it must not impede the interactions or disrupt the workflow of others working concurrently on the surface. At the same time, single copy-and-paste interactions must be attributable to individual users. This requires techniques that immediately identify users while they interact with a surface.

We present three systems that each demonstrate personal clipboards based on a different strategy for personalization on shared surfaces. For each system, we chose a user identification technique that implements the particular personalization strategy.

Context Menu Clipboards

Context menu clipboards build on an implicit personalization strategy, which immediately associates any finger touch to a user. Therefore, users do not need to change familiar multi-touch interaction styles for identified input. We implemented these clipboards using IdWristbands as the underlying identification technique [12]. Users wear IdWristbands like common wristbands (at the hand used for surface interaction). Based on textile sports wristbands, IdWristbands do not impede hand movement. Each IdWristband continuously emits a unique identification code using infrared LED. The shared surface detects and decodes the resulting infrared light flashes. Based on proximity, it then associates finger touches to wristbands and, in turn, users.

Context menus provide immediate access to copy-and-paste anywhere on the surface, without occupying permanent screen space. We used the established Windows 7 press-and-tap gesture to invoke context menus (i.e., "Press the item with one finger, then quickly tap with another finger, while continuing to press the item with the first finger." [13]). As IdWristbands implicitly associates finger touches to corresponding users, attributing individual copy-and-paste interactions to personal clipboards is straightforward.

Figure 2 illustrates copying and pasting with context menu clipboards. To copy an item to the personal clipboard, users perform the press-and-tap gesture on top of the item and select "Copy" from the appearing menu, which closes automatically. The remaining two context menu options are "Clipboard" (to inspect the current clipboard content) and "Cancel" (to close the menu). Performing press-and-tap on the empty background brings up the clipboard right away. Users can select any of the clipboards items for pasting by touching them. Items are inserted directly at the touch location; the clipboard closes automatically after pasting.

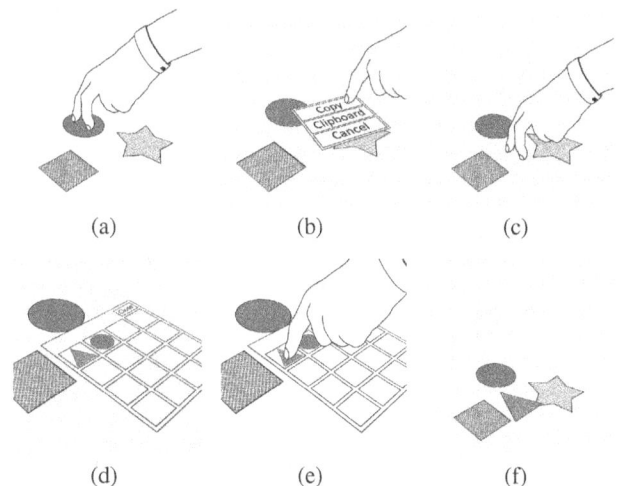

(a)   (b)   (c)

(d)   (e)   (f)

Figure 2. Copying and pasting with *context menu clipboards*, based on implicit user identification with IdWristbands. **(a)** Press-and-tap on item to access menu. **(b)** Select "Copy" to add selected item to personal clipboard. **(c)** Press-and-tap on background to access clipboard directly. **(d)** Current content of clipboard is shown. **(e)** Touch item to be pasted. **(f)** Pasted item appears where touched.

Subarea Clipboards

Subarea clipboards use the personalization strategy of dynamically associating subregions of the surface to individual users on demand. Any touch input within a personal subarea is associated to the corresponding user. This strategy relies on social protocols to prevent interaction within another user's space. We use HandsDown [22], a biometric user identification technique, to access subarea clipboards. Here, users identify by performing a particular hand gesture: After placing a hand flat onto the surface, with the fingers kept apart, the surface takes a snapshot of the hand and identifies users based on differences in hand shape (e.g., by comparing finger lengths and widths). The area surrounding an identified hand is assigned to the corresponding user as long as the hand stays on the surface. Users interact with their other hand inside this personal area, which automatically closes when removing the identified hand.

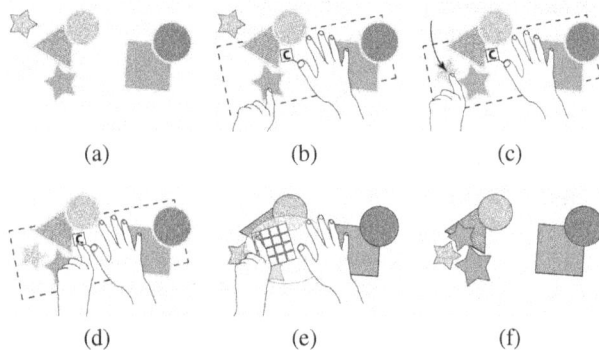

Figure 3. Copying and pasting with *subarea clipboards* enabled by HandsDown. (a)–(b) After identification, touch any item inside the clipboard area to copy it. (c) Moving items inside or outside the clipboard area. (d) Access the current clipboard content. (e) Select items for pasting. (f) Pasted items appear where touched.

As illustrated in Figure 3, we appropriate the identification gesture for immediate access to personal clipboards. To copy, users identify next to the items they intend to copy. A dotted rectangle visualizes the personal clipboard area. Any item inside this area is highlighted with a border and can be copied by touching it with the free hand. Users can move items inside the personal area for copying, or move them outside to reduce clutter. The "C" button brings up the current clipboard content, the "X" button switches back to copy mode. To paste, users touch the item to paste, which is inserted right in place. The clipboard stays open while the identification gesture is active, but closes when removing the identified hand.

Handheld Clipboards

Handheld clipboards use a personalization strategy based on touch input with mobile devices. Similar to using a stylus, users directly touch the surface with the corner of their smart phone. Only touches with the mobile device are identified; finger touches remain anonymous. We used PhoneTouch for touch identification [21]. PhoneTouch is based on simultaneous sensing of touch events on phones (using accelerometers) as well as on the surface (using the integrated camera), and time-based matching of these distributed events. Consequently,

each touch performed with a phone is associated to the corresponding device and its user in turn, while phone and finger touches co-exist.

Phone touches provide another modality in addition to finger touches, which we use for direct access to copy-and-paste. We permanently show the clipboard content on the phones' screen without occupying surface space. As illustrated in Figure 4, users touch an item with the phone to copy it, using either of the phone's two top corners. The copied item instantly appears in the clipboard shown on the phone. To paste, users first select items on the phone screen and then perform a phone touch on the surface; pasted items appear where touched. Moving, resizing, or rotating items on the surface (e.g., to bring them closer or align them) requires finger input; phone touches are reserved for clipboard interactions.

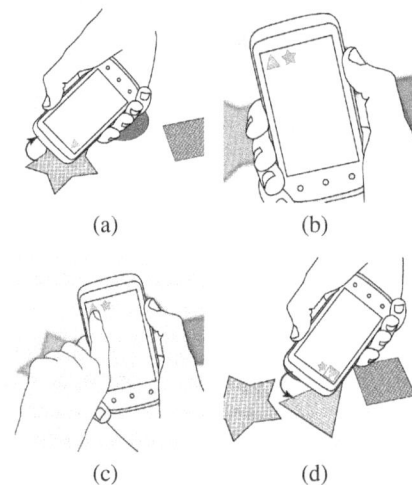

Figure 4. Copying and pasting with *handheld clipboards* enabled by PhoneTouch. (a) Touch an item with the phone for copying. (b) The clipboard content is permanently shown on the phone. (c) Select items for pasting on the phone screen. (d) Touch with the phone to paste items back to the surface.

STUDY DESIGN

The goal of the following user study is to demonstrate the effectiveness of the proposed systems, and to explore how users interact with them. We are particularly interested in how the traditional clipboard concept carries over from single-user devices to multi-user surface computing. At the same time, we compare different personalization strategies in order to gain insights into their impact on interaction characterstics.

To this end, we recruited nine pairs of participants from our local campus through posters and mailing lists (eight female; aged 19 to 29 years, $M = 22.35, SD = 3$). Participants of five groups (56 %) were acquaintances, the others did not know each other beforehand; two groups were mixed-gender. All but one participant were right-handed. Most participants reported a "high" experience (i.e., 4 on a 5-point rating scale) with computers in general and touch interfaces in particular. Only three participants had used a large multi-touch surface before, but many were familiar with direct touch smart phones (67 %) or tablets (22 %). Each participant received £8 for their time.

Apparatus

We implemented all three clipboards with off-the-shelf surface hardware, using the Samsung SUR40 device (Microsoft PixelSense). The SUR40 has a height of 73 cm and a surface diagonal of 120 cm at a resolution of 1920 pixel × 1080 pixel. Only the context menu clipboard, based on IdWristband, requires users to wear custom hardware for identification. The subarea clipboad is self-contained in the surface, and the handheld clipboard integrates off-the-shelf mobile phones for user identification (i.e., iPhone 3GS equipped with protective rubber bumpers). We developed the study task application in C# using Microsoft's .NET framework, Windows Presentation Framework (WPF), and the Surface 2.0 SDK. In each condition, participants sat at the longer table sides opposite each other (see Figure 5).

Figure 5. Participants during the study (using context menu clipboards)

Task

The study consists of a copy and a paste sub-task, carried out one after the other. We asked participants to first copy and then paste a series of geometric shapes. These items differed in three features (see Figure 6(a)): color (×2), pattern (×4), and shape (×4). We presented each unique combination of features twice, resulting in 64 items available for copying. Before starting, we asked participants to choose a color.

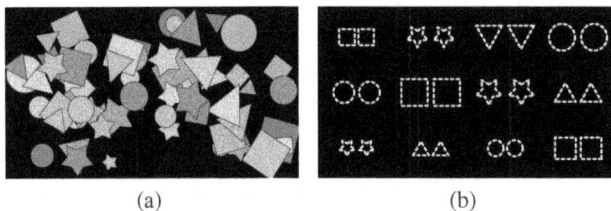

(a) (b)

Figure 6. Copy and paste tasks: (a) First, participants copied 16 items of the same color but different in pattern and shape. (b) In the second step, 12 target locations indicated where to paste the just copied items.

Copy

During the copy task, participants had to search for and copy multiple items into their personal clipboards. We instructed them to find all 16 unique combinations of shape and pattern of their chosen color. As shown in Figure 6(a), we randomly arranged items in the beginning. Participants could move, rotate, and resize any item using typical multi-touch interactions.

Items flashed as confirmation after copying them. We did not allow copying of duplicate items (i.e., same color, pattern, and shape) to prevent participants from rushing through the task by copying random items. Any attempt to copy duplicates was visualized with a shaking animation. To remove an item from the clipboard, participants had to tap and hold it (i.e., on the surface in case of context menu and subarea clipboards, and on the phone in case of handheld clipboards).

Paste

Once participants had copied the requested items, we switched to a second screen. Here, participants had to paste a selection of their copied items, matching the 12 target locations shown in Figure 6(b). For each target location, participants had to select and arrange two items that differed in both color and pattern, but had the same shape, as indicated by the dotted outlines. This was to foster collaboration: Each participant had to contribute one item to every target location. In addition, participants had to coordinate to ensure they selected different patterns.

Conditions

We used a within-subject repeated-measures design with the independent variable *system* (context menu, subarea, or handheld clipboard). Participants performed copy and paste tasks for all three systems, sitting opposite each other (see Figure 5). The presentation of systems was counter balanced.

Procedure

Participants first signed research consent forms. Then, the experimenter explained the copy and paste tasks. Before using each system, the experimenter demonstrated the identification technique and how to perform copy-and-paste interactions; participants tested the system until they felt comfortable using it. In case of subarea clipboards, we asked participants to register for HandsDown beforehand by placing their hands repeatedly on the surface. The copy task was completed once both participants had collected 16 different items of their color. The paste task was completed once both participants had pasted and arranged items matching the indicated target locations. Task completion was not automatically registered but determined by the experimenter.

Throughout the task, we observed participants and took notes. We video-taped all sessions for detailed post-hoc analysis using an open coding approach [31] and ChronoViz to facilitate annotations [34]. Our field notes provided a starting point for initial coding categories. A detailed system interaction log complements this video analysis.

After completing the tasks with each system, we asked participants to state their agreement with eight items selected from the *IBM Computer Usability Satisfaction* questionnaire[1] on a seven-point Likert scale ranging from "strongly agree" to "strongly disagree". Further, using three items from the *NASA Task Load Index*, we asked participants to rate the amount of mental demand required to fulfil the task as well as their frustration level, and to give a self-assessment of their performance. After completing all conditions, we asked participants

---

[1]Statements 2, 4, 5, 6, 7, 9, 17, and 19 of the *Post-Study System Usability Questionnaire* were selected as applicable here.

to rank systems according to several criteria, including general preference as well as their perception regarding execution time, efficiency, enjoyment, learnability, and responsiveness. Finally, we conducted an open-ended interview to gain additional insights into particular interaction patterns we had observed.

RESULTS

Participants readily understood the study tasks, and were able to successfully complete tasks independent of the system. They could instantly identify to access their clipboards when and where required. We did not observe any fundamental difficulties in using copy-and-paste with any of the tested systems. In the following analysis, we first summarize and analyze the collected user feedback and then report on results from our video and system log analysis.

User Feedback

The quantitative user feedback provided a balanced picture of the three systems and did not reveal differences of substance. We did not find significant differences amongst the responses to the 11 selected items from the usability and task load questionnaire (using Friedman's ANOVA). Neither did the system ranking reveal clear preferences for one of the systems, as shown in Figure 7.

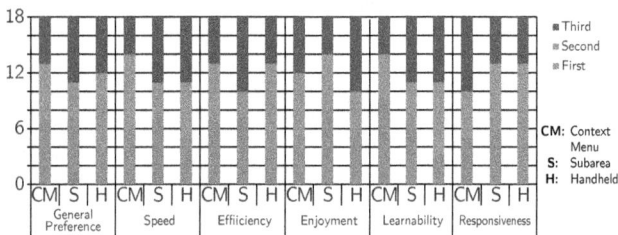

Figure 7. Ranking results show the number of participants who picked a particular system as first (green), second (orange), or third choice (red); they do not reveal clear preferences.

The qualitative user feedback, on the other hand, provided more insights into differences between the three systems. Using context menu clipboards, none of the participants felt impeded by the wristbands, and nine participants explicitly mentioned that wearing wristbands was not cumbersome or uncomfortable. Some compared the experience to wearing regular accessories, such as wrist watches, or perceived wristbands as being "invisible" (participant 9A). We received positive comments from nine participants about the implicitness and subtleness of identified interaction enabled by IdWristbands. Three emphasized the consistency with regular touch screen interaction, as familiar touch styles could be used without having to adapt for identification (8A: "it's like normal finger motion").

Using subarea clipboards, seven participants appreciated the fact that no user instrumentation or additional devices were required for identification. None of the participants brought up privacy issues with respect to using biometrics. Two participants, however, raised concerns about the available surface space; one of them found the overlapping of lenses "irritating" (3B). Another participant felt more comfortable using subarea

compared to context menu clipboards as it was possible to put the "hand down to rest" to open up an identification area, rather than having to "keeping hands up", which was considered tiring (6A). Five other participants would have preferred having both hands available.

Using handheld clipboards, four participants appreciated the mobile phone as a familiar and readily available device. Two participants actually preferred interacting with the phone on the surface compared to using fingers, while another one commented that replacing finger touch entirely by phone touch was not desirable. The same participant felt that using the phone for touch interaction was not intuitive (6B). None of the participants raised concerns with respect to potential damage to the phone or the surface. One participant saw the phone as dedicated tool and highlighted that there were "no gestures or sequences to remember" to copy and paste (3A). The additionally available phone screen was welcomed by 10 participants, as it allowed them to permanently see and quickly inspect what had already been copied. Five participants gave positive feedback about the instantaneous transfer of data between devices (3B: "transferring objects to the telephone was very cool"). None of the participants commented about having to alternate hands for interaction on the surface or on the phone.

Completion Times

Figure 8 summarizes completion times for each system and subtask. The system had a significant effect on copy times ($\chi^2(2) = 12.6, p < .05$; using Friedman's ANOVA due to non-normal data distribution), but not on paste times. We used Wilcoxon tests to follow up on these findings and applied a Bonferroni correction, hence all effects are reported at a .017 significance level. The only significant difference emerged for copying with handheld clipboards, which was significantly faster compared to context menu ($T = 0, p < .017, r = -.62$) and subarea clipboards ($T = 1, p < .017, r = -.6$).

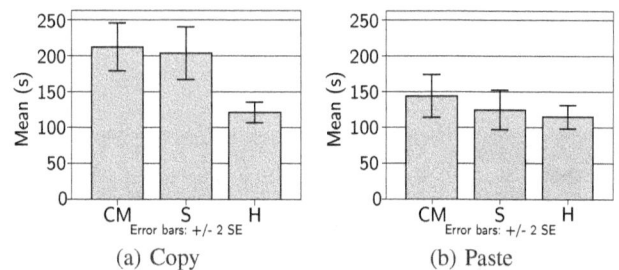

(a) Copy   (b) Paste

Figure 8. Mean completion times of copy and paste tasks are similar for all systems; only copying with handheld clipboards was significantly faster than copying with the other systems (CM: Context Menu, S: Subarea, H: Handheld).

Surface Utilization

To explore possible impacts of the different personalization strategies on interaction characteristics, we analyzed the spatial distribution of copy and paste activities (i.e., activities that required the user to be known) with respect to the following two indicators: *vicinity*—i.e., percentage of copy or paste activities within the surface half closest to a participant—and *coverage*—i.e., percentage of covered surface area based on

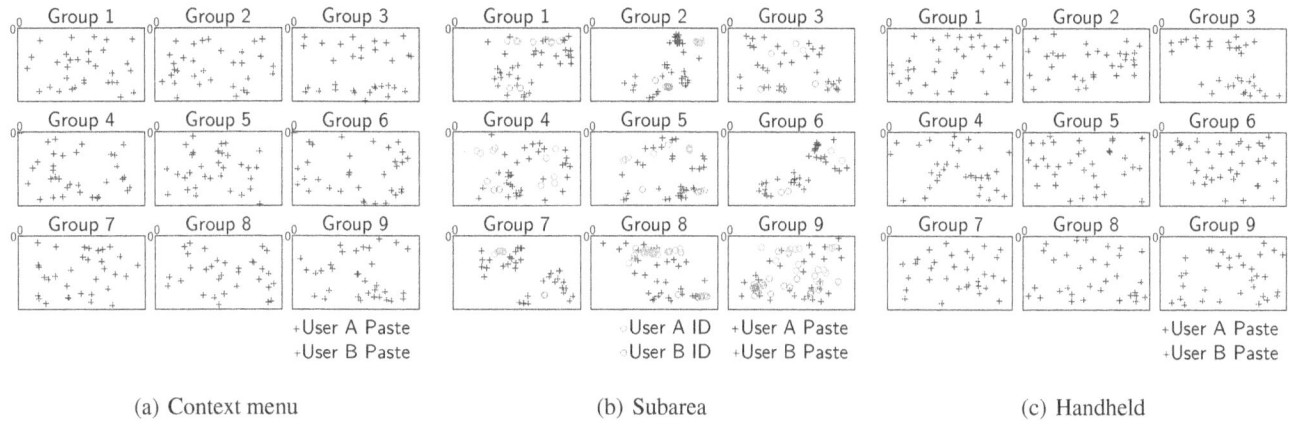

+User A Paste   User A ID +User A Paste   +User A Paste
+User B Paste   User B ID +User B Paste   +User B Paste

(a) Context menu   (b) Subarea   (c) Handheld

Figure 9. Locations at which participants copied items. Crosses indicate copied items, circles HandsDown identification gestures. Participants spread out the most using (c) handheld clipboards followed by (a) context menu clipboards; using (b) subarea clipboards, items were moved before copying.

the convex hull (the smallest convex set) of copy or paste locations. Figure 10 summarizes space utilization for the three systems.

Copy

Figure 9 plots locations of all copy activities for each system and participant group. Using context menu clipboards, six participants (groups 4, 7, and 8) spread out more than average and performed at least 25 % of copy activities within the opposite table half. In contrast, participants of group 3, who had sorted items by color prior to copying, stayed within their respective halves throughout.

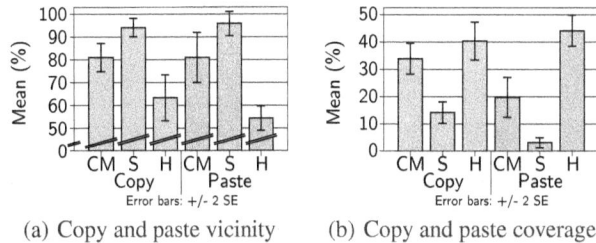

(a) Copy and paste vicinity   (b) Copy and paste coverage

Figure 10. Surface utilization was most spread out for handheld clipboards, followed by context menu and subarea clipboards, independent of copy or paste (CM: Context Menu, S: Subarea, H: Handheld).

Unlike context menu clipboards, subarea clipboards required an explicit identification gesture for access. We found that participants accessed their clipboard 7.94 times on average ($SD = 6.93$). All but two participants (4A and 9A) did so within their half of the table. In general, identification areas were respected. Five participants, however, occasionally dragged items directly out of the other participant's area. This was generally accepted except for once when the disadvantaged participant removed his hand from the surface. We observed two prevalent approaches to copying with subarea clipboards: Half of the participants primarily dragged items towards the identified hand, keeping its position mostly unchanged, while the other half frequently varied the identification location, bringing the hand closer to items in question.

Using handheld clipboards, all but two participants had the phone screen generally facing them. We also observed that

participants frequently had a closer look at their phone to inspect copied items. Compared to the other two systems, participants used more of the available surface area.

Paste

Figure 11 plots locations of all paste activities for each system and participant group, revealing similar distributions as for copying. Using context menu clipboards, half of the participants pasted most items close to the designated target locations, while the remaining half accessed clipboards at seemingly arbitrary positions, arranging items only after inserting them. Some following the latter approach, however, decided on a rough location before accessing the clipboard.

Using subarea clipboards, participants placed their hand for identification 4.56 times on average ($SD = 3.31$). Participants did not vary identification locations much and pasted items grouped together independent of target locations. They performed all HandsDown gestures within their own table half. Most participants (72 %) pasted one or multiple items at a time to then arrange them before proceeding, while three participants pasted all items at once to arrange them in a separate step.

Having the handheld clipboard on a separate screen allowed participants to inspect both remaining items on the phone and targets to fill on the surface at the same time, without occluding the shared work space. Two participants pasted most items in batches to arrange them together. The majority, however, interleaved paste and (finger-based) arrange interactions to directly insert items at the intended target locations, even if close to the other participant, resulting in a clearly visible pattern (see Figure 11(c)).

Analysis

Copy-and-paste interactions typically took place closer to the corresponding participant for subarea than for handheld clipboards; context menu clipboards lie in between. Likewise, copy-and-paste interactions of subarea clipboards covered the smallest area, followed by context menu and then handheld clipboards. Applying a Friedman ANOVA, we found that all four measures were significantly affected by the system: copy vicinity ($\chi^2(2) = 20.49, p < .05$), copy coverage ($\chi^2(2) =$

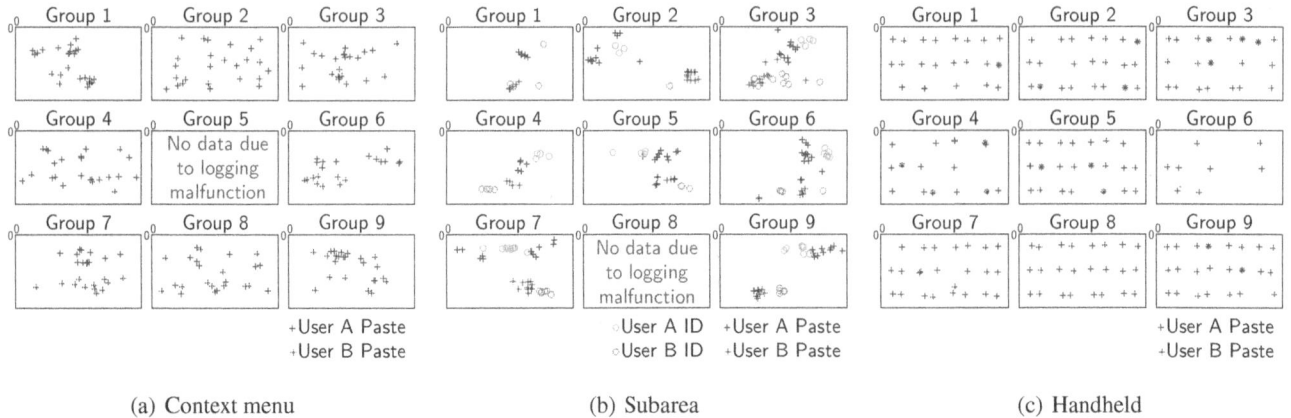

(a) Context menu   (b) Subarea   (c) Handheld

Figure 11. Locations at which participants pasted items. Crosses indicate copied items, circles HandsDown identification gestures. The target location pattern is clearly visible for pasting with (c) handheld clipboards, while participants pasted in clusters using (b) subarea clipboards.

$16.44, p < .05$), paste vicinity ($\chi^2(2) = 17.33, p < .05$), and paste coverage ($\chi^2(2) = 22.43, p < .05$). Wilcoxon post-hoc tests revealed (Bonferroni-corrected significance level of .017) that there were no significant differences between handheld and context menu clipboards for copy coverage and between subarea and context menu clipboards for paste vicinity; all other pairwise tests showed significant effects. Applying Mann-Whitney tests on coverage and vicinity results, we found that participants who knew each other beforehand did not differ from those who were not acquainted with respect to their surface space utilization.

Handedness

Using context menu clipboards, all but one participant choose to wear wristbands on the dominant hand. Although the other hand was available for (anonymous) touch input (e.g., to move or resize items), all but two participants limited themselves to one-handed input.

Using subarea clipboards, participants could perform Hands-Down gestures with either of their hands. Including both copy and paste tasks, we observed that 12 participants (67 %) consistently stayed with the same hand for identification (seven used the dominant and five the non-dominant hand), while the remaining six alternated at least once.

Using handheld clipboards, all but one participant set out using the dominant hand to hold the phone and copy items. While copying, six participants switched hands, for example to delete an item they had copied by mistake, to better reach the opposite table side, or to use the hand for a finger-based interaction on the surface. Participants seldom used finger touch input on the surface when copying. In fact, six participants (33 %) exclusively relied on phone touches. Even if items were partially occluded, participants could copy them directly by touching visible parts with the phone corner.

Unlike copying, pasting required both phone and finger interaction to align items with target locations on the surface. Participants also had to select items to paste on the phone screen. We observed various approaches with regard to hand preferences and alternating hands for the different interaction

types. Eight participants (33 %) kept the phone primarily in one hand. The remaining 10 participants (67 %) frequently alternated hands as they saw fit. To illustrate a possible interaction flow, we describe the approach consistently followed by two participants (see Figure 12): Keeping the phone in their non-dominant hand, they selected items to paste using fingers of the dominant hand (a). Before touching the surface with the phone, they turned it over to the dominant hand (b), pasted items (c), and handed it immediately back to the non-dominant hand (d) for arranging the just pasted item using finger input on the surface (e). This sequence was repeated for the remaining items (f). Approaches varied greatly amongst participants, however. For example, some switched hands only occasionally for finger interaction with the dominant hand on the surface, while otherwise performing such input with the non-dominant hand.

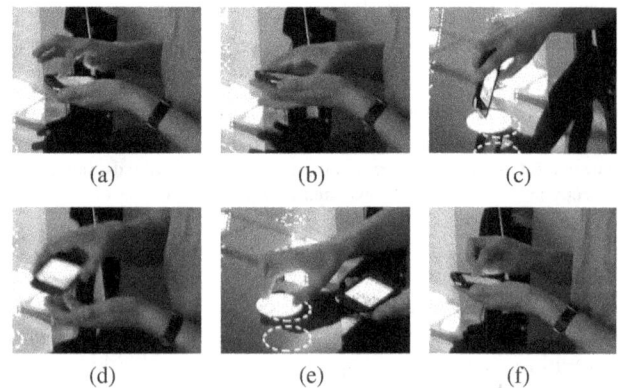

Figure 12. Interleaving finger and phone touches using handheld clipboards: (a) Selecting an item on the phone before (b) changing hands (c) to paste it on the surface. (d) Changing hands (e) to arrange the item on the surface. (f) Continuing with the next item.

DISCUSSION

Participants immediately grasped the idea of personal clipboards and were able to efficiently use the three systems with only minimal training. We showed that user identification allows for directly transferring the familiar clipboard concept from single-user devices to multi-user surface computing. It was apparently taken for granted that each participant could copy to, and paste from, their own clipboard without interference. This implies that participants seemed to expect interactions to be associated to individual users.

Personal clipboards make advantages of traditional clipboards available on shared surfaces. Source and target of copy-and-paste actions do not have to be reachable or even visible at the same time. Therefore, clipboards provide a convenient alternative to drag-and-drop over long distances, or when pasting does not immediately follow copying. This enables users to perform other activities in between. Unlike the shared surface, personal clipboards provide a space exclusive to their owners to collect content without interference.

Despite their different approaches, all tested personalization strategies successfully enabled individual copy-and-paste. In general, the strategy did not influence task completion times significantly. The only exception was the faster copying with handheld clipboards. In contrast to the other systems, handheld clipboards did not require selecting the copy option before each interaction (this could be done once on the phone), resulting in a simple pointing interaction for copying. While no general preference for any of the systems emerged, the underlying identification strategies had a clear impact on interaction characteristics.

Limitations
Regardless of its abstract nature, we are confident that our study task reveals interaction qualities that also apply to typical surface applications. In fact, we chose an abstract task so that the study results are independent of specific applications. The task is designed to feature the kind of copy-and-paste interactions that occur in realistic usage scenarios. In particular, participants had to sift through and consider multiple items before copying, leading to a frequent interleaving of browsing and copying interactions. Similarly, participants interleaved pasting and aligning items, while working closely together to achieve the set goals, resembling a typical collaborative task.

While the chosen setup of two users sitting on opposite table sides is common, we did not study other settings (e.g., side by side or additional users). However, we expect that our findings still apply, as personal clipboards are accessible from any surface location. Nevertheless, the closer users sit together, or the more users share the same table, the more likely are interferences—just as with regular surface interactions. Application designers therefore need to carefully choose size and orientation of context menu and subarea clipboards.

Implications
Users typically organize their workspaces, form different territories, and coordinate collaboration. Unlike the territories identified by Scott et al. [26], personal clipboards are not a permanent part of the workspace, but represent a complementary concept. Therefore, copy-and-paste needs to be accessible independent of surface regions. This was best supported by handheld clipboards, which encouraged participants to widely spread out their copy-and-paste activities, thereby covering the entire surface. Here, users could make selections in advance on the phone; interaction on the surface then narrowed down to a single touch. In contrast, both context menu and subarea clipboards required additional selection steps on the surface.

Surface interaction benefits from the freedom of using multiple fingers and hands for expressive input. Subarea and handheld personalization strategies require supplementary interactions and limit how hands can be used for input. Our analysis of handedness revealed, however, that both strategies were seamlessly integrated into the interaction flow. Moreover, the dedicated HandsDown identification gesture can be overloaded with additional functions (e.g., invoking a clipboard). Similarly, using the phone for touches is comparable to using a configurable tool, like a Swiss army knife: Users can pre-select options (using the built-in GUI) to be applied to the next surface touch (e.g., selecting the item to paste). In comparison to implicitly associating finger touches, assigning regions and using handheld devices allows users to control the scope of identified input; remaining anonymous is as simple as performing a regular finger touch.

Copy-and-paste with subarea clipboards has the highest costs with respect to identification time and surface space utilization. Further, it is difficult to perform HandsDown gestures far from where users are located. Therefore, users need to be able to easily move items they wish to copy into reach. Alternatively, lenses can stay open when lifting off the hand. They can then be moved around and eventually be closed manually (i.e., after copy or paste interactions are completed). As a third of our participants alternatively used both their left and right hand to access clipboards, application designers need to ensure that lens shapes and layouts adapt accordingly.

The separate screen of handheld clipboards was frequently used by participants. Therefore, information presented on the phone needs to be also legible when interacting on the surface (e.g., layout, size, or orientation of content can be changed during copy-and-paste interactions). Furthermore, participants often used phones in lieu of fingers for direct pointing. As pointing with phones results in a larger occlusion of the surface, applications may need to increase the minimum size of user interface elements.

CONCLUSION
We have introduced personal clipboards for shared surfaces and demonstrated that this familiar concept directly transfers to individual copy-and-paste operations in multi-user environments, once users can be identified. Based on three system implementation, our study showed that personal clipboards can be realized with different personalization strategies. We demonstrated that implicitly identifying any finger touch is not required for fluid interaction. Therefore, choosing a personalization strategy may be guided by practical considerations (e.g., available hardware) or required functionalities (e.g., presenting content on separate devices). We leave the exploration of how further GUI concepts that are familiar from single-user devices can be transferred to shared surfaces capable of user identification for future work.

REFERENCES
1. Bederson, B. B. Interfaces for staying in the flow. *Ubiquity 2004* (September 2004), 1–1.

2. Block, F., Gellersen, H., and Villar, N. Touch-Display Keyboards: Transforming keyboards into interactive surfaces. In *Proc. CHI* (2010), 1145–1154.

3. Block, F., Villar, N., and Gellersen, H. A malleable physical interface for copying, pasting, and organizing digital clips. In *Proc. TEI* (2008), 117–120.

4. Chapuis, O., and Roussel, N. Copy-and-paste between overlapping windows. In *Proc. CHI* (2007), 201–210.

5. Deutsch, L. P., and Lampson, B. W. An online editor. *Commun. ACM 10*, 12 (Dec. 1967), 793–799.

6. Dietz, P. H., and Leigh, D. DiamondTouch: A multi-user touch technology. In *Proc. UIST* (2001), 219–226.

7. Dix, A., Catarci, T., Habegger, B., Ioannidis, Y., Kamaruddin, A., Katifori, A., Lepouras, G., Poggi, A., and Ramduny-Ellis, D. Intelligent context-sensitive interactions on desktop and the web. In *Proc. AVI* (2006), 23–27.

8. Everitt, K., Shen, C., Ryall, K., and Forlines, C. Modal spaces: spatial multiplexing to mediate direct-touch input on large displays. In *CHI Ext. Abstracts* (2005), 1359–1362.

9. Hartmann, B., Ringel Morris, M., and Cassanego, A. Reducing clutter on tabletop groupware systems with tangible drawers. Poster UbiComp, 2006.

10. Hutama, W., Song, P., Chi-Wing, F., and Goh, W. B. Distinguishing multiple smart-phone interactions on a multi-touch wall display using tilt correlation. In *Proc. CHI* (2011), 3315–3318.

11. Kjeldskov, J., Skov, M., Als, B., and Høegh, R. Is it worth the hassle? exploring the added value of evaluating the usability of context-aware mobile systems in the field. In *Proc. MobileHCI* (2004), 61–73.

12. Meyer, T., and Schmidt, D. IdWristbands: IR-based user identification on multi-touch surfaces. Poster ITS, 2010.

13. Microsoft. Using touch gestures. 27 April 2012. `http://windows.microsoft.com/en-US/windows7/Using-touch-gesture`.

14. Miller, R. C., and Myers, B. A. Synchronizing clipboards of multiple computers. In *Proc. UIST* (1999), 65–66.

15. Myers, B. A., Miller, R. C., Bostwick, B., and Evankovich, C. Extending the windows desktop interface with connected handheld computers. In *Proc. USENIX Win. Sys.*, vol. 4 (2000), 8.

16. Pinelle, D., Stach, T., and Gutwin, C. TableTrays: Temporary, reconfigurable work surfaces for tabletop groupware. In *Proc. TableTop* (2008), 41–48.

17. Rekimoto, J. Pick-and-Drop: A direct manipulation technique for multiple computer environments. In *Proc. UIST* (1997), 31–39.

18. Richter, S., Holz, C., and Baudisch, P. Bootstrapper: Recognizing tabletop users by their shoes. In *Proc. CHI* (2012), 1249–1252.

19. Rofouei, M., Wilson, A., Brush, A., and Tansley, S. Your phone or mine?: fusing body, touch and device sensing for multi-user device-display interaction. In *Proc. CHI* (2012), 1915–1918.

20. Roth, V., Schmidt, P., and Güldenring, B. The IR Ring: authenticating users' touches on a multi-touch display. In *Proc. UIST* (2010), 259–262.

21. Schmidt, D., Chehimi, F., Rukzio, E., and Gellersen, H. PhoneTouch: A technique for direct phone interaction on surfaces. In *Proc. UIST* (2010), 13–16.

22. Schmidt, D., Chong, M., and Gellersen, H. HandsDown: Hand-contour-based user identification for interactive surfaces. In *Proc. NordiCHI* (2010), 432–441.

23. Schmidt, D., Chong, M., and Gellersen, H. IdLenses: Dynamic personal areas on shared surfaces. In *Proc. ITS* (2010), 131–134.

24. Schmidt, D., Seifert, J., Rukzio, E., and Gellersen, H. A cross-device interaction style for mobiles and surfaces. In *Proc. DIS* (2012), 318–327.

25. Scott, S., Carpendale, S., and Habelski, S. Storage bins: Mobile storage for collaborative tabletop displays. *IEEE Comp. Graph. and App. 25* (2005), 58–65.

26. Scott, S., Carpendale, S., and Inkpen, K. Territoriality in collaborative tabletop workspaces. In *Proc. CSCW* (2004), 294–303.

27. Shen, C., Ryall, K., Forlines, C., Esenther, A., Vernier, F., Everitt, K., Wu, M., Wigdor, D., Morris, M., Hancock, M., and Tse, E. Informing the design of direct-touch tabletops. *IEEE Comp. Graph. and App. 26* (2006), 36–46.

28. Smith, D. C., Irby, C., Kimball, R., Verplank, B., and Harslem, E. Designing the star user interface. *Byte 7*, 2 (1982), 242–282.

29. Stolee, K., Elbaum, S., and Rothermel, G. Revealing the copy and paste habits of end users. In *IEEE Symp. on VL/HCC* (September 2009), 59 –66.

30. Stylos, J., Myers, B. A., and Faulring, A. Citrine: providing intelligent copy-and-paste. In *Proc. UIST* (2004), 185–188.

31. Tang, A., Tory, M., Po, B., Neumann, P., and Carpendale, S. Collaborative coupling over tabletop displays. In *Proc. CHI* (2006), 1181–1190.

32. Tesler, L. A personal history of modeless text editing and cut/copy-paste. *interactions 19*, 4 (July 2012), 70–75.

33. Wallace, G., Biddle, R., and Tempero, E. Smarter cut-and-paste for programming text editors. In *Proc. AUIC* (2001), 56–63.

34. Weibel, N., Fouse, A., Hutchins, E., and Hoolan, J. Supporting an integrated paper-digital workflow for observational research. In *Proc. IUI* (2011), 257–266.

35. Wu, M., Shen, C., Ryall, K., Forlines, C., and Balakrishnan, R. Gesture registration, relaxation, and reuse for multi-point direct-touch surfaces. In *Proc. TableTop* (2006), 185–192.

Collaborative Sensemaking on a Digital Tabletop and Personal Tablets: Prioritization, Comparisons, and Tableaux

James R. Wallace
Systems Design Engineering
University of Waterloo
Waterloo, Ontario Canada
james.wallace@uwaterloo.ca

Stacey D. Scott
Systems Design Engineering
University of Waterloo
Waterloo, Ontario, Canada
stacey.scott@uwaterloo.ca

Carolyn G. MacGregor
Systems Design Engineering
University of Waterloo
Waterloo, Ontario, Canada
carolyn.macgregor@uwaterloo.ca

ABSTRACT

We describe an investigation of the support that three different display configurations provided for a collaborative sensemaking task: a digital table; personal tablets; and both the tabletop and personal tablets. Mixed-methods analyses revealed that the presence of a digital tabletop display led to improved sensemaking performance, and identified activities that were supported by the shared workspace. The digital tabletop supported a group's ability to prioritize information, to make comparisons between task data, and to form and critique the group's working hypothesis. Analyses of group performance revealed a positive correlation with equity of member participation using the shared digital table, and a negative correlation of equity of member participation using personal tablets. Implications for the support of sensemaking groups, and the use of equity of member participation as a predictive measure of their performance are discussed.

Author Keywords

CSCW; Sensemaking; Process; Equity of Participation;

ACM Classification Keywords

H.5.3 Information Interfaces and Presentation (e.g. HCI): Collaborative Computing

General Terms

Human Factors; Design; Experimentation; Performance;

INTRODUCTION

Today technology is deployed to a growing number of environments for supporting co-located, collaborative work. Sensemaking in particular has often been a subject for research (e.g. [27, 25, 28, 1, 4, 23, 17]) due to its growing importance in the modern economy [3], and the inherent difficulty of developing appropriate technological support for knowledge work [32]. While many research projects have investigated the use of specific hardware and software support for collaborative sensemaking, few studies have investigated

how alternative designs might impact a group's sensemaking activities (e.g. [27, 31]). In our work, we aim to understand how different devices support sensemaking activities to develop a theoretical understanding of the types of support that can assist sensemaking groups and to inform the design of future systems. In this work, we consider the role that personal and shared devices play in supporting a group's sensemaking activities, and investigate how an individual's interactions with those devices contribute to the group's overall sensemaking performance and process.

To explore this issue, we conducted a mixed-methods evaluation of groups performing a collaborative sensemaking task using various combinations of personal (i.e. tablet) and shared (i.e. digital table) devices. This research provides two primary contributions. First, we identified a performance improvement for groups performing the sensemaking task with the digital tabletop and linked the presence of the digital tabletop to activities performed within a sensemaking process model. Second, our analyses revealed a positive correlation between equity of participation on a shared device, and a negative correlation between equity of participation on personal devices, with sensemaking performance. In other words, the presence and equitable use of a digital tabletop was associated with improved sensemaking, whereas more equitable use of the provided tablets was detrimental to sensemaking. These results suggest that care should be taken when considering the devices that are provided to support group work, as they may subtly, yet significantly, impact group performance.

To set the context for this research, we first define sensemaking, describe related literature, and potential opportunities for personal and shared devices to support a group's sensemaking process. Next, we describe our methodological approach and an empirical study that compared group work under three display configurations: a digital tabletop, a digital tabletop and handheld tablets, and tablets only. Finally, we present the results of this study, and discuss how the results can inform the design of co-located collaborative environments.

SENSEMAKING

Sensemaking can be defined as understanding information [38], or gaining insight [6]; and involves a user, or group of users, who 'make sense' of a data set in order to make better decisions. That is, they must explore data provided to them, gain an understanding of underlying trends, and make some determination of how those trends should influence future decisions. As sensemaking is so broadly defined it can be a challenging activity to support. Dervin [8] describes sensemakers as using ideas, emotions, and memories to bridge a 'gap' in understanding. Klein et al. [21] discuss how creativity, curiosity, mental modelling, and situation awareness all play roles in sensemaking. Sensemaking also represents a significant portion of the work conducted in the workplace today, yet is poorly supported by current software [31]. The CHI and CSCW communities have investigated sensemaking in domains such as healthcare [28, 1, 4] and rescue work [23].

Building on work by Pirolli and Card [30], Yi et al. [39] identified four fundamental activities that groups perform while sensemaking: overview, adjust, detect pattern, and match mental model. In the overview step, people look at the "big picture", survey the information available, and prioritize that information for future explorations. During the adjust step, people filter and explore the data at different levels of abstraction, with the goal of setting themselves up for the detect pattern step where trends are identified. Finally, once trends have been identified, sensemakers work to reconcile newly identified information with their own mental models, thus making sense of the data. Vogt et al. [35] describe a similar series of five basic activities: extract, cluster, record, connect, review. This model closely resembles the one proposed by Yi et al. [39], where cluster and record would both be considered aspects of the adjust steps.

Sensemaking, especially in collaborative settings, is an ongoing activity. When groups are making sense of available data, work is done in an iterative fashion. Furthermore, individuals within a group may not all perform the same types of work while sensemaking. Vogt et al. [35] reports that in a study of pairs performing a sensemaking task, individuals tended to take on one of two distinct roles as their task progressed: *sensemakers* and *foragers*. The sensemaker was the dominant participant, who stood at a provided whiteboard to direct the group effort and take notes, and often asked the forager to find documents. On the other hand, the forager questioned the sensemaker's active hypothesis, found information, and maintained an overall awareness of the task information.

Support for Collaborative Sensemaking

Given the complexity of sensemaking tasks, and the various activities that groups and individuals engage in, providing appropriate support for sensemaking groups can be a challenging design problem [32]. To address this design problem, the literature has explored the support that a variety of technologies can provide groups. In particular, large, shared displays have been shown to benefit sensemaking groups in a number of contexts. For example, Sharoda and Madhu [28] conducted an ethnographic study of healthcare providers' use of a shared display, and identified their support of activities such as the prioritization of information in Yi et al's model. Vogt et al. [35] investigated the use of a large shared display for an analytics task that simulated intelligence agents gathering evidence of a terrorist attack, and found that the ability to gain an overview of task materials on the shared display was also beneficial to groups. These identified strengths have led to an interest in the development of digital tabletops de-

signed to support sensemaking. For example, Cambiera [17] is a digital tabletop designed to support document search, exploration of search results, and document analysis. Similarly, WeSearch [25] allows users to conduct web searches and share 'clips' from search results with one another on the shared tabletop. However a disadvantage of this approach is that the shared display may not facilitate individuals' exploration of the problem space, as awareness of others' activities may prove distracting [11].

An alternative approach for supporting sensemaking groups is to allow interaction across multiple personal devices, such as laptops and tablets, that each support different sensemaking activities. For example, a personal tablet might support an individuals' exploration of the problem space, whereas a shared, digital tabletop may better support a group's overview and discussion activities. The development of techniques such as pick-n-drop [33], stitching [16], and spilling [26] that enable seamless connectivity between personal and shared devices has prompted the use of integrated collaborative environments to support collaborative sensemaking. For example, Plaue and Stasko [31] found that the availability of whiteboards and side-by-side projected displays improved group sensemaking performance. CoSearch [2] was developed to explore co-located, collaborative sensemaking across a combination of PCs and personal phones, and found that communication was improved relative to searches conducted on an individual PC. However, research has suggested that when compared to the use of a single, shared display, the addition of personal devices may reduce a group's effectiveness at communicating and coordinating their activities. For example, Chung et al. [7] and Wallace et al. [37] report that the presence of personal displays may lead to decreased collaboration in co-located settings. Our research aims to elucidate the different types of support that these two approaches provide by investigating how personal and shared devices are used to support sensemaking activities.

Equity of Participation in Sensemaking

There is a growing consensus in the literature that closely coupled collaboration improves a group's collaborative sensemaking outcomes. Isenberg et al. [17] reported that the amount of time that groups spent working closely together was positively correlated with their performance at the task. Vogt et al. [35], in a subsequent study of collaborative sensemaking, were consistent with these findings. The authors of these studies argue that in supporting sensemaking, designers must design for transient behaviour and encourage closely coupled work. That is, sensemaking environments should facilitate transitions between individual and group work, and provide tools to allow individuals to easily share information with their collaborators. Jetter et al. [20] claim that sensemaking environments should support *low viscosity interaction* [5], or interaction that can evolve with minimal effort as groups progress. While these studies have suggested that closely coupled collaboration leads to better sensemaking outcomes, they do not provide a quantitative, objective measure that reflects this relationship. Our work builds on these previous observations, and applies Harris et al.'s [15] equity of participation quantitative metric to explore the relationship between equity of participation on shared and personal displays and sensemaking performance.

STUDY: PERSONAL AND SHARED DEVICES

To explore the role that personal and shared devices play in supporting collaborative sensemaking activities, we conducted a mixed-methods study that combined quantitative and qualitative data. Quantitative measures were selected based on the teamwork and taskwork framework proposed by [29] and more recently adopted by Wallace et al. [37, 36]. *Taskwork* is the work performed by individuals as they complete the task, whereas *teamwork* is the work required to coordinate individuals' activities within the group. Qualitative data were collected to assist in interpreting the influence of personal and shared devices on the teamwork and taskwork.

Participants

84 students (51 male, 33 female) were recruited from a local university as 21 groups of 4. Participants ranged in age from 17 to 33 years old, with a average age of 22.6 years ($\sigma = 3.69$). 22/84 of the participants reported owning a tablet, and using them on a 'daily' or 'bi-daily' basis.

The Bonanza Paper Forms Task

During the study, participants performed the Bonanza Paper Forms task [19], a collaborative sensemaking task previously used by Gallupe and DeSanctis [10] and Plaue and Stasko [31] to study technological support for collaborative sensemaking. Participants played the role of consultants hired to determine why the fictional Bonanza Paper Forms company has experienced an increase in sales and a decline in profits over the past three financial quarters. To determine the cause of the company's financial difficulties, participants were provided with relevant economic, financial, operational, and company background data.

Plaue and Stasko's [31] task design, which studied groups of 6, was adapted for use with groups of 4 participants for our study. Participants in each group were randomly assigned to one of four investigative roles: Sales Consultant, Advertising Consultant, Financial Consultant, and Domain Research Consultant. For this study, PowerPoint presentations were created that were similar to those utilized by Plaue and Stasko [31], however graphs and data were re-designed to render appropriately on both the shared digital tabletop and personal tablets provided in the study. Information was provided to participants in the form of bulleted information, charts, and graphs. The slides provided to each participant were unique, so it was not possible for the group to determine the most correct solution without individuals sharing their personal information with the rest of the group. The number of slides provided to each participant also varied from 6-10, so not all participants had an equal amount of data with which to work.

Experimental Design

The study utilized a single between-subjects factor for display configuration with 3 levels of control: *Tablets Only*, *Table Only*, and *Table Plus Tablets* (Figure 1). These display configurations incorporated combinations of both personal and shared devices, allowing us to evaluate the impact of each

Figure 1. The Table Only condition (left), consisted of a digital tabletop. The Table Plus Tablets condition (middle), consisted of the digital tabletop and four tablets, provided to each participant. The Tablets Only condition (right) consisted of only four tablets, and the digital tabletop (not shown) was disabled and provided only a physical surface.

type of device on a group's sensemaking performance and process. Groups of 4 completed the experimental task using one of the three display configurations, for a total of one session each.

To investigate the impact that each of these configurations had on groups' sensemaking performance and process, independent variables included measures of taskwork, teamwork, and the group's sensemaking outcomes. The number of pen interactions made on each device by each participant were measured to assess the amount of taskwork performed by individuals. To assess teamwork, the equity of participation of those interactions was calculated using Gini coefficients, in addition to calculations of how many participants interacted with each tablet and the number of slides that each group placed on the digital tabletop. Gini Coefficients have historically been used in studies of economics and sociology as a measure of dispersion of income or wealth, but have recently been adopted in CSCW research as a measure of equity of participation (e.g. [24, 15]). Gini coefficients provide a mechanism by which researchers can quantify the degree to which groups work collaboratively, and to identify settings in which collaborative work is dominated by a subset of group members.

To assess performance, task time and the insight-based evaluation scheme developed by Plaue and Stasko [31] were used. The evaluation scheme consists of two performance measures: *key facts* and *insights*. Key facts are pieces of information contained on the slides provided to participants, whereas insights require groups to synthesize key facts to produce a new piece of information. In this respect, key facts can be considered a measure of the breadth of information that a group has explored, whereas insights measure the depth of the group's understanding of that information. An example of a key fact is "The current investigation points to a problem in marketing". An example insight requires a group to put the two key facts "Small business sales are profitable" and "Small business sales are low" to determine that "Small business sales are not contributing to the company's financial health". The list of 12 key facts and 5 insights developed by Plaue and Stasko [31] through an expert evaluation of the Bonazna Paper Forms Task was used to evaluate group performance in this study.

Hypotheses

We tested the following two hypotheses based on identified trends in display use and closely-coupled work. First, we

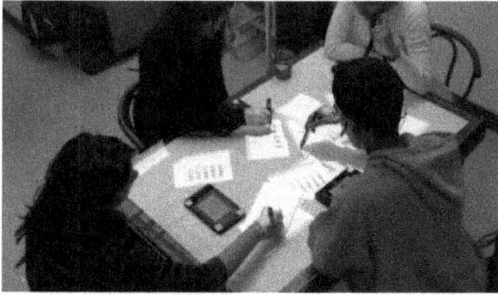

Figure 2. Participants sat on stools around a digital tabletop display. For the Tablets Only conditions the display was set to be inactive.

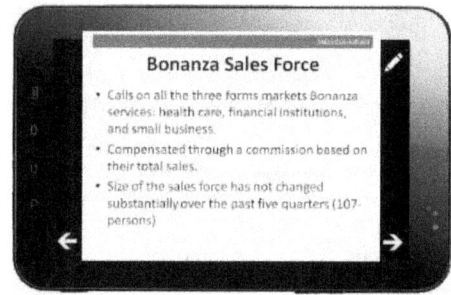

Figure 3. A "virtual tablet", as viewed in the Table Only condition. Participants iterated through slides via forward and back buttons (left/right arrows) in the lower corners of the tablet, or pick-n-drop slides between tablets and digital tabletop via the pen button in the upper right corner.

expected groups working with a large, shared display space to more fully explore task materials than those working with only personal tablets, and that groups provided with personal tablets and a shared table would outperform both groups. In particular, the degree to which groups explore data can vary in two dimensions:

Hypothesis 1a (H1a): Groups with access to personal displays will discuss more key facts (breadth).

Hypothesis 1b (H1b): Groups with access to a digital tabletop will discuss more insights (depth).

Our second hypothesis explored the relationship between closely-coupled collaboration and sensemaking. We hypothesized that equity of participation measures would correlate with the previously observed performance benefits of closely coupled collaboration:

Hypothesis 2 (H2): More equitable interaction by group members will correspond to improved sensemaking performance.

Equipment and Setting

The study was conducted in a controlled university laboratory (See Figure 2). Participants were seated on stools around a 80 x 120 cm table and two projectors located above the table output 1024 x 1536 pixels over an area of 57 x 82 cm onto the table's surface. Groups working in the Table Only and Table Plus Tablets conditions could manipulate slides on the table using Anoto pen technology [12], where each participant could manipulate task materials via the Rotate-and-Translate (RNT) [22] and pick-n-drop [33] metaphors using a provided Anoto pen. Our implementation of pick-n-drop allowed for cut-and-paste functionality, not copy-and-paste, so each slide was always unique across all devices.

In the Tablets Only and Table Plus Tablets conditions, participants were each provided a Samsung Galaxy Tab 7.1. The tablet software displayed a single slide at a time, and participants were able to move through their personal list of slides via forward and back buttons on the tablet. The tablets were also outfitted with small pieces of Anoto paper at three of the four device corners to enable the pick-n-drop and slide navigation functionality, and custom software that enabled users to interact with both the digital tabletop and tablets using the provided Anoto pen. A pick-n-drop button on each tablet allowed participants to transfer slides between tablets, and be-

tween tablets and the digital tabletop in the Table Plus Tablets conditions. In the Tablets Only condition, the tabletop display did not respond to participant's pen interactions, and no task materials could be placed on the digital tabletop.

Groups in the Table Only condition were provided 'virtual tablets' (Figure 3). The virtual tablets emulated the physical tablets that were provided to groups in the other conditions, and were designed to make the task of managing a slide deck more manageable on the digital tabletop. As with the physical tablets, participants could iterate through slides on the virtual tablets, and a pick-n-drop metaphor allowed participants to move slides between virtual tablets. However, unlike in the Tablets Only conditions, participants could pick-n-drop slides from the virtual tablets onto space on the digital tabletop.

Software running on the shared digital tabletop was implemented in C#, and ran on an Intel Core 2 Duo system with 4GB RAM. Software running on the tablets was implemented using the Android SDK, and communicated with the tabletop server via a secured wireless local area network.

Procedure

After arriving at the laboratory and being greeted, participants individually completed an informed consent form and a background questionnaire that gathered demographic and collaborative work experience data. Participants were then introduced to the study software and given time as a group to familiarize themselves with its use and ask any clarifying questions about the interface. Participants then collaboratively completed the Bonanza Paper Forms task, and were given as much time as they required to come to a consensus. Before starting the experimental trial, groups were reminded to work towards the most correct solution they could find, in the shortest amount of time possible. After each groups' trial, participants individually completed a post-trial questionnaire that gathered their opinions on the interface and their collaborative experience. Participants were each paid $10 for their participation in the study, with each member of the group who found the most correct solution in the least amount of time receiving a $20 bonus. Experimental sessions took approximately 1 hour to complete.

Data Collection and Analysis

Participant interaction data were logged to computer files. Since each participant used a different Anoto pen, the logs identified the participant who performed each action, which device it occurred on, and which task materials were manipulated. Audio and video were also captured for each session via a digital camcorder positioned above the table. Participants individually completed post-trial questionnaires that gathered participants' opinions on the advantages and disadvantages of the task interface, their satisfaction with the task, and how well they felt the group performed. The questionnaire consisted of 7-point Likert scales, as well as open-ended questions that assessed their group experience and utility of the study hardware and software during the trial.

One-way analysis of variance (ANOVA) statistical tests were conducted to examine differences between display conditions for the interaction data. To analyze equity of participation for logged interaction data, Gini Coefficients were computed for the number of pen interactions. A correlational analysis was conducted on equity of participation data to investigate potential links to sensemaking performance identified in the literature [35, 17]. Questionnaire data were analyzed using repeated measures analysis of variance (RM-ANOVA) tests to take into account the dependence between responses of group members, with post-hoc pairwise comparisons made using the Bonferroni adjustment. All statistical tests used an alpha-value of 0.05. Finally, the video, questionnaire, and interview data were reviewed to identify any interesting behavioural or conversational patterns and participant opinions.

RESULTS

Our quantitative analyses of taskwork and performance revealed important differences between display conditions, and are reported first. We then present a qualitative analysis of how digital tabletops and tablets were used to support groups' sensemaking process, which aids in explaining the quantitative differences between conditions. An overview of performance and taskwork measures are provided in Table 1, and an overview of teamwork measures are provided in Table 2.

Taskwork and Performance

The 21 groups spent an average of 27.9 minutes exploring and discussing the slides before reaching consensus. However, the time it took for a group to reach consensus varied largely, with the shortest time being 11.4 minutes and the longest time being 42.2 minutes. No significant differences between display conditions were found for task completion time ($F_{(2,18)} = .63, p = .543$). While exploring the provided data slides, groups discussed an average of 6.5 key facts. No significant differences were found between display conditions for the number of key facts discussed ($F_{(2,18)} = 1.3, p = .296$), however, significant differences were found for the number of insights discussed ($F_{(2,18)} = 4.92, p = .019$), with groups in the Tablets Only condition ($\bar{x} = 0.714, \sigma = 0.83$) discussing significantly fewer insights than both those in the Table Only ($\bar{x} = 1.86, \sigma = 1.38, p < 0.05$) and Table Plus Tablets ($\bar{x} = 1.86, \sigma = 1.51, p < 0.05$) display configurations. No significant difference was found between the Table Only and Table Plus Tablets configurations ($p = 1.00$).

The amount of taskwork performed by individuals as they interacted with the digital tabletop and tablets was also analysed. No significant differences were found between display configurations for the average number of pen interactions with the digital tabletop and tablets ($F_{(2,18)} = 2.5, p = 0.110$). However, differences approaching significance were found for the average number of interactions on the digital tabletop ($F_{(1,12)} = 3.63, p = 0.080$), with participants in the Table Only configuration ($\bar{x} = 295, \sigma = 187$) interacting with the tabletop less on average than those in the Table Plus Tablets configuration ($\bar{x} = 483, \sigma = 183$). No digital tabletop was present in the Tablets Only condition, so no comparison was made.

A significant difference was found between display conditions for the number of tablet interactions ($F_{(2,18)} = 14.53, p = .001$), where participants in the Table Only ($\bar{x} = 238, \sigma = 67$) and Table Plus Tablets ($\bar{x} = 224, \sigma = 67$) conditions made significantly fewer interactions with the tablets than those in the Tablets Only configuration ($\bar{x} = 491, \sigma = 141.9$). No significant differences were found between the Table Only and Table Plus Tablets conditions ($p = 1.00$).

Teamwork

In order to investigate how the different types of devices were used by groups as they completed the task, the sharing of slides and devices between participants was also investigated. When the digital tabletop was available, groups placed an average of 15.4 slides on that display. However, groups in the Table Plus Tablets configuration ($\bar{x} = 18.4, \sigma = 2.76$) placed significantly more slides ($F_{(1,12)} = 6.16, p = .029$) onto the shared tabletop space than those in the Table Only conditions ($\bar{x} = 12.3, \sigma = 5.93$). For the Tablets Only configuration, no digital tabletop was available, so no comparison was made.

A comparison of equity of the interactions on the digital tabletop revealed no significant differences between display conditions ($F_{(1,12)} = 2.27, p = .158$). However, correlational analyses revealed that equity of pen interactions on the shared table space (i.e. not including virtual tablets) was positively correlated with the number of key facts and insights discussed by groups ($r = 0.584, p = 0.028$). Further, equity of interaction on the tablets, including virtual tablets in the Table Only conditions, was negatively correlated with the number of key facts and insights discussed by groups ($r = -.548, p = .01$).

Additionally, an analysis was conducted to investigate the degree to which tablets were shared in each display condition, revealing a significant difference between display conditions ($F_{(2,18)} = 16.16, p < 0.0001$). An average of 2.86 ($\sigma = .377$) of the 4 participants interacted with each tablet in the Tablets Only condition, compared to an average of 1.68 ($\sigma = .760$) in the Table Only condition, and an average of 1.32 ($\sigma = .345$) in the Table Plus Tablets condition. No significant difference was found between the Table Only and Table Plus Tablets configurations ($p = .223$).

Finally, an analysis of the post-session questionnaire found a significant difference for participant agreement with the statement "I felt it was easy to compare data between slides" ($F_{(2,18)} = 5.907, p = 0.011$), with participants in the Table

Condition	Taskwork and Performance Measures					
	Solution Quality			Pen Interactions		
	Key Facts	Insights	Task Time (seconds)	Total	Shared Table	Tablet
Table Only	6.71 (1.39)	1.86 (0.83)	1486 (544)	542.7 (170.1)	295 (187)	238 (67)
Table Plus Tablets	7 (1.51)	1.86 (0.83)	1734 (560.3)	707.8 (210.8)	483 (183)	224 (67)
Tablets Only	5.857 (0.83)	0.714 (0.451)	1755 (406.3)	491.3 (141.9)	n/a	491.3 (141.9)
ANOVA Results	$F_{(2,18)} = 1.3$, $p = .296$	$F_{(2,18)} = 4.92$, $p = .019*$	$F_{(2,18)} = .63$, $p = .543$	$F_{(2,18)} = 2.5$, $p = .110$	$F_{(1,12)} = 3.63$, $p = .08$	$F_{(2,18)} = 14.53$, $p = .0001*$

Table 1. Mean values and standard deviations (in parentheses) for performance and taskwork measures, and ANOVA results for comparisons between experimental conditions. Significant results denoted by *.

Only ($p = .016$) and Table Plus Tablets ($p = .04$) configurations agreeing more than those in the Tablet Only configurations. No significant differences were found between participant responses in the Table Only and Table Plus Tablets configurations ($p = 1.00$).

Qualitative Analyses

The initial quantitative analyses revealed that groups working with the digital tabletop performed better at the sensemaking task than those without. To more fully investigate how the table facilitated group discussion of the task information a qualitative analysis of group information sharing activities was conducted. The analyses focused on the use of the shared digital tabletop and tablet computers, and found that three primary activities defined the sensemaking process for groups in this study: finding and bringing attention to relevant task information, making comparisons between slide information, and the formation of tableaux, or grids of task slides, that describe the group's current understanding of the problem.

Sensemaking Process with Digital Tabletops
Post-hoc analysis of the sensemaking groups revealed 3 common activities involving the digital tabletop that facilitated groups' sensemaking processes. First, $11/14$ groups with a digital tabletop display (i.e. the Table and Table Plus Tablet conditions) began by placing materials on the shared table space as they foraged through their personal slide deck. This placement of slides on the table established a pattern by which the shared space acted as a cache for the most relevant materials. Less relevant materials were relegated to the outside of the table, and materials that were deemed irrelevant were left on the tablets or pushed towards the outside of the table where their content was no longer visible. While most groups made this decision implicitly, without any verbal agreement, the process was verbalized by one participant to their collaborators in a Table Plus Tablets trial as "Anything important we should keep it on the table ... and once we rule it as insignificant, take it back."

Second, as materials were moved to the digital tabletop, participants were able to see and work with multiple slides at once. The digital tabletop's flexibility in manipulating digital artefacts played a significant role in facilitating both com-

parisons between slides and foraging through new materials. Participants frequently commandeered space for one activity, only to later clear and repurpose it for another. Third, as participants progressed through the sensemaking task, the table's contents evolved into a tableau of the materials that each group viewed as most relevant to their decision making process. These tableaux served to embody and support the critique of a group's working hypotheses, and to assist in consensus building.

For one group in the Table Plus Tablets condition, these activities were demonstrated in the evolution of how their workspace was partitioned throughout the trial. At the beginning of their session, individuals pulled slides from their tablets and placed single relevant slides directly in front of themselves to share with the group (Figure 4, top). As the table began to fill up, participants made comparisons on one side of the table, while using the rest of the table to store potentially relevant materials (Figure 4, middle). By the end of their session, the group had formed a tableau that spanned nearly their entire workspace (Figure 4, bottom).

Sensemaking Process with Tablets
Groups working in the Tablets Only conditions were more limited in their ability to share and organize materials, but followed a three stage process that closely resembled the process groups utilized when the table was present. Participants started by exploring data on their personal tablets (Figure 5, top). However, as they were unable to set aside slides that they deemed relevant, participants offloaded much of the work of 'discovering' relevant information to a talk-aloud protocol. That is, participants would discuss slide content as they came across it, and then move on to viewing other slides on their tablets.

While comparing data between slides, participants used their tablets as shared, rather than personal, devices. This sharing was reflected in the quantitative analysis, where an average of 2.86 users ($\sigma = .350$) interacted with each tablet display in the Tablets Only conditions, compared to an average of 1.68 users ($\sigma = .703$) in the Table Only condition and an average of 1.32 users ($\sigma = .319$) in the Table Plus Tablets condition. Frequently, participants would push one or more tablets into the shared space in the middle of the table to compare slides

Condition	Teamwork Measures			
	Equity of Participation		Avg. Num. Participants	Slides Placed on Table
	Shared Table	Tablet	Interacted with each Tablet	
Table Only	.478 (.0259)	.468 (.031)	1.68 (.703)	12.3 (5.93)
Table Plus Tablets	.444 (.0478)	.451 (.0585)	1.32 (.319)	18.4 (2.76)
Tablets Only	N/A	.410 (.0384)	2.857 (.350)	n/a
ANOVA Results	$F_{(1,12)} = 2.27$, $p = .158$	$F_{(2,18)} = 2.76$, $p = .090$	$F_{(2,18)} = 16.16$, $p < .0001*$	$F_{(1,12)} = 6.16$, $p = 0.029*$

Table 2. Mean values and standard deviations (in parentheses) for teamwork measures, and ANOVA results for comparisons between experimental conditions. Significant results denoted by *.

Figure 4. (top) Groups often started by sharing relevant slides with their collaborators on the shared surface. (middle) Groups would repurpose display space to facilitate the comparison of slides. (bottom) As groups shifted towards the end of the trial, a tableau was formed that encompassed the groups' current understanding of the task materials.

(Figure 5, middle). Four out of seven groups went so far as to pass their tablets around the table, so that each participant had a chance to inspect the data on each tablet. In an extreme case (Figure 5, bottom), one group decided to move all relevant slides to a single tablet, and to discuss the data together via that tablet. The strategy of moving all task materials to a single tablet may have proven disadvantageous, as the group tied for the worst performance out of all groups who participated in the study (5 key facts and no insights).

It was found that as the group progressed through the task, tablets fluidly transitioned between different regions of the table. A relationship was identified between participants' placement of their individual tablets towards the centre of the table and periods of closely coupled work. This placement of the tablets towards the centre of the table facilitated comparisons between adjacent tablets, much as did the placement of slides in the Table Only and Table Plus Tablets conditions. Conversely, when participants were reviewing task materials individually, tablets were typically placed towards the outside of the table, and enabled individuals to review their task materials in a relatively sheltered work environment. These tablet placements appear to be associated with territoriality [34], where tablets placed in personal territories primarily supported independent work, and tablets placed in shared territories supported collaborative work.

Finally, only 2/7 groups in the Tablets Only condition used a combination of tablets to explain their decision to the investigator at the end of their trial, and groups did not typically form tableaux as was observed in the other two conditions. Unlike the Table Only and Table Plus Tablets conditions, participants tended to either review slides on a single tablet, or recite the group's working hypothesis from memory when explaining their rationale to the investigator.

DISCUSSION

Our analyses revealed that providing groups a large, shared workspace led to the discussion of approximately 20% more insights during the sensemaking task, and that individuals also perceived that data were more easily shared in these conditions. The qualitative analysis of group process further suggests that these performance gains were facilitated by the tabletop's support of three sensemaking activities: the prioritization of slides, the ability to compare multiple slides at once, and the formation of tableaux to embody the group's working hypotheses. We now discuss how these activities contributed to group performance and process, and how our findings contribute towards understanding personal and shared devices' support for collaborative sensemaking process. In particular, we discuss the benefits of accommodating flexible work processes, the benefits of supporting the communication of relationships between task materials, and

Figure 5. Participants reviewed materials individually on tablets near the edge of the shared table (top). When discussing materials collectively, participants pushed tablets towards the centre of the table (middle), or in one case, moved task materials onto a single tablet that was placed in the middle of the table and viewed as a shared space (bottom).

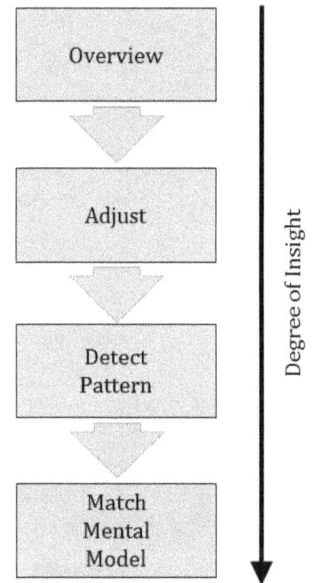

Figure 6. Individuals' prioritization of task materials appeared to support transitions between 'overview' and 'adjust' processes. The ability to fluidly compare materials assisted individuals as they moved from 'adjust' to 'detect pattern' modes of work. The formation of tableaux aided in transitioning between 'detect pattern' and 'match mental model' modes of work.

identified correlations between equity of participation measures and group performance.

Support for Sensemaking Processes

In their investigation of collaborative sensemaking, Isenberg et al. [18] argue that sensemaking tools need to support flexible temporal sequences of work process. Grounding of our analyses in the sensemaking process model by Yi et al. [39] provided an opportunity to elucidate the role that personal and shared devices played in supporting a group's collaborative sensemaking activities. In particular, Figure 6 illustrates how the manipulation of task materials facilitated transitions between different activities. The prioritization of task materials assisted groups in moving between the overview and adjust phases of work; the comparison of task materials aided in detecting patterns in the task materials; and the formation of tableaux helped groups form active hypotheses from detected patterns, and to transition into the 'match mental model' phase of work. The ease with which individuals and groups could manipulate slides on the digital tabletop provided a flexible workspace that accommodated transitions between these phases of work, despite their nonlinear nature. Moreover, our findings show that each of these activities were performed less effectively in the Tablets Only configurations, and that the ability to manipulate task artefacts in the shared space provided a more effective workspace for groups.

Plaue and Stasko [31], report similar findings in their previous study of groups performing the Bonanza Paper Forms task. In particular, they report that groups using vertical, projected screens that could display a maximum of two slides at once overwhelmingly requested "more" display space. Our analyses suggest that this additional display space could be used to facilitate the prioritization and comparison of slides. However, as the projected displays provided limited capacity to manipulate slide data and utilize spatial relationships to communicate, they would not likely support the formation of tableaux to the degree that the digital tabletop did in our study. Interestingly, in Plaue and Stasko's work whiteboard displays were also used to prioritize and organize content as the group made sense of the data and to segue conversation between slides. The use of specialized secondary displays, such as a shared whiteboard for taking notes, was not investigated in our study, however based on Plaue and Stasko's report, they appear to support sensemaking activities. We suggest that the use of Vogt et al.'s model [35], that includes an additional work phase for 'recording' data, may be useful to ground future analyses of such technologies, identify additional activities related to the 'recording' work phase, and elucidate how devices may support those sensemaking activities.

Sensemaking Breadth vs. Depth

The insight-based analysis utilized in our study also provided an opportunity to refine our understanding of how personal and shared displays impact sensemaking performance. In particular, we observed that groups were able to more effectively discuss insights when the digital tabletop was present (H1b), but found no differences in the number of key facts that were discussed (H1a). This finding suggests that while groups explored task materials with equal breadth regardless of the tools provided them, groups with access to a digital tabletop were able to explore the dataset in more depth. Two characteristics of the digital tabletop may help to explain these differences. First, the use of RNT and pick-n-drop metaphors allowed participants to express spatial relationships between task materials through their physical placement and manipulation. Second, the work performed on the digital tabletop may have contributed to more closely-coupled collaboration, as interactions in the shared space were accessible to the entire group.

Groups working with the digital table were better able to compare slides and form tableaux; two activities that were facilitated by the table's use of the pick-n-drop [33] and rotate-and-translate [22] metaphors, which enabled users to manipulate task artefacts with relative ease. The ability to manipulate slides, and to form tableaux, was particularly important as they facilitated interactions between a group's *sensemakers* and *foragers* [35]. Sensemakers could establish an active hypothesis by building a tableau on the digital tabletop, which could then be observed, amended, and critiqued by the group's foragers. While groups working in the Tablets Only condition were able to manipulate materials in a similar manner, the limited number of tablets available to the group may have restricted their ability to communicate effectively.

This ability to share and discuss relationships between task materials while closely-coupled has been shown to benefit group performance for sensemaking tasks [13]. However, Harper and Sellen [14] report that social interaction is more important for sharing interpreted information (i.e. insights) than it is for objective information (i.e. key facts). Thus, one possible explanation for the improved performance of groups working around the tabletop was their support for communicating relationships between task materials in a closely coupled manner. Groups working in the Tablets Only condition were able to explore the task materials as well as groups working with the shared table, however the digital tabletop better facilitated closely-coupled collaboration between sensemakers and foragers. This ability to work closely enabled groups to more effectively engage in the sensemaker and forager activities, such as forming and amending tableaux, and henceforth allowed groups to explore task materials in more depth.

Equity of Participation and Sensemaking

Finally, our use of equity of participation measures may provide a useful measure for predicting a group's sensemaking performance. Our quantitative analyses revealed that more equitable participation on the shared portions of the tabletop display (i.e. not including the virtual tablets) correlated with a higher number of key facts and insights discussed by a group ($p = .028$), supporting H2. Moreover, we identified a *negative* correlation between equity of tablet interactions, including interactions with the virtual tablets, and the number of key facts and insights discussed by groups ($p = .01$). That is, more equal interaction on both virtual and physical tablets was associated with decreased sensemaking performance.

Our results also indicate that despite there being an unequal

distribution of task materials, groups with more equitable participation on the shared display tended to perform better at the task. One might have expected that groups would be better served by the participants with more task materials taking on a more significant role in the task, however our results show otherwise. In the Tablet Only conditions, where insights were discussed the least, the tablets were shared to a much higher degree than they were in the other conditions, which should reduce the impact of the unequal distribution of task materials. Further, no correlation was found between the amount of interaction on the shared tabletop and the number of key facts and insights discussed. That is, it was not how much groups were using the shared space that contributed to their performance, but that they were using the shared space equitably.

Our findings suggest that Gini coefficients, as a measure of equity of participation, may correlate with the trends of "closely coupled" collaboration described by Vogt et al. [35] and Isenberg et al. [17]. Further, equity of participation as a dependent measure does not rely on time consuming video analysis, the subjectivity of inter-coder reliability, or being able to identify relevant task materials. Thus, the use of such easily captured, quantitative measures may be useful as a rapid analysis technique for future studies, and may support or replace the use of time-consuming measures such as discourse analysis. Moreover, equity of participation measures can be captured and visualized in realtime, and potentially be used to predict collaborative outcomes, lending themselves to use in participatory displays (e.g. DiMicco [9]).

CONCLUSION

Our investigation of groups' use of tablets and a shared, digital tabletop for the Bonanza Paper Forms task revealed that the presence of digital tabletops led to improved performance, and identified activities that were supported by the shared workspace. In particular, the digital tabletop supported a group's ability to prioritize information, to make comparisons between task data, and to form tableaux which embodied the group's working hypothesis. Our analysis also revealed correlations between equity of participation measures and group performance. A positive correlation between the use of shared devices and group performance, and a negative correlation between the use of personal devices and group performance were identified.

These results provide insight into the impact that personal and shared devices can have on collaborative sensemaking processes. Our qualitative analyses, grounded in Yi et al.'s [39] process model, revealed how personal and shared devices supported a group's sensemaking activities. Our quantitative analyses demonstrated that access to a digital tabletop enabled groups to explore data in more depth, but with equal breadth. The identification of correlations between equity of interaction measures for personal and shared devices reveals a potential use in predicting group performance. Our results demonstrate the importance of developing a more in-depth understanding of the types of support that personal and shared devices provide groups, and suggest that future studies of sensemaking may benefit from an understanding of the relationship between equity of member participation, closely-coupled collaboration, and sensemaking performance.

ACKNOWLEDGMENTS

We thank the Natural Sciences and Engineering Research Council of Canada (NSERC) and the NSERC Surfnet research alliance for supporting this research.

REFERENCES

1. Albolino, S., Cook, R., and O'Connor, M. Sensemaking, safety, and cooperative work in the intensive care unit. *Cognition, Technology, & Work 9* (July 2007), 131–137.

2. Amershi, S., and Morris, M. R. Cosearch: a system for co-located collaborative web search. In *Proc. CHI 2008*, ACM (New York, NY, USA, 2008), 1647–1656.

3. Baldwin, J. R., and Beckstead, D. Insights on the canadian economy. Tech. rep., Statistics Canada, 2003.

4. Billman, D., and Bier, E. A. Medical sensemaking with entity workspace. In *Proc. CHI 2007*, ACM (New York, NY, USA, 2007), 229–232.

5. Blackwell, A., and Green, T. Notational systems – the cognitive dimensions of notations framework. In *HCI Models, Theories and Frameworks.*, J. M. Carroll, Ed. Morgan Kaufmann, USA., 2003, 103–133.

6. Card, S. K., Mackinlay, J. D., and Shneiderman, B., Eds. *Readings in information visualization: using vision to think.* Morgan Kaufmann Publishers Inc., San Francisco, CA, USA, 1999.

7. Chung, C.-W., Lee, C.-C., and Liu, C.-C. Investigating face-to-face peer interaction patterns in a collaborative web discovery task: the benefits of a shared display. *Journal of Computer Assisted Learning* (2012).

8. Dervin, B. *From the mind's eye of the user: The Sense-Making qualitative-quantitative methodology. In Sense-Making methodology reader: Selected writings of Brenda Dervin.* Hampton Press Inc, Cresskill, NJ, USA, 2003.

9. DiMicco, J. M. *Changing Small Group Interaction through Visual Reflections of Social Behavior.* PhD thesis, Massachusetts Institute of Technology, 2005.

10. Gallupe, R. B., and DeSanctis, G. Computer-based support for group problem-finding: An experimental investigation. *MIS Quarterly 12*, 2 (1988), 276–297.

11. Gutwin, C., and Greenberg, S. Design for individuals, design for groups: tradeoffs between power and workspace awareness. In *Proc. CSCW 1998*, ACM (New York, NY, USA, 1998), 207–216.

12. Haller, M., Leithinger, D., Leitner, J., Seifried, T., Brandl, P., Zauner, J., and Billinghurst, M. The shared design space. In *Proc. SIGGRAPH 2006*, ACM (New York, NY, USA, 2006), 29.

13. Hansen, P., and Järvelin, K. Collaborative information retrieval in an information-intensive domain. *Inf. Process. Manage. 41*, 5 (Sept. 2005), 1101–1119.

14. Harper, R., and Sellen, A. Collaborative tools and the practicalities of professional work at the international monetary fund. In *Proc. CHI 1995*, ACM Press/Addison-Wesley Publishing Co. (New York, NY, USA, 1995), 122–129.

15. Harris, A., Rick, J., Bonnett, V., Yuill, N., Fleck, R., Marshall, P., and Rogers, Y. Around the table: are multiple-touch surfaces better than single-touch for children's collaborative interactions? In *Proc. CSCL 2009*, International Society of the Learning Sciences (2009), 335–344.

16. Hinckley, K., Ramos, G., Guimbretiere, F., Baudisch, P., and Smith, M. Stitching: Pen gestures that span multiple displays. In *Proc. AVI 2004* (2004).

17. Isenberg, P., Fisher, D., Morris, M., Inkpen, K., and Czerwinski, M. An exploratory study of co-located collaborative visual analytics around a tabletop display. In *Proc. IEEE VAST 2010* (oct. 2010), 179 –186.

18. Isenberg, P., Tang, A., and Carpendale, S. An exploratory study of visual information analysis. In *Proc. CHI 2008*, ACM (New York, NY, USA, 2008), 1217–1226.

19. Jarvenpaa, B., and Dickson, G. Bonanza business forms company: A mystery in declining profits. In *Marketing Decision Making*, A. Ruppel, W. O'Dell, R. Trent, and Kehoe, Eds. South-Western Publishing Company, Cincinatti, OH, 1988.

20. Jetter, H.-C., Gerken, J., Zöllner, M., Reiterer, H., and Milic-Frayling, N. Materializing the query with facet-streams: a hybrid surface for collaborative search on tabletops. In *Proc. CHI 2011*, ACM (New York, NY, USA, 2011), 3013–3022.

21. Klein, G., Moon, B., and Hoffman, R. Making sense of sensemaking 1: Alternative perspectives. *Intelligent Systems, IEEE 21*, 4 (july-aug. 2006), 70 –73.

22. Kruger, R., Carpendale, S., Scott, S. D., and Tang, A. Fluid integration of rotation and translation. In *Proc. CHI 2005*, ACM (New York, NY, USA, 2005), 601–610.

23. Landgren, J., and Nulden, U. A study of emergency response work: patterns of mobile phone interaction. In *Proc. CHI 2007*, ACM (New York, NY, USA, 2007), 1323–1332.

24. Lopes, G. R., da Silva, R., and de Oliveira, J. P. M. Applying gini coefficient to quantify scientific collaboration in researchers network. In *Proc. WIMS 2011*, ACM (New York, NY, USA, 2011), 68:1–68:6.

25. Morris, M. R., Lombardo, J., and Wigdor, D. Wesearch: supporting collaborative search and sensemaking on a tabletop display. In *Proc. CSCW 2010*, ACM (New York, NY, USA, 2010), 401–410.

26. Olsen, D. R., Clement, J., and Pace, A. Spilling: Expanding hand held interaction to touch table displays. In *Proc. TABLETOP 2007*, IEEE Computer Society (Los Alamitos, CA, USA, 2007), 163–170.

27. Paul, S. A., and Morris, M. R. Cosense: enhancing sensemaking for collaborative web search. In *Proc. CHI 2009*, ACM (New York, NY, USA, 2009), 1771–1780.

28. Paul, S. A., and Reddy, M. C. Understanding together: sensemaking in collaborative information seeking. In *Proc. CSCW 2010*, ACM (New York, NY, USA, 2010), 321–330.

29. Pinelle, D., and Gutwin, C. Evaluating teamwork support in tabletop groupware applications using collaboration usability analysis. *Personal Ubiquitous Comput. 12*, 3 (2008), 237–254.

30. Pirolli, P., and Card, S. The sensemaking process and leverage points for analyst technology as identified through cognitive task analysis. In *Proc. of Int. Conf. on Intelligence*, McLean (VA, USA, May 2005), 2–4.

31. Plaue, C., and Stasko, J. Presence & placement: Exploring the benefits of multiple shared displays on an interactive sensemaking task. In *Proc. GROUP 2009*, ACM Press (2009), 179–188.

32. Reinhardt, W., Schmidt, B., Sloep, P., and Drachsler, H. Knowledge worker roles and actions—results of two empirical studies. *Process Management 18* (2011), 150–174.

33. Rekimoto, J. Pick-and-drop: a direct manipulation technique for multiple computer environments. In *Proc. UIST 1997*, ACM (1997), 31–39.

34. Scott, S. D., Sheelagh, M., Carpendale, T., and Inkpen, K. M. Territoriality in collaborative tabletop workspaces. In *Proc. CSCW 2004*, ACM (New York, NY, USA, 2004), 294–303.

35. Vogt, K., Bradel, L., Andrews, C., North, C., Endert, A., and Hutchings, D. Co-located collaborative sensemaking on a large high-resolution display with multiple input devices. In *Proc. INTERACT 2011*, Springer-Verlag (Berlin, Heidelberg, 2011), 589–604.

36. Wallace, J., Scott, S., Lai, E., and Jajalla, D. Investigating the role of a large, shared display in multi-display environments. *Computer Supported Cooperative Work (CSCW) 20* (2011), 529–561.

37. Wallace, J., Scott, S., Stutz, T., Enns, T., and Inkpen, K. Investigating teamwork and taskwork in single- and multi-display groupware systems. *Personal and Ubiquitous Computing* (2009).

38. Whittaker, S. *HCI Remixed: Reflections on works that have influenced the HCI community,*. MIT Press, 2008, ch. Making Sense of Sensemaking.

39. Yi, J. S., Kang, Y.-a., Stasko, J. T., and Jacko, J. A. Understanding and characterizing insights: how do people gain insights using information visualization? In *Proc BELIV 2008*, ACM (New York, NY, USA, 2008), 4:1–4:6.

A Comparative Evaluation of Touch-Based Methods to Bind Mobile Devices for Collaborative Interactions

Tero Jokela, Andrés Lucero
Nokia Research Center
P.O. Box 1000, FI-33721 Tampere, Finland
{tero.jokela, andres.lucero}@nokia.com

ABSTRACT

We present a comparative evaluation of two touch-based group-binding methods, a leader-driven method and a peer-based method, against a more conventional group-binding method based on scanning and passwords. The results indicate that the participants strongly preferred the touch-based methods in both pragmatic and hedonic qualities as well as in the overall attractiveness. While the leader-driven method allowed better control over the group and required only one participant to be able to form a group, the peer-based method helped to create a greater sense of community and scaled better for larger group sizes and distances. As the optimal group-binding method depends on the social situation and physical environment, the binding methods should be flexible, allowing the users to adapt them to different contexts of use. For determining the order of the devices, manual arrangement was preferred over defining the order by touching.

Author Keywords

Collocated interaction; mobile phones; user interfaces; device ecosystem binding; group association; pairing.

ACM Classification Keywords

H.5.m. Information interfaces and presentation (e.g., HCI): Miscellaneous.

INTRODUCTION

Mobile devices were originally conceived as, and have traditionally been, very personal devices targeted at individual use. Recent advances in sensor and short-range communication technologies offer new opportunities for collaborative use of mobile devices. Groups of collocated users can couple their devices together and create ecosystems of interaction [21]. This allows the users to engage in collaborative activities and experiences with their mobile devices, thus shifting from *personal-individual* towards *shared-multi-user* interactions. Examples of applications that would benefit from such collaborative use of mobile devices include sharing of digital content,

collaborative creation and editing of content, and different kinds of games. In many of these applications, it would be natural to utilize spatial interactions in the shared space, for example, throwing virtual objects such as files between devices. However, finding the positions of the devices has presented a challenging problem, requiring the use of special tracking equipment or dedicated infrastructure.

Before a group of users can engage in collaborative interactions with their mobile devices, the multi-device ecosystem must first be set up. This involves initiating the necessary system and application software in all devices. The devices must become aware of the other devices existing in the proximity, and the devices intended to participate in the ecosystem must be identified. A communication channel then needs to be established between the devices participating in the ecosystem, in order to allow exchange of data and coordination of the interactions. Wireless short-range communication technologies such as WLAN or Bluetooth are typically used to exchange data between devices. The process of setting up the ecosystem is generally known as device binding or ecosystem binding [21] (also known as device association, pairing, or coupling [3]). As the intention is to enable spontaneous interactions, it should be possible to bind devices having no prior knowledge of each other in a fast and easy way. If the process of binding devices is too complicated or tedious, the users might lose interest in using multi-device interactions in the first place. As the wireless connections provide no physical indications (for example, cables) of which devices are actually connected, the binding process should provide sufficient security and cues so that the users can ensure that the right devices are connected.

In this paper, we are concerned with device-binding methods for establishing an ecosystem of mobile devices to support collaborative interactions within small-to-medium-sized groups of collocated users. While the problem of a single user pairing two devices has been extensively studied in prior research, researchers have started to address more complex scenarios involving multiple users and devices only recently. In particular, we focus on methods based on device proximity and touch interactions, which have been found to be intuitive and easy to explain, but which have been little explored in the literature [2]. We present a comparative evaluation of two touch-based group-binding methods, a leader-driven method called Host and a peer-based method called Ring, against a more conventional method called Seek, which is based on scanning the available devices in the proximity and passwords for security. While most earlier studies on device binding have focused on pragmatic aspects such as security and usability, we approach the problem from a broader user experience perspective, covering also hedonic aspects such as social and emotional factors, which have been shown to be important considerations when users select binding methods in real-life situations [10, 18]. We consider the complete group creation process in a realistic application context, including identification of the devices to participate in the group, initiation of the application software in all devices, and authentication of the connection. We also explore options to determine the device order during the group creation phase, in order to allow spatial interactions without dedicated tracking equipment. The evaluation results indicate that the participants strongly preferred touch-based methods over Seek. Several important differences were identified between leader-driven and peer-based methods. The optimal group-binding method was found to depend on various social and environmental factors, suggesting that the binding methods should be flexible to allow users to adopt different group creation strategies in different contexts of use. For determining the order of the devices, manual arrangement was preferred over defining the order by touching.

The rest of this paper is structured as follows. First, we provide a brief overview of the related work. We then give a detailed description of the three group-binding methods and the evaluation procedure. Finally, we present the results of the evaluation, followed by conclusions.

RELATED WORK
The problem of device binding has been extensively studied in the fields of human-computer interaction and security research. A wide range of methods for device binding has been proposed – in security research alone, over 20 different methods have been identified [17]. These methods vary in terms of device hardware requirements, amount of user involvement, and level of provided security.

The problem of device binding can be divided into two subproblems: device *identification* and *authentication*. Device identification involves selecting which of the devices available in the proximity should be bound with each other. The need for device authentication originates from the invisibility of wireless communications. As the users cannot see the wireless communication channels, they cannot be sure that they are really connecting to the other devices intended to, opening the possibility for so-called Man-in-the-Middle attacks. To counter this threat, a wide variety of methods have been proposed that authenticate the wireless connection over auxiliary communication channels (also known as Out-of-Band Channels), which can be perceived and managed by human users.

The most common device-binding methods today, such as those typically used in Bluetooth and WLAN networks, are based on scanning the environment for available devices and then presenting a list of the found devices to the user for selecting the other device to bind with. The authentication is based on short strings (also known as PIN codes) that the user is expected to copy or compare between devices. The authentication strings can be represented as numbers, words, graphical images, or audio signals in the user interface.

The proposed alternative methods include a variety of techniques based on synchronous user actions, for example, pressing buttons on both devices [19] or touching both devices [23] simultaneously, shaking the devices together [8], or bumping the devices together [6]. Bumping is also used in the popular commercial service Bump[1]. Further, device binding can be based on continuous gestures spanning from one device display to another [7]. Methods based on spatial alignment of the devices include pointing, for example, with laser light [15], touching [20], or placing the devices in close proximity of each other [12]. It is also possible to bind devices with various auxiliary devices, for example, tokens [1] or cameras [16]. Some of the proposed methods cover only device identification or authentication, while others combine both identification and authentication into a single user action.

The development of new binding methods has been largely technology-driven with little user involvement. As an example of a more user-centered approach, Chong and Gellersen [2] present a study on users' spontaneous actions for device binding. In the study, the users' were asked to invent methods for binding together low-fidelity acrylic prototypes of different devices. Device proximity and touch based methods were found to be among the most commonly proposed methods, and the physical contact of devices was also considered as the easiest method to describe and teach to another person. Still, there has been little work exploring such techniques in the literature.

Binding methods are not just means for connecting devices – they have strong social and emotional aspects. In real-life situations, the users do not always use the easiest or fastest method available, nor the one they like best. Many factors influence their choice of binding method, including the place, the social setting, the other people present, and the sensitivity of data [10, 18]. Users are willing to take security risks to comply with social norms [10].

The vast majority of prior research has focused on scenarios of a single user binding two devices with each other (for example, binding a headset with a mobile device). Only recently have researchers started to consider more complex scenarios involving multiple users and devices. Such multi-user scenarios differ in many respects from single-user

---

[1] http://bu.mp/

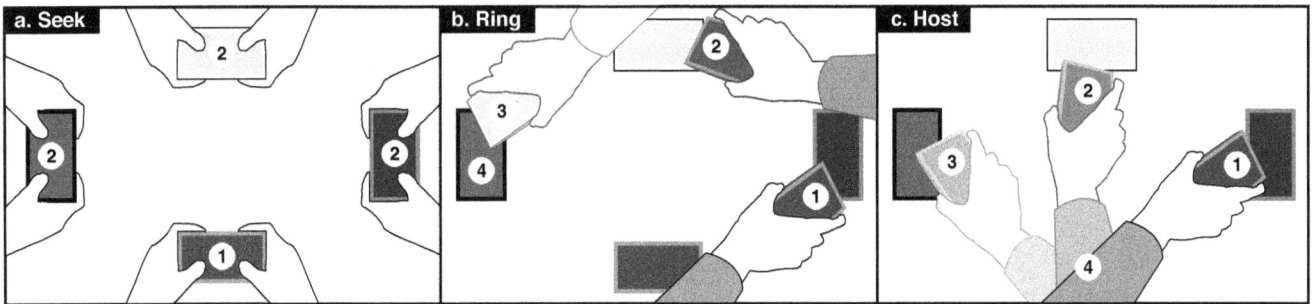

Figure 1. Three group-binding methods. a) Seek: a leader creates a group and shares a password (1), which is then entered in parallel by the other participants (2). b) Ring: one person starts the app and touches the next device to their right to add it (1), then others continue adding the next person to their right (2,3), and the last person completes the group (4). c) Host: a leader starts the app, adds people by touching all devices in counter-clockwise order (1-3), and puts the device on the table to complete the group (4).

scenarios, making the single-user device-binding methods not necessarily applicable to multi-user scenarios. In multi-user scenarios, communication between group members provides an additional source for potential errors. On the other hand, the users are typically willing to help each other and make decisions by mutual agreement, which reduces the amount of errors [11]. Methods that involve physical exchange of devices have been found to be unacceptable unless the users know each other very well, as the users are unwilling to hand in their devices to strangers [22].

Chong and Gellersen [3] present a framework that summarizes and classifies the different factors that influence the usability of spontaneous device binding, identifying technology, user interaction, and application context as the three most important criteria.

EVALUATION OF GROUP-BINDING METHODS

Objectives
In this study, we were primarily interested in three research questions. First, we wanted to compare touch and proximity-based methods for group binding against more conventional methods based on scanning and passwords. Second, we wanted to explore different ways to divide the group-binding task between the participants – in particular, we were interested in differences between leader-driven and peer-based methods. Third, we wanted to investigate possibilities to define the device order as a part of the group creation process, in order to allow implementation of spatial interactions without extensive tracking equipment.

Group-Binding Methods
To study these research questions in practice, we designed three different group-binding methods called Seek, Ring, and Host. The Seek method represented the conventional approach used, for example, in network games and was based on scanning for device identification and passwords for authentication. Both the Ring and Host methods used touch for device identification and authentication. The main difference between Ring and Host was that Ring was peer-based, distributing the group creation task between all participants, while Host was leader-driven, concentrating

the group creation task on one participant. Additionally, Host utilized device gestures for some interactions. The Host method was based on the EasyGroups method [14] reported earlier. While all the methods were generic, we decided to study them in the context of a simple photo sharing application in order to provide a more realistic goal for the group creation task during the evaluation. The photo sharing application was a simplified version of Pass-Them-Around [13] and it allowed the users to browse a collection of photos stored in their own devices and supported spatial interactions of throwing photos between devices.

Seek
To set up a new group, one person (the leader) should start the Seek application on their device and create a new group (Fig. 1a). The application prompts the leader to join a WLAN network and enter a name for the new group. The application automatically generates a six-digit password for the group. The application then moves to the Table Overview (Fig. 2) showing all devices that are currently part of the group and their order as well as the group name and password. As new devices join the group, an animation shows how the device order changes on the table. To enable the users to identify the devices, the color of each device is indicated on the screen. The other persons can then join the group in parallel by starting the Seek application, joining the same network as the leader, and selecting the existing group from the list. The application then prompts the user to enter the password. If the password is correct, the device joins the group and moves to the Table Overview. If the order of the devices presented on the screen is different from the order of the devices on the table, the leader can correct it by dragging the devices to the right positions on the screen. The users can move to the Photo Sharing Mode by tapping their own piles of photos on the screen.

If a new person wishes to join an existing group, the person should start the Seek application and join the group in the same way as during the initial group creation phase. The leader can check the order of the devices on the screen and correct it if necessary. To leave the group, the person should press the "Exit" button on the screen.

Figure 2. The Table Overview during Seek.

Ring

To begin group formation, one person should start the Ring application on their device (Fig. 1b). This device automatically enters Discovery Mode and visual feedback is shown in portrait view to suggest holding the device vertically for a more comfortable grip. The person holding the device is instructed to touch the next device to their right. When the person moves their device close to the next device, the device detects the new device and the person holding the device is asked to hold their device still while the new device is added to the group. When the new device has been added to the group, the device exits Discovery Mode and moves to the Table Overview, which shows all devices that are currently part of the group and their order. The new device that was just added to the group now automatically starts the application and enters the Discovery Mode. The owner of that device is instructed to continue in the same way and touch the next device to their right. By asking the user always to connect to the next device to their right, we are able to define the order of the devices on the table based on the touching order. When all the devices around the table have been added to the group, the owner of the last device can complete the group by pressing the "Complete" button on screen. The users can move to the Photo Sharing Mode and start sharing pictures.

If a new person wishes to join an existing group, the person on the left side of the new person can press the "Add Device" button on the screen and touch the incoming person's device. The new person is then added to the right side of the person who just added them. The new group member can then continue adding new devices, or press the "Complete" button if there are no more devices to add. To leave the group, the person should press the "Exit" button.

Host

To set up a new group, one person (the leader) should start the Host application on their device (Fig. 1c). When the device is picked up from the table, it detects the pick-up gesture and enters Discovery Mode, which allows the leader to add new people to the group. The leader should then touch the other devices one by one in counter-clockwise order around the table (Fig. 3). The order of the

devices on the table is automatically defined based on the touching order. A similar procedure (and visual feedback) as the one described for Ring is used to detect, connect, start the application, and join the group. When all the other devices have been added to the group, the leader should put their device back on the table. The device detects the gesture and exits the Discovery Mode and completes the group set-up. The persons can then start sharing photos between devices.

If a new person wishes to join an existing group, the person on the left side of the new person should pick up their device to enter Discovery Mode and touch the new person's device. The new person is then added next after the person who just added them. To leave the group, the person should pick their device up from the table and flip it upside down. The device detects the gesture and exits.

Prototype Implementation

We built prototypes of the three group-binding methods on Nokia N9[2] mobile devices running the MeeGo operating system. The prototypes were implemented in C++ on top of the Qt 4.7 software framework. QML and Qt Quick with OpenGL ES hardware acceleration were used for fluent animated user interface graphics. The N9's internal accelerometer was used for gesture detection in Host.

In all methods, the objective was to establish a WLAN connection between the devices. In Seek, each device was manually connected to the WLAN network. The device then scanned the network for available groups and presented a list to the user to choose from. In Ring and Host, touching was detected with Bluetooth-based radio technology, which was able to detect other devices at ranges closer than 20 cm in approximately 5 seconds. While the technology generally worked reliably, there were occasionally longer delays before the other devices were detected or detections of devices further away. The necessary connectivity and initialization information was then sent to the discovered device over Bluetooth. A daemon, which listened to a Bluetooth socket, received the

Figure 3. The Host method. The user holding the cyan device has connected the black (right) and magenta devices (top).

[2] http://swipe.nokia.com/

connectivity information on the discovered device and started the actual application, which connected to the correct WLAN network and joined the group. The prototypes were fully functional with real network communication, except for the security protocols, which were only simulated in the user interface.

Participants

We recruited a total of 24 participants for the evaluation by posting an advertisement on a local mailing list. Of the 24 participants, 20 were pairs of users, while the remaining four were individual participants. We preferred to recruit pairs of people who knew each other, so that the participants would feel more comfortable during the evaluation session. We assigned the participants into six groups of four users in the order they registered for the study. Each participant typically knew one other participant in the group, while the two others were strangers. Eight of the participants were female and 16 male. The ages of the participants varied between 23 and 45 years (M=33.6, SD=6.0). Three of the participants were left-handed and 21 right-handed. The participants represented a variety of different backgrounds, with eight participants having a software engineering background, 10 other technical background (for example, mechanical engineering), and six non-technical background (for example, administration or linguistics). The participants were fairly advanced users of technology: on a scale between 1 and 7 (1=novice, 7=expert), the participants rated their familiarity with technology above average (M=5.1, SD=1.2). All participants were active smartphone users and six of the 24 participants had used a Nokia N9 before the study.

Procedure

We organized a series of six evaluation sessions. The evaluation sessions were arranged in a usability laboratory of approximately 40 m^2 (430 sq ft) in size. Fig. 4 shows the evaluation setup. In each session, there were four participants and a moderator present. We used devices of four different colors (black, white, magenta, and cyan) and each participant was assigned a device with a different color. This provided a practical method of identifying the devices of the different participants during the evaluation session. The participants were given seats around a rectangular table of approximately 150x70 cm (60x27 inches) in size, one on each side of the table. The table was carefully selected so that there would be different distances between the participants and that the participants sitting on the short edges would have some difficulty reaching each other. The total durations of the evaluation sessions varied between 100 and 120 minutes.

As the participants arrived in the laboratory, the moderator guided them to their seats around the table and asked them to fill in a background questionnaire form. When all the participants had completed the forms, the moderator introduced the participants to the idea of collaborative use

Figure 4. Evaluation setup with four participants.

of mobile devices and demonstrated it with the photo sharing application. The participants were then given their own devices and they were encouraged to try throwing photos between devices. This small introductory task provided the users with an opportunity to become familiar with their devices. The moderator then explained to the participants that before they could share photos between devices by throwing, they first had to bind their mobile devices together into a group and the objective of the session was to evaluate different methods for that task. Before the actual evaluation started, the moderator informed the participants that some of the methods might require touching other devices and demonstrated how to do it in practice. The participants were then asked to practice touching with their own devices. We saw this training step necessary, because while many of the participants were aware of touching as an interaction technique, few had tried it in practice.

To begin the actual evaluation, the moderator showed a short video clip demonstrating the first group-binding method. The videos were prepared so that they simulated a situation of a participant observing another group of users using the method to create a group. We used video recordings to minimize the variations between the instructions that the different groups received. After the participants had watched the video, the moderator gave them the following task: "By using the method that was just demonstrated to you, create a group so that you can throw photos between your devices." The moderator then observed as the participants tried out the method and only intervened if the participants clearly could not proceed with the method or there were some technical problems with the devices. The task was considered complete, when the participants could successfully throw photos between all devices. The moderator then asked everybody to leave the group and create another group with a different participant initiating the group creation. The moderator also asked at least one person to leave the group and rejoin it. Overall, each group tried each method two to four times.

After testing the method, the moderator asked the participants to fill in two validated questionnaires. The first questionnaire was NASA-TLX [4], which measures the subjective workload experience when performing a task. To gain a broader view of the methods, we extended the questionnaire with four additional scales: learnability, quickness, security, and overall preference. The second questionnaire was AttrakDiff [5], which measures the attractiveness of interactive products.

The same procedure was then repeated for the second and the third methods. We systematically varied the order in which the six groups were exposed to the three methods to counter-balance any learning effects.

After the participants had tested all the methods, the moderator interviewed the participants about their experiences with the methods. The interview was semi-structured and covered a variety of themes including general feedback about the different methods, perceptions about their learnability and security, as well as specific interaction techniques like touching and hand gestures. The moderator also showed the participants three pictures representing different scenarios and asked them to consider what would be the most appropriate method for creating a group in each scenario. The scenarios were: 1) meeting other family members in the living room at home, 2) meeting representatives of another company in a meeting room at the office, and 3) meeting friends in a busy café. The objective was to encourage the participants to think about different situations and environments and their social and physical characteristics. After the interview was completed, the moderator thanked the participants and gave them a movie ticket each to compensate them for their time.

All sessions were video recorded and interaction with the devices was logged. Two researchers independently analyzed the video recordings and wrote notes about their observations. The same two researchers then analyzed the data and built an Affinity Diagram [9] in a series of interpretation sessions. Each researcher individually studied the notes and grouped them into clusters of related items. The clusters then evolved to broader categories that were naturally revealed and were jointly revisited, discussed, and refined. In the end, the categories were processed into more general findings that form the core of the Results section.

RESULTS

We first give an overview of the quantitative results. We then present the qualitative results and contrast them with the quantitative results when relevant.

Extended NASA-TLX

Fig. 5 illustrates the results of the extended NASA-TLX questionnaire [4]. The main bars indicate the means for each subscale, while the error bars indicate standard errors. The original six subscales of NASA-TLX are presented on the left and the four subscales that we added for the purposes of this study (learnability, quickness, security, and overall preference) are on the right. As the participants were observed in groups, the responses of each participant were influenced by the other participants in the same group.

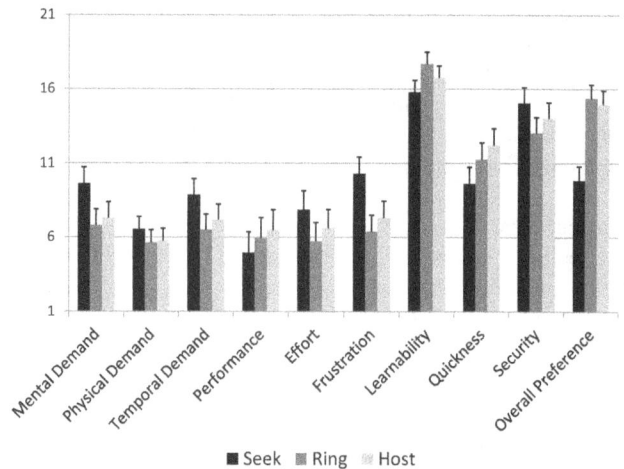

Figure 5. Extended NASA-TLX results.

Therefore, we used mixed model techniques to analyze the data with the binding method as a fixed factor and the groups and the participants nested in the groups as a random component. The results indicate that the binding method had a significant effect on mental demand ($F(2, 44.54) = 8.39$, $p = .001$), frustration ($F(2, 36.92) = 9.54$, $p < .001$), and overall preference ($F(2, 37.18) = 22.16$, $p < .001$). Pair-wise comparisons with Bonferroni correction show that the levels of mental demand ($p = .001$) and frustration ($p < .001$) for Seek were significantly higher compared to Ring, and that the level of overall preference was significantly higher for both Ring ($p < .001$) and Host is ($p < .001$) compared to Seek. There were no significant differences between Ring and Host on any of the subscales.

AttrakDiff

Fig. 6 illustrates the results of the AttrakDiff questionnaire [5] for the three group-binding methods. Pragmatic quality (PQ) refers to the product's ability to support the achievement of behavioral goals (usability). Hedonic quality refers to the users' self: stimulation (HQ-S) is the product's ability to stimulate and enable personal growth, while identification (HQ-I) is the product's ability to address the need of expressing one's self through objects one owns. Perceived attractiveness (ATT) describes a global value of the product based on the quality perception.

We analyzed the AttrakDiff data with the same methodology as the extended NASA-TLX data. The results

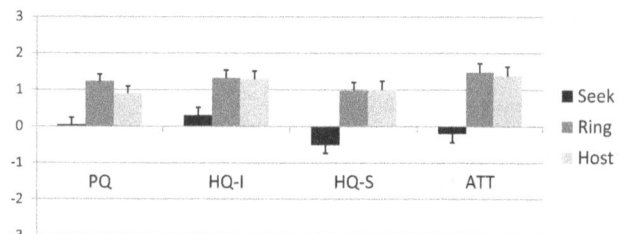

Figure 6. AttrakDiff results.

indicate that the binding method had a significant effect on all dimensions PQ ($F_{(2, 35.63)}$ = 15.74, p < .001), HQ-I ($F_{(2, 32.70)}$ = 60.37, p < .001), HQ-S ($F_{(2, 41.98)}$ = 52.66, p < .001), and ATT ($F_{(2, 31.52)}$ = 55.79, p < .001). Pairwise comparisons with Bonferroni correction show that the levels of PQ for Ring (p < .001) and Host (p = .002) were significantly higher compared to Seek, and that the levels of HQ-I, HQ-S, and ATT for both Ring and Host were significantly higher compared to Seek (all p < .001). There were no significant differences between Ring and Host on any of the dimensions.

Performance

Seek was the most reliable method with all group creation attempts succeeding without moderator assistance. With Ring, two of the six groups failed their initial attempts because several participants started the application simultaneously. With Host, two groups failed their initial attempts because of multiple participants starting the application and two groups because of incorrect touching order. After solving these initial difficulties, all groups were able to successfully create groups with all the methods.

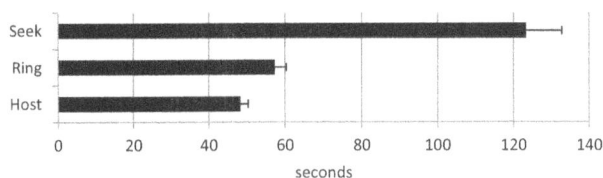

Figure 7. Completion times.

We measured the fastest completion time for the group creation task for each method in each of the sessions from the video recordings and device logs. The participants were instructed to create a group as they would in a real-life situation. If the participants clearly performed the group creation task in a non-optimal way, for example, encountered problems or started to explore different features, the moderator asked them to repeat the task until the process was completed smoothly. Fig. 7 illustrates the mean completion times, with the error bars showing the standard errors. The fastest method was Host, followed by Ring. Seek was clearly slower than the two touch-based methods. While the questionnaire results on perceived quickness show similar order, the distinctions are smaller with no statistically significant differences.

Attractiveness

Half of the participants (12/24) commented that Seek was old-fashioned and boring. *"[P23] Seek was so 90's, engineering style."* Further, many participants (10/24), especially the ones that were less technologically oriented, commented that Seek was far too technical for them. They felt that Seek had too many steps and it was too complicated to use. *"[P16] Seek is too technical. Predictable but not intuitive. Not fun to use."* Compared to Seek, the touch based methods, especially Ring, were

considered to be novel, intuitive, and simple to use. *"[P20] I think Ring is very stylish. It is new... I am not a very technical person, but Ring was simple to use and understand what was happening."*

These qualitative findings are supported by the quantitative results. In NASA-TLX (Fig. 5), Seek was rated significantly higher in mental effort and frustration compared to Ring. On the AttrakDiff questionnaire (Fig. 6), both Host and Ring were rated significantly more attractive (ATT) than Seek.

Acting as a Group

During the group creation task, the participants clearly acted together as a group instead of individuals. There was rich interaction between the participants, suggesting and agreeing the next actions and confirming the results. The participants were eager to help each other, if they noticed that some other participant was experiencing problems with the system. This contributed to the high success rate of the group creation tasks. The attention of the participants was divided between their own devices, and the devices and actions of the other participants. In touch-based methods, the touching actions were clearly visible to everybody, making it easier to follow the situation already before the participants' own devices joined the group and started to provide feedback about the system status. In Seek, the participants were forced to check the status by asking verbally or by peeking on the other users' screens.

Leader-Driven vs. Peer-Based Group Creation

One of the main differences between Ring and Host was that in Host, the group-binding process was driven by one person (the leader) who did most of the work, while in Ring, all participants contributed to the group-binding process as equal peers. This had several interesting effects.

Host provided the leader with control over who could join the group. Many participants (13/24) considered that this would be an important feature in some situations. *"[P20] If there were people [around] that I didn't know so well, like at my workplace, Host would be the best [method] because I could control with whom I share."* Some participants (5/24) suggested that the leader should also be able to force participants to leave the group. Further, Host allowed one person to create a group for everybody, so that the others did not have to do anything. Some participants (9/24) commented that it was good that only one person who was able to create a group was required, for example, if some of the participants were less technologically oriented than the others, or if some of the participants were not fully able to use their devices because of some situational factors (for example, because they had children sitting on their knees).

During the evaluation sessions, the participants were very polite towards each other in selecting the leader. However, as commented by one of the participants, selecting the leader might be more challenging in real-life situations, involving complex group dynamics and cultural factors. *"[P12] How can this guy be the leader, if [another person] is the senior? Or if the oldest guy is the leader, he might not know much about technology. Or with youngsters, if there is one who is the leader of the group, how does the group creation go?"* On the other hand, Host was considered as natural in situations where there was a clear leader, for example, in official meetings.

Almost half of the participants (11/24) felt that Ring brought people more together and helped to create a greater sense of community, because everybody was equally involved in creating the group and was forced to interact with the others by touching their devices. *"[P5] Ring makes a spiritual chain between participants. It makes you feel better."* Participants compared Ring to *"[P14] passing the torch"* or *"[P12] shaking hands"*, and commented that it helped to *"[P10] break the ice"* and *"[P9] take down the barriers."* Ring was considered to be particularly suitable for informal situations where there was no strict hierarchy, for example, when meeting a group of friends.

While Host worked well for small groups with all participants located near each other, most participants (16/24) commented that it would not work for larger groups because it would be tiring for the leader to touch a large number of devices, nor longer distances because the leader could not reach all other devices without moving around. Also other factors, for example, having dinnerware on the table, might make it difficult for the leader to touch the other devices. Some participants (10/24) commented that Ring would scale better to larger groups and distances. One participant contrasted the difference between Host and Ring with distributing handouts in meetings. *"[P6] In large meetings, there is no time to give handouts to everybody one at a time. You circulate them."* On the other hand, in a large scattered group, it might be difficult to know who is the last person and should complete the group.

Touching

In Ring and Host, identification of the devices intended to participate in the group was based on touching. Almost half of the participants (11/24) commented that touching was an easy and intuitive way to add participants to the group. *"[P19] Touching to join was a clear, physical, easy, natural way to bring someone into the group."* On the other hand, some participants (9/24) commented that touching could be socially awkward, for example, in formal situations, and brought about privacy issues. *"[P13] Touching is the same as using the other person's phone myself."* In the case of group creation, however, there was a clear reason to touch the other person's phone, so it did not feel like an invasion of privacy. Many participants (10/24) spontaneously pushed their devices forward when another user approached to touch it. This might simply have been a polite gesture to make it easier for the other participant to reach the device, but it could also have indicated giving a permission to touch one's personal device. Finally, some

participants (6/24) stressed that to be useful, touching should be detected fast and work very reliably.

Other Gestures

In addition to touching, Host also used gestures for two other purposes. The first gesture allowed the participants to leave the group by flipping their devices upside down. Most participants (19/24) flipped their devices by putting them upside down on the table – only a few flipped their devices in their hands. Some participants (8/24) commented that flipping was a novel, simple, and entertaining way to leave the group. On the other hand, some participants (9/24) raised concerns that it was difficult to know and remember the gesture and it was easy to do it accidentally.

The second gesture enabled the participants to move between Photo Sharing and Discovery Modes by putting their devices on the table and picking them up. Half of the participants (12/24) commented that they did not like this feature because holding the device in their hands was the natural way to use the device and allowed them to control the privacy and viewing angle of their screens and because there might not always be a table available to put the device on. *"[P21] Keeping the device on the table is not something I usually do. I usually hold the device in my hand."*

Ordering

In order to allow throwing of photos between devices, the participants had to define the order of the devices on the table. In Seek, this was done manually by the leader, while in Ring and Host, the participants were expected to touch the devices in counter-clockwise order and the order of the devices was automatically determined based on the touching order. Almost all participants (20/24) considered the requirement to touch the devices in a specific order too restrictive, difficult to remember, and unforgiving to errors. *"[P17] I did not like that you had to go in [counter-]clockwise order. Why not the other way? It should work both ways. It is difficult to remember and learn."* Instead, the participants liked the flexibility and robustness that the manual reordering provided to them. *"[P12] Being able to easily change the order would be the number one feature for me."* The participants pointed out several cases, where manual reordering would be beneficial, for example, if there was a human or technical error in the initial group creation phase, or if the participants moved or changed places. Almost half of the participants (11/24) considered the colored dots, which identified the devices on the screen inadequate, and proposed that textual names should be used in addition to the color.

Perceived Security

In Seek, security was based on six-digit authentication strings that were automatically generated by the system. The participants who wanted to join the group had to manually copy and enter the authentication string into their devices. The participants considered the authentication strings as passwords that they were familiar with in other systems. The dominant way of sharing the password was that the leader read the password aloud. Typically, the password had to be repeated many times as not all the participants were ready to enter it at the same time, or some of the participants missed parts of it. In only one of the six sessions, the participants shared the password by putting the device of the leader at the center of the table, so that everybody could read the password from the screen. However, also in this case some of the participants sitting further away from the leader had difficulties in obtaining the password because they could not clearly see the screen. Most participants (14/24) considered the passwords awkward and would have preferred some other security mechanism. *"[P18] If you need that security level, there must be a better way than [passwords]."* Some participants proposed improvements to the passwords used, for example, making the passwords shorter, using common words, or allowing the participants to define the passwords. Half of the participants (12/24) considered sharing the password verbally as a security risk as anybody in the proximity could hear it. In that sense, the passwords were thought to provide a false sense of security. *"[P14] Password is a complication without any security element."*

In Seek and Ring, security was based on physical proximity enforced by the short range of the touch detection technology. Compared to passwords, which were familiar to all, this was a new concept to the participants. Most participants (13/24) considered that touching provided adequate security for scenarios like sharing photos, provided that the detection technology works reliably and the range is not too long. *"[P22] If phones have to touch, it is quite safe. If somebody I don't know comes so close, I would be alert anyway."* This finding is also supported by the extended NASA-TLX results, which indicate no significant differences in perceived security between Seek and the touch-based methods. Still, some participants (8/24) raised concerns over unauthorized persons accessing their devices by touching, for example, when they had their devices in their pockets in a crowded bar or in a queue.

DISCUSSION

Seek vs. Touch-Based Methods
Both quantitative and qualitative results of the user evaluation show that touch-based methods provide a promising alternative to dominant scanning and password based group-binding methods. While Seek was familiar and reliable in practice, it was considered to be technical, complicated, old-fashioned, and boring. Overall, the participants clearly preferred the touch-based methods and considered them to be simple and intuitive as well as novel and enjoyable to use. The touch-based methods were also faster and they allowed the participants to better maintain awareness of the status of the group formation task as the touching actions could easily be perceived by everybody. Regarding security, touching was considered to be equally

secure to passwords. However, to work well in practice, touch detection should be fast and it should work reliably only within the defined distance.

Leader-Driven vs. Peer-Based Methods
The group-binding task can be divided in different ways between the participants. The study results show that different approaches have different strengths and weaknesses. The leader-driven methods, which concentrate the task on a single participant, enable the leader to have strong control over the group and require only one person who is able to create a group. On the other hand, selecting the leader may add more complexity to the group creation process. The peer-based methods, which distribute the work between all participants, help to create a stronger sense of community and scale better to larger numbers of participants and distances. The study results indicate that there is no single optimal method, but the best method depends on the application, social situation, and physical environment. Therefore, the group-binding methods should not strongly enforce a single group creation procedure, but allow for flexibility, so that the participants could adapt the method to the particular needs of each situation.

Device Ordering
The group-binding methods also allowed the determination of the device order using two different approaches: arranging the devices manually or defining the order by touching. The study results indicate that the participants found the requirement to touch the devices in a specific order too restrictive and preferred to touch the devices in a free order and then arrange the devices manually. Again, the optimal touching order depends on social and environmental factors and the group-binding methods should allow the participants to adapt the touching order to each situation. Also, flexible touching order allows the participants to better recover from human and technical errors that may occur during group creation. A well-defined relationship between the touching order and the initial positions of the participants might still be useful for advanced users who want to optimize the group creation process for efficiency.

Supporting Self-Expression and Playfulness
We observed an overall positive mood where participants collaborated and helped each other during group creation. On top of that, we also noticed participants were often laughing, making jokes by creating funny group names, celebrating their collective successes by cheering when they had successfully created a group, and describing the touch-based methods as *"[P8] this is like some Enterprise stuff from Star Trek."* These situations bring to our attention that we are not purely dealing with connecting devices together, but that people are looking for an overall experience that allows them to express themselves and be playful. Therefore, the group-binding methods should look beyond the purely functional task of connecting devices and sharing

information, and aim to also engage users on other aspects such as supporting self-expression and playfulness.

CONCLUSION

We have presented a comparative evaluation of two touch-based group-binding methods, a leader-driven method called Host and a peer-based method called Ring, against a more conventional method called Seek, which was based on scanning the available devices in the proximity and passwords for security. The results indicate that the participants strongly preferred the touch-based methods in both pragmatic and hedonic qualities as well as in overall attractiveness. In terms of perceived security, touching was considered equally secure to passwords. While Host allowed better control over the group and required only one participant to be able to form a group, Ring helped to create a greater sense of community and scaled better for larger group sizes and distances. As the optimal group-binding method depends on the social and physical environment, the binding methods should be flexible, allowing the users to adapt them to different contexts of use. For determining the order of the devices, manual arrangement was preferred over defining the order by touching.

ACKNOWLEDGMENTS

We would like to thank Juha Riippi, Iiro Vidberg, Arttu Pulli, Markus Rinne, and Mikko Tolonen for implementing the software prototypes. We would also like to thank Johan Kildal for helping with NASA-TLX, and Susan Fussell for helping with the statistical analysis.

REFERENCES

1. Ayatsuka, Y. and Rekimoto, J. tranSticks: physically manipulatable virtual connections. In *Proc. CHI '05*, 251-260.

2. Chong, M. and Gellersen, H. How users associate wireless devices. In *Proc. CHI '11*, 1909-1918.

3. Chong, M. and Gellersen, H. Usability classification for spontaneous device association. *Personal and Ubiquitous Computing*, published online (2011).

4. Hart, S. G. and Staveland, L. E. Development of NASA-TLX (Task Load Index): Results of empirical and theoretical research. In Hancock and Meshkati (eds.) *Human Mental Workload*, North Holland Press, 1988.

5. Hassenzahl, M. The Interplay of Beauty, Goodness, and Usability in Interactive Products. *Human-Computer Interaction* 19, 4 (2004), 319-349.

6. Hinckley, K. Synchronous gestures for multiple persons and computers. In *Proc. UIST '03*, 149-158.

7. Hinckley, K., Ramos, G., Guimbretiere, F., Baudisch, P. and Smith, M. Stitching: pen gestures that span multiple displays. In *Proc. AVI '04*, 23-31

8. Holmquist, L.E., Mattern, F., Schiele, B., Alahuhta, P., Beigl, M. and Gellersen, H. Smart-Its friends: a technique for users to easily establish connections between smart artefacts. In *Proc. UbiComp '01*, 116-122

9. Holtzblatt, K., Wendell, J. B. and Wood, S. *Rapid Contextual Design*. Morgan Kaufmann, 2004.

10. Ion, I., Langheinrich, M., Kumaraguru, P. and Čapkun, S. Influence of user perception, security needs, and social factors on device pairing method choices. In *Proc. SOUPS '10*.

11. Kainda, R., Flechais, I. and Roscoe, A. Two heads are better than one: security and usability of device associations in group scenarios. In *Proc. SOUPS '10*.

12. Kray, C., Rohs, M., Hook, J. and Kratz, S. Group coordination and negotiation through spatial proximity regions around mobile devices on augmented tabletops. In *Proc. TABLETOP 2008*, 1-8.

13. Lucero, A., Holopainen, J. and Jokela, T. Pass-Them-Around: collaborative use of mobile phones for photo sharing. In *Proc. CHI '11*, 1787-1796.

14. Lucero, A., Jokela, T., Palin, A., Aaltonen, V. and Nikara, J. EasyGroups: binding mobile devices for collaborative interactions. In *CHI EA '12*, 2189-2194.

15. Mayrhofer, R. and Welch, M. A human-verifiable authentication protocol using visible laser light. In *Proc. ARES '07*, 1143-1148.

16. McCune, J.M., Perrig, A. and Reiter, M.K. Seeing-is-believing: using camera phones for human-verifiable authentication. In *Proc. SOUPS '05*, 110-124.

17. Nithyanand, R., Saxena, N., Tsudik, G. and Uzun, E. Groupthink: usability of secure group association for wireless devices. In *Proc. Ubicomp '10*, 331-340.

18. Rashid, U. and Quigley, A. Interaction techniques for binding smartphones: a desirability evaluation. In *Proc. HCD '09*, 120-128.

19. Rekimoto, J. SyncTap: synchronous user operation for spontaneous network connection. *Personal and Ubiquitous Computing* 8, 2 (2004), 126-134.

20. Rekimoto, J., Ayatsuka, Y., Kohno, M. and Oba, H. Proximal interactions: a direct manipulation technique for wireless networking. In *Proc. INTERACT '03*, 511-518.

21. Terrenghi, L., Quigley, A. and Dix, A. A taxonomy for and analysis of multi-person-display ecosystems. *Personal and Ubiquitous Computing* 13, 8 (2009), 583-598.

22. Uzun, E., Saxena, N. and Kumar, A. Pairing devices for social interactions: a comparative usability evaluation. In *Proc. CHI '11*, 2315-2324.

23. Zimmerman, T. G. Personal area networks: near-field intrabody communication. IBM Systems Journal 35, 3-4 (1996), 609-617.

The Design Space of Body Games: Technological, Physical, and Social Design

Elena Márquez Segura[*], **Annika Waern**[**], **Jin Moen**[***], **Carolina Johansson**[*]

[*]Mobile Life @ SICS Swedish ICT AB
Kista, Sweden
elena@mobilelifecentre.org,
carolina.v.b.johansson@gmail.com

[**]Mobile Life @ Stockholm
University
Kista, Sweden
annikaw@dsv.su.se

[***]Movinto Fun
Åre, Sweden
jin.moen@movintofun.com

ABSTRACT

The past decade has seen an increased focus on body movement in computer games. We take a step further to look at *body games*: games in which the main source of enjoyment comes from bodily engagement. We argue that for these games, the physical and social settings become just as important design resources as the technology. Although all body games benefit from an integrated design approach, the social and physical setting become particularly useful as design resources when the technology has limited sensing capabilities. We develop our understanding of body games through a literature study and a concrete design experiment with designing multiplayer games for the BodyBug, a mobile device with limited sensing capabilities. Although the device was designed for free and natural movements, previous games fell short in realizing this design ideal. By designing the technology function together with its physical and social context, we were able to overcome some of the device limitations. One of the games was subsequently incorporated in its commercial release.

Author Keywords

Body Game; Exertion Game; Gesture; Movement; Design; Sensing; Game; Dance; Children; Play; Interactive Toy; BodyBug; Oriboo; Social Play.

ACM Classification Keywords

H.5.m. Information interfaces and presentation (e.g., HCI): Miscellaneous.

General Terms

Design, Human Factors, Measurement.

INTRODUCTION

There exists a long tradition of games that tap into the players' social and movement experience as their main source of enjoyment. Such games predate the computer game, including many traditional children's games and games from the New Games movement [10]. Common for

such games is that they encourage their players to move in strange, fun, and often almost silly ways.

Although the traditional computer game bears little resemblance to such games, the introduction of movement-based interaction has led to a renewed interest in the social and corporeal experience of play. Many researchers have argued that movement brings about a positive emotional and social response [5, 27, 16]. Developers have striven for an interaction model that is more direct and 'natural', e.g. the Kinect platform is marketed with slogans such as: "*You are the controller*", or "*Technology evaporates, letting the natural magic in all of us shine*" [22]. Paradoxically, to make technology "evaporate", movement-based games need elaborate technology solutions. Commercial games in this genre rely on powerful sensing mechanisms and complex calculations embedded in the game platform.

We see two problems with this approach. First, the technology is in many cases not ready for this responsibility. This happens even with high-tech platforms. To continue using the Kinect as our example, the renowned game developer Peter Molyneux has reported on appreciating the sense of freedom the platform is able to create while at the same time struggling with its technical limitations [36]. This problem is even more severe for platforms that do not use the traditional videogame setup with a stationary device and a TV screen. For mobile devices, the opportunities for precise sensing and visual feedback are severely reduced, since the small size of these devices constrains both hardware and software.

Second, striving for precise sensing also leads to the technology controlling the users' body. Below, we will review literature to show that too precise control may hamper enjoyment, as the social environment and corporeal experience lie at the core of the experience in body games.

We argue that many movement-based games are better seen as *body games*: games in which the body is brought to focus and becomes the main source of enjoyment. This may very well include both digital games with movement-based interaction, like exertion games, and non digital games and activities, such as games like 'Twister', or sports. Taking inspiration from traditional games, we propose to look at the physical and social setting of the game as important design resources complementing the technology.

Our goal is to develop a design approach where all three factors are considered in the design of the game in a systematic manner.

Similar ideas have been proposed for exertion games, as in Mueller *et al.*'s [33]. However, we want to emphasize the importance of the body over the exertion experience, which typically focuses more on the physical effort and precise performance.

To us, three questions surface as critical. The first concerns the physical design of the game, including the role of technology as a physical artefact. The second concerns the distribution of control over the game, between players and technology so that some functions remain stable whereas others can be subject to social agreement among the players. Finally, it is important to understand how an integrated design approach can serve to alleviate sensing limitations of a device.

BACKGROUND

Movement-based interaction in games has received increased attention both commercially and in research. We have witnessed successful commercial examples such as the exertion games developed for the Nintendo Wii, the Sony Eye-toy games, the Konami Dance Dance Revolution [23], and the Dance Central for Kinect [7]. Many of these games seem to share a premise of "*the more the user moves, the better*" - as can be seen in commercial campaigns of some of these exertion games [47].

All these games rely on a powerful sensing platform that supports the whole game. The manufacturers compete to deliver the latest, most precise, and most sophisticated movement recognition system. The technology used in these exertion games has rapidly developed from the early pressure reactive mat in Dance Dance Revolution and the web camera used in the Eyetoy, to the sophisticated infrared camera based Kinect [22], the Sony Playstation Move [37] or the Wii nunchuk accessory [47].

Commercial products have been subject to numerous studies, many of them leveraging the connection between movement and positive socio-emotional responses, such as increased arousal [16], energy level [17], social interaction [27, 16], and increased engagement [27, 5]. In parallel with the studies of commercial games, many researchers have also developed games for research purposes. A major research area has been health and exertion games [24, 13, 41, 32].

Isbister *et al.* [17] compared a range of Nintendo Wii games that require low, medium, or high intensity movements from the players, and showed that there is indeed a significant relationship between how much you move and the level of energy and engagement reported by the players. In terms of engagement, Bianchi-Berthouze *et al.* concluded that an increase in body movement resulted in an increase in the player's engagement level [5].

Bianchi-Berthouze *et al.* argued that the kind of engagement that increases with movement is related to Lazzaro's concept of 'easy fun', where intrigue and curiosity are at focus rather than winning, in contrast with 'hard fun' games (when challenge, strategy, and problem solving are at focus) [25]. They noticed that a strong focus on achievement was correlated with a decrease in body movements, and intervened with the emotional and social experience [5].

Many authors have also emphasized the co-located social aspects of motion-controlled games, highlighting how the physical performative aspects of these games help to create a playful social context [14, 46, 39].

Gestural excess

One concept that is particularly important for our approach is *gestural excess*. The term was coined by Bart Simon in his studies of exertion games with the Wii [42]. He observes that for many players, the fun lies in moving the body and performing funny or silly gestures in front of other players, quite independently of what can be sensed. The gestures performed by the users are excessive, compared to what can be recognized by the game software. For this to happen it is important that the sensing technology is not too precise and leaves some room for improvisation.

In the Wii games that Simon studied, the game design does not reward the gestural excess. In fact, challenge focused players may short cut and perform small movements by flicking a wrist, rather than large expressive movements. By contrast, the research prototype game 'Wriggle' [16] was designed to stimulate corporeal emotions and social play, rather than to achieve precise scoring. The designers found higher emotional arousal when the game allowed for free movement.

Co-Located Social Games

The other aspect of body games that we wish to highlight is that they are also predominantly *co-located social* games. As pinpointed by Voida and Greenberg [46], a major motivation for group console gaming is the social interaction that affords co-located play. De Kort [8] argues that multiplayer games are as much about social interaction as about interaction with the software. Everything, from spatial organization, to co-players, audience, and the game content, shape the player experience. Ravaja [38] argues that social play leads to similar effects as physical play, such as higher engagement, arousal, and positive emotions.

Jakobs *et al.* argue that co-location is not the only element that explains how the social context affects the gameplay experience and performance [19]. De Kort [8] has analyzed this further, highlighting the socially secluded character of traditional computer games, result of the social affordances of the game interface and the spatial characteristics of the player's physical environment. In essence, most co-located digital gaming takes place in playing, seating, and viewing arrangements that hinder mechanisms such as mutual eye contact, natural reciprocation of approach or avoidance cues and mirroring, or emotionally relevant communication signals.

Technology-Supported Body Games

As discussed in the introduction, body games have a long-standing tradition that predates computer technology. Many interactive body games retain something of this non-technological nature, and are for this reason *technology-supported* [48] rather than fully implemented computer games. In this section we will focus on games that either use physical space as a design resource, or games that have deliberately incomplete or open-ended implementations.

Designing space around technology

One category of games that use physical space as a design resource are those designed to be played in a physical space with certain properties. For example, the game 'Weather Gods and Fruit Kids' [20] was is played in a gym hall and uses multiple means of feedback, including both staged sound and light sources. The game was based on Wii technology, but abandoned screen based interaction in favor of social interaction. When it comes to dance games, 'Yamove' [15] is a particularly interesting design experiment. It is based on a critique of the interaction patterns [11] that most commercial dance games use, which are very different from the interaction patterns that happen when dancing in a club. A particular effort was spent on taking players away from screen-based interaction. The spatial design of 'Yamove' is complex and includes the dance space itself as well as a distribution of roles among a mesh-up of people and devices. The game is played with mobile phones and can include a 'master of ceremony', a DJ, a dance model, players.

There also exist technology-sustained approaches to games and play spaces. A very elaborate example is presented in [40]. In this project, a wiimote device is connected to a multiwall virtual theatre and connected to multiple (rather than the normal singular) sensor bars, creating a landscape where the player can interact with the room in any direction and not just towards a single screen. The difference is that while 'Yamove' and 'Weather Gods and Fruit Kids' leave the control of the game setup to the players, the interactive theatre captures and reacts on how the players move in space, and can implement rules concerning spatial movement. Following Bianchi-Berthouze *et al.* [5], this is likely to be more appropriate for skill-based games than for social games, and may thus lead to less engagement in the social and corporeal experience of play.

Incomplete and open-ended rules

There have also been several direct attempts to create games or gaming platforms inspired by traditional body games. A common feature of these games is that the games are not fully implemented, leaving some of the instructions and rules for players to decide.

The explorations by Bekker *et al.* [2] are illuminating. The goal for them was to design games that had no overarching goals, in order to stimulate children to be creative in constructing their own goals, and stimulate social interaction in the form of rule negotiation. One example is the game device 'LEDtube' and its successor 'ColorFlare'[2]. Both of them are cylinders that emit light at each end and that react to movement by changing the color and behavior of the light. Bekker *et al.* tested the former in two different settings: with given rules, and in an open-ended play exploration, and saw that the children tended to prefer open-ended sessions. She also saw several examples of social negotiations concerning the creation of rules and goals, as well as whether the goals had been fulfilled.

Bekker's approach is related to Gaver's concept of self-effacing play [12]:

"This is an engagement that has no fixed path or end, but instead involves a wide-ranging conversation with the circumstances and situations that give it rise. Rules may emerge and goals may be sought, but these will be provisional inventions, makeshift tools to help the advance of curiosity and exploration"

Bekker's work shows that children can – and do - create their own rules and goals. Bekker *et al.* also highlighted that it is not only the functionalities and interactional behavior of the device but also its *shape* that influences the play activity and the invented games.

It is also possible to provide complete rules for a game, but leave some of them out of the implementation. The art game 'B.U.T.T.O.N' (Brutally Unfair Tactics Totally O.K. Now) [49] is a particularly interesting example of this. This game has one single game goal: players compete for being the first player to press a button on a controller according to some rules shown on a screen. 'B.U.T.T.O.N' does not in any way sense if people actually follow those rules - that is entirely left to social control between the players. Drawing upon DeKoven [9], Wilson points out that rules are *"made for the convenience of those who are playing. What is fair at one time or in one game may be inhibiting later on"* [49]. In leaving some of the rules over to social negotiation, games like 'B.U.T.T.O.N.' are focused on being fun to play, rather than important to win.

While 'ColorFlare' is an open play device leaving the game to be defined by its players, 'B.U.T.T.O.N' is a fully defined but *broken* game. By constraining the players to rules that cannot be controlled, it deliberately encourages them to cheat to one another and the game platform. The name itself illustrates this, and this together with the playful artwork of the game design creates a festive context for the play activity in which, essentially, anything goes.

TAKING PHYSICAL AND SOCIAL DESIGN INTO ACCOUNT

From the discussion above, we can see that many design projects have relied not only on the technology, but also on a spatial layout or other physical properties of the setting, or have varied the level of social control that players exert over the game. We take one step further to explicitly include these as *design resources* for body games. Our goal is to develop a design approach in which all three factors, the technology, the physical properties, and the social setting, are systematically included in the design of body games.

We illustrate our approach with a concrete design exploration of the BodyBug, a device with limited sensing capabilities. Our goal was to design multiplayer games for the device; a challenging goal given its limitations. The setting serves to illustrate the design possibilities of placing greater focus on physical and social factors in body game design.

UNDERSTANDING THE TECHNOLOGY

In any project dealing with a limited device, it is important to first understand the technology, its capabilities and limitations. The BodyBug, now commercially launched as Oriboo [34], is intended to be a tool for exploring movement and dance, devised by Jin Moen. She described it as *"an artefact that initiates and maintains bodily movements through its need to be fed with movement input"*, and that would give *"the user the possibility to create and explore 3D movements within a personal interaction space, both individually and in groups"* [30]. The design focus was therefore put on the use of natural movements and the personal space.

Physically, the BodyBug is a sphere slightly larger than a tennis ball, made of hard plastic. The sphere is assembled on a plastic leash, along which the sphere can move by means of a built-in motor (see Figure 1). It takes input from a small touch screen on its 'back' side and built-in sensors (like a 3-axis accelerometer), and it presents the output in the form of sound, light (two 'eyes' composed of 6 LED each), and the touch screen. Finally, it can move along the leash (see more technical information in [29]).

The physical design of the BodyBug was already the result of a user-centered design process [30, 31]. The goals were to support mobility, ease of use, and openness for appropriation. For example, the leash can be held in different ways, each introducing different constraints to body movement. The output methods of sound, light, and the BodyBug's own movement on the leash were intended to support 'head up' interaction [43]: while playing with the BodyBug, players should be free to look at and interact with each other.

However, the technical limitations of the BodyBug were quite relevant, as we will discuss below. At the time when this project was carried out, the only movement sensor in

Figure 1. The BodyBug; front and back.

the device was a 3-axis accelerometer[1], and although its hardware included an antenna for wireless communication, it was not functional at the time. All implemented functionalities therefore targeted single users. The purpose of our project was to develop multiplayer games, since wireless communication was potentially going to be included in the next version of the platform.

First step: Analysis of the situation at hand

Our first goal was to understand how the already existing BodyBug games worked in practice. At the time, there was only one dance game implemented for the device, the game 'Dance It'. This is a single-player game in which the BodyBug instructs the player to perform movements from a repertoire of eight different movements[2]. The dancer/player is given a limited time for performing each of them, indicated by beep sounds. If the movement is done correctly, the player scores and the game continues; if the movement is done incorrectly (or the BodyBug fails to recognize it), the game ends and a result score is displayed on the BodyBug's screen.

The game 'Dance It' has been studied by Tholander and Johansson [44, 45]. They reported two major issues with its interaction model: Firstly, participants were found to keep their visual focus mostly directed at the BodyBug.

The use of visual cues for instructions and feedback made the players keep their eyes on the display, losing contact with the physical and social environment of the play activity. This 'artefact-focused' mode of interaction [44, 45] goes against the design ideals of the BodyBug (free and natural movements, space around the player, etc. [30]). Another issue with the game laid in the way the movement recognition interfered with the players' dance activity. In order for a movement to be registered as correct, it needed to be performed in a 'clean' way. Hence, the players felt forced to stay still and just move in a constraint way.

---

[1] The commercial BodyBug, the Oriboo, also includes a gyroscope.

[2] Tug up/down, sideways, forwards, spin, twist, jump [29].

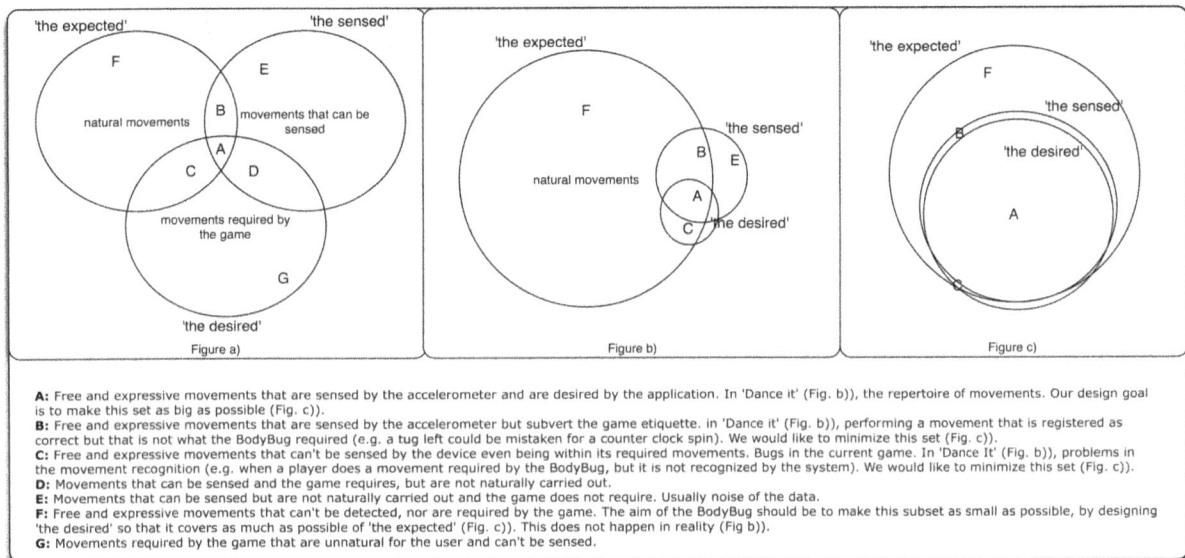

A: Free and expressive movements that are sensed by the accelerometer and are desired by the application. In 'Dance it' (Fig. b)), the repertoire of movements. Our design goal is to make this set as big as possible (Fig. c)).
B: Free and expressive movements that are sensed by the accelerometer but subvert the game etiquette. in 'Dance it' (Fig. b)), performing a movement that is registered as correct but that is not what the BodyBug required (e.g. a tug left could be mistaken for a counter clock spin). We would like to minimize this set (Fig. c)).
C: Free and expressive movements that can't be sensed by the device even being within its required movements. Bugs in the current game. In 'Dance It' (Fig. b)), problems in the movement recognition (e.g. when a player does a movement required by the BodyBug, but it is not recognized by the system). We would like to minimize this set (Fig. c)).
D: Movements that can be sensed and the game requires, but are not naturally carried out.
E: Movements that can be sensed but are not naturally carried out and the game does not require. Usually noise of the data.
F: Free and expressive movements that can't be detected, nor are required by the game. The aim of the BodyBug should be to make this subset as small as possible, by designing 'the desired' so that it covers as much as possible of 'the expected' (Fig. c)). This does not happen in reality (Fig b)).
G: Movements required by the game that are unnatural for the user and can't be sensed.

Figure 2: a) The expected, sensed and desired by Benford, b) applied to the game 'Dance It', and c) our design goal

Analyzing 'Dance It' from a movement perspective
Benford *et al.* [3] have developed an analytic model of user movement in relation to a moveable, physical or mobile system (Figure 2a). They distinguished between what is

i) *'expected'* (movements independent of any specific application, naturally performed by the users), ii) *'sensed'* (movements that can be measured by the system, due to the available sensing technologies), and iii) *'desired'* (movements required by a given application). These three categories do not necessarily overlap [28], leading to potential problems in the interaction.

As an interaction concept, the BodyBug aims to encourage the user's natural and free movements, i.e. 'the expected' [29] (see Figure 2). Hence, 'the desired' or the movements allowed by the game 'Dance It' should have been intended to circumscribe 'the expected'. However, the technical limitations of the device constrained the game design and in 'Dance It' only a set of several simple movements are allowed, i.e. within 'the desired'. Moreover, even those movements are not properly identified and classified by the BodyBug. This happens in cases in which those movements are not performed 'clean'. The 'Dance It' game also presents an ample opportunity for cheating (subset B in Figure 2) through performing a simpler movement than required that is registered as correct (e.g. a counter-clockwise spin, for instance, is easily mistaken for a 'tug up' movement [29]).

To summarise, it is both the interaction design of the 'Dance It' game and the computational capabilities of the BodyBug that makes 'Dance It' appear as a rather stale and private game, compared to other body games such as 'Twister' or 'B.U.T.T.O.N.'.

With our game designs, we aim to extend the movements that the BodyBug allows, i.e. 'the desired' so that to embrace as much as 'the expected' or the user's natural movements as possible (see Figure 2c). We also aim to avoid artefact-focused interaction as much as possible.

CORE DESIGN PRINCIPLES

Social Control
Our first decision was to design technology-supported rather than technology-sustained games [48]: Instead of implementing a game maintained and supported by the BodyBug in all its facets, from control over the outcome to feedback and monitoring of the rules, we aimed to design games in which the BodyBug was responsible for just a few of these tasks. By doing so, we expected both to expand 'the desired' beyond the limitations of the BodyBug capabilities ('the sensed'), and address the artefact-focused interaction issue.

It should be noted that the game 'Dance It' to some extent already affords this. When we let children try that game during our project, they would frequently take turns in using the device to see who could score the highest. In this usage of the game, children expanded the game from a single player to a multiplayer competitive game through the social agreement of maintaining a high-score list.

A question we deliberately left open was to what extent the games would be goal-oriented or self-effacing. As illustrated by the comparison between 'ColorFlare' and 'B.U.T.T.O.N', both approaches are possible and can lead to games that are open for appropriation and social control. In both cases, we wanted to design 'head up' games, and we would do so by designing roles maintained outside the technology. A related issue was if win conditions could be judged by players rather than the BodyBug, as this would help in extending 'the desired'.

Physical design

It became a goal of its own for us to not use any visual display. The goal was driven by a desire to move players' focus away from the tiny screen, avoiding the artefact-focused interaction from 'Dance It' [44, 45].

We hypothesized that this issue could be mitigated by a technology-supported approach to game design. If players were made responsible for maintaining parts of the game, the attention of players would at least need to shift between the players and the device. Also, our designs emphasized *social mirroring* [21] –when your actions are mirrored in what other players do. In this sense, our example games were still heavily dependent on visual information, but from what surrounds the player rather than from screens. For device output, we focused on the use of sound.

BODYSTORMING BODY GAMES

The first step in our process was to explore the design space provided by the physical features of the game setup and the affordances of the BodyBug. For this purpose, we selected to use bodystorming [35]. However, rather than just bodystorm ways of playing with the BodyBug, we designed a set of games (both goal-oriented and self-effacing) that utilized the social and physical setting as well as the device, and played them out with children in a workshop. The participants were instructed to play as if the device was functioning in a specific way, or to play a game with and without the BodyBug. Throughout the bodystorming workshop, the device itself was turned off.

The games we designed for this purpose were inspired by traditional body games for children (mainly outdoor games), as well as by 'Heads Up Games'[43] in our desire to keep the players' focus away from the device. In taking inspiration from children's games, the games became similar to games from the New Games movement [10], in that the rules were open for interpretation and negotiation within the group.

One example of the games we used was 'The Mirror'. The children were paired up facing each other. One was told to play as 'the leader' coming up with movements; the other one played as the 'follower', mimicking the former. This game was very open in that there was no real 'winning' condition and we did not tell the children what the BodyBug would measure. We played this game in multiple versions: with and without the BodyBug, music, and beeps for timing. Our aim was to understand how these elements helped in shaping the activity.

Another example game was 'The Bomb'. In this game, the players were placed in a big circle and were told to pass an imaginary bomb to each other. To pace the game, we used contextual beep sound; a beep that increased in frequency over time, ending in an explosion. In this game, each child was holding a BodyBug and was told that the device would eventually keep track of who was holding the bomb. The aim was to explore whether a sound cue would be enough

to trigger the children's imagination and create, as suggested by [26], an immersive game experience. Part of the enjoyment of this game came from the use of contextual sound cues simulating a bomb about to explode.

The bodystorming workshop took place in a dance school and was carried out with 20 children aged 8 – 14. The age range reflects the target audience for the BodyBug. We included both games that focused on fun and playful activities reported to be enjoyed by children aged 8-12 [1], as well as games that opened up for personal performance and expression that the older were expected to enjoy [4].

Capturing data for analysis of physical aspects is a challenge. We used two cameras, and placed them in roughly 90 degrees angle from each other. Furthermore, we made good use of the fact that one wall had a big mirror: altogether, we created a recording where the events in the room could be seen from four directions. The videos were analyzed exhaustively to the level of physical description of the movements of singular players in relation to the physical planes in which they were performed, as well as in relation to the unfolding activity in the group.

Observations

We saw that some movements transcended the local space where they were performed. For example, in 'The Mirror' the children looked every now and then at other pairs and acknowledged their performance, sometimes mimicking particularly cool movements. Movements are contagious in much the same way as emotions are in social play [18].

Another important observation was the difference in proprioceptive skills between children in different age groups. We realized that the youngest children were unable to fully mirror each other's movements. For example, a movement of the shoulders up and down could be mimicked as a forwards/backwards movement by 'the follower'. This information became important in designing 'the desired' set of movement for our games. The observation made us discard game designs in which there was a fixed set of 'desired' movement to be measured by the BodyBug. (At the very least, we would not go beyond what was already present in 'Dance It'.)

Players would both collaborate and compete. There was a lot of cooperation in 'The Mirror' to cope with the fast-paced beats of the game. For example, 'the leader' would repeat sequences of movements, or the players would take turns in controlling the game. In 'The Bomb' we saw a child enjoying taking control over the game, playing strategically and holding 'the bomb' until the very end to make it explode on a girl. She revenged passing the bomb back to him, whom eventually tried passing it to someone else in the group. However, the whole group seemed to agree on 'punishing' him and passed the bomb back until eventually it exploded. This all brought excitement and enjoyment.

Regarding the use of the BodyBug, we could confirm that a core strength of the device is the way its physical design interacts with the users' body movements, in that it both constrains movement and encourages the user to explore movements that are slightly out of the ordinary. For instance, 'the leaders' in 'The Mirror' were seen to include new movements to their repertoire, and also extend their use of the surrounding space around them (their kinaesthetic sphere) when using the BodyBug, compared to when performing without the device. This in turn influenced 'the followers', who also incorporated those movements into their 'repertoire'. When taking over as 'leaders', they would often continue using them.

The BodyBug was also useful for the players in that it provided them with an excuse to perform 'embarrassing' movements, allowing them to not dance 'well' (this was a dance school after all), and to explore new movements. Finally, the device would trigger the players' imagination (they used it as if it was a bomb, and it also became a jumping rope or a lasso in 'The Mirror').

EXPLORING THE ROLE OF TECHNOLOGY
Next, we turned to the question of how to distribute the tasks/responsibilities within the games among players and technology. To get adequate feedback on this issue from participants, we needed to give them a good understanding of the function of the technology. Hence, in these tests we placed an increased focus on simulating what the technology would actually do.

Fullerton [11] highlights the usefulness of playtesting to test whether the player experience goals are achieved and to refine a model of the game before "*a single programmer, producer, or graphic artist is ever brought to the project*" [11]. In keeping with this, the games used in this test were designed to be *implementable* on the next version of the BodyBug (which would feature wireless communication). One of the games (that did not require wireless communication) was fully implemented. For the rest of the games we used a combination of implemented functions in the BodyBug, and Wizard of Oz techniques [6] to simulate the functionalities that relied on wireless communication.

Three game designs were put to test: 'Make My Sound', 'The Blind Mirror', and 'Join My Move'. From the bodystorming session, the mirroring element transcended and was reflected in different degrees in all three games. From 'The Bomb', we maintained the configuration of placing the players in a circle for most of the new games. The distribution of responsibilities between players and technology was however varied over the games.

The game 'Join My Move' is an extension of the game 'Dance It' into multiplayer mode. In this game, there is a 'leader' placed in front of the rest of the players who performs the movement that they should mimic. To conform to the capabilities of the device, we restricted the game to the movements that were already implemented in

'Dance It'. The main difference between this game and 'Dance It' is that it is the leader, rather than the device, who instruct the participants on which move to perform. Just as in 'Dance It', we gave the role of judging the movements to the BodyBug. This game was tested in a Wizard of Oz setup. The children were told that the BogyBugs were sensing their movements and would communicate who had done a mistake to a computer. The result was shown on the wall using a projector connected to the computer. In reality, the researcher controlled this functionality by controlling what was projected on the wall.

This was the only game that was not meant to extend 'the sensed': we deliberately kept the mistakes in the movement recognition, since we wished to understand how the multiplayer nature of the game would affect the players' reaction towards errors. We intentionally introduced mistakes in the simulated judgements, roughly corresponding to the BodyBug's accuracy in 'Dance It'.

In the game 'The Blind Mirror' we placed the participants in a circle. The BodyBug would mark slots of time during which each player would perform one movement. At the end of the round, the BodyBugs selects a 'leader' from the group, whose movement had to be remembered and mimicked by the rest of the players as fast and accurately as possible. The 'leader' decides who wins. This game requires very limited functionality in the BodyBug, in that it only paces the game and selects the leader. Still, selecting the leader would require wireless communication and was therefore simulated in our experiment. Since the BodyBug does not evaluate the movements, the game manages to expand 'the desired' to overlap entirely with 'the expected'. The only restriction the children have in terms of performance lies in the duration of their movements. The goal for playtesting this game was to see how accepting the children would be towards having another player, rather than the device, judging the outcome of a game.

Finally, we tested one fully implemented game 'Make My Sound'. This was the most playful and self-effacing design. The BodyBug would play one of a repertoire of three music loops, depending on the movement quality of the player. To create a game challenge, the players were placed in a circle and told to try to generate the same music as a randomly selected 'leader'. The BodyBug distinguished between slow, fast, and jerky movements, and adapted its music feedback to reflect these qualities (e.g. slow music for slow movements). In contrast to 'Dance It', this game does not restrict the players' movements to a limited repertoire, but is able to provide feedback on anything within 'the expected'. The role of the BodyBug is that of giving feedback on the movement qualities. This feedback is not a judgement of success or failure, but open for interpretation.

The three game designs were playtested in a workshop at the same dance school. In total we had 13 participants, all of them had previously participated in our bodystorming session. In order to compare 'Join My Move' to 'Dance It', we also playtested the latter. Just as in the bodystorming session, we used a two-angle videotaping setup. However, as this playtest was less focused on the physical aspects of the games we only did a coarse analysis of the videos. To evaluate our games, we asked the participants to fill in a questionnaire with prepared questions concerning their preferences and their focus of attention during play. We also conducted a post-game interview.

Evaluation

From the evaluation it was clear that the new games were able to overcome two limitations of the previous game 'Dance It'. First, our games did not cause artefact-focussed interaction. As the new game designs placed part of the responsibility of the game outside the device, the children's attention was directed towards what surrounded them. The difference was clearly visible in the video recordings, as well as reflected in the questionnaire. We explicitly asked the participants to describe where they placed their focus. For 'Join My Move', the two most frequent top choices were 'My own movements' and 'Things and people around me'. By contrast, the two top responses for 'Dance It' were 'The Bodybug's display' and 'the Bodybug'. In a similar manner, we asked the children what resources they used to attune themselves to the leader in 'Make My Sound'. We received answers like: *"I listened to the music", "I looked at the others", "I just shacked it!"*, all of them indicating that the focus of attention was on sound and on movements of others rather than on the device.

Secondly, the sensing limitations of the BodyBug that had previously constrained the game design were addressed in two ways: through reinventing the sensor mapping of player movements to movement qualities ('Make My Sound') rather on accuracy of performance, and also through designing games which did not rely on sensor data at all ('The blind mirror'). The video analysis showed that both games afforded a big and varied palette of movements.

The evaluation also brought important insights into the desired distribution of roles between technology and the social setting. Two of our games were goal-oriented: 'Join My Move' and 'The Blind Mirror'. By contrast, 'Make My Sound' was more playful. All three games brought fun and enjoyment; however, the game 'The Blind Mirror' was rated as the least fun of the three. The difference lied in the role attributed to the BodyBug, which ranged from just pacing the game in 'The Blind Mirror', to providing feedback in 'Make My Sound', and to 'judging' the movements in 'Join My Move'. The children (specially the youngest) preferred to be judged by the BodyBug (as in 'Join My Move') rather than by another participant (as in 'The Blind Mirror'). This happened even though they understood that the BodyBug made more mistakes than the 'leader' in the judgment. By contrast, the open feedback in 'Make My Sound' allowed the players to negotiate socially if the game was to be seen as a competition at all.

LESSONS LEARNED

In this section, we would like to highlight three main lessons learned from our design experiment.

The role of technology

The distribution of responsibilities between players and technology is not completely arbitrary. In particular, the requirements are different if we design for goal-oriented or self-effacing play. As discussed above, our participants (in particular the youngest children) preferred that the BodyBug would judge the success of the game, even if it made more mistakes in this judgment than a human referee would make. The most likely explanation is that when a win condition was at stake, the children opted for a judge outside the social and affective bounds of the group. For the more self-effacing game 'Make My Sound', the stakes were lower and the children were happy with social control over any 'win' conditions.

The problem with implementing win conditions in technology is that players may focus their play activity towards a more goal-oriented behavior, which in turn has been shown to limit the social and body engagement [5]. However, the experience from B.U.T.T.O.N. and our playtests show that by making the technology *less* precise, or 'broken' in Wilson's terminology, the game can still leave plenty of space for gestural excess and social negotiation.

Sensed, Expected and Desired

In our analysis of the designed games, we made extensive use of Benford's framework for analyzing our sensor-based application. The approach proved useful in framing the limitations of our technology, our design goals, and the possibilities for design.

In particular, we set our goal to extend 'the desired' to cover as much as possible of 'the expected' (See Fig 2, c)). We did so by extending 'the sensed' *socially* instead of technologically. For example the game 'The Blind Mirror', allowed 'the leader' to assess the movements in a way that would be impossible for the technology to do. The framework was also useful in order to evaluate our game designs in comparison with former games, by comparing to what extent 'the desired' overlapped with 'the expected'.

Bodystorming versus Playtesting

It is worth commenting on the convenience of combining bodystorming with more realistic playtesting. Bodystorming proved useful for exploring the design space of physical affordances, space, and movements, and is also very easy to set up. However, to thoroughly understand the results of the bodystorming session we needed a careful setup of video recording tools and a fine-grained analysis of the recordings. By contrast, playtesting proved to be a very useful method to explore how players would organize themselves socially around an implemented functionality. Playtesting required more implementation (or simulation) than bodystorming, but it was easier to analyze. While we employed the same configuration of video cameras in the playtest session, the analysis of social negotiation required less detailed video analysis and relied to a larger extent on post-game interviews and a questionnaire.

CONCLUSIONS

By introducing the concept of body games, we have shifted the focus from movement as an interaction method with a computer game, to the social and corporeal experience of the players in a game. When designing such games, the social and physical setting of the game become as important design resources, as the technology that supports the game.

Since the technology is responsible only for some of the tasks related to the gameplay in these games, designing the role of technology becomes a central design issue. The path towards making body games fun and engaging is not necessarily that of making sensors and feedback systems more and more advanced. In our work, we identified two design approaches that both allow players to appropriate the technology and the games. The first (well illustrated by the game 'Make My Sound') is to use the technology for qualitative feedback, leaving it open for players to decide if the function is used as a win condition or in a self-effacing, playful exploration. The second (well illustrated by the game B.U.T.T.O.N.) is to include win conditions in the technology but deliberately limit the technology's ability to recognize whether the rules were followed or not. From a technology perspective, such games may appear as 'broken', but from a social and corporeal perspective they leave room for playful exploration and social negotiation in quite the same way as self-effacing designs do.

ACKNOWLEDGMENTS

This project was financed by the Swedish funding agency Vinnova and carried out in collaboration with Movinto Fun and the Stepz dance school. We wish to thank our workshop participants and assistants for their effort, engagement, and feedback. Special thanks to Katherine Isbister for feedback and encouragement.

REFERENCES

1. Acuff, D.S. *What Kids Buy and Why. The Psychology of Marketing to Kids*. The Free Press, NY, USA, 1997.

2. Bekker, T., Sturm, J., and Eggen, B. 2010. Designing playful interactions for social interaction and physical play. In *Pers. Ubiq. Comp. 14(5)*, 385-396.

3. Benford, S., Schnädelbach, H., Koleva, B., Anastasi, R., Greenhalgh, C., Rodden, T., Green, J., Ghali, A., Pridmore, T., Gaver, B., Boucher, A., Walker, B., Pennington, S., Schmidt, A., Gellersen, H., and Steed, A. Expected, sensed, and desired: A framework for designing sensing-based interaction. *ACM Trans. Comp.-Hum. Interact. 12(1)*, 2005, 3-30.

4. Bergen, D. and Fromberg, D.P. *Play from Birth to Twelve and Beyond: Contexts, Perspectives, and Meanings*. Garland Pub., Inc., NY and London, 1998.

5. Bianchi-Berthouze, N., Kim, W.W., and Patel, D. Body. 2007. Movement Engage You More in Digital Game

Play? and Why?. In *Proc. ACII'07*, Springer-Verlag,, 102-113.

6. Dahlbäck, N., Jönsson, A., and Ahrenberg, L. 1993. Wizard of oz studies: why and how. In *IUI'93*, 193–200.

7. *Dance Central, Xbox360.* http://www.dancecentral.com/

8. De Kort, Y. A. W., IJsselsteijn, W. A., and Gajadhar, B. J. 2007. People, Places, and Play: A research framework for digital game experience in a socio-spatial context. In *Situated Play: Proc. of DIGRA'07*, 823 - 830.

9. De Koven, B. 2011. Coliberation continued. Blog post, Sept. 2011.http://www.deepfun.com/coliberation-continued/

10. Fluegelman, A., and Tembeck, S. *The New Games Book. Play Hard, Play Fair, Nobody Hurt.* A Headlands Press Book, Dolphin/Doubleday, 1976.

11. Fullerton, T., Swain, C., Hoffman, S. *Game design workshop*. CMP Books, San Francisco. Published by CMP Books an imprint of CMP Media LLC, 2004.

12. Gaver, W. Designing for homo ludens, still. In Binder, Löwgren, and Malmborg. Eds., *(Re)searching the Digital Bauhaus*. London: Springer, 2009,163-178.

13. Graves, L., Stratton G., Ridgers N.D., Cable N.T. 2007. Comparison of energy expenditure in adolescents when playing new generation and sedentary computer games: cross sectional study. *BMJ 335(7633)*, 1282–1284.

14. Harley, D., Fitzpatrick, G., Axelrod, L., White, G., and McAllister, G. 2010. Making the Wii at home: game play by older people in sheltered housing. *In Proc. Int. Conf. on HCI in work and learning, life and leisure*, USAB '10, Springer-Verlag, Berlin, 156-176.

15. Isbister, K. 2012. How to Stop Being a Buzzkill: Designing Yamove!, 2012. A Mobile Tech Mash-up to Truly Augment Social Play. Speaker *in MobileHCI'12.*.

16. Isbister, K., Schwekendiek, U., and Frye, J. 2011. Wriggle: an exploration of emotional and social effects of movement. In *CHI EA '11*, ACM Press, 1885-1890.

17. Isbister, K., Rao, R., Schwekendiek, U., Hayward, E., and Lidasan, J. 2011. Is more movement better? A controlled comparison of movement-based games. In *FDG'11*. ACM Press, 331-333.

18. Isbister, K. Enabling Social Play: A Framework for Design and Evaluation. In *Evaluating User Experience in Games. Concepts and Methods*, R. Bernhaupt, Ed. Springer-Verlag, London, 2010.

19. Jakobs, E., Fischer, A., and Manstead, A. Emotional experience as a function of social context: The role of the other. *Journal of Nonverbal Behavior* 21 (2), 1997, 103-130.

20. Johansson, C., Ahmet, Z., Jonsson, M., Tholander, J., Aleo, F., Sumon, S. 2011. Weather Gods and Fruit Kids

– Embodying abstract concepts using tactile feedback and Whole Body Interaction. In *CSCW'11* ACM Press.

21. Kavanagh, L.C, Suhler, C.L., Churchland, P.S., and Winkielman, P. When It's an Error to Mirror: The Surprising Reputational Costs of Mimicry. *Psychological Science SAGE*, 22 (10), 2011, 1274 - 1276.

22. *Kinect for Xbox 360. Free Xbox Life.* http://www.xbox.com/ar-AE/kinect?xr=shellnav

23. *Konami Dance Dance Revolution.* http://www.konami.com/ddr

24. Lanningham-Foster, L., Jensen, T. B., Foster, R. C., Redmond, A. B., Walker, B. A., Heinz, D., and Levine, J. A. Energy expenditure of sedentary screen time compared with active screen time for children. *Pediatrics 118 (6)*, 2006.

25. Lazzaro, N. Why we play games: Four keys to more emotion without story. In *Player Experience Research and Design for Mass Market Interactive Entertainment*. Technical report, XEO Design Inc, Oakland, 2004.

26. Liljedahl, M. Sound for Fantasy and Freedom. In *Game Sound Technology and Player Interaction: Concepts and Developments*, Ed. M. Grimshaw, Information Science Reference 2010, 22 - 44.

27. Lindley, S.E., Le Couteur, J., and Berthouze, N.L. 2008. Stirring up experience through movement in game play: effects on engagement and social behaviour. In *Proc. CHI'08*, ACM press (2008), 511-514.

28. Loke, L., Larssen, A.T., Robertson, T., and Edwards, J. 2007. Understanding movement for interaction design: frameworks and approaches. In *Pers. Ubiq. Comp. 11(8)*, 691–701.

29. Márquez Segura, E. Engaging in gesture-based multiplayer games for children. Turning limitations in sensing technologies into opportunities for a rich game experience. Master thesis at KTH, Sweden, 2013.

30. Moen, J. *KinAesthetic Movement Interaction. Designing for the Pleasure of Motion.* PhD thesis, KTH, 2006.

31. Moen, J. 2007. From hand-held to body-worn: embodied experiences of the design and use of a wearable movement-based interaction concept. In *TEI'07*, ACM Press, 251–258.

32. Mueller, F., Agamanolis, S., and Picard, R. 2003. Exertion interfaces: sports over a distance for social bonding and fun. Proc. In *CHI'03*, ACM press, 561-568.

33. Mueller, F., Edge, D., Vetere, F., Gibbs, M.R. Agamanolis, S., Bongers, B., Sheridan, J.G. Designing sports: A framework for exertion games. In *CHI'11*, ACM press, 2651-2660.

34. *Oriboo.* Available from http://www.oriboo.com/

35. Oulasvirta, A., Kurvinen, E., and Kankainen, T. Understanding contexts by being there: case studies in bodystorming. In *Pers. Ubiq. Comp. 7(2)*, 2003, 125-134.

36. Pakinkis, T. *Kinect has 'some real problems' – Molyneux. But has a sense of "freedom and emotion".* Computer and videogames.com, 2011. Available from http://www.computerandvideogames.com/308315/kinect-has-some-real-problems-molyneux/

37. PlayStation Move.

    http://us.playstation.com/ps3/playstation-move/

38. Ravaja, N., Saari, T., Turpeinen, M., Laarni, J., Salminen, M., and Kivikangas, M.. Spatial Presence and Emotions during Video Game Playing: Does It Matter with Whom You Play? *Presence 15(4)*, 2006, 381-392.

39. Reynolds, L., Ibara, S., Schwanda, V., and Cosley, D. 2011. Does it know I'm not maintaining good posture?: an in-home play study of wii fit. In *CHI EA '11*, ACM Press, 1687-1692.

40. Schou, T., and Gardner, H.J. 2007. A Wii remote, a game engine, five sensor bars and a virtual reality theatre. In *OZCHI'07*, ACM Press, 231-234.

41. Siegel, S.R., Haddock, B.L, Dubois, A.M. and Wilkin, L.D. Active Video/Arcade Games (Exergaming) and Energy Expenditure in College Students, *International Journal of Exercise Science 2(3)*, 2009, 165-174.

42. Simon, B. 2009. *Wii are Out of Control: Bodies, Game Screens and the Production of Gestural Excess*. Loading 3(4) (2009). http://journals.sfu.ca/loading/index.php/loading/article/viewArticle/65

43. Soute, I., Markopoulos, P., and Magielse, R. Head Up Games: combining the best of both worlds by merging traditional and digital play. In *Pers. Ubiq. Comp. 14(5)*, 2010, 435-444.

44. Tholander, J., and Johansson, C. Bodies, boards, clubs and bugs: a study of bodily engaging artefacts. In *CHI EA'10*, ACM Press (2010), 4045-4050.

45. Tholander, J., and Johansson, C. 2010. Design qualities for whole body interaction: learning from golf, skateboarding and BodyBugging. In *Proc. NordiCHI'10*, ACM Press, 493-502.

46. Voida, A., and Greenberg, S. Wii all play: the console game as a computational meeting place. In *Proc. CHI'09*, ACM Press (2009), 1559-1568.

47. *Wii controllers.* http://www.nintendo.com/wii/what-is-wii/#/controls

48. Waern, A. Information technology in pervasive games. In Montola, Stenros and Waern. In *Pervasive Games: theory and design*, Ed. M. Kaufmann, 2009.

49. Wilson, D. Brutally Unfair Tactics Totally OK Now: On Self-Effacing Games and Unachievements. *International journal of computer game research 11(1)*, 2011.

Seeing Movement Qualities

Helena M. Mentis
Socio-Digital Systems
Microsoft Research
Cambridge, United Kingdom
hementis@microsoft.com

Carolina Johansson
Mobile Life Centre
Swedish Institute of Computer Science
Kista, Sweden
lina@sics.se

ABSTRACT

With the increased availability of movement based interactive devices there is a growing interest in exploring the potential design space for engaging movement-based interactions. This has led to the exploration of different ways to sense and model movement such as Laban Movement Analysis' Effort qualities. However, little is understood in how movement qualities are perceived and experienced by users. We explored this in an interactive improvisational dance performance setting. From video analysis with a Laban Movement expert and post-performance interviews with audience members, we discuss the differences in how a movement quality was perceived. From these findings, we discuss implications for further efforts in designing interactive movement-based systems that strive to capitalize on movement qualities.

Author Keywords

Movement qualities; Laban; Vision; Kinect

ACM Classification Keywords

H.5.m. Information interfaces and presentation (e.g., HCI): Miscellaneous.

INTRODUCTION

The last few years have seen a tremendous increase in the popularity of movement-based interfaces. With the engaging experiences available with sensors such as the Nintendo Wii and Microsoft Kinect, movement sensing has taken on a new level of investigative importance, raising questions on the potential design space for engaging movement-based interactions. The driving force behind the design and development of these new sensors has been on capturing the nuances of human movement and expression in order to provide natural user interaction (NUI). This has been done by sensing evermore fine-grained movement and to determine the most common or universal movement. As argues in O'Hara et al [23] and Harper et al [9] the focus of NUI has been on the interface as the reason for naturalness. That naturalness is not constituted within context, but is brought

to it. However, this is simply treating naturalness as a representational concern – one that ignores the in situ and embodied construction of movement meaning and the possibility for differences in what is construed as natural or even what is perceived.

We feel this has been a problem plaguing a particular design area of movement interaction within HCI – the sensing and use of movement qualities – that are most often based on the Laban Movement Analysis (LMA) category of Effort. Movement qualities refer to the expression and intentions in how we perform a movement. Compare the pushing of a baby stroller while Sunday shopping to starting a car by pushing it to a roll. Are they of the same movement categorized as 'push'? They may very well be, but the characteristics of them are decidedly different. In this example the force of the movement is what makes them quite different from each other. These two movements that are experienced so differently could mistakenly be said to be one and the same by just describing the action taken – in this case, 'pushing'. Assessing *how* the movement is done – the *quality* of the movement – rather than just simply *what* movement is done, will, on the other hand, describe them as embodying two different qualities and, thus, imparting two different connotations – light nudging versus exerted shoving, perhaps.

However, there is a large and growing body of philosophical, sociological, and cognitive science studies showing that perceiving movement is a product of active interventions and not merely passive representations of some stable reality out there (see for example, [14, 16]). There is no ground truth for saying that everyone would or must perceive the body's movement in a particular manner. This has particularly been a point by Robertson & Loke [23] who have highlighted the importance of situatedness in movement-based design and the difficulties in machine vision of situated characteristics of movement and gesture.

With that being said, the contribution of this study is to do with the introduction of gestural interfaces for perceiving the qualities of bodily movement. More to the point, this paper aims to situate the perception of movement qualities – both in terms of perceiving one's own movement qualities as well as perceiving the qualities in another's movements. We accomplish this through a study of a Kinect-based system for an improvisational dance performance where audience members move to influence the music. The system is designed to 'see' audience member movement qualities as defined by the LMA category of *Effort*. After the performance, we probe the audience members' for their descriptions and interpretations of their own and other's movements. We then employ the professional vision of a LMA expert to provide her own judgment as to what qualities the audience members' movements are imbuing. We do this is order to explore the differing phenomenon of seeing movement as embodying a quality. In doing so, we hope to convey something of the embodied vision that occurs and discuss the opportunities this has for the design of movement sensing systems.

BACKGROUND

Constructive Vision of Movement

There is a long tradition of work articulating how experience and perception are situated and interactional. A number of these have found particular influence within the CHI community (see [5, 6, 7, 10, 11, 21, 28]). It is beyond both the scope and purposes of this paper to offer complete coverage of this work. Our intent here is to highlight some of the key theoretical works that particularly influence, motivate, and inform the contributions in this paper.

The significance of this for us is that vision is not purely the psychological process of an individual (see also [6, 21, 21]). Vision and perception are largely socially situated processes where individual differences in how something should be seen can be negotiated (see [7]).

Influential theoretical contributions to our understanding of bodily experience and perception of bodily movement come from the range of work within phenomenology. Within this philosophical study, one's bodily interactions are situated in a physical, social, and temporal space – shaping and guiding all that we experience [26]. In describing the difference between how one perceives movement qualities, the concern is with understanding perception in terms of the meaning it has for the subjects – the qualitative or phenomenal features of their experience or 'what it is like' to experience something [19].

For this study in particular, it is important to note that there are two ways that we can experience and see the body: as the objective body and as the lived body [4]. Merleau-Ponty [17] distinguished between Le Corps Objectif and Corps Proper referring to the phenomenological distinction between the body as seen from an observer's point of view, which is an abstracted description of muscular performance that can be defined and represented, and the body understood from the first-person perspective, which is made meaningful through constant interaction and perception of the world and its actions within it. This view emphasizes the subjective nature of meaning through praxis. Thus, in order to address the difference in phenomenological perception, attention is paid to how those perceptions appear to the observer as well as she who is expressing that quality.

Central to our discussion of perception of movement qualities through the lens of the Laban Effort framework is Goodwin's [5] discussion of professional vision, which is the "socially organized ways of seeing and understanding events that are answerable to the distinctive interests of a particular social group" (p.606). In essence, as one becomes a part of a professional discipline, they learn to see a certain set of phenomena in a particular way. This is partially achieved through the process of classification where knowledge structures are produced for a community of practice to abide by. What is important to note is that not only is professional vision socially constructed, but it is also deeply intertwined with its instruments [3, 5] – that one sees with rather than through the instruments of their trade. Instruments, though, do not refer simply to a material manifestation, but can also refer to the experiences and knowledge one brings to bear on the perception of what is before them.

Designing For and With Movement Qualities

These works raise the question as to the design of interactive systems that rely on sensing or seeing a quality in movement. Qualities can be seen very differently between different people. They are evocative of experience and intentions but reside outside of formal explanation or descriptive vocabulary. You see them rising out of our subconscious through adjectives such as strong, hurried, graceful, but, with regards to computer vision, we resign ourselves to computationally focusing on the movement parameters that lend themselves to finite delimitations.

Much work within the Bodily Interaction/Whole Body Interaction area of HCI has touched upon frameworks such as Emio Greco | PC and the LMA category of Effort in various depths in order to provide those finite delimitations [1, 25, 27]. In Laban, a movement quality refers to the way a movement is performed with respect to inner intention. So one's intention can change the dynamics of a movement, which are perceived as different movement qualities. We cannot perceive one's intention or dynamics behind a movement, but we can see the resulting quality that is manifest in a movement. Examples of such use in interactive system design include imparting personality on robots [18], creating a more engaging aspect of interaction with an intelligent lamp [25], and translating dance into a colourful visualization on a large screen display [27].

A more recent study investigated the user experience of interacting with a light installation through movement qualities. In the design of that system, Alaoui et al. used movement qualities defined by the dance company, Emio Greco | PC as opposed to LMA [1]. They compared a movement quality based system for controlling the light's behaviours (e.g. movement energy is mapped to light intensity) to a position based system (e.g. intensity of the light is mapped to the height of the hand). The simple study was concerned with demonstrating the perceived enhanced experience of interacting with the movement quality interac-

Effort Quality	Effort Element: Fighting	Effort Element: Yielding
Weight	Strong: Wrist joint below hip joint	Light: Wrist joint above hip joint
Time	Sudden: Wrist joint between points A&B stopped quickly	Sustained: Wrist joint between points A&B had continual velocity
Space	Direct: Wrist joint between points A&B had little deviation from straight trajectory	Flexible: Wrist joint between points A&B had a large deviation from straight trajectory
Flow	Bound: Wrist joint was close to hip joint	Free: Wrist joint was far from hip joint

Table 1. Kinect Measurable Aspects of Qualities.

tive system over that of the position-based system. It is important to note for our study and findings that the researchers chose to explain to the participants how to use the system by showing them a two-minute video that contained an explanation of the movement qualities and the corresponding light behaviours. As we shall soon show, this meant that the method of seeing movement qualities was prescribed to the participants. Thus investigating how the participants saw and perceived movement qualities was not explored.

It seems like a fruitful area of design to use movement qualities as an aspect of interaction. It allows for the perception of more expressiveness in the movements of users beyond direction and speed. However, beyond the definitions and oftentimes descriptive notations of the frameworks that describe movement qualities, we have little to go by in terms of how they relate to the perceptive experience of the mover her or himself.

That is the basis of the contribution of this paper. We are motivated to explore how one perceives and describes movement qualities in order to then discuss what it means to sense and interpret movement from this perspective. We also discuss how our findings shed light on the place for movement qualities in the design of interactive systems.

SYSTEM AND RESEARCH METHODS

Laban Movement Analysis (LMA)
LMA was founded by the dancer, Rudolf Laban, as a system for interpreting, describing, visualizing, and notating human movement. LMA comprises of four main categories: Body, Effort, Shape, and Space. Whereas Body, Shape, and Space are concerned with the location and direction of movement, our focus was on the category of *Effort*, which is concerned with the expressive aspect of movement [12, 13, 20]. The Effort system is composed of four factors (Space, Weight, Time, and Flow), which each have two opposing elements. **Space** describes the path of a movement, which can be categorized as either *direct* or *flexible*. A hand moving in a straight line from the shoulder out is an example of a direct quality. Flexible would entail a meandering path between the same two points. **Weight** describes

how *strong* or *light* a movement is. In the earlier example: pushing the baby stroller is a movement of light weight while pushing the car a movement of strong weight. **Time** describes how *sudden* or *sustained* a movement is performed. Drawing a circle in the air with your arm, over and over again, is of sustained quality, while suddenly raising your arm to stop someone from stepping on your foot is a movement of sudden quality. **Flow** deals with the complex notion of whether the movement is *free* or *bound*. Movements that are uncontrolled entail free flow whereas those movements that are bound feel controlled.

The System and Performance
In order to engage audience members in motivated movement that was fun and engaging, but also analysable, we developed a system for an interactive dance performance. Although the system's design was integral in engaging users to move and then reflect on their movement, the specific contribution of this paper entails the use of the system as a technology probe and thus our description of the system is complete yet brief.

The movement detection system was designed with the Xbox Kinect sensor and Kinect for Windows SDK Beta. The Kinect is a depth sensor and skeletal recognition system for movement recognition most commonly used for the Xbox 360 video game console. It enables users to interact with no additional controller or device for input but their moving bodies in front of the sensor. For interaction design, the SDK provides major joint location in XYZ coordinates for up to three skeletons.

By working with a teacher from the Trinity Laban Conservatoire of Music and Dance (Laban Centre) who is an LMA expert and choreographer, we translated the Effort qualities into something we could use the Kinect system to detect. Due to the inaccuracy of the ankle joint tracking, we focused our analysis on the upper body. Table 1 explains how the different movement qualities were recognized by the Kinect by calculating acceleration, pathways, velocity, levels and relationship of limbs to the body.

Qualities intrinsically mean that an element of time is involved in the performance of movement. This might entail a short burst of activity – a flick of a finger at a fly – or a longer action – a slow and long kiss – before the quality is made clear. Thus, a requirement of the system was to analyse movement over a period of time. This proved to be a challenge. On the one hand, that time period could not be too long or the audience member would have too much of a gap and disconnect from their ability to influence the music. On the other hand, if the time period was too short, a dynamic phrase of the music may be cut off. In addition, we were cognizant of the dancers who would be faced with the challenge of continuously changing their dancing to reflect the changing music. After we participated in a series of tests of different detection and music intervals, an interval of 15 seconds was agreed as a balance between the needs of the LMA expert, dancers, and system developer. Whether this was the right decision is up for debate.

During each 15-second interval, the system would (1) analyse the XYZ coordinates to determine if a quality is present, (2) whether a found quality was clear or weak, and (3) determine the most dominant quality of those found in order to play one of the eight musical pieces. Step 1 entailed the computations described in Table 1. Step 2 entailed finely-tuned thresholds for determining whether a found quality was clear or weak – in other words, how much of the 15-second interval was characterized by that quality. A clear quality meant that the system saw this quality during a large portion of the 15-second interaction sequence. A weak quality meant that the system saw this quality during the interaction sequence but for not that much of it. The thresholds for a clear or weak quality were carefully set and calibrated after movement samples of a movement professional performing the different qualities.

For Step 3, the dominant quality was determined by picking the one that was most clearly distinguished by the system. For example, in a 15-second interval, a person might move with a constant speed down to the floor and then move in constant speed high up on his toes. This would be found by the Kinect to be both at a low degree of strong and light. However the Time aspect was the same throughout the sequence: sustained; and so would entail a high degree. Thus, 'sustained' would be determined as the dominant quality by the system. The 15-second music piece depicting that quality would then be played.

A Laban Centre composer created the eight music tracks that represented each of the movement qualities. Being well oriented and knowledgeable of the LMA Effort qualities he composed 15-second music pieces that specifically depicted the eight different qualities. For instance the music piece depicting the time quality 'sudden' would have sharp, uneven, sounds while the 'sustained' music piece was more like an evenly flowing wave of sound.

The four dancers, who were current or former students of the Laban Centre, would then reflect the quality represented by the music back to the audience members through their improvisational dance. The dancers had a structure of rules

Figure 1. Professional dancers improvising under the main spotlight in the middle of the theatre and an audience member interacting with the Kinect in the spotlight on the right.

provided by the LMA expert determining how changes in music should change their movement, but the exact way in which they moved was up to each dancer to decide. For instance when the music piece depicting 'bound' was played their movement would become more inwards, more oriented close to the body, in a slightly unpleasant manner as if being constantly restrained and held back whereas 'free' would be danced in rather large sweeping movements that was free to travel in any new direction at any time.

The Study and Setting
Nineteen participants were recruited by email through the two research labs of the authors as well as through the Laban Centre and private networks. The participants were only told to come wearing clothes that allowed for movement and that they would be able to, as audience members, interact with the dance performance through a Kinect, but were not given any more information. The audience consisted of a very wide range of participants including those that were and were not familiar with the technology, those with a background in dance and those with no experience in the performing arts.

The interactive dance performance was conducted in a cleared, single level theatre at the Laban Centre. Through lighting, staging, and dance costumes, we provided an ambiance for movement, entertainment, and exploration. Lighting was rigged so as to provide one large bright spotlight in the middle of the room where the dancers performed. Another smaller and slightly dimmer spotlight was off to one side of the room for the Kinect interaction area. The rest of the room lights were off. The Kinect camera was placed on a tripod in front of the small, dim spotlight area in a manner that allowed the audience members to move in front of it while still being able to see the dancers in the centre of the room.

When the participants arrived, they were provided programs (as is the custom for attending a dance performance) and then, while standing as a group outside of the theatre, were provided a short explanation of how the music that the dancers would perform to would be triggered by the audience's freely expressed dance movements in front of the Kinect. There was no explanation as to the use of LMA qualities or what movements mapped to what music. We were encouraging a free exploration of the system. The participants then entered the darkened theatre to find the dance performers standing at attention in the middle of the room. As the first audience member entered the Kinect interaction area, her movements subsequently cued the first relevant music clip to play.

The performance lasted for a total of 20 minutes resulting in 80 different interactions slots throughout the performance. At the end of the performance, the music and lights faded out and then the main spotlight was brought up again for the performers to take their bow. Afterward, the participants took a seat in the centre of the room and completed an individual questionnaire that asked them to (1) describe how they moved in front of the Kinect, (2) what happened as a result of their movements, and (3) what would they have wanted to have happen. Thereafter a loosely structured group interview was held, where the participants were asked to describe their experience and in their own words, how they were moving when interacting with the Kinect and what they expected to happen as a result.

Data Collection & Analysis

In addition to the questionnaires and group interview, we collected video of the study, the Kinect output, and the judgment of the LMA expert.

Four video cameras were set up to capture a range of perspectives. One overarching camera high on the wall captured the entire scene, one camera in the far end of the room primarily captured the professional dancers, one camera off to the side of the Kinect interaction area captured the audience interaction, and finally a handheld camera was used to capture other aspects of the performance.

We also collected the Kinect-based system output. This included, for each time-stamped interaction segment, the qualities the system detected, how these qualities were weighted, which quality was selected as the dominant one and the music track that was subsequently played.

The day after the performance we reviewed the video of the participant's interactions with the system for each interaction segment. The LMA expert provided us with her interpretation of the qualities that were evident during each interaction segment. Her judgments were then compared to the judgments of the Kinect-based system. During this process we also had the opportunity to interview the LMA expert as to how she sees the movements and different qualities and how they are manifest in the movements of the participants. This review session was also video recorded.

Our analysis entailed a comparison of what movement qualities the system saw the audience members doing (Kinect data), what movement qualities people said they were doing or what they thought they were doing (individual questionnaire and group interview data), and what qualities the LMA expert saw the participants doing. However, the focus of our understanding the ways of seeing movement qualities relied on an iterative reading and viewing of the interviews of the participants and LMA expert.

It is important to note that, in seeing movement qualities, the audience members were not engaging in the same act as the Laban expert. The Laban expert was watching as an observer, whereas the audience were watching others as well as using their bodies as an actor. Both were then asked to articulate their perception of movement – both of others, but for the audience members, also of themselves. Although a traditional comparative study would have the various participants engaging in the same act of viewing, with this study, we were interested in this difference in perception between the Corps Objectif and Corps Proper.

FINDINGS

A Professional Vision of Movement Qualities

Comparing the Kinect judgments to what our Laban expert saw when watching the video of the sequences shows that in 65.7% of the cases there was an agreement between the two. Although within the field of machine vision this is fairly good (and we were very happy to do this well), it does highlight the difference in seeing between the LMA movement expert and the Kinect system built on the LMA Effort framework with significant guidance by the LMA expert. And so we begin at this point to understand where the vision of movement qualities lies.

The LMA expert's fluency with this particular visual form certainly demonstrates her acquisition of the professional vision with respect to the identification of movement qualities: that is, she applies a discipline-specific way of seeing in her visual interpretation. In general, the LMA expert asserted that, for her judgment, she was watching the whole person moving. As she explained, "*I'm not trying to isolate it to one particular body area.*" This worked well 80% of the time. It led to a clear assessment of the movement quality, stating her judgment quite matter-of-factly, such as "bound and light." However, often there was a moment of hesitation; a moment that required a deeper look and consideration of the movement qualities the body was exuding. In the following example, for instance, she is commenting on an audience member who had been circling her arms around her body.

> LMA expert: "*Free. But, um...there is a little boundness in her.*"
> Interviewer: "*She was a little bound, really?*"
> LMA expert: "*Well, on the free scale... Her movement in space had a freedom to it, but her energy is bound. As a person.*"

In these moments, the movement of limbs played an integral part in how the LMA expert saw the body exude a quality of movement. Particularly for those moments when there was a 'contradiction' between the movement of the body and the movement of the limbs. As the LMA expert explained later on in our discussion:

"In certain things I was looking for the predominance of the arm gesture. For instance, for the woman who had the very bound quality in her torso but was moving the arms in a way, which had a free use but there was a contradiction there. I said that. I said there was a contradiction there but that it was free. The reason I said it was free was because of her arm movements. Not because of her whole body."

These moments expose an interesting aspect of seeing one's movement qualities from one with a trained eye. Despite one's supposed intention – despite their external expression with, for instance, their open and free arms – an aspect of one's movement quality is still reliant on their bodily tendencies.

"There were certain ones where … it is clear because the whole body attitude is there. So some of the judgments were slightly tentative but with some of them I said 'well it's free but it's not that free'; it is somewhere on the scale but there is a little bit of boundness. It is somewhere on that [side of the scale], but it's not completely dramatically one end of the scale. So that is always harder because [movement qualities are on] a spectrum. So some of them are very clear and definite. Some of them I was making a judgment because you were asking me to make a judgment."

In a way, this is how the Kinect system we devised behaved as well. It was being asked to make a judgment no matter what sort of contradictions were presented or no matter how minimal the expressed quality was. Whether it detected both boundness and free, it had to make a judgment as to which side of the spectrum was more predominant in order to play the next music track.

But these moments of contradiction also showed another strategy in applying professional vision to the perception of movement qualities. During moments of intense vision, we can see the LMA expert using her body to 'see' the movements on the screen.

In the interaction clip, the audience member is raising one arm at a time in front of her with loose hands and wrists as if she is enacting up and down brushstrokes. While watching the video, the LMA expert begins to mime these movements in her hands and wrists. When the clip has ended, she states, "Mmm, free and light."

In using her own body to see the movements she is exposing the link between feeling the movement through her own bodily ability and seeing the movement as it resides in another's body. This was not a sporadic occurrence, but in fact occurred often during both the viewing of the video clips and during the discussion afterwards. Mimed actions such as chopping with her hands, whipping her head around, and arching her back all signalled her vision through her own bodily ability.

Thus, the perception of movement qualitites by the LMA expert through the lens of the LMA framework was noticeably full of negotiation and interpretation. This was

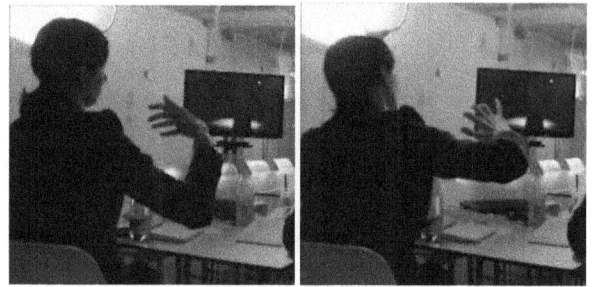

Figure 2. The body work of seeing movement.

achieved primarily through enactment through her own body to make a clear judgment.

Seeing Movement Qualities in the Wild

Out of the total 80 interaction slots during the performance 'sudden', 'light', 'bound', and 'flexible', were quite predominant while 'free', 'sustained', 'direct', and 'strong' were much more infrequent. Knowing this spread of the LMA effort qualities found, how well did they cover the intended qualities that the participants afterwards talked of having done? As expected, the participants did not use the exact same word for the qualities as those in the LMA framework. But still, their explanation of how they moved and what they would have wanted to have happen in the music as a result thereof, indicated whether the perception of the system was congruent with the self-perception of the mover.

One example of when the system's perception was in line with an audience member's was when participant, Sara, stepped in front of the camera for the first time.

As Sara walks into the interaction space, the music for 'direct' was playing. This is a very staccato, jarring musical piece. She stands directly in the middle of the spotlight and then, with a noticeably slower speed, begins to windmill her arms around her body. She turns around in a circle and bends her torso so one arm can sweep the ground. When the music changes into 'flexible' she continues the sweeping arm movement now with the same tempo as the music.

Afterwards she described the movements of her body as *"slow"* and *"flowy"* specifically because she wanted to change the heavily staccato music to something that she described as more *"lovely"*.

"I tried to do these slow movements, and I was completely out of synch with the music because I wanted it to change, it was playing something fast. And when the track changed it changed into something that I thought matched my movement really well."

This was one of a few rare cases where the participant was able to talk about and recognize their movement quality and how to express this in movement that did change the music in the intended way. It points to how people actually can in some cases think about movement qualities in how they move their bodies.

However, this was certainly not typically the case. Many of the participants pointed out they struggled to use qualities as a conscious method for interacting. One participant talked about being uncomfortable in *"moving [his] body like a dancer"* and how he had preferred a more specific gesture rather than this free mode of movement interaction. The crux of the concern on the part of the participants was the knowledge that there was something that they could do that would change the music.

> *"In this scenario there was kind of something that was leading us to ... not that there was a formula, but that there was a possibility of us having that control and, so, thus ... I wanted a bit more control I guess."* [Margaret]

Because of this knowledge of control, the motivation of the audience members were to watch one another very intently to determine the *"key"* or *"essence"* of a movement that would lead to a particular musical piece to play.

> *"It is as if it was not movement, it was like keys, like I have to find the right key. I ended up searching for the thing that was a key."* [Ralph]

> *"I noticed someone walk forward towards it and the tempo of the music got faster, more alive. And I noticed, 'ah!' I think that particular track came on twice and I was wanting it more. I was trying to figure out what movement that was. Was it going forward? Was it the sharpness of the movement? Or how close – how close the body was to the camera."* [Kane]

This seemed to be a focus of many of the participants. In some ways there was an assumption that spatial dimensions are what made the system work. They would watch the other users of the system to see what might be the trigger, they watched the dancers for some insight as to what the essence of a movement associated with a particular music piece could be, and they would sometimes try the system out themselves, going in with a clear intention to try something they had seen before.

But this was not actually the motivation behind the system in the way we envisioned 'controlling' it. As there was no specific gesture for each musical piece, one could do a number of different types of movements that all imbue a certain quality, which would result in the same piece of music playing. There was not meant to be a 'key' per se, but rather, the movements that a user envisioned would be reminiscent of a certain musical score, and then they would perform those movements in order to call up that score. For those that, in essence, did use the system in that manner, it worked quite well for them. As Jill explains during the group interview, the strategy of consciously looking for the 'key' to control the system was not fruitful.

> *"At first I was looking for patterns, but in the end it is like it doesn't really matter. It is about the flow between [the audience music]. ... Once you found out what types of music there were, it was more interesting to see the connection between the person in front of the Kinect and the dancers."*

Figure 3. A 'flowy' movement that led to the music changing to represent the 'flexible' Laban Movement quality.

The crux of the disconnect between how people wanted to use the system and how movement qualities were used comes down to a fundamental aspect of movement qualities themselves. For instance, many of the users were thinking, 'I'm going to go forwards or backwards and that is going to make a difference' when in fact, it was not as simple, or, perhaps, more to the point, not as complex as that. It is subtler and not so obvious. Movement qualities are typically not a conscious aspect of movement. We think about the action we are going to take or we think about the gesture we want to make, but the quality that resides within the execution of that movement is in fact fairly subconscious because it is the expression of one's intention.

But as the audience members began to look at the dancers to 'teach' them what they needed to do to control the system they began to realize it is an expressive act opposed to a semantic gesture that they needed to perform.

> *"I feel as if I can't express as they do, but I was hoping to be able to give them a vehicle, so I was hoping that I could paint the music and then they would teach me what I meant. ... I was hoping to shape the music in a certain way. A big shape or a little shape. And then they would express then I would be 'wow its a fantastic way of expressing."* [Ralph]

But the motivation to learn to perceive and act outside of their own bodily abilities was striking as this was not the point of our attention to movement qualities. Qualities are meant to be an aspect of any movement. Not something that needs to be learned, but something that resides in how we enact a movement in the world we all live in.

Thus being able to 'see' these qualities in another's movements was very difficult for the audience members. Being a subconscious aspect of movement meant that audience members could not consciously discern them in others' movement and, thus, discern a suitable conceptual pattern to map movement qualities to musical scores.

A Chasm of Vision Dimensions

Besides the earlier discussed difference in vocabulary (of the participants not using exactly the same semantics as the

LMA Effort quality's names) we also identified a gap in between what LMA thinks of as movement qualities and what the participants thought of as movement qualities.

This was exemplified in the following example when Beth interacted with the Kinect, which had much attention by the other participants.

The 'light' music track was playing. This is a flirty, up-beat, but calm track. Beth walks into the interaction area and starts jumping vigorously in front of the Kinect camera. When the same music file is repeated and played again, she stops and looks around with a surprised face and the people standing around the Kinect area are heard laughing. She begins jumping even more and begins to windmill her arms around her body. The music changes again and this time it has changed to 'flexible', which is a quick, meandering, but also fairly calm piece.

Afterwards both she and other participants described this as not being the music file they had expected after the movement she had done. They talked about the energy in the jumping, of the intensity of the movement, of how they *"saw energy"* and how they had expected the speed of the music to change. In this case, however, the Kinect system determined the dominant quality to be 'light' because of the height of her arms and therefore continued playing the 'light' musical track. This was a case that was in fact correctly judged by the Kinect system, as also agreed on by the LMA expert but the participant and her fellow participants did not agree to this analysis.

This brings up questions on how to match the everyday language we use to the expert language and, more importantly, to the concept of qualities. In the example of energy the LMA expert talked about energy as being part of every quality; qualities are about the *type* of energy that is used. The quality, also called dynamic expression, is about the energy that is perceived, this is generated by dynamic intent or what Laban called "inner attitude" towards movement, which is a choice about how to use one's energy. There can be a distinction between felt energy, or the actual energy input of the body, and the dynamic expression that is perceived. For example, ballet dancers appear light but only because they are very strong, the expression of lightness is something that they have become practiced at through training and is an aesthetic choice. Untrained bodies may sense the physical effort in the muscles needed to create an action, particularly if that action is against gravity, much more than sensing the potential expressive quality of the action.

Thus, qualities are something that are perceived through interpretation of many sources of perceivable information. It is an accumulation of information to the perceptual systems coupled with an understanding of physical being-ness that we relate to. We see muscle tone and facial expression as well as the action of the body; we see what happens before an action – its preparation energy in the body for example. In this case we can easily see the energy as part of

Figure 4. The Quality of 'Energy'. (top) Seen by the Kinect as 'light' and (bottom) seen by the Kinect as 'flexible'.

the movement, as in the case with the jumping girl in the performance.

Thus, when seeing other's movement qualities, the audience members see different dimensions than the LMA Effort category is based on (not different words, but actually different dimensions) and even though they try to learn what the vocabulary is through trial and error, the preconceived dimensions they hold preclude them from uncovering the LMA Effort dimensions. Thus, this is not just a difference in wording between the expert (or LMA framework) and audience members, but it is really a difference between conceptual dimensions when discussing the qualities of one's movements. For instance, the audience members saw things like energy as lying on a continuum, which is not how the LMA Effort Category views energy. This does not mean they could not perceive of the LMA Effort qualities, but rather that they also saw and felt other aspects of movement that might not be a part of a particular movement framework. For instance, the Emio Greco | PC also embodied energy as an aspect of each of its different qualities: breathing, expanding, and reducing; not as its own separate dimension.

DISCUSSION

Within our findings, we presented a perspective on how seeing movement qualities can be very different depending on experience and background of a viewer. Furthermore, the way one calls on experiences and embodied enaction to construct one's vision, even by the expert, points to the need to embody a movement quality before 'seeing' it. We also learned that the audience members' conceptualization of movement qualities lay on some very different dimensions than what was defined by the LMA Effort qualities.

When observing the LMA expert making a judgment as to what movement quality was being expressed during each 15-second interaction interval, it was striking how often she used her own body to see, discuss, and explain the performance of others. It was reminiscent of studies of scientists', physicians', and other professionals' embodied process of seeing and understanding diagrams and images (e.g. [2].

This is a fundamental aspect of phenomenology's perspective on the way a person can perceive another's movement and, more importantly, see another's movements as embodying meaning [4]. It is because we are experiencing, living bodies that we can recognize the movements in others as being movements. It is the common bodily intentionality that is shared between the perceiving subject and the perceived other. As Gopnik and Meltzoff indicate, "we innately map the visually perceived motions of others onto our own kinesthetic sensations" ([8], p. 129).

This is how the LMA expert saw movement as well. She would recognize the movements in others as the movements in herself. However, the focus of her analysis and description was constrained by her training in LMA. She has learned to see her own bodily movements with regards to the descriptive parameters of LMA. This is what has allowed her to bridge the divide between the movements of the participants and the necessary categories of the LMA Effort qualities.

This, on the other hand, is not how our participants perceived their movement qualities and the movement qualities of others. They tried to embody the movements they saw in the dancers to learn the movement qualities necessary for control, but what they saw before them was coloured by their experience, their language, and their expectations – all which deviate from the dimensions of the LMA Effort dimensions – and, thus, did not yield a suitable model for use with our system. And unfortunately, they could not change their mechanism of 'seeing' movement without further explicit training.

Revisiting Designing For and With Movement Qualities

What we learn from the difference in perception and the need for definition in the movement qualities for controlling a system is that we are faced with two paths in using movement qualities in interactive system design. That is, either have movement qualities as a conscious interactive mechanism where participants are told how to move in order to control or command a system, or we must consider a different realm of interaction for movement qualities that are not about controlling or commanding.

For the latter solution, this could entail using movement qualities as a mechanism for reflection on one's own body – a background process of monitoring and awareness that provide a mirror to one's bodily habits or reactions, but does not require one to learn a new movement vocabulary. The non-trivial and obviously related issues is raised, of course, on how to represent this reflection to a user to let them 'see' their movement qualities as seen by the system, but a system along these lines allows movement qualities to still be seen through the lens of a framework such as LMA, while at the same time, not requiring the user to have

knowledge of this framework when enacting their movements.

For the former, a move towards training users to 'see' and express with a framework such as LMA has yielded positive results. Consider our findings in relation to that of Alaoui et al [1]. In the use of their movement qualities-based system, they presented participants with a two-minute video of how to command the system and the participants had a positive and successful experience with the system. As both experiences were aimed at controlling the system (a light in Alaoui et al's case and music in our case), the basis for a good experience required a 'key' of sorts.

A number of still open problems exist for this tactic, though. First, if a predefined framework is to be used and taught to a user, then the question is how to best teach such a method of 'seeing' one's own movement qualities. Hints towards achieving this is through the embodied manifestation of movements the LMA expert used in seeing the audience member movements within the confines of the LMA Effort dimensions. However, another way to attack this problem may be through the tactic of dialogical control. In other words, having the system and user define together a descriptive framework of movement qualities based on the needs of the situation. This is more in line with Merleau-Ponty's perspective of the lived body, which concerns the way people experience actions within a situated circumstance. Wittgenstein [28] claimed that through action, people create shared meanings and that these shared meanings are what enable one's individual perception to be cohered into socially shared experiences. Along these lines, Loke et al have been attempting to address how to build up these shared meanings between machines, observers, and mover [15].

CONCLUSION

Through this study we have described the mechanism in which the expert entails her professional vision and the audience member's difficulties and mechanisms of entailing their vision – both of which lead to a description of how seeing movement qualities is manifest and thus a critique on the oversimplification and misuse of movement quality frameworks in design. There are a number of limitations to this study to consider. Most importantly are the system design decisions we employed such as the 15-second basis for seeing and interaction as well as, methodologically, that the Laban expert and participants were not engaging in the same act. However, the findings do provide a strong indication of how one can see movement qualities and how this leads us to further consider how movement qualities can be integrated into the design of interactive systems.

ACKNOWLEDGMENTS
We would like to extend our immense thanks to Choreographer Melanie Clarke; Dancers Artemise Ploegaerts, Audrey Rogero, Adam Gain, & Oliver Hornsby-Sayer; Composer Ronen Kozokaro; Light & Sound Technician Janine De Weerd;

and the Head of the Laban Theatre, Brian Brady, for their support along with the creative audience for their beautiful participation. Special thanks to Linden Vongsathorn and Simon Fothergill for support in the development of the system; Sian Lindley for thoughtful review and comments; and Bob Corish for photos.

REFERENCES

1. Alaoui, S.F., Caramiaux, B., Serrano, M., Bevilacqua, F. (2012). Movement qualities as interaction modality. *Proceedings of DIS*, Newcastle, UK, p.761-769.

2. Alač, M. (2008). Working with brain scans: Digital images and gestural interaction in fMRI laboratory. *Social Studies of Science, 38*(4), 483-508.

3. Böscher, M. (2005). Social life under the microscope. *Sociological Research Online, 10*(1).

4. Gallagher, S. & Zahavi, D. (2008). *The phenomenological mind: An introduction to philosophy of mind and cognitive science.* New York: Routledge.

5. Goodwin, C. (1994). Professional vision. *American Anthropologist, 96*(3), 606-633.

6. Goodwin, C. (2003). The semiotic body in its environment. In J. Coupland & R. Gwyn (Eds.), *Discourses of the body.* New York: Macmillan.

7. Goodwin, C. (2003). "Pointing as Situated Practice." In Sotaro Kita (Ed). Pointing: Where Language, Culture and Cognition Meet. Mahwah, NJ: Lawrence Erlbaum, pp. 217-41.

8. Gopnik, A., & Meltzoff, A.N. (1997). *Words, thoughts, and theories.* Cambridge, MA: MIT Press.

9. Harper, R. & Mentis, H.M. (2013). The mocking gaze. The social organization of Kinect use. Proc. of CSCW, San Antonio, TX.

10. Heath, C. (2000). Configuring action in objects: From mutual space to media space. *Mind, Culture and Activity, 7*(1-2), 81-104.

11. Hindmarsh, J. & Heath C. (2000). Embodied reference: A study of deixis in workplace interaction. *Journal of Pragmatics, 32*, 1855-1878.

12. Laban, R. & Lawrence, F.C (1947) *Effort.* London: McDonald and Evans Ltd.

13. Laban, R. & Ullmann, L. (1971). *Mastery of Movement.* London: McDonald and Evans Ltd.

14. Latour, B. (1990). Drawing things together. In M. Lynch & S. Woolgar (Eds.), *Representation in Scientific practice* (pp. 19-68). Cambridge, MA: MIT Press.

15. Loke, L. & Robertson, T. (2013). Moving and making strange: An embodied approach to movement-based interaction design. *Embodied Interaction. Spec. issue of ACM Transactions on Computer-Human Interaction (TOCHI).*

16. Lynch, M. (1985). Discipline and the material form of images: An analysis of scientific visibility. *Social Studies of Science, 15*, 37-66.

17. Merleau-Ponty, M. (1962). *Phenomenology of perception.* Routledge.

18. Masuda, M., Kato, S., Itoh, H. (2010). A Laban-Based Approach to Emotional Motion Rendering for Human-Robot Interaction. *Lecture Notes in Computer Science, 6243*, pp. 372-380.

19. Nagel, T. (1974). What Is it Like to Be a Bat? *Philsophical Review*, pp. 435-50.

20. Newlove & Dalby (2005) *Laban for All.* London: Nick Hern Books.

21. Nishizaka, A. (1997). The Neglected Situation of Vision. :Sage.

22. Nishizaka A. (2000). Seeing what one sees: Perception, emotion and activity. *Mind, Culture, and Activity, 7*(1-2), 105-123.

23. O'Hara, K., Harper, R., Mentis, H., Sellen, A., & Taylor, A. (2013). On the naturalness of touchless: Putting the "interaction' back into NUI. *Embodied Interaction. Spec. issue of ACM Transactions on Computer-Human Interaction (TOCHI).*

24. Robertson, T. & Loke, L. (2009). Designing situations. *Proc of OZCHI*, Melbourne, Australia.

25. Ross, P.R. & Wensveen, A.G. (2010). Designing behavior in interaction: Using aesthetic experience as a mechanism for design. International Journal of Desigh, 4(2), 3-13.

26. Sheets-Johnstone, M., (1999). Emotion and Movement – A beginning empirical-phenomenological analysis of their relationship. *Journal of Consciousness Studies, 6*(11-12), pp. 259-277.

27. Subyen, P., Maranan, D.S., Carlson, K., Schiphorst, T., & Pasquier, P. (2011). Flow: Expressing movement quality. *The User in Flux Workshop at CHI 2011*, Vancouver, BC.

28. Suchman, L. (2000). Embodied practices of engineering work. *Mind, Culture and Activity, 7*(1-2), 4-18.

29. Wittgenstein, L. (1968). *Philosophical Investigations.* Blackwell, Oxford.

CrashAlert: Enhancing Peripheral Alertness for Eyes-Busy Mobile Interaction while Walking

Juan David Hincapié-Ramos
University of Manitoba
Winnipeg, MB, Canada
jdhr@cs.umanitoba.ca

Pourang Irani
University of Manitoba
Winnipeg, MB, Canada
irani@cs.umanitoba.ca

ABSTRACT

Mobile device use while walking, or *eyes-busy mobile interaction*, is a leading cause of life-threatening pedestrian collisions. We introduce CrashAlert, a system that augments mobile devices with a depth camera, to provide distance and location visual cues of obstacles on the user's path. In a realistic environment outside the lab, CrashAlert users improve their handling of potential collisions, dodging and slowing down for simple ones while lifting their head in more complex situations. Qualitative results outline the value of extending users' peripheral alertness in eyes-busy mobile interaction through non-intrusive depth cues, as used in CrashAlert. We present the design features of our system and lessons learned from our evaluation.

ACM Classification: H.5.2 [Information interfaces and presentation]: User Interfaces. - Graphical user interfaces.

Keywords: Eyes-busy interaction, obstacle avoidance, texting and walking, walking user interfaces.

INTRODUCTION

Mobile device users habitually multi-task (e.g. texting, web browsing) while walking. Researchers have introduced walking user interfaces (WUIs) [5] to improve mobile usage *efficiency* with tasks that require significant visual attention or *eyes-busy mobile interaction*. These interfaces include audio feedback [2], enlarged soft buttons [5], two-handed chorded keyboard input [12], and adaptive methods to compensate for extraneous movement [4].

WUIs primarily focus on task efficiency instead of user safety. Eyes-busy mobile interactions limit much of the user's peripheral vision, resulting in users tripping on curbs, walking into traffic or deviating from their intended path [6,7,11]. The year 2008 registered a twofold increase from the previous year in eyes-busy interaction-related accidents [9,8]. This has forced municipalities to consider safety policies that ban mobile device usage while walking [11]. Policy

making aside, technological support for safer walking and multi-tasking is at large unexplored.

We introduce *CrashAlert*, a system aimed at improving safety while on the move. CrashAlert captures and displays information beyond the user's peripheral view using a depth camera attached to a mobile device (Figure 1). The depth camera's field-of-view is orthogonal to that of the eyes-busy operator for increased peripheral awareness. Unlike navigation aids for the visually-impaired which rely on audio or vibro-tactile cues [13, 14], CrashAlert displays a small slice of the depth camera's image as a minimal-footprint display on the mobile's screen. With an extended field-of-view, users can take simpler and early corrective actions upon noticing a potential collision. The display also alerts users of obstacles immediately in front of the user through a red alert, prompting users to immediately stop or lift their heads.

Figure 1 – (left) CrashAlert senses obstacles through a depth camera and informs the user of their positions using various visual transformations. (right) CrashAlert uses limited space on the display and shows nearby obstacles with a red alert.

To the best of our knowledge CrashAlert is one of the first explorations of a safety-aware WUI. Our contribution is threefold: (1) a prototype implementation of CrashAlert, a system designed for safer eyes-busy interaction, (2) a set of visualizations aimed at minimizing screen real-estate and optimizing information about obstacles outside the user's field-of-view, and (3) a study of CrashAlert showing improved handling of potential collisions and an increased perception of safety, without loss of task performance.

INFORMATIVE FIELD OBSERVATIONS

CrashAlert's design emerged from informal observations of pedestrians walking and interacting with their mobiles in a university cafeteria. We noted the holding angle of the device, the number of hands used, the number of steps taken before users lift their heads (to detect on-comers and obstacles), the type of obstacles commonly avoided, patterns in walking speed and how many steps users took while typing.

We noticed that when walking, people handle potential collisions with varying degrees of safety 'cost': from slowing down to dodging obstacles, then lifting their heads and/or ultimately coming to a full stop to avoid a crash. Users rely on their peripheral awareness to notice obstacles early on and to take simpler corrective actions (slowdown/dodge). As their walking continues, the obstacle is reevaluated and, if needed, further corrective actions are taken (heads-up). Limited peripheral vision means that obstacles are noticed later on, restricting the suitable corrective actions to higher cost ones (full stop or a crash). These observations led to the following design requirements (R). A WUI supporting safer walking should therefore prompt users to take simpler corrective actions early on by **encouraging dodges (R1)**, and **alerting on imminent collisions (R2)**.

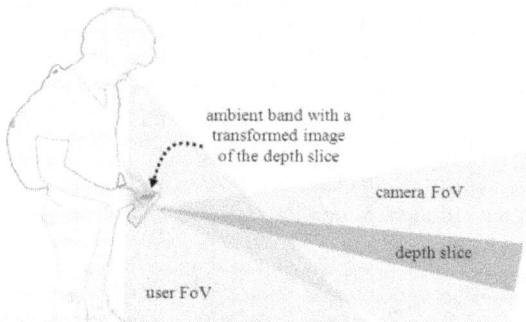

Figure 2 – A visualization based on depth-camera infomation extends the users' limited peripheral alertness.

CRASHALERT DESIGN

We designed CrashAlert (Figure 2) to let users act safely in eyes-busy mobile interaction. CrashAlert has two main components: an ambient visual band and visual alerts for near-by objects. Our system uses both a depth and a regular camera to capture the region in front of the user but outside their eyes-busy field-of-view (FoV). We extract only a small slice of the camera's image and process this to present obstacle positions and distances on the small footprint ambient band. The band conveys a glance-able representation of the elements in front of the user and outside their FoV (R1). Visual alerts are generated from the depth image for objects that are 2 meters away or less from the user. Their appearance (a bright red square in the position of collision, Fig 3) is quite salient, prompting the user to raise her head to better cope with obstacles (R2). We explicitly excluded other feedback modalities (tactile or auditory) due to their limitations in the wild [3] and need of headphones, and to isolate the effects of our visual approach on safety.

We generated different visualizations for the ambient band through a design workshop with eight participants who interacted with 11 different visualizations. Figure 3 presents the three most preferred ambient bands: a) color image, b)

depth image where closer objects are brighter (black at >5m), and c) the color image masked using the depth data. The *color* image is a slice of the picture taken with the color camera (figure 3a). The *depth* image is obtained by applying a binary threshold to the depth capture for a fixed distance (5 meters) and assigning the max value of each column to all of its pixels (figure 3b). The *masked* image uses the depth image (from figure 3b) as a mask on the color image; this way it shows the full color version of the closest objects on a black background (figure 3c). All bands presented a red alert when the obstacle was <2 m away.

Figure 3 – Ambient band visualizations based on a given scene (best seen in color).

Implementation Details

The CrashAlert prototype operates on an Acer A100 7" tablet computer, a laptop computer, and a Microsoft Kinect (Figure 4). The laptop is carried in a backpack together with a 12 volt battery to power the Kinect in a mobile setting. The laptop receives images from the Kinect via USB, processes and transforms them, and sends them to the tablet via Bluetooth. The tablet receives images at approximately 10-11 frames per second. The application is written in C#.NET. It interfaces with the Kinect, processes the images with OpenCV, and communicates them over Bluetooth. The tablet software is an Android 2.3.3 application.

Figure 4 - CrashAlert prototype: Acer A100 + Kinect.

EVALUATION AND USER FEEDBACK

We conducted our experiment to observe participants' safety behaviors using CrashAlert. We recruited eight university students, from various disciplines, who habitually text and walk (6 male, 2 female, mean age of 25.5 years). All participants text while walking, but agreed that such practice is dangerous. On average, our participants reported having a dozen collisions over the last year. We designed a within-subjects experiment in which participants were exposed to four conditions: (1) No feedback (None), (2) Camera Alone (CA), (3) Depth Image (DI) and (4) Image with Mask (IM). Conditions were counter-balanced with an incomplete Latin-square design. The camera was fixed at a 0° angle (Figure 4) and participants were asked to hold the tablet in a natural way. The depth slice covered the middle-low 2/5 of the camera image.

Task and Procedure

We asked participants to play a whack-the-mole game while walking through the university cafeteria. Each trip (or trial) consisted of starting the walk at the near-by bookstore and looping around the entire food court (180 meters). Participants were asked to walk as normally as possible while playing the game. Their objective was to tap on as many moles as possible during their trajectory. Participants were asked to naturally avoid collisions with people and obstacles. We ensured that participants would face *at least* four collisions during each trial. This was achieved by asking an 'actor,' unknown to the participant to provoke potential collisions. The 'actor' would do one of the following: cut the participants' path orthogonally, would stop right in front of them, would come toward them at a fast pace, or would walk beside them but then immediately swerve in their lane. None of our participants suspected the presence of the 'actor'. Participants also faced obstacles from other people and objects in the cafeteria. The experimenter recorded participants' behavior during any potential collision.

We captured the user's total walking time, the number of moles they hit, as well as the number of times they performed a 'dodge/slow down,' a 'heads-up,' a 'full stop,' or a 'crash'. Each experiment lasted roughly 30 minutes. Each condition was done twice, resulting in 8 participants ×4 conditions ×2 trials = 64 trials in total. We also interviewed the participants between trials and had a longer debriefing at the end of the experiment to collect data (5-step Likert-like scale) about their perceived safety, efficiency, alertness, walking speed, understandability and glance-ability of each condition. If a mole was not hit within 2.5s we recorded an error and the mole was shown as being destroyed.

Participants wore a backpack containing the battery pack to which the Kinect was connected. We first explained the task and briefly explained the visualizations. We did not inform them of the planned collisions and asked them to behave naturally while trying to hit moles in the game as efficiently as possible. Participants walked through the cafeteria as per the assigned path.

Results and Discussion

Each trial lasted 130.5 seconds on average ($sd = 20.8$) with an average number of 246.25 moles whacked per trial ($sd = 42.4$), and an average error rate of 0.64% (moles missed, $sd = 1.37\%$). Participants whacked moles at an average rate of 1.91 moles/second ($sd = 0.04$). There were no significant differences between conditions on the number of moles hit,

error rate or completion time. For the total 64 trials, we registered 721 instances of possible collisions with an average of 11.26 ($sd = 2.96$) per trial (only 4 per trial were caused by the actor) and 180.25 ($sd = 8.84$) per condition.

We used the univariate ANOVA test and the Bonferroni correction for post-hoc pair-wise tests for our analysis. Figure 5-left-top shows the percentage distribution of collision handling maneuvers (dodge/slow-down, heads up, stop before crash, near crashes) for each condition. The results showed a main effect of feedback style on the number of dodge/slow-downs ($F_{3,21} = 3.694$, $p < 0.03$) and head ups ($F_{3,21} = 10.553$, $p < 0.01$). Post-hoc analysis showed differences only between the no-feedback (None) condition and all the others, but not between the various visualizations. The apparent increase in near crashes was not significant. These results show that with CrashAlert participants avoided more obstacles by dodging and slowing down, rather than by heads up. Moreover, this better handling came at no cost in playing the game (no significant difference in error rate – figure 5-left-bottom or completion time $F_{3,21} = 0.7$, $p = 0.4$). These results show that CrashAlert induced simpler corrective actions (i.e. dodging and slowing down) to avert possible collisions, providing users additional time and space for other more complex corrections (i.e. heads-up and full stops), and thus leading to safer walking.

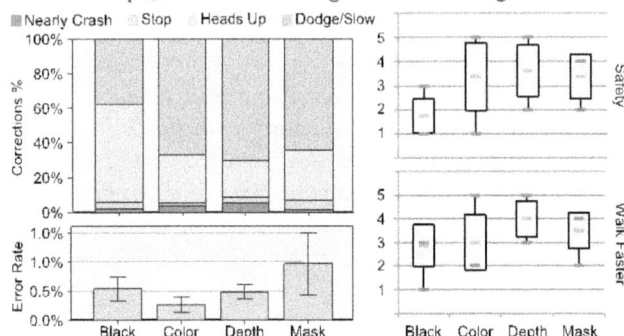

Figure 5 – (left-top) User corrective actions broken down into % of the total actions taken. (left-bottom) No significant difference in error rates among techniques. (right) User rankings for their perception of Safety and Walking Speed.

For subjective ratings we used the Friedman χ^2 test. Results (figure 5-right) showed that with CrashAlert, participants felt safer ($\chi^2(3) = 9$, $p = 0.029$) and had a perception of walking faster ($\chi^2(3) = 10.385$, $p = 0.016$). There were no main effects on the other factors.

We coded their answers (19 tags) into 3 topics: *abstraction*, *navigation*, *alerts*. In terms of the *abstraction* level, participants said that even though the color and the masked images provide higher levels of detail, they were harder to read, requiring more attention and generating more stress when executing the task (even though we did not find any significant impact in performance); for example P8 said "*I have to check the [color] image much more and longer*". In contrast, the depth images were found easier to read "at a glance"; for example P7 indicated that "*[with the depth im-*

age] I can see the [thin] veranda which I couldn't in the color image". Moreover, participants reported depth images as falling into the background to the point where some were convinced they had used them unconsciously.

Participants talked about the different ways that CrashAlert enhances their *navigational* senses (sound, peripheral view and knowledge of the environment) beyond simply alerting about obstacles and potential collisions, by: (1) allowing participants to walk within the dark regions shown on the ambient band, and (2) by interpreting the alert in unforeseen ways. Some participants found it useful to simply relax and follow the darker areas of the depth images, as they trusted that these areas would not have obstacles. In a different situation, when walking through a narrow and crowded corridor, a participant knew the person in front of her (shown with an alert due to proximity) was walking in the same direction and so she decided to follow the position of the alert to way-find through the crowd.

Finally, participants noted that a system based only on depth *alerts* (just the red box with no color, masked, or depth images) would be a marked advantage over current systems. Moreover, participants indicated the need for different *alert types*. One such type are alerts based on direction and speed; for example, participant 1 said *"I couldn't tell whether people where coming toward me or moving further away"*. Another type of alert would be based on the type of object (static or moving object) and their related hazard estimation; for example P3 noted *"[I would like to see] a significant level indication of obstacles like how much danger if collision occurs"*, and P5 said *"perhaps I could be alerted about different objects in different ways... moving people and static chairs require me to take action differently considering time and predictability"*.

Lessons Learned

We summarize three key benefits of CrashAlert:

- Depth and color images orthogonal to the user's FoV can facilitate safe navigation (dodging, slowing down and heads-up if necessary);
- Only a slice of the camera's image is needed to observe a benefit in extending users' peripheral alertness;
- Visual alerts based on depth information can support safer walking when interacting with a mobile device.

Limitations and Future Work

This initial exploration was limited by a low image rate (10-11 fps), a bulky hardware set-up, and naïve detection of obstacles (distance-based). However limited, our system demonstrated the value of considering safety in WUIs. Future work should investigate alternative visualizations (bands, full-screen, abstract, off-screen marks like halo [1]), varying alert styles, such as a growing or shrinking boxes based on distance and speed, other feedback modalities, impact on complex tasks, dynamic selection of the image slice, scene analysis and object recognition (type, speed).

CONCLUSIONS

We presented CrashAlert, a mobile device augmented with a depth sensing camera that shows users out-of-periphery objects in their path while walking. CrashAlert shows salient information such as distance and position about potential obstacles. The information is displayed on a minimal footprint ambient band on top of the device's display. Study results show that users took simpler corrective actions early on in their path upon noticing an obstacle, felt safer with our system and use it in unexpected ways to help navigate around the environment. This improvement came with no negative impact on performance, showing that even minimal environment information outside the user's periphery can provide for safer usage of mobiles while walking.

REFERENCES

1. Baudish, P., Rosenholtz, R., (2003) Halo: a technique for visualizing off-screen objects. CHI 2003.
2. Brewster, S. (2002) Overcoming the lack of screen space on mobile computers. Personal and Ubiquitous Computing.
3. Brewster, S., Chohan, F., Brown, L. (2007) Tactile feedback for mobile ineractions. CHI 2007.
4. Goel, M., Findlater, L., Wobbrock, J.O. (2012) WalkType: Using Accelerometer Data to Accommodate Situational Impairments in Mobile Touch Screen Text Entry. CHI 2012.
5. Kane, S.K., Wobbrock, J.O. and Smith, I.E. (2008) Getting Off the Treadmill: Evaluating Walking User Interfaces for Mobile Devices in Public Spaces. Proc. MobileHCI'08.
6. Nasar, J., Hecht, P., Wener, R. (2008) Mobile telephones, distracted attention, and pedestrian safety. Accident Analysis & Prevention 40, 69–75.
7. Neider, M.B., McCarley, J.S., Crowell, J.A., Kaczmarski, H., Kramer, A.F. (2010) Pedestrians, vehicles, and cell phones, Accident Analysis & Prevention, 42(2).
8. San Diego News (2012) How Risky Is Texting While Walking? http://www.10news.com/news/30530401/detail.html, last accessed: September 2012.
9. Stavrinos, D., Byington, K.W., Schwebel, D.C. (2011) Distracted walking: Cell phones increase injury risk for college pedestrians, Journal of Safety Research, 42(2).
10. Stewart, J., Bauman, S., Escobar, M., Hilden, J., Bihani, K., & Newman, M. W. (2008). Accessible contextual information for urban orientation. UbiComp '08.
11. TIME Magazine (2011), Friedman, M. http://newsfeed.time.com/2011/01/27/can-lamakers-ban-texting-while-walking/, last accessed: September 2012.
12. Yatani, K. and Truong, K.N. 2009. An Evaluation of Stylus-based Text Entry Methods on Handheld Devices Studied in Different Mobility States. Pervasive and Mobile Computing, Vol. 5, No. 5, 496-506.
13. Yatani, K. and Truong, K.N. (2009) SemFeel: a user interface with semantic tactile feedback for mobile touch-screen devices. UIST 2009, 111-120.
14. Uddin, M.S. and Shioyama, T. (2005) Detection of pedestrian crossing and measurement of crossing length - an image-based navigational aid for blind people. Trans. on Intelligent Transportation Systems. IEEE, 2005.

Three Perspectives on Behavior Change for Serious Games

Joshua G. Tanenbaum
Simon Fraser University
Surrey BC, Canada
joshuat@sfu.ca

Alissa N. Antle
Simon Fraser University
Surrey BC, Canada
aantle@sfu.ca

John Robinson
University of British Columbia
Vancouver, BC, Canada
john.robinson@ubc.ca

ABSTRACT

Research into the effects of serious games often engages with interdisciplinary models of how human behaviors are shaped and changed over time. To better understand these different perspectives we articulate three cognitive models of behavior change and consider the potential of these models to support a deeper understanding of behavior change in serious games. Two of these models – Information Deficit and Procedural Rhetoric – have already been employed in the design of serious games, while the third – Emergent Dialogue – is introduced from the field of Environmental Studies. We situate this discussion within a context of designing games for public engagement with issues of environmental sustainability.

Author Keywords

Serious Games; Sustainability; Behavior Change; Procedural Rhetoric; Emergent Dialogue

ACM Classification Keywords

H.5.m. Information interfaces and presentation: Misc.;

INTRODUCTION

In the games research community the power of games to influence behavior is subject to ongoing debate. Researchers invested in games as a significant medium of cultural expression often are faced with the conundrum of wanting to be on two sides of an argument at once. On one side, games are defended against the critiques of myriad advocacy groups who seek to scapegoat them as a cause of youth violence [3]. On the other side, games are lauded as powerful vehicles for learning and persuasion [6]. Researchers interested in advocating for either of these perspectives had best be prepared to accept the ethical implications of the other. We contend that a more nuanced understanding of interdisciplinary perspectives on behavior change can productively broaden the conversation around games, particularly as it applies to "serious games", "games for change", and "game-based-learning".

We are conducting this research within the context of Vancouver's *Greenest City Conversations (GCC) Project* : an interdisciplinary collaboration aimed at fostering and evaluating multiple channels for public engagement on sustainability policies. In this paper we present three perspectives on persuasion and behavior change and consider how they may be used to inform the design of serious games and other digital media for sustainability. The first perspective–the Information Deficit Model–is in common use in current approaches to sustainability education, and can also frequently be seen in many learning games. The second perspective–Procedural Rhetoric– derives from recent theories around persuasive games and is employed in what have been termed "newsgames" (most notably Gonzalo Frasca's *September the 12th*) [4, 13]. The final perspective–Emergent Dialogue–is an approach from Environmental Studies to public engagement that emphasizes bottom-up local solutions arrived at through participation in a dialogic process [9]. These three perspectives are by no means the only (or even the *best*) strategies for affecting behavior change, however we contend that they represent a useful continuum for designers to take into consideration when developing serious games.

THE INFORMATION DEFICIT MODEL

The Information Deficit model of behavior change operates on the premise that unsustainable behaviors occur because people don't know any better. This model posits that providing information changes values; value change drives changes in attitudes; attitude change drives changes in behaviors [7]. For example, it is common for local governments and organizations to run community workshops and lectures intended to educate participants about the benefits of recycling, conservation, reuse, and other environmentally friendly practices. These types of workshops work on the assumption that unsustainable behaviors arise from a lack of education. This same assumption also dominates current K-12 curriculum design and pedagogy. This model assumes a top-down model of sustainable behavior where some entity or organization (such as a national government, NGO, educational institution, or other authority) has already determined what the optimal behavior is for the individual to adopt (Figure 1a). This persuasive model depends on the intellectual commitment that what the public is largely lacking is

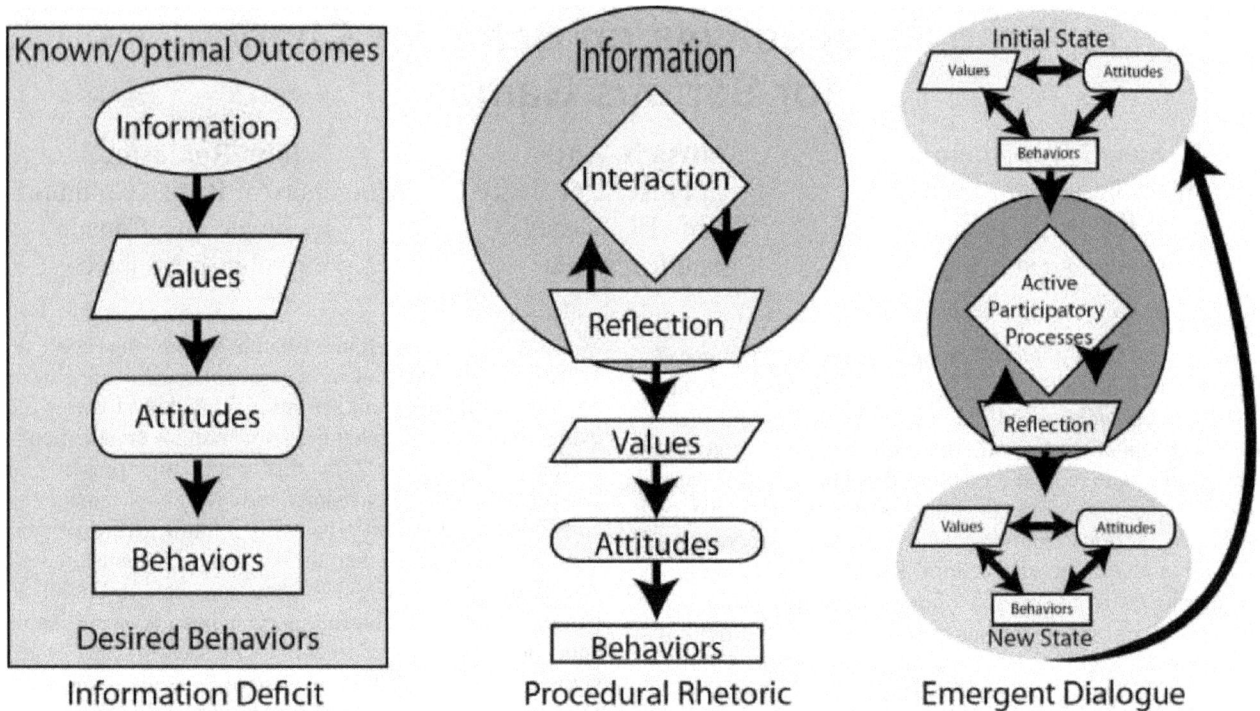

Figure 1 Three models of behavior change (left to right) a. Information Deficit, b. Procedural Rhetoric, c. Emergent Dialogue

information. This approach suffers when confronted with topics that do not yield easy answers. As John Robinson points out:

> "Multiple conflicting views of sustainability exist [that] cannot be reconciled in terms of each other. In other words, no single approach will, or indeed should be, seen as the correct one. This is not a matter of finding out what the truth of sustainability is by more sophisticated applications of expert understanding ... Instead we are inescapably involved in a world in which there exist multiple conflicting values, moral positions and belief systems that speak to the issue of sustainability." [9]

Games designed from the perspective of the Information Deficit model excel at delivering facts, but facts alone are insufficient to persuade. In situations where facts are unclear, or subject to disagreement, this approach breaks down. In these cases, the information deficit model does not reliably produce significant behavior change.

PROCEDURAL RHETORIC

In the field of Serious Games, one of the biggest areas of interest is sustainability and environmental issues (as evidenced by the substantial proportion of environment themed games listed on the *Games For Change* website) [5]. As interest in serious and persuasive games has risen, new models of persuasion in games have evolved. One current theory for how games persuade their players is Ian Bogost's concept of *Procedural Rhetoric* [1]. Procedural Rhetoric is based on the notion that the processes and activities that interactors engage in during play are more

persuasive than the information that is layered on top of those processes.

> "Procedural rhetoric is a general name for the practice of authoring arguments through processes...Procedural rhetoric entails expression—to convey ideas effectively...its arguments are made not through the construction of words or images, but through the authorship of rules of behavior, the construction of dynamic models." [2]

An excellent example of Procedural Rhetoric in action can be found in Gonzalo Frasca's newsgame *September the 12th* [4]. In it the player is presented with a cartoon depiction of a city in the Middle East. The streets are populated with civilians going peacefully about their daily lives. Interspersed among the civilians are armed terrorists. The player has control to move a mouse cursor shaped like a targeting reticle around over the busy streets. When the player clicks the mouse button there is a brief pause and then a missile strike hits the section of the city that was targeted, killing any of the virtual inhabitants that may have wandered into the line of fire during the delay. When this action results in the death of a civilian, another civilian will stop and weep over his or her dead friend or family member, before picking up a gun and transforming into a new terrorist. Through this simple combination of rules and simulational logic, *September the 12th* makes a very pointed claim about collateral damage and the "war on terror".

Unlike the Information Deficit model, Procedural Rhetoric grounds itself in interactive cycles of experience and reflection, similar to those advocated by James Gee [6]. Information and values are still present in this model, but the delivery of facts is not the basis for behavior change. Instead, information underlies the design of a set of simulated processes: it is the experience of interaction and reflection that motivates any changes in values, attitude and behavior (Figure 1b). Although for different reasons, Procedural Rhetoric and the Information Deficit model both employ a top-down approach. For Procedural Rhetoric, this emerges out of the necessarily asynchronous medium of communication: an author or designer must encode a procedural system with a set of potential activities which are then enacted by the interactor.

EMERGENT DIALOGUE

The final model of behavior change is a relatively new one from within sustainability research, based on extensive critiques of the Information Deficit model. As articulated by Robinson et al. [9-11], this model suggests that what is needed is not *information* but *participation* in meaningful processes exploring sustainability issues. Unlike the previous two models, this approach deals specifically with *groups* of people participating in some sort of civic activity.

Robinson's group argues that the previous conception of a unidirectional flow from information and values to attitudes to behaviors is inaccurate. Instead, they contend that information flows in a bi-directional manner, and that often the flow is in reverse: that people bring their attitudes in line with the behaviors they are already accustomed to, as is the case when an individual uses statistics about an increase in recycling to justify not turning off the light when leaving a room.

In participatory processes, the information content is not predetermined in a top down manner: instead it emerges through dialogue. This then leads to new understandings, which then feed back into the loop in an iterative process of ongoing negotiation and reevaluation. From this perspective, the goal of public engagement is not to *educate* people about correct or incorrect behavior but instead to *motivate* people to generate their own views about the type of world they want to live in. Unlike the previous two models, which focus on the decision making process of individuals, Robinson's Emergent Dialogue model positions people as social actors, collectively negotiating a shared vision of their desired future. The Emergent Dialogue model is not focused on individual behavior change but instead on social mobilization in support of collective behavior change. This emerges from the judgment that the most important changes are those (like land use, density, urban form, settlement patterns, transportation infrastructure, energy and water systems) that do not occur at the individual level but at the collective level (and indeed deeply constrain individual behavior change). Participating in these dialogical processes provides individuals and communities with a path to shaping civic policies, while also providing local governments and other stakeholders with a more direct mechanism for communicating their goals and constraints to the public.

Figure 1c shows one way of conceptualizing the Emergent Dialogue model, highlighting the iterative processes of feedback and reevaluation that it introduces.

Unlike the Information Deficit model, which is communicating a preset story about sustainable practices, processes of engagement which employ the Emergent Dialogue model create a context for individuals and stakeholders to imagine their own story for the future. The potential benefit of this model is that participants recognize the complex, multi-level nature of ecological, social and economic problems, and the consequent need for innovation, creativity and adaptive response.

Unlike the Procedural Rhetoric model, which is limited by what can be encoded within a computational system, the Emergent Dialogue model operates under the assumption of multiple human participants, all of whom are capable of creating new information through the process of engagement. This model is thus the only one of the three that fully supports the creation of new outcomes and information about sustainable practices. However, this strength also limits the approach, as the applicability and viability of these outcomes is a function of the commitment and effort of the participants. The biggest challenges faced in implementing this approach are establishing buy-in from a wide range of stakeholders with often very different needs and objectives, and finding ways to scale the process to accommodate a range of communities.

ANALYSIS OF THE MODELS

Each of these models has certain advantages and disadvantages for the design of serious games for sustainability. For many years the Information Deficit model dominated educational game design, which resulted in many games where the content being delivered by the game had very little to do with the gameplay itself. This is still a very common problem for educational games, with a proliferation of games with either game mechanics that are abstracted from the intended lesson, such as NASA's "Recycle This!", or games with no gameplay or game mechanics whatsoever, such as the EPA's "Dumptown" [8, 12]. Our biggest critique of the Information Deficit model is that it has historically failed to result in behavior change. From the perspective of Emergent Dialogue, this is because the Information Deficit model does not provide any avenue along which the recipient may arrive at her own conclusions. Both the Procedural Rhetoric and Emergent Dialogue models provide participants with opportunities to experience the issues through an active process and to arrive at their own conclusions about what is required to move themselves, their community, and their culture towards a more sustainable future. While Procedural Rhetoric still relies on a top-down asynchronous model of information, it does have the distinct advantage of being more easily communicated and transmitted via procedural systems such as games and simulations. Where Emergent Dialogue really stands out is in its ability to reincorporate personal and local approaches to sustainability back into the dialogical process, however there are significant challenges in eliciting buy-in from relevant stakeholders, as well as scaling issues that make it difficult to engage larger communities. Emergent Dialogues can benefit from new methods of facilitation that do not require large scale community events in order to succeed, or that can incorporate a broader subset of community members.

We thus see these three models as existing along a spectrum from the most authoritarian top-down approach on one end (the Information Deficit model) to the most participatory and bottom-up approach on the other end (the Emergent Dialogue Model). Procedural Rhetoric represents the current limit of our ability to design and conceptualize computational systems that support participatory meaning making processes.

Serious Games for Sustainability

A full survey of the current state of serious games for sustainability is outside the scope of this paper, The specific challenge faced by the GCC project is how to implement and incorporate elements of the Emergent Dialogue approach within a games design. We contend that games utilizing Procedural Rhetoric can be used as part of a larger process of public engagement, by contextualizing them within a broader conversation about sustainability. Games and simulations provide configurable tools that can serve as shared points of reference and negotiation for intergenerational conversations and small scale workshop participation. If a Procedural Rhetoric is made sufficiently entertaining, it has the potential to engage members of the public who might not otherwise be motivated to participate in a dialogue about sustainability issues. In spite of their limitations, we see serious games as playing an important role in an emergent process of public dialogue, which we see as essential to a process of behavioral change.

CONCLUSION

Designers of serious games may employ each of these three strategies in parallel, depending on the desired outcome. For example, games that incorporate the Information Deficit model can provide participants with detailed access to facts, opinions, and other materials related to the issue, but may not provide the participant with an experience that is similarly relevant. Games designed using the Procedural Rhetoric model may not include as much factual information; however the activity of playing them should create a state of mind in the participant that communicates a message about the related issues. Finally, games designed with Emergent Dialogue in mind need to provide the participant with the ability to create her own models and potential outcomes by configuring different variables within a domain of concern. Any one of these approaches is going to incorporate elements of the other two: a game rooted in Emergent Dialogue will still require information to manipulate, and any interactive system is going to include a

Procedural Rhetoric of some sort. By incorporating an awareness of these modes of engagement into our designs we are able to create game experiences that more specifically serve a particular approach to facilitating public engagement.

ACKNOWLEDGMENTS
This work is supported by the GRAND NCE Program

REFERENCES

1. Bogost, I. (2007). *Persuasive Games: The Expressive Power of Video Games*. The MIT Press, Cambridge.
2. Bogost, I. (2008). *The Rhetoric of Video Games*.In The Ecology of Games: Connecting Youth, Games, and Learning, K. Salen, eds. The MIT Press, Cambridge, MA.117 - 140.
3. Engelhardt, C. R., Bartholow, B. D., Kerr, G. T. and Bushman, B. J. (2011). This Is Your Brain on Violent Video Games: Neural Desensitization to Violence Predicts Increased Aggression Following Violent Video Game Exposure. *Journal of Experimental Social Psychology*, 47, 5, 1033-1036.
4. Frasca, G. (2003). *September the 12th*.Retrieved from http://www.newsgaming.com/games/index12.htm on September 12, 2012
5. Games for Change. (2011). *Games for Change: Play*.Retrieved from http://www.gamesforchange.org/game_categories/envir onment/ on July 10, 2011
6. Gee, J. P. (2007). *What Video Games Have to Teach Us About Learning and Literacy*. Palgrave Macmillan, New York, NY, USA.
7. He, H. A., Greenberg, S. and Huang, E. M. (2010). One Size Does *Not* Fit All: Applying the Transtheoretical Model to Energy Feedback Technology Design. *Proc. CHI 2010* 927-936
8. Nasa. (2012). *Recycle This!*Retrieved from http://climate.nasa.gov/kids/games/recycleThis/index.cf m on September 14, 2012
9. Robinson, J. (2004). Squaring the Circle? Some Thoughts on the Idea of Sustainable Development. *Ecological Economics*, 48, 369-384.
10. Robinson, J. (2008). Being Undisciplined: Some Transgressions and Intersections in Academia and Beyond. *Futures*, 40, 1, 70-86.
11. Salter, J., Robinson, J. and Wiek, A. (2010). Participatory Methods of Integrated Assessment - a Review. *Climate Change*, 1, 5, 697-717.
12. The United States Environmental Protection Agency. (2012). *Dumptown Game*.Retrieved from http://www.epa.gov/recyclecity/gameintro.htm on September 14, 2012
13. Treanor, M. and Mateas, M. (2009). Newsgames: Procedural Rhetoric Meets Political Cartoons. *Proc. DiGRA 2009*

Privacy as Part of the App Decision-Making Process

Patrick Gage Kelley
University of New Mexico
pgk@cs.unm.edu

Lorrie Faith Cranor
Carnegie Mellon University
lorrie@cs.cmu.edu

Norman Sadeh
Carnegie Mellon University
sadeh@cs.cmu.edu

ABSTRACT

Smartphones have unprecedented access to sensitive personal information. While users report having privacy concerns, they may not actively consider privacy while downloading apps from smartphone application marketplaces. Currently, Android users have only the Android permissions display, which appears after they have selected an app to download, to help them understand how applications access their information. We investigate how permissions and privacy could play a more active role in app-selection decisions. We designed a short "Privacy Facts" display, which we tested in a 20-participant lab study and a 366-participant online experiment. We found that by bringing privacy information to the user when they were making the decision and by presenting it in a clearer fashion, we could assist users in choosing applications that request fewer permissions.

Author Keywords

Privacy; Android; Mobile; Interface; Decision-making

ACM Classification Keywords

H.5.2. Information Interfaces and Presentation (e.g. HCI): User Interfaces

INTRODUCTION

In the past five years Android and iOS, the two now-largest smartphone operating systems, have transformed phones from devices with which to call others into true pocket computers. This has largely been accomplished through smartphone applications, often small, task-focused, executables that users can install on their phones from software markets. However, with each application a user downloads they may be sharing new types of information with additional app developers and third parties. Easy access to hundreds of thousands of applications from a diverse and global set of developers and the large amount of personal and sensitive data stored on smartphones multiply the privacy risks.

In Google Play, the current Android application marketplace, users are shown a series of "permissions" only after they have elected to download an application. Previous research suggests that users are likely to ignore the permissions display because it appears after they have decided to download a particular app [4, 12]. Furthermore, even users who pay attention

to permissions displays have trouble using them because the screens are jargon-filled, provide confusing explanations, and lack explanations for why the data is collected.

Our research aims to provide an alternative permissions and privacy display that would better serve users. Specifically, we address the following research question: Can we affect users' selection decisions by adding permissions/privacy information to the main app screen?

To answer this question, we created a simplified privacy checklist that fits on the main application display screen. We then tested it in two studies: a 20-participant laboratory exercise and a 366-participant Mechanical Turk study. In each study we asked our participants to role-play selecting applications for a friend who has just gotten their first Android phone. Participants were assigned to use either our new privacy checklist or the current permissions display found in the Android market. Our results suggest that our privacy checklist display does affect users' app selection decisions, especially when they are choosing between otherwise similar apps. We also found that both the timing of the privacy information display and the content of the display may impact the extent to which users pay attention to the information.

RELATED WORK

We outline previous research on the security model of the Android operating system, the current permissions model, and users' expectations regarding their phones. We focus on Android due to its historically more detailed permissions system and its large user base.

Android as a Major Application Provider

As of May 2012, Android has had over 15 billion application downloads, and over 500,000 applications, with both these numbers continuing to grow at an increasing rate [19].

Applications are not pre-screened for quality. Android app rating and recommendation site AppBrain reports that 33% of the applications in the Android Market are rated "low quality" by users. Additionally, a 2011 Juniper Networks report found "a 472% increase in Android malware samples" between July and November 2011 [11]. Similar studies from McAfee [16], Kaspersky Lab [20], and Symantec are all reporting continued exploits. The types and quality of this malware vary widely, ranging from attacks that collect user data (normally IMEI and other identifiers), to attacks that delete user data or send premium SMS messages.

To combat malicious applications Google internally developed a malware blocking tool codenamed Bouncer. Google announced that Bouncer had been checking "for malicious apps in Market for a while now," and as a result malware was declining [18]. However, there are reports of Bouncer's limitations, such as applications existing in the market for weeks without being noticed [21].

Android Security Research

While Android has only existed publicly since 2008, a significant amount of work has been conducted on studying the Android permissions/security model. Much of this work focuses on creating theoretical formalizations of how Android security works or presents improvements to system security, and is largely out of scope. Enck et al.'s TaintDroid has bridged the gap between system security and user-facing permissions, focusing on analyzing which applications are requesting information through permissions and then sending that data off phone [5].

Vidas et al. also studied how applications request permissions, finding prevalent "permissions creep," due to "existing developer APIs [which] make it difficult for developers to align their permission requests with application functionality" [25]. Felt et al., in their Android Permissions Demystified paper, attempt to further explain permissions to developers [6]. However, neither of these papers explore end-users understanding of permissions.

There is also a growing body of work on the complexity of the current permissions schemes users must deal with. Researchers have discovered novel attack vectors for applications to make permission requests that are not reported to users [3]. Others who have looked at Android permissions have attempted to cluster applications that require similar permissions to simplify the current scheme [2] or have attempted a comparison of the differences between modern smartphone permission systems [1].

Android Permissions and Privacy Research

Android permissions are a system controlled by the Android OS to allow applications to request access to system functionality through an XML manifest. As these permissions are shown to the user at install time, this system as a whole forms a Computer-Supported Access Control (CSAC) system, as defined by Stevens and Wulf [24].

The majority of work done on user expectations related to this Android access control system has been done by our own group at Carnegie Mellon [12, 17] and two separate teams at Berkeley.

Felt and her colleagues have published a series of papers on the Android permission model, and how users understand it. They found that most users do not pay attention to the permissions screens at install time (83%) and that only three percent of their surveyed users had a good understanding of what the permissions were actually asking for access to [9]. They also performed a large risk-assessment survey of users' attitudes towards possible security and privacy risks, and possible consequences of permission abuses [8]. These results influenced our selection of items to include in a privacy checklist. Felt also performed work detailing other possible methods for asking for permission, with a set of guidelines for presenting these privacy and security decisions to users [7].

Moving away from permissions, the work of King et al. has explored user expectations across the entire use of their smartphones. This broader work, which included interviews with both iPhone and Android users, highlighted difficulties in recognizing the difference between applications and websites, personal risk assessments of possible privacy faults, and how users select applications in the application marketplaces [14].

Research in privacy policies, financial privacy notices, and access control have all similarly shown that privacy-related concepts and terms are often not well understood by users expected to make privacy decisions [13, 15, 22]. No work we are currently aware of has proposed and tested alternative permissions displays, or other ways to help users select applications in Google Play, or other application markets, as we do here.

PRIVACY INFORMATION IN THE ANDROID MARKET

This section details how Google Play currently presents privacy information and other information to consumers to help them select new applications to download to their Android smartphone. We then discuss the privacy facts display we designed to make privacy- and security-related information more central to users' selections.

Privacy currently in Google Play

Google Play users are presented with a number of ways to search and browse for new applications. Featured applications, top charts, categories, a search tool, and similar application lists each direct users to a common "Application Display Screen" (Figure 1A. Standard Market).

This screen provides users with a long list of information about each application. This includes (but is not limited to), a series of navigational items, application information, screenshots, a series of market-assigned labels (top developer, editor's choice), free-test descriptions, a series of reviews, and a series of other types of applications that users may have viewed or chosen. The current market application display screen is very long, yet completely lacks privacy information.

Privacy/security information appears on the above screens only when it is mentioned in free-form text by developers or when it appears in text reviews (almost always in a negative context). Market-provided (and by extension, system-verified) privacy/security information appears only on the secondary screen shown after a user has clicked the download button.

This secondary screen, where permissions are displayed (Figure 1, A. Standard Permissions), again displays the application name, icon, developer, and top developer status icon. This is followed by a very large accept button, which is followed (thus after the action target) by a list of grouped permissions. Only some permissions are shown initially, followed by a "See all" toggle that expands to display the remainder of the permissions an application requests. Each of these permission groups can be selected to see a pop-up window that contains the definitions for each of the permissions in the selected group. Because there may be several grouped

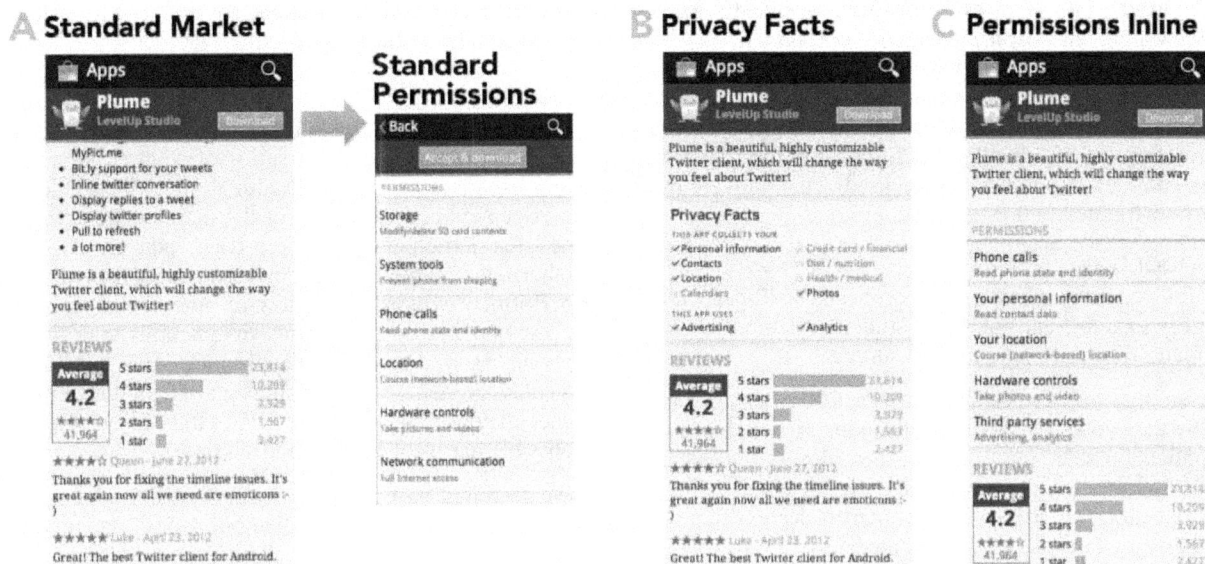

Figure 1. The three privacy/permissions display conditions we tested in our experiments.

permissions, the pop-ups may have to be scrolled to be read completely.

Reasons for modifying the Android application display

We posit that by the time a user selects to move forward by tapping the Download button, they have already made their purchase decision. We will see that this is true within our interview study below. For privacy information to be a salient part of the decision process, it must be presented to the user earlier in the process. Privacy information could be included in the long list of other application aspects on the standard application screen. Instead the current market places permissions on a secondary screen. While some might argue that placing permissions on their own screen draws users' attention to them, our results suggest that it actually does a disservice to users because they are unable to consider permissions as they consider other app characteristics.

Prototype privacy facts checklist design

We created a series of several possible locations and distinct styles of display in an ideation round. The custom privacy display that we decided to test is the Privacy Facts Checklist display shown in situ (Figure 1B. Privacy Facts). The display has several features:

Information— The display has two areas of information. The first with the header "THIS APP COLLECTS YOUR," describes eight types of information the app may collect: Personal information, contacts, location, calendars, credit card/financial, diet/nutrition, health/medical, and photos. The second header specifies "THIS APP USES" and lists advertising and analytics. Each of these ten items has a checkbox next to it, indicating use.

Display Style— The display is 270 pixels tall and the full width of the device (matching other standard application display sections). For comparison, the rating histogram is 162 pixels tall and the screenshots are the same as our privacy

display at 270 pixels.[1] The display has a bold header "Privacy Facts" in a non-Android-standard type.[2] The remainder of the display is presented in the standard Android Market typeface. The items are each displayed at the standard size, with the headers in capital text in a lighter font color.

Location— The display is shown immediately after the Description section (and Video and What's New sections, if present, which they were not in our studies) and always immediately before the Reviews section. This means when participants first see each app screen there is no visual difference from the market as it is currently displayed, as the Privacy Facts section appears below the fold (as it would on most phone models).

Permission mapping— For this display we strayed from the current Android permissions by:

- Including types of information being collected that fall outside of the scope of the current permission model (health information, other financial information).

- Including the use of third-party modules, specifically advertising and analytics.

- Removing permissions that are nearly always used (Internet) and those that are irrelevant to most users such as networking protocols and rarely used permissions.

- Including photographs, which are currently accessible to applications.

The final selection of the checklist items we used was strongly influenced by the work of Felt et al. [8] as well as our earlier work [12], and a series of online pilots. The checklist includes

---

[1]There is variation in screenshot size on different Android phone models. The measurements above, and throughout this paper, are from a Google Nexus One.

[2]The font used is Exo from the Google Font Library.

both Android permissions as well as user-provided information. We wanted this display to include both, for a more holistic privacy summary. Also, by including an item like photos, we create a display that is more in line with users' expectations (which universal accessibility of photos is not). A more complex form of this display could include information that explains how these permissions are used, what they are used for, or how frequently they are used.

METHODOLOGY

We will discuss two phases of experiments: a 20-participant laboratory exercise and interview study, and an online 366-participant MTurk app comparison survey.

In our studies we ask participants to actively consider how and why they download applications in the market, complete our application selection task, and then discuss that experience. In both studies, the core of the experiment was an application selection task using different market designs that vary in how privacy information is presented.

Our study design was based on a similar study run by a team of researchers at Berkeley. The researchers had participants decide whether to install applications on a computer to see whether people read license agreements at install time. Their users evaluated the software tools as complete packages, based on brand, design, functionality, and also End User License Agreements [10]. Similarly, we seek to understand whether people read the permissions display or our updated privacy facts display when installing software on an Android smartphone, and whether we can manipulate their decisions through improved design and information.

Application selection task

The main task asked participants to select one application from each of six pairs of applications we presented in our "custom Android market." We presented two applications for each of the six categories (below). All of the applications we used were real applications that could be found and downloaded in the market. Their names, screenshots, descriptions, features, ratings, and reviews were all authentic. However, we picked most applications in the 1,000 to 10,000 download range, such that the applications would not have been seen or used by most participants. We displayed three text reviews per application, one 2- or 3-star, one 4-star, and one 5-star review.

In four of the comparisons we tested applications that were roughly equivalent (Twitter, document scanning, word game, nutrition app). In each of these four cases participants were presented with two applications with different permissions requests, detailed in Table 2. In each of these choices one of the applications requested less access to permissions and personal information (low-requesting v. high-requesting).

We also tested two special-case comparisons, to begin to explore the effects of rating and brand. In the flight-tracking comparison, we modified one of the applications (Flight-Tracker, low-requesting), to have an average rating of 3-stars. All of the other applications in all categories had 4-star average ratings. In the case of streaming music apps, we tested Spotify, a highly-known (shown in pre-tests) application with

over 50 million downloads. Nearly all of our participants recognized this application.

Lab Study

To test the privacy facts display, and explore our research question, we conducted a series of semi-structured laboratory exercises in July 2012 with 20 participants. This was a between-subjects design. For the main application selection task ten participants saw the privacy facts checklist, and the other ten saw the current Android permissions display. We performed exploratory follow-up interviews seeking broad understanding of participants' interactions with their smartphones as well as diving deeply into issues surrounding the display of permissions, understanding of the terms in the checklist/permissions display, the safety of Google Play, and possible harms of information sharing.

We recruited participants through flyers and local Craigslist postings. Each candidate filled out a short pre-survey online before the exercise, which allowed us to confirm they used an Android-enabled smartphone. We performed the study in an on-campus lab and audio recorded the interviews. Participants were assigned randomly to conditions (without any balancing for gender, time-using android, technical knowledge, or age). They were paid $20 for successful completion of the interview, in the form of their choice of Target, Starbucks, or Barnes & Noble gift cards.

Exercise and Interview focus

The lab study followed a semi-structured format, outlined here:

- *Android introduction*: Questioned participants about general Android experience

- *General new smartphone advice*: Asked for advice to give to a hypothetical friend and new smartphone owner

- *Specific new smartphone advice*: Requested advice framed around a desire for six specific types of apps

- *Application selection task*: Had participants select applications with a Google Nexus One smartphone on our modified market

- *Post task explanation*: Requested explanations for why each app was selected

- *Android in the news and malicious activity*: Inquired on awareness of Android and apps in the news or on the Internet, then on malicious apps

- *Android permissions and privacy displays*: Drilled down to the privacy and permissions issues, asking if they had noticed the new display or used the current permissions display, depending on condition

Online Study

We conducted an online survey, a 366-participant MTurk test of the same application selection task used in the laboratory study. Because this was performed on MTurk the application selection task had a more structured survey format, as well as some other methodological differences that will be discussed

	Gender	Age	Occupation	Phone Model	Time Using Android	# of Apps Downloaded	# of Apps Frequently Used
P1	Female	21	Student	Motorola Droid	1–2 years	11–25	1–5
P2	Male	21	Student	Motorola Photon	7 months–1 year	101+	6–20
P3	Female	29	Other	Motorola Droid	1–2 years	11–25	6–20
P4	Female	39	Non-Profit	T-Mobile MyTouch 4G Slide	More than 2 years	11–25	20+
P5	Female	44	Marketing	Pantech Breakout Droid	7 months–1 year	11–25	6–20
P6	Female	30	Research / Science	Motorola Droid	1–2 years	11–25	6–20
P7	Male	43	Other	Motorola Droid	1–6 months	1–10	None
P8	Male	20	Student	Motorola Defy	1–2 years	1–10	6–20
P9	Male	31	Healthcare / Medical	Motorola Droid	More than 2 years	1–10	1–5
P10	Female	23	Research / Science	Samsung Galaxy	1–2 years	11–25	1–5
A1	Female	20	Student	Motorola Droid	7 months–1 year	11–25	1–5
A2	Female	23	Don't work	T-Mobile G2/HTC Desire Z	More than 2 years	1–10	1–5
A3	Female	20	Student	LG Ally / Optimus	1–2 years	26–100	6–20
A4	Female	28	Student	Samsung Galaxy	More than 2 years	11–25	6–20
A5	Female	24	Student	HTC rezound	More than 2 years	11–25	1–5
A6	Female	24	Research / Science	LG Ally / Optimus	1–2 years	11–25	1–5
A7	Male	21	Student	Motorola Droid	1–2 years	26–100	6–20
A8	Female	23	Research / Science	T-Mobile HTC G2	1–2 years	11–25	1–5
A9	Female	26	Research / Science	HTC Status	1–2 years	26–100	6–20
A10	Female	44	Healthcare / Medical	Motorola Droid	1–2 years	26–100	6–20

Table 1. Basic demographics of our lab study participants. Participant numbers beginning with P saw the privacy facts checklist, those with A saw the standard Android system. All the information above is self reported.

below in the limitations section. We again used a between-subjects design, but with three conditions. Participants saw one of: the privacy facts checklist (Figure 1B); the current android permissions display (Figure 1A); or the current android permissions display style and terms, presented in the application display screen with additional terms to cover categories from the privacy facts display (Figure 1C). In each case they were asked to pick six from the same 12 applications that our participants in the lab study were given, and then were asked to write a short sentence explaining their choice. For successful completion of the survey turkers were paid $0.30.

We used MTurk's user filtering system (95% success required) and required English speakers and Android users. The survey was front loaded with questions about the turker's Android device to discourage users who did not use Android phones. We manually inspected free-response questions to check for participants who were answering randomly, but removed no participants in that stage, only filtering (12) users who had not used the Android market.

LAB STUDY RESULTS

In this section we detail the results from our lab study. We cover the basic demographics of our participants, their experience with Android, their advice both general and specific to their hypothetical friend, the results of their application selection, and their post-task interview responses.

Demographics

As shown in Table 1, 25% of our 20 participants were male and 75% were female. Participants were between 20 and 44 years old, with an average of 28; 30% were undergraduates. All of our participants had downloaded Android applications from the market and were neutral or satisfied with the Google Play experience.

Application selection

The Privacy Facts display appears to have influenced participants in two of the four standard comparisons and in both of the special comparisons. Full selection percentages can be found in the first two columns of Table 3 (alongside the online study results).

In two of the four standard comparisons (word game, and Twitter) participants who saw the privacy facts display were, on average, more likely to pick the application that requested fewer permissions. In Document scanning, only one participant in each condition did not pick DroidScan Lite (the low-requesting app). In the diet application choice, no participants in the Android condition picked Doc's Diet Diary (the high-requesting app), while three with the Privacy Facts display did. In both the two special comparisons more of the participants who saw the privacy facts display picked the low-requesting app.[3]

Participants placed substantial weight on the design and perceived simplicity of using the application. Participants continued to surprise us with ever more idiosyncratic reasons for selecting certain applications. One participant preferred applications with simplistic names, saying "I like to download the apps that have a name that I can easily find. So Calorie Counter, I know where that is gonna be on my phone. I don't have to be like, oh, what is this called."

Participants reported wanting to try the apps out, often saying they would download many and see which was the best (which our study prevented them from doing). One said "And I might try things out and see... I just kind of see how well it works, because some things are more glitchy."

---

[3]Given the small numbers of participants we did not expect differences to be statistically significant and only the Twitter application choice was significant (Fisher's Exact test, $p = 0.023$, the odds ratio is 11.64).

	Personal	Contacts	Location	Calendars	Financial	Diet/nutrition	Health/medical	Photos	Advertising	Analytics	Total
Wordoid!	–	–	–	–	–	–	–	–	–	–	0
Word Weasel	✓	–	✓	–	–	–	–	–	–	✓	3
Twidroyd	✓	–	–	–	–	–	–	✓	–	–	2
Plume	✓	✓	✓	–	–	–	–	✓	✓	✓	6
DroidScan Lite	–	–	–	–	–	–	–	✓	–	–	1
M. Doc Scan Lite	✓	✓	–	–	–	–	–	✓	–	✓	4
Calorie Counter	✓	–	–	–	–	–	–	–	–	✓	2
Doc's Diet Diary	✓	✓	✓	–	–	✓	–	✓	–	✓	6
Rdio	✓	✓	–	–	–	–	–	–	–	–	2
Spotify (brand)	✓	✓	✓	–	✓	–	–	✓	✓	✓	7
Flight Tracker	✓	–	✓	–	–	–	–	–	–	–	2
iFlights (rating)	✓	–	✓	✓	✓	–	–	–	–	✓	5

Table 2. The boxes checked in the privacy facts checklist for each application are shown above. In each application category, one of the two applications requested access to fewer permissions (low-requesting always shown first).

Possible hidden costs also impacted application selection. Several participants noted that while the music streaming applications were free (as were all the applications we tested), they might have to purchase a subscription, or be unable to access certain functionality after a trial period ended. Participants generally wanted to avoid applications where features would expire or that would require later costs, but more importantly they expected the details of these arrangements to be extremely clear in the descriptions.

Android in the news and malicious activity
Most participants reported not seeing much about Android in the news, and most of what they did see being comparisons between Apple's iOS and Android. When we asked about reports of malicious apps, or apps doing unintended things, participants said they had not heard about this. Many believed that it could be hypothetically possible. One participant said "Like, I have wondered, oh could an app be a virus," another "I've heard about viruses, that they can actually shut your computer or phone down. Spyware."

Permissions and Privacy terminology
To test whether the terms we selected for the Privacy Facts display were understandable, we asked participants to explain what each term meant. While most were very clear, Personal Information and Analytics were the two that participants had the most trouble with. Personal Information answers were often too broad, encompassing things we did not intend. For example, one participant defined it as "That would mean like... interactions within the phone, Gmail, Messaging, Calling different people."

Participants generally preferred the checklist and its terminology. One participant said, "[Privacy Facts is] very straightforward to me. And that is something I noticed, I was thinking, Oh this is cool, is this what they are doing now. That is why I didn't say anything about it. I can immediately go: No, Yes, No, Yes."

Only two participants explicitly mentioned privacy information in their application selection decisions, both in the privacy facts checklist condition. One participant, said, "If this one is offering the same thing and they want less of your information, I would go with the one that wants less of your information." This comment shows her awareness of the privacy information, but also that the functionality must be matched between apps.

Task time and permission views
Overall, the entire laboratory exercise ranged from 29 minutes to 59 minutes (average 39:53). Participants spent between 3 minutes and 47 seconds to 25 minutes and 6 seconds on the application selection task. There was no statistically significant difference between conditions (two-tailed t-test, $p = 0.726$), although participants who saw the privacy facts checklist took on average 50 seconds more (11:40 v. 10:51) to complete the task.

Across all participants in the Android permissions condition, the permissions screen was used by participants for about half the selection decisions. Four participants decided which applications they would select without ever looking at any permissions screens. Another four participants looked at permissions for all the applications they selected. A6 looked at both Twitter applications permissions, but did not look at the permissions for either of the flight applications. A9 looked at only the permissions for the Twitter application she selected and no other applications.

Across all 31 permission screen views, participants spent between 1 and 11 seconds looking at the Android permissions display. On average they viewed the permissions display for 3.19 seconds (median 2 seconds), including page load time, a minuscule amount compared to time spent on the applications display screen.

ONLINE STUDY RESULTS
In our online study, the application selection task was conducted on MTurk through a participant's computer, not a smartphone. Participants saw the applications presented at smartphone size, side-by-side in iframes. Participants selected the application they thought was better for their friend, provided a short text reason, and then rated each of the two presented applications on the likelihood that they would personally acquire it.

With this study, we introduce a third condition, called Permissions Inline. This treatment was designed to separate the location of the privacy information from its format. It showed the standard Android Permissions Display, but positioned on the app display screen (where Privacy Facts is located) rather than in the standard location after the user tapped "Download." This condition tested whether it was only the existence of any privacy information on the application screen that changed behavior, or the checklist format and position.

We used the graphic design of the permissions display from the current Google Play store; however, we modified the labels to present the same information as our Privacy Facts display (including health, nutrition, advertising, and analytics).

	Lab Study		Online Study							
	Privacy Facts (n=10)	Android Display (n=10)	*Android Display (n=120)*	Privacy Facts (n=123)	Diff. from Android	p-value	Permissions Inline (n=123)	Diff. from android	p-value	Inline v. Facts
Wordoid!	60%	50%	40.8%	61.0%			49.6%			
Word Weasel	30%	50%	59.2%	39.0%	**20%**	**0.002**	50.4%	9%	0.198	0.095
Twidroyd	70%	20%	25.0%	52.9%			35.8%			
Plume	30%	80%	75.0%	47.2%	**28%**	**< 0.001**	64.2%	11%	0.051	**0.014**
DroidScan Lite	90%	90%	73.3%	60.2%			62.6%			
M. Doc Scan Lite	0%	10%	26.7%	39.8%	−13%	0.031	37.4%	−11%	0.076	0.784
Calorie Counter	70%	100%	55.8%	73.2%			73.2%			
Doc's Diet Diary	30%	0%	44.2%	26.8%	**17%**	**0.005**	26.8%	**17%**	**0.005**	1
Rdio	40%	30%	17.5%	28.5%			22.8%			
Spotify *(brand)*	60%	70%	82.5%	71.5%	**11%**	**0.048**	77.2%	5%	0.340	0.381
Flight Tracker	40%	20%	40.8%	35.0%			37.4%			
iFlights *(rating)*	50%	80%	59.2%	65.0%	−6%	0.358	62.6%	−3%	0.601	0.791

Table 3. Application selections in the laboratory and online studies. The application that requested access to fewer permissions (the privacy-protective choice) is always displayed on top. Statistics for the online study are comparisons to the base Android display. The right-most column shows the significance between the checklist and the inline permissions. Differences in bold, Fisher's Exact. Comparisons with the Android display were planned contrasts. The final comparison between the permissions inline and privacy facts display is Holm-corrected with an adjusted alpha of 0.01667.

An example of this is shown in Figure 1C.

Demographics

Of our 366 MTurk participants 59% were male and 41% were female (markedly different from our lab study). Our participants were between 18 and 63 years old, with an average of 28. All of our participants had experience downloading Android applications from the market (the 12 who did not were removed from this analysis).

Application selection

Overall the privacy facts display (changed format and position) had a stronger effect on participants application selections than only moving the permissions inline (changed position).

Privacy Facts display

In three of the four standard comparisons, significantly more privacy facts participants than Android participants chose the low-requesting app. Only for the document scanner did more participants in the standard Android condition choose the low-requesting app, and this difference was not significant.

For the Twitter choice, nearly three-quarters of the Android display participants chose Plume (high-requesting). One participant captured many of the common reasons for making this choice, reflecting, "Plume has 35,000 more reviews, which suggests to me that this is the more popular, more frequently used application. The description includes a list of everything you can do with the app and those all seem like useful features." However when presented with the privacy facts checklist, the two applications were selected at almost the same rate, with slightly more selecting Twidroyd. Here participants noted and cited the permissions information. One stated, "I picked the one that respects privacy more. The other gets too much personal info." Another participant wrote, "Plume collects too many personal facts."

For the special comparisons, rating and brand recognition outweighed privacy. However, even when one of the choices

was a well-known brand privacy facts participants were significantly more likely than Android participants to select the relatively-unknown, low-requesting choice. For the flight tracking choice, more participants chose iFlights (high-requesting) over Flight Tracker. Although participants thought iFlights "sounds like an iPhone port," many believed it had a cleaner UI, but the top reason given was the rating difference. Flight Tracker's 3-stars seems to have outweighed all other factors. For the streaming music choice, Spotify (high-requesting) had much higher brand recognition (although again, both are real services). In the Android permissions display condition over half of the people (66/104) who selected Spotify explicitly stated that they had already heard it was very good or that they or friends use Spotify. One participant said "Spotify is pretty popular and I have never heard of Rdio." Spotify collected much more information than Rdio. but in this case we see that brand information trumps privacy concerns, though there is still a significant shift (11%) in favor of Rdio in the privacy facts condition.

Permissions Inline

As shown in in Table 3, the permissions inline display, while in the same place and often more space-consuming than the checklist, did not have as large an effect on users' decisions. In only one of the four standard comparisons, the nutrition application, was this change significant, and in most cases it underperformed the checklist display (significantly underperforming for twitter apps). This suggests that in addition to moving privacy information to the application display screen, it is important to present that information in a holistic, clear, and simple way if it is to impact users' app selections.

Free responses

Across the free-text responses for why applications were selected by participants in the Android display conditions, privacy was only mentioned by one participant, and permissions were mentioned by four others. Across the privacy facts checklist condition privacy was mentioned by 15 participants, and permissions were mentioned by seven more. Information or info were mentioned by 49 people in the privacy facts checklist condition, but by only six participants using the Android display. Based on these responses privacy and personal information seem to have factored more strongly into the decisions of those who saw the privacy facts checklist.

Similar to our lab study, many participants, when directly asked, said they did not notice the privacy facts checklist. Of the 125 participants who were shown the privacy facts checklist, 49 (39.2%) reported in a free-text response having not noticed or paid any attention to the display. Both those people who did and those who did not notice the display provided reasons for why they ignored it, or believed it was not necessary:

- "I noticed the Privacy Facts but it really didn't influence me that much. I feel like with social networking it's so much easier to get contacts, photos, or information of someone."

- "It didn't influence my decision even though i noticed it. I tend to pay more attention to ratings and usefulness then anything else."

- "No, not really. It's not the most important factor. I don't keep a bunch of vital personal info on my phone, so no worries. I think people who do are really stupid."

There were also users who found the privacy facts display helpful and made their decisions based on it:

- "Yes. I believe the privacy information is helpful. It would only bother me if I saw something that didn't make sense for the app to use. However, I am not terribly concerned about privacy."

- "Yes. It only influenced me if it seemed to be the only thing to distinguish between the two apps."

- "Yeah, I always check that stuff. I want to know exactly what is happening to and with my data from that program when I use it. It was useful though I wish some apps would go into greater detail."

Participants who both used and didn't use the display still had misconceptions about companies, sharing information, and the market. Many assumed that all applications collect the same information. One participant who didn't look at the display said she did not because, "I assume they always say the same thing...."

Participants also continued to believe external forces protect them. One said, "Yes I saw the privacy facts. That didn't really affect my decision as companies are required to protect consumer's information and companies don't really wanna get sued for breach of security so I am not worried about all that." Another stated the continued belief that the market is internally well-regulated, "I think it is trustworthy, I would assume google play keeps a tight leash on that stuff."

Finally, one participant gave an answer that applies quite broadly, and mirrors work by Staddon et al. [23], "Yes, I noticed the privacy facts but it didn't effect [sic] my decision because I don't really know what the negative impacts of the

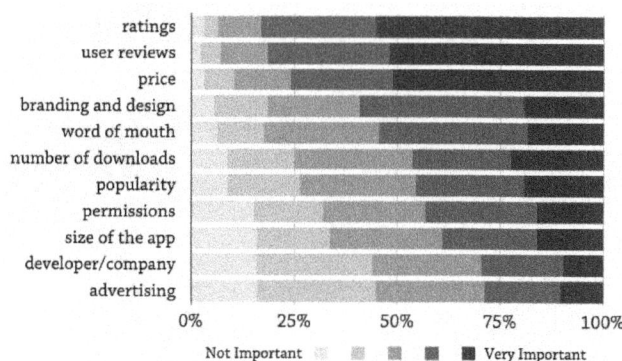

Figure 2. A series of factors users consider when decided on applications. Ranked by the number of users reporting a 4 or 5, where 5 is "Very important."

information they obtain would be." Understanding the potential harm in allowing access to certain types of data remains difficult for consumers both in smartphones and other digital domains.

Self-reported decision factors

We also asked our online participants to rank a series of factors in their personal application-selection process from "Not important" to "Very important." The results of this are presented in Figure 2. Permissions ranked 8th (of 11), just below two metrics of popularity and just above the size of the application. 80% of participants said ratings and reviews were important or very important, compared with only 43% who said that permissions were important or very important.

This result seems to align with how often participants across our tests tended to ignore permissions.

Limitations

Our short checklist display had items that consumers were able to explain in most cases. Analytics and Personal Information were the most problematic. Participants were generally correct when defining Analytics, but often created more invasive definitions that were not intended. Personal Information was more difficult, as it was too vague and many participants listed other types of data that they then realized were covered by another item on the list. We will continue to further refine the terms and types of information that is most important to people.

One more significant design flaw with the display was that participants do not view permissions displays in the same way as they view privacy policies. They see this information only as items the phone can *take*, not things that they personally input. While we believe a complete privacy display should cover both user-provided information that is stored (i.e., medical or diet) *and* automatically collected information like location, this was not explained well by the current design.

Our lab study has many more female participants than male participants, and due to random condition assignment they were not evenly distributed. We note this as a potential limitation, though our results from the two studies are aligned, and we did not see such a similar gender imbalance in our online study.

Mechanical Turk also has its own set of limitations and biases, which we attempted to counter through a careful survey design. While we compared our two survey phases, they did not follow identical methodologies. Our lab study was more realistic, with users using actual cell phones, when on MTurk users saw the applications side by side, and could make direct and visual comparisons. While the reasoning and behavior given seems similar, it is possible that our online survey users had an easier time making decisions, not due to our improved permissions display, but due to the side-by-side display. The only evidence we have to counter this is the permissions-in-place display did not perform as well as the privacy facts display, implying that the side-by-side display alone is not responsible for all the improvements we saw.

Finally, we tested only 12 applications in the studies described above (and an additional 12 in early pilots). We picked applications that seemed similar, functional, and would be unrecognized, but we would like to expand this work in the future to consider larger application datasets.

DISCUSSION
Our goal was to better understand how users select Android applications, and to make privacy and permission information a salient part of that process.

We found that users did not use the current permissions display. By moving privacy/permissions information onto the main screen and presenting it clearly and simply we could affect user decisions in cases where applications were similar. Users mostly appreciated the new privacy facts display, said they would use it to help make their decisions or at least glance at it, and found comparing applications in the market to be a difficult task where better displays would assist them.

Can we affect users' decisions?
The short answer, is yes—the privacy information on the application display screen affected user behavior. In laboratory responses and our online test we saw behavioral differences as well as differences in quality and tone of responses relating to private information.

We also found most people do not consider permissions when downloading new applications. Even when instructed to download applications, most users made decisions without ever pushing the button that would take them to the permissions display. Both our lab participants and our online participants also self-reported that they were aware of the display, but did not look at it. This was confirmed by our lab study participants who, when they did fully "download" applications, spent a median time of 2 seconds on the permissions display. While this was expected based on other research and our own earlier work, we now have evidence that the permissions are, at least partially, disregarded due to their position in the application selection process.

In online testing we found that having a privacy display would in cases of equivalent applications change user application selection, and do so more strongly than simply moving the permissions display to the main screen. We also seem to have initial results that indicate even relatively sizable privacy differences cannot outweigh some other factors such as very

popular applications (significant change, but not a majority) or differences in average ratings (3-star vs. 4-star apps, almost no change).

All of our participants had never seen a privacy facts display before, but were immediately able to make comparisons when specifically instructed to do so after the selection task. However, some simply did not believe privacy information was important or relevant to their decision. Some said it would depend on how much their friend (as part of the role-play) cared about his or her own privacy.

These results are similar to those seen in other labeling efforts. Consumers who care more about privacy, whether they have had a credit card stolen or have started receiving spam text-messages, are more likely to take advantage of labeling information. Even if the impact is not drastic, we see the privacy information on the main screen having an affect on selection behavior.

Do users enjoy, notice, and trust permissions information?
Participants in our studies reported being familiar with permissions displays and being aware that there are differences between applications. While this may seem unimportant or obvious, leveraging the awareness of privacy differences means creating interfaces, like checklists, that help consumers identify and compare differences should benefit users who want to make privacy-preserving decisions.

The terms on the current Android Permissions display remain difficult to understand and participants believed that there was little they could do as most of their information was already exposed. Participants reported that they did not, in most cases, read the information in the displays, and they did not select the permission groupings to see more details or try to better understand the terms. Even when the display was moved to the main screen, it does not have the impact of the privacy facts display.

Participants continued to report not being concerned with data sharing generally, partially due to a belief that companies are following laws and a strong belief that Android/Google is watching out for their safety as a consumer. While this is accurate in a very general sense, the specifics are quite far off from reality. Correcting the ubiquitous idea of Google Play as a safe, protected marketplace, must necessarily be changed if consumers are to protect themselves through understanding privacy and security in their decision-making process.

From both the lab and online studies we found that participants continued to report that other characteristics of applications are as important or more important than permissions, including: cost, functionality, design, simplicity, rating, number of ratings, reviews, downloads, size, and others. Continuing to understand how much privacy can compete and offset other aspects is important future work as consumers battle with a crowded and complex market.

When asked why an application was collecting a type of information, participants most often stated they did not know, but would occasionally venture possibilities. All of our lab study participants wanted to better understand why applications required the permissions they did.

Finally, participants overwhelmingly trusted the application in both the privacy facts display and the permissions display. The question of trusting the information was one most had never considered, and actually gave some participants pause as they realized for the first time that this information might not be accurate. Again, users believe this information is correct, is being verified, and will assume they misunderstand something before they would believe the displays are incorrect. Mistakes in the permissions are not recognized, even when directly discussed. Users will assume they themselves are wrong, not the policy.

CONCLUSION

Smartphones have unprecedented access to sensitive personal information. While users are aware of this, generally, they may not be considering privacy when they select applications to download in the application marketplace. Currently, users have only the Android permissions displays to help them make these application selection decisions, screens which are placed after the main decision occurs, and are not easily understood. We sought to investigate how we could make permissions and privacy play a true part in these decisions. We created a short "Privacy Facts" display, which we then tested in 20 in-lab exercises and an online test of 366 participants. We found that bringing information to the user *when* they are making the decision and by *presenting* it in a clearer fashion, we can assist users in making more privacy-protecting decisions.

ACKNOWLEDGEMENTS

We acknowledge our colleagues at Carnegie Mellon University, and would like to thank Alessandro Acquisti and Sunny Consolvo. This work was supported by the National Science Foundation under Grant DGE-0903659 (IGERT: Usable Privacy and Security). Additional support was provided by NSF grants CNS-1012763, CNS-0905562 and DGE 0903659, by CyLab at Carnegie Mellon under grants DAAD19-02-1-0389 and W911NF-09-1-0273 from the ARO as well as Google.

REFERENCES

1. Au, K., Zhou, Y., Huang, Z., Gill, P., and Lie, D. Short paper: a look at smartphone permission models. In *Proceedings of the 1st ACM workshop on Security and privacy in smartphones and mobile devices (SPSM '11)* (2011).

2. Barrera, B., Kayacik, H., van Oorschot, P., and Somayaji, A. A methodology for empirical analysis of permission-based security models and its application to android. In *In Proceedings of the 17th ACM conference on Computer and communications security (CCS '10)* (2010).

3. Barrera, D., Clark, J., McCarney, D., and van Oorschot, P. C. Understanding and improving app installation security mechanisms through empirical analysis of android. In *2nd Annual ACM CCS Workshop on Security and Privacy in Smartphones and Mobile Devices (SPSM)* (2012).

4. Egelman, S., Tsai, J., Cranor, L., and Acquisti, A. Timing is everything?: the effects of timing and placement of online privacy indicators. In *Proceedings of the 27th international conference on Human factors in computing systems*, ACM (2009), 319–328.

5. Enck, W., Gilbert, P., Chun, B., Cox, L., Jung, J., McDaniel, P., and Sheth, A. Taintdroid: an information-flow tracking system for realtime privacy monitoring on smartphones. In *In Proceedings of the 9th USENIX conference on Operating systems design and implementation (OSDI'10)* (2010).

6. Felt, A., Chin, E., Hanna, S., Song, D., and Wagner, D. Android permissions demystified. In *In Proceedings of the 18th ACM conference on Computer and communications security (CCS '11)* (2011).

7. Felt, A. P., Egelman, S., Finifter, M., Akhawe, D., and Wagner, D. How to ask for permission. In *USENIX Workshop on Hot Topics in Security (HotSec) 2012* (2012).

8. Felt, A. P., Egelman, S., and Wagner, D. I've got 99 problems, but vibration ain't one: A survey of smartphone users' concerns. In *2nd Annual ACM CCS Workshop on Security and Privacy in Smartphones and Mobile Devices (SPSM)* (2012).

9. Felt, A. P., Ha, E., Egelman, S., Haney, A., Chin, E., and Wagner, D. Android permissions: User attention, comprehension, and behavior. In *Symposium on Usable Privacy and Security (SOUPS) 2012* (2012).

10. Good, N., Dhamija, R., Grosssklags, J., Thaw, D., Aronowitz, S., Mulligan, D., and Konstan, J. Stopping spyware at the gate: A user study of privacy, notice and spyware. In *In Proceedings of the 5th Symposium on Usable Privacy and Security (SOUPS 05)* (2005).

11. Juniper Networks. Mobile malware development continues to rise, android leads the way, 2011. http://globalthreatcenter.com/?p=2492.

12. Kelley, P., Consolvo, S., Cranor, L., Jung, J., Sadeh, N., and Wetherall, D. A conundrum of permissions: Installing applications on an android smartphone. In *Financial Cryptography and Data Security*, vol. 7398. 2012, 68–79.

13. Kelley, P. G., Bresee, J., Cranor, L. F., and Reeder, R. W. A "Nutrition Label" for Privacy. In *Proceedings of the 2009 Symposium On Usable Privacy and Security (SOUPS)* (2009).

14. King, J. "How come i'm allowing strangers to go through my phone?"- Smartphones and privacy expectations, 2013. http://jenking.net/mobile/.

15. Kleimann Communication Group Inc. Evolution of a prototype financial privacy notice., February 2006. http://www.ftc.gov/privacy/privacyinitiatives/ftcfinalreport060228.pdf.

16. Labs, M. Mcafee threats report: Third quarter 2011, 2011. http://www.mcafee.com/us/resources/reports/rp-quarterly-threat-q3-2011.pdf.

17. Lin, J., Sadeh, N., Amini, S., Lindqvist, J., Hong, J. I., and Zhang, J. Expectation and purpose: understanding users' mental models of mobile app privacy through crowdsourcing. UbiComp '12, ACM (2012), 501–510.

18. Lockheimer, H. Android and security, 2012. http://googlemobile.blogspot.com/2012/02/android-and-security.html.

19. Lunden, I. Google play about to pass 15 billion app downloads? pssht! it did that weeks ago, 2012. http://techcrunch.com/2012/05/07/google-play-about-to-pass-15-billion-downloads-pssht-it-did-that-weeks-ago/.

20. Namestnikov, Y. It threat evolution: Q3 2011, 2011. http://www.securelist.com/en/analysis/204792201/IT_Threat_Evolution_Q3_2011.

21. Rashid, F. Y. Black hat: Researchers find way to "bounce" malware into google app store, 2012. http://www.scmagazine.com/black-hat-researchers-find-way-to-bounce-malware-into-google-app-store/article/252098/.

22. Smetters, D., and Good, N. How users use access control. In *In Proceedings of the 5th Symposium on Usable Privacy and Security (SOUPS 09)* (2009).

23. Staddon, J., Huffaker, D., Brown, L., and Sedley, A. Are privacy concerns a turn-off? engagement and privacy in social networks. In *Symposium on Usable Privacy and Security (SOUPS)* (2012).

24. Stevens, G., and Wulf, V. Computer-supported access control. *ACM Trans. Comput.-Hum. Interact. 16*, 3 (Sept. 2009), 12:1–12:26.

25. Vidas, T., Christin, N., and Cranor, L. F. Curbing android permission creep. In *W2SP 2011* (2011).

"Everybody Knows What You're Doing": A Critical Design Approach to Personal Informatics

Vera Khovanskaya[1], Eric P.S. Baumer[2,1], Dan Cosley[1], Stephen Voida[1], Geri Gay[2,1]

[1]Department of Information Science
Cornell University
Ithaca, NY 14850 USA

[2]Department of Communication
Cornell University
Ithaca, NY 14850 USA

{vdk9, ericpsb, drc44, svoida, gkg1}@cornell.edu

ABSTRACT

We present an alternative approach to the design of personal informatics systems: instead of motivating people to examine their own behaviors, this approach promotes awareness of and reflection on the infrastructures behind personal informatics and the modes of engagement that they promote. Specifically, this paper presents an interface that displays personal web browsing data. The interface aims to reveal underlying infrastructure using several methods: drawing attention to the scope of mined data by displaying deliberately selected sensitive data, using purposeful malfunction as a way to encourage reverse engineering, and challenging normative expectations around data mining by displaying information in unconventional ways. Qualitative results from a two-week deployment show that these strategies can raise people's awareness about data mining, promote efficacy and control over personal data, and inspire reflection on the goals and assumptions embedded in infrastructures for personal data analytics.

Author Keywords
Personal informatics; critical design; design strategies

ACM Classification Keywords
H.5.m. **[Information interfaces and presentation (e.g., HCI)]:** Miscellaneous.

INTRODUCTION

Users of modern technology live in an environment filled with logging technologies that gather information about them, both with and without their knowledge. Personal informatics systems invite users to reflect on and use these data, notionally to understand themselves better. The conventional approach driving personal informatics systems in the field has been self-betterment through self-knowledge: the fruits of data mining should be presented to users to promote personal optimization and self-improvement in various aspects of their lives [16].

This conventional approach to personal informatics design is facilitated by data-mining infrastructures through which data about measurable behaviors are gathered, interpreted, and reflected back to users. These infrastructures process vast amounts of personal data but often go unnoticed. Just as functioning infrastructure is embedded and transparent in regular use [24], the values of self-optimization through quantification built into these infrastructures similarly disappear into the background.

Using data for self-betterment, however, represents but one possible approach to designing personal informatics. Focusing on self-betterment may affirm and reinforce mainstream or socially predominant values, such as efficiency and optimization, at the expense of others. These systems typically present charts and graphs based on numerical information, and insights based on "the quantified self" are only one kind of insight people might seek [16]. Uncritical use of data-mining infrastructures may reinforce growing trends toward ubiquitous surveillance. Relatively few personal informatics systems encourage people to reflect on or to challenge the values embedded within them or the larger context of data mining. A number of design approaches, such as value-sensitive design [11], reflective design [22], and critical design [8], have been developed specifically to identify ways that social values are embedded in system design and to encourage consideration of alternative relationships between these systems and their users.

This paper applies critical design to personal informatics, with the goal of revealing infrastructure and engaging the users of these systems in a dialogue about the values embedded in data-mining systems. We present a set of strategies for designing personal informatics systems that draw attention to the scope and limitations of data-gathering and data-mining infrastructures. These strategies lead to the design of systems that promote an alternative to the "know thyself" rhetoric by drawing users' attention to other relationships with personal data. We demonstrate these strategies in an interface for collecting and reflecting web browsing data using text-based personal informatics visualizations embedded within the browser. To evaluate the interface and strategies, we conducted a qualitative field study in which participants used our interface for two weeks and participated in interviews about their experiences. Data from these interviews demonstrate a number of ways that critical designs can promote reflection on and an increased critical awareness of the implications and limitations of data-mining infrastructures.

RELATED WORK
Personal Informatics and Self-Knowledge
Past research in personal informatics has shed light on the ways that users interact with and interpret their data. Most of this research has been carried out with the understanding that data-driven self-reflection can be used to help people become more aware of their own behavior [3] and change their behavior for the better [9]. These values have shaped research about the questions that individuals might ask of their data and uses for personal informatics interfaces [17].

The justification for personal informatics systems often rests on arguments about the limitations of human self knowledge: unassisted, knowing oneself is difficult because we often have incomplete data and limited ability to monitor ourselves [27]. Personal informatics augment a person's self-knowledge by breaking down human barriers to personal data management [17]. In this reading, as the infrastructures supporting ubiquitous computing continue to evolve, the promise of the field of personal informatics also grows, as increasingly rich information sources can support new levels of self-understanding and self-optimization.

In addition to the trend of gathering and analyzing more data in personal informatics interfaces, it is also becoming more common to consolidate and integrate data from a variety of sources. This tactic supports users' simultaneous exploration of multiple facets of their lives through their data [15]. As an example, popular commercial products such as Mint and Nike+ consolidate and display information from multiple data sources to help people find patterns in their financial and exercise data [17].

It is important, however, to recognize the role that the underlying value of self-optimization through self-knowledge has had in shaping the field of personal informatics. It has influenced the goals and questions of personal informatics researchers and embedded itself into the nature of data-mining infrastructure. And though there has been interest in applying personal informatics interfaces to other ends, such as reminiscing [19] and personal information management [13], there have been few studies of using personal informatics to raise awareness of the data-mining infrastructures, themselves.

Information Infrastructure and Critical Design
These infrastructures play a major role in how, what, and why people might use personal informatics. In her work on the ethnography of infrastructure, Star notes that infrastructure is, by default, "invisible, buried in semi-private settings and squirreled away in inaccessible technical code" [24]. Embedded in those systems, though, lie the socio-technical standards, aesthetics, and values of the people who build and use them. Star argues for the ethnographic examination of infrastructure, offers several

dimensions of infrastructure that should be examined, and describes the feeling of "embedded strangeness" when invisible processes are brought to light [24].

Several design initiatives have sought both to make infrastructure visible and to support alternative relationships between users and the technologies that make use of such infrastructure. In critical design, Dunne and Raby have been proponents of "developing alternative and often gently provocative artifacts which set out to engage people through humor, insight, surprise and wonder" by adopting alternative values that are not typically designed for in mainstream design [8]. In their Placebo project, eight prototype objects were created with the goal of engaging users with electromagnetism through electromagnetic interference and malfunction. For example, among the objects was a table that "reminds you that electronic objects extend beyond their visible limits" by showing twenty-five compasses on its surface that twitch and spin when electronics are placed near them. They were designed to act on users' existing suspicions and elicit stories about the secret life of electronic objects as seen by their users [8]. Similarly, Redström's Chatterbox system explores various visualization techniques for reflecting on information technology use in the workplace [19].

Data visualization techniques have also been used to draw attention to power infrastructures. For instance, the *Oil Standard* modifies and augments web browsing with the tactic of revealing power and hegemony by translating the prices of consumer goods into units of oil and embedding those translations into the browser window, itself [7, 18]. In personal informatics systems, visualizations are aimed at highlighting elements of users' data, but the visualizations can also be turned on the data-mining infrastructures, themselves, to draw attention to their size and scope. For example, the Mozilla browser extension *Collusion* shows the extent to which websites cooperate to track people's behavior by visualizing cookies and the relationships among the websites that issue them [5]. By displaying the resulting network of data-mining monetization campaigns, it encourages reflection on these infrastructures.

In examining the infrastructure of personal informatics and the values and value systems embedded therein, we approach personal informatics as an arena for subjective engagement. Proponents of a subjectivist approach to personal informatics argue for balancing the presentation of objective data signals with the human ability to make sense of this information and interpret it [14]. In particular, we focus on encouraging people to playfully engage with their personal data through the idea of "making strange" [1], presenting personal informatics data in unusual ways to stimulate the values of "curiosity, play, exploration, and reflection" called for by ludic design approaches [12].

In promoting multiplicity of engagement in personal informatics interfaces, our goal is not to suggest that designing personal informatics for self-optimization

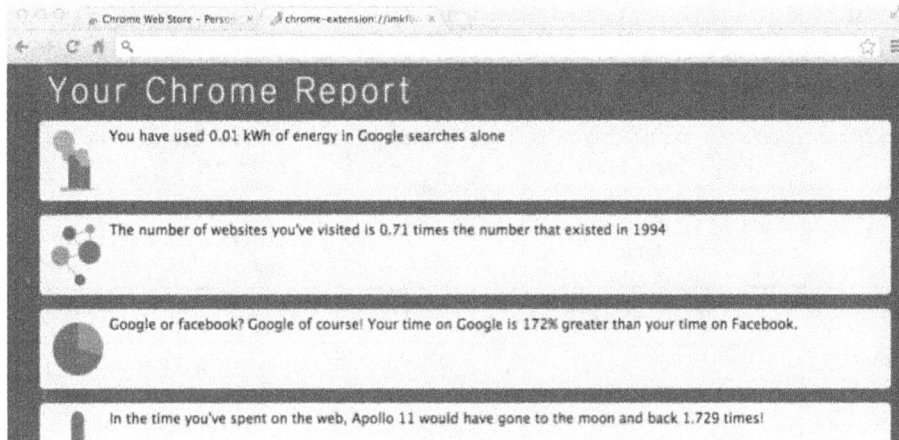

Figure 1. Screenshot of the interface.

through self knowledge is wrong; rather, it is one among a range of possibilities that can be explored. We demonstrate how raising awareness of information infrastructures is a design motivation that can challenge *and* complement personal informatics interfaces [20].

DESIGN PROCESS AND STRATEGIES

Our design goals were to raise awareness of the data-mining process, to highlight its scope and limitations, and to expose predominant values embedded in personal informatics interfaces and data-mining infrastructures. Our design process led to the articulation of three strategies, each of which addressed one of these goals.

Choosing a Data Source and Platform

We began by exploring the kinds of personal data that would be feasible to mine and would provide grist for provoking reflection. After considering potentially personal data sources such as health or biometrics information, we settled on web browsing as a data source. Web browsing activities can be highly personal, meaning that analyzing a user's browsing data both aligns with the traditional focus of personal informatics (i.e., "know thyself") and has significant provocative potential. Further, it is a kind of data that, while passively collected, is easily viewable through browsers' history listings, and it is a kind of data with known risks caused by its collection, evidenced by mass-media coverage of problems caused by the release of search histories and online identity theft.

We developed an extension to the Chrome web browser to collect browsing data and to present personal informatics visualizations of those data. Not only is Chrome a popular browser [26], but building a Chrome extension is not much more difficult or complex than building a web page, and we wanted the techniques we used to be appropriable by other designers who may not have a background in machine learning or data mining. This approach also allowed us to store and process the web browsing data on participants' machines, without having to download it to a server, allowing us to respect participants' privacy.

Creating Provocative Facts

We then examined the Chrome API to see what data it made available and how those data might be used. These available data included the URL of pages visited and the associated time stamps, with additional events for opening tabs and accessing bookmarks. This API became source material and inspiration for an extensive list of "provocative facts," specific presentations of personal information that we might be able to implement and deploy. We focused on text-based presentations rather than the graphs and charts common in conventional personal informatics interfaces, both to facilitate prototyping and to create a simple implementation that designers with other datasets could easily emulate.

We shared this list with colleagues, noting which designs provoked the strongest responses as well as the nature of those responses. The most promising designs served as templates for the final set of facts that the system presented about the users' web browsing. Opening the extension presents the user with a randomly selected subset of these facts, as shown in Figure 1.

During the implementation process, we also organized the facts into rough conceptual groups based on the nature of the provocation that they inspired. We iteratively combined, divided, and recombined these groups, along with their connections and resonances with Star's dimensions and properties of infrastructures, until each stood as both conceptually coherent and distinct from the others.

By examining the facts that ended up in each of these groups, asking what they had in common that made them provocative, and considering what sorts of discussions they evoked, we articulated a set of strategies for designing personal informatics systems. These strategies serve two roles. First, they provide concrete guidance for designers who might wish to apply critical design to the domain of personal informatics. Second, we suggest that these strategies describe an effective means for promoting critical reflection about data-mining infrastructures.

Design Strategy	Infrastructure dimension	Motivation
Make it Creepy: Display the sensitive and highly personal aspects of gathered data.	Reach or scope of data infrastructure	Raise implications of data-gathering systems for surveillance and individual privacy.
Make it Malfunction: Deliberately display gaps in gathered data	Infrastructure becomes visible upon breakdown	Promote reflection on the limitations of data gathering.
Make it Strange: Show information in unconventional ways	Infrastructure links with conventions of practice	Highlight the role of personal informatics systems in perpetuating dominant social norms in data gathering and presentation.

Table 1. Three general strategies for designing provocative facts, their relationship to Star's infrastructures, and their design goals.

Three Design Strategies

Our design strategies describe a means for achieving several goals: to raise awareness of the broad scope of personal data mining, to reveal the limitations of the data-mining process, and to expose the predominant social values embedded in personal informatics infrastructure. Table 1 presents the relationships between these strategies, Star's perspective on infrastructure, and specific design goals we hoped would help raise awareness of key aspects of data-mining infrastructures.

Make It Creepy. "Creepy" informatics highlight the scope of personal data mining and the highly personal nature of the data being collected. To make our interface creepy, we looked for personal data that might be uncomfortable for the user to confront. We did not seek data that were necessarily uncomfortable in and of themselves, but rather data that, when collected and mined, contrasts with the commonly perceived and valued anonymity of web users' behavior. For example, the fact "Did you know that we've been recording your activity for 5 days? In that time, we've seen you online for 200 total hours, and recorded more than 200 sites you've visited" calls attention to the scale and continuous nature of web data logging, as well as the extensive infrastructure that exists for gathering and manipulating users' data. The goal is not to force the user to confront uncomfortable or shameful aspects of their data, but rather to make visible the effect of being under constant surveillance, contrasting the socially normative values of logging and self-tracking with the privacy implications of personal informatics infrastructures and interfaces.

Make It Malfunction. "All models are wrong" [2], and data are always incomplete. Our second design strategy involves highlighting this incompleteness. In some ways, this strategy resonates with Chalmers' notion of "seamful design," an approach that highlights the places where ubiquitous computing technology is not perfectly seamless and explicitly incorporates such seams meaningfully into the design [4]. Similarly, "malfunctioning" informatics highlight gaps in the data and the ways that those gaps can lead to an imperfect picture of the self.

We looked for stories that seemed plausible based on the data alone, but actually were slight misinterpretations, somewhat inaccurate, or completely ridiculous. For example, the Chrome API reports how long every tab has been open but not how long it has held focus; if a user has five tabs open for one hour, a naïve reading of the data provided by the API makes it appear that the user has been online for five hours and has spent one hour on each site. This aspect of the data led to situations in which the system told the user that s/he had been online for longer than 24 hours in a single day. In another example, if the proportion of .edu websites exceeded that of other websites, users were addressed by the interface as being a "scholar." In this case, not only do many scholarly activities take place on non-edu websites, but simply visiting .edu websites does not a scholar make.

These examples show conclusions that are obviously wrong, but that wrongness is the point. By intentionally interpreting the data in incorrect or implausible ways, we engineer breakdowns that make "the normally invisible quality of working infrastructure...visible" [24]. Thus, malfunctioning informatics use satire and incorrectness to draw attention to hidden infrastructures and the assumptions made in the data-mining process.

Make It Strange. Personal informatics collect, analyze, and curate data for a specific purpose, often in the interest of persuasion or behavior change [17]. That purpose shapes the user's relationship with her or his data. Personal informatics rarely highlight the role that these interfaces play in affirming mainstream relationships between individuals and their data. Making strange informatics draws attention to the embedded norms of such systems by suggesting alternative genres of personal informatics that emphasize humor and ludic engagement over behavior change and personal optimization, while still using the metrics and vocabulary of the existing infrastructure.

Making it strange is not a matter of gamification [6] or making personal informatics "fun." Rather, it more closely resembles making fun of personal informatics. To make it strange, we followed a number of approaches. For example, one fact told the user, "You visited 592 websites this week. That's .5 times the number of webpages on the whole internet in 1994!" This historical comparison draws attention to the abundant nature of modern web browsing as collected through unique URLs, but presented in a somewhat obtuse and non-judgmental way. A similar fact stated, "In the time you've spent on the web, Apollo 11 would have gone to the moon and back 1.5 times."

Comparing the user's web browsing data with other data or known quantities measured in different units added a playful dimension, upending social convention and normative values by allowing the design to poke fun at the data or, at times, at itself.

Note that the design strategies were not explicitly described to participants, e.g., no part of the system was labeled or described as being "creepy." Rather, the strategies provide categorization, for our own design process and provide concepts that may be useful to other interested designers.

USER STUDY

To explore the potential value of our strategies, we conducted a user study to evaluate the effectiveness of each strategy at promoting critical reflection about personal informatics and their infrastructures.

Methods

We tested our interface over the course of two weeks with 23 participants, recruited using local university department listserv emails and snowball sampling from those emails. Participants received a mid-point questionnaire that asked them to talk about their experience and general use of the system, as well as their specific reactions to the responses generated by the system (e.g., which facts did you like, which did you find confusing, etc.). Participants were asked to complete an exit interview at the conclusion of the study, featuring more open-ended, interpretive questions and clarifications of responses in the mid-point questionnaire. We did an affinity analysis of our exit interview data, iteratively grouping and regrouping responses to different questions based on thematic similarity. The analysis focused on reactions such as awareness of data-mining infrastructure, criticism and rejection of the dominant personal informatics narrative, and consideration of alternative narratives and values. We used that analysis to loosely code the interviews and questionnaire responses for recurrent themes, which we organize and present in the results section below.

Results

19 (6 female) of the 23 participants returned the mid-point questionnaire and agreed to be interviewed. Our participants were mostly undergraduate students studying at a large research university in the northeastern United States. Two thirds of participants described themselves as studying in technology-oriented fields. Despite the potential bias from technology-focused students, our participant population enabled us to elicit feedback about how people reacted to the design strategies operating on their own data. It also enabled insights about how people who anticipate working in the technology sector think about the effects of designing personal informatics systems that collect and mediate data of other (often non-technical) individuals.

Analysis of our interviews revealed a consistent first impression of the interface. Participants typically saw the tool as a lighthearted and imperfect tool for introspection or—less often—a tool to contemplate one's data traces as they are seen by other online entities. The interview process often had a transformative effect. Initially, users often described the interface as being an optimization tool. After being prompted to describe their experiences of the interface, they arrived at various critical conclusions about broader privacy policy disclosure issues, the inherent limitations of data mining, and the norms and standards embedded into personal informatics. Users also recalled experiences with other personal informatics interfaces outside the traditional "self-optimization through self-knowledge" narrative. We organize the results by our three design strategies.

Make It Creepy. When asked about the scope of the data that users thought their browser collected about them, many participants "just assumed they logged everything" [P17]. 11 participants expressed awareness of and passiveness toward ubiquitous online surveillance and were not surprised about the invasive nature of the creepy informatics because "Google already knows everything about me" [P10]. When prompted to define "everything" in more detail, one user described how he imagined that Google was logging his mouse movements and keystrokes, as per his experience of using Google's built-in chat service, which "knew" whether users were idle or typing: "Chrome knows when you are sleeping, Chrome knows when you're awake…" [P3].

However, the creepy informatics prompted participants to try to identify which infrastructure recorded the number of websites visited and time spent online. One participant commented on the difference between "Chrome history, which is not to be confused with Google history… your Google search history"—where the participant explained that the latter was "going to Google" while the former was only stored locally on their computer [P12]. Participants wondered whether the data gathered in Chrome was still personally identifiable if they "don't use any Google account," and whether it was associated instead by IP address [P8]. Several participants commented on the implications of data tracking outside of our interface; one participant questioned whether Google used any identity information to affect her browsing experience:

> One thing that kind of bothers me is their personalization of your search results without them telling you […] I understand why they narrow down search results, so that people see what they want. But at the same time, it's a little strange that we can all Google the same thing and get different results…. [P10]

These later reactions demonstrate increased concern about specific aspects and implications of the data-mining process and underlying infrastructure. This attitude was also echoed by two participants who, after completing the interview, sent the researchers documents and discussions detailing Google's and Chrome's privacy policies in attempts to clarify aspects of data-mining policy. Attempts to disambiguate the structure of personal data traces also led to critiques of the incongruity between the design motivations of the systems that gather personal data and the systems that present it back to users. When asked with whom they might share facts from our interface, users wanted to give them to other people with the intention of raising the same kinds of awareness:

> I think [my friend] would just find something like this very interesting because we have talked about these same issues before [...] Oh well, everybody tracks all of your information. Everybody knows what you're doing. [P15]

Specifically, individuals who identified themselves as people with technical knowledge thought that the interface could be useful for raising awareness about data mining among non- or less-technical users:

> I would give it to a non-CS [computer science] major friend of mine, because I'd be curious in seeing how they'd respond to it... I don't think they would take the same kindness to a tool collecting statistics about them. [P16]

We hoped to use the creepy informatics to raise awareness of the scope of data mining, yet many participants expressed a general sense of complacency toward Google's ubiquitous data-mining infrastructure. However, participants speculated widely about the actual capabilities of personal informatics systems and the types of data we collected. They attempted to clarify their understanding of the personal data infrastructure, e.g., which entities had access to their information, where that information went, and the extent of the logging. Finally, users speculated on how the data-mining process affected their browsing experiences and how it might affect others' experiences.

Make It Malfunction. In response to informatics built with unreliable data, participants, understandably, did not agree with many of the representations generated in response to their behavior. In response to the system's incorrect identification of their most-visited page on Facebook (by counting time spent at a unique URL), one participant described the discrepancy:

> When I've been on Facebook, my most-visited site was the checkpoint to confirm it was you if you were using a new computer. And I've probably spent more time stalking people than just I have just pressing 'Remember this computer' or whatever. [P2]

Such reactions not only cast doubt on the rest of the interface but also prompted recounting instances of doubting other technologies:

> [On] a treadmill, even if you enter your weight and your age, it's not going to give you your exact heart rate, or...the exact number of calories burned, but you still get a sense... But the treadmill that I've been using in New York [City], I don't think it's me that's better, but it seems that I'm doing better on it than I was at home. [P4]

This reaction bounds the traditional personal informatics narrative of self-optimization through self-knowledge by recognizing that the technologies that gather data could be wrong. In particular, both knowing these limitations and having more information outside of the data presented can help people interpret the results of data mining. Presenting misinformation motivates critical discussion about the limitations of data-mining tools and their potential for error, as well as alternative roles for the user in interpreting these informatics interfaces.

15 participants also attempted to reverse-engineer the erroneous facts to explain how they were computed. This reverse engineering is a form of critical thinking where the subject disambiguates a process that would otherwise be invisible to them. One participant described a reverse-engineering process in response to a fact about her Facebook usage:

> The first time I looked at it, it said that the site on Facebook I'm most likely to visit was my friend [name]'s Facebook [...] I know I've been on my own at least twice that day. So, maybe I accidentally left that tab open... and it does it by time. [P7]

Some reverse-engineering attempts were very technical, such as the participant who described his usage of the interface as "I read the analytics and then thought about which parts of my HTML headers you were collecting" [P18]. Such attention to technical detail may be due in part to our technology-heavy participant sample. However, participants from non-technical backgrounds also engaged in this reverse-engineering process:

> Unless I've discovered a wormhole, I don't see how I could have spent over 1,000 hours online in five days [...] I'm not techie at all, so I only thought of that when I got a weird answer like that. So I realized it was probably calculating all my tabs or taking all my tabs into account or something. [P11]

Such results suggest that designing misinformation can encourage reverse-engineering attempts not just for "techies," but also for people who do not describe themselves as having a technical background. These attempts lead to interrogation of a process that is often invisible or regarded as being value-neutral by non-specialists.

Finally, misinformation prompted several abstract discussions about the inherent limitations of data gathering. One participant criticized the analysis present in the interface and commented that "the same pitfalls of data mining are also true of a lot of statistical manipulation in general.... A big joke in the field is when somebody asks 'what do these numbers mean,' you say, 'what do you want them to mean?'" [P6].

Another participant asserted that web-browsing data "couldn't describe me because it only describes my browsing habits.... It just wouldn't be perfect because I have experiences outside of the web world that would influence my web behavior" [P16]. By drawing attention to and calling into question the methods used to present the data, misinformation undermined the expectation that users are supposed to confront their data and, as a result, change their behavior. Instead, they suggested that the data could be gathered in ways that are biased and that the data presents an inherently limited subset of the users' experiences.

Thus, showing users faulty representations of their personal data provoked a variety of critical reactions about the limitations of personal informatics systems. Users responded with personal narratives around the misinformational facts and how they came into conflict with their own perceptions. Users also attempted to reverse engineer the process of the malfunctioning informatics to explain how they came to show the information that they did, and in that process demonstrated awareness of data-mining structures. More broadly, participants reflected on the effect that misinformation has on their experience of personal informatics and whether misinformation was an inherent and inevitable outcome of data-mining processes, themselves. This contentious attitude toward data-driven persuasion became more central in participants' experiences around the third strategy.

Make It Strange. Several of the facts in our interface showed data in unexpected ways. Participants referred to the strange informatics as "the random ones" and as the ones that they didn't expect to be included in the interface. Specifically, many users reported finding these facts to be unexpected because they did not present users' behavior in familiar units (such as hours or number of pages visited). Participants questioned why certain points of data were chosen and calculated in that way. In response to the fact that incorporated comparisons to the size and scope of the internet, one user looked up how many sites existed in 1994, and said in response:

> I'm actually surprised. I consider myself kind of an Internet power user, and back in 19-something-or-other... there were like ten thousand pages on the Internet, and I haven't even come close to that. [P14]

Instead of reflecting on ways to optimize his web browsing, the participant expressed being impressed by the historical size of the web.

Playful informatics drew attention to the non-neutrality of personal informatics interfaces: one participant referred to them as "sassy" [P16], and another commented that while it "seems like it's spitting out facts... it's clearly intending to get at me, somehow, and be provoking" [P4]. Several users expressed frustration toward facts that were deliberately obtuse. One fact, for example, calculated how long a user has been on their most visited site without disclosing which site it was; this fact infuriated several participants who wanted to know "where they wasted the most time" and expected our interface to show them this information. By

presenting unexpected information, we saw evidence that our strategies may have helped to uncover the expectations and standards embedded in the infrastructure.

Similarly, when a participant was asked why the system chose to show Google searches in kilowatt-hours, they added, "It's not the system, this is you!" [P13]. By making it strange, we created a space where users' expectations (the normative mainstream values of the system) fell into conflict with the interface, drawing attention to the role of the designer as a mediator of data infrastructure.

Over half of our participants responded to the ludic informatics with similarly playful appropriations. One participant proudly described his "extra browser" where he kept several tabs open and stagnant because he wanted to see how many times he "could make Apollo 11 go to the moon" [P13]. Other participants talked about "training" the interface, and doing certain superficial behaviors like closing extra tabs to get what they saw as a more favorable result from the interface (i.e., less time spent online) [P7]. One participant admitted to "fantasizing about opening all the .edu sites, so it would tell me I'm a scholar" [P3]. Similarly, participants' playful responses also extended beyond our interface to other systems, such as when a participant expressed a desire to "log one calorie" into a calorie tracker tool that predicted how much she would weigh in the future because "then it'll tell me [...] you're going to weigh negative two pounds by Friday!" [P4].

One user projected her relationship to the system over time:

> I've been on Facebook for 27.83 hours, right? [...] Well, I kind of don't care. Probably in another month, it telling me about how much time I spend on Facebook is just going to be kind of meaningless to me because it's like, what do those hours mean in any case? But what I do like is the one that's like you've used, mine says .03 kilowatt-hours... that and the fraction of the Internet that existed in 1994. That's kind of interesting because over time it will amount to something meaningful. [P15]

In this case, the participant dismisses the longevity of the persuasive element of personal informatics, instead adopting an alternative relationship based not on self-optimization but on a detached curiosity in watching obtuse units growing over time. These unconventional appropriations of existing infrastructure, such as logging time online in unusual units, promote long-term relationships between personal informatics and their subjects that are not part of the mainstream personal informatics narrative.

Participants' experiences and reactions to ludic informatics involved questioning the content of the interface, undertaking creative engagement, and tampering with the data-gathering infrastructure. These informatics also raised broader issues about the nature of the relationship between personal data and its subject, and the role of the designer and the data infrastructure in forming that relationship. Ludic informatics supported alternative relationships toward personal data and prompted critical reflection on the goals and motivations of mainstream personal informatics.

DISCUSSION

The Rhetoric and Scope of Personal Informatics

Our deployment provoked discussions that problematized the "know thyself" rhetoric of personal informatics systems [16] by drawing attention to limitations to the "knowledge" that personal informatics systems can provide. These limitations were expressed in users' corrective and dismissive reactions to malfunctioning informatics, and in the acknowledgement of the incongruity between the motivations of data-gathering systems and the personal informatics interfaces that use them, as reflected by creepy informatics. Finally, as has been observed in other work around Facebook, even sophisticated and frequently used data-gathering systems can present only a part of the picture of a person's behavior [23]. Our results highlight the ways that the limitations of human self-knowledge that often motivate personal informatics are balanced by the limitations of data gathering in the informatics, themselves, and that the data presented in personal informatics systems are shaped by the infrastructures that are used to gather and present the data (as well as the fact that these data represent a subset of all possible data).

Though the "know thyself" approach has been one effective method for affecting behavior change in fields ranging from health to power usage [17], our deployment highlights a different user relationship with personal informatics systems: that the user can engage with the infrastructures underlying personal informatics by questioning the processes and the values embedded within them. Through creative tampering and dismissal of the self-optimization narrative, our interface supports ludic engagement and reflection on the values, possibilities, and limits of self-optimization.

We do not think that these alternative modes of engagement are in fundamental opposition to the "know thyself" rhetoric that dominates the personal informatics research domain; instead, we recommend that designers consider the strategies we have proposed as a method for designing and building multifaceted personal informatics systems. It is our view that these strategies can be used to complement traditional personal informatics interfaces by providing users with awareness of the underlying infrastructures and alternative ways of interpreting their outputs.

Further, just as Fogg argued that persuasive technologies bear an ethical responsibility [10], personal informatics systems may also be subject to the same ethical burden, particularly since most existing personal informatics systems have been created with the aim of persuading individual behavior change through self-reflection. Pragmatically speaking, because these systems process imperfectly collected and interpreted user data, they will always exhibit some degree of creepiness and malfunction; their output will always be framed with respect to some pre-existing set of values. Our strategies can serve as one resource for designers to acknowledge and communicate the limitations, motivations, biases, and values embedded in personal informatics systems to these systems' users [22]. In contexts in which these somewhat provocative approaches might not be appropriate for deployment in a final product, they can still exist as a design resource for encouraging designers' reflection about how to communicate the boundaries and seams in personal informatics systems that might otherwise not be visible to the systems' users.

Personal Informatics for Data Justice

Our experiences of deploying the interface also call to attention the foggy mysticism, deep uncertainties, and lack of knowledge that surround data-mining infrastructure. Like the participants in Dunne and Raby's project who heard stories of people picking up radio broadcasts in their dental filings and felt their skin tingle when they sat near a TV [8], our participants were largely aware of data mining, and many expressed concerns about its implications. However, overwhelmingly—even among technical audiences—users are unsure of exactly which processes are happening, what data are collected, where those data are stored, and what is being done with them. One participant described our interface as a form of "white-hat hacking":

> If you can log all of this stuff, then maybe just about any other Chrome extension can.... What you're doing [...] is [showing] this what we could have tracked and this is what we could have possibly done with it.... It's like white-hat hacking in that way. [P13]

When we asked participants for design suggestions, they recommended changes that would facilitate understanding of the data-mining infrastructure: "There should be descriptions of where the calculations came from" [P14].

Several participants pointed out a major difference between our interface and other data-mining practices. As one participant put it, "I gave you god powers to do this because I trusted you.... I want you to show me things that I didn't opt into" [P16]. That is, our attempts to be creepy and reveal infrastructure may have been dampened by the fact that our participants "trusted us" with using their data and were fully aware of what we were doing. This is in contrast to other data-mining systems, where users are generally not fully cognizant of or complicit in the tracking of their web-browsing data. Our design strategies promote visibility of the scope of data collection carried out in data-mining infrastructures; this kind of visibility can either help to build users' trust in these infrastructures or raise important questions about where these systems might introduce risks.

Another role that an interface like ours could play, in addition to raising awareness of data mining infrastructures and opening them up for critical discussion, is to explicitly promote personal data efficacy and control. This idea is related to work in the area of usable privacy, where concrete visualizations of personal location data over time can highlight privacy concerns compared to less revealing representations [25]. In our case, instead of describing the infrastructure in static text, interactive and personalized computations might serve as mediators between users and the infrastructure that surrounds them.

Or Not: Staying Open to Interpretation

An alternate relationship that critical personal informatics might facilitate between users and their data is that of a playful but slightly disinterested observer, one who uses the system as an object of curiosity rather than as a tool for self-mastery or data efficacy. For some users, the sense of complacency toward data mining continued after they acknowledged the extensive and poorly understood infrastructure behind the interface. Users continued to use and enjoy our system for other reasons: some users enjoyed tampering with the results, others humorously engaged with and appropriated misinformation, and still others described the joy of watching numbers grow: "I refreshed it every now and then just to see. Probably just as often as I refresh Gmail... because I'm totally a stats guy. I just like looking at numbers [...] Once I look at my numbers for long enough, they're just numbers" [P12]. Participants commented that they would enjoy the interface much less if it had a clearer persuasive agenda: "It says that I've been on Facebook for 27.83 hours.... Well, I kind of don't care" [P15].

These relationships might evolve over time. Participants described being initially surprised by the unexpected aspects of the interface, but then gradually became accustomed to it. In their interviews in *Design Noir*, Dunne and Raby asked a participant if she saw the table-shaped critical object as a kind of gadget. The participant responded that she saw it as a gadget now, but maybe if she used it enough, it would "turn into a piece of furniture" [8]. There might be a similar role for our interface: initially, it could be an instigator of data infrastructure awareness and a proponent of privacy settings, but as the radical nature wears off, it could become as much of an everyday object as the infrastructure it aims to reveal. Maybe not a kitchen table, in the sense that the interface itself is not regularly used, but as something our participants "won't uninstall... but might sporadically come back to check my favorite [data reflections]" [P11].

LIMITATIONS AND FUTURE WORK

We recognize that the reactions to our interface were specific to the audience we recruited, their age and technical capabilities, as the culture in which they live and study. While our study participants are not necessarily representative of all technology users (and did not include hard-to-reach populations), it was representative of the audience to whom traditional "quantified self" applications are generally marketed. However, as Star notes [24], things that may be visible in infrastructure for some are invisible

to others; in the future, we hope to deploy critical personal informatics to people with less technical expertise, less familiarity with data-mining techniques, and less prior exposure to personal informatics tools.

Since our approach of applying critical design techniques to personal informatics systems is relatively new, we chose to approach data gathering in an open-ended and qualitative fashion. This research approach also introduces some limitations on the kinds of data that we were able to gather. Our goal with this research was not to produce universal or generalizable findings but rather to demonstrate that the approach of applying critical design to personal informatics is a useful thing to do, and hope that future work in this field will explore different methods for evaluating the efficacy of critical personal informatics tools.

We have also taken a narrow definition of informatics: as mentioned before, our visualization is text-based, and the computations that we perform on the web-browsing data do not utilize intensive machine learning techniques. Our approach was motivated in part by feasibility—both for the researchers implementing the interface used here and for others who might use our strategies—and in part by the desire to focus our contribution on participants' engagement with our provocative design strategies and to not get distracted by the interface itself or its computational aspects (through complex data mining and pattern finding). However, we recognize that these pursuits are not antithetical to the idea of revealing infrastructure. We have suggested that perceived simplicity invites reverse engineering; further work in this area could reveal whether computational intensity promotes higher or lower levels of critical engagement.

We hope that our design strategies could be used in conjunction with traditional personal informatics approaches to draw users' attention to the processes of data collection and data presentation, as well as the implications and limitations of those processes. Because we intended our strategies to be generalizable, we are continuing to explore their applicability both to different contexts, such as with health and emotion data. We are also interested in combining personal data sets across different settings, and a breadth of "personal" data, such as data shared among several people or, even more broadly, across social and political networks.

CONCLUSION

Personal informatics represents a significant class of applications built atop ubiquitous data-gathering and data-mining infrastructures. While these systems have the potential to allow people to reflect on their own behaviors and habits, existing systems do a poor job of communicating the scope of data collected to build models of human activity, owning up to the errors possible when making sense of mined data, or explicitly acknowledging the values embedded in decisions about which data are collected and how they are reflected back to the user.

In this paper, we argue for the role of critical design in challenging the status quo of personal informatics. We present three design strategies that encourage outward reflection on the data-mining infrastructures and personal informatics interfaces, themselves—as well as the kinds of relationships that these technologies typically afford—by suggesting the possibility of alternative relationships between personal data and its subjects. Our approach challenges the designers of personal informatics systems to incorporate representations of their systems' limitations by foregrounding their potential creepiness, their potential for malfunctions, and the strangeness revealed when systems embody values different from those prescribed by mainstream systems. An analysis of how users experienced a system built around these provocative strategies affirms that personal informatics systems can be used to raise awareness about data mining, can promote efficacy and control over personal data, and can also challenge the role of data analytics as persuasive agents.

ACKNOWLEDGEMENTS

This research was supported by Cornell's Information Science and Communication Departments and the Hunter R. Rawlings III Cornell Presidential Research Scholarship. Thanks to the Interaction Design Lab, Saeed Abdullah, Alistair Ballantine, and Yang Yang Zheng, as well as our study participants. Special thanks to the anonymous reviewers for their helpful feedback and suggestions.

REFERENCES

1. Bell, G., Blythe, M. and Sengers, P. Making by making strange: Defamiliarization and the design of domestic technologies. *ACM Trans. Computer-Human Interaction 12*, 2 (June 2005), 149–173.

2. Box, G.E.P. and Draper, N.R. *Empirical model building and response surfaces*. Wiley, Hoboken, NJ, 1987.

3. Carver, C. and Scheier, M.F. *On the self-regulation of behavior*. Cambridge University Press, Cambridge, UK, 2001.

4. Chalmers, M., MacColl, I. and Bell, M. (2003). Seamful design: Showing the seams in wearable computing. *Proc Eurowearable*, IEE (2003), 11–16.

5. Collusion. http://www.mozilla.org/en-US/collusion/

6. Deterding, S., Sicart, M., Nacke, L., O'Hara, K. and Dixon, D. (2011). Gamification: Using game-design elements in non-gaming contexts. *Ext. Abstracts CHI '11*, ACM Press (2011), 2425–2428.

7. DiSalvo, C. *Adversarial Design*. MIT Press, Cambridge, MA, 2012.

8. Dunne, A., and Raby, F. *Design noir: The secret life of electronic objects*. Birkhäuser, Basel, Switzerland, 2001.

9. Endsley, M.R. The Role of Situation Awareness in Naturalistic Decision Making. In Zsambok, C.E. and Klein, G.A. (Eds.), *Naturalistic decision making*. Erlbaum, Hillsdale, NJ, 1997, 269–282.

10. Fogg, BJ. Persuasive computers: Perspectives and research directions. *Proc. CHI '98*, ACM Press (1998), 225–232.

11. Friedman, B. Value-sensitive design. *interactions 3*, 6 (1996), 16–23.

12. Gaver, W.W. (2002). Designing for Homo Ludens. *I3 Magazine, 12* (June 2002).

13. Jones, W. and Teevan, J. *Personal information management*. UW Press, Seattle, 2007.

14. Leahu, L., Schwenk, S. and Sengers, P. Subjective objectivity: Negotiating emotional meaning. *Proc. DIS '08* ACM Press (2008), 425–434.

15. Li, I., Dey, A.K. and Forlizzi, J. A stage-based model of personal informatics systems. *Proc. CHI 2010*, ACM Press (2010), 557–566.

16. Li, I., Dey, A.K. and Forlizzi, J. Know thyself: Monitoring and reflecting on facets of one's life. *Ext. Abstracts CHI '10*, ACM Press (2010), 4489–4492.

17. Li, I., Dey, A.K. and Forlizzi, J. Understanding my data, myself: Supporting self-reflection with ubicomp technologies. *Proc. UbiComp '11*, ACM Press (2011), 405–414.

18. Mandiberg, M. *Oil Standard* (2006), http://turbulence.org/works/oil/

19. Peesapati, S.T., Schwanda, V., Schultz, J., Lepage, M., Jeong, S. and Cosley, D. Pensieve: Supporting everyday reminiscence. *Proc. CHI '10*, ACM Press (2010), 2027–2036.

20. Redström, J., Jaksefic, P. and Ljungstrand, P. The ChatterBox. Proc. HandheM and Ubiquitous Comp. '99, Springer, 1999.

21. Sengers, P. and Gaver, B. Design for Interpretation. Proc. HCII '05. Lawrence Erlbaum Associates (2005).

22. Sengers, P., Boehner, K., David, S. and Kaye, J. Reflective design. *Proc. Critical Computing*, ACM Press (2005), 49–58.

23. Sosik, V.S., Zhao, X. and Cosley, D. See friendship, sort of: How conversation and digital traces might support reflection on friendships. *Proc. CSCW '12*, ACM Press (2012), 1145–1154.

24. Star, S.L. The ethnography of infrastructure. *American Behavioral Scientist, 43*, 3 (1999), 377–391.

25. Tang, K.P., Hong, J.I. and Siewiorek, D.P. Understanding how visual representations of location feeds affect end-user privacy concerns. *Proc. UbiComp '11*, ACM Press (2011), 207–216.

26. Top 5 Browsers. *StatCounter* (2012). http://gs.statcounter.com/#browser-ww-monthly-201107-201206

27. Wilson, T.D. and Dunn, E.W. Self-knowledge: Its limits, value, and potential for improvement. *Annual Review of Psychology, 55* (2004), 493–518.

Shifting Dynamics or Breaking Sacred Traditions? The Role of Technology in Twelve-Step Fellowships

Svetlana Yarosh
AT&T Research Labs
180 Park Ave,
Florham Park, NJ 07392
lana@research.att.com

ABSTRACT

Twelve-step fellowships are the most common long-term maintenance program for recovery from alcoholism and addiction. Informed by six months of participatory observation of twelve-step fellowship meetings and service structure, I conducted in-depth interviews with twelve members of Alcoholics Anonymous (AA) and Narcotics Anonymous (NA) about the role of technology in recovery. I found that there are a number of tensions in how technology is perceived and adopted. As technology and twelve-step fellowships interact, issues of anonymity, identity, consensus, access, unity, autonomy, and physical presence are foregrounded. I relate these findings to the broader research landscape and provide implications for future design in this space.

Author Keywords

Recovery; addiction; twelve-step fellowships; spirituality.

ACM Classification Keywords

H.5.2. [Information Interfaces and Presentation]: User Interfaces: *User-Centered Design*.

INTRODUCTION

Substance use disorders are characterized by needing increasing amounts of a chemical substance to achieve desired effect, consistent use of larger amounts than intended, and persistent unsuccessful attempts to cut down or stop use despite increasingly severe consequences to the user. These disorders are a medical condition (recognized by the DSM), which are estimated to cost the United States $374 billion per year [33]. 2004 estimates show that 67% of Americans drink alcohol, with 11.9% developing dependence to the substance; 45.8% of Americans try illicit substances during their lifetime, with rates of dependence between 10.3% and 67.8%, depending on the substance [24]. Immediate treatments for substance abuse involve medical intervention such as detox and rehabilitation therapy, but are rarely effective in the long-term unless

paired with a maintenance program [24]. The most common type of a maintenance program is the twelve-step approach, such as Alcoholics Anonymous (AA) and Narcotics Anonymous (NA). Various investigations have shown twelve-step interventions to be as or more effective than alternative approaches and they are frequently the intervention recommended by the medical community [27].

Twelve-step programs are characterized as a social movement that "has become the prototype of a burgeoning category of mutual-help organizations" [22]. In 2012, AA service structure included 114,070 groups and NA included 58,000 groups worldwide [1,2]. Independent studies have hypothesized that these numbers may be understated since only about 50% of groups participate in the general service structure [22]. Some estimates show that as much as 3.1% of the U.S. population may be involved in AA [22].

Though there have been a number of studies examining twelve-step communities from the psychological, sociological, cultural, and clinical perspectives (e.g. [4,13,14,22,27]), the role of technology in twelve-step recovery has not been explicitly examined. In this paper, I report on a series of in-depth interviews, informed by six months of participant observations of AA and NA, conducted with twelve members of twelve-step programs. Three goals drove this investigation: (1) characterizing the perceptions and use of technology by members of twelve-step communities, (2) identifying the unique needs of this community when considering appropriate technological interventions, and (3) describing the opportunities and challenges of working with twelve-step communities to design appropriate interventions to support recovery from addiction and alcoholism. I found that although members of twelve-step fellowships do use technology to support their recovery, there are a number of tensions between the use of technology and the traditions of twelve-step programs.

I begin by providing some background on twelve-step recovery and related work. Next, I provide a detailed description of the methods and present the thematic results of my qualitative investigation. Finally, I discuss the implications of this investigation and how it may provide a unique lens for thinking about technology in other contexts.

ELEMENTS OF 12-STEP RECOVERY

There are over 200 different types of twelve-step programs (known as fellowships) focusing on specific issues of substance dependence (e.g., Crystal Meth Anonymous) and behavioral compulsion (e.g., Gamblers Anonymous). Though my focus in this paper is on the two most established twelve-step groups (NA and AA have the most meetings worldwide and thus provided ample opportunities for participatory observation), all twelve-step fellowships advocate a similar process for recovery, which includes the following elements:

- Abstaining from the Problematic Behavior: twelve-step programs are based on the idea that recovery requires complete abstinence from the problem behavior. Substance-based programs advocate abstinence from all mind-altering substances (e.g., an NA member in recovery does not drink alcohol). Milestones in recovery (e.g., three months clean) are celebrated with a public gifting of a small token such as a poker chip or a keychain. Abstaining is seen as a byproduct of addressing underlying addiction issues (e.g., resentments, loneliness) by following the three classes of suggestions below.

- Meeting Attendance: regularly (daily to weekly) attending meetings where time is devoted to reading the fellowship-approved literature, listening to a member speaker share, and sharing experiences in recovery. Each group meeting is autonomous and non-professional (ran by current members of the fellowship). The groups' relationship to individuals and other groups is governed by the Twelve Traditions[1].

- Sponsorship and Service: working with a member of the program who has had a longer time in recovery (a sponsor) to get an outside perspective one's recovery process and providing the same service to newer members in the program (sponsees). Additionally, service involves participating in outreach meetings at hospitals and institutions, helping with the logistics of running a meeting, and participating at the regional and national levels of the fellowship.

- Stepwork: working with guidance of a sponsor and the fellowship literature to continually progress through the Twelve Steps[1] of the program (after doing Step Twelve, focus again shifts to Step One). The steps include suggestions for admitting the problem, establishing a relationship with a "higher power" (e.g., God), understanding personal character defects through a written inventory, making amends to others, establishing spiritual maintenance practices, and reaching out to newcomers.

[1] An example of the Twelve Steps and Twelve Traditions of one fellowship (AA) can be found here: http://www.aa.org/1212/

Twelve-step programs are considered to be programs of suggestions (rather than rules or requirements) and the only requirement for membership is "a desire to stop" the behavior being addressed. Thus, each individual member's program may include some or all of these elements to varying degrees.

Though the research community has not examined the role of technology in twelve-step recovery, there are a number of currently available technological interventions aimed at this audience. These include specialized social networking sites, repositories of speaker tapes and program literature, mobile apps for locating nearby meetings, services for the delivery of daily meditation or reflection readings, and apps for tracking specific behaviors in recovery (e.g., meeting attendance). Neither AA nor NA officially endorses any of these tools, as all of these are for-profit endeavors.

RELATED WORK

Though there have been no previous studies on the role of technology in twelve-step fellowships, this work is relevant to a number of existing lines of investigation including designing for behavior change, technology for recovery from addiction, examinations of AA as a culture and as a clinical intervention, and the role of technology in spirituality.

Self-Management and Behavior Change

It is reasonable to think about substance use disorders as a chronic medical condition. There is evidence of the success of peer-lead self-management programs on the outcomes of other chronic conditions [18] and twelve-step fellowships may simply be an early, non-professional example of a similar intervention. Recovery from addiction or alcoholism is also an example of radical behavior change. Behavior change is of interest to HCI, with many studies focusing on supporting personal health informatics (e.g., [16]) and persuading individuals to adopt healthy behaviors (e.g., [17]). However in this study, I focus on established members of twelve-step fellowships who are familiar with the traditions and practices of these groups. In the context of the Transtheoretical Model of behavior change [21], all of the participants could be said to have reached the *maintenance* stage of behavior change. In the context of the Health Belief Model, these participants can be said to have sufficiently resolved the three classes of factors to understand that their addiction/alcoholism is a relevant health concern, a threat to their wellbeing, and that a twelve-step fellowship reduces this perceived threat for a subjectively acceptable cost [23]. This work discusses the role of technology in maintaining recovery, rather than persuading addicts/alcoholics to seek recovery or the early process of physical detoxification.

Technology for Recovery from Addiction

Computer-based interventions for substance addiction have been shown to be more effective than assessment-only interventions [19]. Most of these systems involve information being delivered to the patient via an on-site computer in a treatment center. Despite the potential to offer such interventions outside of a treatment center, only one study in the review attempted to do so. Lenert et al. compared an automated email intervention sent to participants who were trying to quit smoking with a single-point-in-time web interaction. While the two interventions had comparable 30-day quit rates, those who received the automated email interventions attempted quitting earlier and more frequently [15]. Computerized interventions are seen as a promising new direction for "less severely dependent" clients [6]. In this study, I focus not on the delivery of initial information to a client who wants to limit their use of a particular substance, but rather on a maintenance program for addicts and alcoholics who have already stopped using and participate in the maintenance program to keep from using again.

As with other maintenance programs for chronic or life-threatening conditions (e.g., [29]), there is a thriving ecosystem of online mutual-support forums and websites for helping the recovering addict or alcoholic. One example is MedHelp alcoholism forum investigated by Chuang and Yang, which was found to help participating individuals receive various forms of support and form a recovery community [5]. Though it seems that most members of the forum were also practicing members of AA, the relationship between these widespread online forums and the practices and policies of 12-step memberships have not been explicitly investigated.

Investigations of Twelve-Step Recovery

Twelve-step fellowships are of interest to both clinical studies of recovery and ethnographic investigations of these fellowships as social structures. Project MATCH, a clinical investigation of recovery from alcoholism, found that AA was no less effective than other interventions on any measures and significantly more effective on the measure of the percentage of participants maintaining abstinence over three years [7]. Other clinical investigations have focused on the effectiveness of twelve-step fellowships for specific subsets of the population (e.g., [11]) and how twelve-step fellowships can be combined with professional interventions for best patient outcomes [30]. Ethnographic investigations of twelve-step fellowships have focused on issues of language and meaning [13], social agency [22], and identity [4]. All of these emphasize that twelve-step fellowships develop a distinct culture, language, and practices that are adopted by new members through participation in these communities. To my knowledge, there have been no formal investigations of how technology fits (or does not fit) into the culture of twelve-step fellowships.

Spirituality

Twelve-step fellowships are spiritual programs of recovery. God is referenced in six of the twelve steps. There is a great

#	Gender	Recovery	Fellowship(s)	Location
P1	M	7 yrs.	NA	GA, USA
P2	M	28 yrs.	NA, OA	GA, USA
P3	M	28 yrs.	NA, EA, CODA	GA, USA
P4	M	5 yrs.	AA	CA, USA
P5	M	2 yrs.	AA, NA	CA, USA
P6	M	3 yrs.	AA	GA, USA
P7	F	19 yrs.	NA, Al-Anon	GA, USA
P8	F	6 yrs.	NA	GA, USA
P9	M	2 yrs.	AA, NA, CMA	GA, USA
P10	F	10 yrs.	NA	GA, USA
P11	M	12 yrs.	NA, Al-Anon	GA, USA
P12	M	21 yrs.	NA	NB, Canada

Table 1. Participants' demographics and fellowships attended (primary listed first). Fellowships included: NA (Narcotics Anon.), OA (Overeaters Anon.), EA (Emotions Anon.), CODA (Co-Dependents Anon.), AA (Alcoholics Anon.), Al-Anon (Families of Alcoholics), and CMA (Crystal Meth Anon.).

deal of controversy about whether twelve-step fellowships are a religious program or even a cult [3], calling into question the constitutionality of twelve-step fellowships as court-ordered or medically-sanctioned interventions. While the use of technology for spiritual or religious purposes is not out of the purview of HCI research (e.g., [31]), taking a stance on the religious aspects twelve-step fellowships is not the purpose of this work. Despite the controversy regarding the twelve-step approach, these are (and will likely continue to be) the most common treatment option for many addicts and alcoholics because AA/NA is free, non-professional, and widespread, making daily meeting attendance practical for most who need it. As in previous work that uses religion as a lens for reconsidering the home [31], this investigation uses twelve-step recovery fellowships as a lens for reconsidering some assumptions of social computing.

METHODS

Informed by participatory observation of AA and NA fellowships, I conducted in-depth interviews with twelve members of twelve-step programs to discuss the role of technology in recovery.

Formative Participatory Observations

Twelve-step fellowships have a distinct culture and language [22]. In order to inform my in-depth interviews, I conducted a six-month participatory observation study of AA and NA. During the course of this time period, I attended 132 meetings (with a roughly even split of AA and NA) in the states of Georgia and California. I also participated in 18 organizational service structure meetings at the group and regional level, conducted a review of currently available technologies for recovery, and reviewed and documented the artifacts of the program such as bulletin boards, information pamphlets, and meeting scripts. This body of work was documented through daily field notes. Discussing the details of this formative phase is outside the scope of this paper; however, this immersion period helped to contextualize and inform the investigation described in this paper, familiarize me with the language and philosophies of twelve-step recovery, and gain access to members of these fellowships for in-depth interviewing.

Interviews

I interviewed twelve participants who were members of AA, NA, or both to understand how they use technology for recovery and the opportunities and challenges of designing for recovery.

Participants

Table 1 provides a description of the participants, including their time in recovery, the fellowships they attend, and their geographic location. Six participants were recruited through an announcement before the start of three meetings: a co-ed NA meeting, a co-ed AA meeting, and a women's NA meeting. Three participants were directly contacted because they expressed the desire to be in the study during the participatory observation investigation. The remaining three participants contacted me on the recommendations of previous study participants. All participants who volunteered had more than one year of continuous recovery. I acknowledge that there is an unfortunate inherent sampling bias in this approach as the people who volunteered for the interviews were more likely to want to share their opinions on technology and thus perhaps hold stronger opinions (either positive or negative) than the larger body of either fellowship.

Procedure

Because of the sensitive nature of the topic approached, informed consent for participation in this study was obtained verbally and the requirement for documentation of consent was waved. Participants were not compensated for their participation. All interviews with Georgia members of AA and NA were conducted in-person, in the location of the participants' choosing (usually recovery clubhouse or coffee shop). The two California interviews were conducted over Skype and the interview with the Canadian participant was conducted by phone (storyboard sketches and consent sheets were emailed to the participants).

Each interview lasted between 50 and 130 minutes. In the first phase, we discussed the participant's background, fellowship participation, and elements of his or her recovery program. In the second phase, we discussed technology used by the participant to aid in his or her recovery process and general opinions about the role of technology in recovery. In the last phase, I elicited more contextualized feedback by presenting six storyboard sketches for potential technology for recovery. These were meant to provoke feedback and generate discussion (rather than serve as actual directions for design):

- **ServiceNet**: an online system for connecting fellowship members who are willing to help with those who need help (especially newcomers), for example rides to meetings, babysitting during a meeting, etc.

- **Meeting Spot**: a searchable list of meetings that is annotated by actual attendees to include information such as meeting size, detailed directions (e.g., which church door to use), and updated time/location.

- **Remote Attend**: a self-contained tablet-like device that can be used to provide remote presence at a meeting through videochat to a member who is currently housebound, hospitalized, or institutionalized.

- **Recovery Trading Cards**: website for making and printing cards that can be given to a newcomer, containing one member's contact information, meeting details, and recovery conversation starters. Includes a QR code for quickly adding new cards to a smart phone or computer contact list.

- **Recovery Tube**: a website that allows members to upload anonymized video (converted to avatar), audio, or text shares tagging them with topic tags. Members looking for a share on a specific topic can search this list and mark contributions as "extra helpful" to allow for recommendations and filtering.

- **GroupAdmin**: an online tool for storing a group's documents, information for trusted servants, and financial information. It can also be used to conduct a "straw poll" of members through email and facilitate communication with regional and national levels (e.g., generate an email to be sent when group info changes).

These ideas were chosen from a larger body of 50 brainstormed ideas because they focused most directly on addressing the major challenges observed in the preceding ethnographic investigation: finding and getting to meetings, forming a social support network, sharing recovery ideas with the larger community of recovering addicts and alcoholics, and organizing the logistics of the meeting.

After explaining each sketch, I asked the participant a number of questions, though the ones that led to most well-articulated responses were: "How can a system like this go wrong?" and "What would keep this from being accepted by your fellowship?" Perhaps this was because many participants knew me from the participatory observation as a technologist, so the negatively phrased questions made it clear that I was interested and open to divergent interpretations of technology.

Analysis

I transcribed all interviews and coded them using the method recommended by Seidman [25]. I began with an open-coding pass through the transcripts. New codes were added whenever I encountered a participant response that did not fit into any previous codes. An independent researcher (who was familiar with qualitative analysis and twelve-step programs, but not a member of any program) and I worked together to cluster these codes thematically using affinity diagramming. Through this process, we identified seven major themes presented below. Once this set of codes was developed, I conducted two additional passes through the transcript data assigning codes to statements where appropriate. The themes reported below were those that appeared consistently across multiple interview participants, though points of contention are also noted to highlight divergent responses and opinions.

RESULTS

I begin with an overview of how currently available technology was used by participants to support recovery from addiction and/or alcoholism. Then, I discuss seven themes that highlight the tensions between twelve-step fellowships and technology for recovery.

Current Perceptions and Use

Interview participants used current technologies to support a number of recovery tasks in their lives. They used technology to find new meetings to attend, to do stepwork with their sponsors or sponsees, to attend online meetings, to find community in social networking site groups, to look for information about recovery and addiction, to keep track of a daily inventory, to read program literature, to coordinate and organize service work, and to listen to archived recovery speakers (see Table 2). Additionally, a number of the participants actually took part in the creation of new technological resources for recovery including creating new mobile apps (P4, P12), creating group webpages (P2) and digital resources (P3, P7), and creating/running online meetings (P11). It was clear that there is some optimism and hope about the potential role that technology could serve in recovery, but participants also acknowledged that there are a number of tensions and challenges related to the topic:

I think as a community, recovering addicts tend to be largely technophobic. (P10)

I have this essential trust that people understand the traditions, whereas ... how can you trust technologies to uphold the traditions? (P5)

Recovery has dealt with shifting dynamics since its inception. We dealt with the shifting dynamics of including women, the shifting dynamics of including gay people, the shifting dynamics of crack cocaine—you will find old timers that refer to themselves as joining NA BC, Before Crack—and you can make the argument that the introduction of technology is nothing more than that same shifting dynamic ... Or, you can choose to take the other side of the argument that technology is breaking traditions and the traditions of NA are sacred and you will have nothing to do with it. (P1)

In the remainder of the results section, I discuss seven themes that highlight some of the tensions in using technology for recovery.

Anonymity and Technology

Anonymity is a primary principle of all twelve-step fellowships, which both protects members from external judgment and protects the fellowship from questionable actions and statements of its members. Both types of anonymity are put at risk through the use of technology.

Participants relayed several examples where individual anonymity was broken through Social Networking Sites or where individuals were concerned about this potentially happening:

Through Facebook, a friend of mine got linked to an NA page, and she didn't do it. Somebody else tagged her, and it was not okay, because not everybody in her life needs to know that she was in NA. (P8)

Even if there are rules that you don't post other people's names, you know somebody will at some point. So what happens then? (P7)

Distrust of technology to be able to protect individual anonymity was also articulated when responding to the idea of remote videochat attendance:

The issue with videochat attendance is that you need to trust about other people not being in the room ... if one member of the group is uncomfortable, the group is just not going to use it. (P4)

As soon as you record your face, there's the possibility to have your own anonymity broken or violate a tradition because a recording might be used in an unintended way. (P12)

This distrust also extended to cloud storage of personal data and committing personal recovery information to any digital form:

I found that committing my personal information to a computer really worried me because there is this idea that everything you type into a computer lasts forever. (P5)

Aside from protecting individual anonymity, twelve-step fellowships worry about members publically identifying as part of the program:

There are Facebook pages devoted to recovery, and people have put themselves out there and I really think that's a violation of traditions ... the danger is in someone becoming identified as a member of a certain fellowship, then perhaps, they relapse. Now, a newcomer might think, "Maybe that AA or NA business is not very effective, so why should I bother trying it?" (P2)

Social Networking Sites and other examples of social computing complicate the process of protecting the fellowship as a whole from the actions of individuals.

Everybody gets on Facebook. And recovery is the core of our existence. What am I going to talk about, except the thing that's most important to me? ... Well, at World Services they met to discuss NA in social media. They talked for two hours and did not come to a consensus. But, NA had a Facebook page before and after that two-hour discussion, without saying that Facebook is wrong or you shouldn't be on Facebook with NA, they took down that page. (P1)

Twelve-step fellowships are still struggling with the relationship between social media and the principle of anonymity.

Principles Before Personalities

Most social computing systems include some notion of persistent identity or reputation, however this idea frequently goes against twelve-step traditions—in particular, the value that all program members are equal and principles come before personalities:

I think for me the biggest issue would be about the spirit of anonymity, in that we are all the same. If you sit there and make a list of what you're good at or what you know about, that totally busts that. (P8)

I can see some people saying that if you have a card with your name and you clean date on it, it sort of sets you apart a little bit ... you could say, "Hey, I have 5 years, I'm better than you." ... You could argue that it goes against the idea of all addicts being equal. (P10)

The whole "celebrity" status thing ... you're almost saying that you're an expert. People may start thinking that this person knows better than somebody else ... this kind of separates us. (P12)

Additionally, one of the basic ideas behind twelve-step programs is that people are capable of change. A persistent state in an online system might hinder this growth, trapping an individual in being seen for who they were instead of who they are:

My first idea is that somebody's past performance might not be a good predictor of their future performance, especially in AA, because people tend to turn a corner. (P5)

This idea extended beyond individuals, to a similar resistance to rating or ranking other aspects of the program, such as meetings or groups:

If somebody just had an isolated experience and writes about it online, then that become the truth ... as soon as you share that, it could be active forever, even though it's relevant only for a moment. (P12)

The interview participants worried that when an impression is committed to publically shared writing, it becomes a "truth" that may be difficult to overcome, which is not in the spirit of recovery.

Membership and Access to Technology

In all twelve-step fellowships, the only requirement for membership is the desire to stop participating in the behavior addressed by the program. Technology is seen to conflict with this tradition because it can potentially introduce additional conditions to central participation in the fellowship:

You could argue that any use of technology goes against the third tradition that the only requirement for membership is the desire to stop using. Now, it's also the desire to start using a computer. (P10)

This concern extends to members who have limited technical ability and would not feel comfortable using technology:

We have a home group member who is really bad with technology. He says, "Don't get me on the Internet, I'll probably crash the whole thing down." So, how would he get a vote in this? (P8)

It also applies to members who may not have the resources to access a type of technology:

The truth is, especially new members of NA, they may not even have computers because they have lost everything they ever had. They're going to be disconnected, disenfranchised... (P12)

My only concern is not to forget about someone that doesn't have technology ... that they're not alienated from a particular resource, really. (P9)

Recovery fellowships do not want to adopt practices that assume any type of technology access on the part of its members, which means that any technical system must have a non-technical alternative for achieving participation.

Building Consensus Remotely

Decisions made by twelve-step groups or organizational structures are supposed to reflect the "group conscience" and so are frequently made through consensus. This is often a frustrating and time-taking process but one that is seen as necessary and better done face-to-face:

Someone might say something with speech that they didn't necessarily feel comfortable writing down or having a record of at all. If you did have discussion on a particular issue, I think it would be more likely to get hostile over the Internet, because you don't have to worry about offending anyone to their face. (P10)

P11 ran an online meeting and experimented with consensus-building through asynchronous online media, but without much success:

In that medium [online forums], and I'm still convinced of this, group conscience is very difficult to formulate. You're not seeing how people are talking, you're not hearing the timbre of their voice ... You know how contentious service can be anyway? Now take away all the human quality of it and it can become very contentious. (P11)

However, it is not always possible to make decisions in person, leading to an approach that combines grassroots input with final decisions made by elected trusted servants. One powerful example is the creation of new literature which is written and approved by the fellowship through a largely consensus driven process. NA has recently approved a new book, titled *Living Clean,* and P12 discussed the process of its creation:

What happens is that there is always an open door for people to input by sending emails or attending workshops. [The 16 people who were responsible for getting it all together] actually took all of the information that was given and they put it on pieces of paper. Then they cut all the lines out and started laying them right on the floor to try and actually see what people said, so they can have all the similar ideas together. (P12)

Chapters of the book grew out of this grounded-theory-like analysis. Each chapter draft was distributed back to the groups for comments and approval. However, this was a complex collaborative process—the 130-page book took more than three years to write and approve.

Message of Recovery and Singleness of Purpose

Twelve-step recovery programs specify standards of behavior using the Twelve Traditions. All interview participants emphasized the importance of "going back and reviewing and keeping the traditions in mind" (P6) while designing for this audience. However, in addition to the Twelve Traditions, each fellowship has a specific culture and message that is supposed to stay consistent to create unity among members: for example, "the Al-Anon message is spoken here, leave all other affiliations outside" (P7). In the rooms, this culture is enforced organically:

You know how people sometimes show up at their first meeting and they share, but they don't understand the customs, culture, and rules of the program ... I've seen it where an old-timer will actually step in and stop their share and tell them to talk to somebody after the meeting instead. (P4)

The culture frequently includes a language, a way of sharing, and the tradition of keeping matters that do not relate to recovery out of the discourse. However, these practices get muddied on social networking sites:

That's when you get people talking about religion and politics in the rooms and that contentious nature is not good for unity ... the traditions have a very loose hold on social media. (P1)

It could go wrong by less focus on singleness of purpose, I could see where you could potentially change the focus. (P6)

Tech-Supported Task	Participants
Finding (Physical) Meetings Online	P1, P2, P4, P5, P6, P7, P9, P8, P10, P12
Remote Sponsorship and Stepwork (Videochat, VoIP, Email)	P1, P2, P6, P7, P8, P10
Online Meetings (Forums, Chat, Audio)	P1, P2, P3, P5, P7, P11, P12
Recovery Social Network Sites (Dedicated SNS, Facebook Groups)	P1, P3, P5, P6, P7, P9, P10, P11
Searching for Info on Recovery	P3, P10, P11
Daily Inventory Using App or Program	P4, P7, P10
Getting Program Literature on a Mobile Device (Apps, PDF, eBooks)	P2, P5, P6, P7, P9, P10, P11, P12
Coordinating for Organizational Service Work (Email, Webinars, Online Surveys)	P2, P7, P8, P10, P11, P12
Speaker Repositories (Online, On CD)	P3, P5, P6, P9, P11, P12

Table 2. Interview participants who explicitly discussed each particular use of currently available technology during the course of the interview.

Participants saw a danger that the message of recovery would be lost in personalities as resentments, negative opinions, and outside issues get played out online:

I'm sure as with any online forum, there's going to be risks ... You might get someone that has a resentment and tries to sabotage a meeting. (P9)

People are far more prone to comment negatively than positively online. So, the problem is that the unity of the program could be broken. (P1)

What about just inappropriate comments, like, "well, if you want to meet hot guys, go to this meeting..." (P7)

Controlling this kind of behavior is inherently subjective and interview participants questioned whether it would ever be possible in an online setting without completely reconsidering how twelve-step fellowships work. "Someone has to be the hall monitor, but this is a program where our leaders do not govern, but only serve," said P11, "so who is going to do that and how is that going to work?"

Group Autonomy

The difficulty of maintaining unity and a single message of recovery is amplified by the tension between the tradition that calls for unity and the tradition that states that each group should be autonomous. Groups interpret the traditions differently due to geographic and demographic differences between groups. For example, in Georgia NA meetings, naming specific drugs is discouraged as it is considered to go against group unity, but:

Every area and every meeting has a different culture and things that are acceptable for sharing. In London, for example, it is not only acceptable, but encouraged to use the names of specific drugs. (P10)

In another example, meetings may face different challenges depending on the demographic of the participants:

In some areas, it's really not a problem because the majority of the members are gay or lesbian, but other areas are still very "men with men" and "women with women" because they try to prevent the very predatory quality of some men in recovery. (P11)

Additionally, NA and AA are grassroots organizations, so there is no requirement for any group to adopt a policy recommended by regional, national, or world levels of the organization:

You will find meetings that won't stock the new book. Even though it was approved unanimously by the World organization, because they don't think that the South had a big enough voice in its approval. (P11)

When most contact between members of the fellowship occurred in person, it was less likely that a participant would run across inconsistent readings of the traditions or conflicting policies. However, as technology connects addicts and alcoholics who would otherwise have never met, unity and autonomy are affected by the response to these inconsistencies.

Importance of Face-to-Face Contact

Every participant emphasized the importance of face-to-face contact for the success of a twelve-step intervention. Participants cautioned that an addict might use online reviews of meetings as an excuse not to attend:

I think there's something positive to be said for going to a meeting and forming your own opinion about it versus listening to the opinions of others and not going. (P6)

There was great resistance to introducing technology that would make an aspect of the program easier or more convenient at the expense of having to take the risk of actually making face-to-face contact with other fellowship members:

Just getting a list of numbers is too easy. People early in recovery need to make a conscious decision to go through the effort of asking for a phone number. They might be terrified to do that, but need to do it ... If it's too easy and you're just spoon-feeding it to people, they're not going to value it. (P1)

Even if online meetings and remote participation could potentially open a meeting to a person who otherwise would not be able attend, participants emphasized that this is "not the same as a regular face-to-face meeting" (P2). The physical aspects of being at a meeting are important:

When I go to a meeting, there is the opportunity to see and be seen, be a part of a fellowship ... I go through a day without touching anyone, but then you go to a meeting and you get to hold people's hands. That's real recovery. (P5)

And remote attendance was seen as just that—remote:

Someone could argue that this encourages a great limitation on face-to-face contact, which could limit empathy, rapport, and unity ... watching a screen is not the same thing as face-to-face contact and it could lead to a level of detachment about your recovery. (P10)

Despite the trouble potentially involved in taking meetings to hospitals and institutions, it was seen as an opportunity to meet in person:

I mean, most people say, "take the meeting to the guy in the hospital." That's going to mean a lot more. You're going to be able to give him a hug and you can cry together, you know. Taking a meeting there is much more meaningful. (P11)

Though participants acknowledged the potential of temporary remote contact for stepwork or sponsorship, there was resistance to technological conveniences that may reduce face-to-face contact in the long run.

Overall Results

All of the participants in this study already used technology for one or more aspects of their recovery. Each person cited one or more of the offered designs as something they would like to see and use in the future, with the most popular designs being Recovery Trading Cards (5 named it "most promising") and GroupAdmin (4 named it "most promising"). However, when asked to consider all the designs from the point of view of the group and AA/NA as a whole, the participants were able to cite a number of issues that may prevent the adoption of such technologies. The main concerns centered around preserving the traditions of each fellowship: keeping participation as open as possible, encouraging in-person contact, supporting group autonomy and unity, and preventing violations of anonymity. Remote Attend was seen as the most potentially problematic idea (8 named it as "most problematic"). It is clear that designing for twelve-step fellowships would require close collaboration with the service bodies of each organization to reach a consensus on what would or would not be appropriate as a technological intervention. However, there are also some considerations that might increase the acceptability of suggested designs. In the next section, I consider five suggestions that may be incorporated into the design of technologies for 12-step fellowships and may also be helpful to other social computing applications.

DISCUSSION

In this section, I present considerations for design that emerged out of my investigation of twelve-step fellowships. Rather than focusing just on specific solutions in designing for recovery, I also draw out themes and design directions that have been foregrounded by this investigation and demonstrate how these ideas may apply to other contexts and existing threads of conversation in the HCI community.

The Social Journey, Not the Information Destination

Though there are a number of ways to make meeting selection, recovery information gathering, and participation in service more efficient in terms of *time*, this may not be helpful to the recovering individual. The interview participants were suspicious of any technology that replaces face-to-face contact with interacting with a system. Getting a list of numbers to call in a twelve-step meeting is not just about gathering contacts, rather it is about making a face-to-face connection and beginning to build a network. While most contact managers try to make it easier to add a contact, one can imagine a technology that makes it more *difficult*, perhaps by requiring you to both meet and to write down a few things about the person you are adding. In recovery, the journey of getting information about new meetings, new people, and new recovery suggestions is just as important as the information gained because it helps build a recovery support network. However, this is not only true of recovery. For example in the workplace, a network of relationships is key to success in an organization [12]. One can imagine that a similar approach to making it harder to contact somebody until making a personal connection might be more difficult in the short-term but more beneficial in the long-term.

Anonymous Social Computing and Democratization

While online interaction allows the users to achieve a certain level of anonymity (e.g., [9]), most social computing approaches rely on the idea of persistent identity and reputation to encourage desired forms of interaction (e.g., posting good posts) and discourage undesired activities (e.g., vandalism). Identity plays an important role in online peer-support communities, but could also interfere with the ability to get emotional support or accountability in times of trouble [20]. The twelve-step spiritual ideas of anonymity and "principles before personalities" challenge the idea that persistent identity is necessary for the health of the community. Twelve-step programs encourage the understanding that all addicts/alcoholics are equal, that there is no such thing as an AA/NA superstar, and that *any* member can be of service regardless of previous reputation. Anonymity has been serving an equalizing purpose in twelve-step fellowships since their inception; perhaps, it can have a similar effect in online communities that are struggling to democratize participation.

Going for the Real Thing
Videochat has been billed as the next best thing to being there in person, as "almost being there" [26]. However, participants in this investigation pointed out that in the hurry to get "the next best thing" to physical presence, one may miss out on the opportunity to feel a sense of loss that might actually drive the search for "the real thing." For example: seeking to stay connected to an old sponsor after a move may prevent looking for a new sponsor who can be physically present; connecting with a hospitalized group member using videochat may actually remove the sense of urgency that might have driven one to visit in person. This is consistent with recent criticisms that communication technology may actually create an illusion of contact while making us feel more disconnected and isolated [28]. This is also consistent with work that shows that children who are separated from their parents focus on the next reunion or substitute in-person contact with another adult, rather than relying on mediated communication that occurs during the separation [32]. Maybe remote contact is at times inevitable and videochat is the next best thing, but it also may be important to work under the assumption that it's still nowhere close the real thing and support achieving in-person contact as the first priority.

High-, Low-, and No-Tech Participation
When access to technology becomes a requirement to full participation, some groups and individuals may become disenfranchised. Communities like AA and NA are particularly sensitive to this possibility and try to provide equivalent no-tech, low-tech, and high-tech ways of participating in important community processes. For example, in the process of writing the *Living Clean* book, an addict could have contributed to the content by participating in a physical book workshop in their area (no-tech), calling in their opinions to the book committee (low-tech), or responding to an online survey (high-tech). There is inherent complexity in having these methods of participation interoperate—in this case, this was achieved only through the service of several individuals who

collected, compiled, and interpreted the input from the various sources. As the differences between those with advanced infrastructure and those without it grow, it may be important to find better ways for high-, low-, and no-tech systems to coordinate. It may be impossible to achieve the same experience when using different levels of technology, but it should be possible to achieve the same goals. This contributes to the ongoing conversation within HCI that maintains that it is important to design technology not only with considerations for those who use it but also for those who might be excluded from its use [8].

Localization, Autonomy, and Polyvocality
There was a great deal of geographic and demographic variety in approaches to recovery and interpretation of traditions within the same fellowship. Groups like AA and NA demonstrate that it is possible to maintain a long-term discussion about the balance between unity and autonomy. This autonomy has always been encouraged in twelve-step fellowships, but may be lost as portions of the fellowship move online. Contact with other perspectives is important, but perhaps the virtual spaces provided by an online community smooth over differences in striving for neutrality in a way that reduces polyvocality in this diverse space. Recent work on post-colonial computing, emphasizes the importance of embracing rather than erasing this diversity of perspectives [10]. The physical metaphor of an autonomous group of a larger fellowship might be an interesting way of considering polyvocality. While an in-person visit to a different physical location holds an implicit understanding of entering a different culture with all of the inherent qualities of being a guest in another's home, online it may be unclear whose perspectives and interpretations are primary for the moment. Introducing the "home" vs. "visiting" metaphor to online communities with diverse subgroups may be a promising direction in design.

CONCLUSION
This work is the first to examine the role of technology in twelve-step fellowships. Through in-depth interviews informed by participant observation, I identified seven major tensions between technology and the fellowships, including challenges in achieving anonymity, equality, universal access, consensus, unity, and autonomy. These findings may serve to inform the design of future technologies for twelve-step recovery, but may additionally highlight alternative ideas and perspectives to help address existing challenges in social computing.

ACKNOWLEDGMENTS
Thank you to Liz Prince for her help with the clinical psychology aspects of this study. Also, I am deeply indebted to the members of the NA and AA groups I have attended, most of all Michael and Kevin without whom I could not have written this paper.

REFERENCES

1. Anon. Estimates Of A.A. Groups And Members As Of January 1, 2012. 2012. www.aa.org.

2. Anon. Facts about NA. 2012. www.na.org.

3. Bufe, C. *Alcoholics Anonymous: Cult or Cure?* 1998.

4. Cain, C. *Becoming a Non-Drinking Alcoholic: A Case Study in Identity Acquisition.* Anthropology Department, UNC. 1991.

5. Chuang, K.Y. and Yang, C.C. Helping you to help me: Exploring supportive interaction in online health community. *ASIST 47*, 1 (2010).

6. Copeland, J. and Martin, G. Web-based interventions for substance use disorders: A qualitative review. *J. of Substance Abuse Treatment 26*, 2 (2004), 109–116.

7. Cutler, R. and Fishbain, D. Are alcoholism treatments effective? The Project MATCH data. *BMC Public Health 5*, 75 (2007).

8. Dantec, C.A. Le and Edwards, W.K. Designs on Dignity : Perceptions of Technology Among the Homeless. *Proc. of CHI*, (2008), 627–636.

9. Donath, J.S. Identity and deception in the virtual community. In *Communities in Cyberspace*. Routledge, New York, 1999, 29–59.

10. Dourish, P. and Mainwaring, S.D. Ubicomp's Colonial Impulse. *Proc. of Ubicomp*, (2012), 133–142.

11. Galaif, E.R. and Sussman, S. For Whom Does Alcoholics Anonymous Work? *Substance Use & Misuse 30*, 2 (1995), 161–184.

12. Granovetter, M.S. The Strength of Weak Ties. *American Journal of Sociology 7*, 6 (1973), 1360–1380.

13. Halloran, S.O. Participant Observation of Alcoholics Anonymous : Contrasting Roles of the Ethnographer and Ethnomethodologist. *The Qualitative Report 8*, 1 (2003), 81–99.

14. Laudet, A.B. Addiction Treatment Clients and Clinitians: Toward Identifying Obstacles to Participation. *Substance Use and Misuse 38*, 14 (2003), 2017–2047.

15. Lenert, L., Muñoz, R.F., Perez, J.E., and Bansod, A. Automated E-mail Messaging as a Tool for Improving Quit Rates in an Internet Smoking Cessation Intervention. *J of the American Medical Informatics Association 11*, (2004), 235–240.

16. Li, I., Dey, A., and Forlizzi, J. A stage-based model of personal informatics systems. *Proc. of CHI*, ACM Press (2010), 557.

17. Lin, J., Mamykina, L., Lindtner, S., Delajoux, G., and Strub, H. Fish'n'Steps: Encouraging Physical Activity with an Interactive Computer Game. *Proc. of Ubiquitous Computing*, (2006), 261–278.

18. Lorig, K.R., Sobel, D.S., Ritter, P.L., Laurent, D., and Hobbs, M. Effect of a self-management program on patients with chronic disease. *Effective Clinical Practice 4*, 6 (2001), 256–62.

19. Moore, B., Fazzino, T., Garnet, B., Cutter, C., and Barry, D. Computer-based interventions for drug use disorders: A systematic review. *J of Substance Abuse Treatment 40*, 3 (2011), 215–223.

20. Newman, M.W., Lauterbach, D., Munson, S.A., Resnick, P., and Morris, M.E. "It's not that I don't have problems, I'm just not putting them on Facebook": Challenges and Opportunities in Using Online Social Networks for Health. *Proc. of CSCW*, (2011).

21. Prochaska, J.O. and Velicer, W.F. The transtheoretical model of health behavior change. *American Journal of Health Promotion 12*, (1997), 38–48.

22. Room, R. Alcoholics Anonymous as a Social Movement. In *Research on Alcoholics Anonymous: Opportunities and Alternatives*. 1993, 167–187.

23. Rosenstock, I., Strecher, V., and Becker, M. Social Learning Theory and the Health Belief Model. *Health Education & Behavior 15*, 2 (1988), 175–183.

24. Sadock, B. and Sadock, V. Substance-Related Disorders. In *Kaplan and Sadock's Synopsis of Psychiatry: Behavioral Science/Clinical Psychiatry*. 2007, 381–464.

25. Seidman, I. *Interviewing as Qualitative Research: A Guide for Researchers in Education And the Social Sciences*. Teachers College Press, New York, 1998.

26. Tarasuik, J.C., Galligan, R., and Kaufman, J. Almost being there: video communication with young children. *PloS one 6*, 2 (2011), e17129.

27. Tonigan, J.S. Alcoholics Anonymous Outcomes and Benefits. In M. Galanter and L.A. Kaskutas, eds., *Research on Alcoholics Anonymous and Spirituality in Addiction*. Springer, 2008, 357–369.

28. Turkle, S. Aspects of the Self. In *Life On the Screen: Identity in the Age of the Internet*. Touchstone, New York, 1997, 177–232.

29. Wang, Y., Kraut, R., and Levine, J.M. To Stay or Leave ? The Relationship of Emotional and Informational Support to Commitment in Online Health Support Groups. *Proc. of CSCW*, (2012), 833–842.

30. White, W.L. Sponsor, Recovery Coach, Addiction Counselor: The Importance of Role Clarity and Role Integrity. *Perspectives on Peer-Based Recovery Support Services*, (2006).

31. Wyche, S.P. and Grinter, R.E. Extraordinary Computing : Religion as a Lens for Reconsidering the Home. *Proc. of CHI*, (2009), 749–758.

32. Yarosh, S. and Abowd, G.D. Mediated Parent-Child Contact in Work-Separated Families. *Proc. of CHI*, ACM (2011), 1185–1194.

33. *National Institute on Drug Abuse. "Addiction Science: From Molecules to Managed Care."* 2008.

Taking Data Exposure into Account:
How Does It Affect the Choice of Sign-in Accounts?

Shahar Ronen
MIT Media Lab
sronen@media.mit.edu

Oriana Riva
Microsoft Research
oriana@microsoft.com

Maritza Johnson
U. of California, Berkeley
maritzaj@cs.berkeley.edu

Donald Thompson
Microsoft Research
donthom@microsoft.com

ABSTRACT

Online services collect personal data from their users, sometimes with no clear need. We studied how users sign-in to web sites using federated IDs, and found that most survey respondents were not aware of the data they expose. However, when presented with the tradeoffs behind each sign-in option, respondents reported a willingness to change how they sign-in to reduce their data exposure or, in fewer cases, to increase it to receive more benefits from the service. Our findings suggest that data exposure is a concern for users, and that there is a need for finding clearer ways for communicating it for each sign-in option.

Author Keywords

Online services; sign in; federated identity; data exposure.

ACM Classification Keywords

H.5.m. [Information Interfaces and Presentation]: Misc.

INTRODUCTION

Many web sites require users to register to enjoy additional benefits: access to premium content (Bloomberg), storage and sharing of media (Flickr), a personalized experience (Monster, The Huffington Post), etc. Registration is the establishment of a relationship with the site using a permanent identity, which can be created on the site or provided by a third party (*federated identity* [4, 9, 11]), such as an e-mail provider (Google, Microsoft, Yahoo!) or a social networking service (Facebook, Twitter). Users can register with Flickr, for instance, using a Facebook, Google, or Yahoo! account. Yet, in addition to benefits, registering with a web site has a cost: personal data are collected by the site and used for its own benefit [1,13]. This is especially true when signing in with federated IDs, which may hold many personal data about users. For example, by registering with Flickr using their Facebook account, users grant Flickr access to information about their Facebook friends.

Some sites support registration through multiple federated IDs, with different data exposure and benefits tradeoffs (Tables 1 and 2). Federated ID providers often inform users of the data they expose to a particular site (yet not necessarily in a clear way), but rarely let users specify upon

registration the types of data made available to the site. Even when users are allowed to decide what to share, they have a hard time choosing, as most sites do not explain why a certain type of data is required and what benefit is provided in return.

In this paper, we present a study that explores how well users are aware of personal data transferred from their federated accounts to sites upon sign-in, and how their sign-in choices change after they are presented with more information about the personal data passed to the site and the benefits received in return. We surveyed 575 people over a two-week period about their sign-in preferences for real and invented sites. We recruited registered and non-registered users to participate using Mechanical Turk. Most of our participants were not aware of the types of personal data they expose to sites upon sign-in, but when given better notice many changed their sign-in choices to reduce data exposure or, in fewer cases, to increase exposure to enable features they perceived as useful. The frequency of both these changes suggests that users do not understand the tradeoffs associated with different sign-in options.

Personal data type	Mons. acct.	Yahoo!	FB
Name and e-mail address	X	X	X
Your picture			X
Gender and birthdate			X
Bio or description		X	X
Interests		X	X
Contacts / friends			X
Education and work history	X		X
Location	X		X
Contacts' info (desc., interests, etc.)			X

Table 1: Data sharing table for Monster, showing for each sign-in option the personal data passed to the site.

Feature	Mons.	Yahoo!	FB
Create your professional profile and notify you about relevant job opportunities	X	X	X
Automatically fill in your professional profile with relevant information			X
Use your friends' education and work info to show you where you have inside connections			X

Table 2: Benefits table for Monster, showing for each sign-in option the features it enables.

RELATED WORK

User misconceptions of data exposure have been studied before, but not in the context of federated IDs. King et al. [8] found that many users were not able to identify the data types exposed by Facebook to third-party apps. Facebook now lists transferred data in the app installation consent form, but these could be misleading [3]. Also, studies on consent forms have shown that users do not understand what they consent to [5, 6]. The use of federated IDs poses additional challenges. First, there are more options to choose from and each may expose different data. Second, users do not understand how federated IDs work: 70% of respondents to Sun et al.'s study [12] thought that the identity provider passed their username and password to the website. Our study goes beyond usernames and passwords and investigates transfer of different types of personal data.

Kelley et al. [7] found that the speed and accuracy of decisions about privacy improved when users were presented a standardized table showing the personal data stored by the site. We use a similar format for communicating to users the data disclosed, but add a table showing the benefits for each option to provide participants complete information about the tradeoffs incurred. This allows us to measure how a better understanding of data exposure affected users' choice of a sign-in account among multiple options.

METHODOLOGY AND SURVEY STRUCTURE

We started by asking our participants how many accounts they have with the following providers: Facebook (FB), Google (G), Microsoft (MS), and Yahoo! (Y), and which of the following data types they believe are stored in each account: basic contact details (phone, e-mail, address, etc.), picture, work and education history, bio/description, location, interests, e-mails, chat history, contacts, events, documents, photos, status updates, contacts' info (description, interests, etc.), and content generated by contacts (documents, status updates, etc.). Then, we presented participants with one of the following sites: Monster, Flickr, The Huffington Post, and Outgo!ng. We selected these sites through a pre-survey, asking 190 Turkers which of 38 sites they were registered with. Flickr ranked first (37% of participants), followed by Monster (15%). We also chose The Huffington Post (6%) because of its wide variety of registration options. Outgo!ng is an invented site, described to participants as "a site for scheduling recreational activities with friends. Given a time frame, Outgo!ng suggests available friends and nearby activities that match your mutual interests".

Participants received one of two questionnaires depending on whether they were registered with the site. Registered users were asked to select from a list the account they used to sign in. The list was populated with accounts supported by the site and also previously specified by the participant. Sign-in options for each site were as follows. HuffPost: FB, G, MS, Y, and a proprietary account that can be created on the site. Flickr: FB, G, Y. Monster: FB, Y, and a Monster account. Outgo!ng: FB, G, MS, Y, and an Outgo!ng account. Finally, we asked participants to select from the list of data types the ones they thought were transferred from the account to the site. Non-registered participants were presented a description of the site, and asked to select from a list the account they would use to register. The list

was similar to the list presented to registered users, with the additional option of creating a new account with one of the identity providers supported by the site.

Then, we presented both groups with two tables: one listed, for each sign-in option, the data types actually transferred from the account to the site, and the other listed the benefits provided by each option (Tables 1 and 2). We then asked participants whether this information made them reconsider their sign-in choice. If so, we asked to select the option that best described why: "I am more comfortable transferring to the site the personal information stored in this account" (interpreted as a concern about data exposure), "I realized I could get a better experience by choosing this account" (desire for better benefits), and "Other (please specify)".

Data Collection

We ran our survey using Amazon's Mechanical Turk over two weeks in August 2012. We aimed for replies from 200 people for each of the real sites (100 registered users) and 50 for Outgo!ng but did not meet the goal (Table 3). We limited participation to US residents with a HIT approval of over 95%, and paid on average $0.45 per survey. Participants were free to choose a HIT (and thus a site) but were limited to submitting one survey. Registered users had to prove they were registered to the site by signing in and copying unique text (e.g., menu options). We received 575 valid responses split almost equally across genders (288 M, 285 F, 2 undisclosed) and from a range of ages (52% aged 18-27, 27% aged 28-37, 21% aged 38+). 86% of our respondents had at least one Facebook account; Google (80%), Yahoo! (64%), and Microsoft (38%) followed.

Site	Registered	Non-registered	Total
Outgo!ng (invented)	N/A	46	**46**
Flickr	61	113	**174**
Huffington Post	49	123	**172**
Monster	67	116	**183**
Total	*177*	*398*	*575*

Table 3: User registration by site.

Site	FB	G	MS	Y	Site acct.	New acct.	Other	Total
Outg NR	12	6	2	6	-	20	-	**46**
Flickr R	2	13	-	40	-	-	6	**61**
Flickr NR	42	35	-	21	-	14	1	**113**
HPost R	9	12	2	7	18	-	1	**49**
HPost NR	18	27	13	20	-	44	1	**123**
Mons R	5	-	-	4	55	-	3	**67**
Mons NR	10	-	-	22	-	79	5	**116**
Total	*98*	*93*	*17*	*120*	*73*	*157*	*17*	*575*

Table 4: Distribution of sign-in accounts by site and registration status: registered (R) and not registered (NR). Numbers for account providers indicate existing accounts; *New acct* is a newly created account with any provider.

RESULTS AND ANALYSIS

Despite the concerns rightfully raised by Sun et al. [12] about user adoption of single sign-on solutions, we found that participants were generally open to using federated accounts when given the option (Table 4). The share of registered users who signed in using federated accounts changed drastically from 13% for Monster to 61% for HuffPost (Flickr supports federated sign-in only). Unregistered users were more open to federated IDs, with 45%, 81%, and 78% choosing a federated account to sign in to Monster, HuffPost, and Outgo!ng, respectively.

Awareness of Personal Data

We compared the number of data types participants (registered and non-registered) thought were associated with each account (Figure 1). Facebook came first with an average of 9.37 data types, followed by Google (5.66), Microsoft (4.71), and Yahoo! (4.32). This indicates that respondents perceive their Facebook accounts as containing more personal data than other providers'. One explanation is that Facebook is a social network whereas the other providers are mostly seen as e-mail services; Google may rank higher than Microsoft and Yahoo! because of its social network, Google+. User perception seems to be correct, as our sites had more data types transferred from Facebook accounts (an average of 8 types per user) than from Yahoo!, Google, or Microsoft, (3.5, 3.3, and 3 types, respectively).

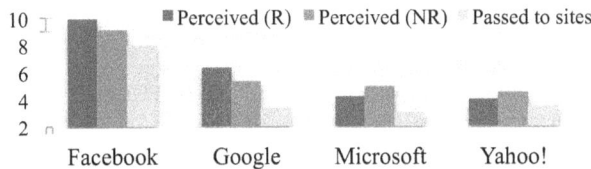

Figure 1: Average number of data types per account. First two bars show what (registered and unregistered) users perceived; the last bar shows the actual number of types passed to sites.

Despite their good intuition about the variety of data stored, participants were not able to correctly identify the data types transferred to the sites. We asked registered users who sign-in with federated accounts (n=94) to select the data types they thought were passed to the site. We compared their answers with the actual data types passed to each site, measuring relevance of responses using *precision* and *recall*. We define precision (P) as the ratio between the number of data types a user named correctly and the number of data types the user named, and recall (R) as the ratio between the number of data types a user named correctly and the number of data types that were actually transferred to the site. For example, if a user specifies that "basic info" and "location" are transferred to a site and the actual data transferred are "basic info", "picture" and "contacts", P=0.5 and R=0.33. The average across all 94 users was P=0.48, and R=0.64 (standard deviation of 0.37 and 0.39, respectively). This means that participants only identified two-thirds of the data types transferred, and that about half the types they guessed were incorrect, showing a rather limited awareness of data types transferred.

Account Reconsideration

Presented with the data sharing and benefit tables, 255 participants (44%) said they would consider changing the sign-in account they had originally chosen. The same rate applied to registered and non-registered users, and we

found similar rates (43%-46%) across all sites. However, only 196 of the 255 (34% of all participants) actually named a different account when asked to select the new sign-in account. We refer to them in the next analysis.

Site	Data exposure	Better benefits	Not resolved	Total
Flickr	43 (21.9%)	18 (9.2%)		**61 (31.1%)**
HuffPost	33 (16.8%)	23 (11.7%)	1 (0.5%)	**57 (29%)**
Monster	36 (18.4%)	27 (13.8%)		**63 (32.2%)**
Outgo!ng	6 (3.1%)	9 (4.6%)		**15 (7.7%)**
Total	*118 (60.2%)*	*77 (39.3%)*	*1 (0.5%)*	*196 (100%)*

Table 5: Reasons for change given by "account changers". "Other" responses were resolved to "data exposure" (16) and "better benefits" (1), but one could not be resolved to either.

Most "account changers" indicated data exposure as the main reason for change (118 participants), while fewer (77) were attracted by the option of more benefits (Table 5). The difference is especially noticeable in the case of Flickr, where the "data-concerned" outnumber the "benefit-concerned" 2.4 to 1. These were mostly Facebook users: 24 (55%) of 44 participants (2 registered, 42 unregistered) who originally chose Facebook to sign in to Flickr changed their decision. A majority of these participants (19, including the two registered users) said they would do so because of a concern about the data Facebook transfers to Flickr; only five mentioned better benefits as the reason for change. Indeed, signing in to Flickr using Google or Yahoo! only transfers a user's e-mail to the site, while a Facebook sign-in transfers e-mail address, picture, gender and birthplace, interests, friends, work and education history, events, status updates, details of friends, and status updates by friends.

	Data exposure	Better benefits	All users
Flickr	-4.19 (43)	+2.22 (18)	**-2.30 (61)**
HuffPost	-1.82 (33)	-0.35 (23)	**-1.21 (57)**
Monster	-0.28 (36)	+1.11 (27)	**+0.32 (63)**
Outgo!ng	-3.50 (6)	-0.44 (9)	**-1.67 (15)**
Total	*-2.30 (118)*	*+0.75 (77)*	*-1.09 (195)*

Table 6: Change in the average number of data types an "account changer" potentially exposed to a site before and after being presented with the tradeoff tables, by reason given for change. Only resolved reasons are shown (n=195).

Change in Data Exposure

We found that participants concerned about their data exposure were able to take effective measures against it. Although the average number of data types potentially exposed to sites decreased for all participants, those who changed account providers because of data exposure exhibited a larger reduction than the benefit-minded participants (-2.30 vs. +0.75, Table 6). It seems that when participants were presented with clearer tradeoffs between data exposure and benefits, they were able to immediately understand them and act accordingly. Decrease in exposure was manifested across all data types and almost all sites (Figure 2). The only site for which data exposure increased was Monster: the 27% increase in the exposure of profile picture, contacts, and contacts' info is the result of a 6% increase in sign-in to Monster using Facebook (Figure 3).

Monster uses the additional data from Facebook to identify "inside connections" in potential work places, and users seem to like it: "better benefits" was the reason given by 9 of the 12 participants who switched to a Facebook account.

	Profile picture	History	Bio	Location	Interests	E-mail content	Contacts	Status updates	Contacts' info	Contacts' content	Events
Flickr	-32%	-32%	-32%	-32%	-32%	N/A	-32%	-32%	-32%	-32%	-32%
Huff. Post	-21%	N/A	-24%	-19%	-24%	N/A	-19%	-30%	N/A	N/A	N/A
Monster	27%	3%	0%	3%	0%	N/A	27%	N/A	27%	N/A	N/A
Outgo!ng	N/A	N/A	N/A	-17%	-15%	-17%	-15%	-13%	-33%	-33%	0%
Total	-19%	-5%	-19%	-7%	-19%	-17%	-18%	-26%	-20%	-32%	-24%

Figure 2: Increase or decrease of "account changer" users per data type exposed to our four sites, after being presented with the data sharing and benefit tradeoff tables (n=196).

A simple measure to limit data exposure is the creation of a new account. A new account holds little or no personal information compared to an existing one, and participants seem to understand this: 42% of "account changers" switched from existing accounts to newly created accounts after they were shown the data sharing and benefit tradeoff tables (see Figure 3). While this trend was found across all sites, the abandoned accounts changed from site to site. For Flickr and Outgo!ng, Facebook exhibited the strongest decrease. For Monster it was the site account that suffered the most, whereas HuffPost exhibited a relatively equal churn rate across all existing accounts.

	Facebook	Google	Microsoft	Yahoo!	Site acct.	New acct.	Other
Flickr	-23%	3%	N/A	-11%	N/A	38%	-7%
Huff. Post	-9%	-7%	-7%	-14%	-11%	47%	0%
Monster	6%	N/A	N/A	-6%	-40%	46%	-6%
Outgo!ng	-27%	7%	-7%	0%	0%	27%	0%
All sites	-10%	-1%	-3%	-10%	-16%	42%	-4%

Figure 3: Increase of decrease of "account changer" users per sign-in account to our four sites, after being presented with the data sharing and benefit tradeoff tables (n=196).

LIMITATIONS

The design of our study allowed us to evaluate users' understanding of data exposure. The results on participant's willingness and reasons to change sign-in methods are subject to limitations. First, we collected self-reported data, which may not correlate to real changes. Second, while the word "privacy" was not mentioned [1, 2], references to data transfer may have increased participants' concern over data. Third, some participants may have felt that we expected them to change their behavior after reading the tradeoff tables and answered accordingly. Also, to facilitate analysis, we limited reasons for account change to "data exposure", "benefits" and "other", which may have biased

participants towards these options. Finally, the use of Mechanical Turk may have introduced a selection bias.

CONCLUDING REMARKS

We studied user sign-in patterns to real sites, using federated and proprietary accounts, and found that the data awareness of most participants was lacking and they could not accurately identify which of their data were transferred from an account to the site. However, given a clear description of their data exposure and benefit tradeoff, participants reported a willingness to change sign-in methods to reduce their data exposure or to get more benefits; this applies to previously registered users and non-users. Our findings suggest that the consent forms currently used by online services do not allow users to make informed choices, and that explaining what data are transferred to a site and why would benefit users. Follow-up studies could evaluate user turnover more accurately, e.g., with participants who were not presented with detailed tradeoff tables as a control. Topics for future study include the effect of trust relationship with sites and account providers on the choice of sign-in account (following [12]), and the efficient presentation of tradeoff tables [7].

REFERENCES

1. Barkuus, L. The Mismeasurement of privacy: Using contextual integrity to reconsider privacy in HCI. In *CHI '12*, ACM (2012), 367-376.

2. Braunstein, A. et al. Indirect content privacy surveys: measuring privacy without asking about it. In *SOUPS '11*, ACM (2011).

3. Charkam, A. 5 design tricks Facebook uses to affect your privacy decisions. *Tech Crunch* (Aug 25, 2012). Accessed Sep. 5, 2012. http://techcrunch.com/2012/08/25/5-design-tricks-facebook-uses-to-affect-your-privacy-decisions/

4. Dhamija, R., and Dusseault, L. The seven flaws of identity management: Usability and security challenges. *IEEE Security & Privacy* 6, 2 (2008), 24-29.

5. Good, N. et al. Stopping spyware at the gate: A user study of privacy, notice, and spyware. *SOUPS '05*, ACM (2005), 43-52.

6. Grossklags, J., and Good, N. Empirical studies on software notices to inform policy makers and usability designers. In *USEC '07*, LNCS, Springer (2007).

7. Kelley, P. G., et al. Standardizing privacy notices: an online study of the nutrition label approach. In *CHI '10*. ACM (2010), 1573-1582.

8. King, J., et al. Privacy: is there an app for that?. In *SOUPS '11*, ACM (2011).

9. Maler, E., and Reed, D. The Venn of identity: Options and issues in federated identity management. *IEEE Security & Privacy* 6, 2 (2008), 16-23.

10. Shehab, M., et al. 2011. ROAuth: recommendation based open authorization. In *SOUPS '11*, ACM (2011).

11. Shim, S. S. Y. et al. Federated identity management. *Computer* 38, 12 (2005), 120-122.

12. Sun, S.-T. et al. What makes users refuse web single sign-on? An empirical investigation of OpenID. In *SOUPS '11*, ACM (2011).

13. What they know. *Wall Street Journal*. http://blogs.wsj.com/wtk.

Understanding the Privacy-Personalization Dilemma for Web Search: A User Perspective

Saurabh Panjwani*, **Nisheeth Shrivastava***, **Saurabh Shukla**[†], **Sharad Jaiswal***

* Bell Labs Research, India. {saurabh.panjwani,nisheeth.shrivastava,sharad.jaiswal}@alcatel-lucent.com
† Indian Institute of Technology, Kharagpur, India. saurabh.shukla@cse.iitkgp.ernet.in

ABSTRACT

Contemporary search engines use a variety of techniques to personalize search results based on users' past queries. While studies have found that users generally prefer personalized search results to non-personalized ones, recent surveys also indicate growing reservations with respect to personalization because of its privacy implications. In this paper, we take a deeper look at privacy considerations of users during web search and explore how users' preferences for privacy and personalization interact when undertaking this activity. We conduct an empirical study over Google search, involving 25 participants in India and their respective web search histories. Our finding is that users exhibit a slight preference for personalization in their search results but are usually willing to "give up" personalization when searching for topics they deem sensitive. We discuss implications of these results for the design of privacy-preserving tools for web search.

Author Keywords

Privacy; personalization; web search; user study.

ACM Classification Keywords

H.5.0 Information Interfaces and Presentation: General

INTRODUCTION

Personalization is a cornerstone of major services on the web today—search engines (Google, Yahoo, Bing), e-retailers (Amazon), content streaming (Netflix) to name a few. As an approach, increased personalization is clearly favored as the way forward by content providers. For example, according to Google[1], personalization in advertisements alone results in a 32% increase in click-through rates and subsequent ad monetization—a significant financial incentive in the multi-billion dollar online ad industry.

Recent research has attempted to gauge user interests and perceived benefits from personalization. Empirical studies often

---

[1]"Opted-in users are 32% more likely to click on ads than opted-out users". (Opted-in users have ad-personalization turned on.) https://www.google.com/settings/ads/preferences/optout

indicate that users prefer personalization in web search [5, 2]. However, somewhat contradictorily, recent surveys have revealed that skepticism and reservation towards personalization and personal data collection is growing amongst users e.g. a recent survey by the Pew Internet research group in the US finds that 66% users would prefer *no* personalization from services like Google and only 29% are in its favor [3]. While instructive, this result is based on a purely binary treatment of personalization and does not capture variations that may exist in user preferences across different search topics. For example, a user may be privacy-sensitive and decline personalized search results about a health condition but, at the same time, like location-based personalization when searching for restaurants that serve his favorite cuisine. To fully understand user preferences for personalization, one must investigate the *trade-offs* users employ between privacy and personalization and how these trade-offs vary with changes in search topics.

Our work focuses on this question. We conducted a preliminary study with 25 users in India in order to understand how they make privacy-personalization trade-offs in the context of Google search. First, based on analyzing and appropriately clustering their search history we asked users to identify search topics that are sensitive to them. Then, we selected a representative subset of queries from their histories and carried out 2 sets of Google searches—one emulating the user themselves, and another a user with no history (a "vanilla" user). Finally, we evaluated user preferences between the personalized and vanilla search results, *while taking into account user sensitivity for particular topics.*

Our study results suggest that users are quite conscious about privacy in web search—84% of users in our sample had queries in their history that they deemed sensitive (with respect to Google), and a vast majority (92%) wanted Google to track only parts of their search history (or not at all). We also learnt that the privacy-personalization dilemma, though real, is a rare phenomenon in practice. On average, only 3.98% of a user's queries are sensitive; and for these queries, users mostly choose privacy over personalization, preferring personalized search results in only 19% of the cases. We believe these results shed new light on user preferences around privacy in web search and, as discussed later, make a case for *simple* tools for privacy-preserving search personalization.

RELATED WORK

Personalization studies. There is rich literature on how personalization leads to improved search experience on the web. Studies have shown that re-ranking search results for users based on their past browsing behavior has a positive effect on user preferences [2, 5]. To add to this, companies like Google report significant monetary benefits they derive from their ad-personalization activities, although the implications of these claims for the benefit of personalized *search results* to companies are not known. Literature on personalization benefits has largely ignored the question of privacy and it is unclear if user preferences for personalization are maintained when privacy constraints are introduced into the picture.

Surveys on privacy vs. personalization. Recent surveys have shown growing concerns among users with respect to personalization, particularly in the context of search results [3]. These surveys indicate that users view personalization strategies as a threat to their privacy and a majority prefer that search engines not personalize their results at all. However, these surveys do not attempt to evaluate user preferences with respect to individual search queries and it is also unclear if experiencing the benefit of personalization (as studied in [2, 5]) can allay some of these negative user perceptions towards personalization. We address both these issues with a carefully-designed user study in this paper.

Privacy in online advertising. There is burgeoning HCI literature on understanding and responding to user perceptions of online behavioral advertising (OBA). Studies have demonstrated that behavioral advertising is perceived as invasive by users [6] and that users desire tighter controls on how and when their data gets shared with advertisers [1]. In our work, we investigate users' privacy perceptions towards data collected by *search providers* (and not advertisers) and find that although privacy concerns remain strong even in this setting, there is expressed willingness to allow providers to track partial data (in particular, non-sensitive portions of the search history) for the benefit of personalization.

Tools for Privacy-Preserving Personalized Search. Finally, numerous researchers have worked on tools to provide personalized search and other services to users while keeping sensitive information in their profiles hidden from service providers [7, 8]. While technically interesting, such work ignores the question of how much personalization matters to users when querying search engines on sensitive information. Our study helps understand the utility of such tools from the users' perspective and takes a fresh look at designing privacy-preserving solutions to search.

STUDY METHODOLOGY
Since our study considered both privacy and personalization preferences of users, we deviated significantly from previous personalization studies in our design. Our design incorporated four steps, executed sequentially as follows:

1. Getting sensitivity data. As a first step, we fetch the entire web search history (a list of all past search queries) of the study participant from Google[2]. These queries are then clustered based on their word similarities using a commercial clustering tool called Lingo3G[3] and shown to the participant.

(Clustering makes history browsing more convenient.) The participant can browse the clusters and view queries inside each cluster. Based on cluster labels and contents, the participant decides which clusters may contain sensitive information where "sensitive" is defined as pertaining to data that she would *not* want Google to store as part of her history. She marks such clusters using a simple labeling UI. We treat all queries inside sensitive clusters as *potentially sensitive*.

2. Querying Google. We augment the participant's potentially sensitive queries with other queries from her history (randomly selected) to form a pool of 1000 queries. Our hope is to arrive at a set of queries for which the participant is likely to view a high degree of personalization from Google. For each query in our pool, we fetch the personalized and "vanilla" results from Google for the query. The personalized results are obtained by making the query by logging into Google as the participant, and vanilla results are the ones that Google returns when no user is logged in. We do both searches while keeping all other parameters except the login information identical, such as IP address, http headers, etc., so that the difference in results is only due to personalization for the user. We then compute the "delta" per query by using the weighted Hoeffding distance across the two types of search results[4]. Out of all the queries made, we select 20 potentially sensitive queries that have large deltaby doing a round-robin across sensitive clusters. If there are not enough potentially sensitive queries with large delta, we pick non-sensitive queries with large delta to fill the gap. These queries are used for gauging user preferences in the next step.[5]

3. Collecting preferences. This is the key step of the study. The participant is shown each of the 20 queries along with the two sets of results (personalized and vanilla) for each query using a split-screen UI, as shown in figure 1. At each step, the order of personalized and vanilla is randomized and *kept hidden from the participant*. The participant is asked the following question for each query:

- Is the query sensitive? (This identifies cases where a potentially sensitive query is not sensitive or a potentially non-sensitive query is.)

- Which set of search results is better? Left, Right or are both equally good? (The last option is marked "Neutral".)

- If the participant selects the personalized result on a sensitive query, a dilemmatic situation arises. Via a dynamic page update, she is notified about this selection and is asked to choose between two options—either continue to prefer the personalized results or switch to the vanilla result instead. The first option models a preference for personalization over privacy, and the second one its converse.

---

[2]http://www.google.com/history
[3]Lingo3G is available at http://carrotsearch.com/lingo3g-overview.h tml. In prior work, we have experimented with different approaches to cluster search queries and collected user feedback as well; these

experiments have influenced our current design for query clustering. We omit details for lack of space.
[4]The weighted Hoeffding distance is a simple measure for comparing two ranked lists and is usually applied on search results [4].
[5]Our motivation for using queries with large delta was to maximize the chances that users choose one set of results from the two that are shown, and not express a "neutral" rating. A post-hoc analysis revealed that participants' preference for neutrality was negatively correlated with the value of delta. The choice of 20 was meant to balance study speed and meaningfulness of results.

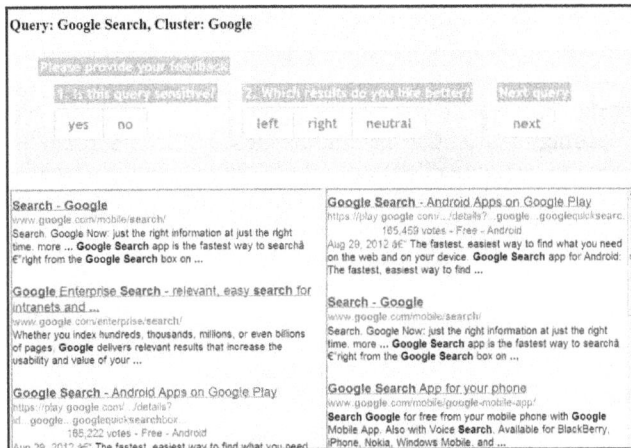

Figure 1. A screenshot of the screen used in step 3 of our study. The query term is displayed in the top left corner, below which there are two questions used to collect participant response on query sensitivity and personalization preference for the query. Below this, two sets of search results for the query—one personalized and one vanilla—are shown. (Font in results enhanced for better readability on paper.)

4. Post-study questionnaire. In the end, participants answer a questionnaire in which we probe them about their online search activities, usage of Google and their overall preference for personalization in search results.

Participants

We recruited 25 participants (21 M, 4 F) for our study, out of which 13 were IT professionals (11 M, 2 F, mean age 29.5 years) working for the same multi-national company in Bangalore (India) and 12 were undergraduate students (10 M, 2 F, mean age 20.5 years) from an Indian Institute of Technology (IIT)—the premier engineering institute of India. Participants were recruited using a combination of word-of-mouth and email fliers and we applied some obvious filters in the selection process—ownership of a Google account and presence of search history on Google. Our participants were all tech-savvy, reporting to spend an average of at least 5.6 hours online everyday and making an average of 25 Google search queries daily. The gender skew in our sample is fairly representative of the overall skew in the two domain institutions we considered. Our sample clearly does not represent the entire Internet population but is nevertheless interesting as a starting point for a wider study because of the high level of web utilization amongst its constituent users.[6]

Protocol

All participants provided informed consent prior to taking part in the study. Our informed consent protocol made it clear that we would not collect any private data about the participant *unless explicitly allowed by her.* The IT professionals ran the study on their own desktop machines (all with identical screen size), the students on dedicated lab machines.

---

[6]Besides these 25 participants, we also ran the study with 9 users who did not have Google history but instead had their search history archived in Chrome, their primary browser. Our study results were unperturbed with the inclusion of these users, modulo the finding that these users received fewer personalized results than the primary ones. For brevity, we exclude their data here.

The procedure for training participants was kept constant throughout the study. Training involved a researcher explaining the study to the participant using an instruction sheet which depicted the study steps with suitable screenshots. (The instruction sheet was left with the participant for later reference.) We stressed the definition of "sensitive" several times during training—a query (resp. cluster) was to be deemed sensitive if the participant did not want Google to store that query (resp. cluster) under his/her account. While training, we also conversed with participants about how search personalization works in search engines and gauged their existing understanding of the phenomenon and the tools available to control it. Training lasted for 10-15 minutes, following which we left the participant. Each participant engaged with the study engine for 30-45 minutes, after which she emailed us the anonymized output of the engine containing all the collected preference data and the responses.

RESULTS

All but one participant in our sample reported Google to be their favorite search engine on the web and were, in general, satisfied with its performance on their queries (an average rating of 4.28 on a Likert scale of 5). Despite their tech-savviness, participants were not fully aware about the incidence of personalization in web search, as became clear during the training sessions. Twelve out of the 25 participants (48%) did not know that Google tracked their search history and used it for personalization and five (20%) did not even know that Google personalizes search results. (Some who thought personalization happened were unaware that search history was a determining factor.) Participants were also not consistently aware about different strategies they could use when making sensitive search queries; for example, 5 participants (20%) did not know that it was possible to log out of Google to avoid the queries to be tracked and 5 (not all the same) did not know about private browsing.

Sensitivity Rate. Nearly all participants in our sample (21 out of 25) found something sensitive in their history as exposed to them during our study. Participants had an average of 1300 queries in their history, which was shown to them in an average of 48 clusters (SD 21.7) by our tool. Out of these, they marked an average of 4.3 clusters as being sensitive (SD 3.56), which in total had an average of 52 potentially sensitive queries. Based on this, our estimate is that about 3.98% of queries in our participants' history were sensitive in nature. Although the variance amongst participants was high, none regarded *every* cluster in their history to be sensitive. Amongst the twenty queries that they were later shown, the sensitivity rate was higher—an average of 3.75 queries (18.75% of 20) marked sensitive—but still, non-sensitive queries dominated our selection.

There are two inferences we made from this: (a) not many topics in participant search histories were sensitive; and (b) for almost all participants in our sample, *some* topics in the search history were sensitive.

Preference for personalization. Despite our query selection strategy (which maximized the gap between personalized and vanilla results), we observed only a mild preference for personalization in participant responses. Participants did choose personalized search results more often than vanilla (38.9% vs. 22.8% across all search queries shown), but they were just as often (38.3%) neutral. No significant differences across sensitive and non-sensitive queries were observed.

Responding to the dilemma. Out of a total of 94 sensitive queries for which participants viewed search results during the study, they preferred personalized results over vanilla only for 41 (43.6%) queries. (This applied to a total of 13 participants in our sample; the rest either did not view sensitive queries or never liked personalized results for them.) When their preference for personalization in these cases was revealed to them, participants switched from personalized to vanilla for 23 queries (56.1% of 41). In sum, out of all the sensitive queries used during the study, only 19.1% of the queries (spread over 6 participants) were those for which participants insisted on personalization even after they were made aware of this selection.

In the post-study questionnaire, participants were asked about the amount of search history they would like Google to maintain for them and given three choices—*store no queries* (no personalization), *store only queries which are not sensitive* (selective personalization) and *store all queries* (full personalization). (Previous work has considered only an all-or-nothing option in such questions [3], while we introduced the possibility of selective query tracking.) An overwhelming majority preferred the first and second options: 17 participants (68%) wanted queries to be stored selectively and 6 participants (24%) wanted Google to maintain no history at all. This includes three out of the four participants who did not find *any* sensitive cluster in the first step of our study.[7]

Overall, it appears that our participants were more willing to suffer a decrease in personalization in their Google searches than to have the provider track their sensitive queries.

Limitations. Even as a preliminary exercise, our study has some limitations which may be addressed in future work. First, we tested user preferences in a fully offline setting, extracting all queries from users' search histories rather than tracking their in situ "real life" Google usage. Previous work has considered the online setting in evaluating personalization preferences [2] but has ignored the question of privacy. While it may be possible to extend these works to study privacy-personalization tradeoffs, given the sparseness of sensitive queries that participants report, this will likely require a study that spans several months. Another limitation of our study is that we tested participant preferences on a small number of queries (20 per participant); this limitation may be possible to remove in an online study but in the offline setting, placing such a bound is necessary for practical reasons. Finally, we re-iterate the sampling bias in our study, which favored male participants in India with a high level of technology exposure; this limitation will need to be addressed in a broader investigation of the subject.

---

[7] These results could potentially differ a bit if we varied the questions to stress personalization outcomes more than the issue of tracking. Such response biases will need to be evaluated in future work.

DISCUSSION AND CONCLUSIONS

The participants in our study were largely privacy-conscious about their search activities, many being aware of mechanisms that would anonymize them from Google and most desiring only partial tracking of their queries. Surprisingly, though, nearly half the users were not aware of the quantity and granularity of data (i.e. search history) that was maintained by Google under their accounts. Other key outcomes from our study were that a majority of the user queries were *not* sensitive (96%), that users were interested in selective personalization of their search results and that even with their leaning towards personalization, only for a small percentage of sensitive queries (19%) did users *persist* with this choice after being fully informed about it.

We believe these findings are interesting both in terms of furthering our understanding of user perceptions of privacy, as well as for guiding the design of privacy-enabling mechanisms for web search. As an example, for the vast majority of users who do not have a preference for personalized results for sensitive queries, an approach that identifies and anonymizes a query falling under a "sensitive" topic should suffice. (Clustering tools, such as what we used in the study, could be used to ease topic selection by users.) For the remaining minority, a mechanism that ensures sensitive queries are not tracked, while allowing personalization to be driven by the large fraction of the search history that is non-sensitive, should offer acceptable results. Past work on privacy-aware web search has largely focused on complex mechanisms [7, 8] that place themselves in the critical path of profiling and personalization (by proposing mechanisms for obfuscating or bundling of *entire* user profiles). Our study indicates that a much simpler approach, relying on cleaving out sensitive aspects of user activity should be sufficient in achieving the right level of privacy preservation. Given that such an approach can be achieved by using existing APIs of search providers also makes it more likely to be deployed in practice. We are in the process of developing such tools, and our experience in deploying them will be presented in future work.

REFERENCES

1. P. G. Kelley, M. Benisch, L. F. Cranor, and N. Sadeh. When are users comfortable sharing locations with advertisers? In *Proc. CHI*, 2011.

2. N. Matthijs and F. Radlinski. Personalizing web search using long-term browsing history. In *Proc. WSDM*, 2011.

3. K. Purcell, J. Brenner, and L. Rainie. Search engine use 2012. http://pewinternet.org/Reports/2012/Search-Engine-Use-2012.aspx.

4. M. Sun, G. Lebanon, and K. Collins-Thompson. Visualizing differences in web search algorithms using the expected weighted hoeffding distance. In *Proc. WWW*, 2010.

5. J. Teevan, S. T. Dumais, and E. Horvitz. Personalizing search via automated analysis of interests and activities. In *Proc. SIGIR*, 2005.

6. B. Ur, P. G. Leon, L. F. Cranor, R. Shay, and Y. Wang. Smart, useful, scary, creepy: Perceptions of online behavioral advertising. In *Proc. SOUPS*, 2012.

7. Y. Xu, K. Wang, B. Zhang, and Z. Chen. Privacy-enhancing personalized web search. In *Proc. WWW*, 2007.

8. Y. Zhu, L. Xiong, and C. Verdery. Anonymizing user profiles for personalized web search. In *Proc. WWW*, 2010.

Slow Design for Meaningful Interactions

Barbara Grosse-Hering[1], Jon Mason[2], Dzmitry Aliakseyeu[2], Conny Bakker[3], Pieter Desmet[3]

	Philips Research[2]	Delft University of Technology[3]
Designit[1]	Human Interaction and	Industrial Design Engineering
Munich, Germany	Experiences Group	Department
grosse.hering@gmail.com	Eindhoven, The Netherlands	Delft, The Netherlands
	{jon.mason,	{c.a.bakker,
	dzmitry.aliakseyeu}@philips.com	p.m.a.desmet}@tudelft.nl

ABSTRACT

In this paper we report on an exploration of how to apply the theory of Slow Design to mass produced products to establish more mindful usage of products; the intention behind this is to promote product attachment and the associated sustainable benefits of long term use. Slow Design is a design philosophy that focuses on promoting well-being for individuals, society, and the natural environment. It encourages people to do things at the right time and at the right speed which helps them to understand and reflect on their actions. Several authors have proposed Slow Design principles and cases have been reported in which these principles were applied in cultural design projects. These applications indicated that Slow Design can indeed have a positive impact on wellbeing. Although promising, this philosophy has not yet been used in the design of mass consumer products. In this paper we present a design case study in which we explored how the Slow Design principles can be applied in the design of an electric fruit juicer. Two studies are reported on where the conditions for implementing Slow Design are explored. The results led to a revision of the principles for use by product designers. The main finding from the case study is that the Slow Design principles can be used to create more 'mindful' interactions that stimulate positive user involvement. This is not from designing interactions that require more time per se, but by stimulating the user to use more time for those parts of the interaction that are meaningful and less for those that are not meaningful.

Author Keywords

Slow design; Product Attachment; Sustainability.

ACM Classification Keywords

H.5.m. Information interfaces and presentation (e.g., HCI): Miscellaneous.

General Terms

Human Factors; Design; Measurement.

INTRODUCTION

A topic of increasing interest in the HCI community has been 'user behavior change' towards being more environmentally conscious and sustainable. One area within this topic is to promote product attachment via the application of emotionally durable design theories [2]. A positive change in the users' behavior can be achieved by creating a stronger bond between users and their products. "When a person becomes attached to an object, he or she is more likely to handle the object with care, repair it when it breaks, and postpone its replacement as long as possible."[18]

For this to occur, people need to be motivated to invest time, money and energy into a product in order to increase their bond with it. Thus far, the numerous theories of product attachment have had their principles applied mostly to unique or artistic orientated objects [2]; only a few examples of applying them to everyday objects can be found [15, 5] and consequently, there is scant knowledge on how to apply such theories to everyday products [9].

With product attachment as a basis for their work, the authors have investigated numerous theories that may contribute and support this area of interest. One of the theories investigated was Slow Design and this paper details how this theory was interpreted and applied to a mass produced product for the purpose of exploring its potential contribution to product attachment.

To date the design principles of Slow Design, as stipulated by Carolyn F. Strauss and Alastair Fuad-Luke are yet to be applied to a mass produced consumer product [4]. The six Slow Design principles are currently quite abstract and use terms such as *"Slow Design processes and outcomes become agents of both preservation and transformation."* How to apply this to a kettle or television is not clear and thus requires a translation phase to assist designers when using these principles. This abstraction may also be a reason why the Slow Design principles have not been used greatly in product design circles. This is certainly unfortunate, since the world in which we live is becoming more chaotic and the need to appreciate our products and conserve resources is more important than ever before. Slow Design could provide designers with an insight into how to design products that promote a more meaningful interaction to promote this reflection and appreciation which may ultimately support product attachment. Meaningful interaction with products shares similarities with Salen' and Zimmerman's definition of meaningful play, where the product is the game that users (the players) are interacting with and responding to. Meaningful play occurs when the relationships between the actions and outcomes are discernible and integrated into the greater context of the game. The meaning resides in this relationship between action and outcome.

The paper begins with a brief overview of product attachment and introduces the theory of Slow Design. The principles of Slow Design are then redefined to make them more applicable for product design and finally we present a case study where they have been applied for the redesign of a juicer.

BACKGROUND

Product Attachment
Many objects initially acquired for their functional, aesthetic or psychosocial benefits are eventually discarded and in some cases these products are still fully functional [1, 2, 3, 21, 22]. One possible strategy for lengthening product life cycles is to increase the attachment people experience towards the products they use and own [20]. A general assumption is that "When a person becomes attached to an object, they are more likely to handle the object with care, repair it when it breaks, and postpone its replacement for as long as possible." [18]. Schifferstein and Zwartkruis-Pelgrim defines consumer-product attachment as the strength of the emotional bond a consumer experiences with a product.

Odom et al. picked up '… the problem of understanding why we preserve some things passionately and discard others without thought [14]. According to them there are three main elements that influence product attachment to digital artifacts: function, symbolism and material qualities. They clustered their research findings from a study 'why people create a stronger attachment with some artifacts' in the following categories: engagement, histories, augmentation and perceived durability. Meanwhile, Zimmerman focused on product attachment with physical artifacts. He "...produced six framing constructs, which work as specific perspectives designers can take when applying product attachment theory in an experience design project." [23]

The discussion on the how to strengthen product attachment has been the work of many researchers [16, 2, 7, 17, 12, 22, 18, 23, 13]. Many of whom differ in opinion with regard to the elements that enable product attachment and their relative importance; however we can identify several common elements that appear in all publications: positive or negative memories [7, 13, 18, 12]; changing over time [16, 18, 17, 13]; self expression [7, 17, 12, 23]; group

affiliation and social interaction [17, 12, 22, 23]; regular involvement [2, 7, 18]; and well functioning [17, 22].

It can be inferred, that product attachment is supported by product and interaction characteristics such as change and evolvement over time (memories, time), and understanding, transparency and involvement (self-expression, involvement, well functioning). These values and goals can also be found within the philosophy of Slow Design. Therefore, it was a reasonable assumption that the principles of Slow Design, when applied to a product, could also be used for enhancing product attachment.

Slow Design
Slow Design is part of the Slow Movement which advocates a cultural shift towards slowing down the pace of life [4]. It began with Carlo Petrini's protest against the opening of a McDonald's restaurant in Piazza di Spagna, Rome, in 1986, resulting in the Slow Food movement. Other sub-movements of the Slow Movement are Slow Technology [6], Slow Cities and Slow Art.

The Slow Technology movement, as described by Hallnäs and Redström [6], state that it is concerned with taking technology applications beyond the efficient and functional to also include expression and reflection in use. Slow Design is not so dissimilar, however its core focus is on promoting the movement to the broad field of product design, which inevitably includes technology and HCI elements.

Alastair Fuad-Luke defines Slow Design as: "Slow Design focuses on ideas of well-being. Wellbeing needs are indirect impacts on health though their relationship to personal fulfillment, quality of life and psychological health. Failure to meet well-being needs results in psycho-social maladjustment and stress-related illnesses. The guiding philosophical principle of Slow Design is to re-position the focus of design on the trinity of individual, socio-cultural and environmental well-being" [4].

Slower human, economic and resource flow metabolisms are integral to the principle of well-being. This encourages those engaged in design to: take a long view; envisage slower rates of production and consumption; stimulate a renewed joy in design (and its outputs); offer new scenarios for the physical, emotional, mental and spiritual durability of design outputs; celebrate diversity and pluralism; envisage slow as a positive sociocultural value; and, focus on the present rather than trying to design the future. [4].

Slow Design Principles
In 2008 Carolyn F. Strauss and Alastair Fuad-Luke published the paper 'The Slow Design Principles - A New Interrogative and Reflexive Tool for Design Research and Practice', [19]. Here they describe the six Slow Design principles with which they wanted to "... posit a new evaluative tool to encourage design practices to orientate towards social, cultural and environmental sustainability

under the rubric of 'Slow Design'". The six principles are [19]:

Reveal: Slow Design reveals spaces and experiences in everyday life that are often missed or forgotten, including the materials and processes that can easily be overlooked in an artifact's existence or creation.

Expand: Slow Design considers the real and potential "expressions" of artifacts and environments beyond their perceived functionality, physical attributes and lifespans.

Reflect: Slowly-designed artifacts and environments induce contemplation and 'reflective consumption.'

Engage: Slow Design processes are "open source" and collaborative, relying on sharing, co-operation and transparency of information so that designs may continue to evolve into the future.

Participate: Slow Design encourages people to become active participants in the design process, embracing ideas of conviviality and exchange to foster social accountability and enhance communities.

Evolve: Slow Design recognizes that richer experiences can emerge from the dynamic maturation of artifacts and environments over time. Looking beyond the needs and circumstances of the present day, Slow Design processes and outcomes become agents of both preservation and transformation.

Several artistic and cultural design projects have been inspired by the Slow Design principles (for an overview see www.slowlab.net). An example is the 'sasa clock' by Icelandic designer Thorunn Arnandottir (http://www.thorunndesign.com). The clock comprises of a sequence of brightly colored beads strung like a necklace, with each color representing an increment of minutes or hours (Figure 1). The string of beads is positioned on a wall-mounted wheel, which turns with an almost imperceptible slowness, releasing one bead every five minutes. Although the beads themselves do represent units of time when positioned on the wheel, they can also be removed from the wheel altogether, representing freedom from time. In doing so, "the clock creates a more emotional perception of time, measured in relation to events in one's life rather than rigid units by which most of us slice up our day." (http://www.thorunndesign.com)

From the literature there appeared to be similarities between the values and goals for enhancing product attachment [2] and the six principles of Slow Design. Based on this an assumption was made that a product developed using the Slow Design principles may also support product attachment. Therefore, the purpose of this investigation was to explore how to interpret the Slow Design principles for use when designing mass produced products via a case study. The first steps towards this were to understand further the effects of slowing people down with regard to everyday products: when is 'slow' a positive or negative

element when interacting with a product? For this purpose an investigation to find out "when is it valuable to slow people down" and "what slows people down positively?" were undertaken.

Figure 1. 'sasa clock' (© Thorunn Arnadottir)

VALUE OF SLOWING PEOPLE DOWN

The philosophy behind the Slow Movement originated from the observation that, in the current world, people live lifestyles that are too fast; a behavior that leads to work overload and stress. By slowing down, focusing, and thinking about what they are doing and why, people will be able to take control and begin to relax.

To explore this philosophy from a product interaction perspective a brief home study was conducted to uncover the positive and the negative aspects of using devices that perform a task more slowly than the participants' conventional means of performing it. This would also identify where the value may be in slowing people down when undertaking the given tasks. Furthermore interviews were conducted to gather more insights into 'What slows people down?'

Driving research questions for the study were:

- How do people feel if they are forced to spend more time on daily activities, such as making coffee?

- Does slowing down the process relax them or cause more stress and irritation?

- To what degree does the time of the day and the context (people around) influence the result?

The five participants of the study were aged between 25 and 60 years and were a mix of Dutch and German nationalities. The participants received the task of using a more time-consuming kitchen device than they would normally use, for one week at home. Two different cases were applied to generate more insights. Two male and one female joined the 'coffee machine vs. Mokka pot' study, while two males participated in the 'bottled juice vs. citrus press' study.

Those given the Mokka stove top coffee maker were asked to use this instead of their coffee machine. The other participants were given a half-mechanical citrus press and were requested to use it whenever they would usually drink a glass of bottled juice. At the end of this one week home study a semi-structured interview was conducted to identify how the participants coped with these alternative situations.

We have observed that time and context is highly important when it comes to the question of whether people perceive slowing a process down as positive/relaxing or negative/stressful. If people have more time available, such as during a weekend, they perceive slower processes as being nice rituals and relaxing. "It takes more time to use the Mokka and is just a burden during the week. On the weekend I would not mind to take more time for preparing coffee or espresso." During the week, or when under time pressure, the opposite applies. The main driver for people to prepare coffee or juice in a more time consuming way is that the quality of the result is often perceived to be better, but even more important, preparing it for someone else (mentioned by 4 participants) - *"I prepared the juice for me and my girlfriend. I know that she is happy about getting something 'special'"*.

To understand further when slowing down makes most sense, ten interviews with participants aging from 24 to 35 were conducted. The participants were asked to share their experience on what slows them down in a positive and relaxing way as well as what they would like to slow down.

The results from these interviews revealed that a diverse range of activities have a 'slowing effect' on people. Physical movement such as sport, stretching, walking or gardening, was mentioned quite often. On the other hand, physical relaxation such as meditating was mentioned, as often as being active. Furthermore, having a structured daily routine or rituals, such as preparing food, tea/coffee or going shopping, was considered as having a 'slowing down effect'. Some people mentioned that focusing on details, creating something, playing instruments or reading a book slows them down. Drinking coffee or tea, or listening to music was most often mentioned as ways to relax during work. The sentence '...doing something else than what I'm doing right now' was mentioned frequently. Such remarks might explain the contradiction of the presence and the absence of physical movement as being equally relaxing.

These insights were compared to the six Slow Design principles [19] in order to determine which of the key slowing down elements can be found there:

- *Reveal* is about discovering things that are often missed or forgotten. Discovery can happen during listening or focusing.
- In the principle *expand* communicating facts that are not expected play an important role. The same can occur during focusing or listening.

- The principle *reflect* seeks to trigger 'reflective consumption', so the user has time to think about his/her actions. This also occurs during listening, focusing or physical relaxation.
- *Engage* is about the sharing of knowledge and cooperation. It is activated when people learn something, such as during listening, creating or focusing.
- *Participate* encourages people to become active. Following the key slowing down elements ensures the application of principles of physical movement, creating, focusing and 'doing something else'.
- *Evolve* implies a change or a growth over time. Learning a skill, such as creating something also grows over time.

As can be seen in the above comparison, most of the slowing down elements from the interviews and home study are covered, with the exception of daily routines and rituals.

Proposed Slow Design Principles

From the previous study on "the value of slowing people down" it was concluded that 'rituals' also appear to be an important element of the slowing down process, thanks to its relaxing and reflection inducing character. Ritual, thus, became the seventh Slow Design principle.

The Slow Design principles are not a design method or tool but a philosophy to inspire designers to stimulate thinking in new ways. Since they are to be used to enhance product attachment it is necessary to understand how designers interpret this philosophy and these principles and ensure there is some consistency so that they can be applied by the wider design community hereafter.

To evaluate the principles a creative session with 4 professional designers and 4 design students was organized. They were asked to use the Slow Design principles to generate ideas for a new juicer. It became apparent that the participants required a demonstration of Slow Design project examples in order to understand and apply the principles. Before these examples were provided, the interpretation of the principles varied greatly from person to person; this confirmed that the SlowLab's definitions of their principles were abstract even to designers. In response to this a more product design related definition was added to every principle and 'ritual' was added as the seventh Slow Design principles. The revised descriptions of the principles are:

Reveal: Creating awareness, uncover the function and essence of a product.

Expand: Give a bigger picture: zoom in (what is it made of) and zoom out (where does it come from).

Reflect: Provide time for the user to think and reflect about his or her actions, visualize processes and create narrative products.

Engage: Create Do-it-yourself concepts; the user becomes a designer; the user is active in the creation of the product.

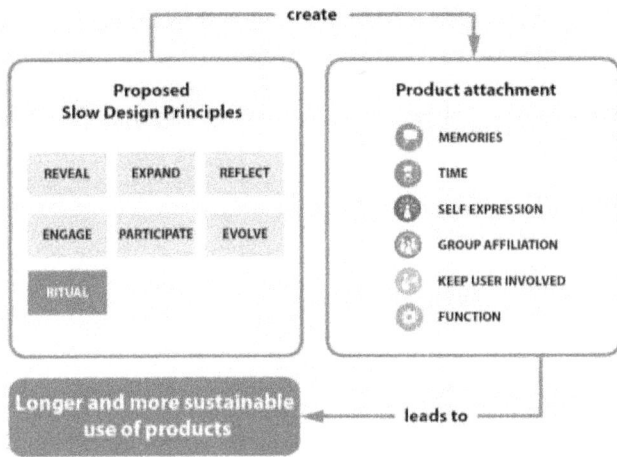

Figure 2: Overview research question

Participate: Create opportunities, supporting the user to personalize and reconfigure the product; the user is active during the use of the product.

Evolve: Create products that are changing or growing over time.

New principle *Ritual:* Create rituals for a better user experience, stimulating social interaction and provide security and stability in a hectic society.

In Figure 2, an overview of the authors' states that the proposed Slow Design principles can inspire designers to create product concepts with an enhanced product attachment, leading to a more sustainable use of products.

CASE STUDY 'JUICYMO'

As we stated in the beginning of the paper our goal was to explore how to apply the Slow Design Principles to mass produced products - which were so far mostly used for craft or artistic projects – for the purpose of potentially increasing product attachment.

The criteria used to select which product would be the focus of the case study was: close user-product interaction; useful life that is longer than two years; and easy to access and evaluate.

A centrifugal juicer was chosen as being the most suitable. This device has a high potential to become a slow product, thanks to, among other reasons, its healthy lifestyle promoting quality and the close interaction between the user and the product. The product's useful life is long enough to provide the requirements needed to build a better product attachment between the user and the juicer. However, the juicer exhibits few Slow Design qualities. For example, its blades turn at a high speed, producing a lot of noise. Equally important is the fact that the actual transformation of the ingredients into juice takes seconds, but the cleaning requires substantial time and effort.

Process

As mentioned previously, there are many ways to apply the Slow Design principles. For the case study of the

centrifugal juicer, the authors will explain their applied design process.

The process began with a research phase, including user research and an analysis of the 'process of use'. With these insights the first ideation cycle was performed using mind mapping as well as a creative session and sketching of first concepts. A selection of the concepts was evaluated during a focus group. The feedback was used for a second ideation cycle, leading to the final concept "JuicyMo" and a prototype. The process ended with a usability test and user feedback on the Slow Design principles.

User research 'centrifugal juicers'

In order to gather information about people's motivations for preparing fresh juice, as well as regarding the perceived advantages and disadvantages of a centrifugal juicer, user research was performed. The research included a product analysis of a Philips centrifugal juicer and interviews. The semi-structured interviews were conducted with 8 participants, all of whom were owners of centrifugal juicers. The insights of the user research are summarized in the 'main drivers' as to why people buy and use such a device, as well as the 'main problems' that occur during use.

The results of the user research showed that the two main drivers for buying and using the juicer are preparing juice for someone else (e.g. for the user's children or a partner). 6/8 participants mentioned this as a reason why they bought and use the juicer – "*Kids like smoothies a lot*". Furthermore, '*feeling healthy while drinking self-prepared fresh juice*' was mentioned by all participants. "*I drink juice every day, because my girlfriend and me are in a Detox diet program.*" or "*Last summer we had a lot of apples in our own garden, so we could just go outside and then prepare a fresh juice.*"

The main problems the participants mentioned were cleaning (some parts are very difficult to clean and the device has too many components), storing the juicer (it is too big for most of the cupboards and too dominant to stay on the kitchen counter), the juicer is too loud, and the pulp is perceived as a waste of ingredients and the amount of pulp in the juice cannot be adjusted to suit their own preferences.

'Process of use' analysis

In order to understand the context of use and to identify the necessary steps, the juicing process was analyzed. The process usually starts with shopping for the ingredients and storing them. The next step is the preparation of the fruits and the actual juicing, followed by serving and cleaning or vice versa. At the end of the process the user can decide if the pulp should be further processed or thrown away. The decision on which combination of ingredients will be used can take place before shopping or it can depend on the fruits the user has at home.

The next step in the design process was perceived as being highly important by the authors when designing with the philosophy of Slow Design. Slow Design is not just about optimizing the product in terms of convenience; rather, the 'right moment' in the 'process of use' should be enriched by increasing the user's experience, joy and fun. Where and when this moment or period is, has to be defined by the designer, supported by the insights of the user research and the 'process of use' analysis. In the case of the juicing process, the 'right moment' or 'focus interaction' was deemed to be when the ingredients are turned into juice, because that is the reason why users buy and use such a device (Figure 3). If it is necessary for the user to understand and reflect about what they are doing, this interaction can take longer than the time currently needed. Consequently, we can also identify the right moments that need to be speed up. In the case of the juicer the moments to reduce or skip were the cleaning time and the 'bring' and 'store' in the cupboard.

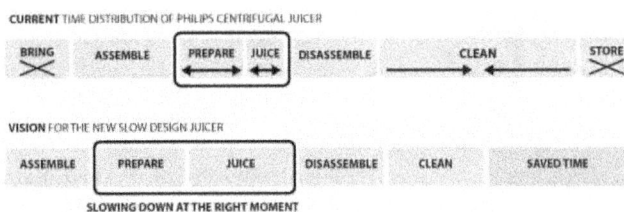

CURRENT TIME DISTRIBUTION OF PHILIPS CENTRIFUGAL JUICER

| BRING | ASSEMBLE | PREPARE | JUICE | DISASSEMBLE | CLEAN | STORE |

VISION FOR THE NEW SLOW DESIGN JUICER

| ASSEMBLE | PREPARE | JUICE | DISASSEMBLE | CLEAN | SAVED TIME |

SLOWING DOWN AT THE RIGHT MOMENT

Figure 3. Analysis and comparison of the current and new juicing processes

Ideation

The ideas generated from the use of mind maps were visualized using scenario sketches. Here are some examples from the first ideation phase:

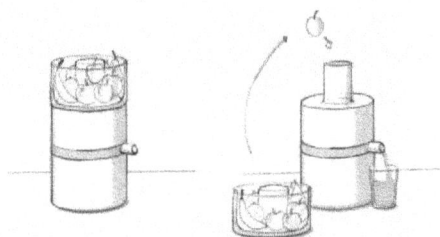

Figure 4 Fruit basket

'Fruit basket' (Figure 4), a concept supporting the juicer's permanent place in a kitchen is a device that doubles as a basket for storing fruits and vegetables. This can also encourage users to prepare a glass of juice from the overripe fruits instead of throwing them away.

Figure 5 Kneading Juice

'Kneading juice'(Figure 5); the user is physically active while feeding the juicer. A soft, pillow like lid contains a small opening where the ingredient can be placed. The next step involves 'kneading' the ingredients like dough towards the blade.

Figure 6 Combined Device

'Combined device'(Figure 6), which offers three devices in one, where only one motor is necessary. The combined device becomes a universal 'juice machine', e.g. for smoothies, clear or pressed orange juice. In addition, the multi-functionality presents the user with three more reasons to keep the device in a visible place in the kitchen.

The concepts were meant to enhance the main drivers and to solve the main problems defined in the user research. The next step after the first ideation cycle was to define strong concepts that incorporated the Slow Design principles.

Many of the developed concepts share in common the physical involvement of the user. Concepts within this category are, for example, 'spinning juice', 'wring like a wet towel' or 'physical effort to make the juice'. They have all been inspired by the Slow Design principle *participate* and all require the user to be physically active in order to produce juice. This concept direction strongly supports the Slow Design philosophy. However, in order to find out to what extent users are willing to be active and still use the device, a creative session about 'physical involvement' was held. The motivation for this extra research was the rationale that when people are not willing to use a physical interaction means, for example by using a crank, they may stop using the device. This leads to weaker product attachment and a less sustainable product.

A creative session was carried out to investigate the possible added value for the user when a kitchen appliance is powered manually. Furthermore to find out to what extent people are willing to be physically active, as well as when and why they perceive this activity as a positive or negative one.

The methods applied during the session were firstly an observation of the participants while they were using provided objects that had a crank, followed by a group discussion about the experience with the tested objects and other kitchen appliances. Four males and four females between the ages of 45 and 60 years participated in the session. None of the participants owned a juicer, but all owned a blender.

The main conclusion from the session was that people like to be active and involved while using a kitchen device, but without exhausting physical effort. Moreover people wanted to be involved in the process of use and to have the feeling of control over the device, though, at the same time, it should not be too exhausting and time consuming.

With this new input, a second ideation cycle was conducted, resulting in the concept 'Engagement and control'. This concept actively involves the user in the process by letting them hold, press or turn the feeding tube in order to keep the motor running. In addition to involvement, this interaction provides a feeling of control over the device. At the exact moment the user releases the hand, the device stops working.

Criteria for the final design
From the 35 concepts, which were developed during the first and second ideation phases, six were selected. They were inspired by five different Slow Design principles. The chosen concepts were translated into a coherent story: the case study 'JuicyMo', with the aim of demonstrating the potential of applying Slow Design principles in one product.

Slow Design can be applied to all aspects of a product, including the mechanical elements, therefore the Single Vertical Auger juicing technique that supports the Slow Design principles was selected. The average rotation speed of this technique is 40 rpm, while the speed of a centrifugal juicer is up to 13.000 rpm. This lower rotation speed will damage the juice less with frictional heat, leading to more nutrients and vitamins in the juice.

Final design
The final design JuicyMo was built as a non-functioning appearance model in order to test and discuss the applicability and suitability of the Slow Design principles for the development of a mass produced product with added consumer value for enhancing product attachment (see Figures 7-12). JuicyMo presents a plain and simple form language; therefore, it is perfect for combining with other kitchen appliances.

The six concepts / aspects of JuicyMo and their relevance to Slow Design are described below:

Kitchen Object (Inspired by the principle REVEAL)
One of the problems encountered in the user research is that users hide their juicers in a cupboard post use. This concept's compact size, of 320 mm height and diameter of 160 mm diameter, reduces its footprint on the kitchen counter increasing the chance that the user will keep the product on display. The next step for this concept was to allow the user to understand the process of juicing by revealing the device's function and internal structure. To use the juicer, one takes off the juice and pulp jar (Figure 7).

Once the device is switched on, its parts slowly become transparent and reveal what is hidden behind the casing: first the auger jar, then the pulp container, and finally the

juicing jar. The aesthetic kitchen object becomes a kitchen device, revealing its function and internal structure. After juicing the device transforms slowly back into a kitchen object. E-Skin technology can be used for implementing this feature [10, 11]; for the prototype we used samples that were provided by Hewlett Packard.

Figure 7. Kitchen Object

Choose Pulp (Inspired by the principle PARTICIPATE)
The user research showed that people have different preferences regarding the amount of fiber they want to have in their juice. Some prefer to have more fibers (a 'smoothie'), while others prefer clear juice. Thanks to the double strainer system this new device offers the possibility to adjust the amount of fiber, as well as combining two devices in one: juicer and blender (Figure 8).

Figure 8. Choose pulp

Another advantage of this strainer concept, as compared to the existing one, is the ease of cleaning. The current vertical auger juicers come with two different strainers, one with larger and one with smaller holes. The hole size is so small that the fibers get stuck and a lot of effort and a special brush are required to clean it. This double strainer can simply be separated and the larger perforations should be easier to clean. Fewer separate components simplify storage and preparation of the juicer. This design element facilitated the reduction in cleaning time that was unanimously considered to be unpleasant by the participants of this investigation.

Second Life for the Pulp (Inspired by the principle EXPAND)
This concept encourages the use of left over pulp. After finishing the juicing process, the user will disassemble the device for cleaning and, while lifting the pulp container from the motor block (cork), they will discover text and

icons printed on the surface, thus information is presented to the user during the decision moment: dispose in the trash or use further (Figure 9).

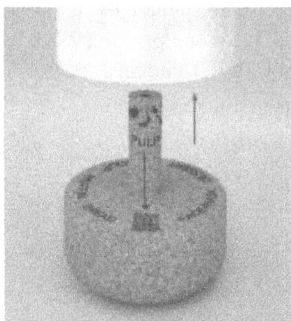

Figure 9. Second Life for Pulp

This concept came from the principle *expand*, which considers the option of 'giving a bigger picture', thus showing how all elements of a process can be used, such as the discarded pulp.

Engagement and Control (Inspired by the principle PARTICIPATE)

As described in the creative session on physical involvement, this concept focused on one of the key elements of product attachment 'keep user involved'. The Slow Design principle used was *participate*, supporting that the user should be active while operating the device. The final 'feeding interaction' with the juicer was solved by using a hollow ¾ sphere on top of the juicer, which represents a bowl where the fruit is placed prior to juicing (Figure 10).

Figure 10. Engagement and Control

When this small fruit bowl is full, the user can turn the sphere around its axis and the fruit slides into the juicer, where they are crushed by the auger. To provide the opportunity to understand and observe this process, these elements were made from a transparent material. In addition to being involved, this interaction gives a feeling of control over the device.

Sharing Stone (Inspired by the principle RITUAL)

This concept was inspired by the principle *ritual*, which supports positive memories and provides security and stability in a hectic society. A ritual can also create or improve a social bond between people. One of the main drivers for people to use their juicer is preparing juice for

someone else, a wife, a husband, a child or a friend. One participant of the user research said: '*It is worth the effort if I see my wife is happy with a glass of juice*'. This motivation led to the action of sharing the juice at the moment when it leaves the juicer. The 'turn and share' concept was translated into 'add stone and share', where the juicer has one big spout, through which the juice leaves the juicer like a waterfall. If someone wants to share the juice, a 'stone' can be added, which divides the 'waterfall' in two streams, one for each glass.

Carefully Serving (Inspired by the principle REFLECT)

The reflect principle stands for animating people to think and reflect about their actions. This was translated into a jar, where the user needs both hands to lift and pour the juice into a glass. The juice jar is made of white glass, encouraging the user to handle it very carefully, taking the time and paying attention during serving (Figure 11).

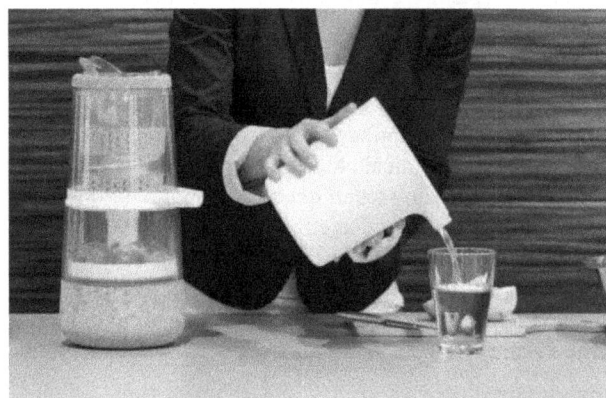

Figure 11. Carefully Serving

User Test

The appearance model was used to determine whether users identified the elements of Slow Design that were designed in. Should the elements be identifiable by the participants then it is a reasonable assumption that the principles of Slow Design were successfully interpreted and realized in a form suitable for a mass produced product. Six participants were invited to the kitchen of Philips' ExperienceLab and asked to explore the Slow Design case study – the JuicyMo.

The prototype employed is a demonstration mock-up, hence, in order to emulate the technique and sound of the JuicyMo as closely as possible, the participants were asked to prepare a glass of juice with the help of an existing vertical auger juicer (Figure 12). During the second task the participants explored the interaction, shape, size, function, and material of the JuicyMo juicer. Additionally, a semi-structured interview was conducted. As a final task the participants were asked, with the help of 'Slow Design feedback cards' (Figure 13), to judge which principles they could see and experience in the new juicer. The testing group consisted of three male participants, who have already joined the user research interviews and three female participants, who have never used a juicer before (gender division of the two groups was not intentional).

Figure 12. Set-up user test

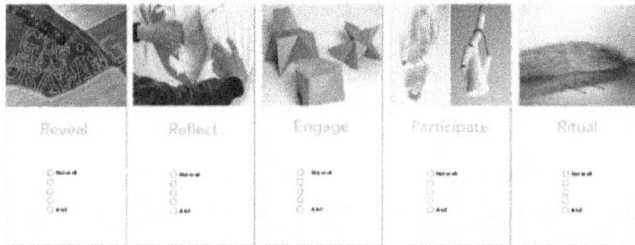

Figure 13. Slow Design feedback Cards

One of the research questions of the user test was "can users find the Slow Design qualities / principles in the final design and if so, which one?" The principles reflect, reveal, and participate were ranked highest with the Slow Design feedback cards. Below are a few excerpts from the comments given by the participants regarding the reasoning behind their choice:

Reflect: *"I would observe the juicing process", "I like the information about the pulp. A nice suggestion on what you can do with it.", "Usually I focus on what I do, so I think I will watch the window of the juicer.", "This transparent thing you showed me in the video... that helps to reflect. Maybe.", or "Yes, ...in this changing effect, I can see 'Reflect' in it."*

Reveal: *"It reveals everything, because it is transparent", or "It reveals the technology."*

Participate: *"...removing the pulp and choosing the filter size", "This is strong, because of the filter and the sharing stone", "This I can see, because I have to assemble the juicer, cut the fruits in smaller parts, but overall it is similar to my Philips centrifugal juicer, just with less noise."*

DICUSSION

Reflection on the Slow Design method

First of all, some words on the name 'Slow Design'. In the course of the project it was identified that term 'Slow' has a negative connotation in our society. It is connected with 'being less productive', laziness, and the opposite of speed and fun. However, the Slow philosophy is not about doing everything at a snail's pace. It's about seeking to do everything at the right speed. [8] In order to communicate well the message of Slow Design, the authors consider

'Design for mindfulness and consciousness' to be a more descriptive and appropriate term.

From the user study with the appearance model JuicyMo it was found that the principles reflect, reveal and participate were identifiable. From this two outcomes can be deduced. Firstly, it was possible to interpret and design using the refined Slow Design principles, since some were noticeable by the end users. Consequently, and secondly, there is room for improvement since not all were clear to the end users; however, this not rule out the potential that they would not have been appreciated following a longer exposure or even subconsciously enjoyed (or not).

The last task of the user test showed that the explanation of the principles, written on the 'Slow Design feedback cards', was, for most of the participants, not easy to understand and they had difficulties to rank them. The researcher had to explain most of them twice. While listening to the participants' comments, it became clear that, in some cases, the principles were interpreted wrongly and needed correction from the researcher. The creation of a testing and feedback tool is the recommendation for further development of the Slow Design principles.

The principles of Slow Design appear to be an inspiring tool for creating product concepts with surprising user interactions and transparent processes, which keep the user involved and lead to an enhanced relationship between user and product. An important outcome that can be drawn from this project is that in order to slow people down the needs of users and living trends of our society have to be taken into account. Balance has to be found between providing product qualities that involve the user more and, perhaps, take even more time to use, learn, and understand them, and, simultaneously offering the convenience of supporting a modern lifestyle. People with busy lives, for example balancing work and children, are willing to spend a few more minutes on interacting with a product they like. However, once 'slow' becomes irritating the product attachment decreases as will the frequency of the product usage. If this happens the goal of creating products that are more sustainable is not achieved. The authors recommend combining the use of the Slow Design principles with the results of a user research and an analysis of the 'process of use'.

The analysis of the juicing process illustrates that some of its segments have to be, and can be, slowed down, while others need to be sped up to create an easier and 'faster' handling, leading to a successful final slow product that supports wellbeing. What the 'right' or the 'important' moment is to slow a process down must be discovered for every Slow Design project as an essential step.

CONCLUSION

From this work we have demonstrated that Slow Design principles can be interpreted by designers and indeed be applied to a mass produced product. In conjunction with literature and this research there are early indications that show Slow Design has the potential to strengthen product attachment when applied with consideration. Slowing products and people down needs to be done at the right time and only then will a more mindful interaction occur that can support the product attachment theories. The original Slow Design principles were written to provide inspiration and direction during a design study; to ensure success when applying them it was found from this study that detailed user centered research into how a product is used is required to identify when it is best to slow people down during use.

ACKNOWLEDGMENTS

We would like sincerely thank Carolyn F. Strauss, on whose work the paper is mostly based and who took the time to explain, in detail, her thoughts on Slow Design. Support for this research was provided by the Innovation Oriented Research Programme 'Integrated Product Creation and Realization IOP-IPCR' of the Netherlands Ministry of Economic Affairs.

REFERENCES

1. DeBell, M. and Dardis, R. Extending Product Life: Technology Isn't the Only Issue. *Advances in Consumer Research 6,* (1979), 381-385.

2. Chapman, J. *Emotionally Durable Design: Objects, Experiences and Empathy.* London: Earthscan, 2005.

3. Cooper, T. Product development implications of sustainable consumption. *The Design Journal, 3(2),* (2000), 46-57.

4. Fuad-Luke, A. *Slow Theory; A paradigm for living sustainably? Fuad-Luke, A., Slow Theory: A paradigm for living sustainably,* 2005

5. Gegenbauer, Silke and Elaine M. Huang. Inspiring the Design of Longer-lived Electronics through an Understanding of Personal Attachment. In *Proc. DIS 2012,* ACM Press (2012), 635-644.

6. Hallnäs, L. and Redström, J. Slow Technology; Designing for Reflection. *Journal of Personal and Ubiquitous Computing 5, 3* (2001), Springer-Verlag , 201-212.

7. Hassenzahl, M. *The Thing and I: Understanding the Relationship Between User and Product.* Blythe, M., Overbeeke, C. Monk, A. F., & Wright, P. C. (Eds.), Funology: From Usability to Enjoyment. Kluwer (2003), 31-42.

8. Krieken, B.'*How to design for emotional durability?'* Master's Thesis. Delft University of Technology, The Netherlands, 2012.

9. Honoré, C. *In praise of Slow.* Orion, London, 2004.

10. Lenssen, K.-M.H., Stofmeel, L., Delden, M.H.W.M. van, Vullers, R.J.M., Visser, H.J. & Pop, V. Zero Energy E-Skin. In *Proc. of the International Display Workshop,* 2010.

11. Lenssen, K.-M.H. 2011. 'Bright e-skin technology and applications: Simplified gray-scale e-paper'. *Journal of the Society for Information Display 19, 1,* (2011), 1-7.

12. Mugge, R. *Product Attachment.* Doctoral Dissertation. Delft University of Technology, The Netherlands, 2007.

13. Norman, D. Memory is more important that actuality. *Interactions, 16, 2,* (2009), 24-26.

14. Odom, W., Pierce, W., Stolterman, E. and Blevis, E. Understanding Why We Preserve Some Things and Discard Others in the Context of Interaction Design. In *Proc. of CHI'09,* ACM Press (2009), 1053-1062

15. Pierce, J. & Paulos, E. Designing for emotional attachment to energy. In *Proc. of Design & Emotion conference,* 2010.

16. Russo, R. *Shoes, Cars and Other Love Stories: Investigating the Experience of Love for Products.* Doctoral Dissertation. Delft University of Technology, The Netherlands, 2010.

17. Savas,Ö. *A perspective on the person-product relationship: attachment and detachment.* McDonagh, D., Hekkert, P., van Erp, J. and Gyi D. (Eds.), Design and Emotion, CRC Press (2003), 317–321.

18. Schifferstein, H. N. J. and Zwartkruis-Pelgrim, E.P. H. Consumer-Product Attachment: Measurement and Design Implications. *International Journal of Design 2, 3* (2008), 1-13.

19. Strauss, C. and Fuad-Luke, A. 2008. The Slow Design Principles - A New Interrogative and Reflexive Tool for Design Research and Practice. *In Proc. of Changing the Change,* Umberto Allemandi & C., Torino, 2008.

20. van Hemel, C. G., & Brezet, J. C. *Ecodesign: A promising approach to sustainable production and consumption.* Paris: United Nations Environmental Programme, 1997.

21. Van Hinte, E. *Eternally Yours: Visions on Product Endurance.* Rotterdam: 010 Publishers, 1997

22. Van Nes, N. *Understanding Replacement Behaviour and Exploring Design Solutions.* in Cooper, T. (Eds.), Longer Lasting Products: Alternatives to the Throwaway Society (107-131). London: Gower, 2010

23. Zimmerman, J. 2009. *Designing for the Self: Making Products that Help People Become the Person they Desire to Be.* In *Proc. of CHI'09,* ACM Press (2009), 395-404.

Making Design Probes Work

Jayne Wallace[1], John McCarthy[2], Peter C. Wright[3], Patrick Olivier[3]

[1]School of Design
Northumbria University
Newcastle upon Tyne, UK
jayne.wallace@northumbria.ac.uk

[2]Applied Psychology
University College Cork
Cork, Ireland
john.mccarthy@ucc.ie

[3]Culture Lab
School of Computing Science
Newcastle University, UK
p.c.wright/patrick.olivier@ncl.ac.uk

ABSTRACT

Probes have been adopted with great enthusiasm in both Design and HCI. The heterogeneity with which they have been used in practice reflects how the method has proved elusive for many. Originators and commentators of probes have discussed misinterpretations of the method, highlighting the lack of accounts that describe in detail the design of probes and their use with participants. This paper discusses our particular use of *Design Probes* as directed craft objects that are both tools for design and tools for exploration across a number of projects, spanning a decade, centered on self-identity and personal significance. In offering an example of what a framework for probe design and use might look like, we attempt to address the identified lacuna, providing a synthetic account of probe design and use over an extended period and conceptualizing the relationship between the properties of probes and their use in design projects.

Author Keywords

Design; Probes; Craft; Interaction Design; Materiality; Empathy; Reciprocity; Trust; Investment.

ACM Classification Keywords

H.5.m. Information interfaces and presentation (e.g., HCI): Miscellaneous.

General Terms

Design

INTRODUCTION

Probes have become a phenomenon within HCI research. Since their creation in 1999 [2] their adoption has become wide in both scope and divergence. In Boehner et al's [1] review of probe use the count was 90 papers cited in the ACM guide to computing literature. The alacrity and enthusiasm with which probes have been adopted in HCI shows that the community saw something new and desirous not only in the method, but also in how it had been used by its originators and the outcomes to which it had led. What is also apparent is that the method has often proved elusive as well as incongruent to other methods used in HCI. In consequence, as Gaver et al [4] and Boehner et al [1]

discuss, probes have often been misunderstood and misappropriated. The results of misinterpretations have in many ways served to muddy the waters further regarding what probes are and how they can be used.

Boehner et al highlight that it is often the case that accounts of probe-use gloss over both the design decisions taken in making probes as well as the detailed use of them. In practice the use of probes has been heterogeneous and both the forms and processes of designing them have reflected this. This is problematic for the research community as it encourages further misappropriation and there are not many accounts or frameworks detailing how probes are designed or used.

We consider the use of *Design Probes* as tools for design and understanding. As such, design probes are objects that are usually small in scale, whose materiality and form are designed to relate specifically to a particular question and context, posing a question through gentle, provocative, creative means offering a participant intriguing ways to consider a question and form a response through the act of completing the probe creatively (Figures 1-9). We regard probes as directed craft objects used in empathic engagements with individuals around issues centered on self-identity and personal significance. Unlike previous accounts that tend to describe one-off uses of probes in a particular design activity by contrast, we reflect on a decade's experience of using probes. We outline properties of our probe design and utilization and give a conceptual and pragmatic framework for qualities of probes and their use in engagement with participants. In doing so we recognize that our approach to designing and using probes is only one of potentially a number of alternatives. Our point is not to prescribe a single probe "methodology', but rather to illustrate what a framework for probe design and use might look like, and in so doing, to provide interested researchers with support for appropriating probes in interesting ways. Thus our contributions in this paper include: addressing the lacuna identified by Boehner concerning the design of probes and the details of their use as designed artifacts; providing a synthetic account of probe design and use over an extended period; and conceptualizing the relationship between the properties of probes and their use in design projects.

With respect to that final contribution, we detail the design properties of thematic openness and boundedness that give a participant space for reflection alongside boundaries that bring clarity and a sense of completability (see Figure 1 for example). The pace of probes is discussed in relation to how different dynamics can be created to facilitate ice breaking in the process or forms of deep reflection (see Figures 4 & 7). We unpick the ways in which materiality can be used to echo a question through innovative forms (see Figure 2), offering a variety of 'ways in' to a particular issue and tangible means to express and represent a response. Our position is that by attending to these elements and dynamics of probes through design it is possible to fully articulate the method; where probes are purposefully designed, inventive and engaging scaffolds for response even in difficult contexts. We further reflect on the use of probes in engagements with participants, in order to reveal how investment leads to a relationship of trust that enables exploration of challenging aspects of experience, and how the reciprocity of the probe method creates a particularly rich, reflective form of communication.

DESIGN AT THE HEART OF THE METHOD

Gaver et al's [2] initial Cultural Probes were born from the pragmatic motivator of researchers in the Presence Project [3] not being able to be with their research participants in person as often as they would have liked, as participants spanned several European countries. The deeper motivation however was to develop a new approach to engaging with the complex and multi-layered realities of experience. Gaver [2, 3] drew on the creative processes of the Situationists, Dadaists and Surrealists appropriating the subversive, playful and at times unsettling nature of processes originating in these art movements to open up a fluid dialogue with participants brokered by objects that explored lived experience at its fullest. As Gaver puts it [2] "…we tried to use, judiciously, tactics of ambiguity, absurdity, and mystery throughout, as a way of provoking new perspectives on everyday life" [p.26].

Probes were designed objects, designed to ask questions and present challenges in an open-ended, often provocative manner, involving a varied set of activities that participants would become involved with and respond to. Gaver et al were able to engage with participants remotely, but more importantly, through the probes they were able to extend themselves into their participants' lives and entice participants into their design process. Probes were curious objects that led in turn to the sharing of unobvious, idiosyncratic and real aspects of the participants' lives and personalities. The probes thus attended to the detail of experience and of individuality.

Notably at a meta-level Gaver [3] saw probes having a wider purpose: "to disrupt expectations about user research and allow new possibilities to emerge" [p.23]. Probes as Boehner [1] discusses were intended to "subvert or undermine, rather than supplement, traditional HCI methods" [p.1080] and importantly design was at the heart of this new approach.

Ideologically, approaches to design in HCI in the 1990s were creating an imbalance in the designer-user relationship. Wright et al [17] discuss how until the early 1990s the idea of design in HCI was taken for granted, and was neither a point of concern nor discussion "Design meant the process of modeling users and systems and specifying system behavior such that it fitted the users' tasks, was efficient, easy to use and easy to learn. In short, design in HCI was about engineering usability." [p.1]. Whilst sections of the HCI community have developed radically from this positioning, as Boehner [1] and Gaver [4] articulate, Probe methods continue to jar with deep-seated considerations of design in HCI. There are examples of probes being used in the Situationist spirit that Gaver described [10] and others emphasizing the use of probes for inspiration foregrounding design sensibilities [6], but although designers such as Mattelmäki [8, 8] and Leitner [5] have emphasized the value and need for design within the Probe method it has nonetheless become something of an umbrella term in HCI under which a wide selection of objects have been ascribed and where design has become somewhat out of focus. Off-the-shelf stationery has become commonplace in Probe kits, for example, lending a veneer of the method without the substance that comes from an engagement through design with the materiality, form and character of Probe artifacts. We unpick our own use of the method over the last decade in fine-grained detail to illustrate the potentials of keeping design at the heart of the method and to refocus attention on what it means to design probes and what the method can afford.

Design Probes for empathetic engagement

Our notion and use of a design probe is to work with individuals to engage deeply with the participant and enquire around her sense of what is personally meaningful. From the experiences and meanings shared with us by a participant we attempt to make digital artifacts that echo fragments of these meanings back to the specific participant. Our research includes the development of digital objects that spur and support reflection, digital jewellery that bears witness to or supports relationships between individuals and artifacts developed through research into the maintenance of a sense of self and relationships to support personhood in dementia.

In working so closely with individuals and making digital artifacts specifically for them, our use of probes is somewhat atypical from the usual group scenario, where probes are used to gain understandings and inspiration to inform designs around a particular theme or issue [8], or from examples of Gaver's practice [4], where individuals respond to probes but where the resulting design ideas are given to different families or individuals to live with. In our practice, probes are part of an intimate relationship and design process that remains with particular individuals throughout. We make a bespoke set of probes for each context or project and a participant lives with these for a number of weeks. The insights we discuss in this paper concerning participant experiences to probes stem primarily from revisiting what participants had done physically to probe objects in responding to them and secondly from revisiting transcripts of discussions around probes from design field studies of projects over the last ten years.

We subscribe to the ethos of Gaver's probes, respecting them for their ability to inspire and "to stimulate our imaginations rather than define a set of problems." [2 p.25] We also agree with his reflections [4] that many in HCI have missed the point of probes, rationalizing them to "produce comprehensible results…[and] even use them to produce requirements analyses" [p.1] We differ from Gaver in that our probes are more deliberately and specifically pointed towards the phenomena we wish to address. Equally our experience differs somewhat from Mattelmäki's descriptions of design probes [8] where "users collect and document the material... [and] Probes are a collection of assignments through which or inspired by which the users can record their experiences as well as express their thoughts and ideas" [p. 40]. In exploring personal significance and identity, at times in extreme contexts such as dementia, we have found that users may struggle to articulate feelings around challenging aspects of their lives and it is not straightforward for them to document these things. Probes need to work hard to facilitate a participant's reflections, deploying a range of multi-angled methods. We see them as objects that enable deep reflection and gentle ways to give a participant access to complex notions and experience. This is important, as a central factor in the probe process is the development of a relationship of trust with participants.

In that we design probes that are purposefully directed towards the phenomenon we are addressing, the ideas for our probe designs are not random; they are forms of tentative hypotheses towards empathic understanding and also future design ideas that are informed by aspects of a particular context that we have hunches about. For example, in recent projects where we have been working with people with dementia [13, 14] (see Figures 1, 2 7 & 9) we have immersed ourselves in the clinical and social aspects of the disease as much as has been possible (volunteer work with Alzheimer's Society day care centers, artist placement with clinicians and philosophers of dementia care, time spent with creative dementia groups, reading texts relating to clinical, social and relational aspects of dementia) and have sought to gain an understanding and empathy for different aspects of how life and self are affected. We create probes that are laden with a particular theory or insight, gained firsthand, and explore specific aspects of this. Consequently probes are evocative of certain issues or what we imagine to be pertinent in a certain context. A set of probes is purposefully structured to relate to a range of such issues. To give an example of what we mean within the *Personhood* project, the term "personhood" speaks to a notion of the self as something socially maintained,

nurtured and constructed at least in part. The role of human relationships in supporting identity for someone with dementia is therefore highly significant. Many of the probes we designed within this project related purposefully to various distinct aspects of these meaningful relationships with other people, self-worth, home, and presentation of the self to others. Without explicitly doing so, each of the probes in the set related to different facets of what we thought might be significant, as informed by theory and our own experiences of dementia.

We use probes as both tools for design and tools for exploration. In the following sections we open up in more detail how we design probes, the roles they take for us in our approach and how we initiate probes with participants. We do this by firstly discussing them as scaffolds for response, which we relate to openness, boundedness, materiality, pace and challenge. Secondly we describe the probe method in terms of a relationship with a participant, the dynamics of which relate to trust and investment as well as reciprocity and communication. Each of these ideas teases out something critical about what the probe process is in terms of design, and underpins the way that we frame and use probes throughout the various stages of our research process.

Scaffolds for response – Designing Probes

It is easy to see that the probe process involves shared making, in that participants complete a probe that was initially made or started by the researcher. But it is less obvious, although we would argue more significant, that the probe process can achieve a form of *co-creativity*. This necessitates more than completion of a probe; it requires a participant to act creatively and invest in the process in order to create a final probe that is an artifact rich in meaning, made whole and unique through the participant's reflections and actions (see Figures 1, 2 & 3). This notion puts emphasis on craft and the completed object, which may be different from a provocative probe object which may focus more on unsettling a participant and encouraging them to think laterally and playfully around a particular issue.

Being creative is not an easy or natural activity for all. One of the first things that most participants say on embarking on a project with us is that they are not creative people. It is not enough to hand over objects to participants and presume that they will respond creatively to them. The design of a probe must involve more than the formation of a question in a three-dimensional form; it must also involve the design of scaffolds for creativity and response. Probes are not an arbitrary set of objects; their materiality is crucial to both framing a question in a particular way and creating a structure that facilitates a participant's creative ability and response.

Form and aesthetic are critical in many senses. Probe design is about the physicality of the probe object, sensitively echoing the question being asked in innovative ways that open up many different channels for creative response and reflection. In this we consider, for example, the feel of the object, how the aesthetics reflect the way we are asking someone to respond, the pace of the probe artifact, the space we are giving someone to reflect within, the era the object feels like it belongs to and the ways that the participant will be able to add their own aesthetic. Such parameters give us scope to share something of ourselves, enable us to bring out specific nuances of a question and facilitate a participant in responding. Through considering probe design in terms of boundedness, materiality and pace, we can explore how the dynamics of probe design function in our experience.

Openness and Boundedness

The openness of our probes is thematic: each probe is made with a theme in mind that is quite specific in some ways. We try to give participants ways of thinking about a theme that they have not experienced before, and in this is the gentle challenge to enter into the probe activity. Here the creativity lies in the challenge to do something new.

Probes are part-made objects explicitly awaiting closure, which offer a participant both openness to share whatever she feels appropriate and clear boundaries to respond within. The significance of both boundaries and a sense of boundedness is that they enable clarity of what the activity to complete a probe needs to be, give a participant the sense that a probe is completable and thus provide an unambiguous context and safe space within which to be creative. The boundedness of a probe balances out the multitude of possibilities facing a participant. It acts like a form of safety net that confirms to the participant how much to do, sets confines within which to be expressive and makes creativity a less fearsome endeavor.

Self Tree probe (Figure 1) allows us to look at these dynamics in more detail.

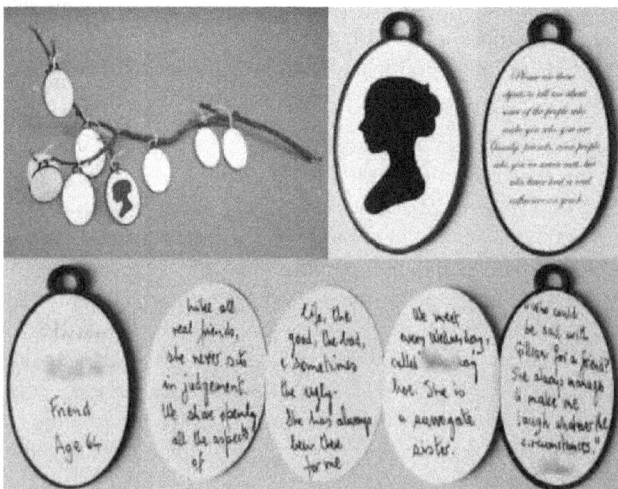

Figure 1. *Self Tree* **probe detailing the group of objects, details of individual elements and examples of participants' responses.**

This probe is made up of a series of oval discs, locket-like in appearance, attached to the branch of a tree. All but one of the discs has paper covering the front, with the word "Name" printed and a small concertina of folded paper on the reverse. The remaining disc is slightly larger than the others and has the silhouette of a woman printed on the front (representing our main participant) with the following instructions on the reverse:

"Please use these objects to tell me about some of the people who make you who you are (family, friends, even people who you've never met, but who have had a real influence on you)."

Self Tree probe is from a set made within the *Personhood* project exploring aspects of self and personhood in dementia. We worked with Gillian, a person with mild stage dementia (at that time) and her husband John.

Gillian and John chose to use the probe to tell us about people who have been close to Gillian: some alive, some dead, some related, some friends. They gave the name of each person on the front of the disc along with a title describing their connection to Gillian (for example daughter, friend) and the person's age. They used the paper on the reverse to give very poignant narrative descriptions of the relationship between Gillian and each individual, where anecdotes and experiences were shared including how each particular relationship had changed over time. On the final section of paper they wrote a quote from each person about their feelings for Gillian. Where possible these quotes were obtained from the individual specifically for the probe and where not possible a quote that Gillian could remember them saying was used.

Gillian and John understood the parameters of the probe; it was the first of the set that they gravitated towards and they found the limitations of paper size to be a positive factor:

"it was, not too big, you hadn't much to write on it. So you had to be quite, selective in what was put on. And I I just thought that was fantastic. (...) I mean compared to you know, if you'd given us a book to write in, well immediately you think I don't have to fill this, you know, but that was so precise that I think that's it's great strength, it worked for us."

The boundedness created by the physicality of the oval forms and the limitations of scale of the paper forced Gillian and John to analyze what the essential aspects of each of these relationships was in order to convey the essence of each in such a focused manner. They were able to get to the heart of what they wanted to say and, once completed, each disc shared a crystallized account of seven rich and meaningful relationships. Within the confines and boundaries of the probe they made it all their own, they were creative and did things with it that we had not prescribed or suggested. They brought in voices of the other people through quotes, posed descriptions of relationships like small stories replete with moral guidance and life lessons learned, and reflected on the changes in these relationships because of dementia.

The physical scale and boundedness of the probe was highly significant in making it feel completable, in suggesting the focused quality for the response, and in making participants feel that they were able to co-create on a level with us. If the *Self Tree* probe had been presented without such focused boundaries (for example, as a blank notebook as John mentioned) there would have been ambiguity surrounding how many people to talk about, how much to say and what kind of dynamic to create through the response. How would a participant know when she had finished? Would the probe be complete only when every page had been filled?

Probes are intentionally designed to be partially complete to create the sense in the participant that to complete a probe feels like finishing something, it is important for a participant to feel that they have done enough, that they have contributed something worthwhile. The expanse and lack of direction of a blank notebook could therefore bring pressure to the response process, create ambiguity around 'how much is enough?' suggest a lack of direction in these matters on the part of the researcher and potentially stymie a participant.

Materiality

Self Tree probe suggested a preciousness that Gillian and John responded to by intimately detailing highly personal experience. More than the boundedness of the probe, this dynamic relates strongly to the aesthetics and physicality of the forms. *Self Tree* was a physical metaphor of what it enquired around: it embodied the context of the question. The discs were locket-like in aesthetic through their oval shape, scale, use of a silhouette of a woman and the concealed space for personal information. Their connection to a tree branch suggested an organic interconnection between the discs in some sense, a "family" of objects. Each of these qualities combined to create a group of objects that suggested a kind of familial and relational preciousness. *Self Tree* placed the participant at the heart of a nexus of rich relationships and as something vital to other people. She could see herself as someone valued, nurtured and supported within this web.

The jewellery-like physicality of the probe related the process to other forms of 'reflection through objects' that we have all experienced: reflection through mementos and souvenirs that draw us back to past experiences and events. Objects like these have always acted as sites and tools for reflection for people. Probes act in similar ways, whether literally as in *Self Tree* or more ambiguously in the case of probes generally. Probes explicitly ask people to use them to reminisce, project and reflect; the object asks to be used as a locus or home for feelings and remembrances. *Self Tree* was challenging as it asked Gillian, a person with dementia, to reflect on her meaningful relationships with people through her life and how they had contributed to the woman she had become. In the context of life with dementia, where change and notions of loss are a constant

backdrop, we were exploring sensitive territory with this probe. However, by designing objects that caringly embodied the question, the forms that the probe took provided gentle ways to do this. They gave Gillian comprehendible structures to explore within, which lent themselves to the subtle, organic contexts that these aspects of self relate to.

The importance of tangibility is not just that the probes can be evocative objects to reflect through, but that the material properties of the probe can structure the reflection itself. If we take two examples, *Home* and *Pillow,* we can explore this point.

The *Home* probe (Figure 2), again designed within the *Personhood* project, is a small (approx 16 x 12 x 15cm), hollow, wooden model of a house with a flag reading *"Please use this object to tell me about what home means to you personally (for instance what are home-like feelings, places, aesthetics, words and objects?) Feel free to draw on/inside the object, stick things onto it or change it in any way you see fit."*

Participants Gillian and John involved their two adult children in their response. They made the probe something their own, not only in the content, but in the way that they used the object physically. They reflected on what home meant to them in relation to the harsh changes to their lives through Gillian's dementia by describing home before and after Gillian's diagnosis.

The structure and form of the probe was, obviously, house-like and the participants reflected this in the way that they interpreted it and changed it physically; areas were compartmentalized, the house was 'decorated' and the roof was 'tiled'. The structure of the form leant itself to being interpreted in this manner and the completed probe actually looked *lived-in* as a result.

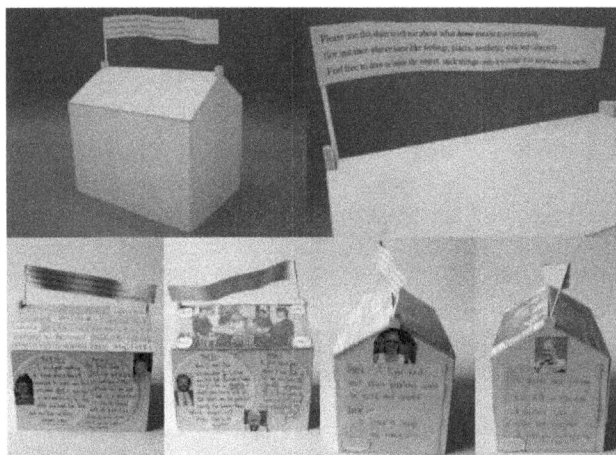

Figure 2. *Home* probe with illustrations of responses.

The heads of the family took the largest sides, whilst the children were allocated the smaller ones. Photographs of each person, titled 'then' and 'now' decorated their side of the object and speech bubbles were used to denote that the written words were their individual voice and opinion. The roof, being split into two and connecting all of the other sides, was selected by the participants to represent the family as a group. It was used to share both abstract concepts of what home means to them (words stuck as multi-colored roof tiles) and something very individual and idiosyncratic (a photograph depicting a family mealtime ritual from when the children were growing up).

The scale of the probe meant that there was a good amount of space on each side for content to be added, but it did not demand a vast amount of content in order to cover all of its surfaces and for the probe to be seen to be complete. It was a strong structure but not heavy, so it could be easily held and manipulated. It was a simple form evocative of a house, but not related to any particular style or suggestive of any particular taste and as such functioned as the symbol of a house, of home. The surfaces were smooth enough to write on and porous enough to take glue easily. These points in the design of probes are important scaffolds to encourage a participant to add to and build on what has been started or laid as a foundation.

The *Pillow* probe (Figure 3) was created to explore issues of personal meaningfulness within a digital jewellery project. It is approximately 9 x 7cm and is made from white cotton with padding like a small pillow. Part of the fabric of the pillow can be folded out from the main body, then tucked away inside the pillow again. The probe asks a participant to keep the pillow with them and to use it to share a dream (which could be a dream from sleep, a daydream, a fantasy or aspiration) by writing on the fold out of fabric and hiding it away again within the main body of the pillow.

Figure 3. *Pillow* probe an example of a completed response.

This probe is evocative of the intimacy of laying your head upon a pillow: the aesthetics are soft and the scale is small and intimate. Each of these physical attributes suggests that this probe could be something to engage with on an intimate level. There are further suggestions of intimacy in the action of writing something and then hiding it away, like the sharing of a secret. The gentleness of the object and the physicality of the action of hiding the shared information both act to suggest that a dream shared by a participant will be safeguarded and handled sensitively. Similarly, the gentleness of the form was an intentional aesthetic designed to be able to carry such a personal and searching question.

The invitation to write on the fabric could be seen as a big commitment. A participant knows that once she is writing on the fabric the words cannot be rethought or removed. In both the uncommonness of writing on fabric and in that the

writing will actually become part of the aesthetics of the object, there is an elevation from writing a response on pieces of paper. Further writing on an artifact is something that we are usually dissuaded from doing and is often thought of as defiling an object. In *Pillow* probe, part of the creative act is a nudging of what someone feels comfortable doing. To scaffold this activity we wanted to give permission to write on the object by starting this process off ourselves in the way we presented the instructions.

We could have embroidered the request to share a dream on the pillow or made a washing label with the instructions sewn into the seam, but we are also always aware of not making a probe feel too finished and potentially alienable. There is a balance to be struck between making the probes too polished (done in an attempt to show a participant your commitment and understanding of a situation, but actually creating objects that seem too well made for a participant to feel she can meet these standards in her own additions) and making probes that leave realistic spaces for completion.

The relative small scale of probes is important because it helps them to remain approachable and manageable. The tangibility of probes means there is something to hold, to touch and to add to in a physical way. When a question is challenging, the physicality of probes becomes a facilitating factor. The tangibility of probes means that there is some*thing* for a participant to focus on. People share ephemeral entities such as their feelings or aspirations and the physicality of the probes enables us to tie these abstract notions to something solid. The dialogue becomes embedded in and mediated by objects in a very concrete sense and these objects become things that we communicate with and through. From the first exchange of probes with a participant, the communication is not only through the responses and questions posed, but also through form and aesthetic.

Our approach to the design of probes is embedded in craft practice, which we describe as an intimate and empathic process that fuses learned knowledge of making with the desire to create objects *for people* [11, 12, 15 & 16]. The human is very present in craft objects, both in the *trace* of the maker in the objects and in the humanizing of various processes and materials, and this holds true in our notion of probe design. A craft approach to the development of probes incorporates an empathic engagement with the theme being explored through each probe in order to concretize and echo sensitive aspects of the theme in physical form.

Pace and Challenge

Probes live with people. They are given to participants for a period of time (usually weeks) during which they inhabit their homes and personal spaces. The probes silently ask questions during this time and the atmosphere around answering them (in our use of the method) is in general an unhurried one. This slowness to the process means that a participant can set her own pace and there is time to reflect, to hold a question in the back of the mind before responding, and further to use her initial response as a reflexive tool. Even if a participant responds to the probes in the last days and hours before returning them the questions have been with her for the duration and even whilst residing in the background have been under consideration by the participant over time.

Within this general pace of the method we find that by creating probes that have a variety of individual paces we can design objects that not only ask a selection of distinct questions, but also act as tools that enable a participant within the various and often challenging acts of response themselves across the probe group.

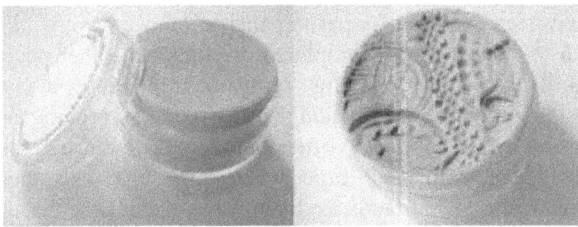

Figure 4. *Pot of Clay* probe with an example of a response.

The faster, lighter weight probes serve as icebreakers in the process. *Pot of Clay* probe (Figure 4) which asked a participant to make an indentation in the clay of something precious, or *Body Mapping* probe (Figure 5) with which a participant attached stickers to areas of the body to show where she wears jewellery at different times and for different purposes were both designed with a faster pace in mind.

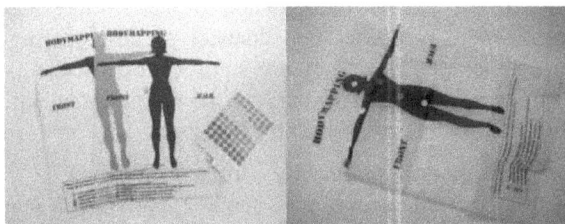

Figure 5. *Bodymapping* probe with an example of a response.

They involve lighter questions and direct, simple, physical acts of response. Such probes can become breathing spaces, offering relief from probes that are proving challenging, and, significantly, they can act as catalysts, the completion of which may trigger further responses to more challenging probes.

Probes that are designed to have fast, lightweight activities and questions often only garner a certain level of intensity and meaning in response, and in many cases the brevity and triviality is not appropriate for certain contexts of question. Some questions or subject matters are difficult to express answers to and we can see how probes that offer space for deeper reflection are needed. When it is hard to get a handle on how you feel about something, it is useful to be able to explore this through a selection of means. As such, a participant may use a few probes to tease out for herself different aspects of what she feels.

Probes that in themselves offer a series of multiple units can be used in distinct stages by a participant, so the difficult or challenging question being posed can be attended to through a series of small steps, breaking it down into something manageable. *Top Trumps* and *Preserves* probes were designed with this in mind.

Top Trumps probe (Figure 6) gave a participant six cards on which to describe objects that were powerful to her; participants could describe the object, draw or glue a photograph onto a window in each card and rate the powers of the object in numerical values out of 100.

Figure 6. *Top Trumps* probe with examples of responses.

Preserves probe (Figure 7) comprised three small jars with the question: *If you could capture anything (for instance any moment, sound, song, smell, view, object, place...) and preserve it in this jar for you to relive what would you choose?* The label could be used to describe the choice (through writing or drawing on it) and/or something could be placed inside the jar to represent their choice.

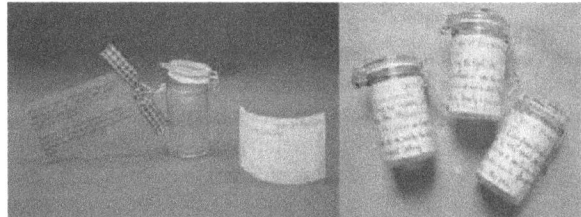

Figure 7. *Preserves* probe with examples of responses.

In their compartmental structure both probes afford a participant the function of segmenting each probe and completing sections over time. This quality can make even a more searching probe feel *completable*; the question being asked may require much searching, but through segmentation the probe doesn't feel over awing and the slow pace of the process helps support this. *Preserves* probe, similarly to *Self Tree*, sets a further slowness of pace in that it enquires around the participant's whole life. This necessitates a certain kind of reflection on the part of a participant relating to their personal biography. We have used metaphors and imagined contexts often in our practice with probes to give participants ways to externalize difficult notions. *Communication Fairytale* and *Self Seeding* probes are useful examples for this discussion.

Figure 8. *Communication Fairytale* probe with example pages.

Communication Fairytale (Figure 8) was a short storybook. The participant, as the central character, was separated from 'loved', a character that the participant relates to someone in her own life. She is then taken through the story and asked to complete sections in the book. Questions range from how a participant felt connected to 'loved' when not with him/her physically, what a good memory of her and 'loved' looked like, what kinds of human communication or modes of technological communication she found precious and if anything were possible, how she would like to communicate with 'loved'.

Self Seeding probe (Figure 9) was a seed packet containing a small number of plant labels.

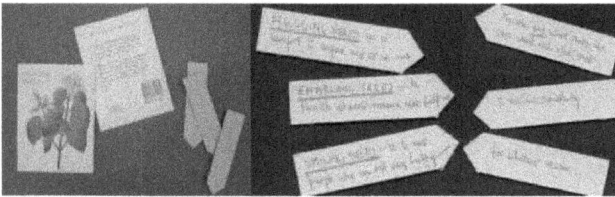

Figure 9. *Self Seeding* probe with examples of responses.

A participant was asked to imagine that she could turn some of her personal qualities or idiosyncrasies into seeds. She is then asked to consider which these would be, where she would plant them and what they would blossom into.

Both probes explore aspects of who the participant is. *Self Seeding* asked a participant to look within herself, enquiring around aspects of her nature and how in turn these qualities extended out into the world to have an impact; to 'blossom' or 'grow'. As a physical metaphor of what it enquired about, *Self Seeding* invoked the context of seeds being planted, which brings with it ideas of something becoming bigger than itself and of something small like a seed holding so much potential that it has the capacity to extend itself and flourish. . It asked a participant to imagine the self continuing over time, and consider what it was about herself that she valued and could see having value for other people. The seeds and seed packet gave us a very useful vehicle to enquire around these complex notions. It provided a recognizable symbol for these things, a simple action through which to convey these complex meanings (writing descriptions of personal qualities and what they would develop into on seed labels) and a simple form into which meaning could be poured. It gave a way to externalize complex aspects of identity, personality, self worth and relationships with things external to self. The process of working with probes can tease out meanings that are seldom explicitly considered, whether through considering a subject in new ways or through expressing meanings in a tangible form. Similarly, *Communication Fairytale* enabled a participant to externalize complex notions through the non-real world context of a fairytale story. Through this medium we were able to create imaginary scenarios and ask the participant to consider situations unencumbered by restraints of what is possible. The freedom afforded us by presenting questions in a

fairytale enables us to sidestep to a degree existing realities and inhibitions. A completed probe can become a reflexive tool that may act to actually show a participant how she feels about something; often externalizing a feeling can bring clarity and a new way of seeing something.

Both *Communication Fairytale* and *Self Seeding* were meant to get participants to think in a broad or lateral way and probes such as these will by association invigorate a probe set with this flexibility and breadth of context. The experiences and feelings that we were asking someone to express may be complex and multi-layered. The heterogeneous nature of probes acts here to offer different ways for a participant to get at what they want to say.

It has been common for participants whom we have worked with to show probes, completed or empty, to other people and discuss their thoughts prior to responding in full. Design probes that are thought provoking, searching and unusual mean that people often want to puzzle through their response and to take time when engaging with them. Conversations that facilitate fresh ways of thinking through a response can happen around them over time. Someone can patiently respond and complete probes piece by piece as the best way for them to respond becomes clear to them.

Thematic openness, boundedness and pace, along with the varied facets of physicality we have discussed, are dynamics of the structural and material properties of probes that can be utilized as scaffolds for creativity and response. They are properties that probes can be imbued with that enable people to engage with them. All of these qualities and scaffolds enable participants to make links across probes, where responses can connect probes together or span a series of them. They are significant components in the process that play a part in how and how far, a participant involves herself in the process.

Relationships and reciprocity – Initiating probes

When done well, probe sets show a participant that a researcher has thought hard about the nature of the enquiry, has designed a set of poignant ways to think about different aspects of the topic, has invested herself in this process and has created a unique environment through which to have a dialogue together. The relationship between researcher and participant is central to the method.

Our first step of the process is to meet with a potential participant to introduce our particular research focus, our methods and ourselves, as a prerequisite to her becoming involved in a project. This initial meeting, although brief, gives us our first insight into the lives of participants and helps us to gain some empathy with them. For us, a sense of investment begins through immersing ourselves in the particular theme of study. This deepens through the creation of probes that attend to different levels of a subject. We design bespoke probes for each project. Some probes (such as disposable cameras) do work in several different themes, but we tailor these tightly to each particular context. We attempt to create a process that is rich and interesting enough that participants will want to enter into it with us and feel that they get something positive out of the process.

Investment and Trust

Gaver [2] pre-empted potential misunderstandings of the method in 1999, suggesting that a generic approach to the production of probe materials would seem "insincere, like official forms with a veneer of marketing" [p.29]. To genuinely understand and use the method, you have to get involved and invest in the process. The method has a very personal aspect to it depending on several things: gaining empathy with your participants' particular situations and environments, the bespoke designing of probes for this particular context and sharing yourself in the process.

In that probes are made in part by each party, there is a sense of shared creation. Probes become a common ground as the process becomes a way of building a relationship in a more democratic manner than the roles of researcher and participant often afford. The level of care that is put into the conceptual and design aspects is palpable and as such evident to a participant communicating the level of investment and respect. Personal engagement around aspects of a participant's life experiences *requires* a relationship of trust to develop and results in the knowledge that what is disclosed will be valued and respected. Reflections can be made together on both poignant (or painful) aspects of experience as well as more enjoyable elements. Probes offer us the means to open up a process of enquiry that is gentle, multi-angled and reciprocal.

Reciprocity and Communication

The probe process is one of bi-directional reciprocity. For this process to really work there needs to be an investment from both researcher and participant. More than a symmetrical activity, the process foregrounds giving and there is a sense of something positive happening here: both parties want to give and invest something of themselves in the endeavor. This aspect of the process is borne out in Gaver et al's [2] descriptions of how participants from the Presence project sent them things above and beyond the tasks asked of them, even greetings cards and messages of goodwill. This kind of investment from both parties is critical to the success of the method.

At first, giving something to someone whom you do not yet know very well is a tentative act. In this context the notion of making a collection of probes is important; we are able to make a set of small artifacts that enable us to give a series of different aesthetics and kinds of objects to test the water and see what fits for the person we are making them for. We can create heterogeneous elements and ensure a good coverage of different activities, media and means to respond. Giving multiple probes helps counter the uncertainty on our part as to which will have poignancy for someone, and means that participants can gravitate towards the probes that they feel they can respond well through

whilst still feeling that they have taken part in the exchange sufficiently. Importantly, a participant is free to respond to as many or as few probes as she wants. We give her the power to reject ones that do not feel right for her. How a participant responds is therefore also a form of editing the probe series and a creative act in itself.

Through reciprocity comes conversation. There are reciprocal gestures, acts of sharing and getting to know one another and an informal nature to the process both within our human interactions and in the participant's interactions with the probes. For us this sense of the conversation is critical; we are not just asking someone a question and gaining an answer, we are asking someone to reflect, share, surprise and reveal things to us in a cycle of atypical gestures. Within this simple premise are rich layers.

Douglas, in summarizing a central insight offered by Mauss' classic The Gift [9] suggests, "A gift that does nothing to enhance solidarity is a contradiction" [Foreword]. In other words, gifts are about the sharing of and sharing in something and, although different from gifts in the traditional sense, probes evoke the notion of giving from both researcher and participant points of view. There is a natural reciprocity to gift giving and undeniably a sense that a giver hopes that her gesture will be reciprocated, but, as Douglas and Mauss argue, this is less to do with pure obligation and more to do with a desire for cohesion between givers. A gift is more than the sum of its parts; it is a representation of how the giver views and understands the recipient, in terms of values and sense of self and how the giver regards the recipient in relation to herself. The reciprocal probes process then is in part a delicate dance where each person shares her own personal values, as well as an understanding of or empathy with those of the other person. Probes, when considered in this context, are far more complex and delicate a method than is often assumed.

It is highly important to us that a participant finds some personal benefit from the process. For us it is not a data gathering exercise; it is a reflective and reflexive process. Empathy is a key element and we work hard to be open as designers to absorbing what a participant tells us about her experiences and to attempt to step into her shoes as far as possible. Probes are enormously valuable tools in gaining empathy as they have the depth and richness to tackle difficult issues from a range of angles and enable engagements with someone around intimate aspects of experience. The cyclical aspect of the method sets probes apart from many research tools and makes their use and value so significant. To be a participant in the probe process is to build up a set of objects, responses and meanings, all from and about yourself. For the participant, the series of completed probes is in a way like a small autobiographical exhibition and offers ways to see her responses and meanings afresh, presented in concrete, tangible forms and in relation to all of the others she has co-created. This dynamic and cyclical process itself begs a participant's attention, re-examination and reflection of what has been shared. As tools for self-reflection, probes have clear and valuable properties. Probe object and action have the means to reveal to a participant something new about her own experiences.

CONCLUSION

Our use of design probes is as embodied questions that exist in a co-creative, empathic and shared context between a participant and a design researcher. Design probes mediate both the relationship between participant and researcher and participant and her own feelings in relation to a question. This process provides more than inspirations for design; it embodies design to enable shared understandings in relation to challenging, intimate and real aspects of lived experience, which enrich the design process through layers of meaning.

We assert that only by keeping design at the heart of probes that the value of the method can be maximized. We have attempted to address the void identified by Boehner, concerning the design of probes and the details of their use, by providing a reflective account of our own approach to probe design and participants' responses to them. Our account describes how the properties of thematic openness and boundedness provide space for reflection; the role of completability; how considerations of pace can enable ice-breaking as well as deep reflection; and also how working with the materiality of a probe can enable questions to be posed in innovative and sensitive ways. In these respects we have sought to offer both a framework for probe design and use, and an initial lexicon of probe qualities.

The original functioning of probes was to go out into the world to capture something of people's lives acting as rich inspiration for designers. Probes were somewhat disembodied, fascinating snapshots of experience and meaning that gave talented designers the stimulus and openness to design in response. This ties in somewhat with how designers tend to work generally making things for a 'person' or 'persons' rather than for someone who they get to know more deeply. We have sought to detail an alternative way of approaching probes that subscribes to Gaver's probes in ethos, but enmeshes the participant and researcher throughout in a multi-layered process of expressing and finding meanings.

ACKNOWLEDGEMENTS

This research was part funded within the SIDE (Social Inclusion through the Digital Economy) RCUK Digital Economy Research Hub.

REFERENCES

1. Boehner, K., Vertesi, J., Sengers, P., and Dourish, P. How HCI interprets the probes. In *Proc. CHI 2007*. ACM Press (2007), 1077-1086.

2. Gaver, W., Dunne, T., and Pacenti, E. Cultural probes. *Interactions* 6, 1 (1999), 21-29.

3. Gaver, W., Hooker, B., & Dunne, A. *The Presence Project* RCA CRD Projects series RCA Research Publications, 2001.

4. Gaver, W., Boucher, A., Pennington, S., and Walker, B. Cultural probes and the value of uncertainty. *Interactions* 11, 5 (2004), 53-56.

5. Leitner, M., Cockton, G., Yee, J., and Greenough, T. The hankie probe: a materialistic approach to mobile ux research In *Proc CHI EA '12* ACM Press (2012), 1919-1924.

6. Mackay, W. E. 2004. The interactive thread. *In Proc. DIS '04*. NY: ACM Press, 103-112.

7. Mattelmäki, T. and Battarbee, K. Empathy Probes. In *Proc PDC2002* Malmo 2002.

8. Mattelmäki, T. *Design Probes*. University of Art and Design Helsinki. 2006.

9. Mauss, M. *The Gift: The Form and Reason for Exchange in Archaic Societies*, trans. W. D. Halls, London: Routledge. ([1923–1924] 1990).

10. Paulos, E. and Beckmann, C. 2006. Sashay. *In Proc. CHI '06*. NY: ACM Press, 881-884.

11. Paz, O. *In Praise of Hands: Contemporary Crafts of the World*. New York Graphic Society. 1974.

12. Sennett, R. *The Craftsman*. Penguin Publishing, 2008.

13. Wallace, J., Wright, P., McCarthy, J., Green, D., Thomas, J. and Olivier, P. A Design-led Inquiry into Personhood in Dementia. In *Proc CHI 2013*, ACM Press (2013).

14. Wallace, J., Thieme, A., Wood, G., Schofield, G. and Olivier, P. Enabling self, intimacy and a sense of home in dementia: an enquiry into design in a hospital setting. In *Proc CHI 2012*, ACM Press (2012), 2692-2638.

15. Wallace, J. and Press, M. All this useless beauty *The Design Journal* 7, 2 (2004), 42-53.

16. Wallace, J. and Press, M. Craft knowledge for the digital age. In *Proc 6th Asian Design Conference* (2003), 14-17.

17. Wright, P., Blythe, M., and McCarthy, J. User experience and the idea of design in HCI *Interactive Systems. Design, Specification, and Verification* Springer Berlin/Heidelberg (2006), 1-14

Indoor Weather Stations: Investigating a Ludic Approach to Environmental HCI Through Batch Prototyping

William W. Gaver, John Bowers, Kirsten Boehner, Andy Boucher, David W. T. Cameron, Mark Hauenstein, Nadine Jarvis, Sarah Pennington

Interaction Research Studio
Goldsmiths, University of London
initial.surname@gold.ac.uk

ABSTRACT

In this project, we investigated how a ludic approach might open new possibilities for environmental HCI by designing three related devices that encourage environmental awareness while eschewing utilitarian or persuasive agendas. In addition, we extended our methodological approach by batch-producing multiple copies of each device and deploying them to 20 households for several months, gathering a range of accounts about how people engaged and used them. The devices, collectively called the 'Indoor Weather Stations', reveal the home's microclimate by highlighting small gusts of wind, the colour of ambient light, and temperature differentials within the home. We found that participants initially tended to relate to the devices in line with two 'orienting narratives' of environmental tools or ludic designs, finding the devices disappointing from either perspective. Most of our participants showed lingering affection for the devices, however, for a variety of reasons. We discuss the implications of this 'sporadic interaction', and the more general lessons from the project, both for environmental HCI and ludic design.

Author Keywords

Research through design; environmental HCI; ludic design; ubiquitous computing; sensing

ACM Classification Keywords

H.5.m. Information interfaces and presentation (e.g., HCI): Miscellaneous.

General Terms

Design

INTRODUCTION

This paper describes our batch production and deployment of a set of three related designs that highlight the home's microclimate, undertaken to explore a ludic approach to

matters of the environment as an alternative to utilitarian or persuasive approaches. A ludic approach to technology design opens up issues to disrupt their reduction to singular narratives. For example, a ludic approach to domestic technology undermines assumptions about 'smart' appliances for the efficient and productive home and presents instead curious systems for exploration and reflection about domestic space [12]. Here we present a ludic approach to designing technology for the environment offering insights into both the development of environmental HCI as a design space and ludic design as an approach.

Opening Up Technology for the Environment

Over the last several years, there has been a growing tendency in HCI to how digital technologies might address environmental issues, for example by making computing more environmentally sustainable [e.g. 2, 31] or, more commonly, promoting 'greener' behaviour on the part of users [e.g.10, 11, 20]. As DiSalvo et al. [7] point out, most of this research works with the logic of persuasive technology, seeking to present information to users in a way that encourages 'correct' behaviour.

There are several challenges to persuasive approaches to environmental issues, e.g. as manifested by resource demand monitors. First, empirical studies indicate that interventions have limited effectiveness [1], producing minor and/or short-lived behaviour changes, for example, or 'boomerang' effects where reduction by some is offset by increased consumption by others [26]. Moreover, critical reflections from social sciences, humanities and the arts, point out broader assumptions and limitations of demand reduction strategies. For instance, Shove [27] paints a compelling picture of how resource use is deeply interwoven with cultural assumptions about cleanliness and consumption. Strengers [28] builds on this, drawing on Bourdieu's [5] notion of 'habitus' and pointing out the constraints many people face in reducing their resource consumption. Dourish [8] points out that the tendency for most environmental HCI work to focus on individual behaviour change reflects the market logic of individual rational actors, and draws attention to the blind spots of this logic, while Brynjarsdóttir et al [6] generalise this argument to link to modernism and its limitations.

Partly inspired by these social, political and cultural critiques, we endeavored to apply a ludic design approach to disrupt the unitary logic of demand reduction technologies. We noted that the uncompromising narrative of ethical sacrifice becomes aversive to people tired of blame and guilt, reifies assumptions about the 'people' and 'the environment' [8], and obscures questions of authority over the discourse they embody [5]. Instead, we sought to create artefacts that complicate simple narratives of responsibility and disrupt a dogmatic logic of self-sacrifice. We wished to encourage people to explore questions about their relationship with the environment but without imposing a pre-established sense of what the right and wrong answers are.

Opening Up Ludic Design

Along with our objective of opening new perspectives on environmental HCI, we also wanted to develop ludic design as a practice. We hoped that applying resources such as *ambiguity* and *interpretation* [14] to the critical and complicated issues of the environment would demonstrate that the playful approach of ludic design does not imply frivolity, but instead that exploration, surprise, improvisation and wonder can be useful tools in approaching complex and serious issues.

In addition, we set out to explore *sensor legibility* [15] as a resource for meaning making. In a previous sensor related project for the home, we had erred on the side of sensors being too opaque, and output thus seeming obvious or wrong [15]. We saw this as an instance of the more general challenge of finding a sweet spot between banality and incomprehensibility. Provocation requires a level of defamiliarization, but this fails if devices are either too familiar, or too alien. In this project, we hoped that making the operation of sensors locally apparent would support people in approaching an unusual system.

Another goal for this project was to test our perception that ludic designs afford multiple perspectives. Whereas in the past, we have sought multiple interpretations of one or a few deployments, for this project we wanted to support multiple views about multiple deployments. In recent environmental HCI work around participatory sensing, citizen science and crowd sourcing [e.g. 10, 11, 21, 22, 25, 28], large numbers of people are drawn into the research and design agenda. Our intention is of a similar spirit, although not toward galvanizing a majority of opinion and behaviour but toward allowing the diversity and richness of multiple views to emerge. Therefore, we proposed to both *batch produce* multiple devices, on the scale of 10-100 devices, and *batch deploy* them to multiple settings, in this case a target of 20 households.

Ludic Design for Environmental HCI

With this dual focus on advancing ludic design and opening environmental HCI, we began our design process. Space precludes a full account (some details may be found

in [4] and [19]) but we highlight some of the ways that our overall objectives informed our eventual design.

Our design process involved many months of delving into the kinds of critical literature described above as well as familiarizing ourselves with a range of environmental issues and responses, from governmental initiatives to grassroots efforts. We conducted two novel Probe studies with several households to understand narrative accounts of energy in the home. Parallel to all these investigations we considered over a hundred historical and contemporary art projects regarding the environment. This survey allowed us to compare art projects that used an aesthetic approach to resource demand monitoring, such as the Power Aware Cord [18] and the Wattson meter (www.diykyoto.com), and projects that used an aesthetic approach in a more open-ended or disruptive manner. The Energy Curtain [9], for instance, creates a conflict rather than advocating a course of action: its owners must choose between closing it on a sunny day so its solar cells can collect energy, or leaving it open to enjoy the natural light.

We were also inspired by contemporary artworks that explore appreciation of environmental aesthetics more directly. For example, Felix Hess makes the swirls and eddies of local drafts visible with arrays of small weathervanes mounted on floors or ceilings [18]. Ackroyd & Harvey covered one of the National Theatre's buildings with grass, suggesting (ackroydandharvey.com/flytower/) that as it faded "it [would] be hard not to think about global warming". Tim Knowles (www.timknowles.co.uk) attaches pencils to the tips of tree branches to produce drawings influenced by the weather. In these works, the sensors – i.e. the weathervanes, the grass, and the tree branches – simultaneously act as the output displays, offering the kind of legibility we wanted to achieve.

Reflecting on these examples, we gravitated toward seeing the home as an instance of 'the environment', imagining that just as someone might reflect upon the rhythms of a natural (and large-scale) landscape like the Grand Canyon, so too might it be possible to reflect on the climactic patterns of one's domestic space, where the noticeable blurs into the unnoticeable and both aesthetic and instrumental appreciation may be evoked. Similar to Hess's weathervanes, we wanted our systems to be small but noticeable, legible but depicting patterns easily ignored or unavailable, batch produced yet still beautiful and curious to behold. We wanted them to intervene in the home climate while becoming part of it. Thus we set about exploring ways that we might build devices that expose *the microclimate of the home* as a topic relevant equally for environmental concern (are there draughts? should we turn down the heating?) and as a domain of aesthetic appreciation (isn't the ambient light beautiful? where are the home's tropical regions?).

THE INDOOR WEATHER STATIONS

Space constraints preclude a detailed account of the process that led from our basic design concept to the realised designs. The process featured innumerable discussions and meetings, the production of six substantial design workbooks [13], sensor tests in the project team's homes, a publicly deployed design experiment, material and electronics tests, and the invention of new processes and tools including a custom fitting that is currently being patented. The result, finally, was three distinct devices collectively referred to as the Indoor Weather Stations: Wind Tunnel, Temperature Tape, and Light Collector.

Wind Tunnel

The Wind Tunnel makes salient the almost imperceptible wind currents of the home. The device consists of a stylized 'forest', made of paper film cut into delicate shapes, enclosed by a transparent, semi-cylindrical canopy. The forest is built on a base, containing electronics to be described later, that allows the device to rest on any flat surface. From one end of the base a tall 'chimney' projects upwards. At its top a wind-sensor, protected by a slotted orange housing, measures tiny gusts of air near the device. This controls a small fan inside the forest's enclosure, which amplifies the gusts to create miniature storms that visibly buffet the 'trees'.

The Wind Tunnel shares two interactional features with all the Weather Stations. On one end (visible in Figure 1) is the *last day* button. When pressed, this reads back through the last 24 hours of logged sensor data, recreating the storms over about two minutes. This allows people to see what the device has been doing in their absence, or overnight. On the other side of the device, under the chimney, the *lull* button stops the output of the device (in this case, the fan), while allowing it to continue collecting data. This is to allow people to stop activities that may be disturbing, e.g. when sleeping. The lull button pauses output for 8 hours, after which it automatically resumes.

Temperature Tape

The Temperature Tape gives people a sense of temperature gradients within the home. Two lengths of 2.5 metre long

fabric ribbon can be wound around or extended from the circular body of the device. The ribbons contain cables that connect to temperature sensors embedded in a plastic hook on one end, and eye on the other. The difference in readings between these sensors is shown by a needle dial on the main body of the device; the needle swings towards the warmer side, with a gauge indicating the relative difference in temperatures. The total span of 5 metres is long enough to allow temperature differences to be measured from floor to ceiling, along stairwells, or between different rooms. In addition, each ribbon is screenprinted with stripes of layered thermochromic ink, arranged so that they fade from yellow to orange to red to black between about 15° - 25° C, to make visible temperature variations along the ribbons' length. Like the Windtunnel, the Tape has both last day and lull buttons.

The Light Collector

The Light Collector shows a history of the changing ambient light colour in the home. The device consists of a small bottle-like main body with a cup shaped 'funnel' on its top. The funnel, which is lined with copper leaf, resembles a radio telescope or radar dish. Inside the base of the funnel is a light sensor. Every five minutes, the device recreates the colour represented by the sensor data as a 1-pixel wide coloured strip at the top of the display; earlier readings are scrolled down. In this way, the device shows a sedimented view of the last two hours of ambient light with oldest readings at the bottom, and most recent ones at the top. As with both other devices, the Light Collector has both lull and last day buttons; the latter, when pressed, causes the display to scroll upwards, revealing readings previously 'hidden' by the bottom of the screen.

Technical and Constructional Features

The three Weather Stations are clearly distinct devices, but they share a number of features that unite them as a family and which made their construction easier. Functionally, they all highlight potentially overlooked aspects of the

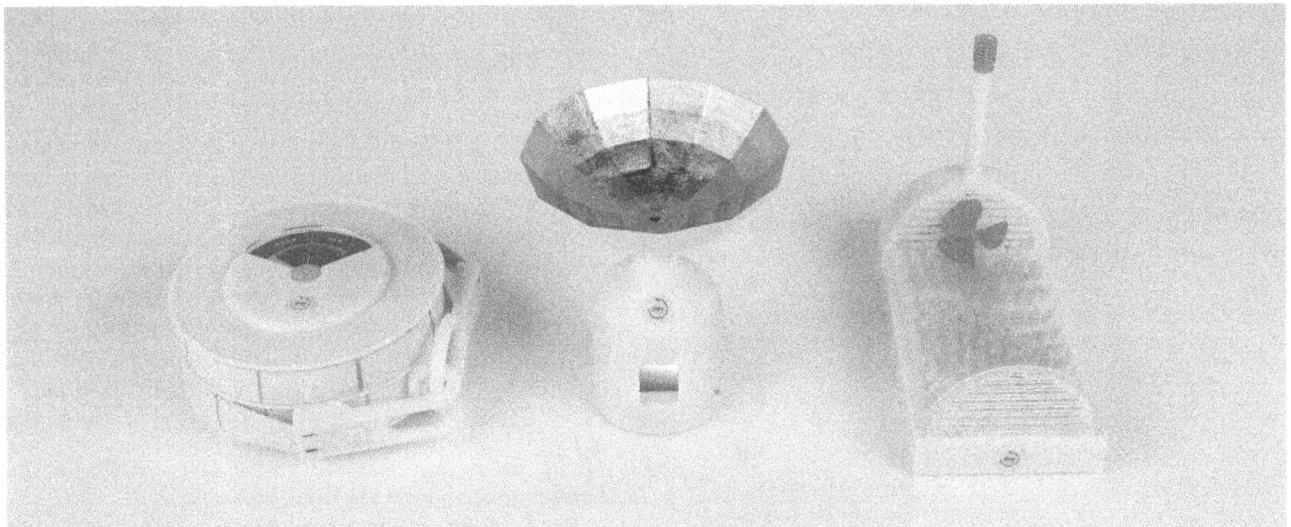

Figure 1. The Indoor Weather Stations: Temperature Tape (left), Light Collector (centre) and Wind Tunnel (right)ç
© Interaction Research Studio

home environment by displaying the outputs of sensor readings taken by the device. They also exhibit sensor legibility, in that they all make clear locally what sensors are reading, an alternative to the common ubiquitous computing tactic of treating sensors as black boxes returning data to remote applications, and one which we thought might mitigate the suspicion and feelings of intrusion which such systems have given rise to in the past.

Several constructional features link the devices as well. The casings, produced using our object printer, were largely left in a relatively unfinished state. Each device includes at least one feature, however – the copper-leafed funnel, the silkscreened ribbon cable, the lasercut 'forest' – that is notably detailed, to indicate the purposefulness of the overall aesthetic.

Each of the devices is built using the Gadgeteer platform ([29]; see also http://research.microsoft.com/en-us/projects/gadgeteer/), a spin-off of Microsoft research that allows rapid prototyping of embedded devices with a range of electronics modules. The modular nature of the hardware accelerated the initial process of experimenting with sensors, actuators and related electronics. Gadgeteer significantly simplified the development of the pieces by providing a development environment (Visual Studio) which allows on-device-debugging as well as writing the embedded software using an object-oriented programming language (C#). A common library could be developed to generically process sensor data, map sensor data to displays, to log data to SD cards, handle the lull and last day functions, and – in a second generation of the devices – to provide wifi and internet connectivity, enabling us to transmit and store the collected sensor data on a database hosted on a central server. This allowed us to access all the devices' real-time and historic data through a web interface. We also had the devices working with rechargeable batteries, but opted for deploying with wired power due to usability and reliability issues

Despite the economy of scale represented by the devices' shared features, there were significant elements of the designs that had to be handled as a matter of repeated craft making rather than batch production. For instance, each of the Light Collectors' funnels was copper leafed by hand. The Temperature Tape's ribbons were produced by screen-printing 10-metre long swathes of cloth, which were then sliced, machine-folded and sewn around ribbon cable. The Wind Tunnel's forest was produced from separate layers of laser-cut paper film, hand laminated between layers of plastic to achieve a topographical effect. These details were arguably crucial to the aesthetics of the pieces, but quite time-consuming to produce.

Batch Production and Deployment

We produced over 60 of the prototype Weatherstations, so that we could batch deploy a complete set of three to each of our 20 volunteer households. One of the reasons that trials of multiple copies of highly finished prototype devices are rare is that they are difficult to achieve. Apart

from SenseCam [23] most of the studies we have reviewed use off-the-shelf hardware with occasional augmentation, whereas our approach involves producing highly finished bespoke computational devices. Batch producing and deploying such devices raised many challenges. In order to achieve the research reported here we built workshop facilities including a Dimension Elite object printer, a laser-cutter, and reflow soldering oven, as well as a team with competencies in CAD software, circuit board design and fabrication, software development for embedded and cloud-based systems, product making, and considerable ingenuity. Despite this, producing the 60+ devices we report here took months even after they were specified: the work to achieve a batch deployment of this kind should not be underestimated.

THE WEATHER STATIONS IN ACTION

To make it possible for us to easily interact with participants and to investigate a sense of community, we recruited local participants via community blogs, coffee shops, and posters in a local park. We revealed that the project concerned questions of community, environment, and design. Our participants were a fairly diverse group in terms of age, backgrounds and occupation (an engineer on the London Underground, a couple working in IT systems, a linguistics analyist, an architect, an urban planner, two journalists, a social science researcher, two teaching artists, a designer, a design student, etc).

Twenty households participated, with many of the homes having more than one person using the stations. Most of the homes had had a representative at an 'orientation session' early in the project, during which they received an overview of the project and a research kit, based on the Cultural Probes [12] approach, to encourage thinking about the home in new ways and also to expose them to kinds of reflective activities that characterize the studio's work. When it came time to deploy the Weatherstations, we chose three distinct settings – their homes (7 participants), our studio (9 Ps) and a local coffeeshop (4 Ps) both for pragmatic reasons (it was impractical to hand them all over separately, but difficult to find times to meet groups of participants together) and to explore strategies for larger deployments in the future. During each handover, we reviewed the project again and introduced the stations. Various levels of interaction followed with the participants including home visits, email/telephone exchanges, and 'prompts' sent via newsletter, website or postal mail. These prompts included things such as 'significant moment forms', photo assignments, weather calendar posters showing their stations' data for a month, and community-wide maps of data collected from the stations. At the time of writing, the Weather Stations have been deployed for over 9 months. The following sections summarise some of our main findings from these deployments.

Accommodating the Weather Stations

Without exception, participants unpacked their stations with a mix of intrigue and excitement, immediately handling the forms and experimenting with forced reactions from the devices. Nick stroked the WT referring to it as a pet. Tim commented about the LC: *"It's like a goblet, a chalice. I love things that are new and haven't quite settled down yet into what they are going to be"*. This mix of attraction and anticipation soon gave way to the task of fitting the Weather Stations into the home.

Finding a place for the Weather Stations raised a number of practical issues: obvious ones such as access to power or a flat surface to rest upon or avoiding awkwardly trailing cabling, and more complicated factors such as what different rooms might reveal or what having a weather station in a certain spot might tell visitors. Several participants described moving the stations around, partly through our encouragement, but partly to find where the stations were "happy". Sumit described how each station took on a different persona for him and this dictated their placement. The LC became a houseplant and was therefore placed amongst other carefully selected pieces in their guest room. The WT felt more like a companion device, and found its way to the dresser in his bedroom. He explained that the Weather Stations: *"have found their place...they gravitated to where they would fit. Now we don't look at them and think 'oh that looks weird' or 'that's taking up space there'."*

Some participants took the approach of deploying the stations to investigate phenomena they suspected existed in their homes, for example putting the WT to work detecting draughts in certain rooms or using the TT to determine if the baby's room really is colder than the neighboring room. Other participants hoped the stations might tell them something new. Rosie wondered, for example, if the stations would reveal some hidden secrets such as whether there were different currents at night while everyone slept.

Working with the Weather Stations
We anticipated that people would work with the Weather Stations to actively investigate the ecology of their home and make comparisons between different locations using the devices. However, after initial enthusiasm, the range of experimentation took on a slower pace than with other systems from our studio. Indeed, as the excitement of discovery wore off, participants sometimes expressed disappointment, perhaps through comparisons with other sensor technology they were familiar with. Pete, for example, felt the stations didn't hold up to the range of real time apps available for measuring *"movement, exercise, sound levels, and anything else you can think of."* Catherine contrasted the stations with her solar panel display's immediate, readable feedback about power generated. *"These,"* she said, referring to the Weather Stations, *"are a bit more secretive about their story."*

Working with the Weather Stations created some dilemmas of readability and expectation. On the one hand, they did not do enough. *"Basically, it's not telling me much I don't already know just being in my house,"* Nick told us. Catherine suspected that her dog was active during the night and, when entering the kitchen, would switch the

Figure 2. A Light Collector in situ.
© Interaction Research Studio

movement-detecting lights on. This she was able to confirm by noting a series of brighter bands on the LC display. However, this was just a minor intrigue, confirming something she already suspected.

On the other hand, what the stations did divulge didn't always match expectations. Meena noted that her family had a major water leak that seemingly went undetected by the stations. Yet, other events took on too much significance without any discernable reason. In trying to make sense of her monthly weather calendar Meena said: *"It looks like we've been very belligerent. We'd like to know what we've done!"*

While the stations only marginally aroused the kind of investigative curiosity of the microclimate of the home we had expected, we found participants using them to make sense of their homes in other ways – particularly when they could see their own data over more extended time periods than the device's replay buttons allowed. While Meena and Tim were unable to decipher specific events on the calendar of LC readings (*"what caused this spike here?"*), the conversation became more animated when referring to the overall patterns she and her partner perceived. Meena joked that her house looked like a *"sludgy cave"*, making her want to turn on more lights – an urge quite contrary to the energy saving motives assumed by many of the participants and an amusing irony Meena was aware of.

This mixed experience of working with the Weather Stations also arose during a field visit with Sumit. After using the stations for several months, Sumit greeted us at his door with the declaration: *"I'm afraid you will find this a negative result."* Yet the conversation quickly proceeded through interesting and desired uses of the Weather Stations. In terms of clear readability and interpretability, Sumit felt the Weather Stations missed the mark, yet he quickly questioned himself as to whether these matters were actually required. *"We have rabbits,"* he reflected, *"and they don't do anything particularly readable either.*

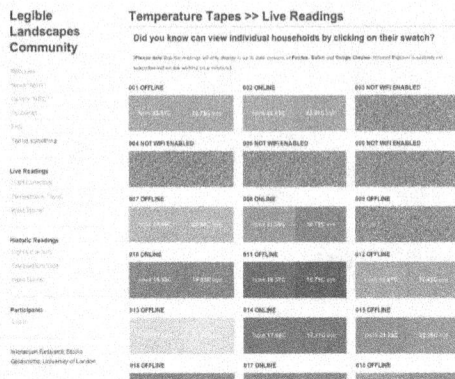

Figure 3. Shared and historical data is available on the web.
© Interaction Research Studio

In fact, it's just this enigmatic behavior that makes them interesting". These furry creatures, Sumit went on to say favorably, *"add a little chaos to an otherwise normal life."*

Engaging with Others

Once we began to realise that participants were not engaging with the Weather Stations in quite the manner we expected, we introduced further resources to offer a richer context in which their data might be interpreted. We had observed that the Weather Stations often acted as talking points for participants in their homes. Families and partners collectively worked with the stations, for example, and the stations were often placed conspicuously to invite visitor questions. That is, the stations and their behaviours were social interactional affairs. It seemed natural, especially considering our batch deployment strategy, to build on this and enable people, through a shared website, to view the data of others. For example, Figure 3 is a screenshot of the live data from all the TTs at a single moment. The site also shows historical data for all the (anonymised) households.

Expanding the project in this way helped people find a new context of interpretation for their own data. Tim explained that awareness of the community made you look at your own stations differently. This led us to further enhance the website as a forum for commenting on each others' data, posting pictures and general project news. While Catherine joked that *"comparative data between households would be like moving back to the 'village' where everyone knows what you are up to: 'what were you doing up at 3 am'"*, in practice, people tended to respond to the community in the same way as the stations, more in terms of appreciating perceptible patterns of aesthetic interest than engaging in more analytic reasoning about their own or other's data or behaviour. For example, Meena's "sludgy cave" remark became particularly salient when she compared her home with the brighter colour palettes detected by other LCs.

One of the most popular views on the website constructed a map of wind readings across households and labeled these as 'gusty', 'light breeze', or 'gale force'. Brett found this map intriguing because he had assumed, yet was mistaken, that his WT would register the windiest given its placement near a window open to heavy breezes across the Thames.

"People must be using hairdryers!" he joked. Others indicated an affinity for this map because it was one of the first views of the data in a geographical context, potentially allowing one to see the wind or the light move across a larger landscape. Both Tim and Meena also noted a more subtle aspect of this map – not only did they see relations between their own home and neighboring ones, but the map effectively drew a boundary around the community they were participating in.

While we were fostering some kind of 'community awareness', what stood out, however, was how people did not propose any kind of community action site to support such affairs as monitoring and reducing consumption. Instead, people used the website for a subtle awareness of differences between homes. Sumit referred to it as an interaction of *"machine ecologies"*, seeing how devices had different experiences in varied settings.

Appreciating the Weather Stations

All participants have been living with the Weather Stations for a period of several months and this has allowed us to see a trajectory of technology adoption and appreciation transpire. After initial excitement, participants settled into troubleshooting and experimenting that eventually gave way to a feeling of disappointment. In an early field visit Meena said, *"you have to get to know these things, you have to play with them"* but at a later field visit she commented, *"it was more interesting early on and then our interest waned...It felt like [they] didn't need us. Just our electricity."* As participants continued to live with the devices, however, we saw a new phase of the trajectory as the stations settled into the home becoming, as more than one participant expressed it, *"part of the furniture"*. Brett, for example, commented that the WT's constant whirring had changed from irritating to soothing, something he noticed now only in its absence.

A big part of the settling into a new appreciation revolved around participants using the stations, most particularly the LC, as an indicator of seasonal changes. The value then was not from a point in time but over time. Sumit recognized that in this regard the stations would appeal more to his wife's sensibilities as a gardener: *"She knows where the light hits the lawn. She thinks more in terms of long time scales...a 10 year plan for the garden or what will flower in 3 months"*. Several participants noted being able to see the days getting longer based on their LC readings. Tim and Meena proposed using the TT to catch varying lengths of sunbeams through their windows. Tim commented: *"If you could record how light comes in and out of your house for a year...who wouldn't be interested in that? It would be seeing time in a different way. I've done that with painting where you feel like you are doing something different [with each iteration] but you aren't. It's like a spiral - you keep coming around."* Catherine noted that the sun's trajectory had become aligned with a stained glass window in her home in just such a way as to send coloured light patches slowly moving across the floor of her hallway. She deployed the LC to record this.

When used over time to explore the quality of light, or currents, or (to a lesser extent) temperature, the Weather Stations came to have new interest and suggested other ways to experiment. Catherine, for instance, decided to take her LC with her on holiday as a means of exploring the quality of light closer to the equator compared to her home. The stations ultimately did not surprise people, a condition that led to initial disappointment, but for some a more subtle surprise, or at least awareness, built up over time.

Tim described this slow creep of surprise when he related how he had made an oil portrait of the LC. In painting the LC, Tim described having to study it, seeing things that might have been unnoticed and to think about it for an extended period. He likened the process as similar to what any painter does, and how the act of painting transforms the object. The painting of the LC and the LC itself went up on display together in the front window he uses as an exhibition space. After its time there, the painting moved to a corner in the home where it sat along with other pairings of a portrait and its artifact. What was interesting here is not that Tim painted the LC. What was interesting was how he rendered it in a similar fashion to the many other curious objects in his home. Through this concentrated appreciation, the LC faded, favorably, into the background.

Relating to the Design Process

It became clear that many aspects of our participants' experience with the Weather Stations are related to their understanding of our design process and our involvement of them in it. In our recruiting material, we described the project as about "developing an awareness of the home's microclimate without directly addressing issues of energy usage or carbon footprint". People told us that they were drawn to participate based on interests in the environment, technology and design, in some combination. At the orientation event, participants were exposed to the studio's way of working and to the project in general. Participants seemed to take immediately to the idea of thinking about the home as an environment and expressing these ideas through the prompts we provided, for example writing notes to appliances, telling secrets about the home, mapping smells, or placing colorful cutouts of animals and robots in 'habitats' around their home. Some participants became more expressive than others through these exercises, but most seemed quite comfortable with exploring their home in a different way.

Our participants were, then, primed to think about the home as a curious place and readily adopted the research agenda. Sumit described himself as *"one of life's participants"*, explaining that he was constantly trying out new things. All of our participants displayed a kind of commitment to the curious as well as a commitment to the process of discovery. Several times we had participants tell us that they had not interacted with the stations as much as they wanted to, yet they continued to keep their stations operating in order to log their data if nothing else. Meena talked about how they had developed an *"allegiance to the*

systems" and despite the stations not being as interactive as she would like she continued to want to work with them. Tim took a long view of the project and could imagine meeting people in a few years time who had later versions of the systems and they'd compare notes.

Several of our participants had orientations towards technology which are redolent of concerns that the studio itself has expressed. For example, there is a sense in which 'the ludic' was a topical concern for participants, not just for ourselves. We had several stories of trying to blow the WT's trees down, making a competitive game out of raising the temperature of the hook versus the eye on the TT, or alternatively flooding and depriving the LC of light. Other participants indicated playfulness through more reflective activities. Elvira commented: *"it feels like we have a ghost in the house, made visible through those weather gadgets"* and John wondered if *"perhaps the Weather Stations were listening to me."* Hing likened the entire project to an exercise in responding to *"intruders in the home"*, a sentiment similar to the one expressed by Brett when he explained the Weather Stations as *"not really for anything...but just about what people do with them."* While we have seen Meena unhappy with the readability of the Weather Stations, she also advocated a bit of uncertainty. *"We like rules but with a bit of a wild card."*

Our participants were not innocent to the world of design, nor of the studio's work, nor did they hold back from reading design intent into the Weather Stations or offering alternative design ideas or orientations to us. We have remarked that, perhaps surprisingly given the discontents expressed over the interpretability of the data from the stations and certain forms of experimentation that were soon abandoned, people persisted with the Weather Stations, at length finding interesting behaviours in them or in comparisons made between their data and other's. We suggest that this persistence, and the favourable backgrounding of the devices that is part of it, was nurtured by participants having a sustained relationship to our design process, its topics and concerns. As Tim provocatively yet appreciatively put it, *"we have become part of a crazy club with no meaning"*.

DISCUSSION

As with most investigations that pursue research through design, our work on the Weather Stations has given rise to an abundance of issues, advances, lessons and speculative conclusions over its course. These range from new perspectives on issues of the environment, to the design of a patentable swivel joint, to new tactics for arranging and maintaining batch deployments, to an appreciation of the difficulties in mapping light sensor data to appropriate colours on an LCD screen. We have touched on some of these outcomes elsewhere [19]; here we focus on participants' experiences of the Weather Stations, and reflect on their implications for environmental HCI and design for ludic engagement.

(Not) Living Up to Orienting Narratives

As described earlier, after an initial period of interest and enthusiasm most of our participants expressed disappointment in the Weather Stations. Nonetheless, for many a lingering affection for the devices persisted. To navigate our way through these somewhat paradoxical results, it is useful to recall that our intention was to disrupt or complicate simple narratives of the environmental. As it turned out, the designs complicated other narratives too.

We had explicitly warned that our designs would not directly attempt to improve environmental impacts (e.g. by promoting demand reduction) throughout our meetings with participants and particularly during deployments. Nevertheless, an *environmental narrative* implying that the devices might offer some benefit with respect to concerns about ecological issues still oriented people's criteria for the success or failure of the Weather Stations. It seemed that raising environmental issues as a context for our designs, even negatively, brought into play a host of assumptions about how designs might properly be expected to address such issues. Thus many of our participants oriented to the devices' potential utility as, e.g., draft detectors or indicators of energy waste due to excess lighting or heating. Not surprisingly, most found them wanting in this regard.

A second narrative also turned out to orient our participants' senses of the success or failure of the Weather Stations. This *ludic narrative* was implied by our previous design work, several examples of which were described to participants in orientation and deployment events and on the project website. Seeing our portfolio seemed to lead our participants to anticipate that the devices built for this project would be similar, e.g. in pacing, in giving access to large amounts of content, and in their interactional possibilities. However, the Weather Stations were slower-paced, simpler, and less interactive than previous designs, only engaging people for short periods of time rather than for extended sessions. While we observed people playfully engaging with the Weather Stations, these activities were not sustained in the long term, leading to a sense of disappointment about the devices.

As the deployment continued, we began to feel that the Weather Stations were failing both in terms of participants' activities with the devices and their conceptual appreciation of them. This pessimistic view was undermined, however, as we became aware that many of our participants were expressing an abiding fondness for at least some of the devices. Moreover, even though it was not uncommon for participants to tell us that they no longer engaged with the devices after a month or two, they were still adamant that they did not want to return them, but preferred for the devices to stay in their homes. They had become part of the home's 'background' and in a desirable way.

The Value of Batch Prototyping

It is doubtful that we would have discovered the modest successes of the Weather Stations, had it not been for our approach of running a relatively large-scale field trial based on the batch production of prototypes. Had we deployed prototype Weather Stations to only a single household, as we have done with previous prototypes, it seems likely we would have attended more to comments about their failure than to any evidence of lingering affection. If this is true, then not only did our multiple deployments allow us to see the range of aesthetic, utilitarian and environmental orientations taken by our participants, but to discern a form of engagement marked by its understatedness and intermittence. It was only because so many of our participants told us of their persisting – if weak – attachment to devices that otherwise seemed unsatisfactory that we took this quotidian relationship seriously.

From this perspective, it may seem that we have rediscovered the ability for large-n studies to reveal patterns in data that would be lost in the noise of smaller ones. There is undoubtedly truth in this, but we do not believe it is incompatible with our interest in varied orientations. If batch deployments allow us to aggregate data to uncover subtle trends, equally, they allow us to uncover multiple, potentially incompatible forms of engagement as well. This capability is important in assessing batch production and deployment as a methodology for research through design. This project marks the first time that we have batch produced highly finished, fully functioning computational devices for field trials with multiple participants. As we have described, this was a costly process, both in terms of money and time. Our results, which illustrate the potential for batch production and deployment to allow both more nuanced and more varied forms of interaction to become evident, lead us to believe the approach a valuable one. In particular, it allowed us to appreciate the subtle but abiding attachment many of our participants formed to the Weather Stations.

Lingering Affection

In our interactions with participants, there appeared to be several sets of reasons for people's continued attachment to the Weather Stations. First, even though the devices were unsatisfactory with respect to the environmental or ludic narratives, it was possible to appreciate them as distinct devices with their own coherent identities. For some this was a matter of aesthetic appreciation, as indicated for instance by Tim's remarks about his painting of the Light Collector. But there were indications of more personal, affective relationships with the devices as well. Several of our participants referred to the intriguing presence the Weather Stations had in the home, as for instance, when Elvira suggested they manifested a *"a ghost in the house"*, or Sumit compared them to his enigmatic rabbits. The devices seemed to become active agents within the home, albeit in understated and easily overlooked ways.

A second source of the fondness we observed for the Weather Stations seemed to involve the way they portray the home as a self-contained ecosystem characterised by seasonal changes. For instance, Sumit described a 'eureka' moment in which thinking about the Weather Stations impelled him to perceive the home as an ecology and not a hermetically sealed box. Several participants remarked the changes of daylight revealed by the website's historical Light Collector data. Moreover, participants seemed to enjoy the way the devices inspired them to imagine new ways to work this design space. Over the course of deployment, we heard numerous suggestions for changes and redesigns. For instance, Brigitte postulated greater engagement if *'the data was translated into something entertaining. Like playing a tune or something. We have a friend who made a symphony from the rise and ebb of the Thames…'* Both directly and through implication, the Weather Stations succeeded in occasioning appreciation of the changing microclimate of the home.

Finally, a third reason participants seemed to find lasting appeal in the Weather Stations had to do with the way the devices tied them to a community of participants and incorporated them into the work of our studio. This became particularly clear when other participants' real-time and historical data were made available online. Many displayed great interest in comparing their own readings with others. In addition, they expressed fascination with seeing that others were also engaged with the devices, with speculating about other peoples' activities and orientations, and with the idea of having joined a larger group of people serving as informants for the design processes of our studio.

Sporadic Engagement

If people retained engagement with the Weather Stations, though, this was of a different character than we've seen in previous deployments. In other work we have discussed how a 'trajectory of appreciation' for a given device can be discerned over the course of long-term field trials, as people's appreciation for and engagement with our prototypes waxes and wanes over time. For instance, in the first days of a deployment an initial excitement at receiving a new device often gives way to disappointment as its limitations become known. In our successful deployments, this downturn is followed by some recovery of enthusiasm and a leveling off of engagement at a moderate level. In unsuccessful deployments, the downturn is not reversed, or not for long, and over time engagement declines more or less completely [15]. This has led us to believe that sustained engagement with our devices is a clear, if somewhat minimal, criterion for their success.

Results of the current deployment require that we take a more nuanced view of potentially successful trajectories of appreciation, on the one hand, and what counts as engagement, on the other. What seems to have emerged for many of our participants are trajectories in which the initial downturn of enthusiasm is not clearly reversed, but engagement never completely dies away, either. Instead, while many of our participants have said things along the lines of 'I never really notice them any more', it becomes clear that they do notice them, periodically, and they do value them, occasionally – and that the occasional pleasure this brings makes the Weather Stations a valued part of the home's furnishings, much as memorabilia, knick-knacks,

artworks and televisions may be ignored for long stretches of time, yet find their value in occasional moments of utility or appreciation.

Moreover, we have seen signs that participants' appreciation of the Weather Stations has evolved with time, as they have seen the devices respond to the changing seasons, and visited the historical data made available on the website. The evolution of appreciation is both intermittent and slow [c.f. 24], but not just because the devices take time to understand and reflect upon, but because their subject, the environment within and around the home, itself evolves slowly.

Enriching Environmental and Ludic HCI

Taking a ludic approach to environmental HCI ultimately leads both to new insights and questions. Participants readily adopted the spirit of using the Weather Stations for open-ended engagement and reflection, even while expressing dissatisfaction with how far the stations went in this regard. We had glimpses of participants using the stations to reflect on the home as 'not hermetically sealed', as a system influenced by seasons, and as a space where their movements and presence contributed to the collected changes – and we also had playful reflections on ghosts, secrets and night-time creatures. Although this speaks to the potential for intertwining environmental and ludic HCI, at least some of us feel, like our participants, that the stations are somewhat lacking. In moving forward, we are considering ways to address the participants' desire for more surprises, reflecting on both the sources and presentation of information. We are also exploring the critical role of framing, as discussed earlier.

With regards to sensor legibility, participants demonstrated an ease with the stations that we attribute to the tight correlation between what was sensed and how it was displayed as well as to their aesthetic quality. Even though the website added a layer of readability to the stations, the devices on their own were accessible and clear. Participants did not regard the stations with suspicion and even positioned them in very private areas of the home such as next to the bed or in the bathroom.

The directness of the displayed information, however, may have resulted in the stations being too simple to sustain interest. One speculation is that although each house had three stations, these represented three very discrete and somewhat disconnected points. Although participants moved the stations around, once they had acquired their spot, they tended to stay put offering a very constrained glimpse of the home's microclimate. This meagreness could be addressed in a number of ways, from adding more points of collection (e.g. multiple Light Collectors to depict patterns within a room or throughout the house) to playing off the single point reading more dramatically.

The question of gathering more points of information manifested as well in our approach of batch production and batch deployment. Much of our learning from this foray revolved around the organizational and technical complexity in moving from singular to multiple deployments. Unsurprisingly, the households with whom we conducted multiple field visits provided the most information, yet those we contacted less frequently reminded us of our objective to bring out multiple narratives and interpretations. In conjunction with the observation that the technical maintenance and development of batch produced systems needs to resemble more of a network without requiring a central organizing hub, so too we are working toward supporting this kind of networked reflection and expression. One looming question, then, is how to gather, make sense of and share with our community a richer multiplicity of views.

Finally, drawing participants into our design process through the research kits and the Weather Stations often produced reflections on environmental and ludic HCI that seem to represent a new twist on participatory design. This sense of collaboration became apparent to us through the many conversations with our participants, through the language they used to describe their experiences, and through their sense of loyalty to the project, including their depiction of 'a crazy club' in which they were members. It was not a collaboration in the sense of designing the stations together, nor did we set out with joint research objectives, nor did we 'sell them' on our agenda. The participants came to the project with their own agenda as we did with ours, and shared their interpretations of the experience just as we did ours. This form of participation – in which designed artefacts both elicit values and evoke ideas for new possibilities – is one we will explore further.

ACKNOWLEDGEMENTS

This research was supported by the European Research Council's Advanced Investigator Award no. 226528, 'ThirdWaveHCI'. Thanks to Nicolas Villar and Microsoft Research for additional support. We also thank André Knörig, Alexandra Antonopoulou and Alex Wilkie for their contributions to the project, and especially the participants for their generous involvement.

REFERENCES

1. Abrahamse et al.: A review of intervention studies aimed at household energy conservation. *Journal of Environmental Psychology* 25(3). (2005).

2. Blevis, E. 2007. Sustainable Interaction Design: Invention & Disposal, Renewal and Reuse. *CHI 2007*, 503-12.

3. Bødker, S. 2006. When second wave HCI meets third wave challenges. *NordiCHI 2006*, 1-8.

4. Boucher, A, Cameron, D, and Jarvis, N. (2012). Power to the people: dynamic energy management through communal cooperation. *DIS 2012*, 612-620.

5. Bourdieu, P. & Wacquant, L. (1992) *An Invitation to Reflexive Sociology*, Polity Press, Cambridge.

6. Brynjarsdottir, H., Hakansson, M., Pierce, J., Baumer, E., DiSalvo, C., and Sengers, P. 2012. Sustainably unpersuaded: How persuasion narrows our vision of sustainability. *CHI 2012*, 947-956.

7. DiSalvo, C., Sengers, P., and Brynjarsdóttir, H. 2010. Mapping the landscape of sustainable HCI. *CHI 2010*.

8. Dourish, P. 2010. HCI and environmental sustainability: The politics of design and the design of politics. *DIS 2010*, 1-10.

9. Ernevi, A., Jacobs, M., Mazé, R., Müller, C., Redström, J., and Worbin, Linda W. (2005) Ambience for energy awareness: The energy curtain. *Ambience 2005*.

10. Froehlich, J., Dillahunt, T., Klasnja, P., Mankoff, J., Consolvo, S., Harrison, B., and Landay, J.A. 2009. UbiGreen: investigating a mobile tool for tracking and supporting green transportation habits. *CHI 2009*, 1043-1052.

11. Ganti, R., Pham, N., Ahmadi, H., Nangia, S., Abdelzaher, T. Green GPS: a participatory sensing fuel efficient maps application. 2010. *MobiSys 2010*, 151-164.

12. Gaver, W. 2009. Designing for Homo Ludens, Still. In *(Re)searching the Digital Bauhaus*. Binder, T., Löwgren, J., and Malmborg, L. (eds.). London: Springer, pp. 163-178.

13. Gaver, W. 2011. Making spaces: How design workbooks work. CHI 2011, 1551-1560.

14. Gaver, W., Beaver, J., and Benford, S. (2003). Ambiguity as a resource for design. *CHI 2003*, 233-240.

15. Gaver, W, Bowers, J, Kerridge, T, Boucher, A, and Jarvis, N. (2009). Anatomy of a failure. *CHI 2009*.

16. Gustafsson, A. and Gyllenswärd, M. 2005. The Power Aware Cord. *CHI 2005*, 1423-1426.

17. Harrison, S., Sengers, P., Tatar, D. 2011. Making epistemological trouble: Third-paradigm HCI as a successor science. *Interacting with Computers*, 23 (5), 385-392.

18. Hess, F. 2001. *Light as Air*. Kehrer Verlag Heidelberg.

19. Jarvis, N, Cameron, D, and Boucher, A. (2012). Attention To detail: Annotations of a design process. *NordiCHI 2012*.

20. Kappel, K., and Grechenig, T. 2009. "Show Me": water consumption at a glance to promote water conservation in the shower. *Persuasive '09*, p. 26, ACM.

21. Kim, S., & Paulos, E. 2010. inAir: Sharing indoor air quality measurements and visualizations. *CHI 2010*, 11861-11870.

22. Kim, S., Robson, C., Zimmerman, T., Pierce, J., Haber, E. 2011. Creek Watch: pairing usefulness and usability for successful citizen science, *CHI 2011*, 2125-2134.

23. Nguyen, D., Marcu, G. Hayes, G., Truong, K.N., Scott, J., Langheinrich, M. and Roduner. C. 2009. Encountering SenseCam: personal recording technologies in everyday life. *Ubicomp 2009*, 165-174.

24. Odom, W., Banks, R., Durrant, A., Kirk, D. and Pierce, J. 2012. Slow Technology: critical reflection and future directions. *DIS 2012*, 816-817.

25. Paxon, M. and Benford, S. 2009. Experiences of participatory sensing in the wild. *Ubicomp 2009*, 265-274.

26. Schultz, P. W., Nolan, J. M., Cialdini, R. B., Goldstein, N. J., & Griskevicius, V. (2007). The constructive, destructive, and reconstructive power of social norms, *Psychological Science*, 18(5), 429–434.

27. Shove, E. (2004). *Comfort, cleanliness and convenience: The social organization of normality*. Berg.

28. Strengers, Y. (2011). Designing eco-feedback systems for everyday life. *CHI 2011*, 2135-2144.

29. Villar, N, Scott, Hodges, Hammil and Miller, (2012). .NET Gadgeteer: A Platform for Custom Devices. *Pervasive 2012*.

30. Whitney, M. and Lipford, H.R. 2011. Participatory sensing for community building. *CHI EA 2011*,

31. Woodruff, A., Hasbrouck, J. and Augustin. S. 2008. A bright green perspective on sustainable choices. *CHI 2007*, 313-322.

Reveal-it!: The Impact of a Social Visualization Projection on Public Awareness and Discourse

Nina Valkanova[1], Sergi Jorda[1], Martin Tomitsch[2], Andrew Vande Moere[3]

[1] Music Technology Group, Universitat Pompeu Fabra
firstname.lastname@upf.edu

[2] Design Lab - Faculty of Architecture, Design and Planning, The University of Sydney
martin.tomitsch@sydney.edu.au

[3] Research x Design - Department of Architecture, Urbanism and Planning, KU Leuven
andrew.vandemoere@asro.kuleuven.be

ABSTRACT

Public displays and projections are becoming increasingly available in various informal urban settings. However, their potential impact on informing and engaging citizens on relevant issues has still been largely unexplored. In this paper, we show that visualizations displayed in public settings are able to increase social awareness and discourse by exposing underlying patterns in data that is submitted by citizens. We thus introduce the design and evaluation of *Reveal-it!*, a public, interactive projection that facilitates the comparison of the energy consumptions of individuals and communities. Our in-the-wild deployment in three distinct physical locations provided insights into: 1) how people responded to this form of display in different contexts; 2) how it influenced people's perception and discussion of individual and communal data; and 3) the implications for a public visualization as a tool for increasing awareness and discourse. We conclude by discussing emerging participant behaviors, as well as some challenges involved in facilitating a socially motivated crowd-sourced visualization in the public context.

Author Keywords

public display; urban screen; urban visualization; energy consumption; sustainability; in-the-wild study; awareness, reflection; captology; persuasive computing; evaluation.

ACM Classification Keywords

H.5.2 Information Interfaces and Presentation: Miscellaneous

INTRODUCTION

Electronic displays are becoming increasingly ubiquitous in our urban environment, ranging from community centers, museums to airports. As display technology is developing rapidly, it is likely that this trend will accelerate, so that people will become more accustomed to this type of situated media [19, 41]. With their visual presence and

opportunistic accessibility, such urban displays form promising communication platforms for citizens [9, 14, 23, 41]. While the majority of urban displays serve mainly civic, commercial, artistic or entertainment purposes, only few works present a civic goal: that of increasing the awareness and discourse on socially relevant topics [1, 38].

One topic of growing public concern is environmental sustainability. Several non-governmental organizations are actively trying to raise awareness on this issue by focusing on making relevant data available in the public media. However, although people are becoming increasingly conscious of the ongoing "Climate Crisis", they are rarely aware of how their own activities contribute to greenhouse gas emissions [24, 36]. As a result, the interaction with energy-consuming appliances tends to occur without any conscious consideration of their environmental impact [33]. Recent initiatives address this problem by providing tools for precise quantitative measures of energy or monetary expenditures. Confined in a private context, these tools negate the potential of social comparison [15] and discussion, which might support people in making sense of, and reflecting on, their personal consumption habits. Furthermore, they tend to not gracefully integrate into the physical environment, and do not typically spark occupants' curiosity [47].

We propose that these opportunities could be addressed by exploiting the unique characteristics of social visualization within the context of the urban environment. Social visualization, in its original definition, describes the enriching of social, electronic communication by making its rich and salient qualities visible in easily accessible and understandable ways [12]. Accordingly, social data exploration offers people the chance to increase their understanding of complex information by the power of collective and collaborative efforts [51]. Recent research in this field has indicated that people seem to become encouraged to create public visualizations for participative purposes, even spurring social activities alongside [11, 17]. While most social visualizations have focused on online environments, little is known on whether they can be successfully deployed in other contexts, such as public spaces. Accordingly, we hypothesize that awareness and discourse about citizen-related issues may benefit from the externalization of contextualized data, for instance by means of social viewing and comparison. As a case study, we thus introduce *Reveal-it!*, a life-size, public visualization that consists of a dynamic infographic illustration to facilitate the comparison of individual and community energy consumption data. *Reveal-it!* is specifically designed as a tool for citizens to explore, reflect and debate on socially-relevant issues, such as energy consumption.

RELATED WORK

A comprehensive taxonomy of the design space and requirements for interactive public displays exists [31], as well as several studies of their real-world deployment in a range of informal public or semi-public contexts: from museums [22] and galleries [46], to urban settings [14]. They have been designed to display information of relevance to a specific group of people [18], support opportunistic conversations [25], provide playful information experience [22, 46], or enrich casual interactions of people sharing an environment [29].

Ambient and Eco-Visualization

Like ambient display [39] and related approaches [34, 35, 48], *Reveal-it!* aims to raise the awareness of people by placing dynamic information in the immediate physical surroundings. While ambient displays communicate at-a-glance information in the periphery of human attention, *Reveal-it!* shifts the idea of an aesthetic, public information display from the peripheral to the center of attention, also by using a more explicit way of representing the data.

Based on the ecological issue of energy consumption, our concept relates to "eco-visualization", originally defined as data-driven animations that display ecological information of any sort [24]. Some eco-visualizations aim to motivate the reduction of consumption by showing abstract yet real-time visual representations of appliance consumption [e.g. 7, 37]. Others constitute unusual interfaces to encourage playful and aesthetic engagement and exploration of energy [2], exploring the experiential and reflective potential of the systems [4]. Research in this field [e.g. 7, 26, 37] has focused mainly on optimizing the effectiveness of energy feedback in terms of measurable reduction of household consumption by supporting different stages of motivation [21]. In contrast, we use the concept of eco-visualization to promote public awareness and discussion outside of the domestic context and shared by many.

Urban Data Projections for Sustainability

Several urban displays have already brought debate on sustainability to the forefront by projecting related data into the public sphere. Some have augmented urban spaces with abstract, metaphorical representations of environmental data, such as future sea water levels [50], CO_2 measurements of the surroundings [5] or the energy consumption of a local nuclear plant [32]. Others have playfully allowed passers-by to form statements on climate change [16]. However, the impact of these visualizations has either not been studied, or little influence on public discussion has been shown, beyond the fascination with the interactive features of the installations [16]. Furthermore, unlike this prior work, *Reveal-it!* represents private and community energy consumptions and allows for data comparison on both individual and public level.

DESIGN PROCESS

The general research objective of our work is to explore how the externalization of contextualized data can influence the reflection and discourse of onlookers. To better inform our design goals, we conducted several design activities including an ethnographic pre-study and a workshop.

Ethnographic Pre-study

We commenced our design process with a pre-study, which helped us better understand the relation between citizens and energy-related information from an individual and community perspective, leading to the design requirements for a shared visualization in public space. The pre-study consisted of seven focus group sessions, each with one to three adults with varying backgrounds and professions. In total we talked to 14 participants (six male and eight female) ranging from 22 to 57 years. Each group shared the same household, among which 4 were home-owners. The focus group sessions lasted from 30 to 55 minutes. The questions probed participants' attitudes and knowledge about their own and public resource consumption. The discussions were based upon a short description of our concept and design examples in the form of sketches.

Pre-study Conclusions

The analysis of the focus group data helped us identify the types of information that seem to capture the interest of people, as well as opinions regarding publicizing this data.

The focus group sessions indicated that the public comparison of individual consumption might spark opportunistic engagement and discussions. However, participants were not interested in the personal data of others in an "isolated" manner. Instead, they were interested in comparing values to averages, which could answer questions like "Am I consuming more or less than others?". The discussions revealed how participants assumed there is a "*good*" average or a "*reasonable*" consumption (even in their local context only) that they found crucial and beneficial to compare on various scales: me vs. neighbors, me vs. neighborhood, neighborhood vs. neighborhood, or neighborhood vs. city. The discussions also revealed that people are only aware of the 'monetary value' - what they actually pay - of their household energy consumption, compared to their consumption expressed as *kWh*, for instance. A majority of focus group participants argued about the "*fair*" positioning of personal data within its context. They often mentioned factors like household size, but also geographical aspects such as climate conditions or living in the same neighborhood or city. Eight out of 14 participants mentioned the importance of "*attractive*" or "*more visual*" representations of consumption data. The discussions suggested that people are interested in non-numeric forms and in 80% of the cases participants found it even unnecessary to talk about "data units".

Design Workshop

We conducted an iterative refinement of design constraints and requirements during a collaborative 3-week workshop with data visualization experts [47]. This process was conducted in an extensive dialogue with paper and digital sketches, interactive prototypes and tests in-the-wild.

Based on the design activities and previous work, we set out to build an urban visualization display that would a) provide awareness on individual and communal data but consider privacy; b) promote socially valid comparisons; c) encourage opportunistic and spontaneous conversations; d) be understandable and enjoyable; and e) be accessible and aesthetically-integrated in the physical environment.

THE URBAN VISUALIZATION DISPLAY "REVEAL-IT!"

To structure and maintain an overview of the design goals, we used the Design Space Explorer Framework for Media Façades [10]. This framework allows us to describe *Reveal-it!* with regards to the key aspects of any urban display system, such as its location and situation, material and form, dataset and data input and visualization design (mapping and animations).

Location and Situation

Considering the situational along with the spatial aspects in the design of public visualization is important, as situations determine the shared understanding and social interpretation of cues in the physical environment [20]. Based on the pre-study and previous work [25] we specifically aimed at creating a situation that supports spontaneous and opportunistic conversations. We thus chose to focus on public and semi-public settings that host informal, opportunistic social activities and encourage informal gathering, dwelling and transition, such as spaces in front of local cafés, inner yards or entrance halls of community centers.

Material and Form

Previous work on visualization in shared settings [37, 43, 45] emphasizes on the seamless aesthetic integration of the display in the physical environment. Therefore, we attempted to mimic the visual style of graffiti, by avoiding the visible rectangular frame of traditional data screens. Our visualization was implemented as a life-size (3x3m) projection, which is suitable to a wide range of physical spaces. This type of low-cost and portable display technology was preferred above alternatives such as LC displays or multi-touch interfaces, as these tend to be too fragile or expensive for a typical public setting.

Dataset

Previous work has used public, comparative feedback to reduce energy consumption by triggering feelings of competition, social comparison or social pressure [45]. Based on our pre-study, which indicated the potential benefits of comparing data averages on several levels, we chose to focus on a dataset that combines private electricity consumption data (i.e. from individual households) with more commonly relevant data, such as the neighborhood and city consumption averages.

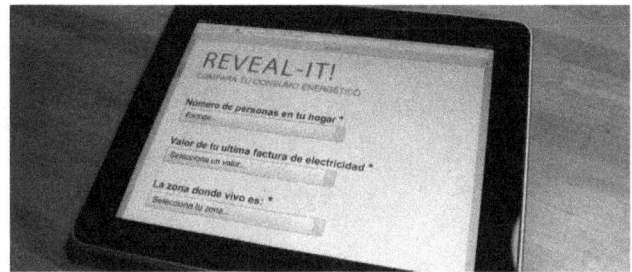

Figure 1. The web-form for private data entry loaded in a table interface.

Private Data Entry

We developed a form of personal, yet public, form of data entry that allows any onlooker to voluntarily input their data into the system. We chose to use a mobile interface, to allow multiple participants to simultaneously interact with our system while still keeping some form of privacy. To this end, we created a web-form, which can be loaded on any tablet or smartphone (Fig. 1). This deliberate act of public data entry is also meant to enhance public engagement, as it provides an opportunistic moment at which participants must dedicate their attention to the topic at hand.

The data entry form requested the participant's monthly energy expense (what she remembers to have paid for her last electricity bill), her neighborhood and the number of co-inhabitants in her household. The participant could also provide her name, however this data entry was not made obligatory. Based on observations from our pre-study, we chose to include a monetary value range instead of electrical usage (kWh). Secondly, we made a list of value ranges available, since people generally do not remember the exact quantitative values. Aiming to address the consideration for fairness, the interface required the input of the number of co-inhabitants. Accordingly, the system normalized the reported electricity bill by the number of co-inhabitants to derive an estimated consumption value per participating household member. While there are admittedly many additional (and difficult to capture) factors that contribute to the real average consumption within a multi-person home, we believe that this estimation proves sufficient to evaluate our research goal.

Visual Mapping

The observations from our pre-study support previous results in literature, which suggest that visually distinct interfaces, visual aesthetics and animation have the potential to promote curiosity and initiate participation [22, 44, 46]. We chose a visualization technique that combines the "seriousness" of the topic with the more accessible style of popular infographics. The visualization consists of an abstract sunburst representation [40], of which each burst (Fig. 2.A) corresponds to the energy bill of an individual household participant. The circular visualization technique allows for scalability and hence an arbitrary number of people to be represented. Upon data entry, the participant's name (if provided) appears in two distinct places: in the center of the sunburst graphic as a textual statement "*X spends Y €!*" and at the end of the corresponding burst, as a

Figure 2. *Reveal-it!*: close-up (left) and two snapshots of the whole visualization interface with 22 (middle) and 56 (right) participants: (A) Burst of a single participant (pink) with her name; (B) Average neighborhood consumption arc (pink); (C) Circle of city-wide consumption statistics; (D)The center as a conversation window with changeable inviting messages.

comparative consumption number: *"Person X: Y €. Neighborhood X: Y €."*. Each neighborhood is represented by a different color, and occupies different parts of the circular shape proportionally to the relative participation rate of the neighborhood.

Animations

The integration of dynamic visual cues can make visualization richer, vivid and more understandable [49]. Accordingly, our visualization shows a dynamically animated arc over each neighborhood portion in order to convey the average consumption of a given neighborhood (Fig. 2.B). The arc representation also allows onlookers to compare neighborhood values to city-wide statistics (Fig. 2.C). This visual feature focuses the attention to one's electricity consumption as a *shared* resource – if an individual consumes more, the average increases and vice versa. In addition, the burst of each new participant visually appears with a smooth animation and bouncing effect, to highlight the recording of fresh data. A new entry is displayed in a white color to unambiguously distinct it from the rest of the graphical representation, which then smoothly takes over the color of its respective neighborhood. To offer an opportunistic "conversational window" between the visualization and the audience, we used the center of the sunburst to occasionally animate inviting messages such as *"Do you know how much you spend?"* or *"N neighborhoods are participating"* (Fig. 2.D).

IN-THE-WILD EVALUATION

We deployed *Reveal-it!* as a public projection at three distinct public locations in two different cities over a total period of 20 days (Fig. 3). The goal of the study was to gain insight into more open-ended questions such as:

- how will onlookers engage with a public visualization of data originating from themselves, in particular in influencing their personal reflections and informal discussions, and

- how well can a social visualization in a public and physical context convey an implicit message (e.g. save energy) that is supported with exact data (e.g. one's energy own consumption).

Location Descriptions

Reveal-it! was first deployed at a public cultural center in the city center of Córdoba, Argentina (location A). The projection was installed for 16 days in a semi-open space within an open-air inner yard of the centers. To expand the diversity of possible overlapping situations [9], *Reveal-it!* was also installed in the entrance lobbies of two community centers (locations B and C) in two different neighborhoods of the city of Barcelona, Spain for one and three consecutive days respectively. The situations *during* deployments varied largely across locations: *Reveal-it!* was installed at location A during an annual festival about arts and technology, and at location B during a local round-table meeting about renewable energies. In contrast, location C hosted various parallel activities at the time of the deployment. In each of the study locations a mobile iPad interface was situated in front of the visualization to facilitate participation. Visitors could dwell around in the spaces, discover and spontaneously approach the visualization. A sign, placed on the wall next to the projection, informed visitors about the study being conducted. Through a contextual inquiry, we identified three distinct types of situational contexts: *daily-basis* activities (e.g. senior social club, daily care for children), *weekly* activities (e.g. workshops, dance classes) and *occasional* special events (e.g. performances, exhibitions or talks on specific topics).

Observations

Two observers watched people for 6 to 8 hours per observation day at location A, and for 3 to 4 hours at locations B and C. Due to ethical constraints, we never recorded video or audio material, but always kept field notes. We observed and listened in to the visitors, capturing their initial behavior towards the projection (e.g. attention and reaction) as well as the visitors' attitudes while interacting with it, discussing among themselves, or contemplating it. To facilitate the process, we devised observational categories that were subsequently refined. In an overall period of 20 days (i.e. 144 observation hours), we took notes of about 442 (out of a total of approximately 558 visitors) unique persons who intentionally approached *Reveal-it!,* alone or in a group.

Figure 3. In-the-wild deployment at location C.

Semi-structured Interviews

The semi-structured interviews typically varied between 7 and 15 minutes and were performed after participants submitted the data entry form in front of the display. Interviews were conducted with individuals or groups, during which we also recorded demographic data, such as age and gender. The interviews included questions regarding the opinions about the *Reveal-it!* in terms of its understandability and experience, as well as its potential usefulness. Visitors were also invited to freely express their suggestions and thoughts in relation to the project. Throughout the 3 study locations, we conducted 18 interviews with 86 visitors overall (47 male and 39 female), who interacted with the visualization and spent at least 2 minutes in front of it. The interviewed people ranged from single individuals or couples to groups of 20 people of approximately 15 to 70 years old.

Participation Logs

At all study locations, we logged the data entries of the visitors who directly interacted with the visualization (N=198) (see subsection *Private Data Entry*). Each participation was digitally time-stamped, allowing us to later map the reported visitors' data to the overall state of the visualization at the moment of participation (Fig. 2).

Questionnaire Test

To quantitatively assess how well the visualization conveyed comparative information, we conducted a post-response questionnaire test with 30 participants in the last deployment day at location C. The questionnaire was integrated in the data entry interface and shown on tablet device. The test followed a simple 2-step procedure:

1. Participation. Participants first entered their personal consumption-related data (like normally). They then observed the visualization and while still standing in front of it, proceeded to the post-response questionnaire.

2. Post-Response. Participants provided a response to the questions "*Compared with my neighbors, my consumption is:*", and "*Compared with my city, my neighborhood's consumption is:*" expressed as a 5-point Likert scale (range: much less - much more).

Data Analysis

We analyzed field notes and visitor opinions using grounded theory to draw bottom-up findings based on the direct quotations and to establish hierarchies and connections among remarkable findings. Apart of descriptive statistics of visitors' participation, we used the logs together with the questionnaire test data to evaluate the comparative understandability of the visualization. We further used this data to triangulate participants' comments and reactions upon participation.

RESULTS

We first uncover factors that influenced participation and discuss patterns and incentives that let visitors explore *Reveal-it!*. We then explain how individual and groups explored the visualization and consider different patterns of interpretation, discussion and comparisons.

Situations

Our study sheds light onto how the actual situational contexts in a public space influence the intrinsic motivation to engage with *Reveal-it!*. The vast majority of visitors at location A and B were interested to actively acquire more knowledge about the installation: approximately 86% at location A (N=344) and all visitors at location B (N=33) intentionally approached the visualization. In contrast, we observed only 52% (N=33) at location C. This result indicates a close connection between the visitors' engagement with the visualization and the degree of situational diversity during the deployment. While the context at locations A and B was a rather constant throughout the study (i.e. an exhibition area and a hosting space for a special talk respectively), location C hosted several co-existing situations: it served as 1) a transit space for people, who were committed to daily tasks, 2) an arriving area for guests of three special events, 3) a recreation area and 4) a waiting area for participants of two weekly workshops. From the overall 52 visitors who directly interacted with *Reveal-it!* at location C, only 8 were daily visitors, 18 were visitors of weekly activities and 26 were visiting a dance spectacle. Previous research discusses that introducing displays into urban spaces transforms the situations specific to these spaces [9]. Accordingly, we analyzed how the interest in *Reveal-it!* unfolded over time versus the variety of situations and visitors.

Temporal Patterns

Weekly Activities. Visitors of weekly activities were more willing to actively engage with the visualization in dwelling periods before and after the activities when they had time to walk around the space, talk and socialize. We measured an average threshold of 8 minutes from the moment when the visitors entered the space until they would intentionally approach the display. In most of the cases (12 out of 18), this occurred upon arriving, when visitors had to wait for their activity to start.

Special Activities. The visualization enticed active interest only *after* the end of the special events people had attended: 48% of the data entries were registered during the last quarter of the daily deployment time. The visitors who approached *Reveal-it!* and entered their data were around

Location	Days	Observed visitors	Visitors intentionally approached	Participation Logs	Interviewed
A	16	400	344	172	67
B	1	33	33	28	5
C*	3	125	65	52	14
Total	20	558	442	198	86

Table 1. Overview of collected data from the three deployments of *Reveal-it!*.
*At location C, we also conducted a questionnaire test with 30 participants

before, and already looked at the visualization when entering. However, they seemed only motivated to closely approach *afterwards*: once the activities were over, visitors would progressively gather in front of the projection, talking and pointing at the visualization.

Generally, our results demonstrate that the use of visualizations in a public setting entails an unfolding *transformation* of the pre-existing situation. In particular, this transformation involves a temporal dimension in that certain 'opportunistic' situations such as idling, dwelling, waiting or gathering [30] are more adequate to engage potential users, in contrast to short-term or goal-oriented situations such as arriving, departing or passing-by.

Evolving Incentives

What were the incentives for these unfolding reactions of people to the public visualization?

Physical Setup and Visual Design. The prominent position and size of the installation were key factors in evoking initial curiosity. All visitors throughout the evaluations *looked* (for more than 2 seconds) at the projection upon entering the space, although some did not approach it. The visual design and the animations further increased people's curiosity. Approximately 86% (N=74) of the interviewed participants (Table 1) mentioned that these features had some persuasive effect on them, e.g. *"I saw the colors, that it [the visualization] is moving."*, *"Cool graphics, I found it intriguing"*. The more dynamic features caused positive, even affective attitudes, such as *"I really liked it, it resembled breathing, which makes you think that it is like something alive."* [V22].

Data-related and Social Factors. The altruistic nature of the data positively influenced people to engage with the visualization, with V16 explaining. *"Of course, it catches the attention visually. [...] But than it gets intriguing, as it is much more different than a boring electricity bill. It is an attractive way to address a serious topic."* Approximately 67% (N=58) of the interviewed visitors described the data visualization as *"intriguing"*, 50% as *"innovative"*, 42% as *"relevant to the community"*. However, 73% (N=145) of the visitors who actually entered their data expressed aloud their doubts about how accurate they could remember their household bill. This might explain why some visitors *did not* directly participate, but observed the display from a distance. Previous studies on public screens have revealed that the implicit expectation to 'perform' in a public context presents a participation barrier [6]. Our observations

indicate that in addition to this "social awkwardness", a public social visualization can suffer from hindrances that relate to the data, such as fear of inaccurate submissions or submitting values that will stand out.

Evolving Reactions. Most of the visitors understood the significance of the visualization only after closer inspection, that is after reading the visualization labels or the information flyers. After a certain time, participants seemed to want to acquire some form of external confirmation of their initial preconception about the goals of the visualization: *"So, this is an ecological project. To promote responsible consumption, right?"* or *"Why do you have this installation, Is it aiming at making people more conscious?"*. People tend to be curious and intrigued first by its prominent visual presence, after which the attention switched to the data that was shown. It was only after further active involvement and reflection that people adopted a more critical perspective towards the visualization and its implications.

Individual Exploration

Approximately 87% (N=172) of the visitors who submitted the data entry form of the visualization (Table 1) reflected on their own consumption behavior afterwards. *Although the installation did not convey any opinion about 'good' or 'bad' energy consumption, the uttered* qualifications varied widely from *"reasonable,"* [V7], *"satisfactory,"* [V12] to *"it could be lower,"* [V6], *"shocking,"* [V4], *"too much for living alone"* [V8]. These interview statements confirm that the comparative features of the visualization provided participants with the opportunity to reflect on their preconceptions about their own energy habits. *"You might think you are fine, because you don't know how the rest is doing. [...] Here [in the visualization] you can see where you stand."* [V20]; *"I thought, that in my house we are big consumers, as we are four and use video consoles, computers, etc. [...] But when I entered the data and saw ourselves in the graphics, actually we are not doing that bad!"* [V14].

Approximately 24% of the interviewed participants (21 out of 86) explicitly claimed that the visualization motivated them to enhance their consumption habits in a positive way. For instance visitor V15 explained: *"I know I use a lot, but now seeing this [the visualization], I would try to do better."*. Often visitors tended to reason on solutions on how to reduce their consumption. *"I see it [his consumption value] is high, and it could be lower. [...] For example, I could disconnect devices such as cell phone chargers, televisions, and others.. they consume minimal but plugged still add to your value."* [V10].

Group and Social Exploration

At all three locations, the participants who explicitly compared their individual consumption to the other bursts in the graphics were mostly part of a group. The relatively private and trusted situational context of a group often empowered people to put (group) pressure on others to participate. For instance, in one of the groups [V16] formed by five elderly women, a participant entered her data, after her friend, and exclaimed happily *"[...] Look, I spend less than you!,"* which directly caused the addressed participant to explain why this might happen *"[...] You live alone, of course you spend less!"*. The women then proceeded to invite a friend of theirs to compare herself as well: *"Come one, come, let me see how much you spend!"*.

The participant names shown in the visualization also seemed to support a playful competition among friends. Participants would often read aloud or comment on those visual sectors that were accompanied with a name-tag. They would cheer up their own name when it appeared in the visualization and would be disappointed when the next participant caused it to disappear. Comments of participants indicate that the infographic visual style combined with this *"social"* [V4] feature seemed to create a more playful situation to engage with this otherwise seemingly boring or impersonal data, with participant V21 saying: *"This graphics and the [participant] names gives a social face to the data, it's not like looking at an impersonal statistics."*

(In)visible Outliers

Visitors explicitly paid attention to 'outliers', patterns in the data that visually stood out within the visualization. For instance, visitors frequently commented on particularly long burst: *"This guy has definitely shot high!"* [V18]. Others reflected on their personal consumption, for instance by comparing it to a low value: *"I thought I am doing fine! [...] But I want to see how this guy is achieving it!"* [pointing at a low burst] [V15]. We observed a similar focus on outliers in the case of neighborhood averages. A vast majority of discussions were concerned with a particularly high neighborhood average, for instance in thinking up its possible causes. People often discussed on the relatively high average consumption of their own neighborhoods, although they never attributed the cause to their own behavior, but instead referred to external factors like construction, infrastructure or city politics: *"[...] Of course, houses here are not so well isolated [...] They cannot be very energy-efficient,"* [V16]; *"Here most of the houses are very old, there is no central heating installed* [V13]; *"[...] There is a lack of general energy awareness, this issue is not really a topic in this neighborhood."* [V14].

We observed that this emergent comparison of neighborhood consumptions triggered critical thoughts, even for neighborhoods which were not even represented in the visualization. For instance, in 11 of the 18 interviews at location A, participants noticed out loud that a certain neighborhood was not included - an economically disadvantaged region with a high unemployment rate and where energy bills are subsidized by the government. These participants argued that people from those regions were the highest consumers of electricity in the city. Their comments were often motivated by preconceived ideas, such as *"they have the whole day the TV on [since they are not working]."* [V2], or *"they steal electricity, so nobody pays."* [V5].

Comparative Understanding

We also analyzed the usability and understandability of the projected sunburst visualization. First, we assessed how people understood comparative information about 1) their own energy consumption and 2) the consumption of their neighborhood, conducting a questionnaire test at location C. As a measure of comparative understanding, we calculated the difference between the reported individual consumption (Fig. 2.A) of the test participant and the current average of her neighborhood's consumption (Fig. 2.B). The neighborhood average in the moment of participation was calculated using the data from the participation logs. A non-parametric Spearman rank test revealed a highly significant correlation between this difference and the post-response of the questionnaire (ρ=0.8142, p<.001). This result demonstrates that participants were able to accurately assess their individual consumption, compared to the average of their neighborhood. In contrast, the Spearman rank test for the difference between participants' neighborhood consumption (Fig. 2.B) and the city average (Fig. 2.C) revealed ρ=0.2215 with p>.01. This suggests that the visualization could not accurately transmit information about participant's neighborhood average, compared to the city-wide statistics. This poor performance could be due to the visualization techniques we used. The distinction between participant's individual consumption and her neighborhood average is supported by several visual features (color, shape, size). In contrast, neighborhood and city-wide statistics have a similar graphical representation and can be distinguished only by color, which can become difficult to differentiate in the uncontrolled setting of a public projection.

The analysis of the questionnaire test data shows that approximately 70% of the test participants, who consumed less than their neighborhood average (10 out of 14) assessed accurately that they are below the average. In contrast, only 30% of the participants who consumed more than their neighborhood average (5 out of 16) reported that they consumed more. This result indicates that participants tend to interpret their own comparative data differently for the different visual "extremes". There may be social factors which influence these different interpretations in a social public setting: high-consumers would feel embarrassed and tend to reject their high consumption, whereas low consumers would acknowledge their "positive" behavior.

DISCUSSION

While data visualization displays have been studied in semi-public and public settings [22, 44, 45, 46], they have not yet been examined in terms of their potential impact on influencing the awareness, discussions, attitudes or opinions of citizens.

Data Comparisons in Social Settings

Our results confirmed the ability of public visualization to convey socially motivated, data-driven information and consecutively inspire both individual reflection and social debate on the underlying topic. Our analysis further uncovered following implications in regard to people's sensitivity to displaying visualizations in a public settings.

Playful Comparisons. The public comparison of normally 'private' information did not cause significant privacy concerns, similar to what was reported in [45]. On the contrary, 93% (N=184), of the visitors who directly participated in the visualization provided a name, which was often a quite long and playful pseudonym. These results suggest that visitors seemed to perceive the public visualization as a harmless social experience. While the potential of play has been recently discussed in the context of participatory urban sensing [28], our results encourage further exploration of playful data dissemination and comparisons by way of public visualizations. The ability to compare data values, enhanced by a playful visual design and the explicit personalization of participants' data can particularly support group exploration of the data, and consequently lead to friendly competition and mutual "nudging".

Interpretation of Comparisons. Both high and low outliers of others were singled out and discussed, the latter causing curiosity on *"how they have done it"*. People were able to self-reflect based on what they perceived on the visualization. When asked where they stood, higher consumers tended to negate their 'negative' behavior, assessing their consumption as lower-than or about-the-average; lower consumers however, assessed their individual consumption more accurately. People also interpreted the apparent averages of their own communities in the context of external factors. Research in psychology has demonstrated that people would try to recognize themselves, and subsequently report about their result more positively than in reality, especially when social comparison is involved [15]. Public visualization researchers should thus be aware of subjectively different interpretations of personal data versus the data of *others*, when designing as well as evaluating public, user-driven visualizations in a social context. It is still an open question whether such systems actually succeed in questioning or reinterpreting, or just affirming the self-image of participants.

Participation Scalability and Visual Complexity
Reveal-it! was designed as a scalable visualization, where an arbitrary number of visitors are able to submit their personal data. In terms of public participation, our observations and activity logs showed that an average of more that 70% of the visitors who intentionally approached the visualization (N=309), entered their own energy bill estimations. However, the specific characteristics of the sunburst visualization technique increases the complexity and density of the graphical representation the more people add data values (and thus increasing and narrowing the individual 'bursts'). While the analysis of the questionnaire test showed a very good performance in participants' understanding of individual comparative data (ρ=0.8142, p-value<.001), it is important to note that the visualization was populated with only 22 visual entries for the first tested visitor, but with 55 for the last tested visitor. A public visualization designer should thus consider the scalability of the chosen representation technique (while keeping each participant's contribution visible), for instance to afford the

efficient and effective displaying of a very large number of participants. Future studies could explore how the explicit presence of the data entries of others influences the entries of following participants. For instance, some people might feel embarrassed to enter a truthful – but relatively higher – value when most previously entered values are much lower.

Combining Opportunistic and Targeted Perspectives
While we designed *Reveal-it!* as an opportunistic yet mediating tool that encourages data-driven social discussion, self-reflection and contemplation, some visitors interacted with the visualization in a rather targeted way. For instance, participants frequently asked whether there existed an online version, so they could later check *"how the data is doing"* [V22]. We therefore suggest supporting alternative ways of engaging with the user-generated data, in addition to the original physical setting. Complementary interfaces can be developed that are aimed at different public and private user-contexts (i.e., web, mobile displays, home-based physical energy-feedback systems) and support complementary objectives [26] of social data exploration and analysis.

Public Visualization as an Urban Communication Tool
In spite of our rather high-tech data entry and display technologies, people often interpreted *"Reveal-it!"* as a tool that provides a bottom-up initiative for the "grass root" collection and broadcasting of citizen data. This often positively influenced their personal motivation, such as to *"help us collect as much data as possible,"* [V18]. Several of the interviewed participants proposed that *Reveal-it!* could be an alternative solution for conducting a public census in community spaces instead of homes as a *"much easier, quicker and accessible way... and [it is] also more secure!"* [V4]. Some suggestions proposed to communicate the data in different public venues such as *"publication of the results in other cultural and educational centers"* [V10]; or *"[to]contact and broadcast this data in the mass-media. [...] It might not be statistically correct but would impact a lot of citizens."* [V8]. These spontaneous visionary ideas from participations seem conceptually similar to those discussed in the context of participatory sensing. Energy (consumption), among others, can be interpreted as a citizen-related urban data activity that acts like a *"social currency within and across communities"* [27]. Consequently, public visualization can be considered as a potential mediator for social communication and constructive feedback among urban stakeholders (i.e. the citizens, the media, the government) on other relevant civic issues, such as, pollution, criminality and beyond.

Dataset, Representation and Trust
Reveal-it! consisted of a relatively simple representation technique in a rather infographic style. Such a visual style might also impact its trustworthiness along with factors like professional appearance of the material or the showing associations with a trustworthy organization reported in [45]. While most of the people appreciated the visual approach and its *"simplicity"* and *"clearness"*, some specifically requested a *"web-interface to look for more*

data", or to discover *"the ideal values"*. Participants who seemed more knowledgeable on energy issues were concerned that the visualization did not capture water or carbon footprint and even meat consumption, some of them proposing to provide us with *"a better"* or *"the right"* data. Therefore, a public visualization should ideally balance the issues of sufficient information capacity and intuitive visual understanding, while still allowing for parallel interaction styles, from an at-a-glance overview to more explorative strategies that allow a deeper sense-making. In addition, public visualization designers should consider that this issue not only relates to aesthetic preferences, but also to the expertise and background of the onlookers and their interest or motivation on the underlying topic.

Unfolding Engagement

Previous research has pointed out that the diversity of situations in the public sphere may pose challenges in urban display design [9]. We showed specifically how the opportunistic engagement promoted by public visualization is influenced by the types [30] and variety of situational contexts. For instance, people engage with public visualizations easier in situations such as idling, dwelling, waiting or gathering, in contrast to short-lived situations such as arriving, departing or passing-by. In addition, our findings suggest that engagement with the visualization involves certain dynamics that tend to unfold over time. While it is well known that prominent visibility [22] and presence of others [6] attracts attention and evokes initial curiosity to public displays, we discovered that the actual engagement with an underlying topic involves a temporal flow, namely first to realize that the display is a visualization, then to understand what the visualization is about, and finally, how to relate to the presented information.

Moral Aspects

Research has highlighted the existence of moral aspects of the public, collective experience of online social media [13]. Observations from our study underline some important moral aspects of how visualization of socially relevant data is collectively interpreted in the public sphere. For instance, specifically high neighborhood consumptions were often attributed to issues related to local urban politics or infrastructure, while economically or socially deprived neighborhoods were publicly discussed as governmentally supported 'outliers'. While these observations confirm the potential of public visualization as a catalyst of critical debate on civic topics, it also calls for awareness of unexpected (and potentially unwanted) group dynamics that may unfold and might even enforce negative social effects, such as stigma. For instance, people or neighborhoods who – intentionally or not – do not take part in the visualization might still be affected due to this uncontrolled social discussion and reflection. This phenomenon implies several implicit responsibilities when designing a public visualization such as its inevitable use as a subjectively interpretive and seemingly data-driven, thus 'accurate', artifact.

CONCLUSION

We investigated a public visualization of crowd-sourced, self-reported energy expenditure as an approach for encouraging awareness and opportunistic discourse on the socially relevant issue of energy consumption. Our in-the-wild deployments in three distinct informal public settings empowered citizens across locations to reflect on their own as well as their communal energy consumption issues. We leveraged our findings to propose social and opportunistic data comparisons as essential to raising awareness and provoking discussion. Our results should encourage future case studies that address the public and visual communication of data as a catalyst for increasing civic awareness. For instance, other urban issues such as air pollution, council expenditures or traffic can benefit from such social visualizations to open up and contextualize the relevant data in the public sphere. In addition, such visualizations could allow opportunistic data entry to encourage voluntary, grass-roots data collection and communication among urban stakeholders for social and political purposes, such as public opinion, census and alike.

We also observed several challenges involved in integrating socially motivated data visualizations into the public context. While the use of abstract aggregate visualization techniques can evoke curiosity and support comparisons among arbitrary individuals and groups, it may impact the accuracy of understanding and the perception of trust. However, the explicit expectation to submit openly one's own data may induce feelings of embarrassment, which may ultimately lead to false data entries and negating the truthfulness of the display. Lastly, our work highlights the challenges of crafting study methods in-the-wild that are able to capture the subtleness of integrating technological means such as visualization projections to encourage an unpredictable, public discourse. Some of the most salient are the discrepancy in self-reflection and the unfolding temporal dimension of engagement with the visualization display.

ACKNOWLEDGMENTS

We would like to thank Medialab Prado, Centro Cultural España Córdoba and both the community centers La Bareloneta and Sant Marti, Barcelona for making this study possible. Special thanks to Juan Pablo Carrascal, Guillermo Malón, Penelope Maldonado, Uta Hinrichs, Martin Inderbitzin, Sytse Wierenga, Andrea Rosales, Ernesto Arroyo, Rodrigo Oliveira and Sebastian Mealla.

REFERENCES

1. Ananny, M. and Strohecker, C. TexTales: Creating Interactive Forums with Urban Publics. In Foth, M. ed. *Handbook of Research on Urban Informatics: The Practice and Promise of the Real-Time City*, IGI Global, Hershey, PA, 2009.

2. Backlund, S., Gustafsson, A., Gyllenswärd, M., Ilstedt- Hjelm, S., Mazé, R. and Redström, J. Static! The Aesthetics of Energy in Everyday Things. In *Proc. DRS 2006*.

3. Blomberg, J., Giacomi, J., Mosher, A. and Swenton-Wall, P. *Participatory Design-Principles and Practices*. Ch. Ethnographic Field Methods and Their Relation to Design, Lawrence Erlbaum, 123–155.

4. Bodker, S. When Second Wave HCI Meets Third Wave Challenges. In *Proc. NordiCHI 2006*, 1-8.

5. Breinbjerg, M., Riis, M. S., Ebsen, T., and Lunding, R. Experiencing the Non-sensuous. *In Proc. NordiCHI 2010*, 611–614.

6. Brignull, H. and Rogers, Y. Enticing People to Interact with Large Public Displays in Public Spaces. In *Proc. INTERACT 2003*, 17-24.

7. Broms, L., Katzeff, C., Beng, Magnus, M., Nyblom, S., Hjelm, S., and Ehrnberger, K. Coffee Maker Patterns and the Design of Energy Feedback Artefacts. In *Proc. DIS 2010*, 93-102.

8. Churchill, E. F., Nelson, L., Denoue, L. and Girgensohn, A. The Plasma Poster Network: Posting Multimedia Content in Public Places. In *Proc. of INTERACT 2003*, 599-606.

9. Dalsgaard, P., and Halskov, K. Designing Urban Media Façades : Cases and Challenges. In *Proc. CHI 2010*, 2277-2286.

10. Dalsgaard, P., Nielsen, R. and Halskov, K.: Towards a Design Space Explorer for Media Facades. In *Proc.OZCHI 2008,* 219-226.

11. Danis, C., Viegas, F., Wattenberg, M. and Kriss, J. Your Place or Mine?: Visualization as a Community Component. In *Proc. CHI 2008*, 275-284.

12. Donath, J., Karahalios, K. and Viegas, F. Visualizing conversations. *Computer-Mediated Communication 4*, 4 (1998).

13. Dourish, P. and Christine, S. The Moral Economy of Social Media. In Foth, M., Forlano, L., Satchell, C. and Gibbs, M. (Eds.) *From Social Butterfly to Engaged Citizen: Urban Informatics, Social Media, Ubiquitous Computing, and Mobile Technology to Support Citizen Engagement* (2011), MIT Press, 21-37.

14. Fatah Gen. Schieck, A., Briones, C. and Mottram, C. The Urban Screen as a Socializing Platform: Exploring the Role of Place within the Urban Space. In F. Eckardt, J. Geelhaar, L. Colini, K.S. Willis, K. Chorianopoulos and R. Hennig (Eds.) MediaCity: Situations, Practices and Encounters (2008), Frank & Timme GmbH, 285-305.

15. Festinger, L. A Theory of Social Comparison Processes. In *Human Relations* 7, 2 (1954), 117-140.

16. Fritsch, J. and Brynskov, M. Between Engagement, Affect and Information - Experimental Urban Media in the Climate Change Debate. In Foth, M., Forlano, L., Gibbs, M., & Satchell, C. (Eds.). *From Social Butterfly to Engaged Citizen: Urban Informatics, Social Media, Ubiquitous Computing, and Mobile Technology to Support Citizen Engagement* (2011), MIT Press, 115-135.

17. Gilbert, E. and Karahalios, K. Using social visualization to motivate social production. In *IEEE Transactions on Multimedia - Special section on communities and media computing 11*, 3 (2009), 413-421.

18. Grasso, A., Muehlenbrock, M., Roulland, F., and Snowdon, D. Public and Situated Displays: Social and Interactional Aspects of Shared Display Technologies, Ch. 11: Supporting Communities of Practice with Large Screen Displays (2003), Springer, 261–282.

19. Greenfield, A., Shepard, M.: Urban Computing and Its Discontents. The Architectural League of New York, New York (2007).

20. Harrison, S. and Dourish, P. Re-place-ing Space: the Roles of Place and Space in Collaborative Systems. In *Proc. CSCW 1996*, 67-76.

21. He, H., Greenberg, S. and Huang, E. One Size Does Not Fit All: Applying the Transtheoretical Model to Energy Feedback Technology Design. In *Proc. CHI 2010*, 927-936.

22. Hinrichs, U., Schmidt, H., and Carpendale, S EMDialog: Bringing Information Visualization into the Museum. *IEEE Transactions on Visualization and Computer Graphics 14*, 6 (2008), 1181–1189.

23. Hinrichs, U., Valkanova, N., Kuikkaniemi, K., Jacucci, G., Carpendale,S. and Arroyo, E. Large Displays in Urban Life. From Exhibition Halls to Media Facades. *Ext. Abstracts CHI 2011*, 2433-2436.

24. Holmes, T. Eco-Visualization: Combining Art and Technology to Reduce Energy Consumption. In *Proc. C&C 2007*, 153-162.

25. Jancke, G. Venolia, G., Grudin, J., Cadiz, J. and Gupta. J. Linking Public Spaces: Technical and Social Issues. In *Proc. CHI 2001*, 530-537.

26. Kim, T., Hong, H. and Magerko, B., Design Requirements for Ambient Display that Supports Sustainable Lifestyle. In. *Proc. DIS 2010*, 103-112.

27. Kuznetsov, S. and Paulos, E. Participatory Sensing in Public Spaces: Activating Urban Surfaces with Sensor Probes. In *Proc. DIS 2010*, 21-30.

28. Kuznetsov, S., Davis, G. N., Paulos, E., Gross, M. D., and Cheung, J. C. Red Balloon, Green Balloon, Sensors in the Sky. In *Proc. UbiComp 2011*, 237-246.

29. McCarthy, F. Public and Situated Displays: Social and Interactional Aspects of Shared Display Technologies, Ch. 12: Promoting a Sense of Community with Ubiquitous Peripheral displays (2003), Springer, 283–308.

30. McCullough, M. On Typologies of Situated Interaction. *Human-Computer Interaction 16*, 2-4 (2001), 336-349.

31. Müller, J., Alt, F., Michelis, D. and Schmidt, A. Requirements and design space for interactive public displays. In *Proc. MM 2010*, 1285-1294.

32. Nuage Vert. http://www.pixelache.ac/nuage-blog/. Visited Sept., 2012

33. Pierce, J., Schiano, D. and Paulos, E. Home, Habits, and Energy: Examining Domestic Interactions and Energy Consumption. In *Proc. CHI 2010*, 1985-1994.

34. Pousman, Z., and Stasko, J. A Taxonomy of Ambient Information Systems : Four Patterns of Design. *In Proc. AVI 2006*, 67–74.

35. Redstrom, J., Skog, T., and Hallanas, L. Informative Art: Using Amplified Artworks as Information Displays. In *Proc. DARE 2000*, 103-114.

36. Roberts, S., Humphries, H., Hyldon, V.: Consumer Preferences for Improving Energy Consumption Feedback. Report to Ofgem, Centre for Sustainable Energy (2004).

37. Rodgers, J., and Bartram, L. Exploring Ambient and Artistic Visualization for Residential Energy Use Feedback. In *Proc. INFOVIS 2011*, 2489-2497.

38. Schroeter, R., Foth, M. and Satchell, C. People, Content, Location: Sweet Spotting Urban Screens for Situated Engagement. In *Proc. DIS 2012*, 146-155.

39. Skog, T., Ljungblad, S. and Holmquist, L.E. Between Aesthetics and Utility: Designing Ambient Information Visualizations. In *Proc. INFOVIS 2003*, 233-240.

40. Stasko, J. SunBurst Project. http://www.cc.gatech.edu/gvu/ii/sunburst/ (2000). Visited Sept. 2012.

41. Struppek, M. The Social Potential of Urban Screens. In *Journal for Visual Communication 5*, 2 (2007), 173-188.

42. Townsend, A., Maguire, R., Liebhold, M. and Crawford, M. The Future of Cities, Information, and Inclusion. Report for the Rockefeller Foundation Institute of the Future. Available at http://www.rockefellerfoundation.org/news/publications/future-cities-information-inclusion

43. Valkanova, N., Arroyo, E. Blat, J. The Visitors: Designing Media Façades to Support Links Between People and Places. In *Proc. IASDR 2011.*

44. Valkanova, N., Moghnieh, A., Arroyo, E., and Blat, J. AmbientNEWS: Augmenting Information Discovery in Complex Settings through Aesthetic Design. In *Proc. IV 2010*, 439–444.

45. Vande Moere, A., Tomitsch, M., Hoinkis, M., Trefz, E., Johansen, S., and Jones, A. Comparative Feedback in the Street: Exposing Residential Energy Consumption on House Facades. In *Proc. INTERACT 2011*, 470-488.

46. Viégas, F., Perry, E. Howe, E. Donath, J. Artifacts of the Presence Era: Using Information Visualization to Create an Evocative Souvenir. In *Proc. INFOVIS 2004*, 105-111.

47. Visualizar'11: Understanding Infrastructures (2011). http://medialab-prado.es/article/visualizar11_taller_seminario.

48. Vogel, D. and Balakrishnan, R. Interactive Public Ambient Displays: Transitioning from Implicit to Explicit, Public to Personal, Interaction with Multiple Users. In *Proc. UIST 2004*, 137-146.

49. Ware, C. *Visual Thinking for Design*. In Morgan Kaufmann Series in Interactive Technologies, 2008.

50. Watermarks Project. http://watermarksproject.org/project.html. Visited Sept. 2012.

51. Wattenberg, M. Babynames, Visualization, and Social Data Analysis. In *Proc. INFOVIS 2005*, 1–7.

Social Media and the Police—Tweeting Practices of British Police Forces during the August 2011 Riots

Sebastian Denef
Fraunhofer FIT
Schloss Birlinghoven
53754 Sankt Augustin
Germany
sebastian.denef@fit.fraunhofer.de

Petra S. Bayerl
Erasmus University Rotterdam – RSM
Burgemeester Oudlaan 50
3062 PA Rotterdam
The Netherlands
pbayerl@composite.rsm.nl

Nico Kaptein
COT
Koninginnegracht 26
2514 AB Den Haag
The Netherlands
n.kaptein@cot.nl

ABSTRACT

With this paper we take a first step to understand the appropriation of social media by the police. For this purpose we analyzed the Twitter communication by the London Metropolitan Police (MET) and the Greater Manchester Police (GMP) during the riots in August 2011. The systematic comparison of tweets demonstrates that the two forces developed very different practices for using Twitter. While MET followed an *instrumental approach* in their communication, in which the police aimed to remain in a controlled position and keep a distance to the general public, GMP developed an *expressive approach*, in which the police actively decreased the distance to the citizens. In workshops and interviews, we asked the police officers about their perspectives, which confirmed the identified practices. Our study discusses benefits and risks of the two approaches and the potential impact of social media on the evolution of the role of police in society.

Author Keywords

Police; Twitter; UK Riots; Crisis Communication; Microblogging

ACM Classification Keywords

H.5.3 Information interfaces and presentation (e.g., HCI): Group and Organization Interfaces – Collaborative computing, Computer-supported cooperative work

General Terms

Human Factors

INTRODUCTION

On Thursday August 4th, 2011, at about 6:15 PM, Mark Duggan, 29, was shot dead by the police in Tottenham in the Greater London area, during an operation aimed to arrest him. Questions about whether or not Duggan shot first and whether this was an act of self-defense started a debate that put the police operation into question. On

Saturday evening, August 6th, a crowd of about 300 people gathered at a police station. What started as a peaceful demonstration, turned into a forceful riot that spread in the following days across neighborhoods and to other cities such as Birmingham, Liverpool and Manchester. Buildings were set on fire and stores were looted. Thousands of people were arrested. Five people died and over 200 people injured; 186 of them police officers [2]. In London alone, 3,443 riot-related crimes were reported [25] which caused damages of over 200 million pounds [18]. During the riots, social media became a contentious topic of public debate, as offenders used different networks and mobile communication services to organize themselves—even leading to a discussion on governmental orders to shut off Twitter [14].

Yet, the UK riots also saw the entry of other users into the social media space. UK police forces likewise used Twitter extensively, in this case as an outreach channel to communicate with the public. During the riots, British police forces not only saw a tremendous growth in the number of Twitter followers. They also, for the first time, engaged with the public on such a large scale via social media, using Twitter as the main platform.

Twitter, as a microblogging system, allows its members to post messages (so-called 'tweets') of up to 140 characters. These tweets are displayed on a member's page as a running stream of messages. Members can choose to follow others. Messages of people they follow are then displayed on their own Twitter page. Tweets usually are posted publicly, giving anybody the chance to access them, regardless of whether they are Twitter members or follow each other. As members can also directly react to tweets of others, Twitter becomes an interactive space of open communication. Given that effective communication is vital in containing and controlling crisis situations, Twitter with its free availability, possibility for dynamic and faced-paced dissemination and unrestricted reach seems imminently well suited for this task.

The appropriation of Twitter, and social media more generally, is, however, not straightforward for the police—not only due to extensive legal frameworks that bind police behavior. The police also have a unique position in society. As the 'coercive arm of the state', they are the only organization that can enforce law and order in a population. At the same time, the police are dependent on the cooperation with the public to fulfill their role successfully. The police thus have to manage a continuous balancing act between repressing problematic elements and supporting and protecting the rest of society. For this balance, aspects such as image and legitimacy are vital for the function of police, yet are affected and challenged by novel computing systems. In this context, the openness of social media for appropriation makes technology adoption and use very challenging.

In the present paper, we investigate police use of Twitter and reactions by followers during the UK riots in August 2011. The events constitute a 'natural experiment' on technology-mediated group interaction during a large-scale incident. Our main focus is here on the appropriation of microblogging by police forces. For this purpose, we compared the Twitter communication of the London Metropolitan Police (MET) and the Greater Manchester Police (GMP). The choice of the two forces was driven by theoretical considerations: MET were at the center of the riots; GMP was less effected by the riots, yet, is known among UK police forces for embracing Twitter and has experimented with its use in campaigns before [8].

In the following, we summarize related work on police and social media in crisis situation more generally. We then describe the methods we applied in our study, followed by an integration of our quantitative and qualitative results. In the discussion we highlight respective benefits and challenges of the two communication approaches identified in our data and end with implications for police and other first-responder organizations, as well as the relevance of our findings for HCI research.

RELATED WORK

Regarding the social media use of police forces, a 2011 trend study on ICT use in European police forces [6] points to social media as a topic with increasing relevance. Only recently have social media emerged as communication channels between the police and the public. While police forces in some European countries, such as the Netherlands and the UK, already made recognizable progress in adopting social media for their daily operations, police forces in other countries consider social media as the most important topic still coming.

Social media possess two potential benefits for police: They can support primary functions such as crime investigations and prevention, and they offer a faster, more direct path of communication with the public [6]. At the same time, social media can be a threat to police: not only do offenders employ social media to organize themselves, but they also open the police up to continuous scrutiny and comment by the general public. Although the police themselves discuss vigorously about the potential of social media for crisis

communication (e.g., [19, 5]), systematic (academic) investigations of social media adoption by public organizations such as police are still rare.

In HCI, there exists a broad set of studies and knowledge about the use of microblogging and social media in crisis contexts. The use of Twitter and comparable systems, for instance, have been described for the 2008 Sichuan earthquake [17], the 2009 earthquake in Haiti [21], the 2010 earthquake in Chile [15], as well as the 2009 Oklahoma grassfires and Red River floods [20, 28]. These studies show how citizens become a resource in crises situations and how systems can support the extraction of this information for emergency responders and others in real-time [9]. They further show that rumors spread and can be identified in social media [15] and how people in crises situations use social media for grassroots coordination and support. Looking beyond specific incidents, researchers have classified the public's reaction on social during disasters [13].

For established crises response organizations, such as the police, these works present insights of what information to expect from the public and possible uses of them. They say, however, relatively little about how professional emergency response organizations can have their own voice and impact in this communication space. One of the main challenges, here, is to communicate successfully with the multitude of groups the police comes in contact with—from suspects to victims to supporting organizations [3]. Managing this *relational complexity* [4] successfully is very challenging, especially in highly dynamic, fast-paced and dangerous situations such as the UK riots. As social media are a very new means of communication—particularly in the repertoire of police forces—there is currently little guidance on how to approach and use them. At present, forces are required to experiment. Studying Twitter usage and its effects during extreme situations such as the UK riots has the potential to add new insights for first responders such as police, but also opens new avenues for research on crisis communication and system design.

METHODS

Data Collection

Messages from the Police

Our empirical database was the complete set of 547 tweets posted by MET and GMP police forces from August 2nd to August 13th that we continuously captured using Twitter search. We decided to include the days immediately prior to and after the riots to investigate whether police use of Twitter altered during the crisis. In addition to these messages, we also followed the further Twitter communication of the forces one month after the events to detect instances, in which previous events from the riots became relevant again.

Messages from the Public

While our primary focus of analysis was on Twitter use by the police, we also captured tweets sent to the two forces by the public to put the police tweets into their context. For this purpose we made use of the Twitter-specific formatting of messages. To direct messages to a specific person, users typically insert an @-symbol before the name of the user. In our case addressees were @metpoliceuk and @gmpolice. Given the large number of messages (the website Peoplebrowsr.com listed 15,000 mentions for MET and 35,000 for GMP for a single day in that period) and the limitations of the Twitter API to search for that many messages, we combined a number of approaches to select public tweets. First, we captured all messages marked as 'top tweets' in Twitter, indicating messages that are especially popular. We further captured all messages that the police chose to reply to, if not already included in the database. A large number of tweets from the public were forwarded tweets ('re-tweets') that we excluded, as they did not provide additional information. Using these methods we captured a total of 6,125 tweets from the public. All these tweets and the ones from the Police had been openly published. They do thus not include direct private messages that people might have sent using Twitter, too.

Number of Followers

We also captured the number of followers for the two forces from beginning of June to beginning of September 2011 as a general indication of popularity of the police forces and the possible spread of their communication. The data was collected using the website twittercounter.com. Interpolated values were removed prior to analysis.

Workshops and interviews with the Police

For a more direct investigation of social media use by the police we used two workshops on social media as a tool for police communication, which included officers from both forces. In addition, we also conducted interviews with officers and a communication strategist from GMP actively twittering during the crisis.

Data Analysis

Our interest in investigating tweets was to identify how police used Twitter to communicate with the public during the crisis. To allow for a comprehensive description, we analyzed messages on three dimensions: content, function, [11], and style. For content, we used open coding [22] to identify topics such as *advice, refute rumors* or *success story*. For function, we used 20 categories adapted from [1] (e.g., *informing, disconfirming, threat, thanks*). For style, we analyzed the *degree of formality* and *type of address,* both of which were coded with two categories (Table 1). We coded all 547 tweets from the police on these aspects.

Our interest in identifying how the police forces used Twitter throughout the crisis focused on two aspects: firstly, whether the two forces differed in their usage of the medium; secondly, whether usage changed over time. To compare the two police forces we operationalized Twitter

use as *quantity* (i.e., frequency of tweets) as well as *form* based on the four coding dimensions described above. Time developments were analyzed in two ways: (1) behavior of a force during the crisis compared to its behavior prior to the crisis and (2) changes within a force across consecutive days. Public messages were not systematically coded, but used in a selective way to illustrate reactions to police communications.

Dimension	Category	Definition
Degree of Formality	Formal	Written language style
	Informal	Close to spoken language, e.g., using slang
	Uncertain	Text is too short for a clear distinction
Type of address	Generic	Tweets do not name a specific addressee
	Direct	Tweets are addressed to a person by name (@x)

Table 1: Definition of style categories

RESULTS

Identifying Differences

Number of Messages Sent

A first glance on the number of messages suffices to see that the two forces used Twitter to a very different extend. From August 4th at 6:15 PM, the beginning of the riots, until Saturday, August 13th at 11:59 PM, MET posted 132 tweets. During the same period GMP posted a total of 371 tweets, almost 3 times as many. Not surprisingly, the frequency of tweets during the crisis increased dramatically in both forces: about one fifths of the messages were sent in the seven days prior to the crisis, the reminder in the seven days after the start of the riots. This ratio was nearly identical for both forces (18% vs. 20% for GMP and MET respectively for pre-riot messages, 82% vs. 80% after the start of the riots).

Communication Style, Content and Function

Comparing communication style, it becomes apparent that MET used a much more impersonal style than GMP. MET's tweets were mostly formal tweets and directed to a generic audience rather than individual followers (cp. Table 2). Interestingly, this difference only emerged after the start of the riots (χ^2-tests MET vs. GMP pre-riot are non-significant.; χ^2-tests MET vs. GMP after the start of the riots significant with p <.001 for both dimensions). This suggests that the two forces did not differ in their communication strategies in general, but developed disparate reactions to the crisis (table 2).

Concentrating on the period after the start of the riots, the forces differed considerably in which topics they approached in tweets, starting with the range of topics. In total, we identified 49 unique topics. GMP covered 46, MET only 25. The same could be observed for function, where GMP covered 19 and MET only 13 functions of the 20 coded. Generally, communications by MET were thus much narrower in intent and much more focused compared to GMP.

MET police used Twitter primarily for informing the public about their own performance (31% of all tweets). To a lesser extent, Twitter was also used for information gathering from the public (17.8%) and information dissemination to the public (13.2%). Nearly one third of MET's tweets reported on arrests made during the riots (29.5%). Tweets with requests for help and reports on police actions accounted for only 7.8% of all messages, and other topics appeared even less.

Formality

	Category	TOTAL	Pre-crisis	During crisis
MET	Formal	151	96.9%	93.0%
	Informal	10	3.1%	7.0%
GMP	Formal	163	80.0%	36.2%***
	Informal	209	20.0%	63.8%***

Type of Address

	Category	TOTAL	Pre-crisis	During crisis
MET	Generic	158	90.6%	100%***
	Direct	3	9.4%	0%***
GMP	Generic	234	92.3	56.7%***
	Direct	138	7.7%	43.3%***

*** pre-post comparison χ2-tests significant at 1%-level

Table 2: Comparison of style dimensions

For GMP, the most important function of Twitter seemed to reassure the public that all was well (25% of all tweets), as the most frequent type of tweets sent by GMP were messages of reassurance, noting that everything was calm and the public should not worry (16.5% or all tweets). Similar to the MET, the secondary function was information gathering and information dissemination (15.1%, 12.5%). This was, followed by indicating police performance (11.5%). Reports of arrests represented 10.3% of all tweets. The third frequent topic was meta-communication about the forces' own Twitter use (7.3%).

The quantitative analysis of messages suggests that the two police forces followed very disparate strategies in their adoption of Twitter during the crisis. MET used Twitter in a rather narrow way, mostly to support primary police functions of keeping law and order. The communication style remained formal and directed at the general public. GMP in contrast used Twitter in a much broader way and also with a much more personal touch. Where MET thus emphasizing the separation between police and public, GMP aimed to establish a close personalized relationship. MET's communication can thus be described as an *instrumental* strategy, while GMP followed an *expressive* approach [26].

Detailed Analysis

To verify the existence of the two disparate approaches and to obtain a deeper understanding of the differences between the two communication strategies, we conducted a further qualitative analysis of the messages. Firstly, we compared how forces formulated their messages when communicating the same topics. Secondly, we also identified unique topics and functions in each force using a qualitative text-based analysis.

Reporting Police Performance

The first tweet from MET dealing with the riots stemmed from Sunday, August 7th at 11:32 AM and reported the number of arrests made following the first riots in the previous night:

MET: *There have been 42 arrests so far following last night's disorder in #Tottenham. Full statement: http://bit.ly/phSbcz*

This type of message became typical for MET over the following days, and—as noted above—the prominent type of communication to the public. During the riots MET soon established a specific format for these messages; only the numbers were changed. These messages provided a constant update on the overall progress of police arrests. Nearly exactly one week after the first message, MET posted the final message of this type in the batch that we reviewed:

MET: *The Met has now arrested 1401 people in connection with violence, disorder and looting. 808 of these have been charged.*

GMP provided similar updates on the arrests, although less frequently. In contrast to MET these messages did not have a fixed format, as these messages from Saturday, August 13th and Wednesday, August 10th show:

GMP: *21 more arrests in last 24hrs. Total arrests now 210 and rising.*

GMP: *Two people already jailed for their part in last night's disorder - swift justice*

As these examples show, GMP used a less formal way of communicating police performance, adding future expectations such as "and rising", in the first, and "already" in the second message. GMP also commented on the progress as "swift justice".

Reports of Police Action on the Street

Related to messages on police performance, were messages reporting concrete police actions on the street. MET, for instance, reported on Monday August 8th, 0:45 AM and Tuesday, August 9th, 2:36 AM:

MET: *Police are responding to a significant amount of criminal activity across London and are deploying officers to tackle it.*

MET: *Armoured vehicles used to support officers on the ground to stop disorder by pushing back over 150 people in Lavender Hill area.*

The function of these tweets can be seen in reassuring the public that the police 'is on top of things', to a smaller extent to demonstrate to potential offenders that police will react if needed (threat function). Equivalent messages were absent in the communication by GMP. Indeed, despite general promises made early in the crisis and later also to followers directly to provide updates on Twitter, the first information message did not appear until Tuesday night at

7:19 PM—and this message pointed only indirectly to the start of the riots:

GMP: *GMP actively trying to arrest anyone involved in disorder. Asking people to stay out of harms way while we apprehend criminals*

The subsequent messages asked the public to report people involved in the disorder and mentioned seven arrests. Two further messages addressed the perpetrators, and one linked to police contact information. At 9:36 PM GMP announced a press conference without giving further detail. At 0:10 AM, GMP issued the message below which points to a video of a traditional police media update:

GMP: *Assistant Chief Constable Garry Shewan said: "Over the past few hours, Greater Manchester Police has been faced ... http://bit.ly/q8C7mW*

Still, during this period of the riots, numerous followers sent supporting messages, such as the following message that became a top tweet:

USR13: *Dear @gmpolice , the good people of Manchester are behind you 100%. Do what it takes to suppress this.*

Followers also positively commented on the response of GMP actions on the street and expressed their gratitude for prompt reactions. Only later (Saturday, August 13th) a tweet asking directly for feedback led followers to express their disappointment. Many would have hoped for more information, such as a journalist who found the Twitter communication during the riots "absolutely invaluable". In reaction to those messages, GMP finally provided an explanation for their silence during the riots on Tuesday.

GMP: *when disorder started it was all hands on deck so couldnt get onto Twitter immediately to update people, but appreciate feedback about this*

In another tweet GMP also commented on a follower's suggestion that the police were trying "to deliberately downplay" the riots on Twitter to stay in control of social media. GMP refutes this accusation, pointing to the difficulty of handing the riots and communicating on Twitter at the same time:

GMP: *@USR16 certainly did not mean to downplay things. Was hard to Tweet and try and deal with disorder, but do take this on board*

Providing Reassurance
GMP put considerable effort into fighting rumors that suggested riots in Manchester and into assuring that 'everything is calm'. Especially, in the beginning of the crisis no clear information existed on whether or not the riots had spread to Manchester. The GMP issued messages such as the following on Monday night that addressed such rumors:

GMP: *No disorder or riots in Manchester. Speculation about ongoing riots totally inaccurate. GMP monitoring the situation.*

In addition to the "all calm" message, they further indicate that the police monitors the situation, thus indicating control of the situation. This message was very well received by followers, who commented on this with "good news", "thank god" or "thankfully". Followers put great trust in such messages, as this reply shows:

USR7: *@gmpolice Thank you much appreciated Will sleep more easily.*

GMP not only issued general messages of reassurance, but also tried to fight rumors. One way was to comment directly on news reports:

GMP: *BBC reports of rioting/disturbances in Greater Manchester inaccurate. No rioting whatsoever, no major disturbances. All quiet at moment.*

Further, GMP addressed concerns of Twitter users directly, as shown in the following dialogue:

USR1: *@gmpolice is it true that chaos has started in town, carphone warehouse has been done over already??*
GMP: *@USR1 nothing at the moment follow us and we will let you know if there is anything to report*

As reported earlier, the promise of updates on Twitter was repeated frequently and reiterated to many people in direct messages. For MET, messages of reassurance were less frequent and not as divers in nature. In their messages, MET rather underlined the strength of their force, for instance, by naming the number of officers available, instead of offering concrete reassurance:

MET: *In the next 24 hours there will now be 16,000 police officers on duty in London.*

Again, for MET reassurance and threat seemed closely linked together.

Crowd Sourcing (Information Gathering, Requests for Help)
Both forces used Twitter extensively to support investigations and to seek information on offenders. Both forces also used the photo sharing site Flickr to publish photos of perpetrators captured on CCTV. The general public was asked to help in the identification of these people. Moreover, they regularly provided phone numbers and websites where citizens could submit information:

MET: *New CCTV images of people police need to identify on our Flickr page http://bit.ly/rnax8U Pls look and RT*
GMP: *Can you you help identify these people? Check our Flickr gallery of wanted suspects and call 0800 092 0410 http://bit.ly/oyfZiN*

The above tweets again highlight the difference in tone between police forces. GMP addresses the reader directly with a question, while the MET message is a formal statement that only indirectly addresses the reader as helper in police's "need to identify". This disparity in addressing followers remained a consistent feature between MET and GMP tweets. On Friday, August 12th, GMP further promoted their crowd sourcing efforts and launched a campaign entitled 'shop a looter'. Large posters in the city showed the faces of suspects and asked people to help with their identification. Twitter was used to announce the campaign and also to introduce the hashtag #shopalooter:

GMP: *GMP launches #shopalooter campaign. Give us info and make the looters pay for their crimes.. Upload info at http://bit.ly/c3q1qk*

Yet, information gathering was not a one-way process. Both forces provided phone numbers or links to their websites where the public could submit information. They also directly asked for hints to be sent via Twitter. In addition, people actively submitted hints as Twitter messages.

USR2:   *@gmpolice gmpolice thought you might be interested in this facebook group http://is.gd/V1JHez*

GMP replied to such information and provided a short notice that the information had been taken into account, often together with a personal thank you note:

GMP: *@USR2 We have seen it and the information has been passed on. Thank you*

A scan of our database indicates that MET received similar messages:

USR3:   *RT this mug! Get him nicked "@USR5: Some dick has taken pics of himself with looted gear in #Tottenham http://[URL anonymized]*

USR4:   *@metpoliceuk http://[URL to the tweet by USR3]*

MET, however, did not reply to such messages in their feed, leaving open the question whether this information had been dealt with.

Disseminating Information
Both forces used Twitter also to disseminate information, mostly as URLs to online resources. MET tweets, for instance, indicated where to apply for compensation or where to new information for businesses:

MET: *DirectGov advice on compensation claims for those who've suffered loss/damage as result of disorder: http://bit.ly/pNe4HW*

GMP issued similar messages, for instance, about the status of public transportation:

GMP: *Anyone wanting to check whether public transport is still running should visit www.tfgm.com and/or metrolink.co.uk*

Most of the tweets by GMP in this category, however, were direct answers to questions from the public. In the following example, a business requested police presence, and GMP provide a phone contact:

USR31:   *@gmpolice As a Manchester Business, I request Police presence stationary in the NQ between 9-11pm. Pls DM me to discuss or call me.*

GMP: *@USR31 0161 872 5050. Thanks*

Comparing this communication with the previous business update by MET again shows a prevalent difference: GMP engaged in one-to-one interactions with their followers, MET did not. Additionally, GMP provided a greater variety of information, such as how to contact the police or how to provide legal information:

USR29:   *@gmpolice Unclear here what the precise criminal offence is of two youths sentenced for 'swearing'. Can you clarify? Thanks*

GMP: *@USR29 an offence under Section Four of the Public Order Act*

This again reiterates the finding in earlier sections that GMP attached a broader role to Twitter than MET.

GMP-Unique Topics
As mentioned above, we found a number of topics in GMP that had no pendants in MET. These were the addressing of perpetrators, name and shame, discussions of GMP's own Twitter use, and purely social promotions of the GMP police force.

Addressing perpetrators: As mentioned above, GMP directly addressed perpetrators in messages with the intention to threaten and thus deter them from further violence. Such threats often warned that perpetrators would be identified through CCTV recordings and online investigations, or simply referred to recent successes:

GMP: *Captured lots of criminals on CCTV - we will identify you and we will be coming for you*

GMP: *If you have been using social networking sites to incite disorder, expect us to come knocking on your door very soon*

GMP: *Just arrested two men found with fuel can, balaclava, ball bearings - if you want to commit disorder, we'll lock you up*

Such messages are without counterparts in MET.

Name and Shame: Another type of tweets only to be found with GMP was a campaign we refer to as "name and shame". In these messages, GMP released full personal details of perpetrators convicted in fast trials after the riots (i.e., name, date of birth, place of residence). GMP announced the naming and shaming on Wednesday night:

GMP: *Criminals still going through the courts now - tomorrow they'll be named and shamed*

On Thursday, GMP released the following messages:

GMP: *We promised we'd name all those convicted for their roles in the disorder - here we go ...*

GMP: *Mark Smith (born 02/02/1980), of Manchester Street, Oldham, jailed for eight months for stealing clothes [name and personal details fictitious]*

As the following messages show, the responses to this campaign were mixed:

USR9:   *In fact @gmpolice tweets are fascinating. Appears some rioters given longer sentences for swearing at police than assault*
USR10: *@USR13 @gmpolice surely this violates human rights. What happened to innocent b4 proven guilty. We are no different to tyrant nations*
USR11: *@gmpolice think it's great your naming & shaming. These people lost any "human rights" the minute they got involved in the riots.*

There are questions about the legality of this approach, the personal content, the choice of publishing them on Twitter, and any many more. GMP addressed these questions by referring to the public nature of court decisions in the UK:

GMP: *Lot of debate about publishing details - courts very clear, justice should be done publicly*
GMP: *@USR12 legally bound to publish address and dates of birth so no-one of the same name can be misidentified as the culprit*

Despite these straight answers, GMP dropped the practice of 'naming and shaming' after the publications of only ten names; without comment. Interestingly, the topic erupted again in messages of followers, long after the event on August 20th, after one of the people named in a GMP tweet was acquitted in second instance, because additional evidence put the identification from CCTV into question. Tragically, during his time in custody, his home had been set on fire—although it remained unclear whether this was indeed a direct reaction to the 'name and shame' campaign. Followers questioned GMP about the issue, and GMP posted the following message:

GMP: *After consulting with CPS, the case of XXX YYY, 18, charged with criminal damage, recklessly endangering life has been discontinued.*

MET, despite direct requests from the public, as shown below, did not engage in a similar campaign:

USR14: *@metpoliceuk You should tweet their names like @gmpolice have been doing. #NameAndShameCriminals*

Meta Communication (Asking for Feedback and Discussing the Right Tone): On Saturday, August 13th, GMP posted the following message:

GMP: *Mum-of-two, not involved in disorder, jailed for FIVE months for accepting shorts looted from shop. There are no excuses.*

This message triggered a massive reaction that made the tweet the most discussed during the riots. It also sparked a discussion on police Twitter communication in general. Out of the many messages of criticism, the following two represent the public opinion fairly well.

USR17: *What abt her kids? RT@gmpolice Mum-of-2, not involved in disorder, jailed for FIVE months for accepting looted shorts. There are no excuses!*
USR18: *That last @gmpolice tweet: wrong sentence, wrong tone, wrong everything. Pissing away goodwill collected over last week.*

A blogger described the reasons for this critique in detail: "The tweet shows enthusiasm, maybe even glee, over the length of the sentence. Particularly with the emphasis of 'FIVE months' and 'There are no excuses!' It is not the place of the police to comment on, recommend or celebrate the length of a sentence or the defence used in court" and continues arguing that the police "should remain detached and professional when it comes to presenting information to the public" [24]. A Google search for the tweet listed 10,300 results ranging from blogs to major newspapers that commented on the event. About an hour after the posting of the original message, GMP deleted the tweet in question and posted the following messages:

GMP: *Apologies for any offence caused from last tweet. Comment was not directed at individual person.*
GMP: *Thanks to all for feedback messages - all your comments have been noted. You are right, it is not our place to comment on sentences.*
GMP: *appreciate all feedback. Changing tack slightly - we really want to know what you think we've got right or wrong this week on Twitter*

In the aftermath, GMP received numerous questions and comments on their Twitter communication. The informal way of communication was discussed, as was the problem of having different officers writing messages that might have different tones. The response was overwhelmingly positive. Users asked for the continuation of the more 'human' police communication approach, showed empathy for making a mistake, and were forgiving about the tweet:

USR19: *Hats off to @gmpolice embracing social media. Someone made a mistake, tweet removed and apology issued. FFS it's human behaviour.*
USR23: *@gmpolice everything right, more transparency = more faith in you guys*

As in the previous example of the contentious name and shame tweet, the sentence for the mother was diminished, and followers asked GMP for a statement. In this case, GMP did not react. While there were positive words of encouragement and gratitude for MET as well, there was no communication about the Twitter messages on a meta level. We could also not find messages by followers that commended the force as 'human'.

Promoting Police Culture: Already before the start of the riots, GMP posted messages that were not directly related to current police operations. For instance, GMP posted a weekly survey question asking followers to vote on police practices via hashtag. The results were then posted the following week:

GMP: *This week's q: Should @gmpolice send a crime scene investigator not PC if it is more likely to lead to arrest? Reply #gmpyes or #gmpno*

GMP also promoted the anniversary of their police museum and other social events related to the police. They posted links to images showing historic police cars and GMP officers of the past. For all these messages, they received some amount of feedback and questions. Noteworthy for the reactions it elicited was another tweet, posted on Saturday, August 13th:

GMP: *It won't be long before Jack is helping out, he is training hard. flic.kr/p/a19R3N*

Jack was a young police dog currently in training. Discussions ensured and followers asked questions about its race and age. Later that evening, after several additional tweets about Jack, GMP also issued a video of the dog. On August 15th, GMP posted a message in which the shooting star Jack could be seen at the anniversary of the museum:

GMP: *So who wants to meet Jack? He will be making an appearance at the museum's 30th anniversary tomorrow at 14:30. flic.kr/p/a19R3N*

Again, this type of personal, purely social use of Twitter did not take place with MET.

Number of Followers

With the start of the riots, both police forces increased their number of followers. MET increased the number of followers from about 4,000 to more than 42,000. GMP increased its followers from below 23,000 to more than 100,000. This record number made the Greater Manchester Police, to the best of our knowledge, the world's second most popular police force on Twitter—only superseded by the U.S. FBI, which moreover operates on a national level, in a country with a much greater population, and is internationally renown. Intriguing about the follower numbers is that GMP, as the smaller police gained, a considerable following nearly 'over night'. Their follower numbers were moreover 2.5 times as high as the ones of MET police. At the time of writing, i.e., twelve months after the events, both forces sustained their followers, with @gmpolice now with 109,000 followers—an indicator for the relevance and interest the public has in police communication. The MET, in the meantime, has seen a larger increase and currently has more than 74,000 followers. This indicates that communication between police and public is also sustainable in the long run, especially when considering the dynamics in unfollow behavior [10]. This is especially remarkable as in our case there is no reciprocity in the relation between poster and follower.

Workshops and interviews with Police Officers

To this point our analyses relied solely on the messages posted on Twitter. This left open, in how far the disparate communication approaches were strategies or 'spur-of-the-moment' decisions. We thus further wanted to learn about the forces' subjective experiences and perspectives and present and discuss our findings with them.

In cooperation with GMP, we organized on-site interviews in the communication offices and also a workshop on the topic of social media as a communication tool for the police at their police academy. The workshop was attended by people of our team as well as by 14 police officers from the UK, other European countries and Canada, including 5 officers from GMP. We asked the officers to share their experiences about the communication during riots and present their overall social media strategies. We also discussed with them our analysis and findings.

At the invitation of the European Police College (CEPOL), the first author participated in CEPOL's first course on social media that took a full week and was attended by about 40 police officers from all over Europe. At the seminar, we had the opportunity to speak to social media specialist officers not only from the MET but also from the National Policing Improvement Agency that oversees and moderates change processes in UK police forces. Again, we listened to the officers' experiences, presented our findings and discussed them.

As a result, we learned that GMP had developed an overall communication strategy that included the comprehensive use of social media not only by using the main Twitter account that we studied but also by operating 60 additional localized Twitter accounts [8]. Using social media, GMP's local officers report about their daily work to their local communities. During the riots, fighting rumors, establishing a trusted voice and the support of intelligence gathering were the main priorities when using Twitter. Here, the #shopalooter campaign was a huge success to support investigations. As also shown in our examples, GMP had to handle issues of overstepping boundaries, the legality of publishing information and to learn when to engage and how to resource it. The need for speedy responses and the availability of respective resources were key challenges in managing the social media communication during the crisis. Yet, for both communication and investigative social media efforts, they could benefit from their past experience with the localized accounts and officers intimately familiar with Twitter communication.

For MET, the use of social media during the riots could not be based on similar extensive prior experience. The way in which social media was used, showed to be highly effective to support their work, nevertheless. Especially the use of Flickr to post images of suspects was highly successful. Here, Twitter served as a means to promote information on Flickr. Tweets using image links were 're-tweeted' at least 8,500 times. Within some hours Flickr images were viewed

4.3 million times. Investigations, especially as press attention decreased, were significantly supported by such identifications through social media.

In discussions at the workshops we also learnt that other forces, including GMP, used social media in the ways that MET did, when first introducing social media. This practice was based closely on ways in which police forces typically publish press information.

DISCUSSION

Instrumental vs. Expressive Usage

Our analysis on police crisis communication during the UK 2011 riots on Twitter identified two different approaches to engage with the public: MET preferred a formal, depersonalized style which emphasized the gap between the police and public. Messages were largely instrumental, either seeking or providing information or demonstrating police performance (e.g., number of arrests made, officers on the street, or requests for information). GMP, in contrast, developed a highly personalized, informal style including direct interactions with individual followers. Social messages of support, reassurance of the public and meta-discussions about the force's way of Twitter use, for instance, were unique to GMP. Based on [26], we refer to these styles as *instrumental* versus *expressive* usage strategies. Interestingly, the different styles only emerged after the start of the crisis. They can therefore be seen as direct expressions of disparate approaches to crisis communication on Twitter.

Benefits and Challenges of the Two Strategies

The police can perceive itself as subservient to the public, emphasize its separation from society as regulated by abstract rule rather than public fiat, or take an active role in influencing public processes [12]. In choosing an instrumental strategy, MET clearly opted for separation in its interaction with society on Twitter, while GMP decided for an active role and therefore adopted an expressive strategy. Our analyses and the subsequent discussions with officers highlighted clear benefits and challenges of the two strategies which are summarized in table 3.

How the public reacts to police actions depends on the relationship between police and public, and more specifically on the image of the police within a society [16, 27]. While in more traditional media, these disparate approaches may not be as visible, the fast-paced, dynamic, and open nature of Twitter throws disparate communication strategies into contrast. Public reactions are strong and first responders such as the police need to be aware of this greater volatility and vulnerability of public relations. The informed choice of a communication strategy is here an important step to prevent loss of legitimacy and trust, as well as public backlashes.

Relevance for HCI

In HCI, researcher have described how users ascribe meaning to technology and called for designs that support

many forms of appropriation (e.g. [7]). Twitter can surely be described as a system that implements this concept with its limited prescriptions for use. In the context of the police, such open system meets an organization with a complex set of rules and trained practice. Our results point to the need for organizational change and practice and policy development, when police forces adopt these interactive tools highly open for appropriation. Aspects such as image and legitimacy are vital for the function of police, yet are continuously affected and challenged by novel computing systems.

	Instrumental	*Expressive*
Benefits	Effective support of primary policing functions; lower maintenance than expressive strategy; no interference in internal decisions by public	Create closer relations to the public; increases following and thus possible reach; creates greater tolerance for mistakes
Challenges	Loose relations with public; lower following, and thus lower potential to harness resources	High maintenance; overstepping of boundaries easy; easy polarization of public opinions

Table 3: Benefits and challenges of strategies

Consequently, HCI for crisis information systems for the police and other emergency responders is not only a technological problem or a problem of immediate men-machine interaction, but requires 'zooming-out' to a wider perspective [23] that takes into account policy designs, culture and the interaction and desired relation with the public. Understanding appropriation practices of social media by early-adopting organizations, such as the British police in our case, needs to inspire and influence the development of future tools and their use.

CONCLUSION

In this paper we analyzed Twitter use by the Metropolitan and Greater Manchester police in the run-up and during the UK riots in August 2011. As we found, even though both forces used the same communication tool, their practices during the crisis differed detrimentally.

Making these different options visible is a basis for future research to widen and deepen our understanding of social media in crisis communications. It also provides a basis to support first responders, such as police forces in our case, to make informed decisions on how to adopt and use social media effectively.

Our study goes a first step into detailing how disparate adoption and usages patterns of Twitter emerge during crises and it further provides a first indication of the effects on image and relationship with the public. Our data indicates that choosing an instrumental versus an expressive strategy may lead to different relationships between police and public. Given the dependence of police on public cooperation, the choice may well impact police performance in the short- and long-term.

For HCI, our study indicates that tools open for appropriation increase the need for professional organizations to develop strategies and policies on how to adopt them and to make them fit within in the given context.

ACKNOWLEDGMENTS

We would like to thank all our interview partners and workshop participants, as well as the respective police forces and our project partners, for their invaluable support in this research. This work is partially funded by the European Commission in the context of the COMPOSITE project (FP7 contract no. 241918).

REFERENCES

1. Bunt, H. The DIT++ taxonomy for functional dialogue markup. Proc. *AMAAS'09 Workshop: Towards a Standard Markup Language for Embodied Dialogue Acts* (2009)

2. CBC News. Getting to the root of the U.K. riots. (2011) http://www.cbc.ca/news/world/story/2011/08/09/f-uk-riots-faq.html

3. Chermak, S. and Weiss, A. Maintaining legitimacy using external communication strategies: An analysis of police-media relations. *J. of Criminal Justice,* 33,(2005).

4. Child, J. and Rodrigues, S. B. How organizations engage with external complexity: A political action perspective. *Organization Studies,* 32(6), (2011), 803-824.

5. Coleman, A. Twitter at the heart of communities. (2011) http://connectedcops.net/?p=3931

6. Denef, S., Kaptein, N., Bayerl, P. S., et al. ICT Trends in European Policing. The COMPOSITE Project. (2011) http://www.fit.fraunhofer.de/content/dam/fit/de/documents/composite_d41.pdf

7. Dourish, P. *Where the Action Is: The Foundations of Embodied Interaction.* The MIT Press (2001).

8. Greater Manchester Police. A day in the life of GMP on Twitter. (2010) http://youtu.be/aulazCNbaDQ

9. Guy, M, Earle, P, Ostrum, C, Gruchalla, K & Horvath, S. Integration and Dissemination of Citizen Reported and Seismically Derived Earthquake Information via Social Network Technologies. Advances in Intelligent Data Analysis IX, *Lecture Notes in Computer Science,* 6065, (2010), 42-53.

10. Haewoon Kwak, Hyunwoo Chun, and Sue Moon. Fragile online relationship: a first look at unfollow dynamics in Twitter. In *Proc. of CHI'11,* ACM (2011).

11. Halliday M.A.K. *Learning how to mean.* Edward Arnold (1975).

12. Herbert, S. Tangled up in blue. Conflicting paths to police legitimacy. *Critical Criminology,* 10(4), (2006), 481-504.

13. Hughes, A., L. Palen, J. Sutton, S. Liu, & S. Vieweg. "Site- Seeing" in disaster: An examination of on-line social convergence. In *Proc. ISCRAM'08.*

14. Hughes, M. and Sanchez R. London riots: Met chief Tim Godwin considered shutting off Twitter. (2011) http://www.telegraph.co.uk/news/politics/8704239/London-riots-Met-chief-Tim-Godwin-considered-shutting-off-Twitter.html

15. Mendoza, M., Poblete, B. and Castillo, C. Twitter under crisis: Can we trust what we RT? *1st Workshop on Social Media Analytics SOMA '10* (2010).

16. Murphy, K., Hinds, L., and Fleming, J. Encouraging public cooperation and support for police. *Policing and Society,* 18(2), (2008), 136-155.

17. Qu, Y., Wu, P. and Wang, X. Online Community Response to Major Disaster: A Case Study of Tianya Forum in the 2008 China Earthquake. In *Proc 42nd Hawaii Int'l Conf. on System Sciences,* (2009), 1-11.

18. Reuters. Riots to cost over £200 million - ABI (2011) http://reut.rs/peJcRx

19. Slater, S. Social media to the rescue When disaster strikes. (2011) http://connectedcops.net/?p=4650

20. Starbird, K, Palen, L, Hughes, A and Vieweg, S. Chatter on the red: What hazards threat reveals about the social life of microblogged information. In *Proc. of CSCW'10* (2010), 241-250.

21. Starbird, K. and Palen, L. (2011). "Voluntweeters": Self-organizing by digital volunteers in times of crisis. In *Proc. CHI'11,* ACM Press (2011), 1071-1080.

22. Strauss, A. and Corbin, J. *Basics of Qualitative Research: Techniques and Procedures for Developing Grounded Theory,* 2nd edition. Sage (1998).

23. Suchman, L. *Human-Machine Reconfigurations: Plans and Situated Actions.* Cambridge Univ. Press (2007).

24. Sumpter, S. Police on Twitter. (2011) http://www.latentexistence.me.uk/police-on-twitter/

25. The Mirror. London riots: More than 2,000 people arrested over disorder. http://www.mirror.co.uk/news/uk-news/london-riots-more-than-2000-people-185548

26. Thomas, J.C. and Kellog, W.A. The Necessity of Expressive Communication in Organizations. (2001). http://www.truthtable.com/ExpressiveCommunicationBuildsMutualTrust.html

27. Tyler, T. R. and Fagan, J. Legitimacy and cooperation: Why do people help the police fight crime in their communities? *Ohio State J. of Criminal Law,* 6, (2008), 231-271.

28. Vieweg, S, Hughes, A, Starbird, K, & Palen, L. Micro-blogging during two natural hazards events: What Twitter May Contribute to Situational Awareness. In *Proc of CHI'10,* ACM Press (2010), 1079-1088.

Whoo.ly: Facilitating Information Seeking
For Hyperlocal Communities Using Social Media

Yuheng Hu
School of Computer Science
Arizona State University
yuheng@asu.edu

Shelly D. Farnham
Microsoft Research
shellyfa@microsoft.com

Andrés Monroy-Hernández
Microsoft Research
amh@microsoft.com

ABSTRACT

Social media systems promise powerful opportunities for people to connect to timely, relevant information at the hyper local level. Yet, finding the meaningful signal in noisy social media streams can be quite daunting to users. In this paper, we present and evaluate Whoo.ly, a web service that provides neighborhood-specific information based on Twitter posts that were automatically inferred to be hyperlocal. Whoo.ly automatically extracts and summarizes hyperlocal information about events, topics, people, and places from these Twitter posts. We provide an overview of our design goals with Whoo.ly and describe the system including the user interface and our unique event detection and summarization algorithms. We tested the usefulness of the system as a tool for finding neighborhood information through a comprehensive user study. The outcome demonstrated that most participants found Whoo.ly easier to use than Twitter and they would prefer it as a tool for exploring their neighborhoods.

Author Keywords

Hyperlocal community; Twitter; Social media; Location-based social networks; Civic engagement; Event detection.

ACM Classification Keywords

H5.3. Information interfaces and presentation: Group and Organization Interfaces – *Collaborative computing*

INTRODUCTION

People rely on multiple sources of information to learn about the communities they live in [28], either for the purpose of community awareness or participation [26]. *Hyperlocal* information is comprised of the news, people, and events that are set within a particular locality, and is of particular interest primarily to the residents of that locality [9]. One of the most important sources of hyperlocal content is social media, such as blogs, microblogs, and social networking sites. Social media has many advantages over traditional media in assisting people's quest for hyperlocal content. With the ubiquity and immediacy of social media, news events often are reported on Twitter or Facebook

ahead of traditional news media. For example, the news of both the 2012 Aurora shootings in Colorado and the 2012 Empire State Building shooting in New York City were reported by social media users earlier than by traditional news outlets [8, 2]. Social media has also become one of the few sources of local news—and life-saving information—where traditional media is sometimes censored by governments or even criminal organizations [24]. Moreover, social media has emerged as a dominant platform for communication and connection. As hyperlocal content is mostly generated by and for a community, seamless communication and networking (through one's social networks) can increase exposure to timely peer-generated content, raise people's community awareness, and potentially foster their sense of community [4].

In spite of these benefits, social media tends to be noisy, chaotic, and overwhelming, posing challenges to users in seeking and distilling high quality content from the noise. It should be no surprise that, regardless of the popularity of social media as a source of hyperlocal information, people are still using television and newspapers (among other traditional sources) as their main channels for local information [28]. People need help leveraging social media as a source of information about their hyperlocal communities. At one extreme are the fast-paced, uncurated social media streams: chaotic and overwhelming. At the other extreme are the traditional, authoritative, news sources: slow and less participatory than social media. In this paper, we present Whoo.ly, a novel web service balanced between these two extremes.

Whoo.ly automatically discovers, extracts, and summarizes relevant hyperlocal information contributed on Twitter to facilitate people's neighborhood information-seeking activities. Inspired by the core journalism questions (what, who, where, and when), Whoo.ly provides four types of hyperlocal content in a simple web-based interface (See Figure 1): (i) *active events* (events that are trending in the locality); (ii) *top topics* (most frequently mentioned terms and phrases from recent Twitter posts); (iii) *popular places* (most frequently checked-in/mentioned); and (iv) *active people* (Twitter users mentioned the most).

It is important to note that it is not our goal with Whoo.ly to replace traditional news media. Instead, we want to provide hyperlocal information that is complementary to what both traditional news media and social media have to offer.

The unique features of Whoo.ly are the novel event detection and summarization algorithms we developed. Active neighborhood events are detected using a novel scalable statistical event detector that identifies and groups trending features in Twitter posts. Top neighborhood topics are inferred using a simple yet effective weighting scheme that finds the most important words and phrases from posts. To identify the most popular places in a neighborhood, we used both template-based information extractors and learning-based information extractors. Finally, to distill a ranked list of the active people in a community, we developed a ranking scheme on the social graph of Twitter users based on their mentioning and posting activities.

To evaluate Whoo.ly's utility as a tool for finding neighborhood information, including its user interface and our algorithms, we performed a user study with thirteen residents from three Seattle neighborhoods. Most of our participants believed Whoo.ly provided them with useful neighborhood information, and rated it easier to use than Twitter's native tools.

The contributions of this work are:

- A novel system for discovering hyperlocal information from the social media site Twitter;
- A novel approach for extracting and summarizing trending events from Twitter posts ; and
- Quantitative and qualitative support that our techniques provide higher quality results than existing solutions.

RELATED WORK

Using new technologies to promote community awareness and participation has long been a research topic for the HCI community and [33, 23]. Web-mediated communities such as Netville and the Blacksburg Electronic Village have demonstrated how the Internet can enhance spatial immediacy, facilitate discussion, and quickly mobilize people around local issues [11, 5].

The prevalence of "Web 2.0" has provided new opportunities for technologies to facilitate better information seeking and communication about local communities. In particular, social media tools have been used to report various activities including breaking news [22], public debates [17], crises like floods [31], earthquakes [29], or even during wartime [24]. Recently, leveraging social media resources for local communities has drawn considerable attention in both research and industry. Such efforts include Livehoods [7] and i-Neighbors [10]. Among them, CiVicinity [14] provides a hyperlocal community portal that integrates information from Facebook, blogs, calendars, and other sources to promote civic awareness and participation. Virtual Town Square (VTS) [20] also aggregates local information from a predefined set of information sources (government, schools, and news organizations) to improve community engagement. Our work uniquely builds on this line of research by exploring automatic solutions to the detection, extraction and summarization of neighborhood information from noisy Twitter posts.

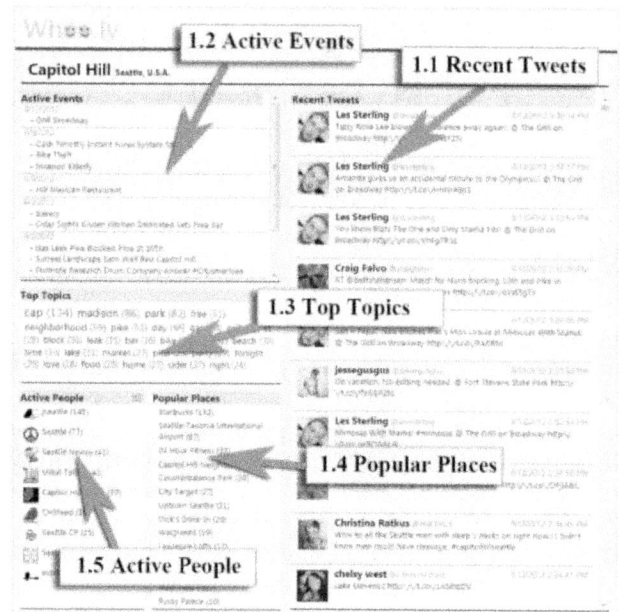

Figure 1. The main Whoo.ly interface, with the recent Twitter posts and summaries of events, topics, places, and people.

The hyperlocal content in Whoo.ly is automatically mined from Twitter, which presents unique challenges not directly addressed by related work: (1) Prior solutions on event detection from social media commonly employ the strategy of clustering similar Twitter posts, using a classifier to predict the event-related clusters, and then extracting events from these clusters [1]. Such an approach may work well on long text documents (e.g., blogs) but perform poorly on Twitter posts, since clustering outcomes can be noisy; at the same time, analyzing sparse and short text can be challenging [15]. In addition, this strategy needs to be trained in advance. In contrast, our proposed event detector finds trending events without any supervision and, more importantly, it is highly scalable, making it feasible to efficiently handle large-scale social media data. (2) Our method of finding top topics was inspired by the TF-IDF statistics that assign scores for terms based on their mentioned frequency within and across documents. Even though there are other efforts to find top topics from Twitter posts [27], such approaches often take a long time to run to discover meaningful topics, and we seek to provide reasonably real-time results. (3) Information extraction has been a long-standing research topic [6]. In Whoo.ly, we use a hybrid approach of both template-based and learning-based extractors to find popular places in Twitter posts.

WHOO.LY OVERVIEW AND DESIGN PROCESS

In this section, we first provide an overview of Whoo.ly and its features. Then, we highlight the motivations underlying the choices we made in the design process.

Whoo.ly is a web service built on top of Twitter. Its goal is to provide people with relevant and reliable hyperlocal news content. By browsing the website, people immediately find what is happening in a specific neighborhood. Whoo.ly provides four hyperlocal content types: active events, top topics, active people, and popular places (See Figure 1). All of them are automatically extracted and summarized from Twitter using various approaches we developed, such as statistical event detector, graph-based ranking algorithm, and information extractors (see the System Design section for more detail).

Early in the design process for Whoo.ly, we examined local newspapers, community blogs, existing hyperlocal sites, and Twitter. The exploratory study revealed several interesting results that we used to motivate the design of Whoo.ly: (1) The majority of the people only consume information—they do not produce it but only read it; (2) People become more active in reporting and disseminating local breaking events (e.g., shooting, water leak) on Twitter by reposting related tweets; (3) People tend to follow neighborhood curators or bloggers who are dedicated to posting hyperlocal content; and (4) Local media and local news services effectively cover important local topics. However, people further seek hyperlocal content generated by people in their communities.

We performed an additional preliminary analysis of Twitter data to help inform our design decisions, answering the following questions: (1) can we find a base of local Twitter posts based on neighborhoods; (2) were there enough messages to seed a neighborhood website; and (3) what do people care to talk about on Twitter regarding their neighborhoods? We first queried for all Twitter messages from people who claimed Seattle as their home town for the month of October of 2011. We then performed a simple extraction of Twitter messages that mentioned one of 83 Seattle neighborhoods. We found 50,609 unique Seattle users and produced 1.2 million messages (about 8% of total Seattle population), out of which 5% explicitly mentioned Seattle, and another 2% mentioned a Seattle neighborhood. On average 132 people posted per neighborhood over the month, averaging 1.8 messages each, which translates into about 8 messages per day per neighborhood. There was great variability across neighborhoods, but we considered the above averages to be a promising start and used them as the volume of neighborhood Twitter messages to expect.

To examine message content, we sampled 24% of the messages (424) from three neighborhoods pre-selected for being diverse from each other. We first coded the messages for whether they were erroneously assigned to the neighborhood. Surprising, only 21 messages (5%) were erroneously assigned, largely because of overlapping neighborhood names and other place names (e.g., the area "Mount Baker" and the mountain "Mount Baker" it was named after). We then looked at how many were personal in nature, of little interest to anyone aside from the author's friends. We found that 13% of messages were of this nature. Places check-ins comprised another 55 messages (10%), which we expect might be interesting when aggregated but not at the individual level. Six items were impossible to interpret and were left unclassified. The remaining messages were 71%

on topic, meaningfully pertaining to the neighborhood. We further inspected and coded by message type and whether or not they were about a current event. We defined a *current event* as a real-world occurrence with an associated time period such that if it is not observed, experienced, or attended in that time period a person will not be able to do so later. Thus a crime, a fire, a festival, or a Friday happy hour are current events. In contrast, a photo shared online, a news story link, a recommendation to try a restaurant, or a shoutout of thanks are not. We found that 55 % of the remaining Twitter messages were about an event.

Types of neighborhood messages	Percent
Neighborhood Affirmations	13%
Local Business Updates	11%
Local News	11%
Recommendations	11%
Civic Activity	10%
Classified Ads	9%
Social Events	8%
Crime, Fire, Emergency, Road Reports	7%
Deals/Coupon	7%
Talks or Classes	4%
Festival or Outdoor Market	4%
Local Sports	2%
Salutations, Thanks, Shoutouts	2%
Acts of Nature	1%

Table 1: Types of neighborhood messages shared on Twitter.

All message types in our data sample were classified as depicted by Table 1. Topics such as crime reports, Yelp-like recommendations, and local news were not surprising. The neighborhood affirmations and salutations were surprising, where people in the community post messages talking about how much they love their neighborhood, or community-affirming, humorous messages reinforcing the neighborhood's stereotypical traits.

Based on these findings, we decided to focus first on detecting events and then to promote community-enabling features such as a list of top users so that people can know and follow each other. To prevent information overload, we also provided top topics so that people can quickly learn the common neighborhood topics in the Twitter posts (tweets).

DATA COLLECTION OF WHOO.LY

Whoo.ly is built on Twitter. We utilized the Twitter Firehose that is made available to us via our company's contract with Twitter. Since we are interested in discovering hyperlocal content for local communities in various geographic regions, we needed to obtain a set of Twitter posts from each region. Twitter offers two possible ways to infer a tweet's location: GPS coordinates associated with a tweet or the user's location in their profile. In this work we used the location information derived from the user profile since the number of Twitter posts found by GPS coordinates is very limited (about 0.6%). From our preliminary analysis using this method, we found a reasonable quantity of on-topic neighborhood messages.

We observed that most Twitter users prefer to mention only their city instead of local community for the profile location, probably due to privacy concerns [13]. As a result, we first obtained Twitter posts from the Firehose, where each associated user profile location matches one of the dictionary strings for a city, e.g., "Seattle" or "Sea". Next, we mapped these Twitter posts into different neighborhood regions by matching their textual content against a list of neighborhoods. Note that the neighborhood list for each city is created by domain experts who have comprehensive experience with the neighborhood development and boundaries in that city.

We used a dataset that included about 2.2 million Twitter posts in English from about 120,000 unique users whose profile location indicated they are from Seattle, over a three-month period from June 1, 2012 to Aug 15, 2012. While we mainly used this static dataset for developing our prototype, our methods may easily be extended to handle real-time tweet streams.

SYSTEM DESIGN OF WHOO.LY

In this section we describe the system design of Whoo.ly (Figure 1), including the interface design of its components and the technical design behind them. Whoo.ly's interface is implemented in HTML, CSS, and Ajax controls toolkits, served by ASP.net on the cloud service Windows Azure.

Whoo.ly first shows a start page, where a user selects his or her country, city, and neighborhood through drop-down lists. After selecting their location, users are taken to the results page (Figure 1), which displays recent Twitter posts, top topics, popular places, and active people.

Recent Twitter Posts

Whoo.ly presents recent Twitter posts in a scrolling list on the right side of the results page (Figure 1.1). Each row in this list contains a detailed Twitter profile for a user on the top, and his or her recent posts at the bottom. The profile includes standard elements retrieved from Twitter such as the user name, screen name, user's profile image, user's profile location, and the posting time of the messages.

Whoo.ly only provides the most recent Twitter posts from a time window of 14 days mainly because people are usually only interested in most recent Twitter posts. Nevertheless, the length of the time span can be easily adjusted through a drop-down list at the bottom of the results page.

Active Events

Whoo.ly presents an active events list calendar (Figure 1.2) on the upper left side of the results page. Each entry shows the events organized by date. Every event is summarized by a list of terms and, by clicking on its name, the user is taken to a page (Figure 2) containing all the posts that are about that event, ranked by their relevance score using vector similarity [22].

A core research question in this component is how can we detect *active events*? Given a tweet stream, where each tweet consists of a set of features F_1, F_2,... (e.g., gas, leak,

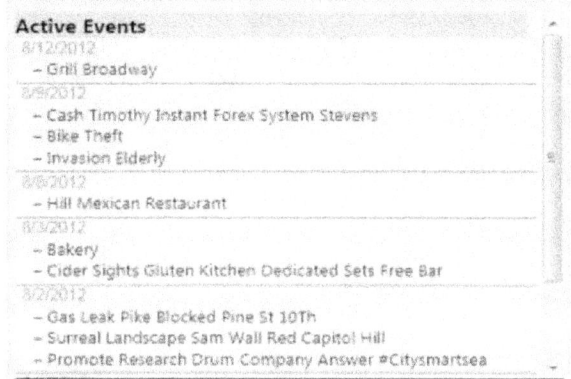

Figure 2: A close-up view of the Active Events pane. Events are organized by date and are represented by a list of terms most associated with each event.

danger, etc.), *active event detection* is finding a set of active events, where an active event consists of a set of *topically-related trending* features, at a given time period. To address this question, we developed a novel event detector, which (1) identifies trending features from Twitter posts using trends indicators; and (2) clusters the topically-related trending features into event-clusters using topic modeling and a clustering scheme. Next, we explain our approach in detail.

Trending Features Identification

To identify trending features from a substantial volume of Twitter posts, we first need to determine what is *trending*. Inspired by the model of theoretical "bursts" in streams of topics [12], we define trending as a time interval over which the rate of change of momentum (i.e., product of mass and velocity) is positive. We further define that *mass* is the current importance of the feature and the *velocity* is the rate of change of the feature's frequency in Twitter posts, during a time period. Since it is hard to directly measure the momentum from these values, we chose to use the trend analysis tools *EMA* (Exponential Moving Average), *MACD* (Moving Average Convergence Divergence), and *MACD* histogram from the quantitative finance literature [25] to yield established measures of momentum. Next, we explain how these tools work to identify trending features from Twitter posts.

Given a feature F and its time series $S(F) = \{f_1, f_2, ... f_m\}$, f_i denotes the frequency that F is mentioned by the Twitter posts posted within the i-th period. For example, the word "morning" can have a time series $S = \{248,305,154,52,24,9\}$ from 8 a.m. to 2 p.m. of the day, in which it was mentioned 248 times by the Twitter posts from 8 a.m. to 9 a.m., 305 times from 9 a.m. to 10 a.m., and so on. Moving averages are commonly used with time series data to smooth out short-term fluctuations and highlight longer-term trend. Here, we compute the n-hour *EMA* for $S(F)$ as: $EMA_i = \alpha \times f_i + (1 - \alpha) \times EMA_{i-1}$, where $\alpha = 2/(n + 1)$ is a smoothing factor, n is a time lag, and $1 \leq i \leq m$ is the index of time period. Essentially, the *EMA* smoothens out noises of F by averaging its time series over a specific number of periods.

Next, to spot changes in the momentum of F, we compute the $MACD$ statistics, which is defined as the difference between the n_1- and n_2- hour EMA for $S(F)$, where n_1 and n_2 are time lags. Finally, to identify whether and when F is trending, we need to quantify the rate of change of its momentum. Therefore, we calculate the $MACD$ histogram, defined as the difference between F's $MACD$ and its signal line (the n-day EMA of $MACD$). As this difference measures the rate of change, the result at a given time period can be either positive (indicating F is trending up) or negative (indicating F is trending down).

In some cases, the trending features may occur repeatedly. For example, "morning" can be trending from 8 a.m. to 11 a.m. every day. Such trending feature may be less interesting compared to the ones which are single occurrences. To resolve this problem, we assign a "novelty" score to the identified trending feature according to their deviation from their expected trend. More specifically, for a trending feature F, we denote $R(h, d, w, F)$ as its $MACD$ histogram result during hour h, day d, and week w. With this notation, we can compare F's trend in a specific day or hour in a given week to the same day or hour in other weeks (e.g., 9 a.m. on Monday, Aug 6, 2012, vs. the trend on other Mondays at 9 a.m.). Let $Mean(h, d, F)$ and $SD(h, d, F)$ denote the *average trend* and the *standard deviation* of F on hour h and day d over week w_1 to w_n, respectively. Then, the novelty score of feature F on hour h, day d, and week w is defined as: $Score(h, d, F) = [R(h, d, w, F) - Mean(h, d, F)]/SD(h, d, F)$. Based on this score, we rank each feature to find the novel trending features.

In practice, to detect the daily active events, we first built a dictionary of features from all the Twitter posts of one day. Then, we created a time series for each feature by counting their frequencies in Twitter posts in every two hours. As a result, we have a 12-hour-long time series for every feature. Then, we applied the EMA, $MACD$, *and* $MACD$ histogram over the time series data to identify whether and when a feature is trending. Finally, for every two hours, we picked the trending feature which (1) is least mentioned 20 times in the Twitter posts from that time period, and (2) has a novelty score among the top 25 scores for all trending features from that time period. Since these steps are computable in an online fashion [12], our approach is highly efficient.

Trending Feature Clustering
To group the trending features into topically-related event-clusters, we use the shared nearest neighborhood (SNN) clustering algorithm [18]. We chose this algorithm because it is scalable and does not require a priori knowledge of the number of clusters (as Twitter posts are constantly evolving and new events get added to the stream over time).

The SNN algorithm is executed as follows: each trending feature is a node of the graph and each node is linked to another by an edge if it belongs to the k neighbor list of the second object. Here, we define feature F_1 is the *neighbor* of feature F_2 only if F_1 and F_2 are topically-related (e.g., "gas" can be a neighbor to "leak" but may not be to "party"). To learn a feature's topic, we use topic modeling [3], a popular machine learning tool for getting topic distributions from text. In order to measure the topical relationship between two features, we use the Jensen-Shannon divergence on their topic distributions. As a result, if the distance is above a threshold, the two features are neighbors.

Top Topics
Below the trending events section, Whoo.ly shows a list of top topics (with their frequencies) that are being discussed in the recent Twitter posts (Figure 1.3). Clicking a topic leads to a page showing all the Twitter posts about it. This component helps people quickly understand and familiarize themselves with the most important topics about the neighborhood appearing in Twitter posts. We design a fast approach by applying normalized TF-IDF statistics for each uni-, bi-, and tri-gram from the recent Twitter posts. We then rank these grams to render this component.

Popular Places
Beyond the event and topics, Whoo.ly shows a list of 15 most popular places (Figure 1.4) that people keep checking into and mentioning in Twitter posts. Similar to other components, clicking a place leads to a page showing all Twitter posts about this place. This component helps people discover interesting places in their neighborhood and learn what is happening there. Extracting these places from Twitter posts requires automated information extraction, which has been a long-standing research topic in NLP and machine learning [6]. In the next sections, we describe two types of extractors we use to build this component, namely a template-based extractor and learning-based extractor.

Template-based Information Extractor
Through our manual inspection of the Twitter posts content (see the Overview section), we found there is a small percentage of Twitter posts (approximately 7%) that were posted by Foursquare check-ins. Such Twitter posts have a specific template in their content: begin with the phase "I'm at", followed by a place name (e.g., *Space Needle*), and followed by its address (e.g., *400 Broad Street, Seattle, WA 98102*). Given this structure, we designed a template-based extractor using regular expressions to distill the place information.

Learning-based Information Extractor
For Twitter posts without explicit format for location inference, we used a statistical information extractor. It is built on top of an n-gram language Markov model and previously trained on Wikipedia pages, Tweets, and Yelp data [32]. We apply it to analyze the Twitter posts to extract entities for places, e.g., restaurants, parks, streets, stadiums, etc.

Active People
Last, Whoo.ly displays a list of top 10 most active people (i.e., Twitter users) for the corresponding neighborhood (Figure 1.5). Each record in the list combines a user's profile and the frequency this user posts or was recently mentioned by other people. In addition, Whoo.ly also presents

the profiles, latest Twitter posts, and activities of all the users who have recently posted Twitter messages (by clicking "All" on the up right corner of this division). With this component, one can easily identify who are the active and influential people in the neighborhood and can decide to follow their activity.

To build this component, we developed a PageRank-like algorithm to rank the Twitter users based on their mentioning and posting activities. Specifically, a directed graph $D(V, E)$ is formed with the users and the "follower-followee" relationships among them. V is the vertex set, containing all the users. E is the edge set. There is an edge between two users if there is "following" relationship between them, and the edge is directed from follower to followee. Our algorithm performs an activity-specific *random walk* on graph D to calculate the rank. It visits each user with certain transition probability by following the appropriate edge in D. The probability is proportional to a linear combination of the interactions between two users (e.g., RT, mentioning, reply) and how many Twitter posts a user has posted recently. The idea is that the more activities a user has, the higher this user's rank is.

USER STUDY

We evaluated Whoo.ly as a tool for users to learn about what is happening in their neighborhood using a within-subjects comparison of Whoo.ly and Twitter, where users completed a series of information-seeking tasks for each platform and then provided feedback. For our user study, we focused only on three Seattle neighborhoods for which we were able to recruit participants.

Participants

We introduced 13 Seattle residents into a private, pre-release version of Whoo.ly through five focus group sessions, with two or three people per session. Participants were recruited from a pre-existing database of people who for the most part had expressed interest in user studies. Potential participants in the database were first filtered for address zip codes in our target neighborhoods. After receiving phone calls to screen for whether they continued to live in the neighborhood and had a Twitter account, they were scheduled to participate in one of five sessions. In exchange for their participation they received their choice of a software gratuity or gift card. Participants were on average 30 years of age (ranging from 23 to 48). 54% of them were female and 46% were male. Ten participants were white, one Asian, one Native American, and one had other ethnic identity. The majority of participants were from the Capital Hill neighborhood (69%), with 23% from Wallingford and 8% from Rainier Valley. These neighborhoods differed in density, SES, and level of existing community infrastructure.

Procedure

During two-hour user sessions participants first completed a preliminary questionnaire. They then briefly discussed their current communication practices for finding and sharing neighborhood information in a semi-structured focused group. Participants then individually completed a series of tasks with both Whoo.ly and Twitter using laptops with an Internet connection we provided. After a brief discussion of participants' experiences, we ended the session by having them rate a series of Twitter messages for neighborhood content.

Preliminary Questionnaire

Participants first completed a brief preliminary questionnaire to assess demographic information, use of Internet, and social media, and measure of their current neighborhood including psychological sense of community, neighborhood communication efficacy, and civic engagement. We measured psychological sense of local community [30], or the feeling of connection, belonging, and loyalty to a local community, with items such as *"I feel loyal to the people in my neighborhood," "I really care about the fate of neighborhood,"* and *"I feel like I belong in my neighborhood."* Civic engagement was measured using items from the Civic Engagement Questionnaire [21], a standard measure asking how often respondents had engaged in various civic activities such as *"Spending time participating in any neighborhood community service or volunteer activity"* and *"playing a leadership role in my neighborhood (such as local government or leadership in a club)."* Neighborhood communication self-efficacy, including communication self-efficacy, was measured with items adapted from the California Civic Index [19] that addressed communication, including *"I know how to collect information and be informed about neighborhood issues,"* and *"I know how to get in touch with members of my neighborhood when I need to communicate with them."* For each measure, items were rated on a Likert scale of 1 to 7, where 1 = *not at all* and 7 = *extremely so*, and then items were averaged for analysis.

Focus Group

To further elucidate existing information-seeking and communication practices, we then had participants discuss their neighborhoods using a semi-structured group interview. Participants first described the character of their neighborhoods, how long they have been living there, and whether they had a sense of connection or community to their neighborhood. We then asked participants to discuss what kinds of information they cared to learn about in their neighborhoods. Participants then described the tools they currently use to seek out information or communicate with others around neighborhood issues and where they would like to see changes or improvements in the tools available.

Neighborhood Information Seeking Task

Following the focus group, participants individually completed a series of four information-seeking tasks, once in Whoo.ly, and once in Twitter. Each participant completed the tasks separately on a laptop with an Internet connection following instructions in a paper packet. The order of the tasks (Whoo.ly vs. Twitter) was counterbalanced across sessions, ending with seven participants completing the Twitter tasks first and six participants completing the Whoo.ly tasks first. Participants were instructed, *"for this part of the study we will have you explore what's happening in your neighborhood using [Twitter or Whoo.ly]."* The four tasks were: 1) find neighborhood events: *"try to find three interesting or significant events that happened in your neighborhood the past couple of weeks"*; 2) find neighborhood reporters: *"imagine you wanted to try to follow three people to help you keep up to date with what's happening in your neighborhood—try to find those three people you would follow"*; 3) find neighborhood topics: *"imagine you wanted to find out what kinds of topics your neighborhood tends to care about—try to find three of these topics;"* and 4) find neighborhood friends: *"imagine you wanted to get to know some people in your neighborhood better—find three people you might want to know more"*.

Participants were instructed to spend only a few minutes on each task, to get a sense for the experience in the system they were evaluating. After completing each task participants rated the ease of the task to complete, how confident they felt about their answers, and how engaged they were by the task (that is, to what extent they found it fun or interesting).

Following the completion of these tasks, participants rated the overall usefulness and ease of each system (Twitter and Whoo.ly), the extent to which it provided a good overview of what is happening in their neighborhood, the extent to which it provided a sense of connection, and which system they would prefer to use for finding out what is happening in their neighborhoods. Finally, participants were asked to rank their preference for individual aspects of the Whoo.ly interface and provide opened-ended feedback to questions about what they liked, disliked, and possible improvements.

Tweet Rating Task
In order evaluate the event-detection algorithms, participants were asked to rate a randomly selected series of Twitter posts from the period spanning two weeks prior to that of the current Whoo.ly system. For each tweet, participants rated if it was a about a neighborhood event and if so, how significant was the event to their neighborhood, where 1 = not at all, few people involved, and 7 = extremely so, entire neighborhood involved.

RESULTS
In analyzing our results, we first examined our participants' existing neighborhood information-seeking and communication practices to better shed light on their experience of Whoo.ly and potential considerations for a real world deployment of this system. We then assessed how well participants completed information-seeking tasks in Whoo.ly, providing a comparison to Twitter as a baseline tool for searching and browsing Twitter messages. Finally, we further examined themes that emerged from participant ratings and discussions that would meaningfully influence the design of Whoo.ly and similar systems.

Existing Practices
In our preliminary questionnaire participants rated themselves as having high levels of overall Internet experience, with 39% categorizing themselves as intermediate, 45% as advanced, and 16% as expert. Seventy-six percent of partic-

ipants reported spending four or more hours a day using the Internet. For communicating and sharing with others, participants reported text messaging ($M = 6.5$, $SD = 0.66$) and e-mail ($M = 6.6$, $SD = 0.65$) to be extremely important, then social networking sites such as Facebook ($M = 5.9$, $SD = 1.00$), blogs ($M = 4.1$, $SD = 1.32$), Twitter ($M = 3.6$, $SD = 1.90$), and mailing lists less so (where 1 = not at all, and 7 = extremely so).

Most of the participants in our study cared very much about their neighborhoods, reporting fairly high levels of psychological sense of community ($M = 5.0$, $SD = 0.83$). The few exceptions made apparent from our interviews were individuals new to the neighborhood, or one participant who felt his neighborhood was too transitional by nature to become attached to it. However, the participants had lower levels of civic engagement (3.0, 1.27) and communication self-efficacy ($M = 3.8$, $SD = 1.8$).

When asked to what extent they could collect information and be informed about neighborhood issues, participants' responses were on average moderate ($M = 3.9$, $SD = 1.8$). An examination of the distribution of this variable suggests it is bimodal, for example people either were low (45% at 2 or 3) or high (39% at 5 or higher) in their ability to find information or communicate with their neighborhood. When participants were asked how exactly they learned about what was happening in their neighborhoods, resources were quite diverse, including local newspapers, local blogs, following business on Twitter, local meetings, Facebook groups, coffee shops, and services such as Reddit, Google, and Yelp. However, local blogs clearly played a prominent role and word of mouth was frequently mentioned as a source of information. Several people mentioned Facebook or Facebook groups, but these were groups of people they knew who were in their neighborhoods, rather than public Facebook groups for the entire neighborhood. Further, it was clear that some neighborhoods had many more resources available than others.

We further asked what kinds of neighborhood information participants wanted to know about. Emerging themes were events such as local festivals and block parties, crime, new restaurants and bars, building developments, people, and local business promotions such as happy hours and coupons. Events and crime were most frequently mentioned, particularly as they impacted the local community. One participant's response was,

Community stuff—like I heard about neighborhood night out but I didn't know about it, my street closed and people were out drinking and barbecuing and I didn't know about it— you know about the big things, but little community stuff, that stuff you should know.

On average, participants were not confident they knew how to get in touch with members of their neighborhood when they needed to communicate with them ($M = 3.5$, $SD = 1.9$). When participants were asked, if they needed to communicate with members of their neighborhood community about neighborhood issues, how would they do so, face-to-face was rated the most highly (M = 5.2, SD = 1.8), followed by Facebook groups. During the interviews across sessions participants similarly exhibited low confidence in how they would go about communicating with their neighbors, and expected they would resort to walking down the street. One participant replied, *"old fashioned way, knock on door. Too many people in the neighborhood to have phone numbers and e-mails."* More tech-savvy participants said they would contact the local blog or access their neighbors' e-mail addresses.

We asked participants to discuss their Twitter usage in particular, given the focus of Twitter as a source of public information in Whoo.ly. All participants had an account, but the majority used it primarily to consume information, either the news or their friends' posts. Only a few used Twitter to follow their neighborhood bloggers or neighborhood businesses.

To summarize, we found that our participants were fairly tech-savvy and felt fairly attached to their neighborhoods. While only a few were more civically engaged, most reported they would want to be more so. However, the participants did not have a strong sense for how to find out about what was happening in their neighborhoods or how to get involved. Particularly, they were not sure how they would go about communicating with others in their neighborhood about issues they cared about. Participants were especially interested in learning about local community events and crimes and relied heavily on one or two hyperlocal bloggers to do so.

Whoo.ly Evaluation

Participants completed four tasks exploring their neighborhood—find recent events, find local neighborhood reporters, find neighborhood topics, and find potential neighborhood friends—using both Whoo.ly and Twitter. We performed an omnibus repeated measures ANOVA (technology X task X type of rating) to test for the impact of type technology across measures of task ease, confidence in completing task, and task engagement. Overall, we found a significant effect of technology (F(1,11) = 3.02, p = 0.05 1-tailed[1]), with participants showing preference for Whoo.ly. As can be seen from Figure 3, people overall found Whoo.ly easy to use and found the tasks easier to complete in Whoo.ly than in Twitter. We found neighborhood communication self-efficacy to be a meaningful covariate interacting with this effect (F(1,11) = 3.3, p = 0.04, for interaction of technology X task X self-efficacy), meaning participants with lower levels of self-efficacy were likely to favor Whoo.ly over Twitter, especially for the find-friends task.

These results suggest that Whoo.ly is particularly easy for users to learn more about their neighborhood if they do not already have effective tools to find information and access people in their neighborhood.

---

[1] Given the small N and a priori predictions, we report 1-tailed p values.

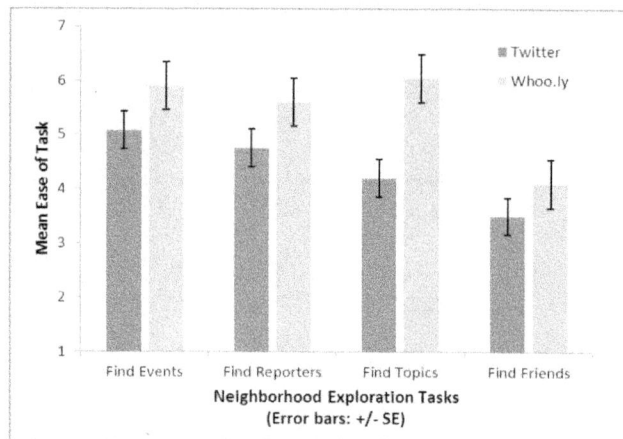

Figure 3: Participants generally found it easier to complete neighborhood exploration tasks using Whoo.ly (where 1 = not at all, and 7 = extremely so.)

Participants also completed overall ratings of Whoo.ly and Twitter, and again using an omnibus repeated measures ANOVA (technology X type of rating) we found an effect of technology (F(1,11) = 3.09, p = 0.06), such that participants reported it as more useful (F(1,11) = 2.24, p = 0.08) and easier to use (F(1,11) = 2.72, p = 9.07), that it provided a better overview (F(1,11) = 2.74, p = 0.07, and that it increased the sense of connection to their neighborhood community (F(1, 11) = 3.5, p = 0.04), as shown in Figure 4. Again, neighborhood communication self-efficacy had a marginally significant interaction such that people with lower levels self-efficacy were more impacted by Whoo.ly in their ratings of sense of connection *(F(1, 11)* = 2.81, p = 0.09).

To assess our event detector, we compared user ratings of 503 Twitter posts in our participants' neighborhoods to the event detectors. Users indicated that 170 of the total Twitter messages were event-related. Among these, the detector also identified 78% of messages as event-related, relative to 17% false positives. A logistic regression shows a strong, significant correspondence (*beta* = 0.53, p < 0.001). The event detector also produced a score for the importance to prioritize events in the user interface, and this score was much higher for Twitter messages the participants identified as events (t = 16.92, p < 0.001). The participants' ratings of the importance of an event was significantly correlated with the event detectors (r = 0.31, p < 0.001).

In order to compare the relative value of the types of summarization provided by Whoo.ly, we asked participants to rank the five main sections by order of preference, where 1 = most preferred and 5 = least preferred. We found that participants rated recent events most highly (M = 1.6), followed by the Tweet stream (M = 2.8), the top topics (M = 3.2), active people (M = 3.5), and popular places (M = 3.5).

After participants completed both sets of tasks, we asked them to choose which application they would prefer to use to find out what is happening in their neighborhood. Eight participants out of 13 preferred Whoo.ly. However, when asked to compare it to their favorite neighborhood blog, eight out of 13 said they would prefer their neighborhood blog. On average, participants indicated they were somewhat likely to actually use Whoo.ly if it were made publicly available ($M = 4.4$, $SD = 1.62$ where 1 = not at all, and 7 = extremely so).

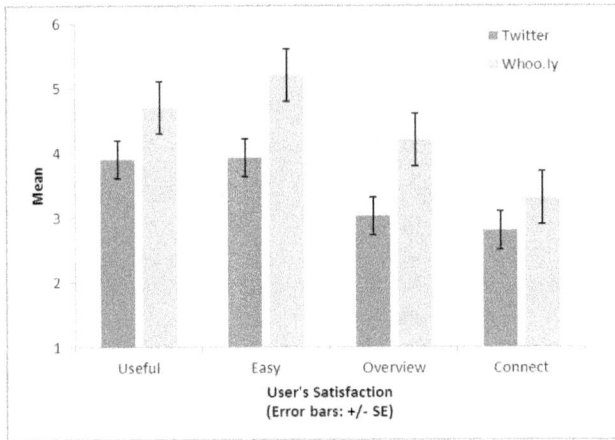

Figure 4: Whoo.ly was found to be more useful, easy to use, with a better overview of the users' neighborhoods, and a sense of connection to their neighborhood communities.

In order to shed light on some of our more quantitative findings, each participant was asked to provide feedback in writing about what they liked and disliked about Whoo.ly and how they would suggest improving it. Then, participants were asked to briefly discuss their experiences. When asked what they most liked about Whoo.ly, participants indicated the summarization and community features. Some of participants' answers were,

"Really liked it overall, definitely a lot easier to find stuff"

"Whoo.ly was set up specifically with the community in mind. It makes community news/events/issues/people etc. easily accessible".

When asked what they disliked, a few participants noted that a lot of the content felt like spam, such as the Craigslist postings, Foursquare check-ins, or overly personal posts, which interfered with participants' ability to access meaningful content. One participant said, *"Results. Mostly the furniture on craigslist. Need to filter out those, and be able to differentiate between the spammy 'top users' and the real top users."*

During the discussions, there were also several requests for further, personalized filters, to focus on the kind of content they cared about.

When asked why they preferred Whoo.ly over Twitter, again participants noted the filtering, summarization, and community features. One participant's answer was,

"Twitter isn't set up for a community. Whool.y functions amazingly for this."

Consistent with our more quantitative findings, we found that participants who preferred Twitter over Whoo.ly did so because they were already well-connected to their neighborhoods and already using Twitter to follow neighborhood reporters. For example, a participant's reply was, *"If I didn't know my neighborhood as well I would use both and compare data. Since I am very embedded in my community Whoo.ly is just another aggregator."*

When asked why they would prefer their local blog over Whoo.ly, participants noted blogs had more extensive features such as calendars and they benefitted from social curation. When asked why they would prefer Whoo.ly, participants mentioned its ease consumption and community feel. Some of the participants' reasons were,

"like that it's short messages...easier than if browsing full blog with full messages; easier to figure what's going on."

"Whoo.ly offers not only news/events, but also connects you with people. Like combining Twitter and a newspaper, I like it".

DISCUSSION

As shown above, the overall reaction to the information provided on Whoo.ly was quite positive. The participants to our study found Whoo.ly easier to use than Twitter and the majority said they would prefer it as a tool for exploring their neighborhoods.

As a prototype system, Whoo.ly has advanced the state of the art for information seeking in hyperlocal communities, but many opportunities for improvement remain. As people cross the line from consuming hyperlocal information to engaging with their local community, they seek to know as much about the people as about the news. Thus, from a hyperlocal community perspective, it is also important to recommend potential similar friends such as "people like me in my neighborhood" as a feature to improve neighborhood connections. Besides, exploring the sentiments behind people's response/reactions to neighborhood issues can be useful [16]. Furthermore, it is interesting to note the unique characteristic of consuming social media when embedded in a geographical location—people could easily walk out their front doors and down the street to experience, for example, the local event they had just read about online.

It is worth noting that we deliberately placed the questionnaire and the focus group prior to the information-seeking user tasks to frame the tasks specifically on neighborhood seeking behaviors. Our intention was to give users the opportunity to have access to each other's neighborhood seeking experiences in evaluating the technology's effectiveness. We recognized a discussion could have systematically and artificially affected preferences towards or against Whoo.ly across all participants. However, there is no indication that this is the case. To further assess potential discussion confound, we tested for group size (2 vs. 3) on preference for Whoo.ly vs. Twitter, and found no effect. Moreover, we also found there were no session and level of Twitter usage effects.

CONCLUSION

Whoo.ly is a web service that facilitates information seeking in hyperlocal communities by finding and summarizing neighborhood Twitter messages. In this paper, we presented several computational approaches used in Whoo.ly to discover hyperlocal content from noisy and overwhelming Twitter posts. In particular, we developed a novel event detector to discover trending events from recent posts. In addition, activity-based ranking algorithms and information extractors provided additional insights into the most active people and popular places in a local community. We performed a user study to evaluate Whoo.ly, and we found that (1) our event detector accurately identified events and (2) the local residents who participated in our study found Whoo.ly to be an easier tool for finding hyperlocal information than Twitter.

Social media such as Twitter has altered society's information and communication fabric and will continue to be increasingly integrated in our daily lives. We believe this paper presents a promising approach to leveraging Twitter messages to better support hyperlocal community awareness and engagement.

REFERENCES

1. Becker, H., Naaman, M., and Gravano, L. Beyond trending topics: Real-world event identification on Twitter. *Proc. ICWSM*, (2011), 438-441.
2. Big Data for Breaking News: Lessons from #Aurora, Colorado. http://blog.socialflow.com/post/7120245507/big-data-breaking-news-aurora-colorado.
3. Blei, D. M., Ng, A. Y., and Jordan, M. I. Latent dirichlet allocation. *Journal of Machine Learning Research*, (2003)
4. Boyd, D.M., and Ellison, N.B., Social Network Sites: Definition, History, and Scholarship. *Journal of Computer-Mediated Communication*, 13 (2007), 210-230.
5. Carroll, J. M., and Rosson, M. B. Developing the Blacksburg electronic village. *Communications of the ACM*, (1996), 69-74.
6. Chang, C. H., Kayed, M., Girgis, M. R., and Shaalan, K. F. A survey of web information extraction systems. *IEEE TKDE*, (2006), 1411-1428.
7. Cranshaw, J., Schwartz, R., Hong, J. I., and Sadeh, N. The livehoods project: Utilizing social media to understand the dynamics of a city. *Proc. ICWSM*, (2012).
8. Fillion R. How Social Media Covered the Empire State Shooting. *The Wall Street Journal*, (2012). http://blogs.wsj.com/digits/2012/08/24/how-social-media-covered-the-empire-state-shooting/.
9. Glaser, M. The New Voices: Hyperlocal Citizen Media Sites Want You (to Write!). *Online Journalism Review*
10. Hampton K. i-Neighbors. http://www.i-neighbors.com.
11. Hampton, K., and Wellman, B. Neighboring in Netville: How the Internet Supports Community and Social Capital in a Wired Suburb. *City & Community*, (2003), 277-311.
12. He, D., and Parker, D. S. Topic dynamics: an alternative model of bursts in streams of topics. *Proc. KDD*, (2010).
13. Hecht, B., Hong, L., Suh, B., and Chi, E. H. Tweets from Justin Bieber's heart: the dynamics of the location field in user profiles. *Proc. CHI* (2010), 237-246.
14. Hoffman, B., Robinson, H., Han, K., and Carroll, J. CiVicinity events: pairing geolocation tools with a community calendar. *Proc. COM.Geo*, (2012).
15. Hu, X., Sun, N., Zhang, C., and Chua, T. S. Exploiting internal and external semantics for the clustering of short texts using world knowledge. *Proc. CIKM*, (2009).
16. Hu, X., Tang, L., Tang, J., and Liu, H. Exploiting Social Relations for Sentiment Analysis in Microblogging. *Proc. WSDM*, (2013).
17. Hu, Y., John, A., Seligmann, D. D., and Wang, F. What Were the Tweets About? Topical Associations between Public Events and Twitter Feeds. *Proc. ICWSM*, (2012).
18. Jarvis, R. A., and Patrick, E. A. Clustering using a similarity measure based on shared near neighbors. *Computers, IEEE Transactions on*, C-22, 11 (1973), 1025-1034.
19. Kahne, J., Middaugh, E., and Schutjer-Mance, K. California civic index. New York: *Carnegie Corporation and Annenberg Foundation*, (2005).
20. Kavanaugh A., Gad, S., Neidig, S., Pérez-Quiñones, M. A., Tedesco, J., Ahuja, A., and Ramakrishnan, N. (Hyper) local news aggregation: Designing for Social Affordances. *Proc. DG.O*, (2012), 1-10.
21. Keeter, S., Zukin, C., Andolina, M., and Jenkins, K. Improving the measurement of political participation. *Annual meeting of the Midwest Political Science Association*.
22. Kwak, H., Lee, C., Park, H., and Moon, S. What is Twitter, a social network or a news media? *Proc. WWW*, (2010)
23. Lewis, S., and Lewis, D. A. Examining technology that supports community policing. *Proc. CHI*, (2012).
24. Monroy-Herndez, A., Kiciman, E., Boyd, D., and Counts, S., Narcotweets: Social Media in Wartime, *ICWSM*, (2012).
25. Murphy, J. Technical Analysis of the Financial Markets. Prentice Hall Press, (1999).
26. Newport, J.K., and Jawahar, G.G.P. Community participation and public awareness in disaster mitigation. *Disaster Prevention and Management* 12, 1 (2003), 33-36.
27. O'Connor, B., Krieger, M., and Ahn, D. Tweetmotif: Exploratory search and topic summarization for twitter. *Proc. of ICWSM*, (2010), 2-3.
28. Rosenstiel, T., Mitchell, A., Purcell, K., and Rainie, L. *How People Learn about their Local Community*. Pew Internet and American Life Project. (2011). http://www.pewinternet.org/Reports/2011/Local-news.aspx.
29. Sakaki T., Okazaki, M., and Matsuo, Y., Earthquake shakes Twitter users: real-time event detection by social sensors. *Proc. WWW*, (2010), 851-860.
30. Sarason, S.B. *The psychological sense of community: Prospects for a community psychology*. Jossey-Bass
31. Vieweg, S., Hughes, A. L., Starbird, K., and Palen, L. Microblogging during two natural hazards events: what twitter may contribute to situational awareness. *CHI*, 2010
32. Wang, C.K,. Hsu, P., Chang, M-W, Kiciman, E., Simple and Knowledge-intensive Generative Model for Named Entity Recognition., *Microsoft Research*, (2013). http://research.microsoft.com/apps/pubs/default.aspx?id=179740.
33. Wellman, B. Community: from neighborhood to network. *Communications of the ACM*, 48, 10 (2005), 53-55.

Author Index

www.ingramcontent.com/pod-product-compliance
Lightning Source LLC
Chambersburg PA
CBHW080130220326
41598CB00032B/5012